Exploring Premium Media Site

Improve your grade with hands-on tools and resources!

- Master *Key Terms* to expand your vocabulary.
- Prepare for exams by taking practice quizzes in the *Online Chapter Review*.
- Download *Student Data Files* for the applications projects in each chapter.

And for even more tools, you can access the following Premium Resources using your Access Code. Register now to get the most out of *Exploring!*

- *Hands-On Exercise Videos* accompany each Hands-On Exercise in the chapter. These videos demonstrate both how to accomplish individual skills as well as why they are important.*
- *Soft Skills Videos* are necessary to complete the Soft Skills Beyond the Classroom Exercise, and introduce students to important professional skills.*

*Access code required for these premium resources

Your Access Code is:

Note: If there is no silver foil covering the access code, it may already have been redeemed, and therefore may no longer be valid. In that case, you can purchase online access using a major credit card or PayPal account. To do so, go to **www.pearsonhighered.com/exploring**, select your book cover, click on "Buy Access" and follow the on-screen instructions.

To Register:

- To start you will need a valid email address and this access code.
- Go to **www.pearsonhighered.com/exploring** and scroll to find your text book.
- Once you've selected your text, on the Home Page, click the link to access the Student Premium Content.
- Click the Register button and follow the on-screen instructions.
- After you register, you can sign in any time via the log-in area on the same screen.

System Requirements

Windows 7 Ultimate Edition; IE 8
Windows Vista Ultimate Edition SP1; IE 8
Windows XP Professional SP3; IE 7
Windows XP Professional SP3; Firefox 3.6.4
Mac OS 10.5.7; Firefox 3.6.4
Mac OS 10.6; Safari 5

Technical Support

http://247pearsoned.custhelp.com

Photo credits: Goodluz/wrangler/Elena Elisseeva/Shutterstock

(ex·ploring)

SERIES

1. Investigating in a systematic way: examining. 2. Searching into or ranging over for the purpose of discovery.

Microsoft®

Office 2013

VOLUME 2

Series Editor **Mary Anne Poatsy**

Davidson | Lau | Lawson | Cameron | Williams | Mulbery

Series Created by Dr. Robert T. Grauer

PEARSON

Boston   Columbus   Indianapolis   New York   San Francisco   Upper Saddle River
Amsterdam   Cape Town   Dubai   London   Madrid   Milan   Munich   Paris   Montréal   Toronto
Delhi   Mexico City   São Paulo   Sydney   Hong Kong   Seoul   Singapore   Taipei   Tokyo

Editor in Chief: Michael Payne
Senior Editor: Samantha McAfee Lewis
Editorial Project Manager: Keri Rand
Product Development Manager: Laura Burgess
Development Editor (Word): Vonda Keator
Development Editor (Excel): Barbara Stover
Development Editor (Access): Lori Damanti
Development Editor (PowerPoint): Linda Harrison
Editorial Assistant: Laura Karahalis
Director of Marketing: Maggie Moylan Leen
Marketing Manager: Brad Forrester
Marketing Coordinator: Susan Osterlitz
Managing Editor: Camille Trentacoste
Production Project Manager: Ilene Kahn
Senior Operations Specialist: Maura Zaldivar
Senior Art Director: Jonathan Boylan
Interior Design: Studio Montage
Cover Design: Studio Montage
Cover Photo: Courtesy of Shutterstock® images
Associate Director of Design: Blair Brown
Digital Media Editor: Eric Hakanson
Director of Media Development: Taylor Ragan
Media Project Manager, Production: Renata Butera
Full Service Project Management: Andrea Stefanowicz/PreMediaGlobal
Composition: PreMediaGlobal

Credits and acknowledgments borrowed from other sources and reproduced, with permission, in this textbook appear on the appropriate page within text.

Microsoft and/or its respective suppliers make no representations about the suitability of the information contained in the documents and related graphics published as part of the services for any purpose. All such documents and related graphics are provided "as is" without warranty of any kind. Microsoft and/or its respective suppliers hereby disclaim all warranties and conditions with regard to this information, including all warranties and conditions of merchantability, whether express, implied or statutory, fitness for a particular purpose, title and non-infringement. In no event shall Microsoft and/or its respective suppliers be liable for any special, indirect or consequential damages or any damages whatsoever resulting from loss of use, data or profits, whether in an action of contract, negligence or other tortious action, arising out of or in connection with the use or performance of information available from the services.

The documents and related graphics contained herein could include technical inaccuracies or typographical errors. Changes are periodically added to the information herein. Microsoft and/or its respective suppliers may make improvements and/or changes in the product(s) and/or the program(s) described herein at any time. Partial screen shots may be viewed in full within the software version specified.

Microsoft® and Windows® are registered trademarks of the Microsoft Corporation in the U.S.A. and other countries. This book is not sponsored or endorsed by or affiliated with the Microsoft Corporation.

---

10 9 8 7 6 5 4 3 2

ISBN 10: 0-13-341212-1
ISBN 13: 978-0-13-341212-3

Dedications

For my husband, Ted, who unselfishly continues to take on more than his share to support me throughout the process; and for my children, Laura, Carolyn, and Teddy, whose encouragement and love have been inspiring.

Mary Anne Poatsy

I dedicate this book in loving memory of my grandmother Earline B. Leggett (Nanny). Your kindness, wisdom, and support have been and will always be an inspiration. I couldn't have made it without you.

Jason Davidson

I dedicate this book to my only child, Catherine Shen, who taught me that there is another wonderful life outside of my work. My life has been more fulfilling and exciting with her in it. I also dedicate this book to the loving memory of my dog, Harry, who was by my side, through thick and thin, for 16 years. I miss him dearly every day.

Linda K. Lau

This book is dedicated to my children and to my students to inspire them to never give up and to always keep reaching for their dreams.

Rebecca Lawson

I dedicate this book to my fiancée, Anny, for encouraging me throughout the writing process and for being the person she is, to Sonny, to Drs. Hubey, Boyno, Bredlau, and Deremer at Montclair State University for educating and inspiring me, and to my students, who I hope will inspire others someday.

Eric Cameron

I offer thanks to my family and colleagues who have supported me on this journey. I would like to dedicate the work I have performed toward this undertaking to my little grandson, Yonason Meir (known for now as Mei-Mei), who as his name suggests, is the illumination in my life.

Jerri Williams

I dedicate this book in memory to Grandpa Herman Hort, who dedicated his life to his family and to the education field as a teacher and administrator. He inspired a daughter and several grandchildren to become passionate educators and provide quality curriculum to students.

Keith Mulbery

About the Authors

Mary Anne Poatsy, Series Editor

Mary Anne is a senior faculty member at Montgomery County Community College, teaching various computer application and concepts courses in face-to-face and online environments. She holds a B.A. in Psychology and Education from Mount Holyoke College and an M.B.A. in Finance from Northwestern University's Kellogg Graduate School of Management.

Mary Anne has more than 12 years of educational experience. She is currently adjunct faculty at Gwynedd-Mercy College and Montgomery County Community College. She has also taught at Bucks County Community College and Muhlenberg College, as well as conducted personal training. Before teaching, she was Vice President at Shearson Lehman in the Municipal Bond Investment Banking Department.

Jason Davidson, Excel Author

Jason Davidson is a faculty member in the College of Business at Butler University, where he teaches Advanced Web Design, Data Networks, Data Analysis and Business Modeling, and introductory MIS courses.

With a background in media development, prior to joining the faculty at Butler, he worked in the technical publishing industry. Along with teaching, he currently serves as an IT consultant for regional businesses in the Indianapolis area. He holds a B.A. in telecommunication arts from Butler University and an M.B.A. from Morehead State University. He lives in Indianapolis, Indiana, and in his free time, enjoys road biking, photography, and spending time with his family.

Dr. Linda K. Lau, Word Author

Since 1994, Dr. Linda K. Lau is an associate professor of Management Information Systems (MIS) at the College of Business and Economics, Longwood University, located in Farmville, Virginia. She received the Outstanding Academic Advisor Award in 2006. Besides teaching and advising, Linda has authored and co-authored several journal and conference articles, edited two books, and sits on numerous editorial boards. Her current research interest focuses on campus ethics, hybrid/online learning, and e-commerce. Linda earned her Ph.D. from Rensselaer Polytechnic Institute in 1993, and her MBA and Bachelor of Science from Illinois State University in 1987 and 1986, respectively. In her younger days, Linda worked as a flight attendant for Singapore International Airlines for six years before coming to America to pursue her academic dream. She also worked as a financial consultant with Salomon Smith Barney from 1999–2000 before returning to the academic world. Linda resides in Farmville and Richmond with her family.

Rebecca Lawson, PowerPoint Author

Rebecca Lawson is a professor in the Computer Information Technologies program at Lansing Community College. She coordinates the curriculum, develops the instructional materials, and teaches for the E-Business curriculum. She also serves as the Online Faculty Coordinator at the Center for Teaching Excellence at LCC. In that role, she develops and facilitates online workshops for faculty learning to teach online. Her major areas of interest include online curriculum quality assurance, the review and development of printed and online instructional materials, the assessment of computer and Internet literacy skill levels to facilitate student retention, and the use of social networking tools to support learning in blended and online learning environments.

Eric Cameron, Access Author

Eric holds a M.S. in computer science and a B.S. degree in Computer Science with minors in Mathematics and Physics, both from Montclair State University. He is a tenured Assistant Professor at Passaic County Community College, where he has taught in the Computer and Information Sciences department since 2001. Eric is also the author of the *Your Office: Getting Started with Web 2.0* and *Your Office: Getting Started with Windows 8* textbooks. Eric maintains a professional blog at profcameron.blogspot.com.

Jerri Williams, Access Author

Jerri Williams is a Senior Adjunct Instructor at Montgomery County Community College in Pennsylvania. Jerri also works as an independent corporate trainer, technical editor, and author. She is interested in travel, cooking, and tending to her colonial farmhouse. Jerri is married (to Gareth for 32 years!), the mother of two beautiful daughters (an Accounting graduate and a budding lawyer), a splendid son-in-law (also a soon-to-be lawyer), and grandmother to a handsome young grandson

Dr. Keith Mulbery, Excel Author

Dr. Keith Mulbery is the Department Chair and a Professor in the Information Systems and Technology Department at Utah Valley University (UVU), where he currently teaches systems analysis and design, and global and ethical issues in information systems and technology. He has also taught computer applications, C# programming, and management information systems. Keith served as Interim Associate Dean, School of Computing, in the College of Technology and Computing at UVU.

Keith received the Utah Valley State College Board of Trustees Award of Excellence in 2001, School of Technology and Computing Scholar Award in 2007, and School of Technology and Computing Teaching Award in 2008. He has authored more than 17 textbooks, served as Series Editor for the Exploring Office 2007 series, and served as developmental editor on two textbooks for the Essentials Office 2000 series. He is frequently asked to give presentations and workshops on Microsoft Office Excel at various education conferences.

Keith received his B.S. and M.Ed. in Business Education from Southwestern Oklahoma State University and earned his Ph.D. in Education with an emphasis in Business Information Systems at Utah State University. His dissertation topic was computer-assisted instruction using Prentice Hall's Train and Assess IT program (the predecessor to MyITLab) to supplement traditional instruction in basic computer proficiency courses.

Dr. Robert T. Grauer, Creator of the Exploring Series

Bob Grauer is an Associate Professor in the Department of Computer Information Systems at the University of Miami, where he is a multiple winner of the Outstanding Teaching Award in the School of Business, most recently in 2009. He has written numerous COBOL texts and is the vision behind the Exploring Office series, with more than three million books in print. His work has been translated into three foreign languages and is used in all aspects of higher education at both national and international levels. Bob Grauer has consulted for several major corporations including IBM and American Express. He received his Ph.D. in Operations Research in 1972 from the Polytechnic Institute of Brooklyn.

Brief Contents

Contents

Microsoft Office Word 2013

Microsoft Office Access 2013

■ CHAPTER FIVE **Data Validation and Data Analysis:** Reducing Errors and Extracting Better Information **581**

■ CHAPTER SIX **Action and Specialized Queries:** Moving Beyond the Select Query **629**

■ CHAPTER SEVEN **Advanced Forms and Reports:** Moving Beyond the Basics **675**

Microsoft Office PowerPoint 2013

■ **Application Capstone Exercises**

Acknowledgments

The Exploring team would like to acknowledge and thank all the reviewers who helped us throughout the years by providing us with their invaluable comments, suggestions, and constructive criticism.

We'd like to especially thank our Focus Group attendees and User Diary Reviewers for this edition:

Stephen Z. Jourdan
Auburn University at Montgomery

Ann Rovetto
Horry-Georgetown Technical
College

Jacqueline D. Lawson
Henry Ford Community College

Diane L. Smith
Henry Ford Community College

Sven Aelterman
Troy University

Suzanne M. Jeska
County College of Morris

Susan N. Dozier
Tidewater Community College

Robert G. Phipps Jr.
West Virginia University

Mike Michaelson
Palomar College

Mary Beth Tarver
Northwestern State University

Alexandre C. Probst
Colorado Christian University

Phil Nielson
Salt Lake Community College

Carolyn Barren
Macomb Community College

Sue A. McCrory
Missouri State University

Lucy Parakhovnik
California State University, Northridge

Jakie Brown Jr.
Stevenson University

Craig J. Peterson
American InterContinental University

Terry Ray Rigsby
Hill College

Biswadip Ghosh
Metropolitan State University of Denver

Cheryl Sypniewski
Macomb Community College

Lynn Keane
University of South Carolina

Sheila Gionfriddo
Luzerne College

Dick Hewer
Ferris State College

Carolyn Borne
Louisiana State University

Sumathy Chandrashekar
Salisbury University

Laura Marcoulides
Fullerton College

Don Riggs
SUNY Schenectady County Community
College

Gary McFall
Purdue University

James Powers
University of Southern Indiana

James Brown
Central Washington University

Brian Powell
West Virginia University

Sherry Lenhart
Terra Community College

Chen Zhang
Bryant University

Nikia Robinson
Indian River State University

Jill Young
Southeast Missouri State University

Debra Hoffman
Southeast Missouri State University

Tommy Lu
Delaware Technical Community College

Mimi Spain
Southern Maine Community College

We'd like to thank everyone who has been involved in reviewing and providing their feedback, including for our previous editions:

Adriana Lumpkin
Midland College

Alan S. Abrahams
Virginia Tech

Ali Berrached
University of Houston–Downtown

Allen Alexander
Delaware Technical & Community College

Andrea Marchese
Maritime College, State University of New York

Andrew Blitz
Broward College; Edison State College

Angel Norman
University of Tennessee, Knoxville

Angela Clark
University of South Alabama

Ann Rovetto
Horry-Georgetown Technical College

Astrid Todd
Guilford Technical Community College

Audrey Gillant
Maritime College, State University of New York

Barbara Stover
Marion Technical College

Barbara Tollinger
Sinclair Community College

Ben Brahim Taha
Auburn University

Beverly Amer
Northern Arizona University

Beverly Fite
Amarillo College

Bonita Volker
Tidewater Community College

Bonnie Homan
San Francisco State University

Brad West
Sinclair Community College

Brian Powell
West Virginia University

Carol Buser
Owens Community College

Carol Roberts
University of Maine

Carolyn Barren
Macomb Community College

Cathy Poyner
Truman State University

Charles Hodgson
Delgado Community College

Cheri Higgins
Illinois State University

Cheryl Hinds
Norfolk State University

Chris Robinson
Northwest State Community College

Cindy Herbert
Metropolitan Community College–Longview

Dana Hooper
University of Alabama

Dana Johnson
North Dakota State University

Daniela Marghitu
Auburn University

David Noel
University of Central Oklahoma

David Pulis
Maritime College, State University of New York

David Thornton
Jacksonville State University

Dawn Medlin
Appalachian State University

Debby Keen
University of Kentucky

Debra Chapman
University of South Alabama

Derrick Huang
Florida Atlantic University

Diana Baran
Henry Ford Community College

Diane Cassidy
The University of North Carolina at Charlotte

Diane Smith
Henry Ford Community College

Don Danner
San Francisco State University

Don Hoggan
Solano College

Doncho Petkov
Eastern Connecticut State University

Donna Ehrhart
State University of New York at Brockport

Elaine Crable
Xavier University

Elizabeth Duett
Delgado Community College

Erhan Uskup
Houston Community College–Northwest

Eric Martin
University of Tennessee

Erika Nadas
Wilbur Wright College

Floyd Winters
Manatee Community College

Frank Lucente
Westmoreland County Community College

G. Jan Wilms
Union University

Gail Cope
Sinclair Community College

Gary DeLorenzo
California University of Pennsylvania

Gary Garrison
Belmont University

George Cassidy
Sussex County Community College

Gerald Braun
Xavier University

Gerald Burgess
Western New Mexico University

Gladys Swindler
Fort Hays State University

Heith Hennel
Valencia Community College

Henry Rudzinski
Central Connecticut State University

Irene Joos
La Roche College

Iwona Rusin
Baker College; Davenport University

J. Roberto Guzman
San Diego Mesa College

Jan Wilms
Union University

Jane Stam
Onondaga Community College

Janet Bringhurst
Utah State University

Jeanette Dix
Ivy Tech Community College

Jennifer Day
Sinclair Community College

Jill Canine
Ivy Tech Community College

Jim Chaffee
The University of Iowa Tippie College of Business

Joanne Lazirko
University of Wisconsin–Milwaukee

Jodi Milliner
Kansas State University

John Hollenbeck
Blue Ridge Community College

John Seydel
Arkansas State University

Judith A. Scheeren
Westmoreland County Community College

Judith Brown
The University of Memphis

Juliana Cypert
Tarrant County College

Kamaljeet Sanghera
George Mason University

Karen Priestly
Northern Virginia Community College

Karen Ravan
Spartanburg Community College

Kathleen Brenan
Ashland University

Ken Busbee
Houston Community College

Kent Foster
Winthrop University

Kevin Anderson
Solano Community College

Kim Wright
The University of Alabama

Kristen Hockman
University of Missouri–Columbia

Kristi Smith
Allegany College of Maryland

Laura McManamon
University of Dayton

Leanne Chun
Leeward Community College

Lee McClain
Western Washington University

Linda D. Collins
Mesa Community College

Linda Johnsonius
Murray State University

Linda Lau
Longwood University

Linda Theus
Jackson State Community College

Linda Williams
Marion Technical College

Lisa Miller
University of Central Oklahoma

Lister Horn
Pensacola Junior College

Lixin Tao
Pace University

Loraine Miller
Cayuga Community College

Lori Kielty
Central Florida Community College

Lorna Wells
Salt Lake Community College

Lorraine Sauchin
Duquesne University

Lucy Parakhovnik (Parker)
California State University, Northridge

Lynn Mancini
Delaware Technical Community College

Mackinzee Escamilla
South Plains College

Marcia Welch
Highline Community College

Margaret McManus
Northwest Florida State College

Margaret Warrick
Allan Hancock College

Marilyn Hibbert
Salt Lake Community College

Mark Choman
Luzerne County Community College

Mary Duncan
University of Missouri–St. Louis

Melissa Nemeth
Indiana University-Purdue University
Indianapolis

Melody Alexander
Ball State University

Michael Douglas
University of Arkansas at Little Rock

Michael Dunklebarger
Alamance Community College

Michael G. Skaff
College of the Sequoias

Michele Budnovitch
Pennsylvania College of Technology

Mike Jochen
East Stroudsburg University

Mike Scroggins
Missouri State University

Muhammed Badamas
Morgan State University

NaLisa Brown
University of the Ozarks

Nancy Grant
Community College of Allegheny
County–South Campus

Nanette Lareau
University of Arkansas Community
College–Morrilton

Pam Brune
Chattanooga State Community College

Pam Uhlenkamp
Iowa Central Community College

Patrick Smith
Marshall Community and Technical College

Paul Addison
Ivy Tech Community College

Paula Ruby
Arkansas State University

Peggy Burrus
Red Rocks Community College

Peter Ross
SUNY Albany

Philip H. Nielson
Salt Lake Community College

Ralph Hooper
University of Alabama

Ranette Halverson
Midwestern State University

Richard Blamer
John Carroll University

Richard Cacace
Pensacola Junior College

Richard Hewer
Ferris State University

Rob Murray
Ivy Tech Community College

Robert Dušek
Northern Virginia Community College

Robert Sindt
Johnson County Community College

Robert Warren
Delgado Community College

Rocky Belcher
Sinclair Community College

Roger Pick
University of Missouri at Kansas City

Ronnie Creel
Troy University

Rosalie Westerberg
Clover Park Technical College

Ruth Neal
Navarro College

Sandra Thomas
Troy University

Sheila Gionfriddo
Luzerne County Community College

Sherrie Geitgey
Northwest State Community College

Sophia Wilberscheid
Indian River State College

Sophie Lee
California State University,
Long Beach

Stacy Johnson
Iowa Central Community College

Stephanie Kramer
Northwest State Community College

Stephen Jourdan
Auburn University Montgomery

Steven Schwarz
Raritan Valley Community College

Sue McCrory
Missouri State University

Susan Fuschetto
Cerritos College

Susan Medlin
UNC Charlotte

Suzan Spitzberg
Oakton Community College

Sven Aelterman
Troy University

Sylvia Brown
Midland College

Tanya Patrick
Clackamas Community College

Terri Holly
Indian River State College

Thomas Rienzo
Western Michigan University

Tina Johnson
Midwestern State University

Tommy Lu
Delaware Technical and Community College

Troy S. Cash
NorthWest Arkansas Community College

Vicki Robertson
Southwest Tennessee Community

Weifeng Chen
California University of Pennsylvania

Wes Anthony
Houston Community College

William Ayen
University of Colorado at Colorado Springs

Wilma Andrews
Virginia Commonwealth University

Yvonne Galusha
University of Iowa

Special thanks to our development and technical team:

Barbara Stover

Cheryl Slavick

Elizabeth Lockley

Heather Hetzler

Jennifer Lynn

Joyce Nielsen

Linda Harrison

Linda Pogue

Lisa Bucki

Lori Damanti

Mara Zebest

Susan Fry

Vonda Keator

Preface

The Exploring Series and You

Exploring is Pearson's Office Application series that requires students like you to think "beyond the point and click." In this edition, we have worked to restructure the Exploring experience around the way you, today's modern student, actually use your resources.

The goal of Exploring is, as it has always been, to go further than teaching just the steps to accomplish a task—the series provides the theoretical foundation for you to understand when and why to apply a skill.

As a result, you achieve a deeper understanding of each application and can apply this critical thinking beyond Office and the classroom.

You are practical students, focused on what you need to do to be successful in this course and beyond, and want to be as efficient as possible. Exploring has evolved to meet you where you are and help you achieve success efficiently. Pearson has paid attention to the habits of students today, how you get information, how you are motivated to do well in class, and what your future goals look like. We asked you and your peers for acceptance of new tools we designed to address these points, and you responded with a resounding "YES!"

Here Is What We Learned About You

You are goal-oriented. You want a good grade in this course—so we rethought how Exploring works so that you can learn the how and why behind the skills in this course to be successful now. You also want to be successful in your future career—so we used motivating case studies to show relevance of these skills to your future careers and incorporated Soft Skills, Collaboration, and Analysis Cases in this edition to set you up for success in the future.

You read, prepare, and study differently than students used to. You use textbooks like a tool—you want to easily identify what you need to know and learn it efficiently. We have added key features such as Step Icons, Hands-On Exercise Videos, and tracked everything via page numbers that allow you to navigate the content efficiently, making the concepts accessible and creating a map to success for you to follow.

You go to college now with a different set of skills than students did five years ago. The new edition of Exploring moves you beyond the basics of the software at a faster pace, without sacrificing coverage of the fundamental skills that you need to know. This ensures that you will be engaged from page 1 to the end of the book.

You and your peers have diverse learning styles. With this in mind, we broadened our definition of "student resources" to include Compass, an online skill database; movable Student Reference cards; Hands-On Exercise videos to provide a secondary lecture-like option of review; Soft Skills video exercises to illustrate important non-technical skills; and the most powerful online homework and assessment tool around with a direct 1:1 content match with the Exploring Series, MyITLab. Exploring will be accessible to all students, regardless of learning style.

Providing You with a Map to Success to Move Beyond the Point and Click

All of these changes and additions will provide you with an easy and efficient path to follow to be successful in this course, regardless of your learning style or any existing knowledge you have at the outset. Our goal is to keep you more engaged in both the hands-on and conceptual sides, helping you to achieve a higher level of understanding that will guarantee you success in this course and in your future career. In addition to the vision and experience of the series creator, Robert T. Grauer, we have assembled a tremendously talented team of Office Applications authors who have devoted themselves to teaching you the ins and outs of Microsoft Word, Excel, Access, and PowerPoint. Led in this edition by series editor Mary Anne Poatsy, the whole team is equally dedicated to providing you with a **map to success** to support the Exploring mission of **moving you beyond the point and click**.

Key Features

- **White Pages/Yellow Pages** clearly distinguish the theory (white pages) from the skills covered in the Hands-On Exercises (yellow pages) so students always know what they are supposed to be doing.

- **Enhanced Objective Mapping** enables students to follow a directed path through each chapter, from the objectives list at the chapter opener through the exercises in the end of chapter.
  - **Objectives List:** This provides a simple list of key objectives covered in the chapter. This includes page numbers so students can skip between objectives where they feel they need the most help.
  - **Step Icons:** These icons appear in the white pages and reference the step numbers in the Hands-On Exercises, providing a correlation between the two so students can easily find conceptual help when they are working hands-on and need a refresher.
  - **Quick Concepts Check:** A series of questions that appear briefly at the end of each white page section. These questions cover the most essential concepts in the white pages required for students to be successful in working the Hands-On Exercises. Page numbers are included for easy reference to help students locate the answers.
  - **Chapter Objectives Review:** Appears toward the end of the chapter and reviews all important concepts throughout the chapter. Newly designed in an easy-to-read bulleted format.

- **Key Terms Matching:** A new exercise that requires students to match key terms to their definitions. This requires students to work actively with this important vocabulary and prove conceptual understanding.

- **Case Study** presents a scenario for the chapter, creating a story that ties the Hands-On Exercises together.

Watch the Video for this Hands-On Exercise!

- **Hands-On Exercise Videos** are tied to each Hands-On Exercise and walk students through the steps of the exercise while weaving in conceptual information related to the Case Study and the objectives as a whole.

- **End-of-Chapter Exercises** offer instructors several options for assessment. Each chapter has approximately 12–15 exercises ranging from multiple choice questions to open-ended projects. Newly included in this is a Key Terms Matching exercise of approximately 20 questions, as well as a Collaboration Case and Soft Skills Case for every chapter.

ANALYSIS CASE
CREATIVE CASE

- **Enhanced Mid-Level Exercises** include a **Creative Case** (for PowerPoint and Word), which allows students some flexibility and creativity, not being bound by a definitive solution, and an **Analysis Case** (for Excel and Access), which requires students to interpret the data they are using to answer an analytic question, as well as **Discover Steps**, which encourage students to use Help or to problem-solve to accomplish a task.

MyITLab® HOE1 Training **MyITLab® Grader**

- **MyITLab** provides an auto-graded homework, tutorial, and assessment solution that is built to match the book content exactly. Every Hands-On Exercise is available as a simulation training. Every Capstone Exercise and most Mid-Level Exercises are available as live-in-the-application Grader projects. Icons are included throughout the text to denote which exercises are included.

Instructor Resources

The Instructor's Resource Center, available at **www.pearsonhighered.com**, includes the following:

- **Instructor Manual** provides an overview of all available resources as well as student data and solution files for every exercise.

- **Solution Files with Scorecards** assist with grading the Hands-On Exercises and end-of-chapter exercises.

- **Prepared Exams** allow instructors to assess all skills covered in a chapter with a single project.

- **Rubrics** for Mid-Level Creative Cases and Beyond the Classroom Cases in Microsoft® Word format enable instructors to customize the assignments for their classes.

- **PowerPoint® Presentations** with notes for each chapter are included for out-of-class study or review.

- **Lesson Plans** provide a detailed blueprint to achieve chapter learning objectives and outcomes.

- **Objectives Lists** map chapter objectives to Hands-On Exercises and end-of-chapter exercises.

- **Multiple Choice and Key Terms Matching Answer Keys**

- **Test Bank** provides objective-based questions for every chapter.

- **Grader Projects** textual versions of auto-graded assignments for Grader.

- **Additional Projects** provide more assignment options for instructors.

- **Syllabus Templates**

- **Scripted Lectures** offer an in-class lecture guide for instructors to mirror the Hands-On Exercises.

- **Assignment Sheet**

- **File Guide**

Student Resources

Companion Web Site

www.pearsonhighered.com/exploring offers expanded IT resources and self-student tools for students to use for each chapter, including:

- Online Chapter Review
- Web Resources
- Glossary
- Student Data Files
- Chapter Objectives Review

In addition, the Companion Web Site is now the site for Premium Media, including the videos for the Exploring Series:

- Hands-On Exercise Videos*
- Audio PPTs*

*Access code required for these premium resources.

Student Reference Cards

A two-sided card for each application provides students with a visual summary of information and tips specific to each application.

Desktop Publishing and Graphic Design

CHAPTER 5

Creating a Newsletter, Working with Graphics, and Linking Objects

OBJECTIVES | AFTER YOU READ THIS CHAPTER, YOU WILL BE ABLE TO:

1. Construct a newsletter p. 2
2. Develop a document design p. 6
3. Insert graphic objects p. 16
4. Manipulate graphic objects p. 22
5. Use OLE to insert an object p. 34
6. Update a linked object p. 37

CASE STUDY | Along The Greenways

Kody Allen is director of The Greenways, a nonprofit organization. The organization was formed to generate interest in outdoor activities, as well as to provide support and funding for additional walking and biking trails in the city and surrounding counties. Maintaining positive public relations is key to generating support for the organization, and providing a quarterly newsletter is one way to do this. Director Allen hired you as the assistant director because you enjoy cycling, have been an outstanding volunteer for this organization, and demonstrate good computer skills.

Director Allen has asked you to create the newsletter in a format that is easy to read but also informative. Director Allen wants to limit the information to only what can be printed on a single page, even though there is much to convey. In addition to mailing the newsletter, it will also be posted on The Greenways' Web site.

Desktop Publishing

Desktop publishing evolved through a combination of technologies, including faster computers, laser and inkjet printers, and sophisticated page composition software that enables users to manipulate text and graphics to produce a professional-looking document. While there are separate applications available for desktop publishing needs, today's generation of word processors have matured to narrow the gap between word processing and desktop publishing. Microsoft Word, for all practical purposes, can offer powerful features that can be used to create all types of documents.

You can enjoy the challenge of creating a document that contains many graphic design techniques. Creating a document can be time consuming and can require an eye for detail, which is why documents such as brochures, newsletters, and flyers are often prepared by skilled professionals. Nevertheless, with a little practice and a basic knowledge of graphic design, you will be able to create effective and attractive documents like the newsletter shown in Figure 5.1.

In this section, you will learn how to develop a simple newsletter that includes a multi-column layout, clip art and other objects, and position those objects within a document.

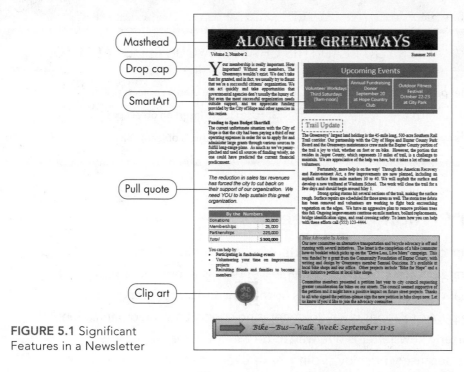

FIGURE 5.1 Significant Features in a Newsletter

Constructing a Newsletter

Microsoft Word can be used to create useful business documents. Documents such as flyers, event calendars, award certificates, and menus are usually one page long, but newsletters or brochures can be one or more pages long. In comparison, a newsletter usually consists of two or three columns, while a brochure is folded into two or three sections. When you use desktop publishing, or Microsoft Word, to create a document, such as a newsletter, there are several techniques to enhance readability and attractiveness. Many features used frequently in word processing are also very effective individually or in combination with one another to emphasize important information within the newsletter. These features include:

- **Images.** A graphic image or photograph can showcase people, events, or topics discussed in a newsletter. They are often reduced in size to take up only a small amount of space. The following are different types of images available in Microsoft Word:
  - **Clip Art.** When used in moderation, clip art will catch the reader's eye and enhance almost any newsletter. It is also used to break up text on a page so that the document does not bore the reader. Images can also help to direct the eye towards the text information. Be careful to have images face toward the text rather than away from the text.

- **WordArt.** WordArt uses some predefined styles to emphasize a major heading that can be placed anywhere in a document.
- **SmartArt.** A SmartArt graphic can be used to represent a process or a hierarchy chart.
- **Shapes.** Microsoft has a set of built-in drawing tools that users can use to create simple shapes and objects to add another visual component to a document.
- **Tables.** Data values can be formally tabulated and presented in a professional-looking table.
- **Charts.** A variety of charts created in a spreadsheet application such as Excel can be inserted into a document to provide a graphical presentation of a data set.
- **Screenshots.** A screenshot is a graphical image captured by the user to show visible displays on the computer screen, such as an output or error message from a software program.
- **Borders.** A line border might surround a paragraph, or a page border might consist of a series of small graphics.
- **Shading.** When used as the background color of an element, such as a text box or as simple vertical and/or horizontal lines, shading is effective for attracting attention. Such techniques are especially useful in the absence of clip art or other graphics and are a favorite of desktop publishers to draw the reader's eye to a location on the document.
- **Lists.** Whether bulleted or numbered, lists help to organize information by emphasizing important topics.
- **Typography.** The arrangement and appearance of information is essential in adding personality to a newsletter. The selection of fonts, font styles, and font sizes that enhance the appearance of a document is a critical, often subtle, element in the success of a document. A good rule of thumb is to stick within one font family for headings, and another complimentary font family for body text that is easy to read. Indeed, good typography goes almost unnoticed, whereas poor typography stands out and detracts the user from a document.
- **Styles.** You can also use predefined styles in desktop publishing to add personality to your newsletter. Remember that a style is a set of formatting options you apply to characters or paragraphs. A style can store formats such as alignment, line spacing, indents, tabs, borders, and shading. You can use the same styles from one edition of your newsletter to the next to ensure consistency. Additionally, the use of styles in any document promotes uniformity and increases flexibility.

No hard and fast rules exist to dictate how many or which features you should include when designing a newsletter. Your objective should be to create a document that is easy to read and visually appealing. You will find that the design that worked so well in one document may not work at all in a different document. An effective presentation is often the result of trial and error, and you should experiment freely to find it.

You can create a newsletter using a newsletter document template or start from scratch. Microsoft provides several templates such as letters, resumes, faxes, newsletters, brochures, labels, cards, and more. To create a newsletter using a template, do the following:

1. Open Word.
2. Type Newsletter in the *Search online templates* search box and press Enter.
3. Scroll down the list of Newsletter templates to locate the design that you like.
4. Click a specific Newsletter selection to view more detailed information about the selection. Click Close to exit the view.
5. Click Create to accept the selected template.

Change Page Setup Options and Column Layout

STEP 1 » The margins of a document can be changed or adjusted from the Margins button in the Page Setup group found on the Page Layout tab. You can create a document with two columns of equal width by clicking the Page Layout tab and clicking Two under Columns in the Page Setup group. Notice that in Figure 5.1, the number of columns varies from one part of the newsletter to another. The masthead is displayed over a single column at the top of the page, whereas the remainder of the newsletter is formatted in two columns of different widths. The number of columns is specified at the section level. When you select one of the column preset designs, Microsoft Word will calculate the width of each column based on the number of columns, the left and right margins on the page, and the specified (default) space between columns. The newsletter shown in Figure 5.1, for example, uses a two-column layout with a wide and narrow column. This design may be preferred over columns of uniform width, as it adds interest to the document. Note, too, that once columns have been defined, text will flow continuously from the bottom of one column to the top of the next. To create columns of different sizes, do the following:

1. Position the insertion point anywhere in the document.
2. Click the PAGE LAYOUT tab.
3. Click Columns in the Page Setup group.
4. Click More Columns to display the dialog box as shown in Figure 5.2.
5. Choose the Left or Right Presets and/or uncheck the option *Equal column width*.
6. Enter the measurement for the column width and column spacing.

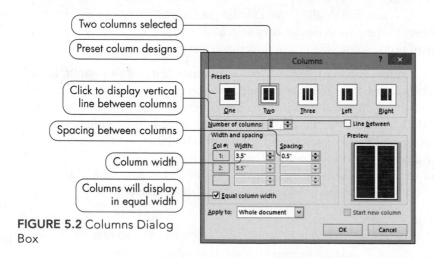

FIGURE 5.2 Columns Dialog Box

Insert Section Break

A section break is required whenever the column specification changes. Also, a section break is required at the end of the last column to balance the text within the columns. Insertion of the continuous section break, as shown in Figure 5.3, enables you to determine where columns start and end on a single page. To insert a continuous section break, do the following:

1. Position the insertion point at the desired location for inserting the section break.
2. Click the PAGE LAYOUT tab.
3. Click Breaks in the Page Setup group, as shown in Figure 5.3.
4. Under *Section Breaks*, click Continuous.

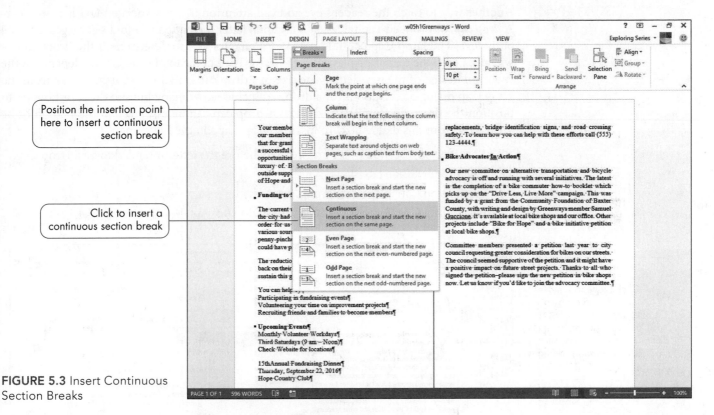

FIGURE 5.3 Insert Continuous Section Breaks

Insert a Column Break

A column break also plays an important role in the development of a newsletter. You use a column break to force paragraph text to start at the top of the next column. This provides control over where the bottom of one column ends before the text wraps to the top of the next column. To insert a column break, do the following:

1. Position the insertion point at the desired location for inserting the column break.
2. Click the PAGE LAYOUT tab.
3. Click Breaks in the Page Setup group.
4. Click Column Page Breaks to force a paragraph to start at the top of the next column.

Create a Masthead and a Reverse

STEP 3》 One technique desktop publishers use to emphasize text is called a *reverse*, and it consists of using light-colored text on a dark-colored background. It is often used in the *masthead*, which is the identifying information at the top of the newsletter or other periodical.

It provides a distinctive look to the publication and often has the characteristics of a banner. The volume number of the newsletter and the date of publication also appear in the masthead in smaller letters. To create a masthead, do the following:

1. Position the pointer at the top of the page to insert a masthead.
2. Use WordArt to create a large text graphic across the top of the document.
3. Insert a one row by two column table under the masthead for information regarding the publication number and date.

Create a Drop Cap

STEP 4 ≫ Another way to catch the reader's eye and call attention to the associated text is a drop cap. A *drop cap*, or dropped-capital letter, is a capital letter formatted in a font size larger than the body text. The Drop Cap command in Word enables you to determine if the dropped cap will align with the text or display in the margin. The choice made will largely depend on the style and design of the newsletter. The size of a drop cap initial is also determined from the Drop Cap dialog box. Options for a drop cap include how many lines to drop, or how far to position the drop cap from the body text. A drop cap can be displayed in the margin or be turned off from this dialog box. To insert a Drop Cap, do the following:

1. Position the insertion point immediately before the letter intended to be a Drop Cap.
2. Click the INSERT tab.
3. Click Drop Cap in the Text group.
4. Click Drop Cap Options to display the dialog box, as shown in Figure 5.4.

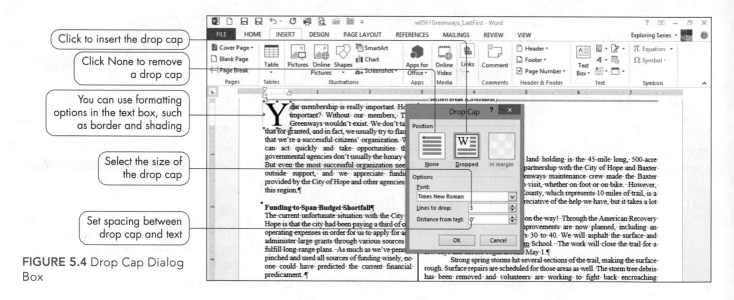

FIGURE 5.4 Drop Cap Dialog Box

Developing a Document Design

The most difficult aspect of creating a newsletter is to develop the design in the first place; the mere availability of a desktop publishing program does not guarantee an effective document any more than a word processor will turn its author into another Shakespeare. Other skills are necessary, and the following text provides a brief introduction to graphic design.

Much of the document layout is subjective, and what works in one situation will not necessarily work in another. Let your eye be the judge and follow your instincts. It also helps to seek inspiration from others by collecting samples of documents that succeed in capturing attention, and then using those document principles as the basic starting point for a design.

The design of a document is developed on a *grid*, an underlying, but invisible, set of horizontal and vertical lines that determine the placement of major elements. A grid establishes the overall structure of a document by indicating the number of columns; the space between columns; the size of the margins; and the placement of headlines, art, and so on. The grid does not appear in the printed document—draw or sketch it out on a piece of paper to solidify the layout prior to creating the newsletter in Word. Figures 5.5 through 5.7 show a document that was developed using different grid designs; the grid design displays on the right side of each completed newsletter document.

A grid may be simple or complex, but it is always distinguished by the number of columns it contains. The three-column grid of Figure 5.5 is one of the most common and utilitarian designs. Figure 5.6 shows an unequal two-column design for the same document. Figure 5.7 illustrates a three-column grid with unequal column widths to provide interest. Many other designs are possible as well. Use a one-column grid for term papers and letters. A two-column, wide-and-narrow format is appropriate for some textbooks and manuals. Two- and three-column formats are often used for newsletters and magazines.

The simple concept of a grid makes the underlying design of any document obvious, and it also helps to determine the page composition. Moreover, the conscious use of a grid will help organize the material and will result in a more polished and professional-looking publication. It will also help to achieve consistency from page to page within a document (or from issue to issue of a newsletter).

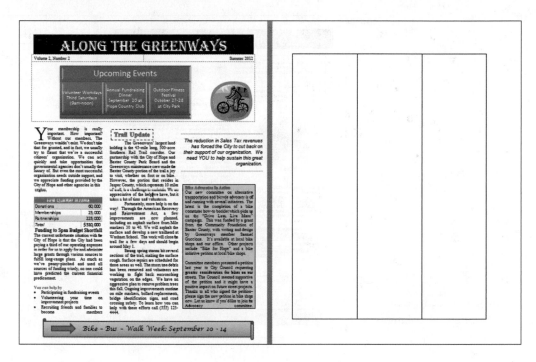

FIGURE 5.5 Three-Column Grid

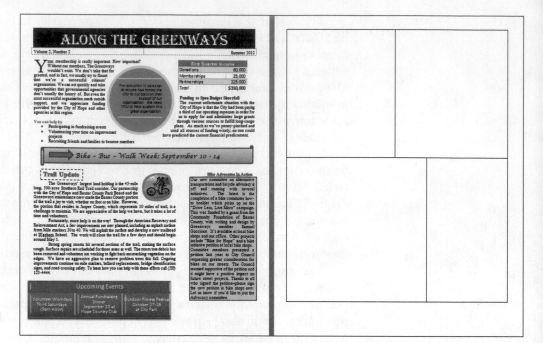

FIGURE 5.6 Two-Column Grid with Unequal Column Widths

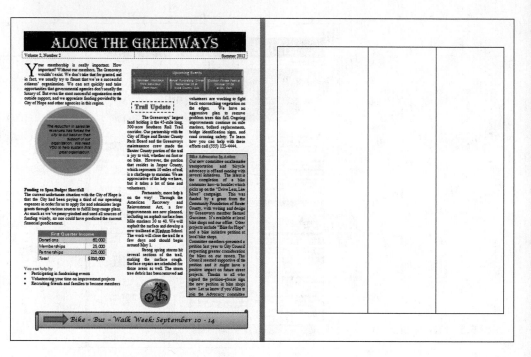

FIGURE 5.7 Three-Column Grid with Unequal Column Widths

Apply Borders and Shading

STEP 5 >> Good design makes it easy for the reader to determine what is important. As indicated earlier, emphasis can be achieved in several ways, the easiest being variations in type size and/or type style. Headings should be set in type sizes at least two points larger than body copy. The use of bold and italic formatting is effective, but both should be done in moderation. UPPERCASE LETTERS and <u>underlining</u> are alternative techniques but are less effective. Uppercase letters are often associated with screaming because that is how you portray a raised voice in e-mail. Uppercase can also be harder to read because of the close spacing. Underlining is often associated with hyperlinks on a Web page, so it should be used on a limited basis, unless you are actually displaying a Web link.

Boxes and/or shading call attention to selected articles. Horizontal lines are effective to separate one topic from another or to call attention to a pull quote. Also recall that a reverse—light text on a dark background—can be striking for a small amount of text. Clip art, used in moderation, will catch the reader's eye and enhance almost any newsletter. Color is also effective, but it is more costly, so the budget allocated may be a factor to consider in designing a document.

All of the techniques and definitions discussed can be implemented with commands you already know, as you will see in Hands-On Exercise 1.

Quick Concepts

1. Describe some of the techniques that can be used to enhance readability and attractiveness of a newsletter. *p. 2*

2. What is the purpose of creating a masthead and a reverse? *p. 5*

3. What is the difference between a continuous section break and a column break? *p. 5*

1 Desktop Publishing

Kody Allen, the director of The Greenways, forwarded you a document with short articles that he would like to include in the newsletter you are preparing. You must design a layout that will display the information in an easy-to-read and visually appealing manner. You will also consider how to display the masthead and other visual elements, then take steps to set up the document and add each feature.

Skills covered: Change Page Setup Options and Column Layout • Modify Column Layout • Create a Masthead and a Reverse • Create a Drop Cap • Apply Borders and Shading and Insert Clip Art

---

STEP 1 >> CHANGE PAGE SETUP OPTIONS AND COLUMN LAYOUT

After opening the file that Director Allen provides, consider the margins needed to display all the information and make appropriate changes to the document. You decide that the newsletter will display in two columns. Refer to Figure 5.8 as you complete Step 1.

FIGURE 5.8 Document Displaying Text in Two Columns

a. Start Word. Open *w05h1Greenways* and save it as **w05h1Greenways_LastFirst**. When you save your files, use your last and first names. For example, as the Word author, I would name my document *w05h1Greenways_LauLinda*.

> **TROUBLESHOOTING:** If you make any major mistakes in this exercise, you can close the file, open *w05h1Greenways* again, and then start this exercise over.

b. Click the **PAGE LAYOUT tab**, click **Margins** in the Page Setup group, and then click **Narrow**.

Because the newsletter contains many items, smaller margins are needed to allow for more working space within the document.

c. Click **Columns** in the Page Setup group and click **Two**.

The text of the newsletter displays in two columns. The column width for each column and the spacing between columns is determined automatically from the existing margins.

d. Click the **Zoom slider**, decrease the zoom to **50%**, and then view the whole page.

You can see both columns.

e. Save the document.

STEP 2 ›› MODIFY COLUMN LAYOUT

In considering the best way to display the articles and information in the newsletter, you decide it would look better if you use unequal column widths for the two columns. You display the Columns dialog box so you can change the preset, set the width to your specifications, and then add a line to separate the columns. Refer to Figure 5.9 as you complete Step 2.

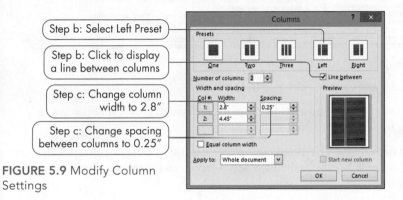

FIGURE 5.9 Modify Column Settings

a. Click the **Zoom slider** and increase the zoom to **80%**. Click the **PAGE LAYOUT tab**, click **Columns** in the Page Setup group, and then click **More Columns** to display the Columns dialog box.

b. Click **Left** under the *Presets* section and click the **Line between check box** to display a line between the columns.

c. Press **Tab** to select the Width list for the first column and type **2.8**. Press **Tab** and type **0.25** in the **Spacing list** for the first column. Uncheck *Equal column width*. Press **Tab** and notice that the width of the second column automatically changes to *4.45*. Click **OK**.

The columns are no longer the same width, and the vertical line displays as a separator.

d. Press **Ctrl+End** to move the insertion point to the end of the document. Click **Breaks** in the Page Setup group. Click **Continuous** under *Section Breaks*.

It is important to move the insertion point to the end of the document so that the continuous section break is inserted at the end of document. The columns are now balanced.

e. Save the document.

STEP 3 ›› CREATE A MASTHEAD AND A REVERSE

The main title of your newsletter is important to design because it is most likely the first element the reader will view. You decide to insert a masthead and use a reverse technique so that it is very distinctive. To make it display properly as one column, you will first need to add a continuous section break at the top of the page. Refer to Figure 5.10 as you complete Step 3.

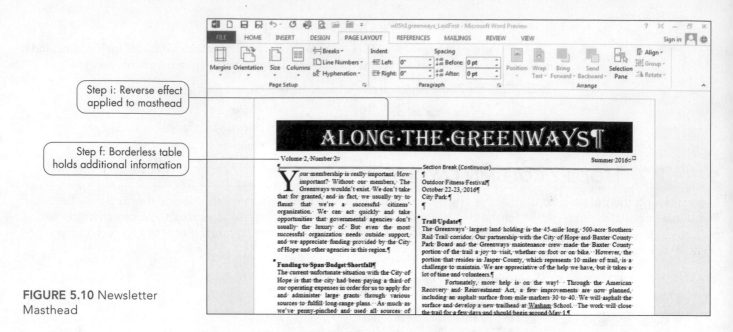

Step i: Reverse effect applied to masthead

Step f: Borderless table holds additional information

FIGURE 5.10 Newsletter Masthead

a. Click the **Zoom slider** and increase the zoom to **110%**.

b. Click the **HOME tab** and click **Show/Hide (¶)** in the Paragraph group, if necessary, to display formatting marks in the document.

c. Press **Ctrl+Home** to move the insertion point to the beginning of the document. Click the **PAGE LAYOUT tab**, click **Breaks** in the Page Setup group, and then click **Continuous** under *Section Breaks*.

You should see a double dotted line, indicating a section break occurs at the top of the left column in the document. Adding this continuous section break enables you to format the area of the document that precedes the section break differently than the section that follows it.

d. Click **Ctrl+Home** to move the insertion point to the top of the page, click **Columns**, and then click **One**.

The section break extends across the top of the document, creating one column at the top of the page. Information you type there will not be split into two columns like the text in the section below the break.

e. Type **Along The Greenways** and press **Enter** twice. Select the text you just typed, click the **HOME tab**, and then click **Center** in the Paragraph group. Click the **Font arrow** on the Mini toolbar, click **Algerian**, click the **Font Size arrow**, and then click **36**.

This large heading is the masthead for the newsletter.

f. Click the left side of the section break, just below the masthead, to move the insertion point. Click the **INSERT tab**, click **Table**, and then drag the pointer over the cells to select two columns and one row (2 × 1 table). Click to insert the table.

A table displays below the masthead and above the section break.

g. Make the following changes in the table:

- Click in the left cell of the table, if necessary, and type **Volume 2, Number 2**.
- Click in the right cell (or press **Tab**) and type **Summer 2016**.
- Press **Ctrl+R** to right align text in the cell on the right.
- Select the entire row, click the **PAGE LAYOUT tab**, and then click the **Spacing Before arrow** until **6 pt** displays.

h. Press **Ctrl+Home** to move the insertion point to the beginning of the masthead. Click the **HOME tab**, click the **Borders arrow** in the Paragraph group, and then click **Borders and Shading**.

The Borders and Shading dialog box displays. The Borders tab is active.

i. Click the **Shading tab**, click the **Style arrow**, click **Solid (100%)**, and then click **OK**. Click in the table to deselect the masthead.

The masthead displays white text on a black background.

j. Click the **Table Move handle** to select the entire table. Click the **Borders and Shading arrow** in the Paragraph group and click **No Border**.

k. Click outside the table and view the masthead.

l. Save the document.

STEP 4 ›› CREATE A DROP CAP

You decide to pull the reader into the articles in your newsletter by adding features such as a drop cap, which is often applied to the very first paragraph of a document. Refer to Figure 5.11 as you complete Step 4.

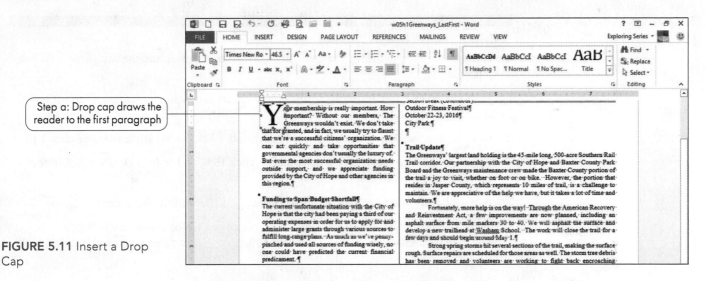

Step a: Drop cap draws the reader to the first paragraph

FIGURE 5.11 Insert a Drop Cap

a. Click to move the insertion point to the left of the first letter for the paragraph at the top left of the page, which reads *Your membership is really important*. Click the **INSERT tab**, click **Drop Cap** in the Text group, and then click **Dropped**.

b. Click anywhere outside the Drop Cap frame.

c. Select the first sentence of the fourth paragraph in the left column, *You can help by*. Click the **HOME tab**, click the **Font Color arrow** in the Font group, and then click **Orange, Accent 6, Darker 50%** (sixth row, tenth column).

d. Select the three paragraph items below the *You can help by* heading and click **Bullets** in the Paragraph group. Click **Decrease Indent** in the Paragraph group to align the bullets with the left edge of the heading.

e. Save the document.

STEP 5 ≫ APPLY BORDERS AND SHADING AND INSERT CLIP ART

Because some of the paragraphs look very similar, you decide to add distinction by using shading and placing a border around one of the paragraphs. You also add clip art to add variety and a little interest to the page. Refer to Figure 5.12 as you complete Step 5.

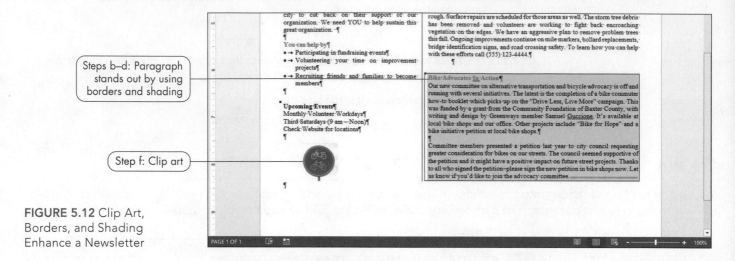

Steps b–d: Paragraph stands out by using borders and shading

Step f: Clip art

FIGURE 5.12 Clip Art, Borders, and Shading Enhance a Newsletter

a. Select the heading in the right column, *Bike Advocates In Action*, and the two paragraphs that follow it.

b. Click the **HOME tab**, if necessary, click the **Borders arrow** in the Paragraph group, and then click **Borders and Shading**.

c. Click **Box** in the *Setting* section of the Borders tab. Click the **Width arrow** and click **1 pt**.

d. Click the **Shading tab**, click the **Style arrow**, click **15%**, and then click **OK**. Click in the article above to deselect the paragraph.

   A black border and gray shading display around and behind the paragraph.

e. Select the heading *Bike Advocates In Action*, click **Font Color arrow** in the Font group, and then click **Dark Blue, Text 2, Lighter 40%** (fourth row, fourth column). Click in the paragraph below to deselect the heading.

f. Insert clip art by completing the following steps:

   • Position the insertion point at the bottom of the left column. Click the **INSERT tab**, click **Online Pictures** in the Illustrations group, and then type **bicycle** in the Office.com **Clip Art Search box**. Click the **Search icon** or press **Enter**.

   • Click the clip art object of the bicycle sign to select this image. Click **Insert** to insert the image into the document. If you do not find the same clip art displayed in Figure 5.12, substitute another appropriate image of your choice.

   When the image is selected, a Layout Options icon appears next to the image. Click the icon to display the Layout Options dialog box.

   • Click **Top and Bottom** (second row, first column) in the Layout Options dialog box.
   • Click **See more** to display the Layout dialog box. Click the **Size tab**. Click the **Absolute arrow** in the *Height* section until **0.8** displays.
   • Click **OK**.

   To deselect the Layout Options dialog box, click **Close** or place the cursor anywhere outside of the dialog box.

   • Drag the clip art to the bottom of the left column and center it under the paragraph text in that column.

- Select the clip art and click the **Layout Options** icon at the top-right corner of the clip art. Click **Fix position on page**.

TROUBLESHOOTING: Use arrow keys to nudge the clip art, if needed, for more exact positioning.

---

g. Click the **HOME tab** and click **Show/Hide** (¶) in the Paragraph group to turn off the formatting marks. Drag the **Zoom Slider** to **50%**.

In viewing the whole document, notice how the changes already improve the look of the newsletter. More enhancements will be added in Hands-On Exercise 2.

h. Save the document. Keep it open if you plan to continue with Hands-On Exercise 2. If not, close the document and exit Word.

Decorative Text and Drawing Tools

Desktop publishing documents, and newsletters in particular, are more appealing to the reader when they display an appropriate level of variety of text and graphic objects. Word provides many graphic and drawing tools that enable you to enhance these documents. You can create text boxes containing text and format them to grab readers' attention, you can create professional-looking diagrams, and you can use predefined shapes or create your own. For each graphic object, you can choose from dozens of options, which you can customize and manipulate to create the effect you want. One thing you should keep in mind when adding graphics to your document—some objects may display better on the computer screen than in print, so view images with a critical eye before you finalize your document.

In this section, you will learn how to insert a variety of graphic objects found on the Insert tab and learn how to use tools to make adjustments such as changing colors, layering, and rotation.

Inserting Graphic Objects

Graphical elements—such as lines, arrows, diagrams, and text boxes—help enhance your documents by adding visual interest. Microsoft Word provides a variety of graphic objects you can use individually or combine to produce a one-of-a-kind drawing. For example, you can insert a shape, which is a geometric or non-geometric object, to represent balloons on strings and format these objects by applying different fill colors. You can position, size, and overlap shapes to achieve the visual effect you desire.

Insert SmartArt

STEP 1 › Using shapes and text allows you to draw attention to your document; however, it is very time consuming to use these tools to create a complex and designer-quality illustration. Word includes **SmartArt**, which is a visual representation of information that can be created to effectively communicate a message or idea in one of many existing and visually appealing layouts. For example, you might insert a SmartArt diagram of an organizational chart, a list, or a process into your document to illustrate an important concept that is difficult to explain with simple text but easier to understand when viewed as an illustration. When you insert a SmartArt diagram in your document, you can select from several existing layouts, and SmartArt will conform to any theme you select for your document (see Figure 5.13). To insert SmartArt into your document, do the following:

1. Position the insertion point at the location where you want to insert the SmartArt.
2. Click the INSERT tab.
3. Click SmartArt in the Illustrations group to display the *Choose a SmartArt Graphic* dialog box as shown in Figure 5.14.
4. Click one of the diagram displays in the gallery. A short description displays in the right gallery pane when you click a diagram choice, as shown in Figure 5.14. After you select the type and subtype of the diagram, click OK.

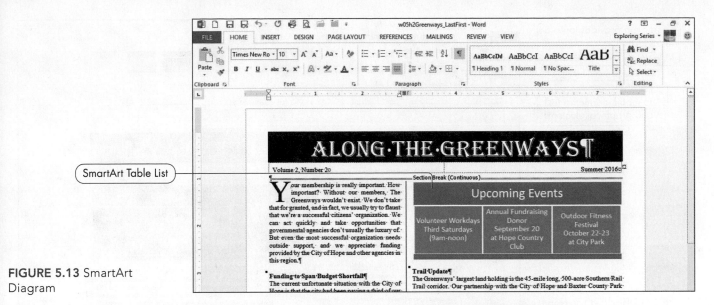

FIGURE 5.13 SmartArt Diagram

SmartArt Table List

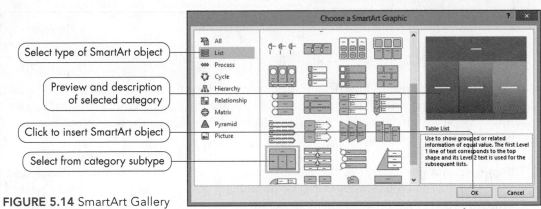

Select type of SmartArt object

Preview and description of selected category

Click to insert SmartArt object

Select from category subtype

FIGURE 5.14 SmartArt Gallery

When a SmartArt diagram is inserted into your document, text placeholders display. You can click a placeholder and type text directly into the desired location in the diagram. Alternatively, you can click the arrow in the middle-left side of the diagram frame to view the Text pane if it is not already visible. The *Text pane* displays an outline view for typing the text items and enables you to type or to insert additional text into the SmartArt. The Design and Format tabs also display on the Ribbon when you select a SmartArt object. The Design tab also provides a toggle button for the Text pane, along with other tools to change the appearance of the diagram, such as adding shapes and changing the style, as shown in Figure 5.15. The Format tab provides tools to modify the appearance of the diagram text.

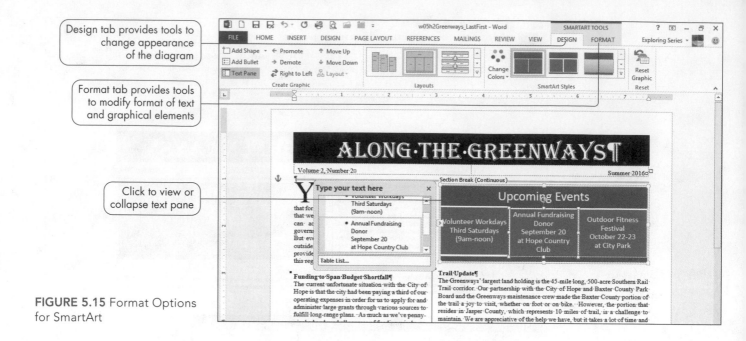

Design tab provides tools to change appearance of the diagram

Format tab provides tools to modify format of text and graphical elements

Click to view or collapse text pane

FIGURE 5.15 Format Options for SmartArt

Insert WordArt

STEP 2 ▸▸

WordArt is a Microsoft Office feature that creates decorative text that can be used to add interest to the text you use in a document. The advantage of using WordArt is that you can rotate text in any direction, add three-dimensional effects, display the text vertically, slant it, arch it, or even display it upside down.

WordArt is intuitively easy to use. You choose a style from the gallery (see Figure 5.16), then enter the specific text in the WordArt text box, after which the results display (see Figure 5.17). The WordArt object can be moved and sized, just like any graphic object. A WordArt Format tab provides many formatting features that enable you to change alignment, add special effects, and change styles quickly. It is fun and easy to create some truly unique documents.

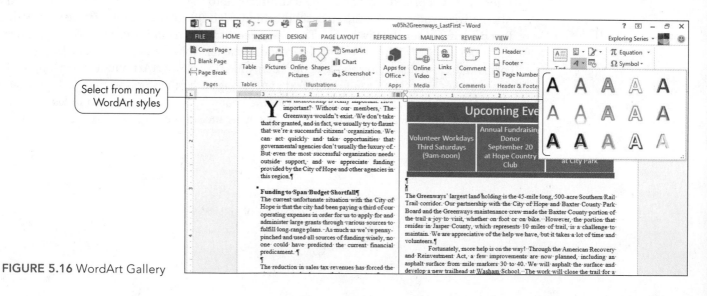

Select from many WordArt styles

FIGURE 5.16 WordArt Gallery

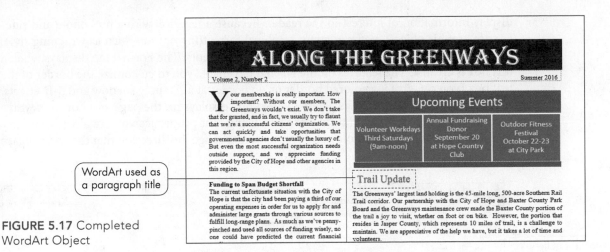

WordArt used as a paragraph title

FIGURE 5.17 Completed WordArt Object

Insert a Text Box

One way to combine the flexibility of a shape object with simple text is to create a text box. A *text box* is simply a graphic object that contains text. Magazine and newspaper articles often use text boxes to help control the placement of text as well as provide a visual tool to entice readers to focus on the contents of the text box. Text boxes can also be layered with other shapes or objects. For example, you can position a text box on a callout shape object and use it as a dialog bubble for a comic strip or clip art, as shown in Figure 5.18.

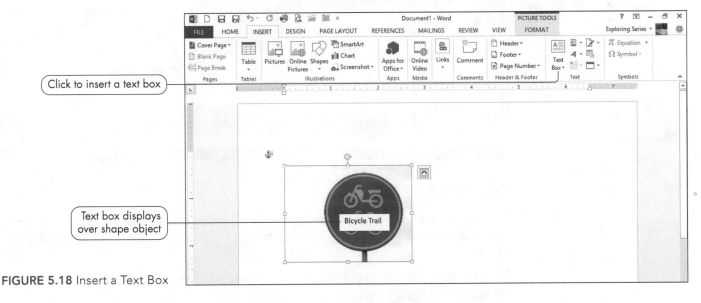

Click to insert a text box

Text box displays over shape object

FIGURE 5.18 Insert a Text Box

To insert a text box, click the Insert tab and click Text Box. A gallery of preformatted text boxes displays, or you can click Draw Text Box to create a custom text box. Several designs in the gallery are suitable for a sidebar or pull quote in a document, as shown in Figure 5.19, but you can also create your own. A *pull quote* is a phrase or sentence taken from an article to emphasize a key point. It is typically set in larger type, often in a different font or in italics, and may be offset with borders at the top, bottom, or on the sides. *Sidebars* also enable you to call attention to information in a document by displaying it in a space along the side of the featured information. Sidebars might display supplementary information, or they can simply display information of interest to the reader. Because a text box with a pull quote and sidebar are graphic objects, you can apply graphical formatting options such as wrapping style, horizontal alignment, outside borders, and font treatments. The Format tab displays when a text box is created. The features on the Format tab enable you to customize the border of the text box (you can give it a colored border or no border at all), apply shadow and 3-D effects, and position attributes, such as where the text box displays on the page and how text wraps around the text box. You can format the text using font properties you are already familiar with, such as size, type, and color, and you also can change the direction that the text displays within the text box.

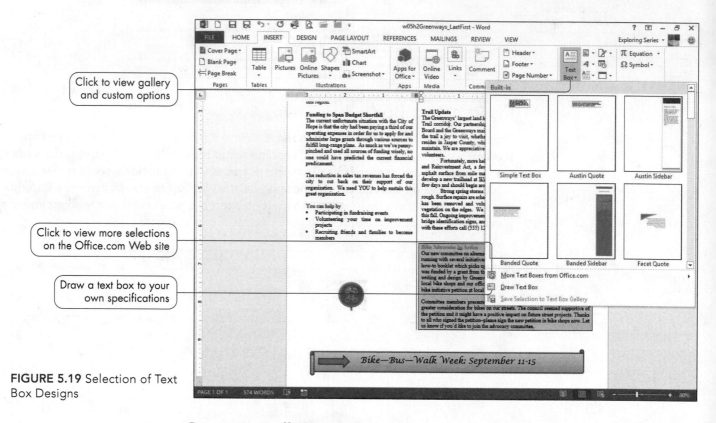

FIGURE 5.19 Selection of Text Box Designs

Create a Pull Quote

STEP 3 » Pull quotes are frequently displayed in professional publications, such as company's monthly newsletters and annual reports, to draw attention to important topics. To create a pull quote, do the following:

1. Position the insertion point at the space where you want to insert the pull quote.
2. Click the INSERT tab and click Text Box in the Text group.
3. Click any of the text boxes given in the Built-in gallery options, as shown in Figure 5.19.
4. Type or copy and paste the desired text quote into the placeholder in the selected text box.
5. Move and position the pull quote text box in the exact location in the document.

Link Two Text Boxes

One text box can be linked to another text box so that when text runs out of space in one box it automatically flows into another box, as shown in Figure 5.20. The best use for linking text boxes is creating a booklet. Each page contains two text boxes that include the booklet text. Because booklets print on both sides of the paper, the text boxes link in such a way so that the text flows from the back of one page to the front of another. When you view the pages in Word, they appear out of order, but when assembled for the booklet, they display correctly.

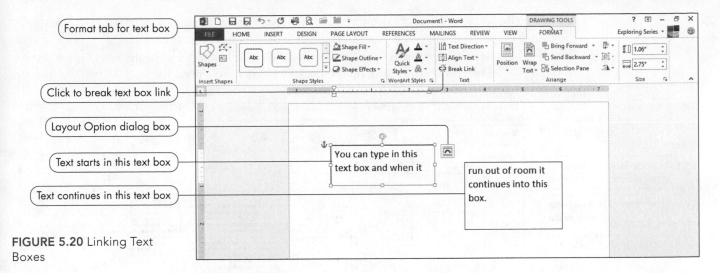

Format tab for text box

Click to break text box link

Layout Option dialog box

Text starts in this text box

Text continues in this text box

You can type in this text box and when it

run out of room it continues into this box.

FIGURE 5.20 Linking Text Boxes

Insert Drawing Shapes

STEP 4 ▶▶ One tool that is especially useful is the Shapes tool located on the Insert tab in the Illustrations group. A shape is an object, such as a circle or an arrow, which you can use as a visual enhancement. Use one shape or combine multiple shapes to create a more complex image. When you click Shapes, the Shapes gallery displays the following categories of shapes:

- Lines
- Rectangles
- Basic Shapes
- Block Arrows
- Equation Shapes
- Flowchart
- Stars and Banners
- Callouts

To insert a shape, do the following:

1. Click the INSERT tab.
2. Click Shapes in the Illustrations group to show the shapes gallery options available.
3. Select the desired shape from the gallery.
4. The pointer changes to a cross-hair, which enables you to define the beginning and ending points of the shape. Click the location where you want to insert the shape and drag the pointer to create the default size for the shape or click and drag to control the desired shape size.

If you need to insert several instances of the same shape, do the following:

1. Click the INSERT tab.
2. Click Shapes in the Illustrations group to choose the desired shape from the gallery options.
3. Right-click the shape object in the gallery.
4. Click Lock Drawing Mode as shown in Figure 5.21.
5. The pointer changes to a cross-hair; position the cross-hair pointer at the desired location in the document for the shape.

6. Click to create the default size for the shape or click and drag to control the cross-desired shape size.

7. Repeat Steps 5 and 6 for as many desired instances of the same shape and press Esc when finished. To turn off the Lock Drawing Mode, press Esc.

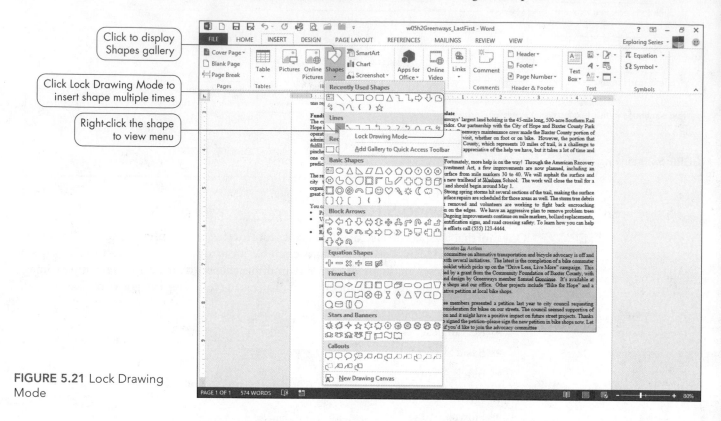

FIGURE 5.21 Lock Drawing Mode

Manipulating Graphic Objects

After you insert a shape, SmartArt, or text box, you can enhance its appearance by using one of the commands available on the Format tab for the object. Shapes display initially with a simple blue border and blue fill. But to capture the attention of the reader, you might want to change the border style, color, or fill effects.

Change Shape Fills and Borders

STEP 2 » Shapes and text boxes have two main components that color can be applied to: the line or border of the object, and the *fill* or interior space of the object. Word provides the Quick Style gallery, which contains a selected list of styles that are predefined using a combination of colors, lines and other effects. On the other hand, you can also apply your personal preferences for the line using the Shape Outline option or adjust the fill colors using the Shape Fill option. Figure 5.22 shows the Shape Fill options you access from the Drawing Tools Format tab and gives examples of several fill and border options. Shapes such as a straight line obviously do not contain an interior area for applying a fill color, but you can change the color, width, and style of the line itself. You can also enhance the shape by adding visual effects such as shadow, reflection, glow, soft edges, bevel, and 3-D rotation listed under the Shape Effects option.

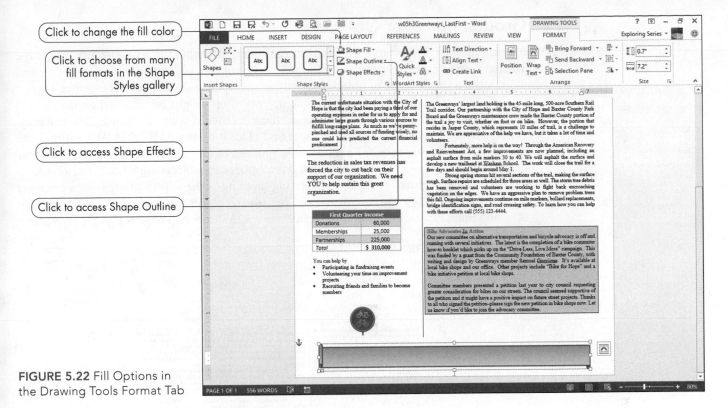

Click to change the fill color

Click to choose from many fill formats in the Shape Styles gallery

Click to access Shape Effects

Click to access Shape Outline

FIGURE 5.22 Fill Options in the Drawing Tools Format Tab

Resize an Object

Any object can be resized—such as a text box, WordArt, image, or shape—manually or precisely using the size group options. In addition, an object can be resized by cropping it. However, the primary purpose of cropping an object is usually to remove unwanted horizontal or vertical edges of the object. Cropping can also be used to hide or remove a part of the object that you do not want to display. Click the Crop tool in the Size group or the dialog box launcher to fine tune the cropping. You can also crop to a shape, use aspect ratio, and *Fill and Fit*. To resize an object manually, click the object to select it and increase or decrease the size by dragging the sizing handle. When you drag away from the object, you will increase the size of the object. Dragging towards the center of the object will decrease the object size. To resize the object precisely to a certain height and width, do the following:

1. Click the object to select it.
2. Click the FORMAT tab.
3. Click the Height and Width options in the Size group to adjust the height and width of the object to a specific measurement.

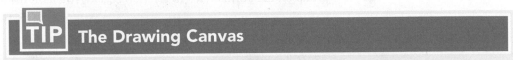

TIP The Drawing Canvas

When combining multiple shapes in one area, you should consider using the Drawing Canvas. The **Drawing Canvas** is a frame-like boundary object in the document to help you arrange parts of a drawing and to keep the parts together. The Drawing Canvas frame has no border or background fill color, but formatting can be applied to the drawing canvas as you would any object. To use the drawing canvas, click the Insert tab, click Shapes, and then click New Drawing Canvas. With the drawing canvas actively selected, insert shapes onto the canvas from the Insert Shapes group on the Drawing Tools Format tab. To delete the drawing canvas, click the frame border to select it and press Delete. The canvas and any shapes it contains are removed.

Group and Layer Objects

STEP 5 » It is fun to work with shapes because you can manipulate them in so many different ways. You have already seen how to change the appearance of a shape. Not only can you format and manipulate a single shape or object, but you can manipulate several objects together.

When you work with several graphic objects, there might be times when the objects need to be arranged so that a part of one overlaps another. It is similar to working on a project on a desk: You pick up a piece of paper and place it on top of another. At any time, you can rearrange the order of the papers, write on one, or add to the stack of papers on your desk. This process is appropriately called *layering* because objects are stacked one on top of another. Another purpose for understanding layering is the ability to separate a complex grouping of objects so you can format and revise each object (or layer) individually without affecting the surrounding graphic objects. Figure 5.23 shows two objects that are layered.

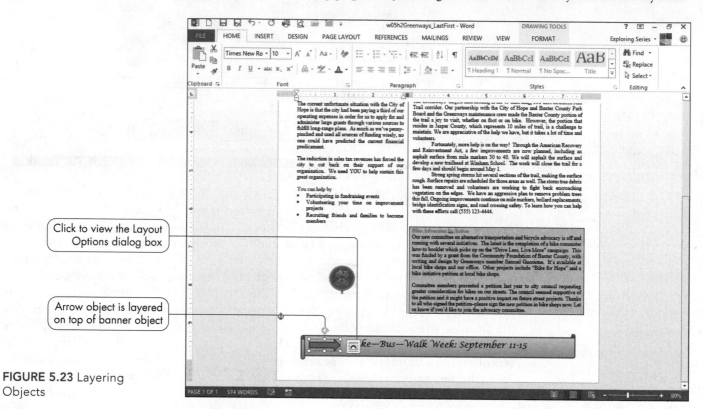

FIGURE 5.23 Layering Objects

When working with layered shapes in Microsoft Word, you can bring a shape to the front by one layer, push a shape back by one layer, move a shape to the front of all layers, or push a shape to the back of all layers. The commands in Table 5.1 are found in the Arrange group on the Format tab. To layer objects together, do the following:

1. Click the first object that you want to layer.
2. Click the FORMAT tab.
3. Click Bring Forward in the Arrange group to place the first object on top of the second object.

TABLE 5.1 Layering Options	
Bring to Front	Moves an object to the top of all other objects
Bring Forward	Moves an object on top of the object directly in front of it
Bring in Front of Text	Moves the object to display in front of text
Send to Back	Moves an object to the back of all other objects
Send Backward	Moves an object below the object directly in back of it
Send Behind Text	Moves the object to display behind text

After you layer objects, it might be useful to group them so they can be moved, resized, and adjusted together as one object. *Grouping* is the process of combining selected objects so that they appear as a single object. When objects are grouped, you can move them together or apply a style to all the grouped objects at one time. To select multiple objects for grouping, do one of the following:

1. Click one object, press and hold Shift, and then click the remaining objects.
2. After all the desired objects are selected, click Group on the FORMAT tab, as shown in Figure 5.24.

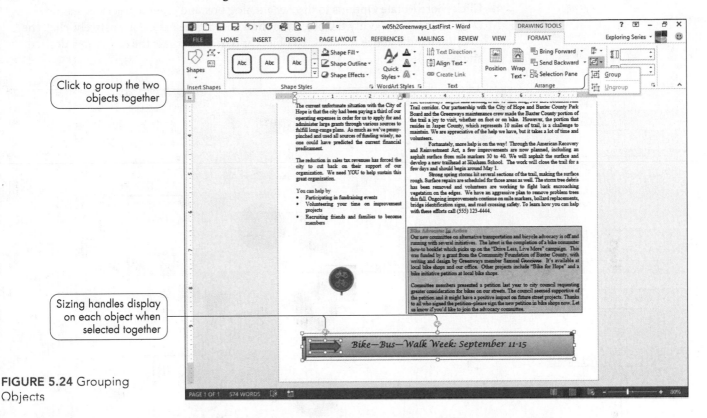

FIGURE 5.24 Grouping Objects

You can separate grouped objects by ungrouping them. *Ungrouping* breaks a grouped object into separate individual objects. You might ungroup objects because you need to make modifications to one individual part of the group rather than to the entire group, such as sizing or repositioning an individual object in the group. Ungrouping also makes it possible to delete an object or add another object to the group. To ungroup an object, click the grouped object to select it. On the Format tab, click Group Objects and click Ungroup in the Arrange group.

TIP **Text Wrapping**

If you encounter difficulties when working with graphic objects, you might need to change the text wrapping option applied to the object. The Wrap Text button can be found in the Arrange group on the Format tab. The Square or Tight text wrapping options are commonly applied settings. Or click Wrap Text and choose More Layout Options to view additional settings available in the Layout dialog box. The *Lock anchor* setting on the Position tab in the Layout dialog box is useful when you want to assign an absolute position to a graphic. In addition, Word 2013 has a new feature called Layout Options. This is an icon located at the top-right corner of the image, and it has an option for you to fix the image's position on the page.

Flip and Rotate Objects

The angle of an object can also be adjusted in several different directions by flipping or rotating the object at various angles. To flip and rotate an object, do the following:

1. Click the object to select it.
2. Click the FORMAT tab.
3. Click Rotate Objects in the Arrange group and select from several commands to rotate the object in a particular direction, or to flip horizontally or vertically.
4. Click More Rotate Options to display a dialog box and enter a precise Rotation measurement to modify the object, as shown in Figure 5.25. Alternatively, click the rotation handle above the selected object and drag to rotate the object to a desired angle.

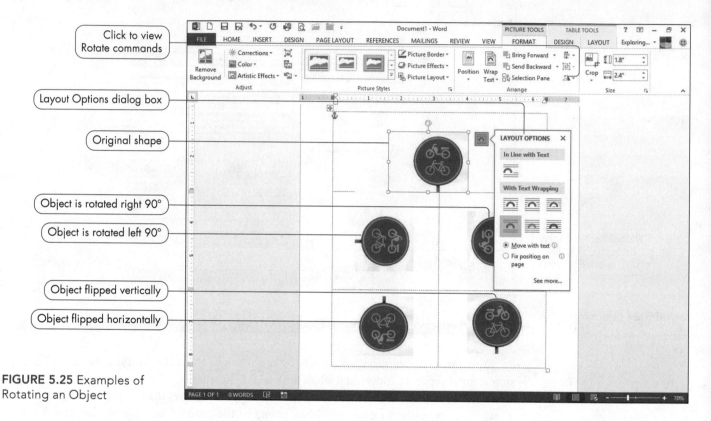

FIGURE 5.25 Examples of Rotating an Object

Quick Concepts ✓

1. Describe the purpose of using some of the graphic objects found on the Insert tab. **p. 16**
2. What is the purpose of creating a pull quote? **p. 19**
3. How can you enhance the appearance of a graphic object? **p. 22**

Hands-On Exercise

Watch the Video
for this Hands-
On Exercise!

MyITLab®
HOE2 Training

2 Decorative Text and Drawing Tools

The Greenways newsletter is coming together nicely. You decide to use graphical features in Microsoft Word to display information about upcoming events. You also decide to display article titles using a combination of graphics and text rather than simply changing the size and color of fonts.

Skills covered: Insert SmartArt • Insert WordArt • Create a Pull Quote • Insert Drawing Shapes and Apply Formatting • Group and Layer Objects

STEP 1 >> INSERT SMARTART

Members of The Greenways should be made aware of several upcoming events. You want to be sure these events stand out in the newsletter, so you decide to use SmartArt to display them. This will give this particular news item a unique look and will fit in the wider right column. Refer to Figure 5.26 as you complete Step 1.

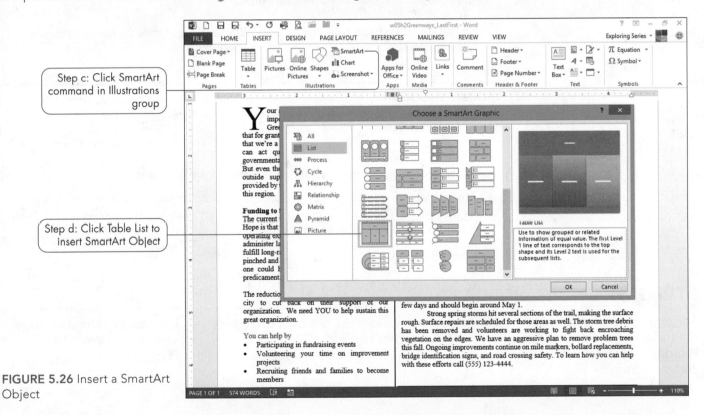

Step c: Click SmartArt command in Illustrations group

Step d: Click Table List to insert SmartArt Object

FIGURE 5.26 Insert a SmartArt Object

a. If necessary, open *w05h1Greenways_LastFirst* and save it as **w05h2Greenways_LastFirst**, changing *h1* to *h2*.

b. Drag the **Zoom slider** to increase the zoom to **80%**. Delete the heading *Upcoming Events* and the event information that follows, up to the blank line above the *Trail Update* heading. Click to position the insertion point on the blank line above the *Trail Update* heading.

> **TROUBLESHOOTING:** If there is no blank line above the *Trail Update* heading, position the insertion point on the left side of *Trail Update* and press **Enter**.

c. Click the **INSERT tab** and click **SmartArt** in the Illustrations group.

The *Choose a SmartArt Graphic* dialog box displays with a list of categories on the left pane of the box.

d. Click **List** on the left pane, scroll down to view the additional designs in the middle pane, and then click **Table List** (eighth row, first column, under *List category*). Click **OK** to close the dialog box.

A representation of the table list displays in your document.

e. Point to the bottom-right corner of the SmartArt shape until the two-headed arrow displays, drag to the right margin, and then release the mouse.

This increases the size of the SmartArt object to create additional space for the information you type next.

f. Click the **Text pane arrow** to expand the Text pane, if necessary, and type **Upcoming Events** in the top bullet.

This places text in the panel that displays at the top of the SmartArt object.

g. Populate the remaining text panels by completing the following steps:

- Click one time in the first sub-bullet, type **Volunteer Workdays**, press **Shift+Enter** to move the insertion point to the next line without a bullet, type **Third Saturdays**, press **Shift+Enter**, and then type **(9am–noon)**.
- Type the following text in the two remaining panels, pressing **Shift+Enter** as needed to move to a new line as shown for each panel.

Annual Fundraising Dinner September 20 at Hope Country Club

Outdoor Fitness Festival October 22–23 at City Park

> **TROUBLESHOOTING:** If you have trouble displaying the information above on multiple lines in each text box, type directly in the text boxes that display in the object instead of typing in the Text pane.

h. Click the **Close (X) button** in the top-right corner of the Text pane.

i. Confirm the entire SmartArt object is selected, click the **DESIGN tab**, and then click the **More button** in the SmartArt group to display a variety of styles for this object. Click **Inset** (second row, second column) under the *3D* heading.

j. Save the document.

STEP 2 ≫ INSERT WORDART

The large article in the middle of the right column looks plain, but it contains some very important information about the trails. You decide that it deserves a more attractive title and will replace the current title text with WordArt. The WordArt can be formatted to coordinate better with the SmartArt added earlier. Refer to Figure 5.27 as you complete Step 2.

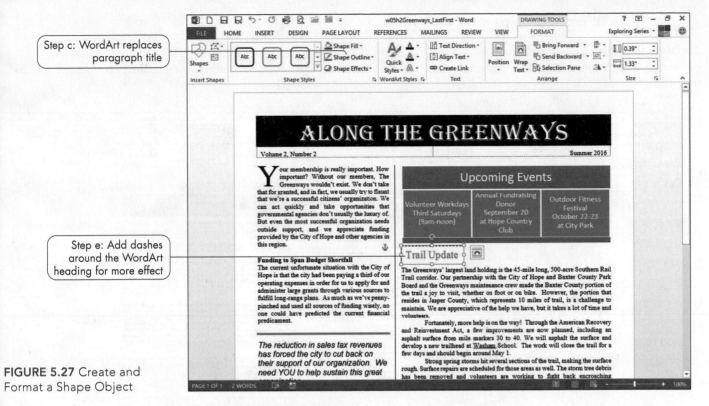

Step c: WordArt replaces paragraph title

Step e: Add dashes around the WordArt heading for more effect

FIGURE 5.27 Create and Format a Shape Object

a. Select the heading *Trail Update* and press **Enter** three times.

This removes the current title and makes room for the WordArt you will insert.

b. Click the **INSERT tab** and click **WordArt** in the Text group. Click **Fill - Blue, Accent 1, Shadow** (first row, second column).

The text box where you type the phrase displays on top of the paragraph. You will relocate the text box later.

c. Press **Backspace** once, type **Trail Update**, click the **Font size arrow**, and then click **16**.

The paragraph heading *Trail Update* displays in the text box in the WordArt style selected. You will move the WordArt heading into the proper position in the next step.

d. Click the **FORMAT tab**, click **Wrap Text** in the Arrange group, and then click **Top and Bottom**. Click the border to display the four-arrow pointer and drag the text box to the right column; position it under the SmartArt object and just above the paragraphs it describes.

> **TROUBLESHOOTING:** Use the arrow keys to nudge the object into exact positioning, if necessary.

e. Click **Shape Outline** in the Shape Styles group, click **Dashes**, and then click **Dash** (fourth item in the list). Click anywhere to deselect the WordArt object.

f. Click the **HOME tab** and click **Show/Hide (¶)**.

g. Save the document and keep it open if you plan to continue with Hands-On Exercise 3. If not, close the document and exit Word.

STEP 3 ≫ CREATE A PULL QUOTE

You decide to move one paragraph into a text box, which has the effect of a pull quote. This is an effective way to display a statement that is so important that you want to make sure the members notice it. Refer to Figure 5.28 as you complete Step 3.

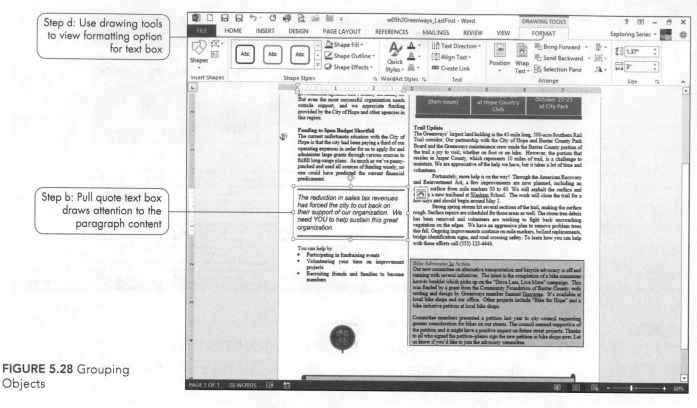

Step d: Use drawing tools to view formatting option for text box

Step b: Pull quote text box draws attention to the paragraph content

FIGURE 5.28 Grouping Objects

a. Click the **HOME tab** and click **Show/Hide (¶)**. Select the paragraph that begins with the text *The reduction in sales tax revenue has forced*, but do not select the paragraph symbol that displays at the end of the last sentence of this paragraph. To modify the format and prepare this text for a pull quote, complete the following steps:

- Click the **Font Size arrow** on the Mini toolbar and click **12**.
- Click the **Font arrow** and click **Arial**.
- Click **Italic**.
- Press **Ctrl+X** to cut the text from the document.
- Press **Backspace** two times to remove the paragraph marks that display between the two paragraphs.

Currently, there is one empty paragraph mark, which is normal, but no more large gaps of white space between the elements in this newsletter. This will enable you to position the pull quote more precisely.

b. Click the **INSERT tab**, click **Text Box** in the Text group, and then click **Austin Pull Quote** from the gallery.

The Text Box gallery includes building blocks that are preformatted for a variety of pull quote styles.

c. Press **Ctrl+V**.

The text you cut earlier displays in the text box.

d. Click the border of the pull quote to select it. To position it more precisely on the page, complete the following steps:

- Click the **FORMAT tab**, if necessary, click **Position** in the Arrange group, and then click **More Layout Options**.
- Click **Absolute position** in the *Horizontal* section and click the arrow until **–0.1** displays, or type in the measurement and be sure to include the negative sign. Click to the right of the arrow and click **Column**.
- Click **Absolute position** in the *Vertical* section and click the arrow until **1.4** displays. Click the **below arrow** and click **Paragraph**.
- Click **Lock anchor**.
- Click **OK** to save the settings.
- Click the **FORMAT tab** and use the Shape Width box in the Size group to resize the pull quote by typing **3.0** and pressing **Enter** so that the pull quote fits within the left column.

e. Save the document.

STEP 4 ≫ INSERT DRAWING SHAPES AND APPLY FORMATTING

You notice there is a significant amount of white space at the bottom of the newsletter and decide to use this space to add a shape object that will span the width of the newsletter and display text to remind readers of an upcoming event. Refer to Figure 5.29 as you complete Step 4.

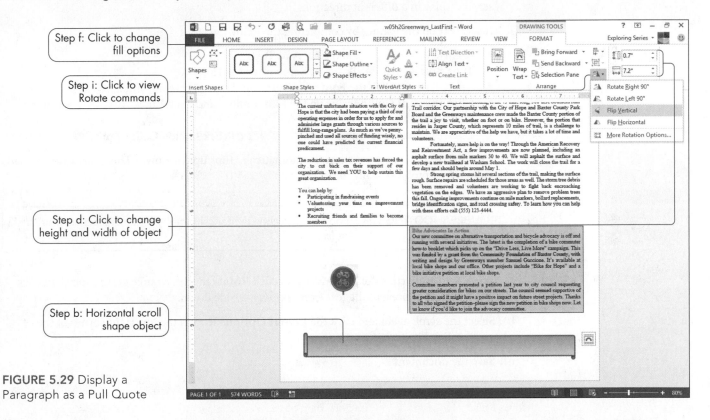

Step f: Click to change fill options

Step i: Click to view Rotate commands

Step d: Click to change height and width of object

Step b: Horizontal scroll shape object

FIGURE 5.29 Display a Paragraph as a Pull Quote

a. Press **Ctrl+End** to move the insertion point to the bottom of the page.

b. Click the **INSERT tab**, click **Shapes** in the Illustrations group, and then click **Horizontal Scroll** (second row, sixth column) in the *Stars and Banners* set.

The insertion point is displayed as a cross-hair.

c. Drag the mouse across the bottom of the newsletter to create a scroll that extends across the width of the page.

The scroll remains selected after releasing the mouse, as indicated by the sizing handles. You can click and drag the yellow square near the top-left corner to change the size of the scroll.

d. Click the **Height arrow** in the Size group on the FORMAT tab until **0.7** displays (or, alternatively, type in the measurement and press **Enter**). Click the **Width arrow** until **7.2** displays.

The height and width can be adjusted more specifically using the sizing controls in the FORMAT tab.

e. Click **Wrap Text** in the Arrange group and click **More Layout Options**. Click the **Position tab** and click **Alignment** in the *Horizontal* section. Click the **Alignment arrow**, click **Centered**, click the **relative to arrow**, and then click **Margin**. Click **OK**.

f. Click the **Shape Fill arrow** in the Shape Styles group. Click the color **Blue, Accent 1, Darker 25%** (fifth row, fifth column).

g. Click the **Shape Fill arrow** again, point to *Gradient*, and then click **Linear Up** (third row, second column) under the *Light Variations* section.

The scroll color changes to display a lighter blue color that gradually lightens as it nears the top of the object.

h. Click the **Shape Outline arrow** in the Shape Styles group, click **Weight**, and then click **2 1/4 pt**.

i. Click **Rotate** in the Arrange group and click **Flip Vertical**.

The two previous steps enhance the outline of the object and flip it so that the edges of the scroll display in a different direction.

j. Insert text on the banner by completing the following steps:

- Right-click the banner and click **Add Text**.
- Type **Bike—Bus—Walk Week: September 11–15**.
- Select the text, click the **Font Size arrow** on the Mini toolbar, and then click **16**.
- Click the **Font Color arrow** on the Mini toolbar and click **Black, Text 1** (first row, second column).
- Click the **Font arrow** on the Mini toolbar and click **Lucida Calligraphy**.

Note that once you type the text, it automatically flips upside down. This is because you had flipped the scroll vertically in the last step.

TROUBLESHOOTING: If you do not have the Lucida Calligraphy font installed on your computer, substitute a different font.

---

k. Select the scroll, click the **FORMAT tab**, click **Rotate** in the Arrange group, and then click **Flip Vertical** to prevent the text from flipping upside down.

l. Select the scroll again and click the **Layout Options icon** at the top-right corner of the scroll. Click **Fix position on page**.

m. Save the document.

STEP 5 ❯❯ GROUP AND LAYER OBJECTS

Shape objects can be displayed together as layered objects, but moving multiple objects for precise placement can become a tedious process. You group the shapes so that, when necessary, you can move them together at the same time. Refer to Figure 5.30 as you complete Step 5.

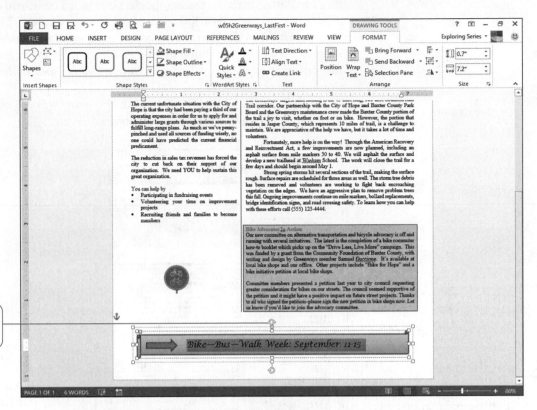

Step e: Only one set of sizing handles displays after grouping items together

FIGURE 5.30 Using WordArt for a Paragraph Heading

a. Click the **INSERT tab**, click **Shapes** in the Illustrations group, and then click **Right Arrow** from the *Block Arrows* section. Drag the pointer to create the arrow on the left side of the scroll before the text that displays in the scroll object at the bottom of the page.

b. Click the **Height arrow** in the Size group on the FORMAT tab until **0.3** displays. Click the **Width arrow** until **0.8** displays or, alternatively, type in the measurements and press **Enter**.

c. Click the **arrow shape object** one time to select it, if necessary, and press the left or right arrow key to nudge the arrow shape into the middle of the scroll shape.

Using the left and right arrow keys will nudge the shape into a more precise position.

d. Press and hold **Shift** and click the banner.

Both objects, the banner and the arrow, are selected and sizing handles for both objects display.

e. Click **Group** in the Arrange group and click **Group**.

If a group object is selected, only one set of sizing handles will display. However, if you click again on one of the shapes in the grouped object, this will drill down to selecting the piece that was clicked and two sets of sizing handles will appear. The inner set of sizing handles belongs to the active shape selected within the group.

f. Save the document.

Object Linking and Embedding

Microsoft Office enables you to create documents that contain objects from other applications. For example, you might create a report in Word that explains the results of a survey. The survey data are saved in an Excel spreadsheet that also includes a chart to summarize the data. Rather than re-creating the data in a Word table, you can insert the spreadsheet and a chart can be inserted or linked into the Word document. The document in Figure 5.31 is a Microsoft Word document that contains objects (a worksheet and a chart) developed in Microsoft Excel. The technology that enables you to insert and link objects or information into different applications is called *Object Linking and Embedding* (abbreviated *OLE*; it is pronounced oh-lay).

In this section, you will learn about the many ways to embed and link an object, and then you will learn to update a linked object.

Linked or embedded from an Excel worksheet

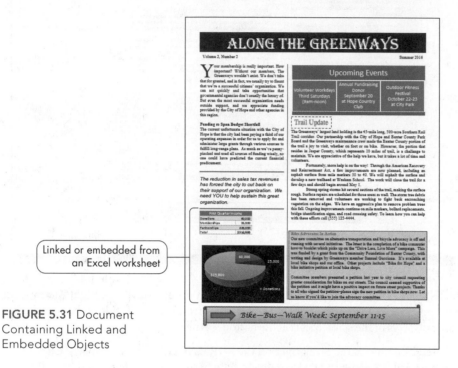

FIGURE 5.31 Document Containing Linked and Embedded Objects

Using OLE to Insert an Object

When you insert objects into a document, there are two options for how the object can be imported into the document. The first option is embedding. *Embedding* imports an object into a document from its original source and allows editing directly in the document without changing the source data file. For example, if you embed a portion of an Excel worksheet, it becomes part of your document; you can make modifications to the copied data at any time, and those changes do not affect the original worksheet. Likewise, any changes to the original Excel file will not display in your document.

The second option for inserting an object or data into your document is by linking the data. *Linking* is the process of importing an object from another program, but the object retains a connection to the original data file. If you change the data in the original source file, the data in the destination file will reflect the changes, and vice versa. A data file used as a linked object may be linked to multiple documents. The same Excel chart, for example, can be linked to a Word document and a PowerPoint presentation. Any changes to the Excel chart are automatically reflected and updated in the document and the presentation to which it is linked.

The advantage of linking over embedding is that a linked object will reflect the most current information. This might be important, for example, when you insert the stock prices for your company into your weekly newsletter—you would always want the most current prices to display. On the other hand, an embedded object is a snapshot of the information at the time the data was embedded into the file; if the desired result is to keep the data constant and any updates are controlled within the document, then this would be a better option to use because you don't have to worry about having access to the source file at a later date. For example, if you want to display the previous year-ending sales figures in the January newsletter, you would embed the data because those numbers will not change.

You can link and embed data into a document using the *Copy and Paste* method in the Paste options.

Use the Copy and Paste Method

When using the *Copy and Paste* method, you first copy a selection from the source, such as an Excel spreadsheet or an object from a PowerPoint slide, and then do one of the following:

1. **To Embed:** Click Paste to insert the copied data into the destination document. When you paste Excel data into Word, the data is pasted into table cells and does not retain Excel spreadsheet capabilities. For example, all pasted formulas and functions convert to actual values; thus if you change one value it will not change any of the other pasted values that use that value. Additionally, the numbers will not align on the decimal points.

2. **To Link:** On the Home tab, click Paste in the Clipboard group, click Paste Special, and then click the *Paste link* option in the Paste Special dialog box, as shown in Figure 5.32, which creates the connection to the original file. Make sure the appropriate object from the *As list* box is selected; for example, if the data is from an Excel file, click the Microsoft Excel Worksheet Object in the listed items. Click OK. If you change a value in the Excel file, it will automatically update in the Word file and vice versa. When the object in the Word file is double-clicked, it opens the source data Excel file to allow editing.

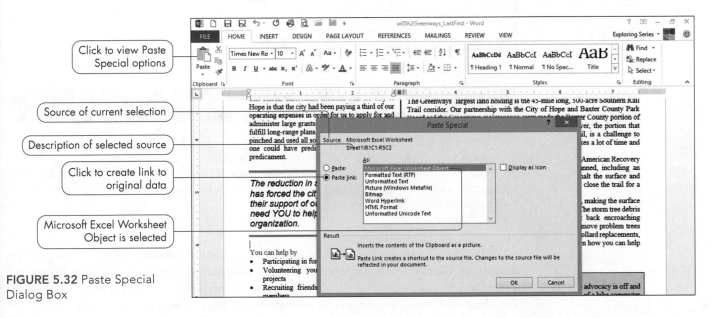

FIGURE 5.32 Paste Special Dialog Box

Use the Insert an Object Method

STEP 1» You can insert an object, such as an Excel workbook, within a Word document without displaying the data contents of the Excel workbook itself. The contents of the entire Excel workbook, which may contain several worksheets, appear as an icon in the document, and when you click the icon, the Excel workbook opens in a separate window. This allows you to associate the data or information with the document without using space to display the data. To use this method, do the following:

1. Click the INSERT tab and click Object in the Text group. The Object dialog box displays, as shown in Figure 5.33, with two tabs at the top.
2. Click the *Create from File* tab, click Browse to navigate to the location of the file, and then double-click the file name.
3. Click the *Link to file* option located on the right side of the dialog box to create a link to the file.
4. Click the *Display as icon* option located on the right to save disk space.
5. Click OK to insert the selected object into the Word document.

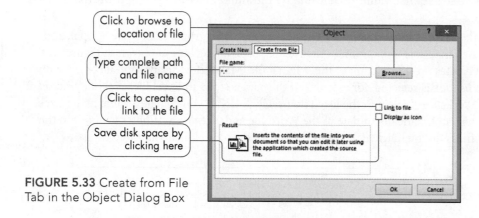

FIGURE 5.33 Create from File Tab in the Object Dialog Box

TIP | **Displaying a Link as an Icon**

You can save disk space by inserting the link as an icon instead of displaying the actual linked data since the data are not repeated or duplicated in the destination file. The *Display as icon* option is available when you are selecting options in either the Paste Special dialog box or the Object dialog box. Double-click the icon in the destination file to open the source data file.

The Object dialog box also has a Create New tab, which is helpful when you do not have an existing file to insert as an object. This tab allows the user to create a new file source that can be linked as an icon. The Object type list box displays the many types of object files that can be created based on the applications installed on your computer, such as Microsoft Excel. When you click the Object type (without clicking the *Display as icon* option), a small window displays in the destination document (see Figure 5.34), and you can create the content for the object that will display in your document. After the object displays in the document, you can edit it by double-clicking the object. If the *Display as icon* option is checked on the Create New tab, the new file displays as an icon and double-clicking opens the object for adding or editing the data.

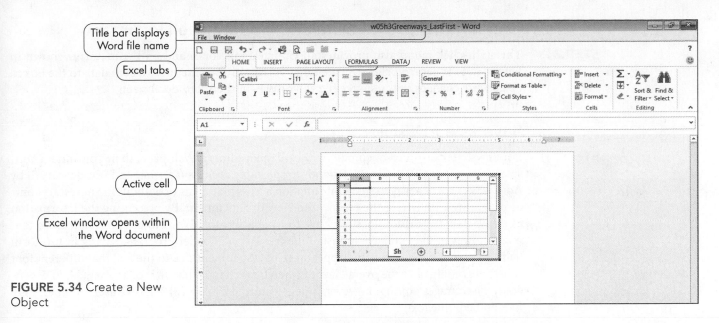

Title bar displays Word file name

Excel tabs

Active cell

Excel window opens within the Word document

FIGURE 5.34 Create a New Object

Updating a Linked Object

After you link an object to your document, you can still make modifications to the source file. At any time, you can open a source file in its native application—Excel, for example—to make modifications. You can also open the application by clicking the linked object in the Word document. To use this method, right-click the linked object, point to Linked Worksheet Object, and then click Edit Link or Open Link, as shown in Figure 5.35. Either option opens the source document to allow for editing or modifications made to the data within the source application.

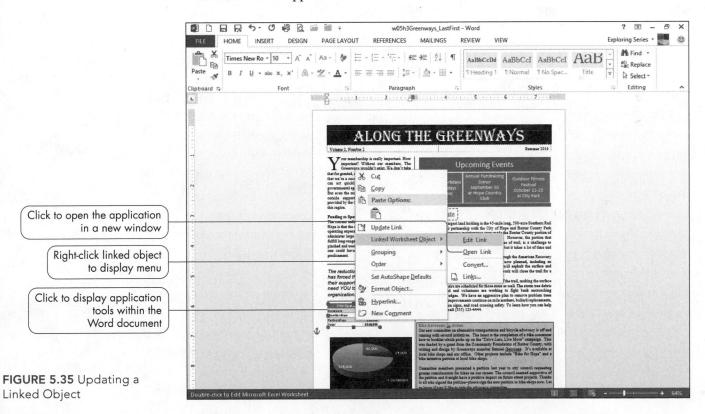

Click to open the application in a new window

Right-click linked object to display menu

Click to display application tools within the Word document

FIGURE 5.35 Updating a Linked Object

Change the Source Data and Update the Document

STEP 2 ▶▶ The right-click menu also provides an Update Link command on the menu, as shown in Figure 5.35. When you click Update Link, Word retrieves the most recent data to the linked object; any changes in the source file will display in the Word document.

Save as a PDF File

STEP 3 ▶▶ If a newsletter or other document will be displayed on a Web page, then you should consider saving it as a PDF file. **PDF** stands for ***portable document format*** and was developed by Adobe Systems as a way to share information across platforms or without the necessary fonts or programs installed for the recipient to view the document. By presenting the information as a PDF file, the reader does not have to have Microsoft Word to open or view the document; however, they do have to install the free Adobe Reader program. Saving in this form helps to preserve the layout and appearance of a document due to the fact that different font substitutes could alter the overall layout when opened in its native Word format. A PDF generally discourages editing; however, a new feature in Word 2013 allows users to open PDF files and edit the text.

Quick Concepts

1. What is the difference between embedding and linking an object? *p. 34*

2. What are some of the objects that can be pasted and then linked back to the source file? *p. 34*

3. Why would you want to link an object? *p. 34*

Hands-On Exercise

3 Object Linking and Embedding

The newsletter for The Greenways is nearly complete. Director Allen requests space to display first-quarter financial information and provides the information in an Excel worksheet. You will add this information by inserting a chart into the newsletter, then save the final copy as a PDF file before leaving for a bike ride!

Skills covered: Copy and Link a Worksheet • Change the Source Data and Update the Document • Save as a PDF File

STEP 1 ≫ COPY AND LINK A WORKSHEET

When Director Allen sends you the Excel worksheet that contains the first quarter income sources, he tells you that it should be added to the newsletter, but some changes to the worksheet might be necessary in the near future. You decide the proper course of action is to insert the information with a link to the original file so you have the option to update the data later. Refer to Figure 5.36 as you complete Step 1.

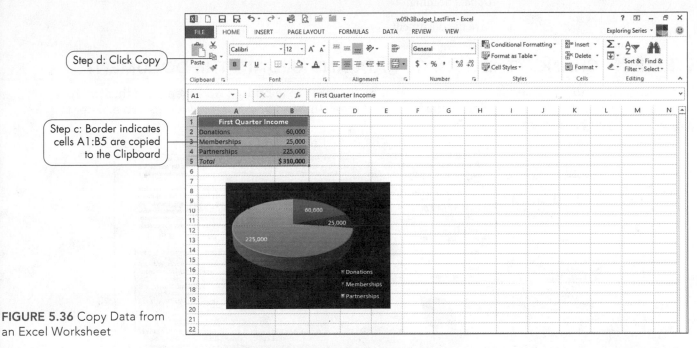

Step d: Click Copy

Step c: Border indicates cells A1:B5 are copied to the Clipboard

FIGURE 5.36 Copy Data from an Excel Worksheet

a. Start Word, and if necessary, open *w05h2Greenways_LastFirst* and save it as **w05h3Greenways_LastFirst**, changing *h2* to *h3*. Click the **HOME tab** and click **Show/Hide (¶)** to display formatting marks if they are not currently turned on.

   In the next step, you will open an Excel workbook. You might find it easier to work with the Excel spreadsheet if you minimize your Word document.

b. Start Excel. Open *w05h3Budget.xlsx* and save it as **w05h3Budget_LastFirst**.

   The file displays in an Excel window. The Windows taskbar now contains icons for both Word and Excel; click either icon to move back and forth between the applications.

c. Drag to select **cells A1 through B5** in the Excel worksheet.

d. Click **Copy** in the Clipboard group (or press **Ctrl+C**).

   A moving border displays around the selection, indicating it has been copied to the Clipboard.

e. Click the **Word icon** on the Windows taskbar to return to the Word document. Place the insertion point on the first blank line above the paragraph that begins *You can help by*. This is where you will insert the Excel worksheet.

> **TROUBLESHOOTING:** If necessary, press **Enter** to insert a blank line before the paragraph heading *You can help by*.

f. Click the **Paste arrow** in the Clipboard group on the HOME tab. Click **Paste Special** to display the Paste Special dialog box. In the As list, click **Microsoft Excel Worksheet Object**.

g. Click **Paste link** on the left side of the dialog box and click **OK**.

> **TROUBLESHOOTING:** If the Update Link option does not display on a right-click menu for the Excel object, that means the object is not linked to the source. Click **Undo** on the Quick Access Toolbar and repeat step g, making sure to click **Paste Special** and check the **Paste link option**.

h. Drag the clip art below the bullets, if necessary. Delete the two blank lines above the *Trail Update* heading.

i. Save the document.

STEP 2 ≫ CHANGE THE SOURCE DATA AND UPDATE THE DOCUMENT

As expected, Director Allen sends the changes you need to make in the budget worksheet, and thus on the newsletter. The changes will be applied to the Excel worksheet and updated in the newsletter table. Refer to Figure 5.37 as you complete Step 2.

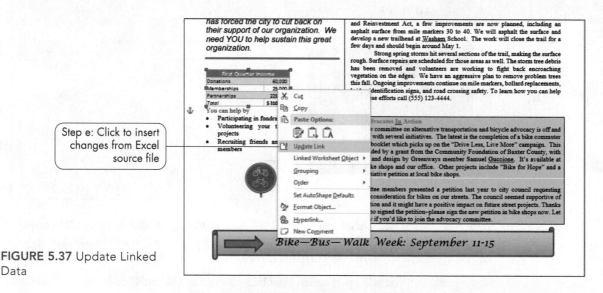

FIGURE 5.37 Update Linked Data

a. Click the **Excel icon** on the Windows taskbar to return to the worksheet. Press **Esc** to deselect the cells.

b. Click **cell A1**, type **First Quarter Income**, and then press **Enter**.

The text typed automatically replaces the original text for cell A1.

c. Click **cell B2**, type **60000**, and then press **Enter**.

d. Save and close the workbook.

e. Click the **Word icon** on the Windows taskbar to return to the Word document. Right-click the **Excel worksheet object** and click **Update Link**.

The linked object reflects the changes you made in the Excel workbook.

> **TROUBLESHOOTING:** If your data table does not reflect the new changes, you need to check and make sure that your Excel workbook is closed.

f. Save the document.

STEP 3 ➤➤ SAVE AS A PDF FILE

Because you will post the newsletter on The Greenways Web site, you decide to save the document as a PDF file. As a result, anyone can view the newsletter, regardless of the type of computer they are using. You can also e-mail the PDF version to members and know they can read it even if they do not have Microsoft Word installed on their PC. Refer to Figure 5.38 as you complete Step 3.

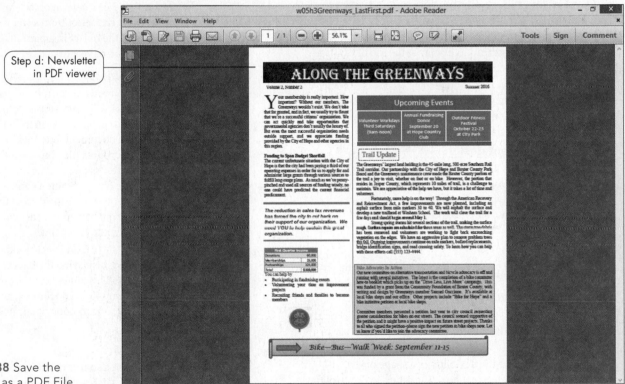

FIGURE 5.38 Save the Newsletter as a PDF File

a. Click **File** and click **Save As**.

b. Click **Browse** and navigate to the folder where you want to save the PDF file.

c. Click the **Save as type arrow** and click **PDF (*.pdf)**.

d. Click **Save**.

An additional window displays the file in Adobe Reader. The file now exists in both Word and Adobe PDF formats.

e. Save and close the file, and submit based on your instructor's directions. Close the Adobe Reader (PDF) version of the file and submit it based on your instructor's directions.

Chapter Objectives Review

After reading this chapter, you have accomplished the following objectives:

1. **Construct a newsletter.**
   - You can create a document with two or more columns of equal width. When you select one of the column preset designs, Microsoft Word will calculate the width of each column based on the number of columns, the left and right margins on the page, and the specified (default) space between columns. A two-column layout with a wide and narrow column design may be preferred over columns of uniform width, as it adds interest to the document.
   - A section break is required whenever the column specification changes and at the end of the last column to balance the text within the columns.
   - Use a column break to force paragraph text to start at the top of the next column. This provides control over where the bottom of one column ends before the text wraps to the top of the next column.
   - You can create a masthead to display at the top of the page to introduce the document and use a reverse to enhance the appearance.
   - Another way to catch the reader's eye and call attention to the associated text is a drop cap. A drop cap is a capital letter formatted in a font size larger than the body text.

2. **Develop a document design.**
   - Good design makes it easier for the reader to determine what is important. Emphasis can be achieved using variations in type size and/or type style, headings, bold and italic formatting, uppercase letters and underlining, boxes and/or shading, pull quote; reverse, clip art, and color.

3. **Insert graphic objects.**
   - SmartArt is a visual representation of information that can be created to effectively communicate a message or idea in one of many existing and visually appealing layouts.
   - WordArt is a Microsoft Office feature that creates decorative text that can be used to add interest to the text you use in a document.
   - One way to combine the flexibility of a shape object with simple text is to create a text box. A text box can control the placement of text and allow for layering with other objects and shapes.
   - A pull quote is a phrase or sentence taken from an article to emphasize a key point. It is typically set in larger type, often in a different font or in italics, and may be offset with borders at the top, bottom, or on the sides. Pull quotes are frequently displayed in professional publications, such as company's monthly newsletters and annual reports, to draw attention to important topics.
   - One text box can be linked to another text box so that when text runs out of space in one box it automatically flows into another box.
   - A shape is an object, such as a circle or an arrow, which you can use as a visual enhancement. You can use one shape or combine multiple shapes to create a more complex image.

4. **Manipulate graphic objects.**
   - After you insert a graphical object, you can enhance the appearance by using one of the commands available on the Format tab for the object, such as fill, outline, and effects.
   - Any object can be resized—such as a text box, WordArt, image, or shape—manually or precisely using the size group options.
   - Grouping is the process of combining selected objects so that they appear as a single object. When grouped, you can move objects simultaneously or apply a Style to all at one time. Layering is the process of placing one shape on top of another. After you layer objects, you might need to group them so you can manipulate them more easily.
   - Word makes it easy to flip or rotate an object. When you click Rotate Objects, you can select from several commands that enable you to rotate the object in a particular direction or flip it along a horizontal or vertical axis.

5. **Use OLE to insert an object.**
   - When you insert objects into your document, you have two options for how the object will work within your document. The first option, embedding, pulls information from its original source into your document, but does not change or maintain a link to that source file. The second option is linking, which is the process of inserting an object from another program, but the object retains a connection to the original data and file. If you change the data in the original source program, you can quickly update the data in the destination program to reflect the changes.
   - You can insert an object, such as an Excel workbook, within a Word document without displaying the data contents of the Excel workbook itself. The contents of the entire Excel workbook appear as an icon in the document, and when you click the icon, the Excel workbook opens in a separate window.

6. **Update a linked object.**
   - At any time, you can open a source file in its native application, for example, Microsoft Excel, to make modifications. You can also open the application by double-clicking the linked object in a Word document. When you click the Update Link option, Word retrieves the most updated form of the object from the source file and displays the changes in the Word document.
   - If a newsletter or other document will be displayed on a Web page, then you should consider saving it as a portable document format (PDF) file. By presenting the information as a PDF file, the reader does not have to have Microsoft Word to open or view the document. A new feature in Word 2013 allows users to open PDF files and edit the text.

Key Terms Matching

Match the key terms with their definitions. Write the key term letter by the appropriate numbered definition.

a. SmartArt
b. Drop cap
c. Embedding
d. Grid
e. Text pane
f. Text box
g. Reverse
h. Pull quote
i. WordArt
j. Ungrouping

k. Linking
l. Drawing Canvas
m. Sidebar
n. Layering
o. Object Linking and Embedding (OLE)
p. Grouping
q. Masthead
r. Fill
s. Desktop publishing
t. PDF

1. _____ A feature that creates decorative text for a document. **p. 18**

2. _____ A frame-like area that helps you keep parts of your drawing together. **p. 23**

3. _____ Pulls an object into a document, where you can edit it without changing the source. **p. 34**

4. _____ A large capital letter at the beginning of a paragraph. **p. 6**

5. _____ The interior space of an object. **p. 22**

6. _____ An underlying, but invisible, set of horizontal and vertical lines that determine the placement of major elements. **p. 7**

7. _____ The process of combining objects so they appear as a single object. **p. 25**

8. _____ The process of placing one shape on top of another. **p. 24**

9. _____ Inserts an object from another program, but retains a connection to the original data. **p. 34**

10. _____ The identifying information at the top of a newsletter or other periodical. **p. 5**

11. _____ A technology that enables you to insert objects into a document regardless of the platform they use. **p. 34**

12. _____ A phrase or sentence taken from an article to emphasize a key point. **p. 19**

13. _____ The technique that uses light text on a dark background. **p. 5**

14. _____ Supplementary text that appears on the side of the featured information. **p. 19**

15. _____ Simply a graphical object that contains text. **p. 19**

16. _____ A special pane that opens up for entering text when a SmartArt diagram is selected. **p. 17**

17. _____ Breaks a combined single object into individual objects. **p. 25**

18. _____ A visual representation of information that can be created to effectively communicate a message or idea in one of many existing and visually appealing layouts. **p. 3**

19. _____ Stands for portable document format and was developed by Adobe Systems as a way to share information across platforms or without the necessary fonts or programs installed for the recipient to view the document. **p. 38**

20. _____ Evolved through a combination of technologies, including faster computers, laser and inkjet printers, and sophisticated page composition software that enables users to manipulate text and graphics to produce a professional-looking document. **p. 2**

Multiple Choice

1. What format do you see when you use a reverse effect on a masthead?

   (a) Light text on a clear background

   (b) Dark text on a clear background

   (c) Dark text on a light background

   (d) Light text on a dark background

2. How do you balance the columns in a newsletter so that each column contains the same amount of text?

   (a) Insert a section break at the end of the last column and use a column break in previous columns to control the flow.

   (b) Insert a page break at the end of the last column.

   (c) Manually set the column widths in the Columns dialog box.

   (d) Press Enter until the text lines up at the bottom of each column.

3. Which feature would not be used to add emphasis to a document?

   (a) Pull Quote

   (b) Borders and Shading

   (c) Paste Link

   (d) Bulleted and Numbered List

4. Which feature enables you to quickly insert an organizational chart, which you can modify and enhance as needed?

   (a) WordArt

   (b) SmartArt

   (c) Shapes

   (d) Clip art

5. You insert an arrow shape in the document that points left, but you need it to point right. You can use the Rotate Objects command under which group to change the direction of your arrow?

   (a) Page Setup

   (b) Paragraph

   (c) Arrange

   (d) Flip

6. To move several shapes as one object, you should:

   (a) Layer the shapes.

   (b) Anchor the shapes.

   (c) Position the shapes.

   (d) Group the shapes.

7. Which of the following processes inserts Excel data in a way that enables you to edit the values in Word, but without changing the source?

   (a) Embedding

   (b) Copying and Inserting

   (c) Linking

   (d) Find and Replace

8. Which process should you use to insert Excel data into Word so that any changes made to the original Excel worksheet can be automatically updated in Word?

   (a) Copying and Pasting

   (b) Linking

   (c) Embedding

   (d) Find and Replace

9. To quickly determine whether spreadsheet data displayed in a Word document is linked to the source file, you can:

   (a) Click the INSERT tab and click Object.

   (b) Single-click the object.

   (c) Click Paste Special.

   (d) Right-click the object and look for the Update Link option.

10. You just inserted two shape objects, a triangle and circle, into the document; the circle is larger and was inserted on top of the triangle, so the triangle cannot be seen. What can you do to display the triangle on top of the circle?

    (a) Click the circle and click *Bring to Front*.

    (b) Click the triangle and click *Bring to Back*.

    (c) Click the circle and click *Send to Back*.

    (d) Click the circle and click *Bring in Front of Text*.

Practice Exercises

1 Personal Computer Consulting

You are a local computer expert who operates a business named Personal Computer Consulting. You are often asked to give advice on purchasing a personal computer. Because the basic considerations are the same for everyone, you decide to create a simple shopping guide to explain those considerations. You want the guide to look professional, so you use several features in Word to develop an attractive document that is easy to read and that will make a good handout for anyone who asks how to buy a PC. This exercise follows the same set of skills as used in Hands-On Exercises 1–2 in the chapter. Refer to Figure 5.39 as you complete this exercise.

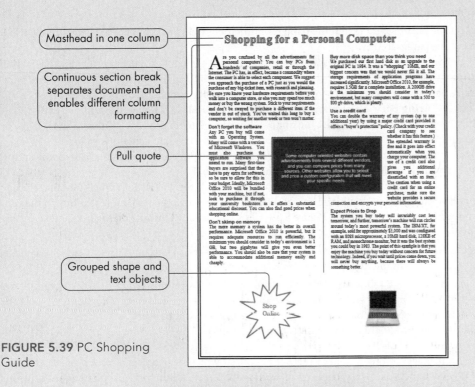

FIGURE 5.39 PC Shopping Guide

a. Open *w05p1PCHandout* and save it as **w05p1PCHandout_LastFirst**.

b. Click the **PAGE LAYOUT tab**, click **Columns** in the Page Setup group, and then click **More Columns**. Click **Two** in the *Presets* section, click the **Line between box**, and then click **OK**. Click **Breaks** in the Page Setup group and click **Continuous.**

c. Click the **HOME tab** and click **Show/Hide (¶)** in the Paragraph group to display formatting marks. Move the insertion point to the right side of the section break. Click the **PAGE LAYOUT tab**, click **Columns** in the Page Setup group, and then click **One**.

d. Create a masthead for this document by completing the following steps:

- Click **Enter** two times and press **Ctrl+Home** to move the insertion point to the beginning of the document.
- Click the **INSERT tab** and click **WordArt** in the Text group. Click the red-colored style named **Fill - Red, Accent 2, Outline - Accent 2** (first row, third column).
- Type **Shopping for a Personal Computer** and select the text. On the Mini toolbar, click **Font size** and click **26**.
- Click the **FORMAT tab** and click the **Size arrow**, if necessary. Click the **Height arrow** until **0.60"** displays and click the **Width arrow** until **6"** displays.
- Click the **Position arrow** and click **Position in Top Center with Square Text Wrapping**.
- Click the **Layout Options dialog box** and select **Fix position on page**.
- Drag the masthead to the space above the text.
- Place the insertion point on the left side of the blank line between the WordArt object and the section break and press **Delete**.

e. Click the **PAGE LAYOUT tab**, click **Margins**, and then click **Custom Margins**. Type **0.7** in each box for **Top**, **Bottom**, **Left**, and **Right**. In the *Apply to:* box, click **Whole document** and click **OK**. Click the **WordArt masthead** and use the arrow keys to nudge it higher on the page, if necessary.

f. Position the insertion point on the left side of the first paragraph in the left column of the page. Click the **INSERT tab**, click **Drop Cap** in Text group, and then click **Dropped**. Click anywhere outside the dropped cap to deselect it.

g. Press **Ctrl+End** to move the insertion point to the end of the document. Click the **PAGE LAYOUT tab**, click **Breaks** in the Page Setup group, and then click **Continuous** to display the content in two equally balanced columns.

h. Insert a text box to display a quote by completing the following steps:

- Select the heading and text in the paragraph titled *Let your fingers do the walking*. Press **Ctrl+X** to cut the paragraph.
- Click the **INSERT tab**, if necessary, click **Text Box** in the Text group, and then click **Grid Pull Quote**. Click **Ctrl+V** to insert the paragraph you cut in this step. Click at the end of the paragraph pasted and press **Delete** to remove the extra empty paragraph mark if necessary.
- Click the **Bring Forward arrow** in the Arrange group and click **Bring in Front of Text**.
- Click the **Size arrow** and adjust the **Shape Height** to **1.69** and **Shape Width** to **3.4**. Click the paragraph heading and text in the pull quote and press **Ctrl+E** to center it.
- Omit the heading, but select the whole paragraph in the pull quote, click the **Font Color arrow**, and then click **White, Background 1** on the Mini toolbar.
- Click **Font** on the Mini toolbar and click **Arial**. Click the **PAGE LAYOUT tab** and click to change the Before spacing in the Paragraph group to **0**. Move the pull quote text box to the center and reposition it as seen in Figure 5.39. Click the **Layout Options dialog box** and select **Fix position on page**.

i. Press **Ctrl+End** to move the insertion point to the end of the document. Insert a clip art, a shape, and a text box by completing the following steps:

- Click the **INSERT tab**, click **Online Pictures** in the Illustrations group, and then type **laptop** in the Office.com **Clip Art Search box** in the Insert Pictures dialog box. Press **Enter**. Select the first image of a laptop computer, or substitute as needed. Click **Insert**.
- Click the **Shape Height arrow** in the Size group until **1.5"** displays. If necessary, click the **Width arrow** until **1.5"** displays.
- Drag the object to the bottom of the right column, which displays on a second page. Click the **FORMAT tab**, if necessary, click **Wrap Text**, and then click **Square**. Click the **Layout Options dialog box** and select **Fix position on page**.
- Click the **INSERT tab**, click **Shapes** in the Illustrations group, and then click the **Explosion 1 shape** in the *Stars and Banners* section (first shape in that section). Click the left side of the bottom of the page to the left of the computer graphic to create a shape clip art. Click the **More button** in the Shape Styles group to display the Quick Styles gallery. Click **Colored Outline—Blue, Accent 1** (first row, second column). Click **Rotate Objects** in the Arrange group and click **Rotate Left 90°**. In the Size group, adjust both the Shape Height and Width to **1.88**.
- Click the **INSERT tab**, if necessary. Click **Text Box** in the Text group and click **Draw Text Box**. Click near the shape to create a text box. Type **Shop**, press **Shift+Enter** to move to the next line, and then type **Online** in the text box. Select the text, click the **Font Color arrow** on the Mini toolbar, and then click **Dark Blue, Text 2, Lighter 40%** (fourth row, fourth column). Click the **Font Size arrow** and click **14**.
- Click the border of the text box. Click the **FORMAT tab**, if necessary, click **Shape Fill**, and then click **No Fill**. Click **Shape Outline** and click **No Outline**.
- Drag the box handles to resize as needed until the box is an appropriate size to fit and display all the text and drag it into a position where the text appears centered in the explosion shape.
- Click the text box, if necessary, press and hold **Shift**, and then click the explosion shape. Right-click, point to *Group*, and then click **Group**. Click the **Layout Options dialog box** and select **Fix position on page**. Click anywhere outside the explosion shape to deselect it.

j. Click the **DESIGN tab**, click **Page Borders**, drag the **Style scroll bar** down until a double line style displays, and then select the double line. Click the **Width arrow** and click **2 1/4 pt**. Click **Box** in the *Setting* section and click **OK**. Click the **HOME tab** and click **Show/Hide (¶)** to remove formatting marks.

k. Save and close the file, and submit based on your instructor's directions.

2 IBC Enterprises

You are the lead financial analyst for IBC Enterprises, a technology manufacturing organization. Each year, you are responsible for preparing a summary of the annual report. After you summarize the main points, you decide the report should include a chart and graph to emphasize certain points, as well as give a visual summary of the information. You begin this exercise by opening the general summary and add data from an Excel spreadsheet that contains the information you want to summarize. You also use SmartArt graphics to display an organization chart of the new administration. This exercise follows the same set of skills as used in Hands-On Exercises 1–3 in the chapter. Refer to Figure 5.40 as you complete this exercise.

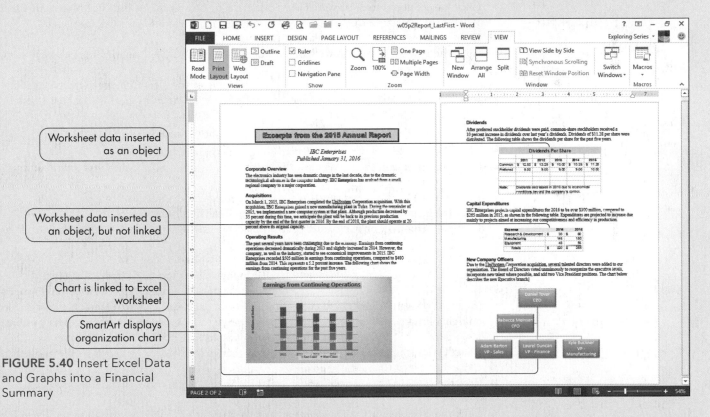

FIGURE 5.40 Insert Excel Data and Graphs into a Financial Summary

a. Open *w05p2Report* and save it as **w05p2Report_LastFirst**. Open *w05p2Dividends.xlsx* and save it as **w05p2Dividends_LastFirst.xlsx**.

b. Insert an Excel object by completing the following steps:
- Place the insertion point on the empty paragraph mark just above the heading *Capital Expenditures* in the Word document. Press **Enter** one time.
- Click the **INSERT tab**, click the **Object arrow** in the Text group, click **Object**, and then click the **Create from File tab**.
- Click **Browse** and select *w05p2Dividends_LastFirst.xlsx*.
- Click **Insert** in the Browse dialog box. Click **OK** in the Object dialog box and scroll down to view the object, if necessary.
- Double-click the worksheet object and click **cell F5**.

- Type **10.00** and press **Enter**.
- Click anywhere outside the object to save the change.
- Right-click the object and click **Format Object**.
- Click the **LAYOUT tab** and click **Tight** under *Wrapping style*. Under *Horizontal alignment*, click **Center** and click **OK**.
- Click to position the insertion point on the left side of the *Capital Expenditures* heading, which has been separated by the object, and press **Enter** seven times to separate the object and the next paragraph.

c. Click one time on the worksheet object to select it. Right-click the object, click **Worksheet Object**, and then click **Open**. To insert and link a worksheet object into the document, complete the following steps:

- Click the **Expenses worksheet tab** at the bottom of the Excel window.
- Position the pointer over **cell A4** and drag down and over to **cell C8**, which contains the total $265.
- Click **Copy** in the Clipboard group on the HOME tab (or press **Ctrl+C**).
- Click the **Word icon** on the Windows taskbar to toggle back and view *w05p2report_LastFirst*. Click once on the empty paragraph mark above the *New Company Officers* paragraph.
- Click the **HOME tab**, if necessary, and click the **Paste arrow** in the Clipboard group.
- Click **Paste Special** to display the Paste Special dialog box. In the As list, click **Microsoft Excel Worksheet Object**. Click **Paste link** on the left side of the window and click **OK**.
- Right-click the object and click **Format Object**.
- Click the **LAYOUT tab** and click **Square** under *Wrapping style*. Under *Horizontal alignment*, click **Center** and click **OK**.
- Click to position the insertion point on the left side of the *New Company Officers* heading, which has been separated by the table, and press **Enter** five times to separate the object and the next paragraph.

d. Insert an Excel chart into the document by completing the following steps:

- Click once on the empty paragraph mark above the *Dividends* heading.
- Click the **Excel icon** on the Windows taskbar to toggle to the *w05p2Dividends_LastFirst* workbook.
- If the moving border remains on the range you copied earlier, press **Esc**.
- Click the **Earnings worksheet tab** at the bottom of the Excel window.
- Position the pointer on the border edge of the chart title *Earnings from Continuing Operations* and click one time to select the entire chart.
- Click the **HOME tab** and click **Copy** in the Clipboard group.
- Click the **Word icon** on the Windows taskbar to toggle back to *w05p2Report_LastFirst*.
- Click the **HOME tab**, if necessary, and click **Paste** in the Clipboard group. Click **Layout Options** (first icon on right of chart) and click **Fix position on page**. Click **Chart Elements** (second icon on right of chart), put your cursor over *Chart Title*, click the arrow, and then click **More options**. Make sure that *Title Options* on the right panel is selected. Click **Gradient Fill** under *Fill*. Click **Chart Styles** (third icon on right of chart) and change the style to the fourth choice on the list. Close the Format Chart dialog box.
- Click the **FORMAT tab**, if necessary, and click the **Shape Height arrow** in the Size group until **3.3"** displays.
- Click the chart below the *Dividends* paragraph and click the **Dividends tab** in the Excel file before closing the Excel file.

e. Create a document title using WordArt by completing the following steps:

- Press **Ctrl+Home** and select the title *Excerpts from the 2015 Annual Report*.
- Click the **INSERT tab** and click **WordArt** in the Text group. Click the style **Fill - Purple, Accent 4, Wireframe - Accent 4** (third row, fifth column). Drag the right middle sizing handle towards the right margin to resize to fit between the margins.
- Select the WordArt text and drag it across the top of the page. Click the **Font Size arrow** on the Mini toolbar and click **20**.
- Click the **FORMAT tab**, if necessary, click **Position** in the Arrange group, and then click **Position in Top Center with Square Text Wrapping**.

- Click **Shape Fill** in the Shape Styles group and click **Yellow**. Click **Shape Outline** in the Shape Styles group, click **Weight**, and then click **2 1/4 pt**.
- Click **Shape Effects** in the Shape Styles group, click **Bevel**, and then click **Cool Slant** (first row, fourth column).
- If necessary, delete additional empty paragraph marks at the heading and the first line of the subheading so that only one paragraph mark displays.

f. Create an organization chart with SmartArt by completing the following steps:

- Press **Ctrl+End** to move the insertion point to the end of the document. Press **Enter** one time.
- Click the **INSERT tab** and click **SmartArt** in the Illustrations group.
- Click **Hierarchy** in the left panel and click **Organization Chart**. Click **OK**.
- Type the following names and positions in the chart, starting from the top and then from left to right on the third level. Press **Enter** to put positions on a new line.

  Daniel Tovar
  CEO
  Rebecca Meinsen
  CFO
  Adam Barton
  VP - Sales
  Laurel Duncan
  VP - Finance
  Kyle Buckner
  VP - Manufacturing

- Click the **DESIGN tab**, click **Change Colors** in the SmartArt Styles group, and then click **Colorful Range - Accent Colors 4 to 5** (second row, fourth column).
- Click the **More button** in the SmartArt Styles and click **Intense Effect** (first row, fifth column).
- Click the **FORMAT tab**, click the **Size arrow**, and then click the **Height arrow** until **2.7** displays. Click the **Width arrow** until **5.5** displays. Click the **Layout Options dialog box** and select **Fix position on page**.

g. Drag the **Zoom slider** in the status bar to **50%**.

h. Save and close the file, and submit based on your instructor's directions.

Mid-Level Exercises

1 Computer Training Association, Inc.

You are preparing a report that announces the implementation of new technology for a computer training company. You need to include a chart that was created in Excel. Because you want the chart in Word to reflect changes in the original Excel workbook, you decide to link the chart.

a. Open *w05m1CTA* and save it as **w05m1CTA_LastFirst**.

b. Open the Excel workbook *w05m1Chart* and save it as **w05m1Chart_LastFirst**.

c. Select the **Projected Costs chart** in Excel and copy it to the Clipboard.

d. Link the Projected costs chart as a chart object to the bottom of the *w05m1CTA_LastFirst* document.

e. Make the following changes in the *w05m1Chart_LastFirst* worksheet:
   - Phase 1 Hardware value: **1.40**
   - Phase 2 Software value: **0.75**
   - Phase 3 Software value: **0.80**
   - Phase 4 Software value: **1.20**
   - Phase 3 Training value: **0.50**
   - Phase 4 Training value: **1.00**

DISCOVER

f. Update the linked chart object in the Word document. Center the chart horizontally on the page.

g. Select the heading *Computer Training Association, Inc.* and display the text as WordArt using **Gradient Fill - Blue, Accent 1, Shadow** (first row, second column). Modify the format of the WordArt by completing the following steps:
   - Change the font size to **24** and bold the text.
   - Use Help to learn how to create a custom fill color. Use the RGB values **196**, **200**, **234** as the custom color.
   - Apply a **10 pt Soft Edges Shape Effect**.
   - Increase width to **6"**.
   - Set the position to display the object in the top center with **square text wrapping**. Delete any blank lines if necessary.

h. Save and close the file, and submit based on your instructor's directions.

2 BRM Online Gift Baskets Sales Newsletter

You are the Web designer for BRM Online Gift Baskets, Inc., and you are in charge of developing the monthly sales newsletter. You have to advertise two sales items, announce the monthly lucky draw, and write a short Tips section, so the layout of the newsletter is important. The text you use for the newsletter is included in a file. Refer to Figure 5.41 as you complete this exercise.

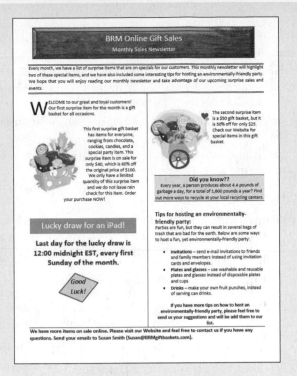

FIGURE 5.41 Online Gift Baskets Newsletter

a. Open *w05m2GiftBaskets* and save it as ***w05m2GiftBaskets_LastFirst***. If you receive a message stating *Your document will be upgraded to the newest file format*, click **OK** to continue.

b. Set a **1.5" top margin** and a **0.18" bottom margin** for the whole document. Change **left and right margins** to **0.5"**. Increase the bottom margin as needed to comply with your printer's capability.

c. Create a two-column newsletter that displays a line between columns. Use a section break after the first paragraph to enable this paragraph and a masthead as a one-column section.

d. Create a masthead for the newsletter by completing the following steps:

- Insert a bevel shape (third row, first column in the Basic Shapes category) that spans the top of the page. Fill the bevel shape with the picture *w05m2Woods.jpg*.
- Add the text **BRM Online Gift Sales Monthly Sales Newsletter** to display on the shape. Change **Spacing after** to **0 pt**.
- Select the text *BRM Online Gift Sales* and change the font size to **20 pt** and have it display on the first line. The font size for *Monthly Sales Newsletter* should be **14 pt**, and it should display on the second line below.

e. Move the first paragraph, which starts *Every month, we have a list of surprise items* to the one-column section and display it just below the masthead. Justify the text and apply a top and bottom double line border to the paragraph. The border should be **3/4 pt** wide and colored **dark blue**.

f. Apply a **drop cap** to the first letter of the word *WELCOME*, which displays on the top of the left column.

g. Format the gift basket image to **Square Wrap Text**. Fix the image's position on the page.

h. Create a text box using the Ion Sidebar 1 style below *Order your purchase NOW!* to emphasize the lucky draw information. Insert **Lucky draw for an iPad!** as the sidebar title, center it, and increase the font size to **20**. Drag the sidebar to the bottom-left corner and change the height to **2.5"**. Increase the text size to **18** and fix the sidebar's position on the page.

i. Insert a diamond shape that is **1.2"** high and **1.5"** wide. Use the rotate handle to display it. Fill the shape using a **yellow color** and group the diamond shape with a text box containing the **16 pt** text **Good Luck!** Display the grouped item below the text in the sidebar.

j. Insert a column break that forces the second surprise sales item to display in the right column. Search for clip art of a gift basket and display it on the left side of the paragraph. Insert at least one line return at the end of the paragraph to add space before the *Did you know??* heading that follows.

k. Select the heading *Did you know??* and the short paragraph that follows it. Apply a black single-line top and bottom border and also apply the shading pattern style **10%**. Bold and center the *Did you know??* heading. Increase the font size to **14**.

l. Create a bulleted list out of the tips for hosting an environment-friendly party. Increase the font size of the *Tips* heading to **14**.

m. Select the paragraph that begins *We have more items on sale online*. Apply a one-column format to the paragraph and apply a single-line top border. Increase the font size to **12 pt** and bold the text in this paragraph. Select the paragraph at the bottom of the right column that begins *If you have more tips* and bold the text and align center.

n. Save and close the file, and submit based on your instructor's directions.

3 Create a Family Tree

CREATIVE CASE

You have decided to begin charting your genealogy. You have a number of different methods for displaying the family tree, but you decide to use SmartArt graphics to show your immediate family. If directed by your instructor, substitute your own personal information and styles for those in the instructions below.

a. Open a new document and save it as **w05m3Family_LastFirst**.

b. Change the document orientation to **Landscape** so you can more easily view the complete family tree.

c. Insert the **Horizontal Hierarchy SmartArt graphic** from the Hierarchy group. Populate the family tree by completing the following steps:
- Click in the first element on the left and type **Michelle** in the first box.
- Type **Gary** and **Sandra** in the second-level boxes to represent Michelle's parents.
- Type **Lester** and **Verdene** in the boxes that represent Gary's parents.
- Type **Sidney** in the box to represent Sandra's father.
- Open the Text pane, add a box for Sandra's mother, and then type **Effie**.
- With the text box open, create sub-bullets so you can add Lester's parents, **Ralph** and **Emma**. Then add sub-bullets to represent Verdene's parents, **George** and **Mary**. Add sub-bullets for Sidney's parents, **Miles** and **Minnie**, and finally, add bullets for Effie's parents, **Jasper** and **Lou**.

d. Modify the chart by completing the following steps:
- Change the height of the chart to **6"** and the width to **9"**.
- Change the color set to your favorite colors.
- Change the Shape Fill to use an appropriate and coordinating color.
- Modify Shape Effects to use some visual effects of your choice.
- Change the position to **Middle Center with Square Text wrapping**.

e. Insert a text box at the top of the document to display the heading **My Family Tree**. Make the following enhancements to the text box:
- Change the size of the text to **28 pt** and center the text in the box.
- Change the font to use any **WordArt Quick Style**.
- Modify the Shape Style to use any style that you like.
- Set the height of the text box to **0.7"** and the width to **3"**.
- Modify Shape Effects to use some visual effects of your choice.
- Change the position so that the text box displays in the top-left corner of the SmartArt diagram.

f. Save and close the file, and submit based on your instructor's directions.

4 Travel Brochure

FROM SCRATCH

A local travel agency is conducting a contest for the best travel brochure. Your instructor wants the class to participate in this contest, and he has divided the students into groups of four. Your group project is to design a three-fold, professional-looking brochure with a country tour theme. Feel free to use any kind of graphical features that you have learned in this chapter to enhance your brochure.

a. Use an online collaboration tool such as Google groups or Skype to conduct a face-to-face meeting with your group members. During this online chat session, you will do the following:
- Choose a name for the group and select a group leader.
- Develop a list of tasks to complete.
- Assign tasks and responsibilities to each group member.

b. The list of tasks will include, but not be limited to, the following:
- Find a specific country to be the main focus of the brochure.
- Develop the tour itinerary and present the tour information in a table.
- Search for several pictures, either online or personal, to illustrate a concept or event.
- Design a masthead for the first page of the brochure.
- Insert a pull quote to highlight key components of the tour.
- Type the agency's contact information, Web site link, and e-mail address on the last page of the brochure.
- Format the final document with a border, narrow margins, and balanced columns.

c. Use the Snipping tool, SnagIt, or the PrtScn key to capture the chat session at several stages as a record of the contribution from team members. Copy and paste all the screenshots into a Word file and save it as **w05m4Travel1_GroupName**.

d. The team leader will create a SkyDrive or Dropbox.com account, where each member can share and open the draft documents while designing the brochure.

e. Save the brochure as **w05m4Travel2_GroupName**.

f. Post the final version of the brochure and the screenshot files to the online storage location.

g. Inform your instructor that the documents are ready for grading and give directions to where they are located.

Beyond the Classroom

Astronomy Is Fun!

RESEARCH CASE

You are a member of the local astronomy club and have been asked to create a monthly newsletter for elementary schools and home-schooled children. Some information and a few short articles have already been provided to you, but it is not enough material for a whole newsletter. You can perform an Internet search to gather information so you can provide a chart of times when they might see shuttles or the ISS pass overhead. You will probably want to use an Excel file to keep track of times so it is easy to update for the next newsletter. Use the techniques from this chapter to organize your facts and present a professional-looking newsletter that children will enjoy reading. Open the Word document *w05b2Stars*, save your changes to **w05b2Stars_LastFirst**, and then submit based on your instructor's directions.

Car Financing Information

DISASTER RECOVERY

You work for a local automotive dealer, and your supervisor requests your help to fix a document he was unable to complete. He attempted to create a document that describes a vehicle, including a spreadsheet calculation for pricing that can be updated automatically. He thinks this will be a great resource for all sales associates, but his first attempt to create the document was not successful. He did not properly link the document with the source file, nor did his graphical enhancements provide the effects he desires. You have been assigned the task of repairing the document so the pricing information from the *w05b3Cooper.xlsx* spreadsheet can be updated easily and automatically. You must also modify the document to display the graphical elements correctly and make any other improvements that create a professional-looking document. Open the Word document your supervisor created, *w05b3Car*, save your changes to **w05b3Car_LastFirst**, and then submit based on your instructor's directions.

Job Fair

SOFT SKILLS CASE

FROM SCRATCH

You will create a professional-looking newsletter describing (a) information of the job fair (date, time, place, and vendors) and (b) strategies for getting an interview. Use the features that you had learned to enhance your document. Some of the recommended features include, but art not limited to, masthead and a reverse, columns, SmartArt or Shapes graphic, and hyperlinks to the recruiters' Websites. Use any of the predefined styles in desktop publishing to add personality to your newsletter. After you have checked the spelling and grammar of your newsletter, save it as **w05b4JobFair_LastFirst**. Submit the document based on your instructor's directions.

Capstone Exercise

You are hired as a marketing manager for a small airline service that provides transportation from Denver to frequently requested locations and vacation cities such as Las Vegas, Orlando, and New York. Your first big assignment is to develop a marketing flyer that can be printed and mailed to potential customers in the Denver area and also in the cities serviced by the airline. From your previous marketing experience, you know that it is important to emphasize the positive attributes of the airline as well as provide information that will generate interest, and eventually revenue for, the company. In this exercise, you will recreate the newsletter as you see it in Figure 5.42.

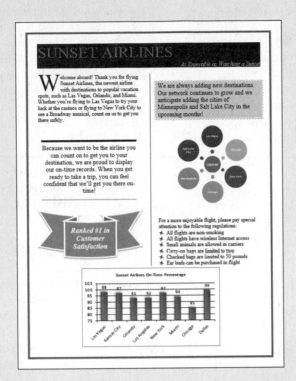

FIGURE 5.42 Sunset Airlines Flyer

Create the Masthead

You have a document with several important pieces of information that should be used in the marketing flyer. You must format the page so it can accommodate the amount of information you display, as well as any graphics you might add later.

a. Open the file named *w05c1Airline* and save it as **w05c1Airline_LastFirst**.

b. Change the margins to **0.7"** on all sides.

c. Set a **Continuous Section Break** at the beginning of the document. Use a single-column format for the masthead.

d. Create a masthead with the main heading **SUNSET AIRLINES**. Use a Reverse on the heading by changing the background to **100% solid black** and use the Text Effect **Gradient Fill - Orange, Accent 6, Inner Shadow** on *Sunset Airlines*. Increase font size to **36 pt**. Left-align the heading.

e. Create a second line for the masthead and type the subheading **As Nice as Riding into the Sunset**. Change the font size to **13 pt** and apply **Italics**. Change the color of the subheading to **Orange, Accent 6, Lighter 40%**. Right align the subheading.

Create Columns and Format Text

You now need to adjust the text to display in two columns below the masthead. You will also make several modifications to that text so that it is visually appealing and conveys all the important information the airline wants to promote to potential customers.

a. Set a two-column format to arrange the text below the masthead. Display a line between the columns and set equal column width. Insert another Continuous Section Break at the end of the text and set the area below to display in one column.

b. Set a dropped cap letter on the first letter of the word *Welcome* in the first paragraph.

c. Cut the paragraph that starts with the phrase *Because we want to be the airline* and display it in a text box in the same place using the Motion Quote design from the Text Box gallery. Add a row of 20 stars at both the top and bottom of the quote. Set the height to **1.9"**, set it to wrap on top and bottom, and then center the text. Adjust the position of the text box so it is centered horizontally in the column and fix on the page.

d. Insert a column break to force the paragraph that starts with the phrase *We are always adding* to display at the top of the second column. Apply a box border around the paragraph using the wavy line style, colored **Orange, Accent 6**, and with a **1 1/2 pt width**. Set shading for the fill of the box using the color **Orange, Accent 6, Lighter 60%**.

e. Insert a page border that uses the style found fourth from the bottom of the style list. Use the **Orange, Accent 6 color** and a **3 pt width**.

f. Use a bulleted list to organize the regulations listed under the paragraph that starts *For a more enjoyable flight*. Customize the bullets to use the airplane symbol, Webdings: 241. Decrease the indent of the bulleted list to display each item on one line.

g. Change the font of the paragraph and bulleted list to **Verdana** and set the size to **11 pt**.

Add Graphics for Visual Effects

You have several ways to make the flyer visually stimulating, but you know that it is easy to add too much and thus defeat the purpose of attracting customers. You decide to use SmartArt, WordArt, and a few shapes to complete the look.

a. Position the insertion point at the bottom of the document. Insert a SmartArt object; use the Diverging Radial from the *Cycle* section. Display the Text pane and type **Denver** on the first line to represent the circle in the middle. Press the down arrow to move to the next bullet and type the next city, **Las Vegas**. Continue to press the down arrow after each city to complete the graphic with the cities **Orlando**, **New York**, **Chicago**. Press **Enter** after you type *Chicago* and type **Minneapolis (Coming Soon!)**. Press **Enter** once again and type **Salt Lake City (Coming Soon!)**.

b. Change the Color scheme of the SmartArt to use **Colorful - Accent Colors**.

c. Format the SmartArt object with **Square Text wrapping** and change the size so the object is **2.5"** high and **3.5"** wide. Display the SmartArt below the shaded paragraph in the second column. Change the Layout properties to center the object horizontally in the column and use a *Lock anchor* setting so it will remain in position.

d. Place the insertion point at the end of the document. Open the Excel workbook *w05c1Flights.xlsx* and save it as **w05c1Flights_LastFirst.xlsx**. Copy the chart from the spreadsheet and link it into the Word document.

e. Reduce the chart size as needed so it fits centered on the bottom of the page, in the one-column section. If necessary, change the wrapping style and use the *Lock anchor* setting for precise placement. Edit the data in the Excel worksheet so the Los Angeles on-time percentage increases to **93%** in **cell D5** and update the chart in the flyer to reflect this change.

f. Insert a **Curved Up Ribbon shape** at the bottom of the first column. Change the shape style to **Light 1 Outline, Colored Fill - Orange, Accent 6**. Display the text **Ranked #1 in Customer Satisfaction** on the Ribbon. Increase the size of the text to **16 pt** and apply bold formatting and center the text. Use the yellow sizing handles on the top of the ribbon object to increase the size of the face of the ribbon so the text fits on it, if necessary.

g. Insert a Sun shape in the bottom-left corner of the flyer. The height and width of the object should be **1.2"**. Change the shape style to **Colored Fill - Orange, Accent 6**. Copy the object and paste it to create a second identical object. Drag the second object to the bottom-right corner of the flyer and use the Align Objects button to align so the two suns appear as bookends to the chart. Fix the position of the two suns on the page using the *Layout options* dialog box.

h. Make adjustments to spacing and line returns as necessary to display all text and objects without overlapping. Save and close all files, and submit based on your instructor's directions.

Time Saving Tools

Using Templates, Multiple Documents, and Themes

CHAPTER **6**

OBJECTIVES AFTER YOU READ THIS CHAPTER, YOU WILL BE ABLE TO:

1. Select a template from the Backstage view p. 58
2. Create a Word template p. 61
3. Use Building Blocks p. 61
4. View documents side by side p. 69
5. Merge documents p. 70
6. Use navigational tools p. 75
7. Customize theme colors, fonts, and effects p. 87

CASE STUDY | Computer Training Concepts, Inc.

Alexandra Caselman is the director of marketing at Computer Training Concepts, Inc., a business that provides technical training on a variety of computer systems to other companies. Alexandra is responsible for collecting information about a potential training event, such as how much time the training will take, how many instructors will be needed, and how much the training event will cost. She collects this information from her staff, then spends a great deal of time copying and pasting the information into a few documents that she can package together and send to a potential client.

During a recent meeting, she mentions this cumbersome task to you, her assistant director, and you mention that Word 2013 has features that will make the process of assembling the information more efficient. Alexandra decides to split the job with you since her method of compiling the information is outdated and slow. She decides to set up some of the documents, then transfer all the files to you. At that point, you will take the information provided from a variety of sources and assemble into one very nice-looking document.

Document Templates

Word is useful for creating very interesting and complex documents because it provides a variety of formatting features that you can apply on your own. You can jump-start the formatting process by using professional designs provided in the form of templates. A *template* is a partially completed document that contains preformatted text and/or graphics. Word provides a variety of templates for common documents, and additional templates can be downloaded from Office.com. You can use Word templates to create letters, memos, reports, resumes, agendas, calendars, and brochures, as well as other documents. Each template contains the framework of formats and text to decrease the time it takes you to create a document. You can also develop your own templates to use when you create certain types of documents that are used frequently, such as specialized reports.

In this section, you will use a template to start a document. You save time using a template because you do not have to set fonts, bullets, or create a style for the document. You also can view and download more templates from Office.com.

TIP Document Template File Extensions

Document templates use the file extensions .dotx or .dotm (if it contains a macro) in Word 2013. Previous versions of Word (2007) use .dot as the extension for templates. When you search for a template on your computer, you must click the *Type of Files* arrow in the Open dialog box to display All Word Templates (*.dotx; *.dotm; *.dot).

Selecting a Template from the Backstage View

Each time you create a new blank document by clicking the New icon on the Quick Access Toolbar, you use the *Normal template*, the framework that defines the 1" left, right, top, and bottom margins, left horizontal alignment, 11 pt Calibri font, 8 pt After spacing, Multiple Line Spacing, and other settings. However, when you click the File tab on the Ribbon and click New, a menu of template options displays in the Backstage view from which you can select, as shown in Figure 6.1. To preview a template, you can click the particular template, click Create on the informational dialog box, and a new document will open with all the features, styles, and placeholders for information that you provide to complete the selected document. A *placeholder* is a field or block of text used to determine the position of objects in a document. If you insert text beside a placeholder instead of replacing it, you should be sure to delete the placeholder before you save the document.

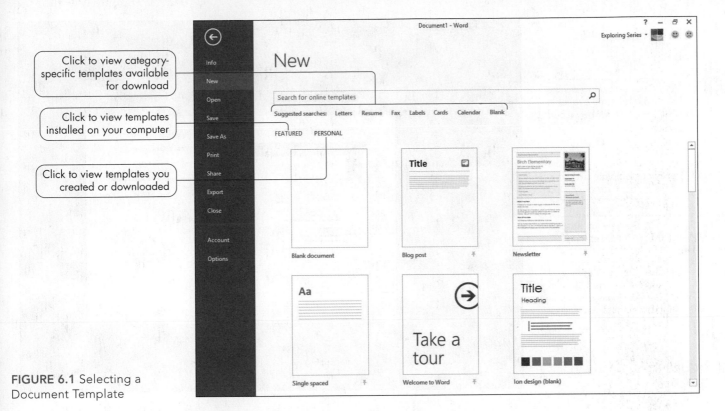

Click to view category-specific templates available for download

Click to view templates installed on your computer

Click to view templates you created or downloaded

FIGURE 6.1 Selecting a Document Template

Select and Download a Resume Template

STEP 1 Templates often help provide assistance with layout for some documents, and Word provides several different templates for different types of documents, as shown in Figure 6.2, such as resumes, curriculum vitae, memos, letters, and faxes. Every person looking for a job should have a resume. A *curriculum vitae (CV)* is similar to a resume; it displays your skills, accomplishments, job history, or other employment information, and is often used by academics. A variety of different ways exist to lay out a resume, and using a template can be an easy way to determine which style best matches your needs. Many of these templates are preformatted using styles or themes such as Facet, Integral, Ion, Organic, Retrospect, Slice, and Whisp. By using templates with a similar style, you can coordinate documents. If the default resume templates do not meet your needs, you can review other choices on Office.com. To select a resume template, do the following:

1. Click the FILE tab.
2. Click New.
3. Click Resume in the *Suggested Searches* section of the Templates pane. A list of resume categories displays.
4. Click any of the resumes to preview it.

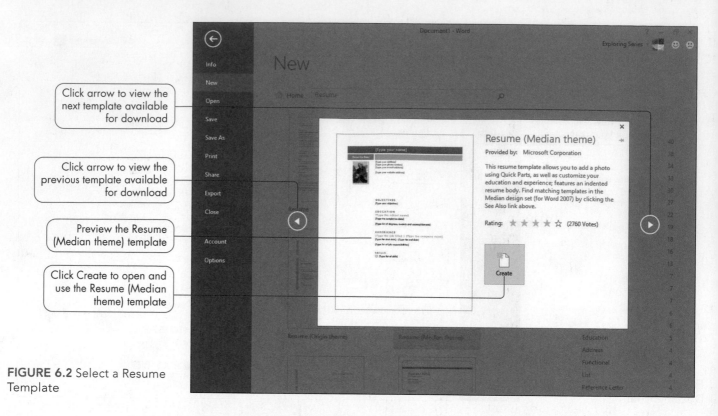

Click arrow to view the next template available for download

Click arrow to view the previous template available for download

Preview the Resume (Median theme) template

Click Create to open and use the Resume (Median theme) template

FIGURE 6.2 Select a Resume Template

After you select a resume template from the long list of choices, you may download the template to your computer. To transfer a selected template to your computer, do the following:

1. Click Create after you select a resume template of your choice from the gallery.
2. After the template downloads, it opens in a new document window to display placeholders and sample text as shown in Figure 6.3.
3. Replace the placeholders with your personal information.
4. Save the document; it will automatically save as a Word document. If you want to save the document as a template, change the *Save as type* to Word Template.

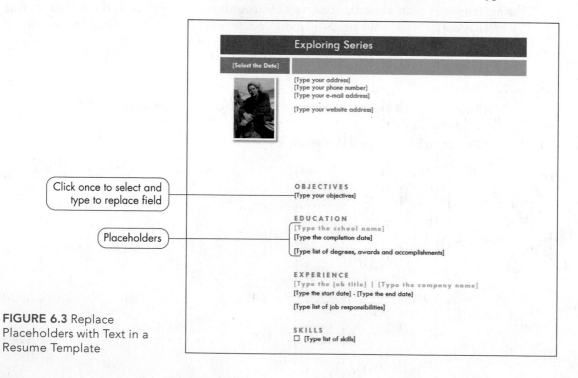

Click once to select and type to replace field

Placeholders

FIGURE 6.3 Replace Placeholders with Text in a Resume Template

After you use or rename a template, it will display in the *Featured* or *Personal* templates category in the Backstage view for a New File. But you can also view other templates installed on your PC or other templates you have created. If you cannot find a template that meets your immediate needs, you can view additional templates available for download from Office.com.

Creating a Word Template

If you create or use a particular document frequently, with only minor modifications each time, you should save the document as a template. When you create the template, you can insert placeholders for the information you change frequently. You can create a document template that contains a company letterhead, greeting, body, and salutation, thereby requiring you to replace only the information for the recipient. Or if you have a report that you update on a regular basis that is contained in a very structured and detailed table, you might consider making the report into a template.

Save a Document as a Template

STEP 2 » To save a document as a template, you should note the location where the template is saved. Word will automatically save the template to a default location for templates. However, you can specify a location on your own hard drive, portable storage device, or SkyDrive account by navigating through the folders of your choice. An appropriate location to store templates on the hard drive would be the Document Library folder. Be aware that templates saved in other locations will not display in the Templates dialog box. To save a document as a template, do the following:

1. Open the selected document.
2. Click the FILE tab.
3. Click Save As.
4. Click Browse.
5. Change the *Save as type* to Word template, as shown in Figure 6.4.
6. The file extension is added for you. Click Save.

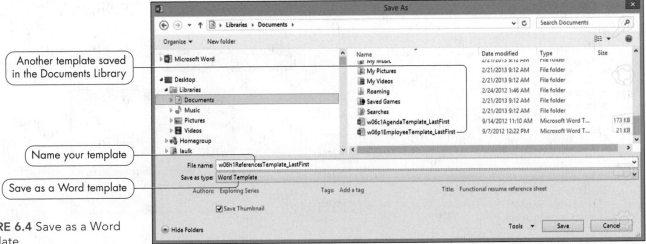

FIGURE 6.4 Save as a Word Template

Using Building Blocks

When you create templates or Word documents that frequently contain particular content or objects, you might want to save the content or objects so that you can use them again without recreating or retyping. Word enables you to create or save objects, called ***Building***

Blocks, which are predefined and can be inserted quickly, easily, and frequently into any document. Building Blocks might include disclaimers that display at the bottom of a document, a company address or logo, a header, or a footer. Other objects that you can save as a Building Block include watermarks, tables, or larger objects such as a cover page to a report, or a whole page with specific tables and formatting. A predefined list of Building Blocks is available in the Building Block Organizer for you to quickly and easily insert into your own documents. A gallery of Building Blocks includes Bibliographies, Cover Pages, Equations, Footers, Headers, Page Numbers, Table of Contents, Tables, Text Boxes, and Watermarks. These Building Blocks can also be accessed from the Insert tab, Design tab, and References tab. You can also save information as AutoText, which is a type of Building Block, to store text or graphics that you want to use again, such as a standard contract clause or a long distribution list. You insert AutoText at a specific location indicated by the cursor, but you can insert building blocks anywhere in the document without having to indicate the specific location—for instance, a cover page or table of contents.

Create and Insert a Custom Building Block

STEP 2 » Each selection of text or graphics that you add to the Quick Part Gallery is stored in the Building Blocks Organizer and is assigned a unique name that makes it easy for you to find the content when you want to use it. You can also assign a name you prefer. Figure 6.5 demonstrates the creation of the AutoText. To save an item as AutoText, which is also a customized Building Block, do the following:

1. Select the item.
2. Click the INSERT tab.
3. Click Quick Parts in the Text group.
4. Select Save Selection to Quick Part Gallery.
5. In the Create New Building Block dialog box, assign a name that reflects the object, select AutoText from the gallery, and then click OK.

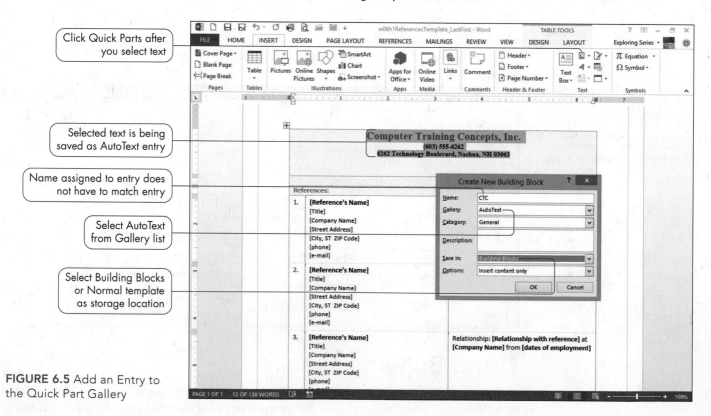

FIGURE 6.5 Add an Entry to the Quick Part Gallery

After you add text to the Quick Part Gallery, you can type the unique name that you assigned to the Quick Part and press F3 to insert the remainder text into your document. Word 2013 contains many Building Blocks already. You can also view and insert the building blocks into your document by doing the following:

1. Position the insertion point where you want to insert the Building Block.
2. Click the INSERT tab.
3. Click Quick Parts in the Text group and do one of the following:
   a. Click AutoText and select the specific AutoText entry.
   b. Click Building Blocks Organizer, as shown in Figure 6.6.
      - Click Name under *Building Blocks* to sort the Quick Parts alphabetically by name.
      - Scroll down the list to select the specific Quick Part that you want.
      - Click Insert.

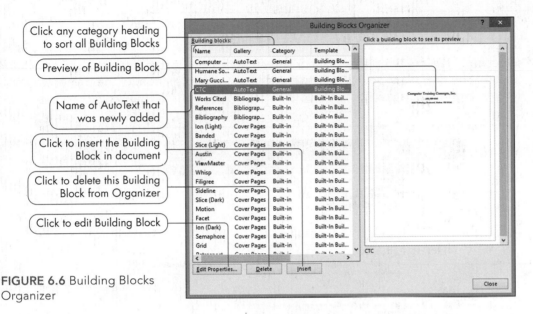

FIGURE 6.6 Building Blocks Organizer

Quick Concepts ✓

1. Why is it important to use the correct extension when saving a file? *p. 58*

2. What are the advantages of using a predefined template? *p. 58*

3. What are the benefits of using a building block? *p. 61*

Hands-On Exercises

1 Document Templates

When Alexandra Caselman assembles a quote for the cost of training, she always includes the instructor's resumes. She also creates a sheet of references—people who have used the services of Computer Training Concepts, Inc. She would like each resume and reference sheet to have a similar look, so she decides to use document templates instead of starting with blank documents each time.

Skills covered: Select and Download a Resume Template • Create and Insert a Custom Building Block • Modify a Template and Save as a Document

STEP 1 >> SELECT AND DOWNLOAD A RESUME TEMPLATE

Alexandra recently found the selection of resume templates that comes with Word and learned that she can search for more templates online at Office.com. She decides to select one style and fill in the information for the trainer whom she will send to the next job. Refer to Figure 6.7 as you complete Step 1.

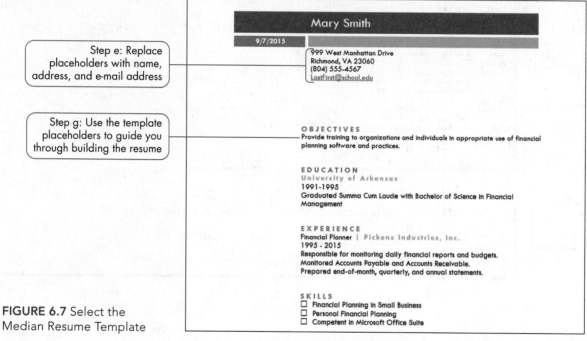

FIGURE 6.7 Select the Median Resume Template

a. Start Word.

The Backstage view displays a list of templates available to users.

b. Click **Resume** in the Suggested Searches box of the Templates pane. In the Resume pane, scroll down and click the **Resume (Median theme) template**. Click **Create** to open the template.

The Resume (Median theme) template opens as a new document, and the User Name specified in Word Options displays at the top.

c. Click one time in the brown bar that displays your name at the top of the resume and click the **Resume Name tab**. Click the **Quick Parts arrow** that displays on the right side of the tab and click **Name**.

This template has two formats—*Name* and *Name with Photo*. When you click Name, you choose the template without a photograph.

> **TROUBLESHOOTING:** If your name does not display at the top of the resume, you can click the name placeholder and type to replace or modify it with your name. If it still does not display, place your cursor on the left side of the placeholder, type your name, and then delete the placeholder.

d. Click the **FILE tab** and click **Save As**. Click **Browse**. Type **w06h1Resume_LastFirst** in the **File name box**. Confirm the *Save as type* box displays *Word Document* and click **Save**.

> **TROUBLESHOOTING:** If the *Save as type* box displays *Word Template (*.dotx)*, click the *Save as type* arrow and click Word Document (*.docx) before you save.

> **TROUBLESHOOTING:** If you receive a message warning you that your document will be upgraded to the newest file format, click OK to accept the upgrade.

e. Replace the next three placeholders (address, phone, and e-mail) with the following information, right-click the **Web site address placeholder**, and then click **Remove Content Control** to delete the placeholder:

999 West Manhattan Drive
Richmond, VA 23060
(804) 555-4567
LastFirst@school.edu

 TIP **Change User Names**

To replace the current User Name with your own, click the File tab, click Options, click General, if necessary, and then type your name in the *User name* box in the *Personalize Your Copy of Microsoft Office* section.

f. Click **Select the Date** in the template to view an arrow control. Click the arrow and click **September 07, 2015**.

g. Type the following information in the resume for each category:

Objectives	[Type your objectives]	Provide training to organizations and individuals in appropriate use of financial planning software and practices.
Education	[Type the school name]	University of Arkansas
	[Type the completion date]	1991–1995
	[Type list of degrees, awards and accomplishments]	Graduated Summa Cum Laude with Bachelor of Science in Financial Management
Experience	[Type the job title]	Financial Planner
	[Type the company name]	Pickens Industries, Inc.
	[Type the start date]–[Type the end date]	1995–2015
	[Type list of job responsibilities]	Responsible for monitoring daily financial reports and budgets. Monitored Accounts Payable and Accounts Receivable. Prepared end-of-month, quarterly, and annual statements.
Skills	[Type list of skills]	Financial Planning in Small Business Personal Financial Planning Competent in Microsoft Office Suite

h. Save and close the file, and submit all files based on your instructor's directions.

The next step in compiling the proposal for a potential client is to generate a list of references. This information changes often, so Alexandra wants to use a template that she can update quickly. She also inserts the company letterhead frequently, so she decides to save that information as a custom Building Block, which can be inserted with only a few key strokes, instead of retyping the information each time. Refer to Figure 6.8 as you complete Step 2.

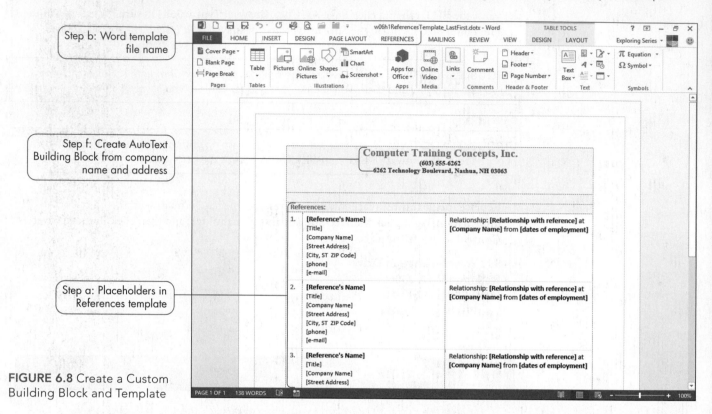

FIGURE 6.8 Create a Custom Building Block and Template

a. Click the **FILE tab** and click **New**. Type **References** in the **Search for online templates search box** and press. **Enter**. Scroll down until you see the Functional resume references sheet. Click to select it and click **Create**.

> **TROUBLESHOOTING:** If a Microsoft Office Genuine Advantage dialog box displays, click *Do not show this message again* and click Continue. If you work in a lab environment, you may not have permission to download document templates from Office.com. If that is the case, read Steps 2 and 3 and continue to the next section.

A download window appears briefly, then the Functional resume reference sheet template displays with placeholders and sample text.

b. Click the **FILE tab** and click **Save As**. Click **Browse**. When the Save As dialog box displays, click the **Save as type arrow**. Click **Word Template**. Type **w06h1ReferencesTemplate_ LastFirst** in the **File name box** and click **Save**.

If a Microsoft dialog box displays with a message about saving in a new file format, click OK. When you save this document as a template, you can open it later and make modifications without changing the original. Be sure to save the file as a template (.dotx) and not a document (.docx).

c. Replace the placeholders at the top of the page by completing the following steps:

• Click the **[Your Name] placeholder** and type **Computer Training Concepts, Inc**.
• Select the **[phone] placeholder** and type **(603) 555-6262**.
• Click one time in the **[Street Address] placeholder** and type **6262 Technology Boulevard**.
• Click the **[City, ST ZIP Code] placeholder** and type **Nashua, NH 03063**.
• Click the **[E-mail] placeholder**, right-click, and then click **Remove Content Control**. Repeat this step for the [Website] placeholder.

d. Select the three lines that contain the company name, phone, and address. Click the **LAYOUT tab** and click **Merge Cells** in the Merge group. Select **Times New Roman** and click **Center** on the Mini toolbar.

e. Select the three lines that display the company name, phone, and address. Click the **INSERT tab**, click **Quick Parts** in the Text group, and then select **Save Selection to Quick Part Gallery**.

f. Complete the following steps within the Create New Building Block dialog box:

- Type **CTC** in the **Name box**.
- Click the **Gallery arrow** and select **AutoText**.
- Click the **Save In arrow** and select **Building Blocks**.
- Click **OK**.

The entry is added to the Normal template and will be available for use in all documents.

TROUBLESHOOTING: If you are in a lab environment, you might not have permission to add this item or save the changes to the Normal template. Consult with your instructor for alternate instructions, if necessary.

---

g. Test your Building Block by selecting the three lines and press **Delete**. On the INSERT tab, click **Quick Parts** in Text group, click **AutoText**, and click **CTC** at the top of the gallery list.

The entry displays just as you had formatted it. Now you can use this Building Block in other documents you design for the company.

h. Save the template.

STEP 3 >> MODIFY A TEMPLATE AND SAVE AS A DOCUMENT

Now that the template is set up, Alexandra forwards it to you so you can add the information about companies that will be used as references in this proposal. After adding the references, you save it as a document instead of a template. Refer to Figure 6.9 as you complete Step 3.

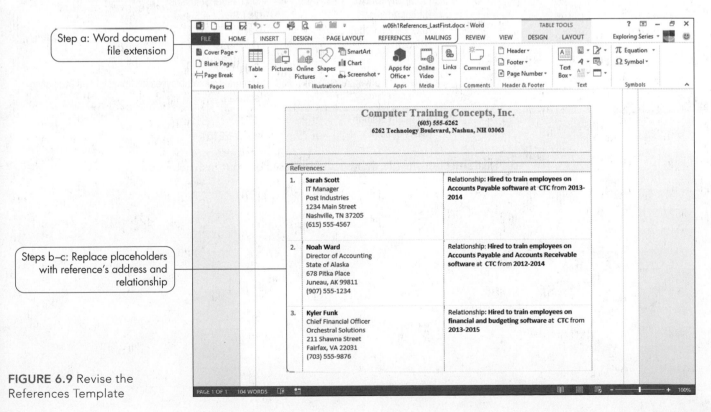

FIGURE 6.9 Revise the References Template

a. Click the **FILE tab** and click **Save As**. Click **Browse**. Click the **Save as type arrow** and select **Word Document**. Type in the file name **w06h1References_LastFirst**.

Be sure to save the file as a document (.docx) and not a template (.dotx).

b. Remove the e-mail placeholders for each reference because they are not used. Also, remove both rows containing the content for Reference #4 and Reference #5 since you only have three references. Select both rows, right-click, and click **Delete Rows**.

c. Type the following information into the respective reference placeholders:

Reference #1	[Reference's Name]	Sarah Scott
	[Title]	IT Manager
	[Company Name]	Post Industries
	[Street Address]	1234 Main Street
	[City, CT Zip Code]	Nashville, TN 37205
	[phone]	(615) 555-4567
	Relationship:	Relationship:
	[Relationship with reference]	Hired to train employees on Accounts Payable software
	[Company Name]	CTC
	[dates of employment]	2013–2014
Reference #2	[Reference's Name]	Noah Ward
	[Title]	Director of Accounting
	[Company Name]	State of Alaska
	[Street Address]	678 Pitka Place
	[City, CT Zip Code]	Juneau, AK 99811
	[phone]	(907) 555-1234
	Relationship:	Relationship:
	[Relationship with reference]	Hired to train employees on Accounts Payable and Accounts Receivable software
	[Company Name]	CTC
	[dates of employment]	2012–2014
Reference #3	[Reference's Name]	Kyler Funk
	[Title]	Chief Financial Officer
	[Company Name]	Orchestral Solutions
	[Street Address]	211 Shawna Street
	[City, CT Zip Code]	Fairfax, VA 22031
	[phone]	(703) 555-9876
	Relationship:	Relationship:
	[Relationship with reference]	Hired to train employees on financial and budgeting software
	[Company Name]	CTC
	[dates of employment]	2013–2015

d. Save and close the file. Submit all files based on your instructor's directions.

Multiple Documents

The collaboration features in Word facilitate an easy exchange of ideas and revisions to a document. But some users do not use the collaboration features, which causes the process of combining information into one document to be less efficient. Fortunately, other features in Word enable you to work with multiple documents simultaneously—you can view multiple documents at one time, as well as combine them into one.

In this section, you will view multiple documents side by side as well as compare and combine them. You will create a document that contains subdocuments and use tools to navigate within lengthy documents. Finally, you will create an electronic marker for a location in a document and use the Go To feature to find that marker.

Viewing Documents Side by Side

The *View Side by Side* feature enables you to display two documents on the same screen. This is a useful tool when you want to compare an original to a revised document or when you want to cut or copy a portion from one document to another.

View Two Documents Side by Side

STEP 1 » To view two documents side by side, you must open both documents. The *View Side by Side* command is grayed out if only one document is open. When the documents are open, click *View Side by Side* in the Window group on the View tab and the Word window will split to display each document as shown in Figure 6.10. If you have more than two documents open, when you click *View Side by Side*, the *Compare Side by Side* dialog box will display and you may select which document you want to display beside the active document.

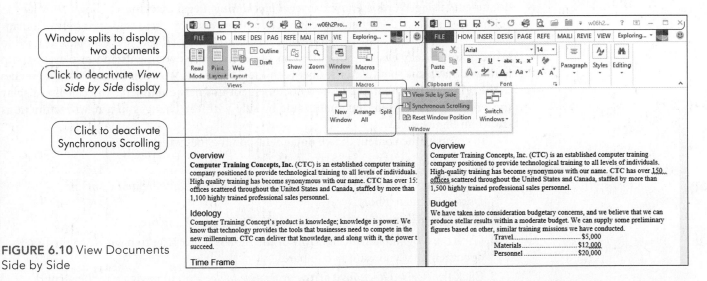

FIGURE 6.10 View Documents Side by Side

When the documents display side by side, synchronous scrolling is active by default. *Synchronous scrolling* enables you to scroll through both documents at the same time. If you want to scroll through each document independently, click Synchronous Scrolling on the View tab to toggle it off. If you are viewing two versions of the same document, synchronous scrolling enables you to view both documents using only one scroll bar. If you scroll through each document asynchronously, you must use the respective scroll bars to navigate through each document.

Resize Documents

While in *Side by Side* view, you can resize and reposition the two document windows. If you want to reset them to the original side-by-side viewing size, click Reset Window Position on the View tab. You can also switch the documents from left to right by clicking the Reset Windows position in the left document. To close *Side by Side* view, click *View Side by Side* to toggle it off. The document that contains the insertion point when you close *Side by Side* view will display as the active document.

Merging Documents

Besides enabling you to view two documents simultaneously, Word also provides different ways to combine multiple documents into one. The particular method you use depends on the purpose of the document. You might simply want to combine two documents, deciding which portions of each to keep and omit. You might need to add the entire contents of one document into another, or you might want to include the entire contents of several documents in one.

Ideally, when you have a document to submit to others for feedback, you want everyone to use the Track Changes feature in Word. However, sometimes it is necessary to have several people edit their own copy of the document simultaneously before they return it to you. When this occurs, you have several similar documents but with individual changes. Instead of compiling results from printed copies or viewing each one in *Side by Side* view to determine the differences, you can use the Compare and/or Combine features.

Compare Two Documents

The comparing of two documents and the displaying of the changes between the two documents using Word is known as **legal blacklining**. Legal blacklining allows attorneys to compare versions of documents or contracts, authors and editors to track progress of a manuscript, and financial managers to review changes in large tables. The **Compare** feature in Word automatically evaluates the contents of two or more documents and displays markup balloons that show the differences between the documents. You can display the differences in the original document, the revised document, or in a new document. You can also display the original and revised documents side by side with the changes in a new document as shown in Figure 6.11.

To compare the content of two documents, do the following:

1. Click the REVIEW tab.
2. Click Compare in the Compare group to display the *Compare and Combine Documents* dialog box.
3. Click Compare to display the Compare Documents dialog box.
4. Click the *Original document* arrow or the *Browse folder* icon to navigate to the first document that you want to compare.
5. Click the *Revised document* arrow or *Browse folder* icon to navigate to the second document that you want to compare.
6. Click the More button to display more options.
7. Click *New document* below *Show Changes in*. Click OK.
8. Click the document choice to keep formatting changes when a dialog box displays a message about keeping formatting changes.
9. Click *Continue with Merge*.
10. Click Compare in the Compare group and click Show Source Documents. You will have the following options regarding the two source documents: Hide Source Documents, Show Original, Show Revised, or Show Both.

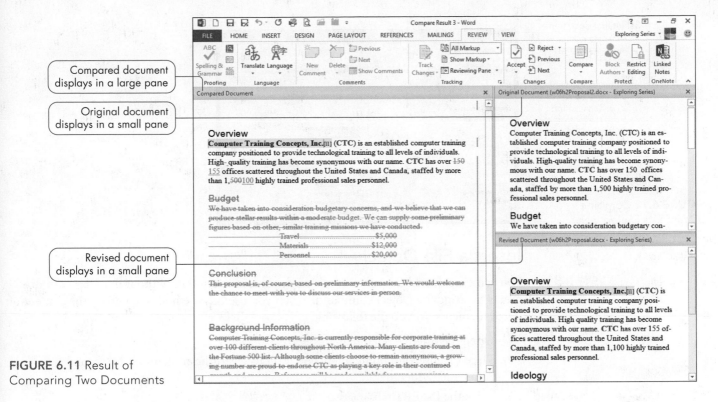

Compared document displays in a large pane

Original document displays in a small pane

Revised document displays in a small pane

FIGURE 6.11 Result of Comparing Two Documents

Combine Two Documents

STEP 2» If you want to go a step further than just viewing the differences, you can use the **Combine** feature to integrate all changes from multiple authors or documents into one single document. To use the Combine feature, click Compare on the Review tab and select Combine. The Combine Documents dialog box contains a variety of options you can invoke, as shown in Figure 6.12; however, options only display after clicking the More button. The option you are most likely to change is in the *Show changes* section where you determine in which document the Combined documents will display—in the original document, the revised document, or in a new document. If you do not want to modify the original documents, you should combine the changes into a new document.

To combine the content of two documents to a blank new document, do the following:

1. Open the target document(s) or a blank new document.
2. Click the REVIEW tab.
3. Click Compare in the Compare group.
4. Click Combine to display the Combine Documents dialog box.
5. Click the *Original document* arrow or the *Browse folder* icon to navigate to the first document that you want to combine.
6. Click the *Revised document* arrow or *Browse folder* icon to navigate to the second document that you want to combine.
7. Click the More button to display more options.
8. Click *New document* below *Show Changes in*. Click OK.
9. Click the document choice to keep formatting changes when a dialog box displays a message about keeping formatting changes.
10. Click *Continue with Merge*.
11. Click anywhere in the left panel box to activate the Revisions tab.
12. Close the Revisions tab.
13. Click Compare in the Compare group and click Show Source Documents. You will have the following options regarding the two source documents: Hide Source Documents, Show Original, Show Revised, or Show Both.

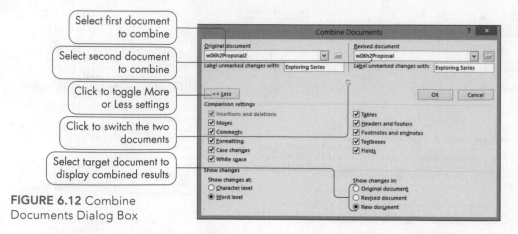

Select first document to combine

Select second document to combine

Click to toggle More or Less settings

Click to switch the two documents

Select target document to display combined results

FIGURE 6.12 Combine Documents Dialog Box

Insert a File Object

STEP 3 You can quickly add the contents of one document to another without opening both documents by using the Object command. When you use this method to combine the content of two documents, you do the following:

1. Open the original document.
2. Place the insertion point where you want to insert the contents of the second (unopened) document.
3. Click the INSERT tab.
4. Click Object in the Text group.
5. Click the *Create from File* tab, as seen in Figure 6.13. You will be prompted to browse to the file that contains the text you want to insert. After you select the file, click Insert and the entire contents will be placed in the open document.

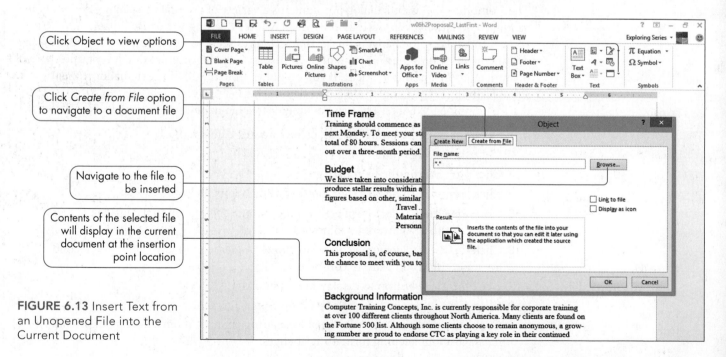

Click Object to view options

Click *Create from File* option to navigate to a document file

Navigate to the file to be inserted

Contents of the selected file will display in the current document at the insertion point location

FIGURE 6.13 Insert Text from an Unopened File into the Current Document

Create Master Documents and Subdocuments

STEP 3 Working with long documents can be cumbersome. If you are working with an older computer system, you may notice your computer slows down when you are working in a lengthy document—scrolling, finding and replacing, editing, and formatting may take longer to process. To improve this situation, you can create a *master document*, a document that acts like a binder for managing smaller documents. A smaller document that is a part of a master document is called a **subdocument**. The advantage of the master document is that you can work with several smaller documents, as opposed to a single large document. Thus, you edit the subdocuments individually and more efficiently than if they were all part of the same document. You can create a master document to hold the chapters of a book, where each chapter is stored as a subdocument. You also can use a master document to hold multiple documents created by others, such as a group project, where each member of the group is responsible for a section of the document. The Outlining tab on the Ribbon contains the Show Document and Collapse and Expand Subdocuments buttons, as well as other tools associated with master documents. Figure 6.14 displays a master document with three subdocuments. The subdocuments are collapsed in Figure 6.14 and expanded in Figure 6.15. The collapsed structure enables you to see at a glance the subdocuments that comprise the master document. You can insert additional subdocuments or remove existing subdocuments from the master document. Deleting a subdocument from within a master document does not delete the actual subdocument file. Look carefully at the subdocuments in Figure 6.14. A padlock appears to the left of the first line in subdocuments. All subdocuments are locked when collapsed.

FIGURE 6.14 Master Document Showing Collapsed Subdocuments

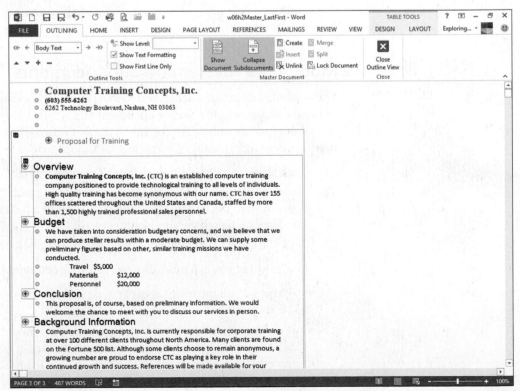

FIGURE 6.15 Master Document Showing Expanded Subdocuments

To work with master and subdocuments, do the following:

1. Open a blank new document.
2. Insert any Building Block if you like, such as a page title, company contact information, a masthead, or a page heading.

 TIP **Printing a Master Document**

If you click Print when a master document is displayed and the subdocuments are collapsed, the message *Do you want to open the subdocuments before continuing with this command?* appears. Click Yes to open the subdocuments so that they will print as one long document. Click No to print the master document that lists the subdocument file names as they display on the screen.

3. Type your headings on separate lines for each of your subdocuments.
4. Select all your headings and click Heading 2 from the Styles gallery on the HOME tab.
5. Click the VIEW tab.
6. Click Outline in the Views group to display the OUTLINING tab on the Ribbon.
7. Click Show Document in the Master Document group to display more master document commands.
8. Click Create in the Master Document group to display the individual subdocuments that were created for the selected headings.
9. Place the insertion point below the first subdocument heading.
10. Click Insert in the Master Document group to insert each subdocument individually into the master document. Navigate and select the first subdocument, and then click Open. Click *Yes to All* when prompted to rename the style in the subdocument.
11. Repeat Step 10 to insert more subdocuments.
12. Click OK to save changes to the master document.
13. Click Collapse Subdocuments in the Master Document group to collapse the subdocuments in the document, and to display the name and path of each saved subdocument.

Modify the Master and Subdocuments

The expanded structure enables you to view and edit the contents of the subdocuments. You can make changes to the master document at any time. However, you can make changes to the subdocuments only when the subdocument is unlocked. You have to issue locks to each subdocument individually. You can lock or unlock a document by doing the following:

1. Click Show Document in the Master Document group.
2. Click Lock Document in the Master Document group. The Lock Document command in the Master Document group is highlighted in a light orange color, and a padlock icon displays below the subdocument icon.
3. Click the Lock Document command again to unlock the subdocument.

Note, too, that you can make changes to a subdocument in one of the following two ways:

- When the subdocument is expanded (and unlocked) within a master document as in Figure 6.15.
- Open the subdocument as an independent document within Microsoft Word. You lock the subdocuments to prevent making changes to their content but also to prevent the subdocument from being deleted from the master document.

Regardless of how you edit the subdocuments, the attraction of a master document is the ability to work with multiple subdocuments simultaneously. The subdocuments are created independently of one another, with each subdocument stored in its own file. Then, when all of the subdocuments are finished, the master document is created, and the subdocuments are inserted into the master document, from where they are easily accessed. Inserting page numbers into the master document, for example, causes the numbers to run consecutively from one subdocument to the next. You also can create a table of contents or index for the master document that will reflect the entries in all of the subdocuments. And finally, you can print all of the subdocuments from within the master document with a single command.

Create Subdocuments from an Empty Master Document

Alternatively, you can reverse the process by starting with an empty master document and using it as the basis to create the subdocuments. This process is ideal for organizing a group project in school or at work, the chapters in a book, or the sections in a report. Start with a new document and type the topics assigned to each group member. Format each topic in a heading style within the master document and use the Create Subdocument command to create subdocuments based on those headings. Saving the master document will automatically save each subdocument in its own file.

Use Master Document and Subdocuments with Extreme Care

Creating a master document and subdocuments is a very useful feature if you want to combine several documents into one large document, for instance, when writing a manuscript. However, since this feature was introduced by Microsoft in Word 6, it had been problematic. Students using this feature must use the following precautions:

1. Backup the original files before creating the master document.
2. The newly created master document must be stored in the same directory as all the subdocuments.
3. If you move or rename a subdocument separately after you create the master document, you will break the link in the master document. You can only restore the link by deleting and recreating the link in the master file with the new file name.
4. If you want to move the master and subdocuments to a new location, you must first open the master file, then save all the subdocuments to the new location.
5. When you make changes to the links in the master document, you must delete all old subdocument files to avoid version confusion.
6. Do not attempt to recreate the master file. If you do, you must delete all the files previously created and used in your last attempt.

Using Navigational Tools

Without a reference source, such as a table of contents, it can be difficult to locate information in a long document. Even scrolling through a long document can be inefficient if you are uncertain of the exact location that you want to view. Fortunately, Word provides navigation tools that assist the author and reader in locating content quickly and easily.

Use the Navigation Pane

STEP 4>> You can use the Find and Go To features in Word to move through a document. Another helpful feature is the *Navigation Pane*, which enables you to navigate through the document by viewing headings, viewing pages, and browsing the results of your last search. The Navigation Pane setting is a toggle, enabling you to turn it on and off. When displayed, the Navigation Pane contains three tabs—one for each type of search.

You may navigate in a document using one of the following two ways:

- If you want to display the headings in a document, be sure the document is expanded to display the text of the whole document. The Navigation Pane will only display headings for a document that uses the styles feature to format headings. The best way to format headings is to apply the built-in title or heading styles from the Styles group on the Home tab. When you are working with long documents, this view provides a way to navigate quickly to a particular topic, as shown in Figure 6.16.

- In lieu of the document headings, you can display *thumbnails*—small pictures of each page in your document—in the Navigation Pane. Thumbnails display when you click the Pages tab in the Navigation Pane. As with the headings, you can click a thumbnail to move the insertion point to the top of that page. This is another method of navigating quickly through a document. Even though you cannot read the text on a thumbnail, you can see the layout of a page well enough to determine if that is a location you want to display (see Figure 6.17). And if you display revision marks and comments, the marks and comment balloons also display in the thumbnails.

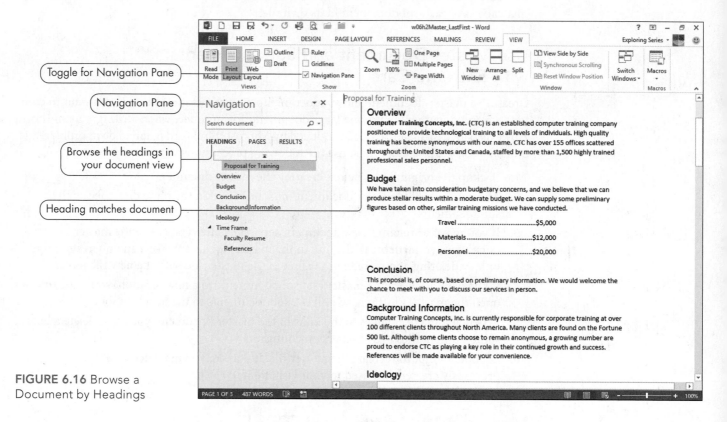

FIGURE 6.16 Browse a Document by Headings

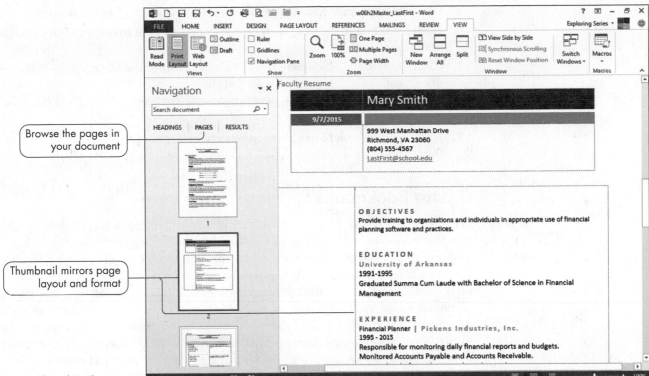

FIGURE 6.17 Thumbnails

The third panel in the Navigation Pane displays the results of a text search. When you type in a word or a string of text, each occurrence displays, as shown in Figure 6.18. You can click the occurrence and the text is highlighted in the document. This pane also enables you to search for other objects in the document, such as graphics and tables.

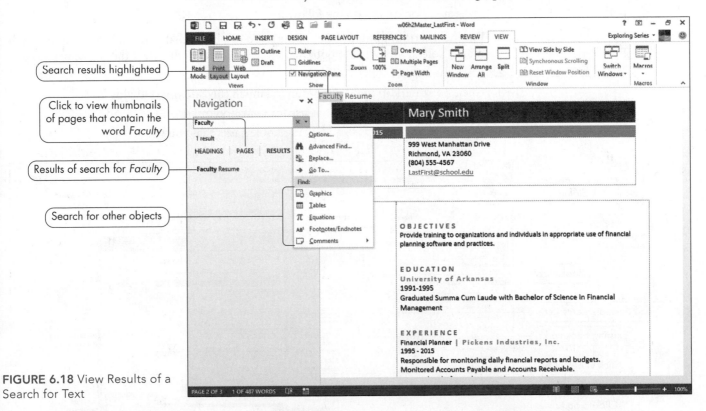

FIGURE 6.18 View Results of a Search for Text

To view your document using the Navigation Pane, do the following:

1. Click the VIEW tab.
2. Click Navigation Pane in the Show group.

3. Click Headings in the Navigation Pane to display headings in the document.

4. Click a heading in the pane to move the insertion point to the location of that heading in the document.

5. Click Pages in the Navigation Pane to display thumbnails of each page in the document.

6. Click a page in the pane to move the insertion point to the location of that page in the document.

7. If you conduct a word or phrase search, click Results in the Navigation Pane to view the results of the search.

Create Bookmarks

STEP 4 › When you read a book, you use a bookmark to help you return to that location quickly. Word provides the *bookmark* feature as an electronic marker for a specific location in a document, enabling you to find that location quickly. Bookmarks are helpful to mark a location where you are working. You can scroll to other parts of a document, then quickly go back to the bookmarked location. In Word, you can bookmark anything, including a heading or a paragraph, an image such as picture, an embedded chart, a table, an audio clip or a video file. Bookmarks are inserted at the location of the insertion point. The Bookmark command is in the Links group on the Insert tab. After you click the command, the Bookmark dialog box displays, and you can designate the name of the bookmark, as shown in Figure 6.19. Bookmark names cannot contain spaces or hyphens; however, they may contain the underscore character to improve readability. Try to use short, concise, and descriptive names to designate your bookmark. You may sort your bookmarks according to the bookmark name (in alphabetical order) or the bookmark location in the document. You may also delete any unwanted bookmarks by clicking the specified bookmark and clicking Delete in the Bookmark dialog box.

To create a bookmark, do the following:

1. Put the insertion point in front of the word or phrase that you want to add to the bookmark. Note: If you want to bookmark a whole paragraph, select the whole paragraph.

2. Click the INSERT tab.

3. Click Bookmark in the Links group to launch the Bookmark dialog box.

4. Type the word that you want to use for your bookmark and click Add.

5. Repeat the above steps to add all the bookmarks that you want.

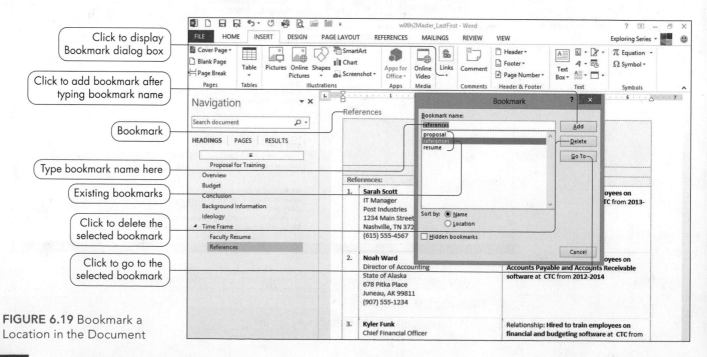

FIGURE 6.19 Bookmark a Location in the Document

Review the List of Bookmarks

STEP 4 >> At any time after creating your bookmarks, you may review the list of bookmarks and navigate to bookmarked content by doing the following:

1. Click the INSERT tab.
2. Click Bookmark in the Links group to launch the Bookmark dialog box.
3. Click a bookmark in the *Bookmark name* list.
4. Click Go To to move the insertion point to the bookmarked location.

Alternately, you may perform the above tasks by using the following method:

1. Press Ctrl+G to open the Go To tab of the *Find and Replace* dialog box.
2. Click Bookmark in the *Go to what* section.
3. Click the *Enter bookmark name* arrow to select the bookmark that you want to view.
4. Click the Go To button to go to the bookmarked location.
5. Click Close if you want to exit the bookmark dialog box without doing anything.

 TIP **Using Numbers in Bookmark Names**

You can use numbers within bookmark names, such as Quarter1. However, you cannot start a bookmark name with a number.

Quick Concepts

1. What are the differences between comparing and combining two documents? *p. 70*
2. Why would you want to create a master and several subdocuments? *p. 72*
3. What is the purpose of creating a bookmark in a document? *p. 78*

Hands-On Exercises

MyITLab®
HOE2 Training

2 Multiple Documents

When setting up a prospective job proposal, Alexandra collects information about the company, the trainers who might work with the clients, and references from previous clients. After collecting this information, she forwards it to you to combine into one or more different documents. The final proposal is created from several files, and it is time consuming to try to number each one so that it looks like they all came from a single document. But you know how to use the master document feature to make that task easier.

Skills covered: View Documents Side by Side • Combine Documents • Create Master Documents and Subdocuments • Use the Navigation Pane and Create Bookmarks

STEP 1 ≫ VIEW DOCUMENTS SIDE BY SIDE

Alexandra has forwarded documents to you which contain information that should be included in the multi-page proposal. Before you start the process of combining information, you decide to view the documents side by side so you can find any overlap in the content. Refer to Figure 6.20 as you complete Step 1.

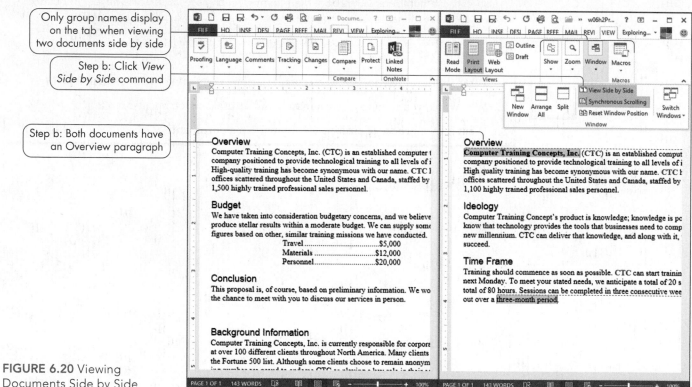

FIGURE 6.20 Viewing Documents Side by Side

    a. Open the files *w06h2Proposal* and *w06h2Proposal2*.

        If necessary, click **Enable Editing** on the yellow bar at the top so that you can edit the document.

    b. Click the **VIEW tab** and click **View Side by Side** in the Window group.

        Two windows display, containing the contents of each file. In the Window group, you see *Synchronous Scrolling* highlighted in light blue to indicate the setting is on. As you scroll in one document, the other will scroll also.

> **TROUBLESHOOTING:** If your view of one or both of the documents is insufficient, you can use the mouse to resize the window. Drag the border of the window until you reach an acceptable size to view the document information.

c. Click the document on the left to make it active and click the arrow at the bottom of the scroll bar in the window on the left to scroll to the bottom of the page.

Both documents scroll down evenly, and you can view the footer of each document.

d. Click **Synchronous Scrolling** in the Window group to turn the toggle off.

Notice that *Synchronous Scrolling* is no longer highlighted in light blue. Now you can scroll through a single document at a time.

e. Close both documents without saving. Do not exit Word.

STEP 2 » COMBINE DOCUMENTS

Now that you know the two files you just viewed are not identical, you decide to use the Combine feature in Word to pull all content into one location. You then make some minor formatting changes, insert the entire contents of another document, and then save the file so that it is ready to accompany the other files in the proposal. Refer to Figure 6.21 as you complete Step 2.

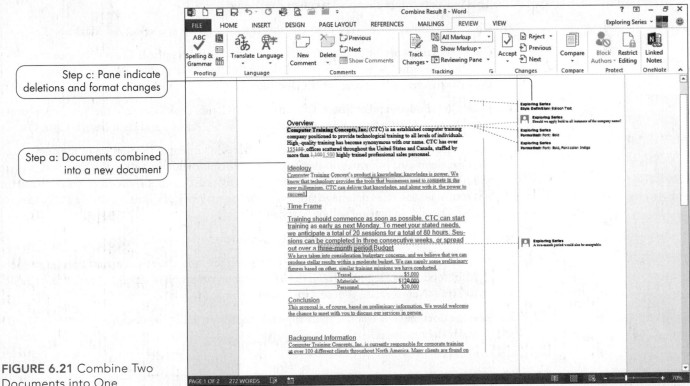

FIGURE 6.21 Combine Two Documents into One

a. Combine the two documents you viewed in the last step by completing the following steps:

- Click the **REVIEW tab**, click **Compare** in the Compare group, and then select **Combine** to display the Combine Documents dialog box.
- Click the **Original document arrow** and select *w06h2Proposal*. If necessary, click **Browse**, navigate to *w06h2Proposal*, and then click **Open**.
- Click the **Revised Document arrow** and select *w06h2Proposal2*. If necessary, click **Browse**, navigate to *w06h2Proposal2*, and then click **Open**.
- Click the **More button**, if necessary, and click **New document** below *Show changes in*, if necessary. Click **OK**. Click **Continue with Merge** to accept the default choice if a Microsoft Word dialog box displays with a message about accepting the tracked changes from both documents.

> **TROUBLESHOOTING:** If the two documents you just merged display in small windows on the screen, select Show Source Documents in the Compare group on the Review tab and click Hide Source Documents to close them.

The document opens in a new window and contains markup balloons to indicate each difference in the two documents. Depending on your Track Changes settings, the balloons might display on either the left or right side of your document.

> **TROUBLESHOOTING:** If the paragraphs in your document do not display in the same order as those in Figure 6.21, close the document and begin the process again. Make sure you select *w06h2Proposal* as the Original document.

b. Click the **Display for Review arrow** in the Tracking group and select **Simple Markup**, if necessary.

The document in this view appears to include information from both files and is what you need to present to the customers. Notice the level of detail in the markup balloons when you switch between Simple Markup and All Markup. After some minor edits, it will be ready for use.

c. Click **Track Changes** in the Tracking group to turn off Track Changes, if necessary.

This prevents future changes from being recorded.

d. Click the **Display for Review arrow** in the Tracking group and select **All Markup**.

e. Click the **Accept arrow** in the Changes group and click **Accept All Changes**. Place the insertion point in the first comment, click the **Delete arrow** in the Comments group, and then click **Delete All Comments in Document**.

f. Press **Ctrl+End** and press **Enter**. Click the **INSERT tab**, click **Object** in the Text group, and then click the **Create from File tab**. Navigate to *w06h2Faculty* and click **Insert**. Click **OK**.

You insert the entire contents of the *w06h2Faculty* document at the bottom of the page because it contains information that you want to display with the rest of the proposal. You will revise the order of the paragraphs later. This feature does not work on PDFs that contain text that was created as an image, however, but the majority of forms and other PDFs that you would want to type on will be supported.

g. Make the following format changes to the document:

- Right-click anywhere in the *Ideology* paragraph text and click the **Format Painter** in the Mini toolbar. Click anywhere in the *Time Frame* paragraph to change the font from Arial to Times New Roman, if necessary.

h. Save the document as **w06h2FinalProposal_LastFirst**. Close the document but leave Word open for the next step.

STEP 3 ≫ CREATE MASTER DOCUMENTS AND SUBDOCUMENTS

You now have the three main pieces of information (*w06h2FinalProposal_LastFirst*, *w06h1Resume_LastFirst*, and *w06h1References_LastFirst*) that you will send to the potential client. You decide to create a master document so that you can insert each piece and make formatting modifications to the subdocuments. Refer to Figure 6.22 as you complete Step 3.

 Backing Up Your Files

Before you create a master document, you should back up all data files you will insert into the master document. Any changes made to the content in the master will alter the originals.

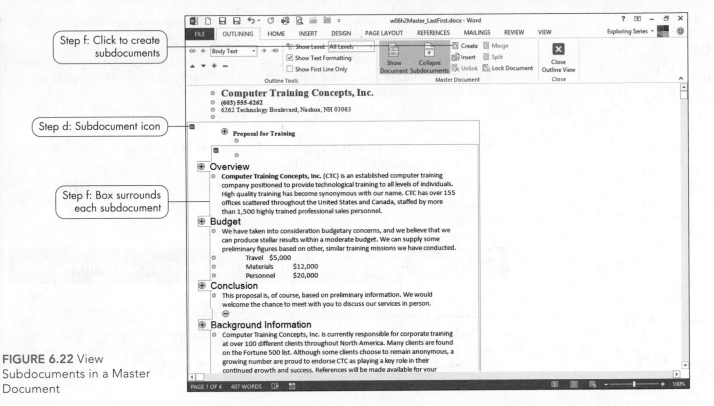

Step f: Click to create subdocuments

Step d: Subdocument icon

Step f: Box surrounds each subdocument

FIGURE 6.22 View Subdocuments in a Master Document

a. Press **Ctrl+N** to open a new document and save it as **w06h2Master_LastFirst**.

b. Type **ctc** and press **F3** to insert the Building Block that contains the company name and address.

c. Press **Enter** one time. Right-align the insertion point. Type the following headings, each on a separate line, for the subdocuments: **Proposal for Training**, **Faculty Resume**, and **References**.

d. Select the three headings you just typed and click **Heading 2** from the Styles group on the HOME tab.

e. Click the **VIEW tab** and click **Outline** in the View group.

> **TROUBLESHOOTING:** If the Heading 2 style does not display in the Styles group, click the Styles dialog box launcher to display the Styles pane, select the Heading 2 style, and then close the Styles pane.

The OUTLINING tab displays and the document text displays in Outline view. Be sure all three headings are still selected before you perform the next step.

f. Click **Show Document** in the Master Document group to display more master document commands. Click **Create** in the Master Document group.

Note that when the Show Document command is selected, it is shaded in light blue.

Individual subdocuments are created for the selected headings. A box surrounds each subdocument, and you see a subdocument icon in the top-left corner of each subdocument box. You also will see section breaks and other formatting marks if the Show/Hide ¶ feature is turned on.

g. Click **Collapse Subdocuments** in the Master Document group to collapse the subdocuments in the document. Click **OK** if prompted to save changes to the master document.

Note that when you click Collapse Subdocuments, it will display the name and path where each subdocument is saved.

h. Click **Expand Subdocuments** in the Master Document group to reopen and display the subdocuments.

i. Place the insertion point on the line directly below the first subdocument heading, *Proposal for Training*. The insertion point will appear to align on the right side of the line. To insert the appropriate subdocument complete the following steps:

- Click **Insert** in the Master Document group to display the Insert Subdocument dialog box.
- Select *w06h2FinalProposal_LastFirst* and click **Open**. If prompted to rename the style in the subdocument, click **Yes to All**.

The entire document displays under the *Proposal for Training* section of the master document.

 Inserting Subdocuments in a Master Document

You need to insert the subdocument in a precise location on the master document. To insert the subdocument into the master document, you need to place the insertion point on the line directly below the subdocument heading. Sometimes it can be difficult to get to the line below. Another way to do this is to click the subdocument heading and press the down arrow to get to the line below.

j. Place the insertion point on the line below the subheading *Faculty Resume*. Repeat the steps above to insert the file *w06h1Resume_LastFirst*. Click **OK** when the Microsoft Word information window displays indicating the subdocument has a different template than its master document. Click **Yes to All** when prompted to rename styles because there are several used in this document.

k. Place the insertion point on the line below the subheading *References*. Repeat the steps above to insert the file *w06h1References_LastFirst*. Click **OK** when the Microsoft Word information window displays indicating the subdocument has a different template than its master document. Click **Yes to All** when prompted to rename styles because several are used in this document.

> **TROUBLESHOOTING:** Be sure to insert the *w06h1References_LastFirst* document, ending in *.docx*, and not the template, which ends in *.dotx*.

 Displaying Subdocuments in a Master Document

After you create subdocuments, the link or path to the location where the subdocument is stored displays in the master document. If you move or rename the subdocument from that original location, the content will no longer display in the master document.

l. Place the insertion point to the right of *Faculty Resume* on page 2 and click **Delete**. Place the insertion point to the right of *References* on the bottom of page 3 and click **Delete**.

m. Save the document.

STEP 4 >> USE THE NAVIGATION PANE AND CREATE BOOKMARKS

You remember that inserting bookmarks is a quick way to get to different pages in a document, so you decide to insert one at the top of each section of the document. You decide to display the Navigation Pane so you can move quickly from one page to another to add those bookmarks. Refer to Figure 6.23 as you complete Step 4.

a. Click the **VIEW tab** and click **Navigation Pane** in the Show group to display the Navigation Pane on the left side of the window. Click **HEADINGS** in the Navigation Pane to display all the headings in the document.

The headings from the master document appear in the pane. A light blue shade appears around the heading of the paragraph where the insertion point displays.

b. Click the **Proposal for Training heading** in the Navigation Pane, if necessary.

Word positions the insertion point at the CTC heading on the first page. Position the insertion point on the first heading.

c. Click the **INSERT tab** and click **Bookmark** in the Links group. Type **proposal** in the **Bookmark name box** and click **Add**.

Word inserts a bookmark with the name you entered. A large, gray I-beam indicates the location of the bookmark.

TROUBLESHOOTING: If you do not see the bookmark indicator, you can change a setting that enables it. Click the File tab and click Options. Click Advanced, scroll down, and then click the *Show bookmarks* check box in the *Show document content* section. Click OK to save the settings and return to the document.

---

d. Click **PAGES** in the Navigation Pane to display thumbnails of each page in the Navigation Pane. Click the thumbnail of page 3, the resume, to display the page and move the insertion point to the top of that page.

e. Click **Bookmark** in the Links group. Type **resume** in the **Bookmark name box** and click **Add**.

f. Type **reference** in the **Search Document box** and press **Enter**. Click **RESULTS** to view the results of the search. Click the second item listed, which is the label *References* that displays at the top of page four.

g. Click **Bookmark** in the Links group. Type **reference** in the **Bookmark name box** and click **Add**.

Notice the brackets that display to show the location of the bookmark. When a block of text is selected at the time you insert a bookmark, brackets display around the text to locate the bookmark instead of a single I-beam, which displays at the location of the cursor.

h. Click the **HOME tab** and click **Replace** in the Editing group. Click the **Go To tab** in the *Find and Replace* dialog box. Click **Bookmark**, if necessary, in the *Go to what* list.

Word displays the *research* bookmark in the *Enter bookmark name* box because it was the last bookmark that you added. If you click the *Enter bookmark name* arrow, the *proposal* and *resume* bookmarks also display in the list.

 TIP **Command to Search for Bookmarks**

You can also access the list of bookmarks by pressing Crl+G to display the Go To tab of the *Find and Replace* dialog box. Click Bookmark, if necessary, in the *Go to what* list.

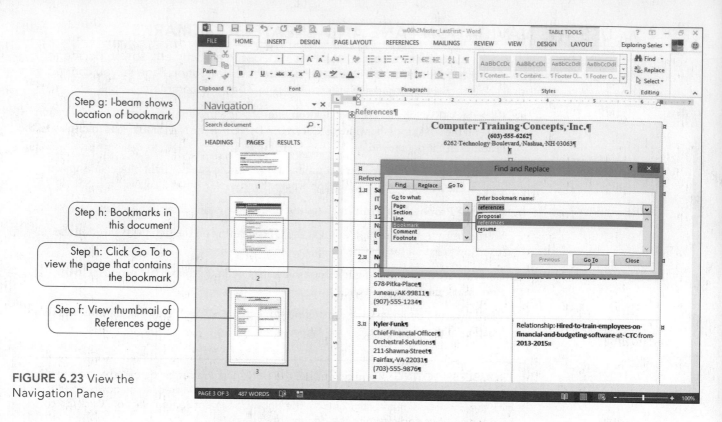

Step g: I-beam shows location of bookmark

Step h: Bookmarks in this document

Step h: Click Go To to view the page that contains the bookmark

Step f: View thumbnail of References page

FIGURE 6.23 View the Navigation Pane

i. Click **Go To**.

The insertion point moves to the bookmark's location and the Bookmark dialog box remains onscreen in case you want to go to another bookmark.

j. Click **Close** to remove the Bookmark dialog box. Click the **Close (X) button** in the top-right corner of the Navigation Pane.

k. Save and close the file. Submit all files based on your instructor's directions.

Document Themes

To create a professional-looking document, you want to select features and styles that coordinate, but creating and managing document design is very time consuming. Word 2013 contains several document themes that enable you to focus on the content of your document instead of spending time creating a design for it. A ***document theme*** is a set of coordinating fonts, colors, and special effects, such as shadowing or glows that are combined into a package to provide a stylish appearance. Microsoft provides consistent document themes across all the Office applications. Therefore, you can use the same theme on different types of files that are used in a project, such as a report created in Word, a worksheet and chart created in Excel, and a slide presentation created using PowerPoint, and even e-mail the files to other users using the same theme in Outlook.

In this section, you will apply themes to a document. You will also create your own theme by customizing the theme elements.

Customizing Theme Colors, Fonts, and Effects

Document themes are formatted with matching color schemes, fonts, and special effects. Currently, ten document themes are available in Word 2013. More themes are available for download at Office.com. Once you download a theme from Office.com, it is saved to your computer, ready to use another time.

When you create a document, it is automatically given a default document theme. If you want to change the document theme, you might want to try several themes before deciding on the best choice for your document. At any time, you may switch back to the original default document theme by clicking the Design tab, clicking the More arrow in the Document Formatting group, and selecting the *Reset to the Default Style Set* selection.

Apply a Theme to a Document

STEP 1 » Everyone has his/her own preferences, so picking the right theme can be a difficult task. But when you are ready to apply a theme to a Word document, do the following:

1. Open the document.
2. Click the DESIGN tab.
3. Click Themes in the Document Formatting group to view a gallery of available themes.
4. You may apply a particular theme to your document by:
   a. Clicking one of the available themes.
   b. Clicking *Browse for Themes* to see themes previously saved to your computer.
5. Click the Themes arrow and click *Reset to Theme from Template* if you decide to revert back to your original theme.
6. Click Page Color in the Page Background group to change the document background to a different color, if you want to use a background color other than white.
7. You can also add the document theme to the Quick Access Toolbar by right-clicking a theme's thumbnail.

Apply a Style Set

STEP 2 » In Word 2013, Microsoft introduces several new features in the Document Formatting group. For instance, a new Style Sets visual gallery allows users to preview a new font style in a title, heading, and text body of a document before applying it. The Style Set also changes the paragraph properties of the document. You may pick a new Style Set as often as you like from one of the nearly twenty style sets available in Word 2013. You can review the full effect of changing each Style Set by clicking the Design tab, clicking the More button to view the

Style Set gallery in the Document Formatting group, and then picking the Style Set selection. The Paragraph Spacing command allows you to quickly change the line and paragraph spacing of your entire document by selecting from a predefined set of values or customizing your own values. Also, the *Set as Default* button will save your current customized theme and will apply the saved settings to all your new documents. This is very helpful to users who have a preferred font type or specified paragraph styling.

To quickly and easily change the look of your document by applying a selected style set, do the following:

1. Click the DESIGN tab.
2. Click Style Set in the Document Formatting group.
3. Click any of the available built-in choices to apply the selected style set.

Revise Theme Colors

STEP 3 › If you wish to make changes to any part of the design, you can modify and customize the theme elements individually. Microsoft Word has more than twenty color schemes and font combinations, in addition to fifteen special effects, resulting in hundreds of combinations available to you. *Theme colors* include four text/background colors, six accent colors, and two hyperlink colors. To create a custom color theme, do the following:

1. Click the DESIGN tab.
2. Click Colors in the Document Formatting group and click Customize Colors. Two text/background colors and four accent colors display, as shown in Figure 6.24.
3. Click any of the available predefined color schemes or the Customize Colors option at the bottom of the gallery to modify the colors in the current theme.
4. Make your color selection for text/background, accents, and hyperlinks.
5. Type a new name for your custom theme in the Name text box.
6. Click Save to save the custom theme with a new name.

The new color theme will then display at the top of the theme color gallery. You may click the Reset button to undo any color changes or the Cancel button to exit the Create New Theme Colors dialog box without saving any changes.

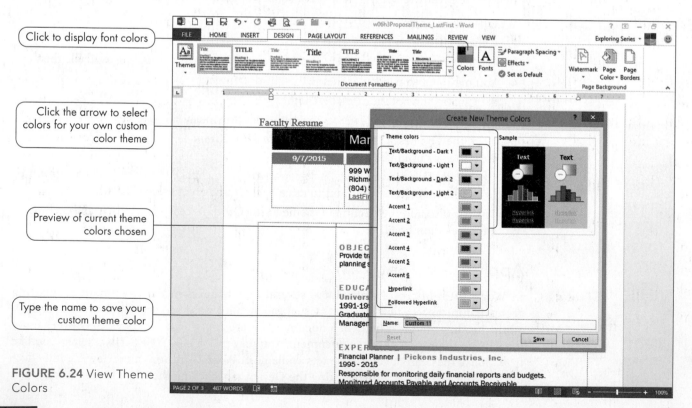

FIGURE 6.24 View Theme Colors

Revise Theme Fonts

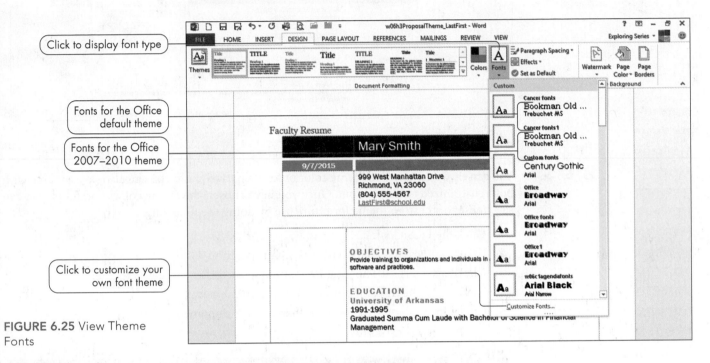

STEP 4 ▶▶ The *theme fonts* contain a coordinating heading and body text font for each different theme. You can view the fonts used in the theme when you click Fonts in the Document Formatting group on the Design tab, as shown in Figure 6.25. Theme fonts display at the top of the font list when you click the Font arrow on the Home tab or on the Mini toolbar. As with theme colors, you can quickly change the text in your document by picking a new font set with a predefined font type. You can also create a new theme font set. Each theme font has the font type for the headings and the body text.

Click to display font type

Fonts for the Office default theme

Fonts for the Office 2007–2010 theme

Click to customize your own font theme

FIGURE 6.25 View Theme Fonts

Customize Theme Effects

Theme effects are another feature that you can incorporate into a document theme. *Theme effects* include lines, fill, and 3-D effects, such as shadowing, glows, and borders. When you apply a theme effect, the theme effects will affect objects such as shapes, SmartArt, and borders around graphics. Unlike theme colors and theme fonts, you cannot create your own set of theme effects, but you can choose from the built-in sets when compiling your own document theme. When a shape or object is created, the theme effects chosen will be reflected in the Shape Styles gallery on the Format tab for the object. When you click Effects in the Document Formatting group found on the Design tab, you will see that the lines, fills and special effects are represented in combinations of three shapes.

A circle represents a line effect applied that includes the width or weight of the line, a rectangle represents the effects applied to an object such as bevels or shadows, and the arrow displays the fill effects that might include gradients, as shown in Figure 6.26.

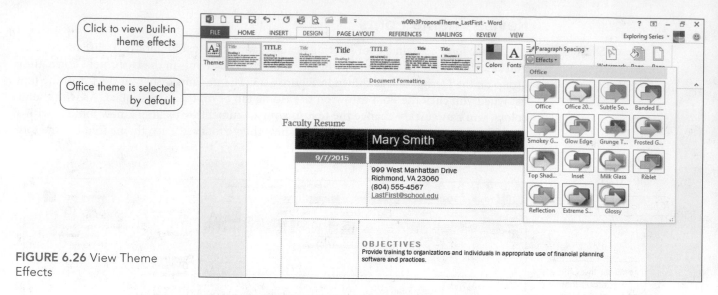

Click to view Built-in theme effects

Office theme is selected by default

FIGURE 6.26 View Theme Effects

Save a Custom Theme

STEP 5 ≫ You can save a customized theme color or font separately, and you can also save a theme with both customized color and font. Once you have chosen the theme colors and fonts, you can save these to a custom theme for future use by doing the following:

1. Click the DESIGN tab.
2. Click Themes in the Document Formatting group.
3. Click Save Current Theme at the bottom of the gallery to save a theme.
4. Navigate to the directory to save the custom theme.
5. Click Open to apply the selected theme to the document.

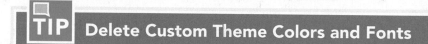

TIP | Delete Custom Theme Colors and Fonts

You can easily delete a custom theme, a custom theme color set, or custom theme fonts. To remove these custom sets, click Themes (or Colors, or Fonts) on the Design tab, right-click the custom set that displays in the top of the gallery, and then click Delete. You will see a confirmation dialog box before the .thmx theme file is removed permanently. You cannot delete the themes, color themes, or font themes that are included in Word.

Quick Concepts

1. What are the advantages of using document themes? ***p. 87***
2. Why would you want to create your own custom themes? ***p. 88***
3. Is it difficult to customize theme effects? ***p. 89***

Hands-On Exercises

Watch the Video
for this Hands-
On Exercise!

MyITLab®
HOE3 Training

3 Document Themes

You are almost ready to print the proposal and send it to the potential client. But each document that you inserted into the master is formatted a bit differently, and you want this document to have a very consistent look. You remember that Microsoft Word enables you to apply a theme to documents so they use the same style of fonts and colors—which is exactly what you need to put the finishing touches on this proposal!

Skills covered: Apply a Theme to a Document • Apply a Style Set • Revise Theme Color • Revise Theme Fonts • Save a Custom Theme

STEP 1 ≫ APPLY A THEME TO A DOCUMENT

Your proposal should have a very professional look to it, so you decide to apply one of the built-in themes in Word. By using the theme, all colors in the resume template and colors used for headings in the other documents will coordinate. The colors in the Organic theme closely match the colors of your business, so you select that theme. Refer to Figure 6.27 as you complete Step 1.

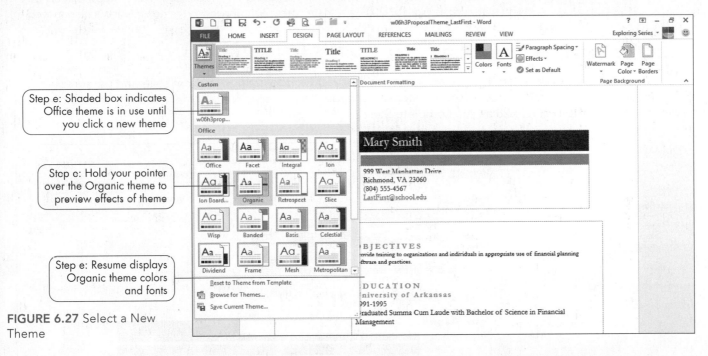

FIGURE 6.27 Select a New Theme

a. Open the *w06h2Master_LastFirst* document and save it as **w06h3ProposalTheme_LastFirst**.

b. Click the **HOME tab** and click **Show/Hide (¶)** in the Paragraph group to turn off formatting marks, if necessary. Click the **VIEW tab** and click **Outline** in the Views group to view the OUTLINING tab and commands. Click **Show Document** in the Master Document group on the OUTLINING tab and click **Expand Subdocuments**, if necessary, to view all of the content in the subdocuments. Click **Close Outline View** to return to Print Layout view.

   When you close the document in the last step, the subdocuments in the master document will be collapsed. Step b will expand the subdocuments so that the whole document will be visible for you to review or modify.

c. Press **Ctrl+G** and click **Bookmark** in the *Go to what* box. Click the **Enter bookmark name arrow** and select **resume**. Click **Go To** and the resume displays. Close the *Find and Replace* dialog box.

d. Click the first **DESIGN tab** and click **Themes** in the Document Formatting group.

The gallery of themes displays and a shaded box surrounds the Office theme. It is active because that is the theme applied to the master document when it was created.

> **TROUBLESHOOTING:** If you see two Design tabs, you will click the first Design tab to format the document themes. The second Design tab is the Table Tools Design tab, which is used to format tables.

e. Click the **Organic theme** to apply the Organic theme to all pages in the master document. Notice how the resume features change to reflect that theme. Also, the content for the *Proposal for Training* section is now on page one only.

f. Save the document.

TIP | Using Themes in Compatibility Mode

If you click the Design tab and notice *Theme* is grayed out, and thus unavailable, your current document is probably open in Compatibility Mode. To use Themes, you must save your document in Word 2013 format (.docx). If you save a Word 2013 document in a compatible format, such as Word 97-2003, any theme previously applied to the document will be removed.

STEP 2 » APPLY A STYLE SET

The Organic theme looks great on the master document, but you want to change the font style and paragraph properties of the document. You decide to take steps to change the font style for the title, heading, and text body of the document. Refer to Figure 6.28 as you complete Step 2.

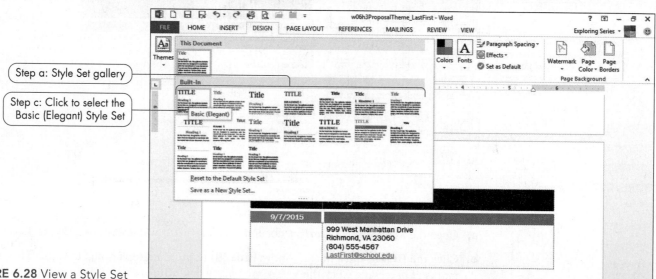

FIGURE 6.28 View a Style Set

a. Click the **DESIGN tab**. Click **Style Set** in the Document Formatting group.

The Style Set gallery appears, with the current Style Set listed at the top and the built-in Style Sets created by Microsoft in the section below. You can select one of the Style Sets from this gallery.

b. Move the insertion point over each of the thumbnail images of the Style Set gallery to reveal the name of the individual Style Set.

c. Click the **Basic (Elegant) Style Set**.

d. Save the document.

STEP 3 ≫ REVISE THEME COLOR

The Organic theme looks great on the master document; however, you would like to change a color that you do not particularly like. You take steps to make a color change in the theme, and you save the changes as a custom theme so you can use it again in other documents. Refer to Figure 6.29 as you complete Step 3.

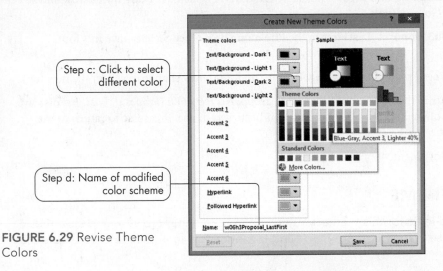

Step c: Click to select different color

Step d: Name of modified color scheme

FIGURE 6.29 Revise Theme Colors

a. Click **Colors** in the Document Formatting group.

   The color gallery appears, with the Custom colors at the top and the Office selections in the section below. You can select the colors for other built-in themes from this gallery.

b. Click **Customize Colors** at the bottom of the gallery.

   The Create New Theme Colors dialog box displays. Now you can customize the colors used in the theme that is currently applied to your document.

c. Click the **Text/Background - Dark 2 arrow** and click **Blue-Gray, Accent 3, Lighter 40%** (fourth row, seventh column).

d. Type **w06h3Proposal_LastFirst** in the **File name box**. Click **Save** to save this color scheme.

   The *w06h3Proposal_LastFirst* color theme is automatically applied to your document. When you click Theme Colors, *w06h3Proposal_LastFirst* displays at the top of the gallery with a box around it.

e. Press **Ctrl+Home** to view the first page of the document. Select the title *Computer Training Concepts, Inc.* and click the **Font Color arrow** on the Mini toolbar.

   Notice the top of the box displays *Theme Colors*, so you know any color you select will coordinate with the document theme.

f. Click **Orange, Accent 5** from the first row.

g. Save the document.

STEP 4 ≫ REVISE THEME FONTS

You notice the same font is used for headings and body text in the theme applied to this document. You would like to make a change so a different, yet coordinating, font is used for the headings. And then the proposal is ready for the printer! Refer to Figure 6.30 as you complete Step 4.

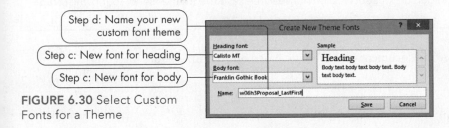

Step d: Name your new custom font theme

Step c: New font for heading

Step c: New font for body

FIGURE 6.30 Select Custom Fonts for a Theme

a. Click the **DESIGN tab**. Click **Fonts** in the Document Formatting group.

The fonts for each theme display. The font style in use for the Organic theme is Garamond.

b. Click **Customize Fonts** at the bottom of the gallery.

c. Click the **Heading font arrow** and select **Calisto MT**. Click the **Body font arrow** and select **Franklin Gothic Book**.

d. Type **w06h3Proposal_LastFirst** in the **File name box**. Click **Save** to save this font scheme.

The headings *Proposal for Training*, *Resume*, and *Resources* change to reflect the new font.

e. Click **Fonts** in the Document Formatting group. Notice *w06h3Proposal_LastFirst* displays at the top of the list with blue shading to indicate it is in use. Press **Esc** to return to the document.

f. Save the document.

STEP 5 ≫ SAVE A CUSTOM THEME

Since you made changes to both colors and fonts for this theme, you decide to take one more step and save the whole theme with a new name so you can use it again without modifying the individual features. Refer to Figure 6.31 as you complete Step 5.

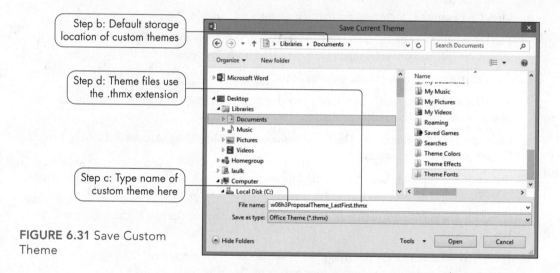

FIGURE 6.31 Save Custom Theme

a. Click the **DESIGN tab**, if necessary, and click **Themes** in the Document Formatting group.

b. Click **Save Current Theme** at the bottom of the gallery.

The Save Current Theme dialog box displays. By default, the new themes are saved in the Document Themes folder for the current user. They are not stored in a folder with the themes that install with Word 2013.

c. Type **w06h3ProposalTheme_LastFirst** in the **File name box**.

d. Click **Save** to save the theme file with the .thmx extension.

> **TROUBLESHOOTING:** If your lab environment does not enable you to save the template to the default folder, or if instructed by your teacher, save the theme file to your own storage media.

e. Save and close the document, and submit it based on your instructor's directions.

Chapter Objectives Review

After reading this chapter, you have accomplished the following objectives:

1. Select a template from the Backstage view.

- Each time you create a new blank document, you use the Normal template. When you use a template, it will display under Blank and Recent documents, but you can also view other templates installed on your PC or templates you have created. Many people will take advantage of the resume templates. By default, resume templates are installed in Word, and they contain placeholders, a field or block of text, to determine the position of objects in a document.

2. Create a Word template.

- If you create or use a particular document frequently, with only minor modifications each time, you should save the document as a template. When you create the template, you can insert placeholders for the information you change frequently.

3. Use Building Blocks.

- Building Blocks are document components you use frequently such as disclaimers, company addresses or logos, or your name and address. Word enables you to create Building Blocks in such a way that they are easy to insert as document parts. Each selection of text or graphics that you add to the Quick Part Gallery is stored in the Building Blocks Organizer and is assigned a unique name that makes it easy for you to find the content when you want to use it.

4. View documents side by side.

- This feature enables you to view two documents on the same screen. It is useful when you want to compare the contents of two documents or if you want to cut or copy and paste text from one document to another. To view two documents side by side, they must both be open in Word.
- While in *Side by Side* view, you can resize and reset the two document windows.

5. Merge documents.

- When you have several copies of the same document submitted from different people, you can use the compare and combine features. The compare feature evaluates the contents of two or more documents and displays markup balloons that show the differences between the documents. You can determine if the differences display in the original document, a revised document, or a new document.
- The combine feature goes a step further and integrates all changes from multiple documents into one.
- Another way to work with multiple documents, especially those that will be combined into one long document, is to create a master document that acts like a binder for managing smaller documents. The smaller document is called a subdocument and can be edited individually at any time.

- You can quickly add the contents of a document to an opened document by using the Object command on the Insert tab.
- You can make changes to the master document at any time but you can make changes to the subdocuments only when they are unlocked.
- If necessary, you can create subdocuments from an empty master document.
- Creating a master document and subdocuments can be very helpful, but they can also be very problematic. Students using this feature must following several precautions.

6. Use navigational tools.

- When you use the Navigation Pane feature *Browse the headings in your document*, only the headings display. You can click a heading in the Navigation Pane to move the insertion point to that heading in the document. The feature is only available when headings are formatted using the Styles feature. You also can use thumbnails to navigate quickly through a document. Thumbnails are small pictures of each page that display in the Navigation Pane when the feature is toggled on. When you click a thumbnail, the insertion point moves to the top of that page. You can also navigate through a document using search keywords or phrases.
- The Bookmark feature is an electronic marker for a specific location in a document. You can designate a bookmark in a particular location in a document and use the Find and Replace dialog box to return to that bookmark.
- At any time after creating your bookmarks, you may review the list of bookmarks and navigate to a bookmarked content.

7. Customize theme colors, fonts, and effects.

- You can select a document theme from the Themes group on the Page Layout tab. When you select a document theme, formatting occurs immediately.
- Style Set allows you to change the font type and paragraph properties of the whole document.
- Theme colors represent the current text and background, accents, and hyperlinks. To create a custom color theme, you can modify the colors in the current theme and save the set with a new name.
- The theme fonts contain a coordinating heading and body text font for each theme. Theme fonts display at the top of the font list when you click the Font arrow on the Home tab or on the Mini toolbar.
- The theme effects include lines and fill effects, such as shadowing, glows, and borders. You cannot create your own set of theme effects, but you can choose from the built-in sets.

Key Terms Matching

Match the key terms with their definitions. Write the key term letter by the appropriate numbered definition.

a. Bookmark
b. Building Block
c. Combine
d. Compare
e. Curriculum vitae (CV)
f. Document theme
g. Legal blacklining
h. Master document
i. Navigation Pane
j. Normal template

k. Placeholder
l. Subdocument
m. Synchronous scrolling
n. Template
o. Theme color
p. Theme effect
q. Theme font
r. Thumbnail
s. View Side by Side

1. _____ A document component used frequently, such as a disclaimer, company address, or cover page. **p. 61**

2. _____ Enables you to display two documents on the same screen. **p. 69**

3. _____ Enables you to simultaneously scroll through documents in side by side view. **p. 69**

4. _____ Evaluates the contents of two or more documents and displays markup balloons showing the differences. **p. 69**

5. _____ Incorporates all changes from multiple documents into a new document. **p. 71**

6. _____ The comparing of two documents and the displaying of the changes between the two documents. **p. 70**

7. _____ A document that acts like a binder for managing smaller documents. **p. 72**

8. _____ A smaller document that is a part of a master document. **p. 72**

9. _____ Enables you to quickly move through documents using text, headings, or pages. **p. 72**

10. _____ A small picture of each page in your document that displays in the navigation pane. **p. 76**

11. _____ An electronic marker for a specific location in a document. **p. 78**

12. _____ A partially completed document containing preformatted text or graphics. **p. 58**

13. _____ The framework that defines the default page settings. **p. 58**

14. _____ A field or block of text used to determine the position of objects in a document. **p. 58**

15. _____ Like a resume, displays your skills, accomplishments, and job history. **p. 59**

16. _____ A set of coordinating fonts, colors, and special effects that give a stylish and professional look. **p. 87**

17. _____ Represents the current text and background, accent, and hyperlinks. **p. 88**

18. _____ Contains a heading and body text font. **p. 89**

19. _____ Includes lines or fill effects. **p. 89**

Multiple Choice

1. If you create new documents every day that contain your company letterhead, which productivity tool would best fit your need?

    (a) Mail merge
    (b) Building Blocks
    (c) Document themes
    (d) Document templates

2. Which of the following is not a way you can obtain a document template?

    (a) Select it from the Styles gallery.
    (b) Download from Office.com.
    (c) Select an installed template on your computer.
    (d) Create a document yourself and save it as a template.

3. What file extension is given to a template?

    (a) .dotx
    (b) .docx
    (c) .xlsx
    (d) .accdb

4. What is another name for the text or fields that display in a document template so you will know where to insert your own information?

    (a) Flag
    (b) Extension
    (c) CV
    (d) Placeholder

5. Why would you use a document theme?

    (a) So you can restrict the use of color in the document
    (b) To merge information from a data source into a document
    (c) To color coordinate elements used in the document and give a professional appearance
    (d) To easily locate bookmarks

6. Which of the following theme elements cannot be customized and saved?

    (a) Theme color
    (b) Theme font
    (c) Theme effect
    (d) Document theme

7. Which of the document elements listed below can you find using the Go To command?

    (a) Hyperlink
    (b) Bookmark
    (c) Table of Contents
    (d) Cross-reference notation

8. After you use the styles feature to format headings, which of the following features can be used to view small pictures of each page in your document?

    (a) Bookmarks
    (b) Navigation Pane—headings
    (c) Navigation Pane—thumbnails
    (d) Navigation Pane—search

9. What comprises a master document?

    (a) Subdocuments
    (b) Templates
    (c) Outline documents
    (d) Combined documents

10. Which feature enables you to evaluate the differences in two documents?

    (a) Side by side view
    (b) Compare documents
    (c) Master documents
    (d) Subdocuments

Practice Exercises

1 My Home Town Cable Services

You work in the Employee Benefits Department of the local cable provider, My Home Town Cable Services. You want to set up a form that all new and existing employees can use to document personal information and emergency contact numbers. Before you create a new form, you decide to look for an existing form in the Word templates gallery. You find just the right form and need to make only minor modifications, adding the company name and logo. You also insert the contents of another document to add insurance information, and the form is ready to be distributed to all employees. This exercise follows the same set of skills as used in Hands-On Exercises 1 and 2 in the chapter. Refer to Figure 6.32 as you complete this exercise.

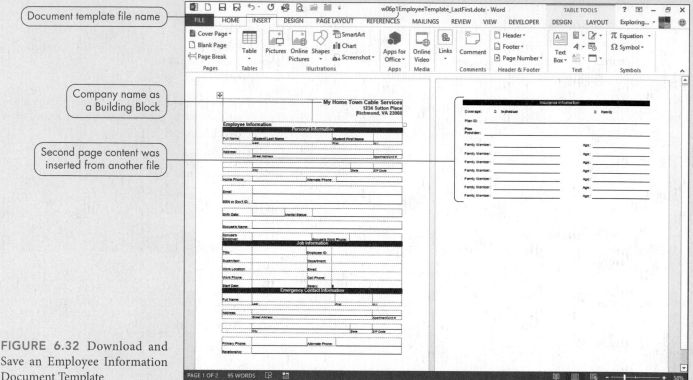

Document template file name

Company name as a Building Block

Second page content was inserted from another file

FIGURE 6.32 Download and Save an Employee Information Document Template

FROM SCRATCH

a. Start Word. Type **Employee Information Form** in the **Search online templates box** and hit **Enter**. Click the first form to preview it and click **Create**. Close the Navigation Pane if it displays.

b. Click the **FILE tab**, click **Save As**, click **Browse**, click the **Save as type arrow**, and then select **Word Template**. Type **w06p1EmployeeTemplate_LastFirst** in the **File name box** and click **Save**.

c. Select the border of the text box that displays *Your Logo Here* and press **Delete**.

d. Select the text **Company Name** to display the text box. Select the text *Company Name* and type the following:

My Home Town Cable Services
1234 Sutton Place
Richmond, VA 23060

e. Insert a blank line after the zip code. Select the two lines that contain the address and press **Decrease Font Size** in the Font group once to decrease the font size.

f. Select the company name and address and click the **INSERT tab**. Click **Quick Parts** in the Text group and select **Save Selection to Quick Part gallery**.

g. Click the **Gallery arrow** in the Create New Building Block dialog box and select **Text Boxes**. Click the **Save In arrow** and select **Building Blocks**, if necessary. Click **OK**.

h. Press **Delete** to remove the text box. Click **Quick Parts** in the Text group, click the **Building Blocks Organizer**, click **Name** to sort the entries by name, scroll down to the *My Home Town Cable Services* entry, click it, and then click **Insert**.

i. Select the whole document. Click the **Paragraph dialog box launcher** in the Paragraph group on the HOME tab and change the Before and After Spacing to **0**. Click **OK**.

j. Press **Ctrl+End** to move to the end of the document. Click the **INSERT tab**, click **Object** in the Text group, and then click the **Create from File tab**. Browse to the location where data files are stored, select *w06p1Insurance.docx*, and then click **Insert**.

k. Position the insertion point on the *Full Name:* line under *Employee Information*, type your last name, press **Tab**, and then type your first name.

l. Save and close the file, and submit it based on your instructor's directions.

2 Anderson High School

You volunteer at the Anderson High School Computer Club and have the opportunity to observe the computer skill level of many students. You decide to create a document that contains new features of Microsoft Word and Excel 2013 that the students can use as a reference. You found two sources of information and want to combine them into one document. You are familiar with the compare and combine features in Word, so you are going to use them to combine the two documents into one document and make modifications so that it is easy to read. This exercise follows the same set of skills as used in Hands-On Exercises 2 and 3 in the chapter. Refer to Figure 6.33 as you complete this exercise.

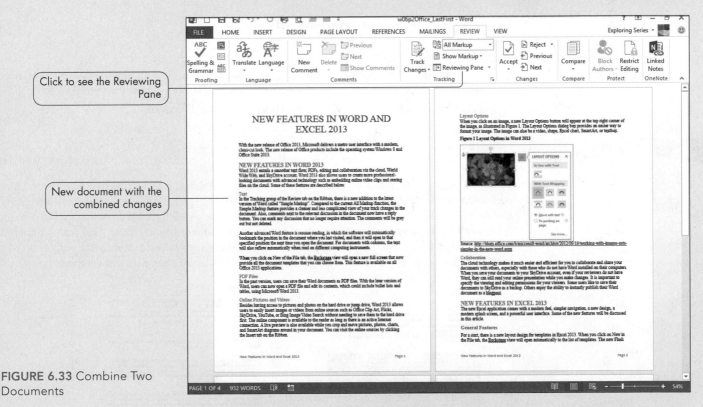

FIGURE 6.33 Combine Two Documents

a. Open both *w06p2Office1* and *w06p2Office2*. Click the **VIEW tab** and click **View Side by Side** in the Windows group. Use Synchronous Scrolling to scroll down to view the contents of each and click **View Side by Side** again to turn off the feature.

b. Click the **REVIEW tab**, click **Compare** in the Compare group, and then click **Combine**.
  - Click the **Original document arrow** and select *w06p2Office1.docx*. If necessary, click **Browse** and navigate to the document. Click **Open**.
  - Click the **Revised document arrow** and select *w06p2Office2.docx*. If necessary, click **Browse** and navigate to the document. Click **Open**.
  - Click the **More button** if necessary and click **New document** below *Show changes in* to select, if necessary. Click **OK**.

c. Save the new document as **w06p2Office_LastFirst**.

d. Click the **REVIEW tab**. If necessary, click **Reviewing Pane** in the Tracking group to show all the changes to your document in a list. Review each of the following tracked changes and accept all of them:

- Two changes in Style Definition for Headings 1 and 2.
- Two changes for the title.
- Four changes for the Layout Options.
- One change for the *NEW FEATURES IN EXCEL 2013* heading.
- Two changes for the FORMULA tab and figure.
- Two changes for the blank line at the end of the document.
- One change for the footnote.

e. Change the first heading *New Features in Word 2013* to all caps and bold it.

f. Click the **DESIGN tab** and format the document as follows:

- Click **Themes** in the Document Formatting group. Click **Retrospect** to apply colors from that theme to the text.
- Click **Colors** in the Document Formatting group and click **Customize Colors** at the bottom of the gallery.
- Click the **Accent 1 arrow** and select **Red** from the Standard Colors group.
- Click in the **Name box**, type **Office colors**, and then click **Save**.
- Click **Fonts** in the Document Formatting group and click **Customize Fonts** at the bottom of the gallery.
- Click the **Heading font arrow** and select **Broadway**.
- Click the **Body font arrow** and select **Arial**.
- Type **Office fonts** in the **Name box** and click **Save**.

g. Click **Themes** and click **Save Current Theme**. Navigate to the location where you save your solution files, type **w06p2OfficeTheme_LastFirst** in the **File name box**, and then click **Save**.

h. Save and close the file. Submit it based on your instructor's directions.

3 Cancer Information

You are a health care professional working at a local hospital, and you receive two documents from co-workers who searched for information about cancer on the Internet. The information is interesting and could be valuable to your patients, so you decide to create a well-formatted document that you can distribute to anyone who expresses an interest in basic information about cancer. And you also apply a document theme so it will look more professional. This exercise follows the same set of skills as used in Hands-On Exercises 1–3 in the chapter. Refer to Figure 6.34 as you complete this exercise.

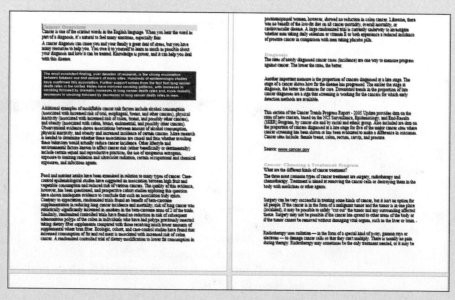

FIGURE 6.34 Theme Applied to Combined Document

a. Open *w06p3Cancer1* and open *w06p3Cancer2*. Click the **VIEW tab** and click **View Side by Side** in the Window group. Use Synchronous Scrolling to scroll down to view the contents of each and click **View Side by Side** again to turn off the feature.

b. Click the **REVIEW tab**, click the **Compare arrow** in the Compare group, and then select **Combine**.
   - Click the **Original document arrow** and select *w06p3Cancer1*. If necessary, click **Browse**, navigate to the document, and then click **Open**.
   - Click the **Revised document arrow** and select *w06p3Cancer2*. If necessary, click **Browse**, navigate to the document, and then click **Open**.
   - Click the **More button** and click **New document** below *Show changes in*, if necessary. Click **OK**.

c. Save the document as **w06p3Cancer_LastFirst**. To accept and reject the tracked changes, complete the following steps:
   - The first three track changes describe the changes in Style Definition - Normal; Heading 1: Font color: Accent 1; and text pattern: Clear (Accent 1). Click **Accept** in the Changes group to accept all three changes.
   - Click **Reject** to remove the extra space below the first paragraph.
   - Click **Accept** to keep the paragraphs with shading.
   - Scroll down until you see a large amount of deleted text, starting with the *What is cancer?* heading. Right-click the selected text and click **Reject Deletion**.

d. Press **Ctrl+Home** to view the first page. Close the Reviewing Pane, if necessary.

e. Click the **DESIGN tab** and click **Themes** in the Document Formatting group. Click **Facet** to apply colors from that theme on the text. Modify theme features by completing the following steps:
   - Click **Colors** in the Document Formatting group and click **Customize Colors** at the bottom of the gallery.
   - Click the **Accent 1 arrow** and click **Dark Green, Accent 2, Lighter 40%** (fourth row, sixth column).
   - Type **Cancer colors** in the **Name box** and click **Save**.
   - Click **Fonts** in the Document Formatting group and click **Customize Fonts** at the bottom of the gallery.
   - Click the **Heading font arrow** and select **Bookman Old Style**.
   - Type **Cancer fonts** in the **Name box** and click **Save**.
   - Click **Themes** and click **Save Current Theme**. Navigate to the location where you save your solution files, type **w06p3CancerTheme_LastFirst** in the **File name box**, and then click **Save**.

f. Save and close the file, and submit it based on your instructor's directions.

Mid-Level Exercises

1 Sidewalk Café

Your friend, Mary Guccione, just purchased the Sidewalk Café restaurant. She prepared an information sheet to distribute to several office buildings within the neighborhood, and she asked you to look at it and offer suggestions. Before you start reviewing the information sheet, she sends another version with new changes. With two different documents, you use the Compare and Combine features to view them, consolidate the documents into one final copy, add your suggested changes, and return it to Mary. Refer to Figure 6.35 as you complete this exercise.

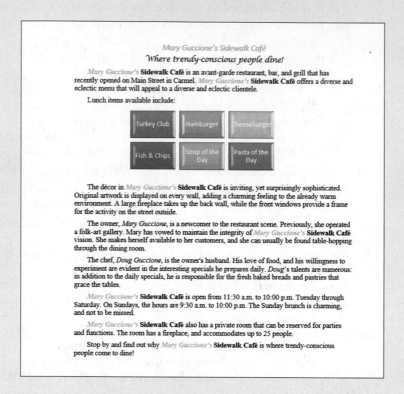

FIGURE 6.35 Information Sheet for Sidewalk Café

a. Use the Compare feature to open the two documents Mary sends, *w06m1Cafe* and *w06m1CafeRevision*, and display the results in a new document. View the differences, save the new document as **w06m1CafeCompare_LastFirst**, and then close the document.

b. Use the Combine feature to combine *w06m1Cafe* (hint: open this as an original document) and *w06m1CafeRevision*. Save the newly combined file as **w06m1CafeCombined_LastFirst**.

c. Accept and reject the following changes that display in the document:
   - Accept the tracked change *Formatted: Space Before: 0 pt.*
   - Reject the tracked change *Formatted: Font: 10 pt.*
   - Reject the addition of text *on a daily basis* that displays above the SmartArt.
   - Reject the insertion of the SmartArt object that includes *Fresh Seafood, Homemade Soup, etc.*
   - Reject the tracked change that displays in the text *is homey and* in the third paragraph.
   - Accept the inclusion of the text *trendy-conscience people.*
   - Accept the tracked change *Deleted: those in the know.*
   - Accept all remaining changes in the document.

d. Apply the **Office theme** to the document.

e. Type **Mary Guccione's** on the title line, so that the title reads *Mary Guccione's Sidewalk Café*. Apply the **Intense Emphasis style** from the style gallery to this text. Change the font color to **Gold, Accent 4**. Select the name, *Mary Guccione's*, and add it as an AutoText entry in the Building Block Organizer.

f. Display the Building Block in front of each occurrence of the *Sidewalk Café* title throughout the document, replacing *The*, where necessary. Bold the AutoText entry, if necessary.

g. Italicize all other instances of Mary Guccione and Doug Guccione, or any variation of their names.

h. Save and close the file, and submit based on your instructor's directions.

2 Creating Themes

CREATIVE CASE

Because you learned about the themes that Word 2013 provides, you decide that you need to use them more often and also create your own custom theme. You download a letter that incorporates a theme already, add a custom Building Block, and then make modifications to create your own custom theme that you can use in other documents.

a. Start Word. Search for and download the Urban Letter template. Save the file as a document template named **w06m2CustomTemplate_LastFirst**. Make certain the *Save as type* box displays *Word Template*.

★ **b.** Delete the image placeholder at the top of the page.

c. Create a Building Block that contains your name and address. Use a style from the Styles group on the HOME tab to format the name and/or address.

d. Delete the placeholders for *[Type the sender name]*, *[Type the sender company name]*, and *[Type the sender company address]*. Insert your new Building Block entry here.

e. Pick today's date in the *[Pick the date]* placeholder.

DISCOVER **f.** Display the Theme gallery and select a theme of your choice.

g. Display the Theme Colors gallery and change the color of any two objects. Save the new color theme as **Custom colors**.

h. Create a new font theme. Change the body font to **Arial font**. Save the font theme as **Custom fonts**.

i. Save the Current Document Theme as **w06m2MyTheme_LastFirst**, since you have personalized several pieces of the theme.

j. Save and close the document template. Submit it based on your instructor's directions.

3 Research on Templates

COLLABORATION CASE

Group collaboration among team members has become more common and easier with the advent of several collaboration tools. There are collaboration tools available in MyITLab, in your campus's course management software, and for free download from the Internet such as Google Docs, Microsoft 365 Web Apps, SharePoint, Sky Drive, Dropbox, OpenOffice, Facebook, Twitter, blogs, chat, and Skype. In this exercise, your group will collaborate on a research paper to describe the various templates available in Word 2013 and at the Microsoft.com Web site. Some of the popular templates are resumes, letters, labels, cards, calendars, award certificates, and announcements.

a. The team will use an online collaboration tool, such as Google groups or Skype, to conduct a face-to-face meeting. During this online chat session, you will do the following:
- Choose a name for the group and select a group leader.
- Develop a list of tasks to complete.
- Assign tasks and responsibilities to each group member.

b. After the initial face-to-face meeting, the team may continue with the discussion using any communication tool, such as Twitter, blogs, Google Docs, or Facebook chat.

c. The team leader will create a SkyDrive or Dropbox.com account where team members can post and share their documents.

d. Each member will review one category of the available templates and will save the individual template as **w06m3Template_LastFirst.dotx**. The team member will then populate the template with the necessary information before saving it as **w06m3Template_LastFirst.docx**, a Word document.

The team member will post his/her own individual template and Word document to the online storage location.

e. The group leader will combine members' files into one master file. The final research report will describe each template in detail.

f. Each team member will be responsible for inserting his/her own Word document as a file object into the research report.

g. Each team member will also take turns to enhance the research report with an appropriate document theme, theme colors, fonts, or effects.

h. Save the research report as **w06m3TemplatesResearch_GroupName**.

i. Inform your instructor that the documents are ready for grading, and also give directions to where they are located.

Beyond the Classroom

Use the Calendar Wizard
RESEARCH CASE

You want to create a monthly calendar for the current year. However, you do not want to manually create and populate 12 tables, one for each month, typing in dates within cells. You know many calendar templates are available on Office.com and decide to find one there. Find and download the Calendar Wizard, and after you complete the steps you can apply Document Themes and modify colors and fonts for a very personalized and custom calendar. Save the calendar as a template, which you can share with others, naming it **w06b2CalendarTemplate_LastFirst.dotx**. For your personal calendar, insert information for important dates such as birthdays and anniversaries; create Building Blocks for frequently used names. Save the calendar as **w06b2Calendar_LastFirst.docx** and submit it based on your instructor's directions.

Repairing Bookmarks
DISASTER RECOVERY

You work in the city's Planning and Zoning department as an analyst. You begin to prepare the *Guide to Planned Developments* document for posting on the city's intranet. The administrative clerk who typed the document attempted to use bookmarks for navigation purposes, but he did not test the bookmarks after inserting them. You must review the document and repair the bookmarks. Additionally, several cross-reference statements are embedded in the document, but appear to be erroneous. The cross-references are highlighted in the document so you can locate them; the highlights should be removed when you have corrected the references. Open *w06b3Bookmarks* and save your revised document as **w06b3Bookmarks_LastFirst**. Close the document and submit it based on your instructor's directions.

Resume and Cover Letter Tips
SOFT SKILLS CASE **S**

You will create a professional-looking resume and cover letter using templates from Microsoft Word to apply for a summer internship. Your resume will display the various types of skills you have, accomplishments you achieved, your job history, or other employment information. Choose a cover letter using a template with a similar style to coordinate your documents. You may also coordinate the appearance of your resume and cover letter by customizing them with an appropriate theme, theme colors, fonts, and effects. After you have checked the spelling and grammar of your documents, save them as **w06b4Resume_LastFirst** and **w06b4CoverLetter_LastFirst**. Submit the documents as directed by your instructor.

Capstone Exercise

You have recently been elected secretary of the local professional chapter of Information Technologist Professionals (ITPs). You decide to send professional-looking documents to the other officers so they can prepare for meetings, as well as collect and distribute information. Your next meeting occurs in one week, so you begin the process of assembling your information. Refer to Figure 6.36 as you complete the exercise.

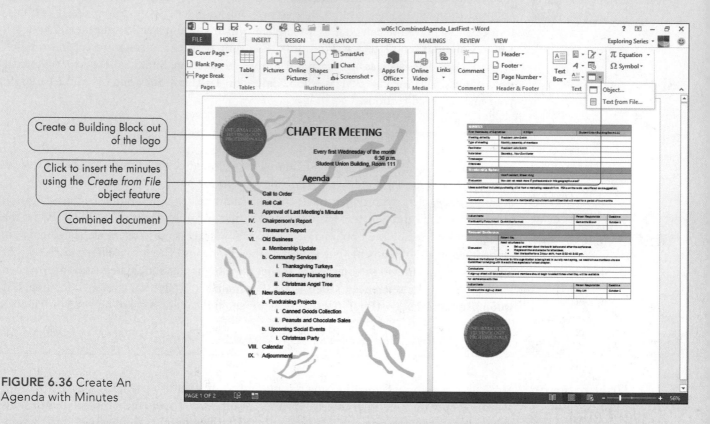

FIGURE 6.36 Create An Agenda with Minutes

Download a Word Template

You want to prepare a meeting agenda that is comprehensive, yet looks attractive and is easy to read. Instead of creating one from scratch, you download a meeting agenda document template from Office.com. Once you personalize these templates with the organization name and logo, you save them as templates so you can use them for each monthly meeting.

a. Open a new document. Conduct a search on online templates using the key term **Agenda** and download the **Community meeting agenda template**.

b. Save the file as a Word template named **w06c1AgendaTemplate_LastFirst**.

c. Replace the word *COMMUNITY* with **CHAPTER**. On the left of this text, insert the graphic *w06c1Logo.png*, which is stored with other data files for this chapter. Position the image so that it is aligned with the upper left corner of the template background color borders and change the wrapping to tight.

d. Remove the bullet points under *Chairperson's Report* and *Treasurer's Report*.

e. Replace the following text in the document template:

Replace This Text	With This Text
[Click to select date]	Every first Tuesday of the month
[Time]	7:00 p.m.
[Location]	Student Union Building, Room 111
VI. a. [Item]	Membership Update
VI. b. [Item]	Community Services
VII. a. [Item]	Fundraising Projects
VII. b. [Item]	Upcoming Social Events

f. Create a Building Block out of the meeting date, time, and place, name it **Meeting_Info**, and then save it to the Quick Part Gallery.

g. Save and close the template.

Combine Documents to Create an Agenda with Minutes

After you create the agenda template, you send it to the president and vice president and ask them to revise it and add their topics for the meeting. When they each return their version to you, you combine them into one final agenda for the upcoming meeting. You also attach the minutes from the last meeting to the end of the agenda.

a. Use the Combine feature to view the returned agendas named *w06c1EileenAgendaTemplate* and *w06c1JohnAgendaTemplate*. Save the combined file as a Word document named **w06c1CombinedAgenda_LastFirst**.

b. Accept all changes to the agenda after the files are combined.

c. Change the date to **Wednesday**. Change the time to **6:30 p.m.**

d. Insert a blank page after the agenda. Use the *Create from File object* feature to add the minutes of the meeting, stored in *w06c1Minutes*, to the end of the agenda.

e. Type your name as Note taker/Secretary for the First Wednesday of September minutes.

f. Insert the logo Building Block at the bottom of the page where you just inserted the minutes. Position the logo so that it is 0.5" from the left margin and 0.2" below the last line.

g. Save and close the file.

Apply a Document Theme to the Meeting Agenda and Minutes

After you combine the agendas and insert the minutes, you decide to customize the document to reflect the national organization's colors. You begin by selecting a theme, but decide to modify it so your colors match and fonts are easier to read. You save your custom settings so that you can use them again on other documents.

a. Change the document theme to **Retrospect**.

b. Modify the colors used in this theme by changing the Accent 1 color to **Orange, Accent 2, Lighter 60%** (third row, sixth column) and changing the Text/Background - Light 1 color to **Black, Background 1** (first row, first column). Save the font colors as **w06c1AgendaColors_LastFirst**.

c. Create new theme fonts by replacing the heading font with **Arial Black** and the body font with **Arial Narrow**. Save the font theme as **w06c1AgendaFonts_LastFirst**.

d. Save the current theme, which includes the revisions you just made, as **w06c1AgendaTheme_LastFirst**.

e. Click the **dark blue-colored logo graphic** on the page where the agenda displays. Change the fill color of that object to **Orange, Accent color 1 Light** (third row, second column under *Recolor*) and apply the **Cement Artistic Effects** (fourth row, first column).

f. Save and close the document.

Add Bookmarks to a Document

After the minutes for each meeting are approved, you are responsible for adding them to a document that holds the minutes for a whole year. The document becomes so lengthy that it is easier to navigate when bookmarks are applied to each month. You will add the minutes from the last meeting and add missing bookmarks.

a. Open *w06c1YearlyMinutes*. Save the document as **w06c1YearlyMinutes_LastFirst**.

b. Add a page break at the beginning of the document and use the *Create from File* object to add the minutes of the September meeting, *w06c1Minutes*.

c. Insert a bookmark named **September** at the left edge of the date *First Wednesday of September*, which displays in the second line of the table holding the minutes.

d. Insert a bookmark named **August** at the left edge of the date *First Wednesday of August*, which displays on the next page. Continue to insert bookmarks for July and June.

e. Press **Ctrl+G** and go to the bookmark named *June*. Close the *Find and Replace* dialog box.

f. Type your name as the Timekeeper. Apply the **w06c1AgendaTheme_LastFirst**.

g. Save and close the document. Submit all files based on your instructor's directions.

Word

Document Automation

Forms, Macros, and Security

OBJECTIVES AFTER YOU READ THIS CHAPTER, YOU WILL BE ABLE TO:

1. Create an electronic form p. 110
2. Insert form controls p. 112
3. Protect a form p. 114
4. Create a macro p. 124

5. Run a macro p. 127
6. Apply document restrictions p. 134
7. Set passwords to open a document p. 137
8. Use digital signatures to authenticate documents p. 140

CASE STUDY | Oak Grove Products, Inc.

Cassie Artman has purchased Oak Grove Products, Inc., a company that sells tulip, hyacinth, and crocus bulbs. Cassie wants to take the company to the next level by automating some of the resources they use. One of the first projects she assigns to you, her technology coordinator, is to create a sales invoice that can be filled out quickly by salespeople who take phone or online orders. The invoice will include check boxes, drop-down menus, and fields that calculate prices automatically. She also wants you to incorporate an informational document about the products sold. She has created a document that she considers complete, so she wants you to password-protect it to prevent any accidental editing. But she also wants you to get feedback from staff before you consider it final and stamp it with a digital certificate.

In the Hands-On Exercises, you will create the invoice form, work with macros, and practice protecting documents.

Forms

Forms are quite common in our society. A form is a document designed for collecting data for a specific situation. For example, you complete a medical history form when you visit a doctor's office; you complete an account application form when you open a bank account; you complete a registration form when you register software and hardware; and you fill out a job application form when you apply for a job. Forms are also used for class registrations, purchase orders, and invoices. The form may be electronic and completed online, or it may exist as a printed document. Figure 7.1 displays a completed form that is an invoice for goods or services.

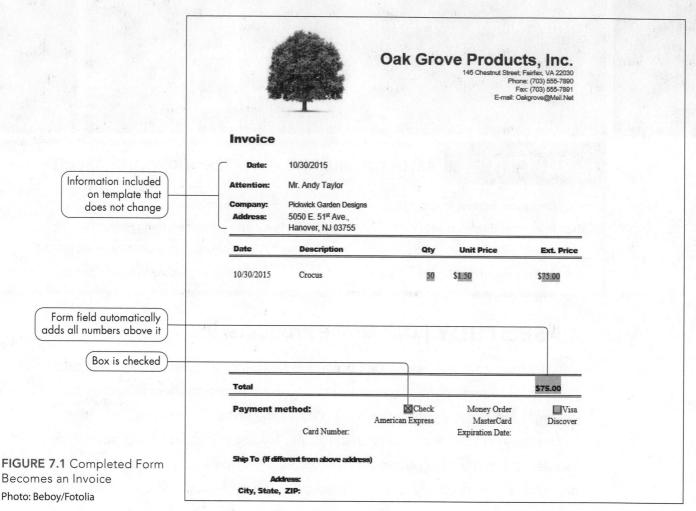

Information included on template that does not change

Form field automatically adds all numbers above it

Box is checked

FIGURE 7.1 Completed Form Becomes an Invoice
Photo: Beboy/Fotolia

In this section, you will create and use a simple form that can be printed and filled in or completed onscreen. You will learn how to create and customize form controls, perform calculations in a table form, and then protect the document so you can use the form.

Creating an Electronic Form

In Word, you can create a *form template*, a document that defines the standard layout, structure, and formatting of a form. You save the document as a Word template and establish settings to enable the user to enter data in specific places, but prevent editing it in any other way. The process requires you to create the form and save it to disk, where it serves as an original template for future documents. Then, when you need to enter data for a specific situation, you open the template form, enter the data, and save the completed form as a document. This process is more efficient than removing old information from a standard document so you can replace it with current data for the new situation. It also minimizes errors that sometimes occur when you intend to replace old information with updated data but overlook some portion of the older data. Using a form enables you to maintain the integrity of an original document or template while also allowing you to customize it.

Figure 7.2 displays a blank form. The shaded fields indicate where a user enters information into a form. To complete the form, the user presses Tab to move from one field to the next and enters data as appropriate. Then, when all fields have been filled in, the form is printed to produce the finished document (an invoice). The data entered into the various fields appear as regular text when printed.

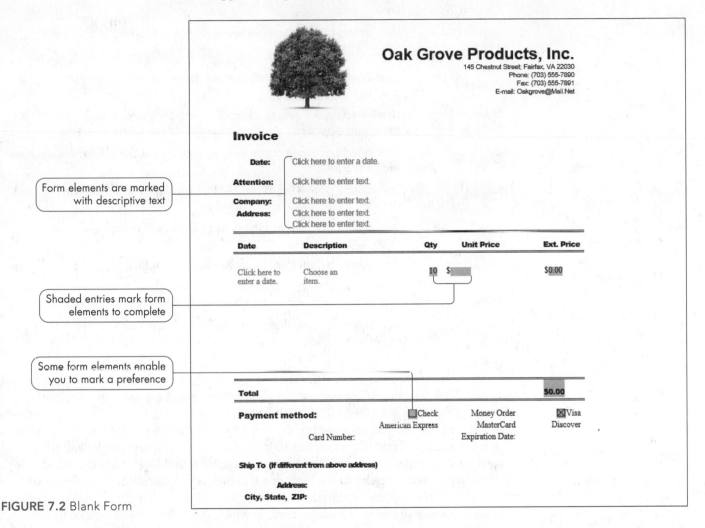

FIGURE 7.2 Blank Form

Create a Document Template

STEP 1 » Before you can create a document template, the Developer tab must be visible on the Ribbon. This tab does not display automatically but is easy to activate. If the Developer tab is not shown on the Ribbon, you may display it by doing the following:

1. Click the FILE tab.
2. Click Options on the left panel.
3. Click Customize Ribbon.
4. Click the Developer (Custom) check box in the *Customize the Ribbon* column.
5. Click OK.

Before you can use the document, you need to save it as a Word template file. This file will have the .dotx instead of the .docx extension. Then, you will add form controls to create a blank form as shown in Figure 7.2.

Inserting Form Controls

You can design forms that will be printed and also forms that will be completed electronically. If you want users to fill out a form electronically, you must insert *form controls*, also called form fields, into the form template. Form controls help the user complete a form by displaying prompts such as drop-down lists and text boxes. Table 7.1 describes the most common types of content controls, located in the Controls group under the Developer tab.

TABLE 7.1 Content Controls	
Control Type	**Description**
Rich Text	User enters text or numbers and modifies the format of the text.
Plain Text	User enters text or numbers but cannot modify the format of the text.
Picture	User inserts a drawing, shape, chart, table, clip art, or SmartArt object in a field.
Building Block Gallery	User selects a building block item to insert in the document, such as a cover page, header, footer, or predefined text, such as a disclaimer.
Check Box	User selects or deselects an item by clicking the check box that displays beside the item.
Combo Box	User selects from a list of choices that displays in a drop-down box, but the user can modify the choices in the list.
Drop-Down List	User selects from a predefined list of choices that displays in a drop-down box.
Date Picker	User selects a date from the calendar that displays.
Repeating Section	User inserts a content control that contains other content controls, and user can repeat the content of the control as needed.
Legacy Tools	User inserts a legacy form content control or ActiveX control from a list of options.

The controls you use most often are text, check boxes, and drop-down lists. The rich text and plain *text content controls* are the most common and are used to enter any type of text into a form. As described in Table 7.1, both the plain and rich text controls allow users to enter text, but users cannot modify the text format for a plain text control. A plain text control is often preferred, but a rich text control allows users to insert images and tables, and to enhance the text entry with features such as highlights and fore and background colors. Text controls usually display in the form of a text box, and they collect information such as name and address and even numerical data such as a phone number. The length of a text box can be set exactly or can be left unspecified, in which case the field will expand to the exact number of positions that are required as the data are entered.

When you have a form that uses numerical information, you can use a text content control to perform calculations. You can use basic formulas, such as those that add or multiply the numbers that display in text form fields. The properties for the text form content control enable you to select the form fields you include in the calculation. You can adjust the format of the numbers; for example, you can use currency format that displays dollar signs and decimal points for a price field.

A *check box form field*, as the name implies, consists of a box that is checked or unchecked. A check box might include the responses *Yes* or *No*, or *Male* or *Female*, for example. You can customize check box form fields so they display checked by default, or not checked. You can also specify the size of the check box.

A *drop-down list* enables the user to choose from one of several existing entries. This type of control should only be used on electronic forms because the list of options will not display on a printed form. A drop-down list enables users to click an arrow and then click one option from the list; the option they click will then display on the form. A list of cities or states is appropriate to display in a drop-down list.

Many forms require a date. The ***Date Picker*** displays a calendar that the user can navigate on an electronic form and click rather than typing in a date. If the user wants to select the current date, the Date Picker calendar has a Today button. The Properties dialog box for the Date Picker enables you to select from several date formats, such as 3/2/2016 or 2-Mar-16.

If you create forms that might be used by people who are not yet using Word 2013, you should remember to use only legacy controls and save the document or template in Compatibility Mode. The Legacy Tools include a list of options for Legacy Forms and ActiveX controls. As the word *legacy* implies, the legacy controls, also called ***legacy form fields***, are created and/or used in Word 2003 or earlier versions. Legacy forms are created using form fields that will only work when the document is in protected mode; that is, all parts of the document are locked and only the form fields can be edited. The legacy form fields can be used in the newer versions of Word documents or templates when you open the files in Compatibility Mode. The controls created for Word 2007 and later versions are called content controls. These controls do not need form protection or macros to work. Unfortunately, content controls cannot be used in Word 2003 or earlier versions. ***ActiveX controls*** are form elements designed for use in Office 2007 and later versions. These controls can be easily inserted into a Word document or template, and especially a Web page. ActiveX controls require macros to work. Figure 7.3 shows the Developer tab and available controls.

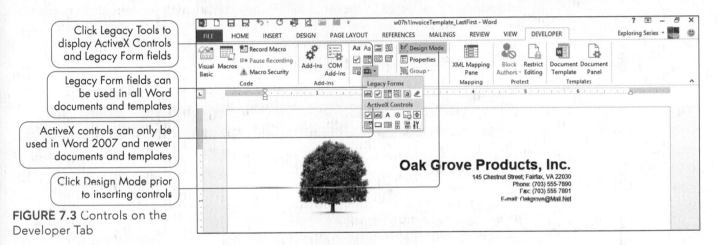

FIGURE 7.3 Controls on the Developer Tab

Insert Form Controls in a Document

STEP 2» On the Developer tab, you see the form controls as well as other commands you use while creating the form. Before you insert the controls in your document, you must enter Design Mode. ***Design Mode*** enables you to view and select the control fields so you can make any necessary modifications to their layout or options. Design Mode is a toggle; click it once to activate Design Mode and click it again to deactivate it. To insert form controls into a form template, do the following:

1. Click the DEVELOPER tab.
2. Click Design Mode in the Controls group. The Properties icon is activated when Design Mode is active.
3. Position the insertion point at the location where you want to insert the form control.
4. Click the specific form control icon in the Controls group to insert it into the document.

Insert Form Controls in a Table

STEP 3» Besides inserting form controls directly into a document, sometimes it is easier to insert form controls using a table to help you align information and to make the form easier for users to fill out. For instance, you can insert a two-column table. You can insert the appropriate content controls in the right column and the label for the corresponding content controls in the left column. Labels for content controls in a form can include Last Name, First Name, Street Address, State, Zip Code, Cell Phone, E-mail Address, Date, and so on. In the right column, you can insert a Drop-Down List content control for the user to select from a list of states, a Date Picker content control for the date, and several plain text content controls for the other labels. All controls already have default settings, but you can redefine the characteristics of any control by clicking Properties in the Controls group. You can also copy and paste a control after you create it.

In addition, you can use the Table feature to format and manipulate the fields and data to improve the form. For example, you can right-align the labels in the left column, such as Last Name and First Name, and then you can left-align the content controls in the right column of the table. This alignment clarifies the instructional information that accompanies the control.

Perform Calculations with Form Control Data

STEP 4 >> Forms can be created to automatically calculate data values or update calculations by clicking a certain button or when exiting from Word. For instance, you can design a form to automatically calculate the sales tax or total price when the user types in the quantity or cost of an item. After you have designed the calculating form, the next step is to determine the data values that will be stored in the form, followed by constructing the formula(s) needed for the calculation. Finally, you will type the formula into the appropriate content control, either directly or using the Formula button in the Data group of the Layout tab. It is important to note that formulas can only be used in tables.

TIP   Planning the Order of Fields

When a user completes an electronic form, Word moves through fields in the order in which you inserted them. Once a form has been completed, the tab order is very difficult to change or modify. Therefore, it is very important that you plan carefully how you want users to fill out the form before you insert the form fields. If you want users to move from left to right across the page, insert form fields from left to right. If you want users to move down the page, insert form fields down the page. You should also keep labels close to the form controls because programs that are used by the visually impaired cannot distinguish which label matches a particular field when they are not positioned closely.

Protecting a Form

STEP 5 >> After the form is created and ready to be distributed to other users to input data, it should be protected to prevent any modification other than data entry. After you have inserted all the necessary content controls into your form, you can protect the form by doing the following:

1. Click the DEVELOPER tab, if it is not selected.
2. Click Design Mode in the Controls group to deactivate it, if necessary.
3. Click Restrict Editing in the Protect group to display the Restrict Editing pane. The Restrict Editing pane displays, as shown in Figure 7.4.
4. Click *Allow only this type of editing in the document* in the Editing restrictions section.
5. Click the arrow and select *Filling in forms* to enable the user to type in, click, or select only the form fields in the form.
6. Click the Yes, Start Enforcing Protection button to activate protection of the form.

Click Restrict Editing to display the Restrict Editing pane

Click to restrict types of editing in form

Click to activate protection of form

FIGURE 7.4 Restrict Formatting and Editing of a Form

After you enforce the protection of a form, you are prompted for a password. You can create a password for the form to serve as another layer of protection and to prevent unauthorized users from deactivating the protection. Without a password, anyone can deactivate the protection. However, if you forget the password, it cannot be recovered. You can skip the password protection by omitting a password in the *Enter new password* box and clicking OK. If you want to revise the form, click Stop Protection in the Restrict Editing pane.

You can protect specific controls on a form without restricting access to the entire document by using the Group command in the Controls group on the Developer tab. When you select a range and apply the Group command, the range is protected from editing. This feature is useful when you want to be able to make modifications to a document that contains form controls, but you do not want to allow any changes to the form controls within that document. After you apply the Group command to the range, click Properties and set one of the two locking options. The first option—*Content control cannot be deleted*—enables you to edit the content of a control but does not enable you to remove the control. The second option—*Contents cannot be edited*—enables you to delete the control, but you cannot edit the content in the control.

Use an Electronic Form

STEP 6 ▶ After an electronic form is created and protected, you may e-mail it to the user or upload it to a Web site. The user will open the form like any other Word document and navigate through the form controls by pressing Tab or the arrow keys, depending on the control types. For instance, the user must use the arrow keys when navigating to the next text box. To insert dates, the user may click the Date Picker arrow to select a date with the date format stipulated in the Properties dialog box. After all the data are entered, the user will save and close the document. If necessary, the user may print the electronic form as a hard copy.

Quick Concepts

1. Describe the reasons for creating a form document. *p. 110*

2. Describe the three most common content controls. *p. 112*

3. What is the main purpose of protecting a form? *p. 114*

Hands-On Exercises

1 Forms

As the new owner of Oak Grove Products, Inc., Cassie Artman wants to improve the resources used by employees in the sales and accounting departments. She asks you to update and automate the invoice form so that it is easier to use. You begin by inserting form controls and using automated calculations from those controls. You then save the document so that employees can open and enter data without affecting the content or structure of the invoice document.

Skills covered: Create a Document Template • Insert Form Controls in a Document • Insert Form Controls in a Table • Perform Calculations with Form Control Data • Add Check Box Controls and Protect the Form • Use an Electronic Form

---

STEP 1 » CREATE A DOCUMENT TEMPLATE

Cassie has passed along an invoice form that you can use as a starting point for your automated invoice. You decide to save it as a Word template so it will be easy and efficient to update for each new customer transaction. Refer to Figure 7.5 as you complete Step 1.

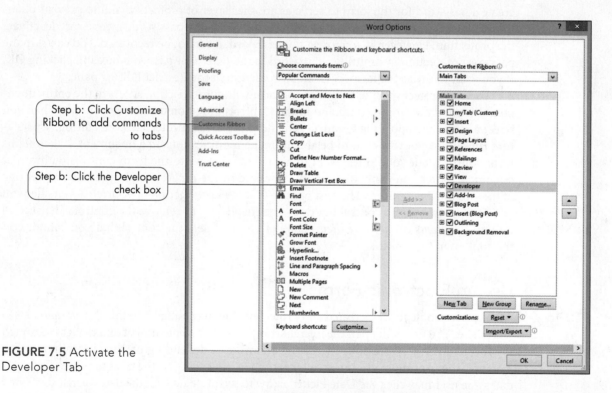

Step b: Click Customize Ribbon to add commands to tabs

Step b: Click the Developer check box

FIGURE 7.5 Activate the Developer Tab

a. Open *w07h1Invoice*. Click **Enable Content** when you see the warning message *Macros have been disabled*.

   This file is saved as a Word 97-2003 document and will open in Compatibility Mode.

> **TROUBLESHOOTING:** If you make any major mistakes in this exercise, you can close the file, open *w07h1Invoice* again, and then start this exercise over.

b. Click the **FILE tab**, if necessary, click **Options**, click **Customize Ribbon**, and then click the **Developer (Custom) check box**, which displays in the *Customize the Ribbon* column on the right. Click **OK**.

This step is necessary to display the Developer tab, which contains all form controls.

c. Click the **DEVELOPER tab** and locate the Controls group.

Notice that most of the controls in the Controls group are grayed out. These ActiveX controls cannot be used in a document that opens in Compatibility Mode.

d. Click the **FILE tab** and click **Save As**. Click **Browse**. Type **w07h1InvoiceTemplate_LastFirst** in the **File name box**. Click the **Save as type arrow** and select **Word Template**. Navigate to the folder where your student files are stored, uncheck the *Maintain compatibility with previous versions of Word* checkbox, and then click **Save**.

Make sure that you uncheck the *Maintain compatibility with previous versions of Word* checkbox or else the content controls will not be available to you.

> **TIP** **Saving a Template Document**
>
> When saving a template, the Save As dialog box will open to a default file folder on the hard drive. Therefore, if needed, you may have to adjust the path by navigating to your preference location to save the template. When saving as a template file type, you will adjust the file type and navigate to the appropriate file directory. You can also change the default directory by clicking Save Options on the Tools drop-down list in the Save As dialog box.

e. Click **OK** to the Microsoft Word dialog box displaying a warning that your document will be upgraded to the newest file format.

f. Click **Yes** to the Microsoft Word dialog box asking if you want to continue to save as a macro-free template.

STEP 2 ≫ INSERT FORM CONTROLS IN A DOCUMENT

Now that the document is saved as a template, you insert form controls for the customer's name, address, and date of the sale. You especially appreciate the Date Picker control, which enables you to click the date from a calendar; this process prevents mistyped dates and should reflect more accurate record keeping. Refer to Figure 7.6 as you complete Step 2.

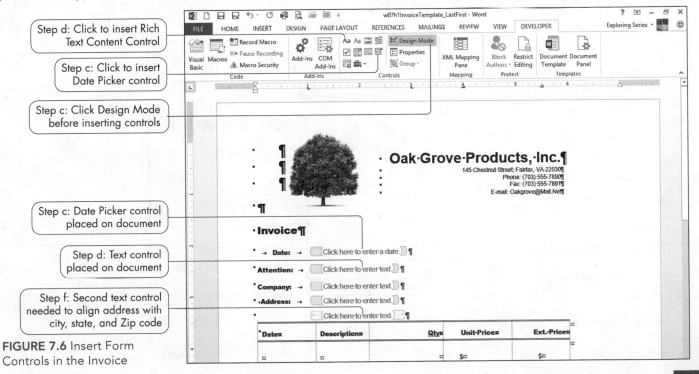

FIGURE 7.6 Insert Form Controls in the Invoice

a. Click the **HOME tab** and click **Show/Hide** (¶) in the Paragraph group, if necessary, to display formatting marks.

b. Click the left side of the paragraph mark that displays at the end of the line for *Date*, which is just below the text *Invoice*.

You are positioning the insertion point prior to inserting a date control.

c. Click the **DEVELOPER tab**, click **Design Mode** in the Controls group, and then click **Date Picker Content Control** in the Controls group.

The control for choosing a date displays with a light blue border and the text *Click here to enter a date*.

> **TROUBLESHOOTING:** If the Date Picker Content Control is grayed out and not available to you, you should repeat Step 1d and make sure that you uncheck the *Maintain compatibility with previous versions of Word* checkbox.

d. Press ⬇ one time to move the insertion point to the end of the line for *Attention* and click **Rich Text Content Control** in the Controls group.

The control for entering text displays with a light blue border and the text *Click here to enter text*.

e. Repeat the process from step d to insert Rich Text Content Controls at the end of the *Company* and *Address* lines.

f. Click the left side of the paragraph mark that displays on the line just below the *Address* line. Click **Rich Text Content Control** in the Controls group.

You must insert a second text control for the city, state, and Zip code portions of the address. The text controls do not align text properly when you press Enter when typing within them, so a second box is necessary to align all the address information.

g. Save the template.

STEP 3 ≫ INSERT FORM CONTROLS IN A TABLE

Customer purchases are recorded in an area of the invoice that is formatted in a Word table. By using a table, you have more control over the placement and alignment of the controls and text that display in the invoice. Because this invoice will be used in digital form, you insert form controls that enable the salesperson to select the product purchased—another way to reduce the possibility of error that occurs when information is typed into a form. Refer to Figure 7.7 as you complete Step 3.

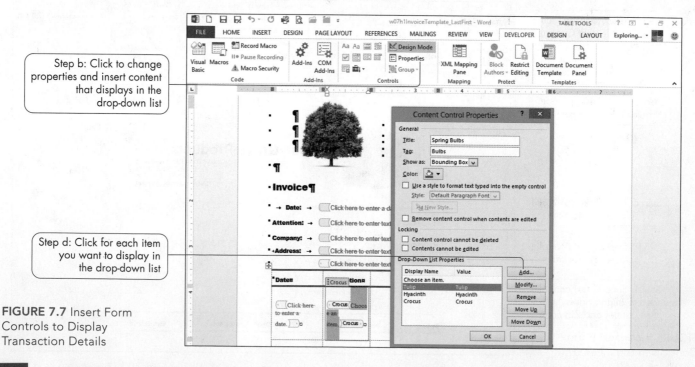

FIGURE 7.7 Insert Form Controls to Display Transaction Details

a. Click the left side of the first blank row in the table, just below the text *Date*. Click **Date Picker Content Control** from the Controls group. Click the left side of the next cell, below the text *Description*.

> **TROUBLESHOOTING:** If you have difficulty positioning the insertion point in the table, click the View tab and click Gridlines in the Show group so you can view each cell border. This border does not display when printed.

b. Click **Drop-Down List Content Control** in the Controls group. Click **Properties** in the Controls group to display the Content Control Properties dialog box.

   Users will select from a predefined list of products when they click this control in the form.

c. Type **Spring Bulbs** in the **Title box**. Type **Bulbs** in the **Tag box**.

d. Click **Add** in the *Drop-Down List Properties* section to display the Add Choice dialog box. Type **Tulip** in the **Display Name box** and click **OK**.

e. Repeat the process in step d to add two more types of bulbs: **Hyacinth** and **Crocus**.

f. Click **OK** to close the dialog box. Save the template.

STEP 4 ≫ PERFORM CALCULATIONS WITH FORM CONTROL DATA

The next few pieces of information entered into the invoice will reflect the quantity and amount paid for the products. Because these fields work with numbers, you use form controls that enable you to format the price entered using currency symbols. The controls also perform calculations using formulas resembling those used in table cell calculations. By using these form controls, you increase the frequency of very accurate sales figures that display on the invoices. Refer to Figure 7.8 as you complete Step 4.

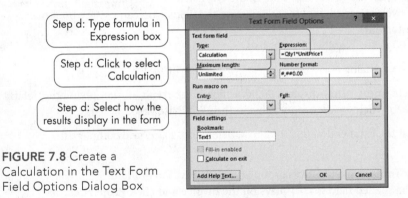

FIGURE 7.8 Create a Calculation in the Text Form Field Options Dialog Box

a. Click in the cell below *Qty*. Click **Legacy Tools** in the Controls group and click **Text Form Field** below the heading *Legacy Forms*.

   A series of small circles displays with a gray background.

> **TROUBLESHOOTING:** If the gray background does not display behind the circles, click Legacy Tools and click Form Field Shading below the heading *Legacy Forms*.

b. Set up the form field by completing the following steps:

   - Click **Properties** in the Controls group to display the Text Form Field Options dialog box.
   - Click the **Type arrow** and select **Number**.
   - Type **10** in the **Default number text box**.
   - Press **Tab** four times and replace the contents of the **Bookmark box** with **Qty1**.

   Make sure that there is no space between Qty and 1 in the bookmark name.

- Click to enable the **Calculate on exit check box**, confirm *Fill-in enabled* is checked, and click **OK**.

By naming the bookmark *Qty1*, you will be able to add more product items to the invoice. The next row can contain a bookmark named Qty2, and eventually, you can use the bookmark names to create formulas to perform calculations within the form. Checking *Calculate on exit* ensures that calculations are updated after users enter numbers.

c. Click in the cell below *Unit Price*, placing your cursor on the right side of the dollar sign, and complete the following steps:

- Click **Legacy Tools** in the Controls group and click **Text Form Field** below the heading *Legacy Forms*.
- Click **Properties** in the Controls group.
- Replace the contents of the **Bookmark box** with **UnitPrice1**.
- Click to enable the **Calculate on exit check box** and confirm *Fill-in enabled* is checked.
- Click **OK** to close the Text Form Field Options dialog box.

d. Click in the cell below *Ext. Price*, placing your cursor on the right side of the dollar sign, and complete the following steps:

- Click **Legacy Tools** in the Controls group and click **Text Form Field**.
- Click **Properties**.
- Click the **Type arrow** and select **Calculation**.
- Type **Qty1*UnitPrice1** after the equal sign in the **Expression box**.
  The equal sign in the Expression box specifies that you are creating a mathematical formula. This formula multiplies the value in the Qty1 field by the value of the UnitPrice1 field. Because you assigned bookmark names to the fields, you can use the bookmark names in the formula.
- Select **#,##0.00** in the Number Format list.

e. Click **OK** to close the dialog box.

The Ext. Price field immediately displays *$0.00*, which is the result of multiplying the default value of 10 in the Qty field by the empty value in the Unit Price field.

f. Click in the cell at the right end of the Total row, below *Ext. Price*, and complete the following steps:

- Click **Legacy Tools** in the Controls group and click **Text Form Field**.
- Right-click the shaded field that displays on the invoice and click **Properties**.
- Click the **Type arrow** and select **Calculation**.
- Click in the **Expression box** and type **sum(above)** after the equal sign.

You do not need to type the formula in all caps; either lowercase or all caps will work.

- Select **$#,##0.00;($#,##0.00)** in the Number Format list.
- Click **OK**.

You want to add all the values in as many fields as appear in the Ext. Price column. You use the SUM function to add values in all fields in this column. You will add more rows to the invoice later. The results display as a dollar value.

g. Save the template.

STEP 5 ›› ADD CHECK BOX CONTROLS AND PROTECT THE FORM

Your changes to the invoice are almost complete. You decide to add only one more form control, a check box for the type of payment, which displays at the bottom of the invoice. You use the document protection tools to prevent editing of the document, allowing only edits that serve to fill out the form. Refer to Figure 7.9 as you complete Step 5.

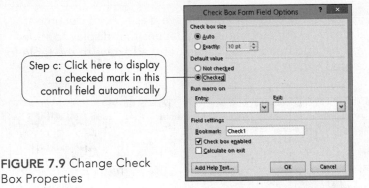

Step c: Click here to display a checked mark in this control field automatically

FIGURE 7.9 Change Check Box Properties

a. Click the left side of the cell containing *Check* in the *Payment method* section of the form. Click **Legacy Tools** in the Controls group and select **Check Box Form Field** below *Legacy Forms*.

This action inserts a check box form field in the cell to the left of the Check payment method. Users can mark the check box next to the payment method they prefer. You use the Legacy form field instead of the ActiveX form field because it enables you to set custom properties for that field, which you complete in a future step.

b. Click the left side of the cell containing *Visa*, click **Legacy Tools** in the Controls group, and then select **Check Box Form Field**.

You do not yet display check boxes next to all the payment methods, but you will add them in a future Hands-On Exercise. However, you do have enough controls to test your form in the next step.

c. Right-click the **Visa check box** and click **Properties**. Click **Checked** in the *Default value* section. Click **OK**.

Because the majority of purchases are charged to the Visa credit card, you decide to check this option automatically. If customers use a different type of payment, they can click the option, but this saves time if they use a Visa card for payment.

d. Click **Design Mode** to turn off Design Mode. Save the document. Click **Restrict Editing** in the Protect group to display the pane.

The Restrict Editing pane displays.

e. Click **Allow only this type of editing in the document**, which displays in the *Editing restrictions* section. Click the down arrow in the box below this option and select **Filling in forms**, if necessary. Click **Yes, Start Enforcing Protection** in the *Start enforcement* section.

> **TROUBLESHOOTING:** If *Yes, Start Enforcing Protection* is grayed out, make sure you are not in Design Mode.

f. Click **OK** when the Start Enforcing Protection dialog box displays.

If you want to password-protect a document, you can insert and confirm the password in this dialog box. Remember that if you forget the password, you cannot recover it and your document cannot be opened. You are going to remove the password so that anyone can open the file to read and edit.

g. Click the **Close button** in the top-right corner of the Restrict Editing pane. Click the **HOME tab** and click **Show/Hide** (¶) to turn off formatting marks.

h. Save and close the template.

STEP 6 ≫ USE AN ELECTRONIC FORM

It is now time to test the electronic invoice. You will open the document template and save it as a Word document prior to entering sales information on the invoice. You will also view the automatic calculations that display to show the full amount of a purchase. If this works as designed, you will update the invoice later and add rows to the table for entering more sales. Refer to Figure 7.10 as you complete Step 6.

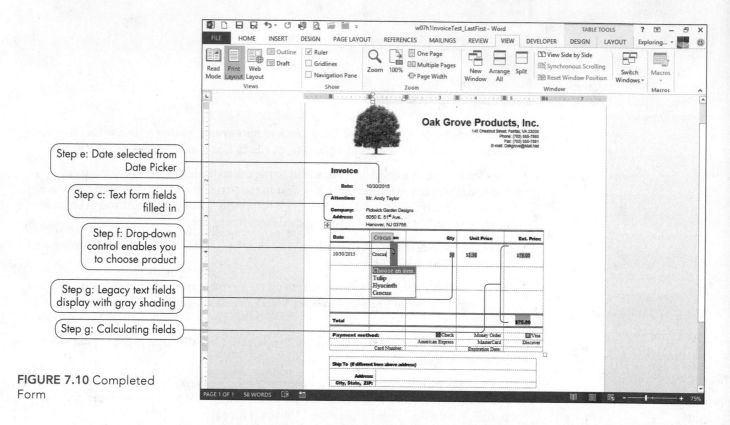

Step e: Date selected from Date Picker

Step c: Text form fields filled in

Step f: Drop-down control enables you to choose product

Step g: Legacy text fields display with gray shading

Step g: Calculating fields

FIGURE 7.10 Completed Form

a. Open the template *w07h1InvoiceTemplate_LastFirst.dotx*. Save it as a Word document and name it **w07h1InvoiceTest_LastFirst**.

Word creates the new Word Document file based on the template. By default, the first form control is selected. Notice the Ribbon is grayed out, preventing you from using the formatting commands, because the document is protected from editing. You will only be able to click and use the form controls.

b. Click the **Date Picker arrow** in the first control. Click **Today**.

c. Click the words **Click here to enter text**, which display next to *Attention*, and type **Mr. Andy Taylor**. Press ⬇.

Word enters the name in the field. You must press the directional arrows to move to the next field for text boxes.

d. Type **Pickwick Garden Designs**, press ⬇, type **5050 E. 51st Ave.**, press ⬇, type **Hanover, NH 03755**, and then press ⬇.

e. Click the **Date Picker arrow** for the date of the first purchase and click **October 30** of the current year. Press **Tab**.

f. Press **Tab** or click one time on the Description field and click the **Description arrow** to display the list of bulbs. Select **Crocus** from the list.

You will click or press Tab to get to the Description field first before the Description arrow will display.

g. Double-click the **Qty control field**, type **50**, and then press **Tab**. Type **1.50** and press **Tab**.

As soon as you press Tab to move out of the Unit Price control field, the Ext. Price and Total fields calculate, and the insertion point moves forward in the form to the check box for the Check method of payment.

h. Press the **Spacebar** to select *Check*. Press **Tab** one time and press **Spacebar** to deselect *Visa*. Press **Tab** two times to cycle through the text fields and update the calculations.

You can also use your mouse to select or deselect a check box.

i. Save and close the file, and submit it based on your instructor's directions.

 TIP Creating Hard Copy Forms

Many offices still use hard copy forms instead of electronic forms. For example, some job application forms are printed, and the job applicants must write or type on the hard copy form. These types of forms contain labels, text boxes, and check boxes. To create a hard copy form, open a document from the form template and print as many copies as you need.

Introduction to Macros

Have you ever pulled down the same menus and clicked the same sequence of commands over and over? If you find yourself performing repetitive tasks, whether in one document or in a series of documents, you should consider using macros. A *macro* is a set of instructions (that is, a program) that executes a series of keystrokes, often to complete a repetitive task, using only a button click or keyboard shortcut. Using a macro in Word is like recording your favorite television show: You turn on the DVR, record the show, and play the show over and over again as often as you want. Examples of useful macros include designating actions to change paragraph format and font styles; insert a page number, header, footer, or watermark such as "Confidential" into a document; change page layout; and format printing procedures.

Office 2013 allows you to save documents with macros automatically enabled or disabled. By default, Word documents with the .docx extension automatically disable any macros the file might contain. If you store a macro in a document, save it as a *Macro-Enabled Document*, which adds the extension .docm to the file and stores VBA macro code in the document to enable execution of a macro.

In this section, you will record a macro that enables you to update and make repetitive modifications to the invoice you are updating for the Oak Grove Products Company. Specifically, you will place additional form controls in the payment section you started in Hands-On Exercise 1. You will run the macro, and you will modify the macro using the editor.

Creating a Macro

Before creating a macro, you should decide what you want to accomplish (such as formatting a letter) and plan exactly which commands and tasks to include (such as margins, alignment, tabs, and so on). Furthermore, you should practice completing the tasks and commands, and make notes of the sequence of steps to perform. Doing so helps you create (record) the macro successfully the first time.

Record a Macro

STEP 1 ❯❯

The process of creating a macro is called *record macro*. When you record a macro, Word records a series of keystrokes and command selections, and converts the tasks into coded statements. The macro commands are located on two tabs—the Developer tab and the View tab—and also in the status bar. You can start recording a macro by clicking Record Macro in the Code group of the Developer tab. You can also perform the same action by clicking the Macros arrow in the Macros group and clicking Record Macro on the View tab. The Record Macro dialog box opens so that you can name the macro, as shown in Figure 7.11. The macro name can consist of up to 80 characters, but no spaces. You have the option of assigning the macro to a button, which can be placed on the Quick Access Toolbar so that it is readily available, or you can assign a keystroke combination that runs the macro. If you do not choose either option, the macro is only available in the Macros dialog box. You also have the choice of storing a macro in a particular file, so that it can only be executed when that file is open, or you can store macros in the normal template so that they can run in all files. To record a macro, do the following:

1. Click the DEVELOPER tab.
2. Click Record Macro in the Code group to activate the Record Macro dialog box.
3. To name or assign a macro, do one or more of the following:

   - Type the selected name of the Macro in the *Macro name* box.
   - If desired, click the Keyboard icon under the *Assign macro to* option to assign a hotkey to this macro.
     i. Place the cursor in the *Press new shortcut key* box and assign a hotkey by pressing the selected key combination.
     ii. Click Assign to assign a hotkey to the macro.

4. Click OK and a recorder-like image with a pointer appears, indicating that the macro is being recorded.
5. Perform the designated tasks for the macro.
6. Click Stop Recording or Pause Recording in the Code group to stop or pause (respectively) the recording at any time.

When you close the Record Macro dialog box, Word records everything—every keystroke and click of the mouse (including any errors and corrections to errors). For this reason, you do not want to perform any unnecessary actions while recording a macro. For example, if you press Ctrl+Home to correct a mistake while recording the macro, Word records the command to move the insertion point to the beginning of the document. This is problematic if you run the macro in an existing document and the macro inserts or formats text in the wrong location. Therefore, it is very important that you take great care in planning the order of the fields on the form. Keep in mind that it is easy to delete a macro that does not function as you intend and record it again.

You may review a macro by clicking the Macros arrow in the Macros group of the View tab. When the Macros dialog box appears, you will see commands for you to run, edit, create, or delete a macro.

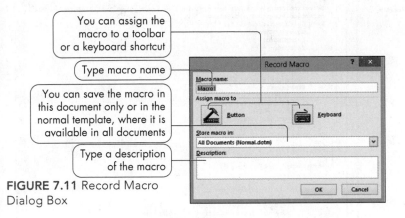

You can assign the macro to a toolbar or a keyboard shortcut

Type macro name

You can save the macro in this document only or in the normal template, where it is available in all documents

Type a description of the macro

FIGURE 7.11 Record Macro Dialog Box

Type Text in a Macro

You can type text to include in a macro. If you want the macro text to contain character attributes, such as bold or font color, you should turn on the attribute before typing that particular text, type the text, and turn off that attribute. While recording a macro, Word does not let you click and drag to select text to be able to apply formatting. If you already have typed text and want to add an attribute while recording, you can select the text by pressing Shift + →. You can apply the attribute you want to the selected text.

Modify a Macro

STEP 3 » Macro instructions are written in *Visual Basic for Applications (VBA)*, a programming language that is built into Microsoft Office. Fortunately, however, you don't have to be a programmer to use VBA. Instead, the macro recorder within Word records your actions, which are translated automatically into VBA. If you need to edit a macro, you can edit the statements after they have been recorded by opening the Visual Basic editor. The Developer tab includes the Visual Basic command in the Code group, which opens the Visual Basic editor and displays the macro contents as programming statements, a set of code written in a specific syntax created by a particular programming language, such as Visual Basic. When editing a macro, it is helpful to have some knowledge of the Visual Basic programming language and how it works. When necessary, you can make minor adjustments to the code to improve the speed and efficiency of the macro. Another way to open the Visual Basic editor is to perform the following steps:

1. Click the VIEW tab.
2. Click Macros in the Macros group to display the Macros dialog box.

3. Click the specific macro that you want to edit in the *Macro name* list.
4. Click the Edit button to open the Microsoft Visual Basic for Applications window to display the programming statements for the macro.
5. Locate the specific task that you want to edit and revise the programming statement accordingly.
6. Click the Save Normal icon to save the change.
7. Close the window.

Each programming statement performs a specific task, such as setting a margin. Every time you choose a dialog box option for a macro, the macro recorder records all dialog box settings, even those you do not change, such as the default font size. Figure 7.12 displays the macro you will create in Hands-On Exercise 2.

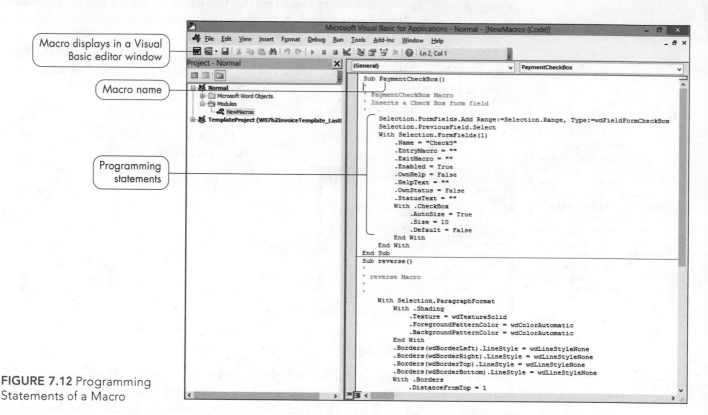

FIGURE 7.12 Programming Statements of a Macro

Copy a Macro

When you record macros, Word saves them in the Normal template by default and stores them in a macro project called NewMacros. Instead of recreating the same macro in multiple documents, you can copy a macro project to another template or document. To copy the NewMacros project to another template or document, do the following:

1. Click the DEVELOPER tab.
2. Click Macros in the Code group.
3. Click Organizer in the Macros dialog box.
4. Specify the destination document or template in the list box on the left side of the dialog box.
5. Click NewMacros in the *In Normal.dotm* list box.
6. Click Copy to copy the macro from the open Word document to the global template named Normal.dotm.
7. Use Help for more specific information on using the Organizer dialog box.

If you no longer need the macros, you can delete them from the Macros dialog box. Select the name of the macro you want to delete and click Delete. Follow the onscreen prompts.

Running a Macro

STEP 2 » The process of playing back or using a macro is called *run macro*. When you run a macro, Word processes the series of commands and keystrokes saved in the macro. Running a macro is faster than manually choosing each command when you need to use a series of commands frequently. You can run a macro by clicking on an object that contains the macro or by pressing the specified hotkey assigned to the macro. You can run, edit, or delete a macro using the Macros dialog box, as shown in Figure 7.13. To open the Macros dialog box, you can use one of the following three options:

- Display the DEVELOPER tab and click Macros in the Code group.
- Display the VIEW tab, click Macros in the Macros group, and then click View Macros.
- Press Alt+F8.

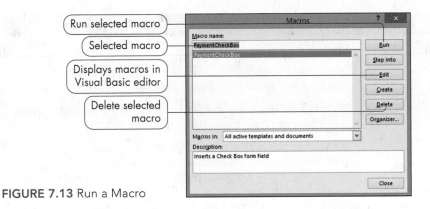

FIGURE 7.13 Run a Macro

If your macro includes a command that types text, that text takes on the current document's format when you run the macro. If you specially formatted the text while recording a macro, that special format is retained when you run the macro, regardless of the document's other formats.

Understand the Security Risks of Macros

Because macros are coded in a Visual Basic application, they are essentially programs. As a program that executes commands, a macro has the potential to include code that imposes harmful viruses onto your computer. Microsoft Office includes a Trust Center to help protect users from unsafe macros. The Trust Center checks for the following scenarios before enabling a macro:

- The macro is signed by the developer using a digital signature.
- The digital signature is valid.
- The digital signature is not expired.
- The certificate associated with the digital signature was issued by a known certificate authority.
- The person who signed the macro is a trusted publisher.

If the Trust Center does not find any of these scenarios, the macro is automatically disabled and a message displays to inform you of the potential risk. You can edit the settings on your computer according to your preference for security. Table 7.2 describes the settings from the Trust Center in the Options dialog box.

Change Macro Security Settings

You can change the macro security settings using the Developer tab. Click Macro Security in the Code group to display the Trust Center dialog box and view the settings. When you change the settings in the Trust Center, they are only valid for the program you are currently using, such as Word 2013. Alternately, you can change the macro security settings in the Trust Center by doing the following:

1. Click the FILE tab.
2. Click Options.
3. Click Trust Center.
4. Click Trust Center Settings.
5. Click Macro Settings, if necessary.
6. Select the Macro Settings that you want, as displayed in Table 7.2.

TABLE 7.2 Macro Security Settings	
Macro Setting	**Description**
Disable all macros without notification	If you do not trust macros, click this option. All macros and security alerts about macros are disabled.
Disable all macros with notification	This is the default setting. All macros are disabled, but it alerts you when a document contains a macro.
Disable all macros except digitally signed macros	This setting works similarly to Disable all macros with notification; however, it enables macros to run if they are digitally signed by a trusted publisher. If you have not included the publisher in your trusted list, you will be alerted about the macro. The alert enables you to allow a macro or to include a publisher in your trusted list. All unsigned macros are disabled and you will not see an alert.
Enable all macros (not recommended; potentially dangerous code can run)	This setting enables all macros to run regardless of their authenticity or signature. This option is not recommended because it exposes your computer to potential attacks by viruses.
Trust access to the VBA project object model	This setting is for use by developers only.

When you open a document that contains macros and you see a *Macros have been disabled* security warning, click the File tab, click Options to display the Microsoft Office Security Options dialog box, click *Enable this content*, and then click OK to return to the document and to use any macros that were stored in the document.

Quick Concepts

1. Explain the reasons for using a macro. *p. 124*
2. Under what circumstances would you want to copy a macro? *p. 126*
3. Why is it important to understand the security risk of macros? *p. 127*

2 Introduction to Macros

After modifying the invoice, you realize it can take several minutes to insert form fields one by one; if a field property needs changing, the time increases even more. But knowing that using a macro can shorten the time it takes for repetitive tasks, you decide to create a macro to update the invoice. After playing the macro to confirm how it works, you might make modifications using the Visual Basic editor, which is faster than re-creating the macro. Finally, you will run it one last time to finish revisions to the invoice.

Skills covered: Record a Macro • Run a Macro • Modify a Macro • Run an Edited Macro

STEP 1 ≫ RECORD A MACRO

After a successful test of the electronic invoice you created, you want to insert additional check boxes in the payment options section of the invoice. Instead of inserting each check box individually, you create a macro to insert them and change the property settings for that form control. Refer to Figure 7.14 as you complete Step 1.

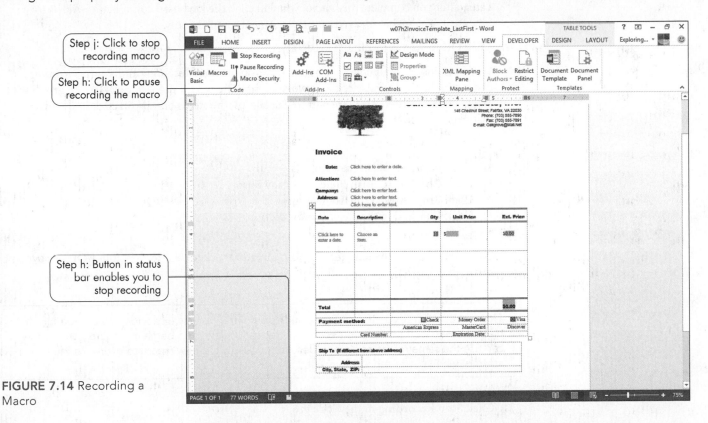

Step j: Click to stop recording macro

Step h: Click to pause recording the macro

Step h: Button in status bar enables you to stop recording

FIGURE 7.14 Recording a Macro

a. Open *w07h1InvoiceTemplate_LastFirst.dotx* and save it as a Word template with the new name **w07h2InvoiceTemplate_LastFirst.dotx**, changing *h1* to *h2*.

b. Click the **DEVELOPER tab** and click **Restrict Editing** to display the Restrict Editing pane. Click **Stop Protection** and close the Restrict Editing pane.

   You must remove the form protection so you can edit the invoice.

c. Click **Design Mode** in the Controls group. Click to position the insertion point on the left side of the Money Order payment method.

d. Click **Record Macro** in the Code group.

The Record Macro dialog box displays so that you can name the macro before you record it. The macro name can consist of up to 80 characters, but no spaces.

> **TROUBLESHOOTING:** If the Developer tab does not display, click the File tab, click Options, click Customize Ribbon, and then click Developer below the *Customize the Ribbon* pane on the right side of the window. Click OK to return to the document.

e. Type **PaymentCheckBox** in the **Macro name box**.

f. Click the **Description box** and type **Inserts a Check Box form field**.

g. Assign a keyboard shortcut to run the macro by completing the following steps:

- Click **Keyboard** to display the Customize Keyboard dialog box.
- Press **Alt+B**.

The dialog box indicates whether the keyboard shortcut is already assigned or not; pay attention to this visual clue of information.

- Click **Assign** and click **Close**.

Later, after you complete the macro, you will click the keyboard combination Alt+B to execute it. The macro is saved in this document template only.

h. Click **OK** to start recording, if necessary.

Word assigns the macro name you entered. You see *Stop Recording* and *Pause Recording* display in the Code group of the Developer tab. The mouse pointer looks like an arrow with an attached recorder. A square button displays on the status bar; if you click it, the macro will stop recording.

i. Perform the following steps to create the macro:

- Click **Legacy tools** in the Controls group.
- Click **Check Box Form Field** in Legacy Forms.
- Click **Properties** in the Controls group.
- Click **Checked** in the *Default value* section.
- Click **OK**.

You insert a check box field that displays already checked next to the Money Order payment method.

> **TROUBLESHOOTING:** If you click something unintentionally or decide you are too far off track for the macro, click Stop Recording. Repeat the steps to begin recording again. You can use the same macro name and description; allow the new macro to overwrite the first attempt when prompted to replace it.

j. Click **Stop Recording** in the Code group.

You can also click the square button in the status bar to stop recording a macro.

k. Save the template.

STEP 2 ≫ RUN A MACRO

Now that you have a macro that inserts the box to check when indicating the form of payment, you want to run the macro to display the box by other forms of payment. Refer to Figure 7.15 as you complete Step 2.

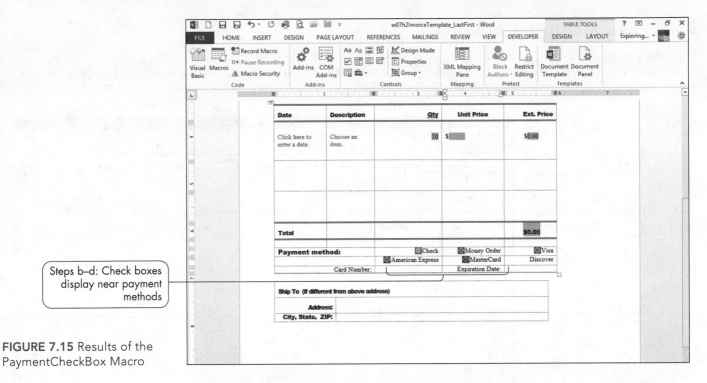

Steps b–d: Check boxes display near payment methods

FIGURE 7.15 Results of the PaymentCheckBox Macro

a. Click to position the insertion point on the left side of the payment method *American Express*.

TIP   Make a Backup

To avoid destroying a document due to macro problems, you should save the document prior to running a macro. If the macro does not provide the desired results, you can close the document and open the original document again.

---

b. Click **Macros** in the Code group.

The macros dialog box displays, and the PaymentCheckBox macro is the only macro available to run.

c. Click **PaymentCheckBox**, if necessary, and click **Run**.

Word runs the macro and inserts a checked box next to the American Express payment method.

TROUBLESHOOTING: The macro security level is too high if you receive a message stating that macros are disabled. A high security level protects you from running a macro that contains a virus. To disable this security so the macro can run, click Macro Security on the Developer tab, click *Enable all macros (not recommended; potentially dangerous code can run)*, and then click OK. Be sure to reset the security to *Disable all macros with notification* after completing this exercise.

---

d. Click to position the insertion point on the left side of the payment method *MasterCard* and click **Alt+B**.

Word runs the macro again and inserts a checked box next to the MasterCard payment method.

e. Save the template.

STEP 3 » MODIFY A MACRO

The macro works well, but you realize that you only want one of the payment methods to be checked by default. Rather than delete each one and start all over, you modify the macro using the Visual Basic editor. Then you run the macro again to replace the incorrectly checked boxes. Refer to Figure 7.16 as you complete Step 3.

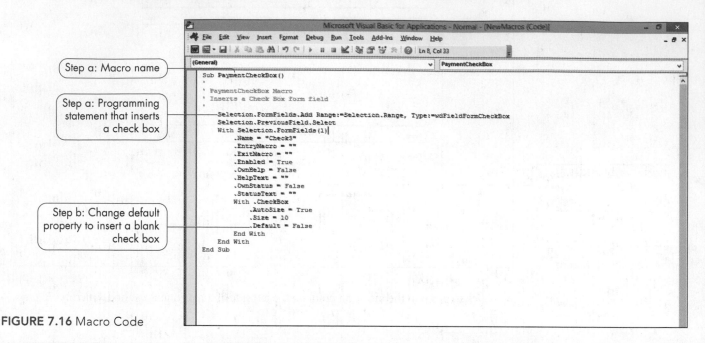

Step a: Macro name

Step a: Programming statement that inserts a check box

Step b: Change default property to insert a blank check box

FIGURE 7.16 Macro Code

a. Press **Alt+F8** to display the Macros dialog box. Select **PaymentCheckBox** in the **Macro name list** if necessary and click **Edit**.

The Visual Basic Editor opens so that you can edit the programming statements. You will modify the Default statement near the end of the code, which shows a *True* value; this causes the box to display as checked.

b. Delete the word *True* at the end of the statement .*Default* = *True* and replace it with the word **False**.

> **TROUBLESHOOTING:** Do not delete any other part of the Default statement or any other statements. If you do, the macro may not run correctly. If you accidentally delete programming statements, refer to Figure 7.16 to retype them and edit the Default statement again.

c. Click the **FILE tab** and click **Close and Return to Microsoft Word**.

You are ready to run the macro again to replace the checked boxes with boxes that are not checked.

d. Save the template.

STEP 4 » RUN AN EDITED MACRO

Now that your macro is revised, you can replace the checked boxes for each payment method on the invoice. You want to leave only one box checked—the one that displays beside the Visa payment method. You select each one individually and run the macro to replace the form field check boxes. Refer to Figure 7.17 as you complete Step 4.

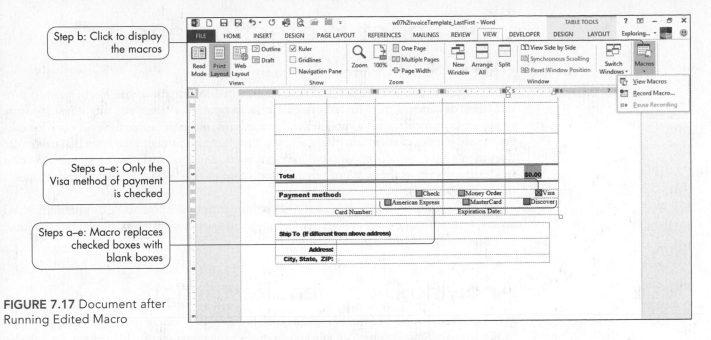

Step b: Click to display the macros

Steps a–e: Only the Visa method of payment is checked

Steps a–e: Macro replaces checked boxes with blank boxes

FIGURE 7.17 Document after Running Edited Macro

a. Select the checked box that displays beside *Money Order*.

> **TROUBLESHOOTING:** If you do not properly select the original check box, the macro will insert a second check box beside the Money Order payment method. Use Shift+→ to select the check box, if necessary.

b. Click the **VIEW tab**, click the **Macros arrow**, and then click **View Macros**.

The Macros dialog box displays so that you can run a macro.

c. Click **PaymentCheckBox** in the *Macro name* box and click **Run**.

The checked box is replaced by a box that does not display as checked.

d. Select the checked box that displays beside *American Express* and press **Alt+B**.

e. Press **Alt+B** to replace the checked box beside *MasterCard*, position the insertion point beside *Discover*, and then run the macro again.

After you run the macro, all payment types display beside a box and only the Visa payment displays beside a checked box.

f. Click the **FILE tab** and click **Save As**. Click **Browse**, click the **Save as type arrow**, and then select **Word Macro-Enabled Template**. If necessary, navigate to the folder where your student files are stored and click **Save** to save the template as **w07h2InvoiceTemplate_ LastFirst**.

g. Save and close the file, and submit it based on your instructor's directions.

Document Protection and Authentication

As you work with documents containing confidential information, you might want to protect those documents from unauthorized access. In other situations, you might need to store reference documents, such as policies and procedures, on an organization's network for others to read but not change. You might also want to assure document recipients that particular documents have come from you and have not been tampered with during transit. To assist in situations such as these, Word provides tools that enable you to protect your documents on many levels.

In this section, you will learn to restrict permissions to documents against unauthorized access, formatting, or content changes. You also will learn how to mark a document as final, set passwords, and add digital signatures.

Applying Document Restrictions

Word provides a variety of ways to save a file to preserve the content or the formatting applied to the content. Some features enable you to protect the contents of a file so that anyone else who opens it cannot change the contents in any way. Other features allow the content to be altered, but restrict the use of formatting tools such as the bold feature or predefined styles. You can use these restrictive features independently or in combination with others.

Mark a Document as Final

STEP 1 » You may have the occasion to share a file with other people, but before you send it you want to make it a read-only file, which prevents others from changing the document. The *Mark as Final* command enables you to create a read-only file and sets the property to Final on the status bar. To alert the reader to this status, it displays an icon in the status bar to indicate the file is in its final form, as shown in Figure 7.18. This is a helpful command for communicating with other people that the document is not a draft but a completed and final version. It also prevents unintentional changes to the document. When marked as final, typing, editing, and proofing marks do not display; all commands in the Ribbon are grayed out; and the document cannot be modified. To use this command, do the following:

1. Click the FILE tab.
2. Click Protect Document.
3. Select *Mark as Final*.

Even though this feature provides a way to communicate the status of the document and enables you to set it as read-only, it does not completely secure the document. *Mark as Final* is a toggle setting and anyone can remove the status from the document as easily as it is set. Additionally, if you use the *Mark as Final* command on a Word 2013 document, it will not retain the read-only status if opened in an earlier version of Word. Therefore, Restricting Editing is a more permanent way of preventing changes from being made to a document.

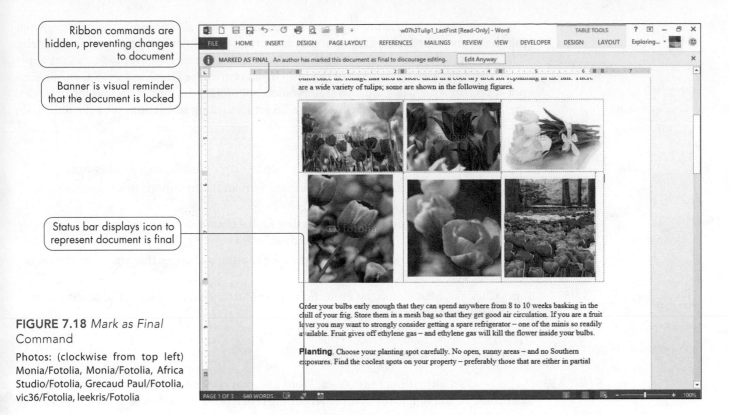

FIGURE 7.18 *Mark as Final Command*

Photos: (clockwise from top left) Monia/Fotolia, Monia/Fotolia, Africa Studio/Fotolia, Grecaud Paul/Fotolia, vic36/Fotolia, leekris/Fotolia

Set Formatting Restrictions

STEP 2 ⟫ Organizations often use specific styles and formatting to ensure consistency among documents. The person who oversees document formatting might create or modify styles that should not be changed by other users. To ensure that others do not modify formatting or styles, you can set *formatting restrictions* on documents. When you set formatting restrictions, character formatting tools, such as bold and font size, are unavailable, as shown in Figure 7.19.

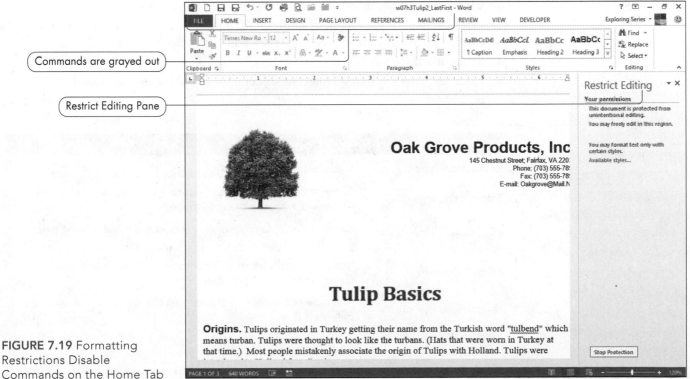

Commands are grayed out

Restrict Editing Pane

FIGURE 7.19 Formatting Restrictions Disable Commands on the Home Tab

In addition to restricting character format tools, Word also prevents users from changing the formats for font, paragraph, column, drop caps, bullets and numbering, and tabs. You may apply approved styles, such as Heading 1, to text. However, you cannot apply styles that have been restricted. For example, if you restrict the Heading 3 style, then you cannot apply that style to text. Furthermore, you cannot modify the format settings for any styles, even those the user is authorized to apply. To set formatting restrictions on a document, do the following:

1. Click the DEVELOPER tab.
2. Click Restrict Editing in the Protect group to display the Restrict Editing pane.
3. Click *Formatting restrictions* to define the formatting limitations to a selection of styles.
4. Click Settings to display the Formatting Restrictions dialog box, where you can specify exactly which formatting options to disable.
5. Click *Editing restrictions* to define the type of editing changes that you allow the users to be able to make.
6. Click Yes, Start Enforcing Protection under *Start enforcement* when the document is ready for distribution.

Set Editing Restrictions

STEP 3

When you set formatting restrictions, Word does not prevent you from changing content in a document. You might also want to set editing restrictions on particular documents. *Editing restrictions* specify limits for users to modify a document. For example, you might set the Tracked changes editing restriction to make sure the Track Changes feature is active when users make any changes to the document. Doing so lets you know what edits are made to collaborative documents, even if the users forget to activate Track Changes themselves. Other types of editing restrictions include limiting users to inserting comments without changing document content, restricting data entry to fields or unprotected areas within a form, and preventing users from making any changes to a letterhead template.

To set editing restrictions on a document, do the following:

1. Click the DEVELOPER tab.
2. Click Restrict Editing in the Protect group to display the Restrict Editing pane.
3. Click the *Allow only this type of editing in the document* checkbox under *Editing restrictions* to show the four editing restrictions, as outlined in Table 7.3.
4. Select one of the four restrictions.
5. Click Yes, Start Enforcing Protection under *Start enforcement* to activate the protection.

TABLE 7.3 Editing Restrictions

Restriction Type	Description
Tracked changes	Enables the track changes feature automatically and marks document with any changes made.
Comments	Users can add comments to the document but cannot make any other changes.
Filling in forms	Users can insert information into form controls or fields but cannot modify other content.
No changes (Read only)	Users cannot make any changes to the document; they can only view it.

Set Exceptions for Restricted Documents

STEP 4 » If you apply the editing restriction *Comments* or *No changes (Read only)*, you can specify user exceptions. A **user exception** is an individual or group of individuals who are allowed to edit all or specific parts of a restricted document. For example, you might want all team members to edit only a particular section of a collaborative document. You can create an exception by enabling users to edit that section only. You can create various user exceptions throughout a document by enabling some individuals to edit particular text, while enforcing the editing restrictions for other individuals. Word color-codes text for which you create different user exceptions.

The default check box in the Exceptions list is *Everyone*. You can add individual users or groups to the list of exceptions by doing the following:

1. Click *More users* to open the Add Users dialog box, as shown in Figure 7.20.
2. Type user names, domains, or e-mail addresses for individuals you want to add, separated by semicolons.
3. Click OK. After you add users, you can continue selecting text and clicking the appropriate user name to create a user exception for editing text.

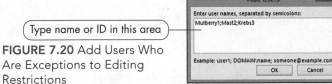

Type name or ID in this area

FIGURE 7.20 Add Users Who Are Exceptions to Editing Restrictions

You must install a special service to add users in the Add Users dialog box. **Information Rights Management (IRM)** services are designed to help you control who can access documents containing sensitive or confidential information. By using an IRM, you can specify different users and the types of permissions you grant to them. If the IRM Services Client is not installed on your computer, a prompt to download it will display when you try to open files that have been rights-managed. Follow the prompts to download and install the software. If you work in a network lab, you might not be able to install it. Use Help to learn more about permissions, IRM, and adding users as exceptions.

Remove Editing Restrictions

If, for whatever reason, you want to remove the editing restrictions, do the following:

1. Click the DEVELOPER tab.
2. Click Restrict Editing in the Protect group to display the Restrict Editing pane.
3. Click Stop Protection at the bottom of the Restrict Editing pane.
4. If the formatting restrictions are password-protected, you must enter the correct password.
5. Click OK. If you did not assign a password, the restrictions are automatically removed. If you applied both formatting and editing restrictions, clicking Stop Protection removes both types of restrictions.
6. If you want to remove only one type of restriction, you must reset the restriction you want to continue to enforce in the Restrict Editing pane.

Setting Passwords to Open a Document

STEP 1 » When creating the form in Hands-On Exercise 1, you had the opportunity to set a password for the document. Setting passwords is one way to secure a document. For example, you might want to password-protect highly confidential documents from being opened by unauthorized users. This is helpful when you need to store a document on a network drive but do not want everyone to be able to open the document. When you assign a password to the document, only those who know the password can open the document. Passwords are case-sensitive, meaning they must match upper- and lowercase letters perfectly. They may consist of letters, numbers, and symbols; a good password will use a combination of all three. You may even use a combination of upper- and lowercase characters, such as EW7_proj_2.

To set a password that must be entered before a document will open, do the following:

1. Click the FILE tab.
2. Click Save As.
3. Click Browse.
4. Click Tools.
5. Click General Options, as shown in Figure 7.21.
6. Type your password in the *Password to open* box.
7. Click OK. The Confirm Password dialog box will prompt you to reenter the password.
8. Retype the password.
9. Click OK to close the dialog box.
10. Save the document.

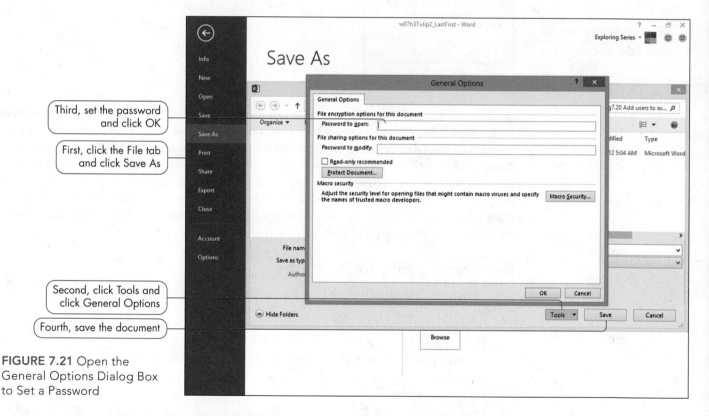

FIGURE 7.21 Open the General Options Dialog Box to Set a Password

Set a Password to Modify a Document

STEP 1 ▶▶ You may want to allow others to open a document but not be able to modify the content. To restrict users from modifying a document, do the following:

1. Click the FILE tab.
2. Click Save As.
3. Click Browse.
4. Click Tools.
5. Click General Options.
6. Type the password in the *Password to modify* box. You can set a password containing up to 15 characters.

7. Click OK.

8. Retype the password into the Confirm Password dialog box.

9. Click OK and you will return to the Save As dialog box.

10. Click Save to save the document. Other users can now open the document, but they must know the password to modify the document.

11. When users attempt to open a document protected against unauthorized modifications, the Password dialog box opens (see Figure 7.22).

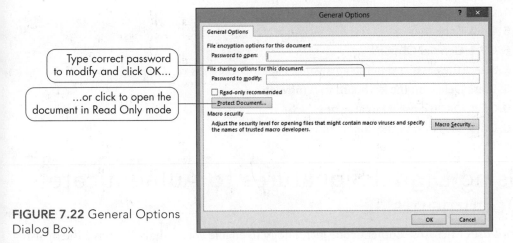

FIGURE 7.22 General Options Dialog Box

Authorized users can type the password in the Password box and click OK. They are able to make changes and save the document with those changes. In Read Only mode, users can make changes; however, they cannot save those changes to the original file. They must choose a different folder or specify a different file name for saving the document through the Save As dialog box.

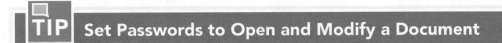

TIP | Set Passwords to Open and Modify a Document

You can assign two passwords to a document—one to open it and another to modify the content. If you choose to use both types, you might prefer to use different passwords for each restriction so that you have the option to authorize another person to open the document but not to modify it by giving them the first password.

Modify a Password to Open or Modify a Document

STEP 2 ❯❯ If you want to change a password, you must know the current password to open or modify the document. With the document open, do the following:

1. Click the FILE tab.

2. Click Save As.

3. Click Browse.

4. Click Tools.

5. Click General Options.

6. Type the replacement password in the *Password to open* or the *Password to modify* box.

7. Click OK.

8. Retype the replacement password into the Confirm Password dialog box.

9. Click OK to close the dialog box.

10. Click Save to save the document.

Delete a Password to Open or Modify a Document

You can remove a password for opening or modifying a document if you decide you no longer want to protect the document with a password. To remove the password, do the following:

1. Open the document using the current password for opening or modifying the document.
2. Click the FILE tab.
3. Click Save As.
4. Click Browse.
5. Click Tools.
6. Click General Options.
7. Select the password in the *Password to open* or the *Password to modify* box.
8. Press Delete on the keyboard to remove it.
9. Click OK to close the dialog box.
10. Click Save to save the document.

Using Digital Signatures to Authenticate Documents

Word uses Microsoft Authenticode technology to enable you to digitally sign a file by using a **digital certificate**—an attachment to a file or e-mail that guarantees the authenticity of the file, provides a verifiable signature, or enables encryption. This authentication is important because as you share files with others, you increase your risk of having files tampered with or infected with a virus. By adding a digital signature to your documents, you confirm through electronic encryption that the information comes from you, is valid, and has not been changed after you signed it. You can use one of the following two ways to use digital signatures to sign Office documents:

- Add an invisible digital signature to a document or
- Add visible signature lines to a document to capture one or more digital signatures.

Attach a Digital Signature to a Document

STEP 5

When you need to confirm the authenticity of a document, you can attach a digital signature. **Digital signatures** are electronic stamps that display information about the person or organization that obtained the certification. You can obtain a digital certificate from a certification authority such as VeriSign by completing an application and paying a fee. Some companies have in-house security administrators who issue their own digital signatures by using tools such as Microsoft Certificate Server.

If you want to create your own digital certificate for personal use, you need to install the *Digital Certificate for VBA Projects* from Microsoft Office. This program allows you to create a self-signed digital signature that you can use for personal macros on the specific machine that you use to create the digital signature. When you sign your document, you are validating its contents, and the document remains signed until it is modified. Therefore, signing a document and attaching the signature should be the last action you take before you distribute it. Adding a digital signature causes the document to be marked as final, so it also becomes a read-only document.

To install the *Digital Certificate for VBA Projects* from Microsoft Office to your computer, do the following:

1. Open File Explorer.
2. Type SELFCERT.EXE in the *Search Programs and Files* box. You do not have to type the file name in all caps.

3. When File Explorer opens and displays the location of the file, double-click it. The SELFCERT.EXE file should be located in the C:\Program Files\Microsoft Office\ Office15 folder.

4. The Create Digital Certificate dialog box opens and provides information about the self-certification program.

5. Type your name in the Your Certificate's Name box.

6. Click OK. A message box appears, stating that you successfully created a certificate. If a system message indicates that your certificate is unauthorized, you can still use it to practice working with digital certificates.

7. Click OK to close the message box.

To use the built-in digital signature feature, you must first save the document and do the following:

1. Click the FILE tab.

2. Click Protect Document.

3. Select *Add a Digital Signature*.

4. Click OK to the Microsoft Word dialog box that explains the feature if this is the first time you use this feature. After that, your signature stamp will attach automatically, as shown in Figure 7.23, but you can change the stamp if more than one certificate is available.

5. Type in the purpose for signing the document, although it is not required.

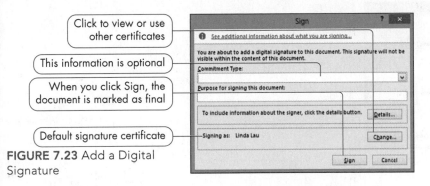

FIGURE 7.23 Add a Digital Signature

If you decide that a digital signature is not needed for a document, you can view and remove the digital signature from a signed document by doing the following:

1. Click the FILE tab.

2. Click View Signatures to display the Signatures pane, which lists all signatures attached to the document.

3. In the Signatures pane, you can click a particular signature to view a menu that includes Signature Details and Remove Signature.

4. When all signatures are removed, the document is no longer marked as final and all formatting commands are available.

Add a Signature Line in a Document

STEP 6 ≫ Word allows you to insert a signature line into a document. The *signature line* enables individuals and companies to distribute and collect signatures, and then process forms or documents electronically without the need to print and fax or mail. The digital signatures, especially if verified by a certifying authority, provide an authentic record of the signer and enable the document to be verified in the future.

When the document opens and the signature line displays, users can type a signature, select a digital image of a signature, or write a signature if they use a tablet PC. After the user inserts his or her signature using one of the options listed above, a digital signature tag is attached to the document to authenticate the identity of the signer and the document becomes read-only to prevent modifications to the content. To insert a signature line, do the following:

1. Click the INSERT tab.
2. Click the Signature Line arrow in the Text group.
3. Click Microsoft Office Signature Line.
4. Click OK to the Microsoft Word dialog box, if it displays.
5. Enter information about the signer when the Signature Setup dialog box displays, as shown in Figure 7.24.
6. Enter the expected signer's name, title, e-mail address, and any additional instructions you want to display near the signature line.
7. Enable signers to add comments to the document and attach the current date to the document when they sign if you prefer.

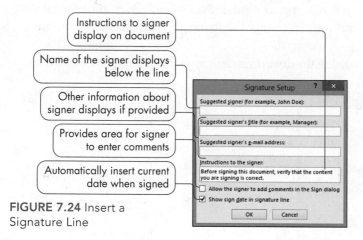

FIGURE 7.24 Insert a Signature Line

Quick Concepts

1. What are the reasons for using editing restrictions on certain documents? *p. 136*
2. Why do you want to set a password to open a document? *p. 137*
3. Explain the reason for using a digital signature. *p. 140*

Hands-On Exercises

3 Document Protection and Authentication

When people purchase tulips, Cassie Artman wants to include information about tulip bulbs in their packages. You have put together a document about tulips, but you want staff members to review it for accuracy. After they return the document to you, edits will be incorporated, a final version will be saved, and you can then mark it with a digital signature. You also want to add a signature line to the invoice so that when it is delivered to a customer he or she will know it has come from the company and is a valid document.

Skills covered: Set a Password to Open a Document and Mark as Final • Set Formatting Restrictions and Modify a Document Password • Set Editing Restrictions • Set Exceptions for Restricted Documents • Attach a Digital Signature to a Document • Insert a Signature Line in a Document

STEP 1 ≫ SET A PASSWORD TO OPEN A DOCUMENT AND MARK AS FINAL

The tulip information document that will accompany all purchases has been created, and you believe it to be in final form. To prevent anyone from opening it, you password-protect the file. Additionally, to prevent any accidental changes to the document when it is open, you mark it as final. Refer to Figure 7.25 as you complete Step 1.

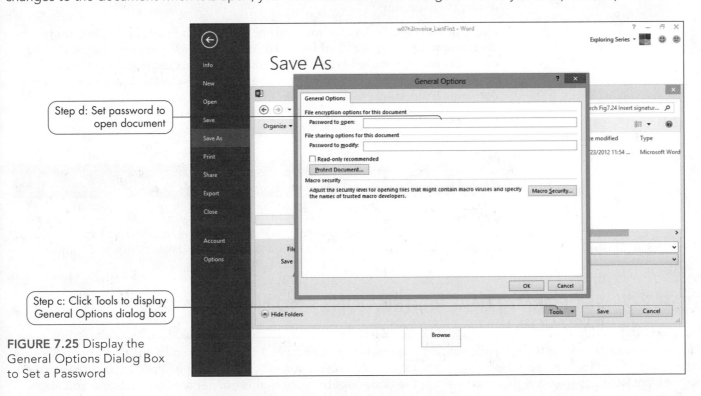

Step d: Set password to open document

Step c: Click Tools to display General Options dialog box

FIGURE 7.25 Display the General Options Dialog Box to Set a Password

a. Open the document *w07h3Tulip*.

This is a draft of the document, and you want to password-protect it until all modifications have been finalized.

b. Click the **FILE tab** and click **Save As**. Click **Browse** and replace the file name with **w07h3Tulip1_LastFirst**. Navigate to the folder where your student files are stored, but do not close the Save As dialog box.

c. Click **Tools** and click **General Options**.

The General Options dialog box displays; this is where you set passwords to open and modify a document.

> **TROUBLESHOOTING:** The Tools menu is located in the Save As dialog box. If you closed that dialog box, click the File tab, click Save As, and then repeat step c.

d. Type **W7h3a** in the **Password to open box**.

Security experts recommend you use a combination of upper- and lowercase letters, numbers, and special characters when you create passwords. Passwords are case-sensitive, meaning they must match upper- and lowercase letters perfectly. For that reason, you must pay special attention to capitalization when setting and using passwords to protect a document.

e. Click **OK**. In the Confirm Password dialog box, type **W7h3a** in the **Reenter password to open box**, click **OK**, and then click **Save** in the Save As dialog box.

> **TROUBLESHOOTING:** If you do not type the same password using the same capitalization, an error message appears stating you have not typed the same password. Click OK to close the message box, delete the passwords in the General Options dialog box, and then type the passwords again.

f. Click the **FILE tab**, click **Protect Document**, and then click **Mark as Final** to avoid accidental editing. Click **OK** in all Microsoft Word dialog boxes. Click the **back arrow** to display the document.

Dialog boxes might display after you mark the document as final. The first informs you the document will be marked as final and saved. The second dialog box informs you that the document has been marked as final and all editing marks are disabled. After these dialog boxes close and you return to the document, the banner displays at the top to indicate the document is *Marked as Final*.

g. Close the document.

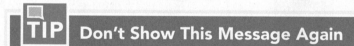

TIP | **Don't Show This Message Again**

If a Microsoft Word dialog box displays *Don't show this message again*, you can click the option so the dialog box will not display in the future. However, if you work in a lab environment, you should ask for instructor permission before changing this type of setting.

STEP 2 » SET FORMATTING RESTRICTIONS AND MODIFY A DOCUMENT PASSWORD

You are now ready to send the tulip information to a marketing manager so she can look over the document. She can make suggestions for changing the format because she will know how best to present the information. However, you do not want her to change any of the content of the document because that is not her area of expertise. You apply restrictions that only enable the marketing manager to change formatting, and you secure the restrictions with a password. Refer to Figure 7.26 as you complete Step 2.

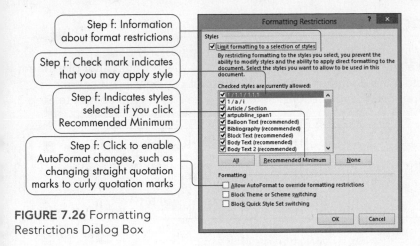

Step f: Information about format restrictions

Step f: Check mark indicates that you may apply style

Step f: Indicates styles selected if you click Recommended Minimum

Step f: Click to enable AutoFormat changes, such as changing straight quotation marks to curly quotation marks

FIGURE 7.26 Formatting Restrictions Dialog Box

a. Open *w07h3Tulip1_LastFirst*, enter the password **W7h3a** when prompted, and then click **OK**. Click **Edit Anyway** in the yellow bar across the top of the page to release the read-only status.

b. Click the **FILE tab** and click **Save As**. Click **Browse**. Type **w07h3Tulip2_LastFirst** in the **File name box** and click **Tools**, and then click **General Options**. Remove the existing password. Click **OK** and click **Save** to return to the document.

If a Microsoft Word dialog box displays with a warning that your document will be upgraded to the newest file format, click OK.

c. Click the **REVIEW tab** and click **Restrict Editing** in the Protect group to display the Restrict Editing pane.

d. Click **Limit formatting to a selection of styles** on the pane. Click **Settings** to display the Formatting Restrictions dialog box.

In this dialog box, you can enable users to apply styles of your choice.

e. Click **None**.

Notice that the check marks beside each style disappear. If you click OK, none of the styles can be used in this document. Next, you reselect the styles.

f. Click **All** and click **OK**. Click **No** in the Microsoft Word dialog box that asks if you want to remove styles that are not allowed.

The user can now apply any style. However, they cannot modify the styles. This option is useful when you want to be sure anyone who edits the document uses a style that is included in Office 2013.

g. Click **Yes, Start Enforcing Protection** on the Restrict Editing pane.

The Start Enforcing Protection dialog box opens. You can use this dialog box to set a password required to remove formatting restrictions.

h. Type **W7h3b** in the **Enter new password (optional) box**. Retype the password in the **Reenter password to confirm box** and click **OK**.

i. Click the **HOME tab**.

Most commands on the Home tab are dimmed, indicating that the document is restricted against formatting changes.

j. Position the insertion point in the title *Tulip Basics* and click **Title** from the Styles gallery.

Word enables you to apply a different style; however, you cannot change character or font attributes or paragraph alignment.

k. Save the document.

STEP 3 » SET EDITING RESTRICTIONS

You want the company botanist to review the tulip information for accuracy. The botanist has only basic computer skills, and you want to make sure he does not make any major changes to the document which would alter placement of information or graphics. You use features to restrict the document so that the botanist can only insert comments, and you add a password so he will not be able to remove the restrictions. Refer to Figure 7.27 as you complete Step 3.

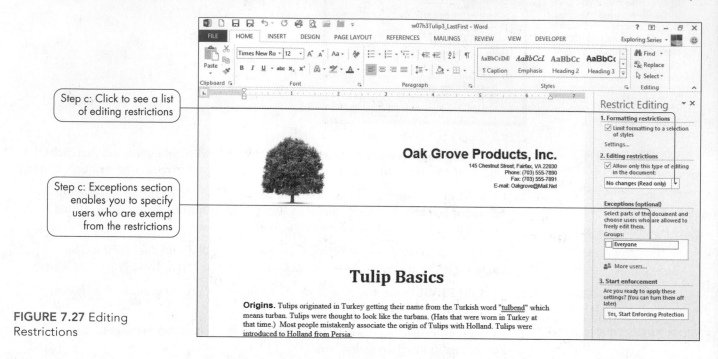

Step c: Click to see a list of editing restrictions

Step c: Exceptions section enables you to specify users who are exempt from the restrictions

FIGURE 7.27 Editing Restrictions

a. Save the document as **w07h3Tulip3_LastFirst**.

b. Click **Stop Protection**, which displays at the bottom of the Restrict Editing pane, type **W7h3b** in the **Unprotect Document dialog box**, and then click **OK**.

   The formatting restriction is removed so that users may use any format features on the document.

TROUBLESHOOTING: If the Restrict Editing pane does not display, click the Review tab and click Restrict Editing.

---

c. Click **Allow only this type of editing in the document** in the *Editing restrictions* section.

   The *Editing restrictions* arrow is available so that you can specify the type of editing to restrict. Additionally, an *Exceptions (optional)* section appears on the pane so that you can apply exceptions to the editing restrictions, as shown in Figure 7.27.

d. Click the **Editing restrictions arrow** and click **Comments**.

e. Click **Yes, Start Enforcing Protection**. Type **W7h3c** in the **Enter new password (optional) box**. Retype the password in the **Reenter password to confirm box**. Click **OK**.

   Users are now restricted from editing the document content. They can only insert comments. The formatting restrictions are also still in place.

f. Press **Ctrl+Home** to move the insertion point to the beginning of the document. Select the title *Tulip Basics* and press **Delete**.

   You cannot delete the text. The status bar displays the message *This modification is not allowed because the selection is locked*. The Restrict Editing pane now displays buttons to show document regions you can edit. However, because you restricted editing to comments only, no regions are available for editing.

g. Click the **REVIEW tab**, click **New Comment**, and then type **Should we call this "Bulb Basics"?**

Because of the type of editing restrictions on the document you can insert a comment. The comment balloon appears on the side of the text.

h. Save the document.

STEP 4 ≫ SET EXCEPTIONS FOR RESTRICTED DOCUMENTS

After reflecting on the situation, you notice one section of the document where you should allow the botanist to modify content. You change the editing restrictions for the document to allow access to that one section, and you reinforce the restrictions for the rest of the document again. Refer to Figure 7.28 as you complete Step 4.

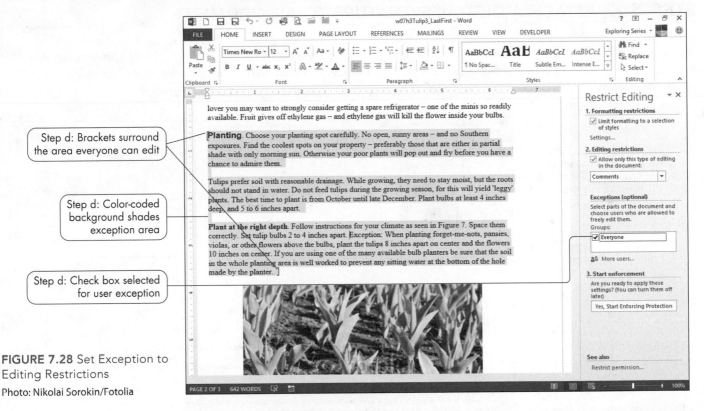

Step d: Brackets surround the area everyone can edit

Step d: Color-coded background shades exception area

Step d: Check box selected for user exception

FIGURE 7.28 Set Exception to Editing Restrictions
Photo: Nikolai Sorokin/Fotolia

a. Display the Restrict Editing pane, if necessary. Click **Stop Protection**. Type **W7h3c** in the **Password box** and click **OK**.

b. Confirm the first two boxes on the pane contain check marks. If they do not, click to mark those boxes.

c. Scroll to the top of page 2 and select the paragraph title *Planting*. Press **Shift+↓** to select the three paragraphs that follow it. Do not select the graphic titled *Figure 7 Planting Tulip Bulbs*.

You want to set a user exception to allow all users to edit this section of the document. You do not want to include the graphic in your selection.

d. Click **Everyone** in the *Exceptions (optional)* section of the Restrict Editing pane. Deselect the text.

The paragraphs you selected display with a light gray background, indicating that the user exception is applied to them.

> **TROUBLESHOOTING:** If you are unable to click the check box for *Everyone* in the *Exception* section of the Restrict Editing pane, make sure you have first selected text in the document.

e. Click **Yes, Start Enforcing Protection**. Type **W7h3d** in the **Enter new password (option) box**. Retype the password in the **Reenter password to confirm box**. Click **OK**.

f. Select the graphic titled *Figure 7 Planting Tulip Bulbs* and press **Delete**.

   You cannot delete the graphic because it is protected against editing.

g. Click the paragraph heading *Planting*, click the **HOME tab**, and then click **Book Title** from the Styles gallery.

   Word enables this editing because you are a part of *Everyone* included in the user exception for the heading.

h. Save the document.

STEP 5 ›› ATTACH A DIGITAL SIGNATURE TO A DOCUMENT

After the document has been reviewed by the experts in the company, you take their changes into consideration and finalize it for distribution. When sent in a digital format, you want it to display a certificate of authenticity from the company; you insert a digital signature in the document, which also marks it as final. Refer to Figure 7.29 as you complete Step 5.

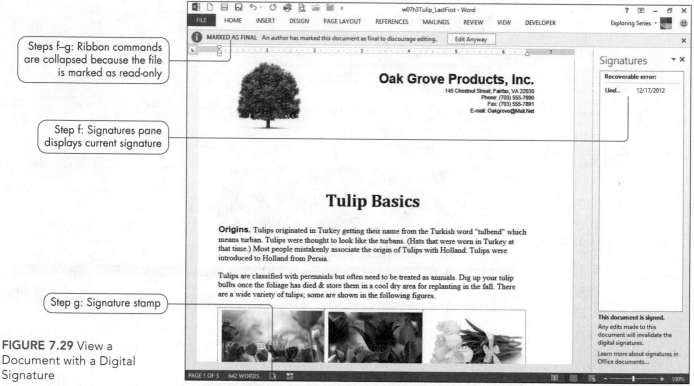

Steps f–g: Ribbon commands are collapsed because the file is marked as read-only

Step f: Signatures pane displays current signature

Step g: Signature stamp

FIGURE 7.29 View a Document with a Digital Signature

a. Open File Explorer. Type **SELFCERT.EXE** in the **Search Programs and Files box**. When Windows Explorer opens and displays the location of the file, double-click it.

   You do not have to type the file name in all caps. The *SELFCERT.EXE* file should be located in the C:\Program Files\Microsoft Office\Office15 folder. The Create Digital Certificate dialog box opens and provides information about the self-certification program.

> **TROUBLESHOOTING:** If you cannot find the *SELFCERT.EXE* file, or if your lab computer will not allow you to install the program, continue to read over the steps in this activity so that you can see how digital signatures work.

b. Type your name in the **Your Certificate's Name box** and click **OK**.

A message box appears, stating that you successfully created a certificate. Although your certificate is unauthorized, you can still use it to practice working with digital certificates.

c. Click **OK** to close the message box.

d. Remove all restrictions and prepare the final version of the document by completing the following steps:

- Click **Stop Protection** in the Restrict Editing pane, enter the password **W7h3d** when prompted, and then click **OK**.
- Remove all check marks from the Restrict Editing pane. When the Microsoft Word dialog box displays and asks if you want to remove the ignored exceptions, click **No**.
- Close the Restrict Editing pane.
- Scroll to the top of page 3. Right-click the **comment balloon** and click **Delete Comment**.

e. Save the document.

f. Click the **FILE tab**, click **Protect Document**, and then click **Add a Digital Signature**. Click **OK** in the Microsoft Word dialog box, if necessary.

The Sign dialog box displays. Your name displays at the bottom of the window because you recently created a digital signature.

> **TROUBLESHOOTING:** If your name does not display in the Sign dialog box, click Change to display the Select Certificate dialog box. Click your name from the *Issued to* column and click OK.

g. Type **To validate contents** in the **Purpose for signing this document box**. Click **Sign** to close the Sign dialog box. Click **OK** to close the Signature Confirmation dialog box and click the back arrow to return to the document.

A yellow information bar displays *MARKED AS FINAL An author has marked this document as final to discourage editing. Edit Anyway* below the ribbon. The Ribbon commands are hidden because the document has been marked as read-only. The signature stamp displays in the status bar.

h. Click once on the signature stamp in the status bar.

The Signatures pane displays on the right side of the document. If you click a signature, a menu arrow displays enabling you to click an option to view details about the signature or to delete the signature.

i. Save and close the file, and submit it based on your instructor's directions.

STEP 6 ≫ INSERT A SIGNATURE LINE IN A DOCUMENT

You decide to add a signature line to the invoice, which will be signed by the person who completes the order. When the invoice is printed, the customer service representative can sign his or her name on the signature line. When he or she sends the invoice in digital format, the representative can type in his or her name or insert a graphic representation of his or her signature. Refer to Figure 7.30 as you complete Step 6.

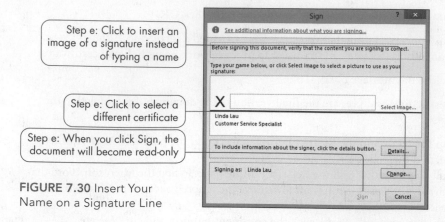

Step e: Click to insert an image of a signature instead of typing a name

Step e: Click to select a different certificate

Step e: When you click Sign, the document will become read-only

FIGURE 7.30 Insert Your Name on a Signature Line

a. Open the document *w07h2InvoiceTemplate_LastFirst.dotm* and save it as a Word Document, **w07h3Invoice_LastFirst**, changing the *h2* to *h3* and removing the word *Template*.

You are opening a template document but saving it as a Word document file.

b. Press **Ctrl+End** to move the insertion point to the end of the document.

c. Click the **INSERT tab** and click **Signature Line**. The Signature Setup dialog box displays.

d. Type your name in the **Suggested signer box**. Type **Customer Service Specialist** in the **Suggested signer's title box**. Type **oakgrove@mail.net** in the **Suggested signer's e-mail address box**. Click **OK**.

The signature line displays in the document, as well as the signer's information that you entered in the Signature Setup dialog box.

e. Insert a signature by completing the following steps:

- Double-click the signature line to display the Sign dialog box. Click **OK** in the Microsoft Word dialog box if necessary.

  If you did not set up the signature ID in the previous step, you will see a dialog box that says *Get a Digital ID*. You need to repeat Steps 5a–c before you can continue with this step.

- Type your own name in the **Type your name below box** or click **Select Image . . .** to select a picture to use as your signature box.
- Click **Sign**.
- Click **OK** in the Signature Confirmation dialog box, if necessary.

The name displays above the signature line, and the date displays in the top-right corner of the *signature line* box. The document is marked as read-only, and formatting features are grayed out.

f. Close the document, exit Word, and then submit it based on your instructor's directions.

Chapter Objectives Review

After reading this chapter, you have accomplished the following objectives:

1. **Create an electronic form.**
   - Before you can create a document template, the Developer tab must be visible on the Ribbon. Then, you need to save the document as a Word template file.

2. **Insert form controls.**
   - If you want users to fill out a form electronically, you must insert form controls, also called form fields, into the form template.
   - Forms can be created to automatically calculate data values or update calculations by clicking a certain button or when exiting from Word.

3. **Protect a form.**
   - After you create a form, you can apply protection that prevents any modification except data entry.
   - After an electronic form is created and protected, you may e-mail it to the user or upload it to a Web site.

4. **Create a macro.**
   - When you record a macro, Word records a series of keystrokes and command selections and converts the tasks into specifically coded statements.
   - Before recording a macro, you should decide what you want to accomplish with your macro, and then you should plan exactly which commands and tasks to include.
   - When you start the macro, you can save it in the current document only or you can save it to the Normal template, where it will be available in all documents.

5. **Run a macro.**
   - The process of playing back or using a macro is called running a macro.
   - A macro has the potential to include code that imposes harmful viruses onto your computer. Fortunately, you can edit the security settings in the Trust Center.
   - You can change the macro security settings using the Developer tab.

6. **Apply document restrictions.**
   - The *Mark as Final* command enables you to create a read-only file, and the status property is set to Final. This is a helpful command for communicating with other people that the document is not a draft but a completed and final version.
   - When you set formatting restrictions, Word does not prevent users from changing content in a document. You might also want to set editing restrictions on particular documents.
   - Editing restrictions specify conditions for users to modify a document. If you set the editing restriction to Comments or *No changes (Read only)*, you can specify user exceptions.
   - A user exception is an individual or group of individuals who is allowed to edit all or specific parts of a restricted document.
   - You can remove all or any type of restrictions from the document any time.

7. **Set passwords to open a document.**
   - Setting passwords is one way to secure a document. When you assign a password to modify the document, only those who know the password can open the document.
   - If you want to change a password, you must know the current password to open or modify the document.
   - You can remove a password to open or modify a document if you decide you no longer want to protect the document with a password.

8. **Use digital signatures to authenticate documents.**
   - When you need to confirm the authenticity of a document, you can attach a digital signature. Digital signatures are electronic stamps that display information about the person or organization that obtained the certification.
   - The signature line enables individuals and companies to distribute and collect signatures, and then process forms or documents electronically without the need to print and fax.

Key Terms Matching

Match the key terms with their definitions. Write the key term letter by the appropriate numbered definition.

a. ActiveX control

b. Check box form field

c. Date Picker

d. Design Mode

e. Digital certificate

f. Digital signature

g. Drop-down list

h. Editing restriction

i. Form control

j. Form template

k. Formatting restriction

l. Information Rights Management (IRM)

m. Legacy form field

n. Macro

o. Macro-Enabled Document

p. Record macro

q. Signature line

r. Text content control

s. User exception

t. Visual Basic for Applications (VBA)

1. _____ A document that defines the standard layout, structure, and formatting of a form. **p. 110**

2. _____ Enables you to view and select the control fields to allow for modifications to the control field layout or options. **p. 113**

3. _____ Helps a user complete a form by displaying prompts such as text boxes and drop-down lists. **p. 112**

4. _____ Used to enter any type of text into a form. **p. 112**

5. _____ Consists of a box that can be checked or unchecked. **p. 112**

6. _____ Enables the user to choose from one of several existing entries. **p. 112**

7. _____ Displays a calendar that the user can click rather than typing in a date. **p. 113**

8. _____ A form element that is created or used in Word 2003 and later. When used in a later version of Word, the document must be opened in Compatibility Mode. **p. 113**

9. _____ A form element designed for use in Office 2007 or later versions that requires a macro to work. **p. 113**

10. _____ A set of instructions that executes a specific task or series of keystrokes that complete a repetitive task. **p. 124**

11. _____ Adds the extension.docm to the file and stores VBA macro code in the document to enable execution of a macro. **p. 124**

12. _____ The process of creating a macro. **p. 124**

13. _____ A programming language that is built into Microsoft Office. **p. 125**

14. _____ Ensures that others do not modify formatting or styles in a document. **p. 135**

15. _____ Specifies limits for users to modify a document. **p. 136**

16. _____ An individual or group that is allowed to edit all or specific parts of a restricted document. **p. 137**

17. _____ Services designed to help control who can access documents containing sensitive or confidential information. **p. 137**

18. _____ An attachment to a file that guarantees the authenticity of the file, provides a verifiable signature, or enables encryption. **p. 140**

19. _____ An electronic stamp that displays information about a person or organization. **p. 140**

20. _____ Enables the user of the document to digitally sign the document. **p. 141**

Multiple Choice

1. Which of the following is true about password protection?

   (a) All documents are automatically saved with a default password.

   (b) The password assigned to a document should use a combination of upper- and lowercase letters, numbers, and special characters.

   (c) A password must be set on a document that is restricted from editing.

   (d) A password cannot be changed after it has been established.

2. When you create a form template that will be broadly distributed outside your organization, you should do all of the following except:

   (a) Insert form controls where needed.

   (b) Protect the template using *Restrict Formatting and Editing* features.

   (c) Save the template with a .dotx extension.

   (d) Set a password to protect the template.

3. Which form control will enable a user to choose from a list of options?

   (a) Drop-Down Box

   (b) Check Box

   (c) Date Picker

   (d) Text

4. Which of the following statements about protecting a form is true?

   (a) The Formatting restrictions of the Restrict Editing pane enable you to prevent users from modifying the content of and the styles used in a form.

   (b) The Formatting restrictions of the Restrict Editing pane enable you to prevent users from adding comments to the document.

   (c) If you forget the password that protects a form, you can recover it by running a macro.

   (d) You cannot specify certain individuals who are exempt from the formatting and editing restrictions placed on a form.

5. Which of the following can you use to authenticate the contents of a document?

   (a) Password

   (b) Digital signature

   (c) Macro

   (d) Form control

6. How can you tell if a document has been digitally signed?

   (a) An icon that looks like a certificate displays on the status bar.

   (b) You must open the Add Digital Signature dialog box.

   (c) A message appears when you open the document.

   (d) A signature line displays at the bottom of the document.

7. When you create a macro in Microsoft Word, where is it stored automatically?

   (a) In the document in which it was created, where it is available only to that document

   (b) In the Normal template, where it is available to every Word document

   (c) In the Macros folder on your SkyDrive account

   (d) In the folder on your hard drive that you are using right now

8. Which of the following is the least appropriate advice to give to someone who wants to learn how to create and run macros?

   (a) Decide what you want the macro to accomplish.

   (b) Make a list of the sequence of tasks you want to perform prior to recording the macro.

   (c) Change your macro security settings to enable all macros all the time.

   (d) Practice completing the steps before actually recording the macro.

9. Before you can insert form controls into a form or display the Visual Basic editor to modify macros, what tab must you display in the Ribbon?

   (a) Add-Ins

   (b) Review

   (c) View

   (d) Developer

10. Which statement about a signature line is false?

    (a) If you specify a name and e-mail address of the signer, they do not display with the signature line.

    (b) You can insert a digital image of a signature on the line.

    (c) If you specify instructions for the signer, they display in the document along with the signature line.

    (d) You can have the date inserted automatically when a signature is inserted on the line.

Practice Exercises

1 White Glove Cleaners

You are the marketing manager for White Glove Cleaners, a small but growing company that offers residential and commercial cleaning services. When potential customers are contacted, they receive a printed document that highlights the cleaning services. You recently decided to update the document so it looks more professional and draws attention to key services. Reversing the shading of the headings will enhance important features of the document. So you create a macro to quickly apply the reverse shading to all the appropriate headings. You also want to include a signature line where clients can sign before they return it and set an appointment for a free estimate. After you make the changes, you mark the document as final to prevent further changes. This exercise follows the same set of skills as used in Hands-On Exercises 2 and 3 in the chapter. Refer to Figure 7.31 as you complete this exercise.

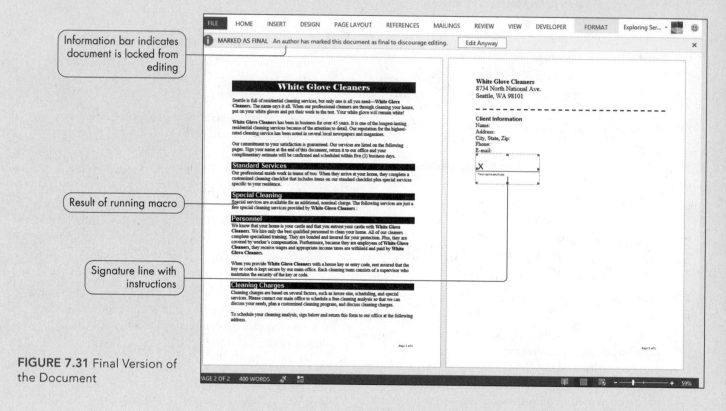

FIGURE 7.31 Final Version of the Document

a. Open the document *w07p1Cleaners*. Click the **FILE tab** and click **Save As**. Click **Browse**. Click the **Save as type arrow** and click **Word Macro-Enabled Document**. Type **w07p1Cleaners_LastFirst** in the **File name box**, navigate to the folder where your student files are stored, uncheck the *Maintain compatibility with previous versions of Word* checkbox, and then click **Save**.

b. Display the **DEVELOPER tab**, if necessary. Click the **FILE tab**, click **Options**, click **Customize Ribbon**, and then check **Developer**, which displays on the right side under the *Customize the Ribbon* section. Click **OK**.

c. Record a macro by completing the following steps:
- Click the left side of the heading *Standard Services* on the first page.
- Click the **DEVELOPER tab**, if necessary, and click **Record Macro** in the Code group.
- Type **reverse** in the **Macro name box**.
- Click **Keyboard** to display the Customize Keyboard dialog box.
- Press **Alt+R** to assign the keystroke combination to the macro.
- Click the **Save changes in arrow**, click **w07p1Cleaners_LastFirst**, and then click **Assign**.
- Click **Close** to return to the document, where the macro recording symbol displays with the pointer. You are now recording the macro.

- Click the **HOME tab**, click the **Border arrow**, and then click **Borders and Shading**.
- Click the **Shading tab**, click the **Style arrow**, click **Solid (100%)**, and then click **OK**.
- Click **Stop Recording** on the status bar.

d. Click the left side of the heading *Special Cleaning* on the first page. Press **Alt+R** to run the macro and apply the reverse effect to the heading. Run the macro on the headings *Personnel* and *Cleaning Charges*.

e. Press **Ctrl+End** to move the insertion point to the bottom of the document. Click the **INSERT tab** and click **Signature Line** in the Text group.

f. Type **Type your name here** in the **Suggested signer box** in the Signature Setup dialog box and click **OK** to insert the signature line in the document.

g. Click the **FILE tab**, click **Protect Document**, and then click **Mark as Final**. Click **OK** in all Microsoft Word dialog boxes that explain the document will be marked as final and saved. Click the back arrow to return to the document.

h. Select the address for White Glove Cleaners and press **Delete**. Because the document is marked as final, it is also protected from any changes and you cannot delete the address.

i. Close the document and submit it based on your instructor's directions.

2 White Glove Cleaners Service Plan

The sales representative for White Glove Cleaners informs you that he would like to use a document that offers more details of the services offered to customers, but he would like it modified as a form. He would like to be able to check off the services that a customer is most interested in contracting from your company. In addition to using a printed form, he indicates that he also communicates with several clients electronically, so he needs an electronic version of the document as well. And he wants it certified to assure the clients that the document is authentic. You make the necessary modifications by replacing bullets with check boxes and adding form controls at the bottom where clients can type their name and address. You protect the form so the clients can only enter their information in the form, and you finish up by adding a digital signature. This exercise follows the same set of skills as used in Hands-On Exercises 1–3 in the chapter. Refer to Figure 7.32 as you complete this exercise.

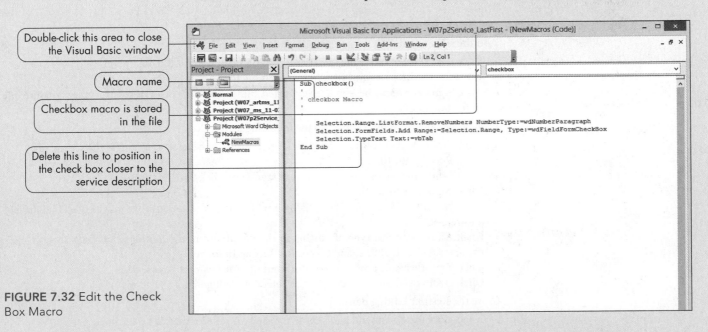

FIGURE 7.32 Edit the Check Box Macro

a. Open *w07p2Service*, click **Edit Anyway**, which displays in yellow at the top of the document, and then save it as a Macro-Enabled document with the name **w07p2Service_LastFirst**.

b. Position the insertion point on the left side of the word *Sweep* that displays in the first bulleted list under the *Entryway* paragraph. Record a macro by completing the following steps:

- Click the **DEVELOPER tab** and click **Record Macro** in the Code group.
- Type **checkbox** in the **Macro name box**.
- Click the **Store macro in arrow**.
- Click **w07p2Service_LastFirst** (document).
- Click **Keyboard**.
- Press **Alt+C**.
- Click the **Save changes in arrow**, click **w07p2Service_LastFirst**, click **Assign**, and then click **Close**.
- Click the **HOME tab**, click the **Bullets arrow**, and then click **None**.
- Click the **DEVELOPER tab**, click **Legacy Tools** in the Controls group, and then click **Check Box Form Field**.
- Press **Tab** and click **Stop Recording** in the Code group.

c. Press ⬇ to move the insertion point to the next bulleted list item that starts *Shine both sides*. Press **Alt+C** to run the macro and replace the bullet with a check box. You adjust the alignment of the check box in the next step.

d. Edit the macro by completing the following steps:

- Click **Macros** in the Code group.
- Click **Checkbox** and click **Edit**.
- Press **Ctrl+End** to move to the bottom of the window and view the programming statements for the checkbox macro.
- Select the third statement, *Selection.TypeText Text:=vbTab*, and press **Delete**.
- Press **Alt+Q** or double-click the top-left corner to close the window.

e. Select the check box and white tab space that follows the first bulleted item (*Sweep*) and press **Delete**. Press **Alt+C** to replay the macro, which removes the space between the check box and the service description. Run the macro and remove any white tab space that follows the bulleted list item on the page (those on the latter pages are completed for you).

f. Move the insertion point to the right side of *Name:* in the *Client Information* section on the last page. Click the **DEVELOPER tab** and click **Design Mode** in the Controls group. Click **Legacy Tools** in the Controls group and click **Text Form Field**. Add a Text Form Field for each of the remaining client information items.

g. Add the signature line by completing the following steps:

- Press **Ctrl+End** to move the insertion point to the bottom of the document.
- Click the **INSERT tab** and click **Signature Line** in the Text group.
- Type **Sign your name here** in the **Suggested signer box** and click **OK** to insert the signature line in the document.

h. Protect the document by completing the following steps:

- Click the **DEVELOPER tab** and click **Design Mode**, if necessary, to toggle the setting off.
- Click **Restrict Editing**.
- Click **Limit formatting to a selection of styles** and click **Settings**.
- Click **None** and click **OK**.
- Click **No** in the Microsoft Word dialog box that asks if you want to remove styles that are not allowed.
- Click **Allow only this type of editing in the document** in the *Editing restrictions* section, click the arrow below that line, and then select **Filling in forms**.
- Click **Yes, Start Enforcing Protection** from the *Start enforcement* section.
- Click **OK** to close the Start Enforcing Protection dialog box.

i. Close the Restrict Editing pane.

j. Save and close the document, and submit it based on your instructor's directions.

Mid-Level Exercises

1 Real Estate Appraisal Report

You are a real estate appraiser who estimates the value of residential homes. At the end of each week, you must submit a report to your supervisor of the properties you appraised during the past seven days. You decide to create a form that you can fill out quickly, even while you are on location with your laptop. You have a document containing a table for the information, but you decide to automate it using form fields; then you will use features to protect the form and create a digital signature prior to submitting it to your boss. Refer to Figure 7.33 as you complete this exercise.

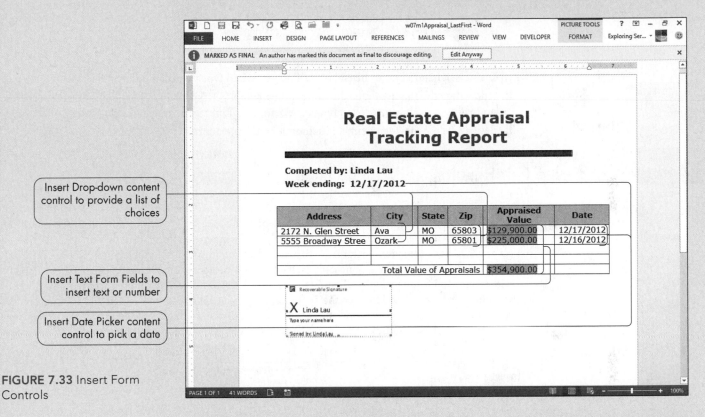

FIGURE 7.33 Insert Form Controls

Insert Drop-down content control to provide a list of choices

Insert Text Form Fields to insert text or number

Insert Date Picker content control to pick a date

a. Open *w07m1Appraisal.dotx* and save it as **w07m1AppraisalTemplate_LastFirst.dotx** (a Word template).

b. Insert a Rich Text Content control on the right side of *Completed by*. This is where you enter your full name.

c. Insert the Date Picker Content control on the right side of *Week ending* and in each cell in the Date column in the table (except for the last Total Value row).

d. Insert Rich Text Content controls in each cell in the Address column (excluding the Total Value row).

DISCOVER

e. Add Drop-Down List Content controls in each cell for City and Zip Code. Since you only assess homes in four cities, populate the *City drop-down list* box with **Ava**, **Salem**, **Ozark**, and **Nixa**. Create a Drop-Down List Content control in the Zip cells for Zip codes using **65800**, **65801**, **65802**, and **65803**. Insert the state abbreviation **MO** in each cell in the state column. *Hint:* You can create one drop-down list control for each category and copy it into other cells in the column.

f. Enter a Text Form Field in each cell of the Appraised Value column. Format the Text Form Field in the last row to calculate the total of the Appraised Value column with dollar formatting. *Hint:* Select the **Calculate on exit property**.

g. Protect the document; allow users to fill in form controls only. Save and close the template.

h. Open the template you just created and save it as **w07m1Appraisal_LastFirst.docx** (a Word document).

i. Fill out the form by entering the following information:
   - Type your name in the **Completed by text form control**.
   - Select **Today** in the date picker control.
   - Type the address and appraised value information below into the table for the first two rows. Select specified dates from the date picker controls.

Address	1387 E. Main Street	8977 N. Fremont Ave.
City	Ava	Ozark
State	MO	MO
Zip	65803	65801
Appraised Value	129,900	225,000
Date	*select* Today	*select yesterday's date*

j. Insert a signature line at the end of the document and type your name above the signature line.

k. Add a digital signature to the document when complete. Type **This report is submitted as correct and valid** as the purpose for signing the document. Type your name in the *Suggested signer* box.

l. Save and close the document, and submit it based on your instructor's directions.

2 Regional Science Fair Results

CREATIVE CASE

After the Regional Science Fair is held on the campus of Missouri State University, the director of the event must document the winners and distribute the awards in each category of the competition. The director's assistant has created an initial list of the winners in the Senior Division and has applied several layers of protection, including a password that you must enter to make modifications. You will open the document, make any necessary changes, and protect the document again. All participants will receive the results via e-mail, and the document should be certifiable for accuracy. You do not want to assign a password to open the document, as that is not appropriate when distributing a public record, but you can use your knowledge of other forms of document protection so that it will be recognized as the official results, which cannot be altered. Refer to Figure 7.34 as you complete this exercise.

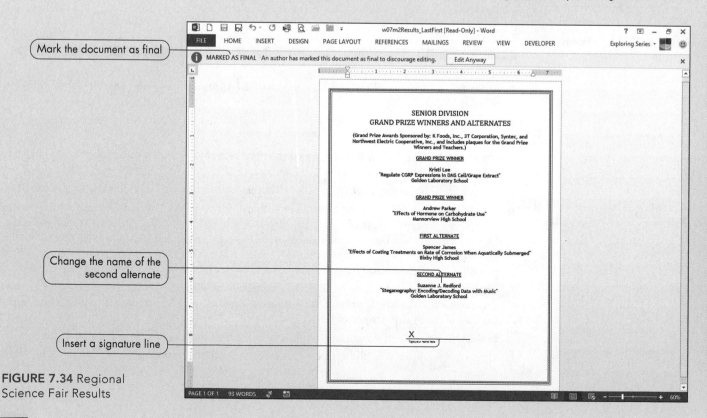

FIGURE 7.34 Regional Science Fair Results

a. Open the *w07m2Results* document and type **Chap7_mid2** as the password to modify the document. Save it as **w07m2Results_LastFirst**.

b. Remove any formatting and editing protection that is applied to the document so you can make the following changes.

c. Change the name of the *Second Alternate*, which is incorrect, to display **Suzanne J. Redford**.

d. Change the main heading of the document to use the **Title style**. Decrease the font size to **20**, center the heading, and then insert a line break so *Senior Division* appears on the first line and the remaining title displays below it.

e. Insert a signature line at the bottom of the page, two lines below *Golden Laboratory School*.

f. Set editing restrictions so the document is read-only and no changes are allowed.

g. Remove the password necessary to open the document.

h. Mark the document as final.

i. Save and close the document, and submit it based on your instructor's directions.

3 Computer Training Concepts

Your company, Computer Training Concepts, was recently purchased, and the new owner is considering a new name for the organization. His first choice for a new name is *Computer Training Solutions*. The new CEO asked you to automate the process of changing the name of the company on all documentation and correspondence. As company documents are used, modifications to reflect the new name should take place. You decide to create a macro that will quickly search each document and replace the old name with the new name. You are also directed to change the appearance of the new name so it is more distinguishable in the documents. Refer to Figure 7.35 as you complete this exercise.

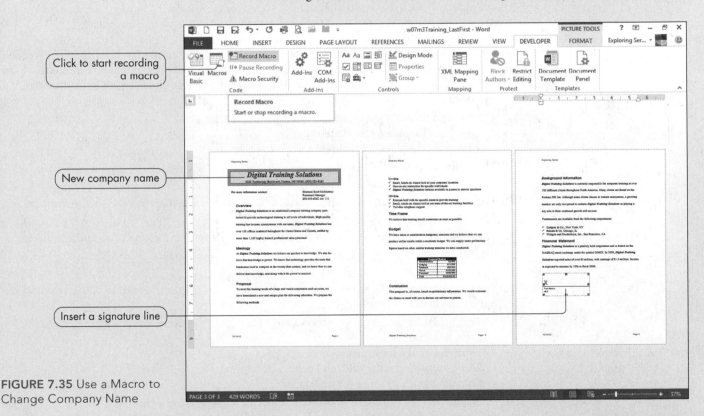

FIGURE 7.35 Use a Macro to Change Company Name

a. Open *w07m3Training* and save it as a Macro-Enabled document named **w07m3Training_LastFirst**.

b. Create a macro named **ReplaceName**. Save it in the *w07m3Training_LastFirst* file. Press **Alt+R** to run the macro and save changes to the macro in the *w07m3Training_LastFirst* Macro-Enabled document.

c. Perform the following steps in the ReplaceName macro:

- Activate the **Find and Replace command**.
- Find occurrences of *Computer Training Concepts* and replace them with **Computer Training Solutions**.
- Change the font attributes of Computer Training Solutions to bold and italic from the *Find and Replace* dialog box.
- Replace all occurrences and close the *Find and Replace* dialog box. Stop recording the macro.

d. Edit the header in each section by replacing *Student's Name* with your name.

e. Restrict formatting of the document to a selection of styles. When you enforce that protection, use a password to secure it. Set the password to modify as **Chap7_mid3**.

f. Edit the macro to reflect the CEO's latest decision to name the company **Digital Training Solutions**. Change the *.Text* statement in the macro to find **Computer Training Solutions** and change the *.Replacement. Text* statement to use **Digital Training Solutions**. Save and close the macro, and run it to make the new corrections. Pay special attention to all the locations in the document where the company name displays, including headers and footers.

g. Insert a Signature Line at the end of the document. The name that displays beneath the line is *Tyler Batten* and his title is *CEO*. Insert **Tyler Batten** in the signature line so that it displays on the document.

h. Save and close the document, and submit it based on your instructor's directions.

4 Electronic Sales Forms

COLLABORATION CASE

You are a member of the university's chess club, and your club organizes several fund-raising events throughout the year to raise money for field trips and community projects. One of the popular fund-raising activities is to sell chocolate bars and cookie dough. It has occurred to you that it would be more efficient to use a standardized form to keep track of the sales items. Several club members volunteered to work together to create and test an electronic fund-raising form with macros.

a. You may use any kind of collaboration tools available to you on the Internet, such as Facebook, Twitter, blogs, Skype, and Google Chat, or the collaboration tools available in your campus's course management content software or the MyITLab, to chat. During the first online chat session, you will do the following:

- Choose a name for the group and select a group leader.
- Develop a list of tasks to complete.
- Assign tasks and responsibilities to each group member.

b. The team leader will create a SkyDrive or Dropbox.com account, where each member can share, upload, view, and open all the documents posted online.

c. Each member will design the form layout by hand, scan it as a PDF file, and then submit it to the online storage location.

d. The group will work together to select an appropriate design for the chess club and also decide on the text labels for the form.

e. The team leader will create the selected form layout.

f. Team members will take turns working on the corresponding form controls, which may include, but are not limited to, the following:

- Text boxes for contact information such as last and first name, street address, city, state, Zip code, and dates.
- Drop-down lists for item selection.
- Text boxes for quantity sold, unit price, and total sales for each buyer.
- Calculating fields to sum the total sales.

g. Each member will also create a macro for a specific activity in the form.

h. The team leader will apply document restrictions by adding the team members to the list of user exceptions to editing restrictions.

i. The team leader will insert a Signature Line at the bottom of the document. Below the line, display the text *Salesperson*.

j. Save the form template as **w07m4FormTemplate_GroupName.dotx**. Then, populate the form with some test data and save it as a form document with the name **w07m4Form_GroupName.docx**.

k. Post all the individual documents and the final version of the research report to the online storage location.

l. Inform your instructor that the documents are ready for grading, and also give directions to where they are located.

Beyond the Classroom

So Many Features to Choose From

RESEARCH CASE

In this chapter, you learned the benefit of using macros to perform a repetitive task. Other features in Word also help you with a repetitive task. Which feature should you use for a particular task? Take this opportunity to create a chart that lists the features and tools in Word such as macros, Format Painter, and Building Blocks, and compare each feature. Consider a scenario that would require the use of each feature and why you would use one instead of the other. Use Microsoft Word Help to learn more about each feature, if necessary. Save your work as **w07b2Features_LastFirst**, close the document, and then submit it based on your instructor's directions.

Calculating Form Fields

DISASTER RECOVERY

A colleague wants to use a form as a purchase order for his small company. He created the form, but it does not work as he expected. The calculating fields do not function properly, the customer information does not appear as a form field, and to top it off, he's no longer able to type anything into his form. His frustration has forced him to call you and ask for advice on solving his problems. Your task is to troubleshoot the form and make corrections or additions that will turn it into a functioning and professional-looking electronic form that is suitable for use. Open the file *w07b3Problem.dotx* and save it as **w07b3Problem_LastFirst.dotx**. Determine the reason why the form fields are not calculating, make corrections to fix the problem, add any other form features that would make this a true digital form, and then save and test the form. When complete, save and close the document, and submit it based on your instructor's directions.

Performance Evaluations

SOFT SKILLS CASE

Students will work as a group to create an employee performance evaluation form that discusses the key points from the video. The electronic form will consist of form controls, document restrictions to protect the form from editing by users, several useful macros, and a digital signature to authenticate the document. Save the form as **w07b4EvaluationForm_GroupName**. Then, each group will conduct mock performance evaluations and record the work performance discussion on the created forms. Save the evaluated performance as **w07b4PerformanceEvaluations_GroupName**. Submit the documents as directed by your instructor.

Many professionals have a job that requires travel. In most organizations, individuals must pay for all travel-related expenses and submit a form in order to receive reimbursement. The form details every expense—from food to hotel to airfare—and at the end of the form the total of all expenses is calculated. The company you

work for has a travel reimbursement form that all employees must print, fill out, and submit via interoffice mail. You are responsible for converting that form so that it can be completed online and e-mailed to the accounting office. Refer to Figure 7.36 as you complete this exercise.

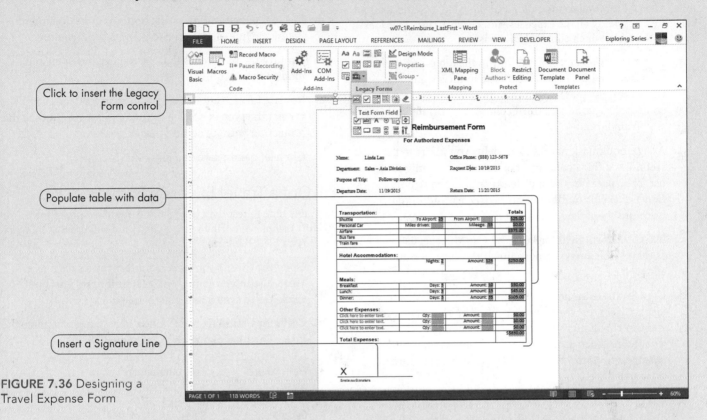

Click to insert the Legacy Form control

Populate table with data

Insert a Signature Line

FIGURE 7.36 Designing a Travel Expense Form

Create a Macro That Inserts Text Controls

The travel expense form will require several text controls to enter information such as name, department, and phone number. To expedite the process of inserting text controls, you create a macro that inserts the field as soon as you press a keyboard combination.

a. Open the file *w07c1Travel*. The password to open is *Chap7_cap* and the password to modify is *2Travel*.

b. Save the file as a Macro-Enabled Document named **w07c1Travel_LastFirst**.

c. Display the DEVELOPER tab, if necessary. Switch to Design Mode. Record a macro named **TextControl**. Store it in the *w07c1Travel_LastFirst* document. Assign the macro to the keyboard combination Alt+L and save changes to the macro in *w07c1Travel_LastFirst*.

d. Click anywhere in the document and perform the following commands in the macro: Click the **DEVELOPER tab** and click the **Rich Text Content Control**. Click **Properties** and select the **Content control cannot be deleted option**. Close the Content Control Properties dialog box and stop the macro.

e. Deselect the control and press **Alt+L** to confirm that the macro runs correctly. Delete all text controls added while recording and testing the macro.

Insert Text and Date Controls on a Form

The Word document you opened in the last steps is the basis for the printed travel reimbursement form. You decide to keep the basic outline of the document and add form controls for users to enter their personal information. The document contains asterisks to mark the location where you want to enter the personal information, so you will delete the asterisks before you insert form controls.

a. Select the asterisks and use the TextControl macro to insert text controls to the right side of *Name*, *Office Phone*, *Department*, and *Purpose of Trip*.

b. Insert Date Picker controls on the right side of *Request Date*, *Departure Date*, and *Return Date*.

c. Save the document.

Insert Controls That Compute Totals

The actual expenses are entered in a table in the document that sorts by category such as transportation, accommodations, and meals. Some expenses, such as Personal Car, might require a calculation of miles driven multiplied by the reimbursement amount per mile. After all information is entered in the table, a grand total is calculated by adding all the expenses. You decide to use legacy text fields in the table, which allow calculations.

a. Insert *legacy text form* fields within the table and apply **Number formats** for each expense in the second and third columns that requires a number to be entered (no controls in second and third column for *Airfare*, *Bus fare*, and *Train fare*).

b. Assign bookmark names to all fields you insert in the second and third columns. For example, you might use *ToAirport* (for the shuttle expense to the airport), *DriveMiles* (for number of miles driven), and *Brkdays* (for number of days you ate breakfast on the trip).

c. Insert the form field for Personal Car Mileage, using **.55** as the default entry, because this is the current mileage allowance.

d. Use Help to learn how to edit field properties so you can display Help text for form controls. The Help message you insert will display on the status bar to tell the user what to do (such as *Enter number of miles driven* or *Enter mileage allowance*) for fields in the second and third columns.

e. Insert a text form field that calculates the total amount in the fourth column. Create formulas that use the form field bookmark names from fields in columns two and three. For example, use *=Brkdays*Brkamt* to calculate the total amount spent for breakfasts during a trip. Notice that some fields will add the results from columns 2 and 3, and others will multiply them. Format calculating fields in the last column with **Currency format** and set them to **calculate on exit**.

f. Insert text form fields in the first column below the Other Expenses category.

g. Insert a calculation field in the last cell with this formula: **=SUM(D2:D16)**. Format the field to display the results as **Currency** to **calculate on exit**.

h. Set right alignment on the text and fields in the second, third, and fourth columns.

i. Save the document.

Protect the Form

To make a true digital form, you wisely decide to add a line for a signature and protect the document so users can only enter information in the control field areas. You remove all passwords and certify the form for authenticity by attaching a digital signature.

a. Insert a Signature Line at the bottom of the document. Below the line, display the text *Employee Signature*.

b. Remove the passwords that are required to open and modify the document.

c. Restrict formatting to a selection of styles (none) and restrict the type of editing to filling in forms. Enforce the protection without setting passwords.

d. Close all panes; save and close the document.

Fill Out a Travel Expense Form

Now, it is time to test the travel expense reimbursement form. You recently completed a trip to visit a client and will use that information to complete the form.

a. Open the travel reimbursement form and save it as a Word document named **w07c1Reimburse_LastFirst**. Click **Yes** to save it as a macro-free document.

b. Use information from the following table to complete the form. The total expenses should equal $830.00.

Form Control	Your information
Name	*enter your name*
Office Phone	(888) 123-5678
Department	Sales - Asia Division
Request Date	October 19, 2015
Purpose of Trip	Follow-up meeting
Departure Date	November 19, 2015
Return Date	November 21, 2015
Shuttle to Airport	25
Airfare	375
Hotel	2 nights @ 125
Breakfast	3 days @ 10
Lunch	3 days @ 15
Dinner	3 days @ 35

c. Sign your name on the digital signature line after you complete the form.

d. Save and close the document, and submit it based on your instructor's directions.

Word and the Internet

wavebreakmedia/Shutterstock

CHAPTER 8

Web Page Creation and Enhancement, and Blogs

OBJECTIVES AFTER YOU READ THIS CHAPTER, YOU WILL BE ABLE TO:

1. Customize the Ribbon p. 166
2. Build and publish a Web page p. 169
3. Create a blog post p. 186
4. Present a Word document online p. 188
5. Enhance a Web page p. 190

CASE STUDY | A Math Tutoring Club

You are working on your bachelor's degree to become a middle school teacher. You know that there is a need for math tutors, so you want to create a Web site to provide online resources to students who want to improve their math skills. It could be just a simple Web site to provide information about your new endeavor, information on how to request tutoring services, sample worksheets for students to practice, and other resources for students to consult. By keeping it simple, you can maintain and update it yourself using tools such as Word 2013.

Your knowledge of the Office suite enables you to set up the Web pages to be multi-functional and to format information about your services in a way that displays well on a Web site. You will use these tools to get started and create a blog where you post more personal notes and links about updates on your Web site.

Web Page Creation

For most students, the Internet is as much a part of their education as books and teachers. The *Internet* is a network of networks that connects computers anywhere in the world. It is easy to connect your computer to the Internet, and that connection enables you to view an abundance of information about every imaginable topic.

The *World Wide Web (WWW)* or, simply, the Web, is a very large subset of the Internet, consisting of those computers that store a special type of document known as a *Web page*. Any document that displays on the World Wide Web is a Web page. Web pages may be self-contained and might provide all the information you need about a topic, or they may offer links to other Web pages. And therein lies the fascination of the Web—you simply click link after link to move effortlessly from one document or resource to the next.

In this section, you will learn to create a Web page using Microsoft Word. However, like any other Microsoft word processors such as WordPad or Publisher, the Web page is best displayed using a Web browser, such as Internet Explorer. You will first customize the Ribbon to display commands you will use for Web page development, then you will format the page, add hyperlinks and bookmarks, and finally save the document as a Web page.

Customizing the Ribbon

The features in Word enable you to create just about any kind of document you could want, and the Ribbon makes it easy to find the commands that you use when creating those documents. But did you know you can create a custom tab for the Ribbon that contains just the commands you want to use? Ribbon customization enables you to include features that you use most frequently or features that are not available on the standard Ribbon. By creating a custom tab, you have access to these features. In addition to creating a new tab, you can change the order of the tabs, change the order of the groups that appear within the tabs, and create new groups within a tab.

To customize the Ribbon, right-click an empty area of the Ribbon and click *Customize the Ribbon*, or do the following:

1. Click the FILE tab to open the Backstage view.
2. Click Options.
3. Click Customize Ribbon.

Figure 8.1 shows the Customize Ribbon options displaying the current arrangement of the Ribbon in the right pane. To expand the view to display the groups within a tab click the plus icon (+), and to collapse the view to hide the groups click the minus icon (−). To change the order of the existing tabs or groups, drag and drop a selected tab and group to a new position.

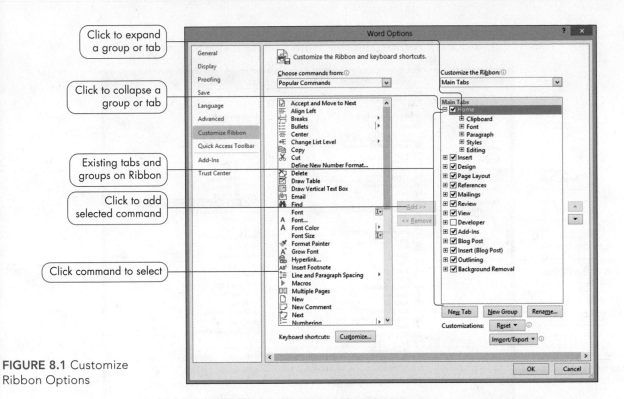

Click to expand a group or tab

Click to collapse a group or tab

Existing tabs and groups on Ribbon

Click to add selected command

Click command to select

FIGURE 8.1 Customize Ribbon Options

TIP **Restore the Ribbon**

You can restore the Ribbon to its original arrangement by clicking *Reset* at the bottom of the *Customize the Ribbon* view and clicking *Reset all customizations*. Reset also enables you to reset individual tabs.

Create a Custom Tab

STEP 1 » To have access to the commands you use most, you can add a new tab to the Ribbon and add the frequently used commands. Below the *Customize the Ribbon* pane, click New Tab. The new tab displays immediately below the tab in the pane that is also the active tab in your document and is named *New Tab (Custom)*. The new tab contains a new group named *New Group (Custom)*. To add additional groups, click New Group below the pane. You can rename tabs or groups by selecting the desired tab or group and clicking Rename. When you rename a group, you can select a colorful symbol to represent the contents of the group. You can reorder the tab in the Ribbon by selecting the desired tab and clicking the Move Up and Move Down arrows on the right side of the pane. Figure 8.2 displays a new tab containing a new group. You may create the new custom tab by doing the following:

1. Click the FILE tab to open the Backstage view.
2. Click Options.
3. Click Customize Ribbon in the left pane.
4. Click New Tab, below the *Customize the Ribbon* pane on the right side of the window.
5. Click to select the New Tab (Custom) and click Rename, which displays below the pane.
6. In the Rename dialog box, give the new tab a name in the *Display name* box.
7. Click OK.
8. Click New Group (Custom) and click Rename.
9. In the Rename dialog box, click a symbol of your choice in the *symbol* section, if one is desired.
10. Give the new group a name in the *Display name* box.

11. Click OK.
12. Click OK again to close the Word Options dialog box.

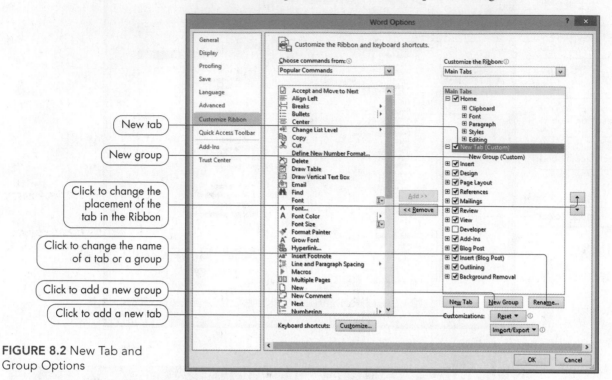

FIGURE 8.2 New Tab and Group Options

Add Commands to a Group

To add commands to an existing tab or group or to a newly created tab, make sure that the tab or group under the *Customize the Ribbon* pane is selected, click a command from the *Choose commands from* pane, and then click Add. Popular commands that you can add are displayed in the default view, but you can also click the *Choose commands from* arrow to choose from additional commands and macros. You will also find a category named *Commands Not in the Ribbon*. For example, you can add commands that are not on the default tabs, such as Web Page Preview, to a group in a personalized tab. Figure 8.3 displays a customized tab with commands you use while creating Web pages.

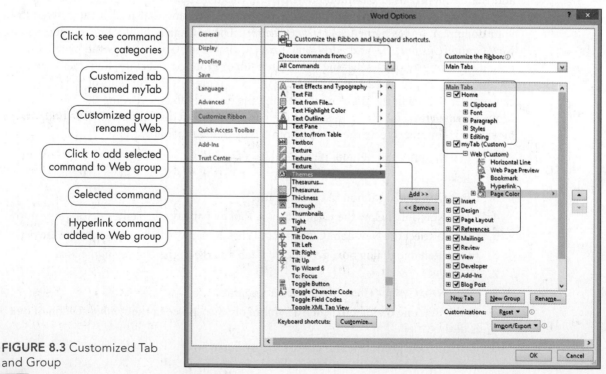

FIGURE 8.3 Customized Tab and Group

You may also add commands not in the Ribbon, such as Horizontal Line and Web Page Preview, to the new tab. If your Web page is relatively long, you may want to insert horizontal lines to separate sections of the document content for easier reading. Add new commands to the custom tab by doing the following:

1. Click to select the desired group below the *Customize the Ribbon* pane on the right.
2. Click the *Choose commands from* arrow and click *Commands Not in the Ribbon*. If you prefer, you may click the All Commands option instead.
3. Scroll down the list of commands, find the desired command, and then click Add.
4. Repeat step 3 to add more desired commands.
5. Confirm that the new tab is checked and click OK to close the Word Options dialog box.

TIP | Export and Import a Custom Tab

If you customize a tab or the Quick Access Toolbar (QAT), that customization will only be applied to the Word application that is installed on that particular computer. You can export the customized tab or the QAT to a file that can be imported to a different computer. Click Import/Export at the bottom of the Word Options dialog box to save your customizations. Copy the file you save onto a different computer and click Import/Export again on the new computer to import your custom tab or QAT.

Building and Publishing a Web Page

Sooner or later, anyone who surfs the World Wide Web wonders if he or she can create a home page or a Web site of his or her own. Word provides all the tools necessary to create a basic Web page. You can use tables and SmartArt graphics to organize and lay out the page elements, add online images and your own pictures to enhance the page with visual elements, use bulleted and numbered lists to organize information on the page, create WordArt for text, and so on. If your Web page design is complex, you will want to use a Web authoring tool such as Microsoft Expression.

Web pages are developed in a special language called *HyperText Markup Language (HTML)*. In the early years of Internet development, the only way to create a Web page was to learn HTML, which is a programming language consisting of a set of codes (or tags) that are assigned to the content and which describe how the document is to appear when viewed in a Web browser.

Office 2013 simplifies the Web page development process because you can create the document in Word from scratch or a template and simply save it as a Web page. Word converts the document and generates the HTML code for you. You can continue to type text or change the formatting just as you can with an ordinary document. Figure 8.4 shows a Web page you will create in the next Hands-On Exercise, and Figure 8.5 displays the HTML code for that page.

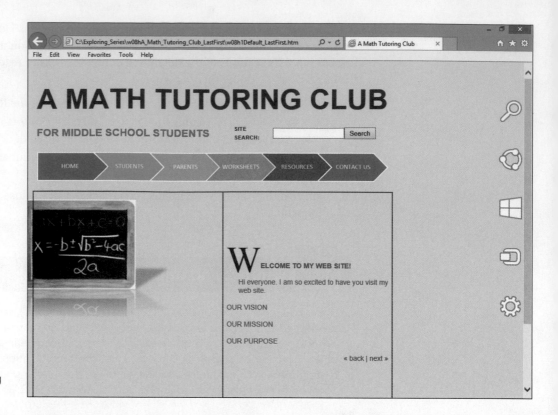

FIGURE 8.4 A Math Tutoring Club Web Page

Code specifies how to format the contents

FIGURE 8.5 HTML Code for A Math Tutoring Club Web Page

Save Document as a Web Page

STEP 2 » When you create a document in Word, you can display it in Web Layout view. This particular view enables you to continue using regular Word formatting features while displaying the document as it will appear in a Web browser. After you create and format documents, you can save them as Web pages. From within the Save As dialog box, click the *Save as type* arrow and choose an appropriate Web format. Table 8.1 lists and describes the three Web file types. When you save your file as a regular Web page, the file will contain all the Word tags and HTML tags, thereby increasing the size of the file. When you save your file as a single file Web page, it will increase the file size because all the images will be embedded and saved in the file. Care must be taken to ensure that the file size does not exceed the maximum size imposed by the e-mail server and that the Web browser used can display this type of file properly. If large file size is a major concern to you, you could save your file as a Web Page, Filtered. All the Word tags are removed, and only the HTML tags remain in the file. Images will be saved in an accompanying folder, which must be located in the same directory as the Web page. This format is often used for Web sites presented on Amazon's Kindle tablet. The downside is that you cannot edit a filtered Web page in Word.

TABLE 8.1   Options for Saving Web Pages

File Type	Description
Web Page (*.htm; *.html)	Create and edit Web page documents and use regular Word editing tools. Keep saving in this format until you are done.
Single File Web Page (*.mht; *.mhtml)	Save all Web site files, including graphics, into one file so that you can send it to someone.
Web Page, Filtered (*.htm; *.html)	Save the final Web page in this format to reduce file size and reduce Word editing options. Upload this file to a Web server.

For a quicker reference, it is a good idea to change the title of each page to reflect the content of the document. You also need to save all the Word documents as individual Web pages in one folder. For instance, to create a Web folder and save the home page for the Web site, do the following:

1. Open the document that will be the designated home page.
2. Click the FILE tab.
3. Click Save As. You can save your Web pages to the following locations:
   a. SkyDrive
   b. Other Web Locations
   c. Computer
   d. Add a Place
   e. Recent Folders
4. If you save your document to your computer, you will click Browse, and in the Save As dialog box, navigate to the drive and folder in which you want to create a folder.
5. Click New folder on the Save As dialog box toolbar or right-click for the shortcut menu and click New.
6. Type a new folder name and click Open.
7. Type Default in the *File name* box. The default name for the home page is either *default* or *index*.
8. Click the *Save as type* arrow and click Web Page (*.htm; *.html).
9. Click Change Title to display the Enter Text dialog box.
10. Type the title of the Web page in the *Page title* text.
11. Click OK.
12. Click Save.

 TIP   Folder and File Names

Many Web servers do not handle spaces well in folder and file names; they might replace each space with the %20 combination. Therefore, it is a good habit to avoid using spaces when naming folders and files by substituting the spaces with underscores. Other options include using the CamelCase notation (a combination of capital and lowercase letters) or hyphens to replace the spaces.

Apply a Theme and Background Color to a Web Page

STEP 3 » Web pages are more interesting when you add design elements such as background images, bullets, numbering, lines, and other graphical features. They also display better when colors and fonts are coordinated among the design elements. You can use the Word themes while developing a Web page, which enables you to coordinate colors and fonts, as shown in Figure 8.6. To make sure themes are as effective as possible, you should format your document by using Word heading styles, such as Heading 1, Heading 2, and so on. You may add a theme by doing the following:

1. Click the DESIGN tab. You may also click the customized new tab/group if you have added selected commands to the customized new tab.
2. Click Themes in the Document Formatting group.
3. Hover the mouse over the theme choices to display a live preview of the individual theme.
4. Click the selected theme to apply the theme features to the Web page.

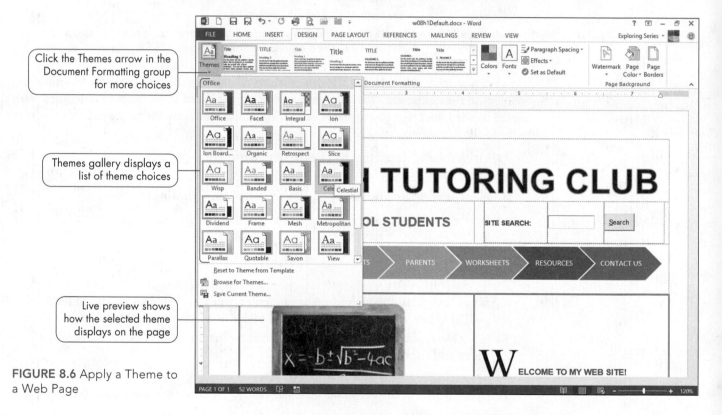

Click the Themes arrow in the Document Formatting group for more choices

Themes gallery displays a list of theme choices

Live preview shows how the selected theme displays on the page

FIGURE 8.6 Apply a Theme to a Web Page

Themes assign colors to the elements on the Web page, such as fonts, numbers, and horizontal lines, which enable you to emphasize key information. However, the theme does not automatically add a background to the Web page. A *background* is a color, design, image, or watermark that appears behind text in a document or on a Web page. A colored background adds visual enhancement to the Web page. You can quickly add a background color to a Web page by clicking the Design tab. If a theme has been selected, the Page Color palette automatically displays colors that coordinate with the theme. To add a background color to a Web page, do the following:

1. Click the DESIGN tab.
2. Click Page Color in the Page Background group.
3. Hover the mouse over any of the theme colors to see a live preview of the selected color.
4. Click the selected color to apply the new color to the Web page.

If you prefer to customize the background color, design, or image, you can click the Page Color command in the Page Background group on the Design tab and select from the commands that display below the Theme Color gallery. The More Colors command displays the Colors dialog box, which enables you to choose from the standard colors or to mix a custom color. The Fill Effects command enables you to apply a gradient, texture, pattern, or picture background. Figure 8.7 shows the Gradient tab of the Fill Effects dialog box, where you can select a gradient design to display on the background of your Web page.

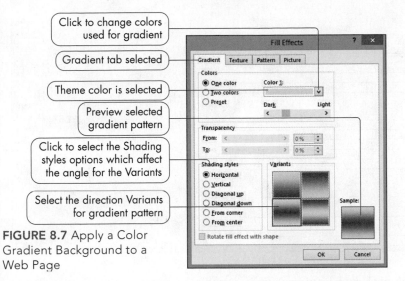

Click to change colors used for gradient

Gradient tab selected

Theme color is selected

Preview selected gradient pattern

Click to select the Shading styles options which affect the angle for the Variants

Select the direction Variants for gradient pattern

FIGURE 8.7 Apply a Color Gradient Background to a Web Page

TIP **Web Page Background**

The size of a Web page is not the same as a Word document; Web pages are wider than a typical 8 1/2" × 11" document using portrait orientation. Therefore, any color, pattern, or image you use as a background will repeat so that it covers the entire Web page. You want to carefully select a background color, pattern, or image so that it is not distracting and does not affect the readability of the contents on the page.

Insert Bookmarks in a Web Page

STEP 4 Some Web pages are very lengthy and require the viewer to scroll a great deal to view all the contents on the page. You can help the viewer to return to the top, bottom, or other location in that page by inserting bookmarks. A *bookmark* is an electronic marker for a specific location in a document, enabling the user to go to that location quickly. A hyperlink takes you to a different page and can even take you to a specific location on a page, but the location must be identified somehow so the hyperlink knows exactly where to go; a bookmark provides that identification. Bookmarks are helpful in long documents because they enable you to move easily from one place to another within that document, without having to manually scroll. They are often used on FAQ (frequently asked questions) Web pages, which help the user to navigate quickly between a question and the respective answer. Another example for the use of bookmarks is shown in Figure 8.8. A bookmark was created for each math category, so that when you click any of the categories at the top of the page, you immediately move to that category and subject topics further down the page. Additionally, the placement of a bookmark at the top of the page enables the user to click a link at the end of each category to return the user to the top of the page to view the list of categories.

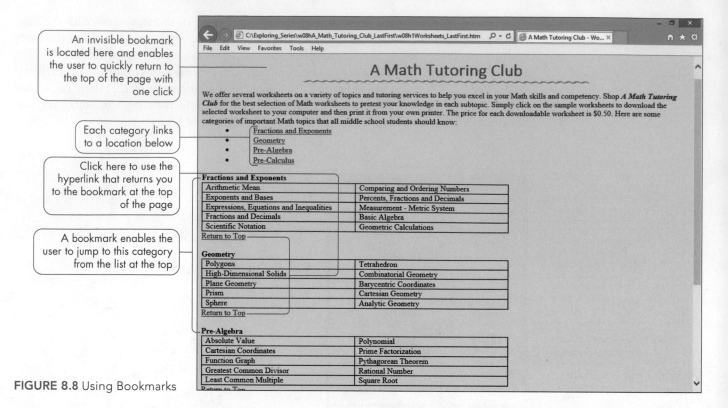

An invisible bookmark is located here and enables the user to quickly return to the top of the page with one click

Each category links to a location below

Click here to use the hyperlink that returns you to the bookmark at the top of the page

A bookmark enables the user to jump to this category from the list at the top

FIGURE 8.8 Using Bookmarks

Creating a bookmark and linking to it is a two-step process. You first create the bookmark(s) throughout the document, and you insert a hyperlink that links to that bookmark. A bookmark for the top of the page is created automatically, so you do not have to create that one manually. To create a bookmark on a Web page, do the following:

1. Click the INSERT tab.
2. Place the insertion point on the left side of the word that you want to use as a bookmark.
3. Click Bookmark in the Links group.
4. Give the bookmark a name in the *Bookmark name* box.
5. Click Add.

 **Bookmark Names**

Spaces and special characters, including hyphens, are not allowed in bookmark names. You can use a combination of capital and lowercase letters, numbers, and the underscore character, but you cannot begin the name of a bookmark with a number. You should create descriptive names so you can identify the bookmark easily when you create a hyperlink to it. For example, a bookmark to question #1 in a FAQ listing might be FAQ1.

Insert Hyperlinks in a Web Page

STEP 5 ▶

One benefit of a Web page is that it contains references, called hyperlinks, to other Web pages. *Hyperlinks* are electronic markers that, when clicked, do one of several actions: move the insertion point to a different location within the same document, open another document, or display a different Web page in a Web browser. Hyperlinks can lead you to Web pages stored on different computers that may be located anywhere in the world.

Hyperlinks can be assigned to text or graphics. For example, consider a Web page you might create to document your visit to several national parks. You display several pictures of the beautiful scenery and provide a summary of the trip. In your summary, you might mention a particular lodge where you spent a few nights, so you create a hyperlink from your Web page to the home page of the lodge. Anyone who reads your page can click the name of the lodge and be directed to the Web site, where they can inquire about reservations for themselves. Additionally, you might want to create a link to a particular park from a picture that was taken there. You can select the picture and assign a hyperlink that, when the picture is clicked, will direct the reader to the Web site for that national park.

To create a hyperlink on your Web page, do the following:

1. Select the text or picture.
2. Click the INSERT tab and click Hyperlink in the Links group.
3. In the Insert Hyperlink dialog box, as shown in Figure 8.9, you have the following options to specify several types of hyperlinks in the *Link to* box:

   - Existing File or Web Page: Links to another Web page by inserting the address (or URL).
   - Place in This Document: Links to another place within the same document. If necessary, click the plus sign (+) next to Bookmarks and select the desired bookmark.
   - Create New Document: Links to a new document that you can edit now or later.
   - E-mail Address: Links to an e-mail address, which opens a new e-mail message when clicked.

4. Click OK.

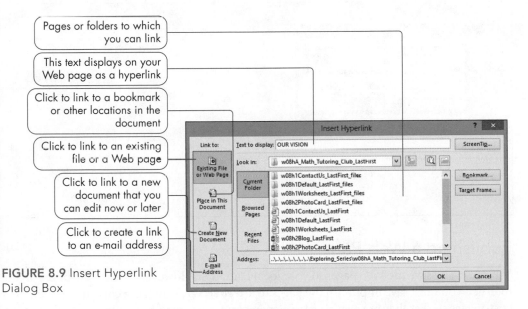

FIGURE 8.9 Insert Hyperlink Dialog Box

When you point to a hyperlink in a Word document, you will see a ScreenTip that directs you to press Ctrl+Click to follow the link, which is not the way you use hyperlinks in a Web page. However, this gives you more control over the link from a developmental standpoint because you are able to select the link and make changes without it automatically opening a new page. If you right-click a hyperlink in a Word document, you will see several options for working with the hyperlink, including Edit Hyperlink (which opens the Edit Hyperlink dialog box), Copy Hyperlink, and Remove Hyperlink (which removes the link but does not remove the text or graphic).

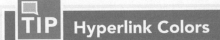

TIP Hyperlink Colors

When you apply a hyperlink to text in a Web page, the text displays in a color that coordinates with the theme in use. After you click the hyperlink, the color of the text changes to the theme or default color for a followed link.

Preview a Web Page

STEP 6 » After finalizing pages for a Web site, you save the document(s) as described earlier. The Web Layout view gives you a very accurate representation of how the page will look when published. You can also preview the page in an actual Web browser before you upload and publish it so that you can confirm it contains the content and is formatted to your specifications. Word contains a Web Page Preview command that you can add to a tab on the Ribbon or to the Quick Access Toolbar before you use it.

You can also open the page from within Internet Explorer, or the browser of your choice, when Word is not active. To view a Web page in Internet Explorer, do the following:

1. Open a Web browser window. Click the File menu.
2. Click Open (or press Ctrl+O if the menu bar does not display), and the Open dialog box displays as shown in Figure 8.10.
3. Click Browse.
4. Navigate and open the folder where the page is stored.
5. Select the file name of your Web page.
6. Click Open.
7. Click OK. The document opens in an Internet Explorer window.

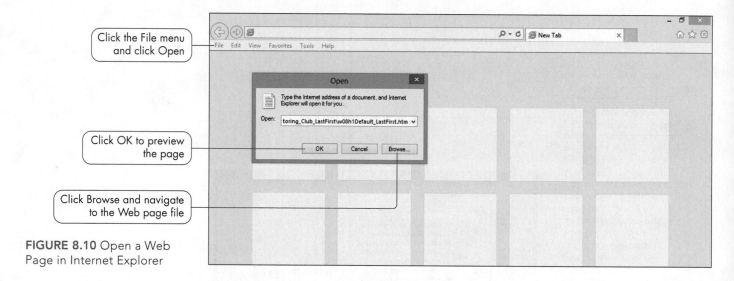

Click the File menu and click Open

Click OK to preview the page

Click Browse and navigate to the Web page file

FIGURE 8.10 Open a Web Page in Internet Explorer

Publishing a Web Page

You can easily save the Web pages to your local computer. However, to view the pages on the Internet, you must save or publish the pages to a *Web server*, which is a computer system that hosts pages so that they are available for viewing by anyone who has an Internet connection. You will need additional information from your instructor about how to obtain an account on a Web server at your school, if available, as well as how to upload the pages from your PC to the server. The most common method of uploading Web pages to the server is by using *File Transfer Protocol (FTP)*, a process that uploads files from a PC to a server or from a server to a PC.

Quick **Concepts**

1. What are the advantages of using Microsoft Word to create a Web page? *p. 166*
2. What are the benefits of using a Word theme in a Web page? *p. 172*
3. What are the benefits of inserting hyperlinks in a Web page? *p. 174*

Hands-On Exercises

1 Web Page Creation

You are designing a Web site for your own math tutoring club. You want a simple design that provides basic information about your service. You have a few documents started but need to refine each one to use a common theme, add color, and add general Web components such as hyperlinks and bookmarks. When complete, you will preview the results to make sure it is ready to go live on the Web.

Skills covered: Create a Custom Tab • Save Document as a Web Page • Apply a Theme and Background • Insert and Hyperlink to Bookmarks • Insert Hyperlinks and a Horizontal Line • Preview a Web Page

STEP 1 ≫ CREATE A CUSTOM TAB

Before you begin designing a Web page, you want to organize the tools that will enable you to work quickly and efficiently. You decide to create a custom Tab to display the commands you will use most frequently while designing the Web site. Refer to Figure 8.11 as you complete Step 1.

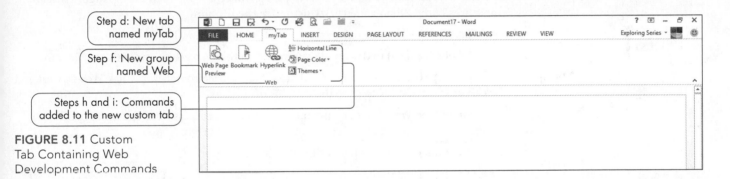

FIGURE 8.11 Custom Tab Containing Web Development Commands

a. Start Word and open a new document.

You can create a custom tab or group in any open document, and it can be used in all documents on the computer on which the software is installed.

b. Click the **FILE tab**, click **Options**, and then click **Customize Ribbon**.

The Word commands available display in the pane on the left side. On the right side, you customize the tabs and groups with the available commands.

> **TROUBLESHOOTING**: If you work in a lab environment where you are unable to customize the applications on your PC, read through the remainder of Step 1.

c. Click **New Tab**, which displays below the *Customize the Ribbon* pane on the right side of the window.

A new tab is created in the Main Tabs list and positioned between the Home tab and the Insert tab. The tab is named *New Tab* (*Custom*) and contains a new group named *New Group* (*Custom*).

d. Click **New Tab (Custom)** and click **Rename**, which displays below that pane. Type **myTab** in the **Display name box** and click **OK**.

The new tab displays as *myTab* (*Custom*).

e. Click **New Group (Custom)** and click **Rename**.

The Rename dialog box opens.

f. Type **Web** in the **Display name box** and click **OK**.

The group displays as *Web (Custom)*. You may select a symbol of your choice from the Symbol gallery if you want.

g. Click the **Choose commands from arrow** and click **Commands Not in the Ribbon**.

All the commands that are not on the Ribbon display in the left panel.

h. Scroll down the list of commands, click **Web Page Preview**, and then click **Add**.

Web Page Preview is added to myTab (Custom) in the Web (Custom) group.

i. Click the **Choose commands from arrow** and click **All Commands**. Select each of the following commands and click **Add** to display them in the Web (Custom) group on the myTab (Custom) tab:

- **Bookmark**
- **Horizontal Line** [Note: Make sure that you select the Horizontal Line, NOT the Horizontal Line…(followed by ellipsis) command]
- **Hyperlink**
- **Page Color**
- **Themes**
- **Web Layout**

j. Confirm that the myTab tab is checked so that it will display on the Ribbon and click **OK** to close the Options dialog box.

k. Click the **myTab tab** and notice the Web group contains seven commands. Right-click an empty area of the Ribbon and click **Customize the Ribbon**.

The Word Options dialog box opens.

l. Click the **plus sign (+)** to display all commands in the Web group under the myTab tab.

m. Click to select **Hyperlink** and drag and drop it above *Horizontal Line*. Click **Web Layout** and click **Remove**. Click **OK** to close the Options dialog box.

This removes the Web Layout command, which you can access from the status bar. It also changes the order in which the commands display on the tab.

n. Leave the blank document open for the next step.

STEP 2 ≫ SAVE DOCUMENT AS A WEB PAGE

You have a few documents prepared as a foundation for the Web site, but before you get started, you first create a folder for storing Web page files. You open each one and save it as a Web page, which places it in the proper format for viewing in a Web browser. You recognize that the name of the page displays in the task bar in Windows and Internet Explorer, so you are careful to change the title for each page. Refer to Figure 8.12 as you complete Step 2.

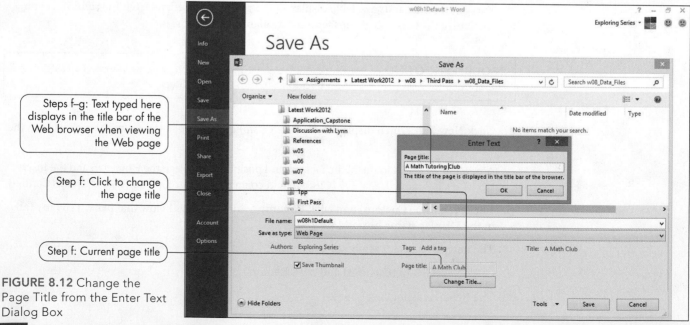

Steps f–g: Text typed here displays in the title bar of the Web browser when viewing the Web page

Step f: Click to change the page title

Step f: Current page title

FIGURE 8.12 Change the Page Title from the Enter Text Dialog Box

a. Open *w08h1Default*.

This document is designed to be the home page for the *A Math Tutoring Club* Web site. In the next step, you create a folder and save the document in that folder.

b. Click the **FILE tab**, click **Save As**, and then click **Browse**. In the Save As dialog box, navigate to the drive and folder in which you want to create a folder.

Before you start creating Web documents, you need to create a folder to store all Web documents for a specific Web site.

c. Click **New folder** on the Save As dialog box toolbar, type **w08hA_Math_Tutoring_Club_LastFirst**, and then press **Enter**. Click **Open** or double-click the new folder to open it.

Be aware that the folder name does not have a *1* after the letter *h*. This is because we will use the same folder name for both Hands-On Exercises 1 and 2. Usually, you will have many files when you create Web pages, so it is a good idea to put all the files and subfolders in the same folder.

 TIP **Naming a Web Site Home Page**

A Web site's home page is typically saved as default.html or index.html so that it loads automatically when you type the main URL in a Web browser address box.

d. Make sure that the same file name [*w08h1Default*] is in the *File name* box and add an underscore, follow by your last name and first name.

e. Click the **Save as type arrow** and click **Web Page (*.htm; *.html)**.

When you save as a Web page, the Save As dialog box displays the *Page title* text area and the Change Title button.

f. Click **Change Title** to display the Enter Text dialog box.

In this dialog box, you can edit the Web page title—the text that appears on the Web browser's title bar when the Web page displays.

g. Place the insertion point before the word *Club*, type **Tutoring**, and then press the **Spacebar** to add a space between words as appropriate in the *Page title* box. Click **OK** and click **Save**.

The page displays in Web Layout view.

h. Open the Word documents listed in the table below. Save each document as a Web page in the w08hA_Math_Tutoring_Club_LastFirst folder. Assign new file names and Web page titles using the information in the following table.

Open This File	Save As Web Page (.htm)	Web Page Title
w08h1Worksheets	w08h1Worksheets_LastFirst.htm	A Math Tutoring Club - Worksheets
w08h1Contact	w08h1ContactUs_LastFirst.htm	A Math Tutoring Club - Contact Us

The *w08hA_Math_Tutoring_Club_LastFirst* folder now contains three Web pages that you use to complete your Web site.

i. Leave each document open for the next step.

 TIP **Naming Pages in Your Web Site**

When you save a folder or page that you plan to use on a Web site, you should refrain from using spaces in the folder or file name. Even though it is possible to include spaces, it forces the Web browser to insert codes in place of the spaces when it displays the file name and path in the Address bar. For example, if you name a Web page *contact info*, it displays as *contact%20info* when viewed in a Web browser. If you need to use a long name, consider using dashes or underscores in place of spaces.

STEP 3 ≫ APPLY A THEME AND BACKGROUND

Now that your Web pages are in the proper form, you select a common theme to use on each one. The theme affects the fonts but not the background. So you also select a background color that gives a dramatic look to your simple pages. Refer to Figure 8.13 as you complete Step 3.

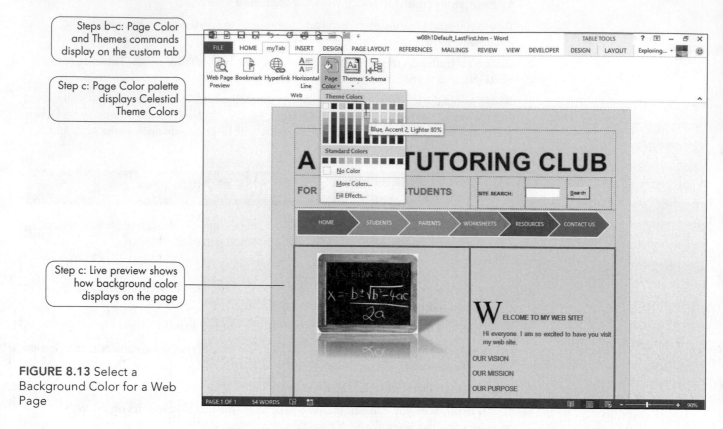

Steps b–c: Page Color and Themes commands display on the custom tab

Step c: Page Color palette displays Celestial Theme Colors

Step c: Live preview shows how background color displays on the page

FIGURE 8.13 Select a Background Color for a Web Page

a. Click the **VIEW tab**, click **Switch Windows** in the Window group, and then click *w08h1Default_LastFirst.htm* from the list of open files.

b. Click the **myTab tab**, click **Themes** in the Web group, and then click **Celestial**.

The *A Math Tutoring Club* title and text below it display in colors represented in the Celestial theme.

c. Click **Page Color** in the Web group. Click **Blue, Accent 2, Lighter 80%** (second row, sixth column).

You applied a light blue background color that covers the entire page.

d. Click **Save** in the Quick Access Toolbar to save the changes to the default.htm document.

e. Press **Alt+Tab** repeatedly until the *w08h1ContactUs_LastFirst.htm* document displays. Repeat steps b and c to apply the same theme and background color to the page. Click **Save** on the Quick Access Toolbar to save the changes.

When you press Alt+Tab, you will move from one open Web page to another.

> **TROUBLESHOOTING:** If you accidentally closed a document, you may open it again by clicking the File tab, clicking Open, and then clicking the document, which should be displayed under *Recent Documents.*

f. Press **Alt+Tab** repeatedly until the *w08h1Worksheets_LastFirst.htm* document displays. Repeat steps b and c to apply the theme and background color to the page. Click **Save** on the Quick Access Toolbar to save the changes.

STEP 4 ▶ INSERT AND HYPERLINK TO BOOKMARKS

The Web page that describes the worksheets is quite lengthy. You know that a good Web design will assist the viewer in navigating up and down the page without having to scroll. With that in mind, you incorporate bookmarks, which are a type of hyperlink, to help the reader move from section to section on the page. Refer to Figure 8.14 as you complete Step 4.

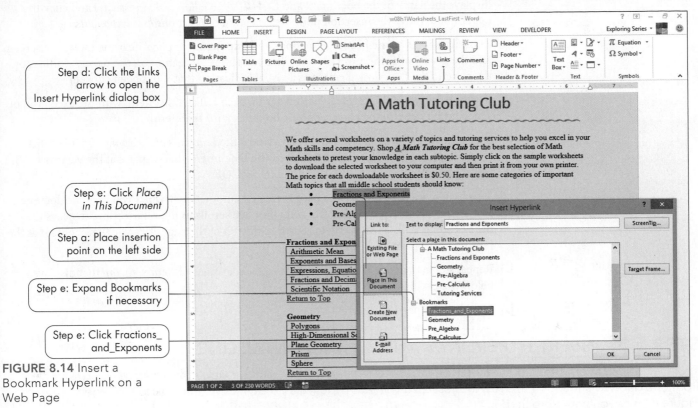

Step d: Click the Links arrow to open the Insert Hyperlink dialog box

Step e: Click *Place in This Document*

Step a: Place insertion point on the left side

Step e: Expand Bookmarks if necessary

Step e: Click Fractions_and_Exponents

FIGURE 8.14 Insert a Bookmark Hyperlink on a Web Page

a. Display the Worksheets page, if necessary. Place the insertion point on the left side of the first table heading, *Fractions and Exponents*.

This table describes the variety of worksheets that are available on the A Math Tutoring Club Web site. Make sure that you do not select *Fractions and Exponents* in the bulleted list.

b. Click **Bookmark** in the Web group, type **Fractions_and_Exponents** in the **Bookmark name box**, and then click **Add**.

> **TROUBLESHOOTING:** If you did not type the underscores, the Add button will not display and you cannot add this bookmark to the Web page. Remember that special characters such as hyphens are not allowed in bookmarks. If you forgot to type the underscore for *Fractions and Exponents*, you will need to recreate the bookmark to meet your specifications, if necessary. Besides underscore, you may choose to use CamelCase notation to replace the hyphenated terms. For instance, you may type PreCalculus to replace Pre-Calculus and PreAlgebra to replace Pre-Algebra.

c. Repeat step b to create bookmarks at the beginning of the table headings that display down the page for *Geometry*, *Pre-Algebra*, and *Pre-Calculus*. The bookmarks should be named to match table heading names. Remember to use the underscore to replace the hyphen (-) sign in Pre-Calculus and Pre-Algebra.

d. Press **Ctrl+Home** to view the top of the page. Select **Fractions and Exponents** in the bulleted list and click **Hyperlink** from the Web group on the myTab tab.

The Insert Hyperlink dialog box displays. You will select the bookmark to create a link from the words *Fractions and Exponents* to the location in the document where the subtopics for Fractions and Exponents display.

e. Click **Place in This Document** in the *Link to* panel of the Insert Hyperlink dialog box. If necessary, click the **plus sign (+)** next to *Bookmarks*. Click **Fractions_and_Exponents** and click **OK**.

Fractions and Exponents displays as a hyperlink and the text color changes to blue.

f. Hover your mouse over the *Fractions and Exponents* hyperlink and view the ScreenTip that displays the name of the bookmark and *Ctrl+Click to follow link*. Press **Ctrl** and click the hyperlink to move the insertion point to the listing of *Fractions and Exponents*.

The page scrolls so the heading Fractions and Exponents displays near the top of the screen, and the insertion point moves as well. This simplifies navigation on the page. Additionally, the color of the hyperlink changes as a visual indication that it has been clicked.

g. Repeat steps d and e to create hyperlinks from each bulleted list item, with the exception of Tutoring Services, to the corresponding bookmark for that item.

h. Select the text *Return to Top* that displays below the *Fractions and Exponents* table. Click **Hyperlink** in the Web group, click **Top of the Document** that displays at the very top of the *Select a place in this document* list, and then click **OK**.

This bookmark to the top of the page is created automatically when you save the document as a Web page. When you click this link, the page scrolls to the very top and displays the page heading. This enables you to return to the top of the page after you view content at the bottom of the page.

i. Repeat step h to create a hyperlink from each occurrence of *Return to Top* that displays below each skill table.

j. Save the Web page.

STEP 5 ≫ INSERT HYPERLINKS AND A HORIZONTAL LINE

Your last modification is the addition of hyperlinks to other pages. You want the viewer to have the ability to click from one page to another in this site with ease, so you add hyperlinks on each page that link to the others. Refer to Figure 8.15 as you complete Step 5.

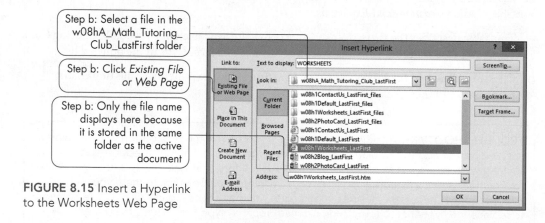

FIGURE 8.15 Insert a Hyperlink to the Worksheets Web Page

a. Click **w08h1Default_LastFirst.htm** on the task bar to display the default Web page. Scroll to the bottom, select **Worksheets** (fourth column in the 1-row table), right-click to display the shortcut menu, and then click **Hyperlink** to display the Insert Hyperlink dialog box.

b. Click **Existing File or Web Page** in the *Link to* panel of the Insert Hyperlink dialog box. Scroll, if necessary, and click the *w08h1Worksheets_LastFirst.htm* file. Click **OK**.

By creating this link, the Worksheets page displays when you click Worksheets on the home page.

c. Repeat step b to create a hyperlink from *Contact Us* on the default page to the w08h1ContactUs_LastFirst.htm Web page. Click **Save** in the Quick Access Toolbar.

You will create a link for *Resources* using the Web page to be created in a future exercise.

d. Click **w08h1ContactUs_LastFirst.htm** on the task bar to display the ContactUs Web page. Complete the following steps to create a link to the default page:

- Press **Ctrl+End** and press **Enter**.
- Type **Return to the Home Page**
- Select the text *Return to the Home Page* and click **Hyperlink** in the Web group on the myTab tab.
- Select *w08h1Default_LastFirst.htm* and click **OK**.

e. Press **Enter** two times to move the insertion point below the hyperlink. Click **Horizontal Line** in the Web group and an orange-colored wavy line displays right below the *Return to the Home Page* link.

Now you have a second wavy line in the document that matches the graphic that displays below the heading.

f. Click **Save** on the Quick Access Toolbar.

g. Click **w08h1Worksheets_LastFirst.htm** on the task bar to display the Worksheets Web page. Press **Ctrl+End** and press **Enter** one time. Type **Return to the Home Page**, select the text you just typed, and then click **Hyperlink**. Select *w08h1Default_LastFirst.htm* and click **OK**.

The ContactUs and Worksheets pages now include a link back to the home page of the Web site.

h. Click **Save** on the Quick Access Toolbar. Minimize all documents.

STEP 6 ≫ PREVIEW A WEB PAGE

With your changes and edits complete, you decide to take a look at the final Web pages. All files are saved in the w08hA_Math_Tutoring_Club_LastFirst folder, so you can open and preview them from within a Web browser. If everything looks acceptable, you will later send them to the company that will host the Web site. Refer to Figure 8.16 as you complete Step 6.

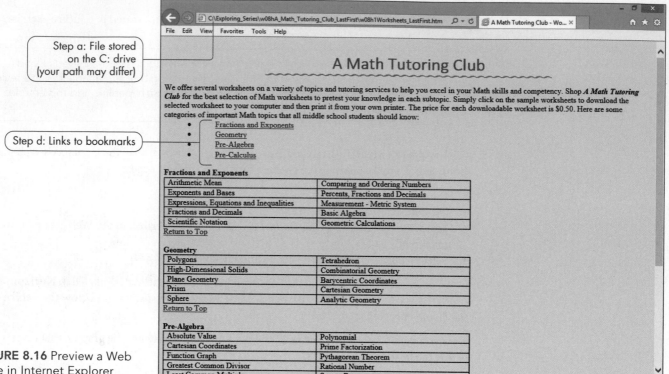

FIGURE 8.16 Preview a Web Page in Internet Explorer

a. Click the **w08h1Default_LastFirst.htm Web page** on the task bar. Click the **myTab tab** and click **Web Page Preview** in the Web group.

   The Web browser window opens and the page displays. Look closely at the components of the URL in the Address bar, reading from right to left. You are viewing the *w08h1Default_LastFirst.htm* document, which is stored in the w08hA_Math_Tutoring_Club_LastFirst folder, which, in turn, is probably stored in one or more folders that are stored on the hard drive (C:). That means you are viewing the site locally, as opposed to seeing it on the Web. Next, you will open and view a page from within the Web browser. If your default Web browser is not Internet Explorer, you can adjust the instructions as needed for your preferred browser.

b. Press **Ctrl+O** with the Web browser open to display the Open dialog box of your Web browser. Click **Browse**, navigate to the w08hA_Math_Tutoring_Club_LastFirst folder, and then double-click *w08h1ContactUs_LastFirst.htm*. Click **OK** in the Open dialog box to display the page.

> **TROUBLESHOOTING**: If the menu bar does not display in Internet Explorer, right-click anywhere in the toolbar area and click Menu Bar. You can also use this same procedure to remove the toolbar. If you do not want to display the menu bar, press Alt+F to display the menu on a temporary basis.

c. Click the **Return to Home Page link** to make sure it works properly.

   The home page, *w08h1Default_LastFirst.htm*, displays.

d. Click the **Worksheets page hyperlink** at the bottom on the home page. Once the Worksheets page displays, click the hyperlinks to navigate from top to bottom and back to top.

You are now in the Worksheets page. When you click each of the hyperlinks in this page, the hyperlinks will bring you to the place where you inserted the bookmarks.

e. Click **Return to the Home Page** to verify the link to the default page works.

You are now back to your home page, *w08h1Default_LastFirst.htm*.

f. Exit your Web browser.

All your opened Web pages in the Web browser will be closed automatically.

g. Click any of the Word documents. Close all the documents (*w08h1Default_LastFirst.htm*, *w08h1Worksheets_LastFirst.htm*, and *w08h1ContactUs_LastFirst.htm*) and exit Word.

h. Open File Explorer and navigate to the w08hA_Math_Tutoring_Club_LastFirst folder. Select all the files and subfolders in this folder, right-click to display the shortcut menu, click **Send to**, and then select **Compressed (zipped) folder**.

All the selected files and subfolders in the w08hA_Math_Tutoring_Club_LastFirst folder are now contained in a zipped file.

i. Select the zipped file name and rename it **w08h1A_Math_Tutoring_Club_LastFirst**. Submit your zipped file based on your instructor's directions.

Notice that you rename the folder with *h1* instead of *h*. This way, your instructor will know that this solution file is for Hands-On Exercise 1. When your instructor downloads the zipped file onto his or her computer, he or she can view all the Web pages that you have created for this exercise using a Web browser.

Web Page Enhancement

Electronic communication and data sharing are common, if not critical, today. People create electronic documents and Web pages and distribute them all over the world using many types of devices such as smartphones, tablets, and computers. The latest release of the Microsoft Office suite was accompanied by a variety of online tools that allow you to work on your own computer or on the cloud via Microsoft's SkyDrive cloud integration technology. Besides the traditional Office 2013 installed on desktop or laptop computers, its online counterpart—Office 365—is available for business or home use via Microsoft cloud services, based on a user subscription. Social media services are made easier when you can quickly post your blog or tweet directly from Word. You can also share and collaborate on your work with anyone, including friends, family, and co-workers, in real time, from wherever you are. By posting any of your Office documents to a virtual storage location, such as Microsoft's SkyDrive account, or to your office's SharePoint work site, you have easy and quick access to them using smartphones, desktop computers, or tablets, across platforms, and without losing any of the Office features or formats. You can even link your non-Microsoft accounts, such as Flickr and YouTube, to your SkyDrive account. When you save your document to SkyDrive, it will also automatically save a copy to your hard drive. If you do not have network access at that point, all changes are automatically synced back to SkyDrive once you are online again.

In this section, you will learn how to create online blogs using the Word blog template, collaborate online with your teammates, save a blank design Word template as a Web page, and embed online pictures and video clips to enhance your Web page.

Creating a Blog Post

Everyone has the ability to post information on the Internet about themselves, their thoughts, their interests, or simply whatever they want to make public. The chronological publication of personal thoughts and Web links is called a *blog*. The term *blog* is derived from the phrase *Web log*, which refers to publishing personal information on the Web. Blogs can provide a vehicle to display the works of current or future journalists and authors, or they can simply reflect the emotions and ideas of an individual at a particular point in time.

Download a Blog Template

STEP 1 » One exciting feature of Word is the Blog post template. These templates benefit users who are accustomed to working in Word, but who also publish blogs on a frequent basis. To download a blog template, do the following:

1. Click the FILE tab.
2. Click New.
3. Type blog in the *Search online templates* search box and press Enter.
4. Click the *Blog post* template.
5. Click Create to download the blog template.
6. Click Register Later in the *Register a Blog Account* dialog box. You will be prompted for this information again the first time you post.

When you open the blog post template, the window looks different because the seven tabs on the Ribbon that you are accustomed to viewing are replaced with only tabs that will provide commands you need to complete the blog post. The Blog Post tab contains commands you use to format text, but also commands that enable you to publish your blog directly to the host server for your blog, as shown in Figure 8.17. The Insert tab displays commands for items you might include in your blog, such as tables, illustrations, hyperlinks, WordArt, and symbols.

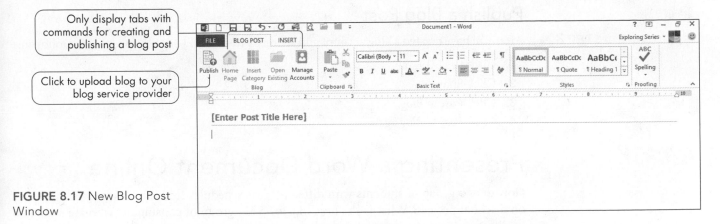

Only display tabs with commands for creating and publishing a blog post

Click to upload blog to your blog service provider

FIGURE 8.17 New Blog Post Window

[Enter Post Title Here]

Create and Set Up a Blog Account

Before you can publish your blog posts, you must have a blog account with one of the several blog service providers. To learn about and find service providers, visit the Microsoft Office Marketplace, perform an Internet search, or ask your friends which service they use. Word supports several blogging sites, including, but not limited to, the following:

- SharePoint Blog
- WordPress
- Blogger
- Telligent Community
- TypePad

Once you have an established blog account with a blog service provider, you can register and publish blogs directly from Word. Click Manage Accounts in the Blog group on the Blog Post tab, and click New in the Blog Accounts dialog box to view the New Blog Account dialog box. From this dialog box, the blog registration wizard prompts you for the service provider information and configures Word to enable you to post your blog directly from Word. If you use a service not listed, you can click Manage Accounts, click New, click Other in the Blog list, click Next, and then type the account information, your user name, and your password. You can register several blog accounts in Word. After they are registered, you can use the Manage Accounts command to change, delete, and set one account as your default blog location.

Include Pictures in a Blog Posting

Some blogs include pictures. Even though they display with the blog post, pictures are stored in a file separate from the blog text. The file that stores the blog text includes a link to the path where the picture is stored. Your blog service provider might supply storage space for images, or you might have a completely different service provider for images. In the New Account dialog box, you can click Picture Options and specify the picture provider location where you store your images that display with the blog.

TIP | **Image Provider Considerations**

If you sign up for an account with an image provider, pay special attention to the terms and conditions for using the service. Some free services might impose a limit on the maximum size of files, total amount of storage, or the types of files you are allowed to store.

Publish a Blog Post

STEP 3》 After you have created a blog account and are ready to publish your blog post, do the following:

1. Click the FILE tab.
2. Click Share.
3. Click *Post to Blog*.
4. Click *Post to Blog* again.

Presenting a Word Document Online

How does a group of students with different class schedules find the time to work together on a school project? What is the best way for a big group of consultants who are stationed in different locations or countries to work together on a request for proposal? What is an effective way that small business owners can present their products or services to potential clients? The Share feature in the Backstage view of Word 2013 enables users to present their Word document online to their target audience. You can use any interactive communication channel, such as Instant Messaging and Skype, to conduct a real-time collaboration with other people. If you have a Microsoft account and Microsoft Office 2013, you can use the Office Presentation Service for free.

Collaborate on a Word Document Online

After you work on your document and you are ready to submit and present it online, do the following:

1. Click the FILE tab.
2. Click Share and you will see the following four options:
   a. Invite People—click to invite and add colleagues, team members, and friends to view and/or work with you online.
   b. Email—click to e-mail your Word document to other people.
   c. Present Online—click to share the link with remote viewers and to start your online presentation.
   d. Post to Blog—click to post your document to a blog service.
3. Click Present Online to open the Present Online dialog box, as shown in Figure 8.18.
4. Click Copy Link to copy and paste the meeting invitation's hyperlink so that your selected viewers can have access to it, or click *Send in Email* if you prefer to send the meeting hyperlink instead.
5. Click Start Presentation when you are ready to start your online presentation. When your audience is ready to watch the presentation, he or she will click the hyperlink and the attached document will display in a Web browser or Skype chat window. Microsoft Office applications are not needed to view the presentation.

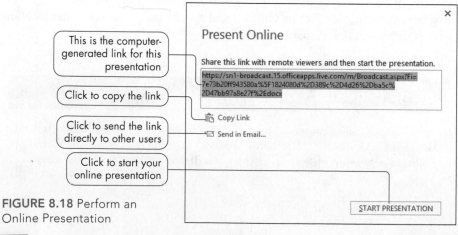

FIGURE 8.18 Perform an Online Presentation

Edit a Word Document Online

During the online presentation, you can quickly and easily make any editorial changes to the document without ending the presentation. When you click Edit in the Present Online group, you will switch into the edit mode as shown in Figure 8.19. You will resume the presentation after you have completed your editing by clicking the Resume Online Presentation button. The attendees can also receive the updated document instantly. If you want to allow attendees to download the document, simply select the *Enable remote viewers to download the document* check box when you start the presentation. You can also share meeting notes with an audience, which can be a particular page or a section of a whole document. You can also create a new document.

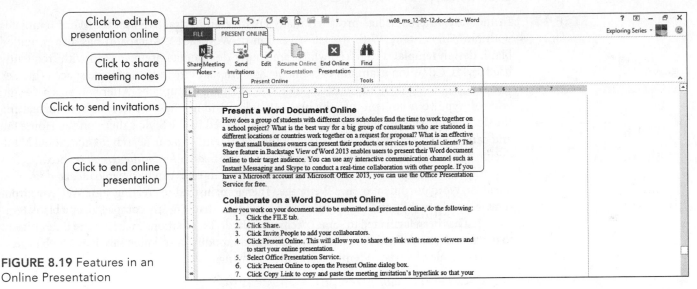

FIGURE 8.19 Features in an Online Presentation

The targeted audience can review the document independently on any electronic devices and at their own time and own pace. A temporary alert and the status bar located at the bottom of the Word document indicate that the reader is no longer following the presenter. The reader can go back to the same place that the presenter is presenting by clicking the Follow Presenter button, as shown in Figure 8.20.

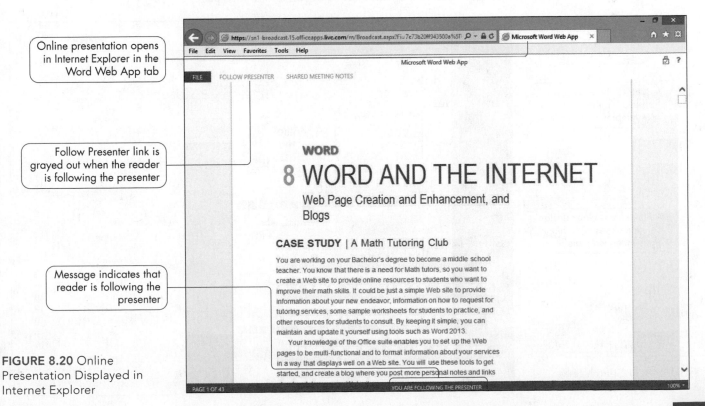

FIGURE 8.20 Online Presentation Displayed in Internet Explorer

Enhancing a Web Page

Besides the professional-looking templates, Microsoft has also provided blank design templates in Word. While Office applications have always made it easy to insert graphics and other assets into documents, Office 2013 is the first version to allow online sources of photos and videos to be embedded into the documents. This is a time saver, and it also allows you to find the items that you need in the places that you often search.

Download a Design Template and Save as a Document or Web Page

STEP 4 » In the past, Microsoft has provided many creative and attractive looking Word templates with built-in content. With the latest version of Word 2013, Microsoft has also provided blank design templates to users, which are empty documents preformatted with frequently used styles. Common examples of blank design templates include the Single spaced (blank), Report design (blank), and Classic double spaced (blank) templates. After you pick a design, you will type your content into the blank template and not have to worry about formatting the document. The predefined heading styles are saved in the Style gallery on the Home tab and can be easily applied to the content of the document. You can search for additional blank design templates by clicking Blank located under the *Search for online templates* box.

Any of the professionally created or blank design templates can be downloaded and saved as a regular Word document or as a Web page. Therefore, instead of creating your Web page from scratch, you have the option of downloading a template that is nearly completed, or a blank template that has been formatted to some specific standards. Both options make it more time efficient to download a predefined template from Office.com, modify it, and then save it as a Web page.

To download a design template, do the following:

1. Click the FILE tab.
2. Click New.
3. Click Blank under the *Search online templates* box to see results as shown in Figure 8.21.
4. Click the thumbnail of the template you want to download.
5. Click Create to download the template.
6. Save the template as a Word document or Web page.

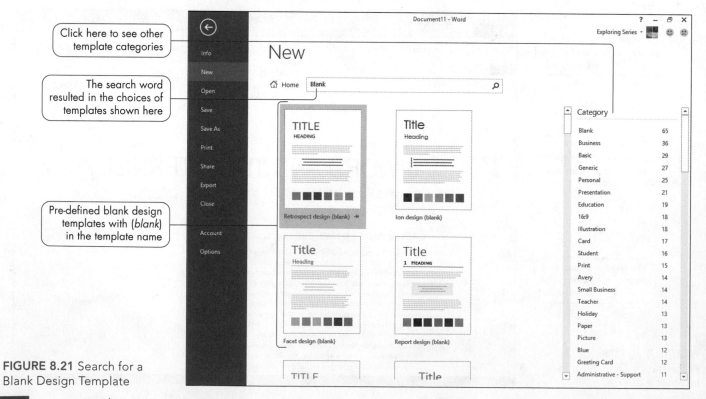

FIGURE 8.21 Search for a Blank Design Template

Insert Online Photos onto a Web Page

STEP 5 ▶▶ For many years, users have been storing their photo albums and video clips on hard drives, CD-ROM, or portable drives. Office 2013 now allows users to insert photos and pictures into a document directly from an online service without having to first download and save the files to a hard drive. Some of the popular online sites where you can obtain or store photos include, but are not limited to, Office.com, Bing Image Search, Flickr, SkyDrive, and Facebook. Sign in to your SkyDrive account to add other accounts and upload photos. You can see a live preview while you resize and move photos and images in your document. The new alignment guides make it easier for you to arrange images such as tables, charts, photos, and diagrams with your text. The Object zoom feature will enlarge the image when you double-click it to zoom in, making sure that the selected image displays in full screen. Click the image to zoom back to the regular size. If you want to add your photos from other sources to your SkyDrive account so that you can access the photos online, do the following:

1. Click the INSERT tab.
2. Click Online Pictures in the Illustrations group.
3. Click the *Also insert from* button in the bottom-left corner of the Insert Pictures dialog box.
4. Click Connect in the *All your photos in one place* dialog box.
5. Sign in to any of your online accounts, such as Flickr or Yahoo.
6. Click Done. You will be connected to your online account.
7. Check to make sure that your selected online account is added to the Insert Pictures dialog box, as shown in Figure 8.22.
8. Click your newly added account to access your photos.
9. Click Insert after you have selected the photos that you want.

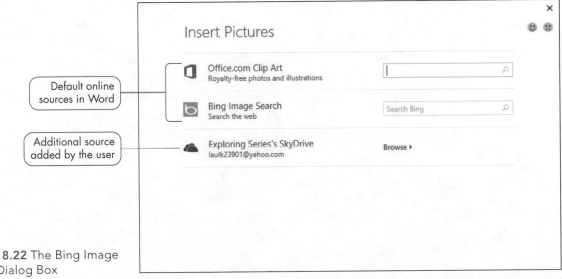

FIGURE 8.22 The Bing Image Search Dialog Box

When you access photos from public sites such as Flickr or Bing Image Search, most of the online photos are subject to Creative Commons licensing, as shown in Figure 8.23. It is very important that you review the specific license for any image to ensure that you comply with the copyright guidelines. Creative Commons is a nonprofit organization located in Mountain View, California, that allows users to share the use of creativity and knowledge through free legal tools. By signing a simple, standardized, copyright license, you give the public the permission to use your creative work under conditions stipulated by you. You can also easily change your copyright terms at any time. Usually, you can use the images for free if it is for personal use. However, you should review the specific license for any image if you want to use it for business or commercial purposes.

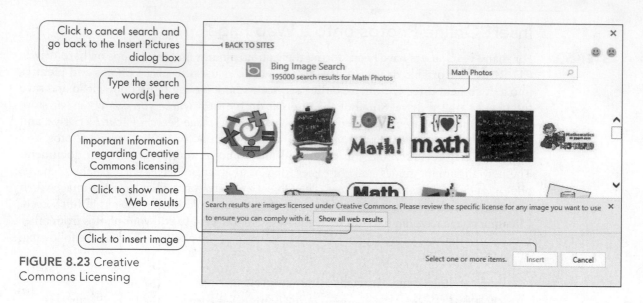

Click to cancel search and go back to the Insert Pictures dialog box

Type the search word(s) here

Important information regarding Creative Commons licensing

Click to show more Web results

Click to insert image

FIGURE 8.23 Creative Commons Licensing

Insert Online Videos onto a Web Page

STEP 6 » One of the most exciting features in Word 2013 is the ability to search and embed online video clips from Web sources, such as YouTube and Bing Video Search, into Office documents and to view the video directly within the context of the document itself. When you do not have to leave your open document to go to another window, you can stay focused on the content itself. From the Insert tab, click Online Video in the Media group. The Insert Video dialog box will appear, and you will have instant access to online video sources such as Bing Video Search, SkyDrive, or YouTube, or you can embed video HTML code manually into the document. You can enlarge the video easily by clicking the embedded item. Figure 8.24 shows a video clip embedded in this Word document. To search for and insert a video into a Web page, do the following:

1. Click the INSERT tab.
2. Click Online Video in the Media group.
3. In the Insert Video dialog box, you may do one of the following:
   a. Type the key search word(s) in the Bing Video Search box and press Enter.
   b. Type the embed code in the *From a Video Embed Code* box and press Enter.
4. Click Insert to insert the video into the document.

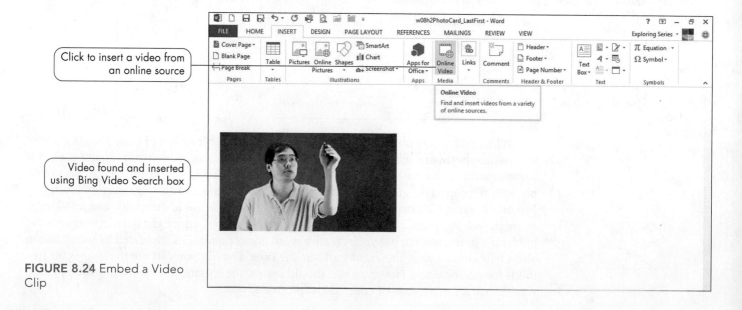

Click to insert a video from an online source

Video found and inserted using Bing Video Search box

FIGURE 8.24 Embed a Video Clip

TIP **Watching an Online Video in a Word Document**

Although an online video clip is embedded into the document, it is not stored on your hard drive. Therefore, you still need to have Internet access to watch the video. Certain Web browsers work better with online videos than others, so you might need to change your default Web browser.

Quick **Concepts**

1. What is the purpose of writing a blog? *p. 186*

2. What are the advantages of presenting a Word document online? *p. 188*

3. Describe the reasons for using a blank design Word template. *p. 190*

4. Why do you want to store your photos online? *p. 191*

5. What are the advantages of embedding a video into a Word document? *p. 192*

Hands-On Exercises

2 Web Page Enhancement

The Web pages for *A Math Tutoring Club* are businesslike, and their purpose is to display information about the math worksheets and online resources that you provide. However, you enjoy a personal relationship with your students and often chat with them about their learning process. You want to start a blog to post some of the conversations and ideas you share with your students, hoping that your students can enjoy them as well. Also, you were very happy with the simple Web site that you built, and you want to present your math tutoring services to a larger group of participants. One of the things you had considered to enhance the Web page is to include a photo page, as well as conceptual and instructional videos that show students how to think critically and solve math problems. You will download a photo template to insert an online photo and to embed an online video. Then you will save the design template, first as a Word document and then as a Web page. Don't forget to link your PhotoCard page back to the home page and also to put the PhotoCard link on the home page. Once the process is complete, you will preview your Web pages using a Web browser.

Skills covered: Create and Set Up a Blog Account • Write a Blog Entry • Publish a Blog Post • Download a Design Template and Save as a Word Document • Insert an Online Photo • Insert an Online Video Clip • Save as a Single File Web Page and Preview Web Page

---

STEP 1 ≫ CREATE AND SET UP A BLOG ACCOUNT

In order to create a blog for the business, you must first set up an account with a service provider. You decide to use Blogger because it is one of the biggest blog providers on the Internet. Refer to Figure 8.25 as you complete Step 1.

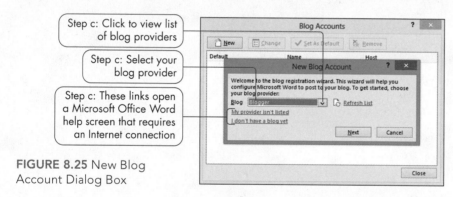

FIGURE 8.25 New Blog Account Dialog Box

a. Start Word. Type **blog** in the *Search online templates* box and press **Enter**. Click the **Blog post template**. Click **Create** to download the blog template. If a *Register a Blog Account* dialog box appears, click **Register Later**.

A new document opens and the Ribbon contains only three tabs: File, Blog Post, and Insert. You might see more tabs if you install programs that create their own tabs or if you created your own custom tabs such as the myTab created in Hands-On Exercise 1. A placeholder prompts you to type the title of your post, and the insertion point is below the horizontal line, ready for you to create your post.

b. Click **Manage Accounts** in the Blog group on the BLOG POST tab. Click **New**.

c. Click the **Blog arrow** in the New Blog Account dialog box. Click **Blogger** and click **Next**.

If you have a different blog service provider, you should click the arrow, select that provider, and then type your personal identification and password in the next step. If you do not have an account with a blog service provider, you can create an account and return to this exercise or read through these steps and continue with Step 2. If you have a Gmail account, you can use the same logon and password to log on to Blogger.

d. Type your blog service user name in the **User Name box**. Type your blog service password in the **Password box**. Click **OK**.

If you have a Google account, you can use the same user name and password for your Google account to log on to your Blogger account.

e. Click **OK** when the Picture Options dialog box displays.

If you have a picture provider, you can click the Picture Provider arrow and select *My own server*. After you choose that option, boxes display where you type the Web address (URL) for the location where you upload your pictures and where the pictures are stored. In this exercise, we will not specify a picture provider.

f. Click **Yes** to the Microsoft Office Word dialog box that tells you a possibility exists that the information you send to your blog service provider could be seen by other people.

The information that passes from Word to your blog service provider is not encrypted, and this does provide the possibility of information being intercepted; however, this possibility is very small.

g. Select your blog in the *Choose a Blog* dialog box and click **OK**. Click **OK** to the Microsoft Office Word dialog box that indicates your account registration was successful.

When you register a blog service successfully, the service will display in the Blog Accounts dialog box.

h. Click **Close** in the Blog Accounts dialog box.

STEP 2 ≫ WRITE A BLOG ENTRY

Now it is time for you to start posting information that your students will enjoy viewing. You are going to write about the How to Learn Algebra I video clip presented by Mr. Jimmy Chang. You remember to use the Spell Check tool, which is an important resource to use before posting information publicly. Refer to Figure 8.26 as you complete Step 2.

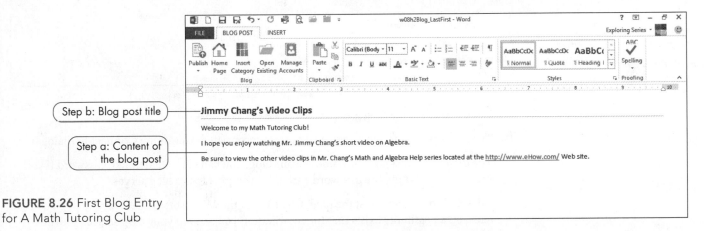

FIGURE 8.26 First Blog Entry for A Math Tutoring Club

a. Type the following text at the insertion point (below the title):

Welcome to my Math Tutoring Club!

I hope you enjoy watching Mr. Jimmy Chang's short video on Algebra.

Be sure to view the other video clips in Mr. Chang's Math and Algebra Help series located at the http://www.ehow.com/ Web site.

After you type the Web site address, notice that it will automatically turned into a hyperlink.

b. Click the placeholder *Enter Post Title Here* and type **Jimmy Chang's Video Clips**. Click anywhere in the document to deselect the post title you just typed.

c. Click **Spelling** in the Proofing group on the Blog Post tab. When spell check is complete, click **OK**.

d. Click the **FILE tab**, click **Save As**, click **Browse** to navigate to the w08hA_Math_Tutoring_Club_LastFirst folder, and then type **w08h2Blog_LastFirst** in the **File name box**. Click **Save** to keep a copy of the post until you are ready to publish.

STEP 3 ≫ PUBLISH A BLOG POST

Now that you have completed the post, it is time to upload it to the Blogger site. You can publish the blog posts right from Word with only a few clicks! Once complete, you display your blog in an Internet Explorer window so you can see the final product. Refer to Figure 8.27 as you complete Step 3.

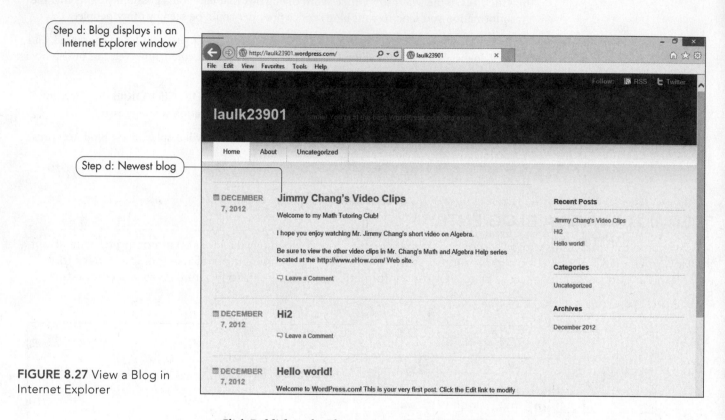

FIGURE 8.27 View a Blog in Internet Explorer

a. Click **Publish** in the Blog group on the BLOG POST tab.

b. Type your user name and password in the appropriate boxes in the Connect to dialog box.

The dialog box displays the name of your blog. You can click Remember Password if you want to avoid typing the password each time you post to the blog server.

c. Click **OK** to save and post the blog. Click **Yes** in the Microsoft Office Word dialog box that tells you a possibility exists that the information you send to your blog service provider could be seen by other people. Click **Don't show this message again** if you want to avoid clicking Yes at this dialog box each time you post a blog entry.

d. Click **Home Page** on the BLOG POST tab to display your blog in a separate Internet Explorer window.

e. Save and close the document. Exit Word. Submit based on your instructor's directions.

STEP 4 ≫ DOWNLOAD A DESIGN TEMPLATE AND SAVE AS A WORD DOCUMENT

Instead of creating a Web page from scratch, you want to take advantage of the design templates available to you. The blank templates, along with other sorted template categories, are available for easy retrieval. For this exercise, you will search Office.com for a photo template, and you will insert an online picture, a text box, and an online video clip. Refer to Figure 8.28 as you complete Step 4.

Step b: Click to download the template

Step b: Click to view the previous template

Step b: Click to view other pages included with the template

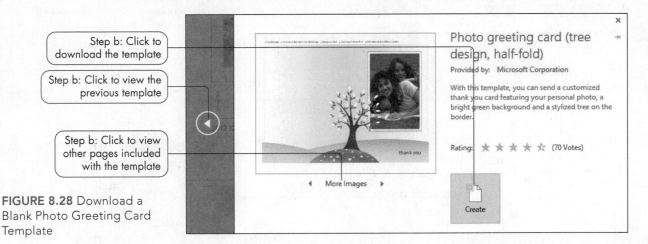

FIGURE 8.28 Download a Blank Photo Greeting Card Template

a. Start Word. Click the **FILE tab**, click **New**, click in the **Search online templates box**, and then type **Photo**.

You have already created several pages for your A Math Tutoring Club Web site. You will now search for a template to use to insert and display your photo instead of creating the Web page from scratch. In the next few steps, you will select and download a photo template, and save the document as a Web page in the Web folder.

b. Scroll down the middle pane template options, click **Photo greeting card (tree design, half-fold)**, and then click **Create** to download the template.

c. Click the **FILE tab**, click **Save As**, and then click **Browse**. Navigate to the w08hA_Math_Tutoring_Club_LastFirst folder.

This is the same folder where you had saved all the other Web pages in Hands-On Exercise 1. You need to save all your documents together in the same folder to keep yourself organized. It would also be easier if you need to upload or email all the Web pages to someone else in a zipped file.

d. Double-click the **w08hA_Math_Tutoring_Club_LastFirst folder** to open it.

TIP | Pin a Design Template

If you find a design template that you would like to use often, you can pin it to the Backstage view by clicking the *Pin to list* button so that it is always at the top portion of your template selection.

e. Type **w08h2PhotoCard_LastFirst** in the **File name box**. Make sure that it is saved as a Word document (.docx) file.

You want to save this file as a Word document file, and you will save it as a Web page later.

f. Click **Save** and click **OK** if a Microsoft Word message box appears to upgrade to the newest file format.

g. Leave the document open for the next step.

STEP 5 ›› INSERT AN ONLINE PHOTO

With a photo template page, you will replace the photo with one of your choice. You will delete the current photo, search for another photo online that is more appropriate for your Web page, and then insert it into the same placeholder. This process is made easy by the design layout that was predefined for you as a template. Refer to Figure 8.29 as you complete Step 5.

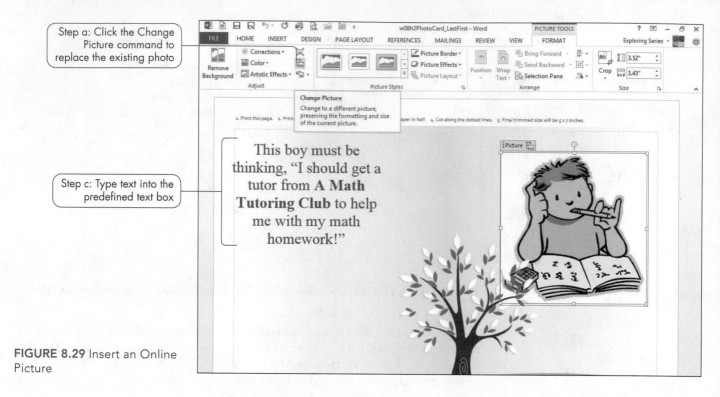

FIGURE 8.29 Insert an Online Picture

a. Insert a picture by completing the following steps:

- Click the photo located on the right side of the first page.
- Click the **FORMAT Tab** and click **Change Picture** in the Adjust group. Type **Math photo** in the **Bing Image Search box**. Press **Enter**.
- Review the list of photos and click the image of the little boy, as seen in Figure 8.29, to insert it into the document. If you do not find the same image that displays in Figure 8.29, you may substitute something different.
- Click **Insert** to insert the image into your document.

You searched for a photo from the Bing Image Search Web site. You can also search other online service photos, which include your own Flickr account.

b. Adjust the size of the image in the Size group of the FORMAT tab, if necessary.

c. Move the *thank you* box and insert your own text by doing the following:

- Select the text box on the second page. Right-click to display the shortcut menu and click **Cut**.
- Move up to the left side of the first page of the document. Press **Ctrl+V** to paste.
- Select the text in the text box and type: **This boy must be thinking, "I should get a tutor from A Math Tutoring Club to help me with my math homework!"**
- Select the text that you just typed and click **Times New Roman** and **26** on the mini toolbar. Select the text *A Math Tutoring Club* and click **Bold** from the mini toolbar.
- Click the **FORMAT tab** and click the **Shape Height arrow** in the Size group until *3.45"* displays.

d. Save the document.

STEP 6 ≫ INSERT AN ONLINE VIDEO CLIP

You know that many kids learn their math by watching someone teach them. So you want to insert an online instructional video on learning algebra in the PhotoCard Web page. You will search online for a video clip on algebra and insert the video onto the second page of the PhotoCard Web page. Refer to Figure 8.30 as you complete Step 6.

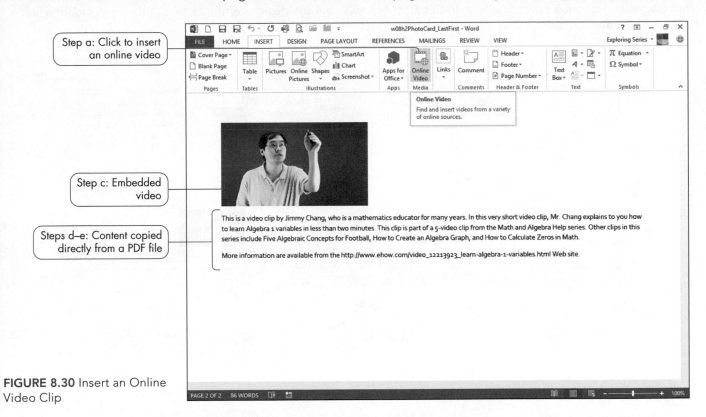

FIGURE 8.30 Insert an Online Video Clip

a. Delete the text box with a green gradient located at the top-left side on the second page. Click the **INSERT tab** and click **Online Video** in the Media group.

b. Type **How to Learn Algebra 1** in the **Bing Video Search box** and press **Enter**.

c. Click the first video, as illustrated in Figure 8.30, and click **Insert**.

You inserted the video from Bing Video Search into your document, but you could also insert a video clip that you created on your own. If you cannot find the same video as that illustrated in Figure 8.30, you may substitute a similar one.

d. Navigate to your student files and open the *w08h2JimmyChang.pdf* file. Press **Ctrl+A** to select all of the text, press **Ctrl+C** or right-click the selected text, and then click **Copy**. Close the PDF file without saving changes if prompted.

You are opening a PDF file in Word 2013, which allows you to open a PDF file without losing any of its formats. If you see a warning sign indicating that the PDF will be converting to an editable Word document, click **OK**.

e. Click **Word** on the task bar to display all the open documents. Click **w08h2PhotoCard_LastFirst**, press **Ctrl+End**, and then press **Enter**. Press **Ctrl+V** to paste.

You are copying the text from the PDF file to Word. If needed, format the text and image layout so that it is more presentable.

f. Save the document.

STEP 7 ►► SAVE AS A SINGLE FILE WEB PAGE AND PREVIEW WEB PAGE

After the video clip is embedded into your Word document, you are ready to save the document as a Web page so that viewers can watch the How to Learn Algebra I video clip from the Web page itself. Besides saving the design template as a Web page, you also want to put it in the w08hA_Math_Tutoring_Club folder together with the other Web pages and give it a new page title. In this step, you will save the design template as a Web page, create a link to the home page, and vice versa. Refer to Figure 8.31 as you complete Step 7.

Step b: Single File Web Page file extension

Step f: Web page showing the online photo and embedded video

Step h: *Return to Home Page* hyperlink

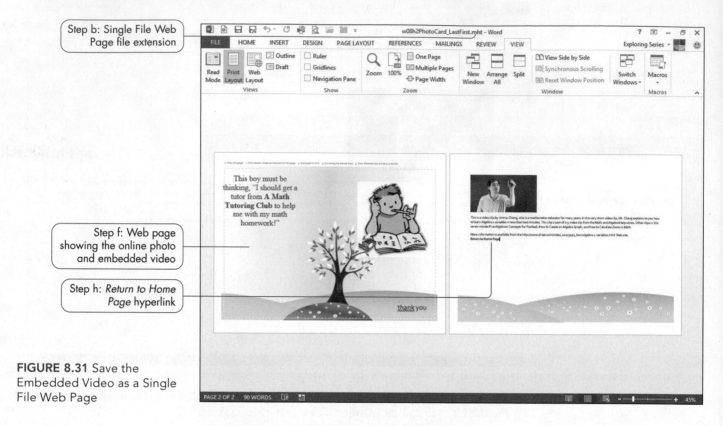

FIGURE 8.31 Save the Embedded Video as a Single File Web Page

a. Click the **FILE tab**, click **Save As**, and then click **Browse**.

b. Navigate to the drive and the w08hA_Math_Tutoring_Club_LastFirst folder in the Save As dialog box to save the file. You will save the document with the same name. Click the **Save as type arrow** and click **Single File Web Page (*.mht; *.mhtml)**.

   When you save as a Web page, the Save As dialog box displays the *Page title* text area and the Change Title button.

c. Click **Change Title** to display the Enter Text dialog box and change the title to **A Math Tutoring Club - Photo Card**. Click **OK**.

   In this dialog box, you can edit the Web page title, which will also appear on the Web browser's title bar when the Web page displays.

d. Click **Save**. If necessary, click **Continue** when you see a dialog box telling you that each video will be converted to an image with a link.

   The page displays in Web Layout view.

TIP Saving an Embedded Video document as a Web Page

If you intend to embed an online video to a Word document or template, you must insert the video *before* you save it as a Web page. Once you save a document or template as a Web page, this immediately disables the Online Video button.

e. Open the *w08h1Default_LastFirst* Web page and save it as **w08h2Default_LastFirst** by changing *h1* to *h2*.

f. Create a link to the home page by completing the following steps:

- Press **Ctrl+End**, press **Enter**, and then type **Return to the Home Page**.

  Pressing Ctrl+End brings you to the end of the image, and pressing Enter inserts a blank line for you to type text.

- Select the **Return to the Home Page text**, click the **INSERT tab**, click **Hyperlink** in the Links group to display the Insert Hyperlink dialog box.
- Click **Existing File or Web Page** in the *Link to* panel of the Insert Hyperlink dialog box. Scroll, if necessary, and click the **w08h2Default_LastFirst.htm file**. Click **OK**.

  By creating this link, the home page displays when you click *Return to the Home Page* on the PhotoCard page.

g. Create a link to the Photo Card page from the home page by completing the following steps:

- Click the *w08h2Default_LastFirst.htm* file on the task bar.
- Scroll to the bottom of the page, select **Resources** in the 1-row table, right-click, and then click **Hyperlink**.
- Click the *w08h2PhotoCard_LastFirst* Web page and press **OK**.

  You will see two *w08h2PhotoCard_LastFirst* files in this folder. One is a Word document and the other is a Web page. Make sure that you select the Web page file.

- Save the document.

  Now the home page has a link to the page that contains the photo and the embedded video clip.

h. Click the **myTab tab** and click **Web Page Preview** in the Web group to view the PhotoCard page in an Internet Explorer window. Click the **Return to Home Page hyperlink page** to navigate back to the home page. Close Internet Explorer.

> **TROUBLESHOOTING:** If you are using a Web Browser other than Internet Explorer, you might notice that the Position Object and Wrap Text features are disabled because they are not compatible with your Web browser. You may want to switch to Internet Explorer instead, which is more user-friendly with Word Web pages.

i. Go back to Word. Click the **FILE tab**, click **Options**, and then click **Customize Ribbon**. Uncheck **myTab tab** to reset the ribbon back to the default ribbon setting. Close all files and exit Word.

j. Open File Explorer and navigate to the w08hA_Math_Tutoring_Club_LastFirst folder. Select ALL of the files and subfolders in this folder, right-click to display the shortcut menu, click **Send to**, and then select **Compressed (zipped) folder**.

Make sure that all the selected files and subfolders in the w08hA_Math_Tutoring_Club_LastFirst folder are now contained in a zipped file. These files and folders include those that you created in Hands-on Exercise 1.

k. Highlight the zipped file name and rename it **w08h2A_Math_Tutoring_Club_LastFirst**. Submit your zipped file based on your instructor's directions.

Notice that you rename the file with *h2* instead of *h1*. This way your instructor will know that this solution file is for Hands-On Exercise 2. When your instructor downloads the zipped file onto his or her computer, he or she can view all the Web pages that you have created for this exercise using a Web browser.

Chapter Objectives Review

After reading this chapter, you have accomplished the following objectives:

1. **Customize the Ribbon.**
   - Create a custom tab: Create a custom tab for the Ribbon that contains only the features that you use most frequently or features that are not available on the standard Ribbon. You can also create new groups within the tab.
   - Add commands to a group: Besides changing the order of the tabs or the groups that appear within the tabs, you can also add commands that are not on the default tabs to a group in your personalized tab, and export and import custom tabs.

2. **Build and publish a Web page.**
   - Save as a Web page: Word provides all the tools necessary to create a basic Web page, converts the document, and generates the HTML (HyperText Markup Language) code for you. You can easily save a Word document as a Web Page to be published to the Internet to be accessed by anyone online.
   - Apply a theme and background color to a Web Page: A colored background adds visual enhancement to the Web page. Use the Word themes to coordinate colors and fonts.
   - Insert bookmarks in a Web page: A bookmark is an electronic marker for a specific location in a document, enabling the user to go to that location quickly. Bookmarks are helpful in long documents because they enable you to move easily from one place to another within that document, without having to manually scroll through the document.
   - Insert hyperlinks in a Web page: Hyperlinks are electronic markers that, when clicked, move the insertion point to a different location within the same document, open another document, or display a different Web page in a Web browser.
   - Preview a Web page: As you prepare a Web page, the Web Layout view gives you a very accurate representation of how the page will look when published. You can preview the page in an actual Web browser before you upload and publish it so that you can confirm it contains the correct content and is formatted to your specifications.
   - Publish a Web page: To view the pages on the Internet, you must save or publish them to a Web server, which is a computer system that hosts pages so that they are available for viewing by anyone who has an Internet connection.

3. **Create a blog post.**
   - Download a blog post template: A blog post template downloaded from Microsoft would be very beneficial to you if you are accustomed to working in Word and also publish blogs on a frequent basis.
   - Create and set up a Blog Account: You must establish a blog account with one of several blog service providers before you can register and publish blogs directly from Word.
   - Include pictures in a blog posting: Word 2013 allows you to post pictures with your blog. However, the pictures are stored in a separate file and can be accessed via a link on the blog text.
   - Publish a blog post: When you are ready, you can publish your blog post from Word by clicking the File tab, Share, and then *Post to Blog*.

4. **Present a Word document online.**
   - Collaborate on a Word document online: After you work on a document, you may collaborate on the work by uploading and sharing the document with others online.
   - Edit a Word document online: Besides sharing your document online with others, you can also make changes to the document instantly and in real time during your presentation.

5. **Enhance a Web page.**
   - Save a blank design Word template as a Web page: Blank design templates are empty documents preformatted with frequently used styles. It is more time efficient to use a predefined template and save it as a Web page.
   - Insert online photos onto a Web page: After you create your Web site, you can go a step further by enhancing it using features such as online photos from any of the online sources or from your own Flickr account.
   - Insert online videos onto a Web page: One of the new features in Word 2013 is the ability to insert and embed an online video into your Word or Web page so that your audience can view the video clips without having to leave the document page.

Key Terms Matching

Match the key terms with their definitions. Write the key term letter by the appropriate numbered definition.

a. Internet
b. World Wide Web (WWW)
c. Web page
d. HyperText Markup Language (HTML)
e. Background

f. Hyperlink
g. Web server
h. File Transfer Protocol (FTP)
i. Blog
j. Bookmark

1. _____ An electronic marker that points to a different location or displays a different Web page. **p. 174**

2. _____ A network of networks that connects computers anywhere in the world. **p. 166**

3. _____ Any document that displays on the World Wide Web. **p. 166**

4. _____ The chronological publication of personal thoughts. **p. 186**

5. _____ A process that uploads files from a PC to a server or from a server to a PC. **p. 176**

6. _____ An electronic marker for a specific location in a document. **p. 173**

7. _____ A color, design, image, or watermark that appears behind text in a document or on a Web page. **p. 172**

8. _____ A very large subset of the Internet that stores Web page documents. **p. 166**

9. _____ Uses codes to describe how a document appears when viewed in a Web browser. **p. 169**

10. _____ A computer system that hosts pages for viewing by anyone with an Internet connection. **p. 176**

Multiple Choice

1. While you are creating and editing documents that will be part of a Web site, you should save them in which format?

    (a) XML
    (b) HTML
    (c) Compatibility Mode
    (d) Text

2. Which of the following is not a legitimate object to use in a hyperlink?

    (a) Schema
    (b) E-mail address
    (c) Web page
    (d) Bookmark

3. What is the advantage of applying a theme to a Web page?

    (a) It adds a background color automatically.
    (b) It cannot be removed after you apply it.
    (c) It applies a uniform design to the links and other objects in a document.
    (d) It is automatically applied to each additional Web page you create.

4. If you view a Web page and hyperlinks display in two different colors, what is the most likely explanation?

    (a) A different theme was applied to each hyperlink.
    (b) One of the hyperlinks is invalid.
    (c) One of the hyperlinks was previously visited.
    (d) One of the hyperlinks is a bookmark.

5. Which of the following is not a format used to save documents as Web pages?

    (a) Web Template
    (b) Single File Web Page
    (c) Web Page
    (d) Web Page, Filtered

6. What information is relayed to the Web browser by HTML tags?

    (a) How to categorize the data on the Web page
    (b) How to save the information on the Web page
    (c) How to transfer the data to a Web server
    (d) How to format the information on the Web page

7. Which of the following statements about online video is not true?

    (a) Once it is embedded into a Web page, it can be viewed without Internet access.
    (b) To insert an online video, click Online Video in the Media group.
    (c) You can insert videos from YouTube.com directly onto your Word document.
    (d) You can manually insert the video HTML code into the Insert Video dialog box.

8. Which of the following statements about online presentations is not true?

    (a) The presenter can share notes with the audience.
    (b) The presenter can start or pause the online presentation at any time.
    (c) The audience must complete the viewing of the whole online presentation at one sitting.
    (d) The audience can retrieve updated documents instantly from the presenter.

9. What type of Web site enables you to view the frequent, chronological publication of personal thoughts?

    (a) Search engine
    (b) FTP
    (c) Web server
    (d) Blog

10. What feature should you change in order to display information about your Web site at the top of the Internet Explorer window?

    (a) XML element
    (b) File name
    (c) Page title
    (d) Document theme

Practice Exercises

1 Dave Meinert Realtors

Dave Meinert owns a large real estate company in New Orleans. The company offers a comprehensive list of services beyond the standard commercial and residential real estate sales and listings, including management of retirement community properties and commercial properties. Although the company is profitable, Dave realizes he should post information about the organization and its services on a Web site. He prefers to establish a very simple Web site in the beginning, and contract a Web site development professional to enhance the site if it generates a lot of business. Dave takes the following steps to turn a few basic Word documents into Web pages. This exercise follows the same set of skills as used in Hands-On Exercise 1 in the chapter. Refer to Figure 8.32 as you complete this exercise.

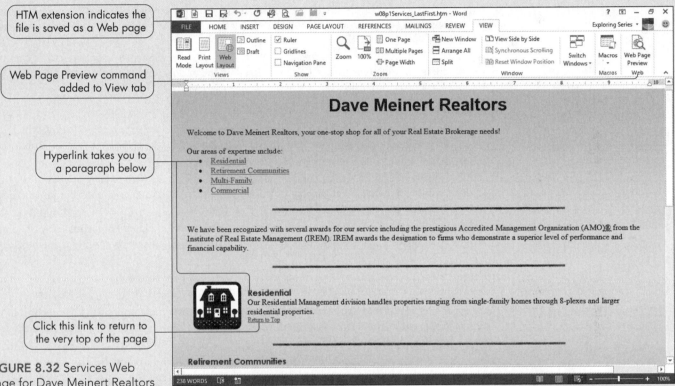

HTM extension indicates the file is saved as a Web page

Web Page Preview command added to View tab

Hyperlink takes you to a paragraph below

Click this link to return to the very top of the page

FIGURE 8.32 Services Web Page for Dave Meinert Realtors

a. Start Word and open *w08p1Default*.

b. Customize the Ribbon by completing the following steps:
- Click the **FILE tab**, click **Options**, and then click **Customize Ribbon**.
- Click the **VIEW tab** in the Main Tabs list on the right. Click **New Group** and click **Rename**. Type **Web** in the **Display name box** and click **OK**.
- Click the **Choose commands from arrow** and select **Commands Not in the Ribbon**.
- Scroll down and click **Web Page Preview**. Click **Add** to add the command to the Web group in the VIEW tab.
- Click **OK** to close the Word Options dialog box.

c. Click the **FILE tab**, click **Save As**, and then click **Browse**. In the Save As dialog box, navigate to the drive and folder in which you want to create a Web folder.

d. Create a folder and save the file as a Web page by completing the following steps:
- Click **New Folder** on the Save As dialog box toolbar, type **w08p1Realtor_LastFirst**, and then press **Enter**. Click **Open**.
- Type **w08p1Default_LastFirst** in the **File name box**. Click the **Save as type arrow** and click **Web Page (*.htm; *.html)**.
- Click **Change Title** to display the Enter Text dialog box. Type **Dave Meinert Real Estate** in the **Page title box** and click **OK**. Click **Save**.

e. Open *w08p1Services* and save it as a Web page named **w08p1Services_LastFirst** in the w08p1Realtor_LastFirst folder. Click **Change Title**, type **Dave Meinert Real Estate Services**, click **OK**, and then click **Save**.

f. Press **Alt+Tab** as needed to display the *w08p1Default_LastFirst* file. Select **Real Estate Services** and click **Hyperlink** in the Links group on the INSERT tab. Click **Existing File or Web Page** in the *Link to* panel of the Insert Hyperlink dialog box. Double-click the **w08p1Realtor_LastFirst folder**, if necessary, click the *w08p1Services_LastFirst.htm* file, and then click **OK**.

g. Apply themes and color to the pages by completing the following steps:
   - Click the **DESIGN tab**, click **Themes** in the Document Formatting group, and then click **Wisp**.
   - Click **Page Color** in the Page Background group. Click **Fill Effects** to display the Fill Effects dialog box and click the **Gradient tab**, if necessary.
   - Click **Two colors** in the *Colors* section. Click the **Color 1 arrow** and select **Orange, Accent 2, Lighter 80%** (second row, sixth column). Click the **Color 2 arrow** and select **Orange, Accent 2, Lighter 60%** (third row, sixth column).
   - Click **Horizontal** in the *Shading styles* section, if necessary. In the *Variants* section, click the square in the top-right corner. Click **OK** to apply the background.

h. Press **Ctrl+S** to save the changes to *w08p1Default_LastFirst.htm*.

i. Repeat step g to apply the theme and background color to the Services page.

j. Place the insertion point on the left side of the second instance of the word *Residential*, which displays as a heading for the paragraph on the Services page. Click the **INSERT tab**, click **Bookmark**, type **res** in the **Bookmark name box**, and then click **Add**.

k. Repeat step j to create bookmarks at the beginning of the headings *Retirement Communities*, *Multi-Family*, and *Commercial* that display down the page. The bookmarks should be named **retire**, **multi**, and **com** respectively.

l. Select **Residential** in the bulleted list near the top of the page and click **Hyperlink** from the Links group. Click **Place in This Document** in the *Link to* panel of the Insert Hyperlink dialog box. Click **res** under *Bookmarks* and click **OK**.

m. Repeat step l to create hyperlinks from each bulleted list item to the corresponding bookmarks retire, multi, and com for bulleted text *Retirement Communities*, *Multi-Family*, and *Commercial*.

n. Select the text *Return to Top* that displays below the *Residential* paragraph. Click **Hyperlink** in the Links group, click **Top of the Document**, which displays at the very top of the *Select a place in this document* list, and then click **OK**.

o. Repeat step n to create a hyperlink from each occurrence of *Return to Top* that displays throughout the Services page.

p. Click the **VIEW tab** and click **Web Page Preview** in the Web group to view the Services page in a Web browser window. Click the hyperlinks in the Services page to navigate up and down the page. Close your Web browser.

q. Save and close all pages. Open File Explorer and navigate to the w08p1Realtor_LastFirst folder. Select all the files and subfolders in this folder, right-click to display the shortcut menu, click **Send to**, and then select **Compressed (zipped) folder**.

r. Select the zipped file name and rename the zipped file **w08p1Realtor_LastFirst**. Submit your zipped file based on your instructor's directions.

2 Create a Blog Post

Jane Stone is participating in a study abroad program at Illinois State University this fall and will spend the semester in China. She is excited about the opportunities to learn about a different country, the people, the language, and the culture. She is also very happy that they do not have classes on Friday, so she can travel and see as much of the country as possible. Her parents are nervous about her time away and want her to write home as much as possible. Her friends are also eager to hear about her experiences. Jane decides the most convenient and efficient way to communicate with everyone is to post blog entries frequently. She can use Word 2013 on her laptop, which she will have with her most of the time, to quickly write and post the blog entries to Blogger—the blog she set up using her Google account. Jane will follow these steps to connect to her blog account and prepare the first entry. Jane can also post photos to her blog. This exercise follows the same set of skills as used in Hands-On Exercise 2 in the chapter. Refer to Figure 8.33 as you complete this exercise.

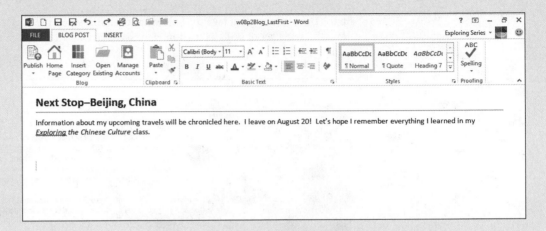

FIGURE 8.33 Blog Post for China Trip

a. Start Word. Type **blog** in the *Search online templates* box and press **Enter**. Click the **Blog post template**. Click **Create** to download the blog template. If the *Register a Blog Account* dialog box displays, click **Register Later**. If you do not have an account with a blog service provider, you can create an account and return to this exercise. If you have a blog account, continue with step b.

b. Click **Manage Accounts** in the Blog group on the BLOG POST tab. Click **New**. Click the **Blog arrow** in the New Blog Account dialog box. Click **Blogger** and click **Next**.

c. Type your blog service user name in the **User Name box**. Type your blog service password in the **Password box**. Click **OK**. Click **OK** when the Picture Options dialog box displays.

d. Click **Yes** in the Microsoft Office Word dialog box that tells you a possibility exists that the information you send to your blog service provider could be seen by other people.

e. Click **OK** in the Microsoft Office Word dialog box that indicates your account registration was successful. Click **Close** in the Blog Accounts dialog box.

f. Type the following text at the insertion point: **Information about my upcoming travels will be chronicled here. I leave on August 20! Let's hope I remember everything I learned in my Exploring the Chinese Culture class.** Select the text *Exploring the Chinese Culture* in the last sentence typed and click **Italic** from the mini toolbar.

g. Click the placeholder *Enter Post Title Here* and insert the text **Next Stop–Beijing, China**.

h. Click the **Spelling arrow** in the Proofing group on the BLOG POST tab.

i. Click the **FILE tab**, click **Save As**, and then navigate to the folder where you store solution files. Type **w08p2Blog_LastFirst** in the **File name box**. Click **Save** to keep a copy of the post until you are ready to publish.

j. Click **Publish** in the Blog group on the BLOG POST tab to publish this blog to your account, if you previously created one. Type your user name and password in the appropriate boxes in the Connect to dialog box.

k. Click **OK** to save and post the blog. Click **Yes** in the Microsoft Office Word dialog box that tells you a possibility exists the information you send to your blog service provider could be seen by other people. Click **Don't show this message again** if you want to avoid clicking Yes at this dialog box each time you post a blog entry.

l. Click **Home Page** on the BLOG POST tab to display the blog in a separate Web browser window.

m. Close the document. Submit it based on your instructor's directions.

1 FlyRight Airways Web Site

The marketing manager at a fledgling airline company is hosting a competition that awards a prize to the employee who designs the best home page for the company's Web site. A document that provides a description of the company is given to each person, and the information on that page should display in the final version. You take the following steps to develop the page you will submit. This exercise follows the same set of skills as used in Hands-On Exercise 1 in the chapter. Refer to Figure 8.34 as you complete this exercise.

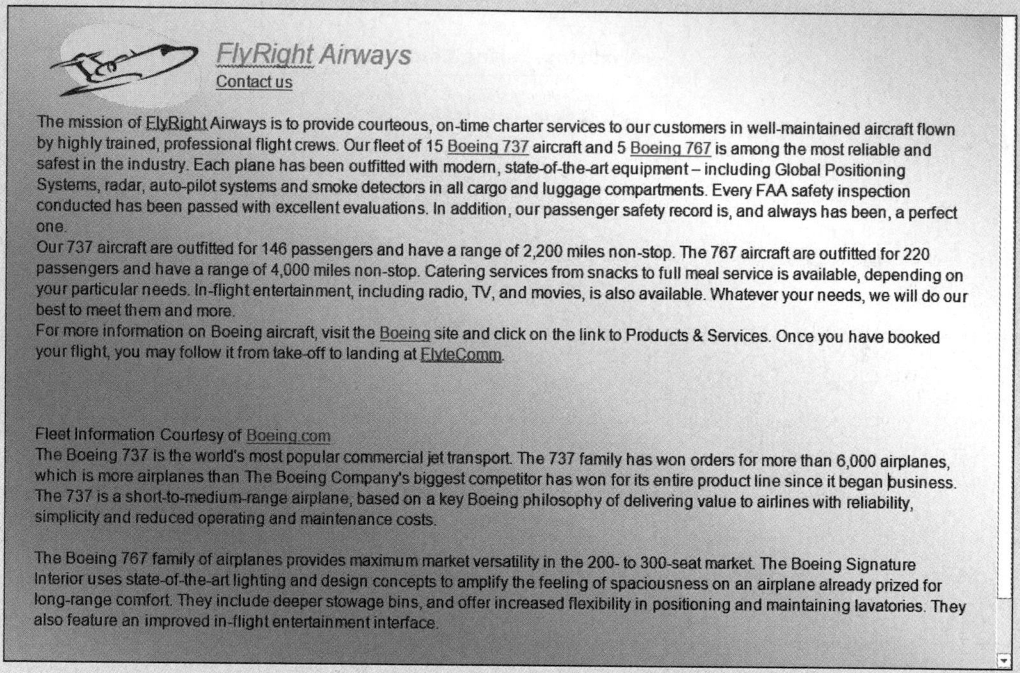

FlyRight Airways
Contact us

The mission of FlyRight Airways is to provide courteous, on-time charter services to our customers in well-maintained aircraft flown by highly trained, professional flight crews. Our fleet of 15 Boeing 737 aircraft and 5 Boeing 767 is among the most reliable and safest in the industry. Each plane has been outfitted with modern, state-of-the-art equipment – including Global Positioning Systems, radar, auto-pilot systems and smoke detectors in all cargo and luggage compartments. Every FAA safety inspection conducted has been passed with excellent evaluations. In addition, our passenger safety record is, and always has been, a perfect one.
Our 737 aircraft are outfitted for 146 passengers and have a range of 2,200 miles non-stop. The 767 aircraft are outfitted for 220 passengers and have a range of 4,000 miles non-stop. Catering services from snacks to full meal service is available, depending on your particular needs. In-flight entertainment, including radio, TV, and movies, is also available. Whatever your needs, we will do our best to meet them and more.
For more information on Boeing aircraft, visit the Boeing site and click on the link to Products & Services. Once you have booked your flight, you may follow it from take-off to landing at FlyteComm.

Fleet Information Courtesy of Boeing.com
The Boeing 737 is the world's most popular commercial jet transport. The 737 family has won orders for more than 6,000 airplanes, which is more airplanes than The Boeing Company's biggest competitor has won for its entire product line since it began business. The 737 is a short-to-medium-range airplane, based on a key Boeing philosophy of delivering value to airlines with reliability, simplicity and reduced operating and maintenance costs.

The Boeing 767 family of airplanes provides maximum market versatility in the 200- to 300-seat market. The Boeing Signature Interior uses state-of-the-art lighting and design concepts to amplify the feeling of spaciousness on an airplane already prized for long-range comfort. They include deeper stowage bins, and offer increased flexibility in positioning and maintaining lavatories. They also feature an improved in-flight entertainment interface.

FIGURE 8.34 FlyRight Airways Web site

a. Open *w08m1Airline* and save the document as a Single File Web page (*.mht; *.mhtml) using the name **w08m1Airline_LastFirst**.

b. Change the Page title to **Take off with FlyRight Airways**.

c. Customize the Ribbon to put the buttons you use most on one custom tab with groups. You can modify the myTab tab you created in Hands-On Exercise 1 or reset the Ribbon to its original state and create a new tab with groups.

d. Apply any theme to the page. Apply the **Intense Emphasis style** to the company name that displays at the top of the document and increase the font size to **20**. Use a different style if you do not find Intense Emphasis on your list of styles.

e. Apply a background color to the page. Use a Gradient Fill Effect that uses two colors. Use a Diagonal down shading style and select **variant effect** in the top-left corner.

f. Select the text *Contact us* that displays near the top of the document. Insert a hyperlink that links to the e-mail address *help@flyrightairways.org* and that contains the subject *Request for Information*.

g. Perform a Web search to find Web site addresses for the two companies mentioned—Boeing and FlyteComm—in the second paragraph. Create hyperlinks to those companies after you find their Web site addresses. The FlyteComm site enables you to track a flight from takeoff to landing.

h. Create bookmarks named **b737** and **b767** at the beginning of the paragraphs at the bottom of the page that describe the two types of aircraft. Create hyperlinks to these bookmarks from the text *Boeing 737* and *Boeing 767* that display in the first paragraph.

i. Save and close the document. Start File Explorer, navigate to the folder containing your Web page, and double-click the file you just created. A Web browser will start automatically because your document was saved as a Web page. Look carefully at the Address bar and note the local address, as opposed to a Web address. Test all links.

j. Close the Web browser. Submit the document based on your instructor's directions.

---

2 Introduce Myself Blog

CREATIVE CASE

FROM SCRATCH

You are enrolled in a social media marketing class at the local university. Companies often use popular social media tools such as Twitter, Facebook, MySpace, LinkedIn, apps, Youtube, Google+, and blogs to advertise products. Therefore, the first assignment in this marketing course is to "sell" yourself to your instructor and your classmates. Your instructor suggests that you use a blog to advertise your first product. You may write about your hobbies, interests, strengths, classes you are taking, and your career goals. Also, to put a face to a name, you need to insert a reasonably sized photo of yourself on a blog post. Since this is a marketing class, feel free to use any kind of Word features to spice up your blog posting. However, you need to remember that you are treading a very fine line in this assignment. On one hand, you want to present enough information to "sell" yourself, but on the other hand, you need to be careful not to reveal information that may be considered private. After all the blogs are posted, students will evaluate the blog postings and will vote on them using "likes" or "dislikes." Your grade for this assignment will be determined by the number of "likes" that you receive from the class.

 a. Download the blog post template and save it as **w08m2Blog_LastFirst**. If you do not have an account with a blog service provider, you can create an account and return to this exercise. If you have a blog account, continue with step b.

b. Write several paragraphs about yourself in your blog that you want others to know about you.

c. Use graphics or a table to tabulate data or information to present your case, if desired.

d. Insert a picture of yourself at the bottom of the blog page. Resize the picture to roughly 2" in height.

e. Type your last name and first name as the Post Title.

f. Proofread your blog entry by clicking the **Spelling arrow** in the Proofing group on the BLOG POST tab.

g. Publish your blog entry online.

h. Close the document. Submit it based on your instructor's directions.

---

3 A Politician Web Site

OLLABORATION CASE

FROM SCRATCH

One of the local politicians is a friend of the instructor of your Web Design class. He was looking for someone to create a Web site for him in order to convey pertinent information to the constituents. This Web site can also help to address important issues, collect suggestions and constructive feedback from citizens, provide local construction updates, and publicize social events. Your instructor divides the class into groups of several students and assigns this request as a class project to replace the final exam. Each group will design a Web site from scratch and will use all the Web design features described in this chapter. For instance, one of the appointed team members will customize the Ribbon to include a new tab and group with commands that the team will use frequently for this project. The Web site will include, but will not be limited to, the following pages:

- Home page with a welcome message from the politician and links to all the other pages
- *Important Issues* page to address pertinent concerns of the constituents
- *Local Updates* page
- *Social Events* page
- *Local Resources Available to Citizens* page
- *Contact Information* page

a. Use an online collaboration tool such as Google Chat or Skype to conduct an online meeting with your group members. During this online chat session, the group will do the following:
- Choose a name for the group and select a group leader.
- Develop a list of tasks to complete, which will include designing a story board and deciding on the number of Web pages.
- Assign tasks and responsibilities to each group member.

b. The team leader will create a SkyDrive or Dropbox.com account, where each member can share, download, and open the submitted documents.

c. Hand draw several Web pages, scan them, and save them as one image file with the name **w08m3WebDesign_LastFirst**. All the students' individual image files will be assembled into one zipped file and posted to the online storage location.

d. Meet online as a group to review all the designs and will decide on the final choice. Each group member, except the team leader, will be responsible for developing one or more Web pages.

e. The group leader will use tools such as Snipping tool, SnagIt, or the PRT SC button on your keyboard to capture the chat session at several stages and to record the contributions from team members. Copy and paste all the screenshots into a Word document and save it as **w08m3WebDiscussion_GroupName**. Make sure to add a caption to your screenshots.

f. After all the individual Web pages are uploaded to the virtual storage location, the group leader will assemble all the Web pages and test all the hyperlinks and bookmarks.

g. Save the Web page as a Single File Web page (*.mht; *.mhtml), using the name **w08m3Default_GroupName**.

h. Post all your files to the online storage location.

i. Inform your instructor that the documents are ready for grading, and also give directions to where they are located.

j. Present your proposed Web site to the client via the Present Online option in Word 2013 since your client is a very busy person and is frequently out of town.

Beyond the Classroom

Track Your Investments

RESEARCH CASE

You are enrolled in a personal finance class this semester. One of the major semester projects for this class is to develop your own retirement plan. The Internet is a great resource for you to research and make a short list of companies in which you would like to invest. You will track stock prices, sales performances, profit margins, and other financial indicators and tabulate the results in a table. Copy and paste several performance charts to your Word document. Save the document as **w08b2Stocks_LastFirst.docx** and submit it based on your instructor's directions. A portion of your course grade requires that you present your proposed retirement plan online to your classmates during the last week of class using the Share option in Microsoft Word 2013. Finally, you will create a blog online to solicit feedback and comments from your classmates on your proposed retirement plan.

Modify a Video Clip

DISASTER RECOVERY

FROM SCRATCH

You are a member of the Web Design team for the Christmas Candle Web site. One of the junior Web designers had embedded a video clip from youtube.com that has since been removed from the Web site. Create a folder named **w08b3ChristmasCandle_LastFirst**. Open the *w08b3Default.mht* file, rename it **w08b3Default_LastFirst.mht**, and then save it to the newly created folder. Search the Internet using a search engine such as Bing or Google for a video clip that emphasizes safety when lighting candles at home. Locate the nonworking video on your Web page and replace it with the new video clip. Test your Web page and the new video. Save and close all files, and submit them based on your instructor's directions.

E-Mail Etiquette

SOFT SKILLS CASE

You will review your own online postings and blogs to see if you adhere to the standards of email etiquette. Also, evaluate your own postings on Facebook and Twitter, the photos that you have attached, and your understanding of the Creative Commons licensing. Summarize your findings in a three-page paper on the etiquette of using social media tools. After you have checked the spelling and grammar of your three-page paper, save it as **w08b4EmailEtiquette_LastFirst**. Submit the document as directed by your instructor.

Joyful Scents Candle Company is a family-owned business that manufactures and sells candles. So far, this company has relied on telephone and fax orders. Because of your extensive experience with Word 2013, the company president hired you to create a Web site. Refer to Figure 8.35 as you redesign the home page.

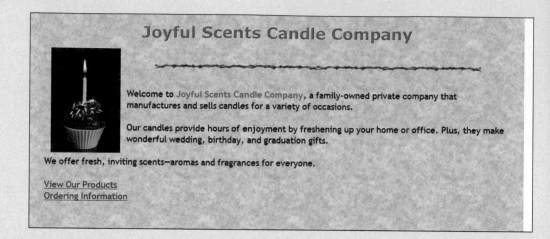

FIGURE 8.35 Joyful Scents Candle Company Web Site

Save a PDF File as a Word Document

The Order page is in PDF format, but you want to save it as a Word document before you link it to the home page.

a. Create a folder named **w08c1Candles_LastFirst** and download the student files to this folder.

b. Start Word. Open the file named *w08c1Order.pdf* and save it as a Word document named **w08c1Order_LastFirst** in the w08c1Candles_LastFirst folder.

Design a Set of Web Pages

You need to convert existing documents to Web pages for Joyful Scents, but before you save them as Web pages, you redesign the pages to incorporate visual enhancements, such as color and graphics.

a. Open the documents *w08c1Default* and *w08c1Products*.

b. Customize the Ribbon to put the buttons you use most on one custom tab with groups. You can modify the myTab tab you created in Hands-On Exercise 1 or reset the Ribbon to its original state and create a new tab with groups.

c. Display the default document, which will become the home page of the Web site. Create a background color with the **Bouquet Texture Fill Effects** (fifth row, fourth column). Apply the **Frame theme**. Increase font sizes of headings to **22 pt** and apply the text effect **Fill - Orange, Accent 4, Soft Bevel** (first row, fifth column).

d. Insert clip art of a candle and display it on the right side of the home page. Use picture format tools to resize the picture to **2" tall** and apply the **Soft Edge Oval effect**. If you do not have access to the Internet, use your judgment on the image you use and use the picture format tools that would be most appropriate for that image.

e. Save this document in the w08c1CandlesLast_First folder as a Web Page named **w08c1Default_LastFirst**.

f. Display the Products document. Apply the **Frame theme** and **Bouquet Texture Fill Effects** to the document. Apply the same text effect and **22-pt font size** used on the default page to the products page heading. Save this document in the w08c1Candles_LastFirst folder as a Web page (*.htm, *.html) named **w08c1Products_LastFirst**.

g. Display the Order document. Apply the **Frame theme** and **Bouquet Texture Fill Effects** to the document. Apply the same text effect and **22-pt font size** used on the default page to the order page heading. Center the text that is currently left justified. Save this document as a Web page in the w08c1Candles_LastFirst folder and change the page title to **Joyful Scents Ordering Information**.

Add Navigation Elements to Web Pages

Your pages are looking good. Now you want to add the ability to navigate within a long page and also to navigate easily between the pages.

a. Display the Default page. Type **View Our Products** and **Ordering Information** on the bottom of the default page. Create hyperlinks to the Products and Order Web pages from these lines of text.

b. Display the Products page. Create the following bookmarks in the appropriate heading location that correspond with the information on the page: **standard, exotic, sizes**, and **descriptions**.

c. Create a list near the top of the page under the paragraph beginning with *Joyful Scents Candle Company provides* for the categories that display down the page. Center the list and create a hyperlink from each item on the list to the appropriate bookmark.

d. Create a **Back to Top hyperlink** at the end of each category that will use a bookmark to navigate back to the top of the document.

e. Type **HOME** at the bottom of the page and create a hyperlink to the default page. Save the page.

f. Display the Order page. Create a hyperlink from *HOME* to the default page. Save the page.

Replace the Photo on the Default Page

You want to replace the photo on the default page with a photo showing a candle on a cupcake.

a. Select the *w08c1Default_LastFirst* document.

b. Select the candle photo on the first page.

c. Conduct a search on Bing Image Search using the key words *a single candle on a chocolate cupcake*. You may substitute the photo with a similar one.

d. Replace the original photo with this new photo.

Add an Online Video to the Order Page

You want to include a video on the safety of burning candles at home on the last page.

a. Go to the last page of the document.

b. Position the insertion point in the paragraph above *HOME*.

c. Conduct a search on youtube.com using the key words *Candle Burning Safety Tips*. You may substitute with a similar video.

d. Insert the video into the document.

Document Progress in a Blog Post

The president of Joyful Scents Candle Company is a strong proponent of documentation. She would like to know how much time you spent on this project and what resources you used. She advocates a casual workplace, so she recommended you just post a blog on the company server so she can read it later. You start the blog and then find the server is down for maintenance, so you save your work and post it at a later time.

a. Open a new blog post document.

b. Note that the title of the blog post is *Preparing the Company Web Site*. Type the following sentence for the post: **I used Word 2013 to design the Web site. Features such as background color, themes, hyperlinks, and bookmarks made the process easy.**

c. Save the blog post in the w08c1Candles_LastFirst folder as **w08c1Blog_LastFirst**.

d. Save and close all files. Preview all your Web pages and test all links. Open File Explorer and send all the files in this folder to a zipped file named **w08c1Candles_ LastFirst**. Submit it based on your instructor's directions.

Subtotals, PivotTables, and PivotCharts

Summarizing and Analyzing Data

Yuri Arcurs/Shutterstock

OBJECTIVES   AFTER YOU READ THIS CHAPTER, YOU WILL BE ABLE TO:

1. Subtotal data p. 216
2. Group and ungroup data p. 219
3. Create a PivotTable p. 224
4. Modify a PivotTable p. 227
5. Filter and slice a PivotTable p. 237

6. Create a calculated field p. 240
7. Format a PivotTable p. 247
8. Use PowerPivot Functionality p. 248
9. Create a PivotChart p. 250

CASE STUDY | Ivory Halls Publishing Company

You are the new Vice President of the Sociology Division at Ivory Halls Publishing Company. The sociology domain has many disciplines, such as introductory sociology, family, research, gender issues, and more. Ivory Halls publishes several textbooks in each discipline to appeal to a vast array of university professors and students.

Your assistant prepared a list of books, their disciplines, and other pertinent data. The current list is not easy to analyze. You need to organize the data so that you can study the sales trends by discipline and area. The list contains current editions of all sociology textbooks. Some books are brand new—in their first edition—while other books are in their 10th edition. All of the books on the list have publication dates between 2014 and 2017.

One of your first tasks in your new position is to analyze sales for all books published in the Sociology Division. To do this, you need to organize data so that you can group data by discipline and then insert subtotal rows. You will also use Excel's PivotTable tool to gain a variety of perspectives of aggregated data. Finally, you will create a PivotChart to depict the aggregated data visually.

Subtotals and Outlines

When you use large datasets, you develop an appreciation for functionality that enables you to manage the data and quickly provide answers to imperative questions. Data alone are meaningless; data translated into meaningful information increase your knowledge so that you can make well-informed decisions. Previously, you used analytical tools such as sorting, filtering, conditional formatting, tables, and charts. These tools help translate raw data into information so that you can identify trends, patterns, and anomalies in a dataset. Now you are ready to explore other functionalities that help you consolidate and analyze large amounts of data.

In this section, you will learn how to insert subtotals for categories. Then you will learn how to group data to create an outline, collapse and expand groups within the outline, and ungroup data to return them to their original state.

Subtotaling Data

Decision makers often want to calculate subtotals by groups within large dataset. You can use the Subtotal feature to insert subtotal rows by categories for a regular data range.

For example, the Ivory Halls Publishing Company's dataset contains a list of sociology textbooks organized by discipline, such as Family. Textbooks are further classified by a specific area within the discipline. For example, the Family discipline contains specific areas such as *Family Interaction* and *Marriage and Family*. You can calculate the number of books sold and the total sales per area. Adding subtotals can help you identify which disciplines and which areas contribute the highest revenue for the company and which disciplines and areas produce the lowest revenue. You can then analyze the data to determine to continue publishing books in high-revenue–generating areas or discontinue the publication of books in low-selling areas. To add subtotals to a dataset, do the following:

STEP 1 ≫

1. Sort the data on a primary category (such as Discipline in the sociology textbook example) that has the same values, such as the same city, state, or department name for several records in one column. **NOTE: If the data are not sorted by a major category, the subtotaled results will not be correct.**
2. Convert the table to range (if the dataset is a table).
3. Click in the dataset and click the DATA tab.
4. Click Subtotal in the Outline group to open the Subtotal dialog box.
5. Click the *At each change in* arrow and select the column by which the data are sorted (see Figure 5.1). **NOTE: You must select the column by which you sorted data in Step 1.**
6. Click the *Use function* arrow and select the function you want to apply.
7. Select the appropriate column heading check boxes in the *Add subtotal to* list for each field you want to subtotal. You can use all functions for columns that contain numeric data. For text columns, you can only count the number of rows within the group.
8. Select any other check boxes you want to use and click OK.

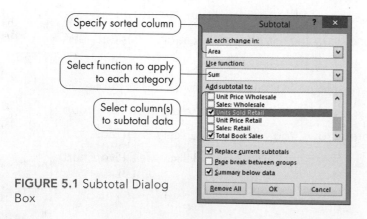

FIGURE 5.1 Subtotal Dialog Box

The dataset must be sorted by categorical labels. For example, the Sociology Textbooks dataset is sorted first by discipline. When you use the Subtotal feature, Excel inserts a *subtotal*, a row within the dataset containing at least one aggregated value when the category you specified in the *At a change in* option changes. For example, when Excel detects a change from Family to Introductory, a subtotal row is inserted on row 35 (see Figure 5.2). (NOTE: Subtotal rows for discipline are highlighted in yellow in the figure; however, the Subtotal feature does not add highlighting.) The subtotal of the number of Family discipline books sold at wholesale was 76,710, and the subtotal of the number of Introductory discipline books sold at wholesale was 179,415, indicating that the number of Introductory books sold is more than double the number of Family books sold. A grand total row is inserted at the end of the dataset to indicate the grand total values (not shown in the figure).

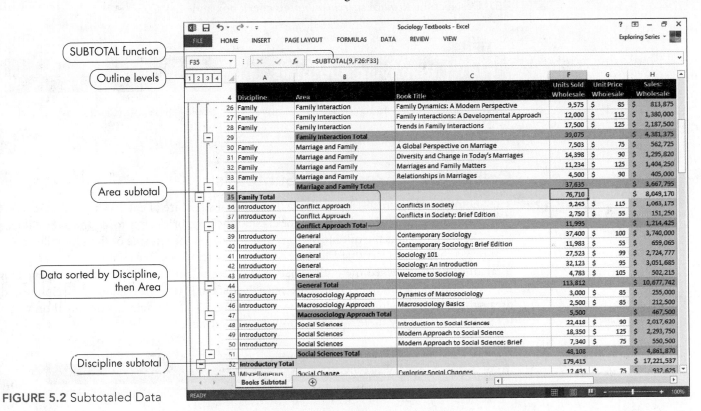

FIGURE 5.2 Subtotaled Data

Excel uses the SUBTOTAL function to calculate the subtotals. Cell F35 contains =SUBTOTAL(9,F26:F33) to sum the values in the range F26:F33. The first argument indicates which summary function is used to calculate the subtotal. Use 1-11 to summarize data including hidden values; use 101-111 to summarize visible data only. Table 5.1 lists some of the summary functions and their respective argument values. For example, 9 sums all values in the range specified in the second argument. If you create a subtotal to average the gross sales, the first argument in the function would be 1 instead of 9.

TABLE 5.1	SUBTOTAL Function_Num Argument	
Summary Function	**Argument to Include Hidden Values**	**Argument to Ignore Hidden Values**
AVERAGE	1	101
COUNT	2	102
COUNTA	3	103
MAX	4	104
MIN	5	105
SUM	9	109

Add a Second Level of Subtotals

You can add a second level of subtotals to a dataset. Adding a second level preserves the primary subtotals and adds another level of subtotals for subcategories. In the Sociology Textbook example, Figure 5.2 shows the discipline subtotals as well as the areas subcategory subtotals. To add a second level of subtotals while maintaining the existing subtotals, do the following:

1. Perform a two-level sort based on primary and secondary categorical data.
2. Click the DATA tab and click Subtotal in the Outline group.
3. Click the *At a change in* arrow and specify the column that was used for the secondary sort.
4. Select the function and columns to be subtotaled.
5. Deselect the *Replace current subtotals* check box and click OK.

> ### TIP | Removing Subtotals
>
> The subtotal rows are temporary. To remove them, display the Subtotals dialog box and click Remove All.

Collapse and Expand the Subtotals

STEP 3 >> The Subtotal feature creates an **outline**, a hierarchical structure of data. When a dataset contains a structured list, you can collapse or expand the categories after using the Subtotal feature. Table 5.2 explains the outline buttons that appear on the left side of the subtotaled data. Figure 5.3 shows a dataset that is collapsed to display the discipline subtotals and the grand total after the user clicked the outline button 2. The number of outline buttons depends on the total number of subtotals created. Because the data in Figure 5.2 contained discipline and area subtotals, four outline buttons appear in Figure 5.3. If the dataset contained only one level of subtotals, only three outline buttons would appear.

TABLE 5.2 Outline Buttons

Button	Description
1	Collapse outline to display the grand total only.
2	Display subtotals by the main subtotal category and the grand total.
3	Displays subtotals by the main subtotal category, the secondary subtotal category, and the grant total.
4	Display the entire list.
+	Expand an outline group to see its details.
–	Collapse an outline group to see its category name only.

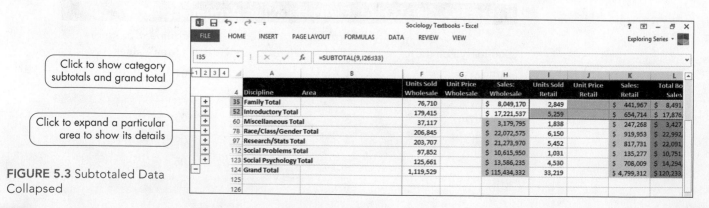

FIGURE 5.3 Subtotaled Data Collapsed

Grouping and Ungrouping Data

STEP 4 » The Subtotals feature outlines data into categories by rows. You can create outlines by columns of related data as well. For Excel to outline by columns, the dataset must contain formulas or aggregate functions. If Excel cannot create the outline, it displays the message box *Cannot create an outline*. To create an outline by columns, do the following:

1. Click the DATA tab.
2. Click the Group arrow in the Outline group.
3. Select Auto Outline.

For more control in creating an outline, you can create groups. *Grouping* is the process of joining rows or columns of related data together into a single entity. After you create groups in the dataset, you can click a collapse button (−) to collapse a group to show the outsider column or click the expand button (+) to expand groups of related columns to view the internal columns of data. Grouping enables you to hide raw data while you focus on key calculated results. To group data, do the following:

1. Select the rows or columns you want to group. For column groups, you often select columns containing details but not aggregate columns, such as totals or averages. (Rows are automatically grouped if you use the Subtotals feature.)
2. Click the DATA tab.
3. Click Group in the Outline group. If the Group dialog box opens, choose the option to group by columns or rows and click OK.

In Figure 5.4, Excel grouped the data by columns. Because the Units Sold Retail and Unit Price Retail columns are grouped, you can click the collapse button above Sales Retail to collapse the columns and focus on the Sales Retail column. Currently, some of the wholesale columns are hidden, showing only the Sales: Wholesale column. You can click the expand button above the Sales: Wholesale column to display the related wholesale columns.

Group related columns

Ungroups the dataset

Click to collapse column groups

Click to expand a group of columns

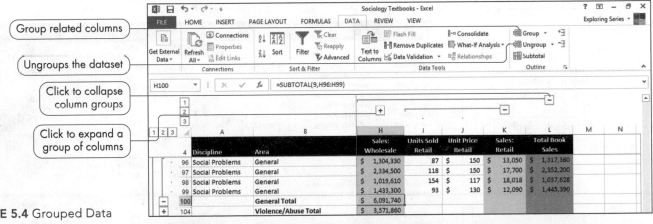

FIGURE 5.4 Grouped Data

TIP Removing Groups

To remove groups, select all grouped columns or rows and click Ungroup in the Outline group.

Quick Concepts

1. Why must a dataset be sorted by a category before using the Subtotal feature? Within the Subtotal dialog box, which option do you set to match the column you used to sort the data? *p. 216*

2. Explain the SUBTOTAL function as it is used by the Subtotal feature. *p. 217*

3. How can you expand or collapse outlined groups of columns? *p. 219*

1 Subtotals and Outlines

As VP of the Sociology Division at Ivory Halls Publishing Company, you want to conduct a preliminary analysis of your current textbook offerings. Each textbook falls within a general discipline, and each discipline is divided into several areas. Details for each textbook include the title, current edition, and copyright year. The company tracks units sold, unit prices, and gross sales by two major types of sales: (1) wholesale sales to bookstores and (2) retail sales to individual consumers. You will organize the data and include area subtotals. Your assistant applied Freeze Panes to keep the column headings in row 4 and the disciplines and areas in columns A and B visible regardless of where you scroll.

Skills covered: Subtotal the Data • Add a Second Subtotal • Collapse and Expand the Subtotals • Group and Ungroup Data

STEP 1 ≫ SUBTOTAL THE DATA

Before you use the Subtotal feature, you must sort the data by discipline and then by area. After sorting the data, you will insert subtotals for each discipline. You want to see the totals for the wholesale sales, retail sales, and combined book sales. Refer to Figure 5.5 as you complete Step 1.

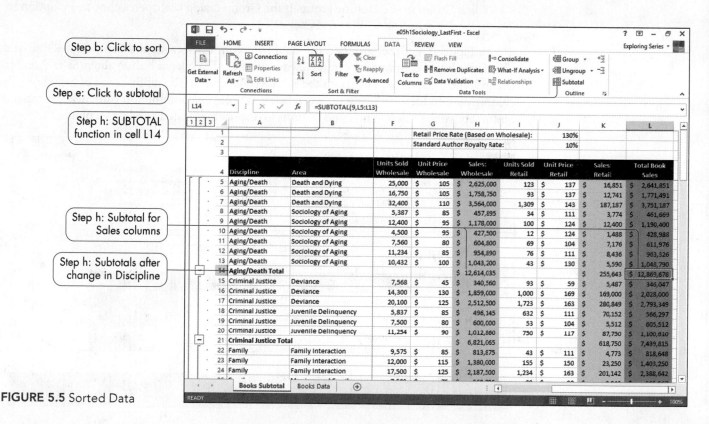

FIGURE 5.5 Sorted Data

a. Open *e05h1Sociology* and save it as **e05h1Sociology_LastFirst**.

> **TROUBLESHOOTING**: If you make any major mistakes in this exercise, you can close the file, open *e05h1Sociology* again, and then start this exercise over.

The workbook contains two worksheets: Books Subtotal for Hands-On Exercise 1 and Books Data for Hands-On Exercises 2–4.

b. Click the **DATA tab** and click **Sort** in the Sort & Filter group.

c. Click the **Sort by arrow** and select **Discipline** in the Sort dialog box.

d. Click **Add Level**, click the **Then by arrow**, and then select **Area**. Click **OK**.

   Excel sorts the data by discipline in alphabetical order. Within each discipline, Excel sorts the data further by area. The data are sorted first by disciplines so that you can apply subtotals to each discipline.

e. Click **Subtotal** in the Outline group.

   The Subtotal dialog box opens. The default *At each change in* is the Discipline column, and the default *Use function* is Sum. These settings are correct.

f. Click the **Sales: Wholesale check box** in the *Add subtotal to* section.

g. Click the **Sales: Retail check box** in the *Add subtotal to* section.

   Excel selected the last column—Total Book Sales—automatically. You selected the other two sales columns to total. You will leave the *Replace current subtotals* and *Summary below data* check boxes selected.

h. Click **OK**. Scroll to the right to see the subtotals and click **cell L14** to see the SUBTOTAL function for the total book sales for the Aging/Death discipline. Save the workbook.

   Excel inserts subtotal rows after each discipline category. The subtotal rows include labels and subtotals for the wholesale sales, retail sales, and book sales columns.

> **TROUBLESHOOTING**: If your subtotals do not match the totals in Figure 5.5, open the Subtotal dialog box, click Remove All, click OK, and repeat steps b through h again.

STEP 2 ≫ ADD A SECOND SUBTOTAL

Displaying subtotals by discipline helps you compare sales data better; however, you want to add another level to see subtotals for each area within each discipline. To insert two levels of subtotals, you must subtotal the primary category first (Discipline) and then add a subtotal to the second category (Area). As you use the Subtotal dialog box, you want to keep the original subtotals intact. Refer to Figure 5.6 as you complete Step 2.

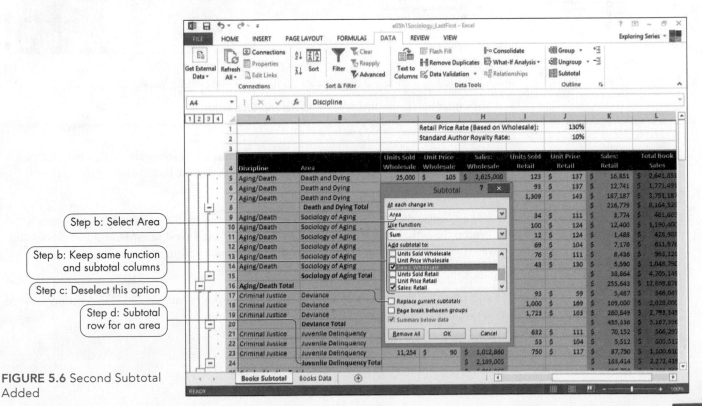

FIGURE 5.6 Second Subtotal Added

a. Click **Subtotal** in the Outline group to open the Subtotal dialog box again.

b. Click the **At each change in arrow** and select **Area**.

The *Use function* is still Sum, and Excel remembers the last columns you selected in the *Add subtotal to* section—Sales: Wholesale, Sales: Retail, and Total Book Sales.

c. Click the **Replace current subtotals check box** to deselect it.

Deselecting this check box will keep the discipline subtotals.

d. Click **OK** and click **cell L15**. Save the workbook.

Excel inserts subtotal rows after each area. The Formula Bar displays =SUBTOTAL(9,L9:L14). Your data have discipline subtotals and area subtotals within each discipline.

> **TROUBLESHOOTING:** If you subtotal the area first and then discipline, Excel adds several discipline subtotals, which repeat the area subtotals. That is why you must subtotal by the primary category first and then subtotal by the secondary category.

STEP 3 ≫ COLLAPSE AND EXPAND THE SUBTOTALS

You want to compare wholesale, retail, and book sales among the disciplines and then among areas within a discipline. Refer to Figure 5.7 as you complete Step 3.

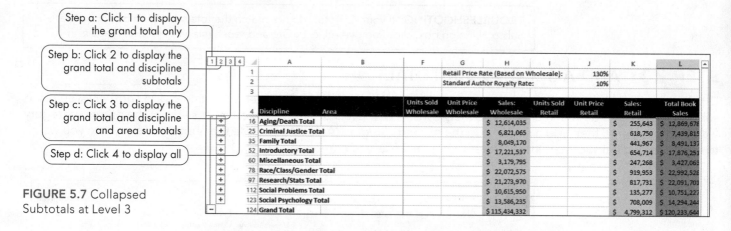

Step a: Click 1 to display the grand total only

Step b: Click 2 to display the grand total and discipline subtotals

Step c: Click 3 to display the grand total and discipline and area subtotals

Step d: Click 4 to display all

FIGURE 5.7 Collapsed Subtotals at Level 3

a. Click the **1** in the top-left outline area (to the left of the column headings).

You collapsed the outline to show the grand totals only.

b. Click the **2** in the top-left outline area.

You expanded the outline to show the grand and discipline subtotals. Which two disciplines had the highest wholesale and retail sales? Which discipline had the lowest total sales?

c. Click the **3** in the top-left outline area.

You expanded the outline to show the grand, discipline, and area subtotals (see Figure 5.7). Within the Introductory discipline, which area had the lowest sales? How do wholesale and retail sales compare? Are they proportionally the same within each area?

d. Click the **4** in the top-left outline area. Save the workbook.

You expanded the outline to show all details again. If you had not added the second subtotal, the outline would have had three levels instead of four.

STEP 4 ≫ GROUP AND UNGROUP DATA

You want to apply an outline to the columns so that you can collapse or expand the units sold and unit prices columns. Refer to Figure 5.8 as you complete Step 4.

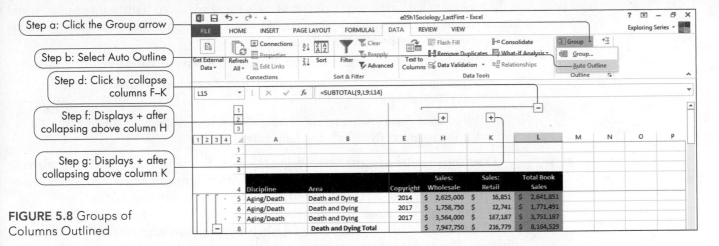

FIGURE 5.8 Groups of Columns Outlined

a. Click the **Group arrow** in the Outline group on the DATA tab.

You want to see if Excel can create a column outline for you so that you do not have to select columns and group them individually.

b. Select **Auto Outline**.

Excel displays the message box *Modify existing outline?* because it recognizes that an existing outline exists—the row subtotals outline.

c. Click **OK**.

Excel maintains the outlined subtotals and adds column subtotals. Horizontal lines and collapse buttons appear above the columns. The formula in column H is =F5*G5, so Excel creates an outline for these columns. The formula in column K is =I5*J5, so Excel creates an outline for these columns. It also creates a hierarchical outline of columns F through K, since the formula in column L sums the values in columns H and K.

d. Click the **collapse (–) button** above column L.

You collapsed columns F through K to display disciplines, areas, and total sales by title.

e. Click the **expand (+) button** above column L.

You expanded the outline to show columns F through K again.

f. Click the **collapse (–) button** above column H.

You collapsed the outline to hide columns F and G so you can focus on the wholesale sales without the distraction of the Units Sold or Unit Price columns.

g. Click the **collapse (–) button** above column K.

You collapsed the outline to hide columns I and J so you can focus on the retail sales without the distraction of the Units Sold or Unit Price columns.

h. Save the workbook. Keep the workbook open if you plan to continue with Hands-On Exercise 2. If not, close the workbook and exit Excel.

PivotTable Basics

Analyzing large amounts of data is important for making solid decisions. Entering data is the easy part; retrieving data in a structured, meaningful way is more challenging. *Data mining* is the process of analyzing large volumes of data, using advanced statistical techniques, and identifying trends and patterns in the data. Managers use data-mining techniques to address a variety of questions, such as the following:

- What snack foods do customers purchase most when purchasing Pepsi® products?
- What age group from what geographic region downloads the most top 10 songs from iTunes?
- What hotel chain and rental car combinations are most popular among Delta Air Lines passengers flying into Salt Lake City?

Questions similar to those above help organizations prepare their marketing plans to capitalize on consumer spending patterns. The more you know about your customer demographics, the better you can focus your strategic plans to increase market share.

A *PivotTable* is a powerful, interactive data-mining feature that enables you to summarize and analyze data, especially helpful when working with large datasets. An advantage of using a PivotTable is that you can group data into one or more categories and perform a variety of calculations without altering the original dataset. The most important benefit of a PivotTable is that it is dynamic. You can easily and quickly *pivot*, or rearrange, data to analyze them from different viewpoints, such as expanding or collapsing details, organizing and grouping data differently, and switching row and column categories. Viewing the PivotTable from different perspectives helps you more easily identify trends and patterns among the variables in the data that might not be obvious from looking at the data from only one viewpoint.

In this section, you will learn how to create a PivotTable by organizing data into columns and rows to aggregate data.

Creating a PivotTable

Before you create a PivotTable, ensure the data source is well structured. Applying the rules for good table design is a start: Use meaningful column labels, ensure data accuracy, and avoid blank rows and columns in the dataset. To consolidate and aggregate data, at least one column must have duplicate values, such as the same city, state, or department name for several records. You then use these columns of duplicate values to create categories for organizing and summarizing data. Another column must have numeric values that can be aggregated to produce quantitative summaries, such as averages or sums.

Create a PivotTable from the Quick Analysis Gallery

You can create a PivotTable from the Quick Analysis gallery. A benefit of this method is that Excel displays recommended PivotTables based on the data. To create a PivotTable using Quick Analysis, do the following:

STEP 1 ≫

1. Select the entire dataset, including the field names (column labels).
2. Click the Quick Analysis button in the bottom-right corner of the selected range.
3. Click TABLES in the Quick Analysis gallery.
4. Position the mouse pointer over the PivotTable thumbnails to see a preview of the different recommended PivotTables (see Figure 5.9).
5. Click the PivotTable thumbnail to create the desired PivotTable.

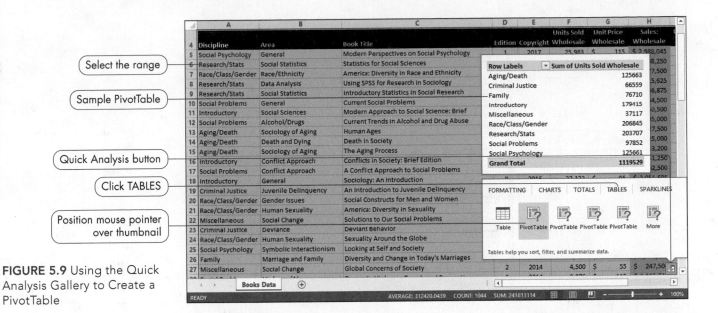

Select the range

Sample PivotTable

Quick Analysis button

Click TABLES

Position mouse pointer over thumbnail

FIGURE 5.9 Using the Quick Analysis Gallery to Create a PivotTable

---

TIP **PivotTable or Subtotals?**

At first glance, PivotTables are similar to subtotals because they both produce subtotals, but PivotTables are more robust. PivotTables provide more flexibility than subtotals provide. If you need complex subtotals cross-referenced by two or more categories with filtering and other specifications, create a PivotTable.

Create a PivotTable from the Ribbon

You can also create a PivotTable by using commands on the Ribbon. The Insert tab contains PivotTable and Recommended PivotTables commands. If you click PivotTable, Excel displays the Create PivotTable dialog box so that you can create a blank PivotTable from scratch. However, if you click Recommended PivotTables, Excel displays a dialog box so that you can select from a gallery of PivotTables. This option is similar to using the Quick Analysis gallery. To create a recommended PivotTable using the Ribbon, do the following:

1. Click inside the dataset (the range of cells or table).
2. Click the INSERT tab and click Recommended PivotTables in the Tables group to open the Recommended PivotTables dialog box (see Figure 5.10).
3. Click a thumbnail in the gallery on the left side of the dialog box to see a preview of the PivotTable on the right side.
4. Click OK to create the desired PivotTable.

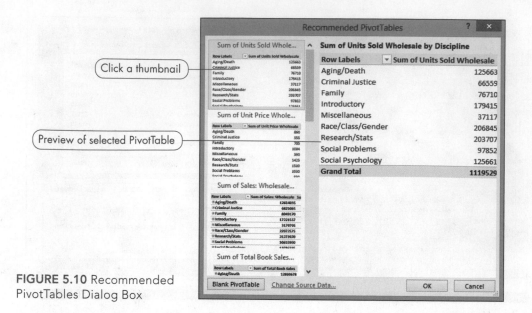

FIGURE 5.10 Recommended PivotTables Dialog Box

After you use the Recommended PivotTables dialog box or the Quick Analysis gallery, Excel creates a PivotTable on a new worksheet (see Figure 5.11). The ROWS area contains the category names of the summarized data. For example, each discipline, such as Family, is listed in only one row, regardless of how many times each category name appears in the original dataset.

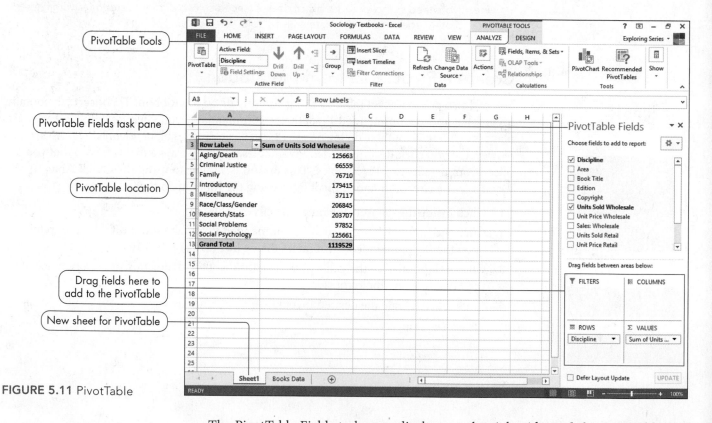

FIGURE 5.11 PivotTable

The PivotTable Fields task pane displays on the right side, and the PivotTable Tools Analyze and Design contextual tabs appear on the Ribbon. If you click outside the PivotTable, the contextual tabs and the task pane disappear. Click within the PivotTable to display these elements again.

The **PivotTable Fields task pane** contains two sections. The *Choose fields to add to report* section lists all the fields or column labels from the original data source. You can click either drag a field to an area in the bottom of the task pane or click the check box to add the field to the PivotTable. Use the *Drag fields between areas below* section to arrange fields in one of the four PivotTable areas. Table 5.3 describes the areas of a PivotTable.

TABLE 5.3   Areas of a PivotTable

Area	Description
Filters Area	Filters the data to display results based on particular conditions you set.
Columns Area	Subdivides data into one or more additional categories.
Rows Area	Organizes and groups data into categories on the left side. Each group name occupies a single row.
Values Area	Displays summary statistics, such as totals or averages.

Modifying a PivotTable

After you create a PivotTable, you might want to modify it to see the data from a different perspective. For example, you might want to add fields to the rows, values, and columns areas of the PivotTable. In addition, you might want to collapse the PivotTable to show fewer details or expand it to show more details.

Add Rows

You can add fields to provide a more detailed analysis. For example, you might want to organize data by discipline by adding the Discipline field to the ROWS area in the PivotTable Fields task pane. To add a field as a row, do one of the following:

STEP 2 »

- Click the field's check box in the *Choose fields to add to report* section. Excel adds the field to a PivotTable area based on the type of data stored in the field. If the field contains text, Excel usually places that field in the ROWS area.

- Drag the field from the *Choose fields to add to report* section and drop it in the ROWS area.

- Right-click the field name in the *Choose fields to add to report* section and select *Add to Row Labels*.

Add Values

A PivotTable has meaning when you include quantitative fields, such as quantities and monetary values, to aggregate the data. For example, you might want to display the total wholesale sales for each discipline and area. To add values, do one of the following:

- Click the field's check box in the *Choose fields to add to report* section. Excel makes it the value aggregate, such as *Sum of Sales*.

- Drag the field from the *Choose fields to add to report* section and drop it in the VALUES area.
- Right-click the field name in the *Choose fields to add to report* section and select *Add to Values*.

Excel sums the values for each group listed in the ROWS area. For example, the total number of units sold wholesale for the Family discipline is 76,710. If you drag a text field, such as Book Title, to the VALUES area, Excel counts the number of records for each group listed in the ROWS area. In this case, Excel counts seven books in the Family discipline.

Add Columns

Although you can create subdivisions of data by adding more fields to the ROWS area, you might want to arrange the subdivision categories in columns. Doing so minimizes the redundancy of duplicating subdivision row labels and helps consolidate data. To subdivide data into columns, drag a field from the *Choose fields to add to report* section and drop it in the COLUMNS area. Excel updates the aggregated values by the combination of row and column categories.

Figure 5.12 shows a PivotTable that uses the Discipline field as rows, the *Sum of Units Sold Wholesale* field as values, and Copyright field as columns. Each discipline label and each copyright year label appears only once in the PivotTable. This added level of detail enables you to see the total sales for each discipline based on its copyright year. The PivotTable includes grand totals for each discipline and grand totals for each year.

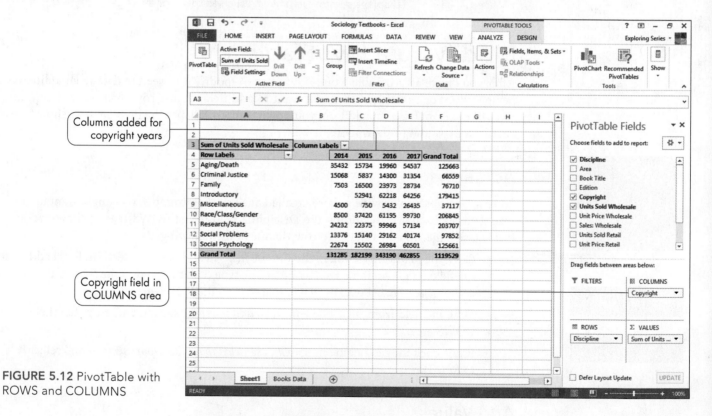

FIGURE 5.12 PivotTable with ROWS and COLUMNS

Collapse and Expand Items

If you include two fields as ROWS, the PivotTable displays more depth but may be overwhelming. You can hide or collapse the secondary field rows. For example, if the PivotTable contains both Discipline and Copyright row labels, you might want to collapse copyright years for some disciplines. The collapse and expand buttons display to the left of the row labels. If they do not, click Show and click the +/− buttons on the Analyze tab. Figure 5.13 shows the collapse and expand buttons.

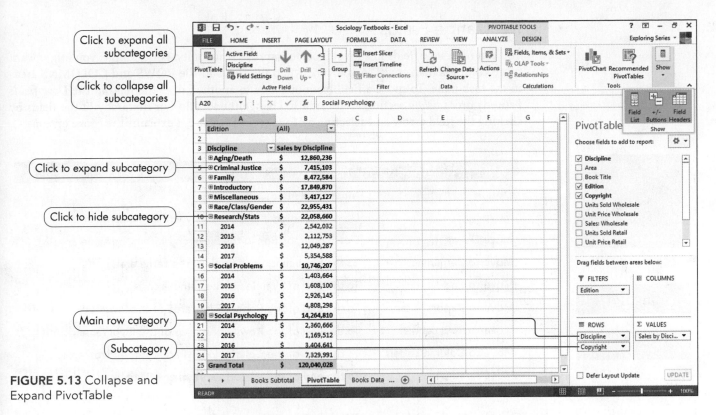

FIGURE 5.13 Collapse and Expand PivotTable

To hide the subcategories for a particular category, click the collapse button (–) on the left side of the specific category you wish to collapse. Excel hides the subcategories for that particular category and shows only the aggregated totals for the category. Continue collapsing other categories as needed to focus on a particular category's details.

To expand the subcategories again, click the expand button (+) on the left side of the category labels.

> **TIP** **Collapse and Expand All**
>
> You can collapse all categories at one time by clicking Collapse Field in the Active Field group on the Analyze tab. To expand all categories at one time, click Expand Field. This approach is faster than collapsing or expanding each category individually.

Remove Fields

You can remove fields to reduce the amount of data to analyze. To remove a field from the PivotTable, do one of the following:

STEP 3»

- Click the field name in the *Drag fields between areas below* section and select Remove Field.
- Deselect the check box next to the field name in the *Choose fields to add to report* section.
- Drag a field name in the *Drag fields between areas below* section outside the PivotTable Fields task pane.

Rearrange Fields

You can rearrange fields in a PivotTable to improve readability. For example, you might want more columns than rows, so you can switch the fields in the ROWS and COLUMNS areas in the task pane. To move a field from one area to another, drag the field in the *Drag fields between areas below* section. You can also change the location or hierarchy of the fields by clicking the field arrow and selecting a Move option. Table 5.4 explains the Move options.

TABLE 5.4 Move Options

Option	Moves the Field...
Move Up	Up one position in the hierarchy within the same area
Move Down	Down one position in the hierarchy within the same area
Move to Beginning	To the beginning of all fields in the same area
Move to End	To the end of all fields in the same area
Move to Report Filter	To the end of the Report Filter area of the PivotTable
Move to Row Labels	To the end of the Row Labels area of the PivotTable
Move to Column Labels	To the end of the Column Labels area of the PivotTable
Move to Values	To the end of the VALUES area of the PivotTable

Change the Values Field Settings

Although Excel uses the SUM function as the default summary statistic for numerical fields, you can select a different function. For example, you might want to calculate the average, lowest, or highest value within each group, or identify the lowest sales for each discipline/copyright year combination to see if the older books have decreased sales. In addition to changing the summary statistic, you might want to change the column label that appears above the summary statistics. By default, words indicate the summary statistic function applied, such as *Sum of Total Sales by Book* or *Average of Total Sales by Book*, depending on the summary statistic applied to the values. Finally, you might need to format the aggregated values. To modify any of these value settings, do the following:

STEP 4 ⟩⟩

1. Click a value in the appropriate field in the PivotTable and click Field Settings in the Active Field group on the ANALYZE tab. Alternatively, click the field's arrow in the VALUES area of the task pane and select Value Field Settings. The Value Field Settings dialog box opens (see Figure 5.14).

2. Type the name you want to appear as the column label in the Custom Name box. For example, you might want the heading to appear as *Total Sales* instead of *Sum of Total Book Sales*.

3. Select the summary statistical function you want to use to summarize the values in the *Summarize value field by* list.

4. Click Number Format to open an abbreviated version of the Format Cells dialog box. Select a number type, such as Accounting, in the Category list; select other settings, such as number of decimal places in the *Decimal places* spin arrow; and then click OK.

5. Click OK in the Value Field Settings dialog box.

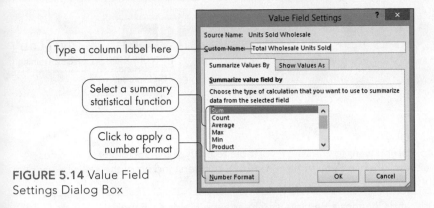

Type a column label here

Select a summary statistical function

Click to apply a number format

FIGURE 5.14 Value Field Settings Dialog Box

 Multiple Summary Statistics

You can display more than one function for a field. For example, you might want to show *both* the total book sales and the average book sales. To display multiple summary statistics, drag another copy of the same field to the VALUES area and set each value setting separately.

Refresh a PivotTable

Although PivotTables are powerful, they do not update automatically if you make any changes to the underlying data in the data source. For example, if you change a sales value or delete a row in the data source, the PivotTable does not reflect the changed data. Unfortunately, this causes PivotTable summary statistics to be outdated with inaccurate results. If you change the data source, you must update the PivotTable by doing the following:

STEP 5 ≫

1. Click in the PivotTable.
2. Click the ANALYZE tab.
3. Click Refresh in the Data group to refresh the current PivotTable only, or click the Refresh arrow and select Refresh All to refresh all PivotTables in the workbook.

If you want to ensure your PivotTable is up to date when you open the workbook, click the Analyze tab, click the PivotTable arrow on the left side of the Ribbon, select Options to open the PivotTable Options dialog box, click the Data tab, select *Refresh data when opening the file*, and then click OK.

Quick **Concepts**

1. What are the advantages of using a PivotTable instead of a subtotal? *p. 224*
2. What is the main benefit of creating a PivotTable using the Quick Analysis gallery or from the Recommended PivotTables dialog box over creating a blank PivotTable? *pp. 224–225*
3. List the four areas of a PivotTable. *p. 227*

Hands-On Exercises

2 PivotTable Basics

After exhausting the possibilities of outlines and subtotals, you want to create a PivotTable to analyze the sociology book sales. You realize you can see the data from different perspectives, enabling you to have a stronger understanding of the sales by various categories.

Skills covered: Create a PivotTable • Add Rows, Values, and Columns • Remove and Rearrange Fields • Change the Values Field Settings • Refresh a PivotTable

STEP 1 ›› CREATE A PIVOTTABLE

Because you want to keep the subtotals you created in the Books Subtotal worksheet, you will create a PivotTable from the Books Data worksheet. Refer to Figures 5.10 and 5.15 as you complete Step 1.

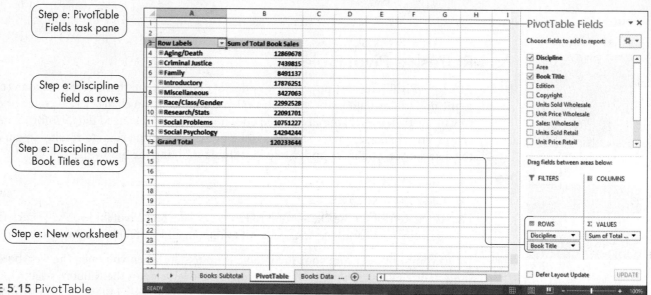

FIGURE 5.15 PivotTable

a. Open *e05h1Sociology_LastFirst* if you closed it at the end of Hands-On Exercise 1 and save it as **e05h2Sociology_LastFirst**, changing *h1* to *h2*.

b. Click the **Books Data worksheet tab**.

   Excel does not let you create a PivotTable using subtotaled data. To preserve the subtotals you created in Hands-On Exercise 1, you will use the dataset in the Books Data worksheet.

c. Click in **cell A5**, click the **INSERT tab**, and then click **Recommended PivotTables** in the Tables group.

   The Recommended PivotTables dialog box opens (see Figure 5.10).

d. Scroll the thumbnails of recommended PivotTables and click the **Sum of Total Book Sales by Discipline thumbnail**. (NOTE: Hover the mouse pointer over the thumbnails to see the full names.)

   You selected this PivotTable to show the overall total book sales for each discipline. The dialog box shows a preview of the selected PivotTable.

e. Click **OK** and click within the PivotTable, if necessary. Rename Sheet1 as **PivotTable**. Save the workbook.

Excel inserts a new Sheet1 worksheet, which you renamed as PivotTable, with the PivotTable on the left side and the PivotTable Fields task pane on the right side (see Figure 5.15).

STEP 2 » ADD ROWS, VALUES, AND COLUMNS

You want to compare sales combinations by discipline, copyright year, and edition. The discipline field is already in the PivotTable, but you need to add the copyright year and edition fields. Refer to Figure 5.16 as you complete Step 2.

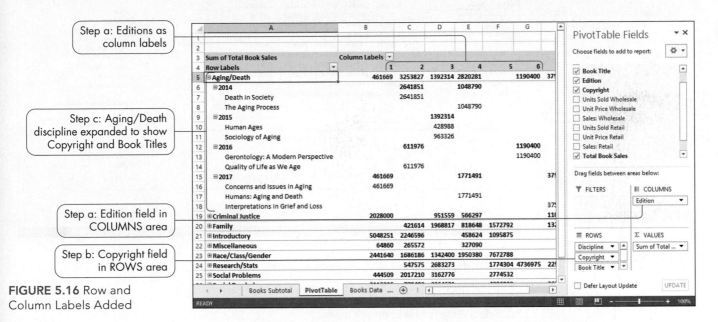

Step a: Editions as column labels

Step c: Aging/Death discipline expanded to show Copyright and Book Titles

Step a: Edition field in COLUMNS area

Step b: Copyright field in ROWS area

FIGURE 5.16 Row and Column Labels Added

a. Drag the **Edition field** to the COLUMNS area in the PivotTable Fields task pane.

Excel displays the total book sales by a combination of discipline and edition. This enables you to compare sales of current editions within each discipline. Blanks appear in the PivotTable when a discipline does not have a specific edition. For example, the Family discipline does not have any first-edition books currently being published.

b. Drag the **Copyright field** to be between the Discipline and Book Title fields in the ROWS area.

The Copyright and Book Titles are not showing because they are collapsed within the Discipline rows.

c. Click the **Aging/Death expand (+) button**. Save the workbook.

You expanded the Aging/Death discipline to show the copyright years and titles.

TIP **Field ScreenTip**

It may be confusing to see *Sum of Total...* in the VALUES box. Position the pointer over a field name in the area to see a ScreenTip with the full name, such as *Sum of Total Book Sales*.

STEP 3 ≫ REMOVE AND REARRANGE FIELDS

Although it is informative to compare sales by edition, you think that the PivotTable contains too much detail, so you will remove the Edition field. In addition, the ROWS area contains the Book Titles field, but those data are collapsed; therefore, you will remove it as well. After you remove the fields, you will rearrange other fields to simplify the PivotTable. Refer to Figure 5.17 as you complete Step 3.

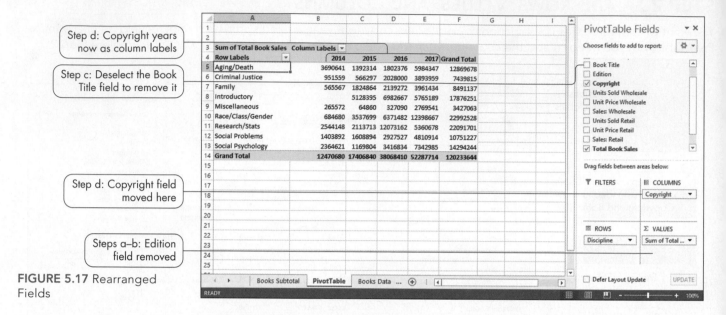

Step d: Copyright years now as column labels

Step c: Deselect the Book Title field to remove it

Step d: Copyright field moved here

Steps a–b: Edition field removed

FIGURE 5.17 Rearranged Fields

a. Click the **Edition arrow** in the Column Labels area.

Excel displays a menu of options to apply to this field.

b. Select **Remove Field** on the menu.

You removed the Edition field from the PivotTable. Instead of several sales columns, Excel consolidates the sales into one sales column. Although you find it helpful to have sales breakdowns by copyright year, you think the PivotTable will be easier to read if you move the Copyright field to the COLUMNS area.

c. Deselect the **Book Title check box** in the *Choose fields to add to report* section of the task pane.

You removed the Book Title field from the PivotTable.

d. Drag the **Copyright field** from the ROWS area to the COLUMNS area. Save the workbook.

This arrangement consolidates the data better. Instead of repeating the copyright years for each discipline, the copyright years are listed only once each at the top of the sales columns.

STEP 4 ≫ CHANGE THE VALUES FIELD SETTINGS

After selecting the PivotTable fields, you want to improve the appearance of the sociology textbook PivotTable. You will format the values for Accounting Number Format and replace the generic Row Labels description with a label that indicates the sociology disciplines. Refer to Figure 5.18 as you complete Step 4.

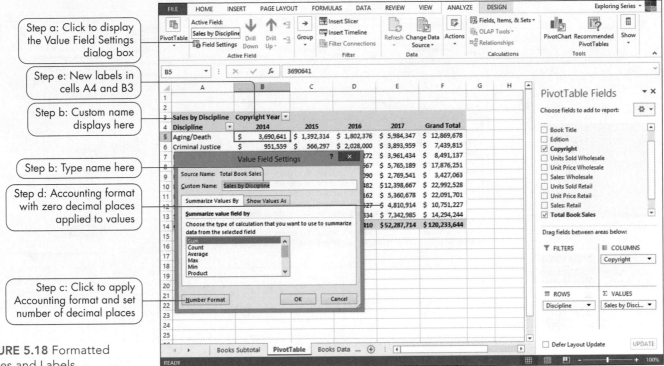

FIGURE 5.18 Formatted Values and Labels

a. Click **cell B5** and click **Field Settings** in the Active Field group on the ANALYZE tab.

The Value Field Settings dialog box opens so that you can format the field.

b. Type **Sales by Discipline** in the **Custom Name box**.

Leave Sum as the selected calculation type in the *Summarize value field by* section.

c. Click **Number Format**.

Excel opens a Format Cells dialog box with only one tab: the Number tab.

d. Click **Accounting** in the Category list, change the **Decimal places value** to **0**, click **OK** in the Format Cells dialog box, and then click **OK** in the Value Field Settings dialog box.

You formatted the values with Accounting Number Format with no decimal places, and the heading *Sales by Discipline* appears in cell A3.

e. Type **Discipline** in **cell A4** and type **Copyright Year** in **cell B3**.

You replaced the generic *Row Labels* heading with *Discipline* to describe the contents of the first column, and you replaced the *Column Labels* heading with *Copyright Year*. Although you can create custom names for values, you cannot create custom names for row and column labels. However, you can edit the labels directly in the cells.

f. Select the **range B4:F4** and center the labels horizontally. Save the workbook.

STEP 5 >> REFRESH A PIVOTTABLE

After consulting with the Accounting Department, you realize that the retail prices are incorrect. The unit retail prices are based on a percentage of the wholesale price. The retail unit price is 30% more than the wholesale unit price, but it should be 25%. You will edit the input cell in the original worksheet and refresh the PivotTable to see the corrected results. Refer to Figure 5.19 as you complete Step 5.

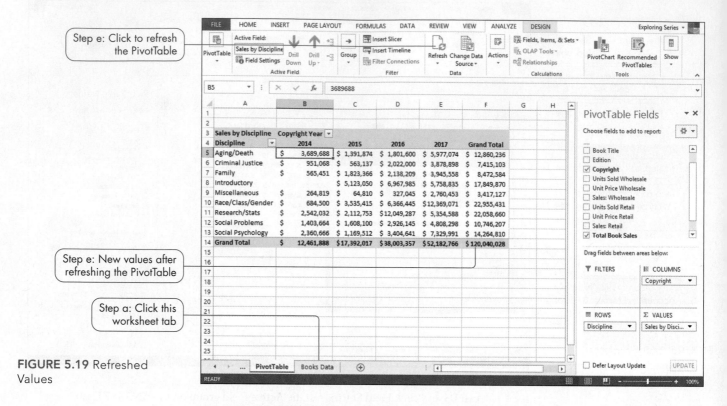

Step e: Click to refresh the PivotTable

Step e: New values after refreshing the PivotTable

Step a: Click this worksheet tab

FIGURE 5.19 Refreshed Values

a. Click the **Books Data worksheet tab**.

   You need to locate and change the retail price percentage.

b. Click **cell J1**, the cell that contains the current retail price percentage.

c. Type **125%** and press **Enter**. Save the workbook to update the formula results on the Books Data worksheet.

> **TROUBLESHOOTING:** If the formula results in the Unit Price Retail, Sales: Retail, and Total Book Sales columns do not change after you edit the data in step c, the workbook may be set for manual calculation. To ensure that formulas update automatically, click the File tab, click Options, click Formulas, click Automatic as the Workbook Calculation setting, and then click OK.

d. Click the **PivotTable worksheet tab**.

   Notice that the PivotTable aggregate values did not change. The grand total is $120,233,644. You must refresh the PivotTable.

e. Click the **ANALYZE tab** and click **Refresh** in the Data group.

   Excel updates the PivotTable values based on the change you made in the Books Data worksheet.

f. Save the workbook. Keep the workbook open if you plan to continue with Hands-On Exercise 3. If not, close the workbook and exit Excel.

PivotTable Options

As you have experienced, PivotTables consolidate and aggregate large amounts of data to facilitate data analysis. You can customize the PivotTable for more in-depth analysis. In the previous section, you used the Analyze tab to display the Value Field Settings dialog box and refresh the PivotTable. However, the Analyze tab contains more ways for you to customize your PivotTable. For example, you can filter groups, display or hide particular groups temporarily, and add subtotals.

In this section, you will learn how to filter data in a PivotTable. In addition, you will create a calculated field and display subtotals.

Filtering and Slicing a PivotTable

By default, PivotTables display aggregated data for each category. However, you may want to set a filter to exclude particular categories or values. You can specify a particular field to use to filter the PivotTable. In addition, you can include slicers to easily set filters to designate which specific data to include in the PivotTable.

Add Filters

Although PivotTables consolidate data from the original data source into groups, the PivotTable might contain more details than you want. You can apply filters to show only a subset of the PivotTable. Drag a field to the FILTERS area in the task pane when you want to engage a filter based on a particular field. For example, you might want to filter the PivotTable to show only aggregates for first- and second-edition books. When you drag a field to the FILTERS area, Excel displays the field name in cell A1 with a filter arrow in cell B1. To set the filter, click the filter arrow and do one of the following and then click OK:

STEP 1 »

- Select the value in the list to filter the data by that value only.

- Click the *Select Multiple Items* check box if you want to select more than one value to filter the PivotTable. Then click the check boxes by each value you want to set (see Figure 5.20).

- Type a value in the Search box if the list is too long and you want to find a value quickly.

Only a subset of the data that meet those conditions appears in the PivotTable; Excel hides the unselected items.

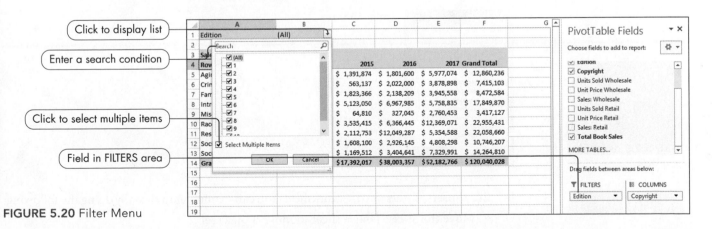

FIGURE 5.20 Filter Menu

Cell B1 displays (All) when no filter is enabled, the value if one filter is enabled, or (Multiple Items) if more than one item is selected. To remove the filter entirely, remove it from the FILTER area. To remove the filter temporarily, click the filter arrow in cell B1, select (All), and then click OK.

You can apply additional filters based on the row and column label groupings. For example, you can apply date filters to display summary statistics for data occurring within a particular time frame or apply filters for values within a designated range. To apply group filters, click the Row Labels or Column Labels arrow in the PivotTable and specify the settings (see Figure 5.21). Excel calculates the summary statistics based on the filtered data rather than the complete dataset.

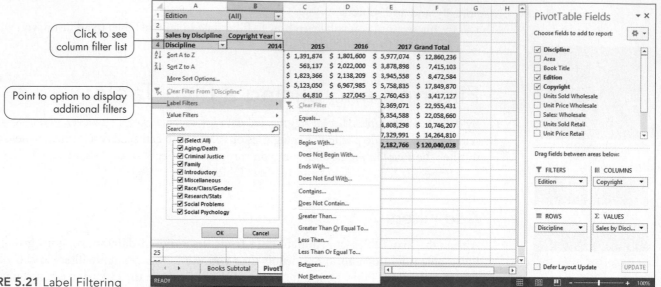

FIGURE 5.21 Label Filtering

Insert Slicers

You can insert a *slicer*, a small window containing one button for each unique item in a field so that you can filter the PivotTable quickly. Slicers are especially helpful to filter data when a PivotTable is based on multiple tables. The visual representation is easier to manipulate than adding more fields to the FILTERS area and then setting each field's filter through drop-down lists. To insert a slicer, do the following:

STEP 2>>

1. Click the ANALYZE tab.
2. Click Insert Slicer in the Filter group to display the Insert Slicers dialog box (see Figure 5.22).
3. Click one or more field check boxes to display one or more slicers and click OK.

FIGURE 5.22 Insert Slicers Dialog Box

Excel inserts slicers into the worksheet. You can manipulate a slicer by doing the following:

- **Move the Slicer.** Drag a slicer to move it onscreen.
- **Filter Data.** Click the slicer button to filter by the value represented by the button. Press Ctrl to select several slicers to apply additional filters. Excel highlights the item to make it clear how you filtered the PivotTable. For example, in Figure 5.23, the Discipline field is filtered by Family, Introductory, and Social Problems. Although

no filter has been enabled for the Edition field, the 6th and 9th edition buttons are unavailable because the three disciplines selected do not have books that are in their 6th or 9th editions.

- **Remove a Filter.** Click Remove Filter in the top-right corner of the slicer window.

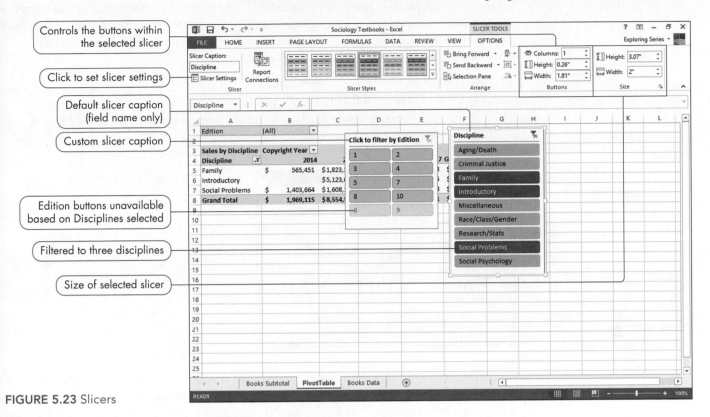

FIGURE 5.23 Slicers

Customize Slicers

When you select a slicer, the Slicer Tools Options tab displays so that you can customize a slicer. The default slicer caption displays the field name only. The *slicer caption* is text that displays in the header at the top of the slicer window. However, you can customize the slicer by changing its caption. In Figure 5.23, the left slicer's caption displays an instruction to the user, whereas the right slicer's caption displays the default field name. Table 5.5 lists and describes the commands on the Slicer Tools Options tab.

TABLE 5.5	Slicer Tools Commands
Group	**Commands**
Slicer	Enables you to change the slicer caption, display the Slicer Settings dialog box for further customization, and manage the PivotTable connected to the slicer. In Figure 5.23, the Edition slicer has been sorted in ascending order. The light blue items 6 and 9 do not apply to the selected disciplines.
Slicer Styles	Applies a style to the slicer by specifying the color of the filtered item in the slicer. For example, given the workbook theme, the default active filters appear in blue and unavailable items appear in light blue. In Figure 5.23, Slicer Style Dark 2 has been applied to the Discipline style.
Arrange	Specifies the slicer's placement in relation to other groups, such as placing a slicer on top of other slicers.
Buttons	Defines how many columns are displayed in the selected slicer and the height and width of each button inside the slicer. For example, the Edition slicer contains two columns, and the Discipline slicer contains one column in Figure 5.23.
Size	Sets the height and width of the slicer window. For example, the Discipline slicer's height is 3.07" in Figure 5.23.

Creating a Calculated Field

You can create a *calculated field*, which is a user-defined field that does not exist in the original dataset. It derives its values based on performing calculations on other original dataset values. For example, you can create a calculated field that converts totals to percentages for easier relative comparison among categories, or you might want to create a calculated field that determines what the number of units a 10% increase in units sold for the upcoming year would be. To create a calculated field, do the following:

STEP 3 >>

1. Select a cell within the PivotTable.
2. Click the PIVOTTABLE TOOLS ANALYZE tab.
3. Click Fields, Items, & Sets in the Calculations group and select Calculated Field to display the Insert Calculated Field dialog box (see Figure 5.24).

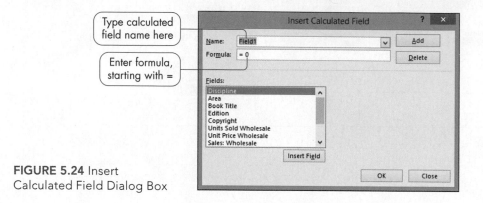

FIGURE 5.24 Insert Calculated Field Dialog Box

Type a descriptive label for the calculated field in the Name box. Build a formula starting with the equal sign (=). Instead of using cell references, insert the field names and other operands. For example ='Total Book Sales'*.1 calculates a 10% royalty amount on the total book sales. Click OK to insert the calculated field in the PivotTable. Format the numerical values in the calculated field column as needed.

Show Values as a Specific Calculation Result

In addition to creating calculated fields, you can apply built-in custom calculations that display relationships between values in rows and columns in the PivotTable. For example, you can show each value as a percentage of the grand total or each value's percentage of the row total. To display values in relation to others, do the following:

STEP 4 >>

1. Click the field in the VALUES area of the task pane and select Value Field Settings (or click within the field in the PivotTable and click Field Settings in the Active Field group on the ANALYZE tab).
2. Click the Show Values As tab within the Value Field Settings dialog box.
3. Click the *Show values as* arrow and select the desired calculation type. Table 5.6 lists and describes some of the calculation options.
4. Click Number Format to set number formats, click OK to close the Format Cells dialog box, and then click OK to close the Value Field Settings dialog box.

TABLE 5.6 Calculation Options

Option	Description
% of Grand Total	Displays each value as a percentage of the grand total.
% of Column Total	Displays each value as a percentage of the respective column total. The values in each column total 100%.
% of Row Total	Displays each value as a percentage of the respective row total. The values in each row total 100%.
% of Parent Row Total	Displays values as: (value for the item) / (value for the parent item on rows).
Running Total	Displays values as running totals.
Rank Smallest to Largest	Displays the rank of values in a specific field where 1 represents the smallest value.
Rank Largest to Smallest	Displays the rank of values in a specific field where 1 represents the largest value.

Quick Concepts

1. What is the purpose of applying a filter to a PivotTable? How do you apply a main filter and additional filters? *p. 237*

2. What is a slicer? What do the three different colors indicate in a slicer? *p. 238*

3. When would you create a calculated field in a PivotTable? *p. 240*

Hands-On Exercises

3 PivotTable Options

The PivotTable you created has been beneficial for you to review sales data by discipline for each copyright year. In addition, you have used the PivotTable to compare grand total sales among disciplines and grand totals by copyright year. Now you want to extend your analysis. You will calculate author royalties from the sales and impose filters to focus your attention on each analysis.

Skills covered: Set Filters • Insert and Customize a Slicer • Create a Calculated Field • Show Values as Calculations

STEP 1 >> SET FILTERS

The level of success of the first two editions especially determines the likelihood of approving subsequent revisions and editions. To display aggregated sales for these editions, you need to set a filter to remove the other editions from being included in the calculated sales data. After you review the first- and second-edition data, you will enable additional filters to review books published in the past two years. Refer to Figure 5.25 as you complete Step 1.

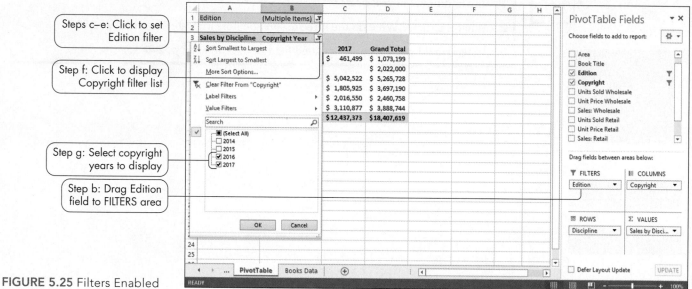

FIGURE 5.25 Filters Enabled

a. Open *e05h2Sociology_LastFirst* if you closed it at the end of Hands-On Exercise 2 and save it as **e05h3Sociology_LastFirst**, changing *h2* to *h3*.

> **TROUBLESHOOTING:** Click in the PivotTable to display the PivotTable Field task pane if necessary.

b. Make sure the PivotTable worksheet tab is active and drag the **Edition field** from the *Choose fields to add to report* section to the FILTERS area.

You can now filter the PivotTable based on the Edition field. Cell A1 displays the field name, and cell B1 displays (All) and the filter arrow.

c. Click the **Edition filter arrow** in **cell B1** and click the **Select Multiple Items check box**.

The list displays a check box for each item.

d. Click the **(All) check box** to deselect it.

e. Click the **1** and **2 check boxes** and click **OK**.

The summary statistics reflect sales data for only first- and second-edition publications. The filter arrow changes to a funnel icon in cell B1.

f. Click the **Copyright Year filter arrow** in **cell B3** and click the **(Select All) check box** to deselect it.

g. Click the **2016** and **2017 check boxes** and click **OK**.

Excel filters out data for years that do not meet the condition you set. The filter arrow changes to a funnel icon in cell B3.

h. Save the workbook.

STEP 2 » INSERT AND CUSTOMIZE A SLICER

You might distribute the workbook to colleagues who are not as skilled in Excel as you are. To help them set their own filters, you insert slicers. Refer to Figure 5.26 as you complete Step 2.

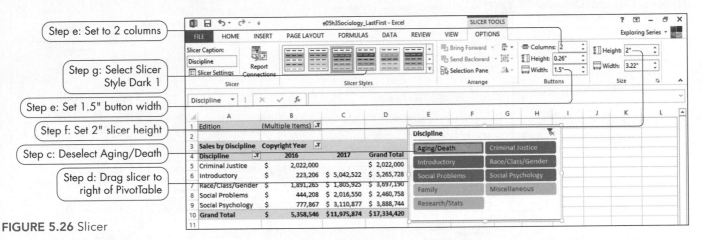

FIGURE 5.26 Slicer

a. Click **Insert Slicer** in the Filter group on the ANALYZE tab.

The Insert Slicers dialog box opens, listing each field name.

b. Click **Discipline** and click **OK**.

Excel inserts the Discipline slicer in the worksheet. Six slicer buttons are blue, indicating that those disciplines are selected. The grayed-out buttons at the bottom of the slicer indicate those disciplines are not applicable based on other engaged filters you set (first and second editions and 2016 and 2017 copyright years).

c. Press and hold **Ctrl** as you click **Aging/Death** in the Discipline slicer.

This deselects the Aging/Death discipline.

> **TROUBLESHOOTING**: Because several disciplines are selected, if you click Aging/Death instead of pressing Ctrl as you click it, you set Aging/Death as the only discipline. The others are filtered out. If this happens, immediately click Undo and repeat step c.

d. Drag the slicer to the right side of the PivotTable.

You moved the slicer so that it does not cover up data in the PivotTable.

e. Change the **Columns value** to **2** in the Buttons group on the SLICER TOOLS OPTIONS tab. Change the button **Width** to **1.5"** in the Buttons group.

The slicer now displays buttons in two columns. You changed the width of the buttons to 1.5" to display the full discipline names within the buttons.

f. Change the slicer **Height** to **2** in the Size group.

The slicer window is now only 2" tall.

g. Click the **More button** in the Slicer Styles group and click **Slicer Style Dark 1**. Save the workbook.

Based on the selected workbook theme, Slicer Style Dark 1 applies a dark blue fill color for selected disciplines, dark gray and black font for available but not currently selected disciplines, and light gray fill with medium gray font for nonapplicable disciplines.

STEP 3 ⟫ CREATE A CALCULATED FIELD

You want to calculate the amount of the sales returned to the authors as royalties. Although the 10% royalty rate is stored in cell J2 in the Books Data worksheet, the value must be used in the calculated field because range names and cell references outside the PivotTable cannot be used. Refer to Figure 5.27 as you complete Step 3.

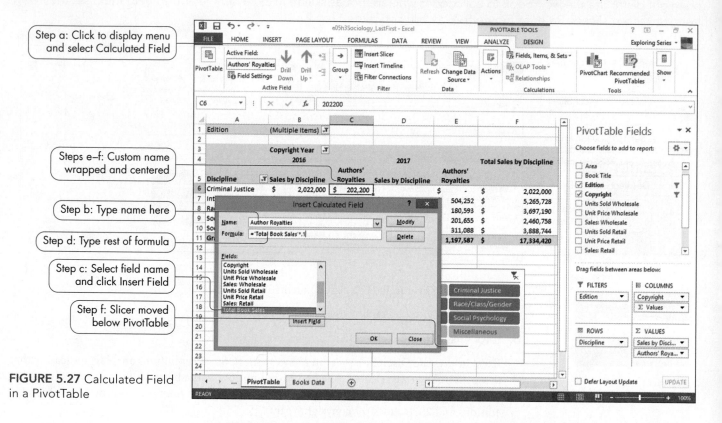

FIGURE 5.27 Calculated Field in a PivotTable

a. Click within the PivotTable, click the **ANALYZE tab**, click **Fields, Items, & Sets** in the Calculations group, and then select **Calculated Field**.

The Insert Calculated Field dialog box opens.

b. Type **Author Royalties** in the **Name box**.

c. Scroll down the Fields list, click **Total Book Sales**, and then click **Insert Field**.

Excel starts to build the formula, which is currently ='Total Book Sales'.

d. Type ***.1** at the end of the **Formula box** and click **OK**.

Excel adds Sum of Author Royalties calculated field columns, one for each copyright year category. It calculates the authors' royalties as 10% of the total sales for each copyright year.

e. Right-click the **Sum of Author Royalties heading** in **cell C5**, select **Value Field Settings**, type **Authors' Royalties** in the **Custom Name box**, and then click **OK**.

f. Move the slicer below the PivotTable. Select **cells C5** and **E5**, wrap text for field names, set **30** row height, **12** column widths, and center column labels.

g. Save the workbook.

STEP 4 ≫ SHOW VALUES AS CALCULATIONS

You want to see what copyright year generated the largest sales for each discipline, which discipline contributes the largest percentage of the total sociology sales, and which introductory book has the largest sales contribution within that discipline. Refer to Figure 5.28 as you complete Step 4.

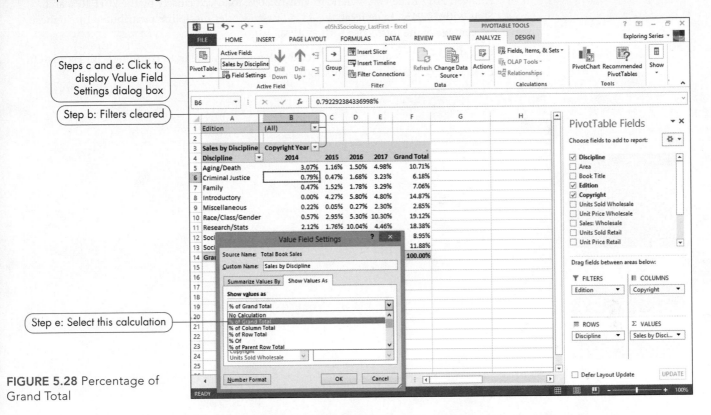

FIGURE 5.28 Percentage of Grand Total

a. Right-click the **PivotTable worksheet tab**, select **Move or Copy**, click **Books Data** in the *Before sheet* list, click the **Create a copy check box**, and then click **OK**.

You copied the PivotTable worksheet to maintain the previous tasks you completed as evidence. You will work with the PivotTable (2) worksheet, which is the active worksheet.

b. Do the following to remove filters, slicer, and Authors' Royalties field:

- Click the **Edition filter** in cell B1, click the **(All) check box**, and then click **OK** to clear the Edition filter.
- Click the **Discipline filter** in cell A5 and select **Clear Filter From "Discipline"**.
- Click the **Copyright Year filter** in cell B3 and select **Clear Filter From "Copyright"**.
- Select the slicer and press **Delete**.
- Click the **Authors' Royalties** in the VALUES area of the task pane and select **Remove Field**.

c. Click within any value in the PivotTable, click the **ANALYZE tab**, and then click **Field Settings** in the Active Field group.

The Value Field Settings dialog box opens.

d. Click the **Show Values As tab**, click the **Show values as arrow**, select **% of Row Total**, and then click **OK**.

Excel displays each copyright year's values as percentages for that discipline. All disciplines except Introductory and Research/Stats had the highest percentage of sales for the books with a 2017 copyright. These two disciplines had their highest percentage of sales for books with a 2016 copyright.

e. Click the **Field Settings** in the Active Field group, click the **Show Values As tab** within the dialog box, select **% of Grand Total**, and then click **OK**.

See Figure 5.28. Each discipline's yearly value displays as a percentage of the total sales. Which discipline and for what copyright year produces the highest percentage of total sales? Answer: 2017 Race/Class/Gender with 10.30%, followed closely by the 2016 Research/ Stats with 10.04%. In general, the Race/Class/Gender discipline contributed the highest percentage of the total sales with 19.12%.

f. Save the workbook and keep the workbook open if you plan to continue with Hands-On Exercise 4. If not, close the workbook and exit Excel.

PivotTable Design and PivotCharts

After you create and modify the structure of a PivotTable, you can focus on the overall appearance and format of the PivotTable. The PivotTable Tools Design tab enables you to control the position of grouped calculations and the PivotTable style. In addition to finalizing the PivotTable's appearance, you might want to create a PivotChart to depict the consolidated data in a visual form.

In this section, you will apply a different style to and change the layout of a PivotTable. In addition, you will create and format a PivotChart.

Formatting a PivotTable

Excel applies basic formatting to PivotTables. For example, it formats primary row labels in bold to distinguish those categories from the subcategories. In addition, the subtotals are bold to offset these values from the subcategory values. The PivotTable Tools Design tab contains commands for enhancing the format of a PivotTable (see Figure 5.29).

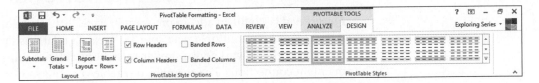

FIGURE 5.29 PivotTable Tools Design Tab

STEP 1 A PivotTable style controls bold formatting, font colors, shading colors, and border lines. To change the style, click the PivotTable Tools Design tab and click the More button in the PivotTable Styles group to display the PivotTable Styles gallery (see Figure 5.30). Select the most appropriate style that accentuates the data in your PivotTable. As you move the pointer over the gallery, Excel shows how that style will affect the PivotTable. Click a style to apply it to the PivotTable.

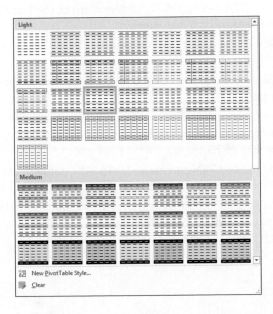

FIGURE 5.30 PivotTable Styles

After you apply a style, you can select which areas of the PivotTable are affected by the style. Select check boxes in the PivotTable Style Options group to apply formats to row headers, column headers, banded rows, and banded columns.

By default, the VALUES area consolidates data by showing subtotals for each category. You can customize the location of subtotals by clicking Subtotals in the Layout group on the

Design tab. For example, when the PivotTable is large, displaying the subtotals at the top of the group draws attention to the totals and enables you to scroll to view all of the supporting data if necessary. Table 5.7 describes the Subtotals options.

TABLE 5.7 PivotTable Subtotals Options

Option	Description
Do Not Show Subtotals	Removes subtotals for each category but retains the category names and displays aggregated values for the subcategories.
Show All Subtotals at Bottom of Group	Displays category subtotals below the last subcategory value within each category. Subtotal labels and values appear in bold.
Show All Subtotals at Top of Group	Displays category subtotals at the top of the list on the same row as the category labels. This approach takes up fewer rows than Show All Subtotals at Bottom of Group.
Include Filtered Items in Totals	Includes values for filtered items in the total rows and columns. (Active only when a filter has been applied.)

Using PowerPivot Functionality

PowerPivot is a built-in add-in program in Excel 2013 that enables you to import millions of rows of data from multiple data sources, create a relationship between two or more related tables within one workbook (similar to creating relationships among tables in Access), and maintain connections. For example, one table contains sales representatives' names and IDs. A related table contains the sales dates and sales amounts but only the sales reps' IDs to avoid mistyping a person's name. You must create a relationship based on a common field (such as ID) between the tables. A *relationship* is an association between two related tables where both tables contain a related field of data, such as IDs.

After you create a relationship between tables, you can use PowerPivot to create a PivotTable from both tables. After you create the relationship, you can use the common field to display the sales reps' names instead of their IDs. To create a relationship, do the following:

1. Click the DATA tab and click Relationships in the Data Tools group to open the Manage Relationships dialog box.
2. Click New in the dialog box to open the Create Relationship dialog box (see Figure 5.31).
3. Click the Table arrow and select the name of the primary table. The primary table in this example is SALES.
4. Click the Column (Foreign) arrow and select the name of the column that contains a relationship to the related or lookup table. For example, the column that relates to the other table is REPS.
5. Click the Related Table arrow and select the name of the related or lookup table. For example, the related table is REPS.
6. Click the Related Column (Primary) arrow and select the name of the column that is related to the primary table. For example, the ID column relates to the Rep column in the SALES table. Click OK.

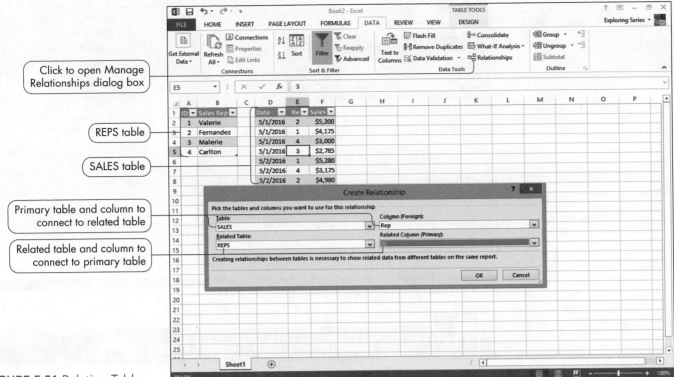

FIGURE 5.31 Relating Tables

After you create a relationship between the tables, you can use PowerPivot to create a PivotTable based on the relationship. Do the following to create a PivotTable using two related tables:

1. Click within the primary table.
2. Click the INSERT tab and click PivotTable in the Tables group to open the Create PivotTable dialog box (see Figure 5.32).
3. Make sure the primary table name displays in the Table/Range box.
4. Click the *Add this data to the Data Model* check box and click OK.

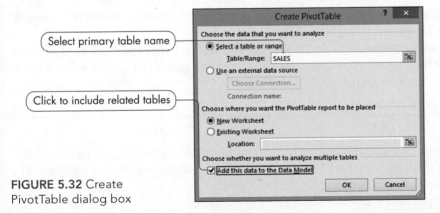

FIGURE 5.32 Create PivotTable dialog box

In the PivotTable Fields task pane, click ALL to display the names of all related tables. Then click the table names to display their field names. From there, you can arrange the fields in the different area boxes at the bottom of the task pane (see Figure 5.33).

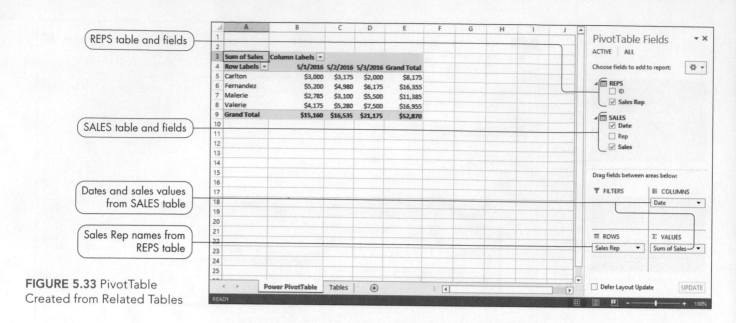

REPS table and fields

SALES table and fields

Dates and sales values
from SALES table

Sales Rep names from
REPS table

FIGURE 5.33 PivotTable
Created from Related Tables

TIP **More Information on Power PivotTables**

Look up the topic *What's new in PowerPivot in Excel 2013* to learn more about the
PowerPivot functionality and how to create PivotTables from related tables. The Help
menu also informs you which versions of Microsoft Office 2013 contain this feature and
how you can enable it.

Creating a PivotChart

Charts display data visually. This visual representation may help you and your audience
understand the data better than merely presenting the data in a spreadsheet. Although
PivotTables help reduce the amount of data to analyze, PivotTables can be overwhelming.
Another way to display a PivotTable's aggregated data is through a PivotChart. A **PivotChart**
is an interactive graphical representation of the data in a PivotTable. A PivotChart presents
the consolidated data visually.

A PivotChart is associated with a PivotTable. When you change the position of a field in
either the PivotTable or the PivotChart, the corresponding object changes as well. To create
a PivotChart, do the following:

STEP 2

1. Click inside the PivotTable.
2. Click the ANALYZE tab and click PivotChart in the Tools group.

Excel creates a PivotChart based on the current PivotTable settings—row labels, column
labels, values, and filters. The PivotChart contains elements that enable you to set filters. The
ROWS area changes to AXIS (CATEGORY) and the COLUMNS area changes to LEGEND
(SERIES) when you select the PivotChart (see Figure 5.34).

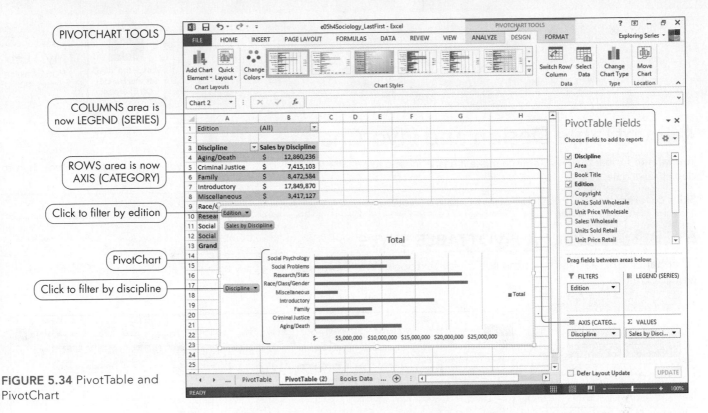

PIVOTCHART TOOLS

COLUMNS area is now LEGEND (SERIES)

ROWS area is now AXIS (CATEGORY)

Click to filter by edition

PivotChart

Click to filter by discipline

FIGURE 5.34 PivotTable and PivotChart

Although Excel creates the PivotChart based on the current PivotTable settings, you can change the settings using the PivotTable Field List. Click the FILTERS arrow and select values to filter the chart. Click the AXIS (CATEGORY) arrows to sort or filter the categories and subcategories in rows. Click the LEGEND (SERIES) to filter the chart representation based on the values. Changes you make to the PivotChart also affect the corresponding PivotTable. For example, if you apply a filter to the PivotChart, Excel also filters the PivotTable.

The Chart Tools Analyze tab contains the same options that you used to customize a PivotTable. In addition, the Actions group contains the Move Chart option so that you can move a PivotChart to a different worksheet.

The Chart Tools Design tab contains options to add a chart element, apply a layout, change colors, and apply a chart style. In addition, you can switch the data between the category axis and the legend, select the data used to create the chart, change the chart type, and move the chart to a different worksheet.

You can further customize PivotChart elements the same way you can customize regular charts—display data labels, change the fill color for a data series, display axis titles, and so forth. Use Help to learn more about customizing PivotCharts.

Quick Concepts

1. What types of specific elements can you select to be controlled by PivotTable styles? *p. 247*

2. What must be done to create a PivotTable from more than one table? *p. 248*

3. What replaces the ROWS and COLUMNS in the task pane when you create a PivotChart? *p. 250*

Hands-On Exercises

 Watch the Video for this Hands-On Exercise!

 MyITLab®
HOE4 Training

4 PivotTable Design and PivotCharts

You want to format the PivotTable to make it easier for you to analyze the sales data. In addition, you want to create a PivotChart to depict sales data.

Skills covered: Apply a PivotTable Style • Create a PivotChart

STEP 1 » APPLY A PIVOTTABLE STYLE

To enhance the readability of the sociology textbook PivotTable, you will apply a style. Refer to Figure 5.35 as you complete Step 1.

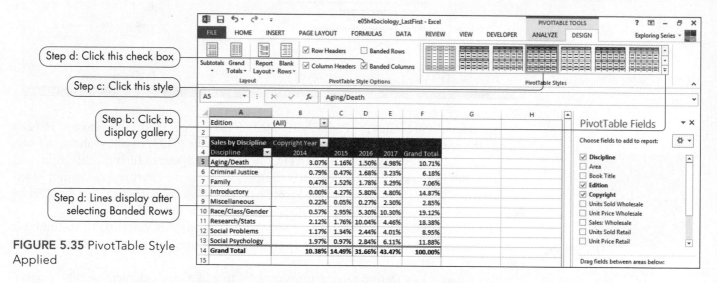

FIGURE 5.35 PivotTable Style Applied

a. Open *e05h3Sociology_LastFirst* if you closed it at the end of Hands-On Exercise 3 and save it as **e05h4Sociology_LastFirst**, changing *h3* to *h4*.

b. Make sure the PivotTable (2) sheet is active. Click a cell within the PivotTable, click the **DESIGN tab**, and then click the **More button** in the PivotTable Styles group.

   The PivotTable Style gallery displays styles that you can apply.

c. Click **Pivot Style Medium 3** to apply a dark red style to the PivotTable.

d. Click the **Banded Columns check box** in the PivotTable Style Options group to add dark red vertical lines between the columns. Save the workbook.

STEP 2 >> CREATE A PIVOTCHART

You want to create a PivotChart to depict the sales data by discipline. Refer to Figure 5.36 as you complete Step 2.

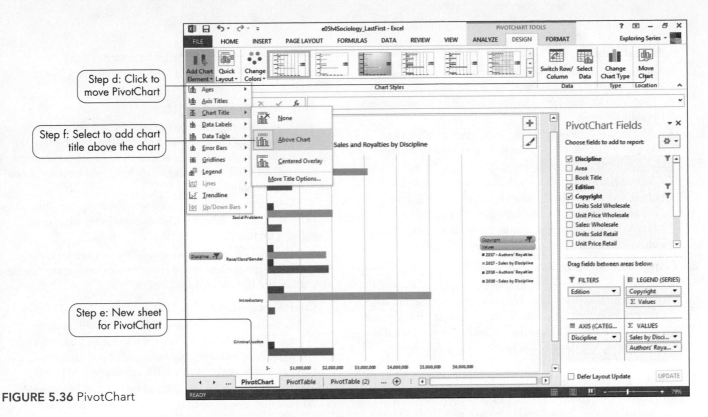

FIGURE 5.36 PivotChart

a. Click the **PivotTable sheet tab** and click inside the PivotTable.

b. Click the **ANALYZE tab** and click **PivotChart** in the Tools group.

The Insert Chart dialog box opens.

c. Click **Bar** and click **OK**.

Excel creates a clustered bar PivotChart based on the PivotTable. Any changes you make to the PivotChart will also affect the PivotTable.

d. Click the **PIVOTCHART TOOLS DESIGN tab** and click **Move Chart** in the Location group.

The Move Sheet dialog box opens.

e. Click **New sheet**, type **PivotChart**, and then click **OK**.

The PivotChart is now on its own sheet.

f. Click the **DESIGN tab**, click **Add Chart Element**, point to *Chart Title*, and then select **Above Chart**.

A Chart Title placeholder displays above the plot area in the PivotChart.

g. Type **Sales and Royalties by Discipline** and press **Enter**.

h. Save and close the workbook, and submit based on your instructor's directions.

Chapter Objectives Review

After reading this chapter, you have accomplished the following objectives:

1. Subtotal data.

- The Subtotal dialog box enables you to insert subtotals, such as sums or averages, based on sorted data. This feature detects changes between categories arranged in rows to insert the subtotal rows.
- Add a second level of subtotals: To keep the first level and add a second level, deselect the *Replace current* subtotals check box in the Subtotals dialog box.
- Collapse and expand the subtotals: Click the outline level buttons to collapse the subtotals to the grand total, grand total and subtotals, or entire dataset. Click a particular collapse button to collapse a category, or click an expand button to expand a particular category.

2. Group and ungroup data.

- If the data contain columns of formulas based on other columns and/or row subtotals, use the auto outline process to create an outline based on the data structure. You can then collapse and expand the outline as you review the data. If you no longer need grouped data, select and ungroup the data again.

3. Create a PivotTable.

- Create a PivotTable from the Quick Analysis Gallery: Select a range, click the Quick Analysis button, click TABLES, and click the desired PivotTable thumbnail.
- Create a PivotTable from the Ribbon: Use the Ribbon to create a blank PivotTable or to display the Recommended PivotTables dialog box to create a PivotTable.

4. Modify a PivotTable.

- Add rows and values: Drag fields to the ROWS and VALUES areas of the PivotTable Fields task pane to add row categories and columns of aggregated values.
- Add columns: Drag fields to the COLUMNS area to add additional columns of details.
- Collapse and expand items: Click the collapse button to collapse subcategory rows and click the expand button to expand a subcategory of details.
- Remove fields: Click a field name in the respective area of the task pane and select Remove Field.
- Rearrange fields: Drag fields from one area to another in the task pane to rearrange fields in the PivotTable.
- Change the value field settings: You can select a different function to calculate the statistics in the PivotTable. You can also apply number formatting and specify a custom column heading for value columns.

- Refresh a PivotTable: PivotTables do not update automatically if you change the original dataset. You must click Refresh to update the PivotTable.

5. Filter and slice a PivotTable.

- Add filters: Drag a field to the FILTERS area of the task pane and click the Filter arrow at the top of the PivotTable to set the filter conditions. You can also click the row labels arrow in cell A4 to set row filters and click the column arrow in cell B3 to set column filters.
- Insert slicers: A slicer is a small window containing the values for a particular field. You click buttons in the slicer to set filters for that particular field.
- Customize slicers: You can specify the slicer's style and size. You can specify how many columns of buttons appear in the slicer and the size of those buttons.

6. Create a calculated field.

- A calculated field is a user-defined field based on other fields. This field does not exist in the original dataset. You can use basic arithmetic operations, but you cannot use cell references or range names in the calculated field syntax.
- Show values as a specific calculation results: You can apply predefined calculations, such as *% of Grand Total*, for displaying the values in the PivotTable.

7. Format a PivotTable.

- The PivotTable Tools Design tab enables you to improve the appearance of a PivotTable by applying a PivotTable style. The style controls the fill color, bold formatting, and other formatting aspects of data in the PivotTable.

8. Use PowerPivot Functionality.

- You can create relationships between two or more related tables within one workbook. After creating the relationships, you can use PowerPivot to create a PivotTable that uses fields from the related tables.

9. Create a PivotChart.

- The PivotChart is similar to creating a regular chart, except it is based on the categories and structure of the PivotTable, not the original dataset. You can customize a PivotChart with the same methods you use to customize a regular chart. If you change fields or sort in either the PivotTable or the PivotChart, Excel automatically adjusts the corresponding pivot object.

Key Terms Matching

Match the key terms with their definitions. Write the key term letter by the appropriate numbered definition.

a. Calculated field
b. Columns area
c. Data mining
d. Filters area
e. Grouping
f. Outline
g. PivotChart
h. PivotTable

i. PivotTable Fields task pane
j. PowerPivot
k. Relationship
l. Rows area
m. Slicer
n. Slicer caption
o. Subtotal
p. Values area

1. _____ An association created between two tables where both tables contain a matching field. **p. 248**

2. _____ A hierarchical structure of data. **p. 218**

3. _____ A row within a dataset that displays the total or another statistic for a particular category. **p. 217**

4. _____ A process of joining related rows or columns of related data. **p. 219**

5. _____ The process of analyzing large volumes of data to identify patterns and trends. **p. 224**

6. _____ An organized structure that summarizes large amounts of data without altering the original dataset. **p. 224**

7. _____ A user-defined field that performs a calculation based on other fields in a PivotTable. **p. 240**

8. _____ A window listing all items in a field and enabling efficient filtering. **p. 238**

9. _____ Drag fields here to display categories horizontally in a PivotTable. **p. 227**

10. _____ Drag fields here to display data as aggregates, such as sums or averages. **p. 227**

11. _____ Drag fields here to be able to specify which values or content to include or exclude in the PivotTable. **p. 227**

12. _____ Drag fields here to add more vertical data to a PivotTable. **p. 227**

13. _____ A graphical representation of aggregated data derived from a PivotTable. **p. 250**

14. _____ A window that enables you to drag fields to particular areas to build and arrange data in a PivotTable. **p. 227**

15. _____ The label that appears at the top of a slicer window. By default, it displays the name of the field used. **p. 239**

16. _____ A built-in add-in program that enables users to create a PivotTable from multiple related tables. **p. 248**

1. A worksheet contains data for businesses that are sponsoring this year's Arts Festival. The worksheet contains these columns in this sequence: Business Name, Address, City, State, and Donation Amount. Data are sorted by State and then by City. What is the default *At a change in* setting within the Subtotal dialog box, and what would be a more appropriate setting?

   (a) Business Name (default field), Donation Amount (correct field)

   (b) Business Name (default field), State (correct field)

   (c) Donation Amount (default field), Address (correct field)

   (d) Address (default field), Donation Amount (correct field)

2. You created an outline for a dataset. What does the + button indicate to the left of a row heading?

   (a) You can add a new row at that location only.

   (b) One or more columns are hidden.

   (c) You can click it to collapse the details of that category.

   (d) You can click it to expand the details of that category.

3. A worksheet contains a PivotTable placeholder and the PivotTable Fields task pane. Where do you drag the State field if you want a list of each state in the first column of the PivotTable?

   (a) FILTERS area

   (b) COLUMNS area

   (c) ROWS area

   (d) VALUES area

4. You just created a slicer for the State field in a PivotTable. Which of the following does *not* characterize the initial slicer?

   (a) The slicer buttons are set to filter out all records.

   (b) The slicer caption is State.

   (c) The slicer contains one column of state names or abbreviations.

   (d) The slicer may display on top of the PivotTable data.

5. You created a PivotTable and made some changes to values in the original dataset from which the PivotTable was created. How does this affect the PivotTable?

   (a) The PivotTable updates automatically when you make changes to the dataset.

   (b) You must create a new PivotTable if you want updated results in a PivotTable.

   (c) Click the DATA tab and click Update to update the PivotTable to reflect changes you made in the dataset.

   (d) Click Refresh in the Data group on the ANALYZE tab to update the PivotTable.

6. You created a PivotTable to summarize salaries by department. What is the default summary statistic for the salaries in the PivotTable?

   (a) Average

   (b) Sum

   (c) Count

   (d) Max

7. What settings should you select for a PivotTable if you want to apply a different color scheme and display different fill colors for main category rows and horizontal lines within the PivotTable?

   (a) Banded Rows and Banded Columns check boxes

   (b) Banded Columns check box and a different PivotTable style

   (c) Banded Rows check box and a different PivotTable style

   (d) A different PivotTable style only

8. Which PivotTable calculated field is correctly constructed to calculate a 20% tip on a meal at a restaurant?

   (a) =Meal Cost * 20%

   (b) ='Meal Cost'*.2

   (c) ="Meal Cost"*.2

   (d) =B5*1.2

9. You have created a PivotChart showing sales by quarter by sales rep. Before presenting it to management, you notice the name of a rep who has since been fired. How do you remove this rep from the chart without deleting the data?

   (a) Filter the Sales Rep field in the PivotChart and deselect the employee's check box.

   (b) Make the employee's data points and axis titles invisible.

   (c) You cannot delete the rep from the chart without first deleting the data.

   (d) Hide that rep's row(s) in the underlying list, which automatically removes that rep from the chart.

10. Currently, the House Types field is in the Row Labels area, the Real Estate Agent field is in the Column Labels area, and Sum of List Prices is in the VALUES area. How can you modify the PivotTable to display the agent names as subcategories within the house types in the first column?

    (a) Drag the Real Estate Agent field from the Column Labels area and drop it above the House Types field in the Row Labels area.

    (b) Drag the House Types field from the ROWS area and drop it below the Real Estate Agent field in the COLUMNS area.

    (c) Drag the House Types field from the ROWS area to the FILTERS area and drag the Real Estate Agent field from the COLUMNS area to the ROWS area.

    (d) Drag the Real Estate Agent field from the COLUMNS area and drop it below the House Types field in the ROWS area.

Practice Exercises

1 | The Men's Store

You work at the Men's Store, a men's department store in Cheyenne, Wyoming. You need to analyze a year's worth of transactions to determine which salesperson had the highest overall sales and which salesperson had the best sales in the Dress Shirts and Ties category. You will use the Subtotal feature and outline the list of transactions for the year. This exercise follows the same set of skills as used in Hands-On Exercise 1 in the chapter. Refer to Figure 5.37 as you complete this exercise.

	Order Date	Salesperson	Category	Sale Item	Total Amount
3	Order Date	Salesperson	Category	Sale Item	Total Amount
22			Accessories Total		$ 8,673.23
70			Casual wear Total		$ 32,870.22
101			Dress Shirts and Ties Total		$ 19,280.39
126			Sport Jackets and Slacks Total		$ 28,679.05
175			Suits Total		$ 71,981.32
188			Underwear Total		$ 1,024.91
189		Adams Total			$ 162,509.12
220			Accessories Total		$ 8,893.02
296			Casual Wear Total		$ 41,884.53
322			Dress Shirts and Ties Total		$ 12,167.17
360			Sport Jackets and Slacks Total		$ 41,201.04
408			Suits Total		$ 80,843.55
421			Underwear Total		$ 1,248.57
422		Baker Total			$ 186,237.88
443			Accessories Total		$ 6,327.99
489			Casual wear Total		$ 22,565.30
511			Dress Shirts and Ties Total		$ 9,878.98
535			Sport Jackets and Slacks Total		$ 24,945.13
576			Suits Total		$ 59,443.75
591			Underwear Total		$ 1,680.33
592		Davis Total			$ 124,841.48
613			Accessories Total		$ 8,595.89
654			Casual Wear Total		$ 19,318.44
687			Dress Shirts and Ties Total		$ 18,170.45
716			Sport Jackets and Slacks Total		$ 29,509.26
763			Suits Total		$ 68,538.25
772			Underwear Total		$ 785.42
773		Goodman Total			$ 144,917.71
774		Grand Total			$ 618,506.18
775					

FIGURE 5.37 Subtotals

a. Open *e05p1MensStore* and save it as **e05p1MensStore_LastFirst**.

b. Sort the list by salesperson and then by category within salesperson.

c. Click the **DATA tab** and click **Subtotal** in the Outline group. Do the following in the Subtotal dialog box:
   - Click the **At each change in arrow** and select **Salesperson**.
   - Click the **Order Amount check box** and the **Sales Tax check box** in the *Add subtotal to* list.
   - Keep the *Total Amount* check box selected. Click **OK**.

d. Add a second-level subtotal by category by doing the following:
   - Click **Subtotal** in the Outline group.
   - Click the **At each change in arrow** and select **Category**.
   - Keep the *Order Total*, *Sales Tax*, and *Total Amount* check boxes selected.
   - Click the **Replace current subtotals check box** to deselect it. Click **OK**.

e. Click **2** to collapse the list to see the salesperson subtotals. Who had the highest order totals for the year? Who had the lowest order totals for the year?

f. Click **3** to expand the list to see category subtotals for each salesperson. Who had the highest dress shirts and tie sales for the year? Is this the same person who had the overall highest order totals for the year?

g. Click the **Group arrow** in the Outline group on the DATA tab and select **Auto Outline**. Click **OK** when prompted to modify the existing outline. Click the **collapse button** above column G to collapse the columns.

h. Create a footer with your name on the left side, the sheet name code in the center, and the file name code on the right side.

i. Save and close the workbook, and submit based on your instructor's directions.

Your college friend Cirio owns a successful Greek restaurant in Denver, Colorado. He tracks daily dinner revenue but needs your assistance to consolidate data for the entire year. Specifically, he wants to compare quarterly totals by weekday, and he wants to take a closer look at the fourth-quarter revenue. You will insert two functions to complete the main worksheet and then create a relationship between that table and a related table of weekday names. You will build a PivotTable and a PivotChart to help Cirio analyze the weekday revenue by quarters. This exercise follows the same set of skills as used in Hands-On Exercises 2–4 in the chapter. Refer to Figure 5.38 as you complete this exercise.

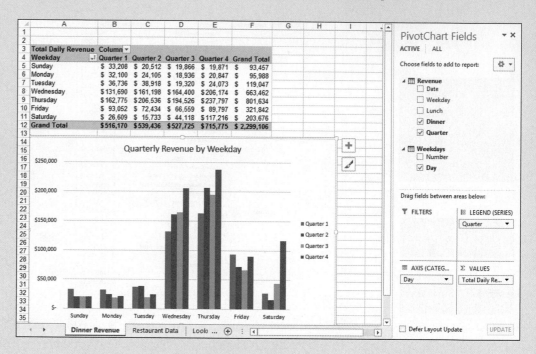

FIGURE 5.38 PivotTable and PivotChart

a. Open *e05p2Dinner* and save it as **e05p2Dinner_LastFirst**. Click the **Lookup Tables worksheet tab** to see the two datasets. The first dataset is a table named Weekdays that will be used to relate the day numbers (such as 2) with the names of the weekdays (such as Monday). The second dataset is a lookup table range-named Quarters so that you can create a VLOOKUP function to look up a value within a breakpoint, identified by month numbers, and return which quarter the month is in. For example, the fifth month (5) returns Quarter 2.

b. Create two formulas to calculate missing values by doing the following:

• Click the **Restaurant Data worksheet tab**, click in **cell B2**, type **=WEEKDAY(A2)**, and then press **Enter**. For 1/1/2016, the WEEKDAY function returns 6, which represents Friday.

• Click **cell E2**, type **=VLOOKUP(MONTH(A2),Quarters,2)**, and then press **Enter**. MONTH(A2) returns the month from the data in cell A2, which is 1. The VLOOKUP function looks up the month number in the lookup table that is range-named Quarters and returns the quarter of the year for that date. For example, months 1 through 3 return Quarter 1.

DISCOVER

c. Create a relationship between the Revenues table in the Restaurant Data worksheet and the Weekdays table in the Lookup Tables worksheet by doing the following:

• Click the **DATA tab** and click **Relationships** in the Data Tools group to open the Manage Relationships dialog box.

• Click **New** to open the Create Relationships dialog box.

• Click the **Table arrow** and select **Revenue** (the main table). Click the **Column (Foreign) arrow** and select **Weekday**.

• Click the **Related Table arrow** and select **Weekdays**. Click the **Related Column (Primary) arrow** and select **Number**.

• Click **OK** to close the Create Relationships dialog box. Click **Close** to close the Manage Relationships dialog box.

d. Use PowerPivot to create a PivotTable using the related tables by doing the following:

- Click the **INSERT tab** and click **PivotTable** in the Tables group to open the Create PivotTable dialog box.
- Click the **Add this data to the Data Model check box** in the *Choose whether you want to analyze multiple tables* section. Click **OK**.
- Click **ALL** at the top of the PivotTable Fields task pane to display all table names.
- Click **Revenue** at the top of the task pane to display the fields for the Revenue table.
- Click the **Dinner** and **Quarter check boxes** in the task pane and drag **Quarter** from the ROWS area to the COLUMNS area.
- Scroll down, if necessary, and click **Weekdays** in the task pane to display the fields for the Weekdays table.
- Click the **Day check box** in the task pane to add this field to the ROWS area.

e. Modify the PivotTable by doing the following:

- Click the **Row Labels arrow** in **cell A4** and select **Sort A to Z**. (Note that this action sorts in sequential order by weekday, not alphabetical order by weekday name.)
- Click **cell A4**, type **Weekday**, and then press **Enter**.
- Click the **DESIGN tab**, click the **More button** in the PivotTable Styles group, and then click **Pivot Style Light 15**.

f. Format the values by doing the following:

- Click **cell B5**, click the **ANALYZE tab**, and then click **Field Settings** in the Active Field group.
- Type **Total Daily Revenue** in the **Custom Name box**.
- Click **Number Format**, click **Accounting**, click the **Decimal places spin arrow** to display *0*, click **OK** in the Format Cells dialog box, and then click **OK** in the Value Field Settings dialog box.
- Set a column width of **9** for column B.

g. Create a PivotChart from the PivotTable by doing the following.

- Click **PivotChart** in the Tools group on the ANALYZE tab and click **OK** in the Insert Chart dialog box to create a default column chart.
- Click the **DESIGN tab**, click **Quick Layout** in the Chart Layouts group, and then click **Layout 1**.
- Click the **Chart Title placeholder**, type **Quarterly Revenue by Weekday**, and then press **Enter**.
- Move the chart so that the top-left corner starts in **cell A14**. Resize the chart to extend through **cell H35**.
- Click the **ANALYZE tab**, click **Field Buttons** in the Show/Hide group, and then select **Hide All** to hide the buttons within the chart area.

h. Rename the Sheet1 worksheet **Dinner Revenue**. Create a footer with your name on the left side, the sheet name code in the center, and the file name code on the right side on each worksheet.

i. Save and close the workbook, and submit based on your instructor's directions.

3 ## Greek Restaurant Combined Revenue

Cirio needs to conduct additional revenue analysis. Now he wants you to create a PivotTable that displays the daily percentage of revenue that contributes to the total lunch and dinner revenues, respectively. Because he has a list of several ways to view the data, you decide to insert slicers so that Cirio can filter the PivotTable data himself. This exercise follows the same set of skills as used in Hands-On Exercises 2–4 in the chapter. Refer to Figure 5.39 as you complete this exercise.

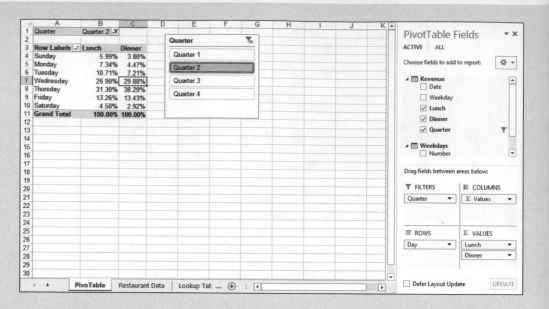

FIGURE 5.39 PivotTable and Slicers

a. Open *e05p3Revenue* and save it as **e05p3Revenue_LastFirst**.

b. Use PowerPivot to create a PivotTable using the related tables by doing the following:

- Click the **INSERT tab** and click **PivotTable** in the Tables group to open the Create PivotTable dialog box.
- Click the **Add this data to the Data Model check box** in the *Choose whether you want to analyze multiple tables* section. Click **OK**.
- Click **ALL** at the top of the PivotTable Fields task pane to display all table names.
- Click **Weekdays** at the top of the task pane to display the fields for the Weekday table.
- Drag **Day** to the ROWS area.
- Click **Revenue** in the task pane to display the fields for the Revenue table.
- Drag the **Quarter field** to the FILTERS area.
- Click the **Lunch** and **Dinner check boxes** to add them to the VALUES area.
- Click the **Row Labels arrow** in **cell A3** and select **Sort A to Z**.

c. Display the daily revenue as a percentage of total weekly sales for lunch by doing the following:

- Click **cell B4** and click **Field Settings** in the Active Field group to open the Value Field Settings dialog box.
- Type **Lunch** in the **Custom Name box**.
- Click the **Show Values As tab** in the dialog box, click the **Show Value As arrow**, and then select **% of Column Total**. Click **OK** in the Value Field Settings dialog box.
- Apply the custom name **Dinner** to **cell C4** and show the values as *% of Column Total*. Click **OK** to close the dialog box.

d. Click **Insert Slicer** in the Filter group, click the **Quarter check box** in the Insert Slicer dialog box, and then click **OK**.

e. Move the slicer to the right of the PivotTable, click the **SLICER TOOLS OPTIONS tab**, enter **1.8** in the **Width box** in the Size group, and then enter **1.77** in the **Height box** in the Size group.

f. Click the **Quarter 2 slicer slice** to filter the PivotTable by the second quarter of the year.

g. Create a footer with your name on the left side, the sheet name code in the center, and the file name code on the right side on each worksheet.

h. Save and close the workbook, and submit based on your instructor's directions.

1 Mountain View Realty

ANALYSIS CASE

You are a real estate analyst who works for Mountain View Realty in the North Utah County area. You have consolidated a list of houses sold during the past few months and need to start analyzing the data. For a simple analysis, you will outline the data and use the Subtotal feature. Then you will create a PivotTable to give you a way to perform more in-depth analysis.

a. Open *e05m1RealEstate* and save it as **e05m1RealEstate_LastFirst**.

b. Make sure the Sales Subtotals worksheet is the active sheet. Insert a column between the Selling Price and Listing Date columns. Enter the heading **% of Asking Price** and double-click between the column G and H headings to increase the column width. Insert a formula in **cell G2** to calculate the selling price percentage of the asking price, format it with **Percent Style** with one decimal place, and then copy the formula down the column.

c. Enter the heading **Days on Market** on the right side of the last column and double-click between the column J and K headings to increase the column width. Calculate the number of days between the listing date and sale date. Copy the formula down the column.

d. Sort the list by city in alphabetical order, then by selling agent in alphabetical order, and finally by listing date in chronological order.

e. Use the Subtotal feature to calculate the average selling price, percentage of asking price, and days on market by city.

f. Apply an automatic outline to the columns. Collapse the outline to hide the listing and sale dates. Click the appropriate button to display the grand average and city average rows only. Format the average days on market to zero decimal places. Apply wrap text, **10.00** column width, and increased row height to **cells G1** and **J1**. Set a print area for the **range C1:J88**.

⭐ g. Go to **cell C95** in the Sales Subtotals worksheet. Read the questions and provide the appropriate answers in the respective highlighted cells in the **range G96:G100**.

h. Click the **Sales Data worksheet** and create a PivotTable on a new worksheet. Name the new worksheet **PivotTable**.

i. Display the cities in the first row of the PivotTable, selling agents in the first column, and asking and selling prices in additional columns.

j. Modify the PivotTable. Display averages rather than sums with **Accounting Number Format** with zero decimal places. Pivot the data by placing the cities in columns and the selling agents in rows.

k. Add a group filter to display only Alpine and Cedar Hills.

l. Adjust column widths, wrap text as needed, insert a bottom border line below the city names, and then add a more descriptive label for the first column and any other columns that need more descriptive labels. Adjust row heights so that column labels fully display.

m. Go back to the Sales Data worksheet. You realize that a selling price is incorrect. Change the selling price for Number 40 from *$140,000* to **$1,400,000**. Refresh the PivotTable.

n. Create a footer with your name on the left side, the sheet name code in the center, and the file name code on the right side for the Sales Subtotals and the PivotTable worksheets. Adjust the margins and scaling to fit on one page.

o. Save and close the workbook, and submit based on your instructor's directions.

2 Fiesta® Collection

Your Aunt Laura has been collecting Fiesta dinnerware, a popular brand from the Homer Laughlin China Company, since 1986. You help her maintain an inventory. So far, you and Aunt Laura have created a table of color numbers, color names, year introduced, and year retired, if applicable. In a second table, you entered color numbers, item numbers, items, current value, and source. Previously, you helped her research current replacement costs from Homer Laughlin's Web site (www.hlchina.com), Replacements, Ltd. (www.replacements.com), and eBay (www.ebay.com); however, you believe the retired colors may be worth more now. Laura is especially interested in the values of retired colors so that she can provide this information for her insurance agent. You will build a PivotTable and add slicers to help her with the analysis.

a. Open *e05m2Fiesta* and save it as **e05m2Fiesta_LastFirst**.

b. Create a relationship between the Items table using the Color Number field and the Colors table using the Number field.

c. Create a blank PivotTable from within the Items table to analyze multiple tables. Place the PivotTable on a new worksheet and name the worksheet **Retired Colors**.

d. Display the names of both tables in the PivotTable Fields task pane.

e. Display the Color names as ROWS and the sum of the Replacement Value field as VALUES.

f. Add a FILTER to display aggregates for retired colors only. Note that current colors do not have a retirement date, so you must filter out the blanks.

g. Apply the **Pivot Style Medium 7**.

h. Format the values with **Accounting Number Format** with two decimal places. Create a custom heading named **Replacement Value**. Change *Row Labels* in **cell A3** to **Retired Colors**.

DISCOVER

i. Add a calculated field by doing the following:

- Display the Excel Options dialog box, click **Customize Ribbon** on the left side of the dialog box, click the **POWERPIVOT check box** in the *Customize the Ribbon* section on the right side, and then click **OK**.
- Use the Calculated Fields command to create a new calculated field.
- Enter the formula to multiply [Sum of Replacement Value] by 1.15.
- Type the custom name **Updated Replacement Values**. Word-wrap and center the label.
- Apply the same number format that you did for the Replacement Values column.

j. Add slicers for the Color field. Select these colors to display: **Apricot**, **Chartreuse**, **Lilac**, **Marigold**, **Pearl Gray**, and **Sapphire**.

k. Apply the **Slicer Style Light 6 style**.

l. Create a footer with your name on the left side, the sheet name code in the center, and the file name code on the right side of the Retired Colors worksheet.

m. Save and close the workbook, and submit based on your instructor's directions.

3 Facebook® Social Phenomenon

COLLABORATION CASE

FROM SCRATCH

Facebook has experienced phenomenal growth since its creation in 2004. What is it that has made Facebook a huge success story, starting a decade after many of the other Web company startups? To understand how people use Facebook, look at its applications. Work with another student to conduct this research, obtain data, and create PivotTables.

a. Open www.checkfacebook.com in a Web browser to read about Facebook's history.

b. Start a new Excel workbook and save it as **e05m3Facebook_LastFirst**.

c. Go to **http://statistics.allfacebook.com** and use this site to build a worksheet that lists at least 200 application leaders for 10 categories, two of which must be Business and Just For Fun. Each student should find 100 different application leaders. Use collaboration tools to make sure you and your team member use the same format and do not duplicate data.

d. Include data for these columns: Category, Name, Daily Average Use (DAU), Monthly Average Use (MAU), and Daily Growth.

e. Copy your team member's worksheet as a new worksheet in your workbook. Then create a third worksheet to combine the data. Name the sheets appropriately.

f. Format the data and headings appropriately in the combined worksheet.

g. Create a PivotTable based on the data to reflect one perspective of analysis. Format the values and apply desired filters.

h. Have your teammate copy the combined sheet and create his or her own PivotTable with a different perspective, formatting, and desired filters.

i. Discuss your analysis with your team member.

j. Create a footer with your name and your team member's name on the left side, sheet name code in the center, and the file name code on the right side of each worksheet.

k. Save and close the workbook, and submit based on your instructor's directions.

Beyond the Classroom

Departing Flights
RESEARCH CASE

You want to research morning flight departures at Oklahoma City Will Rogers Airport. Find the airport's departing flight schedule and copy the morning departing flight information to a new worksheet. Name the workbook as **e05b2OKC_LastFirst**. Clean up the data after copying it. Name the worksheet as **Morning Departures**. Create a PivotTable using the *Count of Departing To by Airline* recommendation. Display the Status field as a column so that you can see canceled, on-time, and delayed flights. Add the Gate information as a secondary row label. Apply **PivotStyle Medium 13 style**. Type **Airlines and Gates** in **cell A4**. Type **Status** in **cell B3**. Adjust column widths as needed. Name the worksheet **PivotTable**.

Create a PivotChart from the original dataset. Use the Airline field as the Axis and the Flight # as the Value. Change the chart type to a pie chart. Add a chart title and percentage data labels. Adjust the chart size and location as needed. Name the sheet as **PivotChart**. Create a footer with your name, the sheet name code, and the file name code on each worksheet. Save and close the workbook, and submit based on your instructor's directions.

Innovative Game Studio
DISASTER RECOVERY

You work as an assistant to Terry Park, the producer for a video game studio in Phoenix, Arizona. The company produces games for the PlayStation®, Xbox®, and Wii™ consoles. The producer tracks salaries and performance for everyone on a particular team, which consists of artists, animators, programmers, and so forth. Terry tried to create a PivotTable to organize the data by department and then by title within department. He also wants to display total salaries by these categories and filter the data to show aggregates for team members who earned only Excellent and Good performance ratings. In addition, he wants to see what the percentages of total salaries for each job title are of each department's budget. For example, the total salary for Senior Artists is $263,300. That represents 50.27% of the Art Department's salary budget for Excellent- and Good-rated employees. However, the percentages are not displayed correctly. Terry called you in to correct his PivotTable.

Open *e05b3Games* and save it as **e05b3Games_LastFirst**. Identify the errors and make a list of these errors starting on row 41 in the PivotTable worksheet. Correct the errors and improve the format, including a medium Pivot Style, throughout the PivotTable. Create a footer with your name, the sheet name code, and the file name code. Save and close the workbook, and submit based on your instructor's directions.

Job Fair
SOFT SKILLS CASE

FROM SCRATCH

You are ready to help your college create a worksheet to organize the companies that will participate. Create a list of companies, the cities in which they are located, and the number of active openings they are advertising. Include any other details that help classify the companies. Sort the list by a major classification and then display subtotals to indicate the total number of jobs by classification. Save the workbook as **e05b4JobFair_LastFirst**. Create a footer with your name, the sheet name code, and the file name code. Save and close the workbook, and submit based on your instructor's directions.

Capstone Exercise

You are an analyst for an authorized Greenwich Workshop® fine art dealer (www.greenwichworkshop.com). Customers are especially fond of James C. Christensen's art. You prepared a list of artwork: art, type, edition size, release date, issue price, and estimated current market value. Studying the data will help you discuss value trends with art collectors.

Sort, Subtotal, and Outline Data

You need to organize data to facilitate using the Subtotal feature. Then you will further outline the list so that you can collapse and expand groups.

a. Open *e05c1FineArt* and save it as **e05c1FineArt_LastFirst**.

b. Click the **Subtotals worksheet**. Sort the data by type and further sort it by the name of the art, both in alphabetical order.

c. Use the Subtotal feature to identify the highest Issue Price and Est. Value.

d. Select and group the first and last name columns.

e. Collapse the names created by the grouping.

f. Study the list to see the Est. Value in each type.

Create a PivotTable

Although creating an outline and subtotaling data are helpful for an initial analysis of the artwork values, you will create a PivotTable for further analysis.

a. Click the **Christensen worksheet** and create a blank PivotTable from the data.

b. Use the Type, Release Date, and Issue Price fields, enabling Excel to determine where the fields go.

c. Remove the Release Date field. Add the Est. Value field.

Format the PivotTable

You will calculate averages within each art type. You will format the values and provide clear headings in the PivotTable.

a. Modify the value fields to determine the average issue price and average estimated market value by type.

b. Insert a calculated field to determine percent change in values by type.

c. Format the three columns of values appropriately, using whole numbers for dollar values and two decimal places for percentages.

d. Edit the custom names for the values columns. Apply these formats to the three values column headings: wrap text, center horizontally, **30** row height, and **9.7** column widths.

e. Enter appropriate labels for the first column and the grand total label.

Filter the PivotTable and Apply a Style

You want to focus on average values for sold-out art because these pieces typically increase in value on the secondary market. In addition, you want to narrow the list to particular types. After filtering the data, you will apply a style.

a. Set a filter to display only sold-out art (indicated by *Yes*).

b. Set a Type filter to *omit* Hand Colored Print, Limited Edition Hand Colored Print, Open Edition Print, and Poster types.

c. Apply **Pivot Style Medium 5**.

d. Display banded columns and banded rows.

Create a PivotChart

To help interpret the consolidated values of the art, you want to create a PivotChart. You realize that displaying both monetary values and percentages on the same chart is like mixing apples and oranges. If you modify the PivotChart, you will change the PivotTable; therefore, you will create a PivotChart from the original data source.

a. Use the Christensen worksheet to create a PivotChart.

b. Use the Type, Issue Price, and Est. Value fields. Find the average issue price and average estimated value.

c. Set filters as you did for the first PivotTable.

d. Apply formatting as you did for the first PivotTable.

e. Change the chart type to **Bar**.

f. Move the PivotChart below the PivotTable, resize the PivotChart, and hide the field buttons in the PivotChart.

g. Insert an appropriate chart title reflecting the contents and the filter. Set a **12-pt font size** for the chart title.

h. Set the upper limit of the value axis to **2000** if needed.

i. Sort the PivotTable in such a way that its effect on the PivotChart is to display the category labels alphabetically.

j. Type **Art Type** in cell A3 and type **Overall Averages** in cell A13.

Finalizing Your Workbook

You need to finalize your workbook.

a. Rename the first PivotTable worksheet **PivotTable**.

b. Rename the second PivotTable/PivotChart worksheet **PivotChart**.

c. Select landscape orientation and adjust the top and bottom margins for the Subtotals worksheet.

d. Create a footer on all four worksheets with your name, the sheet name code, and the file name code.

e. Save and close the workbook, and submit based on your instructor's directions.

What-If Analysis

Using Decision-Making Tools

OBJECTIVES AFTER YOU READ THIS CHAPTER, YOU WILL BE ABLE TO:

1. Create a one-variable data table p. 266
2. Create a two-variable data table p. 270
3. Identify an input value with Goal Seek p. 277
4. Use Scenario Manager p. 278
5. Generate scenario summary reports p. 280
6. Load the Solver add-in p. 286
7. Optimize results with Solver p. 287

CASE STUDY | Personal Finance: Buying Your First Home

After several years of living with friends after college, you have decided to purchase your first home. After doing some preliminary research on prices, you developed a spreadsheet to help you calculate your monthly mortgage payment, total amount to repay the loan, and the total amount of interest you will pay. Your total budget for the home is $150,000 including taxes, closing costs, and other miscellaneous fees. You plan to take $10,000 out of your savings account for a down payment. You are currently investigating loan interest rates at various banks and credit unions. You realize that you may need to find a less expensive home or increase your down payment. Although you can change input values to see how different values affect the monthly payment, you want to be able to see the comparisons at the same time. In addition, you want to look at your budget to review the impact of purchasing a new home on your income and expenses.

You will use Excel to help you analyze the variables that affect the mortgage payment, total amount to repay the loan, and the total interest paid. To help you make a decision, you will use several tools, each with specific purposes, benefits, and restrictions. With these tools, you will have a better understanding of how a mortgage payment will affect your overall budget.

One- and Two-Variable Data Tables

You are now ready to explore Excel's powerful what-if analysis tools. *What-if analysis* enables you to experiment with different variables or assumptions so that you can observe and compare how these changes affect a related outcome. A *variable* is an input value that can change to other values to affect the results of a situation. People in almost every industry perform some type of what-if analysis to make educated decisions. For example, business people perform what-if analysis to see the impact that producing different quantities of a product will have on revenue. Remember that these what-if analysis tools are just that—tools. While these tools do not provide the definitive, perfect solution to a problem, they will help you analyze data and interpret data, but you or another human must make ultimate decisions based on the data.

In this section, you will learn how to create one- and two-variable data tables to perform what-if analysis. You will design the data tables, insert formulas, and complete the data tables to compare the results for different values of the variables.

Creating a One-Variable Data Table

A *one-variable data table* is a structured range that contains different values for *one variable* to compare how these values affect one or more calculated results. For example, you can use a one-variable data table to compare monthly payments on a mortgage. As you recall, monthly payments are based on the interest rate, the number of payment periods, and the amount of the loan. Holding the number of payment periods and loan amount constant, you can compare how different values of the interest rate (the one variable) affect the calculated results: monthly payment, total amount to repay the loan, and total interest paid.

When setting up a one-variable data table, you must decide which one variable you want to use. After you decide on an input variable, then you select one or more formulas that depend on that input variable for calculations.

Set Up the Substitution Values

STEP 1》 Your first step is to decide which one variable, such as the interest rate, to manipulate. Then you need to specify the substitution values. A *substitution value* is a value that replaces the original input value of the variable in a data table. For example, the original interest rate is 4.5%, but you might want to substitute 5%, 5.5%, 6%, 6.5%, and 7% to see how changing the interest rate affects the results.

Locate a range to the right of or below the regular worksheet data to create the one-variable data table. Leave at least one blank row and one blank column between the dataset and the data table. Enter the substitution values down one column or across one row. With one variable and several results, a vertical orientation for the substitution values is recommended because people often look up a value in the first column of a table and then read across to see corresponding values.

You can enter the substitution values yourself or use the Series dialog box to help complete a series of values. To use the Series dialog box, do the following:

1. Type the first substitution value (such as 5%) in cell D4 and keep that cell as the active cell (see Figure 6.1, cell D4).
2. Click the HOME tab, click Fill in the Editing group, and then select Series to open the Series dialog box (see Figure 6.1).
3. Click Rows to place the series of substitution values in a row or click Columns to place the series of substitution values down a column.

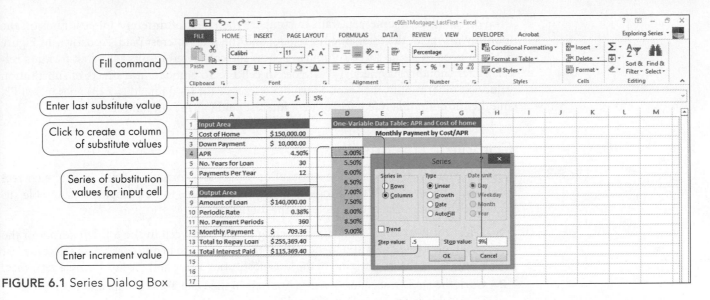

Labels pointing to the figure:
- Fill command
- Enter last substitute value
- Click to create a column of substitute values
- Series of substitution values for input cell
- Enter increment value

FIGURE 6.1 Series Dialog Box

4. Enter the value increment in the *Step value* box and enter the ending value for the series in the *Stop value* box. For example, if you want to create a list of incremental interest rates, such as 5%, 5.5%, and 6% up to 9%, then enter 0.5% in the *Step value* box and 9% in the *Stop value* box.

5. Click OK. Excel fills in a series of values, as shown in Figure 6.1. You may need to format the percentages to show one or more decimal places. If decimal places are not displayed, the interest rate values will appear rounded to the nearest integer.

TIP Auto Fill a Series of Substitution Values

Instead of using the Series dialog box, you can use Auto Fill to complete a series of substitution values. To do this, enter the first two substitution values (such as 5% and 5.5%). Select the cells containing these two values and drag the fill handle down until the ScreenTip displays the last substitution value you want. Excel sets the increment pattern based on the difference between the first two values.

Add Formulas to the Data Table

STEP 2 After you enter the substitution values in either a column or row, you must add one or more formulas that relate mathematically to the variable for which you are using substitution values. Although you can create formulas directly in the data table, referencing cells containing existing formulas outside the data table is preferable because the formulas are often already created. You can save time and reduce errors by referencing the original formula. Within the data table range, the formula references must be entered in a specific location based on the location of your substitution values (see Table 6.1).

TABLE 6.1 Locations for Formula References

Location of Substitution Values	Enter the First Formula Reference	Enter Additional Formula References
Vertically in a column	On the row above and one column to the right of the first substitution value	To the right of the first formula reference
Horizontally in a row	On the row below and one column to the left of the first substitution value	Below the first formula reference

For example, assume you want to compare the effect of different interest rates on the monthly payment, the total amount repaid, and the total interest paid. As shown in Figure 6.2, you need to set up three columns to show the calculated results. The first formula reference for monthly payment (=B12) goes in cell E3. To compare the effects of substitution values on other results, the second formula reference for total repaid (=B13) goes in cell F3, and the third formula reference for total interest paid (=B14) goes in cell G3.

Complete the Results

STEP 3 ▶▶ It is important that you enter the substitution values and formula references in the correct locations. This sets the left and top boundaries of the soon-to-be-completed data table. To complete the one-variable data table, do the following:

1. Select the data table boundaries, starting in the blank cell in the top-left corner of the data table. Drag down and to the right, if there is more than one column, to select the last blank cell at the intersection of the last substitution value and the last formula reference.

2. Click the DATA tab, click What-If Analysis in the Data Tools group, and then select Data Table to open the Data Table dialog box (see Figure 6.2).

3. Enter the cell reference of the cell containing the original variable for which you are substituting values. If you listed the substitution values in a row, enter the original variable cell reference in the *Row input cell* box. If you listed the substitution values in a column, enter the original variable cell reference in the *Column input cell* box. In Figure 6.2, for example, click cell B4—the original interest rate variable—in the *Column input cell* box because you entered the substitution interest rates in a column. Note that the cell reference is automatically made absolute so that Excel always refers to the original input cell as it performs calculations in the data table.

4. Click OK.

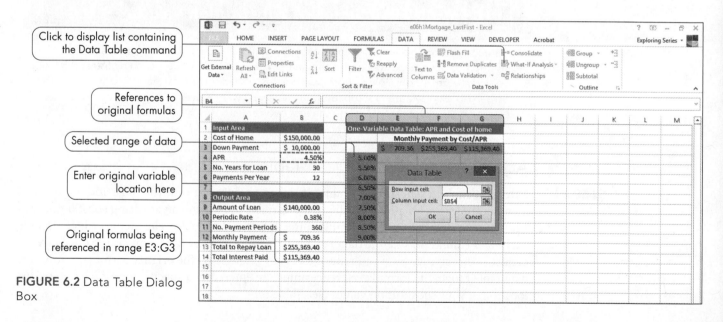

FIGURE 6.2 Data Table Dialog Box

When you create the one-variable data table, Excel uses the substitution values individually to replace the original variable's value, which is then used in the formulas to produce the results in the body of the data table. In Figure 6.3, the data table shows the substitution values of different interest rates, whereas the formulas produce the monthly payments (column E), total payments (column F), and total interest paid (column G) for the respective interest rates.

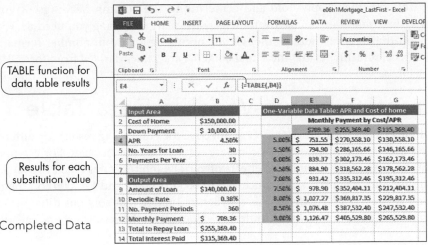

TABLE function for data table results

Results for each substitution value

FIGURE 6.3 Completed Data Table

Format the Data Table

After creating the data table, you should format the values with Accounting Number Format. To reduce confusion, you should also create custom formats to disguise the formula references as column labels. To create custom formats, do the following:

1. Click in the cell containing a formula reference in the data table.
2. Click the Number Dialog Box Launcher in the Number group on the HOME tab to open the Format Cells dialog box with the Number tab active.
3. Click Custom in the Category list, scroll up in the Type list, and then select General in the list.
4. Select General in the Type box above the Type list and type what you want to appear as a column heading. Enter the text within quotation marks, such as "Payment," and click OK. Note that you must include the word to be displayed within quotation marks or the custom format will not display properly (see Figure 6.4).
5. Click OK.

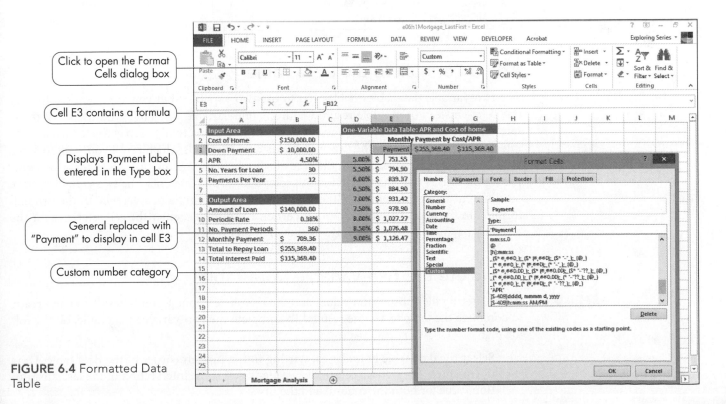

Click to open the Format Cells dialog box

Cell E3 contains a formula

Displays Payment label entered in the Type box

General replaced with "Payment" to display in cell E3

Custom number category

FIGURE 6.4 Formatted Data Table

You can then apply bold and centering to the column headings. If you see pound signs, the column is too narrow to display the text, indicating you need to wrap the text or expand the column width. Although you are using a custom number format that displays text, Excel remembers that the actual contents are values derived from formulas.

Creating a Two-Variable Data Table

Although a one-variable data table is effective for comparing results for different values for one variable, you might want to compare results for two variables. For example, you might want to compare the combined effects of various interest rates (such as 5%, 5.5%, and 6%) and different down payments (such as $10,000, $15,000, and $20,000) on the monthly payment. A *two-variable data table* is a structured range that contains different values for *two variables* to compare how these differing values affect the results for one calculated value.

Set Up the Substitution Values for Two Variables

STEP 4 » Create the two-variable data table separate from regular worksheet data, similar to the method used for a one-variable data table. For a two-variable data table, you use the top row for one variable's substitution values and the first column for the other variable's substitution values. Figure 6.5 shows substitution interest rates in the first column (range D4:D12) and substitution down payments in the first row (range E3:G3).

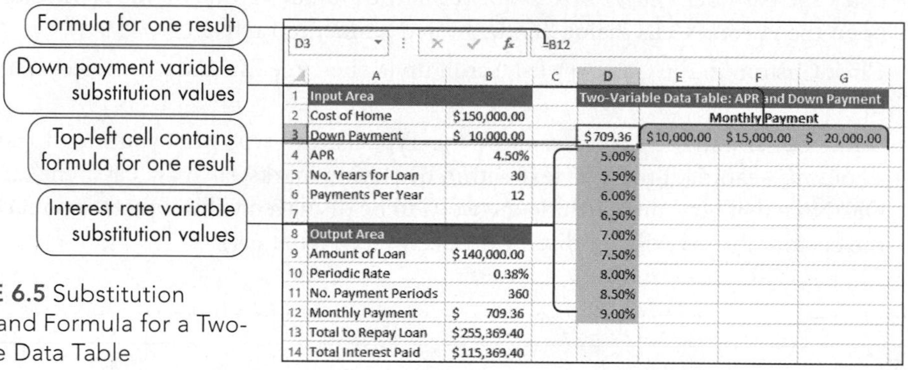

FIGURE 6.5 Substitution Values and Formula for a Two-Variable Data Table

Add a Formula to the Data Table

The two-variable data table enables you to use two variables, but you are restricted to only one result instead of multiple results. With the one-variable data table, you use the interest rate variable to compare multiple results: monthly payment, total to repay the loan, and total interest paid. However, for the two-variable data table, decide which result you want to focus on based on the two variables. In the case of a home loan, you might want to focus on comparing the effects that changes in interest rates and down payments (the two variables) have on different monthly payments (the result). Enter the formula or reference to the original formula in the blank cell in the top-left corner. For example, enter the cell reference for the monthly payment (=B12) in cell D3 as shown in Figure 6.5.

Complete the Two-Variable Data Table

STEP 5 » After entering the substitution values and the reference to one formula result, you are ready to complete the table to see the results. To complete the two-variable data table, do the following:

1. Select the data table boundaries, starting in the top-left corner of the data table. Drag down and to the right to select the last blank cell at the intersection of the last substitution value for both the column and the row.

2. Click the DATA tab, click What-If Analysis in the Data Tools group, and then select Data Table. The Data Table dialog box opens.

3. Enter the cell that contains the original value for the substitution values in the first row in the *Row input cell* box. Enter the cell that contains the original value for the substitution values in the first column in the *Column input cell* box. For example, the original row (down payment) variable value is stored in cell B3, and the original column (APR) variable value is stored in cell B4.

4. Click OK.

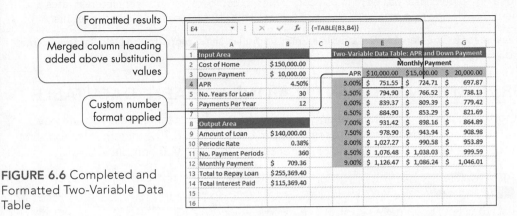

FIGURE 6.6 Completed and Formatted Two-Variable Data Table

After you complete the data table, to reduce confusion, you should format the results by applying a custom number format to the formula cell to appear as a heading and add a merged heading above the row substitution values (see Figure 6.6).

Quick Concepts

1. What is the first step to creating a one-variable data table? *p. 266*

2. Why is it preferable to reference formula cells outside of a one-variable data table versus entering the formula manually? *p. 267*

3. What is the difference between a one- and two-variable data table? *p. 270*

Hands-On Exercises

Watch the Video for this Hands-On Exercise!

MyITLab®
HOE1 Training

1 One- and Two-Variable Data Tables

As you consider different options for a home purchase, you want to use data tables to compare how different interest rates and price will affect your monthly payment. You decide to create both one- and two-variable data tables to analyze the results.

Skills covered: Enter Substitution Values for a One-Variable Data Table • Enter Formulas and Complete the Data Table • Format the One-Variable Data Table • Set Up the Structure for a Two-Variable Data Table • Complete the Two-Variable Data Table

---

STEP 1 ▸▸ ENTER SUBSTITUTION VALUES FOR A ONE-VARIABLE DATA TABLE

You want to compare monthly mortgage payments, total amounts to repay a loan, and total interest you will pay based on several interest rates—the variable. The interest rates range from 4% to 6% in 0.25% increments. Your first step is to enter a series of substitution values for the interest rate. Refer to Figure 6.7 as you complete Step 1.

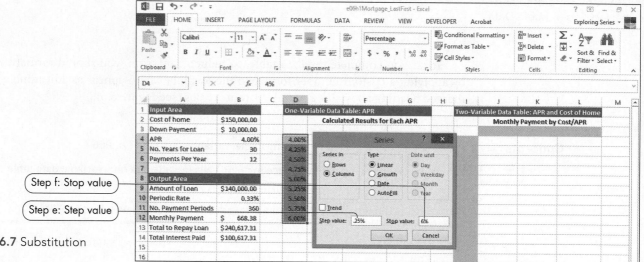

FIGURE 6.7 Substitution Values

a. Open the *e06h1Mortgage* workbook and save it as **e06h1Mortgage_LastFirst**.

> **TROUBLESHOOTING:** If you make any major mistakes in this exercise, you can close the file, open *e06h1Mortgage* again, and then start this exercise over.

b. Click **cell D4**, type **4%**, and then press **Ctrl+Enter**.

    Cell D4 is the first cell containing a substitution value. Make sure cell D4 is still the active cell.

c. Click **Fill** in the Editing group on the HOME tab and select **Series**.

    The Series dialog box opens.

d. Click **Columns**.

    You changed the *Series in* option to Columns because you want the series of substitution values listed vertically in column D.

e. Delete the existing value in the **Step value box** and type **0.25%**.

f. Type **6%** in the **Stop value box** and click **OK**.

Excel fills in the series of values; however, you need to increase the number of decimal points to see the full percentages.

> **TROUBLESHOOTING:** If you forget to type the decimal point in step e and/or the percent sign in steps e or f, the series will be incorrect. If this happens, click Undo and repeat steps c through f.

STEP 2 ≫ ENTER FORMULAS AND COMPLETE THE DATA TABLE

In the next steps, you will enter references to the monthly payment, total amount to repay the loan, and total interest formulas. Then, you will complete the table to compare the results for different interest rates ranging from 4% to 6%. Refer to Figure 6.8 as you complete Step 2.

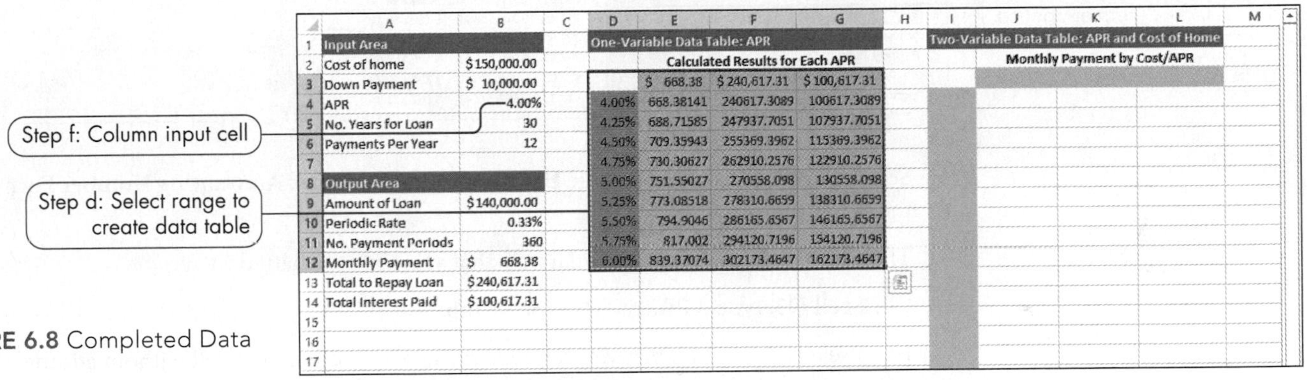

Step f: Column input cell

Step d: Select range to create data table

FIGURE 6.8 Completed Data Table

a. Click **cell E3**, type **=B12**, and then press **Tab**.

You entered a reference to the original monthly payment formula. When the results of cell B12 change, they are reflected in cell E3.

b. Type **=B13** in **cell F3** and press **Tab**.

You entered a reference to the original total amount to repay the loan.

c. Type **=B14** in **cell G3** and press **Enter**.

You entered a reference to the original total interest paid.

d. Select the **range D3:G12**.

You select the entire range of the data table, starting in the blank cell in the top-left corner. Note that you did not select the titles or headings in cells D1:G2.

e. Click the **DATA tab**, click **What-If Analysis** in the Data Tools group, and then select **Data Table**.

f. Click in the **Column input cell box**, click **cell B4**, and then click **OK**. Save the workbook.

Because the substitution values are in a column, you reference cell B4 in the *Column input* box. Excel inserts the TABLE array function in the empty result cells and substitutes the values in range D4:D12 individually for the original APR to calculate the respective monthly payments, total amounts, and total interest payments. The higher the APR, the higher the monthly payment, total amount to repay the loan, and total interest.

STEP 3 ›› FORMAT THE ONE-VARIABLE DATA TABLE

You want to format the results to show dollar signs and to display rounded values to the nearest penny. In addition, you want to add column headings to provide more detail to the data table and add custom formats to the cells to appear as column headings. Refer to Figure 6.9 as you complete Step 3.

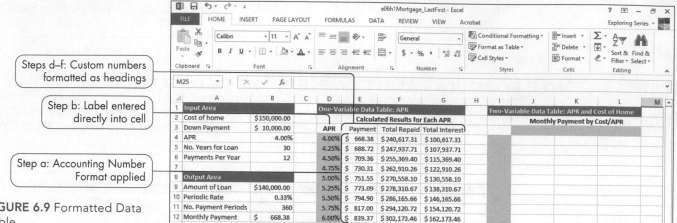

FIGURE 6.9 Formatted Data Table

a. Select the **range E4:G12**, click the **HOME tab**, and then click **Accounting Number Format** in the Number group.

The values look more professional now that you have formatted them.

b. Click **cell D3**, type **APR**, and then press **Tab**.

Because cell D3 was empty, you can type the label directly in the cell without adding a custom format. Cell E3 should now be the active cell.

c. Click the **Number Dialog Box Launcher** in the Number group on the HOME tab of the Ribbon.

d. Select **Custom** in the **Category list**, scroll up through the Type list, and then select **General** in the list.

e. Select **General** in the **Type box**, type **"Payment"**, and then click **OK**.

The formula result $668.38 now appears as Payment in cell E3.

f. Repeat and adapt steps c through e to enter the following custom number formats: **"Total Repaid"** for **cell F3** and **"Total Interest"** for **cell G3**.

> **TROUBLESHOOTING:** If you forget the quotation marks, the cell contents will contain a mix of numbers and characters. If this happens, open the Format Cells dialog box again and edit the contents of the Type box to display the text surrounded by quotation marks.

g. Center and bold the **range E3:G3**. Save the workbook.

STEP 4 ≫ SET UP THE STRUCTURE FOR A TWO-VARIABLE DATA TABLE

Now you want to focus on how a combination of interest rates and different costs will affect just the monthly payment. The interest rates range from 4% to 8% at .25% increments with costs of $200,000, $225,000, and $250,000. Refer to Figure 6.10 as you complete Step 4.

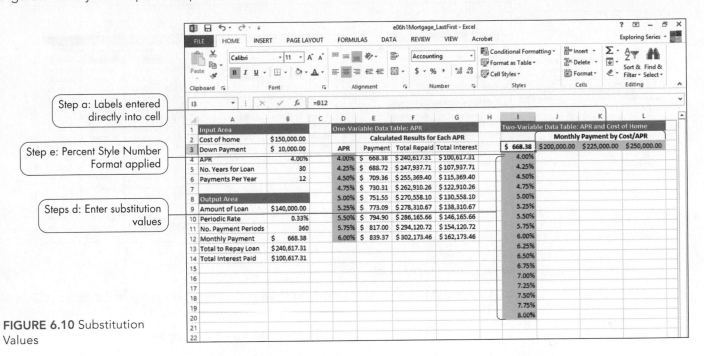

FIGURE 6.10 Substitution Values

- Step a: Labels entered directly into cell
- Step e: Percent Style Number Format applied
- Steps d: Enter substitution values

a. Enter **200000**, **225000**, and **250000** in the **range J3:L3**. Format these values with **Accounting Number Format**.

> **TROUBLESHOOTING:** After formatting the numbers, you may see ### displayed in the cells. The pound signs indicate the number is larger than the width of the column. To automatically expand the column to the proper width, click the HOME tab, click Format from the Cells group, and then select Auto Fit Column Width.

b. Click **cell I4**, type **4%**, and then press **Ctrl+Enter**.

c. Click **Fill** in the Editing group, select **Series**, and then click **Columns**.

d. Replace the existing value in the **Step value box** with **0.25%**, type **8%** in the **Stop value box**, and then click **OK**.

e. Format the **range I4:I20** with **Percent Style** with two decimal places.

f. Click **cell I3**, type **=B12**, and then press **Ctrl+Enter**. Save the workbook.

You inserted the reference to the formula in the top-left cell of the two-variable data table. The cell displays pound signs, indicating the column is too narrow to display the value; you will apply a custom number format in Step 5.

You complete the data table, format the monthly payment results, and apply a custom number format to the cell containing the formula reference so that it displays the text APR. Refer to Figure 6.11 as you complete Step 5.

Step e: Custom number format

Step c: Row input value

Step d: Column input value

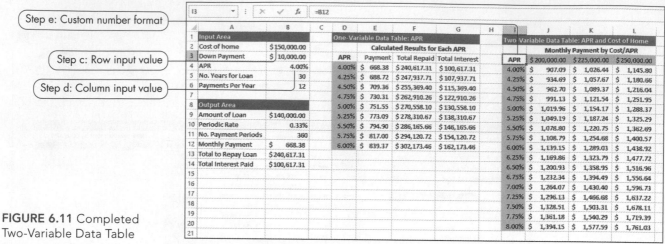

FIGURE 6.11 Completed Two-Variable Data Table

a. Select the **range I3:L20**.

b. Click the **DATA tab**, click **What-If Analysis** in the Data Tools group, and then select **Data Table**.

c. Click **cell B2** to enter that cell reference in the **Row input cell box**.

Because you entered the purchase price substitution values in the top row of the data table, you entered the reference to the cell containing the original cost in the Row input cell box.

d. Click in the **Column input cell box**, click **cell B4**, and then click **OK**.

Because you entered the interest rate substitution values in the left column of the data table, you entered the reference to the cell containing the original APR variable in the Column input cell box.

e. Click **cell I3** and apply a custom number format to display *APR*. Center and bold the contents in **cell I3**.

f. Save the workbook. Keep the workbook open if you plan to continue with Hands-On Exercise 2. If not, close the workbook and exit Excel.

Goal Seek and Scenario Manager

Although data tables are useful for particular situations to compare effects of different values for one or two variables, other what-if analysis tools such as Goal Seek and Scenario Manager are better suited for other situations. For example, you might want to use Goal Seek to determine exactly the down payment required to acquire a desired payment. In this situation, you would not need all of the data provided by a data table. You may also want to weigh the options between various options of down payments, purchase costs, and interest rates. If more than two variables are required, data tables would not be a viable option.

In this section, you will learn when and how to use both Goal Seek and Scenario Manager to assist you in making decisions. These tools enable you to perform what-if analysis to make forecasts or predictions involving quantifiable data.

Identifying an Input Value with Goal Seek

STEP 1》 Suppose the most you can afford for a monthly payment on a mortgage is $800. How can you determine the down payment amount needed to meet that monthly payment? *Goal Seek* is a tool that enables you to specify a desired result from a formula ($800 monthly payment) without knowing what input value achieves that goal. Goal Seek works backward to identify the exact value for a variable to reach your goal. In this case, you can use Goal Seek to determine the required down payment. Unlike variable data tables, Goal Seek uses the original worksheet data to change an input instead of displaying various combinations of results in a separate table. Goal Seek manipulates only one variable and one result; it does not produce a list of values to compare. To use Goal Seek, do the following:

1. Click What-If Analysis in the Data Tools group on the DATA tab.
2. Select Goal Seek to open the Goal Seek dialog box.
3. Enter the cell reference for the cell to be optimized in the *Set cell* box. This cell must contain a formula, such as the monthly payment.
4. Enter the result you want to achieve (such as the $800 goal) in the *To value* box.
5. Enter the cell reference that contains the variable to adjust (such as the down payment) in the *By changing cell* box as shown in Figure 6.12. This cell must be a value, not a formula, which has a mathematical relationship with the cell containing the formula or goal.
6. Click OK.

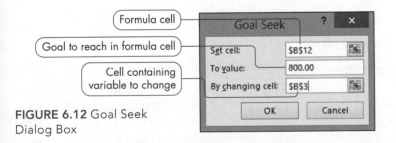

FIGURE 6.12 Goal Seek Dialog Box

Excel varies the input value until the desired result is achieved, if possible, and displays the Goal Seek Status dialog box. Click OK to accept the target value and change the value of the input cell you entered in Step 5 to achieve the goal you specified in Steps 3 and 4. Click Cancel to keep the original input cell value instead of changing it. If Excel cannot determine a solution given the input cell and the desired results, it displays a message box.

Using Scenario Manager

You may want to compare several variables and their combined effects on multiple calculated results. This type of analysis involves identifying and setting up *scenarios*, which are detailed sets of values that represent different possible situations. Business managers often create a best-case scenario, worst-case scenario, and most likely scenario to compare outcomes. For example, a best-case scenario could reflect an increase in units sold and lower production costs. A worst-case scenario could reflect fewer units sold and higher production costs.

Scenario Manager is a what-if analysis tool that enables you to define and manage up to 32 scenarios to compare their effects on calculated results. You can perform more sophisticated what-if analyses with Scenario Manager than with data tables with the increased number of variables and results. The Scenario Manager dialog box (see Figure 6.13) enables you to create, edit, and delete scenario names. Each scenario represents different sets of what-if conditions to assess the outcome of spreadsheet models. Each scenario is stored under its own name and defines cells whose values change from scenario to scenario.

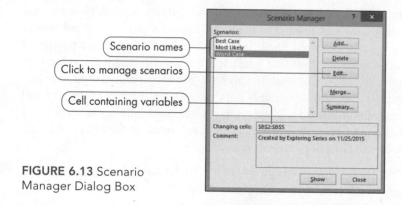

FIGURE 6.13 Scenario Manager Dialog Box

TIP **Scenarios on Different Worksheets**

When you create scenarios, Excel maintains those scenarios on the worksheet that was active when you created them. You can create scenarios for each worksheet in a workbook. The Scenario Manager dialog box displays only those scenarios you have created on the active worksheet.

Create and Edit Scenarios

Before you start the Scenario Manager, identify cells that contain the variables you want to change or manipulate. For example, in evaluating home loans, you might want to manipulate the values for these variables: cost, down payment, interest rate, and the duration of the loan. You enter the cell references for these variables as the changing cells because you change the values to compare the results. After identifying the variables you want to change, identify one or more cells containing formulas that generate results you want to compare. Note these formulas must directly impact the change cell. To create a scenario, do the following:

1. Click What-If Analysis in the Data Tools group on the DATA tab.
2. Select Scenario Manager to open the Scenario Manager dialog box.
3. Click Add to open the Add Scenario dialog box (see Figure 6.14).
4. Enter a meaningful name in the *Scenario name* box.
5. Enter the input cells for the scenario in the *Changing cells* box. These are the cells containing variable values that Scenario Manager will adjust or change. The changing cells must be identical cell references across all scenarios.

6. Click in the Comment box. Excel enters the name of the person who created the scenarios in the Comment box; however, you can change the name and enter additional descriptions and rationales for the scenarios.

7. Click OK to open the Scenario Values dialog box (see Figure 6.15), which lists the changing cell references that you specified in the previous dialog box. In each respective box, type the value you want to use for that particular scenario.

STEP 3 »

8. Click Add to add another scenario and specify its values. After you enter values for the last scenario, click OK to return to the Scenario Manager dialog box.

FIGURE 6.14 Add Scenario Dialog Box

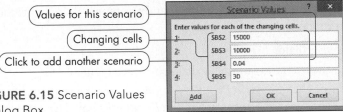

FIGURE 6.15 Scenario Values Dialog Box

TIP Range Names

To help you know what data to enter for the changing cells, you might want to assign a range name to the variable cells before using Scenario Manager. If you do this, the range names, rather than the cell references, appear in the Scenario Values dialog box.

If you need to modify the parameters of a scenario, such as the name or input values, open the Scenario Manager dialog box, select the scenario you want to modify in the Scenarios list, and then click Edit. The Edit Scenario dialog box opens so that you can change the values. Click OK after making the necessary changes.

If you have scenarios in several worksheets or workbooks, you can combine them. Click Merge in the Scenario Manager dialog box to open the Merge Scenarios dialog box. Select the workbook and worksheet and click OK. Use Help to learn more about merging scenarios.

View Scenarios

After you create the scenarios, you can view each of them. To view your scenarios, click What-If Analysis in the Data Tools group on the Data tab, select Scenario Manager, select the name of the scenario you want to view in the Scenarios list, and then click Show. Excel places the defined values in the respective changing cells and displays the results.

Generating Scenario Summary Reports

TIP Updated Scenario Reports

Unlike one- and two-variable data tables that update results if you change other values in the input area, scenario reports do not update. If you change other values or assumptions, or if you add, edit, or delete scenarios, you will have to generate a new scenario report. To avoid this problem, do your best to double-check the scenarios to ensure they are perfect before you generate a scenario summary report.

Although you can view the defined values and their results individually, you will probably want to compare all scenarios in a table. A *scenario summary report* is an organized structured table of the scenarios, their input values, and their respective results. The summary report appears in the form of a worksheet outline and enables you to compare the results based on different values specified by the respective scenarios. Excel can produce two types of reports: scenario summary and scenario PivotTable report. PivotTable reports summarize the data in a pivot table. This provides the same functionality as any other pivot table. Scenario summary reports display the results of each scenario in a new worksheet. The data reported in the summary are formatted without gridlines, and the report is easily printable. To create a scenario summary report, do the following:

1. Open the Scenario Manager dialog box.
2. Click Summary to open the Scenario Summary dialog box (see Figure 6.16).
3. Click *Scenario summary* or click *Scenario PivotTable report*. Enter the reference for the cell(s) whose values change in the scenarios in the *Result cells* box. Drag to select a range of adjacent results cells, or press Ctrl as you click cells in nonadjacent ranges. For example, in Figure 6.16, the result cells are monthly payment (B12) and total interest (B14).
4. Click OK. Excel creates the Scenario Summary on a new worksheet (see Figure 6.17).

FIGURE 6.16 Scenario Summary Dialog Box

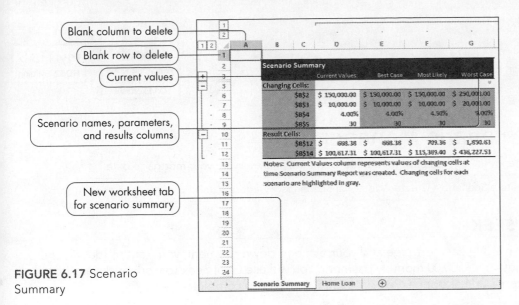

Blank column to delete

Blank row to delete

Current values

Scenario names, parameters, and results columns

New worksheet tab for scenario summary

FIGURE 6.17 Scenario Summary

The scenario summary contains a column listing the changing and result cell references, current values and result values, and a column of values and results for each defined scenario. This organized structure helps you compare the results as you analyze the scenarios. You should modify the structure and format the data for a more professional look. Typically, you should do the following:

- Delete the blank row 1 and the blank column A.
- Delete the Current Values column if it duplicates a defined scenario or if you do not want that data.
- Replace cell reference labels with descriptive labels in the first column.
- Delete the explanatory paragraph below the table and replace it with a narrative analysis relevant to the data.

Quick **Concepts**

1. What is the difference between Goal Seek and Scenario Manager? *p. 278*

2. What is the difference between a scenario summary report and a PivotTable report? *p. 280*

3. Will scenario summary reports automatically update when variables are changed? *p. 280*

Hands-On Exercises

2 Goal Seek and Scenario Manager

You want to use Goal Seek and Scenario Manager to perform additional what-if analyses with your mortgage data.

Skills covered: Use Goal Seek • Create a Scenario • Create Additional Scenarios • Generate and Format a Summary Report

STEP 1 ≫ USE GOAL SEEK

Given the current interest rate with a 30-year mortgage and your planned down payment, you want to identify the most that you can afford and maintain a $600.00 monthly payment. You will use Goal Seek to work backward from your goal to identify the ideal home purchase price. Refer to Figure 6.18 as you complete Step 1.

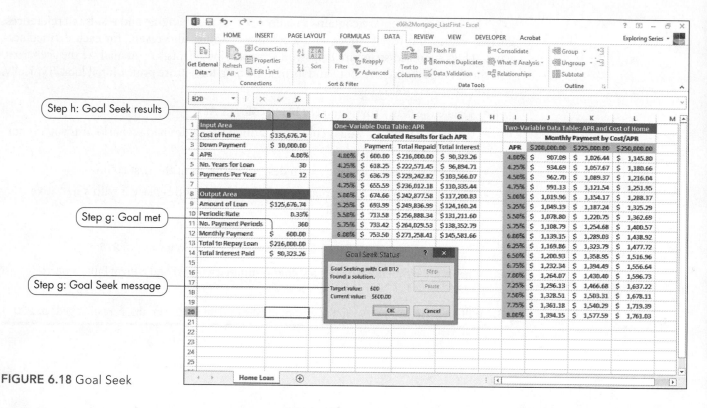

FIGURE 6.18 Goal Seek

a. Open the *e06h1Mortgage_LastFirst* workbook and save it as **e06h2Mortgage_LastFirst**, replacing *h1* with *h2*.

b. Click the **DATA tab**.

c. Click **What-If Analysis** in the Data Tools group and select **Goal Seek**.

   The Goal Seek dialog box opens.

d. Click **cell B12** to enter the cell reference in the **Set cell box**.

   You indicated which cell contains the formula that produces the goal.

e. Click in the **To value box** and type **600**.

   You want the monthly payment to be $600.

f. Click in the **By changing cell box** and click **cell B2**, the cell containing the cost of the home.

   Cell B2 is the cell whose value will be determined using the Goal Seek analysis tool.

g. Click **OK**.

The Goal Seek Status dialog box opens, indicating that it reached the target monthly payment goal of $600.

h. Click **OK** to accept the solution and to close the Goal Seek Status dialog box. Save the workbook.

To achieve a $600 monthly mortgage payment, you need to purchase a home that costs up to $135,676.74, instead of the original $150,000, assuming the other variables (down payment, interest rate, and term of loan) stay the same.

STEP 2 ≫ CREATE A SCENARIO

You want to use Scenario Manager to explore different scenarios. Your first scenario is a best-case scenario with these parameters: $250,000 home, $10,000 down payment, special no-interest financing for 30 years. Refer to Figure 6.19 as you complete Step 2.

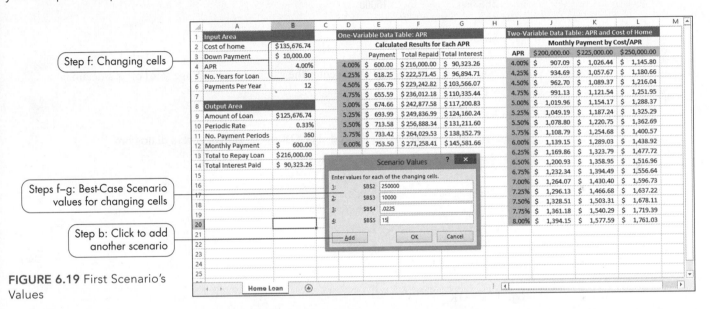

FIGURE 6.19 First Scenario's Values

a. Click the **DATA tab**, if necessary, click **What-If Analysis** in the Data Tools group, and then select **Scenario Manager**.

The Scenario Manager dialog box opens.

b. Click **Add**.

The Add Scenario dialog box opens so that you can assign a scenario name and select the changing cells.

c. Click in the **Scenario name box** and type **Best-Case Scenario**.

d. Delete existing contents in the *Changing cells* box and select the **range B2:B5**.

Excel enters this range in the *Changing cells* box.

e. Edit the Comment box, if needed, to display your name and the date the scenario is created, such as *Created by Jason Davidson on 8/01/2015*, and click **OK**.

The Scenario Values dialog box opens so that you can enter the parameters for the scenario.

f. Type **250000** in the **$B$2 box** and press **Tab** twice to accept the current $10,000 down payment.

You entered 250000 as the cost of the home.

g. Type **.0225** in the **$B$4 box**, press **Tab**, and then type **15** in the **$B$5 box**.

h. Click **OK** and click **Close**. Save the workbook.

While you could have kept the Scenario Values dialog box open to continue to the next step, you closed it so that you could save the workbook.

STEP 3 ≫ CREATE ADDITIONAL SCENARIOS

You will add two more scenarios: a worst-case scenario and a most likely scenario. In the worst-case scenario, you assume you will have to settle for a higher down payment, higher interest rate, and a longer loan period. In the most likely scenario, you will enter values that are between those in the other two scenarios.

a. Click **What-If Analysis** in the Data Tools group and select **Scenario Manager**.

b. Click **Add**, type **Worst-Case Scenario**, and then click **OK**.

The *Changing cells* box displays *B2:B5*, the range you selected for the first scenario.

c. Type the following values in the respective changing cells boxes:

Changing Cell Box	Value
$B$2	250000
$B$3	15000
$B$4	6%
$B$5	45

For the cell $B$4 box, you can enter the value as a percentage (6%) or as a decimal equivalent (0.06).

d. Click **Add**.

e. Type **Most Likely Scenario** and click **OK** in the Add Scenario dialog box.

f. Type the following values in the respective changing cells boxes:

Changing Cell Box	Value
$B$2	250000
$B$3	8500
$B$4	4.25%
$B$5	30

g. Click **OK**.

The Scenario Manager dialog box lists the three scenarios you created.

TROUBLESHOOTING: If you believe you made any data entry errors, or if you want to double-check your values, select a scenario and click Edit. You can then change values in the Edit Scenario dialog box and click OK.

---

h. Click **Close** to close the Scenario Manager dialog box. Save the workbook.

STEP 4 ≫ GENERATE AND FORMAT A SUMMARY REPORT

You want to generate a scenario summary report to compare the three home loan scenarios you created. Refer to Figures 6.17 and 6.20 as you complete Step 4.

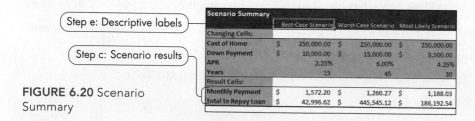

FIGURE 6.20 Scenario Summary

a. Click **What-If Analysis** in the Data Tools group and select **Scenario Manager**.

b. Click **Summary**.

Excel may select a range within a data table.

c. Select the **range B12:B14** to enter it in the *Result cells* box and click **OK**.

Excel generates the summary on a new worksheet named Scenario Summary. The results are similar to Figure 6.17 except your summary also includes $B$13 results. You need to make a few deletions and add descriptive labels.

d. Delete the following:

- Column A
- Row 1
- Current Values column
- Notes in the **range A12:A15**

e. Enter descriptive labels in the following cells:

- **Cost of home** in **cell A5**
- **Down Payment** in **cell A6**
- **APR** in **cell A7**
- **Years** in **cell A8**
- **Monthly Payment** in **cell A10**
- **Total to Repay Loan** in **cell A11**
- **Total Interest Paid** in **cell A12**

The labels describe data contained in each row. Now you can delete column B, which displays the cell references.

f. Delete column B and increase the width of column A.

The Best-Case Scenario provides the lowest monthly payment.

g. Save the workbook. Keep the workbook open if you plan to continue with Hands-On Exercise 3. If not, close the workbook and exit Excel.

 TIP **Scenario Worksheets**

Each time you generate a summary, Excel inserts another Scenario Summary worksheet. You can delete a summary worksheet if you no longer need the data.

Solver

Add-ins are programs that can be added to Excel to provide enhanced functionality. **Solver** is an add-in application that searches for the best or optimum solution to a problem by manipulating the values for several variables within restrictions that you impose. You can use Solver to create optimization models. **Optimization models** find the highest, lowest, or exact value for one particular result by adjusting values for selected variables. Solver is one of the most sophisticated what-if analysis tools, and people use Solver in a variety of situations and industries. For example, a cellular phone manufacturing facility can use Solver to maximize the number of phones made or minimize the number of labor hours required while conforming to other production specifications. A financial planner might use Solver to help a family adjust its expenses to stay within its monthly income.

In this section, you will learn how to load the Solver add-in. Then, you will use Solver to set a target, select changing cells, and create constraints.

Loading the Solver Add-In

STEP 1 » Because other companies create the add-ins, they are not active by default. You must load the Solver add-in before you can use it. To load Solver, do the following:

1. Click the FILE tab and select Options.
2. Click Add-Ins to see a list of active and inactive add-in applications. The Active Application Add-ins list displays currently enabled add-ins, and the Inactive Application Add-ins list displays add-ins that are not currently enabled.
3. Click the Manage arrow, select Excel Add-ins, and then click Go to open the Add-Ins dialog box (see Figure 6.21).
4. Click the Solver Add-in check box in the *Add-Ins available* list and click OK.

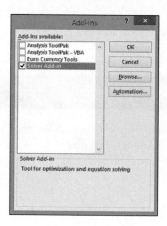

FIGURE 6.21 Add-Ins Dialog Box

When you load Solver, Excel displays Solver in the Analysis group on the Data tab (see Figure 6.22), where it remains until you remove the Solver add-in. However, if you are in a campus computer lab that resets software settings when you log off, you will have to load Solver again each time you log into the lab's network.

FIGURE 6.22 Solver on Data Tab

Optimizing Results with Solver

Solver may be the best what-if analysis tool to solve complex linear and nonlinear problems. You can use it for complex equation solving and for constrained optimization where a set of constraints is specified and you want the outcome to be minimized or maximized. With Solver, you are able to change the values of several variables at once to achieve the desired result. For example, a business analyst might want to use Solver to maximize profits by changing selected variables while adhering to required limitations. Or a fulfillment company might want to determine the lowest shipping costs to transfer merchandise from a distribution center to retail stores.

Identify the Objective Cell and Changing Cells

STEP 2 Before using Solver, review your spreadsheet as you specify the goal, identify one or more variables that can change to reach the desired goal, and determine the limitations of the model. You will use these data to specify three parameters in Solver: objective cell, changing cells, and constraints.

The *objective cell* specifies the cell that contains a formula that produces a value that you want to optimize (that is, maximize, minimize, or set to a value) by manipulating values of one or more variables. The formula in the objective cell relates directly or indirectly to the changing cells and constraints. Using the mortgage case study as an example, the objective cell is B14 (the cell containing the total interest paid formula), and your goal is to minimize the total interest.

The *changing variable cells* are the cells containing variables whose values change within the constraints until the objective cell reaches its optimum value. The changing variable cells typically contain values, not formulas, but these cells have a mathematical relationship to the formula in the objective. In the home loan example, the changing variable cells are B3 (down payment) and B5 (number of years). You can select up to 200 changing variable cells. To specify the objective and changing cells, do the following:

1. Click Solver in the Analysis group on the Data tab to open the Solver Parameters dialog box (see Figure 6.23).
2. Enter the cell containing the formula for which you want to optimize its value in the Set Objective box.
3. Click an option in the *To* section to specify what type of value you need to find for the target cell. Click Max to maximize the value, Min to find the lowest value, or Value Of, and then specify the value in the Value Of box.
4. Enter the cell references that contain variables in the By Changing Variable Cells box. These are the variables that you want to change to reach the objective.

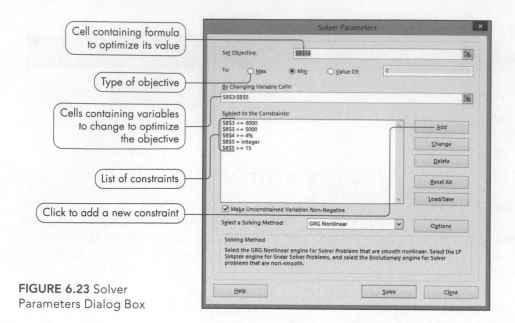

Cell containing formula to optimize its value

Type of objective

Cells containing variables to change to optimize the objective

List of constraints

Click to add a new constraint

FIGURE 6.23 Solver Parameters Dialog Box

Define the Constraints

The *constraints* specify the restrictions or limitations imposed on a spreadsheet model as Solver determines the optimum value for the objective cell. Rules govern every business model, based on historical requirements, physical limitations, and other decisions. Probably the most challenging process in using Solver is identifying all legitimate limitations. You may identify limitations through conversations with your supervisor, by reading policy statements, gathering information in meetings, and so on. Even after you enter data into Solver and run a report, you may gain knowledge of other limitations that you must build into the model. Using the home loan example, a constraint might be that the down payment must be between $5,000 and $8,000.

To add constraints to the Solver, do the following inside the Solver Parameters dialog box:

1. Click Add to the right of the *Subject to the Constraints* list to open the Add Constraint dialog box.

2. Enter the cell reference, the operator to test the cell references, and the constraint the cell needs to match (see Figure 6.24). The cell reference contains a variable whose value you want to constrain or restrict to a particular value or range. The operator defines the relationship between the variable and the constraint. For example, cell B3 (the down payment) is restricted to being less than or equal to $8,000. Solver will not allow the cost to be higher than this value.

3. Click OK to add the constraint and return to the Solver Parameters dialog box, or click Add to add the constraint and create another constraint.

TIP Integer Constraint

One of the constraint operators is integer. This constraint requires the changing variable cell to be an integer, or whole number. For example, a manufacturing plant does not produce partial units such as 135.62 units, and a department store does not sell 18.32 shirts. To ensure that Solver produces realistic results, you should create integer constraints for these types of quantities. In Figure 6.23, the constraint $B$5 = integer limits the number of years for the loan to be a whole number.

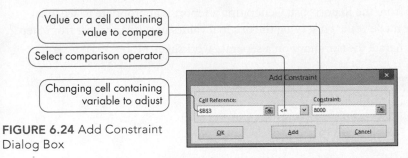

Value or a cell containing value to compare

Select comparison operator

Changing cell containing variable to adjust

FIGURE 6.24 Add Constraint Dialog Box

To modify a constraint's definition, select the constraint in the *Subject to the Constraints* list and click Change. Make changes in the Change Constraint dialog box and click OK to update the definition. If you no longer need a constraint, select it in the *Subject to the Constraints* list and click Delete. Be careful when using Delete; Solver does not prompt you to confirm the deletion. Solver deletes the selected constraint immediately, and you cannot restore the deleted constraint.

TIP | Greater-Than-Zero Constraint

Another often-overlooked constraint is the requirement that the value of a variable cell be greater than or equal to zero. Physically, it makes no sense to produce a negative number of products in any category. Mathematically, however, a negative value in a changing variable cell may produce a higher value for the objective cell. By default, the Make Unconstrained Variables Non-Negative check box is selected to ensure variable values are greater than or equal to zero. If you want to allow the lower end of a variable's value to be a negative value, you can create a constraint such as B2>=−100. That constraint takes priority over the Make Unconstrained Variables Non-Negative check box.

Create a Solver Report

STEP 4 After defining the objective, changing variable cells, and constraints, select a solving method. Solver uses the selected solving method to determine which type of algorithms it executes to reach the objective. The Solver add-in for Excel 2013 contains these solving methods: GRG Nonlinear, Simplex LP, and Evolutionary. Look up *Solver* in Help to link to a specific set of descriptions of these methods. You can also review additional information and download additional add-ins on www.solver.com. For the purposes of this chapter, accept the default option, GRG Nonlinear.

You are now ready to use Solver to find a solution to the problem. Solver uses an iterative process of using different combinations of values in the changing variable cells to identify the optimum value for the objective cell. It starts with the current values and adjusts those values in accordance with the constraints. Once it finds the best solution, given the parameters you set, it identifies the values for the changing variable cells and shows you the optimum value in the objective value. If Solver cannot determine an optimum value, it does not enable you to generate summary reports. To create a Solver report, do the following:

1. Click Solve in the Solver Parameters dialog box. When Solver completes the iterative process, the Solver Results dialog box appears (see Figure 6.25). If it finds a solution, the Reports list displays available report types. If Solver cannot reach an optimal solution, no reports are available. Solutions are unattainable if a logic error exists or if the constraints do not allow sufficient elasticity to achieve a result. For example, a constraint between 10 and 11 may not allow sufficient flexibility, or a constraint greater than 20 but also less than 10 is illogical. If this happens, check each constraint for range constraints or errors in logic.

2. Click Keep Solver Solution to keep the changed objective and variable values, or click Restore Original Values to return to the original values in the worksheet. If you keep the changed values, Excel makes those changes to the actual worksheet. Do this if you are comfortable with those changes. If you want to maintain the original values, you should restore the original values.

3. Select a report from the Reports list. Generating a report is appropriate to see what changes Solver made while preserving the original values in the worksheet from Step 2.
4. Click OK to generate the summary on a separate worksheet.

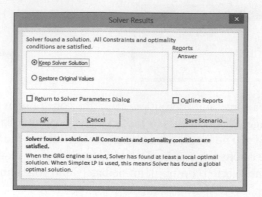

FIGURE 6.25 Solver Results Dialog Box

Solver creates a new worksheet for the Solver summary report containing four major sections (see Figure 6.26). The first section displays information about the Solver report. Specifically, it displays the report type, file name and worksheet containing the dataset, date and time the report was generated, Solver Engine details, and Solver Options that were set at the time the report was generated.

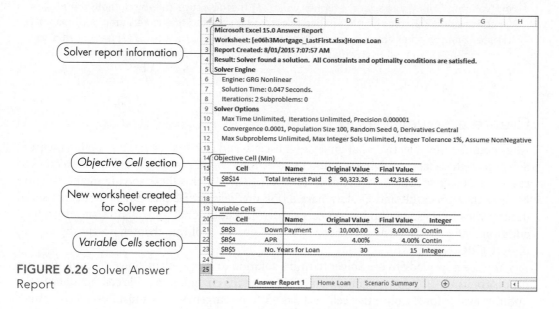

FIGURE 6.26 Solver Answer Report

The remaining sections of the report help you analyze the results. The section displays the objective cell information. Specifically, this section shows the original and final objective cell values. For example, using the original worksheet values, the original total interest paid in cell B14 was $100,617.31. The final minimized total interest paid is $47,064.23.

The third section displays the variable cells. Specifically, it displays the cell references, the variable cell names, original values, and final values. For example, the original down payment was $10,000, and the final value is $8,000.

The final section lists the constraints. Specifically, it displays the cell reference, description, new cell value, formula, status, and slack for each defined constraint. In this case, the down payment slack ($3,000) is the difference between the lower constraint ($5,000) and the final value ($8,000). The Status column indicates Binding or Not Binding. A ***binding constraint*** is a rule that Solver has to enforce to reach the objective value. That is, the value hits the maximum allowable value for a less-than-or-equal-to, minimum allowable value for a greater-than-or-equal-to, equal to, or integer constraint. For example, $B$3<=8000 is a binding constraint. That is, the down payment was raised to its maximum limit of $8,000 to identify the optimal least amount of total interest paid. If this constraint had not been set, Solver could have identified a higher down payment to obtain a lower value for the objective cell. A *nonbinding constraint* is one that does not restrict the target value that Solver finds. For example, $B$3>=5000 is nonbinding. Solver did not have to stop at a lowest down payment of $3,000 to reach the optimal total interest paid value.

If you change any of the Solver parameters—objective cell, changing variable cells, or constraints—you need to generate another report. Solver does not update the report automatically. Each time you generate a report, Solver creates another new worksheet with names like Answer Report 1, Answer Report 2, and so on. Delete any reports you no longer need to minimize the file size of your workbook.

TIP | Save Scenario

If you want to save the solution parameters to use in Scenario Manager, click Save Scenario in the Solver Results dialog box and type a name for the scenario in the *Scenario name* box.

Configure Solver

You can closely monitor the trial solutions prior to reaching the final solution. Solver is a mathematical modeling operation, and you can determine solutions using the associated mathematics. However, stepping through Solver enables you to view the steps Solver performs. To step through trial solutions, do the following:

1. Click Options in the Solver Parameters dialog box to open the Options dialog box.
2. Select the Show Iteration Results check box to see the values of each trial solution and click OK.
3. Click Solve in the Solver Parameters dialog box.
4. When the Show Trial Solution dialog box appears, either:
   - Click Stop to stop the process and open the Solver Results dialog box, or
   - Click Continue to continue the process and display the next trial solution.

You can also use the Options dialog box to customize Solver further. Because Solver uses an iterative approach, you can specify the number of iterations to try, how much time to take to solve the problem, and how precise the answer should be (i.e., accuracy to what number of decimal places), among other settings.

Save and Restore a Solver Model

When you use Solver, Excel keeps track of your settings and saves only the most recent Solver settings. In some cases, you may want to save the parameters of a model so that you can apply them again in the future. Saving a Solver model is helpful if the original data source might change and you want to compare results by generating multiple Solver answer reports. When you save a Solver model, you save the objective value, the changing variable cells, and the constraints.

Saving a Solver model places the information in a small block of cells on a worksheet. The number of cells required to save the Solver model is dependent on the number of constraints in the model. To save Solver settings, do the following:

1. Click Load/Save in the Solver Parameters dialog box.
2. Click in the worksheet where the first cell is to be placed. Make sure the worksheet has sufficient empty cells so the Solver information does not overwrite Excel data.
3. Click Save to return to the Solver Parameters dialog box.

If you want to use an existing Solver model with new or updated data, you must return to a previous Solver model. When you want to use a Solver model that you saved, do the following:

1. Click Load/Save in the Solver Parameters dialog box.
2. Select the worksheet cells that contain the Solver data. You must select all cells with the Solver data.
3. Click Load to load the model's values and return to the Solver Parameter dialog box.

Quick Concepts

1. Is Solver preloaded in Excel? *p. 286*
2. What three optimization goals can Solver calculate? *p. 286*
3. What is the advantage of Solver over Goal Seek? *p. 287*

Hands-On Exercises

Watch the Video for this Hands-On Exercise!

3 Solver

Although Goal Seek and Scenario Manager were helpful in further analyzing your home purchase, you want to ensure the spreadsheet model imposes constraints on the situation. Therefore, you will continue your analysis by using Solver.

Skills covered: Load the Solver Add-In • Set the Objective and Variable Cells • Define the Constraints • Generate a Report

STEP 1 >> LOAD THE SOLVER ADD-IN

Before you can use Solver to analyze your home loan model, you need to load Solver. If Solver is already loaded, skip Step 1 and start with Step 2. Refer to Figure 6.27 as you complete Step 1.

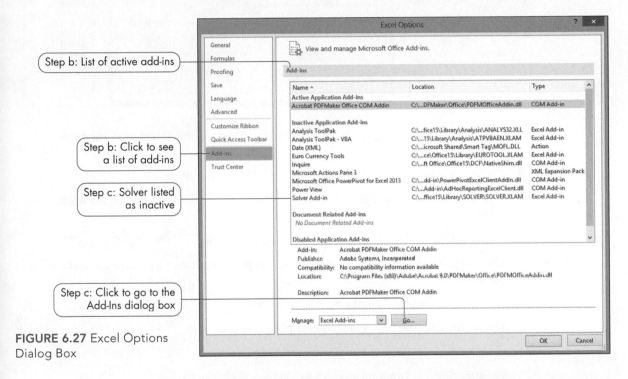

Step b: List of active add-ins

Step b: Click to see a list of add-ins

Step c: Solver listed as inactive

Step c: Click to go to the Add-Ins dialog box

FIGURE 6.27 Excel Options Dialog Box

a. Click the **FILE tab** and click **Options**.

The Excel Options dialog box opens so that you can customize Excel settings.

b. Click **Add-Ins** on the left side of the Excel Options dialog box.

The Excel Options dialog box displays a list of active and inactive application add-ins.

c. Check to see where Solver is listed. If Solver is listed in the Active Application Add-ins list, click **OK**, and then skip step d. If Solver is listed in the Inactive Application Add-ins list, click the **Manage arrow**, select **Excel Add-ins** if necessary, and then click **Go**.

The Add-Ins dialog box opens, containing a list of available add-in applications.

d. Click the **Solver Add-in check box** in the **Add-Ins available list** and click **OK**.

Before using Solver, you want to reset the variables to their original values. After entering the original variable values again, you will specify the monthly payment cell as the objective cell and the home cost, down payment, APR, and number of years for the loan as the changing variable cells. Refer to Figure 6.28 as you complete Step 2.

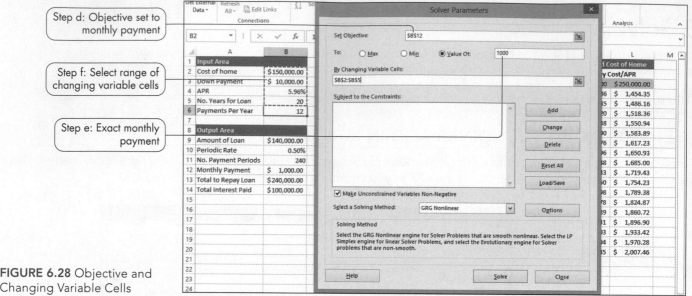

FIGURE 6.28 Objective and Changing Variable Cells

a. Open the *e06h2Mortgage_LastFirst* workbook and save it as **e06h3Mortgage_LastFirst**, replacing *h2* with *h3*.

b. Click the **Home Loan worksheet tab** and type **150000** in **cell B2**.

Now that you have reset the values to your original spreadsheet model, you are ready to use Solver.

c. Click the **DATA tab** and click **Solver** in the Analysis group.

The Solver Parameters dialog box opens so that you can define the objective and changing variable cells.

d. Click **cell B12** to enter it in the **Set Objective box**.

You set the objective cell as the monthly payment.

e. Click **Value Of** and type **1000** in the **Value Of box**.

You specified that you want an exact $1000 monthly home payment.

f. Click in the **By Changing Variable Cells box** and select the **range B2:B5**. Click **Close** and save the workbook.

TROUBLESHOOTING: Be careful to select the correct range. If you accidentally select cell B6, Solver might produce inaccurate results.

STEP 3 ≫ DEFINE THE CONSTRAINTS

You define the constraints: $100,000 to $300,000 cost, $5,000 to $10,000 down payment, 4% to 6% APR, and 15- to 30-year loan. In addition, you set an integer constraint for the years so that Solver does not produce a fractional year, such as 5.71. Refer to Figure 6.29 as you complete Step 3.

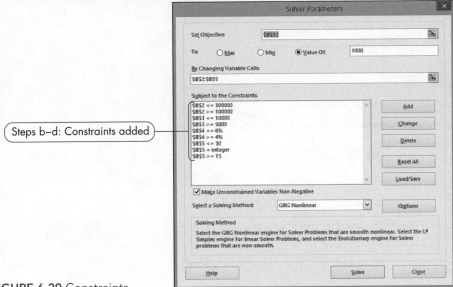

Steps b–d: Constraints added

FIGURE 6.29 Constraints

a. Click **Solver** in the Analysis group and click **Add**.

   The Add Constraint dialog box opens so that you can define the first constraint.

b. Click **cell B2**, make sure <= is selected, click in the **Constraint box**, and then type **300000**.

   You defined a constraint that the total home cost cannot exceed $300,000.

c. Click **Add** to define another constraint. Click **cell B2**, click the **operator arrow**, select >=, click in the **Constraint box**, and then type **100000**.

   The second constraint specifies that the cost of the home must be at least $100,000.

d. Add the following constraints in a similar manner. After you enter the last constraint, click **OK** in the Add Constraint dialog box.

   * B3<=10000
   * B3>=5000
   * B4<=6%
   * B4>=4%
   * B5<=30
   * B5>=15
   * B5 int

   > **TROUBLESHOOTING:** Click Add to complete the current constraint and open an Add Constraint dialog box to enter another constraint. Click OK in the Add Constraint dialog box only when you have completed the last constraint and want to return to the Solver Parameters dialog box to solve the problem.

e. Check the constraints carefully against those shown in Figure 6.29 and step d. Click **Close** and save the workbook.

STEP 4 >> GENERATE A REPORT

Now that you have completed the parameters for restricting the result based on the cost of the home, the down payment, the APR, and the number of years for the loan, you are ready to generate a Solver report. Refer to Figure 6.30 as you complete Step 4.

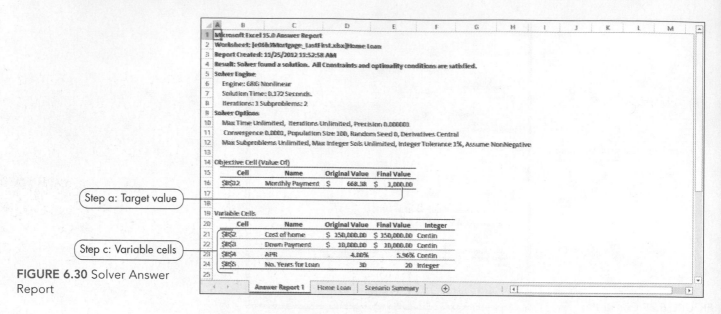

Step a: Target value

Step c: Variable cells

FIGURE 6.30 Solver Answer Report

a. Click **Solver** in the Analysis group and click **Solve**.

The Solver Results dialog box opens. If you look at the worksheet data, the new values appear in the changing cells, and the $1000 target monthly payment appears in cell B12.

b. Select **Answer** in the **Reports list** and click **OK**.

Solver generates a report and displays it in a new worksheet named Answer Report 1.

> **TROUBLESHOOTING:** If you see the error message, *Solver: An unexpected internal error occurred, or available memory was exhausted*, close Solver, click Undo, remove Solver as an add-in, save and close the workbook, open the workbook again, and then enable the Solver add-in again. Then click Solver in the Analysis group, click Solve, select Answer Report, and then click OK.

c. Click the **Answer Report 1 worksheet tab**.

Solver adjusts the values in the changing cells B2:B5 to obtain the exact value of $1000 for the objective cell B12. The report shows the previous and final values of the objective and variable cells. *Your final values may vary slightly from those shown in the figure.*

d. Scroll down through the worksheet to see the constraints.

In addition, the report displays the constraints—cell references, descriptive labels, current cell values, formulas, status (binding/not binding), and slack. Although not specified, integer constraints are always binding. Had you not constrained the years to a whole number, Solver might have found different values for the variable cells. However, you need to enforce that constraint because the term of the mortgage is a whole year. The 4% APR constraint is binding, meaning that Solver found the lowest possible APR to produce its answer. Finally, the 30-year limit is binding, meaning that Solver could not use a larger number of years for the loan to derive its answer.

e. Save and close the workbook, and submit based on your instructor's directions.

Chapter Objectives Review

After reading this chapter, you have accomplished the following objectives:

1. **Create a one-variable data table.**
   - A one-variable data table enables you to compare different values for one variable to compare their effects on one or more results.
   - Set up the substitution values: Substitution values replace the original value of a variable in a data table.
   - Add formulas to the data table: After entering a substitution value, a formula must be added to relate mathematically to the substation values.
   - Complete the results: Excel uses the substitution values individually to replace the original variable's to populate the data table.
   - Format the data table: After completing the data table, all values should be appropriately formatted.

2. **Create a two-variable data table.**
   - A two-variable data table enables you to compare results for two variables at the same time but for only one result.
   - Set up the substitution values for two variables: Use the top row for one variable's substitution values and the first column for the second variable's substitution values.
   - Add a formula to the data table: Enter the required formula in the top-left corner of the data table.
   - Complete the two-variable data table: Select the data table boundaries, then choose Data Table from the What-If Analysis menu on the Ribbon.

3. **Identify an input value with Goal Seek.**
   - Use Goal Seek to work backward with a problem when you know what you want for the result but you do not know the value of a variable to achieve that goal. If you accept the results, Excel enters the identified input value directly in the variable cell.

4. **Use Scenario Manager.**
   - Use Scenario Manager to create a set of scenarios, each with multiple variables.
   - The Scenario Manager dialog box enables you to add, delete, and change scenarios.
   - For each scenario, you specify a name, the changing cells, and the values for those changing cells.
   - Create and edit scenarios: Click What-If Analysis in the Data Tools group of the Data tab. Select Scenario Manager. Click Add to open the scenario dialog box.

   - View scenarios: To view a created scenario, click What-If Analysis in the Data Tools group of the Data tab. Select Scenario Manager, click the name of the scenario you would like to review, and then click show.

5. **Generate scenario summary reports.**
   - After you create the scenarios with specific values, you can generate a summary report.
   - Excel creates the summary report in a structured format on a new worksheet and displays the values for the changing cells and their effects on the results cells so that you can compare the results easily.

6. **Load the Solver add-in.**
   - Solver is an add-in program for Excel. When you enable Solver, Excel places Solver in the Analysis group on the Data tab.

7. **Optimize results with Solver.**
   - Solver is an optimization technique that enables you to maximize or minimize the value of an objective function, such as profit or cost. Solver uses an iterative process to use different values for variable cells until it finds the optimum objective value within the constraints you set.
   - Identify the objective cell and changing cells: The objective cell contains the information that is to be set to value of, minimum, or maximum by Solver.
   - Define the constraints: Set in the Solver dialog box, constraints are limitations that are imposed on Solver.
   - Create a Solver report: In the Solver Results dialog box, choose an option under Reports to have Excel create a report on a new worksheet.
   - Configure Solver: Solver's calculation settings can be configured by clicking the Options button in the Solver Parameters dialog box.
   - Save and restore a Solver model: A Solver model can be imported or exported by clicking Load/Save in the Solver Parameters dialog box.

Key Terms Matching

Match the key terms with their definitions. Write the key term letter by the appropriate numbered definition.

a. Add-in
b. Binding constraint
c. Changing variable cell
d. Constraint
e. Goal Seek
f. Nonbinding constraint
g. Objective cell
h. One-variable data table
i. Optimization model

j. Scenario
k. Scenario Manager
l. Scenario summary report
m. Solver
n. Substitution value
o. Two-variable data table
p. Variable
q. What-if analysis

1. _____ A constraint that Solver enforces to reach the target value. **p. 290**

2. _____ A cell containing a variable whose value changes until Solver optimizes the value in the objective cell. **p. 287**

3. _____ An add-in application that manipulates variables based on constraints to find the optimal solution to a problem. **p. 286**

4. _____ A data analysis tool that provides various results based on changing one variable. **p. 266**

5. _____ A set of values that represent a possible situation. **p. 278**

6. _____ The cell that contains the formula-based value that you want to maximize, minimize, or set to a value in Solver. **p. 287**

7. _____ Finds the highest, lowest, or exact value for one particular result by adjusting values for selected variables. **p. 286**

8. _____ A constraint that does not restrict the target value that Solver finds. **p. 291**

9. _____ The process of changing variables to observe how changes affect calculated results. **p. 266**

10. _____ A value that you can change to see how that change affects other values. **p. 266**

11. _____ Replaces the original value of a variable in a data table. **p. 266**

12. _____ A limitation that imposes restrictions on Solver. **p. 288**

13. _____ A program that can be added to Excel to provide enhanced functionality. **p. 286**

14. _____ A worksheet that contains scenario results. **p. 280**

15. _____ A data analysis tool that provides results based on changing two variables. **p. 270**

16. _____ A tool that identifies the necessary input value to obtain a desired goal. **p. 277**

17. _____ Enables you to define and manage scenarios to compare how they affect results. **p. 278**

Multiple Choice

1. Which what-if analysis tool is the best option for complex calculations requiring constrained optimization?

   (a) Goal Seek
   (b) Scenario Manager
   (c) Data Tables
   (d) Solver

2. Which tools are best suited to calculate the impact of multiple interest rates on an auto loan? (Check all that apply.)

   (a) Goal Seek
   (b) Scenario Manager
   (c) One-variable data table
   (d) Solver

3. Which tool is most effective when comparing the impacts of various combinations of interest rates and down payments on a mortgage?

   (a) Goal Seek
   (b) Solver
   (c) Two-variable data table
   (d) Scenario Manager

4. This tool calculates the value required in a single cell to produce a desired result with in a related cell.

   (a) Goal Seek
   (b) Solver
   (c) One- or Two-variable data table
   (d) Scenario Manager

5. This analysis tool has the ability to handle multiple adjustable cells while minimizing, maximizing, or meeting goals.

   (a) Goal Seek
   (b) Solver
   (c) One- or Two-variable data table
   (d) Scenario Manager

6. Which of the following is an Excel add-in?

   (a) Goal Seek
   (b) Solver
   (c) One- or Two-variable data table
   (d) Scenario Manager

7. Doug would like to purchase a new automobile. He has budgeted for $600 per month. If the interest and number of payments are constant variables that cannot change, which analysis tool should Doug use to calculate the amount to spend on a car?

   (a) Goal Seek
   (b) Solver
   (c) One- or Two-variable data table
   (d) Scenario Manager

8. Which dialog box enables you to specify the result cells for a scenario summary report?

   (a) Scenario Summary
   (b) Scenario Values
   (c) Add Scenario
   (d) Solver Options

9. Which of the following tools can incorporate constraints?

   (a) Goal Seek
   (b) Solver
   (c) Data Tables
   (d) Scenario Manager

10. How can you determine if the Solver add-in is active? (Check all that apply.)

    (a) Solver is an option in the Home tab of the Ribbon.
    (b) Solver is available via right-click.
    (c) Solver appears in the Data tab of the Ribbon.
    (d) Solver appears in the Goal Seek dialog box to make it appear as a label.

Practice Exercises

1 Annual Bonuses

You manage a software development company in Portland. Employees earn an annual bonus that ranges from 0.5% to 5% of their gross salary. You are required by law to withhold applicable income taxes. To minimize employee disappointment from knowing what their qualified bonus is versus seeing the bonus on their paychecks, you developed a model that you can distribute to employees to help them predict their net bonus amount. You create a one-variable data table to list various bonus rates and their effects on the gross bonus, taxes withheld, and net bonus. Then you create a two-variable data table that compares combinations of various bonus rates and sample gross salaries to show net bonuses. This exercise follows the same set of skills as used in Hands-On Exercise 1 in the chapter. Refer to Figure 6.31 as you complete this exercise.

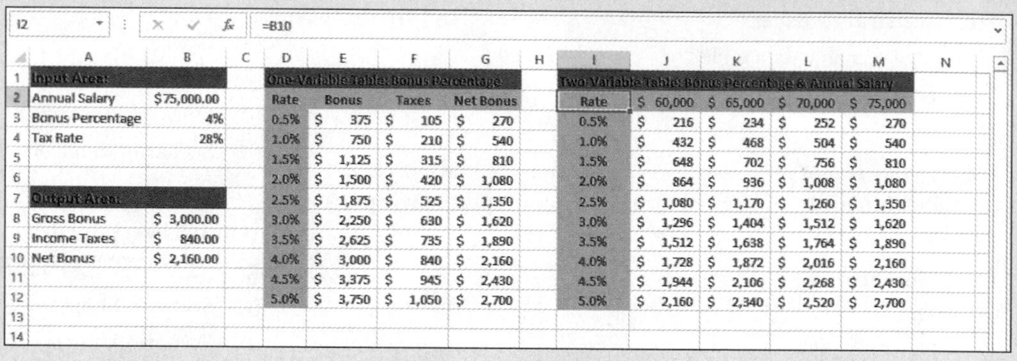
I2 =B10

	A	B	C	D	E	F	G	H	I	J	K	L	M	N
1	Input Area:			One-Variable Table: Bonus Percentage					Two-Variable Table: Bonus Percentage & Annual Salary					
2	Annual Salary	$75,000.00		Rate	Bonus	Taxes	Net Bonus		Rate	$ 60,000	$ 65,000	$ 70,000	$ 75,000	
3	Bonus Percentage	4%		0.5%	$ 375	$ 105	$ 270		0.5%	$ 216	$ 234	$ 252	$ 270	
4	Tax Rate	28%		1.0%	$ 750	$ 210	$ 540		1.0%	$ 432	$ 468	$ 504	$ 540	
5				1.5%	$ 1,125	$ 315	$ 810		1.5%	$ 648	$ 702	$ 756	$ 810	
6				2.0%	$ 1,500	$ 420	$ 1,080		2.0%	$ 864	$ 936	$ 1,008	$ 1,080	
7	Output Area:			2.5%	$ 1,875	$ 525	$ 1,350		2.5%	$ 1,080	$ 1,170	$ 1,260	$ 1,350	
8	Gross Bonus	$ 3,000.00		3.0%	$ 2,250	$ 630	$ 1,620		3.0%	$ 1,296	$ 1,404	$ 1,512	$ 1,620	
9	Income Taxes	$ 840.00		3.5%	$ 2,625	$ 735	$ 1,890		3.5%	$ 1,512	$ 1,638	$ 1,764	$ 1,890	
10	Net Bonus	$ 2,160.00		4.0%	$ 3,000	$ 840	$ 2,160		4.0%	$ 1,728	$ 1,872	$ 2,016	$ 2,160	
11				4.5%	$ 3,375	$ 945	$ 2,430		4.5%	$ 1,944	$ 2,106	$ 2,268	$ 2,430	
12				5.0%	$ 3,750	$ 1,050	$ 2,700		5.0%	$ 2,160	$ 2,340	$ 2,520	$ 2,700	
13														
14														

FIGURE 6.31 Bonus Variable Data Tables

a. Open *e06p1Bonus* and save it as **e06p1Bonus_LastFirst**.

b. Click **cell D3** and do the following to enter a series of substitution values for the bonus percentage:
- Type **0.5%** and press **Ctrl+Enter** to keep **cell D3** active.
- Click **Fill** in the Editing group on the HOME tab and select **Series**.
- Click **Columns** in the *Series in* section, type **0.5%** in the **Step value box**, type **5%** in the **Stop value box**, and then click **OK**.

c. Enter the references to formulas in the following cells:
- **Cell E2: =B8**
- **Cell F2: =B9**
- **Cell G2: =B10**

d. Complete the one-variable data table by doing the following:
- Select the **range D2:G12**.
- Click the **DATA tab**, click **What-If Analysis** in the Data Tools group, and then select **Data Table**.
- Click in the **Column input cell box**, click **cell B3**, and then click **OK**.
- Select the **range E3:G12**, click the **HOME tab**, and then apply **Accounting Number Format** with zero decimal places.

e. Create column headings for the data table by doing the following:
- Type **Rate** in **cell D2**.
- Click **cell E2** and click the **Number Dialog Box Launcher** in the Number group.
- Click **Custom** in the **Category list**, scroll up in the **Type list**, and then select **General**.
- Select **General** in the Type box, type **Bonus**, and then click **OK**.
- Adapt the above steps to create a custom number format to display *Taxes* in **cell F2** and **Net Bonus** in **cell G2**.
- Center and bold the **range D2:G2**.

f. Set up the variables for the two-variable data table by copying the **range D3:D12** and pasting it in the **range I3:I12**. Enter **60000** in **cell J2** and use the Series dialog box to fill the row data to **75000** in steps of **5000**.

g. Enter **=B10** in **cell I2**.

h. Complete the two-variable data table by doing the following:

- Select the **range I2:M12**.
- Click the **DATA tab**, click **What-If Analysis** in the Data Tools group, and then select **Data Table**.
- Click **cell B2** to enter that reference in the **Row input cell box**.
- Click in the **Column input cell box**, click **cell B3**, and then click **OK**.
- Select the **range J3:M12** and apply **Accounting Number Format** with zero decimal places.
- Create a custom number format to display *Rate* in **cell I2**. Bold and center data in this cell.

i. Select **landscape orientation** and set **0.4"** left and right margins.

j. Create a footer with your name on the left side, the date code in the center, and the file name code on the right side.

k. Save and close the workbook, and submit it based on your instructor's directions.

2 Sue's Bakery

Sue has opened a bakery specializing in cupcakes. Her budget must account for fixed expenses, such as her facility lease, utilities, and credit card equipment fees. In addition, she accounts for variable costs including cost of goods sold and credit card processing fees. You will use Goal Seek to determine how many cupcakes she must sell to earn a net profit of $3,500. Then you will use Scenario Manager to evaluate several possible situations. This exercise follows the same set of skills as used in Hands-On Exercise 2 in the chapter. Refer to Figure 6.32 as you complete this exercise.

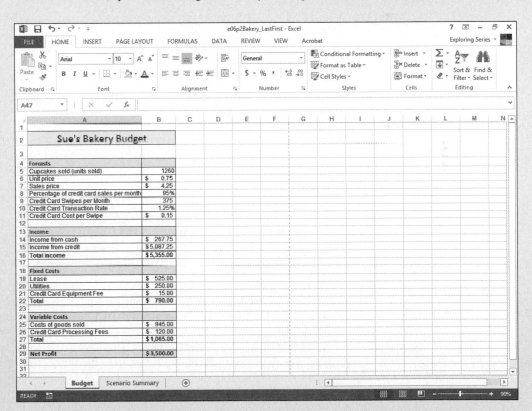

FIGURE 6.32 Sue's Bakery Budget

a. Open *e06p2Bakery* and save it as **e06p2Bakery_LastFirst**.

b. Enter the following formulas:

- **Cell B14**: **=B16-B16*B8** to calculate the projected cash sales amount of the total sales.
- **Cell B15**: **=B16-B14** to calculate the amount of income from credit card transactions.
- **Cell B25**: **=B5*B6** to calculate the cost of goods sold, which is the product of the units sold and unit cost.
- **Cell B26**: **=(B10*B15)+(B9*B11)** to calculate credit card processing fees, which are currently 1.25% of credit card amounts and $0.15 cents per transaction.
- **Cell B29**: **=B16-B22-B27** to calculate the net profit.

c. Click the **DATA tab**, click **What-If Analysis** in the Data Tools group, and then select **Goal Seek**.

d. Complete the Goal Seek by doing the following:

- Click **cell B29** to add the cell reference to the *Set cell* box.
- Click in the **To value box** and type **3500**.
- Click in the **By changing cell box** and click **cell B5**.
- Click **OK** in the Goal Seek dialog box and click **OK** in the Goal Seek Status dialog box. How many cupcakes must Sue sell to reach her net profit goal of $3,500? Answer: 1,260.

e. Click **What-If Analysis** in the Data Tools group and select **Scenario Manager**.

f. Create the first scenario by doing the following:

- Click **Add** and type **Current Conditions** in the **Scenario name box**.
- Click in the **Changing cells box**, select the **range B5:B7**, and then press and hold **Ctrl** while you select the **range B9:B10**.
- Click in the **Comment box** edit it to reflect your name, such as *Created by Jason Davidson on 9/4/2015*, and then click **OK**.
- Type **700** in the **$B$5 box**, leave the other current values intact, and then click **OK**.

g. Create the following three scenarios, clicking either **Add** or **OK** as indicated:

Scenario Name	Ideal Case	Increased Costs	Low Sales
$B$4	1,260	700	500
$B$5	.75	.75	.75
$B$6	4.25	4.50	4.00
$B$8	375	275	150
$B$9	1.25%	2.49%	1.25%
Button	Add	Add	OK

h. Click **Summary**, select and delete the suggested range in the **Result cells box**, press and hold **Ctrl** as you click **cells B16, B22, B27,** and **B29** to enter these cells, and then click **OK**.

i. Make these changes to the summary on the Scenario Summary worksheet:

- Delete the blank column A, the Current Values column, the blank row 1, and the notes in the **range A16:A18**.
- Click in **cell A5**, type **Units Sold**, and then press **Enter**.
- Enter **Unit Cost, Sale Price, Credit Card Swipes,** and **Card Transaction Rate** in the **range A6:A9**.
- Enter **Gross Sales, Fixed Costs, Variable Costs,** and **Profit** in the **range A11:A14**.
- Increase the width of column A to display the labels.
- Delete column B containing the cell references because these references would have no meaning if you distribute only the scenario summary worksheet to others.

j. Create a footer with your name on the left side, and the file name code on the right side for both worksheets.

k. Save and close the workbook, and submit it based on your instructor's directions.

Mid-Level Exercises

1 Housing Construction Cost Variables

Your friends, Elijah and Valerie Foglesong, want to build their dream house. They identified tentative costs, but they cannot afford the $414,717 estimated cost. You will use Goal Seek to determine an estimate of the total finished square footage they can afford. To help provide more flexibility in their decision making, you will create a data table listing various finished square footages and their effects on the base house cost and total cost. Finally, you will create another data table showing combinations of square footages and lot prices to identify total costs. Although a builder's overall house design specifies the square footage, the Foglesongs can use your data tables to help guide them in their decision.

a. Open *e06m1House* and save it as **e06m1House_LastFirst**.

b. Use Goal Seek to determine the total finished square footage to meet the total cost goal of $350,000.

c. Enter a series of total square footages ranging from 1,800 to 3,600 in increments of 200 in the **range D6:D15**. Apply **Blue font** and **Comma Style** with zero decimal places to the series. Enter references to the base cost and total cost in the appropriate cells on row 5.

d. Complete the data table using the appropriate input cell. Apply custom number formats to give appropriate descriptions to the second and third columns. Apply these formats to the headings: bold, center, and **Blue font**.

e. Identify the square footage, base price, and total cost that come closest to their goal. Apply **Blue, Accent 1, Lighter 40% fill color** to those cells in the data table.

f. Copy the square footage substitution values to the **range H6:H15** and remove the fill color. Enter these lot price substitution values in the **range I5:K5: 90000, 96000**, and **102675**. Format these values with **Accounting Number Format** with zero decimal places and **Blue font**.

g. Enter the reference to the total cost formula in the appropriate location for the second data table. Complete the data table using the appropriate input cells. Apply a custom number format to the reference to the formula cell. Apply bold and **Blue font color** to that cell. Apply **Blue, Accent 1, Lighter 40% fill color** to the total price in each column that comes closest to their goal.

h. Format results in both tables with **Accounting Number Format** with zero decimal places.

i. Create a footer with your name on the left side, the sheet name code in the center, and the file name code on the right side. Adjust the orientation, margins, and scaling to fit on one page.

j. Save and close the workbook, and submit it based on your instructor's directions.

2 Ray's Heating and Air

ANALYSIS CASE

You are the Chief Financial Officer for Ray's Heating and Air. You have been given the task of increasing gross income from $91,000 to $120,000 per year. Ray's income is earned through service calls. Customers are charged trip and hourly charges as pictured in the table below. Your goal is to create a spreadsheet to allow you to evaluate the most economically feasible option for increasing gross income while adhering to the following constraints. The maximum amount of hours billed without hiring additional technicians is 2,500. The trip charge may not exceed $50.00, and the service hourly rate/trip charge must all be whole numbers. The calls/hourly rate/trip charge must all be whole numbers.

Current Service Calls	Hourly rate	Trip Charge	Hours Billed
640	$30.00	$25.00	2500

a. Open *e06m2RaysAC* and save it as **e06m2RaysAC_LastFirst**.

b. Use the formula service calls * trip charge + hours billed * hourly rate to determine gross income.

c. If not loaded, load the Solver add-in.

d. Set the objective cell to $120,000.

e. Set constraints to ensure service calls, hourly rate, and trip charge are integers.

f. Set a constraint to ensure hours billed cannot exceed 2,500.

g. Set a constraint to ensure the trip charge does not exceed $50.00.

h. Set a constraint to ensure hourly rate does not drop below $30.00

i. Create an Answer Report to outline your findings.

j. After solving, answer the questions in the Q&A section.

3 College Budget

COLLABORATION CASE

FROM SCRATCH

You are beginning your freshman year of college. Prior to leaving for school, you worked a summer job and were able to save $1,500 for expenses such as books, supplies, and a university parking pass. After arriving on campus, you discovered your computer was out of date, and you need to purchase a newer model. Your books cost $700, a mini fridge for your room costs $250.00, and you are estimating your parking pass will cost $350.00. After researching pricing for newer computers, you determine a new computer will cost $750.00. Your parents have agreed to give you the additional money required to purchase the computer; however, they will only do so if you send them an Excel workbook outlining your expenses and the amount of money that they must contribute to the purchase. You have decided to create this document and then share the file with your parents through your family's SkyDrive account.

Student 1:

a. Open Excel and create a blank document. Save this document as **e06m3CollegeBudget_LastFirst**.

b. Click in **cell A1** and type item **Description**. Press **Tab** and type **Expense** in **cell B1**.

c. Click in **cell A2**, type the name of your first expense—for example, **Parking Pass**—and then enter the corresponding cost in **cell B2**.

d. Continue entering your expenses in **cells A3:B3** for books and in **cell A4:B4** for the mini fridge. Type **Total expenses** in **cell A5** and enter a SUM function in **cell B5** to total your expenses.

e. Highlight **cells A5:B5** and apply the **Bad style** from the styles group located in the HOME tab of the Ribbon.

f. Click **cell D1**, type **Summer Savings**, and then type **1500** in **cell D2**. Then complete the following tasks:

- Type **Savings after expenses** in **cell A6**.
- Type **Computer cost** in **cell A7**.
- Type **Parental contribution** in **cell A8**.
- Type **Deficit** in **cell A9**.
- Type **750** in **cell B7**.
- Type **0** in **cell B8**.

g. Click in **cell B9** and enter the following formula: **=B7-B6-B8**. This calculates the financial deficit after the computer has been purchased. The goal is for this cell to have a value of zero after your parents' contribution.

h. Use Goal Seek to set the deficit to **0** by changing your parents' contribution amount.

i. Format the worksheet with the font and color of your choice. Apply **Currency format** to all numbers.

j. Save the workbook to SkyDrive.

Student 2:

k. Open the worksheet and review the proposed budget.

l. Based on the budget, navigate to www.amazon.com and research the going rates on a college size mini fridge. If you are able to locate a better price, update the dollar amount and upload back to sky drive.

Beyond the Classroom

Too Cold to Snow
RESEARCH CASE →

Have you ever wondered whether it could be too cold to snow? Actually, it is much more likely to snow if the temperature is close to freezing than if it is much below. The reason is because the air gets too dry to snow. As the air gets colder, it holds less water vapor for making snow. This explains why Nashville, Tennessee, typically gets more snowfall each year than frigid Barrow, Alaska! Because snow in northern Alaska does not melt as quickly as snow in Nashville, the area appears to get more snow.

You are a high school science teacher preparing a lesson on the effect of temperature and water vapor on snowfall. The dew point is the temperature at which water vapor condenses and forms into liquid or frozen precipitation, and the wet bulb temperature is the lowest temperature that can be reached by the evaporation of water only. Typically, the greater the difference between wet bulb and air temperatures, the drier the air. Because drier air is less likely to produce snow, you will use the wet bulb temperature to approximate the dryness of the air and the potential for snow. Use the Internet to find the temperature and dew point of Nashville on January 6 of the current year and develop an estimate of the wet bulb temperature.

Open *e06b2Snow* and save it as **e06b2Snow_LastFirst**. Use Scenario Manager to create a Most Likely and Least Likely projection of wet bulb temperature for Nashville. The Most Likely statistics are those that you identified for January 6. The Least Likely statistics are a temperature of 18° and a dew point of 5°. Wet bulb temperature is calculated by subtracting dew point from temperature and dividing the result by 3. Edit the summary as specified in the *Generating Scenario Summary Reports* section in the chapter. Insert a text box and write an analysis about your results. Create a footer with your name, the sheet name code, and the file name code. Save and close the workbook, and submit it based on your instructor's directions.

Mining Company
 **DISASTER RECOVERY**

You work for an investment corporation that is considering purchasing a coal mine. One of your colleagues developed a spreadsheet model and started a what-if analysis using Solver. Unfortunately, Solver is unable to solve the problem given the parameters entered. You need to identify and correct the errors and then generate an answer report. Open *e06b3Mining* and save it as **e06b3Mining_LastFirst**. Make sure that Solver is loaded. If not, load the Solver add-in. The objective is to maximize the rate of return by the end of the fifth year. The investment firm is considering paying between $20 and $25 million for the mine with an anticipated 1 to 1.5 million tons sold in the first year. Research indicates the price per ton to be between $12.35 and $14.50 initially. The price-per-ton increase should range from 0.5% to 1.25%. Before you run the Solver report, change the number of iterations to 1,500 in the Solver Options dialog box. Insert notes to describe the parameter errors, correct the errors, and run a Solver answer report. Create a footer with your name, the sheet name code, and the file name code on the report. Adjust the left and right margins on the Answer Report 1 worksheet so that the data can print on one page. Deselect the options that print gridlines and headings on the Forecast worksheet. Save and close the workbook, and submit it based on your instructor's directions.

Payment Options

SOFT SKILLS CASE S

You have been hired by a debt management company and given the task of working with recent graduates to help manage student loan debt. While the goal of your company is to make money, they value the importance of transparency in payment options. As part of your daily tasks, you will use Excel to build scenarios based on payment options to determine the best repayment choice for each graduate.

Open the file *e06b4Repayment*. Save the file as **e06b4Repayment_LastFirst**. Use Scenario Manager to create three scenarios to share with your client. Name the first scenario **Early payment**. Select **cell C5** as the change cell and use the value **8**. Create a second scenario named **Normal payment**. Select **cell C5** as the change cell and use the value **10**. Create a third scenario named **Extended payment**. Select **cell C5** as the change cell and use the value **20**. Create a scenario summary report using **cells C7** and **F3**. Be sure to format the scenario report accordingly, removing the extra row and column created by Excel. The client has expressed that he is most comfortable with a repayment plan that is no more than 7% of his monthly income. Based on the scenarios you created, enter the repayment plan you recommend in **cell E12.** Once completed, save and close the workbook, and submit it based on your instructor's directions.

Capstone Exercise

You are on the budget committee for the formal Valentine's Day Ball at your university. The ball includes dinner and dancing. Your committee prepared a tentative budget outlining income and expenses. The primary sources of income are contributions from student organizations and ticket prices. Expenses include the actual cost of the dinner, facilities, parking, and other costs at a luxurious hotel in the city. Your goal is to balance the income and expenses, decide on the most appropriate ticket price per student, and ensure your budget falls within the limitations you must work with.

Goal Seek

Currently, the estimated budget has a deficit. The fastest way to try to reconcile the income and expenses is to use Goal Seek. The goal is to break even, that is, to have a zero balance. Your instinct is to adjust the ticket price per person to reach the goal.

a. Open *e06c1Dance* and save it as **e06c1Dance_LastFirst**.

b. Use Goal Seek to achieve a $0 balance by changing the ticket price per person.

c. Enter the value of the ticket price per person variable in the Q&A worksheet.

One-Variable Data Table

You believe that between 200 and 500 students will attend. Because the ticket revenue, chair setup, catering cost, and valet parking expenses are dependent on the number of students, you decide to create a one-variable data table to compare the budget effects based on different numbers of students attending.

a. Start in **cell E3**. Complete the series of substitution values ranging from 200 to 500 at increments of 20 students vertically down column E.

b. Enter references to the total revenue, total expenses, and balance formulas in the correct location for a one-variable data table.

c. Complete the one-variable data table, and then format the results with **Accounting Number Format** with two decimal places.

d. Apply custom number formats to make the formula references appear as descriptive column headings. Bold and center the headings and substitution values.

e. Answer questions 2 through 4 on the Q&A worksheet. Save the workbook.

Two-Variable Data Table

The break-even point for the one-variable data table is identical to the current model because all other variables are held constant. You want to compare the balances of different combinations of attendees and ticket prices per person using a two-variable data table.

a. Copy the number of attendees substitution values from the one-variable data table, and then paste the values starting in **cell E22**.

b. Type **$50** in **cell F21**. Complete the series of substitution values from $50 to $100 at $10 increments.

c. Enter the reference to the total income formula in the correct location for a two-variable data table.

d. Complete the two-variable data table and format the results with **Accounting Number Format** with two decimal places.

e. Apply a fill color to the cells closest to break-even without creating a deficit.

f. Apply a custom number format to make the formula reference appear as a descriptive column heading. Bold and center the headings and substitution values.

g. Answer questions 5 and 6 on the Q&A worksheet. Question 6 requires three combinations to list. Save the workbook.

Scenario Manager

You negotiated different cost per meal and ballroom rental rates based on 500, 400, 300, or 200 attendees. You estimated tentative ticket prices per attendee. To help you decide the target number of attendees, you need to use Scenario Manager.

a. Create a scenario named **500 Attend**, using the number of attendees, meal cost per person, ticket price per person, and ballroom rental variables as the changing cells. Enter these values for the scenario: **500, 15.95, 75**, and **12500**.

b. Create a second scenario named **400 Attend**, using the same changing cells. Enter these values for the scenario: **400, 17.95, 85**, and **12500**.

c. Create a third scenario named **300 Attend**, using the same changing cells. Enter these values for the scenario: **300, 19.95, 90**, and **11995**.

d. Create a fourth scenario named **200 Attend**, using the same changing cells. Enter these values for the scenario: **200, 22.95, 95**, and **11995**.

e. Generate a scenario summary report using the total revenue, total expenses, and balance as the results.

f. Clean up the summary as discussed in the chapter.

g. Answer questions 7 through 9 on the Q&A worksheet. Save the workbook.

Use Solver

You realize a perfect break-even point may be unrealistic, but you will donate any positive balance to charity. For this analysis, you will use Solver to keep the expenses constant while changing the number of attendees and ticket price per person.

a. Load the Solver add-in if it is not already loaded.

b. Set the objective to calculate the highest balance possible.

c. Use the number of attendees and the ticket price per person as changing variable cells.

d. Look at the *Limitations* section of the spreadsheet model.

e. Set a constraint for the number of attendees.

f. Set constraints for the ticket price per person.

g. Set an appropriate integer constraint.

h. Set a constraint that ensures the valet parking expense is less than or equal to the product of the number of parking stalls and the valet price per vehicle.

i. Solve the problem, but keep the original values in the Budget worksheet. Generate the Answer Report. If you get an internal memory error message, remove Solver as an add-in, close the workbook, open the workbook, add Solver in again, and finish using Solver.

j. Answer questions 10 through 13 on the Q&A worksheet. Apply **landscape orientation** to the Q&A worksheet. Save the workbook.

k. Create a footer on all four worksheets with your name on the left side, the sheet name code in the center, and the file name code on the right side.

l. Save and close the workbook, and submit it based on your instructor's directions.

Specialized Functions

CHAPTER 7

Logical, Lookup, Databases, and Finances

Yuri Arcurs/Shutterstock

CASE STUDY | Transpayne Filtration

You are an assistant accountant in the Human Resources (HR) Department for Transpayne Filtration, a company that sells water filtration systems to residential customers. Transpayne has locations in Atlanta, Boston, and Chicago, with a manager at each location who oversees several account representatives. You have an Excel workbook that contains names, locations, titles, hire dates, and salaries for the 20 managers and account representatives. To prepare for your upcoming salary analyses, you downloaded salary data from the corporate database into the workbook.

The HR manager wants you to perform several tasks based on locations and job titles. You will use logical functions to calculate annual bonus amounts and database functions to help analyze the data. Finally, you will review financial aspects of automobiles purchased for each manager.

Logical and Lookup Functions

Logical functions enable you to test conditions to determine if the condition is true or false. You have used the IF function, which is the most popular logical function, to perform different actions based on whether the logical test is true or false. Lookup and reference functions are valuable when you need to look up a value contained elsewhere in a workbook. For example, the VLOOKUP and HLOOKUP functions enable you to take an identified value, such as the number of months for a certificate of deposit (CD) to mature, look up that value in a vertical or horizontal lookup table, and then obtain a related value, such as the annual percentage rate (APR). Excel contains additional logical and lookup functions to perform more complex calculations and analyses.

In this section, you will learn how to create a nested logical function using the IF function. In addition, you will learn how to use the MATCH and INDEX lookup functions.

Creating a Nested Logical Function

The IF function contains three arguments: logical_test, Value_if_true, and Value_if_false. You can enter formulas within both the Value_if_true and Value_if_false arguments to perform calculations. For situations with multiple outcomes based on conditions, you can nest IF functions within the Value_if_true and Value_if_false arguments. A nested function is a function that is embedded within an argument of another function. Excel permits up to 64 IF statements in one formula.

Nested IF Within an IF Function

STEP 1 » Figure 7.1 illustrates three bonus rates based on employee hire date. If a representative was hired before 1/1/2005, the rep receives 9% of her or his total salary as a bonus. If a representative was hired between 1/1/2005 and 1/1/2010, the rep earns a 5% bonus. Lastly, anyone hired after 1/1/2010 receives a 3% bonus.

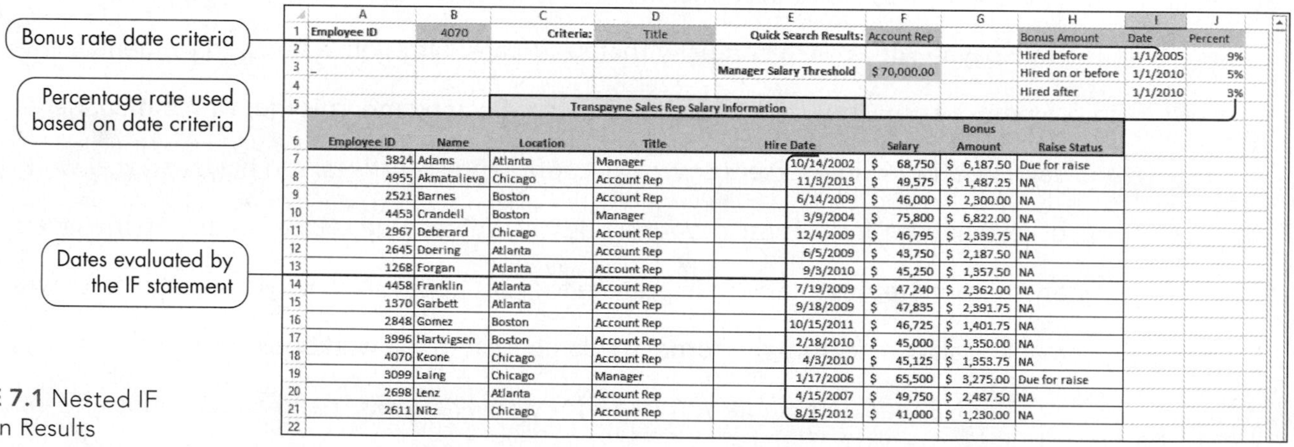

Bonus rate date criteria

Percentage rate used based on date criteria

Dates evaluated by the IF statement

FIGURE 7.1 Nested IF Function Results

Figure 7.2 illustrates the process as a flowchart. Diamonds are logical_test arguments and rectangles are Value_if_true and Value_if_false arguments. The second IF function is stored in the outer Value_if_false argument. Figure 7.3 illustrates the process with cell references.

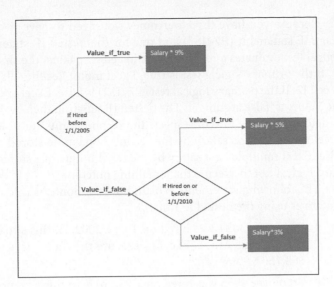

FIGURE 7.2 Nested IF Function Flowchart

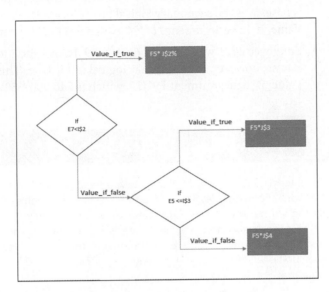

FIGURE 7.3 Nested IF Function Flowchart with Cell References

Figure 7.4 shows the nested IF function as the argument in the Value_if_false box in the Function Arguments dialog box. The function uses relative cell references for the hire date (cell E7) so that the cell reference will change to the next sales rep's hire date when you copy the formula down the column. The formula uses mixed references for the date thresholds (I$2 and I$3) and for the bonus percentages (J$2, J$3, and J$4) so that the references will point to the same rows when you copy the formulas down the column. You could use absolute instead of mixed references, such as $J$4, but doing so creates a longer formula and makes it a little more difficult to read. In the Formula Bar, the nested IF statement looks like this:

=IF(E5<J$7, F5*K$7,IF(E5<=J$8,F5*K$8,F5*K$9))

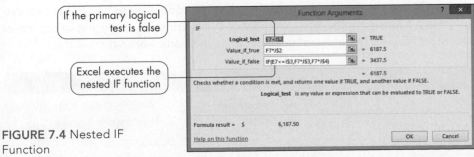

FIGURE 7.4 Nested IF Function

Because you have three outcomes, you need to have two logical tests: one for the primary IF statement (E7<I$2) and one for the nested IF statement (E7<=I$3). The primary logical test evaluates a rep's hire date in cell E7 against the first hire date cutoff stored in cell I2. If the primary logical test is true, Excel multiplies the salary in cell F7 by the rate stored in cell J2. If the primary logical test (E7<I$2) is false, Excel executes the nested IF function in the Value_if_false argument. The nested IF function then evaluates its logical test (E7<=I$3) to determine if the hire date meets the second bonus cutoff level. If that logical test is true, Excel multiplies the salary by the second bonus rate stored in cell J3. If that logical test is false, Excel multiples the salary by the third bonus rate stored in cell J4. You do not need a third logical test to execute the remaining outcome.

The following statements explain how the bonus is calculated for the individual representatives using the nested IF function:

- Employee 3824 was hired on 10/14/2002. In this situation, the logical test (E7<I$2) is true. This causes Excel to execute the Value_if_true argument J2*F$7, which is $68,750 * 9%.

- Employee 4955 was hired on 11/3/2013. In this situation, the logical test (E8<I$2) is false, as is the secondary logical test (E8<=I$3). This causes Excel to execute the Value_if_false argument F8*J$4, which is $49,575 * 3%.

- Employee 2521 was hired on 6/14/2009. In this situation, the logical test (E9<I$2) is false; however, the secondary logical test is true. This causes Excel to execute the Value_if_true argument F9*J$2, which is $46,000 * 5%.

TIP How Many Logical Tests?

To determine how many logical tests you need, count the number of outcomes and subtract one. For example, if you have three outcomes (such as Exceeds Expectations, Meets Expectations, and Below Expectations), you need only two logical tests. The first logical test produces one outcome (Exceeds Expectations). The nested logical test produces a second outcome (Meets Expectations) if true or produces the third outcome (Below Expectations) if false. Therefore, you do not need a third logical test to produce the third outcome.

Nest AND, OR, and NOT Functions

STEP 2>> At times, you might need to evaluate *multiple* conditions *at the same time* to determine the result. For example, you might want to evaluate all employees that make less than $50,000 and who are managers for an equity-based salary increase. Excel contains three additional functions to determine whether certain conditions are true or false. These functions are AND, OR, and NOT. You can use these functions individually (which has limited usefulness) or nest them inside another function, such as inside an IF statement (which can increase the capabilities of the function).

The *AND function* accepts two or more logical tests and displays TRUE if *all* conditions are true or FALSE if *any* of the conditions are false. You can test up to 255 conditions. Programmers often create truth tables to help analyze the conditions to determine the overall result. Table 7.1 illustrates the AND truth table that a professor might use to determine whether a student earns a bonus based on attendance and homework submissions.

TABLE 7.1 AND Truth Table		
	All Homework Submitted	**Missing One or More Homework Scores**
Perfect Attendance	TRUE	FALSE
Absent 1 or More Days	FALSE	FALSE

The bonus is awarded (TRUE) only when a student has perfect attendance *and* has completed all homework assignments, as shown in column D in Figure 7.5. Only Zach had perfect attendance and completed all assignments. All other combinations of attendance and homework submissions result in FALSE. Although Bill had perfect attendance, he missed one assignment, so he does not get the bonus.

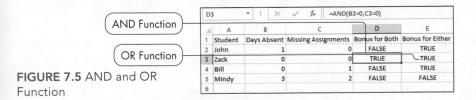

FIGURE 7.5 AND and OR Function

=AND(logical1,logical2)

You can nest the AND function inside the logical_test argument of an IF function to test to see if multiple conditions are met. For example, =IF(AND(B2=0,C2=0),10,0) where B2 contains the number of days absent, C2 contains the number of homework assignments missed, 10 represents the number of bonus points if both conditions are met, and 0 represents that no bonus points are awarded if either condition is false.

TIP **AND Results**

If the logical argument contains text or empty cells, those values are ignored. If no values exist in the logical argument, the AND function returns the #VALUE! error.

The **OR function** also accepts two or more conditions and returns TRUE if any of the conditions are true. It returns FALSE only if all conditions are false. You can test up to 255 conditions. Table 7.2 illustrates the OR truth table that a professor might use to determine whether a student earns a bonus based on attendance and homework submissions.

TABLE 7.2 OR Truth Table	All Homework Submitted	Missing One or More Homework Scores
Perfect Attendance	TRUE	TRUE
Absent 1 or More Days	TRUE	FALSE

In column E in Figure 7.5, the bonus is awarded (TRUE) when the student had either perfect attendance *or* if the student completed all assignments. The only time the student does not earn a bonus is if the student is absent one or more days and is also missing one or more homework scores. Mindy was the only student who did not earn the bonus using the OR condition. See Table 7.3 for more detail on the differences between AND and OR functions.

=OR(logical1,logical2)

Table 7.3 displays the differences between AND and OR functions.

TABLE 7.3 AND vs. OR

	All conditions are true	At least one condition is true	At least one condition is false	All conditions are false
AND	TRUE	FALSE	FALSE	FALSE
OR	TRUE	TRUE	TRUE	FALSE

The **NOT function** reverses the truth value of its argument. You use the NOT function when you want to make sure a value is not equal to a particular value. If the logical argument is false, the NOT function returns TRUE, and if the logical argument is true, the NOT function returns FALSE. Unlike the AND and OR functions that require two or more logical arguments, the NOT function contains only one logical argument.

=NOT(logical)

Using MATCH and INDEX Lookup Functions

You have used the VLOOKUP and HLOOKUP functions to look up a value, compare it to a lookup table, and then return a result from the lookup table. Two other lookup functions that are helpful when the order of data is not conducive to VLOOKUP or HLOOKUP are MATCH and INDEX. Figure 7.6 demonstrates the MATCH, INDEX, and nested functions.

	A	B	C
1	Agent	Sales	
2	Judy	$10,251.00	
3	Randy	$14,147.00	
4	Bill	$ 8,454.00	
5	Jack	$ 9,254.00	
6			
7	Condition	Results	Formula
8	High Sales amount	$14,147.00	=MAX(B2:B5)
9	Position of High Sales	2	=MATCH(B8,B2:B5,0)
10	Rep w/ Highest Sales	Randy	=INDEX(A2:B5,B8,1)
11	Rep w/ Highest Sales	Randy	=INDEX(A2:B5,MATCH(MAX(B2:B5),B2:B5,0),1)

FIGURE 7.6 MATCH, INDEX, and Nested Functions

Use the MATCH Function

The **MATCH function** returns the position of a value in a list. Think of it like a reverse phone number lookup. Instead of using directory assistance to look up a person's phone number, it would be like using the phone number to look up the person. You should use the MATCH function, not the VLOOKUP function, when you have the value, such as $14,147, but want to identify its row position within a list, such as third row. Whereas the MATCH function is often nested inside other functions, you should understand how it works on its own. The MATCH function contains three arguments: lookup_value, lookup_array, and match_type. In Figure 7.6, the MATCH function in cell B9 returns 2, the position of $14,147 within the sales range. The following list explains the arguments of the MATCH function.

=MATCH(lookup_value,lookup_array,[match_type])

- **Lookup_value.** The lookup_value argument is the value that you want to find in the array or list. It can be a value, label, logical value, or cell reference that contains one of these items. In Figure 7.6, the lookup_value argument for the MATCH function in cell B9 refers to the cell containing the MAX function: B8.

- **Lookup_array.** This argument is a range of contiguous cells that contain potential lookup values. In Figure 7.6, the lookup_array argument for the MATCH function in cell B9 is the range of cells containing the sales values: B2:B5.

- **Match_type.** This argument is 1, 0, or -1 to indicate which value to return. Use 1 to find the largest value that is less than or equal to the lookup_value when the values in the lookup_array are arranged in ascending order. Use -1 to find the smallest value that is greater than or equal to the lookup_value when the values in the lookup_array are in descending order. Use 0 to find the first value that is identical to the lookup_value when the values in the lookup_array have no particular order. In Figure 7.6, the match_type is 0 to find an exact match of the highest sales amount.

Use the Index Function

The *INDEX function* returns a value or the reference to a value within a range based on X and Y coordinates. So, for example, it will return the value in the intersection of a specific row and column such as the 3rd value in the 2nd column of a worksheet. When you select this function, the Select Arguments dialog box opens so that you can select an array form or a reference form. The array form is the more commonly used option. It displays the value of an element in a table based on either a row or column number.

`=INDEX(array,row_num,[column_num])`

- **Array.** This argument is one or more ranges. In Figure 7.6, the array argument in the INDEX function in cell B10 is the range containing the agents and their respective sales: A2:B5.

- **Row_num.** This argument identifies the row number within the array range. In the INDEX function in cell B10 in Figure 7.6, the row_num argument is B9, the cell containing the MATCH function results. Recall that the MATCH function in cell B8 determined the position of the highest sales amount from the list of Sales values in cells B2:B5. Therefore, the INDEX function refers to cell B10, which then uses the second row of the array in the range A2:B5.

- **Column_num.** This argument identifies the column within the reference that contains the value you want. In Figure 7.6, the column_num is 1 to identify the first column within the range A2:B5. The first column contains the agent names. So, after the MATCH function identifies the row (2) containing the highest sales value ($14,147.00), the column_num argument (1) identifies the name (Randy) in the first column that corresponds to the highest sales value.

The array in the range A2:B5 contains more than one row and column; therefore, row_num and column_num arguments were required. If an array contains only one row, the column_num is required, and if the array contains only one column, the row_num is required.

 TIP | **INDEX Function in Reference Form**

The reference form displays the cell reference of a row and column intersection. The syntax for the reference form is =INDEX(reference,row_num,[column_num],[area_num]). Use Help to learn about the arguments and to see an example of its usage.

You can reduce the number of cells containing functions by nesting the MATCH function inside the INDEX function. For example, cell B11 in Figure 7.6 contains a nested MAX function inside the MATCH function, which is then nested inside the INDEX function to identify which sales rep had the highest amount of sales.

Nest Functions in Other Functions

STEP 3 » You can use the Insert Function and Function Arguments dialog boxes to insert functions as arguments for another function instead of typing the entire nested function directly in the Formula Bar. For example, to create =INDEX(A2:B5,MATCH(MAX(B2:B5),B2:B5,0),1) in dialog boxes, do the following:

1. Click Insert Function, select the outer function, such as INDEX, and then click OK to display the Function Arguments dialog box.

2. Click in the argument box where the nested function is needed, click the Name Box arrow on the Formula Bar, and then select the desired function from the list of recently used functions, or select More Functions from the Name Box drop-down list, select the function, such as MATCH, in the Insert Function dialog box, and then click OK to open the Function Arguments dialog box for the nested function.

3. Enter the arguments for the nested function. Click in the outer function's name—INDEX—in the Formula Bar to display the Function Arguments dialog box for the outer function again.

4. Continue entering or nesting other arguments. When the entire function is complete, click OK in the outer function's Function Arguments dialog box.

Quick **Concepts**

1. What is the difference between a single IF statement and a nested IF statement? *p. 310*

2. In what situation would you use an AND function over a nested IF statement? *p. 312*

3. What is the benefit of nesting the MATCH function inside the INDEX function? *p. 315*

Hands-On Exercises

Watch the Video
for this Hands-
On Exercise!

MyITLab®
HOE1 Training

1 Logical and Lookup Functions

As the Transpayne accounting assistant, you have been asked to identify underpaid account representatives to bring their salaries up to a new minimum standard within the corporation. In addition, you want to calculate annual bonus amounts based on hire date as well as create a quick search lookup field to allow for instant access to individual information.

Skills covered: Create a Nested IF Function • Nest an AND Function Inside an IF Function • Create a Lookup Field Using INDEX and MATCH Functions

STEP 1 ≫ CREATE A NESTED IF FUNCTION

Your first task is to calculate the annual bonus amount for each employee. The company uses a tiered bonus system that awards a specific percentage of salary based on hire date. Employees hired before 1/1/2005 receive 9%. Employees hired on or before 1/1/2010 receive 5%, and employees that were hired after 1/1/2010 receive 3%. You plan to use a nested IF function to calculate each employee's bonus. You will then use the fill handle to replace the function in the rest of the column. Refer to Figure 7.7 as you complete Step 1.

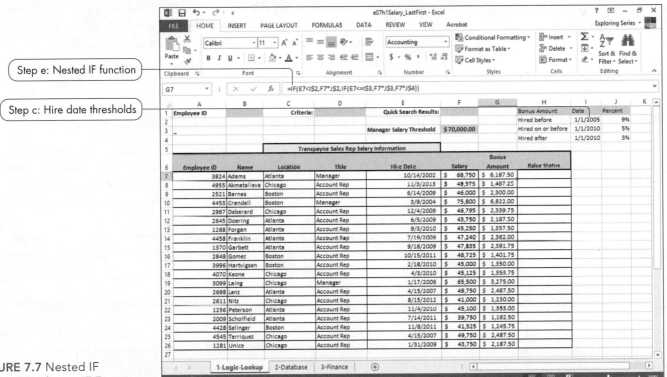

FIGURE 7.7 Nested IF Function Within an IF Function

a. Open *e07h1Salary* and save it as **e07h1Salary_LastFirst**. Click the **1-Logic-Lookup worksheet tab**.

> **TROUBLESHOOTING:** If you make any major mistakes in this exercise, you can close the file, open *e07h1Salary* again, and then start this exercise over.

b. Click **cell G7**, click the **FORMULAS tab** if necessary, click **Logical** in the Function Library group, and then select **IF**.

c. Type **E7<I$2** in the **Logical_test box**.

The logical test compares the hire date to the first bonus threshold, 1/1/2005. Because you will copy the formula down the column and want to make sure the reference to the employee's hire date changes, use a relative cell reference to cell E7. To ensure that the reference to the date threshold remains constant, use a mixed cell reference to cell I$2. You could use an absolute reference, but because you are copying the formula down, the column letter I will remain the same. Using a mixed reference keeps the formula shorter and easier to read.

d. Type **F7*J$2** in the **Value_if_true box**.

This will multiply the salary by the bonus percentage if the logical test provided is true. If the logical test is not true, it will move on to the next argument created in step e.

e. Type **IF(E7<=I$3,F7*J$3,F7*J$4)** in the **Value_if_false box**.

By entering an IF statement in the Value_if_false box, you have created a nested function that evaluates the second threshold, 1/1/2010 (cell I3). If the hire date does not fall within the first or second thresholds defined by the primary and secondary logical tests, it will then by default trigger the Value_if_false, (F7*J$4). This will calculate the bonus based on the lowest bonus amount, 3% (cell J4). Use relative cell references for the employee's hire date (cell E7), because it should change when you copy the formula down the column. Use a mixed (or an absolute) reference for the threshold date (cell I$3) to ensure it does not change as you copy the formula down the column. Again, using mixed references keeps the formula shorter and easier to read than absolute references, but both produce the same results.

f. Click **OK** in the Function Arguments dialog box.

The function returns the value 6,188. This is calculated by multiplying the current salary, $68,750 (cell F7), by the bonus percentage rate of 9% (cell J2).

g. Double-click the **cell G7 fill handle** to copy the function down the column.

h. Select the **range G7:G26** and apply **Accounting Number Format**.

i. Save the workbook.

STEP 2 >> NEST AN AND FUNCTION INSIDE AN IF FUNCTION

The Human Resources Director recommends that the company pay managers at least $70,000. You would like to nest an AND function inside an IF function to determine which managers should receive pay raises based on their current salary level. The salary threshold is located in cell F3 in the 1-Logic-Lookup worksheet. Refer to Figure 7.8 as you complete Step 2.

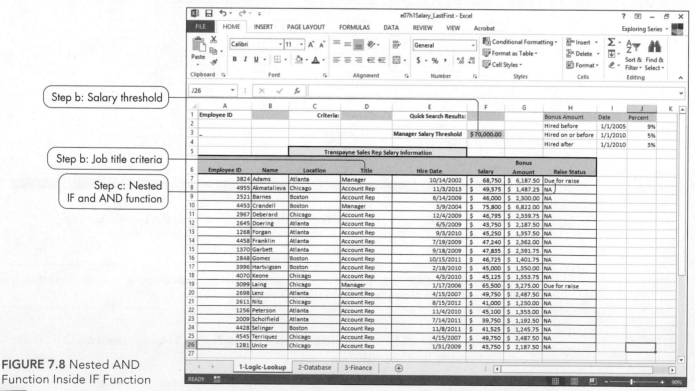

FIGURE 7.8 Nested AND Function Inside IF Function

a. Click **cell H7**, click the **FORMULAS tab**, click **Logical** in the Function Library group, and then select **IF**.

b. Type **AND(D7="manager",F7<F$3)** in the **Logical_test box**.

Using the AND function nested in the logical test of the IF statement gives you the ability to add multiple arguments. In this scenario, you have the criteria if the employee is a manager (D7="manager" and makes less than $70,000 (F7<F$3).

c. Type **"Due for raise"** in the **Value_if_true box**.

If both conditions specified in the AND function are true, the employee is eligible for a raise. You use a mixed reference in cell F3 to ensure that row number 3 does not change when you copy the formula down the column.

d. Type **"NA"** in the **Value_if_false box**.

> **TROUBLESHOOTING:** Do not make cells D7 or F7 absolute or mixed. If you do, the function will use the incorrect values and return the first person's salary of $68,750, in the range H7:H26.

e. Click **OK**, double-click the **cell H7 fill handle** to copy the formula down the column, and then save the workbook.

The function now evaluates the employee's title and salary. If both arguments in the AND function are true, then *Due for raise* is displayed; if not, *NA* is displayed.

STEP 3 ≫ CREATE A LOOKUP FIELD USING INDEX AND MATCH FUNCTIONS

You want to provide a simple search feature so that users can enter an employee number in cell B1 and then display employee title information in cell F1. For example, if Employee ID 4070 is entered in cell B1, cell F1 displays "Account Rep." Refer to Figure 7.9 as you complete Step 3.

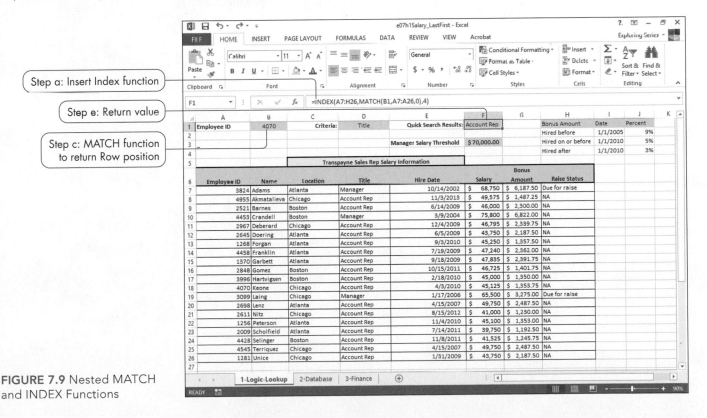

FIGURE 7.9 Nested MATCH and INDEX Functions

a. Click **cell F1**, click **Lookup & Reference** in the Function Library group, and then select **INDEX**. Choose **array, row_num, column_num** from the Select Arguments dialog box and click **OK**.

b. Select **range A7:H26** in the Array box.

This defines the data pool from which Excel will pull information.

c. Type **MATCH(B1,A7:A26,0)** in the **Row_num box**.

If you nest the MATCH function in the Row_num box of the index function, Excel will look up the position of the employee number in cell B1 within the range A7:A26 and return the relative position, which for employee 4070 is 12. Currently, the function returns #N/A because cell B1 is blank.

d. Type **4** in the **Column_num box**. Click **OK**.

If you enter the number 4 in the Column_num box, the function returns information from the fourth column in the data set.

e. Type **4070** in **cell B1**.

Cell F1 now displays the current position of employee 4070. It does this by matching the Employee ID in column A to the Title in column D.

f. Save and leave the workbook open if you plan to continue with Hands-On Exercise 2. If not, save and close the workbook, and exit Excel.

Database Filtering and Functions

Databases are prevalent in most organizations today to store and manipulate data, such as inventory details about automobiles at a particular dealership or financial transaction details for your credit card. Whereas Microsoft Access is more appropriate for relational database modeling, people often use Excel for basic database storage and manipulation. You have some experience in using Excel tables to perform basic database tasks, such as sorting and filtering data. However, you may need to perform more advanced filtering or calculations.

In this section, you will learn how to use advanced filtering techniques and insert database functions. Specifically, you will define a criteria range and extract data that meet certain criteria. Then you will insert the DSUM and DAVERAGE functions to calculate results based on filtered data.

Using Advanced Filtering

Data become more useful in decision making when you reduce the records to a subset of data that meets specific conditions. For example, a manager might want to identify account reps who earn more than $30,000 in Chicago. The manager can use the filter arrows to filter the table data by job title, salary, and location, and Excel will filter the original dataset by hiding records that do not meet the conditions. Sometimes, however, it may be important to keep the original dataset visible and create a copy of only those records that meet these conditions in another location of the worksheet. To do so, the manager can use advanced filtering techniques.

Define a Criteria Range

STEP 1 ▸ Before you apply advanced filtering techniques, you must define a criteria range. A **criteria range** is a separate range of cells—often several rows above or below the table—that specifies the conditions used to filter the table. A criteria range must contain at least two rows and one column. The first row contains the column labels as they appear in the table, and the second row contains the conditions (e.g., values) for filtering the table. Figure 7.10 shows the original table, criteria range, and copy of records that meet the conditions.

	Employee ID	Name	Location	Title	Salary	Bonus Amount	Raise Status
6							
7	3824	Adams	Atlanta	Manager	$ 68,750	$ 6,187.50	Due for raise
8	4955	Akmatalieva	Chicago	Account Rep	$ 49,575	$ 1,487.25	NA
9	2521	Barnes	Boston	Account Rep	$ 46,000	$ 2,300.00	NA
10	4453	Crandell	Boston	Manager	$ 75,800	$ 6,822.00	NA
11	2967	Deberard	Chicago	Account Rep	$ 46,795	$ 2,339.75	NA
12	2645	Doering	Atlanta	Account Rep	$ 43,750	$ 2,187.50	NA
13	1268	Forgan	Atlanta	Account Rep	$ 45,250	$ 1,357.50	NA
14	4458	Franklin	Atlanta	Account Rep	$ 47,240	$ 2,362.00	NA
15	1370	Garbett	Atlanta	Account Rep	$ 47,835	$ 2,391.75	NA
16	2848	Gomez	Boston	Account Rep	$ 46,725	$ 1,401.75	NA
17	3996	Hartvigsen	Boston	Account Rep	$ 45,000	$ 1,350.00	NA
18	4070	Keone	Chicago	Account Rep	$ 45,125	$ 1,353.75	NA
19	3099	Laing	Chicago	Manager	$ 65,500	$ 3,275.00	Due for raise
20							
21							
22	Employee ID	Name	Location	Title	Salary		
23			Chicago	Account Rep	>30000		
24							
25	Employee ID	Name	Location	Title	Salary		
26	4955	Akmatalieva	Chicago	Account Rep	$ 49,575		
27	2967	Deberard	Chicago	Account Rep	$ 46,795		
28	4070	Keone	Chicago	Account Rep	$ 45,125		
29	2611	Nitz	Chicago	Account Rep	$ 41,000		
30	4545	Terriquez	Chicago	Account Rep	$ 49,750		

Callouts: Criteria set on the second row of the criteria range; Original data; Labels on the first row of the criteria range; Copy of records meeting criteria

FIGURE 7.10 Data, Criteria Range, and Output

Because you want to display records that meet all three conditions, you enter the conditions on the second row of the criteria range, immediately below their respective labels: Chicago below Location, Account Rep below Title, and >30000 below Salary. By default, Excel looks for an exact match. If you want to avoid an exact match for values, enter relational operators. For example, entering >30000 sets the condition for salaries that are greater than $30,000. You can use <, >, <=, >=, and <> relational operators, similar to using relational operators in the logical_test argument of an IF function. Excel copies only the records that meet all three conditions. Therefore, Adams earning $68,750 from Atlanta is excluded because Adams is a manager, not an account rep, and is not from Chicago. You can set an OR condition in the criteria range. For example, you want to display (a) Chicago account reps who earn more than $30,000 *or* (b) Atlanta account reps regardless of salary. Figure 7.11 shows the conditions in the criteria range. Notice that the criteria range contains three rows: column labels on the first row, the first set of conditions on the second row, and the second set of conditions on the third row. Each column of conditions sets an AND condition; that is, each criterion must be met. Each additional row sets an OR condition.

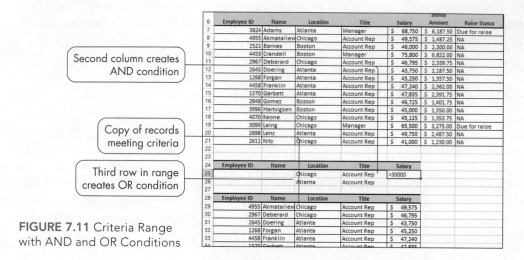

Second column creates AND condition

Copy of records meeting criteria

Third row in range creates OR condition

FIGURE 7.11 Criteria Range with AND and OR Conditions

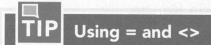

TIP Using = and <>

Using equal (=) and unequal (<>) symbols with the criteria values selects records with empty and nonempty fields, respectively. An equal with nothing after it will return all records with no entry in the designated column. An unequal (<>) with nothing after it will select all records with an entry in the column. An empty cell in the criteria range returns every record in the list.

Apply the Advanced Filter

STEP 2 ▶

After you create the criteria range, you are ready to apply the advanced filter using the Advanced Filter dialog box. This dialog box enables you to filter the table in place or copy the selected records to another area in the worksheet, specify the list range, specify the criteria range, or display unique records only. To apply the advanced filter, do the following:

1. Click a cell in the data table.
2. Click Advanced in the Sort & Filter group on the DATA tab.
3. Click the desired action: *Filter the list, in-place* to filter the range by hiding rows that do not match your criteria or *Copy to another location* if you want to copy the rows that match your criteria instead of filtering the original dataset.
4. Make sure the *List range* displays the range containing the original dataset, including the column headings.
5. Enter the criteria range, including the criteria labels, in the *Criteria range* box. To perform the advanced filter for the OR condition in Figure 7.11, you must select all three rows of the criteria range: the column labels, the row containing the criteria for Chicago account reps earning more than $30,000, and the row containing criteria for Atlanta account reps.

6. Specify the *Copy to* range if you selected *Copy to another location* in Step 3. Notice that you enter only the starting row. Excel will copy the column labels and fill in the rows below the heading with the records that meet the conditions you set. Make sure the *Copy to* range contains sufficient empty rows to accommodate the copied records. If you do not include enough rows, Excel will replace existing data with the copied records. Click OK.

Figure 7.12 shows the Advanced Filter dialog box with settings to produce the advanced filter shown in Figure 7.11.

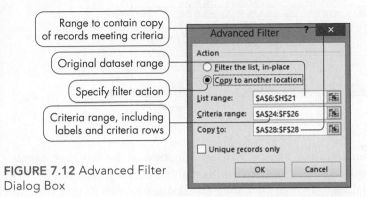

Range to contain copy of records meeting criteria

Original dataset range

Specify filter action

Criteria range, including labels and criteria rows

FIGURE 7.12 Advanced Filter Dialog Box

TIP Auto Range Names

When you use the Advanced Filter dialog box, Excel assigns the range name *Criteria* to the criteria range and *Extract* to the output range.

Manipulating Data with Database Functions

Database functions analyze data for selected records only in a database table. These functions are similar to statistical functions (SUM, AVERAGE, MAX, MIN, COUNT) except that database functions are exclusively used for database tables; these functions affect only records that satisfy the specified criteria. Data not meeting the specified criteria are filtered out. All database functions use a criteria range that defines the filter parameters. Using range names can simplify the construction of database functions.

Database functions have three arguments: database, field, and criteria.

- **Database.** The database argument is the entire table, including column labels and all data, on which the function operates. The database reference may be represented by a range name. In Figure 7.13, the Database argument is A6:H21.
- **Field.** The field argument is the database column that contains the values operated on by the function. You can enter the name of the column label in quotation marks, such as "Salary," or you can enter the number that represents the location of that column within the table. For example, if the Salary column is the fifth column in the table, you can enter a 5 for the field argument. You can also enter a cell reference, for example, F6, as shown in Figure 7.13.
- **Criteria.** The criteria argument defines the conditions to be met by the function. This range must contain at least one column label and a cell below the label that specifies the condition. The criteria argument may include more than one column with conditions for each column label, indicated by a range such as A24:F25 or a range name.

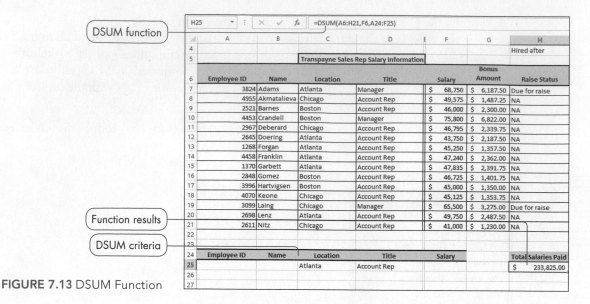

DSUM function

Function results

DSUM criteria

FIGURE 7.13 DSUM Function

To insert a database function, you can click Insert Function in the Function Library group or Insert Function between the Name Box and Formula Bar. Then click the *Or select a category* arrow, select Database, and then click the desired database function in the *Select a function* list.

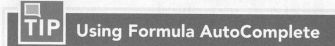

Using Formula AutoComplete

Alternatively, to begin using a database function, you can type =D in a cell. Excel displays the Formula AutoComplete list, showing a list of functions that start with the letter D. Select the appropriate database function from the list.

Use DSUM and DAVERAGE Functions

STEP 3 » The **DSUM function** adds the values in a numeric database column based on conditions you specify in a criteria range. In Figure 7.13, the criteria range sets conditions for Boston and account rep. You then use the criteria range to calculate the total salaries for records meeting those two conditions.

=DSUM(database,field,criteria)

The DSUM function is shorter and easier to read than other conditional summary functions, but you must create a criteria range to complete the conditions first. Note that the criteria argument does not need to include the entire database range A6:H21; it only needs to include the column labels and conditions such as A24:F25.

The **DAVERAGE function** determines the arithmetic mean, or average, of numeric entries in a database column that match conditions you specify. For example, you might want to determine the average salary of account reps in Boston using =DAVERAGE(A6:H21, "Salary",A24:F25).

=DAVERAGE(database,field,criteria)

Identify Values with DMAX and DMIN

STEP 4 » The *DMAX function* identifies the highest value in a database column that matches conditions you specify. For example, you can use the DMAX function to determine the highest salary ($49,750) of account reps in Boston. The *DMIN function* identifies the lowest value ($43,750) in a database column that matches conditions you specify. For example, you can use the DMIN function to determine the lowest salary for account reps in Boston.

=DMAX(database,field,criteria)

=DMIN(database,field,criteria)

Identify the Total Number with DCOUNT

STEP 5 » The *DCOUNT function* counts the cells that contain numbers in a database column that match conditions you specify. For example, you can use the DCOUNT function to count the number of account reps in Boston, which is four. However, if one of the records is missing a value, DCOUNT excludes that record from being counted. If after completing the DCOUNT, you decide you would like to change the match conditions, you can do so by altering the information entered in the criteria area. To count records containing an empty cell, use DCOUNTA instead.

=DCOUNT(database,field,criteria)

=DCOUNTA(database,field,criteria)

Quick Concepts

1. Why would you use advanced filtering over basic filtering? *p. 321*
2. What are the benefits of database functions? *p. 323*
3. Why would you use a database function over advanced filtering? *p. 323*

Hands-On Exercises

Watch the Video
for this Hands-
On Exercise!

MyITLab®
HOE2 Training

2 Database Filtering and Functions

Other assistant accountants want to be able to enter criteria to see a list of records that meet the conditions they specify. In addition, these assistants then want to calculate summary statistics based on the filtered results.

Skills covered: Create Criteria and Output Ranges • Perform an Advanced Filter • Insert a DAVERAGE Function • Use DMIN, DMAX, and DCOUNT Functions • Change the Filter Criteria

STEP 1 ≫ CREATE CRITERIA AND OUTPUT RANGES

You want to set up the workbook with a criteria range and an output range. This will enable other assistant accountants to enter criteria of their choosing to filter the list of salary data. Refer to Figure 7.14 as you complete Step 1.

Step c: Pasted label range

Step d: Second copy of label range for output range use

FIGURE 7.14 Criteria and Output Ranges

a. Open *e07h1Salary_LastFirst* and save it as **e07h2Salary_LastFirst**, replacing *h1* with *h2*. Click the **2-Database worksheet tab**.

b. Select the **range A2:F2** and copy the range.

c. Paste the data in **cell A25**.

d. Click **cell A30**, paste another copy of the data, and then press **Esc**. Save the workbook.

You copied the original column labels and pasted them in the range A25:F25, the area for the Criteria Range, and another copy of the headings for the Output Range in cells A30:F30.

STEP 2 ≫ PERFORM AN ADVANCED FILTER

You are ready to enter conditions to restrict the output list to Account Reps in Boston. Refer to Figure 7.15 as you complete Step 2.

Step a: Advanced filter criteria

Step g: Advanced filter results

FIGURE 7.15 Conditions and Output

a. Type **Boston** in **cell C26** and type **Account Rep** in **cell D26**.

You entered the conditions on the first row below the labels in the criteria range. Because you entered both conditions on the same row, you created an AND condition. Both conditions must be met in order to display employee data in the output range.

b. Click in **cell D19** (or any cell within the dataset).

c. Click the **DATA tab** and click **Advanced** in the Sort & Filter group.

The Advanced Filter dialog box opens so that you can specify the desired filter action, the list, the criteria range, and other details.

d. Click **Copy to another location**.

e. Click in the **List range box** and select the **range A2:F22**.

f. Click in the **Criteria range box** and select the **range A25:F26**.

You selected the labels and the row containing the conditions for the criteria range.

g. Click in the **Copy to box**, select the **range A30:F30**, and then click **OK**.

Make sure you select only the labels for the output range.

h. Scroll down to see the output records. Save the workbook.

Four employees are account reps in Boston.

STEP 3 ≫ INSERT A DAVERAGE FUNCTION

Regardless of the criteria entered in the criteria range A25:F26, you want to calculate the average salary for the records that meet those conditions. You will insert a DAVERAGE function to perform the calculation. Refer to Figure 7.16 as you complete Step 3.

FIGURE 7.16 DAVERAGE Function

a. Click **cell I25** and click **Insert Function** in the Function Library group on the FORMULAS tab.

b. Click the **Or select a category arrow**, select **Database**, select **DAVERAGE** in the *Select a function* list if necessary, and then click **OK**.

c. Select the **range A2:F22** to enter that range in the Database box.

The database argument must include the column labels and original dataset.

d. Click in the **Field box** and type **Salary**.

Excel enters the quotation marks for you within the dialog box. If you want, you can enter the field name in quotation marks yourself, or you can enter the column number (6) of the column that contains the data you wish to average.

e. Click in the **Criteria box** and select the **range A25:F26**.

Excel might display *Criteria* instead of the range in the Criteria box.

f. Click **OK**. Save the workbook.

The average salary of account reps in Boston is $44,813.

STEP 4 ≫ USE DMIN, DMAX, AND DCOUNT FUNCTIONS

The other accounting assistants would like to see the lowest and highest salaries based on the database conditions. In addition, you want to insert the DCOUNT function to count the number of records that meet the specified conditions. Refer to Figure 7.17 as you complete Step 4.

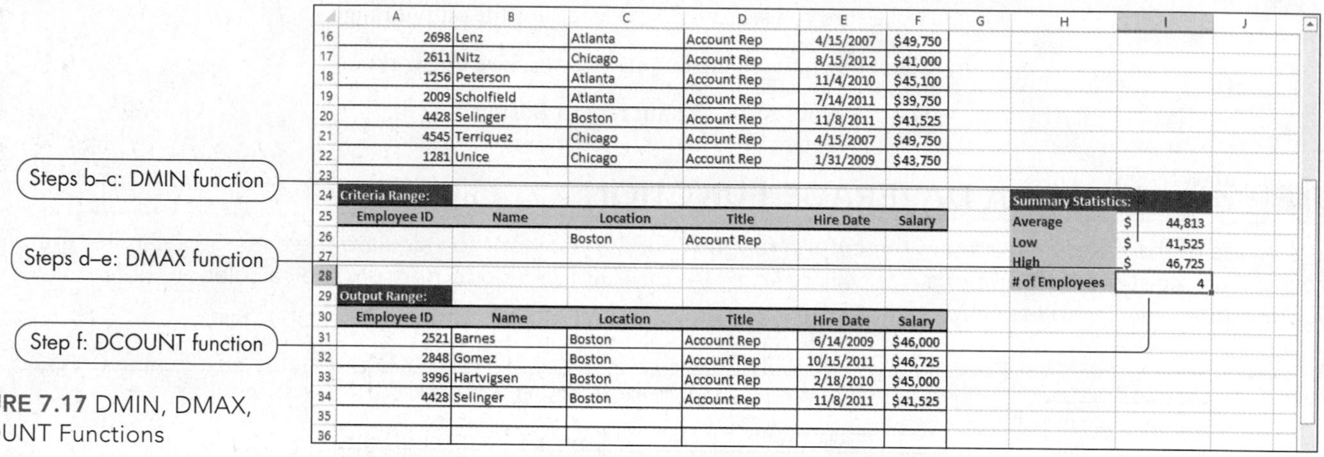

Steps b–c: DMIN function
Steps d–e: DMAX function
Step f: DCOUNT function

FIGURE 7.17 DMIN, DMAX, DCOUNT Functions

a. Click **cell I26** and click **Insert Function** in the Function Library group.

The Database functions should be listed because that was the last function category you selected.

b. Select **DMIN** in the *Select a function* list and click **OK**.

c. Select the **range A2:F22** in the Database box, select the **cell F2** in Field box, select the **range A25:F26** in the Criteria box, and then click **OK**.

The lowest salary for account reps in Boston is $41,525.

d. Click **cell I27** and click **Insert Function** in the Function Library group. Select **DMAX** in the *Select a function* list and click **OK**.

e. Select the **range A2:F22** in the Database box, select the **cell F2** in Field box, select the **range A25:F26** in the Criteria box, and then click **OK**.

The highest salary for account reps in Boston is $46,725.

f. Type **=DCOUNT(A2:F22,"Salary",A25:F26)** in **cell I28**. Save the workbook.

The company has four account reps in the Boston location.

STEP 5 ≫ CHANGE THE FILTER CRITERIA

You want to change the criteria to see the managers' salary data. Refer to Figure 7.18 as you complete Step 5.

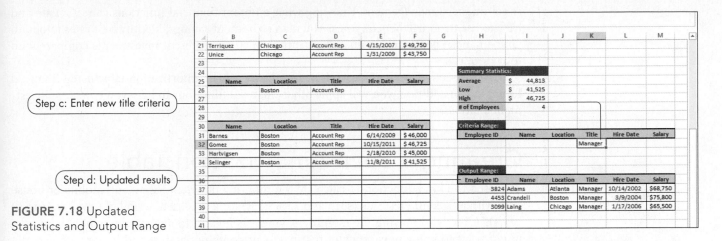

Step c: Enter new title criteria

Step d: Updated results

FIGURE 7.18 Updated Statistics and Output Range

a. Copy the data in the **range A24:F26** and paste the copied data in **cell H30**.

b. Delete the contents in **cells J32** and **K32**.

c. Type **Manager** in **cell K32** and press **Enter**.

d. Copy **cell A29** and paste it in **cell H35**.

e. Click anywhere in the original dataset. Repeat Steps 2c through f using the **data range A2:F22**.

   Excel updates the filtered list in the output range.

f. Save the workbook. Keep the workbook onscreen if you plan to continue with Hands-On Exercise 3. If not, close the workbook and exit Excel.

Financial Functions

Excel's financial functions are helpful for business financial analysts and for you in your personal financial management. Knowing what different financial functions can calculate and how to use them will benefit you as you plan retirement savings, identify best rates to obtain your financial goals, and evaluate how future values of different investments compare with today's values.

In this section, you will learn how to prepare a loan amortization table using financial functions. In addition, you will apply other financial functions to help you complete investment analyses.

Creating a Loan Amortization Table

STEP 2 >> You used the PMT function to calculate the monthly payment for an automobile or house loan with a fixed interest rate (such as 5.75% APR) for a specified period of time (such as 30 years). Although knowing the monthly payment is helpful to analyze a potential loan, you might want to know how much of that payment contains interest and how much actually goes toward paying off the loan balance. Interest is not identical for every month of the loan. Interest is calculated on the balance of the loan. As you continue making monthly payments, the loan balance continually decreases; therefore, the amount of interest decreases and the principal increases each month. Because your monthly payments are constant throughout the life of the loan, with each payment, more of the payment goes toward paying off the loan. To see the interest and principal portions of each monthly payment and the reduction in the loan amount, you can create a *loan amortization table*, which is a schedule that calculates the interest, principal repayment, and remaining balance.

Figure 7.19 shows the top and bottom portions of an amortization schedule (rows 22:51 are hidden) for an automobile loan of $30,000 with an APR of 5.25% for a four-year loan with a monthly payment of $694.28, rounded to the nearest penny. The borrower pays a total of $33,325.51 (48 payments of $694.28). These payments equal the principal of $30,000 plus $3,325.51 in interest over the life of the loan.

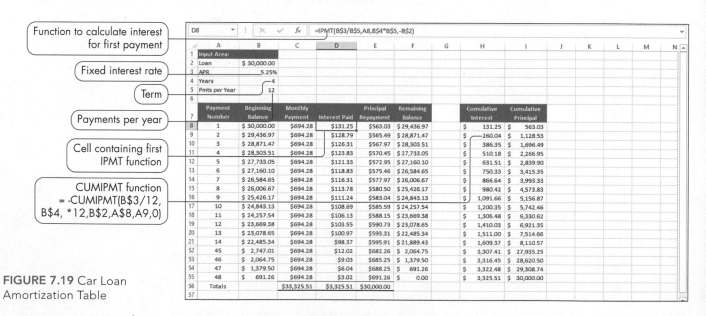

FIGURE 7.19 Car Loan Amortization Table

Perform Internal Calculations

The body of the worksheet shows how principal and interest comprise each payment. The balance of the loan at the beginning of the first period is $30,000. The monthly payment includes interest and principal repayment. The interest for the first month ($131.25) is calculated on the beginning balance for the period, which is the original loan amount ($30,000) for the first payment at a monthly interest rate (5.25%/12).

The principal repayment is the amount of the monthly payment that is left over after deducting the monthly interest. For the first payment, the principal repayment is $563.03 ($694.28 – $131.25).

The remaining balance is the difference between the previous remaining balance and the principal repayment. For the first month, subtract the principal repayment from the original loan amount ($30,000 – $563.03).

The interest for the second month ($128.79) is less than interest for the previous period because the remaining balance to start that period is less ($29,436.97 * 5.25%/12). As each month's beginning balance decreases, so does the monthly interest. The principal repayment is higher for the second month because the interest is less than for the first month.

TIP Extra Principal Payment

Many homebuyers choose a 30-year mortgage to keep the monthly payment low but opt to pay extra toward the principal each month to reduce the length of the mortgage and the total interest paid. This reduction in interest can be substantial. For example, paying an extra $100 a month on a 30-year, $350,000 mortgage with an interest rate of 3.24% APR can save more than $40,000 in interest over the life of the mortgage and pay off the mortgage before its original payoff date.

Calculate Interest and Principal Payments with IPMT and PPMT Functions

The financial category contains additional functions to calculate results for loan payments: IPMT and PPMT. You can use these functions in isolation or within the body of a loan amortization table if the table does not allow additional principal payments. If your loan amortization enables users to pay additional principal, these functions will not provide accurate results.

The *IPMT function* calculates the periodic interest for a specified payment period on a loan or an investment given a fixed interest rate, term, and periodic payments. In Figure 7.19, you use the IPMT function to calculate the interest payment for each period (for example, the calculation for interest for the first period is: =IPMT(B$3/B$5,A8,B$4*B$5,-B$2)). A benefit of the IPMT function is that you can use it to identify the interest for any given payment without having to create a loan amortization table. The IPMT function has four required arguments and two optional arguments:

=IPMT(rate,per,nper,pv,[fv],[type])

- **Rate.** The rate argument is the periodic interest rate. If the APR is 5.25% (cell B3) and monthly payments are made, the rate is 5.25%/12 (B3/12), or 0.438%.

- **Per.** The per argument is the specific payment or investment period to use to calculate the interest where the first payment period is 1. It is best to include a payment number column as in Figure 7.19. You can use a relative cell reference to avoid having raw numbers in the argument.

- **Nper.** The nper argument represents the total number of payment or investment periods. With a four-year loan consisting of monthly payments, the nper is 48. You should perform the calculation using the input cells, such as $B$4*$B$5, in the nper argument instead of typing the value 48 in case the number of years or number of payments per year changes.

- **Pv.** The pv argument represents the present value of the loan or investment. Enter a minus sign in front of the cell reference to avoid having a negative interest payment returned. In this example, pv would be –B$2.

- **Fv.** The optional fv argument represents the future value of the loan or investment. If you omit this argument, Excel defaults to 0. For loan payments, the balance should be zero after you pay off your loan.

- **Type.** The optional type argument represents the timing of the payments. Enter 0 if the payments are made at the end of the period, or enter 1 if the payments are made at the beginning of the period. If you omit this argument, Excel assumes a default of 0.

The ***PPMT function*** calculates the principal payment for a specified payment period on a loan or an investment given a fixed interest rate, term, and periodic payments. In Figure 7.19, you can use the PPMT function to calculate the principal repayment in column E. For example, cell E8 contains =PPMT(B$3/B$5,A8,B$4*B$5,-B$2). The first month's total payment of $694.28 includes $563.03 principal repayment. The PPMT function has the same four required arguments and two optional arguments as the IPMT function:

`=PPMT(rate,per,nper,pv,[fv],[type])`

Calculate Cumulative Interest and Principal Payments with CUMIPMT and CUMPRINC Functions

STEP 3 »
Although the IPMT function calculates the amount of interest paid in one particular loan payment, it does not determine the amount of interest paid over a specific number of payments. You can use the ***CUMIPMT function*** to calculate the cumulative interest throughout a loan amortization table. This function accumulates the interest paid between selected payments or throughout the entire loan. For the first payment, the cumulative interest is the same as the periodic interest. From that point on, you can calculate the cumulative interest, such as the sum of the interest paid for the first two periods, as shown in cell H9 in Figure 7.19. If you do not want to calculate a running total for the entire loan, you can specify the interest between two periods, such as between payment periods 5 and 10, to calculate the total interest paid for the second year of the loan. The CUMIPMT contains six arguments:

`=CUMIPMT(rate,nper,pv,start_period,end_period,type)`

The rate, nper, pv, and type arguments are the same arguments that you use in the IPMT and PPMT functions. The start_period argument specifies the first period you want to start accumulating the interest, and the end_period argument specifies the last payment period you want to include. In Figure 7.19, the first cumulative interest payment formula in cell G8 uses 1 for both the start_period and end_period arguments. From that point on, the start_period is still 1, but the end_period changes to reflect each payment period, using the payment numbers in column A.

STEP 4 »
You can use the ***CUMPRINC function*** to calculate the cumulative principal throughout a loan amortization table. This function accumulates the principal repayment between selected payments or throughout the entire loan. For the first payment, the cumulative principal paid is the same as the first principal repayment. From that point on, you can calculate the cumulative principal payment, such as the sum of the principal repayment paid for the first two periods, as shown in cell H9 in Figure 7.19. If you do not want to calculate a running total for the entire loan, you can specify the principal repayment between two periods, such as between payment periods 5 and 10, to calculate the total principal repaid for the second year of the loan. The CUMPRINC contains six arguments:

`=CUMPRINC(rate,nper,pv,start_period,end_period,type)`

Performing Other Financial Calculations

In addition to using financial functions to calculate monthly payments on a loan and to build a loan amortization table, you might want to make other investment-related calculations. For example, you can calculate present or future values, rates, and number of payment periods. Figure 7.20 illustrates the results of several financial functions.

	A	B	C	D	E	F	G	H	I	J	K
1	Present Value			Number of Periods							
2	Lump Sum	$1,000,000.00		Loan	$ 30,000.00						
3	Present Value	$1,246,221.03	$1,246,221.03	APR	5.25%						
4	Per Year	$ 100,000.00		Number of Periods in Year	12						
5	No. of Years	20		Monthly Payment	694.28						
6	Rate	5%		Number of Periods	48.0001	48.0001					
7											
8	Future Value			Rate							
9	Yearly Contributions	3000		Loan	30000						
10	No. of Years	40		Monthly Payment	694.28						
11	APR	7%		Number of Periods in Year	12						
12	Future Value	$598,905.34	$598,905.34	Years	4						
13	Total Contributed	120000		Periodic Rate	0.44%	0.44%					
14	Interest	$ 478,905.34		APR	5.25%						
15											
16	Net Present Value										
17	Invest End of Year	3000									
18	Yearly Income	1200									
19	Rate	3%									
20	Net Present Value	$382.85	$382.85								

FIGURE 7.20 Financial Functions

Calculate Present and Future Values

STEP 1

The **PV function** calculates the total present (i.e., current) value of a series of payments that will be made in the future. This function illustrates the time value of money in which the value of $1 today is worth more than the value of $1 received at some time in the future, given that you can invest today's $1 to earn interest in the future. For example, you might want to use the PV function to compare a lump-sum payment versus annual payments if you win the lottery to see which is better: receiving $100,000 per year for the next 20 years or $1 million now. The PV function has three required arguments (rate, nper, and pmt) and two optional arguments (fv and type). The rate, nper, and type arguments have the same definitions as in other financial functions. The pmt argument is the fixed periodic payment. The fv argument represents the future value of the investment. If you do not know the payment, you must enter a value for the fv argument. In Figure 7.20, cell B3 contains the PV function. The yearly payments of $100,000 invested at 5% yield a higher present value ($1,246,221.03) than the $1 million lump-sum payment.

=PV(rate,nper,pmt,[fv],[type])

The **FV function** calculates the future value of an investment, given a fixed interest rate, term, and periodic payment. You can use the FV function to determine how much an individual retirement account (IRA) would be worth at a future date. The FV function has three required arguments (rate, nper, and pmt) and two optional arguments (pv and type). If you omit the pmt argument, you must enter a value for the pv argument.

=FV(rate,nper,pmt,[pv],[type])

Assume that you plan to contribute $3,000 a year to an IRA for 40 years and that you expect the IRA to earn 7% interest annually. The future value of that investment—the amount you will have at age 65— would be $598,905.34! In Figure 7.20, cell B12 contains the FV function. You would have contributed $120,000 ($3,000 a year for 40 years). The extra $478,905.34 results from compound interest you will earn over the life of your $120,000 investment!

The **NPV function** calculates the net present value of an investment, given a fixed discount rate (rate of return) and a set of given cash inflows. Specifically, it considers periodic future income and payments. The NPV and PV functions are very similar in concept. The difference is that the PV function requires equal payments at the end of a payment period, whereas the NPV function can have unequal but constant payments. The NPV function contains two required arguments (rate and value1) and additional optional arguments (such as value2). If an investment returns a positive net present value, the investment is profitable. If an investment returns a negative net present value, the investment will lose money.

=NPV(rate,value1,value2,)

- **Rate.** The rate argument is the discount rate for one period. It is also called the rate of return or the percentage return on your investment. If an investment pays 12% per year and each period is one month, the rate is 1%.

- **Value1.** The value arguments represent a sequence of payments and income during the investment period. To provide an accurate net present value, the cash flows must occur at equally spaced-out time periods and must occur at the end of each period.

Assume you invest $3,000 at the end of the first year and receive $1,200 during the second, third, and fourth years with a 3% discount rate. In Figure 7.20, cell B20 contains the NPV function. The net present value would be $382.85. However, if you pay the $3,000 at the beginning of the first year instead of the end of the first year, you cannot discount the $3,000 since it is already in today's value. You would then subtract it after the function: =NPV(B19,B18,B18,B18)–B17. By investing $3,000 immediately, the net present value is higher at $394.33.

Use NPER and RATE Functions

The **NPER function** calculates the number of payment periods for an investment or loan given a fixed interest rate, periodic payment, and present value. You can use NPER to calculate the number of monthly payments given a car loan of $30,000, an APR of 5.25%, and a monthly payment of $694.28. In Figure 7.20, cell E6 contains the NPER function. The NPER would be 48.0001, or about 48 payments. The NPER function contains three required arguments (rate, pmt, and pv) and two optional arguments (fv and type).

=NPER(rate,pmt,pv,[fv],[type])

The **RATE function** calculates the periodic rate for an investment or loan given the number of payment periods, a fixed periodic payment, and present value. You can use RATE to calculate the periodic rate of a four-year car loan of $30,000 and a monthly payment of $694.28. In Figure 7.20, cell E13 contains the RATE function. The periodic rate would be 0.44%. Keep in mind that this is the periodic or monthly rate. The APR is then found by multiplying the periodic rate by 12: 5.25%. The RATE function contains three required arguments (nper, pmt, and pv) and two optional arguments (fv and type).

=RATE(nper,pmt,pv,[fv],[type])

Quick Concepts

1. In what situation would you use IPMT and PPMT? *p. 331*
2. What is the difference between IPMT and CUMIPMT? *p. 332*
3. What is the difference between PV and NPV calculations? *p. 333*

Hands-On Exercises

Watch the Video
for this Hands-
On Exercise!

MyITLab®
HOE3 Training

3 Financial Functions

The location managers want new company cars. Angela Khazen, the chief financial officer, has determined that the company can afford $450 monthly payments based on a 5.25% APR for four-year loans. She wants you to prepare a loan amortization table and running totals for interest and principal repayment.

Skills covered: Calculate the Present Value of the Loan • Enter Formulas in the Amortization Table • Calculate Cumulative Interest • Calculate Cumulative Principal Paid

STEP 1 ›› CALCULATE THE PRESENT VALUE OF THE LOAN

Because Angela determined the monthly payment for an automobile, you must use the PV function to calculate the loan amount. Other variables, such as trade-in value of the current vehicle, need to be considered, but you will exclude those variables at the moment. Refer to Figure 7.21 as you complete Step 1.

	A	B	C	D	E
E2			fx	=PV(E3,E4,-B2)	
1	Input Area:			Basic Output Area:	
2	Payment	$ 450.00		Loan	$ 19,444.57
3	APR	5.25%		Periodic Rate	0.438%
4	Years	4		# of Payments	48
5	Pmts per Year	12			
6					

Steps d–e: Enter PV function

FIGURE 7.21 PV Function

a. Open *e07h2Salary_LastFirst* and save it as **e07h3Salary_LastFirst**, replacing *h2* with *h3*. Click the **3-Finance worksheet tab**.

   You will calculate the periodic interest rate and number of payment periods before you can calculate the present value of the loan.

b. Click **cell E3**, type **=B3/B5**, and then press **Enter**.

   The periodic rate, 0.438%, is the result of dividing the APR by the number of payments per year.

c. Type **=B4*B5** in **cell E4** and press **Enter**.

   The total number of monthly payments, 48, is the product of the number of years the loan is outstanding and the number of payments per year.

d. Click **cell E2**, click **Financial** in the Function Library group on the FORMULAS tab, scroll through the list, and then select **PV**.

e. Click **cell E3** to enter that cell reference in the Rate box, click in the **Nper box**, and then click **cell E4**. Click in the **Pmt box**, type **-B2**, and then click **OK**. Save the workbook.

   The result is $19,444.57 based on four years of $450 monthly payments with an APR of 5.25%. You entered a negative sign to the left of the B2 reference. If you do not enter a negative sign, Excel will display the loan as a negative value.

STEP 2 ›› ENTER FORMULAS IN THE AMORTIZATION TABLE

Angela wants you to create an amortization table. The column labels and payment numbers have already been entered into the worksheet. Now you will enter formulas to show the beginning loan balance for each payment, the monthly payment, interest paid, and principal repayment. Refer to Figure 7.22 as you complete Step 2.

Step a: Reference to the original loan amount

Step h: Total repaid

Step h: Total interest paid

	A	B	C	D	E	F	G	H	I
1	Input Area:			Basic Output Area:					
2	Payment	$ 450.00		Loan	$ 19,444.57				
3	APR	5.25%		Periodic Rate	0.438%				
4	Years	4		# of Payments	48				
5	Pmts per Year	12							
6									
7	Payment Number	Beginning Balance	Monthly Payment	Interest Paid	Principal Repayment	Ending Balance		Cumulative Interest	Cumulative Principal
8	1	$ 19,444.57	$ 450.00	$ 85.07	$ 364.93	$ 19,079.64			
9	2	$ 19,079.64	$ 450.00	$ 83.47	$ 366.53	$ 18,713.11			
10	3	$ 18,713.11	$ 450.00	$ 81.87	$ 368.13	$ 18,344.98			
48	41	$ 3,530.15	$ 450.00	$ 15.44	$ 434.56	$ 3,095.59			
49	42	$ 3,095.59	$ 450.00	$ 13.54	$ 436.46	$ 2,659.13			
50	43	$ 2,659.13	$ 450.00	$ 11.63	$ 438.37	$ 2,220.77			
51	44	$ 2,220.77	$ 450.00	$ 9.72	$ 440.28	$ 1,780.48			
52	45	$ 1,780.48	$ 450.00	$ 7.79	$ 442.21	$ 1,338.27			
53	46	$ 1,338.27	$ 450.00	$ 5.85	$ 444.15	$ 894.13			
54	47	$ 894.13	$ 450.00	$ 3.91	$ 446.09	$ 448.04			
55	48	$ 448.04	$ 450.00	$ 1.96	$ 448.04	$ 0.00			
56	Totals		$ 21,600.00	$ 2,155.43	$ 19,444.57				
57									
58									
59									
60									
61									

FIGURE 7.22 Loan Amortization Table

a. Click **cell B8**, type =E2, and then press **Tab**.

You entered a reference to the original loan amount because that is the beginning balance to start the first payment period. Referencing the original cell is recommended instead of typing the value directly in the cell due to internal rounding. Furthermore, if you change the original input values, the calculated loan amount will change in both cells B8 and E2.

b. Type =**B$2** in **cell C8** and press **Ctrl+Enter**. Use the fill handle to copy the payment down the column ending in **cell C55**.

The monthly payment is $450.00. You entered a reference to the original monthly payment so that if you change it in cell B2, Excel will update the values in the Monthly Payment column automatically. The cell reference must be a mixed (B$2) or absolute ($B$2) reference to prevent the row number from changing when you copy the formula down the column later.

c. Type =**IPMT** in **cell D8**, press **Tab**, and click the **Insert Function button**. Type **E$3** for the rate, **A8** for per, **E$4** for the NPER, and **-E$2** for the PV and click **OK**. Use the fill handle to copy the function down the rest of the column.

The IPMT function calculates the interest of a specific payment based on the starting balance of $19,444.57 with a periodic interest of .438% over 48 payments. By not making cell A8 absolute, the function is able to adjust the period to match the specific period of evaluation.

d. Type =**PPMT** in **cell E8** and press **Tab**. Click the **Insert Function button**. Type **E$3** for the rate, **A8** for per, **E$4** for the NPER, and **-E$2** for the PV and click **OK**. Use the fill handle to copy the function down the rest of the column.

To manually calculate interest, the interest of the first payment $85.07 is subtracted from the monthly payment of $450. The remaining portion of the payment $364.93 goes toward paying down the principal owed. Using the PPMT function automatically completed these calculations.

e. Click in **cell F8** and type **=B8-E8**.

This calculates the ending balance after the first payment is made. The ending balance is calculated by subtracting the amount of principal in the payment $364.93 from the balance currently owed $19,444.57.

f. Click in **cell B9**, type **=F8**, and then press **Ctrl+Enter**.

The beginning balance of the second payment is also the ending balance of the first payment. The easiest method to populate the column is by referencing the ending balance from the prior month (cell F8). However, this can also be calculated by subtracting the previous principal repayment value (such as $364.93) from the previous month's beginning balance (such as $19,444.57).

Refer to Figure 7.23 as you complete Step 3.

g. Use the fill handle to copy the cell reference in **cell B9** down the rest of the column, ending in **cell B55**.

h. Click **cell F8** and use the fill handle to copy the formula down, ending in **cell F55**.

i. Type SUM functions in **cells C56, D56,** and **E56**. Select the **range A56:F56** and apply the **top and double bottom border**. Save the workbook.

You calculated totals for the appropriate columns, noting that column B is a running balance and cannot be logically totaled. Figure 7.22 shows the top and bottom portions of the amortization table using Freeze Panes.

STEP 3 ≫ CALCULATE CUMULATIVE INTEREST

The loan amortization table shows how much of each payment is interest and how much pays down the principal. However, Angela wants you to include a column to show the cumulative interest after each payment. Refer to Figure 7.23 as you complete Step 3.

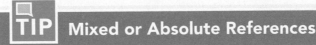

Steps a–b: Enter CUMIPMT function

	A	B	C	D	E	F	G	H	I
1	Input Area:			Basic Output Area:					
2	Payment	$ 450.00		Loan	$ 19,444.57				
3	APR	5.25%		Periodic Rate	0.438%				
4	Years	4		# of Payments	48				
5	Pmts per Year	12							
6									
7	Payment Number	Beginning Balance	Monthly Payment	Interest Paid	Principal Repayment	Ending Balance		Cumulative Interest	Cumulative Principal
8	1	$ 19,444.57	$ 450.00	$ 85.07	$ 364.93	$ 19,079.64		$ 85.07	
9	2	$ 19,079.64	$ 450.00	$ 83.47	$ 366.53	$ 18,713.11		$ 168.54	
10	3	$ 18,713.11	$ 450.00	$ 81.87	$ 368.13	$ 18,344.98		$ 250.41	
48	41	$ 3,530.15	$ 450.00	$ 15.44	$ 434.56	$ 3,095.59		$ 2,101.02	
49	42	$ 3,095.59	$ 450.00	$ 13.54	$ 436.46	$ 2,659.13		$ 2,114.57	
50	43	$ 2,659.13	$ 450.00	$ 11.63	$ 438.37	$ 2,220.77		$ 2,126.20	
51	44	$ 2,220.77	$ 450.00	$ 9.72	$ 440.28	$ 1,780.48		$ 2,135.92	
52	45	$ 1,780.48	$ 450.00	$ 7.79	$ 442.21	$ 1,338.27		$ 2,143.71	
53	46	$ 1,338.27	$ 450.00	$ 5.85	$ 444.15	$ 894.13		$ 2,149.56	
54	47	$ 894.13	$ 450.00	$ 3.91	$ 446.09	$ 448.04		$ 2,153.47	
55	48	$ 448.04	$ 450.00	$ 1.96	$ 448.04	$ 0.00		$ 2,155.43	
56	Totals		$ 21,600.00	$ 2,155.43	$ 19,444.57				

FIGURE 7.23 Cumulative Interest

a. Click **cell H8**, click **Financial** in the Function Library group on the FORMULAS tab, and then select **CUMIPMT**.

The Function Arguments dialog box displays so that you can enter the arguments for the CUMIPMT function.

b. Type the following arguments: **E$3** in the **Rate box**, **E$4** in the **Nper box**, **E$2** in the **Pv box**, and **A$8** in the **Start_period box**.

Make sure the cell references you enter in Rate, Nper, Pv, and Start_period boxes are mixed as shown to prevent the row number from changing as you copy the formula down the column.

> **TIP** **Mixed or Absolute References**
>
> You can also use absolute references; however, the entire formula is easier to read (and is shorter) in the Formula Bar when you use mixed instead of absolute references.

c. Type **A8** in the **End_period box**.

This reference should be relative so that it reflects the current month's payment number as you copy the formula down the column.

d. Press **Tab**, type **0** in the **Type box**, and then click **OK**.

The cumulative interest for the first payment is the same as the first payment's interest. However, the formula displays a negative result, as indicated by the parentheses.

e. Edit the function by typing - between = and *CUMIPMT* to convert the results to a positive value.

Unlike other functions, placing a - before the PV variable of the function will not return the intended result. To circumvent the issue, you place the - before the start of the CUMIPMT function after the = sign.

f. Copy the formula through **cell H55**. Save the workbook.

The cumulative interest in cell H55 should match the total interest paid calculated in cell D56: $2,155.43.

STEP 4 ≫ CALCULATE CUMULATIVE PRINCIPAL PAID

Angela wants to see the cumulative principal paid after making each loan payment. You will use the CUMPRINC function to calculate the cumulative principal paid. Refer to Figure 7.24 as you complete Step 4.

Steps a–b: Enter CUMPRINC function

	A	B	C	D	E	F	G	H	I	J	K	L
1	Input Area:			Basic Output Area:								
2	Payment	$ 450.00		Loan	$ 19,444.57							
3	APR	5.25%		Periodic Rate	0.438%							
4	Years	4		# of Payments	48							
5	Pmts per Year	12										
6												
7	Payment Number	Beginning Balance	Monthly Payment	Interest Paid	Principal Repayment	Ending Balance		Cumulative Interest	Cumulative Principal			
8	1	$ 19,444.57	$ 450.00	$ 85.07	$ 364.93	$ 19,079.64		$ 85.07	$ 364.93			
9	2	$ 19,079.64	$ 450.00	$ 83.47	$ 366.53	$ 18,713.11		$ 168.54	$ 731.46			
10	3	$ 18,713.11	$ 450.00	$ 81.87	$ 368.13	$ 18,344.98		$ 250.41	$ 1,099.59			
48	41	$ 3,530.15	$ 450.00	$ 15.44	$ 434.56	$ 3,095.59		$ 2,101.02	$ 16,348.98			
49	42	$ 3,095.59	$ 450.00	$ 13.54	$ 436.46	$ 2,659.13		$ 2,114.57	$ 16,785.43			
50	43	$ 2,659.13	$ 450.00	$ 11.63	$ 438.37	$ 2,220.77		$ 2,126.20	$ 17,223.80			
51	44	$ 2,220.77	$ 450.00	$ 9.72	$ 440.28	$ 1,780.48		$ 2,135.92	$ 17,664.08			
52	45	$ 1,780.48	$ 450.00	$ 7.79	$ 442.21	$ 1,338.27		$ 2,143.71	$ 18,106.29			
53	46	$ 1,338.27	$ 450.00	$ 5.85	$ 444.15	$ 894.13		$ 2,149.56	$ 18,550.44			
54	47	$ 894.13	$ 450.00	$ 3.91	$ 446.09	$ 448.04		$ 2,153.47	$ 18,996.53			
55	48	$ 448.04	$ 450.00	$ 1.96	$ 448.04	$ 0.00		$ 2,155.43	$ 19,444.57			
56	Totals		$ 21,600.00	$ 2,155.43	$ 19,444.57							

FIGURE 7.24 Cumulative Principal Paid

a. Click **cell I8**, click **Financial** in the Function Library group, and then select **CUMPRINC**.

The Function Arguments dialog box displays so that you can enter the arguments for the CUMPRINC function.

b. Type the following arguments: **E$3** in the **Rate box**, **E$4** in the **Nper box**, **E$2** in the **Pv box**, **A$8** in the **Start_period box**, **A8** in the **End_period box**, and **0** in the **Type box**.

c. Click **OK** and edit the function by typing - between = and *CUMPRINC*.

d. Copy the formula through **cell I55**.

The cumulative principal in cell I55 should match the total principal repayment calculated in cell E56: $19,444.57.

e. Save and close the workbook, and submit based on your instructor's directions.

Chapter Objectives Review

After reading this chapter, you have accomplished the following objectives:

1. **Create a nested logical function.**
   - A nested IF function is one that contains one or more additional IF functions nested inside one or more arguments. This type of nested function helps derive calculations for complex situations with multiple outcomes.
   - Nested IF within an IF function: When more than two outcomes are possible, you can nest additional IF statements within an IF statement.
   - Nest AND, OR, and NOT functions: Nested AND, OR, and NOT statements give you the ability to evaluate multiple conditions at the same time.

2. **Use MATCH and INDEX lookup functions.**
   - Use the MATCH function: The MATCH function returns the position of a value in a list.
   - Use the INDEX function: The INDEX function returns a value or the reference to a value within a range.
   - Nest functions in other functions: Nest the MATCH function inside the INDEX function to identify a location and then return related data.

3. **Use advanced filtering.**
   - Create a criteria range that is separate from the table or list, contains column labels, and lists the conditions.
   - If multiple conditions must be met, enter those criteria on the same row.
   - If the advanced filter should be an either/or case, enter the second set of criteria on the row below the first row of criteria.
   - Define a criteria range: Before you apply advanced filtering, you must define the criteria range.
   - Apply the Advanced Filter: Once applied, the Advanced Filter only displays information that meets predefined criteria.

4. **Manipulate data with database functions.**
   - Database functions help calculate aggregates for databases in which you have created an advanced filter.
   - Use DSUM and DAVERAGE functions: The DSUM functions adds the values in a numeric database column based on predefined conditions. The DAVERAGE function averages the values in a numeric database based on predefined conditions.
   - Identify values with DMAX and DMIN: The DMAX function returns the highest value in a database column that matches predefined criteria. In contrast, the DMIN function returns the lowest value in a database column that matches predefined criteria.
   - Identify the total number with DCOUNT: The DCOUNT function counts the cells that contain numbers in a database column that match predefined criteria.

5. **Create a loan amortization table.**
   - A loan amortization table is a schedule of monthly payments, interest per period, principal repayment per period, and balances.
   - Perform internal calculations: Use basic arithmetic operations to manually calculate interest and principal payments.
   - Calculate interest and principal payments with IPMT and PPMT functions: The IPMT function calculates the periodic interest for a specified payment period on a loan or investment. The PPMT function calculates the principal payment for a specified payment period on a loan or investment.
   - Calculate cumulative interest and principal payments with CUMIPMT and CUMPRINC functions: The CUMIPMT function calculates the cumulative interest throughout a loan. The CUMPRINC function calculates the cumulative principal throughout a loan.

6. **Perform other financial calculations.**
   - Several financial functions are available to calculate payment or investment values.
   - Calculate present and future values: The FV function calculates the future value of an investment. The PV function calculates the present value of an investment.
   - Use NPER and RATE functions: Use the NPER function to calculate the number of payment periods for a loan or an investment if the other variables are given. Use the RATE function to calculate the periodic interest rate if other variables are given.

Key Terms Matching

Match the key terms with their definitions. Write the key term letter by the appropriate numbered definition.

a. AND function
b. CUMIPMT function
c. CUMPRINC function
d. Database function
e. DAVERAGE function
f. DCOUNT function
g. DMAX function
h. DMIN function
i. DSUM function
j. FV function

k. INDEX function
l. IPMT function
m. Loan amortization table
n. MATCH function
o. NOT function
p. NPER function
q. NPV function
r. OR function
s. PPMT function
t. PV function

1. _____ Calculates the number of periods for an investment of loan. **p. 334**

2. _____ Calculates the future value of an investment. **p. 333**

3. _____ Calculates the net present value of an investment with periodic payments and a discount rate. **p. 333**

4. _____ Calculates cumulative principal for specified payment periods. **p. 332**

5. _____ Calculates the present value of an investment. **p. 333**

6. _____ Calculates cumulative interest for specified payment period. **p. 332**

7. _____ A schedule showing monthly payments, interest per payment, amount toward paying off the loan, and the remaining balance for each payment. **p. 330**

8. _____ Calculates the principal payment for a specified payment period given a fixed interest rate, term, and periodic payments. **p. 332**

9. _____ Calculates periodic interest for a fixed-term, fixed-rate loan or investment. **p. 331**

10. _____ Counts the cells that contain a number in a database column based on specified conditions. **p. 325**

11. _____ Identifies the highest value in a database column based on specified conditions. **p. 325**

12. _____ Identifies the lowest value in a database column based on specified conditions. **p. 325**

13. _____ Averages values in a database column based on specified conditions. **p. 324**

14. _____ Adds values in a database column based on specified conditions. **p. 324**

15. _____ Analyzes data for selected records in a table. **p. 323**

16. _____ Returns a value or reference to a value within a range. **p. 315**

17. _____ Identifies a searched item's position in a list. **p. 314**

18. _____ Returns TRUE if the argument is false and FALSE if the argument is true. **p. 314**

19. _____ Returns TRUE if any argument is true and returns FALSE if all arguments are false. **p. 313**

20. _____ Returns TRUE when all arguments are true and FALSE when at least one argument is false. **p. 312**

Multiple Choice

1. A workbook contains a list of university students. You want to identify the total number of students who are seniors and who are majoring in biology. Without modifying the original student dataset, what function can you use to find the answer to your question?

    (a) Nested IF
    (b) COUNTA
    (c) DCOUNT
    (d) COUNT

2. The original mortgage loan was for $300,000 with a 5% APR for 30 years. You want to calculate the interest on the last monthly payment at the end of the 15th year. What value should be referenced for the *per* argument in the IPMT function?

    (a) 15
    (b) 180
    (c) 30
    (d) 0.05/12

3. A local police office wants to create a rule that if an officer pulls over a person for exceeding the speed limit by at least five miles per hour or if that person has two or more speeding violations on record, the officer will fine the speeder the higher of $200 or $50 for each mile over the speed limit. Otherwise, the fine is $45. The speed limit is entered in cell B5, the person's speed is entered in cell B10, and the person's number of previous tickets is entered in cell B11. What function derives the correct answer?

    (a) =IF(AND(B10>B5,B11>=2),200,45)
    (b) =IF(AND(B10-B5>=5,B11<2),MAX(200,
       (B10-B5)*50),45)
    (c) =IF(OR(B10-B5>=5,B11>=2),MAX(200,
       (B10-B5)*50),45)
    (d) =IF(OR(B10>B5,B11>=2),MAX(200,50),45)

4. How much interest is paid on the first payment of a $15,000 auto loan financed at 3.25% interest paid monthly over 6 years?

    (a) $50.25
    (b) $40.63
    (c) $47.55
    (d) None of the above

5. A worksheet contains the times in which runners completed a race, with the times organized from fastest to slowest. You will use the MATCH function to identify what place a runner came in given a time of 4:05 (four minutes and five seconds). Which argument should contain the specific runner's time?

    (a) Lookup_value
    (b) Lookup_array
    (c) Match_type
    (d) Row_num

6. What function would you use to calculate the total principal paid on a loan over a specific start and end date?

    (a) CUMIPMT
    (b) IPMT
    (c) PPMT
    (d) CUMPRINC

7. Which database function would you use to count a range of cells that have some cells that are blank without excluding the blank cells?

    (a) DCOUNT
    (b) DCOUNTA
    (c) COUNT
    (d) DSUM

8. Which function should you use to calculate the total interest paid for all monthly payments for the second year of a four-year automobile loan?

    (a) CUMPRINC
    (b) PPMT
    (c) IPMT
    (d) CUMIPMT

9. In the Advanced Filter dialog box, where do you enter the location for placing the output?

    (a) Copy to
    (b) List range
    (c) Criteria range
    (d) Unique records only

10. What function would you use to calculate the total number of periods in a loan or investment?

    (a) NPER
    (b) RATE
    (c) PV
    (d) FV

Practice Exercises

1 Financial Investments

Some of your friends are in a business finance class. They are studying for their first test and will have to use financial calculators. As they practice for the test, they want to make sure they are calculating investment variables correctly. You volunteered to set up an investment model in which they enter the input variables to check their answers against formula calculations you will enter. This exercise follows the same set of skills as used in Hands-On Exercise 3 in the chapter. Refer to Figure 7.25 to complete this exercise.

	A	B	C	D	E	F	G	H	I
1	**Instructions:**	Enter input values in cells with light blue.							
2									
3	**Investment Variable**	PMT/FV	PV	NPER/FV	RATE/FV				
4	Payments Per Year	12	12	12	12				
5	Present Value	$ 100,000.00	$ 100,000.00	$ 100,000.00	$ 100,000.00				
6	APR	10.00%	10.00%	10.00%	10.00%				
7	Rate	0.83%	0.83%	0.83%	0.83%				
8	Term	20	20	20	20				
9	No. of Payments	240	240	240	240				
10	Periodic Payment	$ 965.02	$ 965.02	$ 965.02	$ 965.02				
11	Future Value	$1,465,614.73	$1,465,614.73	$1,465,614.73	$1,465,614.73				
12									
13									

FIGURE 7.25 Financial Functions

a. Open *e07p1Finance* and save it as **e07p1Finance_LastFirst**.

b. Calculate the periodic rate, number of periods, periodic payment, and future value in column B by completing the following:
   - Click **cell B7** and type =B6/B4 to calculate the periodic rate.
   - Click **cell B9** and type =B8*B4 to calculate the number of payment periods.
   - Click **cell B10**, click the **FORMULAS tab**, click **Financial** in the Function Library group, scroll down, and then select **PMT**. Type **B7** in the **Rate box**, type **B9** in the **Nper box**, and then type -B5 in the **PV box**. Click **OK** to calculate the monthly payment.
   - Click **cell B11**, click **Financial** in the Function Library group, and then select **FV**. Type **B7** in the **Rate box**, type **B9** in the **Nper box**, type **B10** in the **Pmt box**, and then type **B5** in the **Pv box**. Click **OK** and edit the formula by typing - on the right side of =.

c. Calculate the number of payments, periodic rate, and present value in column C by completing the following:
   - Click **cell C9** and type =C8*C4 to calculate the number of payment periods.
   - Click **cell C7** and type =C6/C4 to calculate the periodic rate.
   - Click **cell C5**, click **Financial** in the Function Library group, and then select **PV**. Type **C7** in the **Rate box**, type **C9** in the **Nper box**, and then type **C10** in the **Pmt box**. Click **OK** and edit the formula by typing - on the right side of =.

d. Calculate the rate, number of payment periods, term, and future value in column D by completing the following:
   - Click **cell D7** and type =D6/D4 to calculate the periodic rate.
   - Click **cell D9**, click **Financial** in the Function Library group, and then select **NPER**. Type **D7** in the **Rate box**, type **D10** in the **Pmt box**, type -D5 in the **Pv box**, and then click **OK**.
   - Click **cell D8** and type =D9/D4 to calculate the term (i.e., number of years).
   - Click **cell D11** and type =-FV(D7,D9,D10,D5) to calculate the future value.

e. Calculate the number of payment periods, rate, APR, and future value in column E by completing the following:
   - Click **cell E9** and type =E8*E4 to calculate the number of payment periods.
   - Click **cell E7**, click **Financial** in the Function Library group, and then select **RATE**. Type **E9** in the **Nper box**, type -E10 in the **Pmt box**, type **E5** in the **Pv box**, and then click **OK**.
   - Click **cell E6** and type =E7*E4 to calculate the APR.
   - Click **cell E11** and type =-FV(E7,E9,E10,E5) to calculate the future value.

f. Create a footer with your name on the left side, the sheet name code in the center, and the file name code on the right side.

g. Save and close the workbook, and submit based on your instructor's directions.

2 Detailed Loan Amortization

You are planning to buy a house soon, so you want to set up a detailed loan amortization table. So far, you have designed a worksheet with a loan parameters area (i.e., input area), a summary area, and amortization table column labels. You want to build in mechanisms to prevent formula errors if input data are missing and to hide zeros from displaying if you take out a shorter-term loan or pay it off early. However, you must keep formulas in place for a traditional 30-year loan. In addition, you will notice overpayments on the last payment if you pay extra toward the principal each month. To make the amortization table as flexible as possible and to avoid errors, you will create several nested IF functions. This exercise follows the same set of skills as used in Hands-On Exercise 3 in the chapter. Refer to Figure 7.26 as you complete this exercise.

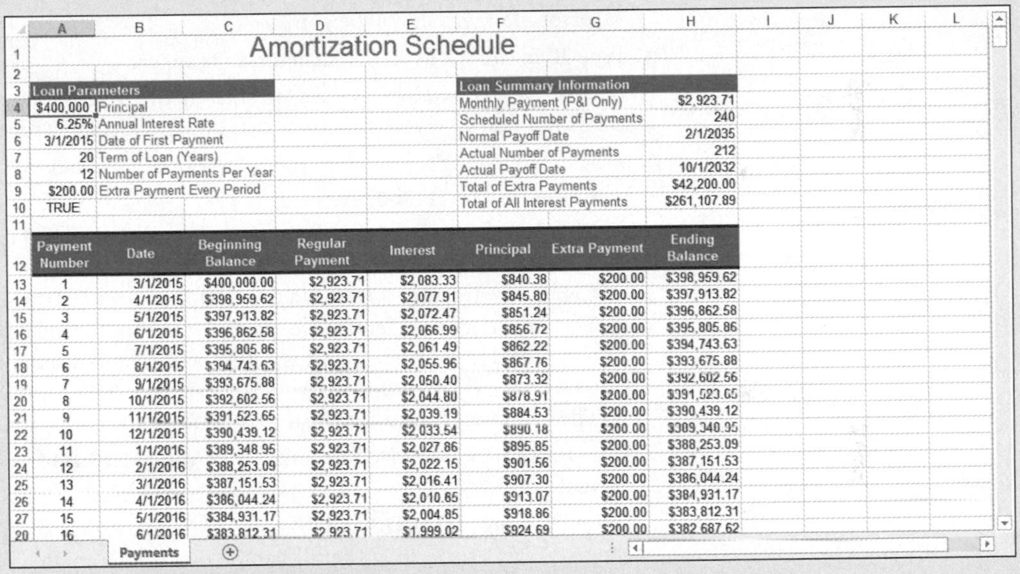

Amortization Schedule

	A	B	C	D	E	F	G	H
3	Loan Parameters					Loan Summary Information		
4	$400,000	Principal				Monthly Payment (P&I Only)		$2,923.71
5	6.25%	Annual Interest Rate				Scheduled Number of Payments		240
6	3/1/2015	Date of First Payment				Normal Payoff Date		2/1/2035
7	20	Term of Loan (Years)				Actual Number of Payments		212
8	12	Number of Payments Per Year				Actual Payoff Date		10/1/2032
9	$200.00	Extra Payment Every Period				Total of Extra Payments		$42,200.00
10	TRUE					Total of All Interest Payments		$261,107.89
12	Payment Number	Date	Beginning Balance	Regular Payment	Interest	Principal	Extra Payment	Ending Balance
13	1	3/1/2015	$400,000.00	$2,923.71	$2,083.33	$840.38	$200.00	$398,959.62
14	2	4/1/2015	$398,959.62	$2,923.71	$2,077.91	$845.80	$200.00	$397,913.82
15	3	5/1/2015	$397,913.82	$2,923.71	$2,072.47	$851.24	$200.00	$396,862.58
16	4	6/1/2015	$396,862.58	$2,923.71	$2,066.99	$856.72	$200.00	$395,805.86
17	5	7/1/2015	$395,805.86	$2,923.71	$2,061.49	$862.22	$200.00	$394,743.63
18	6	8/1/2015	$394,743.63	$2,923.71	$2,055.96	$867.76	$200.00	$393,675.88
19	7	9/1/2015	$393,675.88	$2,923.71	$2,050.40	$873.32	$200.00	$392,602.56
20	8	10/1/2015	$392,602.56	$2,923.71	$2,044.80	$878.91	$200.00	$391,523.65
21	9	11/1/2015	$391,523.65	$2,923.71	$2,039.19	$884.53	$200.00	$390,439.12
22	10	12/1/2015	$390,439.12	$2,923.71	$2,033.54	$890.18	$200.00	$389,348.95
23	11	1/1/2016	$389,348.95	$2,923.71	$2,027.86	$895.85	$200.00	$388,253.09
24	12	2/1/2016	$388,253.09	$2,923.71	$2,022.15	$901.56	$200.00	$387,151.53
25	13	3/1/2016	$387,151.53	$2,923.71	$2,016.41	$907.30	$200.00	$386,044.24
26	14	4/1/2016	$386,044.24	$2,923.71	$2,010.65	$913.07	$200.00	$384,931.17
27	15	5/1/2016	$384,931.17	$2,923.71	$2,004.85	$918.86	$200.00	$383,812.31
28	16	6/1/2016	$383,812.31	$2,923.71	$1,999.02	$924.69	$200.00	$382,687.62

Payments

FIGURE 7.26 Detailed Amortization Table

a. Open *e07p2House* and save it as **e07p2House_LastFirst**.

b. Click in each cell in the **range B13:H13** to look at the formulas in the Formula Bar. Delete the contents of **cell A7** and look at the #NUM! errors.

c. Click **cell A10**, click the **FORMULAS tab**, click **Logical**, and then select **AND**. Do the following in the Function Arguments dialog box:

- Type **A4>0** in the **Logical1 box**.
- Type **A5>0** in the **Logical2 box**.
- Type **A6>0** in the **Logical3 box**.
- Type **A7>0** in the **Logical4 box**.
- Type **A8>0** in the **Logical5 box** and click **OK**.

The arguments ensure that if any required input value is missing, the AND function returns FALSE. You will use cell A10's results to avoid error messages in calculated cells. Currently, the result is FALSE because you deleted the contents of cell A7.

d. Assign the range name **DataEntered** to **cell A10** so that you can use a range name in formulas that refer to this cell.

e. Enter the following replacement functions on row 13 to test if data have been entered or if cell A13 contains a value greater than zero. If data have been entered, calculations occur. If not, the functions return zeros:

- **Cell A13: =IF(DataEntered,1,0)**

    If DataEntered (cell A10) is TRUE, display **1** for first payment number. If DataEntered is FALSE, display **0** for first payment number.
- **Cell B13: =IF(A13>0,A6,"")**

    If DataEntered (cell A13) is TRUE, display date of first payment as entered in cell A6. If DataEntered is FALSE, an empty cell displays.
- **Cell C13: =IF(A13>0,A4,0)**
- **Cell D13: =IF(A13>0,H$4,0)**
- **Cell E13: =IF(A13>0,C13*A$5/A$8,0)**
- **Cell F13: =IF(A13>0,D13-E13,0)**
- **Cell G13: =IF(A13>0,A$9,0)**
- **Cell H13: =IF(A13>0,C13-F13-G13,0)**

f. Edit the formula in **cell H4** to be =IF(DataEntered,PMT(A5/A8,H5,-A4),0). Edit the formula in **cell H5** to be =IF(DataEntered,A7*A8,0).

All error messages should be gone now.

g. Type **30** in **cell A7** to see calculated results appear.

Because all required input values are entered, the AND function in cell A10 indicates TRUE, which is then used in several IF functions that display calculated results if all required inputs are entered.

h. Type the following formulas on row 14 to calculate values for the second payment:

- **Cell A14: =IF(H13>0,A13+1,0)**

    This function calculates the next payment number only if the previous ending balance is greater than zero.
- **Cell B14: =IF(A14>0,DATE(YEAR(B13),MONTH(B13)+1,DAY(B13)),0)**

    The date functions identify the specific year, month, and day and add 1 to increase each due date to the next month. The result is 42095 because it is a serial date so far. You will format it soon.
- **Cell C14: =IF(A14>0,H13,0)**

    The beginning balance is equal to the ending balance from the previous period.

i. Format **cell B14** as **Short Date** and format **range C13:H14** as **Currency** (not Accounting Number Format).

j. Select the **range D13:H13** and drag the fill handle down to copy the formulas to row 14. Select the **range A14:H14** and drag the fill handle down to copy the formulas to row 372—the end of the 360th payment in which the 30-year loan is paid off.

k. Click **cell A7** and change the value to **20** years. Scroll down the amortization table to row 252—the end of the 240th payment in which the 20-year loan is paid off. Notice that row 253 contains a negative balance (due to rounding) and rows 254 through 372 contain zeros because the loan is paid off.

l. Click the **FILE tab**, click **Options**, and then click **Advanced** to see *Advanced Options for working with Excel.*

m. Scroll through the options to see *Display options for this worksheet: Payments*, click the **Show a zero in cells that have zero value check box** to deselect it, and then click **OK**. Deselecting this option hides the zeros in rows 254 through 372, but Excel keeps the formulas intact in case the results change, and the negative values on row 253 still display. If you change the term to 30 years again, the results will display in the otherwise empty cells. Also note that if you used Accounting Number Format, you would see $ - instead of empty cells.

n. Type **200** in **cell A9** and format it as **Currency**. Scroll down and notice that you have a negative balance, indicating that you overpaid. You need to modify the regular payment and extra payments to prevent overpayment on the last payment.

o. Click **cell D13** and type =IF(A13>0,IF(C13>$H$4,$H$4,C13*A$5/A$8+C13),0). If cell A13 is 0, then the result shows zero. If the logical_test is true, the nested IF statement checks the current balance against the regular monthly payment. If the balance is greater, you pay the monthly payment.

If the monthly payment is higher, you pay the balance plus the interest on the balance only to avoid overpayment. Double-click the **cell D13 fill handle** to copy the formula down the column through **cell D372**.

p. Click cell G13 and type: =IF(AND(A13>0,C13-F13>=A$9),A$9,0). The nested AND in the logical_test makes sure that the payment number is greater than 0 *and* the difference between the beginning balance and principal is greater than or equal to the extra payment. If so, you pay the extra payment. If not, the extra payment is zero. This prevents paying an extra principal payment during the last payment and overpaying the final balance. Double-click the **cell G13 fill handle** to copy the formula down the column through **cell G372**.

q. Click **cell H6**, type =IF(DataEntered,DATE(YEAR(A6),MONTH(A6)+(A7-1)*A8+11,DAY(A6)),0), and then format it as **Short Date** to determine the normal payoff date if you do not make any extra payments.

r. Click **cell H7** and type =IF(DataEntered,MATCH(0,EndingBalance,-1),0). The MATCH function searches the existing range name EndingBalance for the smallest value that is greater than or equal to zero. The balance never goes exactly to zero because of a rounding error. Thus, the row above the match corresponds to the number of actual payments.

s. Click **cell H8** and type =IF(DataEntered,INDEX(AmortizationTable,H7,2),0). Apply the **Short Date format** to **cell H8**. The INDEX function returns the date from column 2 of the row within the table that was returned by the MATCH function in the above step.

t. Click **cell H9**, type =SUM(ExtraPayment), and then format it as **Currency**.

This calculates the total of all extra payments made. Note the ExtraPayment range name used in this step and Interest range name used in the next step were predefined in the student data file.

u. Click **cell H10**, type =SUM(Interest), and then format it as **Currency**. Note that you cannot use the CUMIPMT to calculate total interest because that function does not incorporate extra payments.

v. Create a footer with your name on the left side, the sheet name code in the center, and the file name code on the right side.

w. Save and close the workbook, and submit based on your instructor's directions.

3 Retirement Planning

FROM SCRATCH

You have recently taken a position as a financial planner, and your first client would like assistance planning for retirement. Your client is currently 30 years old and would like to retire at the age of 60. Your client would like to contribute $300.00 a month until retirement. You plan on investing the $300 in an interest-earning savings account that earns 2.75% APR. Your client would like you to create a worksheet that details the investment and calculates the future value of the investment.

a. Open Excel and create a new document. Save the document as **e07p3Retirement_LastFirst**.

b. Click **cell A1** and type **Retirement Goal**. Press **Enter** and type the following headings in column A:

- **Cell A2: Current Age**
- **Cell A3: Retirement Goal**
- **Cell A4: Monthly Investment**
- **Cell A5: APR**
- **Cell A6: Periodic Rate**
- **Cell A7: NPER**
- **Cell A8: Number of payments per year**
- **Cell A9: Future value at retirement**

c. Click **cell B2** and type **30**. Press **Enter** and type the following data:

- **Cell B3: 60**
- **Cell B4: 300**
- **Cell B5: 2.75%**
- **Cell B6: =B5/12**, if necessary format to display two decimal positions.
- **Cell B7: =(B3-B2)*12**
- **Cell B8: 12**

d. Type the following function in **cell B9**: =FV(B6,B7,-B4).

e. Increase the width of column A and apply **Accounting Number Format** to **cell B9**.

f. Create a footer with your name on the left side, the sheet name code in the center, and the file name code on the right side.

g. Save and close the workbook, and submit based on your instructor's directions.

Mid-Level Exercises

1 West Coast University Admissions Office

You work in the Admissions Office for West Coast University, a mid-sized regional university in California. Your assistant entered a list of college applicants for the Fall 2015 semester. You determine if a student qualifies for early admission or early rejection based on SAT and GPA. After determining the immediate admissions and rejections, you calculate a total score based on SAT and GPA to determine regular admissions and rejections.

a. Open *e07m1Admissions* and save it as **e07m1Admissions_LastFirst**.

b. Enter a nested logical function in the Admit Early column to display either Yes or No. The university admits a student early if that student meets *both* the early admission criteria for the SAT and GPA. That is, the student's SAT score must be 2000 or higher, and the GPA must be 3.80 or higher. Use appropriate references to the cells in the Admission Criteria range. Based on the requirements, the first student, Julie Alevy will be admitted early.

c. Enter a nested logical function in the Reject Early column to display either Yes or No. The university rejects a student early if that student has *either* an SAT score less than 1000 *or* a GPA below 1.80. Use appropriate references to the cells in the Admission Criteria range.

d. Enter a formula in the Score column to calculate an applicant's admission score. Apply the multiplier (found in the Miscellaneous Standards & Filter range) to the student's GPA and add that score to the SAT. Julie Alevy's score is 4700.

e. Enter a nested IF function inside a main IF function in the Final Decision column. The decision text should be one of the following: Early Admission, Early Rejection, Admit, or Reject. *Hint:* Two logical tests are based on the Yes/No displayed in the Admit Early and Reject Early columns. For regular admission, a student must have a combined admission score that is 2900 or higher. A student is rejected if his or her score is lower than the threshold. Use appropriate references to the cell in the Miscellaneous Standards & Filter range.

f. Copy the formulas down the Admit Early, Reject Early, Score, and Final Decision columns.

g. Enter a database function to count the total number of admissions with >= threshold scores.

h. Enter a database function to count the total number of in-state early admissions.

i. Enter database functions to calculate the average SAT and GPA for all early admits with admissions scores at or above the threshold. Note that you cannot merely average the existing averages because the counts are different for Early Admits and Regular Admits. You can use the database function without performing an advanced filter with an output range.

j. Calculate the average GPA for all in-state early admits.

k. Create a footer with your name on the left side, Page 1 of 28 codes in the middle, and the file name code on the right side.

l. Save and close the workbook, and submit based on your instructor's directions.

2 Artwork Database

You are an analyst for an art gallery that is an authorized Greenwich Workshop fine art dealer (www.greenwichworkshop.com). Customers in your area are especially fond of James C. Christensen's art. You prepared a list of artwork: art, type, edition size, release date, issue price, and estimated market value. You want to identify highly sought-after pieces based on age, percentage of value increase, and sold-out status. In addition, you want to perform an advanced filter and identify specific details from the filtered data.

a. Open *e07m2Art* and save it as **e07m2Art_LastFirst**.

b. Make sure the Valuable worksheet is active and enter a nested logical function in the Comments column to display *Highly Valuable* if either condition is met:

- The release date is on or before December 31, 1989, *or*
- The sold-out status is Yes, the percentage increase in value is at least 500%, or the Edition Size was less than 400.

Enter an empty text string if the conditions are not met. Hint: You will need to nest two logical functions within the logical test argument. Use cell references to the two conditions.

c. Enter conditional math and statistical functions in the **range N8:N10** to calculate the number of pieces, average estimate value, and total estimate value of the highly valuable pieces of artwork indicated in column K.

d. Display the Database worksheet. Assign a range name called **database** to the **range A14:J178**. Assign a range name called **Criteria** to the **range A7:J9**.

e. Create column labels for the Criteria range and replace the Edition Size with a second Release Date column label. Set the following conditions in the Criteria range:

- Sold-out limited-edition canvases released after 1/1/2000 and before 12/31/2003
- Sold-out limited-edition prints released after 1/1/2000 and before 12/31/2003

f. Create an advanced filter using the database list and Criteria range. Filter the records in place.

g. Enter the appropriate database function in **cell C2** in the Summary Statistics area to calculate the highest estimated value of the filtered records. Apply **Currency format** and left-align the value.

h. Enter a nested function using INDEX and MATCH to display the title (in cell C3) and the release date (in cell C4) for highest estimated valued filtered artwork. Left-align and format the date.

i. Create a footer with your name on the left side, the sheet name code in the center, and the file name code on the right side on each worksheet.

j. Save and close the workbook, and submit based on your instructor's directions.

3 | Personal Financial Management

COLLABORATION CASE

ANALYSIS CASE

An out-of-state family member asked for your assistance with financial planning. First, he is considering purchasing a house and would like you to create a detailed amortization table and calculate cumulative principal paid, as well as cumulative interest throughout the loan, total amount of interest, and interest for selected years. In addition, he is considering a five-year investment in which you invest $75 per month. He would like you to calculate the interest earned per month and the ending values. Once you have completed the work, you will upload your file to SkyDrive to allow for review.

Student 1:

a. Open *e07m3Personal* and save it as **e07m3Personal_LastFirst**.

b. Enter formulas on the Loan worksheet to complete the Calculations area.

c. Enter values 1 through 360 in the Payment Number column.

d. Calculate values for the first payment using appropriate relative, mixed, and absolute references:

- Beginning Balance: Create a reference to the appropriate value above the amortization table.
- Monthly Payment: Enter a reference to the calculated monthly payment.
- Interest Paid: Use the appropriate financial function to calculate the interest payment for the given period.
- Principal Repayment: Use the appropriate financial function to calculate the principal repayment for the given period.
- Ending Balance: Enter the formula to calculate the ending balance after you make the first payment.

e. Type a reference to display the beginning balance for the second period. Copy formulas down their respective columns. Apply **Accounting Number Format** to the monetary values.

f. Calculate the following cumulative values:

- Total Interest: Enter the appropriate function to calculate the total interest for the entire loan in **cell I6**.
- Cumulative Interest: Use the appropriate financial function to calculate the cumulative interest for each period, starting in **cell H10**. The final value in cell H369 should be identical to the value calculated in cell I6.
- Cumulative Principal: Use the appropriate financial function to calculate the cumulative principal for each period, starting in **cell I10**. The final value in cell I369 should match the loan amount in cell E3.
- Interest Paid Summary: Enter individual financial functions to calculate total interest paid during specific years in the **range I2:I5**. The first function calculates total interest for the fifth year only, which is $13,441.15.

g. Format monetary values with **Accounting Number Format**.

h. Set appropriate margins and page scaling to fit one page so that if you decide to print the Loan worksheet, all columns fit across each page. Repeat the headings on row 9 on all pages. Create a footer with your name and the worksheet tab code on the right side of the Loan worksheet.

i. Display the Investment worksheet and in **cell A12**, enter a reference to the original start of the first investment period date. In **cell A13**, enter the DATE function with nested YEAR, MONTH, and DAY functions with appropriate arguments. Ensure that the month number represents the next month. Copy the formula down the column and apply different but complementary shading, such as progressive shading of blue, to each 12-month period of dates. Apply right horizontal alignment and increase the indent three times for the dates in column A.

j. Enter formulas for the first period:

- Beginning Value: Type **0**.
- Interest Earned: Enter a formula to calculate the interest for the first period. Use relative and mixed references only.
- End-of-Period Invest: Enter a reference to the Deposit per Period found in the Input Area.
- Ending Value: Calculate the Ending Value, which includes the beginning Value, Interest Earned, and End-of-Period Investment.

k. Calculate the second period's Beginning Value by referencing the previous period's Ending Value. Copy formulas down the columns.

l. Enter the appropriate financial function in **cell E75** to calculate the final value of the investment. This value should be identical to the value shown in cell E71.

m. Format monetary values with **Accounting Number Format**.

n. Adjust margins and insert a page break so that the first three years of investment display on page 1. Center the worksheet data between the left and right margins, and repeat the column headings at the top of page 2. Create a footer with your name on the left side, the sheet name code in the center, and the file name code on the right side of the Investment worksheet.

o. Save the file to SkyDrive to share with student 2.

Student 2:

p. Open *e07m3Personal_LastFirst*.

q. Click the Loan worksheet and change the value in **cell B2** to **$350,000**.

r. Click the Investment worksheet and change **cell B5** to **$125.00**

s. Answer the questions on the Q&A worksheet.

t. Save and close the workbook, and submit based on your instructor's directions.

Home Renovation

RESEARCH CASE

You are considering a home renovation project. You plan on investing in a mixed-market savings account (MMA) to reach your monetary goal faster. You will invest $100.00 a month for three years to save for the project. You will research the interest rates of MMA accounts and use the data to calculate the future value of your investment. Open *e07b2Renovation* and save it as **e07b2Renovation_LastFirst**. Research current MMA interest rates online and populate the **range F4:F8** with the names of the top five institutions offering MMA savings accounts. Enter the interest rates for each of the institutions in the **range G4:G8**. In **cell I4**, enter a future value function to calculate the value of your investment at the end of the three-year period. Use the fill handle to copy the function down to fill the **range I5:I8**. Fill the top cells containing the two highest values with green. Create a footer with your name, the sheet name, and the file name on each worksheet. Save and close the workbook, and submit based on your instructor's directions.

Cruises

DISASTER RECOVERY

You just started working for a travel agency that specializes in working with cruise companies departing from Miami and travelling to the Caribbean and Mexico/Central America. Carter, your predecessor, created a database in Excel that lists details about each cruise, such as number of days of the cruise, departure date, destination, cruise line, ship name, and posted rates by cabin type. In addition, Carter calculated 10% discounts on Outside and Balcony cabins and discounts for Interior and Deluxe cabins based on these rules:

- 15% discount on Deluxe/Suite cabins for either 4- OR 5-day cruises
- 20% discount on Interior cabins with both (a) 7 or more day cruise AND (b) 4 rating
- 25% discount on Interior cabins with both (a) 7 or more day cruise AND (b) 3.5 rating

Open *e07b3Cruises* and save it as **e07b3Cruises_LastFirst**. Correct the errors with the discount formula in the Adj-Suite column and in the Adj-Interior column. Insert comments in **cells K10** and **N10** describing the errors and what you did to correct the errors. Carter also created a Criteria Range to be able to filter records for seven-day cruises to the Caribbean that depart before May 1, 2012, with a rating of either four or five. Correct and document errors in this range and perform the advanced filter again, copying the results in the Output Range. Carter created an Adjusted Rate Statistics area using database functions to identify the lowest, highest, and average adjusted rates for the four cabin types. In addition, he calculated the number of cabins meeting the criteria. Correct and document errors in this section. Create a footer with your name, the sheet name, and the file name. Save and close the workbook, and submit based on your instructor's directions.

Course Evaluation

SOFT SKILLS CASE

You are helping create a course-assessment survey for your university. Open *e07b4Evaluation* and save it as **e07b4Evaluation_LastFirst**. Enter a function in **cell C18** to total the cells C7, C9, C11, C13, C15. In **cell D18**, enter a nested IF function that returns *Eligible for teaching award* if the total score is 50 and *Forward to Dean* if the value is less than or equal to 20; all other scores should return the text *Forward to instructor*. Create a footer with your name, the sheet name, and the file name on each worksheet. Save and close the workbook, and submit based on your instructor's directions.

Capstone Exercise

You work for a company that owns five apartment complexes in Nevada. The owners want some specific information about rentals by apartment size (e.g., number of bedrooms per apartment). The owners are also considering purchasing a sixth apartment complex and asked you to perform some financial calculations and analyses.

Apartment Unit Statistics

The owners decided that unoccupied units should be remodeled if the last remodel took place before 2005. Furthermore, they have decided to calculate the pet deposit based on the number of bedrooms and remodel date.

a. Open *e07c1Apartment*, click the **Summary worksheet**, and then save it as **e07c1Apartment_LastFirst**.

b. Insert functions in the Pet Deposit column to calculate the required pet deposit for each unit. If the unit has two or more bedrooms and was remodeled after 2008, the deposit is $125; if not, it is $75.

c. Enter a nested function in the Recommendation column to indicate *Need to remodel* if the apartment is unoccupied and was last remodeled before 2005. For all other apartments, display *No change*.

Create a Search

The owners would like to be able to perform a simple search by ranking to identify which apartment complex is at that ranking.

a. Type **101** in **cell B2**; this is the cell the owners will use to research apartment unit prices.

b. Insert a nested lookup function in **cell E2** that will look up the rental price in column D using the apartment number referenced in cell B2.

Manage a Database List

The Database worksheet contains an identical list of apartments. One of the owners wants to know how many two- and three-bedroom apartments should be remodeled, the value of lost rent,

and the year of the oldest remodel on those units. You need to perform an advanced filter and enter some database functions to address the owner's concerns.

a. Click the **Database worksheet tab**.

b. Enter conditions in the Criteria Range for unoccupied two- and three-bedroom apartments that need to be remodeled.

c. Perform an advanced filter based on the criteria range. Filter the existing database in place.

d. Enter database functions to calculate the database statistics in the **range C8:C10**.

Loan Amortization

The owners are considering purchasing a sixth apartment complex for $850,000 with a down payment of $375,000 for 30 years at 5.75%, with the first payment due on March 20, 2015. You will perform internal calculations and build a loan amortization table.

a. Click the **Loan worksheet tab**.

b. Enter the loan parameters in the Input Area and insert formulas to perform calculations in the Summary Calculations.

c. Complete the loan amortization table. Use a date function for the Payment Date column and financial functions for the Interest Paid and Principal Payment columns.

d. Create a footer with your name on the left side, the sheet name code in the center, and the file name code on the right side of each worksheet. Adjust page setup options as needed.

e. Save and close the workbook, and submit based on your instructor's directions.

Statistical Functions

Analyzing Statistics

OBJECTIVES   AFTER YOU READ THIS CHAPTER, YOU WILL BE ABLE TO:

1. Use conditional math and statistical functions p. 354
2. Calculate relative standing with statistical functions p. 357
3. Measure central tendency p. 367
4. Load the Analysis ToolPak p. 374
5. Perform analysis using the Analysis ToolPak p. 374
6. Perform analysis of variance (ANOVA) p. 374
7. Calculate COVARIANCE p. 376
8. Create a histogram p. 376

CASE STUDY | Education Evaluation

You are the superintendent of schools for Banton School System, a K–12 school district in Erie, Pennsylvania. You and your team have the task of evaluating student and teacher performance across schools in your district. As part of your evaluation you would like to perform several statistical calculations based on location, age, and test scores.

First, you will evaluate teachers' performance rankings and salary quartiles. You then plan to assess middle school students' standardized testing performance. As part of this analysis, you will perform basic descriptive statistical calculations. You will also compare performance to attendance and test the correlation between test scores and daily turnout. Last, you will perform more advanced evaluation of high school students' performance using the Analysis ToolPak.

Math and Statistical Functions

Do not let the term *statistics* scare you. Every day, you rely on statistics to make routine decisions. When you purchase a car, you compare the miles per gallon (MPG) among several vehicles. The automobile manufacturer conducted multiple test drives, recorded the MPG under various driving conditions, and then calculated the MPG statistic. Statistics involves analyzing a collection of data and making inferences to draw conclusions about a dataset. You already have learned to use the SUM, AVERAGE, MIN, MAX, MEDIAN, and COUNT statistical functions.

However, sometimes you might want to calculate a statistic based on a particular condition. Excel's math and statistical function categories contain functions that enable you to perform conditional calculations, such as calculating a total only when a particular circumstance or set of circumstances exists. In addition, you might want to analyze individual values against others in a dataset to determine relative standing.

In this section, you will use math and statistical functions—SUMIF, AVERAGEIF, COUNTIF, SUMIFS, AVERAGEIFS, and COUNTIFS—to perform conditional statistical calculations. In addition, you will use relative-standing functions, such as RANK, PERCENTRANK, PERCENTILE, and QUARTILE.

Using Conditional Math and Statistical Functions

When you use SUM, AVERAGE, and COUNT functions, Excel calculates the respective total, the mathematical average, and the number of values for all values in the range specified in the function's arguments. The math and statistical function categories contain related functions—SUMIF, AVERAGEIF, COUNTIF, SUMIFS, AVERAGEIFS, and COUNTIFS—that perform similar calculations but based on a condition. These functions are similar to the logical function IF. As you recall, the IF function evaluates a logical test to determine if it is true or false. If the logical test is true, Excel returns one result; if the logical test is false, it returns a different result. In a way, these conditional math and statistical functions are a hybrid of math/statistical and logical functionality. Figure 8.1 shows a salary table for educators in the district and the results of these math and statistical functions.

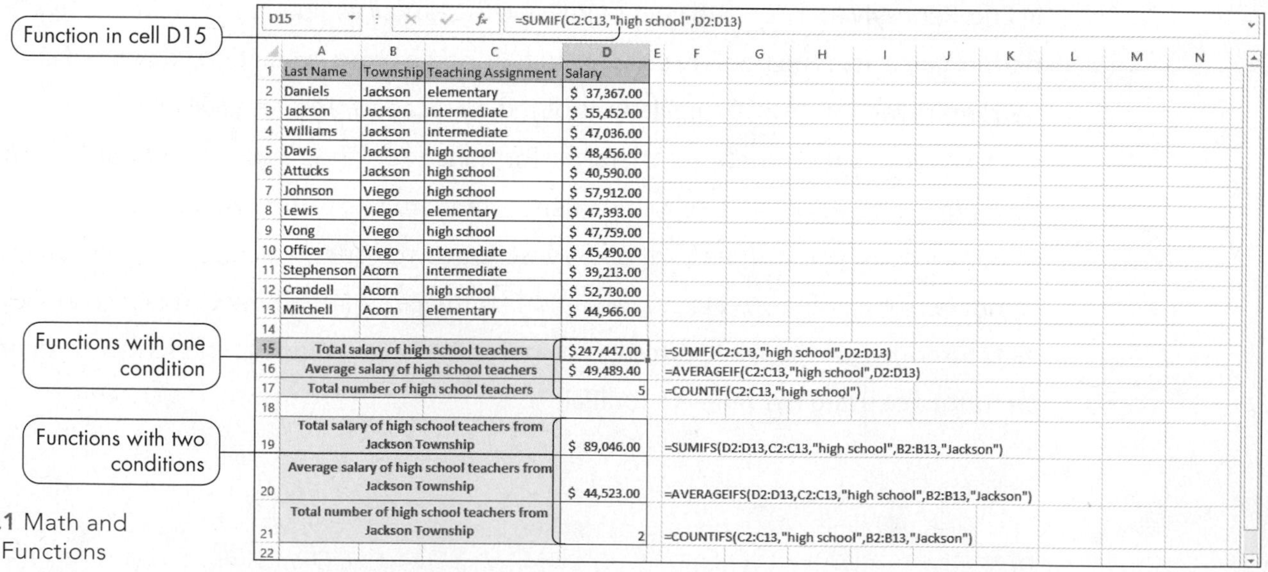

FIGURE 8.1 Math and Statistical Functions

Use the SUMIF, AVERAGEIF, and COUNTIF Functions

STEP 1 » The *SUMIF function* is similar to the SUM function except that it calculates a sum of values in a range only when related data meet a specific condition instead of calculating the sum of an entire range. For example, in Figure 8.1, if you want to calculate the total salaries for all high school teachers in the district, you cannot use the SUM function because it would calculate the total salaries for teachers in the district's elementary and intermediate schools as well. However, you can complete the task using the SUMIF function. In Figure 8.1, cell D15 contains the results of the function =SUMIF(C2:C13,"high school",D2:D13) to sum the Salary column (D2:D13) if the Teaching Assignment column (C2:C13) contains the text *high school*. The total value of salaries for high school teachers is $247,447.00. The SUMIF function contains three required arguments:

=SUMIF(range,criteria,sum_range)

- **Range.** The range argument specifies the range of cells you want to evaluate to determine if the values meet a particular condition. In Figure 8.1, the SUMIF function's range is C2:C13, the range containing the job titles.

- **Criteria.** The criteria argument specifies the condition that imposes limitations on what values Excel sums. The criteria can be a value, date, text, or another cell containing a value, date, or text. In Figure 8.1, the SUMIF function's criterion is the text *high school*. Excel restricts the totaling to rows in which the range contains only *high school*. When you use text as a criterion, you must enclose it within quotation marks. When you use values as criteria, do not use quotation marks. You can also create an input range to specify the condition and then simply use a cell reference as the criteria argument in the SUMIF function.

- **Sum_range.** The sum_range argument designates the cells containing values to add if the condition is met. In Figure 8.1, the SUMIF function's sum_range is D2:D13, the range containing the salaries.

The *AVERAGEIF function* calculates the average, or arithmetic mean, of all cells in a range that meet a specific condition. In Figure 8.1, cell D16 contains =AVERAGEIF(C2:C13,"high school",D2:D13) to calculate the average value in the Salary column (D2:D13) when the Teaching Assignment column (C2:C13) contains the text *high school*. The average high school teacher's salary is $49,489.40.

=AVERAGEIF(range,criteria,average_range)

The AVERAGEIF function contains three required arguments: range, criteria, and average_range. The range and criteria arguments have the same meanings as the same arguments in the SUMIF function. The average_range argument specifies the range containing values that you want to average if the condition is met. In the AVERAGEIF function, the average_range is D2:D13.

TIP Referencing the Input Range

When using the SUMIF, AVERAGEIF, and COUNTIF functions, you can create an input range to specify the condition and then simply use a cell reference as the criteria argument in the function. This allows the user the flexibility to change the criteria and receive instant calculation updates.

The *COUNTIF function* is similar to the COUNT function except that it calculates the number of cells in a range that meet a condition you specify instead of calculating the count of an entire range. In Figure 8.1, cell D17 contains =COUNTIF(C2:C13,"high school") to count the number of high school teachers, which is five.

=COUNTIF(range,criteria)

The COUNTIF function contains only two arguments: range and criteria. Similar to the SUMIF and AVERAGEIF functions, the range argument for the COUNTIF function specifies the range of cells you want to evaluate to see if the values meet a particular condition. The criteria argument specifies the condition to be met in order to count cells in the designated range.

Use the SUMIFS, AVERAGEIFS, and COUNTIFS Functions

STEP 2 ≫

Whereas the previously described functions enable you to perform conditional calculations, they can address only a single condition. Similar math and statistical functions enable you to specify more than one condition: SUMIFS, AVERAGEIFS, and COUNTIFS.

The **SUMIFS function** calculates the total value of cells in a range that meet multiple criteria. In Figure 8.1, cell D19 contains =SUMIFS(D2:D13,C2:C13,"high school",B2:B13,"Jackson"). This function sums the Salary range if the teaching assignment range contains *high school* and if the township range contains *Jackson*. The total salary of high school teachers in Jackson Township is $89,046.00. The SUMIFS function contains at least five arguments: sum_range, criteria_range1, criteria1, criteria_range2, and criteria2. Additional ranges and their criteria may be included. All conditions must be met in order to include values in the sum_range in the total.

=SUMIFS(sum_range,criteria_range1,criteria1,criteria_range2,criteria2…)

- **Sum_range.** The sum_range argument designates the cells containing values to add if the condition is met. In the SUMIFS function, the sum_range argument is the first argument instead of the last argument as in the SUMIF function. In Figure 8.1, the SUMIFS function's sum_range is D2:D13, the range containing the salaries.

- **Criteria_range1.** The range argument specifies the first range of cells you want to evaluate to see if the values meet a particular condition. The range must contain values, range names, arrays, or references that contain numbers, dates, or text. In Figure 8.1, the criteria_range1 is C2:C13, the range containing the teaching assignments.

- **Criteria1.** The criteria1 argument specifies the condition for the criteria_range1 argument that imposes limitations on what values are summed. In Figure 8.1, the SUMIFS function's criteria1 argument is *high school*.

- **Criteria_range2.** The range argument specifies the second range of cells you want to evaluate to see if the values meet a particular condition. The range must contain values, range names, arrays, or references that contain numbers, dates, or text. In Figure 8.1, the SUMIFS function's criteria_range2 is B2:B13, the range containing the township.

- **Criteria2.** The criteria2 argument specifies the condition that imposes limitations on what values are summed. In Figure 8.1, the SUMIFS function's criteria2 is *Jackson*.

The **AVERAGEIFS function** calculates the average value of cells in a range that meet multiple criteria. In Figure 8.1, cell D20 contains =AVERAGEIFS(D2:D13,C2:C13"high school",B2:B13,"Jackson"). This function calculates the average value in the Salary range if the teaching assignment is *high school* and if the township is *Jackson*. The average salary of high school teachers in Jackson Township is $44,523. The AVERAGEIFS function contains at least five arguments. The average_range argument specifies the range of cells containing values that will be averaged when multiple conditions specified by the criteria ranges and criteria are met.

=AVERAGEIFS(average_range,criteria_range1,criteria1,criteria_range2,criteria2…)

The **COUNTIFS function** counts the number of cells in a range that meet multiple criteria. In Figure 8.1, cell D21 contains =COUNTIFS(C2:C13,"high school",B2:B13,"Jackson"). This function counts the number of high school teachers in Jackson Township, which is two. The COUNTIFS function contains at least four arguments: two ranges and their respective criteria.

=COUNTIFS(criteria_range1,criteria1,criteria_range2,criteria2…)

Whereas the syntax shows only two criteria for SUMIFS, AVERAGEIFS, and COUNTIFS, you can continue adding criteria ranges and criteria. If you type the function in a cell, separate criteria ranges and criteria with commas. If you use the Function Arguments dialog box, it expands to display another Criteria box as you enter data in existing boxes, or you can press Tab within the dialog box to see additional criteria ranges and criteria boxes.

Enter Math and Statistical Functions

Excel organizes the conditional functions in the math and statistical function categories. The SUMIF and SUMIFS functions are math functions. To enter these functions, click Math & Trig in the Function Library group on the Formulas tab and select either SUMIF or SUMIFS. Enter the arguments in the Function Arguments dialog box and click OK.

The AVERAGEIF, AVERAGEIFS, COUNTIF, and COUNTIFS functions are statistical functions. To enter these functions, click More Functions in the Function Library group on the Formulas tab, click Statistical, and then select the desired function name. Enter the arguments in the Function Arguments dialog box and click OK.

Calculating Relative Standing with Statistical Functions

Often people analyze a dataset based on an individual value compared to the rest of the dataset. You do not have to be a statistician to need to use statistical calculations. For example, a professor might want to rank students in a chemistry class, or a medical doctor might want to identify diabetic patients' blood sugar levels based on what quartile they fall in. You can use the RANK.EQ, PERCENTRANK, QUARTILE, and PERCENTILE functions to analyze data.

Use the RANK and PERCENTRANK Functions

STEP 3 » Excel 2013 contains two rank functions: RANK.EQ and RANK.AVG. The *RANK.EQ function* identifies a value's rank within a list of values. For example, the rank of 1, E7 in Figure 8.2, indicates that the $57,912.00 salary is the highest-ranking salary in the list, $55,452.00 is the second-highest-ranking salary, and so on. If the range of values contains duplicate numbers (such as $44,966.00 in cells D8 and D13), both values receive the same rank (8), the next ranking (9) is skipped, and the next value ($40,590) is assigned the ranking of 10.

The *RANK.AVG function* identifies the rank of a value but assigns an average rank when identical values exist. Column F shows the results of the RANK.AVG function in which both $44,966 values have a ranking of 8.5—the average of rankings 8 and 9—instead of a rank of 8. Some statisticians consider the RANK.AVG function results to be more accurate than the RANK.EQ function results.

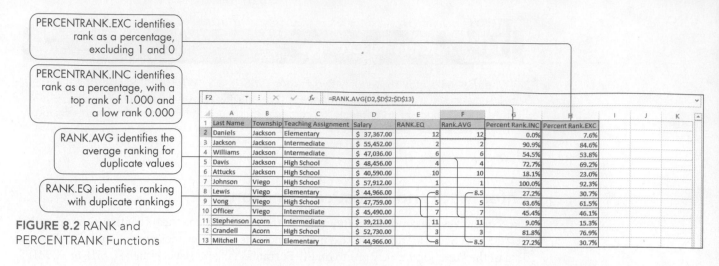

FIGURE 8.2 RANK and PERCENTRANK Functions

Both the RANK.EQ and RANK.AVG functions contain two arguments (number and ref) and one optional argument (order).

=RANK.EQ(number,ref,[order])

=RANK.AVG(number,ref,[order])

- **Number.** The number argument specifies the cell containing the value you want to rank, such as cell D2.

- **Ref.** The ref argument specifies the range of values, such as D$2:D$13, that you want to use to identify their rankings. Mixed references are used so that the row numbers do not change as the formula is copied down the column.

- **Order.** The optional order argument enables you to specify how you want to rank the values. The implied default is 0, which ranks the values as if the values were listed in descending order. Because the order argument was omitted in Figure 8.2, the first-rank salary is the highest salary value of $57,912. If you enter any nonzero value for the order argument, Excel ranks the values as if the values were listed in ascending order (i.e., low to high). If the order argument were 2, the first-ranked salary would be the lowest value, which is $37,367.

Some functions have a descriptor added to the function name to further clarify the function's purpose and to distinguish functions that perform similar tasks but have subtle differences. The .INC descriptor indicates *inclusive* functions, that is, the functions *include* particular parameters. The .EXC descriptor indicates *exclusive* functions, that is, functions that *exclude* particular parameters. The **PERCENTRANK.INC function** displays a value's rank as a percentile of the range of data in the dataset. In other words, you can use this function to identify a value's relative standing compared to other values in the dataset. Excel displays ranks as decimal values between 0 and 1, but you can format the results with Percent Number Style. The first rank is 1.000, and the lowest percent rank is 0.000, because the .INC descriptor *includes* 0 and 1. The percent rank correlates with the rank of a value. For example, in Figure 8.2, the $57,912 salary is the highest-ranking salary; its percent rank is 1.00 or 100% percentile. The $55,452 value is the second-highest-ranking salary; its percent rank is 0.909, indicating that this salary is the 90.9% percentile.

Excel 2013 contains a similar function—PERCENTRANK.EXC. The **PERCENTRANK. EXC function** is similar in that it returns a value's rank as a percent. This function adheres to best practices in that a percent rank is between 0 and 1 because the .EXC descriptor *excludes* the 0 and 1. For this function, the $57,912 salary has a percent rank of 0.923 or is in the 92.3% percentile.

Both PERCENTRANK.INC and PERCENTRANK.EXC functions contain two required arguments (array and x) and one optional argument (significance).

=PERCENTRANK.INC(array,x,[significance])

=PERCENTRANK.EXC(array,x,[significance])

- **Array.** The array argument specifies the range that contains the values to compare, such as D$2:D$13.

- **x.** The x argument specifies an individual's salary, such as cell D2.

- **Significance.** The optional significance argument designates the number of significant digits for precision. If you omit the significance argument, Excel displays three significant digits.

Use the QUARTILE and PERCENTILE Functions

STEP 4 »

A *quartile* is a value used to divide a range of numbers into four equal groups. The **QUARTILE.INC function** identifies the value at a specific quartile for a dataset, *including* quartile 0 for the lowest value and quartile 4 for the highest value in the dataset. The **QUARTILE.EXC function** is similar in that it returns the value at a specific quartile but *excluding* quartiles 0 and 4. These functions contain two required arguments: array and quart. The array argument specifies the range of values. The quart argument is a number that represents a specific quartile (see Table 8.1).

TABLE 8.1   Quart Argument

Argument Value	Description
0	Lowest value in the dataset. Identical to using the MIN function. Allowed in QUARTILE.INC only.
1	First quartile of the dataset. Identifies the value at the 25th percentile.
2	Second quartile or median value within the dataset. Identifies the value at the 50th percentile.
3	Third quartile of the dataset. Identifies the value at the 75th percentile.
4	Fourth quartile or highest value within the dataset. Identical to using the MAX function. Allowed in QUARTILE.INC only.

=QUARTILE.INC(array,quart)

=QUARTILE.EXC(array,quart)

In Figure 8.3, cell B24 contains =QUARTILE.INC(D$2:D$13,A24), where cell A24 contains the quartile of Salary. The function returns $37,367, which is the lowest salary in the range. Cell B25 contains =QUARTILE.INC(D$2:D$13,A25) to identify the top salary in the first quartile, which is $43,872. Look at column G, which contains the PERCENTRANK.INC function, and column H, which contains the PERCENTRANK.EXC function. Any salaries with 25% or less fall in the first quartile, salaries above 25% and up to 50% fall in the second quartile, salaries above 50% and up to 75% fall in the third quartile, and salaries above 75% fall in the fourth (or top) quartile. The dataset is sorted in ascending order by salary, and the data in columns D and H are color coded to help you identify values within each quartile.

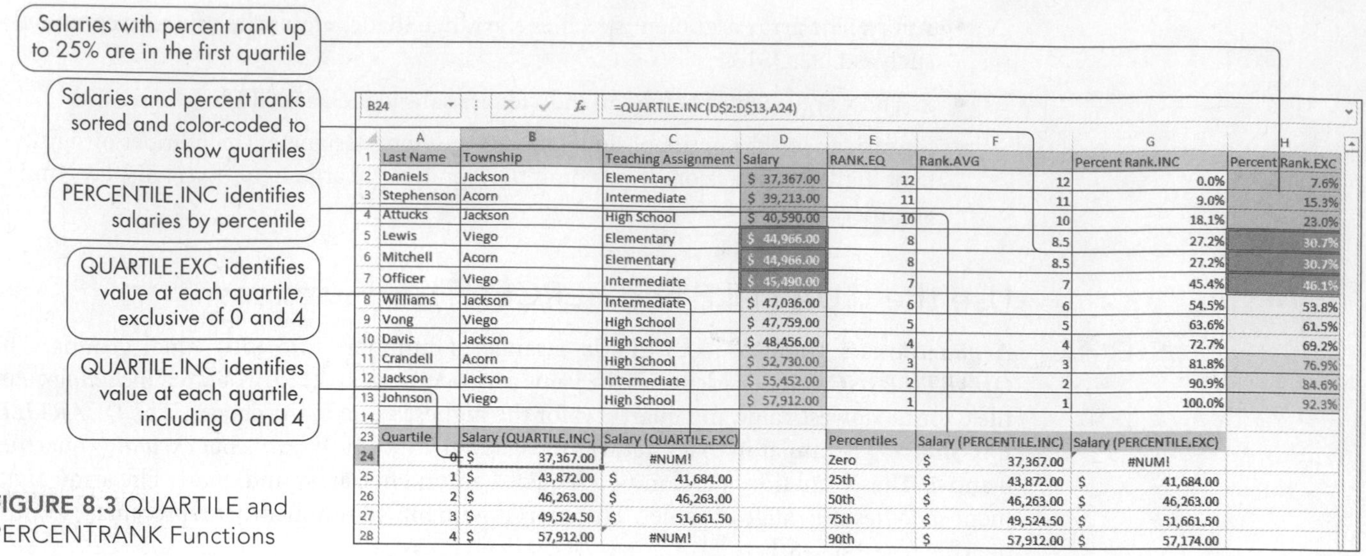

Salaries with percent rank up to 25% are in the first quartile

Salaries and percent ranks sorted and color-coded to show quartiles

PERCENTILE.INC identifies salaries by percentile

QUARTILE.EXC identifies value at each quartile, exclusive of 0 and 4

QUARTILE.INC identifies value at each quartile, including 0 and 4

FIGURE 8.3 QUARTILE and PERCENTRANK Functions

Range C24:C28 contains the QUARTILE.EXC function. For example, cell C24 contains =QUARTILE.EXC(D$2:D$13,A24). Because QUARTILE.EXC excludes 0 and 4, the function returns #NUM! error messages when 0 and 4 are used as the quart argument in cells C24 and C28. The salaries at the first and second quartiles are identical for either QUARTILE function; however, the salaries for the third quartile differ based on which function you use. Table 8.2 summarizes the findings from the QUARTILE.EXC functions.

TABLE 8.2 Quartile Grouping

Quartile	Salary at Top of Quartile	Salaries
1 (0.25 or lower)	$41,684	$37,367
		$39,213
		$40,590
2 (between 0.251 and 0.5)	$46,263	$44,966
		$44,966
		$45,490
3 (between 0.501 and 0.75)	$51,661.50	$47,036
		$47,759
		$48,456
4 (above 0.75)	$57,174.00	$52,730
		$55,452
		$57,912

The *PERCENTILE.INC function* identifies the kth percentile of a specified value within a list of values, including the 0th and 100th percentiles. College admissions offices find this function helpful when identifying college applicants' percentiles to determine which candidates to admit to their college. For example, a college might have a policy to admit only candidates who fall within the 80th percentile. The *PERCENTILE.EXC function* also identifies a value at a specified percentile; however, the .EXC *excludes* 0th or 100th percentiles.

The PERCENTILE functions contain two required arguments: array and k. The array argument specifies the range containing values to determine individual standing. For the PERCENTILE.INC function, the *k* argument specifies the percentile value from 0 to 1.

For the PERCENTILE.EXC function, the *k* argument *excludes* values 0 and 1. For example, 0.25 represents the 25th percentile. In Figure 8.3, cell F25 contains =PERCENTILE.INC(D$2:D$13,0.25) to identify the value at the 25th percentile. Note that this salary ($43,872) is the same as the value returned by =QUARTILE.INC(D$2:D$13,A25). However, unlike the QUARTILE.INC function that has distinct quartiles (0, 1, 2, 3, 4), you can specify any decimal value for the *k* argument in the PERCENTILE functions, such as =PERCENTILE.INC(D$2:D$13,0.9) to find the value at the 90th percentile. The PERCENTILE.EXC returns different values than PERCENTILE.INC at the higher percentiles. Also, =PERCENTILE.EXC(D$2:D$13,0) returns an error since the .EXC descriptor excludes 0 as a legitimate parameter.

=PERCENTILE.INC(array,k)

=PERCENTILE.EXC(array,k)

Quick Concepts

1. When would you use SUMIFS instead of SUMIF? *p. 356*
2. When would you use RANK.AVG instead of RANK.EQ? *p. 357*
3. What is the difference between PERCENTRANK.INC versus PERCENTRANK.EXC? *p. 358*

Hands-On Exercises

1 Math and Statistical Functions

For the first step of your assessment, you need to calculate summary statistics of the teachers' salaries. First, you want to calculate statistics, such as average salary for teachers hired before 2005. Then you will turn your attention to the Acorn Township, the township with the fewest teachers, as you perform statistical calculations. Finally, you want to rank each person's salary compared to the other salaries and identify the salary ranges for each quartile.

Skills covered: Use SUMIF, AVERAGEIF, and COUNTIF Functions • Enter SUMIFS, AVERAGEIFS, and COUNTIFS Functions • Calculate Salary Ranks • Identify Salary Ranges by Quartile

STEP 1 >> USE SUMIF, AVERAGEIF, AND COUNTIF FUNCTIONS

You want to calculate the number of high school teachers that were hired before 1/1/2005. You also want to calculate the average salary and total payroll for all high school teachers hired before 1/1/2005. You will use SUMIF, COUNTIF, and AVERAGEIF to complete the calculations. Refer to Figures 8.4 and 8.5 as you complete Step 1.

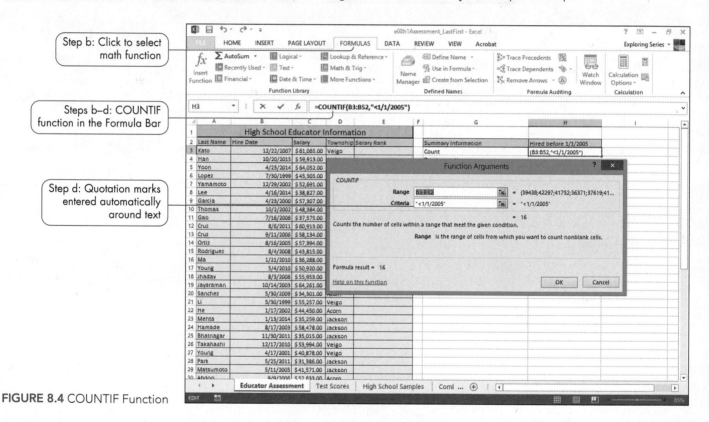

FIGURE 8.4 COUNTIF Function

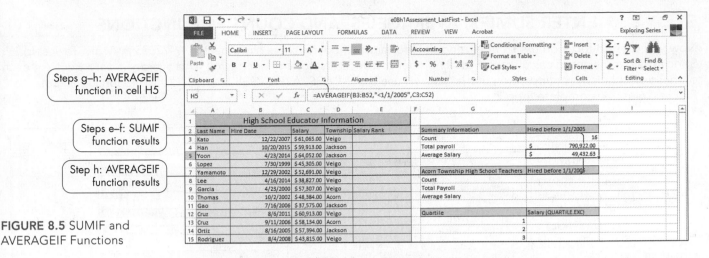

FIGURE 8.5 SUMIF and AVERAGEIF Functions

a. Open *e08h1Assessment* and save it as **e08h1Assessment_LastFirst**. If necessary, click the **Educator Assessment worksheet**.

> **TROUBLESHOOTING**: If you make any major mistakes in this exercise, you can close the file, open *e08h1Assessment* again, and then start this exercise over.

b. Click **cell H3**, click the **FORMULAS tab**, click **More Functions**, select **Statistical** in the Function Library group, scroll through the list, and then select **COUNTIF**.

Cell H3 is the cell in which you want to calculate the total number of high school teachers hired before 1/1/2005.

The Function Arguments dialog box opens so that you can enter the range and criteria arguments.

c. Drag to select the **range B3:B52** to enter it in the Range box.

d. Click in the **Criteria box**, type **<1/1/2005**, and then click **OK**.

The newly created function indicates there are 16 teachers that meet the criteria requirements.

e. Click **cell H4**, click **Math & Trig** in the Function Library group, and then select **SUMIF**.

The Function Arguments dialog box displays so that you can enter the range, criteria, and sum_range arguments.

f. Type **B3:B52** in the **Range box**, type **<1/1/2005** in the **Criteria box**, type **C3:C52** in the **Sum_range box**, and then click **OK**.

The total salaries paid to high school teachers hired before 1/1/2005 is $790,922.

g. Click **cell H5**, click **More Functions** in the Function Library group, click **Statistical**, and then select **AVERAGEIF**.

h. Type **B3:B52** in the **Range box**, type **"<1/1/2005"** in the **Criteria box**, type **C3:C52** in the **Average_range box**, and then click **OK**.

The average salary for high school teachers hired before 1/1/2005 is $49,432.63.

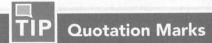 **Quotation Marks**

When entering criteria that contain text, a date, or an operator such as <, you must surround the criteria with quotation marks. If you enter the criteria using the insert function box, Excel will automatically add quotation marks. If you type the function from scratch instead of using the insert function, you must type the quotation marks manually.

STEP 2 >> ENTER SUMIFS, AVERAGEIFS, AND COUNTIFS FUNCTIONS

Now you want to focus on the summarizing data for high school teachers hired before 1/1/2005 in Acorn Township. Specifically, you want to calculate the total number of educators, total salary payroll, and average salary. Because each of these calculations requires two criteria, you will use the SUMIFS, AVERAGEIFS, and COUNTIFS functions. Refer to Figure 8.6 as you complete Step 2.

Steps a–c: COUNTIFS function in cell H8

Steps d–e: SUMIFS function results

Step f: AVERAGEIFS function results

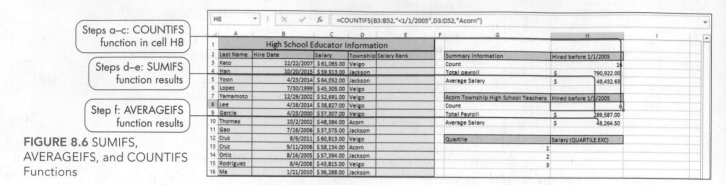

FIGURE 8.6 SUMIFS, AVERAGEIFS, and COUNTIFS Functions

a. Click **cell H8**, click **More Functions – Statistical** in the Function Library group, scroll through the list, and then select **COUNTIFS**.

b. Type **B3:B52** in the **Criteria_range1 box**, click in the **Criteria1 box**, and then type **<1/1/2005**.

c. Click in the **Criteria_range2 box** and type **D3:D52**. Type **"Acorn"** in the **Criteria 2 box** and click **OK**.

The function returns 6, the total number of high school teachers in Acorn Township hired before 1/1/2005, by using the criteria "<1/1/2005" and "Acorn" to filter the data ranges B3:B52 and D3:D32.

d. Click **cell H9**, click **Math & Trig** in the Function Library group, and then select **SUMIFS**.

e. Type **C3:C52** in the **Sum_range box**, type **B3:B52** in the **Criteria_range1 box**, type **"<1/1/2005"** in the **Criteria1 box**, type **D3:D52** in the **Criteria_range2 box**, type **"Acorn"** in the **Criteria2 box**, and then click **OK**.

The total payroll for high school teachers in Acorn Township hired before 1/1/2005 is $289,587.00.

TROUBLESHOOTING: If you misspell criterion text, such as the township name, the results will be inaccurate. Always check the criterion text to make sure it matches text in the respective column.

---

f. Click **cell H10** and type **=AVERAGEIFS(C3:C52,B3:B52,"<1/1/2005",D3:D52,"Acorn")** manually or by selecting the function from the More Functions list and entering the arguments similarly to how you entered the SUMIFS function in step e.

The average salary of high school teachers in Acorn Township hired before 1/1/2005 is $48,264.50.

g. Save the workbook.

STEP 3 >> CALCULATE SALARY RANKS

You want to identify the rank of each teacher's salary. Doing so will enable you to later compare salaries with classroom performance. Refer to Figure 8.7 as you complete Step 3.

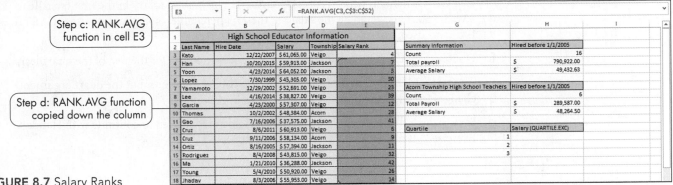

Step c: RANK.AVG function in cell E3

Step d: RANK.AVG function copied down the column

FIGURE 8.7 Salary Ranks

a. Click **cell E3**, click **More Functions** in the Function Library group, click **Statistical**, and then select **RANK.AVG**.

b. Click **cell C3** to enter it in the Number box.

Excel uses the individual salary to compare it to a list of salaries to identify its rank.

c. Click in the **Ref box**, type **C$3:C$52**, and then click **OK**.

You use the mixed reference C$3:C$52 to prevent the row numbers from changing when you copy the functions down the column. You do not have to use absolute references since the column letters will be the same as you copy the function down the same column.

Kato's salary of $61,065 is ranked fourth out of the entire list of salaries.

d. Double-click the **cell E3 fill handle** to copy the function down the rank column. Save the workbook.

STEP 4 >> IDENTIFY SALARY RANGES BY QUARTILE

You want to see what salary ranges fall within each quartile. You will use the QUARTILE function to identify the ranges and to identify the lowest and highest salaries. Refer to Figure 8.8 as you complete Step 4.

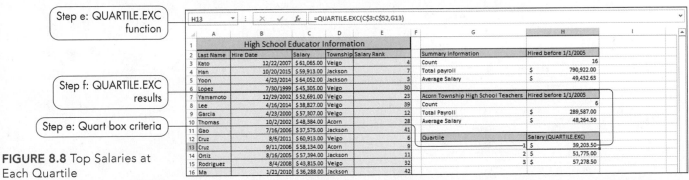

Step e: QUARTILE.EXC function

Step f: QUARTILE.EXC results

Step e: Quart box criteria

FIGURE 8.8 Top Salaries at Each Quartile

a. Click **cell H13**, the cell to contain the top salary for the first quartile.

b. Click **Insert Function** on the **FORMULAS tab** on the Ribbon. In the function Library group, click the **Or select a category arrow** and select **Statistical** if necessary.

c. Scroll through the *Select a function* list, select **QUARTILE.EXC**, and then click **OK**.

The Function Arguments dialog box opens so that you can enter the array and quart arguments.

d. Drag to select the **range C3:C52** to enter it in the Array box. Edit the range to reflect mixed references so that the row numbers remain the same as you copy the function down: **C$3:C$52**.

e. Click in the **Quart box**, type **G13**, and then click **OK**.

Cell G13 contains 1, which reflects Quartile 1. The highest salary in the first quartile is $39,203.50. This would be the salary at the 25th percentile. Note that because QUARTILE. EXC was used, quartiles 0 and 4 were omitted.

f. Double-click the **cell H13 fill handle** to copy the function for the rest of the quartiles.

The array argument remains the same in the copied functions, but the quart argument changes to reflect the correct quartile values in column G.

g. Save the workbook. Keep the workbook onscreen if you plan to continue with Hands-On Exercise 2. If not, close the workbook and exit Excel.

Descriptive Statistical Functions

Attempting to make decisions based on datasets with hundreds if not thousands of entries can be a daunting task. Analyzing, summarizing, and describing a large dataset would be close to impossible without a methodology of approach. Descriptive statistics provide the tools that help analyze and describe large datasets into pockets of manageable and usable information. While descriptive statistics like average and quartile are useful in defining the characteristics of a specific dataset, they are only descriptive and do not provide insight that is applicable into data outside the dataset. For example, a survey of high school teachers' opinions on dress code in Ohio would not provide any insight into high school teachers' opinions in Arkansas.

Measuring Central Tendency

Functions used earlier in the chapter such as AVERAGEIF, QUARTILE, and RANK.AVG are all tools to measure central tendency. To add to these functions, Excel offers FREQUENCY, VARIANCE, standard deviation (STDEV), and CORREL to help define the shape and variation of a population or a sample of data. A *population* is a dataset that contains all the data you would like to evaluate. A *sample* is a smaller, more manageable portion of the population. For example, all educators in the state of Pennsylvania comprise an example of a population. A survey of 10% of the educators of each city in Pennsylvania is a sample.

Use the Standard Deviation and Variance functions

STEP 1 ≫

Variance is a measure of a dataset's dispersion, such as the difference between the highest and lowest test scores in a class. *Standard deviation* is the measure of how far the data sample is spread around the mean, which is also referred to as μ when using statistics. If calculated manually, the standard deviation is the square root of the variance.

Standard deviation and variance are two of the most popular tools to measure variations within a dataset. Recall that when working in descriptive statistics, the statistician can utilize data from the entire population or from a portion of the population, called a sample. Excel offers a variety of functions for these calculations based on the use of a sample or a population. Table 8.3 details the options available in Excel 2013.

TABLE 8.3 Standard Deviation and Variance		
	Function	**Description**
Standard Deviation	STDEVA	Standard deviation of a sample including logical values and text
	STDEVPA	Standard deviation of a population including logical values and text
	STDEV.P	Standard deviation of a population
	STDEV.S	Standard deviation of a sample
Variance	VARA	Variance of a sample including logical values and text
	VARPA	Variance of a population including logical values and text
	VAR.P	Variance of a population
	VAR.S	Variance of a sample

The STDEV.S function calculates the standard deviation of a sample. This is the measure of how far the sample is spread around the mean. This value is calculated mathematically by determining the square root of the variance. The variance of a sample is the summation of the squared deviations divided by the amount of the sample ($n - 1$). While calculating standard deviation and variance mathematically may seem daunting, in Excel the functions are no more complicated than using a SUM function.

=STDEV.S(number1,number2)

=VAR.S(number1,number2)

The STDEV.S and VAR.S functions return values for a data sample rather than a population; however, Excel does contain functions to calculate population variation as well, as described in Table 8.3 and as displayed in syntax below.

=STDEV.P(number1,number2)

=VAR.P(number1,number2)

Use the CORREL Function

STEP 2»

The **CORREL function**, short for correlation coefficient, helps determine the strength of a relationship between two variables. When used to compare datasets, the function will return a value between –1 and 1. The closer the value is to 1, the stronger the relationship. For example, Figure 8.9 depicts the strength of the relationship between salary and credit score. Cell D3 contains a calculated correlation of .913135908. This would indicate a strong correlation between salary and a high credit score.

The input variables for the CORREL function are entered in arrays.

=CORREL(Array1,Array2)

To use the CORREL function to calculate correlation, complete the steps below.

1. Click a cell.
2. Click the FORMULAS tab on the Ribbon and choose More Functions – Statistical – CORREL.
3. Select the range for the first data array.
4. Select the range for the second data array.
5. Click OK.

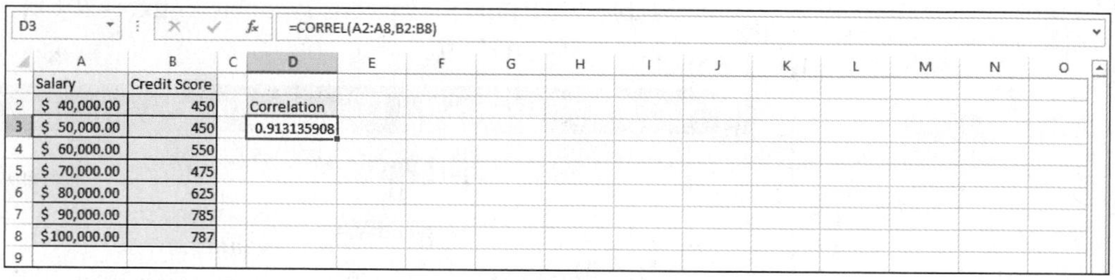

FIGURE 8.9 CORREL Function

Calculate Frequency Distribution

STEP 3»

The **FREQUENCY function** is a descriptive static function in Excel that determines the frequency distribution of a dataset. The frequency distribution is a meaningful descriptive tool because it determines how often a set of numbers appears within a dataset. For example, you may want to determine how many student GPAs fall within a specific range. FREQUENCY could determine how many students earned As, Bs, and Cs. Using the FREQUENCY function is somewhat unique because it returns a vertical array of data based on data bins that you determine. For example, in Figure 8.10, the FREQUENCY function returns the number of occurrences of each salary in the dataset as determined by quartiles. In this scenario, there are 12 occurrences of the salary that are less than or equal to $39,203.50.

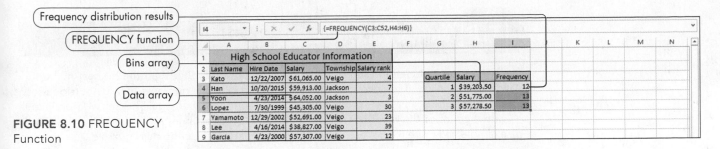

Frequency distribution results

FREQUENCY function

Bins array

Data array

FIGURE 8.10 FREQUENCY Function

As shown in Figure 8.11, the FREQUENCY function requires two input variables, the data_array and the bins_array.

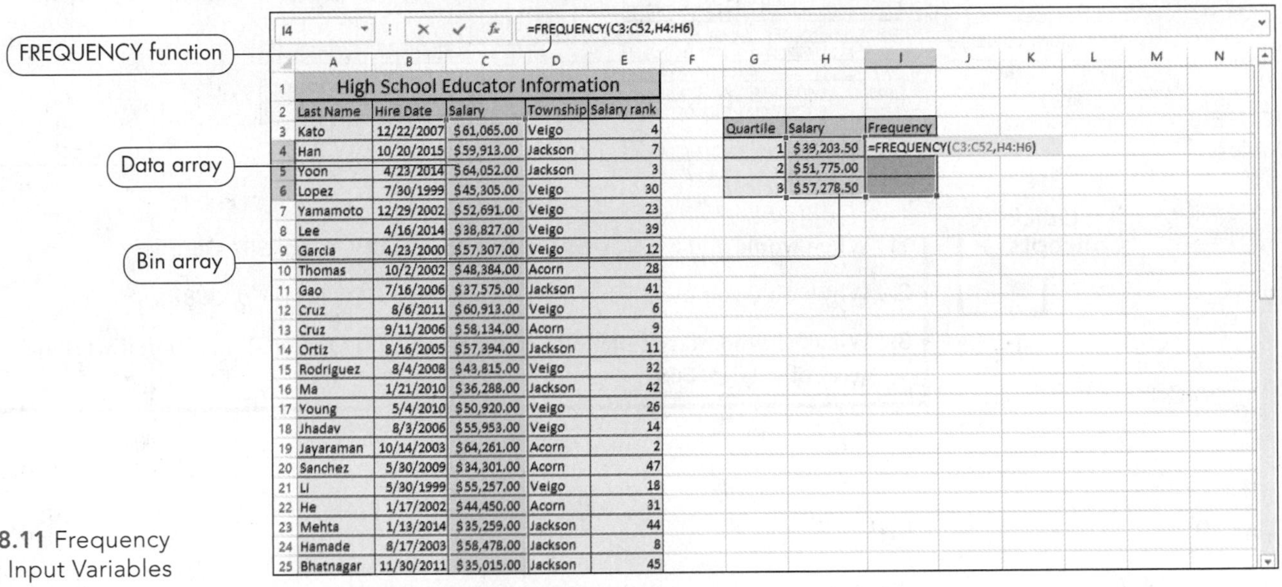

FREQUENCY function

Data array

Bin array

FIGURE 8.11 Frequency Function Input Variables

=FREQUENCY(Data_array,Bins_array)

- **Data_Array.** The data_array is the range of cells that contain the values that are being evaluated for frequency of occurrence. In Figure 8.11, the Data_Array C3:C52 is being evaluated to determine how many salaries fall within the first, second, or third quartile.

- **Bins_Array.** The bins_array is a predefined set of numerical values that are used to organize and count the data. In Figure 8.11, the range H4:H6 displays the quartile values that will be used to determine frequency of occurrence within the Data_Array.

Unlike other Excel functions, you do not simply type the FREQUENCY function in a cell and press Enter. Instead, you must first select the cells in which you want to put the FREQUENCY function, type the formula, and then press Ctrl+Shift+Enter. If you simply press Enter, then FREQUENCY will only calculate the frequency of the data that fall in the first cell bins_array. To use the FREQUENCY function, do the following:

1. Select a range to output results.
2. Type =FREQUENCY and press Tab.
3. Select the data_array.
4. Select the bins_array.
5. Press Ctrl+Shift+Enter.

TIP | Numerical Outliers

The frequency function will not return values that are higher than the highest number in the bins_array. If you are interested in documenting the numbers that fall outside the predefined bins_array, select one additional cell to the return range. This cell will populate with a count of the numbers that fall outside the highest number in the bins_array. For example, in Figure 8.12, there are 12 salaries that are outside the third quartile.

FREQUENCY function

Outlier return value

FIGURE 8.12 Numerical
Outliers

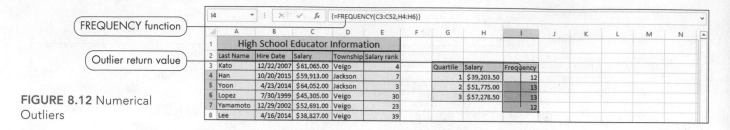

| I4 | | | × ✓ fx | {=FREQUENCY(C3:C52,H4:H6)} | | | | | | | | | | | |

	A	B	C	D	E	F	G	H	I	J	K	L	M	N
1	High School Educator Information													
2	Last Name	Hire Date	Salary	Township	Salary rank									
3	Kato	12/22/2007	$61,065.00	Veigo	4									
4	Han	10/20/2015	$59,913.00	Jackson	7		Quartile	Salary	Frequency					
5	Yoon	4/23/2014	$64,052.00	Jackson	3		1	$39,203.50	12					
6	Lopez	7/30/1999	$45,305.00	Veigo	30		2	$51,775.00	13					
7	Yamamoto	12/29/2002	$52,691.00	Veigo	23		3	$57,278.50	13					
8	Lee	4/16/2014	$38,827.00	Veigo	39				12					

Quick Concepts ✓

1. When would you use STDEV.S instead of STDEV.P? *pp. 367–368*

2. Why would you use FREQUENCY instead of COUNTIF? *p. 368*

3. What is keyboard command to complete the FREQUENCY function if working with an array of data? *p. 369*

Hands-On Exercises

2 Descriptive Statistical Functions

As the superintendent, you have been tasked with evaluating student performance. You have decided to base your assessment on standardized test scores and total attendance. You would also like to test the correlation between test scores and attendance. You plan to base your calculations on a sample of 50 students from the district.

Skills covered: Calculate Standard Deviation and Variance • Calculate Correlation Coefficient • Determine Frequency Distribution

STEP 1 » CALCULATE STANDARD DEVIATION AND VARIANCE

The sample you have collected contains scores as well as attendance information of sixth- through eighth-grade students across the district. You will calculate the standard deviation of the test scores within the sample. Refer to Figure 8.13 as you complete Step 1.

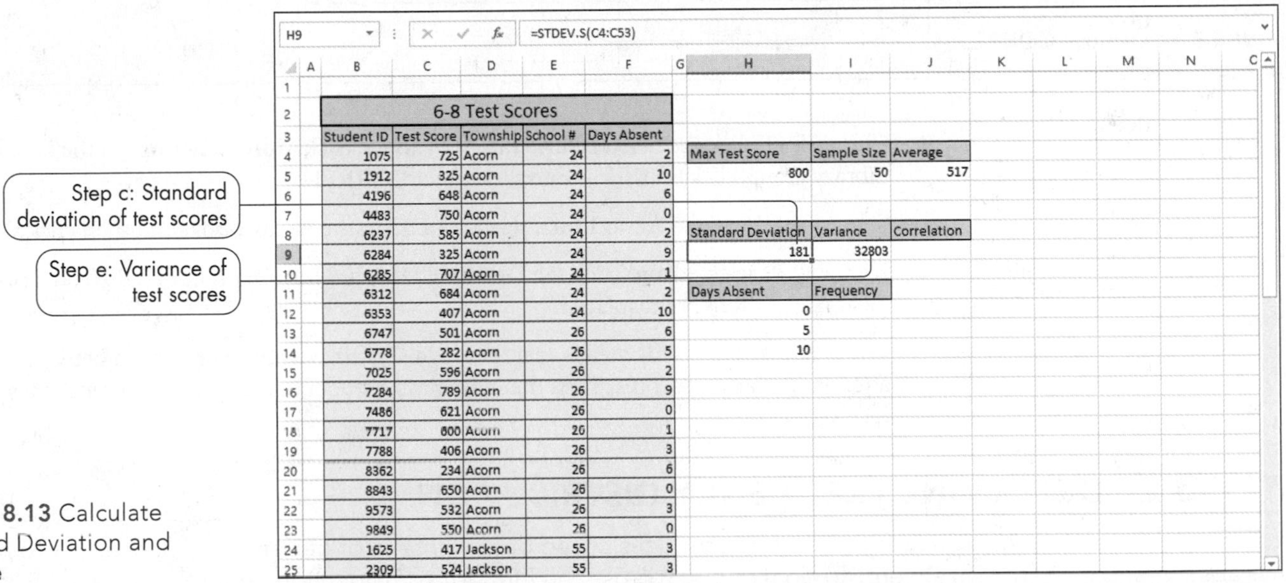

Step c: Standard deviation of test scores

Step e: Variance of test scores

FIGURE 8.13 Calculate Standard Deviation and Variance

a. Open *e08h1Assessment_LastFirst*, click the **Test Scores worksheet**, and then save it as **e08h2TestScores_LastFirst**.

b. Click **cell H9**, click the **FORMULAS tab** if necessary, click **More Functions** in the Function Library group, select **Statistical**, and then click **STDEV.S**.

   STDEV.S is being used because the data is a random sample of 50 test scores. If every test score were included in the dataset, STDEV.P would be used.

c. Select the **range C4:C53** and click **OK**. Then with **cell H9** still selected, click the **Decrease Decimal button** in the Number group on the HOME tab until no decimal points are displayed.

   The standard deviation for the sample is 181. Therefore, assuming the distribution is normal, about 66% of students will receive a test score between 336 and 698. This is calculated by adding the standard deviation, 181, to the average test score of 517 to determine the high end of the range and subtracting 181 from 517 to determine the low end of the range.

d. Click **cell I9**, click the **FORMULAS tab** if necessary, click **More Functions** in the Function Library group, click **Statistical**, and then select **VAR.S**.

e. Type **C4:C53** in the **Number box** and click **OK**. With **cell I9** still selected, click the **Decrease Decimal button** located on the HOME tab until no decimal points are displayed.

The larger the variance, the greater the dispersion of data around the mean test score. The results of the VAR.S function (32803) would indicate a large dispersion.

STEP 2 ≫ CALCULATE CORRELATION COEFFICIENT

After calculating the standard deviation and variance to help determine the data points' distance from the mean, you would like to test for a correlation between test scores and attendance. Refer to Figure 8.14 as you complete Step 2.

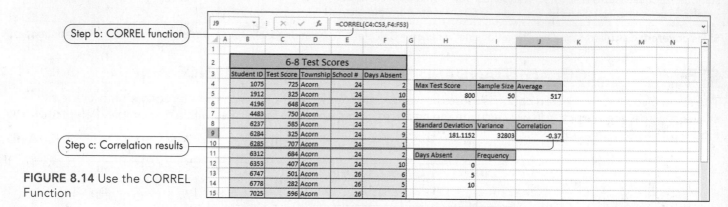

FIGURE 8.14 Use the CORREL Function

a. Click **cell J9**, click the **FORMULAS tab** if necessary, click **More Functions** in the Function Library group, click **Statistical**, and then select **CORREL**.

b. Select **C4:C53** in the **Array1 box**, select **F4:F53** in the **Array2 box**, and then click **OK**.

c. Keep **cell J9** selected and click the **Decrease Decimal button** on the HOME tab until two decimal positions are displayed.

The result is –0.37. This means that there is a slightly negative correlation between attendance and test scores. Thus the more days a student is absent, the lower the test scores received.

STEP 3 ≫ DETERMINE FREQUENCY DISTRIBUTION

You want to determine the frequency of student absences based on the criteria of perfect attendance, 0, 1 to 5 days absent, and 6 to 10 days absent. To do this, you will use the FREQUENCY function. Refer to Figure 8.15 as you complete Step 3.

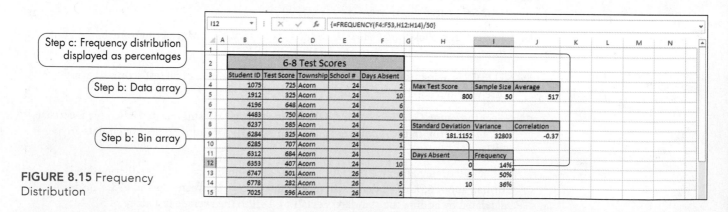

FIGURE 8.15 Frequency Distribution

a. Select the **range I12:I14** and type **=FREQUENCY(F4:F53**. Press **comma (,)**, type **H12:H14)/50**, and then press **Ctrl+Shift+Enter**.

The range I12:I14 was selected in order to return all results. If only I12 were selected, the function would return data just for students with 1 to 5 absences. You divided the frequency function by the number of data points in the sample (50) so that the results are calculated as percentages.

> **TROUBLESHOOTING**: Make sure you add the right parenthesis after the Bins_Array but before adding /50. This will complete the frequency function before dividing the results by 50 to calculate the percentage.

b. Select the **range I12:I14**, if necessary, and apply the **Percentage number format**.

From the results, you can determine that 14% of the students had perfect attendance, 50% missed between 1 to 5 days, and 36% missed between 5 and 10 days.

c. Save the workbook. Keep the workbook onscreen if you plan to continue with Hands-On Exercise 3. If not, close the workbook and exit Excel.

Inferential Statistics

Descriptive statistics help define characteristics of a population such as mean, standard deviation, and variance. However, in many situations, you may want to research a population that you may not have the time or resources to evaluate—for example, evaluating test scores for every student in the state of Pennsylvania. In situations in which the population is too large to acquire every point of data needed, samples must be used. The limitation of dealing with samples is that they do not contain all the information available. Furthermore, depending on the sample set selected, the relationship between the sample set and the entire population may or may not be very strong. Inferential statistics help analyze differences between groups and relationships within groups of data. They can be applied to samples to help make more informed statements about a population within a certain margin of error. In the following section, you will use the Excel add-in Data Analysis ToolPak to calculate inferential statistics on the school system's high school students.

Loading the Analysis ToolPak

STEP 1 » The *Analysis ToolPak* is an add-in program that provides statistical analysis tools. For example, you can use Analysis ToolPak to perform ANOVA, Correlation, F-Tests, T-Tests, and Z-Tests for analyzing a dataset (see Figure 8.16). To enable the Analysis ToolPak add-in, do the following:

1. Click the FILE tab and click Options.
2. Select Add-Ins on the left side.
3. Make sure that Excel Add-ins is selected in the Manage box and click Go.
4. Click the Analysis ToolPak check box and click OK.

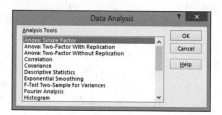

FIGURE 8.16 Analysis ToolPak

Performing Analysis Using the Analysis ToolPak

The Analysis ToolPak offers 19 tools that fit a variety of needs across all professions. There are alternate options to many of these tools, such as the FREQUENCY function versus the Histogram summary in the ToolPak. The difference in using the Analysis ToolPak versus the corresponding function is that the ToolPak will generate reports while the function equivalents only return values.

Performing Analysis of Variance (ANOVA)

STEP 2 » In statistics, it is common to compare the means between two or more sample groups of data—for example, comparing test scores from a cross-section sample of multiple high schools in the same district or comparing test scores in a time-series sample over a period of years from the same high school. A common tool to compare these samples is analysis of variance, also abbreviated as ANOVA.

ANOVA is a statistical hypothesis test that helps determine if samples of data were taken from the same population. In practical use, it can be used to accept or reject a hypothesis.

There is no one function to calculate ANOVA in Excel; however, you can create an ANOVA report using the Analysis ToolPak.

Three types of ANOVA calculations can be performed:

- Single-factor
- Two-factor with replication
- Two-factor without replication

The most commonly used option is single factor. To use the Analysis ToolPak to create a single-factor ANOVA report on a cross-section sample of high school SAT scores from the district, do the following:

1. Click the DATA tab and select Data Analysis in the Analysis group.
2. Select ANOVA: Single Factor from the Data Analysis dialog box and click OK.
3. Click the Input Range selection box and select the range of data you want to analyze.
4. Select either Grouped By Columns or Grouped By Rows based on your data layout.
5. Choose the default alpha 0.05 (meaning there is a 5% chance of rejecting the null hypothesis).
6. Select an output option.
7. Click OK.

Excel places the results on a new worksheet in the same workbook. The results of the sample test scores can be viewed in Figure 8.17. The summary portion of the report provides basic descriptive statistics of each group analyzed. The ANOVA portion of the report breaks the data into two sets, between groups and within groups. ANOVA analysis within groups measures random variation. ANOVA analysis between groups measures variation due to differences within the group. Table 8.4 provides further detail on the ANOVA summary information.

TABLE 8.4 ANOVA Summary Report

Abbreviation	Full name	Explanation
SS	Sum of squares	Sum of the squares of the data points in the sample
df	Degrees of freedom	The number of data points in the sample – 1 (*N* – 1)
MS	Mean square	The means of the sample squared
F	F ratio	Equal to the mean square between/mean square within
P-value	Probability	Probability of population being similar to the sample
F crit	Critical value of F	Used to determine if the F_Test is significant

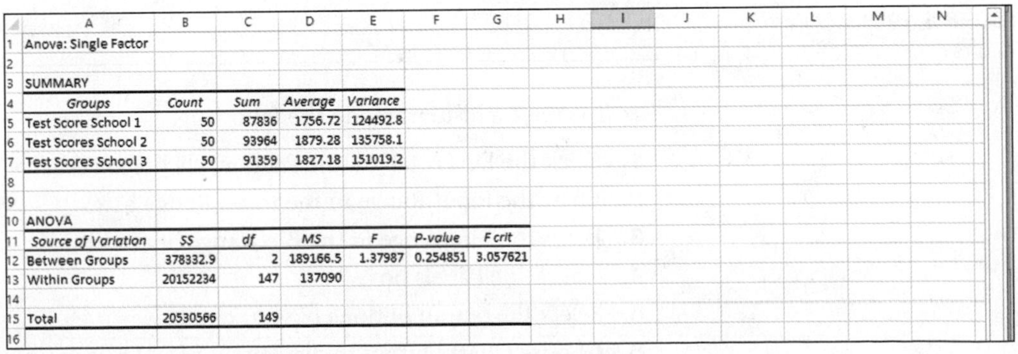

	A	B	C	D	E	F	G
1	Anova: Single Factor						
2							
3	SUMMARY						
4	*Groups*	*Count*	*Sum*	*Average*	*Variance*		
5	Test Score School 1	50	87836	1756.72	124492.8		
6	Test Scores School 2	50	93964	1879.28	135758.1		
7	Test Scores School 3	50	91359	1827.18	151019.2		
8							
9							
10	ANOVA						
11	*Source of Variation*	*SS*	*df*	*MS*	*F*	*P-value*	*F crit*
12	Between Groups	378332.9	2	189166.5	1.37987	0.254851	3.057621
13	Within Groups	20152234	147	137090			
14							
15	Total	20530566	149				
16							

FIGURE 8.17 ANOVA Results

Calculating COVARIANCE

STEP 3 » *Covariance* is similar to correlation. It is a measure of how two sets of data vary simultaneously. It is calculated by taking the average of each product of the deviation of a data point. In Excel, there are COVARIANCE.P and S functions that can calculate covariance, and there is also a covariance reporting feature included in the Analysis ToolPak. While both the Analysis ToolPak and COVARIANCE functions will return the covariance, the Analysis ToolPak will also calculate the variance in the output in a preformatted report.

For example, you may hypothesize that the more days of school missed by a student, the lower the SAT scores. The CORREL function would return a numerical value that analyzes the strength of the relation. The covariance analysis will produce a matrix that shows how the datasets change together (see Figure 8.18). To create a covariance report, do the following:

1. Click the DATA tab and choose Data Analysis in the Analysis group.
2. Select Covariance and click OK.
3. Click the Input Range selection box and select the range of the data you want to analyze.
4. Select Grouped By Columns or Grouped By Rows depending on the organization of the dataset.
5. If the first row contains labels, check Labels in the First Row checkbox.
6. Choose the Output Range or choose to place the output in a new workbook or worksheet and click OK.

	SAT Score	Absences			SAT Score	Absences
	1436	6				
	2014	0				
	2308	0				
	1763	3		SAT Score	136870.4431	
	1544	7		Absences	-30.13666667	10.58333
	1347	3				
	1383	7				
	1504	1				

FIGURE 8.18 COVARIANCE Results

Creating a Histogram

STEP 4 » A *histogram* is a visual display of tabulated frequencies (see Figure 8.19). There are several ways to create a histogram in Excel; however, one of the simplest methods is using the Analysis ToolPak. Creating a histogram is somewhat similar to using the frequency function in that it requires bins to tabulate the data and will return a frequency distribution table. Figure 8.19 depicts a completed histogram.

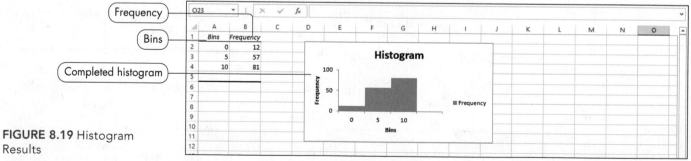

FIGURE 8.19 Histogram Results

To create a histogram, do the following:

1. Click the DATA tab on the Ribbon, click Data Analysis, and then choose Histogram.
2. Enter the Input Range in the Input Range box.
3. Enter the Bin Range in the Bin Range box.
4. Check the Labels box.
5. Select the output options of your choice.
6. Choose Chart Output to display the visual histogram in the output.
7. Click OK.

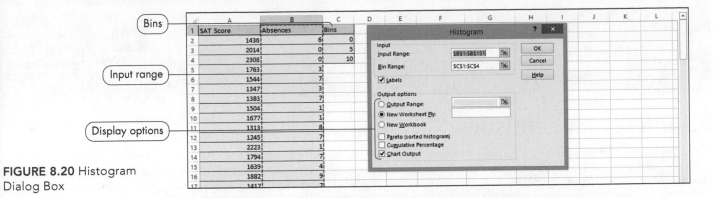

FIGURE 8.20 Histogram Dialog Box

TIP Additional Features and New Functions

The Analysis ToolPak offers 19 total tools. To further explore the possibilities, click the ? icon in the Data Analysis start screen. Furthermore, Excel 2013 has added six new statistical functions that can be used outside the Analysis ToolPak. See Table 8.4 for more details.

TABLE 8.5   New Functions in Excel 2013

Name	Description
Binom.dist.range	Calculates the probability of trial result using a binomial distribution
Gamma	Returns gamma value
Gauss	Returns 0.5 less than the standard normal cumulative distribution
PermutationA	Returns the number of permutations for a given number of objects (with repetitions) that can be selected from the total objects
PHI	Returns the value of the density function for a standard normal distribution
Skew.P	Returns the skewness of a distribution based on a population

Quick Concepts ✓

1. What is the difference between inferential statistics and descriptive statistics? *p. 374*

2. What is the benefit of using the Analysis ToolPak over a regular Excel function? *p. 374*

3. What is the difference between COVARIANCE and CORREL? *p. 376*

Hands-On Exercises

 Watch the Video for this Hands-On Exercise!

 MyITLab® HOE3 Training

3 Inferential Statistics

For the last portion of your educational assessment, you would like to analyze SAT data across multiple high schools in the district. As part of the analysis, you are going to use the Analysis ToolPak to calculate an ANOVA report as well as test the variation of test scores and SAT results using covariance. Last, you will create a histogram of all SAT scores in the sample.

Skills covered: Load the Analysis ToolPak Add-In • Performing Analysis of Variance • Calculate Covariance • Create a Histogram

STEP 1 >> LOAD THE ANALYSIS TOOLPAK ADD-IN

Before you begin your calculations, you need to enable the Analysis ToolPak add-in. If the ToolPak is already loaded, skip to Step 2. Refer to Figure 8.21 as you complete Step 1.

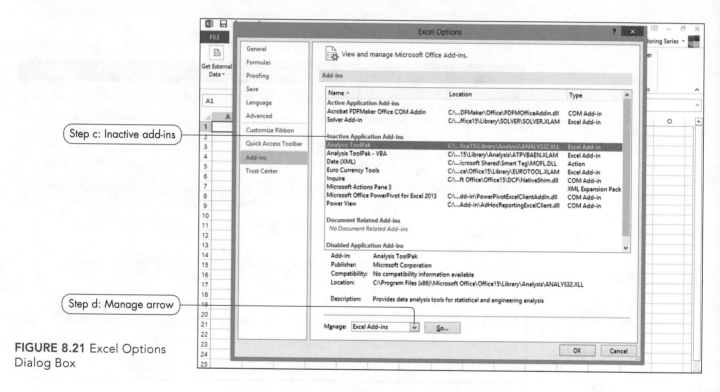

Step c: Inactive add-ins

Step d: Manage arrow

FIGURE 8.21 Excel Options Dialog Box

a. Open *e08h2TestScores_LastFirst*, make the *High School Samples* worksheet active, and then save it as **e08h3Analysis_LastFirst**.

b. Click the **FILE tab** and select **Options**.

c. Click **Add-Ins** on the left side.

The Excel Options dialog box displays a list of active and inactive application add-ins.

d. Click the **Manage arrow**, select **Excel Add-ins** if necessary, and then click **Go**.

The add-ins dialog box opens, containing a list of available add-in applications.

e. Click the **Analysis ToolPak check box** in the *Add-Ins available* list and click **OK**.

STEP 2 ≫ PERFORMING ANALYSIS OF VARIANCE

You are ready to create an analysis of variance using the Analysis ToolPak. You will analyze a cross section data sample of SAT scores from three high schools in the school district. Refer to Figure 8.22 as you complete Step 2.

Step e: ANOVA summary

Step c: Input range

	Sample High School SAT Scores		
	SAT Score High School 1	SAT Score High School 2	SAT Score High School 3
4	1436	2065	1944
5	2014	1229	2163
6	2308	2134	2010
7	1763	1431	1965
8	1544	1710	2243
9	1347	1727	1815
10	1383	1310	2005
11	1504	2150	1250
12	1677	2163	1835
13	1313	1225	2172
14	1245	2309	2037
15	2223	2155	1673
16	1794	1581	2273
17	1639	2343	1375
18	1882	1519	1444
19	1417	1938	2222
20	1698	1839	1669
21	2042	1513	1601
22	1691	1878	1702
23	2324	1778	2120
24	1224	1204	1311
25	1674	2255	2098
26	1963	1821	1259
27	1834	1941	2174
28	2344	1585	2220

Anova: Single Factor

SUMMARY

Groups	Count	Sum	Average	Variance
Column 1	50	87836	1756.72	124493
Column 2	50	93964	1879.28	135758
Column 3	50	91359	1827.18	151019

ANOVA

Source of Variation	SS	df	MS	F	P-value	F crit
Between Groups	378332.92	2	189166	1.37987	0.25485	3.0576
Within Groups	20152233.54	147	137090			
Total	20530566.46	149				

FIGURE 8.22 ANOVA Summary

a. Click the **DATA tab** and select **Data Analysis** in the Analysis group.

b. Select **Anova: Single Factor** from the Analysis Tools options box and click **OK**.

c. Type **B4:D53** in the **Input Range box**.

   This selects the entire dataset to be utilized for the ANOVA.

d. Click **Columns** if necessary to select it. Confirm that *Labels in first row* is not checked and leave the *alpha* setting at the default 0.05.

e. Click **Output Range** in the *Output options* section and type **F7** in the **Output Range box**. Click **OK**.

   This embeds the ANOVA output on the current worksheet.

f. Select the **range F7:L21**, click the **HOME tab** on the Ribbon, and then select **Auto-Fit Column Width** from the Format menu in the Cells group.

STEP 3 ›› CALCULATE COVARIANCE

Your next assessment is an analysis of trends between SAT scores and attendance. To complete this task, you will create a covariance summary. Refer to Figure 8.23 as you complete Step 3.

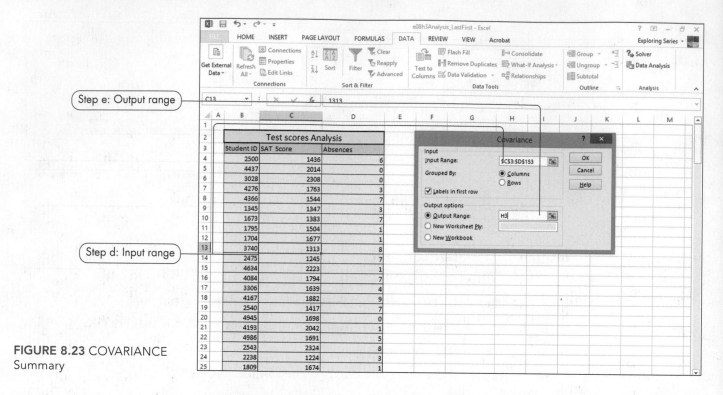

FIGURE 8.23 COVARIANCE Summary

a. Select the **Combined Score Samples worksheet**.

b. Click the **DATA tab** and select **Data Analysis** in the Analysis group.

c. Choose **Covariance** from the Analysis Tools options box and click **OK**.

d. Click in **Input Range selection box** and type **C3:D153**.

   This selects the entire dataset to be utilized for the covariance summary.

e. Select **Columns**, select **Labels** in the first row, click **Output Range** in the *Output options* section, type **H3** in the **Output Range box**, and click **OK**.

   By selecting cell H3 for the output range, you place the summary starting in cell H3 on the current worksheet.

f. Save the workbook.

STEP 4 ≫ CREATE A HISTOGRAM

Your last task is creating a histogram to document the frequency of absences in the high school. To complete the task, you will organize the data into bins for perfect attendance, 1 to 5 absences, and 5 to 10 absences. Refer to Figure 8.24 as you complete Step 4.

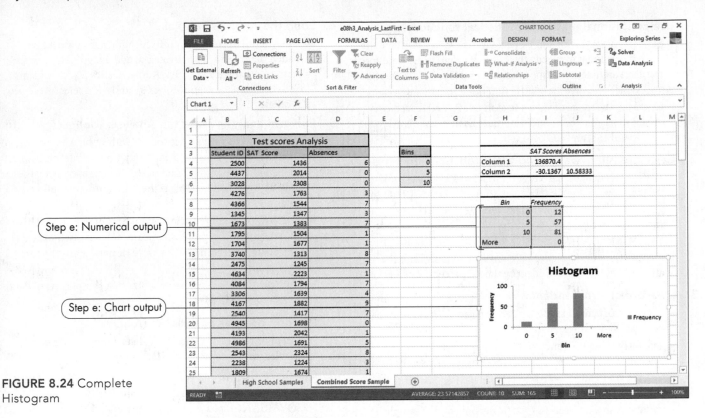

FIGURE 8.24 Complete Histogram

a. Click the **DATA tab** and select **Data Analysis** in the Analysis group.

b. Choose **Histogram** from the Analysis Tools options box and click **OK**.

c. Type **D4:D153** in the **Input Range box**.

d. Type **F4:F6** in the **Bin Range box**.

e. Select **Output Range** in the *Output options* section, type **H8**, select the **Chart Output option**, and then click **OK**.

f. Move the newly created histogram chart so that the top-left corner is in cell H15.

g. Save the workbook and submit based on your instructor's directions.

Chapter Objectives Review

After reading this chapter, you have accomplished the following objectives:

1. **Use conditional math and statistical functions.**
   - SUMIF, AVERAGEIF, and COUNTIF: These functions require a range argument to specify the range of values to evaluate and a criteria argument that specifies the condition for the range.
   - The SUMIF and AVERAGEIF: functions contain arguments to specify the range of values to sum or average, respectively. When more than one condition must be met, use SUMIFS, AVERAGEIFS, and COUNTIFS.

2. **Calculate relative standing with statistical functions.**
   - The RANK.EQ and RANK.AVG functions calculate ranking for individual values within a list. PERCENTRANK.INC and PERCENTRANK.EXC calculate rank as a percentage for each value in a list.
   - The QUARTILE.INC and QUARTILE.EXC functions identify the value at a specific quartile. PERCENTILE.INC and PERCENTILE.EXC identify the kth percentile of a value.

3. **Measure central tendency.**
   - Measures of central tendency define basic characteristics of a population or sample of data.
   - The FREQUENCY function is an array function that calculates the number of occurrences of specific sets of data that appear in a data series.
   - The STDEV.S and STDEV.P functions help determine variations in a data series, specifically how far the sample is spread around the mean.
   - The VAR.S and VAR.P functions determine the summation of the squared deviations divided by the amount of the sample – 1 or the total population.
   - The CORREL function determines the correlation coefficient. The value returned will be between –1 and 1. The closer the value is to 1, the stronger the positive relationship between datasets.

4. **Load the Analysis ToolPak.**
   - The Analysis ToolPak is an Excel add-in that must be loaded before use. To activate the add-in, go to Options on the Backstage view, click Add-Ins, click Excel Add-ins from the Manage menu, click Go, and then select Analysis ToolPak.

5. **Perform analysis using the Analysis ToolPak.**
   - There are 19 tools available for use within the Analysis ToolPak. Many of the tools have function counterparts that can be used in drafting functions. The benefit of using the ToolPak over the functions is the final summary options in the ToolPak.
   - ANOVA, is an abbreviation of analysis of variance. This statistical tool compares the means between two data samples to determine if they were derived from the same population.
   - COVARIANCE is a measure of how two sample sets of data vary simultaneously.

6. **Perform analysis of variance (ANOVA).**
   - Accept or reject a hypothesis by determining if two or more samples were taken from the same population.

7. **Calculate COVARIANCE.**
   - COVARIANCE.P can be used to calculate the COVARIANCE of a dataset that encompass the entire population.
   - COVARIANCE.S calculates the COVARIANCE of a sample datasets.

8. **Create a histogram.**
   - A histogram is a tabular display of data frequencies organized into bins. The histogram feature of the Analysis ToolPak is comparable to the FREQUENCY function. It will return the number of occurrences of data points based on predefined bins. It also has charting capabilities.

Key Terms Matching

Match the key terms with their definitions. Write the key term letter by the appropriate numbered definition.

a. Analysis ToolPak
b. ANOVA
c. AVERAGEIF function
d. CORREL function
e. COUNTIF function
f. Covariance
g. Frequency function
h. Histogram
i. PERCENTILE.EXC function
j. PERCENTILE.INC function

k. PERCENTRANK.EXC function
l. PERCENTRANK.INC function
m. QUARTILE.EXC function
n. QUARTILE.INC function
o. RANK.AVG function
p. RANK.EQ function
q. Standard Deviation
r. SUMIF function
s. Variance

1. _____ A tabular display of data that displays the frequencies of occurrence organized into bins. **p. 376**

2. _____ Measure of how two sample sets of data vary simultaneously **p. 376**

3. _____ A statistical tool that compares the means between two data samples to determine if they were derived from the same population. **p. 374**

4. _____ An add-in program that contains tools for performing complex statistical analysis. **p. 374**

5. _____ A descriptive statistics tool that determines the summation of the squared deviations divided by the amount of the $n - 1$. **p. 367**

6. _____ Measures how far the data sample is spread around the mean. **p. 367**

7. _____ Determines the number of occurrences of numerical values in a dataset based on predetermined bins. **p. 368**

8. _____ Calculates the correlation coefficient of two data series. **p. 368**

9. _____ Calculates the total of a range of values when a specified condition is met. **p. 355**

10. _____ Identifies the rank of a value, omitting the next rank when tie values exist. **p. 357**

11. _____ Identifies the rank of a value, providing an average ranking for identical values. **p. 357**

12. _____ Identifies the value at a specific quartile. **p. 359**

13. _____ Identifies the value at a specific quartile, exclusive of 0 and 4. **p. 359**

14. _____ Identifies a value's rank as a percentile between 0 and 1 of a list of values. **p. 358**

15. _____ Identifies a value's rank as a percentile, excluding 0 and 1, of a list of values. **p. 358**

16. _____ Counts the number of cells in a range when a specified condition is met. **p. 355**

17. _____ Calculates the average of values in a range when a specified condition is met. **p. 355**

18. _____ Identifies the kth percentile of a specified value within a list of values, including the 0th and 100th percentiles. **p. 360**

19. _____ Identifies a value at a specified percentile; however, the .EXC *excludes* 0th or 100th percentiles. **p. 360**

Multiple Choice

1. A workbook contains a list of university students. You want to identify the total number of students who are seniors and who are majoring in biology. Without modifying the original student dataset, what function can you use to find the answer to your question?

   (a) SUMIF

   (b) AVERAGEIFS

   (c) DCOUNT

   (d) COUNTIFS

2. What function would you use to identify a values rank as a percentile, excluding 0 and 1?

   (a) QUARTILE.INC

   (b) PERCENTRANK.EXC

   (c) PECENTRANK.INC

   (d) RANK.EQ

3. A worksheet contains a list of traffic stops over the past 12 months. The police chief wants to determine the total dollar amount of all traffic tickets written in the ZIP code 46208. What function derives the correct answer?

   (a) SUMIF

   (b) AVERAGEIFS

   (c) DCOUNT

   (d) COUNTIFS

4. A worksheet contains test scores for students in an aviation class. The scores are 95, 90, 90, 85, 80, 75, 75, 70, and 60. Using the RANK function that is considered a best practice, what is the rank of the second student who scored 90?

   (a) 2

   (b) 3

   (c) 2.5

   (d) None of the above

5. What function would you use to calculate the spread of data around the mean in a data sample?

   (a) STDEV.S

   (b) CORREL

   (c) STDEV.P

   (d) FREQUENCY

6. You hypothesize that there is a relationship between lack of regular exercise and illness. To research this theory, you have compiled a sample set of data that contains numbers of days in which an hour or more of exercise is completed as well as numbers of days sick within a calendar year. What tools in Excel could you use to investigate the relationships between the data? Select all that apply.

   (a) CORREL

   (b) PERCENTRANK.INC

   (c) COVARIANCE

   (d) SUMIFS

7. Which of the following tools is not a part of the Data Analysis ToolPak add-in?

   (a) Covariance

   (b) ANOVA

   (c) Histogram

   (d) RANK.EQ

8. What is the difference between STDEV.S and STDEV.P?

   (a) STDEV.S calculates standard deviation of a sample; STDEV.P calculates the standard deviation of a population.

   (b) STDEV.P calculates the standard deviation of a population; STDEV.S calculates average variation.

   (c) STDEV.P calculates the standard deviation of a population; STDEV.S calculates variance.

   (d) There is no difference.

9. What is the difference between a sample and a population?

   (a) A sample contains all data possible for evaluation, while a population contains a portion of data available.

   (b) A population contains all data possible for evaluation, while a sample contains a portion of the data.

   (c) A sample contains all data from the population except statistical outliers.

   (d) There is no difference.

10. What keystroke combination is required to calculate a Frequency data array?

    (a) Ctrl+Enter

    (b) Alt+Enter

    (c) Ctrl+Shift+Enter

    (d) Ctrl+Shift+Delete

Practice Exercises

1 Sociology Textbooks

As vice president of the Sociology Division at Ivory Halls Publishing Company, you monitor sales of textbooks published by your division. The division categorizes textbooks by discipline (such as criminal justice and family) and then further classifies books by an area within the discipline. Your assistant downloaded and formatted the latest sales figures. Now you want to calculate some summary statistics for the introductory discipline and then, more specifically, the general area. This exercise follows the same set of skills as used in Hands-On Exercise 2 in the chapter. Refer to Figure 8.25 as you complete this exercise.

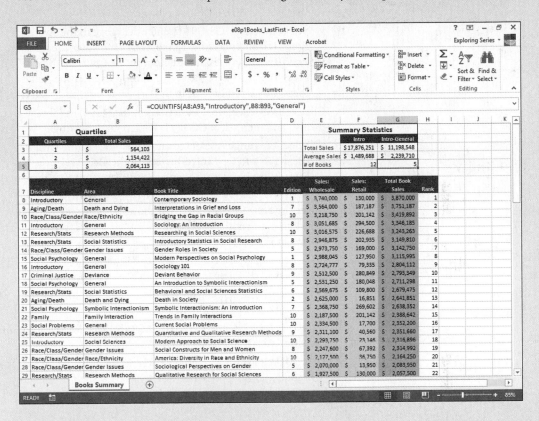

FIGURE 8.25 Sociology Statistics

a. Open *e08p1Books* and save it as **e08p1Books_LastFirst**.

b. Click **cell F3** and click the **FORMULAS tab**.

c. Click **Math & Trig** in the Function Library group, scroll through the list, and then select **SUMIF**. Do the following:
   - Select the **range A8:A93** to enter the range in the Range box.
   - Press **Tab** and type **Introductory** in the **Criteria box**.
   - Press **Tab**, select the **range G8:G93** to enter the range in the Sum_range box, and then click **OK**.

d. Click **cell F4**, click **More Functions** in the Function Library group, click **Statistical**, and then select **AVERAGEIF**. Do the following:
   - Select the **range A8:A93** to enter the range in the Range box.
   - Press **Tab** and type **Introductory** in the **Criteria box**.
   - Press **Tab**, select the **range G8:G93** to enter the range in the Average_range box, and then click **OK**.

e. Click **cell F5**, click **More Functions** in the Function Library group, click **Statistical**, and then select **COUNTIF**. Do the following:
   - Select the **range A8:A93** to enter the range in the Range box.
   - Press **Tab**, type **Introductory** in the **Criteria box**, and then click **OK**.

f. Click **cell G3**, click **Math & Trig** in the Function Library group, scroll through the list, and then select **SUMIFS**. Do the following:
- Select the **range G8:G93** to enter the range in the Sum_range box.
- Press **Tab** and select the **range A8:A93** to enter the range in the Criteria_range1 box.
- Press **Tab** and type **Introductory** in the **Criteria1 box**.
- Press **Tab** and select the **range B8:B93** to enter the range in the Criteria_range2 box.
- Press **Tab**, type **General** in the **Criteria2 box**, and then click **OK**.

g. Click **cell G4**, click **More Functions** in the Function Library group, click **Statistical**, and then select **AVERAGEIFS**. Do the following:
- Select the **range G8:G93** to enter the range in the Average_range box.
- Press **Tab** and select the **range A8:A93** to enter the range in the Criteria_range1 box.
- Press **Tab** and type **Introductory** in the **Criteria1 box**.
- Press **Tab** and select the **range B8:B93** to enter the range in the Criteria_range2 box.
- Press **Tab**, type **General** in the **Criteria2 box**, and then click **OK**.

h. Click **cell G5**, click **More Functions** in the Function Library group, click **Statistical**, scroll through the list, and then select **COUNTIFS**. Do the following:
- Select the **range A8:A93** to enter the range in the Criteria_range1 box.
- Press **Tab** and type **Introductory** in the **Criteria1 box**.
- Press **Tab** and select the **range B8:B93** to enter the range in the Criteria_range2 box.
- Press **Tab**, type **General** in the **Criteria2 box**, and then click **OK**.

i. Select the **range F3:G4**, apply **Accounting Number Format** with zero decimal places, and then adjust column widths as needed.

j. Click **cell H8**, type **=rank**, and then double-click **RANK.AVG** from the Formula AutoComplete list. Click **G8**, type a comma, select the **range G8:G93**, press **F4** to make the range absolute, and then press **Ctrl+Enter** to enter =RANK.AVG(G8,$G$8:$G$93).

k. Double-click the **cell H8 fill handle** to copy the formula down the Rank column. Sort the list in ascending order by the Rank column.

l. Click **cell B3**, click the **FORMULAS tab**, click **More Functions** in the Function Library group, click **Statistical**, and then scroll through the list.

m. Select **QUARTILE.EXC** and type **G$8:G$93** in the **Array box** to create a mixed reference in which row numbers will not change when you copy the formula down. Press **Tab**, type **A3** in the **Quart box** to refer to the first quartile, and then click **OK**. Copy the formula to the **range B4:B5**. The array argument does not change, but the quart argument changes to reflect the correct quartile.

n. Format the **range B3:B5** with **Accounting Number Format** with zero decimal places. Apply the **Bottom Border style** to **cell B5**, if necessary.

o. Create a footer with your name on the left side, the sheet name code in the center, and the file name code on the right side.

p. Save and close the workbook, and submit based on your instructor's directions.

2 Customer Satisfaction

You have been hired to analyze the effectiveness of a local restaurant's drive-thru service. As part of your analysis, you plan to evaluate customer satisfaction. You hypothesize that customer satisfaction decreases as wait time increases. You have collected a cross-section sample of 20 customers' wait time and satisfaction levels based on the ordinal range of 1 to 5, with 1 being least satisfied and 5 being most satisfied. You will use the Analysis ToolPak to complete the next steps. This exercise follows the same set of skills as used in Hands-On Exercises 2 and 3 in the chapter. Refer to Figure 8.26 as you complete this exercise.

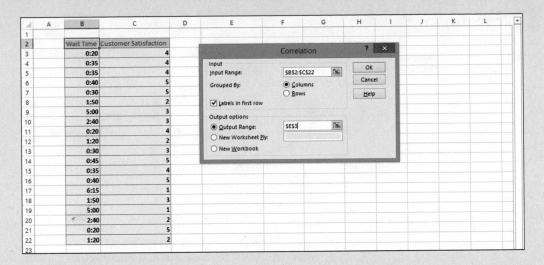

FIGURE 8.26 Correlation Coefficient

a. Open *e08p2WaitTime* and save it as **e08p2WaitTime_LastFirst**.

b. Load the Analysis ToolPak, if necessary, by completing the following:
   - Click the **FILE tab** on the Ribbon.
   - Click **Options** and select **Add-Ins** on the left side of the Excel Options Window.
   - Select **Excel Add-ins** from the Manage box and click **Go**.
   - Click **Analysis ToolPak** from the Add-Ins window and click **OK**.

c. Click the **DATA tab** and click **Data Analysis** from the Analysis group.

d. Select **Correlation**, click **OK**, and then complete the following:
   - Type **B2:C22** in the **Input Range box**.
   - Click the **Columns radio button** to group by columns if it is not selected.
   - Click the **Labels in first row check box** if it is not selected.
   - Click the **Output Range radio button** and type **E3** to place the results beginning in that cell.
   - Click **OK**.

e. Select **columns E, F, and G**, click the **HOME tab**, and then choose **AutoFit Column Width** from the Format menu in the Cells group.

   The correlation results of –0.73034472 indicates a fairly strong negative relationship between wait time and satisfaction. This supports your hypothesis that the longer the wait, the less satisfied customers become.

f. Create a footer with your name on the left side, the sheet name code in the center, and the file name code on the right side.

g. Save and close the workbook, and submit based on your instructor's directions.

Mid-Level Exercises

1 Investment Banking

FROM SCRATCH

You are an investment banker and you would like to put together a brief statistical report of the most viewed stock quotes for the day. To complete this task, you will research stock prices at www.nasdaq.com/quotes and create a report using the Analysis ToolPak.

a. Open Excel and create a new workbook. Save the workbook as **e08m1Stocks_LastFirst**.

b. Navigate to **www.nasdaq.com/quotes/real-time.aspx** and locate the five most-viewed stock prices for the day.

c. Type **Symbol** in **cell B2** and type **Last Sale Price** in **cell C3**.

d. Type the corresponding stock symbols and prices in **columns B** and **C**.

e. Load the Analysis ToolPak add-in, if necessary, as described in the chapter.

DISCOVER

f. Use the Data Analysis command and select **Descriptive Statistics**. Use the following specifications:
   - Select the **range C2:C7** as the input range.
   - Select or deselect the **Labels in first row check box**, based on the input data you selected.
   - Select the **output range E2**.
   - Select **Summary statistics**.

g. Create a footer with your name on the left side, the name of the worksheet in the middle, and the file name code on the right side.

h. Save and close the workbook, and submit based on your instructor's directions.

2 Reading Comprehension Scores

ANALYSIS CASE

As an elementary school principal, you are concerned about students' reading comprehension. You brought in a reading consultant to help design an experimental study to compare the current teaching method (the control group), a stand-alone computer-based training (CBT) program, and a combination of the traditional teaching method and CBT (hybrid). The consultant randomly assigned 72 third-grade students into three groups of 24 each. During the two-week study, students were taught reading comprehension skills based on the respective methodology. At the end of the two-week period, students completed a standardized reading comprehension test. The consultant prepared a worksheet listing the test scores for each group. No student names or IDs were reported to you.

Now you want to calculate some general statistics and then conduct a one-way analysis of variance (ANOVA). Doing so will enable you to compare the three sample group means and evaluate the variances within each group compared to the variances among the three groups. The null hypothesis is that sample means are equal.

a. Open *e08m2Stats* and save it as **e08m2Stats_LastFirst**.

b. Calculate the descriptive statistics in the **range F2:H8**. For the variance and standard deviation, use the functions that include the *.S* descriptor. Format the values with **Comma format** with three decimal places.

c. Check the DATA tab to see if it contains the Data Analysis command. If not, load the Analysis ToolPak add-in program as directed in the chapter.

d. Use the Data Analysis command and select the **Anova: Single Factor tool**. Use the following specifications:
   - Select the **range A1:C25** as the input range.
   - Select the **Labels in first row check box**.
   - Confirm the alpha value is *0.05*.
   - Place the **Output Range** starting in **cell E11**.

e. Apply **Comma format** with three decimal places to the averages and variances in the ANOVA table. Verify that the averages and variances in the ANOVA table match those you calculated in the *General Stats* section. If they do not match, correct the functions in the *General Stats* section. If needed, format the P-value with **Comma format** with six decimal places.

DISCOVER

f. Use a statistics book or the Internet to research how to compare and interpret the 0.05 alpha and the calculated P-value to determine if you accept or reject the null hypotheses. Insert a comment in the **P-value cell** on your decision and interpretation.

★ **g.** Answer the questions on the Q&A worksheet.

h. Apply **landscape orientation** to the Reading Performance Scores worksheet.

i. Create a footer with your name on the left side, the sheet name code in the center, and the file name code on the right side.

j. Save and close the workbook, and submit based on your instructor's directions.

3 Portfolio Analysis

COLLABORATION CASE

You are a financial advisor, and a client would like you to complete an analysis of his portfolio. As part of the analysis, you will perform basic analysis of value by type of commodity, calculate basic descriptive statistics with the Analysis ToolPak, and answer client questions. Your client is located in DC and you are in New York, so you have decided to send him the completed file via SkyDrive after completion for review.

Student 1:

a. Open *e08m3Portfolio* and save it as **e08m3Portfolio_LastFirst**.

b. Use the RANK.AVG function to calculate the rank of the current values of each investment in **cell F6**. Use the fill handle to complete the column.

c. Use the COUNTIF function to determine the total number of bonds in the portfolio in **cell I6**.

d. Use the fill handle to copy the function down the **range I7:I8**. Be sure to use the appropriate absolute or mixed cell references.

e. Use the SUMIF function to determine the total value of bonds in the portfolio in **cell J6**.

f. Use the fill handle to copy the function down the **range J7:J8**. Be sure to use the appropriate absolute or mixed cell references.

g. Load the Analysis ToolPak, if necessary.

h. Create a descriptive statistics summary based on the current value of investments in column E. Display the output in **cell H11**.

i. Format the mean, median, mode, standard deviation, minimum, maximum, and sum in the report as **Accounting Number Format**.

j. Answer the questions in the Q&A worksheet.

k. Save the document to your SkyDrive account and share the file with Student 2.

Student 2:

l. Open the workbook located on SkyDrive and save it as **e08m3PortfolioReview_LastFirst**.

m. Sort column F from smallest to largest.

n. Locate the three lowest-valued commodities and apply the **Bad Cell Style** to the entire range.

o. Type **Sell assets highlighted in red** in **cell D25**.

p. Save and close the workbook, and submit based on your instructor's directions.

Stock Market Research

RESEARCH CASE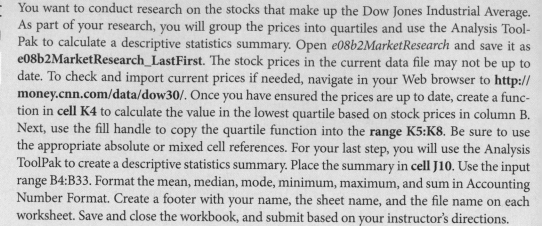

You want to conduct research on the stocks that make up the Dow Jones Industrial Average. As part of your research, you will group the prices into quartiles and use the Analysis Tool-Pak to calculate a descriptive statistics summary. Open *e08b2MarketResearch* and save it as **e08b2MarketResearch_LastFirst**. The stock prices in the current data file may not be up to date. To check and import current prices if needed, navigate in your Web browser to **http://money.cnn.com/data/dow30/**. Once you have ensured the prices are up to date, create a function in **cell K4** to calculate the value in the lowest quartile based on stock prices in column B. Next, use the fill handle to copy the quartile function into the **range K5:K8**. Be sure to use the appropriate absolute or mixed cell references. For your last step, you will use the Analysis ToolPak to create a descriptive statistics summary. Place the summary in **cell J10**. Use the input range B4:B33. Format the mean, median, mode, minimum, maximum, and sum in Accounting Number Format. Create a footer with your name, the sheet name, and the file name on each worksheet. Save and close the workbook, and submit based on your instructor's directions.

Taste Test

DISASTER RECOVERY

After receiving negative feedback on their older menu items, Lecxe Bakery decided to create a new menu of desserts. Before taking their desserts to production, they decided to conduct a taste-test survey based on a random cross-section sample of their client base. Your task as production manager is to analyze the results. You will calculate the frequency of responses as percentages as well as complete an ANOVA summary of the data using the Analysis ToolPak. Open *e08b3Survey* and save it as **e08b3Survey_LastFirst**. Using the response options in the range F6:F10, create a frequency that calculates the percentage of respondents that answered 1 through 5. Be sure to format the results with **Percentage number format**. Next, set columns G and H to **AutoFit Column Width**. Create a pie chart with the appropriate labels to visually document the information.

Your last step is to complete an ANOVA summary using the Analysis ToolPak. Create an ANOVA report starting in **cell F23** using the **range B5:D35**. Create a footer with your name, the sheet name, and the file name on each worksheet. Save and close the workbook, and submit based on your instructor's directions.

Performance Evaluation

SOFT SKILLS CASE S

You are an HR associate and have been given the task of analyzing employee performance. As part of the task, you will calculate the percentage rank based on salary as well as the frequency of occurrence based on quartiles.

Open the workbook *e08b4Performance* and save it as **08b4Performance_LastFirst**. Create a function in **cell D4** that calculates the percent rank excluding 0, then use the fill handle to complete the column. Sort the column from smallest to largest. Create a function in **cell G5** that calculates the salary range of the first quartile. Use the fill handle to populate **cells G6:G7**, making sure to use appropriate cell referencing. Calculate the frequency of salaries based on the quartile ranges in the range G5:G7. Craft the frequency function to display results as percentages. Change the fill color of each range of cells in column C based on quartile. Create a footer with your name, the sheet name, and the file name on each worksheet. Save and close the workbook, and submit based on your instructor's directions.

Capstone Exercise

You are the HR director for a Fortune 500 marketing company. You would like to research employees' overall salaries as they affect job satisfaction. To complete this task, you administered a survey to a cross-section sample of all employees across the company.

Use Conditional Math and Statistical Functions

You would like to calculate basic demographic information about the sample you have collected. You will calculate the average job satisfaction and salary by position, as well as specific information regarding directors and managers.

a. Open *e08c1Satisfaction* and save it as **e08c1Satisfaction_LastFirst**.

b. Enter a conditional function in **cell I5** to calculate average satisfaction for support staff. Format the results with the **Number format** and two decimal positions.

c. Use the fill handle in **cell I5** to copy the function down through the **range I6:I9**. Be sure to use the appropriate mixed or absolute referencing.

d. Enter a function in **cell J5** to calculate the average salary of all support staff in the survey.

e. Use the fill handle in **cell J5** to copy the function down through the **range J6:J9**. Be sure to use the appropriate mixed or absolute referencing.

f. Enter a function in **cell I12** to calculate the number of directors in the survey that have a job satisfaction level of 4 or higher.

g. Enter a function in **cell I13** to calculate the average salary of directors in the survey that have a job satisfaction level of 4 or higher.

h. Adapt the process used in steps f and g to calculate the total number and average salary of managers that have a job satisfaction of 4 or higher.

Calculate Relative Standing with Statistical Functions

To continue your analysis, you will calculate salary rankings as well as salary quartile thresholds.

a. Enter a function in **cell F4** that calculates the rank of the salary in **cell D4** against the range of salaries in the dataset.

b. Use the fill handle to copy the function down **column F**. Be sure to include the appropriate absolute or mixed cell references.

c. Enter a function in **cell I20** to calculate the minimum quartile value in the list of salaries.

d. Use the fill handle to complete the remaining quartile values in **range I21:I24**. Be sure to include the appropriate absolute or mixed cell references.

Measure of Central Tendency

You would like to test the strength of the relationship between satisfaction and salary. You will use the CORREL function to complete your calculation.

a. Enter a function in **cell H27** to calculate the correlation of columns D and E.

b. Format the results as **Number Format** with two decimal positions.

Using the Analysis ToolPak

To complete your analyses, you will create a summary of descriptive statistics using the Analysis ToolPak. Be sure to activate the Analysis ToolPak add-in before beginning the next steps.

a. Click the **DATA tab** and select **Data Analysis**. Select **Descriptive Statistics** and click **OK**.

b. Complete the input criteria using the salary data in **column D**.

c. Set the output functions to display on a new worksheet.

d. Name the newly created worksheet **Descriptive Statistics**.

Create a Histogram

Your last step is to create a histogram with the Analysis ToolPak, based on the quartile criteria determined earlier.

a. Click the **DATA tab** and select **Data Analysis**. Select **Histogram** and click **OK**.

b. Use the salaries in **column D** as the input range.

c. Use the quartiles in the **range I20:I24** as the bin range.

d. Output the data in **cell H29**. Be sure to include a chart with the output.

e. Format the chart and output table accordingly.

f. Save and close the workbook, and submit based on your instructor's directions.

Multiple-Sheet Workbook Management

Ensuring Quality Control

OBJECTIVES AFTER YOU READ THIS CHAPTER, YOU WILL BE ABLE TO:

1. Work with grouped worksheets p. 394

2. Manage windows and workspaces p. 397

3. Insert hyperlinks p. 399

4. Insert a 3-D formula p. 407

5. Link workbooks p. 409

6. Audit formulas p. 417

7. Set up a Watch Window p. 419

8. Validate data p. 420

CASE STUDY | Circle City Sporting Goods

You are the regional manager of Circle City Sporting Goods (CSG), which has locations in Indianapolis, Bloomington, and South Bend. CSG is a comprehensive retailer that sells athletic apparel, exercise equipment, footwear, camping gear, sports gear, and sports nutrition items. Each store manager gathers data for every department monthly and prepares a quarterly worksheet. Because each store contains the same departments, the worksheets are identical. Having an identical structure helps you consolidate sales data for all three locations.

You want to review sales data for the past fiscal year. Before consolidating data, you need to format the worksheets, copy data to the summary sheet, and then insert hyperlinks from the summary sheet back to the individual quarterly sheets in the Indianapolis workbook. Later, you will consolidate data from the Indianapolis, Bloomington, and South Bend workbooks into a regional workbook. Finally, you will use auditing tools to identify errors in the Bloomington workbook and add validation to ensure users enter correct data.

Multiple Worksheets

A workbook can contain one or more worksheets of related data. Deciding how to structure data into multiple worksheets and how to manage these worksheets is important. You should determine how much data to enter on each worksheet, when to divide data among several worksheets, and how to format worksheets efficiently. You might also want to create links among the worksheets to enable efficient navigation. For example, you can create a documentation worksheet and then insert links to each worksheet.

After you design multiple worksheets in a workbook, you might want to display worksheets side by side or in a particular arrangement. You can also save the worksheet view layout so that it retains a specific view when you open the workbook again.

In this section, you will work with multiple worksheets and insert hyperlinks from one worksheet to other worksheets. In addition, you will group worksheets together to enter data and apply formatting. Finally, you will manage windows by controlling worksheet visibility, opening and arranging windows, splitting a window, and saving a workspace.

Working with Grouped Worksheets

You often work with workbooks that contain several worksheets. For example, a workbook might contain sales data on one worksheet, a column chart on another sheet, and a PivotTable on a third sheet. In addition, you might create scenarios with Scenario Manager, generate a scenario summary report on a new worksheet or create a Solver model, and then generate a Solver answer report on a new worksheet. In these situations, in order to organize data, the original data are separated into separate worksheets from the consolidated analysis.

Worksheets within a workbook often contain similar content and formatting. For example, a budget workbook might contain detailed monthly data on separate worksheets. By placing monthly data on separate worksheets, you can focus on one month's data at a time instead of presenting the entire year's worth of data on only one worksheet. When worksheets contain similar data but for different time periods—such as months—or different company locations—such as department store locations in various states—you should structure and format the data the same on all worksheets. For example, each monthly worksheet in the yearly budget workbook should contain an identical structure and format for the list of income and expenses. The only differences among the worksheets are the actual values and the column labels that identify the respective months.

Creating worksheets with identical structure and formatting provides consistency and continuity when working with the same type of data on multiple worksheets. In addition, it helps you locate particular items quickly on all worksheets because you know the structure is identical.

Group and Ungroup Worksheets

STEP 1 Although you can design and format worksheets individually, you can improve your productivity by designing and formatting the worksheets as a group. *Grouping* is the process of selecting two or more worksheets so that you can perform the same action at the same time on all selected worksheets. Table 9.1 describes how to group worksheets. Excel displays grouped worksheet tabs with a white background color and green line spanning the length of all grouped worksheets, and [Group] appears in the title bar.

TABLE 9.1 Grouping Worksheets	
To Group:	**Do This:**
All worksheets	Right-click a worksheet tab and select Select All Sheets.
Adjacent worksheets	Click the first worksheet tab, press and hold Shift, and then click the last worksheet tab.
Nonadjacent worksheet tabs	Click the first worksheet tab, press and hold Ctrl, and then click each additional worksheet tab.

Ungrouping is the process of deselecting grouped worksheets so that actions performed on one sheet do not affect other worksheets. To ungroup worksheets, click a worksheet tab for a sheet that is not grouped. If you grouped all worksheets, right-click a worksheet tab and select Ungroup Sheets.

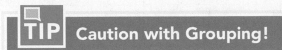

TIP Caution with Grouping!

Make sure that you ungroup worksheets when you want to perform a task on only one worksheet. If you forget to ungroup sheets, you could potentially ruin several worksheets by overwriting data on all worksheets instead of just the active worksheet.

Enter Data and Format Grouped Worksheets

STEP 2 >> Grouping worksheets enables you to improve your productivity by performing the same tasks on the grouped worksheets at the same time instead of performing the tasks individually on each worksheet. Grouping worksheets helps you enter data, change the worksheet structure, apply page layouts, and print worksheets. Whatever you do to the active worksheet also affects the other grouped worksheets.

Data Entry

You can enter labels, values, dates, and formulas efficiently on grouped worksheets, saving you from entering the same data on each worksheet individually. For example, if you enter row labels in the range A5:A10 to describe the different types of monthly income and expenses, Excel enters the same data in the same location (the range A5:A10) on the other grouped worksheets. When you enter a formula on grouped worksheets, Excel enters the formula in the same cell address on all grouped worksheets. For example, if you enter =A4-B4 in cell C4 on the active worksheet, Excel enters =A4-B4 in cell C4 on all grouped worksheets. The formulas use the values on the respective worksheets.

Structural Changes

If you insert a row between rows 4 and 5 and widen column B on the active worksheet, Excel inserts a row between rows 4 and 5 and widens column B on all grouped worksheets. You can cut, copy, and paste data to the same locations and delete cell contents, rows, and columns on grouped worksheets. You can also copy, delete, or hide a group of worksheets.

Formatting

You can apply font formats (e.g., font, font size, bold, font color), alignment settings (e.g., top-left vertical alignment, center horizontal alignment, wrap text), and number formats (e.g., Accounting Number Format, Percent Style, and decimal points) in the same cells on grouped worksheets. Figure 9.1 shows worksheets that were grouped to enter and format data.

Page Layouts and Printing

You can group worksheets, and then apply identical headers, set the page orientation, set the print areas, and adjust the scaling all at one time instead of applying these page layouts individually to each worksheet. After grouping worksheets, you can display them in Print Preview, select print settings, and then finally print the grouped worksheets.

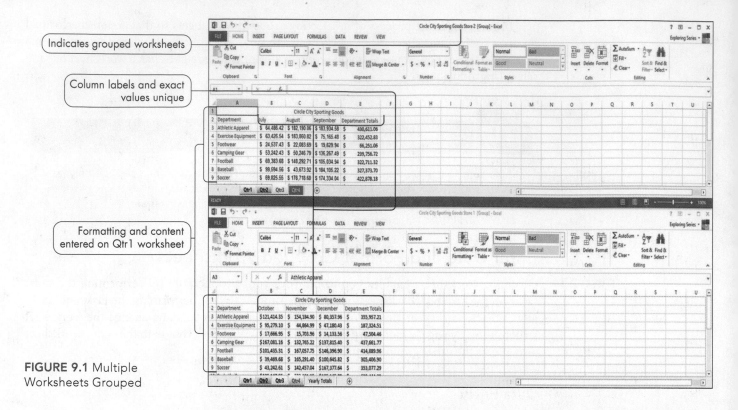

Indicates grouped worksheets

Column labels and exact values unique

Formatting and content entered on Qtr1 worksheet

FIGURE 9.1 Multiple Worksheets Grouped

TIP | **Unavailable Tasks**

Some tasks are not available on grouped worksheets. These tasks appear grayed out on the Ribbon or in menus. For example, you cannot apply conditional formatting or format data as a table on grouped worksheets. Most commands such as PivotTable on the Insert tab are unavailable for grouped worksheets.

Fill Across Worksheets

The previous discussion assumes you are entering new data or formatting existing data across several worksheets at the same time. However, you might have created and formatted only one worksheet, and now you want to copy the data and formats to other worksheets. Instead of using the Copy and Paste commands or copying the entire worksheet, you can fill the data to other worksheets to save time and reduce potential errors, such as formatting the wrong area or forgetting to format a worksheet. To fill data and/or formats from one sheet to other sheets, do the following:

1. Click the worksheet tab that contains the data and/or formats you want to copy. Select the range that you want to fill across the worksheets.
2. Press Ctrl while you click the destination worksheet tabs—the worksheets that you want the data and/or formats applied to.
3. Click the HOME tab, click Fill in the Editing group, and then select Across Worksheets to open the Fill Across Worksheets dialog box (see Figure 9.2).
4. Click All to copy data and formats, click Contents to copy the data only without the formatting, or click Formats to copy only the formatting to the other grouped worksheets. Click OK.

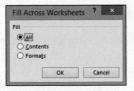

FIGURE 9.2 Fill Across Worksheet Dialog Box

Excel copies the data and/or formatting to the same cells in the other worksheets. For example, if cell A1 in the original worksheet contains the text *Heartland Department Store* bold, centered, and in 14-pt font, Excel copies this text and formatting to cell A1 in the grouped worksheets.

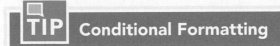

> **TIP** Conditional Formatting
>
> Excel disables the Conditional Formatting feature when you group worksheets. You cannot group worksheets and then create and manage conditional formats. However, you can create a conditional formatting rule on one worksheet, group the worksheets, and then use the Fill Across Worksheets command to replicate the conditional formatting rule to a range on other worksheets.

Managing Windows and Workspaces

Because a workbook may contain several worksheets, you need to be able to manage the worksheets onscreen to help you focus on particular worksheets and reduce information overload. To help you manage worksheet windows, you can control worksheet visibility, open and arrange windows for ease of use, split a window to see different parts of a worksheet, and save the layout of the worksheet windows.

Control Visibility of Worksheets

STEP 4 » If a workbook contains so many worksheets that each corresponding tab is not visible, use the worksheet scroll buttons on the left side of the worksheet tabs to find the worksheet you need. If you do not need to view a worksheet, you can hide it. Hiding worksheets is helpful to keep visible only those worksheet tabs that you are currently working on to minimize scrolling through worksheet tabs or when you want to display worksheets on a projector in a meeting but you do not want to accidently click a worksheet containing confidential data. To hide a worksheet, right-click a worksheet tab and select Hide, or do the following:

1. Select the worksheet or worksheets you want to hide. If you want to hide a single worksheet, click the respective worksheet tab. If you want to hide two or more worksheets, select their tabs in a similar way to that with which you group worksheets.
2. Click the HOME tab and click Format in the Cells group.
3. Point to Hide & Unhide and select Hide Sheet.

When you need to display a hidden worksheet again, click Format in the Cells group, point to Hide & Unhide, and then select Unhide Sheet. Excel then opens the Unhide dialog box (see Figure 9.3). Select the worksheet that you want to display and click OK.

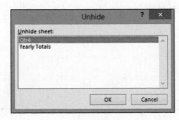

FIGURE 9.3 Unhide Dialog Box

Open and Arrange Windows

You might want to see the contents of two worksheets in the same workbook at the same time. For example, you might want to compare the Qtr1 and Qtr2 worksheets simultaneously. Instead of clicking back and forth between worksheet tabs, you can open another window of the same workbook, and then display different worksheets within each window.

Open Another Window. To open another window of the current workbook, click the View tab, and then click New Window in the Window group. Excel opens another window of the workbook. The title bar adds *:1* to the original workbook view and *:2* to the second window. Although only one window appears maximized, both windows are open. There is no limit to the number of windows that can be opened.

Arrange the Windows. To see all windows of the same workbook, click Arrange All in the Window group. Select one of the options from the Arrange Windows dialog box (see Figure 9.4). You can display windows in a tiled arrangement, horizontally, vertically, or in a cascaded view. If you have other workbooks open when you click Arrange All, Excel includes those workbook windows. To display windows for the current workbook only, click the *Windows of active workbook* check box.

FIGURE 9.4 Arrange Windows Dialog Box

Split a Window

When you work with very large, complex worksheets, you may need to view different sections at the same time. For example, you may need to look at input data on rows 5 and 6 and see how changing the data affects overall results on row 150. To see these different worksheet sections at the same time, split the worksheet window. *Splitting* is the process of dividing a worksheet window into two or four resizable panes so you can view separate parts of a worksheet at the same time (see Figure 9.5). All panes are part of the one worksheet. Any changes you make to one pane affect the entire worksheet.

To divide a worksheet into panes, click Split in the Window group on the View tab. Depending on which cell is the active cell, Excel splits the worksheet into two or four panes with *split bars*—vertical and horizontal lines that frame the panes—above and to the left of the active cell. If the active cell is in row 1, the worksheet appears in two *vertical* panes. If the active cell is in column A, the worksheet appears in two *horizontal* panes. If the active cell is cell A1 or any cell besides in the first row or first column, the worksheet appears in four panes.

Once the window is split, you can further customize the display by dragging the horizontal or vertical line that appears. Drag the vertical split bar to divide the worksheet into left and right (vertical) panes. Drag the horizontal split bar to divide the worksheet into upper and lower (horizontal) panes. While the active cell will be mirrored across all split panes, you can scroll each pane to the desired range you wish to see.

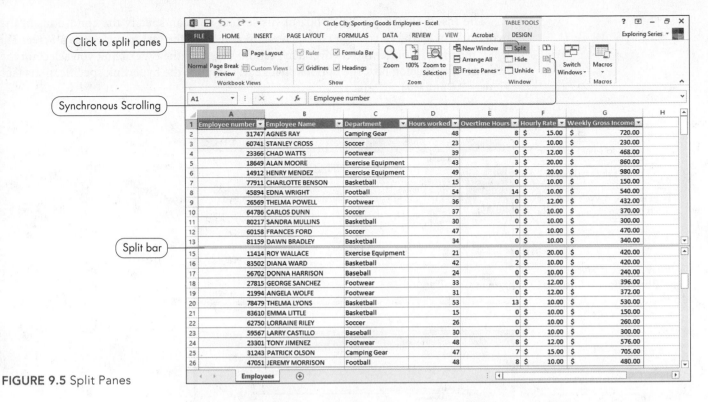

Click to split panes

Synchronous Scrolling

Split bar

FIGURE 9.5 Split Panes

To remove panes, click Split in the Window group, or double-click the split bar, or drag a vertical split bar to the left or right edge of the worksheet window or a horizontal split bar to the top or bottom of the worksheet window.

> **TIP | Other Window Settings**
>
> The Window group on the View tab contains options to enable you to view two worksheet windows side by side and synchronize the scrolling for both windows or enable separate scrolling. If you have adjusted the window sizes, you can reset the open worksheet windows to share the screen equally. In addition, you can hide a worksheet if you do not want to display it, or you can display a previously hidden worksheet window. However, you cannot use the Freeze Panes settings and split bars at the same time.

Inserting Hyperlinks

STEP 3 ⟫

When you create a workbook that has multiple worksheets, you might want to include a documentation worksheet that is similar to a table of contents. On the documentation worksheet, enter labels to describe each worksheet, and then create hyperlinks to the respective worksheets. A *hyperlink*, or link, is an electronic marker that, when clicked, connects to another location in the same or a different worksheet, another file, a Web page, or an e-mail. To create a hyperlink, click the cell that will contain the hyperlink or select an object, such as an image, that you want to use as the hyperlink, and then do one of the following:

1. Click the INSERT tab and click Hyperlink in the Links group.
2. Right-click the cell or object and select Hyperlink.
3. Click a cell or object and press Ctrl+K.

The Insert Hyperlink dialog box opens so that you can specify the conditions of the hyperlink. In addition, you can click ScreenTip and enter the text to appear as a ScreenTip when the mouse pointer hovers over a hyperlink. Based on the type of link you select on the left side of the dialog box, the options change to complete the hyperlink specifications (see Figures 9.6 and 9.7).

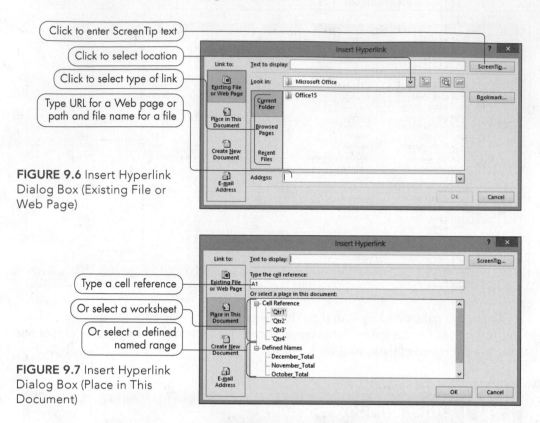

FIGURE 9.6 Insert Hyperlink Dialog Box (Existing File or Web Page)

FIGURE 9.7 Insert Hyperlink Dialog Box (Place in This Document)

Hyperlink Objects

You have the ability to add hyperlinks to more than just text. You have the ability to add links to inserted images and objects as well.

Workbook hyperlinks are similar to Web page hyperlinks. Textual hyperlinks appear blue with a blue underline. When you position the mouse pointer over a hyperlink, the pointer looks like a hand, and Excel displays a default ScreenTip indicating where the link will take you or the custom ScreenTip if you created one in the Set Hyperlink ScreenTip dialog box (see Figure 9.8). Click the link to jump to the link's destination. After you click a hyperlink, the color changes to purple so that you can distinguish between links you have clicked and links you have not clicked. The hyperlink color changes back to blue after a period of time.

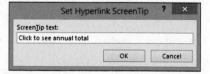

FIGURE 9.8 Set Hyperlink ScreenTip Dialog Box

To modify a hyperlink, right-click it, and then select Edit Hyperlink to open the Edit Hyperlink dialog box, which is similar to the Insert Hyperlink dialog box. Make the desired changes and click OK. To remove a hyperlink, right-click it and select Remove Hyperlink. This action removes the hyperlink but does not delete the cell contents or object.

Quick **Concepts**

1. What are the benefits of grouping worksheets? *p. 394*

2. What are the benefits of using Split window? *p. 398*

3. Besides linking inside a worksheet, where else can hyperlinks lead the user? *p. 399*

Hands-On Exercises

1 Multiple Worksheets

After reviewing last year's fiscal data, you need to improve the appearance of the worksheets for Circle City Sporting Goods. You need to enter a missing heading on the summary worksheet and enter formulas across the quarterly worksheets. To save time, you will group the worksheets to perform tasks to all grouped worksheets at the same time. After you complete the quarterly worksheets, you will insert hyperlinks from the yearly worksheet to the quarterly worksheets.

Skills covered: Group and Fill Across Worksheets • Enter and Format Data Across Worksheets • Insert Hyperlinks • Open and Arrange Worksheets

STEP 1 ≫ GROUP AND FILL ACROSS WORKSHEETS

You noticed that the main title and the row headings are displayed only in the Qtr1 worksheet in the Indianapolis workbook. You need to fill in the title and row headings for the other three quarterly and the yearly worksheets. Refer to Figure 9.9 as you complete Step 1.

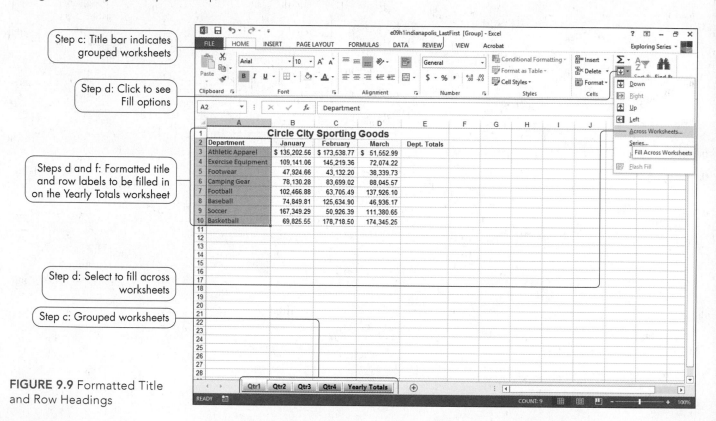

FIGURE 9.9 Formatted Title and Row Headings

a. Open *e09h1Indianapolis* and save it as **e09h1Indianapolis_LastFirst**.

> **TROUBLESHOOTING:** If you make any major mistakes in this exercise, you can close the file, open *e09h1Indianapolis* again, and then start this exercise over.

b. Click the **Qtr1 worksheet tab** and click each worksheet tab to see the differences.

The Qtr1 worksheet contains a title and row labels, whereas the Qtr2, Qtr3, and Qtr4 worksheets are missing the title, row labels, and number formatting. The Yearly Totals worksheet is empty.

c. Click the **Qtr1 worksheet tab**, press and hold **Shift**, and then click the **Yearly Totals worksheet tab**.

> You grouped all worksheets together. Anything you do now affects all grouped worksheets. The title bar displays *[Group]* after the file name.

d. Click **cell A1** in the Qtr1 worksheet to select it, click **Fill** in the Editing group on the HOME tab, and then select **Across Worksheets**.

> The Fill Across Worksheets dialog box opens so that you can select what to fill from the active worksheet to the other grouped worksheets. The default option is All, which will fill in both the content and the formatting.

e. Click **OK**.

> Excel fills in the formatted title from the Qtr1 worksheet to the other worksheets.

f. Select the **range A2:A10** on the Qtr1 worksheet, click **Fill** in the Editing group on the HOME tab, select **Across Worksheets**, and then click **OK**.

> **TROUBLESHOOTING:** Do not select the range A1:D9 to fill across worksheets. If you do, you will overwrite the other worksheet data with the January, February, and March labels and data. If this happens, click Undo to restore data in the other worksheets.

g. Right-click the **Yearly Totals worksheet tab** and select **Ungroup Sheets**. Click each worksheet to review the results. Save the workbook once review is complete.

> You ungrouped the worksheets. Now all grouped worksheets contain the formatted title and row labels that were copied across worksheets.

STEP 2 >> ENTER AND FORMAT DATA ACROSS WORKSHEETS

You need to regroup the worksheets so that you can increase the width of column A. In addition, you want to insert monthly and department totals for the quarterly worksheets. Refer to Figure 9.10 as you complete Step 2.

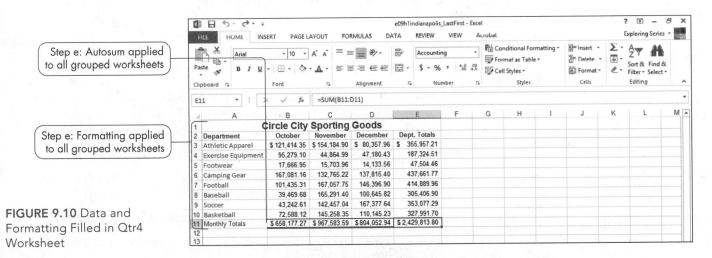

FIGURE 9.10 Data and Formatting Filled in Qtr4 Worksheet

a. Right-click the **Yearly Totals worksheet tab** and select **Select All Sheets**.

b. Click **cell A2**, click **Format** in the Cells group, select **Column Width**, type **18** in the **Column width box**, and then click **OK**.

> You set the column width to 18 for the first column in the grouped worksheets, ensuring that column A's width is identical among the worksheets.

c. Right-click the **Qtr1 worksheet tab** and select **Ungroup Sheets**.

d. Press and hold **Shift** and click the **Qtr4 worksheet tab**.

> You have to ungroup sheets and group only the four quarterly worksheets to perform the next few steps.

e. Do the following to the grouped quarterly worksheets:

- Select the **range B3:E11** and click **AutoSum** in the Editing group to insert department totals in column E and monthly totals in row 11.
- Apply **Accounting Number Format** to the **ranges B3:E3** and **B11:E11** to display $ and commas for the first and total rows.
- Type **Monthly Totals** in **cell A11**. Apply bold, increase indent, and **Purple font color**.
- Type **Dept. Totals** in **cell E2**. Use Format Painter to copy the formats from **cell D2** to **cell E2**.
- Select the **range B11:E11**, click the **Border arrow** in the Font group, and then select **Top and Double Bottom Border**.

You applied the Top and Double Bottom Border style to the monthly totals to conform to standard accounting formatting practices.

f. Right-click the **Qtr4 worksheet tab**, select **Ungroup Sheets**, click each quarterly worksheet tab to ensure the formats were applied to each worksheet, and then save the workbook.

STEP 3 ≫ INSERT HYPERLINKS

You want to insert hyperlinks on the Yearly Totals worksheet so that you can click a hyperlink to jump back to the respective quarterly worksheet quickly. Refer to Figure 9.11 as you complete Step 3.

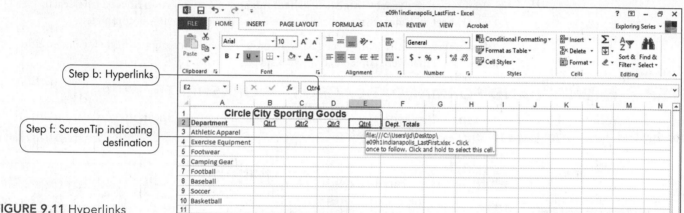

FIGURE 9.11 Hyperlinks

a. Click the **Yearly Totals worksheet tab**, type **Qtr1** in **cell B2**, and then use the fill handle to fill in the remaining quarter labels in the **range C2:E2**. Type **Dept. Totals** in **cell F2**. Center the labels. Increase the width of column F to **12**.

b. Click **cell B2**, click the **INSERT tab**, and then click **Hyperlink** in the Links group.

The Insert Hyperlink dialog box opens so that you can specify the destination when the user clicks the hyperlink.

c. Click **Place in This Document** in the *Link to* section on the left side of the dialog box.

d. Type **E2:E11** in the **Type the cell reference box**, click **'Qtr1'** in the **Or select a place in this document list**, and then click **OK**.

You created a hyperlink to the range E2:E11 in the Qtr1 worksheet. Note that if you do not specify a reference cell for the link it will default to cell A1.

e. Create the following hyperlinks by adapting steps b through d:

- **Cell C2**: Create a hyperlink to the **range E2:E11** in the Qtr2 worksheet.
- **Cell D2**: Create a hyperlink to the **range E2:E11** in the Qtr3 worksheet.
- **Cell E2**: Create a hyperlink to the **range E2:E11** in the Qtr4 worksheet.

f. Position the mouse pointer over cell E2.

The ScreenTip informs you where the hyperlink's destination is (see Figure 9.11). The path and file name shown on your screen will differ from those shown in the figure. If you had created a ScreenTip in the Insert Hyperlink dialog box, that text would appear instead of the destination.

g. Click the hyperlink in **cell E2**.

The hyperlink jumps to the destination: the range E2:E11 in the Qtr4 worksheet.

h. Click the **Yearly Totals worksheet tab** and click the other hyperlinks to ensure they work. When you are done, click the **Yearly Totals worksheet tab** and save the workbook.

> **TROUBLESHOOTING:** If a hyperlink does not jump to the correct range and worksheet, right-click the cell containing the wrong hyperlink, click Edit Hyperlink, and then edit the hyperlink in the Edit Hyperlink dialog box.

STEP 4 ➤➤ OPEN AND ARRANGE WORKSHEETS

You want to see the four quarterly sales data worksheets at the same time. To do this, you need to open additional windows of the workbook, and then arrange them. Refer to Figure 9.12 as you complete Step 4.

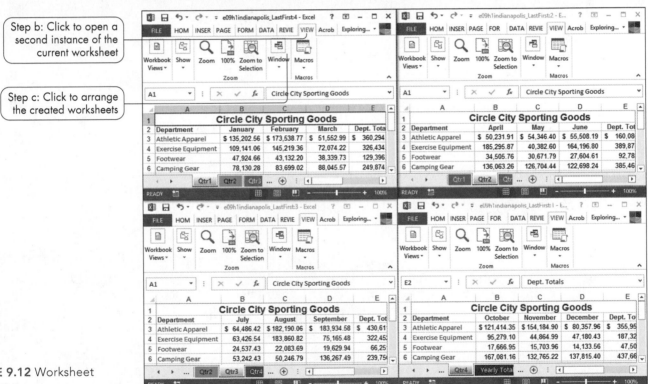

FIGURE 9.12 Worksheet Windows

a. Click the **VIEW tab** and click **New Window** in the Window group.

You opened another window of the same workbook. The title bar displays the same file name with *:2* at the end of the name.

b. Click **New Window** on the **VIEW tab** in the Window group twice.

Two new windows open with *:3* and *:4* at the end of each file name. You now have four windows open.

c. Click **Arrange All** in the Window group on the VIEW tab.

The Arrange Windows dialog box opens so you can specify how you want to arrange the open worksheet windows.

d. Click **Tiled**, if necessary, click the **Windows of active workbook check box**, and then click **OK**.

Clicking the *Windows of active workbook* check box ensures that the windows display for the active workbook. If you have other workbooks open, those windows do not display.

Excel arranges the four windows of the same workbook. Currently, all the windows display the Yearly Totals worksheet, but you will display a different worksheet in each window.

e. Click the **Qtr1 worksheet tab** twice in the top-left window, click the **Qtr2 worksheet tab** twice in the top-right window, click the **Qtr3 worksheet tab** twice in the bottom-left window, and click the **Qtr4 worksheet tab** twice in the bottom-right window.

f. Save the workbook. Keep the workbook open if you plan to continue with Hands-On Exercise 2. If not, close the workbook and exit Excel.

3-D Formulas and Linked Workbooks

Excel workbooks often contain data from different time periods, geographic regions, or products. For example, a workbook might contain a worksheet to store data for each week in a month, data for each location of a chain of department stores, or data for sales of each type of automobile produced by one manufacturer. While you have experience creating formulas and functions to perform calculations within one worksheet, you need to be able to consolidate, or combine, data from multiple worksheets into one. For example, you might want to consolidate sales data from all of your department store locations into one worksheet for the year.

Additional data analysis occurs over time. To avoid overloading a workbook with detailed sales data for several years, you might have detailed sales data in individual worksheets in one workbook for a specific year. You then might want to determine the average yearly sales for the past 10 years.

In this section, you will create a 3-D formula to consolidate data from several worksheets. In addition, you will learn how to link data from several workbooks to one workbook.

Inserting a 3-D Formula

STEP 1 You have referenced other cells in the same worksheet. For example, when you created a one-variable data table, you entered a reference, such as =B12, to display the contents of a formula in cell B12 instead of performing the calculation again in the one-variable data table. At times, you need to consolidate data from multiple worksheets into one worksheet. For example, you might want to create a yearly budget by consolidating values from monthly worksheets, or you might want to calculate average daily occupancy rates for a hospital from detailed weekly occupancy worksheets. When you create formulas that involve reference cells on different worksheets, you include worksheet references. A *3-D reference,* is a pointer to a cell in another worksheet, such as October!E3, which references cell E3 in the October worksheet. An exclamation point separates the worksheet name and the cell reference. If the value in cell E3 in the October worksheet changes, you do not have to edit the value in another worksheet; the reference does that for you automatically.

'Worksheet Name'!RangeOfCells

You can use worksheet references in formulas. For example, a formula that adds the values of cell E3 in the October, November, and December worksheets looks like this: =October!E3+November!E3+December!E3. If a worksheet name contains words separated by a space such as *October Sales*, single quotation marks surround the worksheet name, such as ='October Sales'!E3+'November Sales'!E3+'December Sales'!E3.

TIP CamelCase Notation

CamelCase notation is a file naming convention that eliminates spaces and capitalizes compound words—for example, OctoberSales.xlsx versus October sales.xlsx. By using a naming convention such as CamelCase, you can reduce some of the complexity of a 3-D formula by eliminating the need for single quotation marks.

Entering this type of formula manually or by using the semi-selection process is time-consuming to ensure you click every worksheet and every cell within the respective worksheets. When individual worksheets have an identical structure (i.e., totals for the Jewelry Department are in cell E7 in each quarterly worksheet), you can improve your efficiency in creating formulas by using a ***3-D formula***, which is a formula or function that refers to the same cell or range in multiple worksheets. The term *3-D formula* comes from having a reference with three dimensions: worksheet name, column letter, and row number. It is a convenient way to reference several identically structured worksheets in which the cells in each worksheet contain the same type of data, such as when you consolidate sales information from different branches into the Summary worksheet. For example, =SUM('Qtr1:Qtr4'!E3) is a 3-D formula that adds the values in cell E3 in each worksheet, starting in the Qtr1 worksheet and ending in the Qtr4 worksheet, including worksheets between those two. You can type a 3-D reference directly into a cell formula or function, but using the semi-selection method is more efficient. To create a 3-D formula, do the following:

1. Click the cell in which you will enter the 3-D formula.
2. Type =, type the name of the function, such as SUM, and then type an opening parenthesis.
3. Click the first worksheet tab, such as Qtr1.
4. Press and hold Shift as you click the last worksheet tab for adjacent worksheets, or press and hold Ctrl as you click nonadjacent worksheet tabs.
5. Click the cell or select the range that contains the value(s) you want to use in the function argument and press Enter. Figure 9.13 shows the process of creating a 3-D formula before you press Enter.

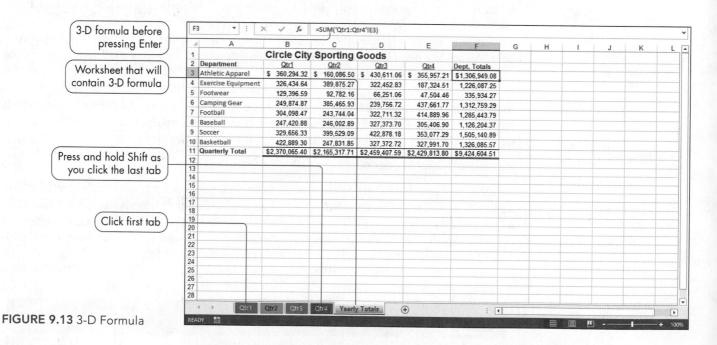

FIGURE 9.13 3-D Formula

=SUM('First Worksheet:Last Worksheet'!RangeOfCells)

You can use a variety of functions for 3-D formulas. Some of these functions include SUM, AVERAGE, COUNT, MIN, and MAX. You can create 3-D formulas using some standard deviation and variance functions. Other functions, such as PMT, VLOOKUP, and COUNTIF, do not work with 3-D formulas.

Linking Workbooks

Workbook linking is another way of consolidating data. When you link workbooks, you consolidate the data from several workbooks into another workbook. *Linking* is the process of creating external cell references from worksheets in one workbook to cells on a worksheet in another workbook. For example, you might have three workbooks—Indianapolis, Bloomington, and South Bend—one for each store location. Each store manager maintains a workbook to record sales by department—such as exercise equipment, footwear, and camping gear—for a particular time period. As district manager, you want to consolidate the data from each workbook into one workbook. Instead of reentering the data, you can create links from specific cells of data in the individual workbooks to your active workbook.

Before creating links, identify the source and destination files. A *source file* is one that contains original data that you need elsewhere. For example, the individual department store workbooks—Indianapolis, Bloomington, and South Bend—are source files. The *destination file* is a file containing a pointer to receive data from the source files—that is, the target file that needs the data. When you link workbooks, you create a connection between the source and destination files. If data change in the source file, the destination file's data update also. Linking ensures that the destination file always contains the most up-to-date data.

Create an External Reference

STEP 3 >> When you create a link between source and destination files, you establish an external reference or pointer to one or more cells in another workbook. The external reference is similar to the worksheet reference that you created for 3-D formulas. However, an external reference must include the workbook name to identify which workbook contains the linked worksheet and cell reference. For example, to create a link to cell E3 in the Qtr3 worksheet in the Indianapolis file, type =[Indianapolis.xlsx]Qtr3!E3. You must type the workbook name, including the file name extension, between brackets, such as [Indianapolis.xlsx]. After the closing bracket, type the worksheet name, such as Qtr3, followed by an exclamation mark and the cell reference, such as E3. Table 9.2 lists additional rules to follow when entering external references.

[WorkbookName]WorksheetName!RangeOfCells

TABLE 9.2	External References	
Situation	**Rule**	**Example**
Workbook and worksheet names do not contain spaces; source and destination files are in the same folder.	Type brackets around the workbook name and an exclamation mark between the worksheet name and range.	[Indianapolis.xlsx]Qtr3!A1
Workbook or worksheet name contains spaces; source and destination files are in the same folder.	Type single quotation marks on the left side of the opening bracket and the right side of the worksheet name.	'[South Bend.xlsx]Qtr3'!A1
Worksheet name contains spaces; source and destination files are in the same folder.	Type single quotation marks on the left side of the opening bracket and the right side of the worksheet name.	'[Bloomington.xlsx]Qtr 3 Sales'!A1
Source workbook is in a different folder than the destination workbook.	Type a single quotation mark, and then the full path—drive letter and folder name—before the opening bracket and a single quotation mark after the worksheet name.	'C:\Data[Indianapolis.xlsx] Sheet1'!A1

Excel displays formulas with external references in two ways, depending on whether the source workbook is open or closed. When the source is open, the external reference shows the file name, worksheet, and cell reference. When the source workbook is closed, the external reference shows the full path name in the Formula Bar. By default, Excel creates absolute cell references in the external reference. However, you can edit the external reference to create a relative or mixed cell reference. To create an external reference between cells in different workbooks:

1. Open the destination workbook and all source workbooks.
2. Select the cell or cells to hold the external reference.
3. Type =. If you want to perform calculations or functions on the external references, type the operator or function.
4. Switch to the source workbook and click the worksheet that contains the cells to which you want to link.
5. Select the cells you want to link to and press Enter.

TIP Drive and Folder Reference

Excel updates an external reference regardless of whether the source workbook is open. The source workbooks must be in the same folder location as when you created the link to update the destination workbook. If the location of the workbooks changes, as may happen if you copy the workbooks to a different folder, click Edit Links in the Connections group on the Data tab.

Manage and Update Linked Workbooks

STEP 4》 If you create an external reference when both the source and destination files are open, changes you make to the source file occur in the destination file as well. However, if the destination file is closed when you change data in the source file, the destination file does not automatically update to match the source file. Excel does not update linked data in a destination workbook automatically to protect the workbook against malicious activity, such as viruses.

When you open the destination file the first time, Excel displays the Security Warning Message Bar between the Ribbon and Formula Bar with the message *Automatic updates of links has been disabled*. If you are confident that the source files contain safe data, enable the links in the destination file. Click Enable Content to update the links and save the workbook. The next time you open the destination file, Excel displays a message box that prompts the user to update, do not update, or select help. Click Update to update the links. Figure 9.14 has been contrived to show you both ways of updating links.

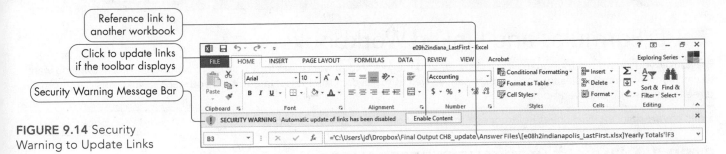

FIGURE 9.14 Security Warning to Update Links

External references identify the workbook names and locations. If you rename or move the source workbook, you must ensure that the external reference in the destination file matches the name of the new source workbook. Otherwise, when you open a destination file that contains external links that cannot be updated, Excel displays an error message, *This workbook contains one or more links that cannot be updated.* Click Edit Links to display the Edit Links dialog box and modify the source links (see Figure 9.15).

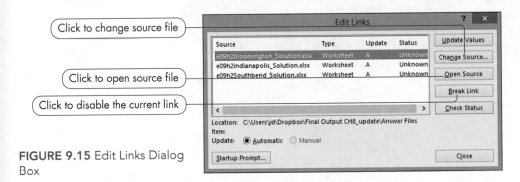

FIGURE 9.15 Edit Links Dialog Box

The Status column displays OK if the external reference link to the source file still works. If a problem exists, the Status column indicates the type of error, such as *Error: Source not found.* Click the source that contains an error and click Change Source to find and select the renamed or moved source file.

Quick Concepts

1. What is a 3-D formula? *p. 408*

2. What are the benefits of 3-D formulas? *p. 408*

3. How do you create an external reference? *pp. 409–410*

Hands-On Exercises

2 3-D Formulas and Linked Workbooks

Previously, you set up the four quarterly worksheets and the yearly total worksheet for Circle City Sporting Goods. Next, you want to calculate total yearly sales for each department as well as the overall total sales. In addition, you want to link sales data from all three locations into one workbook.

Skills covered: Insert Worksheet References • Insert 3-D Formulas • Link Workbooks • Complete the Linked Workbook

STEP 1 ≫ INSERT WORKSHEET REFERENCES

Each quarterly worksheet calculates the quarterly sales totals for a three-month period for each department. You want to insert references from each quarterly worksheet to consolidate the quarterly sales on the Yearly Totals worksheet. Refer to Figure 9.16 as you complete Step 1.

Step c: Reference to cell E3

Step f: Results of linking Quarterly worksheet data to Yearly Totals worksheet

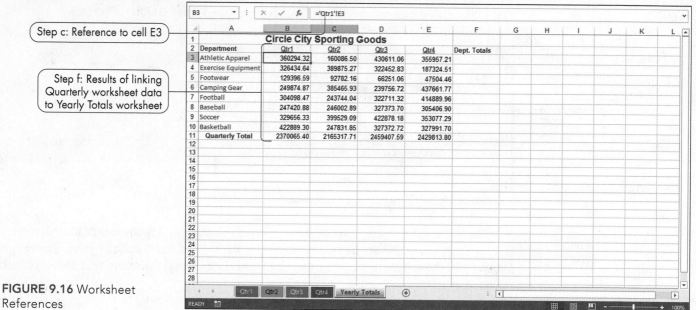

FIGURE 9.16 Worksheet References

a. Open *e09h1Indianapolis_LastFirst* and save it as **e09h2Indianapolis_LastFirst**, changing *h1* to *h2*.

b. Click the **Yearly Totals worksheet tab**. Type **Quarterly Total** in **cell A11**. Bold, indent, and apply **Purple font color** to the label.

c. Click **cell B3**, type =, click the **Qtr1 worksheet tab**, click **cell E3** in that worksheet, and then press **Ctrl+Enter**.

Look at the Formula Bar. The formula is ='Qtr1'!E3, where Qtr1 refers to the worksheet, and E3 refers to the cell within that worksheet.

d. Double-click the **cell B3 fill handle** to copy the formula down the column.

The formula's cell reference is relative, so it changes as you copy the formula down the column. The formula in cell B4 is ='Qtr1'!E4.

e. Click **cell C3** in the Yearly Totals worksheet, type **=**, click the **Qtr2 worksheet tab**, click **cell E3** in that worksheet, and then press **Ctrl+Enter**. Double-click the **cell C3 fill handle** to copy the formula down the column.

Look at the Formula Bar. The formula is ='Qtr2'!E3, where Qtr2 refers to the worksheet and E3 refers to the cell within that worksheet.

f. Adapt step e to enter references to the appropriate totals in the Qtr3 and Qtr4 worksheets.

g. Increase the four quarterly column widths to **13**. Save the workbook.

STEP 2 ≫ INSERT 3-D FORMULAS

You want to calculate the total annual sales by department. Although you could simply sum the values in the Yearly Totals worksheet, you want to use a 3-D formula to provide a cross-check that the totals are correct. Refer to Figure 9.17 as you complete Step 2.

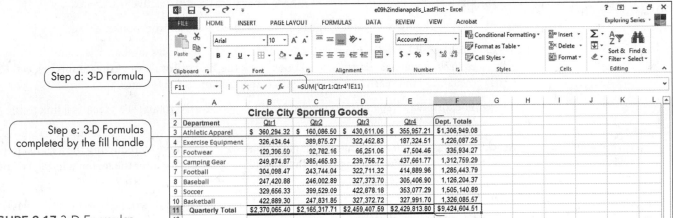

FIGURE 9.17 3-D Formulas

a. Click **cell F3** in the Yearly Totals worksheet.

This cell needs to calculate the total yearly sales for the Men's Clothing Department.

b. Type **=SUM(**

You start the 3-D formula with =, the function name, and the opening parenthesis.

c. Click the **Qtr1 worksheet tab**, press and hold **Shift**, and then click the **Qtr4 worksheet tab**.

You grouped the worksheets together so that you can use a common cell reference for the range of cells to sum.

d. Click **cell E3**, the cell containing the quarterly sales, and press **Ctrl+Enter**.

Look at the Formula Bar. The formula is =SUM('Qtr1:Qtr4'!E3). If you select the range B3:E3, the status bar shows that the sum is $1,306,949.08, the same value that appears when you inserted the 3-D formula.

e. Double-click the **cell F3 fill handle** to copy the formula down the column.

The cell reference is relative, so it changes as you copy the 3-D formula.

f. Apply **Accounting Number Format** to the **ranges B3:F3** and **B11:F11**. Apply **Comma Style** to the **range B4:F10**. Increase the width of column F to **13**. Apply the **Top and Double Bottom Border** to the **range B11:F11**. Bold **cell F2** and change the color to **purple**. Save the workbook.

STEP 3 ≫ LINK WORKBOOKS

You need to link the Indianapolis, Bloomington, and South Bend workbooks to display their totals in the Indiana workbook. The South Bend and Bloomington workbooks have the same structure as the Indianapolis workbook on which you have been working. Refer to Figure 9.18 as you complete Step 3.

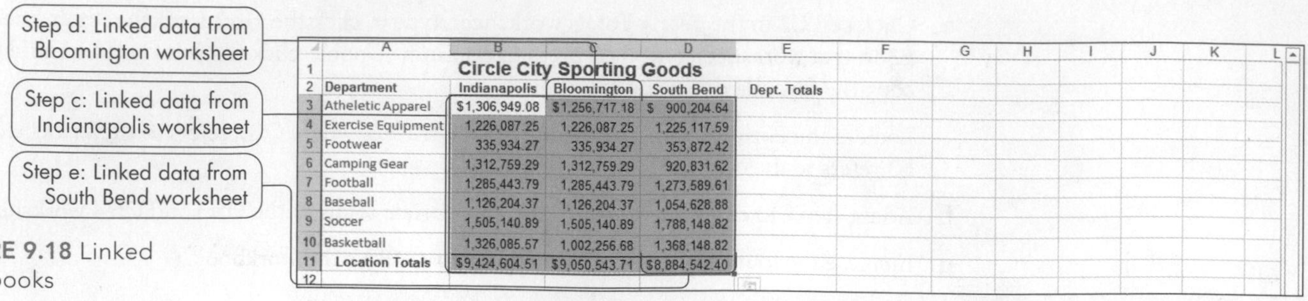

Step d: Linked data from Bloomington worksheet

Step c: Linked data from Indianapolis worksheet

Step e: Linked data from South Bend worksheet

FIGURE 9.18 Linked Workbooks

a. Open *e09h2Bloomington* and save it as **e09h2Bloomington_LastFirst**; open *e09h2SouthBend* and save it as **e09h2SouthBend_LastFirst**; and then open *e09h2Indiana* and save it as **e09h2Indiana_LastFirst**, making sure you save the workbooks in the same folder as your *e09h2Indianapolis_LastFirst* workbook.

b. Click *e09h2Indiana_LastFirst* on the taskbar to make it the active workbook.

This workbook will contain the links to the three location workbooks.

c. Click **cell B3**, type =, point to the Excel icon on the Windows taskbar, select the *e09h2Indianapolis_LastFirst* workbook, click the **Yearly Totals worksheet tab**, click **cell F3** containing the yearly department totals, and then press **Ctrl+Enter**.

The formula =‘[e09h2Indianapolis_LastFirst.xlsx]Yearly Totals’!$F$3 creates a link to the Indianapolis workbook.

d. Edit the cell reference in the formula to make cell F3 relative by removing the $ signs in the Formula Bar and pressing **Ctrl+Enter** or placing the cursor after the formula in the Formula Bar and pressing **F4** three times.

You must make this cell reference relative before copying it down the column. Otherwise, the results will show the value for cell F3 for the other Indianapolis departments.

e. Click **cell C3**, type =, point to the Excel icon on the Windows taskbar, select the *e09h2Bloomington_LastFirst* workbook, click the **Yearly Totals worksheet tab**, click **cell F3**, and then press **Ctrl+Enter**.

You created a link to the Bloomington workbook. The formula appears as =‘[e09h2Bloomington_LastFirst.xlsx]Yearly Totals’!$F$3.

f. Edit the cell reference in the formula to make cell F3 relative.

g. Adapt steps e and f to create a link to the South Bend workbook's yearly totals.

h. Copy the formulas down the columns in the *e09h2Indiana_LastFirst* workbook. Save the workbook.

STEP 4 ❯❯ COMPLETE THE LINKED WORKBOOK

You need to insert department totals for all three locations and format the linked workbook. Refer to Figure 9.19 as you complete Step 4.

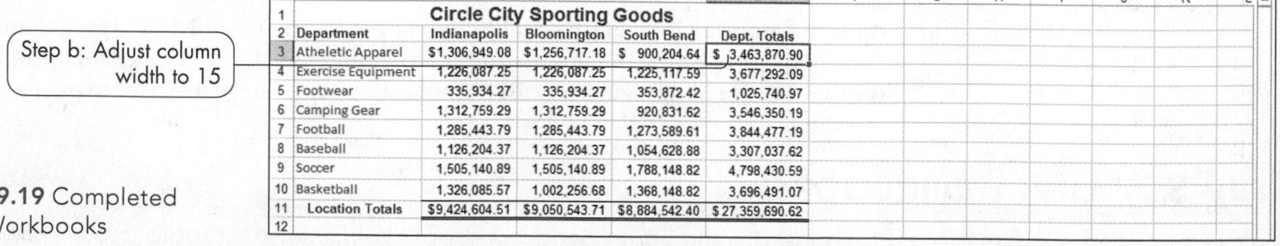

Step b: Adjust column width to 15

FIGURE 9.19 Completed Linked Workbooks

a. Click **cell E3** in the *e09h2Indiana_LastFirst* workbook.

b. Insert the SUM function to enter **=SUM(B3:D3)**. Copy the formula down column E. Adjust the width of column E to **15**.

You calculated the total yearly sales across all three locations by department.

c. Format the **range B4:E10** with **Comma Style**.

d. Apply **Top and Double Bottom Border** to the **range B11:E11**.

e. Save and close all open workbooks, and submit based on your instructor's directions.

Formula Audits and Data Validation

Errors can occur in a worksheet in several ways. Sometimes, an error may occur with a function name, such as =AVG(B1:E1) when the formula should be =AVERAGE(B1:E1). A *syntax error* is an error that occurs because a formula or function violates correct construction, such as a misspelled function name or illegal use of an operator. Syntax errors also include illegal mathematical construction, such as attempting to divide a value by zero. You must correct syntax errors to obtain a viable result. Excel helps you detect and correct syntax errors. For example, Excel displays #DIV/0! if the formula divides a value by zero to inform you that a result cannot be calculated. Table 9.3 lists some common syntax errors and the reasons for those errors.

TABLE 9.3   Syntax Errors Explained

Error	Reasons
#DIV/0!	Formula attempts to divide a value by zero or an empty cell
#NAME?	Misspelled or invalid range name or function name, such as VLOKUP instead of VLOOKUP
	Parentheses missing for function, such as =TODAY instead of =TODAY( )
	Omitted quotation marks around text, such as using *text* instead of *"text"* in the function =IF(A4="text",A5,A6)
	Missing colon in a range reference, such as =SUM(A1A8)
#N/A	Function is missing one or more required arguments, or VLOOKUP, HLOOKUP, or MATCH functions do not return a match
#NULL!	Incorrect range separator
	Formula requires cell ranges to intersect and they do not
#NUM!	Invalid arguments used in a function
#REF!	Reference to cell that contains no data or deleted data
#VALUE!	Incorrect type of data used in an argument, such as referring to a cell that contains text instead of a value

More difficult to detect are errors that appear to be correct but are not because an incorrect range was entered, such as =AVERAGE(B1:D1) when the range should be =AVERAGE(B1:E1). *Logic errors* are the result of a syntactically correct formula but logically incorrect construction, which produces inaccurate results. Logic errors occur when a formula contains the wrong operator or cell reference.

You can design worksheets to help facilitate correct data entry, such as ensuring that a user enters a value, not text. Doing so helps prevent formula errors because the user must enter valid data. Although you can design workbooks to require valid data, you might work with workbooks that other people created that contain errors in the formulas.

In this section, you will learn how to use formula auditing tools to detect errors. In addition, you will apply data validation rules to make sure users enter correct data into input cells.

Auditing Formulas

Recall that you can press Ctrl+` (grave accent key) to display cell formulas instead of cell results. Displaying the formulas may help you identify some errors, but you might not be able to detect all errors immediately. Especially challenging to detect are errors in 3-D formulas or formulas that link workbooks. To help you detect and correct formula errors, you can use *formula auditing*, a set of tools that enable you to display or trace relationships for formula cells, show formulas, check for errors, and evaluate formulas. The Formula Auditing group on the Formulas tab contains commands to help you audit a workbook (see Figure 9.20).

FIGURE 9.20 Formula Auditing Group

TIP | Green Triangle

Excel detects potential logic errors even if the formula does not contain a syntax error. For example, Excel might detect that =SUM(B2:B5) contains a potential error if cell B1 contains a value, assuming the possibility that the function might need to include B1 in the range of values to add. When this occurs, Excel displays a green triangle in the top-left corner of the cell. Click the cell containing the green triangle and click the error icon, the yellow diamond with the exclamation mark, to see a list of options to correct the error.

Trace Precedents and Dependents

STEP 1 » Although Excel displays error messages, you might not know what cell is causing the error to appear in the formula cell. Even if your worksheet does not contain errors, you might want to use formula auditing tools to identify which cells are used in formulas. Formulas involve both precedent and dependent cells. *Precedent cells* are cells that are referenced in a formula. For example, assume an hourly pay rate ($10.25) is stored in cell A1, hours worked (40) is stored in cell A2, and the formula =A1*A2 is stored in cell A3 to calculate the gross pay. Cells A1 and A2 are precedent cells to the formula in cell A3. *Dependent cells* contain formulas that refer to other cells. These cells *depend* on other cells to generate their values. For example, if cell A3 contains the formula =A1*A2, cell A3 is a dependent of cells A1 and A2.

You use Trace Precedents and Trace Dependents to display *tracer arrows* that show the relationship between cells and formulas (see Figure 9.21). The tracer starts in a precedent cell with the arrowhead ending in the dependent cell. To trace precedents, select the cell that contains the formula for which you will find precedent cells and click Trace Precedents in the Formula Auditing group. To trace dependent cells, click the cell for which you will find dependents and click Trace Dependents in the Formula Auditing group. The tracer arrows help you identify cells that cause errors. Blue arrows show cells with no errors. Red arrows show cells that cause errors.

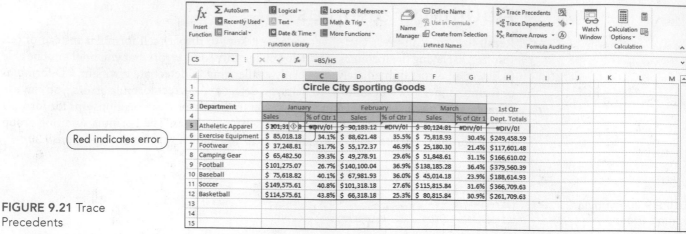

FIGURE 9.21 Trace Precedents

Red indicates error

> **TIP** ☐ **Remove Tracer Arrows**
>
> Click Remove Arrows in the Formula Auditing group on the Formulas tab to remove all tracer arrows, or click the Remove Arrows arrow and select Remove Arrows, Remove Precedent Arrows, or Remove Dependent Arrows.

Check For and Repair Errors

STEP 2 » When the tracing of precedents or dependents shows errors in formulas, or if you want to check for errors that have occurred in formulas anywhere in a worksheet, you can use Error Checking in the Formula Auditing group. When Excel identifies an error, the Error Checking dialog box opens (see Figure 9.22) and identifies the cell containing an error and describes the error.

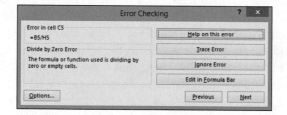

FIGURE 9.22 Error Checking Dialog Box

Click *Help on this error* to see a description of the error. Click Show Calculation Steps to open the Evaluate Formula dialog box (see Figure 9.23), which provides an evaluation of the formula and shows which part of the evaluation will result in an error. Clicking Ignore Error either moves to the next error or indicates that Error Checking is complete. When you click *Edit in Formula Bar*, you can correct the formula in the Formula Bar.

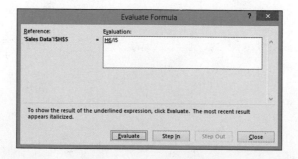

FIGURE 9.23 Evaluate Formula Dialog Box

Evaluate a Formula

Using nested formulas can make it difficult to understand the formula evaluation. Understanding how a nested formula calculates is hard because intermediate calculations and logical tests exist. You can use the Evaluate Formula dialog box to view different parts of a nested formula and evaluate each part. To use the Evaluate Formula dialog box, do the following:

1. Select the cell you want to evaluate.
2. Click Evaluate Formula in the Formula Auditing group to see the Evaluate Formula dialog box (see Figure 9.23).
3. Click Evaluate to examine the value of the reference that is underlined.
4. If the underlined part of the formula is a reference to another formula, click Step In to display the other formula in the Evaluation box.
5. Click Step Out to return to the previous cell and formula.
6. Continue until you have evaluated the entire formula and click Close.

Use the IFERROR Function to Detect Errors

If you create a workbook for others to use, you should anticipate errors the users will introduce so that you can provide a way to identify and correct those errors. The **IFERROR function** is a logical function that checks a cell to determine if that cell contains an error or if a formula will result in an error. If no error exists, the IFERROR function returns the value of the formula. The *value* argument contains the value being checked for an error, and the *value_if_error* argument is the value to return if the formula evaluates to an error. IFERROR detects the following types of errors: #N/A, #VALUE!, #REF!, #DIV/0!, #NUM!, #NAME?, and #NULL, although the output does not indicate the type of error.

Typically, you use a text string enclosed in quotation marks to return an error message. For example, if you divide the contents of cells in row 2 by cell B1 and anticipate that a #DIV/0! error might occur when copying the formula, you can use =IFERROR(A2/B1,"You cannot divide by zero. Change the value of cell B1 to a value higher than 0.").

=IFERROR(value,value_if_error)

TIP Information Functions

The Information functions contain additional functions you can use for error checking. Of particular interest are the ERROR.TYPE and ISERROR functions. Use Help to learn how to incorporate these functions in error-checking tasks.

Setting Up a Watch Window

STEP 3» When you are working with a worksheet containing a large dataset, formulas in cells that are not visible can be "watched" using the Watch Window. You do not need to keep scrolling to different parts of the worksheet if you are using a Watch Window. The **Watch Window** enables you to create a small window so you can conveniently inspect, audit, or confirm formula calculations involving cells not immediately visible on the screen. You can double-click a cell in the Watch Window to jump to that cell quickly. To add cells to the Watch Window, do the following:

1. Click Watch Window in the Formula Auditing group.
2. Click Add Watch in the Watch Window toolbar.
3. Select the cells to watch in the Add Watch dialog box and click Add. The Watch Window shows the cells and formulas you selected to watch (see Figure 9.24).

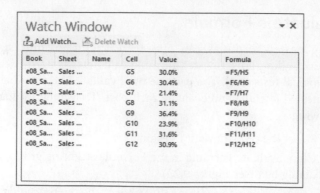

FIGURE 9.24 Watch Window

STEP 4

> **TIP** Changes to Watched Cells
>
> Any time you make a change to the watched cell(s), the Watch Window shows you the current value of the watched cell(s).

Validating Data

Data validation enables you to control the data that can be entered into a cell. It warns and prevents people from entering "wrong" data in a cell, or it can provide a list of valid data from which to choose. Data validation enables you to specify and correct the kind of data that can be entered, specify an input message alerting users when they click a cell that only specific types of data can be entered in that cell, and specify error messages that appear when others persist and attempt to enter incorrect data. To set up a data validation rule, click the cell for which the rule will be applied, and then click Data Validation in the Data Tools group on the Data tab.

Specify Data Validation Criteria

In the Data Validation dialog box, use the Settings tab to specify the *validation criteria*—the rules that dictate the type of data that can be entered in a cell. Click the Allow arrow to specify what type of data you will allow the user to enter, such as a whole number, a value that is part of a specific list, or a date that is within a particular date range. For example, if you specify whole number and the user attempts to enter a decimal, Excel displays an error message. You can also specify that the data must be between two values and specify the minimum and maximum values permitted. Figure 9.25 shows a validation rule in which the cell contents must be (a) a whole number and (b) between a minimum and maximum value, which are stored respectively in cells G5 and G6.

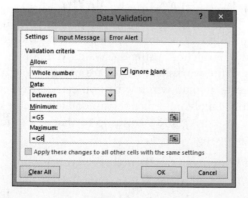

FIGURE 9.25 Data Validation Settings Tab: Criteria

To make data entry easier or to limit items to certain defined items and thereby be more accurate, you can create a list of valid entries from data contained in cells. When you create a list, Excel displays an arrow in the cell. The user clicks the arrow, and then selects the desired entry. The user cannot enter invalid data. To create a list, do the following:

1. Create a list of valid entries in a single column or row without blank cells.
2. Click the cell for which you want to create a validation rule.
3. Click the DATA tab and select Validation in the Data Tools group to show the Data Validation dialog box.
4. Click the Settings tab, click the Allow arrow, and then select List.
5. Enter a reference to the list in the Source box (see Figure 9.26).
6. Make sure that the *In-cell dropdown* check box is selected and that the *Ignore blank* check box is clear and click OK.

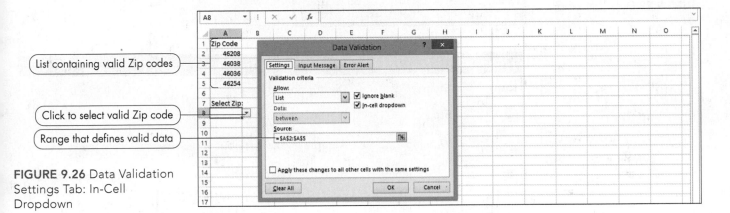

FIGURE 9.26 Data Validation Settings Tab: In-Cell Dropdown

Create an Input Message

STEP 5 ▶▶

Input messages are descriptive text or instructions for data entry that can be entered in the Data Validation dialog box. You add input messages to cells, and Excel displays these messages when a user moves to a cell that has a data-entry restriction. Input messages consist of two parts: a title and an input message (see Figure 9.27). These messages should describe the data validation and explain or show how to enter data correctly. For example, an input message might be *Enter hire date in the form: mm/dd/yyyy* or *Enter Employee name: last name, first name.*

FIGURE 9.27 Data Validation Input Message Tab

Create an Error Alert

Sometimes, no matter how descriptive you are with an input message, users will attempt to enter invalid data in a cell. Instead of using Excel's default error message, you can create an *error alert*, a message that displays when a user enters invalid data in a cell that has a validation rule applied to it. To create an error alert, specify the style, title, and error message on the Error Alert tab (see Figure 9.28). The error alert message should be polite and clearly state what the error is. Cryptic, nondescriptive alert messages do not help users understand the data-entry problem. Table 9.4 shows the error styles that control the icon that appears with the error message.

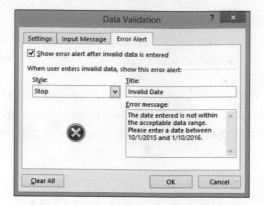

FIGURE 9.28 Data Validation Error Tab

TABLE 9.4 Error Style

Icon	Style	Description
	Stop	Prevents the user from entering invalid data
	Warning	Accepts invalid data but warns user that data are invalid
	Information	Accepts invalid data but provides information to user

TIP Circle Text

After defining data validation rules, you can display circles around invalid text. To display circles for invalid data, click the Data Validation arrow in the Data Tools group and select Circle Invalid Data. When the user corrects the invalid data, the circles disappear.

Quick Concepts

1. What is the difference between precedent and dependent cells? *p. 417*

2. What is the benefit of the Watch Window? *p. 419*

3. What is the benefit of data validation? *p. 420*

Hands-On Exercises

3 Formula Audits and Data Validation

A colleague prepared a worksheet based on projected data if the company opened a store in Fort Wayne. Unfortunately, your colleague introduced several errors. You will use auditing tools to identify and correct the errors. In addition, you will insert validation rules to ensure only valid data are entered in the future.

Skills covered: Trace Precedents and Dependents • Check for Errors • Set Up a Watch Window • Create a Validation Rule • Specify Inputs and Alerts

STEP 1 ≫ TRACE PRECEDENTS AND DEPENDENTS

You want to display precedent and dependent arrows to identify sources and destinations for cells being used in formulas in the Fort Wayne workbook. Refer to Figure 9.29 as you complete Step 1.

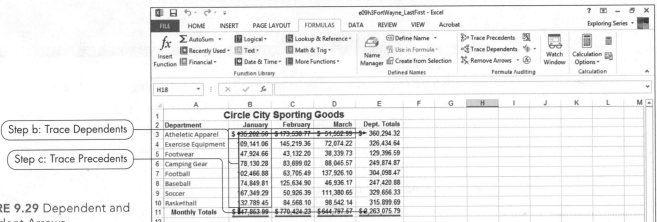

FIGURE 9.29 Dependent and Precedent Arrows

a. Open *e09h3FortWayne*, click **OK** when prompted to fix a circular error, and then save it as **e09h3FortWayne_LastFirst**.

b. Click **cell B3**, click the **FORMULAS tab**, and then click **Trace Dependents** in the Formula Auditing group.

Excel displays a tracer arrow from cell B3 to cells E3 and B11, indicating that cell B3's value is used in formulas in cells E3 and B11.

c. Click **cell E11** and click **Trace Precedents** in the Formula Auditing group.

Excel displays a tracer error showing that the values in the range B11:D11 are used within the current cell's formula.

d. Click **Remove Arrows** in the Formula Auditing group. Save the workbook.

STEP 2 ≫ CHECK FOR ERRORS

The Qtr2 worksheet contains errors. You will use the Error Checking dialog box and trace precedents to identify the errors. Refer to Figure 9.30 as you complete Step 2.

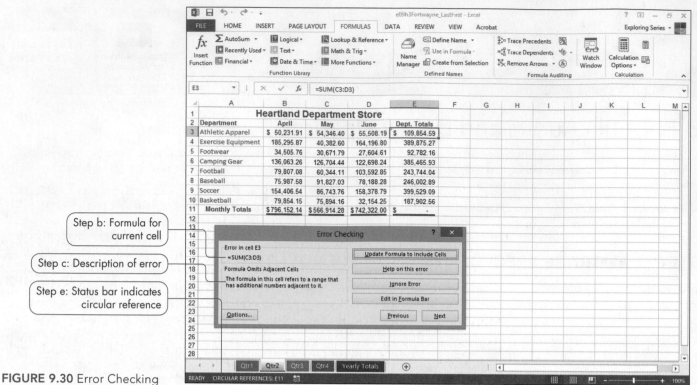

FIGURE 9.30 Error Checking

Step b: Formula for current cell

Step c: Description of error

Step e: Status bar indicates circular reference

a. Click the **Qtr2 worksheet tab**, look for the green error checking error in cell E3, and then click **cell A1**.

b. Click the **Error Checking arrow** in the Formula Auditing group and select **Error Checking**.

The Error Checking dialog box opens, indicating an error in cell E3. Excel detects that the formula omits an adjacent cell.

c. Click **Update Formula to Include Cells**.

Excel modifies the formula from =SUM(C3:D3) to =SUM(B3:D3) to include the April sales.

d. Click **OK** in the message box that informs you that error checking is complete.

When you opened the workbook, an error message stated that the workbook contains a circular reference. However, the Error Checking dialog box did not locate that circular reference. The status bar still indicates that a circular reference exists.

e. Click the **Error Checking arrow** in the Formula Auditing group, point to *Circular References*, and then select **$E$11**.

A circular reference occurs when a formula refers to itself. In this case, cell E11's formula includes itself in the function argument.

f. Edit the formula to be **=SUM(B11:D11)**. Save the workbook.

The circular reference notation on the status bar disappears.

STEP 3 ≫ SET UP A WATCH WINDOW

You want to set up a Watch Window to watch the results of formulas in the Yearly Totals worksheet when you change values in another worksheet. Refer to Figure 9.31 as you complete Step 3.

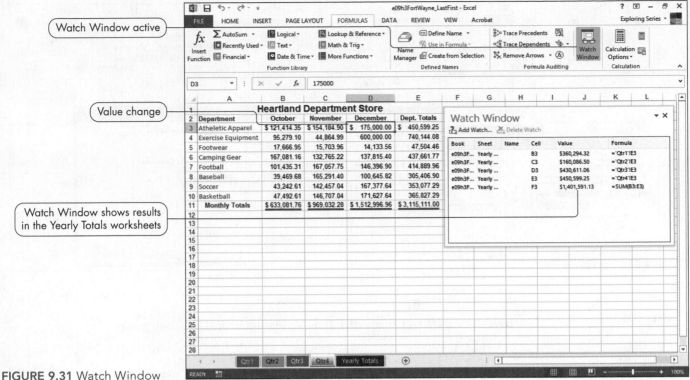

FIGURE 9.31 Watch Window

a. Click the **Yearly Totals worksheet tab**.

b. Select the **range B3:F3**.

You selected the range you want to watch to ensure formulas work correctly.

c. Click **Watch Window** in the Formula Auditing group and click **Add Watch** in the Watch Window.

The Add Watch dialog box opens, indicating the worksheet and cells you selected.

d. Click **Add**.

The Watch Window adds a watch for every cell in the selected range. It shows the workbook name, worksheet name, cell address, current value, and formula.

e. Click the **Qtr4 worksheet tab**.

The Watch Window remains onscreen. The current Athletic apparel total is $355,957.21, shown in cell E3 and in the Watch Window. The Watch Window also shows the total Athletic Apparel sales to be $1,306,949.08.

f. Click **cell D3**, enter **175000**, and then press **Ctrl+Enter**.

The Qtr4 Athletic Apparel total changed to $450,599.25 in cell E3 and in the Watch Window. The Watch Window also shows that the total Athletic Apparel sales are now $1,401,591.13.

g. Click **Watch Window** in the Formula Auditing group to hide the Watch Window. Save the workbook.

STEP 4 》 CREATE A VALIDATION RULE

You want to insert a validation rule for the Exercise Equipment, Footwear, and Camping Gear values on the Qtr4 worksheet. Based on projections, you believe the maximum revenue would be no more than $500,000. Refer to Figure 9.32 as you complete Step 4.

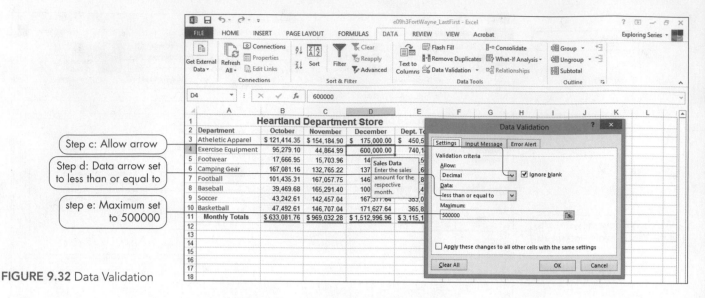

FIGURE 9.32 Data Validation

a. Select the **range B4:D4** on the Qtr4 worksheet.

b. Click the **DATA tab** and click **Data Validation** in the Data Tools group.

The Data Validation dialog box opens.

c. Click the **Allow arrow** and select **Decimal** to allow for dollar-and-cent entries.

The dialog box displays Data, Minimum, and Maximum options.

d. Click the **Data arrow** and select **less than or equal to**.

e. Type **500000** in the **Maximum box**. Keep the Data Validation dialog box open for the next step.

STEP 5 >> SPECIFY INPUTS AND ALERTS

You will specify the input message and an alert if a user enters more than 500,000 however, you will let the incorrect value be entered. Refer to Figure 9.33 as you complete Step 5.

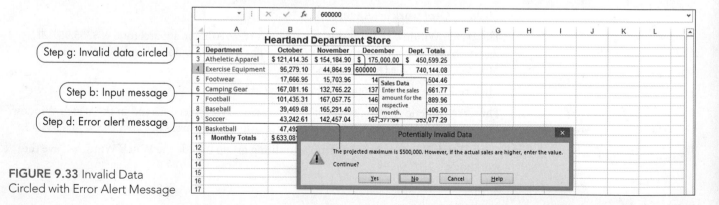

FIGURE 9.33 Invalid Data Circled with Error Alert Message

a. Click the **Input Message tab** in the Data Validation dialog box.

> **TROUBLESHOOTING:** If you wish to edit the validation message that was set up after completing the prior step, you can edit the validation rule by reentering the data validation menu.

b. Type **Sales Data** in the **Title box** and type **Enter the sales amount for the respective month.** in the **Input message box**.

c. Click the **Error Alert tab** in the Data Validation dialog box, click the **Style arrow**, and then select **Warning**.

The stop style would prevent values outside the acceptable maximum from being entered. However, your sales projections might be wrong, so you want to allow values over the maximum.

d. Type **Potentially Invalid Data** in the **Title box** and type **The projected maximum is $500,000. However, if actual sales are higher, enter the actual value.** in the **Error message box**. Click **OK**.

e. Click **cell D4**, notice the input message you created from step b, type **600000**, and then press **Enter**.

The error message you created appears (see Figure 9.33).

f. Click **Yes**. Note that even though 600000 is beyond the validation limit, the user is still able to enter the number by clicking **Yes**.

g. Click the **Data Validation arrow** in the Data Tools group and select **Circle Invalid Data**.

Excel circles the value in cell D4, indicating that the value violates the validation rule.

h. Save and close the workbook, and submit it based on your instructor's directions.

Chapter Objectives Review

After reading this chapter, you have accomplished the following objectives:

1. **Work with grouped worksheets.**
   - Group and ungroup worksheets: Allows you to perform the same action simultaneously to grouped worksheets.
   - Enter data and format grouped worksheets: Data entry, structural changes, formatting, and page layout can be edited on grouped worksheets.
   - Fill across worksheets: Selecting Fill Across Worksheets from the Fill button on the Ribbon will copy formatting across all grouped worksheets.

2. **Manage windows and workspaces.**
   - Control visibility of worksheets: You have the ability to hide or unhide worksheets from the Format drop down in the cells group located in the Home tab.
   - Open and arrange windows: The Arrange Window dialog box allows you to display multiple windows as tiled, horizontal, vertical, or cascade.
   - Split a window: Divides the current worksheet window into resizable panes.

3. **Insert hyperlinks.**
   - Insert hyperlink: Hyperlinks are markers that connect one cell to another cell in the same worksheet, different worksheet, or different worksheet in another workbook. You can also create hyperlinks to link to Web pages or e-mail.

4. **Insert a 3-D formula.**
   - Insert a 3-D formula: A 3-D formula is used to consolidate data among two or more worksheets.

5. **Link workbooks.**
   - Create an external reference: An established external reference or pointer to one or more cells in an external worksheet.
   - Manage and update linked workbooks: When a destination file is first opened, you will be prompted to enable automatic link updates.

6. **Audit formulas.**
   - Trace precedent and dependents: Shows arrows that depict the relationships between precedent and dependent cells.
   - Precedent cells are cells referenced in a formula, dependent cells contain formulas that refer to other cells.
   - Check for and repair errors: Check and repair errors by selecting *Error checking* from the Formula Auditing group on the Formulas tab.
   - Evaluate a formula: Provides an evaluation of a formula that shows the portion that returns an error.
   - Use IFERROR function to detect errors: Checks a value and returns the results if possible or an error message.

7. **Set up a Watch Window.**
   - Set up a Watch Window: When you work with large datasets, you can watch formulas in cells that are not visible by using the Watch Window feature. Click Watch Window in the Formula Auditing group and then select Add Watch.

8. **Validate data.**
   - Specify data validation criteria: To specify criteria, use the Settings tab in the Data Validation dialog box.

Key Terms Matching

Match the key terms with their definitions. Write the key term letter by the appropriate numbered definition.

a. 3-D formula
b. Data validation
c. Dependent cell
d. Destination file
e. Error alert
f. Formula auditing
g. Grouping
h. Hyperlink
i. IFERROR function
j. Input message

k. Linking
l. Logic error
m. Precedent cell
n. Source file
o. Split bar
p. Splitting
q. Syntax error
r. Tracer arrow
s. Ungrouping
t. Validation criteria

1. _____ Occurs when formula construction rules are violated. **p. 416**

2. _____ An electronic marker to another location in a worksheet, workbook, file, Web page, or e-mail. **p. 399**

3. _____ Rules that dictate the data to enter a cell. **p. 420**

4. _____ Checks a value and returns the result if possible or an error message. **p. 419**

5. _____ A file that contains a pointer to the source file. **p. 409**

6. _____ Requires that rules be followed in order to allow data to be entered in a cell. **p. 420**

7. _____ Tools to enable you to detect and correct errors in formulas by identifying relationships among cells. **p. 417**

8. _____ A colored line that indicates relationships between precedent and dependent cells. **p. 417**

9. _____ The process of connecting cells between worksheets. **p. 409**

10. _____ The process of selecting worksheets to perform the same action at the same time. **p. 394**

11. _____ The process of dividing a worksheet window. **p. 398**

12. _____ The process of deselecting worksheets that were grouped. **p. 395**

13. _____ A vertical or horizontal line that frames panes in a worksheet and enables the user to resize the panes. **p. 398**

14. _____ A cell containing a formula that is dependent on other cells to obtain its value. **p. 417**

15. _____ Occurs when a formula adheres to syntax rules but produces inaccurate results. **p. 416**

16. _____ A formula or function that refers to the same range in multiple worksheets. **p. 408**

17. _____ A file that contains original data. **p. 409**

18. _____ A cell that is referenced by a formula in another cell. **p. 417**

19. _____ A message that appears when the user enters invalid data in a cell containing a validation rule. **p. 421**

20. _____ A description or instructions for data entry. **p. 421**

Multiple Choice

1. You have a workbook that contains sales data for different regional sales reps of a company. Which task is the least likely to be done while the worksheets are grouped?

   (a) Fill the sales categories across the worksheets.

   (b) Format the column and row labels at the same time.

   (c) Enter specific values for the first sales rep.

   (d) Format the values with an appropriate number style.

2. Your manager sent you a workbook that contains data validation rules. One rule specifies a maximum value of 15% with a warning alert. You try to enter 22% in that cell. What happens?

   (a) Excel enters the 22% with no message boxes.

   (b) Excel enters the 22% and provides a message box to inform you that your entry violates the validation rule.

   (c) Excel displays a message box and prevents you from entering 22%.

   (d) Excel displays a message box informing you the value is above the maximum value and lets you choose to go ahead and enter that value or a different value.

3. The function =FV(D10,D8,-D5) is entered in cell D12. Which cell is a dependent of cell D8?

   (a) D10

   (b) D12

   (c) D5

   (d) D1

4. If you want to display a portion of all three worksheets in a workbook, what should you do?

   (a) Open two new workbook windows, arrange windows, and then click a different worksheet tab in each window.

   (b) Use the Freeze Panes option and cascade the title bars of all open workbooks.

   (c) Double-click the split boxes to display four window panes, click within each pane, and then click the worksheet tab to display its content.

   (d) Use the Split, Freeze Panes, and Arrange All commands at the same time.

5. Which function cannot be used in a 3-D formula?

   (a) SUM

   (b) AVERAGE

   (c) MIN

   (d) PMT

6. A personal trainer stores how much weight each person can lift in several categories. Each week's data are stored in a separate worksheet within the same workbook, and each worksheet has an identical structure. Assume cell F5 contains the weight the first person can bench press. What function can identify that person's highest amount bench-pressed in all worksheets?

   (a) =COUNT(Week 1,Week4:F5)

   (b) =SUM(Week 1:Week4:F5)

   (c) =MAX('Week 1:Week 4'!F5)

   (d) =MAX(Week1:Week4:'F5')

7. You want to create a hyperlink within your document to the SEC Web site. Which type of link do you create?

   (a) Existing File or Web Page

   (b) Place in This Document

   (c) Create New Document

   (d) E-Mail Address

8. To study the results of a formula on the Summary worksheet when you change an input value on the Input worksheet, what can you do?

   (a) Create a watch for the formula and display the Watch Window while changing the input value on the Input worksheet.

   (b) Create a watch for the input cell and display the Watch Window on the Summary worksheet.

   (c) Display the trace precedents and dependents arrows on both worksheets as you change the input value.

   (d) Create a hyperlink from the results to the input cell and from the input cell to the formula.

9. You are preparing an accreditation report for your university. You have several workbooks of data for each college, such as Arts, Sciences, and Business. Assuming the individual workbooks are stored in the same folder as the University workbook, how would a link to cell B15 in the Digital Media worksheet in the School of Computing workbook appear in the University workbook?

   (a) =Computing.xlsx:Digital Media:B15

   (b) ="School of Computing"!'Digital Media'!B15

   (c) ='[School of Computing.xlsx]Digital Media'!$B$15

   (d) ='School of Computing'![Digital Media]:$B$15

10. Which dialog box specifies a cell containing an error and the type of error, such as *Divide by Zero Error*?

    (a) Watch Window

    (b) Circular Reference

    (c) Evaluate Formula

    (d) Error Checking

Practice Exercises

1 Range Free Foods Corporation

The Range Free Foods Corporation began operation last year in Phoenix by opening three stores in different areas of the city. The manager of each store prepared a workbook that summarizes the first-quarter results. As the assistant to the general manager, you need to complete the Downtown workbook, and then link data from the three workbooks to a consolidated workbook. This exercise follows the same set of skills as used in Hands-On Exercises 1 and 2 in the chapter. Refer to Figure 9.34 as you complete this exercise.

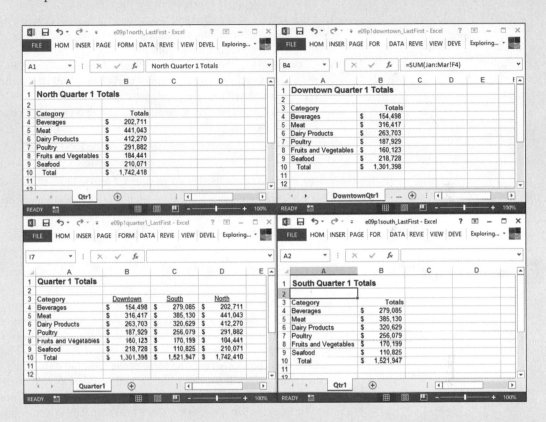

FIGURE 9.34 Range Free Foods Corporation

a. Open *e09p1Downtown* and save it as **e09p1Downtown_LastFirst**. Click each worksheet tab to see what work has been done and what work you will do.

b. Click the **Jan worksheet tab**, press and hold **Shift**, click the **Mar worksheet tab**, and then do the following:
   - Click **cell A1**, click the **HOME tab**, click **Fill** in the Editing group, and then select **Across Worksheets**. Click **Formats** in the Fill Across Worksheets dialog box and click **OK**.
   - Select the **range B4:F10** and click **Sum** in the Editing group.

c. Click the **DowntownQtr1 worksheet**, click **cell B4**, and then insert a 3-D formula by doing the following:
   - Type **=SUM(**
   - Click the **Jan worksheet tab**, press and hold **Shift**, and then click the **Mar worksheet tab**.
   - Click **cell F4** and press **Ctrl+Enter**.
   - Double-click the **cell B4 fill handle** to copy the formula down the column.

d. Open *e09p1South* and save it as **e09p1South_LastFirst**, open *e09p1North* and save it as **e09p1North_LastFirst**, and then open *e09p1Quarter1* and save it as **e09p1Quarter1_LastFirst**.

e. Click the **VIEW tab**, click **Switch Windows** in the Window group, and then select *e09p1North_ LastFirst*.

f. Click the **Jan worksheet**, hold **Shift**, click the **Mar tab** to group the worksheets, and then select **Hide**.

g. Adapt steps e and f to hide the Jan, Feb, and Mar worksheets in *e09p1South_LastFirst*.

h. Click **Switch Windows** in the Window group and select *e09p1Quarter1_LastFirst*.

i. Click **Arrange All** in the Window group, click the **Windows of active workbook check box** to deselect it if necessary, and then click **OK** in the dialog box.

j. Add links by doing the following:

- Click **cell B4** in the Quarter1 worksheet. Type =, display *e09p1Downtown_LastFirst*, click **cell B4** in the DowntownQtr1 worksheet, and then press **Ctrl+Enter**. Edit the formula to change *$B$4* to **B4**. Copy the formula down the Downtown column.

- Click **cell C4** in the Quarter1 worksheet. Type =, display *e09p1South_LastFirst*, click **cell B4** in the Qtr1 worksheet, and then press **Ctrl+Enter**. Edit the formula to change *$B$4* to **B4**. Copy the formula down the South column.

- Click **cell D4** in the Quarter1 worksheet. Type =, display *e09p1North_LastFirst*, click **cell B4** in the Qtr1 worksheet, and then press **Ctrl+Enter**. Edit the formula to change *$B$4* to **B4**. Copy the formula down the North column.

- Format the monetary values with **Accounting Number Format** with zero decimal places in the Quarter1 worksheet.

k. Click **cell B3** in the Quarter1 worksheet, click the **INSERT tab**, click **Hyperlink** in the Links group, scroll through the list of files, select *e09p1Downtown_LastFirst.xlsx*, and then click **OK**.

l. Adapt step k to create hyperlinks in **cells C3** and **C4** to their respective files.

m. Create a footer with your name on the left side, the sheet name code in the center, and the file name code on the right side of the Quarter1 worksheet.

n. Save and close the workbooks, and submit based on your instructor's directions.

2 Retirement Planning

An associate created a worksheet to help people plan retirement based on a set of annual contributions to a retirement account. A user indicates the age to start contributions, projected retirement age, the number of years in retirement, and the rate of return expected to earn on the money when the user retires. The worksheet determines the total amount the user will have contributed, the amount the user will have accumulated, and the value of the monthly retirement amount. However, the worksheet contains errors. You will use the auditing tools to identify and correct errors. Then you will specify validation rules to ensure users enter valid data. This exercise follows the same set of skills as used in Hands-On Exercise 3 in the chapter. Refer to Figure 9.34 as you complete this exercise.

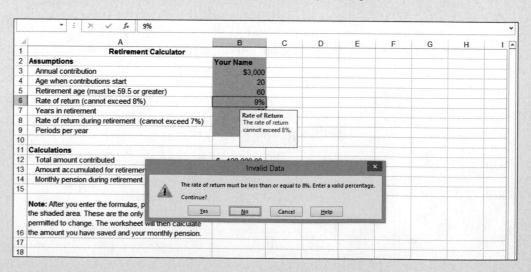

FIGURE 9.34 Retirement Planning

a. Open *e09p2Retire* and save it as **e09p2Retire_LastFirst**.

b. Click **cell B14**, click the **FORMULAS tab**, and then click **Trace Precedents** in the Formula Auditing group.

c. Click the **Error Checking arrow** in the Formula Auditing group and select **Error Checking**.

d. Click **Show Calculation Steps** in the Error Checking dialog box. The Evaluate Formula dialog box opens, showing the formula and stating that the next evaluation will result in an error. Click **Evaluate** to see the error replace the argument in the function: #DIV/0!. Click **Step In** to see the value and click **Step Out** to return to the evaluation. Repeat the Step In and Step Out process and click **Close**. Click **Next** in the Error Checking dialog box and click **OK** in the message box. Find the 0 in **cell B9** and change it to **12**.

e. Click **Remove Arrows** in the Formula Auditing group to remove the precedents arrow.

f. Click **Watch Window** in the Formula Auditing group and click **Add Watch**. Move the dialog boxes so that you can see the data, select the **range B12:B14**, and then click **Add**.

g. Create a data validation rule to ensure the retirement age is greater than 59.5 by doing the following:
   - Click **cell B5**, click the **DATA tab**, and then click **Data Validation** in the Data Tools group.
   - Click the **Settings tab**, click the **Allow arrow**, and then select **Decimal**.
   - Click the **Data arrow** and select **greater than or equal to**.
   - Type **59.5** in the **Minimum box**.
   - Click the **Input Message tab** and type **Retirement Age** in the **Title box**.
   - Type **Federal law does not permit payout prior to 59.5.** in the **Input message box**.
   - Click the **Error Alert tab**, click the **Style arrow**, and then select **Warning**.
   - Type **Invalid Data** in the **Title box**, type **Age must be greater than 59.5.** in the **Error message box**, and then click **OK**.

h. Adapt step g to create a validation rule for **cell B6** to ensure the rate of return will not exceed 8%. Include appropriate titles and messages.

i. Adapt step g to create a validation rule for **cell B8** to ensure the rate of return during retirement will not exceed 7%. Include appropriate titles and messages.

j. Type **50** in **cell B5**. Click **No** when the error message displays, change the value to **60**, and then press **Enter**.

k. Type **8.5%** in **cell B6**. Click **No** when the error message displays, change the value to **8%**, and then press **Enter**.

l. Type **7.5%** in **cell B8**. Click **No** when the error message displays, change the value to **7%**, and then press **Enter**. Close the Watch Window.

m. Create a footer with your name on the left side, the sheet name code in the center, and the file name code on the right side.

n. Save and close the workbook, and submit it based on your instructor's directions.

Mid-Level Exercises

1 Sales Data

ANALYSIS CASE

You are an accountant for a pharmaceutical sales company. As part of your tasks, you compile an annual report that documents regional sales information into one standardized worksheet. As part of this process, you group the worksheets and insert descriptive rows and columns, apply formatting, and insert functions. Your last step is to create a sales summary worksheet and provide basic information for management to evaluate.

a. Open *e09m1Sales* and save it as **e09m1Sales_LastFirst**.

b. Group the five regional worksheets and do the following:
- Insert a new row above row 1 of the existing data. Type **Agent** in **cell A1**. Apply the **Heading 2 style** from the styles group.
- Type **Qtr1** in **cell B1**. Use the fill handle to add Qtr2-Qtr4 in **cells C1:E1**. Apply **Heading 3 format** to **cells B1:E1**.
- Type **Total** in **cell F1**. In **cell F2**, enter the following function: **=SUM(B2:E2)**. Use the fill handle to complete the summary information for the rest of column F.

c. Keep the five worksheets grouped (not including the Summary sheet) and do the following:
- Type **Total** in **cell A20**. In **cell B20**, insert a function to total Qtr1 sales. Copy the function to the **range C20:F20**.
- Format **cells B2:F20** with the **Accounting Number Format**. Set the column width for the **range B1:F20** to 20.
- Apply **Heading 2 style** to **cell F1**. Add Top and Double Bottom Borders to **cells B20:F20**.

d. Ungroup the worksheets, click the **Summary worksheet tab**, and then apply **Accounting Number Format** to **cells B2:E6**. Select **cells F2:F6** and press **ALT =** to add totals to column F. Set the column width to **18**.

e. Highlight **cells F2:F6** and apply flag indicator conditional formatting.

f. Using the data in the Summary sheet answer the summary questions in the worksheet labeled **Q&A**.

g. Save and close the workbook, and submit it based on your instructor's directions.

2 Temperature Comparisons

As a weather analyst, you have been tracking daily high and low temperatures for Oklahoma City, Tulsa, and Lawton during June, July, and August. Each month's data are stored in their own workbooks, with each city's data stored in its own worksheet. You need to apply consistent formatting and enter formulas for all worksheets. On each workbook, you need to create the summary worksheet to identify the record high and low temperatures by day and identify the respective cities. Finally, you will link the data to a master workbook.

a. Open *e09m2June* and save it as **e09m2June_LastFirst**.

b. Group the city worksheets and do the following:
- Fill the formatting of **cells A1, A2**, and **A5:C5** from the OKC worksheet to the other city worksheets.
- Enter dates 6/1 to 6/30 in this date format (no year) in the Date column. Apply **Orange, Accent 6, Lighter 60% fill** to the dates.
- Split the window after 6/10. Scroll down in the second window to see the Monthly Records section. Note that only the active window in the grouped worksheets is split.
- Enter a function in **cell B39** to calculate the highest temperature of the month. Enter a function in **cell C39** to calculate the lowest temperature of the month.
- Use a nested MATCH function within the INDEX function in **cell B40** to identify the date for the highest temperature. The dataset may contain several identical highest temperatures, but the nested function will identify the first date containing the match.
- Use a nested MATCH function within the INDEX function in **cell C40** to identify the date for the lowest temperature.
- Right-click the **OKC worksheet** and select **ungroup**.

DISCOVER

DISCOVER

c. Use a Web browser to go to **www.wunderground.com**, a weather Web site. Locate and click the **History Data link** below the Local Weather menu and do a search for **OKC**. Copy the URL and create a hyperlink to this Web page for **cell A3** in the OKC worksheet. Add a ScreenTip stating **Click to see weather history for Oklahoma City.**

d. Adapt step c to create hyperlinks for the Tulsa and Lawton worksheets as well. Continue to use **www.wunderground.com** for the weather link. Check each hyperlink to ensure it works correctly.

e. Enter the following 3-D formulas in the appropriate cell in the Summary worksheet:

- Calculate the highest temperature from the three cities for 6/1. Copy the formula down the High column.
- Calculate the lowest temperature from the three cities for 6/1. Copy the formula down the Low column.

DISCOVER

- Enter a nested IF function in **cell C6** to determine which city had the highest temperature. Remember to enclose city names in double quotation marks. Use Help if needed to help you understand a nested IF statement. Copy the formula down the High-City column.
- Enter a nested IF function in **cell E6** to determine which city had the lowest temperature. Copy the formula down the Low-City column.

f. Enter formulas in the shaded *Monthly Records* section (below the daily data) on the summary worksheet to identify the highest and lowest temperatures. Enter nested INDEX and MATCH functions to identify the dates and cities for the respective highest and lowest temperatures.

g. Create a footer with your name on the left side, the sheet name code in the center, and the file name code on the right side of each worksheet. Select the option to center the worksheet data horizontally on each sheet. Save the workbook.

h. Open *e09m2July* and save it as **e09m2July_LastFirst**. Open *e09m2August* and save it as **e09m2August_LastFirst**. Study the workbooks and adapt steps b and e above as necessary to enter formulas on grouped city worksheets and to enter 3-D formulas on the Summary worksheets for these two workbooks. The formatting and hyperlinks are done for you. Add your name on the left side of the footer for each worksheet.

i. Open *e09m2Summer* and save it as **e09m2Summer_LastFirst**. Insert external reference links to the respective cells on the monthly Summary worksheets. Format dates and labels appropriately. Enter your name on the left side of the footer. Save the workbook.

j. Save and close the workbooks, and submit them based on your instructor's directions.

3 Book Club

You have decided to join a book club. As part of the book club, each member has the ability to choose a book from any popular genre. To help make the decision process easier, you have decided to create an Excel spreadsheet that has links to popular media Web sites to allow members of the club to browse the options. You will save this file on SkyDrive to allow each member to access the links as needed.

Student 1

a. Log in to your SkyDrive account using your Windows ID. Do the following to create a shared folder for the rest of the participants.

- Click **Create**, click **Folder**, and then type **Book Club shared folder**.
- Click the newly created folder and click **Excel workbook** from the Create menu.
- Save the newly created file as **e09m3BookClub_LastFirst**.

b. Type **Popular media websites** in **cell A1**.

c. Expand the width of column A to allow the full text to be seen.

d. Name the worksheet **Movie Links**.

e. Close the worksheet to return to the SkyDrive home screen. From the home screen, complete the following steps:

- Right-click the *e09m3BookClub_LastFirst* file and click **Sharing**.
- Type the e-mail address of a student you will be collaborating with in the pop-up window and click **Share**.

Student 2

a. Open the e-mail that contains the shared Excel workbook.

b. Click **Edit in Excel Web App** from the Edit Workbook menu.

c. Click **cell A2**. Click the **INSERT tab** on the Ribbon and create a hyperlink to **www.amazon.com**.

d. Click **cell A3** and create a hyperlink to **www.barnesandnoble.com**.

e. Click **cell A4** and create a hyperlink to **www.ebookstore.sony.com**.

f. Click **cell A5** and create a hyperlink to **www.apple.com/apps/ibooks**.

g. Save the file as **e09p3BookClub_LastFirst** and close.

h. Save and close the workbooks, and submit them based on your instructor's directions

Beyond the Classroom

Europe Trip

RESEARCH CASE →

Your grandparents are giving you a trip to Europe as a graduation present. You need to plan your trip and get cost estimates for their approval. Open *e09b2Trip* and save it as **e09b2Trip_LastFirst**. This workbook will summarize your trip expenditures. You will visit two countries, with two major excursions in each country. Open *e09b2Country* and save it as **e09b2Country1_LastFirst** for the first country you plan to visit. Open *e09b2Country* again and save it as **e09b2Country2_LastFirst**. Each workbook should contain a worksheet for each excursion and a country cost summary worksheet where the cost fields are linked in case your projections change. Convert all costs to U.S. dollars.

Include hyperlinks to Web sites from which you obtained your information in case your grandparents have questions. For ease of visibility, display the Summary worksheet for each country workbook and the trip summary from the trip workbook. Link the country workbook's key financial fields to the overall trip workbook summary area. Set a Watch Window on the total expenditure cell to oversee that a formula error does not occur. Close the Watch Window. Create a footer with your name on the left side, the sheet name code in the center, and the file name code on the right side of each worksheet. Save and close the workbooks, and submit them based on your instructor's directions.

Gradebook Errors

DISASTER RECOVERY +

You are taking a teaching methods course at your college to prepare you to be a secondary education teacher. One course module teaches students about gradebook preparation, in which you learn how to create formulas to assign grades based on course assessment instruments. Your methods professor assigned a flawed gradebook to see how well you and the other future teachers will do in identifying and correcting the errors. Open *e09b3Grades*, and then save it as **e09b3Grades_LastFirst**. Set validation rules for the range of quiz and final exam scores to accept scores between 0 and 100 only. Create appropriate input and error messages. Use the feature to circle invalid data. Start Microsoft Word, click the Insert tab, and then click Screenshot in the Illustrations group to capture a screenshot for the Excel window. Copy the screenshot in Word, and then paste it on the right side of the worksheet data. Adjust the screenshot sizes as needed so that the entire worksheet will print on only two pages. Insert a comment in each cell containing invalid data describing what is wrong with the data and how to fix it. Then fix the data-entry errors.

Use the auditing tools to find errors, and then display precedents and dependents to identify errors. From Microsoft Word, insert a screenshot of the Excel window, and then copy the screenshot in Word and paste it below the first screenshot in the workbook. Correct the errors in the formulas. Insert comments indicating the errors found and how you corrected the formulas. Create a footer with your name on the left side, the sheet name code in the center, and the file name code on the right side of the worksheet. Save and close the workbook, and submit it based on your instructor's directions.

Managing Your Personal Space

You work for E&L Financial, a large financial management company that specializes in department store management. You have been assigned as the account manager of Dickson's department store. As part of your task, you will review the past year's earnings. Moving forward you will continue to manage their earnings, therefore you have decided to create a custom workspace to help manage the data.

Open the file *e09b3Workspace*. Save the file as **e09b4Workspace_LastFirst**. Click New Window in the View tab three times to open three additional copies of the document. Arrange the four workbooks in tiled view. Make the Qtr2 worksheet active in the worksheet located in the top-right corner. Make the Qtr3 worksheet active in the bottom-left corner and the Qtr4 worksheet active in the bottom-right corner. Save the layout as a workspace with the name **e09b4Workspace_LastFirst**. Close the workbook and submit it based on your instructor's directions.

Capstone Exercise

You are an accounting assistant for Downtown Theater in San Diego. The theater hosts touring Broadway plays and musicals five days a week, including matinee and evening performances on Saturday. You want to analyze weekly and monthly ticket sales by seating type.

Data Validation

You notice a few occurrences in which it appears more tickets were sold than seats were available. Therefore, you decide to set a validation rule for Week 1.

a. Open *e09c1Theater10* and save it as **e09c1Theater10_LastFirst**.

b. Select the number of daily Orchestra Front tickets sold for Week 1 in the **range C3:G3**.

c. Create a validation rule to accept only numbers that are less than or equal to the available value in cell B3 (i.e., whole numbers between 0 and 86). The input message should display the ticket type in the title bar and should instruct the user to **Enter the number of tickets sold per day.** Use a Stop icon for invalid data, with a title and specific instructions on what to do to correct invalid data entry.

d. Create respective validation rules for the number of tickets sold for the remaining ticket types.

e. Circle invalid data entry. Change each invalid entry to the maximum number of available seats. Save the workbook.

Group Worksheets and Enter Formulas

You need to calculate the daily revenue by seating type (such as Orchestra Front), the weekly seating totals, and the total daily revenue in the weekly worksheets.

a. Group the four weekly worksheets.

b. Enter a formula to calculate Sunday's Orchestra Front revenue, which is based on the number of seats sold and the price per seat found in cells B15:B22. Use relative and mixed cell references correctly.

c. Copy the formula for the Sunday column to the other weekdays. If you constructed the formula correctly, you should not have to edit the copied formulas.

d. Insert formulas to calculate the weekly seating totals in column H and the total daily revenue in row 23. Include the revenue grand total for the week. Save the workbook.

Format Grouped Worksheets

You want to indent the word *Totals*, format the monetary values in the revenue area, and then insert underlines for readability. You also realize the October worksheet needs similar formatting for the descriptions for each section.

a. Indent and bold the word *Totals* in **cells A11** and **A23** on the grouped worksheets.

b. Apply **Accounting Number Format** with zero decimal places to the Orchestra Front revenue and the Total revenue row.

c. Apply **Comma Style** with zero decimal places to the remaining seating revenue rows.

d. Apply a regular underline to the Balcony Level 2 revenue and apply a **Double Underline** for the total revenue values on Total row.

e. Use Format Painter to copy the formats from **cells A2:H2** to **cells A14:H14**.

f. Ungroup the worksheets. Look at the October worksheet to see that the titles above the column headings lack formatting. Fill the formats of **cells C1** and **C13** from the Week 4 worksheet to the October worksheet *without* copying the content. Save the workbook.

Create Hyperlinks

Because several accountants will review the workbook, you want to add hyperlinks from the documentation worksheet to the other worksheets.

a. Select the **Documentation worksheet**, enter your name and the current date in the respective cells, and then create a hyperlink from the Week 1 label to the Week 1 worksheet.

b. Create the hyperlinks from the Documentation worksheet to the other worksheets.

c. Select the **Week 1 worksheet**. Create a hyperlink in **cell A1** back to the Documentation worksheet. Group the weekly and October worksheets and use the Fill Across Worksheets command to copy the link and formatting for the other weekly and summary worksheets.

d. Test all hyperlinks and make any necessary corrections. Save the workbook.

Create 3-D Formulas

You need to consolidate data from the weekly worksheets to the October worksheet to see the percentage of total daily sales and the total revenue by day/seat type.

a. Insert a 3-D formula that calculates the total Sunday Orchestra Front revenue for all four weeks in **cell C15** in the October worksheet. Copy the formula for the remaining seating types, weekdays, total row, and total column.

b. Use the Week 4 worksheet to fill the revenue number formatting to the October revenue.

c. Enter a 3-D formula in **cell C3** on the October worksheet that calculates the overall percentage of total Sunday Orchestra Front tickets sold based on the total available Orchestra Front seating. The result is 97.7%, based on the sum of 336 Sunday Orchestra Front tickets sold (86+84+80+86) out of 344 (86 available for each performance) available tickets. The 3-D formula must perform several internal calculations, avoid raw numbers, and use an appropriate mix of relative and mixed references to derive the correct percentage. Format the result with **Percent Style** with one decimal place.

d. Copy the formula down the Sunday column through the Avg. Daily Capacity row and then across to the Saturday Evening column.

e. Calculate the average daily revenue for each seating type. Format the results with **Percent Style** with one decimal place and copy the formula down the column. Save the workbook.

Audit a Workbook

You need to identify and correct some errors in the November workbook using the Auditing Tools.

a. Open *e09c1Theater11*, click **OK** to acknowledge the error, and then save the workbook as **e09c1Theater11_LastFirst**.

b. Show precedents for **cell H15** and fix the error in the formula.

c. Activate the Error Checking dialog box to find the first potential error. Display the precedent arrows for that formula. If the formula is correct, click **Ignore Error**. If the formula contains an error, fix it. Continue ignoring correct formulas and fix the error in **cell H23** when detected.

d. Use Error Checking to identify a circular reference. Display the precedents arrow and fix the error. Save the workbook.

Link Workbooks

You need to consolidate monthly revenue into the fourth quarter workbook using links. To make it easier to create the links, you will tile windows.

a. Open *e09c1Theater12* and save it as **e09c1Theater12_LastFirst**.

b. Open *e09c1TheaterQ4* and save it as **e09c1TheaterQ4_LastFirst**.

c. Tile the four windows, making sure the monthly totals worksheets are active.

d. Create links in the *e09c1TheaterQ4_LastFirst* workbook to the individual monthly seat revenue and monthly totals. Save the workbooks.

e. Set up a Watch Window to watch the formulas in the quarterly workbook. Close the Watch Window.

Finalize the Workbooks

You are ready to finalize the workbooks.

a. Create a footer on all worksheets with your name on the left side, the sheet name code in the center, and the file name code on the right side.

b. Apply **landscape orientation** and center the worksheet horizontally on the printouts. Save the workbooks.

c. Save and close the workbooks, and submit them based on your instructor's directions.

Imports, Web Queries, and XML

Managing Data

OBJECTIVES AFTER YOU READ THIS CHAPTER, YOU WILL BE ABLE TO:

1. Import data from external sources p. 442
2. Create a Web query p. 446
3. Manage connections p. 448
4. Convert text to columns p. 456
5. Manipulate text with functions p. 457
6. Use Flash Fill p. 459
7. Understand XML syntax p. 463
8. Import XML data into Excel p. 464

CASE STUDY | Stock Analysis

You are a junior financial analyst for a stockbroker. One of your new clients, Angie Warner, wants you to analyze stock patterns for 10 companies in which she is interested. She e-mailed you a list of the company names and stock symbols, which you will import into an Excel worksheet. You need to create links to stock data on the Web so that you can prepare a thorough analysis for her next week. However, you do not want to simply create hyperlinks to a Web site; you want to import current data into an Excel worksheet so that the data are always up to date. Angie wants a comparison table of basic stock data, which you can import from a Web site. In addition, you need to do in-depth research on two particular stocks by connecting to a Web site containing historical stock data. Your assistant compiled some historical data and saved it in an XML format. You will import those data into your workbook for additional analysis.

In addition to creating links to external data, you need to format the worksheet data. One challenge you will face is to separate the company names (such as BEST BUY CO., INC.) from the stock symbols (such as BBY) that currently share one column into two columns. After separating the data, you will use text functions to display the data in title or proper case, such as Best Buy Co., Inc., because title case is easier to read than all capital letters. Using text functions will save time so that you do not have to retype the data in the desired format. Finally, you will import data containing open, high, low, and close stock prices from an XML file.

External Data

Data originate from and are stored in a variety of locations and formats. When you use Excel to manipulate data and perform quantitative analyses, you might obtain data that originate in an external source—somewhere besides an Excel workbook. For example, you might download customer data from a large database stored on your organization's server, or you want to receive a text file containing data you need to manipulate in Excel.

External data may not be properly formatted for your Excel worksheet, but importing external data and formatting them in Excel maintains greater accuracy than if you manually enter the data. Furthermore, importing external data into a worksheet enables you to update the worksheet data based on changes from the external source.

In this section, you will learn how to import external data into an Excel workbook. Specifically, you will learn how to import text files and Access database tables. In addition, you will learn how to create Web queries.

Importing Data from External Sources

Importing is the process of inserting external data—data created or stored in another format—into the current application. Excel enables you to import a variety of data formats directly into Excel either by opening the file using the Open dialog box or by creating a connection or a link to the original data source. Two of the most common file types you can easily import into Excel are text files and Access database files.

When you import external data into Excel but do not maintain a link to the original data source, you *embed* the data within the Excel worksheet. That is, you can edit the data directly within Excel because they do not have a connection to the original data source. Changes in the original data source or the embedded data in Excel do not change the other data; they are two separate datasets.

When you import external data as a connection, you create a link to the original data source. You can refresh the Excel worksheet so that the imported data are updated if any changes are made to the original data source. Before importing data into Excel, decide whether you need to manage the data as a separate dataset in Excel or if you want to maintain a connection to the original data source.

Import a Text File

A *text file* (indicated by the .txt file extension) is a data file that contains characters, such as letters, numbers, and symbols, including punctuation and spaces. However, a text file does not contain formatting, sound, or video. You can use a text editor, such as Notepad, to create a text file, or you can download data from an organization's database or Web server as a text file. The benefit of a text file is that you can import a text file easily into a variety of programs, such as Excel or Access. After importing data from a text file, you can format the data within Excel.

Text files contain *delimiters*, special characters (such as a tab or space) that separate data. A *tab-delimited file* uses tabs to separate data into columns; a *newline character* is a special character that designates the end of a line and separates data for the next line or row. Figure 10.1 shows a tab-delimited file in Notepad and the imported data in Excel. In the tab-delimited file, the columns do not align; only one tab separates columns. If the user had pressed Tab multiple times to align the data, the data would not have imported correctly into Excel because Excel counts the number of tabs to determine what column the data imports into. An extra tab in a text file imports as a blank cell in Excel.

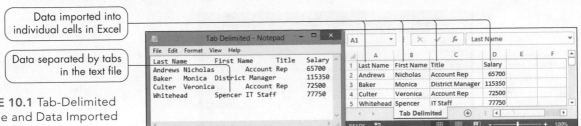

FIGURE 10.1 Tab-Delimited Text File and Data Imported into Excel

The ***comma separated values (CSV) file*** uses commas to separate data into columns and a newline character to separate data into rows. Many Web sites, such as census.gov, contain links to download a text file directly into Excel. When you click the download link from a Web site, the data download into a new Excel workbook or the File Download dialog box opens so that you can open the data in Excel or save the dataset. Figure 10.2 shows a CSV file in Notepad and the imported data in Excel. In the CSV file, commas are used only to separate data; commas are *not* used as the thousands separators in values or as punctuation marks. Otherwise, Excel would separate data at the commas used for punctuation or in values.

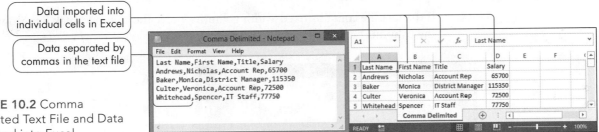

FIGURE 10.2 Comma Delimited Text File and Data Imported into Excel

To import data from a text file into a new Excel workbook, do the following:

STEP 1 »
1. Open the Open dialog box.
2. Click the File Type arrow that currently displays *All Excel Files* and select Text Files.
3. Navigate to the folder that contains the text file, select it, and then click Open.

If you open a file with the .CSV file extension, Excel opens the data immediately in Excel. Because commas delimit the data, data between commas in the CSV file import into individual cells in Excel. Each line within the CSV file becomes a row within Excel.

If you open a file with the .txt file extension, the Text Import Wizard opens, prompting you to specify the data type and other instructions for importing the data during these three major steps:

Step 1: Select Delimited or *Fixed width* based on how the data are structured in the text file. Most text files use delimiters to separate data; therefore, you usually select Delimited to import text data. If data in each column contain the same number of characters and spaces are used only to separate columns, you can choose *Fixed width*. A ***fixed-width text file*** is a file in which each column contains a specific number of characters, such as 5 characters for the first column, 20 for the second column, and so on, to separate the fields.

Set the *Start import at row* value to where you want the data to begin (see Figure 10.3). Look at the *Preview of file* section to see the data in the text file and how they will import based on the *Start import at row* setting. If the text file contains a title or extraneous data extending across multiple columns, do not import from row 1; start importing from the row that contains the actual data.

If the text file contains column headings that describe the contents of each column, click the *My data has headers* check box.

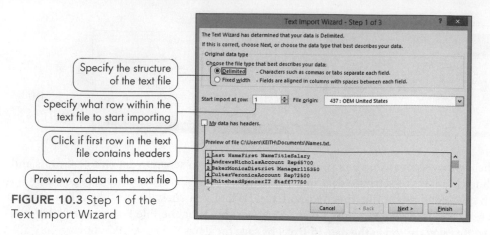

Specify the structure of the text file

Specify what row within the text file to start importing

Click if first row in the text file contains headers

Preview of data in the text file

FIGURE 10.3 Step 1 of the Text Import Wizard

Step 2: Do one of the following in the Text Import Wizard (see Figure 10.4).

- If the text file is delimited, click the appropriate delimiter check box, such as Tab. If the text file contains a different delimiter, click the Other check box and type the specific character in the box.
- If the text file contains fixed-width columns, move the column break lines to where the columns begin and end.

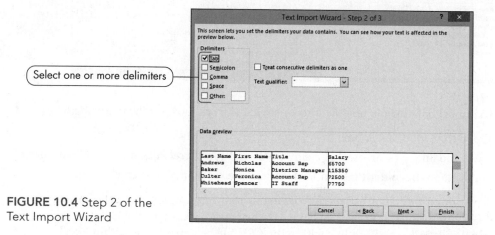

Select one or more delimiters

FIGURE 10.4 Step 2 of the Text Import Wizard

Step 3: Select an option in the *Column data format* section for each column you want to import in the Text Import Wizard (see Figure 10.5).

Click the column heading in the *Data preview* window and select an option in the *Column data format* section. If you do not want to import a column, select it and click *Do not import column (skip)*. The default column data format is General, but you can apply a different format. For example, you might want a column of dates to have the Date format.

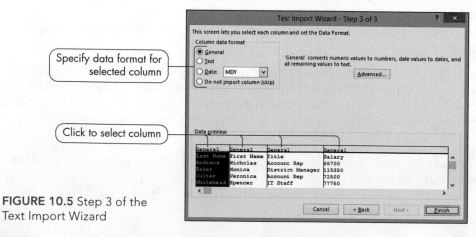

Specify data format for selected column

Click to select column

FIGURE 10.5 Step 3 of the Text Import Wizard

After you import data from a text file, review the data in Excel. Typically, you will need to adjust column widths and format the data, such as centering column labels and applying Accounting Number Format to monetary data. Check for and correct any data errors if the data did not import correctly.

Import an Access Database Table or Query

Large amounts of data are often stored in databases, such as an Access database table. However, database programs are less intuitive about manipulating data for quantitative analyses or do not contain the capabilities to do so. For example, Access 2013 does not contain a PivotTable feature. However, you can import database tables or queries into Excel for further analysis. For example, a car dealership uses a database to maintain an inventory of new cars on the lot, but to analyze monthly sales by car model, the manager uses Excel and creates a PivotTable.

When importing an Access database table or query into Excel, you can maintain a connection to the Access data so that the Excel worksheet data are always current. To import an Access database table or query into Excel:

STEP 2 1. Start Excel, start a new workbook or open an existing workbook, and then click the appropriate worksheet tab to which you want to import the data.

2. Click the DATA tab and click From Access in the Get External Data group to open the Select Data Source dialog box.

3. Select the Access database file that contains data you need to import and click Open.

4. Choose a table or query from the list in the Select Table dialog box (see Figure 10.6). A rectangle icon in the Name column and TABLE in the Type column indicate a table object. The two overlapping rectangles icon in the Name column and VIEW in the Type column indicate a query object. If you want to import more than one table or query, click the *Enable selection of multiple tables* check box and click the check box for each table and query you want to import. Click OK to display the Import Data dialog box (see Figure 10.7).

5. Select how you want to view the data in your workbook, such as Table or PivotTable Report. Select where you want to import the data, such as starting in cell A1 in an existing worksheet or in a new worksheet. Click OK.

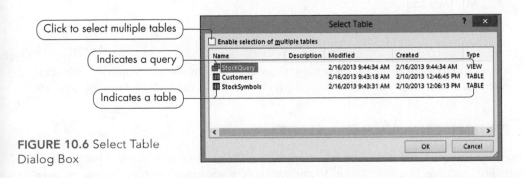

FIGURE 10.6 Select Table Dialog Box

FIGURE 10.7 Import Data Dialog Box

If you import the data as a table, Excel formats the data using a default Excel table style. In addition, Excel displays the Table Tools Design tab as well as the filter arrows so that you can sort and filter data. The Table Name box indicates the data type, such as Table, an underscore, and the name of the Access object (see Figure 10.8).

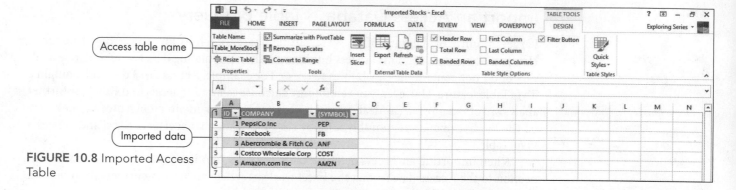

Access table name

Imported data

FIGURE 10.8 Imported Access Table

> **TIP** **Copying Data from an Access Table**
>
> If you do not want to create a link to the Access database table, you can open the table in Access, select the table including field names, copy it, and then paste the data in Excel.

Import Data from Other Sources

You can import data from sources other than text files and Access databases. Click From Other Sources in the Get External Data group to display a list of additional sources:

- SQL Server
- Analysis Services
- Windows Azure Marketplace
- OData Data Feed
- XML Data Import
- Data Connection Wizard
- From Microsoft Query

Use Help to learn about each source and the type of data you can import. Some services require a username and password. Some marketplace datasets require a fee to obtain.

Creating a Web Query

You might need to frequently update worksheet data you imported from a particular Web page. For example, you might want to analyze daily stock prices, traffic accident reports, or airport delays. You can create a **Web query** to set up a connection to a table on a Web page.

The Web query creates a link to the Web page so that you can update the results in Excel without importing the data again. To create a Web query, do the following:

STEP 3 »
1. Click the DATA tab in Excel and click From Web in the Get External Data group to display the New Web Query dialog box (see Figure 10.9).

STEP 4 »
2. Type or paste the URL in the Address box and click Go to display the Web page. Click Yes if the Script Error dialog box opens. If a Security Warning message box opens, click the appropriate button to respond.

3. Scroll within the Web page to the specific data you want.

4. Click the yellow selection icon with a right-pointing arrow to select the table you want. The icon changes to a green box with a check mark, and the table data are selected.

5. Click Options to display the Web Query Options dialog box. Select desired formatting. *None* imports the data without any formatting. Select *Rich text formatting only* or *Full HTML formatting* to maintain formatting, such as bold for the imported data. Click OK.

6. Click Import at the bottom-right corner of the New Web Query dialog box to open the Import Data dialog box.

7. Click either *Existing worksheet* and enter a cell reference of the top-left cell where you want the data to import or click *New worksheet* and click OK.

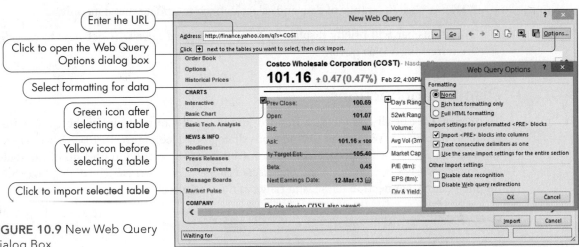

FIGURE 10.9 New Web Query Dialog Box

 TIP Limitations of a Web Query

Before setting up a Web query, you should be aware of its limitations. First, not all Web pages contain data that are structured as a table. Data may *appear* to be in a table format, but if they are not formatted a particular way, you will not be able to create a Web query to the data. Second, Excel connects a Web query to a specific URL. If the URL changes, you must change the URL specified in your Web query to prevent errors. Third, if you have to log in to a Web site, the query generally will not work because it has no built-in feature to store your login and password.

 TIP Copying or Downloading Data from a Web Page

If you do not want to create a link to a Web page, you can select the data on the Web page in a Web browser, copy them, and then paste the data in Excel. Some Web pages have links that will download a CSV file that directly opens into Excel or one you can save to your computer and then open from within Excel.

Managing Connections

When you import data using the options in the Get External Data group, Excel creates a link to the original data source so that you can update the data quickly in Excel. After you create the initial connection, you might want to view or modify the connection. The Connections group on the Data tab contains options to manage your external data connections.

Refresh Connections

Data on a Web page or data in an external database may change periodically. Although you created a connection to the external data within Excel, the data in the database or on a Web page may have changed. For example, if you created a connection to a Web page containing hourly weather, the weather may have changed after you created the connection. To ensure that the Excel data are current, you need to *refresh* the connections to the original external data source periodically. Do one of the following to refresh data:

STEP 5 »

- Click Refresh All in the Connections group to refresh all connections in the active workbook.
- Click the Refresh All arrow in the Connections group and select Refresh to update data for the range containing the active cell.
- Right-click in a range of data and select Refresh to update that data only.

The status bar will briefly display *Running background query...(Click here to cancel)* if you are refreshing a Web query.

Display Connections

To display a list of all connections in a workbook, click Connections in the Connections group to display the Workbook Connections dialog box (see Figure 10.10). To see where a specific connection is located, select the connection name in the top portion of the dialog box and click *Click here to see where the selected connections are used*. The dialog box shows the sheet name, connection name, and range in the worksheet.

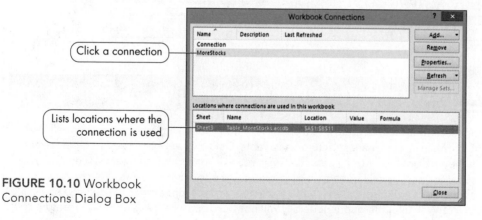

FIGURE 10.10 Workbook Connections Dialog Box

You can remove a connection if you no longer want to link the data to the external data source. After you disconnect the data in Excel from the external data source, you will not be able to refresh the data. To remove a connection, do the following:

1. Select it in the Workbook Connections dialog box.
2. Click Remove.
3. Click OK in the warning message box and click Close in the Workbook Connections dialog box.

Set Connection Properties

Data range properties are settings that control how imported data in cells connect to their source data. These properties also specify how the data display in Excel, how often the data are refreshed, and what happens if the number of rows in the data range changes based upon the current data in the external data source. To display the properties, do one of the following:

- Click Properties in the Connections group.
- Click the Refresh All arrow and select Connection Properties.
- Click Connections in the Connections group and click Properties.

When you click Properties in the Connections group, the External Data Range Properties dialog box displays (see Figure 10.11). This dialog box looks slightly different based on the type of external data you imported and based on which option you use to display the dialog box. For example, the dialog box has fewer options for a connection to an Access database table than it does for a Web query.

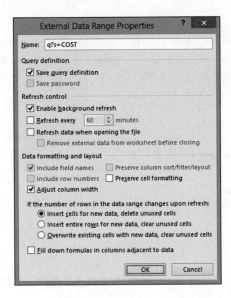

FIGURE 10.11 External Data Range Properties Dialog Box

Quick Concepts ✓

1. What is the purpose of delimiters in a text file? Name two common text file delimiters. **pp. 442–443**

2. What is the difference in opening a text file directly in Excel and using the Get External Data option to import text file data? **p. 445**

3. What is the purpose in creating a Web query? Give two examples of Web pages for which it would make sense to create a Web query. **pp. 446–447**

Hands-On Exercises

Watch the Video for this Hands-On Exercise!

MyITLab®
HOE1 Training

1 External Data

Angie e-mailed a list of 10 companies for you to research. In addition, you want to include a list of 10 other companies that is stored in an Access database table for her further consideration. You will research five companies on each list and then create a Web query to a specific company's historical stock information. Each day, you will need to refresh the connection to import the most up-to-date data into your worksheet.

Skills covered: Import a Text File • Import an Access Database Table • Create Web Queries for Multiple Stocks • Create a Web Query for Historical Stock Data • Maintain Connections

---

STEP 1 ≫ IMPORT A TEXT FILE

Angie created her list of companies in Notepad, so your first task is to import the data into Excel. You do not need to create a connection to the text file because Angie does not plan to update the text file, so you will simply open the file directly from the Open dialog box in Excel. Refer to Figure 10.12 as you complete Step 1.

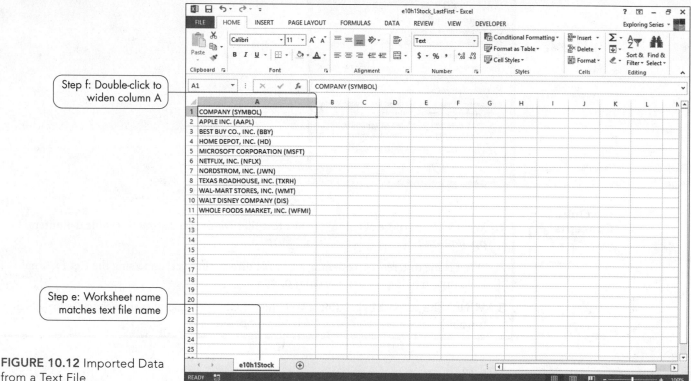

Step f: Double-click to widen column A

Step e: Worksheet name matches text file name

FIGURE 10.12 Imported Data from a Text File

a. Start Excel, click **Open Other Workbooks** in the bottom-left corner of the start window, and then double-click **Computer** to display the Open dialog box.

b. Click the **File Type arrow** that currently displays *All Excel Files*, select **Text Files**, select *e10h1Stock*, and then click **Open**.

The Text Import Wizard dialog box opens. Accept the defaults: Delimited and 1 as *Start at row number*.

c. Click the **My data has headers check box** and click **Next**.

The *Text Import Wizard – Step 2 of 3* dialog box contains options to specify the type of delimiter(s) contained in the text file. This text file does not contain delimiters. You could use the opening parenthesis as a delimiter, but you will use text functions in Hands-On Exercise 2 to separate the company names from the stock symbols.

> **TROUBLESHOOTING**: If you select Space as a delimiter, you will import company names into separate columns. For example, the text *Home Depot, Inc.*, will appear in three separate cells. You cannot use the comma as a delimiter for a similar reason: Home Depot will appear in one cell and Inc. will appear in a separate cell.

d. Deselect all check boxes in the *Delimiters* section and click **Next**.

The *Text Import Wizard – Step 3 of 3* dialog box lets you select each column and specify its data type.

e. Click **Text** in the *Column data format* section and click **Finish**.

Excel imports the data from the text file into the first column of the worksheet. The worksheet name matches the name of the text file: *e10h1Stock*.

f. Double-click between the column A and B headings to widen column A.

g. Click the **FILE tab**, click **Save As**, double-click **Computer**, type **e10h1stock_LastFirst** in the **File name box**, click the **Save as type arrow**, select **Excel Workbook**, and then click **Save**.

STEP 2 》 IMPORT AN ACCESS DATABASE TABLE

You created an Access database table that contains additional company names and their stock symbols. You want to import that into the Excel workbook so that you will be able to analyze more stock options for Angie. Refer to Figure 10.13 as you complete Step 2.

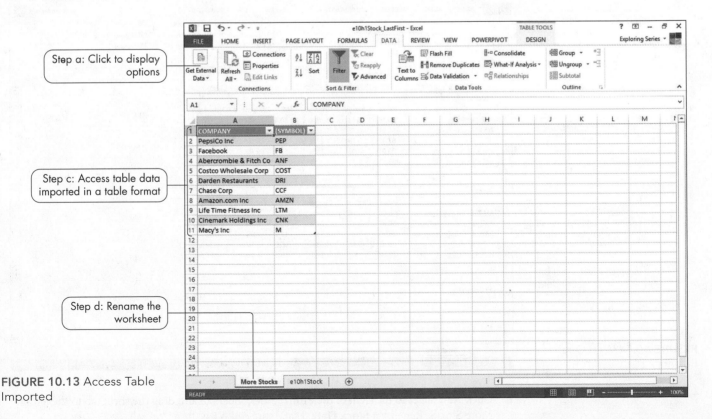

FIGURE 10.13 Access Table Imported

a. Click the **DATA tab**, click **Get External Data** (if necessary), and then click **From Access**.

b. Select **e10h1MoreStocks** in the Select Data Source dialog box and click **Open**.

The Import Data dialog box opens so that you can specify how to the view data and where to place it.

c. Make sure *Table* is selected, click **New worksheet**, and then click **OK**.

You imported the Access data in a new worksheet. Notice that when you import data from a text file, the data import into a range of cells, whereas the Access import formats data as a table.

> **TROUBLESHOOTING**: If you accepted the default set to *Existing worksheet* and =$A$1, Excel will import the data starting in cell A1 and move the existing data to the right. If this happens, select columns A and B, delete them, and then start step a over again.

d. Double-click the **Sheet1 tab**, type **More Stocks**, and then press **Enter** to rename the worksheet.

e. Save the workbook.

STEP 3 ≫ CREATE WEB QUERIES FOR MULTIPLE STOCKS

Based on your past analysis, you selected five stocks from Angie's list and five stocks from your list for further analysis. You want to create a worksheet that compares data for these 10 stocks. However, you will create two separate Web queries of five stocks each. You know from experience that if you try to enter more than five stock symbols at a time, the results will show fewer details than if you limit the Web query to five queries. Refer to Figure 10.14 as you complete Step 3.

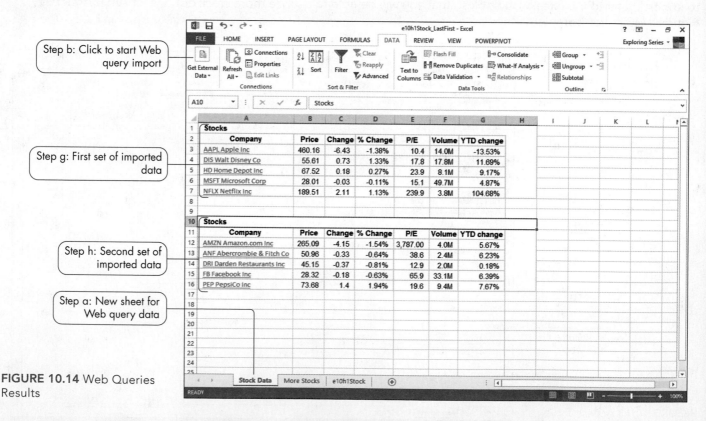

FIGURE 10.14 Web Queries Results

a. Click **New sheet** to the right of the e10h1_Stock sheet tab and drag the sheet tab to the left of More Stocks. Rename it **Stock Data**. Make sure **cell A1** is the active cell.

b. Click the **DATA tab**, click **Get External Data** (if necessary), and then click **From Web**.

The New Web Query dialog box opens, similar to a Web browser window. Maximize the dialog box if you want.

c. Type **www.money.cnn.com** in the **Address box** and click **Go**.

The Web page loads within the New Web Query dialog box.

d. Type **AAPL,DIS,HD,MSFT,NFLX** in the **Enter symbol or keyword box** on the right side of the Web page and click **Search**.

TROUBLESHOOTING: Make sure you spell the symbol names correctly and separate them with commas. If you mistype a stock symbol or leave out a comma, the results will be inaccurate or will produce an error message.

The Web page loads the stock results below the heading *Multiquote results*. A yellow selection icon with a right-pointing arrow displays to the left of the subheading *Stocks*.

e. Click the **yellow selection icon** to the left of the *Stocks* subheading to select the table of multistock data.

The icon is now green with a check mark, indicating you selected this table to import.

f. Click **Options** in the top-right corner of the dialog box to open the Web Query Options dialog box, click **Full HTML formatting**, and then click **OK**.

The Full HTML formatting option maintains hyperlinks to individual company data, header formatting, and other Web page formatting.

g. Click **Import** in the bottom-right corner of the dialog box and click **OK** in the Import Data dialog box.

The headings and table data are imported into the range A1:H7, with column H appearing empty.

h. Click **cell A10**. Repeat steps b through g, substituting **AMZN,ANF,DRI,FB,PEP** in step d. Save the workbook.

The headings and table data are imported into the range A10:H16, with column H appearing empty. Figure 10.14 shows that Netflix had the highest positive year-to-date (YTD) change. (Note: Your results will differ based on the day you perform the Web query.)

STEP 4 ≫ CREATE A WEB QUERY FOR HISTORICAL STOCK DATA

You want to create a Web query to display historical data for Netflix since it has the highest positive year-to-date (YTD) change. The money.cnn.com Web site does not have a built-in table to display historical data for a particular stock, so you will use finance.yahoo.com. Refer to Figure 10.15 as you complete Step 4.

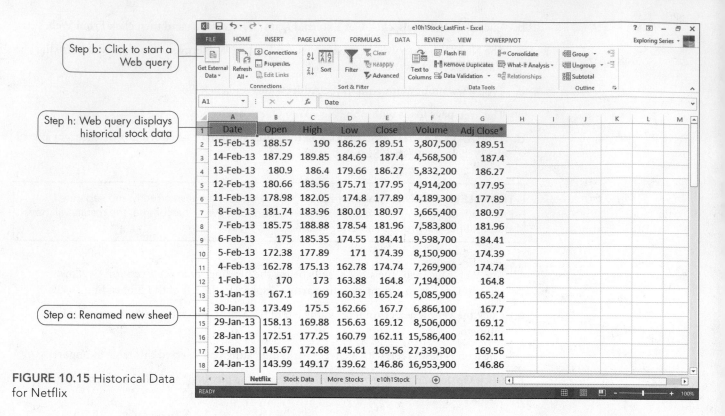

FIGURE 10.15 Historical Data for Netflix

a. Click **New sheet**, move it to the left of Stock Data, and rename it **Netflix**. Make sure **cell A1** is the active cell.

b. Click **Get External Data** and click **From Web**.

The New Web Query dialog box opens.

c. Select any existing text in the **Address box**, type **www.finance.yahoo.com**, and then click **Go**.

> **TROUBLESHOOTING**: If a Script Error dialog box opens, click Yes to continue running scripts on this page. This error may occur several times.

d. Click in the box to the left of *Get Quotes*, type **NFLX**, and then click **Get Quotes**.

A Web page containing information about Netflix, Inc. displays.

e. Scroll down and click **Historical Prices** on the left side.

f. Scroll down to see the *Prices* section and click the **yellow selection icon** next to the Date column heading to select the table containing the data.

The icon changes to a green box with a check mark.

> **TROUBLESHOOTING**: Make sure you click the yellow selection arrow to the top-left of the Date column heading; do not click the yellow selection arrow to the left of the PRICES heading.

g. Click **Options** in the top-right corner of the dialog box to open the Web Query Options dialog box, click **Full HTML formatting**, and then click **OK**.

h. Click **Import** in the bottom-right corner of the dialog box and click **OK** in the Import Data dialog box. Save the workbook.

You will review the historical stock data with Angie during your next meeting.

STEP 5 » MAINTAIN CONNECTIONS

You want to change the refresh property so that it will refresh every 30 minutes for the Web queries you imported for Angie's potential stock investment. This change will enable you to monitor stock price changes throughout the day. Refer to Figure 10.16 as you complete Step 5.

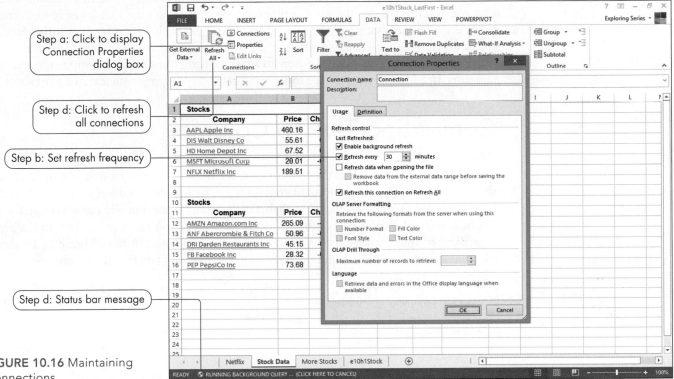

FIGURE 10.16 Maintaining Connections

a. Click the **Stock Data worksheet** and click **cell A10**, if necessary. Click the **DATA tab** (if necessary) and click **Properties** in the Connections group.

A dialog box opens so that you can modify the properties for the Web query.

b. Click the **Refresh every check box**, type **30** in the **minutes box**, and then click **OK**.

The second Web query should update every 30 minutes to reflect any changes that occur on the Web page.

c. Click **cell A1**, set its refresh setting to **30** minutes, and then click **OK**.

The first Web query should update every 30 minutes to reflect any changes that occur on the Web page.

d. Click **Refresh All** in the Connections group.

The status bar displays *Running background query* and the connected data update.

e. Save the workbook. Keep the workbook open if you plan to continue with Hands-On Exercise 2. If not, close the workbook and exit Excel.

Text Manipulation

When you import data from external sources or need to modify a workbook created by someone else, the data may not be structured in a way that meets your needs. For example, data might import into one column instead of multiple columns, which would facilitate sorting and filtering at deeper levels. Furthermore, external data might be in all capital letters, and you want to display the data in title case—text in which the first letter of each major word is capitalized but prepositions such as *in* and *on* are lowercase—so that the data are easier to read. Excel contains features to help you manipulate text to fit your needs.

In this section, you will learn how to separate text stored in one column into multiple columns. In addition, you will use some text functions to manipulate text in a worksheet.

Converting Text to Columns

Whether you use someone else's workbook or import data from external sources, data might display in one column when they would be more useful if separated into two or more columns. For example, a column might contain titles, first names, and last names, such as Mr. John Doe. You need to sort the list alphabetically by last name, but you cannot do that when the first and last names are combined in the same cell. You can use the Text to Columns command to split the contents in one column into separate columns. Figure 10.17 shows combined data in column A and the results after converting text into three columns.

	A	B	C
1	Original Data	Empty Columns	
2	Mr. John Doe		
3	Dr. Jackie Doe		
4	Ms. Jill Doe		
5	Dr. Jay Doe		

	A	B	C
1	Original Column	Originally Empty	
2	Mr.	John	Doe
3	Dr.	Jackie	Doe
4	Ms.	Jill	Doe
5	Dr.	Jay	Doe

FIGURE 10.17 Combined and Separated Data

 STEP 1

The *Convert Text to Columns* Wizard is very similar to the Text Import Wizard. To convert combined text into multiple columns, do the following:

1. Select the column containing the text you want to separate.
2. Click the DATA tab and click *Text to Columns* in the Data Tools group.
3. Use the *Convert Text to Columns* Wizard to distribute the data. Specify the file type, such as Delimited or *Fixed width*, and click Next.
4. Specify the delimiters, such as a Tab or Space, in the *Convert Text to Columns* Wizard—Step 2 of 3. The data shown in Figure 10.17 are delimited by spaces. The wizard can use the space to separate the title and first and last names in this example. Click Next.
5. Select the column data format, such as Text, in the *Convert Text to Columns* Wizard—Step 3 of 3, and click Finish.

TIP Allow Room for Separation

Allow enough columns to the right of the column containing text to separate to avoid overwriting data. Excel does *not* insert new columns. It separates data by placing them into adjoining columns. If you have a first name, middle name, and last name all in one column and you separate to get a first name column, middle name column, and last name column, you must have two empty columns. If the columns on the right side of the original column to split are not empty, Excel will overwrite existing data.

Manipulating Text with Functions

Excel has 24 functions that are specifically designed to change or manipulate text strings. The Function Library group on the Formulas tab contains a Text command that, when clicked, displays a list of text functions. You can also access the text functions from the Insert Function dialog box. Some of the most commonly used text functions are CONCATENATE, PROPER, UPPER, LOWER, and SUBSTITUTE.

Combine Text with the CONCATENATE Function

Text labels are often called text strings. A text string is not used for calculation. You can combine text strings stored in two or more cells into one cell. For example, you might want to combine a last name (e.g., Doe) and first name (e.g., John) stored in two cells into one text string to look like this: *Doe, John*. In this example, you included a comma and a space after the last name. The ***CONCATENATE function*** joins between 2 and 255 individual text strings into one text string. In Figure 10.18, the first name is in cell B2, the last name is in cell C2, and cell E2 contains the =CONCATENATE(C2,", ",B2) function. The comma and space included inside quotes produce *Doe, John*. When constructing a CONCATENATE function, place any data (such as commas and spaces) correctly within quotation marks so that you get the desired result. The text items can be strings of text, numbers, or single-cell references.

=CONCATENATE(text1,text2)

	A	B	C	D	E	F
D2				=CONCATENATE(C2,", ",B2)		
1	Title	First	Last	Concatenated		
2	Mr.	John	Doe	Doe, John		
3	Dr.	Jackie	Doe	Doe, Jackie		
4	Ms.	Jill	Doe	Doe, Jill		
5	Dr.	Jay	Doe	Doe, Jay		

FIGURE 10.18 Concatenation: Join Text Strings

TIP Another Way to Concatenate

Use the ampersand (&) operator instead of the CONCATENATE function to join text items. For example, =A4&B4 returns the same value as =CONCATENATE(A4,B4).

Change Text Case with Text Functions

Data come in a variety of case or capitalization styles, such as ALL CAPS, Title Case, and lowercase. Depending on your usage of data, you may need to change the case in a worksheet. Excel contains three functions to change the case or capitalization of text: PROPER, UPPER, and LOWER. Figure 10.19 illustrates the results of these three functions.

	A	B	C	D	E	F
1	Original	Proper	Upper	Lower		
2	jOHn dOE	John Doe	JOHN DOE	john doe		
3	JACKIE doe	Jackie Doe	JACKIE DOE	jackie doe		
4	jill DOE	Jill Doe	JILL DOE	jill doe		
5	Jay Doe	Jay Doe	JAY DOE	jay doe		

FIGURE 10.19 Results of Text Functions

STEP 2>> Large amounts of capitalized text are difficult to read. Use the ***PROPER function*** to capitalize the first letter of each word in a text string, including the first letter of prepositions (such as *of*) and articles (such as *a*). The PROPER function converts all other letters to lowercase. The text argument is a text string that must be enclosed in quotation marks, a formula that returns text, or a reference to a cell that contains text that you want to partially capitalize. In Figure 10.19, cell B2 contains =PROPER(A2) to change the case to proper case, such as *John Doe*.

=PROPER(text)

The **UPPER function** converts text strings to uppercase letters. The text argument is the text to be converted to all capitals and can be a reference or text string. Use this function when a cell or range contains text in lowercase letters and you need the text to be formatted in all uppercase letters. In Figure 10.19, cell C2 contains =UPPER(A2) to change the case to uppercase letters, such as *JOHN DOE*.

=UPPER(text)

The **LOWER function** converts all uppercase letters in a text string to lowercase. The text argument is text you want to convert to lowercase. In Figure 10.19, cell D2 contains =LOWER(A2) to change the case to lowercase letters, such as *john doe*.

=LOWER(text)

Use the SUBSTITUTE Function

STEP 3 » The **SUBSTITUTE function** substitutes or replaces new text for old text in a text string. For example, if a company changes its name, you can use the SUBSTITUTE function to replace the old company name with the new company name.

=SUBSTITUTE(text,old_text,new_text,instance_num)

Text is the original text or reference to a cell that is to be substituted, *old_text* is the text to be replaced, and *new_text* is the text you want to replace old_text with. *Instance_num* specifies which occurrence of old_text you want to replace with new_text. When instance_num is specified, only that instance is changed. If you do not include instance_num, all occurrences are changed.

Use Other Text Functions

Other text functions help you achieve a variety of text manipulations. Table 10.1 lists a few other common text functions and their descriptions.

TABLE 10.1	Additional Text Functions
Function	**Description**
TRIM(Text)	Removes leading and trailing spaces in a text string but maintains spaces between words in a text string
LEFT(Text,Num_chars)	Returns the specified number of characters from the start of a text string
RIGHT(Text, Num_chars)	Returns the specified number of characters from the end of a text string
MID(Text,Start_num,Num_chars)	Returns the specified number of characters from the middle of a text string, based on a starting position and length

 Nested Text Functions

Text functions are often used in nested functions. You can nest text functions, such as nesting the CONCATENATE function inside an UPPER function argument. For example, =UPPER((CONCATENATE(A2,", ",A3)) concatenates the contents of cells A2, a comma and a space, and the contents of cell A3. The concatenated result is then converted to uppercase.

Using Flash Fill

Flash Fill enables you to enter data in one or two cells to set an example, and Excel completes the data entry for you. Often, you use Flash Fill in conjunction with data in existing columns. Data within a column must be structured in a similar way for Flash Fill to recognize data patterns. For example, in Figure 10.20, column A contains cities and state abbreviations. Instead of using Text to Columns, you can type the first city name in a column adjacent to the dataset and use Flash Fill to create a column of city names only. To use Flash Fill, do the following:

STEP 4 »

1. Enter data that use part of existing data in a column in the dataset.
2. Press Enter and start typing the second sample data. Flash Fill should identify the pattern and complete the column.

   If you type only one sample entry and leave that as the active cell, you can click Fill in the Editing group on the Home tab and select Flash Fill to complete the rest of the column. If Excel can detect a pattern, it will fill in the data in the rest of the column. If Excel cannot detect a pattern, it displays an error message. In order for Flash Fill to work, the existing data must be structured in some pattern Excel can recognize. Flash Fill can often perform the same tasks as some of the text functions, such as PROPER and CONCATENATE.

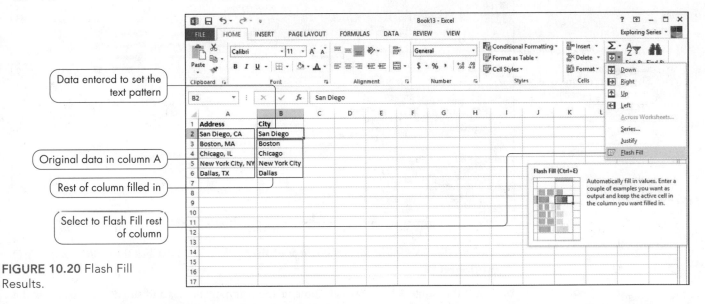

FIGURE 10.20 Flash Fill Results.

 Quick Concepts

1. What is the purpose of the Text to Columns feature? Provide one example of when it would be useful. ***p. 456***

2. What is the difference among the PROPER, UPPER, and LOWER functions? ***pp. 457–458***

3. How must data be structured in order for Flash Fill to work? ***p. 459***

Hands-On Exercises

Watch the Video
for this Hands-
On Exercise!

MyITLab®
HOE2 Training

2 Text Manipulation

After importing the stock data from the text file that Angie gave you, you want to use text functions to manipulate the text within the worksheet. You want to make the data easier to access and display in multiple formats for future usage.

Skills covered: Convert Text to Columns • Use the PROPER Function • Use the SUBSTITUTE Function • Use Flash Fill

---

STEP 1 ≫ CONVERT TEXT TO COLUMNS

Currently, the e10h1Stock worksheet contains the company name and stock symbol in the same column. You want to separate the company names and stock symbols so that you can sort or filter by stock symbols more easily in the future. Refer to Figure 10.21 as you complete Step 1.

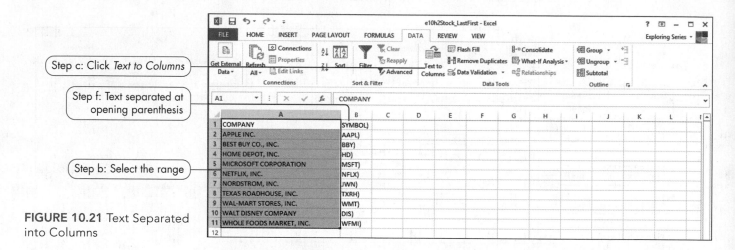

Step c: Click *Text to Columns*

Step f: Text separated at opening parenthesis

Step b: Select the range

FIGURE 10.21 Text Separated into Columns

a. Open *e10h1Stock_LastFirst* and save it as **e10h2Stock_LastFirst**. Click the **e10h1stock worksheet tab**.

b. Select the **range A1:A11**, which contains the company names and stock symbols. Copy the data and paste them starting in **cell A20**. Press **Esc** and select the **range A1:A11** again.

Before using Text to Columns, you copied the data so that you can use Flash Fill later in this exercise.

c. Click the **DATA tab** if necessary and click **Text to Columns** in the Data Tools group.

The Convert Text to Columns Wizard dialog box opens.

d. Leave *Delimited* selected and click **Next**.

Because the selected text has multiple-word company names with spaces and commas such as *Home Depot, Inc.*, you cannot use the space or comma as a delimiter. The best option is to create a custom delimiter character: the opening parenthesis.

e. Deselect all check boxes, click the **Other check box**, and then type (in the **Other box**.

The *Data preview* shows the data in two columns: company names and symbols. Because you used the opening parenthesis as the delimiter, Excel removes that symbol from the text. The closing parenthesis remains at the end of the stock symbol.

> **TROUBLESHOOTING**: If you do not deselect all but the Other check box, the data may not separate correctly into columns.

f. Click **Next**, click **Text** in the *Column data format* section, click the **second column** in the *Data preview* section, click **Text**, and then click **Finish**.

g. Save the workbook.

STEP 2 » USE THE PROPER FUNCTION

You want to improve the readability of the company names by displaying the data in title case using the PROPER function. Refer to Figure 10.22 as you complete Step 2.

FIGURE 10.22 PROPER Function Results

a. Type **COMPANY** in all capital letters in **cell C1** and press **Enter**.

b. Click the **FORMULAS tab**, click **Text** in the Function Library group, and then select **PROPER**.

    The Function Arguments dialog box opens.

c. Click **cell A2** to enter it in the Text box and click **OK**.

    The results of the PROPER function return the proper case of APPLE INC. as Apple Inc.

d. Double click the **cell C2 fill handle** to copy the formula down the column.

e. Increase the width of column C. Save the workbook.

STEP 3 » USE THE SUBSTITUTE FUNCTION

You notice that the second column containing the stock symbols still shows the closing parenthesis. The opening parenthesis was removed when you used it as the delimiter to separate the company names from the symbols in Step 1. Now you will use the SUBSTITUTE function to remove the closing parenthesis. Refer to Figure 10.23 as you complete Step 3.

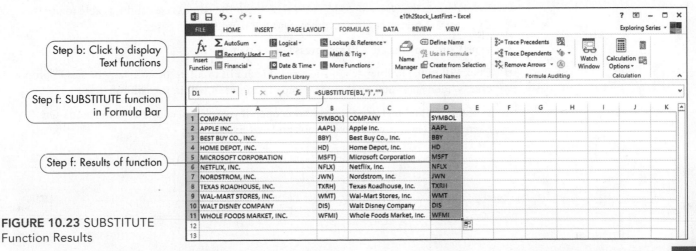

FIGURE 10.23 SUBSTITUTE Function Results

a. Click **cell D1**.

b. Click **Text** in the Function Library group and select **SUBSTITUTE**.

   The Function Arguments dialog box opens so that you can specify the arguments for the SUBSTITUTE function.

c. Click **cell B1** to enter it in the Text box.

d. Press **Tab** and type) in the **Old_text box**.

e. Press **Tab** and type " " in the **New_text box**.

   You are replacing the closing parenthesis with a null or empty string, indicated by the two double quotation marks.

> **TROUBLESHOOTING**: If you attempt to leave the New_text argument blank, an error will occur.

f. Click **OK** and double-click the **cell D1 fill handle** to copy the formula down the column. Save the workbook.

STEP 4 ≫ USE FLASH FILL

While you have been using text functions, you want to experiment with using Flash Fill on the company names and stock symbols. Refer to Figure 10.24 as you complete Step 4.

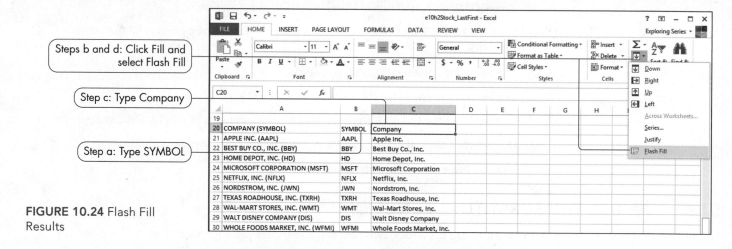

FIGURE 10.24 Flash Fill Results

a. Type **SYMBOL** in **cell B20** and press **Ctrl+Enter**.

b. Click the **HOME tab**, click **Fill** in the Editing group, and then select **Flash Fill**.

   Excel detects that you entered SYMBOL without the parentheses and was able to use that data entry to fill in the stock symbols without parentheses.

c. Type **Company** in **cell C20** and press **Ctrl+Enter**.

d. Click **Fill** in the Editing group and select **Flash Fill** to fill in the company names in proper case. Widen column C so that the company names fit within the column.

e. Save the workbook. Keep the workbook open if you plan to continue with Hands-On Exercise 3. If not, close the workbook and exit Excel.

XML

Organizations run a variety of applications on different hardware and operating systems. Individuals access the same data from different cities or countries, using laptops, desktops, smartphones, and other mobile devices. The hardware and software vary greatly, but they share a common element: They access and manipulate data. Faced with the challenge of creating data that people can use on these various systems, the World Wide Web Consortium (W3C) developed a solution to standardize file formats using eXtensible Markup Language.

eXtensible Markup Language (XML) is an industry standard for structuring data across applications, operating systems, and hardware. It enables data to be sent and retrieved between otherwise incompatible systems. XML describes the structure of data but not the appearance or formatting. Individual users, rather than a central authority, create the XML elements.

In this section, you will learn how to interpret XML tags and how to import XML data into an Excel worksheet.

Understanding XML Syntax

You are probably asking: What is markup language and what makes it extensible? Why is it flexible? Consider the following example:

```
3bedrooms/2bathrooms–$1,000permonth–(305)555-1234
```

You probably recognize the text as an advertisement for an apartment. Although you recognize the advertisement, the computer needs a method to interpret it. Using XML, the advertisement would appear as this, with no space between the tags and the data:

```
<Apartment>
    <Bedrooms>3</Bedrooms>
    <Bathrooms>2</Bathrooms>
    <Rent>$1,000</Rent>
    <Telephone>(305) 555-1234</Telephone>
</Apartment>
```

The data have been marked up with various tags (enclosed in angled brackets) to give it structure. A *tag* is a user-defined marker that identifies the beginning or ending of a piece of data in an XML document. Various tags are nested within one another; for example, the Bedrooms, Bathrooms, Rent, and Telephone tags are nested within the Apartment tag. The tags are relatively obvious and can be read by any XML-compliant application for further processing. The XML document does not contain any information about *how* to display the data; XML *describes* the data itself rather than the formatting of the data.

HTML uses a finite set of predefined tags, such as <b></b> and <i></i> for bold and italic, respectively. XML, however, is much more general because it has an infinite number of tags that are defined as necessary in different applications. In other words, XML is *extensible*, meaning it can be expanded as necessary to include additional data, such as adding elements for the apartment number.

Figure 10.25 displays an XML document that was created in Notepad. The XML declaration in the first line specifies the XML version and the character encoding used in the document. The question mark and angled brackets are part of the optional *XML declaration*, which specifies the XML version and character encoding used. The document also contains a comment in the second line to identify the author. The indentation throughout the document makes it easier to read but is not required.

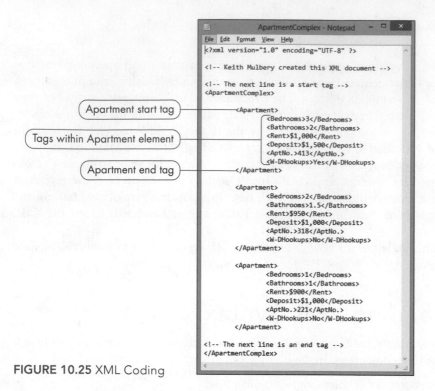

Apartment start tag

Tags within Apartment element

Apartment end tag

FIGURE 10.25 XML Coding

- An XML document is divided into elements. Each **element** contains a start tag, an end tag, and the associated data. The **start tag** contains the name of the element, such as Rent. The **end tag** contains the name of the element preceded by a slash, such as /Rent.

- XML tags are case sensitive. In Figure 10.25, <Rent> and </Rent> use the same case. However, <Rent> $1,000 </rent> would be incorrect because the start and end tags are not the same case.

- XML elements can be nested to any depth, but each inner element (or child) must be entirely contained within the outer element (or parent). For example, the Bedrooms and Rent elements are nested within the Apartment element.

- Indenting indicates the hierarchy structure. For example, elements for a particular month are indented one or two levels so that the start <Month> and end </Month> tags stand out. The outer element tags are aligned for readability.

- An XML comment is optional data that provide explanatory information about the coding. An XML comment starts with <!-- and ends with -->.

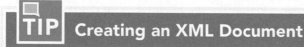

TIP | **Creating an XML Document**

Typically, people use Notepad, or any text editor, to create an XML document, switch to a Web browser, such as Internet Explorer, to view the XML document, and then switch back to Notepad to make any changes.

Importing XML Data into Excel

Excel is designed to analyze and manipulate data, but the source of that data is irrelevant. Data may originate within a worksheet, be imported from an Access table or query, come from a text file, or come from an XML document. Like a text file, an XML document can be opened directly from the Open dialog box or imported with a connection to the original document. To open an XML file, do the following:

1. Display the Open dialog box.
2. Click the File Type arrow and select XML Files.
3. Select the XML file you want and click Open. The Open XML dialog box opens (see Figure 10.26).
4. Select the option that describes how you want to open the file and click OK. If the Microsoft Excel message box appears stating *The specified XML source does not refer to a schema. Excel will create a schema based on the XML source data.* Click OK.

FIGURE 10.26 Open XML Dialog Box

The *As an XML table* default option opens the XML file as a table with each element as a column label or field. Excel imports all records from the source file without any connection to the original XML document. If the original XML document is changed, those changes will not be updated in the Excel workbook. You may have to format some imported XML data. For example, if you import the XML data shown in Figure 10.25, the monetary values import as text. You will then have to apply a number format to use the data as values.

If you select the *Use the XML Source task pane* option, Excel opens a new workbook and displays the XML Source task pane on the right side (see Figure 10.27). The data do not import by default. To map XML elements to worksheet cells and import data, do the following:

1. Drag an element to the desired cell in the worksheet. You do not have to use all XML elements, and you can drag them in any sequence. Notice the different sequence and the omission of the W-DHookups element.
2. Right-click a cell in the XML area and select XML.
3. Select Import, find the XML file containing the data you want to import, and then click OK. Excel imports the data that match the elements and sequence you specified.

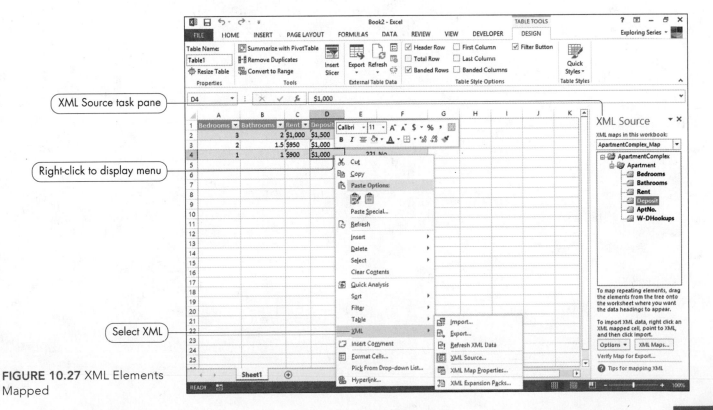

FIGURE 10.27 XML Elements Mapped

STEP 1 ▶ If you want to maintain a connection to the original XML data file, do the following to import the data instead of using the Open dialog box:

1. Click the DATA tab, click From Other Sources in the Get External Data group, and then select From XML Data Import.

2. Select the XML document you want to import in the Select Data Source dialog box and click Open.

3. Select the desired options in the Import Data dialog box and click OK. Excel imports the XML data in the sequence of the original XML file and displays the XML Source task pane on the right side.

Quick
Concepts

1. What is the benefit of XML? *p. 463*

2. What is the standard formatting for elements within an element? *p. 464*

3. If you want to maintain a connection to the original XML file, how should you import it? *pp. 464–465*

Hands-On Exercises

Watch the Video for this Hands-On Exercise!

MyITLab®
HOE3 Training

3 XML

One of your assistants researched a five-month period (October 1, 2012, through February 15, 2013) to identify the open, high, low, and closing prices of Amazon.com, Inc. and Netflix, Inc. stock for the first trading day of each month. She saved the data in XML format. You will need to import that data into your workbook that contains other stock data that you are using to analyze stocks for your client Angie.

Skills covered: Import XML Data • Change the XML Document • Refresh the XML Data in Excel

STEP 1 >> IMPORT XML DATA

You want to import the XML document that contains historical data about Amazon.com and Netflix into a new worksheet in your stock analysis. You will create a connection so that as you or your assistant add more data, you can refresh the Excel worksheet. Refer to Figure 10.28 as you complete Step 1.

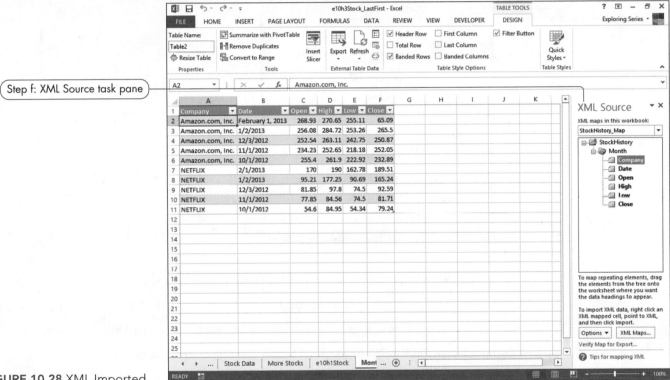

FIGURE 10.28 XML Imported

a. Open *e10h2Stock_LastFirst* and save it as **e10h3Stock_LastFirst**.

b. Start Notepad, select **File**, and then select **Open**. Click the **File Type arrow**, currently indicated as Text Documents (*.txt), and select **All Files**. Open *e10h3HighClose.xml* in Notepad and save it as **e10h3HighClose_LastFirst.xml**. Keep Notepad open.

c. Display the Excel workbook, click **New sheet**, and then rename the worksheet **Monthly Data**.

d. Click the **DATA tab**, click **Get External Data**, click **From Other Sources**, and then select **From XML Data Import**.

The Select Data Source dialog box opens.

e. Select *e10h3HighClose_LastFirst.xml* from your data files, click **Open**, click **OK** in the message box informing you that the XML source does not refer to a schema, and then click **OK** in the Import Data dialog box.

The data import into the Monthly High Close worksheet.

f. Right-click within the imported data, point to *XML*, and then select **XML Source**. Save the workbook.

The XML Source task pane displays on the right side of the worksheet.

STEP 2 » CHANGE THE XML DOCUMENT

You notice that the name NETFLIX is in all capital letters and that a February date is in a different format from the other dates. In addition, the first Close price for Amazon.com is 65.09, which seems low compared the rest of the February 1, 2013, values. You realize it contains an error and needs to be corrected. You need to modify the original XML document and save the changes. Refer to Figure 10.29 as you complete Step 2.

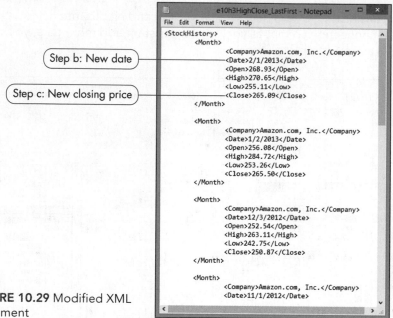

FIGURE 10.29 Modified XML Document

a. Display the *e10h3HighClose_LastFirst.xml* document in Notepad.

b. Change *February 1, 2013* to **2/1/2013** on the fourth line in the XML file.

You changed the date to be consistent with the other dates in the XML document.

c. Change *65.09* to **265.09** for the 2/1/2013 Close price for Amazon.com.

> **TROUBLESHOOTING:** Be careful when editing the XML document that you do not delete any of the tags. If so, you will need to retype the tags to avoid error messages.

d. Click **Edit** and select **Replace** to open the Replace dialog box.

e. Type **NETFLIX** in the **Find what box**, type **Netflix** in the **Replace with box**, click the **Match case check box**, and then click **Replace All**.

You replaced the capitalized company name with one in title case.

f. Click **Cancel**, save the XML document in Notepad, and then close Notepad.

> **TROUBLESHOOTING:** If you are unable to save the XML file in Notepad, close the Excel workbook, save the XML file in Notepad, and then open the Excel workbook again.

STEP 3 ≫ REFRESH THE XML DATA IN EXCEL

Now that you have modified the XML document with the correct data, you will need to refresh the imported data in the Excel workbook. Refer to Figure 10.30 as you complete Step 3.

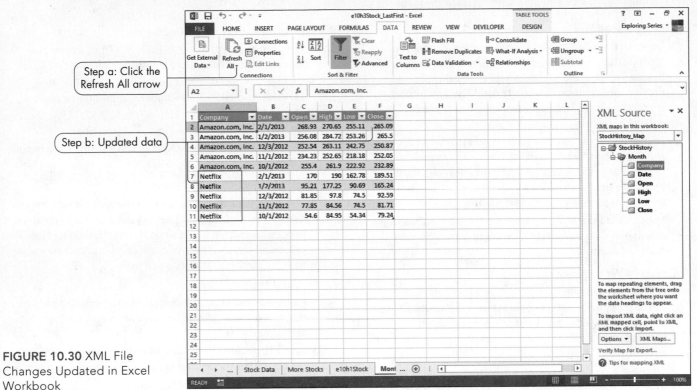

FIGURE 10.30 XML File Changes Updated in Excel Workbook

a. Click **cell A2**, click the **DATA tab** in Excel, and then click the **Refresh All arrow** in the Connections group.

b. Select **Refresh**.

   Excel refreshes only the XML data in the workbook.

c. Save and close the workbook, and submit based on your instructor's directions.

Chapter Objectives Review

After reading this chapter, you have accomplished the following objectives:

1. Import data from external sources.

- Import a text file: Text files usually contain delimiters to separate data. A tab-delimited file is a text file that uses tabs to separate data, and a comma-separated value file is a text file that uses commas to separate data. The Text Import Wizard guides you through importing data and selecting the delimiter.
- Import an Access database table or query: You can copy data from an Access table into Excel. If you want to maintain a connection to the Access table, import it through the Get External Data command. You can then select the table or query, how to view the data, and where to place it.
- Import data from other sources: You can import data from other sources, such as an SQL server or from Windows Azure Marketplace.

2. Create a Web query.

- A Web query sets up a connection to a particular table on a Web page, such as stocks or other data that might change frequently. You can update the results in Excel without having to complete the import process every time you want current data.
- To create a Web query, type the URL in the Address box of the New Web Query dialog box. Click a selection icon to select a table within a Web page.
- Click Options to specify if you want to maintain formatting.

3. Manage connections.

- Refresh connections: Click Refresh All to refresh all connections or click the Refresh All arrow to select a specific refresh option.
- Display connections: The Workbook Connections dialog box lists the connections within the workbook. You can click a connection to see where it is located in the workbook.
- Set connection properties: Display the external Data Range Properties dialog box to specify the query definition, refresh control, and other attributes for a specific data import.

4. Convert text to columns.

- When you import data or receive a workbook, data might be stored in one column. Use the Text to Columns command to separate data into multiple columns. Specify a delimiter and format the columns in the Wizard.

5. Manipulate text with functions.

- Combine text with the CONCATENATE function: This function joins two or more text strings into one text string.
- Change text case with text functions: Use the PROPER, LOWER, and UPPER functions to control the case of text.
- Use the SUBSTITUTE function: The SUBSTITUTE function substitutes new text for old text in a text string.
- Use other text functions: Other useful text functions include TRIM, LEFT, RIGHT, and MID.

6. Use Flash Fill.

- The Flash Fill feature enables you to enter data into one cell that uses part of data in a previous column. The data in the previous column must be similarly structured. The Flash Fill command can then be used to quickly fill the new column with the same type of data typed in the first cell.

7. Understand XML syntax.

- eXtensible Markup Language (XML) is a standard file format that enables data sharing across hardware, operating systems, and applications.
- An XML document contains user-defined tags to mark up the beginning and ending of data elements, such as a person's name.
- The start tag contains the name of the element, such as <Rent>, and the end tag contains a slash and the element name, such as </Rent>. Tags are case sensitive; that is, <Rent> is different from <rent>.

8. Import XML data into Excel.

- Use the Open dialog box to import XML data into a new blank workbook.
- Click Get External Data, click From Other Sources, and then select XML Data Import to import XML data into an existing or new workbook but maintain a connection to the actual XML file.

Key Terms Matching

Match the key terms with their definitions. Write the key term letter by the appropriate numbered definition.

a. Comma separated values (CSV) file
b. CONCATENATE function
c. Delimiter
d. Element
e. End tag
f. eXtensible Markup Language (XML)
g. Fixed-width text file
h. Flash Fill
i. Importing
j. LOWER function
k. PROPER function
l. Refresh
m. Start tag
n. SUBSTITUTE function
o. Tab-delimited file
p. Tag
q. Text file
r. UPPER function
s. Web query

1. _____ A function that converts all uppercase letters to lowercase. **p. 458**

2. _____ An XML component, including the start tag, an end tag, and associated data. **p. 464**

3. _____ An XML code indicating an element's starting point and element's name. **p. 464**

4. _____ A file that uses commas to separate text into columns. **p. 443**

5. _____ A file that contains letters, numbers, and symbols only; it does not contain formatting, sound, or video. **p. 442**

6. _____ A character used to separate data in a text file. **p. 442**

7. _____ A function that capitalizes the first letter in a text string and any other letters in text that follow any character other than a letter. **p. 457**

8. _____ A file that uses tabs to separate text into columns. **p. 442**

9. _____ An XML code indicating an element's ending point and name. **p. 464**

10. _____ A function that joins two or more text strings into one text string. **p. 457**

11. _____ A data connection that links an Excel worksheet to a particular data table on a Web page. **p. 446**

12. _____ A data-structuring standard for sharing data across applications, operating systems, and hardware. **p. 463**

13. _____ A user-defined marker that identifies the beginning or ending of a piece of XML data. **p. 463**

14. _____ A file that stores data in columns that have a specific number of characters designated for each column. **p. 443**

15. _____ The process of updating data in Excel to match current data in the external data source. **p. 448**

16. _____ The process of inserting data from one application or file into another. **p. 442**

17. _____ A function that substitutes new text for old text in a text string. **p. 458**

18. _____ A feature that fills in data or values automatically based on one or two examples you enter. **p. 459**

19. _____ A function that converts text to uppercase letters. **p. 458**

Multiple Choice

1. A text file separates data by a special character called a:
   - (a) Position holder.
   - (b) Delimiter.
   - (c) Column spacer.
   - (d) Start tag.

2. You created a Web query to determine how many bushels of corn were harvested in your state last year. You referenced a USDA Web page. You need to view that page again and cannot remember the URL. You should:
   - (a) Open the Excel workbook and use the Data Import Wizard to find the URL.
   - (b) Use the Find command to locate the URL.
   - (c) Create a hyperlink to the URL.
   - (d) Open the Excel workbook and open the Connection Properties dialog box where the URL is listed.

3. Last week, you created a Web query in Excel to import price and volume data about the stocks that interest you from a Web site. You open the file today and refresh the data. What will your spreadsheet show?
   - (a) The values you saved in the file last week and any calculations based on that data.
   - (b) The new values of the stock, but the calculations will need to be updated to reflect the current values.
   - (c) The new values with the calculations reflecting the current values of the stocks.
   - (d) The values you saved in the file last week, but you cannot create calculations based on a Web query.

4. Your coworker created a workbook with a list of names and addresses. The state abbreviation and ZIP code are stored in one cell per customer, such as NC 27215. You need to be able to sort these data by postal code to use bulk-rate mailing. The appropriate Excel action is to:
   - (a) Type 27215 in the cell to the right of NC 27215 and use Flash Fill.
   - (b) Copy the data to another column and edit each cell to delete the state abbreviations.
   - (c) Use the BREAK APART function to separate the state abbreviation and zip code.
   - (d) Insert a new column and retype the postal codes.

5. A workbook contains addresses in column C. The addresses use commas after the street, city, and state, such as 129 Elm Street, Burlington, NC, 27215. Column D contains the phone number. You instruct Excel to divide the data into multiple columns using comma delimiters. You successfully divide the column into four columns. What happens to the phone numbers in column D?
   - (a) Excel inserts new columns for each comma so the phone number will move to column G.
   - (b) The phone numbers are overwritten by the cities.

   - (c) Nothing will happen to the phone numbers.
   - (d) The phone numbers will convert to commas.

6. The text in column D is in uppercase letters. You want to convert the text to an initial capital letter followed by lowercase letters. You should use the _____ function.
   - (a) CONCATENATE
   - (b) UPPER
   - (c) LOWER
   - (d) PROPER

7. You received an inventory report showing what items and the quantities of each your store has in stock. All merchandise has a unique inventory number stored in column B. All items' eight-digit inventory numbers begin with 9890. You want to remove the 9890 prefix to better sort and manage the list. In a new column, insert the _____ function to show just the final four digits of the data in column B.
   - (a) LEFT(B2,9890)
   - (b) RIGHT(B2,9890)
   - (c) RIGHT(B2,4)
   - (d) LEFT(B2,4)

8. One advantage of using XML data is that:
   - (a) Data are not dependent on a specific operating system.
   - (b) XML contains instructions on how the data should be formatted.
   - (c) People must use identical tag names.
   - (d) Once coded, XML data cannot be expanded.

9. When using the XML Source task pane option, you may not:
   - (a) Select only some of the desired elements.
   - (b) Change the elements' order.
   - (c) Map the XML elements to a specific worksheet.
   - (d) Import all elements by default.

10. Examine the following XML code and select the TRUE statement.
    ```
    <internship>
        <position>Help Desk Trainee</position>
        <pay>10.50</pay>
        <payperiod>hour</payperiod>
        <hours>mornings</hours>
    </internship>
    ```
    - (a) The tag names should use all capital letters.
    - (b) The nested tags (position, pay, payperiod, and hours) have no connection to the internship.
    - (c) Only applicants available in the mornings will be considered.
    - (d) Adding <b> before and after <hours> will create boldfaced type.

Practice Exercises

1 Seattle Travel Time

FROM
SCRATCH

You own a company that provides legal document delivery to attorneys and clients in Seattle. You need to know the estimated travel time before you send your couriers out with the legal documents. You will create a Web query to the Travel Times table on the Washington State Department of Transportation Web site. This exercise follows the same set of skills as used in Hands-On Exercise 2 in the chapter. Refer to Figure 10.31 as you complete this exercise.

	State Route/ Interstate	Route Description	Distance (miles)	Average Travel Time	Current Travel Time	Via HOV (min.)	G	H	I	J	K
4	I-405	Alderwood to Southcenter	29.4	33	30	N/A					
5	I-5	Alderwood to Southcenter	27.97	36	30	N/A					
6	I-5	Arlington to Everett	13.32	13	13	N/A					
7	SR 167	Auburn to Renton	9.76	10	10	10					
8	I-405	Bellevue to Bothell	9.61	10	10	10					
9	I-405 I-5	Bellevue to Everett	26.04	29	27	27					
10	I-405 I-5	Bellevue to Federal Way	24.56	28	25	25					
11	I-405 I-90	Bellevue to Issaquah	9.55	10	10	10					

FIGURE 10.31 Web Query for Travel Times

a. Start a new blank workbook and save it as **e10p1Travel_LastFirst**.

b. Import data from WSDOT's Web page by doing the following:
- Click the **DATA tab** and click **From Web** in the Get External Data group.
- Type **http://www.wsdot.com/traffic/traveltimes/default.aspx** in the **Address box** and click **Go**.
- Click the **yellow selection arrow** in the top-left of the State Route/Interstate column label.
- Click **Options** in the top-right corner of the dialog box, click **Full HTML formatting** in the Web Query Options dialog box, and then click **OK**.
- Click **Import** in the New Web Query dialog box.
- Accept the default settings in the Import Data dialog box and click **OK**.

c. Rename Sheet1 as **Seattle Travel Times** and save the workbook.

d. Start Word, save the new document as **e10p1Travel_LastFirst**, and then do the following:
- Click the **INSERT tab** and click **Screenshot** in the Illustrations group.
- Click **Microsoft Excel - e10p1Travel_LastFirst** in the Available Windows gallery to insert a screenshot of the Excel workbook.
- Click **Picture Border** in the Picture Styles group and click **Black, Text 1**.
- Insert a footer with your name on the left side, **Seattle Travel Times** in the center, and a file name field on the right side of the document. Save the Word document.

e. Display the Excel workbook, set **0.2"** left and right margins, and select **rows 1:3** to repeat at the top.

f. Create a footer with your name on the left side, the sheet name code in the center, and the file name code on the right side of the worksheet.

g. Save and close the workbook. Wait a few hours, open the workbook, click the **DATA tab**, and then click **Refresh All** in the Connections group.

h. Insert another screenshot on the second page in the Word document. Apply the **Black, Text 1** picture border. Save and close the Word document.

i. Save and close the workbook, and submit based on your instructor's directions.

2 New Employees

One of your jobs in the IT Department is to create e-mail addresses for new employees. You received a text file containing a list of new employees. You will use text functions to convert the data to columns, create a list with surnames first in proper case, create a list of e-mail addresses, and then create a list of alternate e-mail addresses since your company provides two e-mail addresses per person: one with an underscore between the first and last names and one with a period between the first and last names. This exercise follows the same set of skills as used in Hands-On Exercises 1 and 2 in the chapter. Refer to Figure 10.32 as you complete this exercise.

FIGURE 10.32 Names and E-Mail Addresses

	A	B	C	D	E	F
1	FIRST	LAST	NAMES	E-MAIL ADDRESS	ALTERNATE E-EMAIL ADDRESS	
2	FRANK	BAILEY	Bailey, Frank	frank_bailey@ourcompany.com	frank.bailey@ourcompany.com	
3	RENA	BERKOWICZ	Berkowicz, Rena	rena_berkowicz@ourcompany.com	rena.berkowicz@ourcompany.com	
4	HEATHER	BOND	Bond, Heather	heather_bond@ourcompany.com	heather.bond@ourcompany.com	
5	JEFF	BOROW	Borow, Jeff	jeff_borow@ourcompany.com	jeff.borow@ourcompany.com	
6	ZEV	BOROW	Borow, Zev	zev_borow@ourcompany.com	zev.borow@ourcompany.com	
7	ARIEL	BOROW	Borow, Ariel	ariel_borow@ourcompany.com	ariel.borow@ourcompany.com	
8	LARRY	BRAGG	Bragg, Larry	larry_bragg@ourcompany.com	larry.bragg@ourcompany.com	
9	HARRY	BUNTING	Bunting, Harry	harry_bunting@ourcompany.com	harry.bunting@ourcompany.com	
10	JEFF	COTTRELL	Cottrell, Jeff	jeff_cottrell@ourcompany.com	jeff.cottrell@ourcompany.com	

a. Open the Open dialog box in Excel, click the **File Type arrow**, select **Text Files**, select *e10p2Names*, and then click **Open**.

b. Do the following in the Text Import Wizard dialog box:
  - Click the **My data has headers check box** and click **Next**.
  - Deselect all check boxes in the *Delimiters* section and click **Next**.
  - Click **Text** in the *Column data format* section and click **Finish**.

c. Click the **FILE tab**, select **Save As**, type **e10p2Names_LastFirst** in the **File name box**, click the **Save as type arrow**, select **Excel Workbook**, and then click **Save**.

d. Convert the data into two columns by doing the following:
  - Click the **column A header**, click the **DATA tab**, and then click **Text to Columns** in the Data Tools group to open the *Convert Text to Columns Wizard* dialog box.
  - Make sure *Delimited* is selected and click **Next**.
  - Select the **Space check box**, deselect the other check boxes, and then click **Next**.
  - Click **Text**, click the **General column** in the *Data preview* section, and then click **Text**.
  - Click **Finish** and widen columns A and B.

e. Combine names and convert the text to proper case by doing the following:
  - Click **cell C1**, type **Last, First**, and then press **Ctrl+Enter**.
  - Click the **HOME tab**, click **Fill** in the Editing group, and then select **Flash Fill** to fill the names down the column. Widen column C.

f. Click **cell D2**, type **=LOWER(CONCATENATE(A2,"_",B2,"@ourcompany.com"))**, and then press **Ctrl+Enter**. Copy the formula down the column and widen column D.

g. Click **cell E2**, type **=SUBSTITUTE(D2,"_",".")**, and then press **Ctrl+Enter**. Copy the formula down the column and widen column E.

h. Type **NAMES** in **cell C1**, **E-MAIL ADDRESS** in **cell D1**, and **ALTERNATE E-MAIL ADDRESS** in **cell E1**. Bold and center the labels on the first row.

i. Select **Landscape orientation**, set **0.3"** left and right margins, and then set titles to repeat the first row.

j. Create a footer with your name on the left side, the sheet name code in the center, and the file name code on the right side for each worksheet.

k. Save and close the workbook, and submit based on your instructor's directions.

3 Years on the Job

You manage a local bank in Kansas City. Employee retention is a concern. You are considering providing incentives to employees who have worked for the bank for more than five years. The HR director provided a list of employees and dates they were hired in an XML document. You will import the data into Excel and create a formula to calculate the number of years each employee has worked. In addition, you will count the number of employees by years on the job and to apply a conditional format for employees who have worked more than five years. This exercise follows the same set of skills as used in Hands-On Exercise 3 in the chapter. Refer to Figure 10.33 as you complete this exercise.

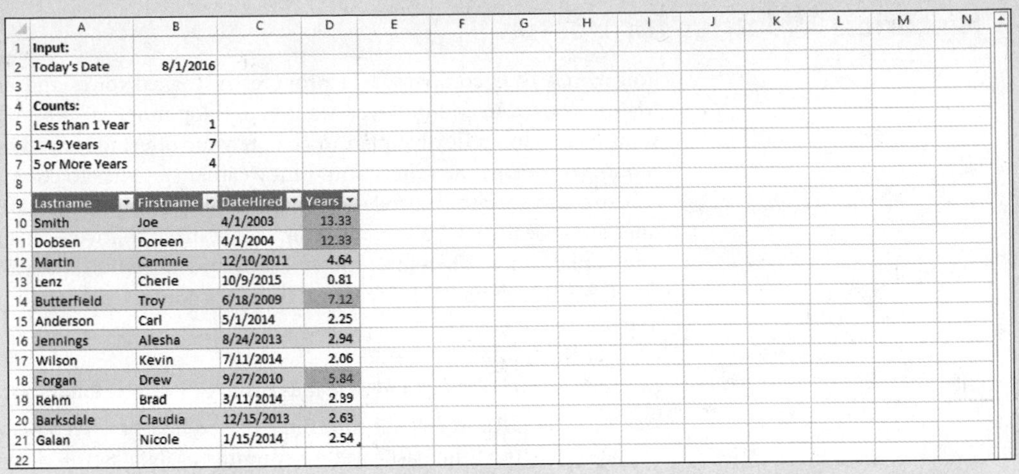

	A	B	C	D
1	Input:			
2	Today's Date	8/1/2016		
3				
4	Counts:			
5	Less than 1 Year	1		
6	1-4.9 Years	7		
7	5 or More Years	4		
8				
9	Lastname	Firstname	DateHired	Years
10	Smith	Joe	4/1/2003	13.33
11	Dobsen	Doreen	4/1/2004	12.33
12	Martin	Cammie	12/10/2011	4.64
13	Lenz	Cherie	10/9/2015	0.81
14	Butterfield	Troy	6/18/2009	7.12
15	Anderson	Carl	5/1/2014	2.25
16	Jennings	Alesha	8/24/2013	2.94
17	Wilson	Kevin	7/11/2014	2.06
18	Forgan	Drew	9/27/2010	5.84
19	Rehm	Brad	3/11/2014	2.39
20	Barksdale	Claudia	12/15/2013	2.63
21	Galan	Nicole	1/15/2014	2.54
22				

FIGURE 10.33 Employee List

a. Copy *e10p3People.xml* and rename the copied file as **e10p3People_LastFirst.xml**.

b. Open *e10p3Employees* in Excel and save it as **e10p3Employees_LastFirst**.

c. Import the XML data by doing the following:
- Click the **DATA tab**, click **Get External Data** if needed, and then click **From Other Sources**.
- Select **From XML Data Import**, select *e10p3People_LastFirst.xml*, and then click **Open**.
- Click **OK** in the Microsoft Excel message box.
- Type **A9** in the **XML table in existing worksheet box** and click **OK**.

d. Type **Years** in **cell D9**.

e. Calculate and conditionally format the number of years by doing the following:
- Type **=YEARFRAC(C10,B$2)** in **cell D10** and press **Ctrl+Enter**.
- Select the **range D10:D21** and apply the **Comma Style**.
- Click **Conditional Formatting** in the Styles group on the HOME tab, point to *Highlight Cells Rules*, select **Greater Than**, type **4.99** in the **Greater Than dialog box**, and then click **OK**.

f. Enter functions to count the number of employees by year by doing the following:
- Type **=COUNTIF(D10:D21,"<1")** in **cell B5**.
- Type **=COUNTIFS(D10:D21,">=1",D10:D21,"<5")** in **cell B6**.
- Type **=COUNTIF(D10:D21,">=5")** in **cell B7**.

g. Double-click between the column A and B column headings to increase the width of column A.

h. Save the workbook. Open *e10p3People_LastFirst.xml* in Notepad. Change Cheri Lenz's hire date to **10/9/2015**. Change Drew Forgan's hire date to **9/27/2010**. Be careful not to delete any XML tags. Press **Ctrl+S** to save the XML document and close it.

i. Click the **DATA tab** and click **Refresh All** in the Connections group. If warning messages appear, click **OK** in each message box and save the workbook. Adjust the width of column A.

j. Create a footer with your name on the left side, the sheet name code in the center, and the file name code on the right side of the worksheet.

k. Save and close the workbook, and submit based on your instructor's directions.

Mid-Level Exercises

1 Historical Weather for Boston

You own a tour company that provides historical tours and activities for vacationers in Boston, Massachusetts. In addition, you want to develop more off-season activities for the colder months. You want to develop a flexible plan to change your offerings based on the day's weather. You track three months of weather at a time. You want weather statistics to compare to your sales for the period to be able to see the weather correlation and fine-tune your product offerings. In the past, you created a Web query to a weather Web site; however, you realized that you can't select the table within the New Web Query dialog box. Therefore, you will copy and paste the data from the Web site into your Excel worksheet. (Although the Web page has a link for a comma-delimited file, the headings will not import into one row in Excel.)

a. Open *e10m1Weather* and save it as **e10m1Weather_LastFirst**.

b. Copy the URL in **cell C2** into the Address box of a Web browser. Select the starting and ending dates to extract the past full three months of data. Scroll down to the Observations table. Drag to select starting with the column labels through the end of the table, press **Ctrl+C**, click **cell A5** in the Raw Data sheet, and then click **Paste**.

c. Set **6.1** column widths for columns A:S, bold the headings on rows 5 and 6, and then apply **Align Right** for the headings on row 6. Apply **Bottom Border** for row 5.

d. Click **cell V7** and create a nested function that displays *sunny* for any day that does not have an event observation and repeats events if listed. Nest the IF statement in a function that displays the results in uppercase letters. After you copy the function down the column, delete functions on heading rows between months. Type **Weather** in **cell V6** and adjust the width for this column.

e. Display the Statistics sheet. In the **range B4:D10**, create functions to display the appropriate results for the number of days by event using data from the Raw Data sheet. Use the * wildcard to count multiple-event days respectively. For example, if the weather is *RAIN, THUNDERSTORM*, make sure the function counts that day for both Rain and Thunderstorm.

f. Insert functions to calculate the average temperatures and precipitation statistics in the **range B11:D16**. Use mixed cell references to enable efficient copying and slight editing of formulas as you copy them. Apply **Comma Style** with the appropriate number of decimal points to the results.

g. Use a formula that replaces the Month 1, Month 2, and Month 3 column labels in the Statistics worksheet with the name of the months in the Raw Data worksheet. Horizontally center the column labels.

h. Use the Raw Data worksheet to create three line charts—one per month—to plot the daily high, average, and low temperatures. Place each line chart on a separate sheet, and name the sheets appropriately, such as **November Temps**. Add an appropriate chart title to each chart.

i. Create a footer for all worksheets with your name on the left side, the sheet name code in the center, and the file name code on the right side.

j. Save and close the workbook, and submit based on your instructor's directions.

2 Animal Shelter

ANALYSIS CASE

FROM SCRATCH

You manage a small animal shelter in Dayton, Ohio. Your assistant created an XML document that lists some of the recent small animals that your shelter took in. In particular, the XML document lists the animal type (such as cat); the age, sex, name, color, and date the animal was brought in; and the date the animal was adopted. You want to manage the data in an Excel worksheet, so you will create a link to the original data source in case they change.

a. Use Windows to copy the *e10m2Animals.xml* file and rename the copied file **e10m2Animals_LastFirst.xml**.

b. Start a new workbook and save it as **e10m2Animals_LastFirst**.

c. Import the XML document *e10m2Animals_LastFirst.xml* into Sheet1 of the workbook. Rename Sheet1 **Animals**.

d. Create a PivotTable from the imported data, placing the animal type and sex as row labels and counting names as values. Use the adoption date as a report filter and set a filter to show those animals that have *not* been adopted. Rename the PivotTable worksheet **PivotTable**. Delete the blank worksheets.

e. Open *e10m2Animals_LastFirst.xml* in Notepad. Edit the XML document by adding **3/25/2016** for the adoption date for Paws the cat. Edit Fido's data by entering his age: **6 months**. Edit Twerpy's color as **Orange**. Edit Misty's adoption date of **3/31/2016**. Save the XML file and close Notepad.

f. Display the Animals worksheet in Excel and refresh the connection. Display the PivotTable worksheet and refresh the PivotTable.

 g. Display the PivotTable worksheet, type labels **Most Available Animals**, **Most Adopted Animals**, and **Cat Gender Most Adopted** in the **range A15:A17**. Type answers to these questions in the **range B15:B17**.

h. Display the Animals worksheet and type **Name, Type** as a column label in **cell H2**. In **cell H3**, type **Paws, Cat**. Use Flash Fill to complete the rest of the data entry in this column.

i. Create a footer with your name on the left side, the sheet name code in the center, and the file name code on the right side of each worksheet.

j. Save and close the workbook, and submit based on your instructor's directions.

COLLABORATION CASE

It is interesting to find out what people's favorite movies are. Work with a classmate to create an Access database table of favorite movies that you can import into an Excel workbook.

FROM SCRATCH

a. Create a blank Access database named **e10m3Movies_LastFirst.accdb**.

b. Create a table with these fields: Movie Title, Genre, Rating, Year Released, Lead Actor, and Lead Actress. Save the table as Favorite Movies_Last First.

c. Enter 10 records in the table, one for each of your favorite 10 movies.

d. Close the Access database and upload it to a SkyDrive where you give your team member privileges to read and write files.

e. Download your team member's Access file and rename it by adding your last name after his or her name in the file name.

f. Start a new Excel workbook and save it as **e10b3Movies_LastFirst.xlsx**.

g. Import your team member's Access database table into your Excel workbook.

h. Create a footer with your name on the left side, the sheet name code in the center, and the file name code on the right side of the worksheet. Save the workbook.

i. Open the Access database file *e10b3Movies_LastFirstLastFirst.accdb*.

j. Add five of your favorite movies to the list. Make sure they do not duplicate any existing data. Sort the table in alphabetical order by movie title. Close the database.

k. Refresh the connection in Excel so that the data are updated to match the changes you made to the database.

l. Upload your completed files to the SkyDrive account so that your team member can access your files to see what movies you added.

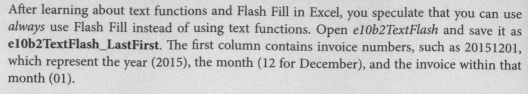

Beyond the Classroom

Text Functions vs. Flash Fill

RESEARCH CASE

After learning about text functions and Flash Fill in Excel, you speculate that you can use *always* use Flash Fill instead of using text functions. Open *e10b2TextFlash* and save it as **e10b2TextFlash_LastFirst**. The first column contains invoice numbers, such as 20151201, which represent the year (2015), the month (12 for December), and the invoice within that month (01).

Research the text functions that were not covered in Hands-On Exercise 2 and use text functions to separate the invoices to display the year, month, and invoice number in the range B4:D16. Answer the question by typing your responses in the range A19:E21. Use Flash Fill to complete data in the range H4:J16. Answer the question by typing your responses in the range H19:J21.

Create a footer with your name on the left side, the sheet name code in the center, and the file name code on the right side of the worksheet. Save and close the workbook, and submit based on your instructor's directions.

Personal Book Library

DISASTER RECOVERY

Your friend Jeromy wants to create a list of books in his personal home library. His brother created an XML document containing data for a few of Jeromy's books. Unfortunately, the document contains errors. Use Windows to copy *e10b3Books.xml* and rename the copied file **e10b3Books_LastFirst.xml**. Open the XML document in Notepad. Identify the errors. Insert XML-style comments that describe the errors. XML-style comments begin with <!-- and end with -->. Also, insert comments on style issues, although these issues are not programming errors. Fix the errors and style issues and save the XML document. Import the XML document into a new Excel workbook and name the workbook **e10b3Books_LastFirst** in the Excel Workbook format. Rename Sheet1 **Book List** and delete the extra worksheets. Create a footer with your name on the left side, the sheet name code in the center, and the file name code on the right side of the worksheet. Save and close the workbook, and submit based on your instructor's directions.

Sexual Harassment

SOFT SKILLS CASE S

FROM SCRATCH

Use a Web browser to read information about sexual harassment and then locate a table that provides statistics on sexual harassment or sexual harassment charges in the United States. Copy the URL. Start a new workbook named **e10b4Harassment_LastFirst**. Create a Web query using the URL you found. Select the option to preserve HTML formatting and import the data. Below the imported data, type a source line and paste the URL. In the next cell, type the date you retrieved this information. Create a footer with your name on the left side, the sheet name code in the center, and the file name code on the right side of the worksheet. Save and close the workbook, and submit based on your instructor's directions.

Capstone Exercise

Whisenhunt Enterprises is located in Oklahoma City. Denise Petrillo and Omar Vincent travel frequently for business. To help plan for flight delays, you will create a workbook that provides airline data with up-to-date arrival and departure information from the Will Rogers World Airport.

Import Text

You need to import airline data (airline names, codes, and URLs) from a tab-delimited file created by one of your colleagues. In addition, you need to separate the airline name from its code.

a. Use Windows to copy the *e10c1Airlines.txt*. Rename the copied file as **e10c1Airlines_LastFirst.txt**.

b. Open *e10c1Departures* and save it as **e10c1Departures_LastFirst**.

c. Display the Airline Codes worksheet. Create a link to *e10c1Airlines_LastFirst.txt*, a tab-delimited file. Select the option that the text file has headers.

d. Edit *e10c1Airlines_LastFirst.txt* in Notepad. Type **Frontier**, **F9**, and **FF5** in alphabetical order, pressing **Tab** between columns. Save and close the text file.

e. Refresh the connection to the text file.

Obtain Data from a Web Site

You want to copy data from the Will Rogers World Airport Web site. You can't create a Web query because Excel is not able to recognize the departures data as a table.

a. Use a Web browser to go to **http://flyokc.com/**, click **Departing**, and then click **Search**.

b. Copy and paste the departure data in the Departures worksheet in Excel.

Insert Text and Logic Functions

You want to use functions to extract data from the Departures worksheet to the Filtered List worksheet. For the first column, you want to insert a function to look up the airline code. For the second column, you want to combine the airline code with the flight number. For the third column, you want to display the city name in title case. For the fourth column, you want to display the time and then format it. For the last column, you want to display the status in title case.

a. Create a table using the **range A1:E51** on the Filtered List worksheet.

b. Click **cell A2**. Use a VLOOKUP function to look up the airline in the Departures worksheet, compare it to the airline table in the Airline Codes worksheet, and return

the IATA code for that airline. For example, United will display as UA.

c. Click **cell B2**. Use a text function to combine the airline code from the previous step with a space and the flight number on the respective row in the Departures worksheet.

d. Click **cell C2**. Use a text function to display the cities from the Departures worksheet in the desired format, such as Houston.

e. Click **cell D2**. Enter a formula to repeat the time from the Departures worksheet. Format the entire column with the **Time format**, such as 1:30 PM.

f. Click **cell E2**. Enter a text function that returns the status in title case, such as On Time.

g. Set a filter for both Houston airports with a status of **On Time**.

Import XML Data

Another employee created an XML file containing city names and airport codes. You want to connect to this XML file. After importing the XML file, you realize one major airport is missing and an airport code is incorrect for another airport.

a. Use Windows to copy *e10c1Airports.xml*. Rename the copied file **e10c1Airports_LastFirst.xml**.

b. Create a connection to the *e10c1Airports_LastFirst.xml* file in the Airports worksheet.

c. Open *e10c1Airports_LastFirst.xml* in Notepad. Copy the first Airport element and paste the copy above the original first airport element. Edit the data by typing **Atlanta** and **ATL** within the proper tags.

d. Change the Chicago airport code to **ORD**.

e. Save the XML file and close it.

f. Refresh the XML connection only.

Finalize the Workbook

You are ready to finalize the workbook.

a. Create a footer with your name on the left side, the sheet name code in the center, and the file name code on the right side of each worksheet. Delete any extra worksheets.

b. Save and close the workbook, and submit based on your instructor's directions.

Collaboration and Workbook Distribution

Sharing Data with Others

OBJECTIVES   AFTER YOU READ THIS CHAPTER, YOU WILL BE ABLE TO:

1. Customize Excel p. 482

2. Change properties p. 485

3. Share and merge workbooks p. 491

4. Insert comments p. 494

5. Track changes p. 496

6. Check for issues p. 505

7. Protect a workbook p. 507

8. Save a workbook in different formats p. 514

9. Send a workbook to others p. 516

CASE STUDY | Marching Band Senior Dinner

You are a senior member of your school's marching band. As a senior gift, you would like to organize a fundraiser to help the band purchase new uniforms. To raise the required funds, you are going to organize a dinner with music provided by the senior members of the band. Each dinner ticket is $100, but you plan to provide a few complimentary tickets to current benefactors of the program. The dinner is held in the university ballroom. The university waives the standard room rental fee, but the Facilities Department charges for table and chair rentals, linen cleaning, and cleanup. A grocery store donates the food ingredients, and a decorator prepares and donates a variety of decorations. Additional expenses include beverages, flowers, table decorations, and various publicity costs.

As the event coordinator, you developed a worksheet that contains an input section for the number of tables, chairs, complimentary tickets, and ticket price. In addition, you itemized revenue, donations, expenses, and net income. To ensure the budget is accurate and complete, you will share the workbook with other students to get their feedback using collaborative tools. After updating the workbook, you will check for issues, protect the workbook from unauthorized modification, save the workbook in several formats, and distribute the final workbook to other people who have a vested interest in the success of the event.

Customization and Personalization

When you move into a new apartment, you want to add your personal touches to it by decorating it to suit your style. Similarly, you might want to personalize Excel to suit your needs. You can customize Excel through the Excel Options dialog box. Think of the Excel Options dialog box as the control center that manages the behavior and settings of Excel—the color scheme, formula rules, automatic corrections, AutoComplete rules, and which items display onscreen. Previously, you used the Excel Options dialog box to load the Solver and Analysis ToolPak add-in applications.

In addition to customizing the Excel program itself, you might want to personalize workbooks that you create. For example, you might want to insert your name as the workbook author or add your company name to the workbook. Adding these attributes to your workbooks gives you the credit for the work you do in an organization.

In this section, you will customize Microsoft Office using your name as the user name. In addition, you will view and add properties to characterize a workbook.

Customizing Excel

The Excel Options dialog box contains a variety of settings that control how Excel behaves. Table 11.1 lists the options categories and some key options that you can customize.

TABLE 11.1   Excel Options Categories

Category	Description	Some Options
General	Controls general Excel options	Interface options, such as the color scheme. Defaults for new workbooks, such as font and number of sheets. Personalization: User name and the newly added customizable office backgrounds.
Formulas	Controls formula calculations, performance, and error handling	Workbook calculation Formula AutoComplete Error checking rules
Proofing	Controls corrections and formatting	AutoCorrect Spelling
Save	Controls how workbooks are saved	File format AutoRecover rules
Language	Specifies language preferences	Editing languages ScreenTip language
Advanced	Controls advanced settings	Editing options Cut, copy, and paste Display settings Formula settings
Customize Ribbon	Enables users to customize the Ribbon	Commands, tabs, and groups Reset Import/Export
Quick Access Toolbar	Enables users to customize the Quick Access Toolbar	Commands Reset Import/Export
Add-Ins	Manages add-in programs	Active and inactive add-ins
Trust Center	Keeps documents safe	Protecting your privacy Security and more Microsoft Excel Trust Center

When you create an Excel workbook, a Word document, or a PowerPoint presentation, the respective program identifies the default user information to code the files. The user name indicates who authored a particular document. You should personalize your copy of Microsoft Office so that the files will automatically indicate that you authored or edited the file. Because people share files with each other on a network or via e-mail within an organization, it is important to know who created or edited a particular file. For example, you want to add your name as the author of the Marching Band Senior Dinner workbook so that others will know that you created the budget. To personalize Microsoft Office, do the following:

1. Click the FILE tab to access the Backstage view.
2. Click Options to open the Excel Options dialog box, which shows the General options for working with Excel (see Figure 11.1).
3. Type your name in the User name box in the *Personalize your copy of Microsoft Office* section. (In Microsoft Word, PowerPoint, or Access, you can also enter your first and last initials in the Initials box.) Click OK.

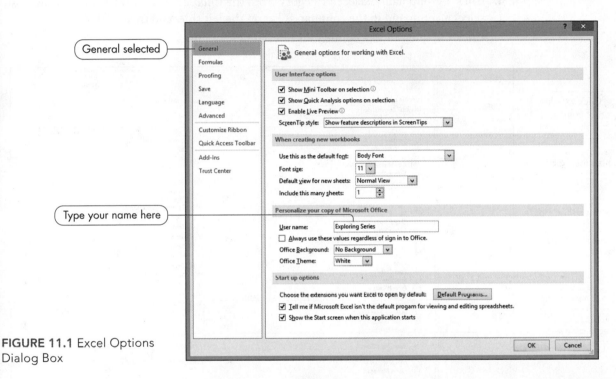

FIGURE 11.1 Excel Options Dialog Box

 TIP **Common Personalization**

Entering your user name and initials in one Microsoft Office program stores that information in the other Microsoft Office programs. On a private computer, changes you make become the default. If you are in a computer lab, however, the lab settings may delete your preferences when you log out.

Customize the Ribbon

When you load an add-in such as Solver, Excel adds a command automatically to a tab on the Ribbon. In addition, if you install software, such as Adobe Acrobat, you might see an Add-Ins tab with commands that interact with those programs. You can customize the Ribbon by creating new tabs and groups, adding and removing commands, and resetting the Ribbon. People customize the Ribbon when they use particular commands frequently, but they do not want to click several original tabs to execute a command. By creating a custom tab with frequently used commands, they can use one tab to do most of their work. To create a new custom tab with commands, do the following:

1. Click the FILE tab, click Options, and then click Customize Ribbon (see Figure 11.2).
2. Click New Tab. Excel adds *New Tab (Custom)* with *New Group (Custom)* to the Main Tabs list.
3. Click New Tab (Custom) in the Main Tabs list, click Rename, type a name in the *Display name* box in the Rename dialog box, and then click OK. The tab now has a unique name. Use Help to learn how to hide a tab or change the order of tabs. Use the same process to rename New Group (Custom).
4. Click New Group to add another new group on the custom tab.
5. Click New Group (Custom) in the Main Tabs list, click Rename, type a name in the *Display name* box in the Rename dialog box, and then click OK. The group now has a unique name. Repeat this process to rename all new groups you add to the tab. Use Help to learn how to change the order of groups on a tab.
6. Click a group name, select a category from the *Choose commands from* drop down list, select a command in the commands list on the left side, and then click Add.
7. Click OK after adding commands to each new group.

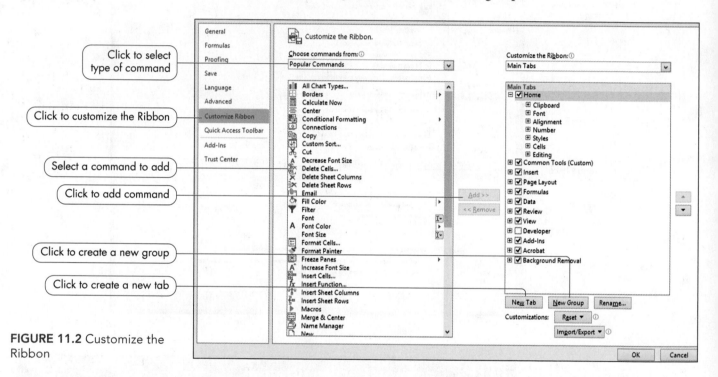

FIGURE 11.2 Customize the Ribbon

TIP Reset the Ribbon

You can reset customizations if you no longer need them. To reset changes made to an original tab, select the tab in the Main Tabs list, click Reset, and then select *Reset only selected Ribbon tab*. To remove all customizations and return to the original settings, including new tabs created and Quick Access Toolbar customizations, click Reset, select *Reset all customizations*, and then click Yes. To remove a custom tab, right-click it in the dialog box and select Remove.

Customize the Quick Access Toolbar

By default, the Quick Access Toolbar contains three commands: Save, Undo, and Redo. You can customize the Quick Access Toolbar to add any frequently used commands. To customize the Quick Access Toolbar, do the following:

1. Click Customize Quick Access Toolbar, the arrow to the right of the Quick Access Toolbar, and select More Commands. Alternatively, click the FILE tab, click Options, and then click Quick Access Toolbar. The list of commands is similar to those for customizing the Ribbon.

2. Do one of the following to customize the Quick Access Toolbar:

   - Choose a command group from the *Choose commands from* drop down menu. Click a command in the list on the left and click Add to add a command to the Quick Access Toolbar.
   - Click a command in the right list and click Remove to remove it from the Quick Access Toolbar.
   - Click Reset and select *Reset only Quick Access Toolbar* to reset it to the default settings.
   - Use Help to learn how to change the order of commands or group commands by adding a separator.

3. Click OK.

 TIP Import and Export Settings

After customizing the Quick Access Toolbar or Ribbon, you can share the custom settings with other people. Click Import/Export, select *Export all customizations*, enter a file name in the File Save dialog box, and then click Save. The file is saved as an Exported Office UI File format. To import the customizations file on another computer, click Import/Export, select *Import customization file*, select the file in the File Open dialog box, and then click Open.

Changing Properties

STEP 1>> When you create or edit a file, *metadata* (data that describe other data) or **document properties** are attached to that file. Document properties that describe or identify a file include details such as the author's name, title, subject, company, creation date, revision date, and keywords. Including document properties for your workbooks helps you organize your files. In addition, you can perform a search to find files that contain particular properties. For example, you can use Windows to perform a search for all files authored by a coworker or all files that contain *marching band* as keywords.

STEP 2>> On the File tab, click Info, if necessary, to display the properties for the current workbook (see Figure 11.3). You can enter or edit standard properties, such as Title, Categories, and Author, by positioning the mouse pointer over the respective property, clicking, and typing the information. You are not able to change automatically updated properties directly, such as Size, Last Modified, and Last Printed. These properties change based on when you last perform an action, such as saving the workbook. When you save the workbook, the document properties are saved as part of the workbook too.

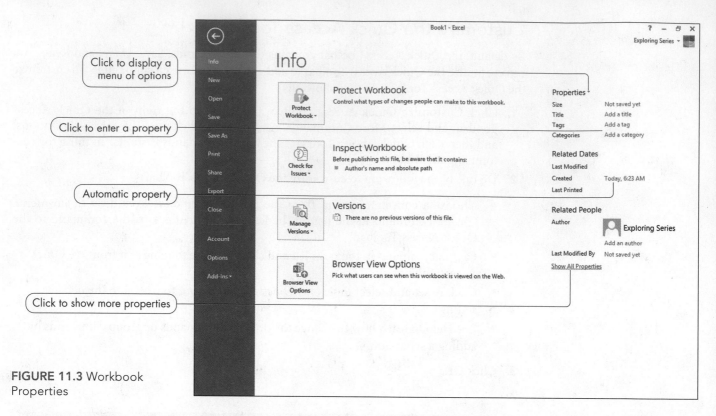

FIGURE 11.3 Workbook Properties

To view workbook properties, do the following. Click the File tab on the Ribbon to access the Backstage view. Click the Show All Properties link in the bottom-right corner to display additional properties, such as Company and Manager. When you display all the properties, the link changes to Show Fewer Properties. You can click Show Fewer Properties to display the original shortened list of properties again.

Use the Properties Dialog Box

The Properties dialog box provides more details than the property list. To display the Properties dialog box, click Properties on the right side of the Backstage view and select Advanced Properties. The dialog box name reflects the current workbook name, such as Marching Band Senior Dinner Properties (see Figure 11.4).

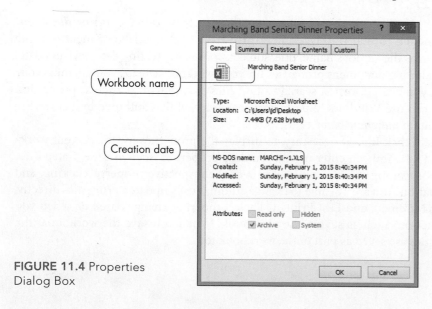

FIGURE 11.4 Properties Dialog Box

The dialog box contains five tabs to organize various properties:

STEP 3»

- **General.** Displays the file name, file type, location, size, creation date, modification date, and last accessed date. In addition, it indicates the attributes, such as Read only or Hidden. General properties are created automatically and cannot be changed directly by the user.

- **Summary.** Displays properties the user can enter and change, such as title, subject, author, manager, company, category, keywords, and comments. Keywords are helpful to add as document properties because they help describe the document, and you can use keywords to search for files that contain particular keywords, such as when you enter keywords to conduct an Internet search.

- **Statistics.** Includes creation, modified, accessed, and printed dates. Also displays the author who last saved the file, revision number, and total editing time, if tracked.

- **Contents.** Displays the worksheet names contained in the workbook.

- **Custom.** Enables the user to create and maintain custom properties for the current workbook, such as Department, Project, and Purpose.

Show the Document Panel

STEP 4»

You can display the Document Panel above the workbook so that you can view and edit properties while reviewing the workbook data. To do this:

1. Click the FILE tab, click Info, if necessary, and then click Properties.
2. Select Show Document Panel.
3. The Document Panel enables you to enter the Author, Title, Subject, Keywords, Category, Status, and Comments properties.
4. To remove the Document Panel, click the Close (X) button in the top-right corner of the Document Panel.

Quick Concepts

1. Why would you add custom tabs to the Ribbon? *p. 483*

2. How do you add your author information to a Document's Properties? *p. 483*

3. How do you show the Document Panel? *p. 487*

Hands-On Exercises

1 Customization and Personalization

You want to personalize Microsoft Office on your computer so that your name will appear in the Author property on new files you create in any Microsoft Office 2013 program. In addition, you want to add some properties to the Marching Band Senior Dinner workbook.

Skills covered: Enter a User Name • Display and Add Properties • Add Advanced Properties • Display the Document Panel

STEP 1 » ENTER A USER NAME

Before working on the Marching Band Senior Dinner workbook, you want to enter your name as the user name for Microsoft Office 2013 on your computer.

a. Open *e11h1Dinner* and save it as **e11h1Dinner_LastFirst**.

> **TROUBLESHOOTING:** If you make any major mistakes in this exercise, you can close the file, open *e11h1Dinner* again, and then start this exercise over.

b. Click the **FILE tab** and click **Options**.

The Excel Options dialog box opens. General is the default category on the left side.

c. Select any existing text in the **User name box**, type your name, and then click **OK**. Save the workbook.

STEP 2 » DISPLAY AND ADD PROPERTIES

You want to display the document properties for the Marching Band Senior Dinner workbook. Because the workbook was created before you entered your name as the user name, you want to edit the Author property. In addition, you want to enter information about the Senior Dinner in the Title property. Refer to Figure 11.5 as you complete Step 2.

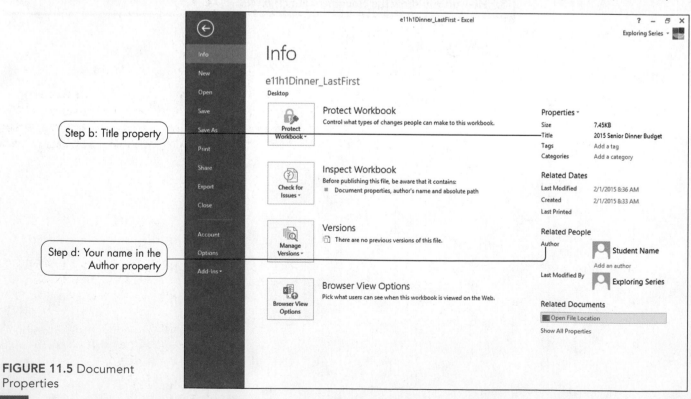

FIGURE 11.5 Document Properties

a. Click the **FILE tab**.

b. Click **Add a title** that displays next to the Title property, type **2015 Senior Dinner Budget**, and then press **Enter**.

The Title property displays the text you entered.

c. Right-click **Exploring Series**, the currently listed Author property, and select **Edit Property**.

The *Edit person* dialog box opens.

d. Select the text in the **Enter names or e-mail addresses box**, type your name, and then click **OK**.

e. Click the back arrow to exit the Backstage view and save the workbook.

STEP 3 ≫ ADD ADVANCED PROPERTIES

You want to add some additional properties to the workbook. Specifically, you want to enter Chef Dan as the manager. In addition, you want to enter keywords, such as donations, ticket prices, and expenses. Refer to Figure 11.6 as you complete Step 3.

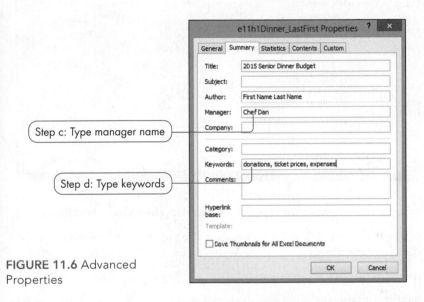

FIGURE 11.6 Advanced Properties

a. Click the **FILE tab**, if necessary, click **Info**, click **Properties**, and then select **Advanced Properties**.

The Properties dialog box for the current workbook opens.

b. Click the **Summary tab**, if necessary.

c. Click in the **Manager box** and type **Chef Dan**.

d. Click in the **Keywords box** and type **donations, ticket prices, expenses**.

e. Click **OK**, click the back arrow to leave the Backstage view, and then save the workbook.

STEP 4 ▶▶ DISPLAY THE DOCUMENT PANEL

You want to look at the Senior Dinner worksheet data as you decide which additional properties to enter. To see the worksheet data and properties at the same time, you will display the Document Information Panel. Refer to Figure 11.7 as you complete Step 4.

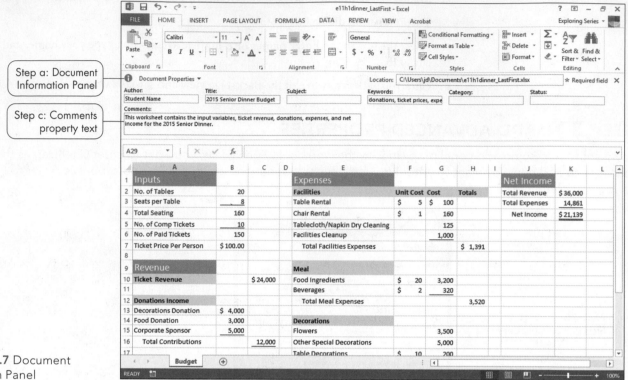

FIGURE 11.7 Document Information Panel

a. Click the **FILE tab**, if necessary, click **Properties**, and then select **Show Document Panel**.

The Document Information Panel displays between the Ribbon and the Formula Bar. It displays properties you have already set, such as Author, Title, and Keywords.

b. Click in the **Comments box** in the Document Information Panel.

c. Type **This worksheet contains the input variables, ticket revenue, donations, expenses, and net income for the 2015 Senior Dinner.**

d. Click **Close the Document Information Panel** in the top-right corner of the Document Information Panel and save the workbook.

You saved the comments along with the other properties.

e. Keep Excel open if you plan to continue with Hands-On Exercise 2. If not, exit Excel.

Collaboration

Collaboration is the process by which two or more individuals work together to achieve an outcome or goal by using software technology and features to share and edit the contents of a file. Often, the contents of a complex workbook result from the collaborative efforts of a team of people. Team members work together to plan, develop spreadsheets, conduct quantitative research, enter data, and analyze the results. For example, you are working with a team of students to prepare and finalize the Senior Dinner workbook. Together, your team obtains cost estimates, facilities expenses, meal expenses, decorations, publicity, projected donations, and revenue from ticket sales to prepare the budget worksheet.

You can share workbooks with other people and merge their workbooks into one workbook. In addition, Excel includes two key features that facilitate the collaborative process: comments and track changes. These features enable you and your team members to provide feedback and identify each other's suggested changes in a workbook.

In this section, you will learn how to share workbooks with others, compare and merge workbooks, and insert and edit comments. In addition, you will learn how to track changes made by team members and how to accept or reject their suggestions.

Sharing and Merging Workbooks

STEP 2 >> One way to collaborate on a workbook is to create a shared workbook. In Excel, a *shared workbook* is a file that is designated as shareable and is stored on a network that is accessible to multiple people who can edit the workbook at the same time. Users can see changes made by other users. The person who creates the workbook and designates it as a shared workbook is the owner. The owner controls user access and resolves any conflicting changes made. To share a workbook, do the following:

1. Click the REVIEW tab and click Share Workbook in the Changes group to open the Share Workbook dialog box.
2. Click the *Allow changes by more than one user at the same time* check box and click the Advanced tab (see Figure 11.8) to specify the settings that control the shared workbook.
3. Specify how long, if at all, you want to keep a history of the changes made in the *Track changes* section.
4. Specify how often to update changes in the *Update changes* section.
5. Select one of the settings in the *Conflicting changes between users* section and click OK. Click OK if a message box opens informing you that the workbook will be saved.

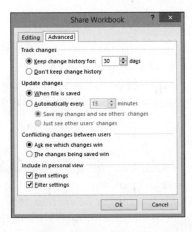

FIGURE 11.8 Share Workbook Dialog Box

After sharing a workbook on a network, you might want to know who is currently working on it. Click Share Workbook in the Changes group on the Review tab and then click the Editing tab. The *Who has this workbook open now* list displays names of people who have the workbook open (see Figure 11.9).

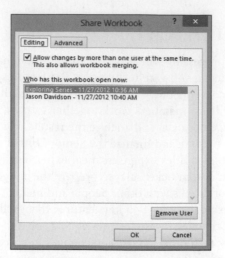

FIGURE 11.9 Share Workbook
Dialog Box: Editing Tab

TIP | **Shared Workbook Limitations**

While sharing workbooks is a powerful collaboration tool, it does have limitations. Workbooks that contain tables may not be shared. Furthermore, the maximum number of users that can access the file at once is 256.

Understand Conflicts and Network Issues

Conflicts can arise when several users are working with shared workbooks. If multiple users attempt to change the same cell at the same time, a Resolve Conflicts dialog box opens for the second user (see Figure 11.10). The change is resolved based on the settings you select in the Share Workbook dialog box. When several people on a network share a workbook and make changes to it, the last person to make changes decides which changes to accept. This becomes a problematic situation when the last person is the least knowledgeable about Excel or the contents of a particular workbook.

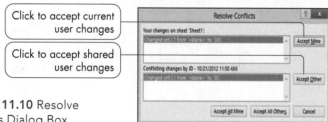

Click to accept current user changes

Click to accept shared user changes

FIGURE 11.10 Resolve
Conflicts Dialog Box

Issues with network permission also may arise when storing and using files on a network. The network permissions control who has rights to open and modify files. Furthermore, workbooks that have not been designated as shareable may still be able to be modified by various users. The next two paragraphs discuss these situations.

Network Permissions

A network drive may be set to Read-Only for some users and as Owner for other users. People who have Owner rights can open, save, delete, and modify files. People who have Read-Only rights can open a file but cannot delete it or save changes back to that location; however, they can save changes to another location such as their own hard drive or a flash drive. If you open a workbook from a network location of which you are not an owner, the title bar displays [Read-Only] after the file name.

Nonshareable Workbook

A workbook may be stored on a network that you can access, but the workbook might not be designated as a shared workbook. If another user has the workbook open and you try to open it, the *File in Use* dialog box will appear. Click Read Only to open the file in Read-Only mode, or click Notify to open the workbook in Read-Only mode and be notified when the workbook is no longer being used, or click Cancel to not open the workbook at this time. If you click Notify, the File Now Available dialog box opens when the other user closes the workbook.

Compare and Merge Workbooks

STEP 3 » When you share a workbook with others, you might want to see what each person changed in the workbook instead of allowing immediate changes to the original workbook. You can use the *Compare and Merge Workbooks* command to combine the shared workbooks into one workbook so that you can compare the changes to decide which ones to keep. The *Compare and Merge* command works only with copies of a shared workbook; it does not work on workbooks that have not been designated as shared.

Each user must save a copy of the shared workbook with a unique name, such as *Senior Dinner Stephen* and *Senior Dinner Cheryl*, so that these names differ from the original file name. These files must be stored in the same folder that contains the shared workbook.

The *Compare and Merge* command is not on the Ribbon by default. However, you can add the command to either the Ribbon or the Quick Access Toolbar. To add the command to the Quick Access Toolbar, do the following:

1. Click Customize Quick Access toolbar on the right side of the Quick Access Toolbar and select More Commands. Alternatively, click the tab, click Options, and then click Quick Access Toolbar on the left side of the Excel Options dialog box.
2. Click the *Choose commands from* arrow and select *Commands Not in the Ribbon*.
3. Scroll through the list and click *Compare and Merge Workbooks*.
4. Click Add and click OK.

The *Compare and Merge Workbooks* command looks like a green circle on the Quick Access Toolbar when you open a shared workbook (see Figure 11.11). It appears dimmed when you work with regular workbooks.

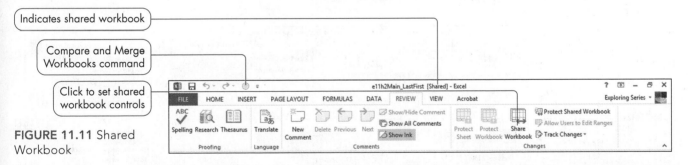

FIGURE 11.11 Shared Workbook

STEP 4 » After adding the *Compare and Merge Workbooks* command to the Quick Access Toolbar, you can use it to merge copies of a shared workbook. To merge the workbooks, do the following:

1. Open the original shared workbook.
2. Click *Compare and Merge Workbooks* on the Quick Access Toolbar.
3. Click OK if the message box *This action will now save the workbook. Do you want to continue?* displays. The *Select Files to Merge Into Current Workbook* dialog box opens.
4. Click the file you want to merge. To select multiple files, press and hold Ctrl as you click the files. Click OK.

Changes are indicated by different color borders and top-left triangles, representing the different users who made changes to the shared workbook (see Figure 11.12).

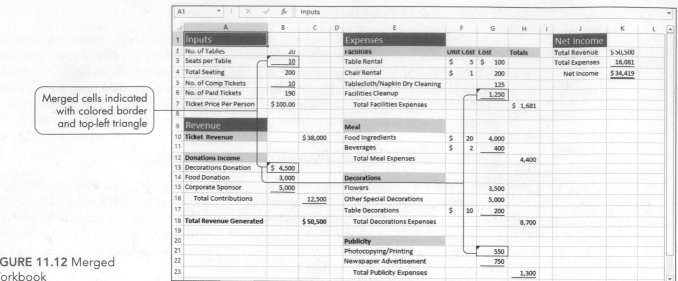

FIGURE 11.12 Merged Workbook

Inserting Comments

You can insert notes to yourself or make suggestions to another team member by inserting comments into a cell. A *comment* is a note or annotation to ask a question or provide a suggestion to another person about content in a worksheet cell. Comments help document a worksheet by providing additional information or clarification of the data, formula results, or labels. For example, in the Senior Dinner workbook, you want to insert the comment in cell C18 regarding income. To insert a comment for a particular cell, do the following:

1. Click the cell in which you want to insert the comment.
2. Click the REVIEW tab and click New Comment in the Comments group or right-click the cell and select Insert Comment. A red triangle, known as a *comment indicator*, appears in the top-right corner of a cell containing a comment. A comment box appears, showing the default user name in bold.
3. Type the text that you want to appear in the comment box and click outside the comment box (see Figure 11.13).

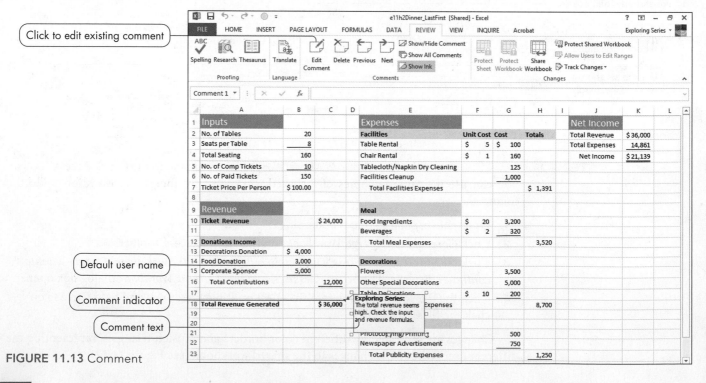

FIGURE 11.13 Comment

Show and Hide Comments

When you click outside the comment box, it closes, but the comment indicator remains in the cell. Position the mouse pointer over that cell to display the comment again. The comment in that cell remains onscreen until the cell selector is moved. Other comments remain hidden unless you show them. Table 11.2 lists steps to show and hide comments onscreen.

TABLE 11.2	Show and Hide Comments	
Action	**Ribbon Method**	**Shortcut Method**
Show a comment	1. Click the cell containing the comment. 2. Click Show/Hide Comment in the Comments group on the Review tab.	1. Right-click the cell containing the comment. 2. Select Show/Hide Comments.
Hide a comment	1. Click the cell containing the comment. 2. Click Show/Hide Comment in the Comments group.	1. Right-click the cell containing the comment. 2. Select Hide Comment.
Display or hide all comments in the entire workbook	1. Click Show All Comments in the Comments group.	Not applicable

Click Previous in the Comments group on the Review tab to go to the cell containing the previous comment, or click Next to go to the next comment. When you click these commands, Excel goes to the respective cell and displays the comment box.

 TIP **Comment Box**

If the comment box obstructs the view of a cell you would like to see, it can be repositioned by clicking the outer edge of the comment box and dragging to a new location. You can also drag a selection handle on the outer edge of a comment box to increase or decrease its size.

Edit and Delete Comments

STEP 1 » You may need to edit the comment text if information changes. You might have originally inserted a general comment such as *Some decorations will be donated*. A few days later, another team member identifies a supply store called Party America that is willing to donate some decorations. Therefore, you can edit the comment to display *Party America will provide $500 worth of decorations*. To edit a comment, do the following:

1. Click the cell that contains the comment you want to edit.
2. Click the REVIEW tab. Click Edit Comment in the Comments group or right-click the cell and select Edit Comment.
3. Edit the comment text.
4. Format the comment text, if desired. Select the comment text, right-click the selected text, select Format Comment, select formats in the Format Comment dialog box, and then click OK. Alternatively, select comment text and apply font attributes, such as bold and font size, from the Font group on the HOME tab.
5. Click outside the comment box when you are done.

You can delete a comment if you no longer need it. To delete a comment, do the following:

1. Click the cell that contains the comment you want to delete.
2. Click the REVIEW tab and click Delete in the Comments group, or right-click the cell and select Delete Comment. Excel immediately deletes the comment without providing a warning. If you need to restore the comment, immediately click Undo on the Quick Access Toolbar.

 TIP | Removing All Comments

To remove all comments at the same time, press Ctrl+G to display the Go To dialog box, click Special, make sure Comments is selected, and then click OK. This selects all cells containing comments in the current worksheet. Click the Home tab, click Clear in the Editing group, and then select Clear Comments.

Print Comments

When you print a worksheet, comments do not print by default. The Sheet tab in the Page Setup dialog box contains two options for printing comments. The default Comments setting is (None). If you choose *As displayed on sheet*, the visible comment boxes appear where they are located onscreen. Hidden comments do not print. Choose *At end of sheet* to print the comments on a separate page (see Figure 11.14). This printout includes the cell reference and the comment text for each comment on the active worksheet, even if the comments are hidden.

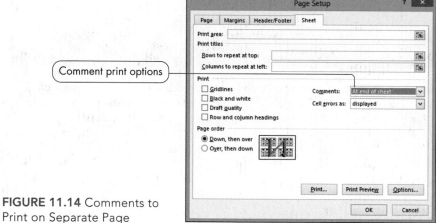

FIGURE 11.14 Comments to Print on Separate Page

Tracking Changes

Although comments are helpful for posing questions or suggestions, you may want to create a log that identifies changes you and other people make in a workbook. *Track Changes* is a feature that records particular changes made in a workbook. It tracks changes to cell contents, row and column insertions and deletions, and copied and moved data. With several team members contributing to the Senior Dinner workbook, you can activate Change Tracking to see who makes what change, such as changing the value of the price per person from $75 to $100.

Excel does not track all changes. For example, it does not track formatting changes such as applying bold or Accounting Number Format or adjusting column width or row height. Because Excel does not track these types of changes, keep a copy of the original workbook. You can compare the original workbook to the workbook your team members changed to see if they made any formatting changes.

To activate the Change Tracking feature, do the following:

1. Click the REVIEW tab.
2. Click Track Changes in the Changes group and select Highlight Changes. The Highlight Changes dialog box opens.
3. Click the *Track changes while editing. This also shares your workbook* check box. The remaining options are now available (see Figure 11.15).
4. Click OK. If prompted, enter the name of the workbook and click Save.

Click to specify other options

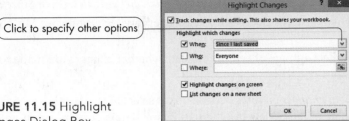

FIGURE 11.15 Highlight Changes Dialog Box

You can track changes only in a shared workbook. When you activate Track Changes, [Shared] appears on the right side of the file name on the title bar. Shared workbooks are often stored on a network server so that several people can simultaneously edit the workbook. However, you can track changes in a workbook stored on a local hard drive or external storage device.

A small triangle appears in the top left corner when an edit is made and Track Changes is enabled. When you position the mouse pointer on that cell, a yellow message box similar to a comment box displays the name of the person who made the change, the date and time the change was made, and the type of change made.

When you share a workbook or activate Change Tracking, some Excel features are disabled, indicated by dimmed commands on the Ribbon. You cannot do the following tasks when you turn on Change Tracking:

- Merge cells together or split merged cells into several cells.
- Add or change conditional formats.
- Format a range as an Excel table.
- Delete, protect, or unprotect worksheets.
- Change the tab color for worksheets.
- Create or change charts, PivotTables, PivotCharts, shapes, pictures, objects, and hyperlinks.
- Apply, change, or remove passwords.
- Import or link external data, display connections, or edit links.
- Add, modify, or remove data validation rules.
- Create, edit, delete, or view scenarios.
- Group, ungroup, or subtotal tables.
- Edit a macro, insert controls, and assign a macro to a control.

 TIP **Turning Off Change Tracking**

After reviewing the changes, you can turn off Change Tracking by clicking Track Changes in the Changes group, selecting Highlight Changes, deselecting the *Track changes while editing* check box in the Highlight Changes dialog box, and then clicking OK. If you turn off Change Tracking, the workbook is no longer shared, the history of changes made is lost, and other users who are sharing the workbook will not be able to save the changes they have made.

Highlight Changes

STEP 5 »
When changes are made with Change Tracking on, each cell changed contains a colored triangle in the top-left corner. If you close the workbook and open it again, the triangles indicating changes are hidden. To display the triangles, do the following:

1. Click Track Changes in the Changes group on the REVIEW tab.
2. Select Highlight Changes.
3. Select which changes to highlight:

   - Click the When arrow to select *Since I last saved*, *All*, *Not yet reviewed*, or *Since date*.
   - Click the Who arrow to select changes made by Everyone, Everyone but Me, you, or another person.
   - Click Where and select a range of cells to indicate whether changes are made to those respective cells.

   By default, the *Highlight changes on screen* check box is selected to ensure that changes display onscreen. You can then review the changes in any sequence by positioning the mouse pointer over the cells containing blue triangles. Click *List changes on a new sheet* to create a list of changes made on a new worksheet.
4. Click OK.

Accept and Reject Changes

STEP 6 »
You can view changes in sequence through a dialog box that enables you to accept or reject changes. When you accept a change, the change is no longer indicated by the colored triangle; the change is accepted as part of the worksheet. When you reject a change, the suggested change is removed from the worksheet. For example, if someone made a change by deleting a row and you reject that change, the row is restored. To accept and reject changes, do the following:

1. Click Track Changes in the Changes group on the REVIEW tab. If you have not saved the workbook, you will be prompted to do so.
2. Select Accept/Reject Changes. The *Select Changes to Accept or Reject* dialog box opens (see Figure 11.16).
3. Click the check boxes for the type of changes to accept and reject and specify their settings. Click OK. The *Accept or Reject Changes* dialog box opens (see Figure 11.17), displaying the change number, who made the change, and what the person changed.
4. Click Accept to accept the change, click Reject to reject that change and move to the next change, click Accept All to accept all changes made, or click Reject All to reject all changes made. The dialog box closes automatically after all changes have been either accepted or rejected.

FIGURE 11.16 Select Changes to Accept or Reject Dialog Box

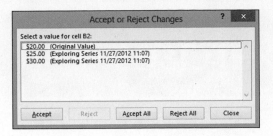

FIGURE 11.17 Accept or Reject Changes Dialog Box

Before accepting or rejecting changes, you might want to create a list of changes in a *history worksheet*. Within the Highlight Changes dialog box, click *List changes on a new sheet*. When you click OK, Excel creates a History worksheet that lists the changes made to the workbook, such as value changes, inserted and deleted columns and rows, and some formula changes. Note that changes made to formulas that are dependent on other cells, also known as dependent values, are not listed. The log does not track font changes or hiding/unhiding columns or rows. Figure 11.18 shows a change log in a new worksheet named History. The change log shows the dates, times, new and original values, and other details about all the changes. The History worksheet is temporary; Excel removes it when you close the workbook.

Action Number	Date	Time	Who	Change	Sheet	Range	New Value	Old Value	Action Type	Losing Action
1	11/27/2012	11:07 AM	Exploring Series	Cell Change	Budget	B2	$25.00	$20.00		
2	11/27/2012	11:07 AM	Exploring Series	Cell Change	Budget	B2	$30.00	$25.00		
3	11/27/2012	11:13 AM	Exploring Series	Cell Change	Budget	B13	$5,000.00	$4,000.00		
4	11/27/2012	11:13 AM	Exploring Series	Cell Change	Budget	F10	$15.00	$20.00		
5	11/27/2012	11:13 AM	Exploring Series	Cell Change	Budget	F3	$10.00	$5.00		
6	11/27/2012	11:14 AM	Exploring Series	Cell Change	Budget	B2	$25.00	$30.00		
7	11/27/2012	11:14 AM	Exploring Series	Cell Change	Budget	B13	$4,500.00	$5,000.00		
8	11/27/2012	11:14 AM	Exploring Series	Cell Change	Budget	F10	$20.00	$15.00		
9	11/27/2012	11:14 AM	Exploring Series	Cell Change	Budget	F3	$15.00	$10.00		

FIGURE 11.18 Change Log

TIP Creating the Change Log

The History worksheet is deleted when you save a workbook; however, you can copy and paste the values into a new worksheet that will remain when the workbook is saved.

Quick Concepts

1. Why do you insert a comment? *p. 494*

2. How do you edit or delete a comment? *p. 495*

3. What are the benefits of Track Changes? *p. 496*

Hands-On Exercises

2 Collaboration

You want to insert some comments and then share the Senior Dinner workbook with Penny and Ian, two other marching band senior students. After they review the workbook, you will merge and combine the workbooks to see what comments they have. Finally, you will accept and reject changes as necessary.

Skills covered: Insert and Edit a Comment • Share the Workbook • Add the Compare and Merge Workbooks Command to the Quick Access Toolbar • Compare and Merge Workbooks • Highlight Changes • Accept and Reject Changes

STEP 1 ≫ INSERT AND EDIT A COMMENT

You notice that the total revenue generated seems high. Because you do not have time to check the worksheet formulas now, you will insert a comment to remind you to review the formulas later. Refer to Figure 11.19 as you complete Step 1.

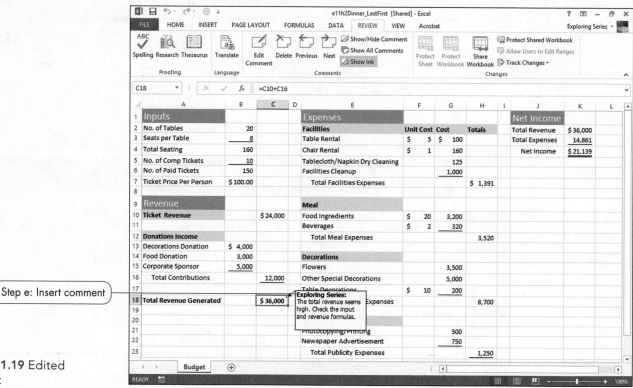

FIGURE 11.19 Edited Comment

a. Open *e11h1Dinner_LastFirst* and save it as **e11h2Dinner_LastFirst**.

> **TROUBLESHOOTING:** If you make any major mistakes in this exercise, you can close the file, open *e11h1Dinner_LastFirst* again, and then start this exercise over.

b. Click **cell C18**.

c. Click the **REVIEW tab** and click **New Comment** in the Comments group.

Excel displays a comment indicator in the top-right corner of cell C18 and a comment box containing your name.

d. Type **This seems high** and click **cell C18** again.

The New Comment command in the Comments group changes to Edit Comment.

e. Click **Edit Comment** in the Comments group and change the comment text to **The total revenue seems high. Check the input and revenue formulas.** Save the workbook.

STEP 2 ≫ SHARE THE WORKBOOK

You want to designate the Senior Dinner workbook as shareable so that other team members can review it and offer suggestions. Refer to Figure 11.19 as you complete Step 2.

a. Click **Share Workbook** in the Changes group on the REVIEW tab.

The Share Workbook dialog box opens.

b. Click the **Editing tab** if necessary and click the **Allow changes by more than one user at the same time check box**.

c. Click **OK** and click **OK** when prompted to save the workbook.

Excel displays [Shared] after the file name on the title bar.

d. Save the workbook.

STEP 3 ≫ ADD THE COMPARE AND MERGE WORKBOOKS COMMAND TO THE QUICK ACCESS TOOLBAR

You received an updated workbook from two team members. Before you can combine the separate workbooks into one workbook, you need to add the Compare and Merge Workbooks command to the Quick Access Toolbar. Refer to Figure 11.20 as you complete Step 3.

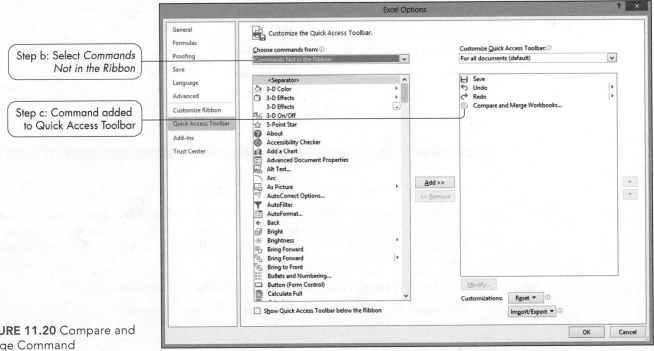

FIGURE 11.20 Compare and Merge Command

a. Click **Customize Quick Access Toolbar** on the right side of the Quick Access Toolbar and select **More Commands**.

The Excel Options dialog box opens, displaying the Quick Access Toolbar options.

b. Click the **Choose commands from arrow** and select **Commands Not in the Ribbon**.

c. Scroll through the commands list, select **Compare and Merge Workbooks**, and then click **Add**.

Excel adds an icon and the *Compare and Merge Workbooks* command to the Customize Quick Access Toolbar list.

d. Click **OK**.

The *Compare and Merge Workbooks* command appears as a green circular icon in the Quick Access Toolbar.

STEP 4 ⟫ COMPARE AND MERGE WORKBOOKS

You need to merge Ian's and Penny's workbooks into your workbook so that you can see the changes they made to the Senior Dinner budget. Refer to Figure 11.21 as you complete Step 4.

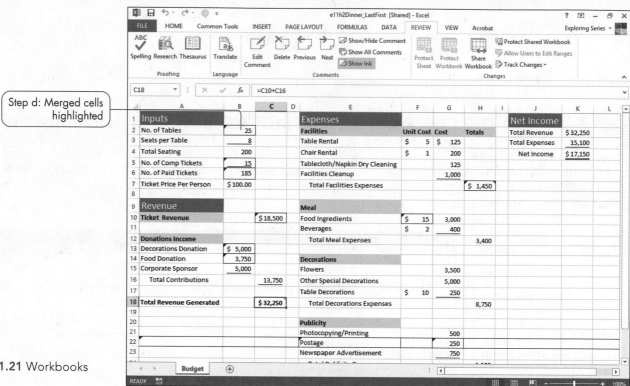

FIGURE 11.21 Workbooks Merged

a. Open *e11h2Main* and save it as **e11h2Main_LastFirst**.

This shared workbook is almost identical to the one you saved and closed. Because you are not sending your workbook to Ian and Penny in real time, the publisher is providing an equivalent workbook that was used to share with the fictitious Ian and Penny so that you can merge three workbooks into one.

b. Click **Compare and Merge Workbooks** on the Quick Access Toolbar.

The *Select Files to Merge Into Current Workbook* dialog box opens.

> **TROUBLESHOOTING:** If *Compare and Merge Workbooks* is grayed out, click Share Workbook in the Changes group on the Review tab.

c. Navigate to the folder containing the Exploring Excel data files.

d. Select *e11h2Main_Ian*, press and hold **Ctrl**, and then click *e11h2Main_Penny* in the *Select Files to Merge Into Current Workbook* dialog box.

The results of each individual worksheet have now been merged into one combined worksheet.

e. Click **Open** and save the workbook.

STEP 5 ≫ HIGHLIGHT CHANGES

You want to highlight the changes that Ian and Penny made to the shared workbook. In addition, you want to generate a change log in a History worksheet. Refer to Figure 11.22 as you complete Step 5.

Step c: History worksheet

Action Number	Date	Time	Who	Change	Sheet	Range	New Value	Old Value	Action Type	Losing Action
1	12/16/2012	11:17 AM	Exploring Series	Cell Change	Budget	B5	$15.00	$10.00		
2	12/16/2012	11:17 AM	Exploring Series	Cell Change	Budget	C10	'=B6*B7	'=B6*B4		
3	12/16/2012	11:17 AM	Exploring Series	Cell Change	Budget	B13	$5,000.00	$4,000.00		
4	12/16/2012	11:17 AM	Exploring Series	Cell Change	Budget	B14	$3,200.00	$3,000.00		
5	12/16/2012	11:17 AM	Exploring Series	Cell Change	Budget	F10	$15.00	$20.00		
6	12/16/2012	11:20 AM	Exploring Series	Cell Change	Budget	B2	$25.00	$20.00		
7	12/16/2012	11:20 AM	Exploring Series	Cell Change	Budget	B6	$185.00	'=B4-B5		
8	12/16/2012	11:20 AM	Exploring Series	Cell Change	Budget	B13	$5,000.00	$4,000.00		
9	12/16/2012	11:20 AM	Exploring Series	Cell Change	Budget	B14	$3,750.00	$3,000.00		
10	12/16/2012	11:20 AM	Exploring Series	Cell Change	Budget	H7	'=SUM(G3:G6)	'=SUM(F3:G6)		
11	12/16/2012	11:20 AM	Exploring Series	Cell Change	Budget	F10	$15.00	$20.00		
12	12/16/2012	11:20 AM	Exploring Series	Row Insert	Budget	'22:22				
13	12/16/2012	11:20 AM	Exploring Series	Cell Change	Budget	E22	Postage	<blank>		
14	12/16/2012	11:20 AM	Exploring Series	Cell Change	Budget	G22	$250.00	<blank>		

FIGURE 11.22 History Worksheet

a. Click **Track Changes** in the Changes group on the REVIEW tab and select **Highlight Changes**.

The Highlight Changes dialog box opens.

b. Click the **When check box** to deselect it.

If you deselect the When check box, all changes will be shown in the history worksheet.

c. Click the **List changes on a new sheet check box** to select it and click **OK**. *Do not save the workbook.*

Excel highlights changes in the Budget worksheet with color-coded outlines and triangles. Excel also creates a History worksheet that lists the changes.

d. Open Word and create a new document. Click the **INSERT tab**, click **Screenshot** in the Illustrations group, and then click **e11h2Main_LastFirst [Shared] – Excel** on the gallery.

You inserted a screenshot of the Excel window into the Word document. This document is evidence that you created a History worksheet.

e. Save the Word document as **e11h2History_LastFirst**. Insert a footer with your name on the left side and a file name field on the right side. Save the Word document and exit Word. Save the Excel workbook.

Excel removes the History worksheet when you save the shared workbook, but the changes remain in the Budget worksheet.

As you review Ian's and Penny's changes, you will accept and reject them, based on your decisions. Refer to Figure 11.23 as you complete Step 6.

Step a: Delete comment

	A	B	C	D	E	F	G	H	I	J	K	L
1	Inputs				Expenses					Net Income		
2	No. of Tables	25			Facilities	Unit Cost	Cost	Totals		Total Revenue	$ 32,250	
3	Seats per Table	8			Table Rental	$ 5	$ 125			Total Expenses	15,100	
4	Total Seating	200			Chair Rental	$ 1	200			Net Income	$ 17,150	
5	No. of Comp Tickets	15			Tablecloth/Napkin Dry Cleaning		125					
6	No. of Paid Tickets	185			Facilities Cleanup		1,000					
7	Ticket Price Per Person	$ 100.00			Total Facilities Expenses			$ 1,450				
8												
9	Revenue				Meal							
10	Ticket Revenue		$ 18,500		Food Ingredients	$ 15	3,000					
11					Beverages	$ 2	400					
12	Donations Income				Total Meal Expenses			3,400				
13	Decorations Donation	$ 5,000										
14	Food Donation	3,750			Decorations							
15	Corporate Sponsor	5,000			Flowers		3,500					
16	Total Contributions		13,750		Other Special Decorations		5,000					
17					Table Decorations	$ 10	250					
18	Total Revenue Generated		$ 32,250		Total Decorations Expenses			8,750				
19												
20					Publicity							
21					Photocopying/Printing		500					
22					Postage		250					
23					Newspaper Advertisement		750					

FIGURE 11.23 Updated Worksheet

a. Place your cursor over **cell C10** to see Ian's comment about the formula. After reading his comment about the inaccurate formula, right-click **cell C10** and select **Delete Comment**. Click **cell H7**, read Penny's comment, right-click **cell H7**, and then select **Delete Comment**.

b. Click **Track Changes** in the Changes group on the REVIEW tab and select **Accept/Reject Changes**. Click **OK** in the *Select Changes to Accept or Reject* dialog box.

This opens the *Accept or Reject* dialog box that you will use to review changes.

c. Click **Accept All** to accept all changes that have been made to the document.

d. Save and close the *e11h2Dinner* workbook if it is still open.

e. Save the *e11h2Main_LastFirst* workbook. Keep Excel open if you plan to continue with Hands-On Exercise 3. If not, exit Excel.

Workbook Information

When you prepare to share an electronic copy of a workbook with others, you should run some checking tools to review your workbook for particular issues that might reveal personal information or create problems with other users. For example, if you are conducting a confidential analysis for a client or if you have a confidentiality agreement with a client, that client probably does not want to reveal that you did some analysis. You should remove your "fingerprints" from the file by removing any properties or identifying attributes that indicate your work on the workbook. After reviewing and updating a workbook, you can protect the integrity of the workbook. For example, you can save the workbook with a password or restrict who is able to edit or print the workbook.

In this section, you will prepare a workbook for sharing and then protect a workbook. In particular, you will use tools to check for issues and then mark a workbook as final.

Checking for Issues

Often, people prepare and distribute workbooks to others inside and outside their organizations. For example, you might distribute the Senior Dinner budget to some of the donors. Excel contains three tools—Document Inspector, Accessibility Checker, and Compatibility Checker—that check the workbook for issues and then alert you so that you can make any necessary changes before distributing the workbook.

Use Document Inspector

Recall that document properties contain details, such as the author and organization, about a workbook, which you may not want publicized. The *Document Inspector* reviews a workbook for hidden or personal data stored in the workbook or personal document properties, such as author, and then informs you of these details so that you can select what data to remove. Document Inspector finds and removes comments, document properties, e-mail headers, user names, document server properties, header and footer information, and hidden rows and columns. However, you cannot remove these data if the workbook is a shared workbook.

 TIP Make a Duplicate!

Before using Document Inspector, you should save the workbook and then run Document Inspector on the duplicate workbook, because you cannot always restore all data that Document Inspector removes.

STEP 1 ≫

To use Document Inspector, do the following:

1. Click the FILE tab and click Info.
2. Click *Check for Issues* and select Inspect Document to open the Document Inspector dialog box (see Figure 11.24). Excel will prompt you to save the workbook if you have made any changes that have not been saved yet.
3. Select the check boxes for the types of document content you want to inspect.
4. Click Inspect to display the inspection results.
5. Click Remove All for the types of content that you want to remove. Keep in mind that you might not be able to undo the changes. Use Help to learn more about hidden data and personal information that can be contained in a workbook.

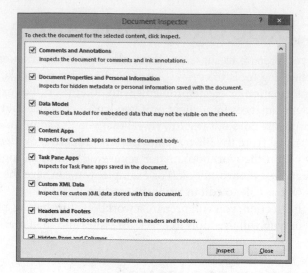

FIGURE 11.24 Document Inspector

Check Accessibility

Many organizations provide electronic documents for the public to download from Web sites or as e-mail attachments. With a diverse audience of people using technology today, you should ensure your documents are accessible by everyone. The *Accessibility Checker* reviews your files for potential issues that could hinder the ability of users who access your public files and then alerts you to these issues so that you can address them. The Accessibility Checker identifies the following types of issues, among other issues:

- Has alt text been assigned to objects so that the object is described when the pointer hovers over it?
- Do tables contain header rows?
- Do tables contain merged cells?
- Do hyperlinks contain meaningful text as ScreenTips?

Accessibility Checker provides three types of feedback for each issue:

- **Error.** Content that creates extreme difficulty or impossibility for persons with disabilities to view correctly.
- **Warning.** Content that is difficult for users to comprehend.
- **Tip.** Content that is understandable but could be presented or organized differently to maximize comprehension.

STEP 2

To use the Accessibility Checker, do the following:

1. Click the FILE tab and click Info.
2. Click *Check for Issues* and select Check Accessibility. The Accessibility Checker task pane opens on the right side of the worksheet window, showing the results.
3. Click a listed issue to see feedback in the Additional Information window. This window tells you why you should fix the problem and how to fix it.

Check Compatibility

When you provide an Excel workbook for others to use, they may have an older version of Excel on their computers. Because each new version of Excel contains new features, you may be using features that are not compatible with previous versions. For example, you may be using a conditional formatting feature or an updated function, such as the newly added Web functions, that was not available in previous Excel versions. You can use *Compatibility Checker* to check the workbook contents to see what data and features are not compatible with previous versions. To use Compatibility Checker, do the following:

1. Click the FILE tab and click Info.
2. Click *Check for Issues* and select Check Compatibility. The Microsoft Excel - Compatibility Checker dialog box opens, showing a list of issues (see Figure 11.25). You have the option to check compatibility against Excel 97-2003, 2007, and 2010. By default, all three options are selected.
3. Click the *Check compatibility when saving this workbook* check box if you want to check compatibility every time you save the workbook. Leave the check box blank if you do not want to check the workbook automatically upon saving.
4. Click *Copy to New Sheet* to create a report on a separate worksheet that lists the issues.
5. Click OK after reviewing the issues so that you can address them in the workbook.

Select version of Excel to review compatibility

Minor loss of fidelity issue

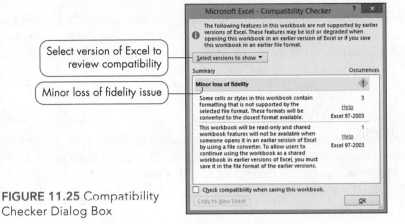

FIGURE 11.25 Compatibility Checker Dialog Box

 TIP **Unsupported Features**

Look up *Check file compatibility with earlier versions* in Help to find out about Excel 2013 features that are not supported in earlier versions. This Help topic provides details about significant loss of functionality, what it means, and what to do to solve the problem.

Protecting a Workbook

You can protect a workbook to ensure the integrity of its contents. Workbook protection includes marking the workbook as final with an easy-to-remove read-only mode and inserting a digital signature that ensures the workbook's integrity and that it has not been changed since it was signed electronically. The type of protection you add depends on the level of security you need to place on the workbook contents.

Mark a Workbook as Final

 STEP 4 »

After completing a workbook, you may want to communicate that it is a final version of the workbook. The *Mark as Final* command communicates that it is a final version and makes the file read-only. Excel prevents users from typing in and editing the workbook, displays a *Marked as Final* icon to the right of Ready on the status bar, and sets the Status document property as Final. If a workbook is shared, you cannot mark it as final; you must first remove the sharing attribute. To mark a workbook as final, do the following:

1. Click the FILE tab and click Info.
2. Click Protect Workbook and select *Mark as Final*. A warning message box appears, stating *This workbook will be marked as final and then saved.*

3. Click OK. If you have note saved the file, you will be prompted to do so. Excel then displays an information message box (see Figure 11.26).
4. Click OK. The Permissions area of the Backstage view displays *This workbook has been marked as final to discourage editing*.

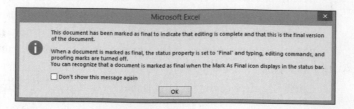

FIGURE 11.26 *Mark as Final* Verification Box

The Message Bar appears below the Ribbon. A user can click Edit Anyway to remove the marked-as-final indication and begin editing the workbook. Furthermore, if a person opens the marked-as-final Excel 2013 workbook in any previous version of Excel, the read-only attribute is removed, permitting the user to edit the workbook.

Encrypt a Workbook with a Password

You can protect a workbook by restricting its access to authorized people only. To do this, you can encrypt the workbook with a password the user is required to enter in order to open the workbook. However, you cannot encrypt a file with a password if you have already marked it as final. To encrypt a workbook with a password, do the following:

1. Click the FILE tab and click Info.
2. Click Protect Workbook and select *Encrypt with Password*. The Encrypt Document dialog box opens (see Figure 11.27) so that you can enter a password in the Password box. If you forget the password, you cannot recover the workbook.
3. Type a password and click OK to display the Confirm Password dialog box. Type the same password in the *Reenter password* box and click OK. The Permissions area of the Backstage view displays *A password is required to open this workbook*.

FIGURE 11.27 Encrypt Document Dialog Box

When you attempt to open a password-protected workbook, the Password dialog box opens. Enter the password and click OK.

TIP | **Problems with Forgotten Passwords**

You should make a note of passwords you use for saving files. If you forget a password, you will not be able to open the file.

Add a Digital Signature

A *digital signature* is an electronic, encrypted notation that stamps a document to authenticate the contents, confirms that a particular person authorized it, and marks the workbook as final. Use a digital signature to ensure that a workbook is authentic and that the content has not been changed since the signature was added. Your digital signature is valid until you make changes and resave the file. For example, an auditor might add a digital signature to a company's year-end financial statements to authenticate that no changes have been made after the audit.

To digitally sign a workbook, you must obtain a certificate from a certified authority who can verify your signature. If you review the links at the Microsoft Office Marketplace Web site, you can choose a signature service. This is similar to having your signature notarized. Digital signatures may be either visible or invisible.

An invisible digital signature means that a signature is not added as a graphic object in the workbook. The digital signature is an electronic tag or attribute added to the workbook. For more information on creating a digital signature through a third-party certificate authority, complete the following steps:

1. Click the FILE tab and click Info.
2. Click Protect Workbook and select *Add a Digital Signature*. If you have not saved the file, you will be prompted to do so. The Microsoft Excel message box appears. Click Signature Services from the Office Marketplace to find a service to issue a digital ID for you, or click OK to continue.

Add a Signature Line

Instead of creating an invisible digital signature, you may want to include a signature line. A *signature line* is similar to a signature line in a printed document, such as a contract or legal document. In Microsoft Office 2013, an author can create a signature line to request someone type a signature, select an image containing a signature, or write a signature using a tablet PC. When the person electronically signs the document, Microsoft Office adds a digital signature indicating the time signed as a means to authenticate the person's identity. In addition, Microsoft Office designates the file as read-only and displays the Marked as Final Message Bar. To create a signature line, do the following:

STEP 3 »
1. Click the INSERT tab and click Signature Line in the Text group. If the Microsoft Excel message box opens, click OK. The Signature Setup dialog box opens (see Figure 11.28).
2. Enter information in the appropriate boxes and click OK.
3. Repeat the process to create additional signature lines in the same workbook.

FIGURE 11.28 Signature Setup Dialog Box

When you save the workbook and open it again, the Signatures Message Bar appears, stating *This document needs to be signed*. Note, you only receive this message after closing and reopening the workbook. Click View Signatures to complete the process. To sign the document, do the following:

1. Right-click the signature line and select Sign. If the Microsoft Excel message box opens, click OK.

2. Add your signature using one of the following methods:

- Type your name next to the X if you want a printed version of your signature.
- Click Select Image on the right side of the dialog box, find and select an image file of your signature in the Select Signature Image dialog box, and then click Select.
- Use the inking feature on a tablet PC to add a handwritten signature.

3. Click Sign.

The Signatures button, which looks like a red ribbon, appears on the status bar.

Quick Concepts

1. What is the functionality of the Document Inspector? *p. 505*

2. Why is it important to check compatibility? *p. 506*

3. How do you edit a workbook that has been marked as final? *p. 508*

Hands-On Exercises

Watch the Video for this Hands-On Exercise!

MyITLab®
HOE3 Training

3 Workbook Information

To prepare your Senior Dinner budget workbook to share the updates with other students, chefs, and donors, you need to check for and resolve issues. Then you will mark the budget as being final and add a digital signature.

Skills covered: Use the Document Inspector • Check Accessibility and Compatibility • Add a Signature Line • Mark as Final

STEP 1 >> USE THE DOCUMENT INSPECTOR

Your budget may contain some items that you do not want to appear in the workbook you distribute to others. In particular, you want to make sure all comments are removed. Refer to Figure 11.29 as you complete Step 1.

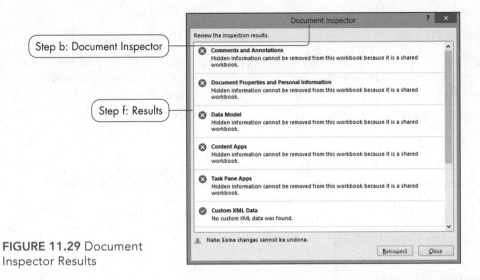

FIGURE 11.29 Document Inspector Results

Step b: Document Inspector

Step f: Results

a. Open *e11h2Main_LastFirst* and save it as **e11h3Main_LastFirst**.

> **TROUBLESHOOTING:** If you closed and reopened *e11h2Main_LastFirst*, make sure the file is still shareable, as indicated by [Shared] on the title bar. If not, complete the process to share the workbook again that was detailed in Hands-On Exercise 2, Step 2.

b. Click the **FILE tab**, click **Info** if necessary, click **Check for Issues**, and then select **Inspect Document**.

The Document Inspector dialog box opens.

c. Ensure all the check boxes are selected and click **Inspect**.

The Document Inspector results indicate that some hidden information cannot be removed because the workbook is shared.

d. Click **Close** to close the Document Inspector and click the back arrow to return to the spreadsheet.

e. Click the **REVIEW tab**, click **Share Workbook** in the Changes group, deselect the **Allow changes by more than one user at the same time check box**, and then click **OK**. Click **Yes** when a message box opens.

f. Click the **FILE tab**, click **Check for Issues**, select **Inspect Document**, and then click **Inspect**.

The Document Inspector results with a red exclamation point indicate that it found document properties and personal information, such as Author.

g. Click **Remove All** in the *Document Properties and Personal Information* section.

h. Click **Close**, click the back arrow, and then save the workbook.

STEP 2 ≫ CHECK ACCESSIBILITY AND COMPATIBILITY

You want to make sure the Senior Dinner budget does not contain any content that might cause difficulties for users. In addition, you know that another senior band member has Excel 2010, so you want to make sure the workbook does not have critical features that might not appear in the workbook when she opens it in Excel 2010.

a. Click the **FILE tab**, click **Check for Issues**, and then select **Check Accessibility**.

The Accessibility Checker task pane displays on the right side. The inspection results indicate that no issues were found.

b. Close the Accessibility Checker task pane.

c. Click the **FILE tab**, click **Check for Issues**, and then select **Check Compatibility**.

The Microsoft Excel - Compatibility Checker dialog box opens. It did not find any critical losses of fidelity. It did find minor compatibility issues with Excel 97-2003 compatibility. This is not an issue, as all members of your project are using at least Excel 2010.

d. Click **OK** and save the workbook.

STEP 3 ≫ ADD A SIGNATURE LINE

You want to add a signature line to indicate that you approve the dinner budget. Refer to Figure 11.30 as you complete Step 4.

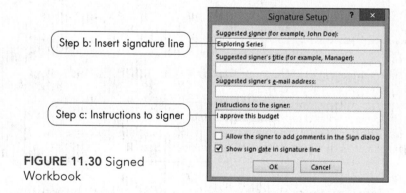

FIGURE 11.30 Signed Workbook

a. Click the **INSERT tab**, click **Add a Signature Line** in the Text group, and then select **Microsoft Office Signature Line**.

b. Type your name and e-mail address in the **Signature Setup dialog box**.

c. Delete the template text in the *Instructions to the signer* input area and type **I approve this budget.**

d. Click **OK**.

You will now see the signature box appear in the spreadsheet.

e. Position the signature box in **cell A23**.

f. Save *e11h3Main_LastFirst*.

STEP 4 ≫ MARK AS FINAL

You want the recipients of your workbook to know that it is a final budget. Refer to Figure 11.31 as you complete Step 3.

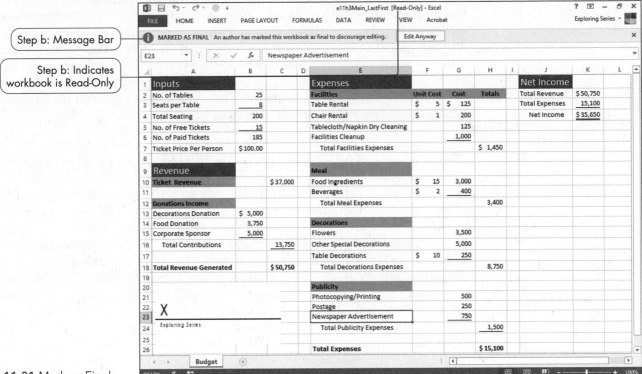

FIGURE 11.31 Mark as Final

a. Click the **FILE tab**, click **Protect Workbook**, and then select **Mark as Final**.

A message box appears, indicating that *This workbook will be marked as final and then saved.*

b. Click **OK**.

Another message box appears, indicating that *This document has been marked as final to indicate that editing is complete and that this is the final version of the document.*

c. Close the workbook.

Workbook Distribution

Some people prefer different formats for files they receive. While you are primarily working in Excel 2013, you might need to save a file in other formats for the convenience of other users. Excel provides the means for you to change the file type and create different types of files from your Excel 2013 workbooks. If you do not provide data in a file format your recipients can manipulate, the data are useless to them. After saving a workbook, you are ready to distribute it. Excel provides a variety of distribution methods so that you can provide others with easy access to your workbooks, whether that is as an e-mail attachment or uploaded to a server.

In this section, you will learn how to save a workbook in different file formats and how to send the workbook to others electronically.

Saving a Workbook in Different Formats

When you save a workbook in Excel 2013, you save the workbook in the default 2013 file format, which ends with the .xlsx extension. Excel 2010 and 2007 also save files in the .xlsx format. However, previous versions of Excel saved workbooks with the .xls extension. The primary reasons that the .xlsx file format is better than the .xls format are that the .xlsx files are smaller in size because the .xlsx format uses a built-in compression feature, and content images and macros are stored separately to enable increased probability of data recovery if a file becomes corrupted. In addition, any Office version beginning with 2007 uses XML (eXtensible Markup Language), a standardized way of tagging data so that programs can automatically extract data from workbooks.

Although you use the default .xlsx file format when you save most Excel 2013 workbooks, you might need to save a workbook in another format. Excel enables you to save workbooks in many different formats. Table 11.3 lists and describes some of the most commonly used file formats.

TABLE 11.3 File Formats		
Format	**Extension**	**Description**
Excel Workbook	.xlsx	Default Office Excel 2007–2013 XML-based file format.
Excel 97-2003 Workbook	.xls	Binary file format used for Excel 97-2003 workbooks.
OpenDocument Spreadsheet	.ods	Format for spreadsheet applications such as Google Docs and OpenOffice.
Excel Template	.xltx	The default Office Excel 2007–2013 file format for an Excel template.
Excel Macro-Enabled Workbook	.xlsm	XML-based and macro-enabled format for Excel 2007–2013.
Excel Binary Workbook	.xlsb	Binary file format for Excel 2007–2013.
Text (Tab delimited)	.txt	Tab-delimited format so that the file contents can be used with other Microsoft Windows programs. Uses the tab character as a delimiter to separate data into columns. Saves only the active worksheet.
CSV (Comma delimited)	.csv	Comma-delimited text file for use with other Windows programs. Uses the comma as a delimiter to separate data into columns. Saves only the active worksheet.
Formatted Text (Space delimited)	.prn	Lotus space-delimited format. Saves only the active worksheet.
Portable Document Format	.pdf	File format that preserves formatting and prevents changes.

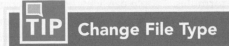

TIP Change File Type

As an alternative method to change the file format, you can choose Change File Type from the Export menu in the Backstage area. This will list all export options and corresponding details.

Save a Workbook for Previous Excel Versions

More people are upgrading from Excel 2007 or Excel 2010 to Excel 2013. However, some people will continue to use previous versions of Excel. You can open a workbook saved in Excel 2003 format within Excel 2013 and save it in the .xlsx format. However, Excel 2013 workbooks are not by default backward compatible with Excel 2003 and previous versions. If you need to send a workbook to someone who is using a previous version of Excel, you can save the workbook in the Excel 97-2003 Workbook format (.xls) by following these steps:

1. Click the FILE tab and click Export.
2. Click Change File Type, located on the left side of the Export menu. The Backstage view displays a third column of File Types (see Figure 11.32).
3. Select Excel 97-2003 Workbook in the *Change File type* list.
4. Navigate to the folder in which you want to store the file and type an appropriate name in the *File name* box.
5. Click Save in the Save As dialog box to save the workbook.

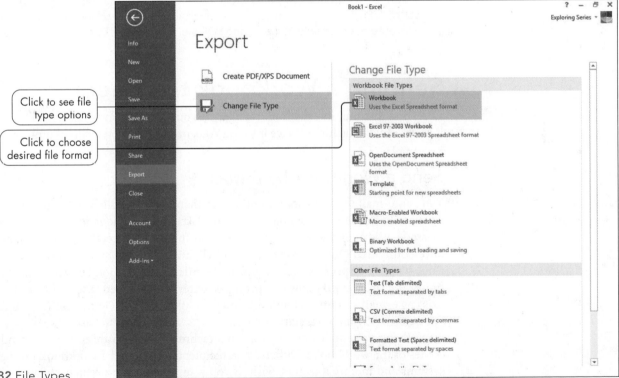

FIGURE 11.32 File Types

Save a Workbook as a PDF File

STEP 1 Sometimes you may want to save an Excel workbook so those who do not have Excel can display and print the file. The most common and best way to enable non–Excel users to display and print Excel workbooks is to save the Excel file in *Portable Document Format (PDF)*, a standard file format that preserves the formatted data, including images, as originally intended in the source program and ensures that other people cannot edit the original data or see proprietary formulas. People can view PDF files correctly on various computer systems and platforms, even if the user does not have the source program. Saving a workbook as a PDF file saves the formatting that you used in an Excel workbook and enables non–Windows users to display and print the file because Adobe Systems Incorporated designed PDF as a universal file format. To save a file in the PDF format, do the following:

1. Click the FILE tab and click Export.
2. Click Create PDF/XPS Document in the *Export* section. The Backstage view displays a third column of *Create a PDF/XPS Document*.
3. Click Create PDF/XPS in the third column to open the *Publish as PDF or XPS* dialog box.
4. Click the *Save as type* arrow and select PDF if it is not already selected.
5. Navigate to the folder in which you want to store the file and type an appropriate name in the *File name* box. If you want to see how the file looks in PDF format after publishing it, click the *Open file after publishing* check box.
6. Click Options to open the Options dialog box. Select appropriate settings, such as the page range, and click OK.
7. Click Publish in the *Publish as PDF or XPS* dialog box to save the workbook in PDF format.

TIP Print to PDF

If you have Adobe Acrobat (not just Adobe Reader) or other third-party applications that create PDF files installed, you can create a file through the Print options. Click the File tab, click Print, click the Printer arrow, select Adobe PDF, and then click Print. You will be prompted to enter a file name for the PDF file.

Sending a Workbook to Others

Excel provides multiple methods for sharing your workbook with other people. You can send it as an e-mail attachment, save it to the Web, or publish it on a SharePoint site.

Send a Workbook by E-Mail

You can e-mail the workbook to others so that they can collaborate on the contents of the workbook. While it is possible to send an Excel workbook as an attachment to an e-mail message, it is often more convenient to send the e-mail directly from Excel, as long as you have configured Outlook as your e-mail client. When you start Outlook 2013 for the first time, you will be prompted to complete the Microsoft Outlook 2013 Startup Wizard to configure the program. Follow the prompts, enter the required information to connect your existing e-mail account to Outlook, download the Outlook Connector (if prompted), restart your computer, and then start Outlook.

When you send a workbook as an attachment, keep in mind you are sending separate copies of the workbook to others. The recipients can save the workbook on their computer systems and modify it as they wish. If you want to incorporate their changes, the recipients will need to e-mail their modified copy back to you so that you can compare and merge the workbook with yours. To send an Excel workbook as an attachment by e-mail, do the following:

1. Click the FILE tab and click Share.
2. Click the E-mail icon in the *Share* section. The Backstage view displays a third column; click *Send as Attachment*.

3. Click *Send as Attachment* or another send option. If a dialog box opens to prompt you to enter your Windows Live ID credentials, enter your credentials.

4. Enter your information in the *E-mail address* and Password boxes and click OK. The workbook file name appears in the Attached box (see Figure 11.33).

5. Type the recipient's e-mail address in the To box.

6. Change the default subject line to an appropriate title.

7. Compose a message that informs the recipient of the workbook attachment and what you want the recipient to do with the workbook.

8. Click Send to send the e-mail message with the attached Excel workbook.

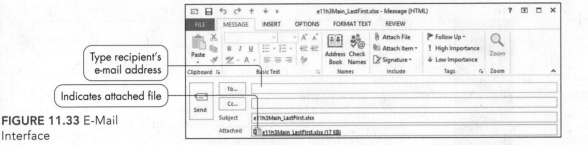

FIGURE 11.33 E-Mail Interface

Type recipient's e-mail address

Indicates attached file

 TIP | Sending an Attached Workbook Without Outlook

If Outlook is not installed as your default e-mail client, you may not be able to use the Send Using E-mail options to start the e-mail program and attach the workbook. Instead, you should close the workbook, open your e-mail client, and then click the Attach button or command in that window to send the workbook as an e-mail attachment.

Save to the Web

STEP 2>> You probably find yourself needing files when you are away from your base computer. For example, you might save your homework for your Excel class on your home computer, but then you need to work on it between classes on campus. However, you might not want to carry a flash drive or external drive with you. You can save a workbook to your Windows Live SkyDrive. *SkyDrive* is a central storage location in which you can save and access files via an Internet connection. Saving to SkyDrive is an effective way to access your files from any device that has an Internet connection, including your smartphone or tablet (see Figure 11.34).

 TIP | Accessing Windows Live Account

When Microsoft Office 2013 is installed, you are required to create or sign in with an existing Windows Live account. This allows you to access SkyDrive without additional logins. If you attempt to access your SkyDrive account remotely, you will need to enter your user name and password. If you forget your SkyDrive password it can be reset at the following URL: https://account.live.com/ResetPassword.

You can create folders on SkyDrive just as you create folders on your computer's hard drive or on a flash drive. Furthermore, you can give other people access to a particular folder and the files it contains so that they can view and edit documents. This approach may be preferable to sending an e-mail attachment and then consolidating changes from multiple workbooks later. Furthermore, saving files to SkyDrive enables you and other people to use Office 365 to view and edit documents in a browser window. To save a workbook to SkyDrive, do the following:

1. Click the FILE tab and click Save As.
2. Select your SkyDrive from the top of the Backstage view Save As list. If prompted to log into SkyDrive, do so.
3. Click the folder, such as Exploring, you want to save the workbook to, or click *New folder* if you want to create a new folder on your SkyDrive.
4. Enter a file name in the *File name* box in the Save As dialog box and click Save. The status bar displays *Uploading to the server*.

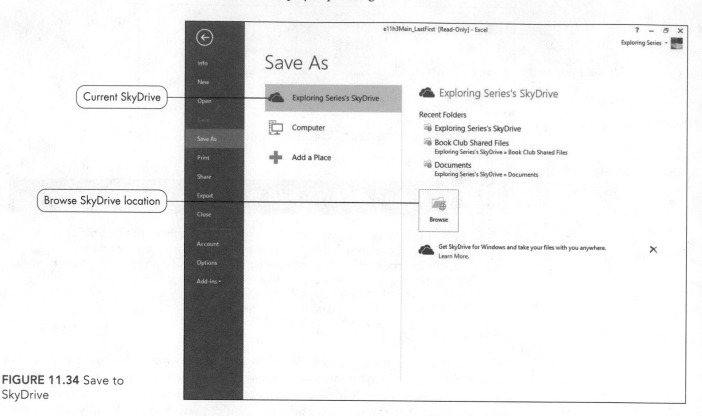

FIGURE 11.34 Save to SkyDrive

After saving files to your SkyDrive, you can access them from any computer that has Internet access. To access your files, do the following:

1. Type www.skydrive.com in your Web browser's Address box and press Enter.
2. Log in using your user name and password.
3. Click Files and select the folder containing the files you want to review.
4. Click the checkbox to select the file you would like to open and then choose Open from the navigation bar at the top of the screen.

Quick Concepts

1. How do you export a PDF? *p. 516*
2. Why do you send a workbook as an e-mail attachment? *p. 516*
3. How do you save to Microsoft SkyDrive? *p. 517*

Hands-On Exercises

4 Workbook Distribution

You want to send the workbook to several people for reference. To ensure the recipients can see the data in the same format and to prevent them from changing the data, you will save the workbook as a PDF file. Then you will save the workbook to SkyDrive.

Skills covered: Create a PDF File • Save to the Web

STEP 1 >> CREATE A PDF FILE

You want to save the workbook as a PDF file so that the Senior Dinner donors can view but not change the budget. Refer to Figure 11.35 as you complete Step 1.

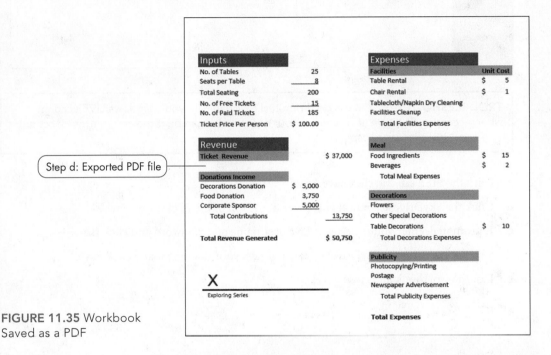

FIGURE 11.35 Workbook Saved as a PDF

a. Open *e11h3Main_LastFirst* and save it as **e11h4Main_LastFirst**.

> **TROUBLESHOOTING:** If you open the *e11h3Main_LastFirst* workbook and try to save it as another file name, Excel will remove the marked-as-final indication and the digital signature. You need to preserve those settings so that your instructor can verify that you completed those steps in Hands-On Exercise 3.

b. Click the **FILE tab** and click **Export**.

c. Click **Create PDF/XPS Document** and click **Create PDF/XPS** on the right side of the Backstage view.

d. Navigate to the folder containing your files, click **Open file after publishing**, and then click **Publish**. Close the newly created PDF and proceed to the next step.

STEP 2 ≫ SAVE TO THE WEB

You want to send the digitally signed workbook to the head chef to review the final dinner budget. Refer to Figure 11.36 as you complete Step 2.

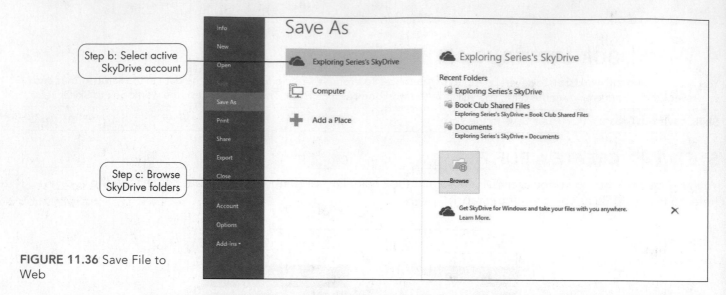

FIGURE 11.36 Save File to Web

TROUBLESHOOTING: You will be prompted to log in with your Windows LIVE account when accessing SkyDrive. If you forget your password, it can be retrieved at https://account .live.com/ResetPassword.aspx.

---

a. Click the **FILE tab** and click **Save As**.

b. Click the SkyDrive account that appears at the top of the Backstage view.

c. If prompted, enter your Microsoft Live user name and password and click **Browse**.

d. Select a folder on the SkyDrive in which to save your document and click **Save**.

e. Exit the workbook and close Excel.

Chapter Objectives Review

After reading this chapter, you have accomplished the following objectives:

1. **Customize Excel.**
   - Customize the Ribbon: Customize the Ribbon by adding tabs, groups, and commands.
   - Customize the Quick Access Toolbar: Customize the Quick Access Toolbar by adding commands.

2. **Change properties.**
   - Use the Properties dialog box: Add various document properties to a workbook to provide efficient searching through files based on properties set.
   - Show the Document Panel: You can display the Document Properties Panel at the top of a workbook.

3. **Share and merge workbooks.**
   - Understand conflicts and network issues: Depending on the network permissions, some users may not be able to edit a workbook.
   - Compare and merge workbooks: Use the *Compare and Merge Workbooks* command to merge the workbooks into one and compare the changes others have made.

4. **Insert comments.**
   - Show and hide comments: Comments can be displayed or suppressed.
   - Edit and delete comments: All comments can be edited or deleted.
   - Print comments: All comments can be optionally printed.

5. **Track changes.**
   - Highlight changes: When selected, all changes will be highlighted in the workbook.
   - Accept and reject changes: When tracking changes, all edits can be accepted or rejected.

6. **Check for issues.**
   - Use Document Inspector: The Document Inspector detects personal and hidden data in a workbook and removes the data to your specifications.

   - Check accessibility: Detects issues that could hinder a user's ability to use a workbook.
   - Check compatibility: Detects data and features that are not compatible with previous versions of Excel.

7. **Protect a workbook.**
   - Mark a workbook as final: Mark a workbook as final to indicate that you approve that particular version of the workbook.
   - Encrypt a workbook with a password: For enhanced protection, you can password-protect a file.
   - Add a digital signature: Add a digital signature to indicate that the workbook is authentic and has not been changed since you added the signature.
   - Add a signature line: A signature line is a visible form of a digital signature.

8. **Save a workbook in different formats.**
   - Save a workbook for previous Excel versions: Save the workbook in a legacy format for compatibility with older versions of Excel.
   - Save a workbook as a PDF file: Save a workbook as a Portable Document Format (PDF) file that can be viewed in Adobe Reader or Adobe Acrobat.

9. **Send a workbook to others.**
   - Send a workbook by e-mail: Use Outlook to send the file as an attachment.
   - Save to the Web: If you have a Windows LIVE account, you can save the file to a folder on your SkyDrive so that you or others can access the workbook.

Key Terms Matching

Match the key terms with their definitions. Write the key term number by the appropriate numbered definition.

a. Accessibility Checker
b. Collaboration
c. Comment
d. Comment indicator
e. Compatibility Checker
f. Digital signature
g. Document Inspector
h. Document property

i. History worksheet
j. Metadata
k. Portable Document Format (PDF)
l. Shared workbook
m. Signature line
n. SkyDrive
o. Track Changes

1. _____ A central storage location where you can save and access files via Internet connection. **p. 517**

2. _____ Enables a person to type or insert a visible digital signature to authenticate the workbook. **p. 509**

3. _____ A universal file format that preserves a document's original data and formatting for multiplatform use. **p. 515**

4. _____ An electronic notation in a document to authenticate the contents. **p. 508**

5. _____ Detects issues that could hinder a user's ability to use a workbook. **p. 506**

6. _____ Detects data and features that are not compatible with previous versions of Excel. **p. 506**

7. _____ Lists particular types of changes made to a workbook. **p. 499**

8. _____ Detects hidden and personal data in a workbook to remove. **p. 505**

9. _____ A colored triangle in the top-right corner of a cell to indicate that the cell contains comments. **p. 494**

10. _____ Records certain types of changes made in a workbook. **p. 496**

11. _____ Occurs when multiple people work together to achieve a common goal by using technology to edit the contents of a file. **p. 491**

12. _____ A file that enables multiple users to make changes at the same time. **p. 491**

13. _____ An attribute, such as an author's name or keyword, that describes a file. **p. 485**

14. _____ A notation attached to a cell to pose a question or provide commentary. **p. 494**

15. _____ Pieces of data, such as a keyword, that describe other data, such as the contents of a file. **p. 485**

Multiple Choice

1. Which statement about comments in Excel is true?

   (a) Comments remain onscreen in the right margin area.

   (b) Position the mouse pointer over the cell containing a comment indicator to display a comment box.

   (c) After you insert a comment, Excel prevents you from changing it.

   (d) Comment boxes display the date and time that the user inserted the comment in the worksheet.

2. Which document property cannot be changed within the Backstage view?

   (a) Author

   (b) Title

   (c) Categories

   (d) Last Modified date

3. What is the default file format for a basic Excel 2013 file?

   (a) .xls

   (b) .pdf

   (c) .xlsx

   (d) .csv

4. Which tool detects issues that could hinder a user's ability to use a workbook?

   (a) Accessibility Checker

   (b) Compatibility Checker

   (c) Change tracker

   (d) Document Inspector

5. The Track Changes feature does not detect what type of change?

   (a) Changing a value of a number from 10 to 25

   (b) Inserting a new row above row 18

   (c) Deleting text within a label

   (d) Applying Percent Style for the range B4:B10

6. A workbook that has been marked as final:

   (a) Opens in Read-Only mode.

   (b) Is password protected to make any changes.

   (c) Displays a nonstop, flashing Message Bar that the workbook is final.

   (d) Must contain a digital signature.

7. The _____ tool detects particular properties, such as Author, and removes those properties from a file that you plan to distribute.

   (a) Compatibility Checker

   (b) Document Inspector

   (c) Advanced Properties

   (d) Accessibility Checker

8. If you want to save a file in a format that preserves worksheet formatting, prevents changes, and ensures that the document looks the same on most computers, save the workbook in the _____ file format.

   (a) .csv

   (b) Excel template

   (c) Excel 97-2003 workbook

   (d) .pdf

9. If you want to save a workbook to a highly secure central location to enable efficient collaboration:

   (a) Send the workbook as an e-mail attachment.

   (b) Save the workbook to a SharePoint site or to a shared SkyDrive folder.

   (c) Save the workbook to a regular Web site.

   (d) Backup the workbook to an external hard drive.

10. You can do all of the following *except* _____ for both customizing the Ribbon and customizing the Quick Access Toolbar.

    (a) Add a command

    (b) Reset the customizations

    (c) Print

    (d) Import and export customizations

Practice Exercises

1 Instructor Evaluation

FROM SCRATCH

You are a student who has recently completed the course Introduction to Information Systems. You received a correspondence from the dean of your college requesting your evaluation of the course based on effectiveness of the teacher, rigor of workload, and overall course value. The dean would like you to create an Excel worksheet answering the questions with values 1 through 5, 1 being strongly disagree and 5 being strongly agree. Once the survey is completed, he would like you to send the worksheet to him via e-mail attachment. This exercise follows the same set of skills as used in Hands-On Exercise 3. Refer to Figure 11.37 as you complete this exercise.

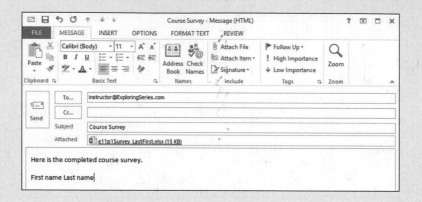

FIGURE 11.37 Send File via E-Mail

a. Open Excel and create a new blank worksheet. Save the worksheet as **e11p1Survey_LastFirst**.

b. Click **cell A1** and type **Intro to Information Systems Survey**.

c. Click **cell B1** and type **Rating**.

d. Enter the following information in the corresponding cells.
- Click **cell A2** and type **Effectiveness of the teacher**.
- Click **cell A3** and type **Rigor of course load**.
- Click **cell A4** and type **Overall course value**.
- Enter the 1–5 rating of your choice in **cells B2**, **B3**, and **B4**.

e. Select the **range A1:B1** and add a thick box border.

f. Select the **range A2:B4** and add **All Borders**.

g. Click the **INSERT tab** and insert a signature line in **cell A6** with the following information:
- Enter your name for *Suggested signer's name*.
- Enter **Student** for *Suggested signer's title*.
- Enter your e-mail address for *Suggested signer's e-mail*.

h. Click the **FILE tab** and click **Share**. Click **E-mail** and click **Send as Attachment**. Do the following in the Outlook window:
- Type your instructor's e-mail address in the **To box**.
- Type **course survey** in the **Subject box**.
- Type **Here is the completed course survey**.
- Press **Enter** twice and type your name.
- Click **Send**.

i. Close the workbook.

2 Valentine's Day Dance

You are on the budget committee for the formal Valentine's Day Ball at your university. The ball includes dinner and dancing. Your committee prepared a tentative budget outlining income and expenses. The primary sources of income are contributions from student organizations and ticket prices. Expenses include the actual cost of the dinner, facilities, parking, and other costs at a luxurious hotel in the city.

Your goal is to balance the income and expenses, decide on the most appropriate ticket price per student, and ensure your budget falls within the limitations you must work with. This exercise follows the same set of skills as used in Hands-On Exercise 2 in the chapter. Refer to Figure 11.38 as you complete this exercise.

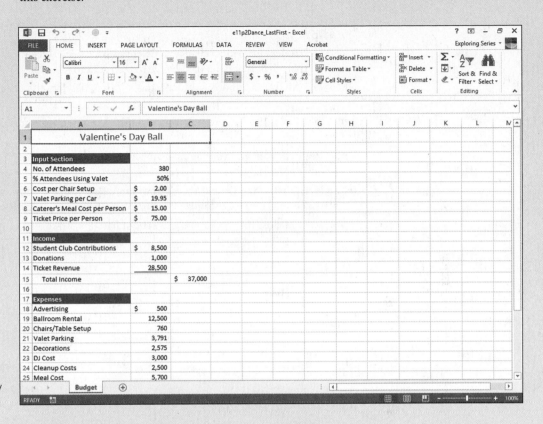

FIGURE 11.38 Valentine's Day Dance Budget

a. Open *e11p2Dance* and save it as **e11p2Dance_LastFirst**.

b. Click the **FILE tab**, click **Options**, select the text in the **User name box**, type your name, and then click **OK**.

c. Look at the Quick Access Toolbar to see if it contains the *Compare and Merge Workbooks* command. If so, continue with step d. If not, click **Customize Quick Access Toolbar** on the right side of the Quick Access Toolbar and select **More Commands**. Do the following in the Excel Options dialog box:

- Click the **Choose commands from arrow** and select **Commands Not in the Ribbon**.
- Scroll through the list, select **Compare and Merge Workbooks**, and then click **Add**.
- Click **OK**.

d. Make the following changes:

- Select and delete **rows 11 through 16**.
- Right-click **row 13** and select **Insert**. Type **Donations** in **cell A13** and **1000** in **cell B13**.
- Type **1500** in **cell B18** and **10000** in **cell B19**.
- Type **=B4*B8** in **cell B25**. Save the workbook.

e. Click **Compare and Merge Workbooks** on the Quick Access Toolbar, select *e11p2Dance_Anita*, and then click **OK**.

f. Click the **REVIEW tab**, select **Track Changes** in the Changes group, select **Highlight Changes**, deselect the **When check box**, click the **List changes on a new sheet check box**, and then click **OK**.

g. Start Word and create a new document. Click the **INSERT tab**, click **Screenshot**, click the **Microsoft Excel – e11e11p2Dance_LastFirst window** in the gallery, save the document as **e11p2History_LastFirst**, insert a footer with your name on the left side and the file name field on the right side, save the document, and then exit Word.

h. Click the **Budget worksheet tab**, click **Track Changes** in the Changes group, select **Accept/Reject Changes**, and then click **OK**.

i. Click **Accept** for all of your changes. When prompted to select a value for cell B18, click **$500.00** by Anita and click **Accept**.

j. Click **Accept** for Anita's change of cell B4 to *380* and click **Accept** on Anita's change of cell B8 to *$15*.

k. Click **Reject** for Anita's change to delete row 19, click **Accept** on her change of cell B22 to *$2,575*, and then click **Reject** on her change for cell A23 to *Live Band*.

l. Click **Share Workbook** in the Changes group, deselect the check box, and then click **OK**. Click **Yes**.

m. Click **cell C29**, click **New Comment** in the Comments group, and then type **The balance should be $0 or greater.**

n. Create a footer with your name on the left side, the sheet name code in the center, and the file name code on the right side.

o. Click **Customize Quick Access Toolbar**, select **More Commands**, select **Compare and Merge Workbooks** in the Customize Quick Access Toolbar list, click **Remove**, and then click **OK**.

p. Save and close the workbook, and submit based on your instructor's directions.

Mid-Level Exercises

1 Lecture Series Expenses

ANALYSIS
CASE

The College of Science at Prestige University hosts a lecture series of guest presenters in the industry. As the fiscal manager, you are responsible for maintaining the budget, which includes the following expenses: lunches for the speakers and select faculty, printing costs for bulletin board fliers, travel accommodations for one out-of-state presenter per semester, and a gift pen set for each speaker. Your predecessor created a workbook containing expenses for the 2014–2015 academic year; however, it contains errors. You and the associate dean, Samantha Young, will review and correct the workbook. Then you will merge the two workbooks and accept and reject changes as needed. In addition, you need to prepare the workbook for distribution to the university's budget office and answer four questions on the data.

a. Open *e11m1Lecture* and save it as **e11m1Lecture_LastFirst**.

b. Make sure your name is the user name in the Excel Options dialog box.

c. Add the *Compare and Merge Workbooks* command to the Quick Access Toolbar, if necessary. Compare and merge *e11m1Samantha* with your workbook.

d. Make the following changes in the workbook:

Worksheet	Cell	Change
Fall	B8	Use the correct cell reference for the total Fall travel from the Travel sheet.
Fall	B9	Use the correct cell reference for the total Fall printing/copies cost from the Printing sheet.
Spring	B9	Use the correct cell reference for the total Spring printing/copies cost from the Printing sheet.
Lunches	C31	77.90
Lunches	C34	117.58
Lunches	C35	104.35

e. Insert the following comment in **cell C13** in the Spring worksheet: **The 2014–2015 budget was $5,000, so we didn't have a deficit. However, we need to trim at least $225 from next year's expenses.**

f. Activate the **Track Changes feature** so that you can accept and reject changes. Accept and reject these changes:

Description of Change	Action
Changed cell C16 from *$77.90* to *$117.58*	Accept
Changed cell C29 from <blank> to *$104.35*	Reject
Changed cell C4 from *$5,000* to *$4,500*	Accept
Changed cell B8 from =Travel!C2 to =Travel!C6	Accept
Changed cell B9 from =Printing!#REF! to =Printing!C4	Accept
Changed cell B9 from =Printing!#REF! to =Printing!C10	Accept
Changed cell C31 from *$91.13* to *$77.90*	Accept
Changed cell C34 from *$124.71* to *$117.58*	Accept
Changed cell C35 from *$114.70* to *$104.35*	Accept

g. Edit your comment in **cell C13** in the Spring worksheet by typing **Updated cut cost: $120** at the end of the existing comment.

h. Create a footer with your name on the left side, the sheet name code in the center, and the file name code on the right side on each worksheet.

i. Edit **cell A10** in the Travel sheet: Spring 2015 and make the semesters specific, such as 2014 and 2015, in cells A1 and A6 in the Gifts sheet.

j. Run Accessibility Checker. Ignore any warnings about merged cells and close the Accessibility Checker task pane.

k. Answer the questions on the Q&A sheet. Then save the workbook.

DISCOVER

l. Create a Windows Live account if you do not already have one. Create a folder on your SkyDrive and name it **Exploring**. Enter your instructor's e-mail address so that you can share that folder with your instructor.

m. Save the workbook to the Exploring folder on your SkyDrive.

n. Save and close the workbook, and submit based on your instructor's directions.

2 Ribbon Customization

COLLABORATION CASE

FROM SCRATCH

You and a coworker have been assigned to a team that manages financial sheets that must be merged and then e-mailed to management. To synchronize your efforts, you have decided to customize your Office Ribbon and then share the settings with your fellow team members. In addition, you will insert before and after screenshots into a Word document and change document properties.

Student 1

a. Start a new workbook and save it as **e11m2Custom_LastFirst**.

b. Make sure your name is the user name in the Excel Options dialog box.

c. Display the Document Panel, add the following document properties, and then close the Document Panel:
- Author: your name
- Title: **Excel 2013 Custom Ribbon**
- Keywords: **Excel, customization, Ribbon, groups, commands**

d. Click the **FILE tab**, select **Options**, and then click **Customize Ribbon**.

e. Click **New Tab** from the *Customize the Ribbon* section.

f. Click **Rename** and name the newly created tab **Group Project**.

g. Create a new group in the Group Project tab named **Common Functions** and do the following:
- Click **Choose commands from** and select **All Tabs**. Click **Review**, select **Changes**, and then add Share Workbook and Track Changes to the newly created Common Functions group.
- Click **Choose commands from** and select **Commands Not in the Ribbon**. Select **Compare and Merge Workbook** and click **Add** to add the option to the Common Functions Group.

h. Click the **Import/Export menu** and select **Export all customizations**. Save the file as **e11m2CustomSet_LastFirst**.

Student 2

i. Open Excel, create a new workbook, click the **FILE tab**, and then click **Options**. Click **Customize Ribbon**.

j. Click **Import/Export** and select **Import customization file**.

k. Import the file *e11m2CustomSet_LastFirst.exportedUI*. Click **Yes** when prompted to replace all existing Ribbon and Quick Access Toolbar customizations. Then display the newly customized tab.

l. Open Microsoft Word and create a new document.

m. Click the **INSERT tab** on the Ribbon and insert a screen shot of your Excel application with the newly added customizations.

n. Save the document as **e11m2ScreenCapture_LastFirst**. Save the document and close Word.

Beyond the Classroom

Cell Phone Plans
RESEARCH CASE →

You and a classmate want to compare individual cell phone plans for three cell phone companies. Open *e11b2CellPhone* and save it as **e11b2CellPhone_LastFirst**. Make sure your name is the user name in Excel Options. Research individual plans in your city. Use the following parameters: 450 anytime minutes, unlimited texting, and a data plan to use the Internet. Enter the cost details in the worksheet. Enter number of weekend minutes used, and enter a formula to calculate the total monthly costs, not including taxes and fees. Save the workbook and send as an e-mail attachment to a classmate. Have that classmate do the same for you.

You and your classmate should save the received workbook with your name, turn on Track Changes, make some changes, and insert comments. Then e-mail the workbooks back to each other and save the updated workbook as **e11b2CellPhone2_LastFirst**. Accept and reject changes as necessary, turn off the shared workbook, and then mark the workbook as final. Close the workbook and submit all files based on your instructor's directions.

Passenger Car Ratings
DISASTER RECOVERY

You work as an analyst for an independent automobile rating company that provides statistics to consumers. You prepared a worksheet containing the test results of five 2015 mid-sized passenger car models. Open *e11b3Autos* and save it as **e11b3Autos_LastFirst**. Make sure your name is the user name in Excel Options. Insert a comment in the cell that indicates the top-ranked car. Insert a footer with your name on the left side, the sheet name code in the center, and the file name code on the right side. Insert a signature line with your name and job title below the worksheet data. Close the workbook and make a copy of it in File Explorer. Open the copied workbook. Use Compatibility Checker to see what features are not compatible with previous versions. Create a memo in Word that includes a full screenshot of the Compatibility Checker's results. Explain how you plan to handle each warning. Save the Word document as **e11b3AutosMemo_LastFirst**. Make appropriate changes in the workbook and save it in Excel 97-2003 Workbook format as **e11b3Autos2_LastFirst**. Submit the three files based on your instructor's directions.

Workplace Etiquette
SOFT SKILLS CASE S

You have recently been hired at CBK Financial, a wealth management company located in Atlanta. CBK has strict etiquette for managing and distributing Excel workbooks. They require each document to be checked for compatibility, free of all personal information, and digitally signed.

Open the file *e11b4Etiquette*. Save the file as **e11b4Etiquette_LastFirst**. Review the document for errors, and after you are satisfied that it is free of anomalies, use the Document Inspector to delete any personal information. Next check the document for ignoring any minor or major issues with any version prior to Excel 2007. Add a digital signature approving the document. Save the workbook and send as an e-mail attachment to a classmate. Have that classmate do the same for you. Close the workbook and submit all files based on your instructor's directions.

Capstone Exercise

You have been hired as an assistant accountant for a small health care IT company. Your role is to merge monthly financial documents from multiple locations, check compatibility, and, after management approval, finalize and distribute your results.

Customize Excel

Since it is your first day on the job, you want to take time to customize Excel. You want enter the user name. You also want to customize the Quick Access Toolbar to add the *Compare and Merge Workbooks* command.

a. Type your name as the user name in the Excel Options dialog box if necessary.

b. Add the *Compare and Merge Workbooks* command to the Quick Access Toolbar if necessary.

Add Document Properties

You want to add document properties to the workbook.

a. Open *e11c1HealthCare* and save it as **e11c1HealthCare_LastFirst**.

b. Display the Backstage view.

c. Enter appropriate data in the Author and Title properties.

Compare and Merge Workbooks

You saved a shareable version of your master document for other offices to use as a template. You need to merge the sales data from Dallas and Atlanta offices into your master document. Then you will compare and merge workbooks.

a. Compare and merge *e11c1Dallas* and *e11c1Atlanta* into your workbook.

b. Click **cell B13**, type **$100,250** to reflect a last-minute addition of $10,000 in sales, and then save the workbook.

c. Activate the **Track Changes feature**, highlight all changes, and then create a History worksheet.

d. Start Word, insert a screenshot of the History worksheet, save the document as **e11c1History_LastFirst**, insert a footer with your name on the left side and a file name field on the right side, save the document, and then exit Word.

Accept and Reject Changes

After studying the History worksheet, you are ready to accept and reject changes.

a. Open the *Select Changes to Accept or Reject* dialog box and deselect all check boxes.

b. Accept all changes.

c. Turn off workbook sharing and save the workbook.

Finalize the Workbook

Although the workbook is intended primarily for you, you want to check the workbook for potential problems. You want to communicate to upper management that the workbook is final and add a signature line to the finalized workbook.

a. Run the Accessibility Checker, identify potential problems, and then fix the warning issues detected. Close the Accessibility Checker task pane.

b. Run the Compatibility Checker, correct any significant loss of fidelity issues, and ignore any minor loss of fidelity issues.

c. Insert a footer with your name on the left side, the sheet name code in the center, and the file name code on the right side.

d. Add a signature line.

e. Mark the workbook as final.

Distribute the Workbook

In case the clients do not have Excel 2013, you want to save the workbook in Excel 97-2003 format.

a. Save the workbook in Excel 97-2003 Workbook format.

b. Save the workbook in PDF format using the same basic file name and close Adobe Reader or Adobe Acrobat.

c. Save the file to your SkyDrive if you have one. Provide rights for your instructor to access it on your SkyDrive.

d. Close all open workbooks and files.

Templates, Styles, and Macros

Standardizing Workbooks

CASE STUDY | Staff Accounting Services

Recently, you took a position as the manager of staff accounting at EBL, Ltd., a regional information technology (IT) company based in Denver, Colorado, with additional offices in Salt Lake City, Utah, and Reno, Nevada. The company provides computer and data network consultation services to individuals, small businesses, and nonprofits. The previous manager used a paper-based system to prepare expense reports, invoices, and payroll statements. However, this was a time-consuming process and required manual recalculation when any values changed.

Because of your extensive experience using Excel, you want to start automating these tasks. You decide to start with the monthly travel expense report form. Because each office utilizes the same procedures, you want to adapt an Excel template to use as a model for travel expense documentation. The template needs to be generic enough to accommodate a range of options, but it also needs to maintain a standard design to facilitate easy data entry.

You will customize the template by applying cell styles to give the form a more polished look and then create macros to perform a series of tasks, such as clearing the values to reset the form if needed and printing the expense report worksheet for management approval.

Templates, Themes, and Styles

Designing the perfect workbook can be time consuming. By now, you know you have to plan the layout before you enter data to minimize data-entry changes later. You decide what column and row labels are needed to describe the data, where to place the labels, and how to format the labels. In addition, you enter and format quantitative data, such as applying Accounting Number Format and decreasing the number of decimal places. The longer you work for the same department or organization, the more you will notice that you create the same types of workbooks. Excel has the right tools to improve your productivity in developing consistently formatted workbooks. Some of these tools include templates, themes, backgrounds, and styles.

In this section, you will select an Excel template. After opening the template, you will apply a theme, display a background, and apply cell styles.

Selecting a Template

STEP 1 ≫ A *template* is a partially completed document that you use as a model to create other documents that have the same structure and purpose. A template typically contains standard labels, formulas, and formatting but may contain little or no quantitative data. Templates help ensure consistency and standardization for similar workbooks, such as detailed sales reports for all 12 months of a year. When you start Excel, you are presented with a gallery of templates. If you are already working within a workbook, click the File tab and click New. The Backstage view displays a gallery of featured templates (see Figure 12.1). You can select from templates you have recently used, sample templates that were installed with the software, or templates you created, or download new templates. To create a workbook based on a template, do the following:

1. Click a sample template, such as *Travel expense report*.
2. A pop-up window will display a sample of the selected template (see Figure 12.2).
3. Click Create to load the template data as a new workbook.

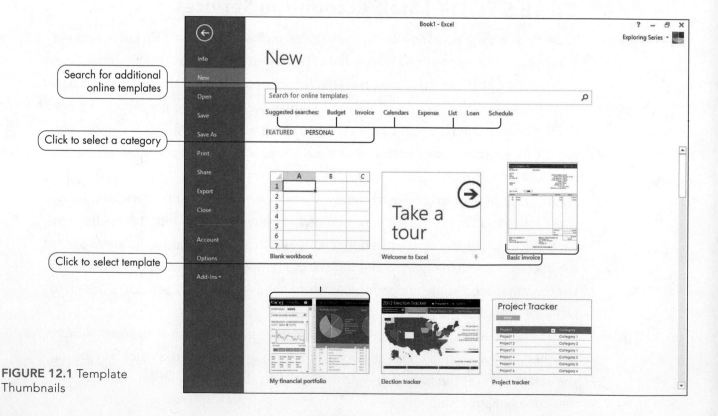

FIGURE 12.1 Template Thumbnails

The *Search for online templates* box allows you to search Office.com for a particular template by entering your search conditions and pressing Enter. Start searching, or you can select a template from a category, such as Budgets. These templates are created by Microsoft, a Microsoft partner, or a member of the Microsoft community. To download an Office.com template, do the following:

1. Click a template category, such as Expense. The Backstage view then displays thumbnails representing the various templates in that category.

2. Click the template thumbnail representing the template you want to download. A pop-up window displays information about the selected template, such as the template name and creator and the download size (see Figure 12.2).

3. Click Create. The Download Template message box displays briefly, after which the template is opened as a workbook in Excel.

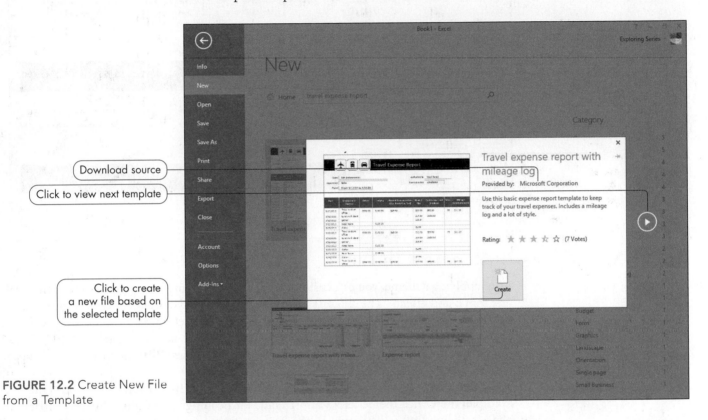

FIGURE 12.2 Create New File from a Template

Downloading the template does not save it to a storage location. You must save the workbook on a storage device. When you save a workbook from a downloaded template for the first time, the Save As dialog box defaults to SkyDrive in Windows 8; however, you can select another location in which to save the workbook.

Applying Themes and Backgrounds

STEP 2» In addition to selecting a template, you might want to apply a theme or insert a background to create a consistent look with the workbooks you create. A *theme* is a collection of formats that include coordinating colors, fonts, and special effects to provide a stylish appearance. You can apply a theme to a workbook to give it a consistent look with other workbooks used in your department or organization. Most organizations have a style that encompasses particular fonts, colors, and a logo or trademark on corporate stationery, advertisements, and Web pages. You can use themes in Excel workbooks to match the corporate "look and feel." Some of the Excel theme names match theme names in other Office applications so that you can provide continuity and consistency in all of your documents. To apply a theme to all worksheets in a workbook, do the following:

1. Click the PAGE LAYOUT tab.
2. Click Themes in the Themes group. The Office theme is presented first; the other built-in themes are listed alphabetically in the Themes gallery (see Figure 12.3).
3. Position the pointer over each theme to display a Live Preview of how the theme would format existing data on the current worksheet.
4. Click a theme to make it active.

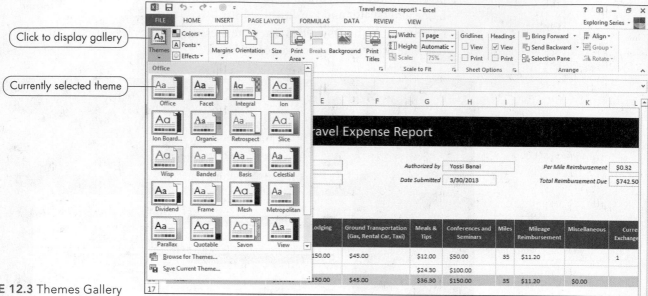

FIGURE 12.3 Themes Gallery

Customize a Theme

After applying a theme, you can customize the three elements that comprise the theme: colors, fonts, and effects. The Themes group on the Page Layout tab contains commands to customize your theme. When you click Colors, you can select from a gallery of colors, or you can select Customize Colors to define the text, background, accent, hyperlink, and followed hyperlink colors. If you create and name your own color theme, that theme name will appear in the *Custom* section of the Colors menu.

Theme fonts contain a coordinating heading and body text font for each theme. For example, the Office theme uses Calibri Light for headings and Calibri for cell entries. To select a theme font, click Fonts in the Themes group and select a theme font, or select Customize Fonts to define your own theme fonts.

Theme effects are special effects that control the design differences in objects, such as shapes, SmartArt, and object borders. To select a theme effect, click Effects in the Themes group, position the mouse pointer over an effect to see a Live Preview of how that effect will affect objects, and click the desired effect to apply it to your workbook.

Apply a Background

STEP 3 » Excel enables you to use graphics as the background of a worksheet. The effect is similar to placing a background on a Web page. A ***background*** is an image placed behind the worksheet data. For example, you might want to use the corporate logo as your background, or you might want a "Confidential" graphic image to remind onscreen viewers that the worksheet contains corporate trade secrets. (If you want an image to appear behind data on a printed worksheet, insert the image as a watermark in a header.) Be careful in selecting and using backgrounds, because the images can distract users from comprehending the quantitative data. A subtle, pale image is less likely to distract a workbook user than a bright, vividly colored image. To add a background to a worksheet, do the following:

1. Click Background in the Page Setup group on the PAGE LAYOUT tab to open the Insert Pictures dialog box.

2. Select the picture file, such as a jpeg or bitmap file, that you want to use as a background.
3. Click Insert.

The image, like background images in Web pages, is tiled across your worksheet (see Figure 12.4). The background image displays only in the worksheet onscreen; it does not print. Notice that Delete Background replaces Background in the Page Setup group after you insert a background for a specific worksheet.

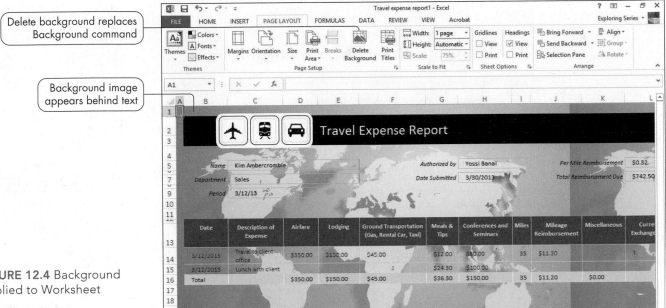

Delete background replaces Background command

Background image appears behind text

FIGURE 12.4 Background Applied to Worksheet

Photo: Kundra/Fotolia

TIP Background Visibility

You can turn off the gridlines to increase the visibility of the background image and the worksheet data. Click the Page Layout tab and deselect the Gridlines View check box in the Sheet Options group.

TIP Delete Background Image

To delete a background picture, click Delete Background in the Page Setup group on the Page Layout tab.

Applying Cell Styles

STEP 4

Different areas of a worksheet have different formatting. For example, titles may be centered in 16-pt size; column labels may be bold, centered, and dark blue font; and input cells may be formatted differently from output cells. A *cell style* is a collection of format settings based on the currently selected theme to provide a consistent appearance within a worksheet and among similar workbooks. Cell styles control the following formats:

- Font attributes, such as font and font size
- Borders and fill styles and colors
- Vertical and horizontal cell alignment

- Number formatting, such as Currency and number of decimal places
- Cell-protection settings

The currently selected theme controls cell styles. If you change the theme, Excel updates cells formatted by cell styles to reflect the new theme. For example, if you change from Facet theme to Integral, particular fill colors change from shades of green to blue. To apply a style to a cell or range of cells, do the following:

1. Click the HOME tab and click Cell Styles in the Styles group to display the Cell Styles gallery (see Figure 12.5).
2. Position the mouse pointer over a style name to see a Live Preview of how that style will affect the active cell.
3. Click a style to apply it to the active cell or range.

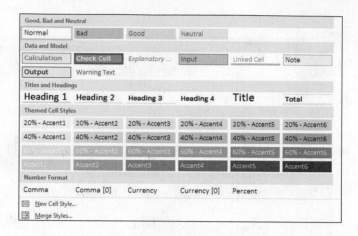

FIGURE 12.5 Cell Styles

The gallery contains the following five predefined cell categories:

- **Good, Bad, and Neutral:** Use to emphasize bad, good, or neutral results, or click Normal to reset a cell to its original default setting.
- **Data and Model:** Use to indicate special cell contents, such as a calculated result, input cell, output cell, or warning.
- **Titles and Headings:** Use to format titles and headings, such as column and row labels, for emphasis.
- **Themed Cell Styles:** Use Accent styles for visual emphasis. These cell styles are dependent on the currently selected theme.
- **Number Format:** Provide the same formatting as commands in the Number group on the Home tab.

Create Custom Cell Styles

You can create your own custom cell styles if the predefined cell styles do not meet your needs. For example, you might want to create custom cell styles that match the color, font, and design of your corporate logo or stationery to help brand your workbooks with the company image. After you create custom cell styles, you can apply them in multiple workbooks instead of formatting each workbook individually. To create a custom cell style do the following:

1. Click the cell that contains the desired formatting.
2. Click the HOME tab and click Cell Styles in the Styles group.
3. Select New Cell Style at the bottom of the gallery to open the Style dialog box (see Figure 12.6).
4. Type the name for your new style in the *Style name* box.

5. Click the check boxes to select the style options you want in the *Style Includes (By Example)* section. (If you are not creating a style using the active cell as an example, click Format to open the Format Cells dialog box and select the formats just as you would format an individual cell.)

6. Click OK to close the Style dialog box.

After you create a custom style, Excel displays another section, *Custom*, at the top of the Cell Styles gallery. This section lists the custom styles you create.

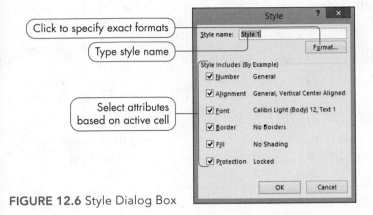

Click to specify exact formats

Type style name

Select attributes based on active cell

FIGURE 12.6 Style Dialog Box

Modify and Remove Custom Cell Styles

After you create and apply custom styles to worksheet cells, you might decide to change the format. For example, you might want to change the font size or fill color. The primary advantage to creating and applying styles is that you can modify the style, and Excel updates all cells for which you applied the style automatically. To modify a style, do the following:

1. Right-click the style in the *Custom* section of the Cell Styles palette.
2. Select Modify to open the Style dialog box.
3. Make the desired format changes and click OK.

If you no longer need a cell style, you can delete it. However, if you delete a cell style that has been applied to worksheet cells, Excel will remove all formatting from those cells. To delete a cell style, right-click the style name in the *Custom* section of the Cell Styles palette and select Delete. Excel does not ask for confirmation before deleting the style.

 TIP | Use Styles in Other Workbooks

When you create your own cell styles, the styles are saved with the workbook in which you created the styles. However, you may want to apply those styles in other workbooks as well. To do this, open the workbook that contains the custom cell styles (the source) and open the workbook in which you want to apply those custom styles (the destination). In the destination workbook, click Cell Styles in the Styles group on the Home tab. Select Merge Styles at the bottom of the Cell Styles gallery to open the Merge Styles dialog box. In the *Merge styles from* list, select the name of the workbook that contains the styles you want and click OK. When you click Cell Styles again, the custom styles appear in the gallery.

 Quick Concepts

1. What are the benefits of using templates? *p. 532*
2. How do you print worksheets with background images? *p. 534*
3. Why would you create a custom cell style? *p. 536*

1 Templates, Themes, and Styles

You need to get up and running quickly since you took over at EBL, Ltd. You decide to use the Travel Expense Report template that is part of the Office 2013 template downloads. After opening the template, you will modify it by applying a theme, theme color, background, and cell styles.

Skills covered: Select a Template • Apply a Theme • Apply a Background • Apply Cell Styles

STEP 1 >> SELECT A TEMPLATE

To save time, you would like to create a new report using a template. After reviewing the templates available in the template gallery, you decided the Travel Expense Report template shown in Figure 12.7 was sufficient to build your company's report. Your first step is to download the Travel Expense Report template. Refer to Figure 12.7 as you complete Step 1.

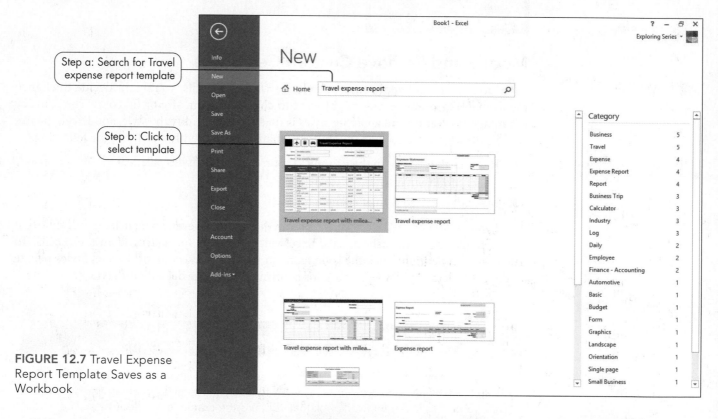

FIGURE 12.7 Travel Expense Report Template Saves as a Workbook

a. Open Excel, type **Travel expense report** in the **Search for online templates box**, and then press **Enter**.

b. Click **Travel expense report with mileage log** to select it; a pop-up window will appear with a brief description of the template.

   Since there are several templates with the same name, choose the template that is the same format as the template shown in Figure 12.7.

> **TROUBLESHOOTING:** Any Microsoft Office user has the ability to submit personally created templates to Office.com. If when searching you discover several templates with the name *Travel Expense Report*, be sure to select the option that resembles the image in Figure 12.7.
>
> If you are unable to locate the required template, a copy of the file *e12h1ExpenseReport* is included with the start files for this chapter.

c. Click **Create** below the preview on the right side of the Backstage view.

   Excel opens a copy of the Travel Expense Report as a new workbook. The template contains labels, fill colors, sample data, and formulas.

d. Save the workbook as **e12h1ExpenseReport_LastFirst**.

STEP 2 ≫ APPLY A THEME

The Travel Expense Report template provides the basic design you need, but you want to apply a different theme to the workbook. Refer to Figure 12.8 as you complete Step 2.

FIGURE 12.8 Theme Applied

a. Click the **PAGE LAYOUT tab** and click **Themes** in the Themes group.

b. Move the pointer over the Banded and Office themes to see the Live Preview of how those themes will affect the workbook.

c. Click **Basis** to apply that theme to the workbook. Save the workbook.

STEP 3 ≫ APPLY A BACKGROUND

To enhance the professional look and feel of the Travel Expense Report, you will add a clip art background image. Refer to Figure 12.9 as you complete Step 3.

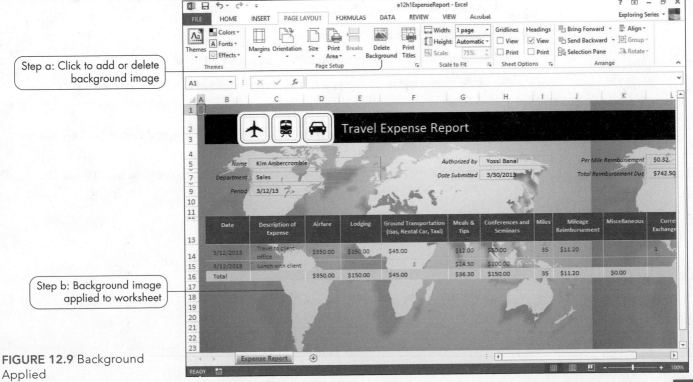

FIGURE 12.9 Background Applied

a. Click the **PAGE LAYOUT tab**, if necessary, and click **Background** in the Page Setup group.

b. Select *e12h1Map.jpg* from the student data file folder and click **Insert**.

The image is tiled across and down the worksheet and appears behind the worksheet data. Because the original template did not include fill colors, the background image can be seen underneath the cells in the worksheet.

c. Save the workbook.

STEP 4 >> APPLY CELL STYLES

You want to further customize the Travel Expense Report workbook by applying different cell styles. For example, you want fill colors in the cells that contain data labels for rows 4:9. You also would like an accent color for rows 14:15 to make the data easier to view. Refer to Figure 12.10 as you complete Step 4.

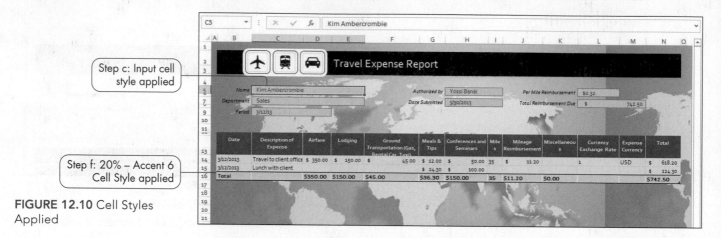

FIGURE 12.10 Cell Styles Applied

a. Select **cell C5**, press and hold **Ctrl**, and then select **cell C7**.

b. Click the **HOME tab** and click **Cell Styles** in the Styles group.

The Cell Styles gallery opens so that you can apply a cell style to the selected cells.

c. Click **Input** in the *Data and Model* section.

d. Adapt steps b and c to apply **Input cell style** to **cell C9**, the **range H5:I5**, **cell H7**, **cell L5**, and **cell L7**.

e. Apply **Short Date number format** to **cell C9**.

f. Select the **range B14:N15**. Apply **20% – Accent 6 Cell Style**.

These ranges had no background. With the cell styles applied, they are now easier to read.

g. Select the **range B16:N16** and apply **Bold** font format.

h. Select the **range B16:N16**, if necessary, click the **HOME tab**, and then apply **Top and Bottom Border** from the Font group.

i. Save the workbook. Keep the workbook open if you plan to continue with Hands-On Exercise 2. If not, close the workbook and exit Excel.

Custom Templates and Workbook Protection

Using Excel templates helps save time when designing workbooks, but these templates will not always meet your needs. When this is the case, you can create a workbook with the specifications you need and save it as a template so that you can use it as a model to create identically structured workbooks for unique data. For example, after downloading the Travel Expense Report template, you applied a theme, a background, and several cell styles. You want the company's employees to be able to use this modified workbook to create individual reports. However, creating a new workbook from scratch for each employee is time consuming. When you find yourself needing the same workbook design for several unique workbooks, you should develop and use a template that can be accessed by each employee and modified as needed.

You can protect cells or worksheets from unauthorized or accidental changes. Doing so ensures that people do not change areas of a worksheet, such as formulas, when you distribute the worksheet on an organization's server.

In this section, you will learn how to save a workbook as a template. In the process, you will learn how to protect cells and worksheets from being changed.

Creating and Using a Template

The Travel Expense Report template you used contains labels, sample values, and formulas. The formulas calculate category totals, such as the total airfare and total of the lodging category expenses. You can remove the sample expenses from the workbook and save it as a template so that you have an empty report for each employee to fill out.

When you create a template from scratch instead of starting with an existing template, adhere to the following guidelines:

- Keep in mind that a template should contain formatted, descriptive labels, empty cells, and formulas.
- Avoid values when possible in formulas; use cell references instead.
- Use an appropriate function to trap errors.
- Include data-validation settings (valid data rules, warning messages, input messages).
- Include instructions for the template.
- Turn off worksheet gridlines, if desired, for clarity.
- Apply appropriate formatting to the template.
- Give worksheets meaningful names and delete worksheets that are not used.

 TIP | **Trap Errors with the IFERROR Function and Set Data Validation**

Formulas used in workbooks display zeros or error messages when you remove values to create a template. You can use the IFERROR function to check a cell to see if it contains errors or if a formula will result in an error. If no error exists, the IFERROR function returns the value of the formula. You can enter an argument in the function to display a customized error message instead of a default error, such as #DIV/0! In addition, you can set validation rules so template users will enter correct data.

After you finalize your workbook, you need to save it. To save a workbook as a template, do the following:

1. Click the FILE tab and click Export.
2. Click Change File Type.
3. Click Template in the Change File Type scrollable list and click Save As at the bottom of the Backstage view to open the Save As dialog box. Notice that the *Save as type* is set to Excel Template.
4. Select the desired location, type a name in the *File name* box, and then click Save. **Note: This method does not default to the "correct" Template folder to provide easy access.**

To save the template so that it automatically is included in the Templates gallery, do the following:

1. From the Backstage view, click Save As and click Computer to open the Save As dialog box.
2. Click the *Save as type* arrow and select Excel Template. Excel then selects the C:\Users\username\Documents\CustomOfficeTemplates folder automatically.
3. Type a name in the *File name* box and click Save.

 Templates Folder

Templates use a different file extension (.xltx) than Excel workbooks (.xlsx). In order for your template to appear in the Template gallery in the Backstage view, be sure to save it in the correct folder, C:\Users\username\Documents\CustomOfficeTemplates in Windows 8 and Windows 7. If you use File Explorer to find the Templates folder, you will need to display hidden folders to do so. If you save your custom templates in the correct location, you can use them to create new workbooks by clicking the File tab, clicking New, and then clicking Personal in the Templates gallery of the Backstage view. The New dialog box displays thumbnails and names for the templates you created.

Protecting a Cell, a Worksheet, and a Workbook

Most templates protect worksheets by enabling users to change only particular cells in a worksheet. For example, users are permitted to enter data in input cells, but they cannot change formulas or alter formatting or worksheet structure. In Hands-On Exercise 2, you will protect the formula cells in the Travel Expense Report template. This will prevent users from changing the formulas. Protecting worksheets prevents modification of formulas and text but enables you to change values in unprotected cells.

Lock and Unlock Cells

 A *locked cell* is one that prevents users from editing the contents or formatting of that cell in a protected worksheet. By default, all cells are locked as indicated by the blue border around the padlock icon for the Lock Cell option on the Format menu in the Cells group on the Home tab. Locked cells are not enforced until you protect the worksheet. Locking or unlocking cells has no effect if the worksheet has not been protected. Before protecting the worksheet, you should unlock the cells that you want users to be able to edit. For example, you will unlock the Per Mile Reimbursement and Date Submitted cells in the Travel Expense Report template so that users can enter unique values. However, you will keep the cells containing formulas locked. To unlock input cells, do the following:

1. Select the cells in which you want users to be able to enter or edit data.
2. Click the HOME tab and click Format in the Cells group (see Figure 12.11). Note that Lock Cell is active by default.
3. Select Lock Cell in the *Protection* section to unlock the active cell or selected range of cells.

To relock cells, repeat the above process.

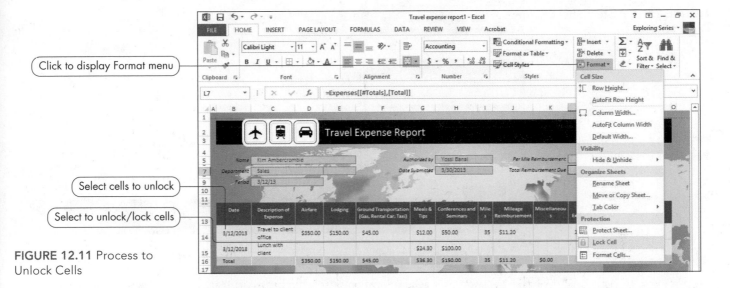

FIGURE 12.11 Process to Unlock Cells

TIP Using the Format Cells Dialog Box

Alternatively, after selecting a cell or range of cells to unlock, you can open the Format Cells dialog box, click the Protection tab, deselect the Locked check box, and then click OK.

Protect a Worksheet

STEP 2» After unlocking cells that you want the users to be able to modify, you are ready to protect the worksheet. When you protect a worksheet, you prevent users from altering the locked cells. During the process of protecting a worksheet, you can enter a password to ensure that only those who know the password can unprotect the worksheet. Protecting the template is typically the final step in the creation of a custom template because you need to enter standard labels, create formulas, and unprotect input cells first. If you protect the worksheet before finalizing the content, you will have to unprotect the worksheet, make content changes, and then protect the worksheet again. To protect a worksheet, do the following:

STEP 3»
1. Click the HOME tab and click Format in the Cells group.
2. Select Protect Sheet in the *Protection* section (or click Protect Sheet in the Changes group on the REVIEW tab) to open the Protect Sheet dialog box (see Figure 12.12).
3. Select the check boxes for actions you want users to be able to do in the *Allow all users of this worksheet to* list.
4. Type a password in the *Password to unprotect sheet* box and click OK. The Confirm Password dialog box opens (see Figure 12.13). Type the same password in the *Reenter password to proceed* box.
5. Read the caution statement and click OK.

TIP Passwords

Passwords can be up to 255 characters, including letters, numbers, and symbols. Passwords are case sensitive, so *passWORD* is not the same as *Password*. Make sure you record your password in a secure location or select a password that you will always remember. If you forget the password, you will not be able to unprotect the worksheet.

After you protect a worksheet, most commands on the Ribbon are dimmed, indicating that they are not available. If someone tries to enter or change data in a locked cell on a protected workbook, Excel displays the warning message and instructs the user how to remove the protection (see Figure 12.14). To unprotect a worksheet, do the following:

1. Click Unprotect Sheet in the Changes group on the REVIEW tab, or click Format in the Cells group on the HOME tab and select Unprotect Sheet. The Unprotect Sheet dialog box opens.

2. Type the password in the Password box and click OK. The worksheet is then unprotected so that you can make changes.

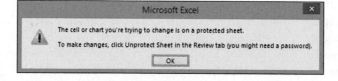

Protect a Workbook

Although locking cells and protecting a worksheet prevents unauthorized modifications, users might make unwanted changes to other parts of the workbook. You can prevent users from inserting, deleting, renaming, moving, copying, and hiding worksheets within the workbook by protecting the workbook with a password. Protecting an entire workbook does not disable the unlocked cells within a workbook; it merely prevents worksheet

manipulation from occurring. That is, individual cells must still be unlocked even if a workbook is unprotected. To protect a workbook, do the following:

1. Click the REVIEW tab and click Protect Workbook in the Changes group. The Protect Structure and Windows dialog box opens (see Figure 12.15).
2. Click the check boxes for the desired action in the *Protect workbook for* section.
3. Type a password in the *Password (optional)* box and click OK. The Confirm Password dialog box opens.
4. Type the same password in the *Reenter password to proceed* box and click OK.

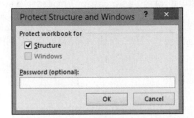

FIGURE 12.15 Protect Structure and Windows Dialog Box

TIP   Unprotect a Workbook

To unprotect a workbook, click the Review tab, click Protect Workbook, type the password in the Password box in the Unprotect Workbook dialog box, and then click OK.

STEP 4 ≫   Once a workbook is completed and the appropriate cells are locked, the last step is to save the file as a template. Saving the file as a template not only stores the files as a template in the Custom Office Templates folder on your computer, it also displays the file as a personal template in the Backstage gallery. To save a workbook as a template, do the following:

STEP 5 ≫
1. Click the FILE tab.
2. Click Save As, click Computer, and then click Browse.
3. Select Excel Template from the *Save as type* menu.
4. Click Save.

Quick
Concepts

1. What is the default file extension for a template? *p. 542*
2. Where are templates saved in Windows 8? *p. 542*
3. Why would you protect a workbook? *p. 544*

Hands-On Exercises

Watch the Video
for this Hands-
On Exercise!

MyITLab®
HOE2 Training

2 Custom Templates and Workbook Protection

After customizing the Travel Expense Report, you want to ensure consistency of use within the company by saving the workbook as a template. As the manager, you do not want your staff deleting formulas or other imperative sections of the expense form you have created. Your next set of steps will include protecting the workbook and then saving it as a template.

Skills covered: Unlock Input Cells • Delete Sample Values • Protect the Worksheet • Save the Workbook as a Template • Use the Template to Create a Sample Expense Report

STEP 1 >> UNLOCK INPUT CELLS

Before protecting the worksheet, you will unlock input cells. You need to ensure the input cells are unlocked so that each employee can enter specific lodging, mileage, and miscellaneous costs. Refer to Figure 12.16 as you complete Step 1.

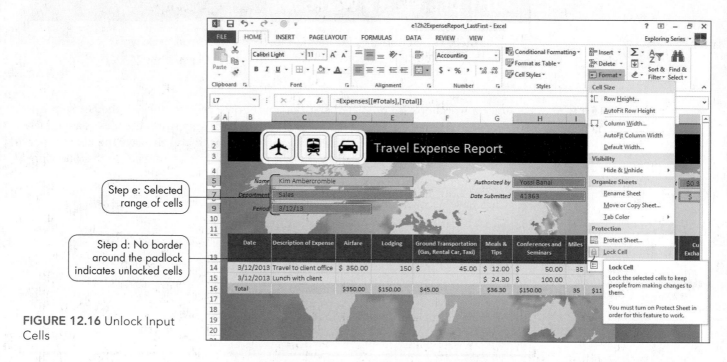

FIGURE 12.16 Unlock Input Cells

a. Open the *e12h1ExpenseReport_LastFirst* workbook and save it as **e12h2ExpenseReport_ LastFirst**, changing *h1* to *h2*.

b. Select **cell C5**.

This cell will be the input area for the name of the creator of the report.

c. Click the **HOME tab**, if necessary, and click **Format** in the Cells group.

The Format menu opens.

d. Select **Lock Cell** in the *Protection* section.

The Lock Cell option does not change to Unlock Cell. However, when you unlock a cell, the Lock Cell command does not have a blue border around the padlock icon on the menu. The selected range of cells is unlocked and will remain unlocked when you protect the worksheet later.

e. Press **Ctrl** while selecting the following cells and range and repeat steps c and d to unlock the cells and range:

- **Cell C7**
- **Cell C9**
- **Cell H5**
- **Cell H7**
- **Cell L5**
- **Range B14:M15**

TROUBLESHOOTING: If you unlock too many cells, select the cells that should be locked, click Format, and then select Lock Cell to lock them again.

---

f. Save the workbook.

STEP 2 ≫ DELETE SAMPLE VALUES

Although you unlocked the input cells for Name, Department, Period, Authorized by, Date Submitted, Per Mile Reimbursement, and Total Reimbursement, you need to delete the sample values to create a ready-to-use empty form before you protect the worksheet and save it as a template. Refer to Figure 12.17 as you complete Step 2.

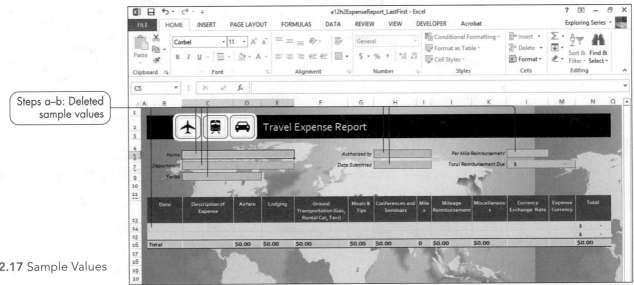

FIGURE 12.17 Sample Values Removed

a. Select **cell C5** and press **Delete**.

b. Delete the sample values in the following cells and range:

- **Cell C7**
- **Cell C9**
- **Cell H5**
- **Cell H7**
- **Cell L5**
- **Range B14:M15**

c. Save the workbook.

STEP 3 ❯❯ PROTECT THE WORKSHEET

Now that you have unlocked input cells and deleted sample expense values, you are ready to protect the Expense Report worksheet. The other cells in the worksheet still have the Lock Cell property enabled. So, after you protect the worksheet, those cells will not be able to be modified.

a. Press **Ctrl+Home**.

b. Click **Format** in the Cells group and select **Protect Sheet**. If not already checked, check *Select locked cells* and *Select unlocked cells*.

The Protect Sheet dialog box opens. The *Protect worksheet and contents of locked cells* check box is selected by default. In addition, the users are allowed to *Select locked cells* and *Select unlocked cells*. Although they can select locked cells, they will not be able to change those cells. Notice that users are not allowed to format data, insert columns or rows, or delete columns or rows.

c. Type **eXploring** in the **Password to unprotect sheet box**.

Remember that passwords are case sensitive and that you must remember the password. If you forget it, you will not be able to unprotect the sheet.

d. Click **OK**.

The Confirm Password dialog box opens with a caution.

e. Read the caution, type **eXploring** in the **Reenter password to proceed box**, and then click **OK**.

f. Click **cell N14** and try to type **1000**.

Excel displays the warning box that the cell is protected with instructions on how to unprotect the worksheet.

> **TROUBLESHOOTING**: If you are allowed to enter the new value without the warning box, the cell is not locked. Click Undo to restore the formula, review Step 1, and then lock this cell.

g. Click **OK** to close the warning box and save the workbook.

STEP 4 ❯❯ SAVE THE WORKBOOK AS A TEMPLATE

You are ready to save the Travel Expense Report workbook as a template. Refer to Figure 12.18 as you complete Step 4.

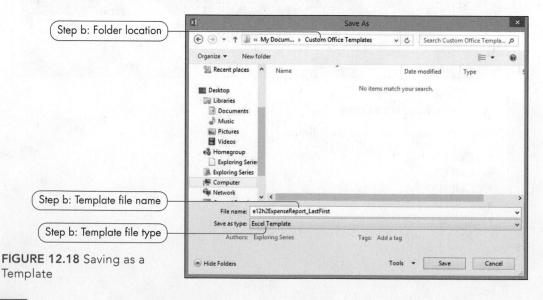

FIGURE 12.18 Saving as a Template

a. Click the **FILE tab**, click **Save As**, click **Browse**, and then click the **Save as type arrow**.

b. Select **Excel Template** and save the file to the default folder, Custom Office Templates, as **e12h2ExpenseReportTemplate_LastFirst**.

The Save As dialog box opens, displaying the current workbook name and Excel Workbook as the default file type.

TROUBLESHOOTING: When saving a template, Excel changes the file location to C:\Users\Username\My Documents\CustomOfficeTemplates. You may not have the ability to save a template to the hard drive of your school's computer lab, or your instructor may request you submit the file. To ensure you do not lose the template, be sure to change the save location to your student data folder. Note that if you do change the default location, the template will not display in the Personal template gallery and you will need to manually open the file from your student data folder to continue.

---

c. Click **Save**.

This will save the workbook as a template and exit the backstage area.

d. Click the **FILE tab** and click **Close**.

STEP 5 ≫ USE THE TEMPLATE TO CREATE A SAMPLE EXPENSE REPORT

Now that you have created a Travel Expense Report template, you are ready to enter data for one of your coworkers. Refer to Figure 12.19 as you complete Step 5.

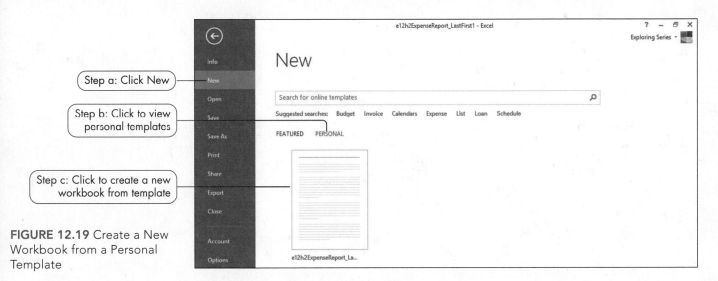

FIGURE 12.19 Create a New Workbook from a Personal Template

a. Click the **FILE tab** and click **New**.

The Backstage view displays a gallery of available templates.

b. Click **PERSONAL** in the *gallery* section.

This displays personal templates saved on your computer.

TROUBLESHOOTING: If you were not able to save the template to the Custom Office Templates folder in Step 4, you will not see the template in the Personal template gallery. If this is the case, the file can be located by searching Recent Workbooks from the Open menu in the Backstage view.

---

c. Click *e12h2ExpenseReportTemplate_LastFirst* and click **OK**.

The template creates a new workbook based on the same file name but with a number appended to the end, such as *e12h2ExpenseReportTemplate_LastFirst1*.

d. Type **Your Name** in **cell C5**.

e. Type the following values in the appropriate cells:

Cell	Value
C7	Finance
H7	1/28/2015
L5	.35
B14	1/3/2015
C14	Sales Conference
D14	250.00
E14	125.00
F14	35.00

f. Press **Ctrl+Home** and save the workbook as **e12h2Sample_LastFirst** in the Excel Workbook file format. Close the workbook and submit based on your instructor's directions.

Macros

By now, you have used most of the tabs on the Ribbon to perform a variety of tasks. Often, you repeat the execution of the same commands as you develop and modify workbooks. Although the sequence to execute commands is easy, you lose productivity when you repeat the same procedures frequently. Previously, you learned how to apply styles and themes and how to create and use templates as models to develop similar workbooks. However, you can automate other routine tasks to increase your productivity. For example, think about how often you set a print range, adjust scaling, set margins, insert a standard header or footer, and specify other page setup options.

You can automate a series of routine or complex tasks by creating a macro. A *macro* is a set of instructions that execute a sequence of commands to automate repetitive or routine tasks. While the term *macro* often intimidates people, you should view macros as your personal assistants that do routine tasks for you! After you create a macro, you can execute the macro to perform all the tasks with minimal work on your part. When you run a macro, the macro executes all of the tasks the same way each time, and faster than you could execute the commands yourself, thus reducing errors while increasing efficiency.

The default Excel Workbook file format (.xlsx) cannot store macros. When you save a workbook containing macros, click the *Save as type* arrow in the Save As dialog box, and select one of the following file formats that support macros:

- Excel Macro-Enabled Workbook (.xlsm)
- Excel Binary Workbook (.xlsb)
- Excel Macro-Enabled Template (.xltm)

In this section, you will learn how to use the Macro Recorder to record a macro. You will also learn how to run a macro, edit a macro, create macro buttons, and review macro security issues.

Creating a Macro

Excel provides two methods for creating macros. You can use the Macro Recorder or type instructions using *Visual Basic for Applications (VBA)*. VBA is a robust programming language that is the underlying code of all macros. While programmers use VBA to create macros, you do not have to be a programmer to write macros. It is relatively easy to use the *Macro Recorder* within Excel to record your commands, keystrokes, and mouse clicks to store Excel commands as VBA code within a workbook. Before you record a macro, keep the following points in mind:

- Remember that once you begin recording a macro, most actions you take are recorded in the macro. If you click something in error, you have to edit the code or undo the action to correct it.
- Practice the steps before you start recording the macro so that you will know the sequence in which to perform the steps when you record the macro.
- Ensure your macros are broad enough to apply to a variety of situations or an action you perform often for the workbook.
- Determine whether cell references should be relative, absolute, or mixed if you include cell references in the macro.

Use the Macro Recorder

You can access the Macro Recorder in a variety of ways: from the View tab, from the Developer tab, or from the status bar. The following list briefly describes what each method includes:

- The View tab contains the Macros group with the Macros command. You can click the Macros arrow to view macros, record a macro, or use relative references.

- The Developer tab, when displayed, provides more in-depth tools that workbook developers use. The Code group contains the same commands as the Macros arrow on the View tab, but it also includes commands to open the Visual Basic editor and set macro security.

- The status bar displays the Macro Recording button so that you can quickly click it to start and stop recording macros.

To display the Developer tab on the Ribbon, do the following:

1. Click the FILE tab and click Options to open the Excel Options dialog box.
2. Click Customize Ribbon on the left side to display the *Customize the Ribbon* options.
3. Click the Developer check box in the Main Tabs list to select it and click OK. Figure 12.20 shows the DEVELOPER tab.

FIGURE 12.20 Developer Tab

Record a Macro

Recording a macro is relatively straightforward: You initiate the macro recording, perform a series of commands as you normally do, then stop the macro recording. Be careful and thorough when recording a macro to ensure that it performs the task it is designed to do and to avoid the need to edit the macro in the VBA Editor. Before recording a macro, you should practice it first and make sure you know the sequence of tasks you want to perform. After planning a macro, you are ready to record it. To record a macro, do the following:

1. Click the VIEW tab, click the Macros arrow in the Macros group, and then select Record Macro; or click the DEVELOPER tab and click Record Macro in the Code group; or click Macro Recording on the status bar. The Record Macro dialog box opens (see Figure 12.21 and Figure 12.22).
2. Type a name for the macro in the *Macro name* box. Macro names cannot include spaces or special characters and must start with a letter. Use CamelCasing (capitalize the first letter of each word but without a space), a programming naming convention, to increase readability of the macro name.
3. Assign a keyboard shortcut, if desired, for your macro in the *Shortcut key* box. Use caution, because many Ctrl+ shortcuts are already assigned in Excel. To be safe, it is best to use Ctrl+Shift+, such as Ctrl+Shift+C instead of Ctrl+C, because Ctrl+C is the existing keyboard shortcut for the Copy command.
4. Click the *Store macro in* arrow and select a storage location, such as This Workbook.
5. Type a description of the macro and its purpose in the Description box and click OK to start recording the macro.
6. Perform the commands that you want to record.
7. Click the VIEW tab, click Macros in the Macros group, and then select Stop Recording; or click the DEVELOPER tab and click Stop Recording in the Code group; or click Stop Recording on the status bar.

TIP **Adding to an Existing Macro**

You cannot append a macro using the macro recorder. Additional steps can only be added using the VBA Editor; however, writing new programming code takes time to learn. Until you are comfortable adding a lot of commands to a macro, you can create a temporary macro, record the commands you need, and then copy the code in the VBA Editor and paste it in the appropriate location in the primary macro code.

Click to record Macro

FIGURE 12.21 Status Bar

FIGURE 12.22 Record Macro Dialog Box

TIP **Record a Personal Macro Workbook**

The default *Store macro in* setting is This Workbook. If you want to create a macro that is available in any Excel workbook, click the *Store macro in* arrow and select Personal Macro Workbook. This option creates Personal.xlsb, a hidden **_Personal Macro Workbook_** containing the macro in the C:\Users\Username\AppData\Roaming\Microsoft\Excel\XLStart folder within Windows 8 and Windows 7. Workbooks stored in the XLStart folder open automatically when you start Excel. When the Personal Macro workbook opens, the macros in it are available to any other open workbook.

Use Relative References

It is important to determine if your macro should use relative, absolute, or mixed references as you record the macro. By default, when you select cells when recording a macro, the macro records the cells as absolute references. When you run the macro, the macro executes commands on the absolute cells, regardless of which cell is the active cell when you run the macro. If you want flexibility in that commands are performed relative to the active cell when you run the macro, click the Macros arrow in the Macros group on the View tab and select Use Relative References *before* you perform the commands. Relative references look like this in the VBA Editor:

ActiveCell.Offset(3,-2).Range("A1").Select

This code moves the active cell down three rows and back to the left by two cells. If the active cell is D1 when you run the macro, the active cell becomes B4 (down three rows; to the left by two cells).

Run a Macro

STEP 3 ⟫ After you record a macro, you should run a test to see if it performs the commands as you had anticipated. When you run a macro, Excel performs the tasks in the sequence in which you recorded the steps. To run a macro, do the following:

1. Select the location where you will test the macro. It is recommended to test a macro in a new, blank workbook if you recorded it so that it is available for multiple workbooks. If you saved it to the current workbook only, insert a new worksheet to test the macro.
2. Click the VIEW tab, click the Macros arrow in the Macros group, and then select View Macros; or click the DEVELOPER tab and click Macros in the Code group. The Macro dialog box opens (see Figure 12.23).
3. Select the macro from the *Macro name* list and click Run.

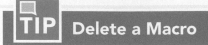

TIP Delete a Macro

If you no longer need a macro, use the Macro dialog box to select the macro and click Delete. Excel will prompt you with a message box asking if you want to delete the selected Macro. Click Yes to confirm the deletion.

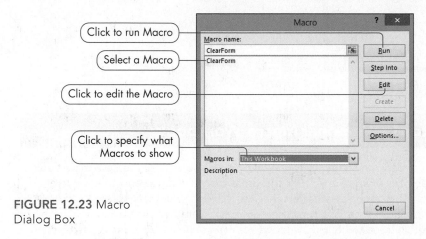

FIGURE 12.23 Macro Dialog Box

Creating Macro Buttons

STEP 4 ⟫ For the most part, it will be a rare macro that is so all-encompassing that it would rate a place on the Quick Access Toolbar. On the other hand, you may create a macro that is frequently used in a particular workbook. The easiest way to access frequently used macros within a workbook is to assign a macro to a button on a worksheet. That way, when you or other people use the workbook, it is easy to click the button to run the macro. To add a macro button to a worksheet, do the following:

1. Click the DEVELOPER tab, click Insert in the Controls group, and then click Button (Form Control) in the *Form Controls* section of the Insert gallery. See Figure 12.24.
2. Drag the crosshair pointer to draw the button on the worksheet. When you release the mouse button, the Assign Macro dialog box opens (see Figure 12.25).
3. Select the macro to assign to the button and click OK.
4. Right-click the button, select Edit Text, delete the default text, and then type a more descriptive name for the button.
5. Click the worksheet to complete the button.
6. Click a cell, if necessary, that should be the active cell when the macro runs and click the button to execute the macro assigned to the button.

FIGURE 12.24 Form Controls

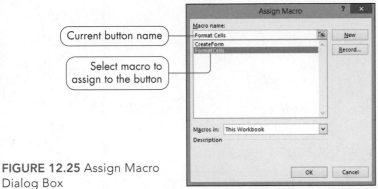

FIGURE 12.25 Assign Macro Dialog Box

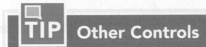

TIP Other Controls

You can insert other controls in a worksheet such as images and artwork and then assign macros to them. For example, you can insert combo boxes, check boxes, and option buttons by clicking Insert in the Controls group on the Developer tab and selecting the desired control. Drag an area on the worksheet to draw the control, right-click the object, and then select Assign Macro to assign a macro action for that particular control.

Setting Macro Security

Macro security is a concern for anyone who uses files containing macros. A macro virus is nothing more than actions written in VBA set to perform malicious actions when run. The proliferation of macro viruses has made people more cautious about opening workbooks that contain macros. By default, Excel automatically disables the macros and displays a security warning that macros have been disabled (see Figure 12.26). Click Enable Content to use the workbook and run macros.

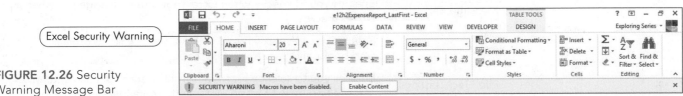

FIGURE 12.26 Security Warning Message Bar

You can use the Trust Center dialog box to change settings to make it easier to work with macros. The Trust Center can direct Excel to trust files in particular folders, trust workbooks created by a trusted publisher, and lower the security settings to allow macros. To open the Trust Center, do the following:

1. Click the FILE tab and click Options.
2. Click Trust Center on the left side of the Excel Options dialog box.
3. Click Trust Center Settings. The Trust Center dialog box displays the sections described in Table 12.1 on the left side of the dialog box (see Figure 12.27).

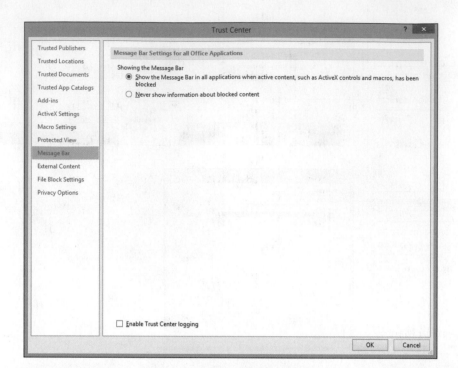

FIGURE 12.27 Trust Center Dialog Box

TABLE 12.1 Trust Center Options

Item	Description
Trusted Publishers	Directs Excel to trust digitally signed workbooks by certain creators.
Trusted Locations	Enables you to select places on your computer to store workbooks securely.
Trusted Documents	Enables you to trust network documents to open without Excel displaying any security warnings.
Trusted App Catalogs	Enables you to trust third-party Office Apps that run inside Excel.
Add-Ins	Enables you to specify which add-ins will be allowed to run given the desired level of security.
ActiveX Settings	Enables you to adjust how Excel deals with ActiveX controls.
Macro Settings	Enables you to specify how Excel deals with macros.
Protected View	Opens potentially dangerous files in a restricted mode but without any security warnings.
Message Bar	Enables you to specify when Excel shows the message bar when it blocks macros.
External Content	Enables you to specify how Excel deals with links to other workbooks and data from other sources.
File Block Settings	Enables you to select which types of files, such as macros, to open in Protected View or which file type to prevent saving a file in.
Privacy Options	Enables you to deal with nonmacro privacy issues.

Quick
Concepts

1. What is the purpose of a macro? *p. 551*

2. How are macros accessed after they have been recorded? *p. 554*

3. What potential risks are associated with macros? *p. 555*

Hands-On Exercises

3 Macros

Because you want all employees to use the Travel Expense Report template to report expenditures each month, you want to create a macro to clear the form. In addition, you want to create a button to run the macro so that other users can easily clear the form if they do not know what a macro is or how to run it.

Skills covered: Display Developer Tab • Record a Macro • Run a Macro • Add a Macro Button

STEP 1 ≫ DISPLAY DEVELOPER TAB

The average employee at your company does not use developer tools; therefore, they are not enabled on your workstation. You would like to display the Developer tab so that you can record the macro.

    a. Open *e12h2ExpenseReportTemplate_LastFirst* and save it with the file name **e12h3ExpenseReportTemplate_LastFirst**, changing *h2* to *h3*.

    When you use Open or Recent to open a template, you open it as a template to edit. When you use New, you make a copy of the template as a workbook.

> **TROUBLESHOOTING:** If you do not see Templates in Recent Places, click Open and navigate to the local directory that contains your student files.

    b. Click the **FILE tab** and click **Options** to open the Excel Options dialog box.

    c. Click **Customize Ribbon**, click the **Developer check box** in the Main Tabs list, and then click **OK**.

    The Developer tab is added to the Ribbon.

STEP 2 ≫ RECORD A MACRO

You do not want to assume the level of Excel expertise throughout your company; therefore, you want to craft a macro that will automate as much as possible. The macro you would like to create needs to automatically clear existing values and then display an instruction for users to enter specific data. Although the template is empty to start, users might open the template, save a workbook, and then want to use that workbook to prepare future months' reports. Therefore, you need the macro to clear cells even though the original template has no values. Refer to Figure 12.28 as you complete Step 2.

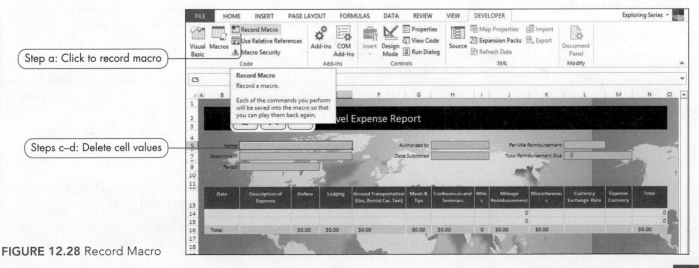

FIGURE 12.28 Record Macro

a. Click the **DEVELOPER tab** and click **Record Macro** in the Code group.

The Record Macro dialog box opens so that you can name and describe the macro.

b. Type **ClearForm** in the **Macro name box**, click in the **Description box**, type **This macro clears existing values in the current Travel Expense Report**, and then click **OK**.

> **TROUBLESHOOTING:** Read through steps c–g in advance before you proceed. Remember most actions taken in Excel are recorded by the macro recorder. Practice the steps below before activating the recorder. If you make a major mistake, delete the macro and repeat steps b through j.

c. Select **cell C5** and press **Delete**.

Even though the cells are empty now, they may contain values at some point. You want the macro to delete any values that might exist in this range.

d. Adapt step c for the following cells and ranges:

- **Cell C7**
- **Cell C9**
- **Cell H5**
- **Cell H7**
- **Cell L5**
- **Range B14:I15**
- **Range K14:M15**

You deleted ranges that might contain values after the user enters data into any workbooks created from the template. It is always good to plan for various possibilities in which data might be entered even if those ranges do not contain values now.

e. Press **Ctrl+G**, type **C5** in the **Reference box** of the Go To dialog box, and then click **OK**.

f. Type **Enter Name Here** in **cell C5** and press **Ctrl+Enter**.

Pressing Ctrl+Enter keeps cell C5 the active cell so that users can immediately enter the label when they open a workbook from the template.

g. Click **cell C7**, type **Enter Department Name**, and then press **Ctrl+Enter**.

h. Click **Stop Recording** in the Code group on the DEVELOPER tab.

i. Save the *e12h3ExpenseReportTemplate_LastFirst* template; click **No** when prompted that the workbook cannot be saved with the macro in it.

Excel opens the Save As dialog box so that you can select the file type.

j. Click the **Save as type arrow**, select **Excel Macro-Enabled Template**, and then click **Save**.

> **TROUBLESHOOTING:** Make sure you select Excel Macro-Enabled Template, not Excel Macro-Enabled Workbook, because you want the file saved as a template, not a workbook. Because the template contains macros, you must save it as an Excel Macro-Enabled Template, not just a template.

STEP 3 ≫ RUN A MACRO

You want to make sure the ClearForm macro does what you want it to do. First, you will add some sample data and run the macro.

a. Type your name in **cell C5**, type **Finance** in **cell C7**, type **1/25/2015** in **cell H7**, type **1/5/2015** in **cell B14**, type **Sales Meeting** in **cell C14**, and then type **$75.00** in **cell G14**.

You entered some sample values in various cells to test the ClearForm macro to verify if it will delete those values.

b. Click the **DEVELOPER tab**, if necessary, and click **Macros** in the Code group.

The Macro dialog box opens and displays the ClearForm macro, which should be selected in the Macro name box.

c. Select **ClearForm**, if necessary, and click **Run**.

The ClearForm macro quickly goes through the worksheet, erasing the values in the specified ranges, goes to cells C5 and C7, enters descriptive labels, and then stops.

> **TROUBLESHOOTING:** If the macro does not delete sample values, delete the macro and rerecord it.

STEP 4 ❯❯ ADD A MACRO BUTTON

Your colleagues are probably not Excel experts and do not know how to run a macro. To make it easier to clear values from the form, you want to assign the ClearForm macro to a button. The users can then click the button to clear the form to use it for another month. Refer to Figure 12.29 as you complete Step 4.

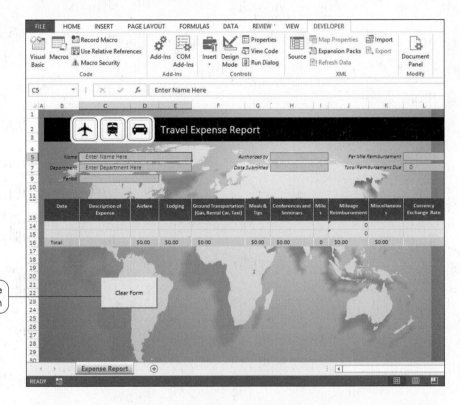

FIGURE 12.29 Macro Button

a. Click the **HOME tab**, click **Format** in the Cells group, select **Unprotect Sheet**, type **eXploring** in the **Password box** in the Unprotect Sheet dialog box, and then click **OK**.

You have to unprotect the worksheet before you can insert a macro button.

b. Click the **DEVELOPER tab**, click **Insert** in the Controls group, and then click **Button (Form Control)** in the *Form Controls* section of the gallery.

c. Click the top of **cell C20** and drag down and to the right to the bottom of **cell D23** to create the area where the button will be placed.

The Assign Macro dialog box opens.

d. Select **ClearForm** in the Macro name list and click **OK**.

This action assigns the ClearForm macro to the button. The button appears in cells C20:D23, is selected, and displays *Button 1*. You will provide descriptive text to appear on the button.

e. Right-click **Button 1** and select **Edit Text**. Select the **Button 1 text**, type **Clear Form**, and then click any cell on the worksheet outside the button.

The button now shows *Clear Form*, which is more descriptive of the button's purpose than *Button 1*.

f. Right-click the **Expense Report worksheet tab**, select **Protect Sheet**, type **eXploring** in the **Password to protect sheet box**, click **OK**, type **eXploring** in the **Reenter password to proceed box**, and then click **OK**.

You need to protect the worksheet after creating the macro button.

g. Type **6/1/2015** in cell **B14** and type **6/29/2015** in **cell B15** to enter sample data.

h. Click **Clear Form** in the worksheet.

When you click Clear Form, Excel runs the ClearForm macro.

i. Save the Macro-Enabled Template. Keep the workbook open if you plan to continue with Hands-On Exercise 4. If not, close the workbook and exit Excel.

Visual Basic for Applications

As you perform commands while recording a macro, those commands are translated into programming code called Visual Basic for Applications (VBA). VBA is a robust programming language that can be used within various software packages to enhance and automate functionality. While many casual users will be able to complete required tasks using just the macro recorder, more advanced VBA macros can be created by authoring code directly into modules within the Visual Basic Editor. A *module* is a file in which macros are stored. The ***Visual Basic Editor*** is an application used to create, edit, execute, and debug Office application macros using programming code. These macros can then be used within a Macro-Enabled Workbook or Template. The two types of VBA macros are sub procedures and custom functions. ***Sub procedures***, which are also created when using the macro recorder, perform actions on a workbook, such as the ClearForm example earlier in the chapter. For example, you can create a sub procedure to insert the current date in a worksheet. Similar to the hundreds of built-in functions in Excel, custom functions have the ability to manipulate input variables and return a value.

Creating a Sub Procedure

STEP 1 » The first step to creating a sub procedure is inserting a new module or editing data in an existing module within the VBA editor. To access the VBA Editor, press Alt+F11 on your keyboard. The left side of the VBA window contains the Project Explorer, which is similar in concept and appearance to the File Explorer except that it displays only open workbooks and/or other Visual Basic projects (see Figure 12.30).

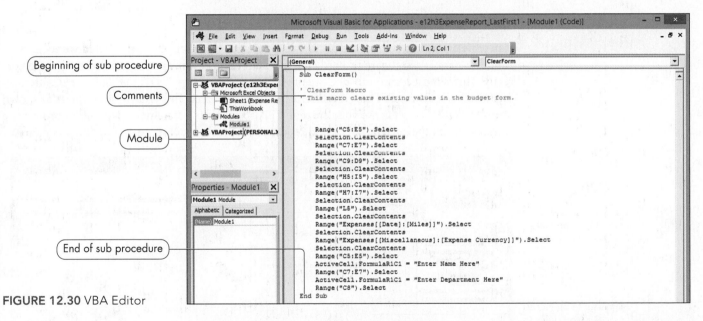

FIGURE 12.30 VBA Editor

The Visual Basic statements appear in the Code window on the right side. A Visual Basic module consists of at least one *procedure*, which is a named sequence of statements stored in a macro. In this example, Module1 contains the ClearForm procedure, which is also the name of the macro created in Excel. Module1 is stored in the Travel Expense Report workbook.

A procedure or macro always begins and ends with the Sub and End Sub statements. The Sub statement contains the name of the macro, such as Sub ClearForm() in Figure 12.30. The End Sub statement is the last statement and indicates the end of the macro. Sub and End Sub are Visual Basic keywords and appear in blue. *Keywords* are special programming syntax that have special meaning with the programming language and must be used for their intended purposes.

Comments, which are indicated by an apostrophe and appear in green, provide information about the macro but do not affect its execution and are considered documentation. Comments can be entered manually or are inserted automatically by the macro recorder to document the macro name, its author, and shortcut key (if any). You can add, delete, or modify comments. To create a basic sub procedure that would enter a date into a cell, complete the following steps:

1. From the VBA Editor, select Module from the Insert menu.
2. Type *sub currentdate()* and press Enter.
3. Type '*This macro will insert the current date in cell H7.*
4. Type *range("H7") = date* and press Enter.
5. Type *range("H7").font.bold = true.*
6. Save and exit the Visual Basic Editor.

Table 12.2 explains some of the lines of code used to create the previous sub procedure. The first word, *range*, refers to an object. An **object** is a variable that contains both data and code and represents an element of Excel such as Range or Selection. A period follows the object name, and the next word is often a behavior or attribute, such as Select or ClearContents, that describes a behavior or action performed on the object.

TABLE 12.2 VBA Editor Code

Code	Explanation
range("H7")	Identifies the range H7
= date	Applies the current date to the cell
font.bold = true	Applies object property, setting the font to bold. To disable, change *true* to *false*.

Use VBA with Protected Worksheets

Run time errors can sometimes occur when running VBA scripts on protected worksheets. A **run time error** is a software or hardware problem that prevents a program from working correctly. This is most commonly due to a procedure such as *range("H7").font.bold = true*, attempting to alter a locked cell. There are several methods to correct this issue. The simplest, as shown in Figure 12.31, is to encase your current VBA script with a statement that will unprotect the worksheet, run the current script, and reprotect the worksheet before ending the procedure.

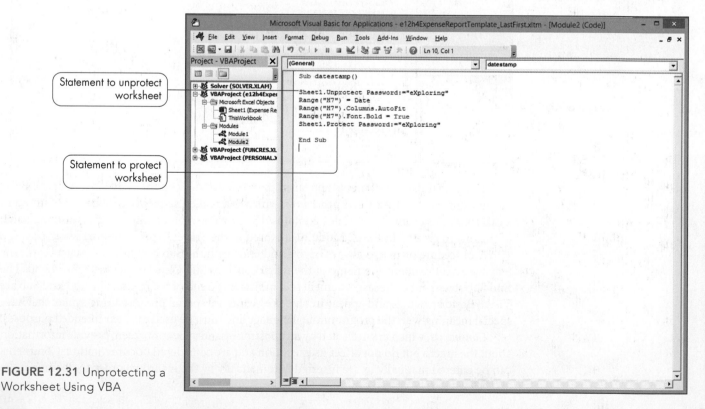

Statement to unprotect worksheet

Statement to protect worksheet

FIGURE 12.31 Unprotecting a Worksheet Using VBA

In the example given, cell H7 is formatted and the column size is altered. However, this will create a run time error because the worksheet is protected. The statement *Sheet1. Unprotect Password:= "eXploring"* unprotects the worksheet to allow the format changes to occur. The statement *Sheet1.Protect Password:= "eXploring"* then reprotects the worksheet.

Edit a Macro in the Visual Basic Editor

STEP 2 》

If you work with a workbook that has macros that were created by a coworker or you used the macro recorder, you can edit the existing macro using the Visual Basic Editor. For example, if you record a macro to apply bold, Arial font, 12-pt size, and Red font color, each command appears in a separate statement (see Figure 12.32). The two statements to apply bold and italic start with Selection.Font, indicating that a font attribute will be applied to the current selection. The statement continues with a period and behavior, such as *Bold = True,* indicating that bold is activated. If the sub procedure is turning off bold, the statement looks like this:

Selection.Font.Bold = False

The With statement enables you to perform multiple actions on the same object. All commands between the With and the corresponding End With statement are executed collectively. Although the font and font size were changed in the macro, the macro also indicates that other attributes, such as superscript and subscript, are turned off. You can delete those lines of code if you want.

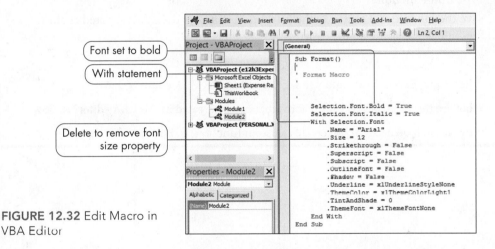

FIGURE 12.32 Edit Macro in VBA Editor

Creating a Custom Function

STEP 4 》

There are several hundred built-in functions in Excel that can perform tasks as simple as capitalizing the first letter of a word, such as the Proper function, or as complex as a multiconditional sum, as created with SumIFs. In the event that one of the numerous built-in functions does not meet your needs, you have the ability to create your own custom function using VBA. Custom functions are virtually limitless. However, like sub procedures, they are still saved in modules. This means that if they are not saved to a Personal Macro Workbook, they will only be available within the Macro-Enabled Workbook in which they were created.

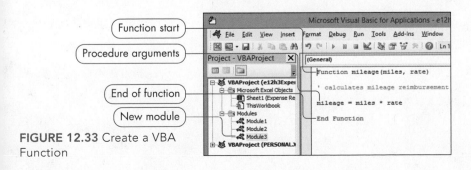

FIGURE 12.33 Create a VBA Function

When creating a custom function in VBA, you must start by creating a new module and typing *function* followed by the name of the function you are creating and the arguments that the function will use inside parentheses (see Figure 12.32).

After entering arguments on the next line, you have the ability to add comments in the same manner they were added to sub procedures. Your next step is to enter the statement that defines your function such as:

Mileage = miles * rate

After completing the statement, you end the function by typing End Function. However, this step should automatically be completed by the VBA editor.

Once a custom function is completed, it can be viewed within Excel under User Defined functions within the Insert Function command in the Function Library. Furthermore, you can access the function by simply typing = in the cell of your choice and the name of the function. This will allow you to use the custom function in the same manner as any of the built-in Excel functions. To create the VBA function described above, complete the following steps:

1. Press Alt+F11 to open the VBA Editor.
2. From the INSERT tab, select Module.
3. Type *Function mileage (rate, miles)* and press Enter.
4. Type *mileage = rate * miles*.
5. Type End Function.
6. Save the module and return to the workbook to access the newly created custom function.

Quick Concepts

1. When using Excel, why would you want to access the VBA editor? *p. 561*
2. What are the two types of VBA macros that can be created in the VBA editor? *p. 561*
3. Why would it be necessary to create a custom function? *p. 563*

Hands-On Exercises

4 Visual Basic for Applications

You would like to automate as much of the Travel Expense Report as possible. Therefore, you will create a sub procedure assigned to a macro button to automatically insert the current date into the worksheet. You would also like to add an additional function that will allow the user to estimate mileage reimbursement prior to submission.

Skills covered: Create a Sub Procedure • Edit a Macro • Assign a Macro to an Image • Create a Custom Function

STEP 1 ≫ CREATE A SUB PROCEDURE

Before you create the sub procedure, you will open the template you created in Hands-On Exercise 3 and save it as a template with another name to preserve the original template in case you make any mistakes.

    a. Open the Macro-Enabled Template *e12h3ExpenseReportTemplate_LastFirst*, click **Enable Content** to activate the prior macro, and save it as **e12h4ExpenseReportTemplate_LastFirst**, changing *h3* to *h4*.

    When you use Open or Recent to open a template, you open it as a template to edit. When you use New, you make a copy of the template as a workbook.

    b. Press **Alt+F11** on your keyboard to open the Visual Basic Editor.

    c. Click the **Insert menu** and select **Module**.

    d. Type *sub datestamp ()* on the first line of the newly created module and press **Enter**.

    e. Type **Sheet1.Unprotect Password:= "eXploring"** and press **Enter**.

    This unprotects the workbook to allow the remaining changes to take place.

    f. Type **range("H7") = date** and press **Enter**.

    This enters the current date.

    g. Type **range("H7").columns.autofit** and press **Enter**.

    This sets the selected column to autofit, which will ensure proper display of the date.

    h. Type **range("H7").Font.Bold = True**.

    This sets the newly entered date to bold.

    i. Type **Sheet1.Protect Password:= "eXploring"** and press **Enter**.

    j. Save the macro and press **F5** to test the newly created macro.

    When run, the newly created sub procedure unprotects the worksheet, adds and formats the current date, sets the column width to auto, and reprotects the document.

STEP 2 ≫ EDIT A MACRO

After running the created sub procedure, you have decided that the newly inserted date should be italicized instead of bold. You will make this change in the VBA Editor by editing the bold property.

    a. Press **Alt+F11** on your keyboard if the VBA Editor is not open.

    Excel opens the VBA Editor so that you can edit the macro programming language.

    b. Click **module 2**, if it is not already selected, to display the sub procedure created in Step 1. Select the line **Range("H7").Font.Bold = True** and replace the word *Bold* with **Italic**.

    This edits the command to set the inserted date to italics instead of bold.

    c. Save and exit the VBA Editor.

STEP 3 >> ASSIGN A MACRO TO AN IMAGE

After creating the sub procedure to insert the current date in the worksheet, you would like to enhance the usability of the document by creating a calendar icon to activate the macro. Refer to Figure 12.34 as you complete Step 3.

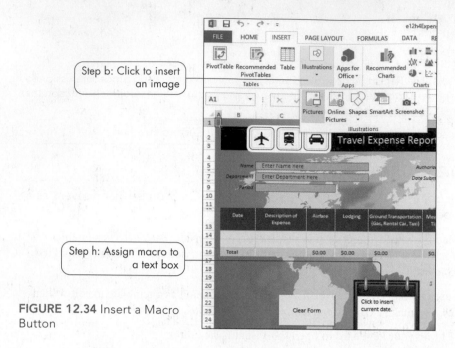

Step b: Click to insert an image

Step h: Assign macro to a text box

FIGURE 12.34 Insert a Macro Button

a. Right-click the **Expense Report worksheet tab**, select **Unprotect Sheet**, type **eXploring** in the **Password to unprotect sheet box**, and then click **OK**.

b. Click the **INSERT tab** and select **Pictures** from the Illustrations group.

c. Insert the image **e12h4Calendar.png** and position the image to the right of Clear Form.

d. Right-click the inserted image and click **Assign Macro**. Click the **datestamp macro**.

e. Click the **INSERT tab**, if necessary, and click **Text Box** in the Text group.

f. Draw a text box inside the image inserted in step b.

g. Type **Click to insert current date** in the text box.

h. Right-click the text box and click **Assign Macro**. Click the **datestamp macro box**.

You decided to assign the macro to both the inserted image and the text box to make sure that the macro activates no matter where the end user clicks on the image.

i. Click the newly created button to verify the current date. Once the date is verified, click **Clear Form** and save the template.

STEP 4 >> CREATE A CUSTOM FUNCTION

Even though the Travel Expense Report has the ability to automatically calculate travel mileage reimbursement, you have decided to create a custom function to allow users to manually calculate their mileage reimbursement if they choose.

a. Press **Alt +F11** on your keyboard to open the Visual Basic Editor.

b. Click the **Insert menu** and select **Module**.

c. Type **function mileage(miles,rate)** on the first line of the newly created module and press **Enter**.

d. Type **This function will calculate mileage reimbursement**. Press **Enter**.

This will appear as a comment in the module. However, it will not impact the calculation of the function.

e. Type the statement **mileage = miles * rate** and press **Enter**.

f. Save and exit the VBA Editor.

This creates a custom function that can be used in a similar fashion to any built-in function within Excel.

g. Click **cell H21** and type **=mileage(32,0.75)**. This returns the value 24.

You entered 32 miles at the rate of $.75 per mile to test the newly created function.

h. Delete the contents of **cell H21**.

i. Right-click the **Expense Report worksheet tab**, select **Protect Sheet**, type **eXploring** in the **Password to protect sheet box**, click **OK**, type **eXploring** in the **Reenter password to proceed box**, and then click **OK**.

j. Save the workbook and submit based on your instructor's directions.

Chapter Objectives Review

After reading this chapter, you have accomplished the following objectives:

1. **Select a template.**
   - A template is a partially created workbook that you can use as a model to create a workbook. You can create a workbook based on sample templates stored on your computer, or you can download a template from Office.com to create a new workbook.

2. **Apply themes and backgrounds.**
   - A theme is a collection of colors, fonts, and special effects. You can apply themes to various workbooks to develop a consistent look for your organization's workbooks.
     - Customize a theme: After applying a theme, you can customize the colors, fonts, and effects.
     - Apply a background: Excel has the ability to use graphics as a background of a worksheet.

3. **Apply cell styles.**
   - A cell style is a collection of format settings to provide a consistent look for fonts, borders, fill colors, alignment, and number formatting.
   - The Cell Styles gallery provides a variety of existing cell styles. If you change the cell style formatting, all cells affected by that style assume the new formatting, thus saving you valuable time so that you do not have to reformat cells individually.
     - Create custom cell styles: You can create a new custom style from the Styles group in the Home tab.
     - Modify and remove custom cell styles: Create custom styles that can be modified or removed by right-clicking the style and selecting the desired change in the Styles group.

4. **Create and use a template.**
   - You can save a workbook as a template when existing templates do not provide the structure you need.
   - When you save a template, Excel saves it in the C:\Users\username\Documents\CustomOfficeTemplates folder so that the templates are available when you click the File tab and click New.
   - Templates have an .xltx file name extension.

5. **Protect a cell, a worksheet, and a workbook.**
   - By default, the Locked property is selected for all cells in all new workbooks you create; however, this property has no effect until you protect the worksheet.
   - Before protecting the worksheet, you should unlock cells that you want a user to be able to change, such as input cells.

   - For greater security, you can assign a password that is required to unprotect the worksheet.
   - For additional protection, you can protect an entire workbook to prevent users from inserting, deleting, renaming, or moving worksheets.

6. **Create a macro.**
   - A macro is a stored procedure that performs multiple, routine, or complex tasks.
   - The Developer tab contains commands to record, run, and edit macros.
     - Use the Macro Recorder: The Macro Recorder translates user actions into VBA. It can be accessed by pressing Alt+F11.
     - Record a macro: When recording a macro, all user actions will be recorded by the Macro Recorder and stored in VBA.
     - Record a Personal Macro workbook: Personal Macro workbooks allow user-created macros to be available at all times. They are stored in the XL Start folder in Windows 8.
     - Run a macro: After macros are created, they can be run from the assigned keyboard shortcut, a macro button, or from the View Macro dialog box.

7. **Create macro buttons.**
   - To facilitate the running of a macro, you can assign a macro to a button. The Developer tab contains controls, such as buttons, you can insert in a worksheet.

8. **Set macro security.**
   - The proliferation of Excel macro viruses has made it dangerous to open workbooks that contain macros. To counter this threat, Excel automatically disables the macros and displays a security warning message that macros have been disabled.

9. **Creating a sub procedure.**
   - Sub procedures can be created using the Macro Recorder or entered manually in the VBA Editor. Sub procedures only perform actions and cannot return values.
     - Edit a macro in the VBA Editor: After a sub procedure has been created, it can be edited in the VBA Editor.

10. **Creating a custom function.**
    - If the built-in Excel functions do not meet your needs, you can create a custom function using VBA. All custom functions are noted in VBA with the Open function and the Close End function.

Key Terms Matching

Match the key terms with their definitions. Write the key term letter by the appropriate numbered definition.

a. Background
b. Cell Style
c. Comment
d. Keyword
e. Locked Cell
f. Macro
g. Macro Recorder
h. Module
i. Object

j. Personal Macro Workbook
k. Procedure
l. Run Time Error
m. Sub Procedure
n. Template
o. Theme
p. Visual Basic for Applications (VBA)
q. Visual Basic Editor

1. _____ A special workbook file used as a model to create similarly structured workbooks. **p. 532**

2. _____ A collection of colors, fonts, and special effects. **p. 533**

3. _____ An image that appears behind the worksheet data onscreen; it does not print. **p. 534**

4. _____ A set of formatting options applied to worksheet cells. **p. 535**

5. _____ Prevents users from making changes to a specific cell in a protected worksheet. **p. 542**

6. _____ A set of instructions that tells Excel which commands to execute. **p. 551**

7. _____ A tool that records a series of commands in the sequence performed by a user and converts the commands into programming syntax. **p. 551**

8. _____ A hidden workbook stored in the XL Start folder that contains macros and opens automatically when you start Excel. **p. 553**

9. _____ The Office application used to create, edit, execute, and debug macros using programming language. **p. 561**

10. _____ A named sequence of statements that can be executed by the user or a macro. **p. 561**

11. _____ A special programming syntax used for a specific purpose that appears in blue in the Visual Basic Editor. **p. 561**

12. _____ Documents programming code, starts with an apostrophe, and appears in green in the VBA Editor. **p. 561**

13. _____ Command lines written in the VBA Editor that have the ability to perform actions in Excel. **p. 561**

14. _____ A file that stores sub procedures and functions. **p. 561**

15. _____ A variable that contains both data and code and represents an element of Excel. **p. 562**

16. _____ A software or hardware problem that prevents a program from working correctly. **p. 562**

17. _____ A robust programming language that can be used within various software packages to enhance and automate functionality. **p. 551**

Multiple Choice

1. Which would you do to start using a calendar template from Office.com Templates?

   (a) Open the Backstage view, click Open, and then choose a template from the Office.com gallery.

   (b) Open the Backstage view, click New, and then click Calendars in the Suggested Searches options.

   (c) Click the Office.com option in the Template Manager on the Developer tab.

   (d) Open the Backstage view, click Options, and then choose the Office.com templates in the Template Manager.

2. You created an invoice template to prepare invoices for your consulting business. In Windows 8, where would you save the template so it is available in the available templates list in the Backstage view?

   (a) C:\Users\user_name\Libraries\Documents

   (b) Submit it to Office.com.

   (c) C:\Users\username\Documents\CustomOfficeTemplates

   (d) None of the above

3. Your company just had a new corporate logo designed. What do you do in Excel to present professional-looking reusable workbooks to share with clients?

   (a) Replace the old logo with the new logo in all templates used by the company.

   (b) Create a theme that complements the colors, fonts, and effects of the new logo and apply the theme to all templates.

   (c) Create a cell style that complements the new logo and update cell styles in all of the templates used by the company.

   (d) All of the above

4. How do you print a background image?

   (a) In Print Options, select Print Background.

   (b) A background image is printable only from the Print Preview options.

   (c) Backgrounds print automatically when the worksheet prints.

   (d) Backgrounds are not printable.

5. What is the keyboard shortcut to access the VBA Editor?

   (a) Alt+F8

   (b) Command-T

   (c) F4

   (d) Alt+F11

6. If you forget the password you used to protect an Excel worksheet, how do you reset it?

   (a) You cannot reset it.

   (b) You can reset it in Excel Options in Backstage view.

   (c) You can e-mail it to Office.com for reset.

   (d) There is a password reset in the Properties pane for each Excel workbook.

7. In which programming language are Excel macros written?

   (a) Java

   (b) C++

   (c) VBA

   (d) SQL

8. When you get ready to write a macro:

   (a) Be careful and thorough as you plan which actions to record so you do not inadvertently record unnecessary steps.

   (b) You can record steps and easily delete extraneous steps while using the Macro Recorder.

   (c) Neither A nor B

   (d) Both A and B

9. Which of the following statements is true about macro security?

   (a) When you add a Macro-Enabled Workbook to the Trust Center, you must enable the content of that file each time you open it.

   (b) Setting your Trust Center options to include files in a specific folder and then saving macro-enabled files in that folder allows you to open those files with the content enabled.

   (c) Set macro security options on the Developer tab to Secured.

   (d) Macro-enabled files cannot contain viruses.

10. Which of the following Workbook file extensions support macros?

    (a) .xlsm

    (b) .xlsb

    (c) .xltm

    (d) All of the above

Practice Exercises

1 Blood Pressure Tracker

FROM SCRATCH

Inner City Health Clinic is located in downtown San Francisco. As a physician's assistant, you help monitor each patient's blood pressure. It is important for some patients to track their blood pressure throughout the week between office visits, so you want to create a template that you can e-mail to them. You will create a template from scratch, select a theme, add a background image, and apply styles. After you are satisfied with the appearance, you will then save the workbook as a new template that you can e-mail to your computer-savvy patients so that they can track their blood pressure at home. This exercise follows the same set of skills as used in Hands-On Exercises 1 and 2 in the chapter. Refer to Figure 12.35 as you complete this exercise.

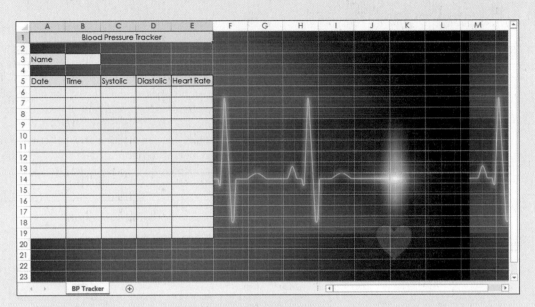

FIGURE 12.35 Blood Pressure Tracker Template

Photo: psdesign1/Fotolia

a. Start Excel and click **Blank workbook** from the Backstage view.

b. Save the workbook as a template with the file name **e12p1BpTracker_LastFirst**.

c. Name the worksheet **BP Tracker**.

d. Click the **PAGE LAYOUT tab**, click **Themes** in the Themes group, and then select **Slice**.

e. Click **Background** in the Page Setup group, click **Browse**, and then navigate to your student data files. Select *e12p1Bpressure.jpg* in the Sheet Background dialog box and click **Insert**.

f. Merge and center the **range A1:E1** and complete the following tasks:
   - Type **Blood Pressure Tracker** in **cell A1** and apply **20% – Accent 5 cell style**.
   - Type **Name** in **cell A3** and apply **20% – Accent 5 cell style**.
   - Apply the **Output cell style** to **cell B3**.

g. Select the **range A5:E5**, click **Borders** in the Font group on the HOME tab, apply **All Borders,** and then apply **20% – Accent 5 cell style**.

h. Enter the following text as column headings in row 5:
   - **Cell A5: Date**
   - **Cell B5: Time**
   - **Cell C5: Systolic**
   - **Cell D5: Diastolic**
   - **Cell E5: Heart Rate**

i. Click **cell E5**, click the **HOME tab**, and then select **Format** from the Cells group. Select **AutoFit Column Width**.

j. Select **range A6:E19** and apply the **Output cell style**.

k. Select **cell B3**, press and hold **Ctrl**, and then select the **range A6:E19**. Click **Format** in the Cells group of the HOME tab and select **Lock Cell**.

l. Protect the worksheet by doing the following:

- Right-click the **BP Tracker sheet tab**, select **Protect Sheet**, type **eXploring** in the **Password (optional) box**, and then click **OK**.
- Type **eXploring** in the **Reenter password to proceed box** and click **OK**.

m. Click the **FILE tab**, click **Save As**, and then navigate to your student data files. Click the **Save as type arrow**, select **Excel Template**, keep the default name, and then click **Save**.

n. Save and close the workbook. Submit based on your instructor's directions.

2 Florida Doctor List

The Florida Medical Referral Agency maintains a list of select doctors, cities, specialties, genders, and board certification data. In addition, the list indicates whether each doctor is accepting new patients (Yes) or not (No). The workbook contains three worksheets: the Doctor List, Criteria Settings to enter advanced criteria, and the Output worksheet to display the results of an advanced filter. You will create range names to use for completing advanced filters. To assist the employees who run the call center, you want to make the workbook easy to use. You want to create three macros: two macros to filter the database to display a list of doctors meeting selected criteria and one macro to clear the output results. You will then assign macros to buttons. This exercise follows the same set of skills as used in Hands-On Exercise 3 in the chapter. Refer to Figures 12.36 and 12.37 as you complete this exercise.

FIGURE 12.36 Results of Running Pediatrics New Macro

	A	B	C	D	E	F	G	H
1	Instructions:		Click a button to display a list of doctors who meet specific needs.					
2								
3		Clear Output	Pediatrics Accepting New Patients	Miami Internal Medicine Accept New				
4								
5								
6	ID	Last Name	First Name	City	Specialty	Gender	Board Certified	New Patients
7	6	Jones	Jeffrey	Coral Gables	Pediatrics	M	10/14/1982	Yes
8	26	Sywolski	Neil	Hollywood	Pediatrics	M	4/22/1978	Yes
9	50	Wall	Jessica	Miami	Pediatrics	F	12/15/1985	Yes
10	58	Staab	Steven	Fort Lauderdale	Pediatrics	M	11/24/1979	Yes
11	67	Pierre	Allberto	Hollywood	Pediatrics	M	6/8/1989	Yes
12	70	Honey	Angela	Miami	Pediatrics	F	2/1/2004	Yes
13	73	Ledon	Francisco	Coral Gables	Pediatrics	M	7/4/1986	Yes
14	79	Baker	Reeva	Coral Gables	Pediatrics	F	8/1/1982	Yes
15	80	Camar	Theresa	Hollywood	Pediatrics	F	12/15/1985	Yes
16	81	McElroy	Tom	Miami	Pediatrics	M	8/22/1977	Yes
17	85	Counts	Annie	Fort Lauderdale	Pediatrics	F	5/15/2009	Yes
18	92	Grotegut	Adam	Fort Lauderdale	Pediatrics	M	12/1/2007	Yes
19	113	Miller	Olena	Miami	Pediatrics	F	6/15/2009	Yes
20	114	Anderson	Paul	Coral Gables	Pediatrics	M	3/4/2003	Yes
21	131	Pederson	Angie	Coral Gables	Pediatrics	F	5/2/1979	Yes
22	135	Fletcher	Brandy	Fort Lauderdale	Pediatrics	F	11/15/2007	Yes
23	142	Phillips	Mary	Coral Gables	Pediatrics	F	8/22/1977	Yes
24	143	Jensen	William	Miami	Pediatrics	M	1/16/1981	Yes
25								

Output | Doctor List | Criteria Settings

```
(General)                                          ▼  MiamiInternalNew                        ▼
Sub PediatricsNew()
'
' PediatricsNew Macro
' Extracts a list of pediatricians who are accepting new patients
'
'
    Sheets("Criteria Settings").Select
    Range("A2:H2").Select
    Selection.ClearContents
    Range("E2").Select
    ActiveCell.FormulaR1C1 = "Pediatrics"
    Range("H2").Select
    ActiveCell.FormulaR1C1 = "Yes"
    Sheets("Output").Select
    Range("B6").Select
    Range("Database").AdvancedFilter Action:=xlFilterCopy, CriteriaRange:=Range _
        ("Criteria"), CopyToRange:=Range("Extract"), Unique:=False
    Range("A1").Select
End Sub
Sub MiamiInternalNew()
'
' MiamiInternalNew Macro
' Extracts a list of Miami doctors who specialize in internal medicine and who are accepting new
'
'
    Sheets("Criteria Settings").Select
    Range("A2:H2").Select
    Selection.ClearContents
    Range("D2").Select
    ActiveCell.FormulaR1C1 = "Miami"
    Range("E2").Select
    ActiveCell.FormulaR1C1 = "Internal Medicine"
    Range("H2").Select
    ActiveCell.FormulaR1C1 = "Yes"
    Sheets("Output").Select
    Range("B6").Select
    Range("Database").AdvancedFilter Action:=xlFilterCopy, CriteriaRange:=Range _
```

FIGURE 12.37 Macro Code in VBA Window

a. Open *e12p2Doctors* and save it as **e12p2Doctors_LastFirst** in the Excel Macro-Enabled Workbook file format.

b. Create range names by doing the following:

- Click the **Output sheet tab**, select the **range A6:H6**, type **Extract** in the **Name Box**, and then press **Enter**.
- Click the **Doctor List sheet tab**, select the **range A1:H151**, type **Database** in the **Name Box**, and then press **Enter**.
- Click the **Criteria Settings sheet tab**, select the **range A1:H2**, type **Criteria** in the **Name Box**, and then press **Enter**.

c. Check the Ribbon to see if it contains the DEVELOPER tab. If not, click the **FILE tab**, click **Options**, click **Customize Ribbon** in the Excel Options dialog box, click the **Developer check box** in the Main Tabs list, and then click **OK**.

d. Click the **Output sheet tab** and create a macro that filters the database to show pediatric doctors who are accepting new patients by doing the following:

- Click the **DEVELOPER tab** and click **Record Macro** in the Code group to open the Record Macro dialog box.
- Type **PediatricsNew** in the **Macro name box**, type **Extracts a list of pediatricians who are accepting new patients** in the **Description box**, and then click **OK**.
- Click the **Criteria Settings sheet tab**, select the **range A2:H2**, and then press **Delete** to delete any existing conditions that might exist later.
- Click **cell E2**, type **Pediatrics**, click **cell H2**, type **Yes**, and then press **Ctrl+Enter**.
- Click the **Output sheet tab** and click **cell B6** to place the active cell in the Extract range.
- Click the **DATA tab** and click **Advanced** in the Sort & Filter group to open the Advanced Filter dialog box.
- Click the **Copy to another location option**, type **Database** in the **List range box**, type **Criteria** in the **Criteria range box**, type **Extract** in the **Copy to box**, and then click **OK**.
- Press **Ctrl+Home** to position the active cell in **cell A1**.
- Click the **DEVELOPER tab** and click **Stop Recording** in the Code group.

e. Create a macro that filters the database to show internal medicine doctors in Miami who are accepting new patients by doing the following:

- Click the **DEVELOPER tab** if necessary and click **Record Macro** in the Code group to open the Record Macro dialog box.
- Type **MiamiInternalNew** in the **Macro name box**, type **Extracts a list of Miami doctors who specialize in internal medicine and who are accepting new patients** in the **Description box**, and then click **OK**.
- Click the **Criteria Settings sheet tab**, select the **range A2:H2**, and then press **Delete** to delete any conditions that a user might enter to perform their own filter.
- Click **cell D2**, type **Miami**, click **cell E2**, type **Internal Medicine**, click **cell H2**, type **Yes**, and then press **Ctrl+Enter**.
- Click the **Output sheet tab** and click **cell B6** to place the active cell in the Extract range.
- Click the **DATA tab** and click **Advanced** in the Sort & Filter group to open the Advanced Filter dialog box.
- Click the **Copy to another location option**, type **Database** in the **List range box**, type **Criteria** in the **Criteria range box**, type **Extract** in the **Copy to box**, and then click **OK**.
- Press **Ctrl+Home** to position the active cell in **cell A1**.
- Click the **DEVELOPER tab** and click **Stop Recording** in the Code group. Save the workbook.

f. Create a macro that clears the criteria range and the output by doing the following:

- Click the **DEVELOPER tab** if necessary and click **Record Macro** in the Code group to open the Record Macro dialog box.
- Type **Clear** in the **Macro name box**, type **Clears the criteria range and the output** in the **Description box**, and then click **OK**.
- Click the **Criteria Settings sheet tab**, select the **range A2:H2**, and then press **Delete** to delete any existing conditions that might exist later.
- Click **cell A2**, type **-100** as a dummy value, and then press **Ctrl+Enter**.
- Click the **Output sheet tab** and click **cell B6** to place the active cell in the Extract range.
- Click the **DATA tab** and click **Advanced** in the Sort & Filter group to open the Advanced Filter dialog box.
- Click the **Copy to another location option**, type **Database** in the **List range box**, type **Criteria** in the **Criteria range box**, type **Extract** in the **Copy to box**, and then click **OK**.
- Press **Ctrl+Home** to position the active cell in **cell A1**.
- Click the **DEVELOPER tab** and click **Stop Recording** in the Code group.

g. Create a macro button and assign the Clear macro to it by doing the following:

- Click the **DEVELOPER tab** if necessary, click **Insert** in the Controls group, and then click **Button (Form Control)** in the *Form Controls* section.
- Click in **cell A2** and create a button that fills the range A2:B4. When you release the mouse button, the Assign Macro dialog box opens.
- Select **Clear** in the *Macro name* list and click **OK**. The button displays *Button 1*.
- Right-click the button, select **Edit Text**, select **Button 1**, type **Clear Output**, and then click in **cell A1**. Save the workbook.

h. Create a macro button and assign the PediatricsNew macro to it by doing the following:

- Click **Insert** in the Controls group and click **Button (Form Control)** in the *Form Controls* section.
- Drag to create a button on the right side of the Clear Output button. Make sure the second button is approximately the same height and width as the Clear Output button.
- Select **PediatricsNew** in the *Macro name* list and click **OK**. The button displays *Button 2*.
- Right-click the button, select **Edit Text**, select **Button 2**, type **Pediatrics Accepting New Patients**, and then click in **cell A1**. If you need to resize the button to display the button text, press **Ctrl** as you click the button to select it. Then resize the button as necessary. Save the workbook.

i. Adapt step h to create a macro button on the right side of the Pediatrics button and assign the MiamiInternalNew macro to it. Display the text **Miami Internal Medicine Accept New** and click in **cell A1**. Save the workbook.

j. Run the macros by doing the following:

- Click **Pediatrics Accepting New Patients**. The Output sheet should display 18 records (see Figure 12.35).
- Click **Miami Internal Medicine Accept New**. The Output sheet should display 4 records.
- Click **Clear Output**.

k. Edit any macro that does not run correctly: Click the **DEVELOPER tab**, click **Macros** in the Code group, select the macro that contains errors, and then click **Edit**. Edit the code as necessary in the VBA Editor (see Figure 12.36), click **Save**, close the VBA Editor, and then run the macro again.

l. Create a footer with your name on the left side, the sheet name code in the center, and the file name code on the right side of all three worksheets.

m. Save and close the workbook, and submit based on your instructor's directions.

Mid-Level Exercises

1 Little League Statistics

You volunteered to coach for your community Little League program. You are working with the Pirates, a team of 10- to 12-year-olds who respond well to seeing their batting statistics. You created a workbook to record the Pirates' batting data and calculate their statistics. The recreation department manager is a friend of yours from high school and is impressed with your workbook. He wondered if you could make something similar for the other coaches when he saw how you were recording statistics.

a. Open *e12m1Pirates* and save it as **e12m1Pirates_LastFirst**.

b. Apply the **Title cell style** to **cell A1**, the **Heading 2 cell style** to the **range A2:R2**, the **Heading 4 cell style** to the **range A4:A20**, and **Output style** to the **range B3:R20**.

c. Apply the **Wood Type theme** and apply the **Red theme colors**.

d. Add *e12m1Pirate.jpg* as a background image for the worksheet.

e. Save the Excel workbook and save it as a template named **e12m1Baseball_LastFirst**.

f. Delete the background from the Statistics worksheet and insert *e12m1Baseball.jpg* as the background image for the template before distributing the template to the other teams.

g. Select the **Game 1 worksheet**, delete all players' names and batting information from the **range A3:M16**. Right-align the labels in the **range C2:M2**.

h. Unlock cells in **cell A1**, the **range A3:M16** of the Game 1 worksheet, and **cell A1** in the Statistics worksheet. Right-align the labels in the **range B2:R2** in the Statistics worksheet.

i. Set **0.2"** left and right margins on both worksheets. Set a width of **6.00** for columns B:H and J:O on the Statistics worksheet.

j. Create a footer with your name on the left side, the sheet name code in the center, and the file name code on the right side of both worksheets.

k. Protect all worksheets with a password of **eXploring**. Allow all users to format cells, columns, and rows.

l. Save and close the template.

m. Create a new workbook from the *e12m1Baseball_LastFirst* template and save the workbook as **e12m1Broncos_LastFirst**.

n. Edit the league name from *Pirates* to **Broncos** in **cell A1** of each worksheet and enter player names and data for 14 players in the Games 1 worksheet.

o. Save the workbook and submit based on your instructor's directions.

2 Jackson Municipal Airport

ANALYSIS CASE

Hulett Enterprises is located in Jackson, Mississippi. In the past, you have created Web queries to find departure and arrival information for your supervisors, Denise Petrillo and Omar Vincent, who travel frequently for business meetings. Because of your Excel experience, other managers are interested in having you develop a workbook with this information they can use. You decide to create macros to update the Web queries, adjust formatting of the imported data, and then print the worksheets. Finally, you will assign the macros to macro buttons.

a. Open *e12m2Airport* and save it as **e12m2Airport_LastFirst** as an Excel Macro-Enabled Workbook file format.

b. Create a Web query in **cell A8** to **http://www.jmaa.com/JAN/FlightInfo_arr.asp** to the arrival schedule table on the Arrivals worksheet.

c. Create a Web query in **cell A8** to **http://www.jmaa.com/JAN/FlightInfo_arr.asp** to the departure schedule table on the Departures worksheet.

d. Apply **conditional formatting** to the Status column (the **range F9:F50**) to highlight DELAYED flights with **Light Red Fill with Dark Red Text formatting** on both worksheets.

DISCOVER

e. Display the Arrivals worksheet and record a macro named **Update** to do the following:
- Refresh all Web queries.
- Bold the column labels on row **8**.
- Set **cell A1** as the active cell.

f. Create a button on each worksheet in the **range A4:C6** that is assigned to the Update macro and displays *Refresh the List* on the button.

g. Click **Refresh the List** on each worksheet to ensure it works.

h. Create a footer with your name on the left side, the sheet name code in the center, and the file name code on the right side on each worksheet.

★ i. Answer the questions on the Q&A worksheet.

j. Save and close the workbook, and submit based on your instructor's directions.

---

3 Fundraiser

COLLABORATION CASE

You work for a regional philanthropic organization that helps raise money for underprivileged youth. To help meet an end-of-the-year fundraising goal, you have decided to deploy regional donation agents to help collect contributions. You would like to make a worksheet to help track donations. Once the worksheet is completed, you will share the file via e-mail with a collaborator in the region who will update the numbers.

Student 1:

a. Open *e12m3FundRaiser* and save it as **e12m3FundRaiser_LastFirst**.

b. Select **cell B2** and apply the **Heading 2 cell style**.

c. Select the **range B3:E10**, click the **HOME tab**, click **Format** and then unlock the cells.

d. Click **Format** and protect the worksheet using the password **eXploring**.

e. Click the **FILE tab** and select **Share** in the Backstage view.

f. Select **EMAIL** and choose **Send as Attachment**.

g. E-mail the worksheet to your collaborator.

Student 2:

h. Open the e-mail and the attachment and enter the following data:

Date	Name	Donation	Collector
12/20/2015	Smith	$350.00	
12/22/2015	Williams	$125.00	
12/23/2015	Wilky	$110.00	
12/23/2015	Barns	$500.00	

i. Type your name as the **collector** in column E.

j. Create a footer with your name on the left side, the sheet name code in the center, and the file name code on the right side on each worksheet.

k. Save and close the workbook, and submit based on your instructor's directions.

Beyond the Classroom

Trust Center

RESEARCH CASE →

So far, you have worked with the default Trust Center settings. You want to learn more about the Trust Center. Open the Trust Center dialog box in Excel and display the Macro Settings options. Start Word and insert a screenshot of the default Macro Settings. Set a **3"** shape height for the screenshot. Save the Word document as **e12b2Trust_LastFirst**. Compose a short explanation of the default Macro Settings option. Display the File Block Settings options and select the Excel 2007 and later Macro-Enabled Workbooks and Templates Open and Save check boxes. Insert a screenshot in your Word document and set a **3"** shape height. Click **OK** in each open dialog box.

In Excel, open *e12h3ExpenseReportTemplate_LastFirst.xltm*, the Macro-Enabled Template. In Word, explain what happens when you open this template and what happens when you try to run the macro by clicking **Clear Form**. Close the Macro-Enabled Template and deselect the check boxes you just selected in the File Block Settings. In the Word document, insert a footer with your name on the left side and a file name field on the right side. Save the document and submit based on your instructor's directions.

Real Estate Listings

DISASTER RECOVERY +

You are a real estate analyst who works for Mountain View Realty in the North Utah County area. Your assistant, Joey, compiled a list of houses sold during the past few months in a Macro-Enabled Workbook. Joey created three macros: (1) a Clear macro to clear the existing Criteria Range and run the filter to empty the Output Range, (2) a CedarHills macro to set a criterion in the Criteria Range to filter the list for Cedar Hills only, and (3) a CityAgentCombo interactive macro with input boxes to prompt the user for the city and agent, enter those in respective cells, and run the advanced filter. In addition, Joey created three macro buttons, one to run each macro. However, the macros and buttons have errors. Open *e12b3RealEstate.xlsm* and save it as a Macro-Enabled Workbook named **e12b3RealEstate_LastFirst**. Find the errors in the macros, document the problems in the macro code using programming comments, and then fix the errors. Find and correct the macro button errors. Create a footer with your name on the left side, the sheet name code in the center, and the file name code on the right side of the Input-Output worksheet. Save and close the workbook, and submit based on your instructor's directions.

Interview Techniques

SOFT SKILLS CASE S

FROM SCRATCH

Soon you will graduate from college and, in preparation for graduation, you will be participating in several job interviews. As part of your preparation, you would like to do research on interview techniques. Your next goal is to create an Excel worksheet to help rate your overall feelings toward your performance during each interview.

After completing your research, create a workbook named **e12b4Evaluation_LastFirst**. Name the worksheet **Interview Notes**. Type the heading **Company** in **cell A1**, **Position** in **cell B1**, **Date** in **cell C1**, and **Notes** in **cell D1**. Format the cells with the **Heading 2 cell style**. Highlight the **range A1:D1** and ensure the cells are locked. Your last step is to protect the worksheet, using the password **eXploring**. Create a footer with your name on the left side, the sheet name code in the center, and the file name code on the right side of the Input-Output worksheet. Save and close the workbook, and submit based on your instructor's directions.

Capstone Exercise

As the department head of the Information Systems Department at a university, you are responsible for developing the class teaching schedules for your faculty. You have a tentative Fall 2015 schedule developed in sequence, but you want to ensure that you are not double-booking classrooms or faculty. To help you review room and faculty schedules, you will need to sort the original list in various ways. In addition, you want to create a model to use as a template for future semesters and to share with other department heads.

Create a Template

You want to convert the existing Fall 2015 schedule into a template so that you can use it to develop future semester schedules. In addition, you want to apply cell styles to format the template.

a. Open *e12c1Schedule* and save it as **e12c1Schedule_ LastFirst** in Macro-Enabled Template file format.

b. Apply the **Retrospect theme**.

c. Apply the **Heading 3 cell style** to the column labels in the **range A4:K4** in the Sequential worksheet.

d. Apply the **Aspect theme color**.

e. Save the template.

Create the RoomSort Macro

You will sort the table by room number to ensure you do not have any room conflicts, such as double-booking a room. To avoid having to create a custom sort each time you want to perform this sort, you will record the steps as a macro.

a. Record a macro named **RoomSort**.

b. Display the Room worksheet data, use the Name Box to select the **range A4:M100**, and then delete the selected range. (This process will delete any existing data to ensure empty cells before copying new data to this worksheet.)

c. Display the Sequential worksheet, use the Go To command to go to **cell A4**, and then press **Ctrl+Shift+End** to select the scheduling data. Copy the selected range and paste it starting in **cell A4** of the Room worksheet. Use the Go To command to go to **cell A4**.

d. Create a custom sort with these settings:

- Sort by Room in alphabetical order.
- Sort then by Days with a custom order by adding entries in this order: MWF, MW, M, W, TR, T, R, S.
- Sort then by Start Time from earliest to latest.
- Perform the sort.

e. Display the Sequential worksheet, use the Go To command to go to **cell A1**, and then stop recording the macro.

f. Save the file as a Macro-Enabled Template.

Create the FacultySort Macro

You want to sort the table by faculty, days, and times to ensure you do not have any scheduling conflicts, such as double-booking a faculty member with two classes at the same time. To avoid having to create a custom sort each time you want to perform this sort, you will record the steps as a macro.

a. Record a macro named **FacultySort**.

b. Display the Faculty worksheet data, use the Name Box to select the **range A4:M100**, and then delete the selected range. (This process will delete any existing data to ensure empty cells before copying new data to this worksheet.)

c. Display the Sequential worksheet, use the Go To command to go to **cell A4**, and then press **Ctrl+Shift+End** to select the scheduling data. Copy the selected range and paste it starting in **cell A4** of the Faculty worksheet. Use the Go To command to go to **cell A4**.

d. Create a custom sort with these settings:

- Sort by Instructor in alphabetical order.
- Sort then by Days with a custom order you created previously.
- Sort then by Start Time from earliest to latest.
- Perform the sort.

e. Display the Sequential worksheet, use the Go To command to go to **cell A1**, and then stop recording the macro. Save the Macro-Enabled Template.

Create Macro Buttons

To create a user-friendly interface for yourself and others who might use your Macro-Enabled Template, you will insert two macro buttons, one for each macro, on the Sequential worksheet.

a. Insert a button at the top of the worksheet and assign it to the RoomSort macro.

b. Edit the text that appears on the button to display appropriate text.

c. Create, place, and edit a button for the second macro.

d. Right-click each macro button and set **0.5"** height and **1.5"** width. Ensure all buttons are the same distance from the top of the worksheet and the same distance apart.

e. Save the Macro-Enabled Template.

Finalize the Template

You will save the current data as a Macro-Enabled Workbook to preserve the data. Then you will prepare the file to be a template without the data.

a. Save the workbook as **e12c1InfoSys_LastFirst** in the Excel Macro-Enabled Workbook file type.

b. Delete the specific scheduling data on all three worksheets, but do not delete the macro buttons or column labels in the Sequential worksheet.

c. Save the file as **e12c1InfoSys_LastFirst** in the Excel Macro-Enabled Template file format. Close the template.

Use the Template

Another department head gave you a copy of her partial schedule. You want to select the template you created, import her data, and run the macros you created.

a. Use the New dialog box to select the *e12c1InfoSys* Macro-Enabled Template you created.

b. Open *e12c1Office*, copy the data, and then paste the data below the column headings in the Sequential worksheet. Center data horizontally in the ID, Prefix, Number, and Section columns.

c. Click the macro buttons to sort the data on the respective worksheets.

d. Save the file as **e12c1Office_LastFirst** in the Excel Macro-Enabled Workbook file format.

e. Close the files and submit based on your instructor's directions.

Data Validation and Data Analysis

Reducing Errors and Extracting Better Information

OBJECTIVES   AFTER YOU READ THIS CHAPTER, YOU WILL BE ABLE TO:

1. Establish data validation p. 582
2. Create an input mask p. 585
3. Create and modify a lookup field p. 587
4. Create a parameter query p. 597
5. Use advanced functions in the Expression Builder p. 601
6. Perform date arithmetic p. 607

CASE STUDY | Implementing a New Database at Tommy's Shelter

Tommy Mariano operates a small animal shelter. He has been keeping records by hand, but due to a large turnover in volunteers, record-keeping has become a problem. He has decided to move to a database solution, and his hope is that this will help reduce errors. Though volunteers may still make mistakes, he believes that a well-designed database will prevent some common errors.

As a volunteer, you have offered to create a database to assist him in this process. You have created the tables and done some data entry, and you will now work to make sure data validation takes place.

In addition to the problem of data entry, Tommy has been examining a lot of the data from his shelter by hand. As someone with some database experience, you know that advanced queries are the answer here. You will use advanced queries to help streamline his data gathering and reporting so Tommy can focus on what is important—finding homes for the animals in his shelter.

Data Validation in Tables

When filling out forms online, you may notice certain pieces of information are required. You may also notice that information you enter is checked for validity and that some fields are menus rather than text fields. For example, you cannot complete a checkout if you leave the credit card information blank. Likewise, on most sites, you cannot enter an e-mail address without the @ sign. Instead of entering Male or Female for a gender box, you may be given a menu offering only those two options. Having a list of options for the user to choose from helps narrow the possible answers as well as eliminates spelling errors.

Access also contains most of the validation features that are found in Web forms. Many of these features are found in the table settings; some are available in forms as well. In this section, you will explore setting data validation in tables in order to create more reliable data in your database. By setting up data validation, you reduce user errors, which is a key reason to use a database.

Establishing Data Validation

Data validation is a set of constraints or rules that help control how data is entered into a field. Access provides some data validation automatically. For example, you cannot enter text into a field with a number data type or add a new record to a table with the same primary key value as another record. Access provides the following data validation methods to help minimize the number of data entry errors:

- **Required**—Sets the Required property of a field to force data entry, such as a last name.

- **Default Value**—Specifies a value that is automatically entered into a field. For example, if most of your customers live in New Jersey, you can set the default value of the State field to NJ. The user can overwrite the default value with a different state abbreviation when needed.

- **Validation Rule**—Limits the type or range of data a user can enter into a field. For example, you could establish a rule for salary to ensure it is greater than zero.

- **Validation Text**—Provides the error message telling users what they did wrong and giving them instructions on what they need to do to fix it. For example, the validation text for the rule violation above might be, "You cannot enter a negative salary amount."

- **Input Mask**—Forces users to conform to a specific data-entry format for a given field. For example, a Social Security number must be entered in the format 123-45-6789. The hyphens would not need to be typed; they can be optionally stored or not stored with the entered data.

- **Lookup List**—Field values are limited to a predefined list of values. For example, a company might have temporary and full-time employees and enable users to choose either *temporary* or *full time* from a menu.

- **Multiple-Value Field**—Accepts multiple values in a single field. For example, an employee might have a status of both full time and temporary.

- **Data Macro**—Enables you to execute programming tasks whenever data in a table is changed. This is similar to a Validation Rule except the logic is more complex and the actions taken are more powerful when table data is changed.

The location of some of these properties is shown in Figure 5.1.

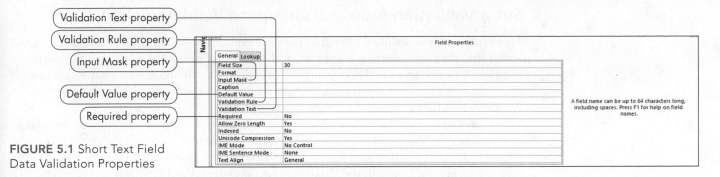

| Validation Text property |
| Validation Rule property |
| Input Mask property |
| Default Value property |
| Required property |

FIGURE 5.1 Short Text Field
Data Validation Properties

Establish Required Fields

A required field is one that cannot be left blank when you create a new record. You have already learned about setting the Required property of a field. Primary keys are required fields by definition. The default Required setting is No for all the remaining fields, which enables you to create a record with no data in those fields. To ensure the integrity of the records in a table, you should set the Required property to Yes for critical fields. To change a field to Required, do the following:

STEP 1 ⟫

1. Open the table in Design view.
2. Click the field you want to set to Required in the table design grid.
3. Click the Required property in the Field Properties pane. When you click in the box, an arrow appears with the options Yes and No.
4. Select Yes. For all new records, Access will require you to enter data into the required field. However, Access enables existing records to have blanks. Save the table.
5. Click No when asked if you want to test existing data with the new rules.

TIP Existing Blank Fields

If you set the Required property to Yes after data has already been entered in a table, you will see the message, "Data integrity rules have been changed; existing data may not be valid for the new rules. This process may take a long time. Do you want the existing data to be tested with the new rules?" If you click Yes and if blank fields exist, you are prompted to keep the new required setting, to revert to the old optional setting, or to stop testing the existing data for the requirement. Keeping the required setting (option 1) does not indicate which records have a blank field. To find existing records that contain empty values for a particular field, create a query and set the field's criterion to null (which means blank).

Set Default Field Values

When a majority of new records contain a common value, such as the same city or state, you can set a default value for that field to reduce data entry time. To change a default value, do the following:

1. Open the table in Design view.
2. Click the field you want to add a default value to in the table design grid.
3. Click the Default Value property in the Field Properties pane.
4. Type the default value you wish to add.

For example, suppose the majority of the animals the shelter handles are cats. If you set the default to Cat, all new records will display Cat. You can enter a different piece of information if necessary.

Set a Validation Rule and Generate Validation Text

A *validation rule* is designed to restrict the data values that can be entered into a field. Data values that do not conform are rejected, and the user is prompted to change the value. As mentioned earlier, you could add *Salary > 0* to a salary field to make sure a pay rate is greater than zero. For most data types, you can enter a validation rule by specifying an expression in the Validation Rule property.

If you violate a validation rule, Access does not let you continue until the data value conforms to the rule. Validation rules can cause frustration when filling out a form, especially if you cannot continue to the next step and you do not know why. Access helps you notify the user by entering an error message in the Validation Text property. Validation text provides feedback to users when a validation rule has been broken. For the salary example, when a user enters a negative value, the validation text displays. The validation text might state, "You have entered a negative value." Though not required, a database designer can be more specific to provide users guidance and tell them how to correct the validation-rule violation. Stating "You entered a negative salary. Salary must be greater than zero." provides the users with better feedback. The validation rule and validation text can be entered in the Field Properties pane, as shown in Figure 5.1. If a field violates a validation rule, the validation text displays as shown in Figure 5.2.

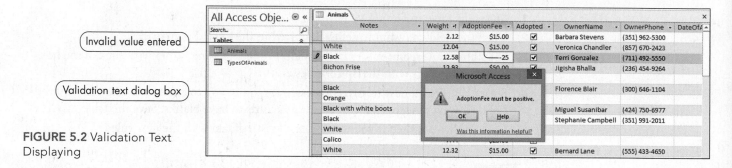

FIGURE 5.2 Validation Text Displaying

To set up a validation rule, do the following:

STEP 2》
1. Open the table in Design view.
2. Click the field you want to add a default value to in the table design grid.
3. Click the Validation Rule property in the Field Properties pane.
4. Enter the validation you wish to add.
5. (Optional, but recommended) Enter a meaningful error message in the Validation Text property in the Field Properties pane.

TIP Existing Data Violates New Validation Rule

If you add a validation rule to a table with existing records, some data in those records may violate the rule. When Access warns you that existing data may violate the new validation rule, you can click Yes to test the data. If existing data is in violation, you will be prompted to do one of three things: to keep the new setting and continue testing (Yes), revert to the old setting and continue testing (No), or stop testing (Cancel). To correct this situation, you can click No to remove the rule, switch to Datasheet view, find and correct the data that violates the new rule, and then return to Design view and add the rule again. Alternately, you can use a query to find and update nonconforming data.

Validation rules only check values entered for a field. They do not prevent users from skipping the field. Unless you set the Required property to Yes, having a validation rule does not force data entry for the field. Therefore, if you add a validation rule to a field, you should also consider setting the Required property to Yes.

Creating an Input Mask

In addition to controlling what users enter into a data table, database designers must also control how users enter data into tables. The first method for controlling data input is by selecting the appropriate data type when adding fields to a table. For that reason, database developers usually design tables with fields that have the most constraining data type. The Date/Time data type restricts input to dates and/or times; the Number data type restricts input to numeric data. Short Text is the most forgiving data type, but it is also the type that can collect the most invalid data. For example, a phone number might be stored in a Short Text field with a size of 14. The database designer might expect users to enter (973) 555-1212. However, users could enter 973.555.1212, 9735551212, 973-555-1212, or even 9999999999999 just as easily. If they are performing data entry through a form, they will not see how other users have entered the numbers and may accidentally create inconsistencies. Sorting, as well as some filters and queries, would not work correctly with such data.

By creating an *input mask* you can further restrict the data being input into a field by specifying the exact format of the data entry. Social Security number and phone number are two common text fields that often use input masks. Figure 5.3 shows a field with a phone number input mask applied.

Input mask for OwnerPhone field

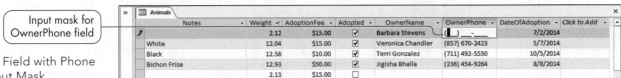

FIGURE 5.3 Field with Phone Number Input Mask

Use the Input Mask Wizard

The *Input Mask Wizard* is frequently used to generate data restrictions (an input mask) for a field based on responses to a few questions. You launch the Input Mask Wizard by opening the table in Design view, and then selecting the field for which you want to create a mask. In the Field Properties pane, in the lower part of the table Design view, click the input mask property. The Build button appears to the right of the field as shown in Figure 5.4; click Build to start the Input Mask Wizard. Figure 5.5 shows the first screen in the Input Mask Wizard dialog box. In this step, you select the type of input mask.

For example, select Social Security number to create the 123-45-6789 input mask format. This type creates an input mask with three digits, then a dash, then two digits, then another dash, and then four more digits. The input mask property for the field would appear as 000\-00\-0000;0; in the table Design view. Users doing data entry will see ###-##-#### to let them know the expected format of the Social Security number.

For phone numbers, the input mask also helps ensure consistency in data entry. As stated earlier, users may enter phone numbers in different ways. Good database design promotes consistent data input, and consistent data input leads to reliable data output. For example, if you query the database and ask for a count of customers who reside in the 973 area code, consistent data entry produces the correct results. If the data were entered in a variety of formats—some in the format (973), some in the format 973-, and some in the format 973.— the results would be unreliable because each of these entries would be perceived as being different by Access, even though users may recognize them to be the same.

To create an input mask, do the following:

STEP 3»

1. Ensure you are in Design view for the table and click the field to which you want to add an input mask.
2. Click the Input Mask Wizard, designated by the ellipsis (…) at the end of the Input Mask row, as shown in Figure 5.4.

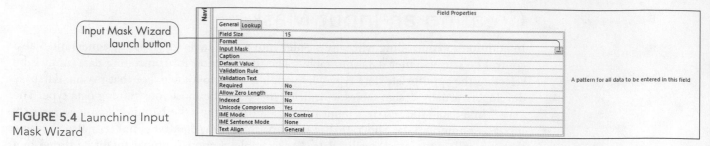

FIGURE 5.4 Launching Input Mask Wizard

3. Choose one of the built-in input masks from the menu. A number of common formats exist, including Phone Number, Social Security Number, and Zip Code, as shown in Figure 5.5. Click Next.

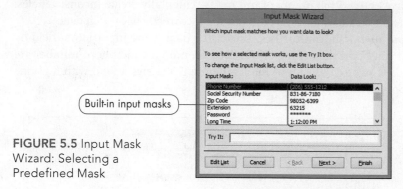

FIGURE 5.5 Input Mask Wizard: Selecting a Predefined Mask

4. The next step in the Input Mask Wizard enables you to select a placeholder character, such as an underscore (_) or the pound sign (#), to display in the field in Datasheet view until you type the data. This tells the user what format is required when entering the information, as shown in Figure 5.6. Click Next.

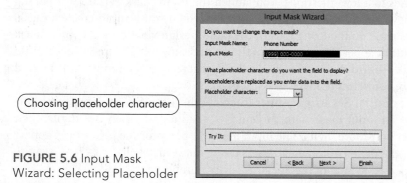

FIGURE 5.6 Input Mask Wizard: Selecting Placeholder

5. The next step enables you to tell Access if you want the symbols, such as the parentheses and hyphens, to be stored with the data. Although a small amount of additional disk space is required, it is a good idea to store the symbols with the data. This helps avoid confusion later when you create queries and enter criteria for that field, as shown in Figure 5.7. Click Next.

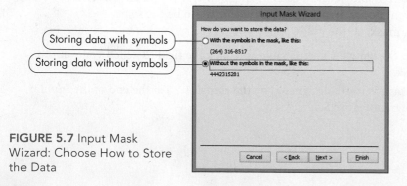

FIGURE 5.7 Input Mask Wizard: Choose How to Store the Data

6. Click Finish. The input mask now appears in the input mask property. For example, a phone number field might appear as !\(999") "000\-0000;0; or something similar. This mask forces you to enter the phone number in a consistent manner in the database table or form (as shown earlier in Figure 5.3). The underscore placeholder appears for each digit as you type the phone number, and the symbols are stored with the data.

TIP Custom Input Masks

Access enables the creation of custom input masks. For example, to have a code start with *PC*, followed by a dash, followed by two required letters, followed by five required numbers, the mask would be:

"PC-"LL00000

As you can imagine, custom input masks can be complex, but they also enable you to control user input. For more information, search Microsoft Help or the Internet for custom input masks.

Creating and Modifying a Lookup Field

Input masks provide good validation for data, but at times you may want even more control. When looking at a datasheet, you may notice repetitive data. A field with a number of repeated values may be better suited as a *lookup field*, which provides the user with a finite list of values to choose from in a menu. For example, the shelter houses three types of animals: cats, dogs, and birds. Data entry would be faster and more accurate if the options for this field were limited to the three values in a list format. Changing the field to a lookup field would present users with the three options and ensure uniformity and consistency of the data.

TIP State as a Lookup Field

State may make sense as a lookup field, as a limited number of options exist. However, if you are using a State field for shipping, do not forget about Washington, D.C. Though it is not a state, DC is as valid an abbreviation as NY or CA.

In addition to DC, the U.S. Postal Service recognizes a number of other abbreviations (such as U.S. territories and countries with free associations with the United States): American Samoa (AS), Guam (GU), the Marshall Islands (MH), Micronesia (FM), the Northern Marianas (MP), Palau (PW), Puerto Rico (PR), and the Virgin Islands (VI).

In addition, three abbreviations are used for the U.S. military. AA represents Armed Forces Central and South Americas, AE represents Armed Forces Europe, and AP represents Armed Forces Pacific.

Each of these areas has its own ZIP code, so these should be considered when creating a lookup field for State. This means that though 50 states exist, 62 different locations have ZIP codes.

Search the Internet for ZIP code 96960 to see an example of this.

Usually, the options in a lookup field are stored in a separate table. For example, if an AnimalType field has the three options listed above, you may want to create a table to store the values. In this case, a *Types of Animals* table would contain three records, one for each option. Storing the options in a separate table makes it easier for users to update the list. To add another option, for example Snakes, the user opens the *Types of Animals* table and adds a new record to the table. The new option automatically appears the next time the list is activated. The other method for lookup field options is to store the lookup values with the lookup field. This method is not recommended because modifications to the list are difficult for end users. Figure 5.8 shows an example of a lookup field.

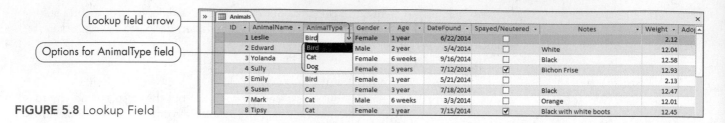

FIGURE 5.8 Lookup Field

Access provides a Lookup Wizard to help you create a lookup field. Before you launch the wizard, it is best to create the new table that will hold the lookup field options (for example, the *Types of Animals* table previously mentioned). The **Lookup Wizard** creates the menu of finite values (lookup field) by asking you six questions and using your answers to create the options list.

> **TIP** **A Lookup Field Creates a Hidden Relationship**
>
> When you use the Lookup Wizard to create a lookup field, Access creates a hidden relationship between two tables—the table that contains the lookup field and the table that holds the options. Access needs this relationship to populate the options list for the lookup field. After you create the lookup field and save the table, click Relationships in the Relationships group on the Database Tools tab. When the Relationships window displays, the new relationship does not appear. Click All Relationships in the Relationships group and the new hidden relationship appears.

Create a Lookup Field

The first step in creating a lookup field is often to create a new table that will hold the options. As mentioned, it is usually best to look up the values in a table because end users can update the list easily. For the AnimalType field in the Animals table, shown in Figure 5.8, the new table is named *Types of Animals* and contains three records, as shown in Figure 5.9. To start the Lookup Wizard, open the Animals table in Design view, select the AnimalType field that will be converted to a lookup field, and then select Lookup Wizard as the data type (see Figure 5.10).

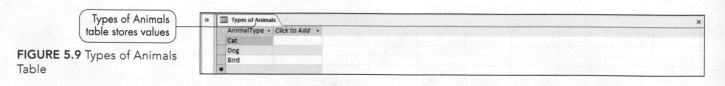

FIGURE 5.9 Types of Animals Table

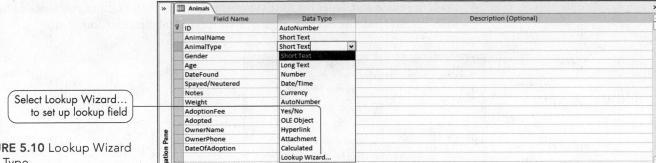

FIGURE 5.10 Lookup Wizard Data Type

Select Lookup Wizard... to set up lookup field

To create a field using the Lookup Wizard, do the following:

STEP 4 »

1. First, you are asked if you want to look up the values in a table or type in the values (shown in Figure 5.11). Select the appropriate option (likely to look up values in a table). Click Next.

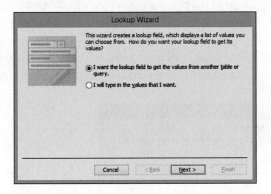

FIGURE 5.11 Lookup Wizard: Choosing Source for Field

2. Next, identify the table that holds the values for the lookup column. Figure 5.12 shows the *Types of Animals* table selected. Click Next.

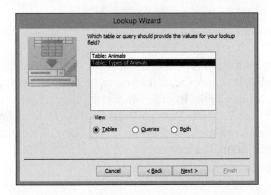

FIGURE 5.12 Lookup Wizard: Select Table

3. Next, select the field or fields from the *Types of Animals* table for the lookup field (see Figure 5.13). These fields help the user determine which option to choose. Click Next.

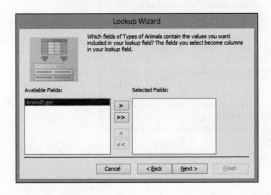

FIGURE 5.13 Lookup Wizard: Select Fields

4. Next, specify a sort order for the list box (see Figure 5.14). Because you will add to and delete items from the list, it is often best to sort alphabetically. Click Next.

FIGURE 5.14 Lookup Wizard: Choose Sort Order

5. Next, adjust the column width for the lookup column. Columns should be wide enough to display the longest value (see Figure 5.15). Use the mouse to resize the column; drag the right column edge to the right or left to the appropriate width. As an aside, there may also be times you are given the option Hide Key Field. In this case, because AnimalType does not have a primary key, you do not see that message, but if your lookup table does have a primary key, this option appears. Click Next.

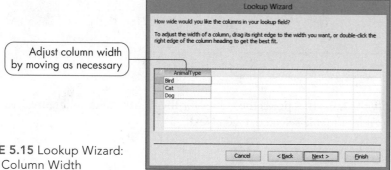

FIGURE 5.15 Lookup Wizard: Adjust Column Width

6. Finally, label the lookup field; usually, the original field name is listed and accepted. See Figure 5.16. Click the check box to Enable Data Integrity and only allow options from the lookup table. In other words, if a user tries to enter a value not found in the table, it is rejected. The Restrict Delete option is the default, which does not enable you to delete a record in the lookup table (e.g., Dog) if related records (Dogs) exist in the table that is doing the lookup.
7. Click Finish.

FIGURE 5.16 Lookup Wizard: Choose a Field Label and Finish

Modify a Lookup Field by Adding and Deleting Values

STEP 5 ▶ You can add, delete, or edit values in the lookup field to accommodate changing data needs. For example, if the shelter expands the types of animals it cares for to include rabbits, you open the *Types of Animals* table and add the new record to the bottom of the table. You also decide to delete Snakes because the shelter cannot properly care for them. When you click the category field the next time, the new option is listed. When making a change to a lookup table, you may need to go through the table data first and reclassify the records prior to changing the lookup values. For example, any animals that are snakes need to be reclassified or removed.

> ### TIP Using a Multivalued Lookup Field
>
> A multivalued field is one that accepts multiple choices in a lookup field. If a local charity received golf lessons as an auction item, you could classify the donation as either *service* or *gift certificate*. The user would have to choose only one. A multivalued field enables you to choose two or more options—the golf lessons could be classified as both a service and a gift certificate. The last step in the Lookup Wizard contains the option Allow Multiple Values, as shown in Figure 5.14. Be cautious using this feature if you plan to migrate your Access database to another database product. The multivalued field is not supported in all database management tools.

In Hands-On Exercise 1, you will practice using the Access features that help validate data entry. You will use the field data type and field properties to restrict the users from entering invalid data. You will use the Lookup Wizard to create an option list to help ensure data consistency.

Quick Concepts ✓

1. Why would you set a default value for a field? *p. 582*

2. What sort of validation rule would you add to a Number field named CustomerAge? Why? *p. 584*

3. What is the purpose of adding an input mask to a field? *p. 585*

4. What would make a field a good candidate to be switched to a lookup field? *p. 587*

Hands-On Exercises

1 Data Validation in Tables

The purpose of the shelter database is to cut down on errors, so you will add some data validation rules to the tables. You will set default field values, set validation rules, create input masks, and establish a lookup field.

Skills covered: Establish Required Fields and Set Default Field Values • Set a Validation Rule and Generate Validation Text • Use the Input Mask Wizard • Create a Lookup Field • Modify a Lookup Field

---

STEP 1 ≫ ESTABLISH REQUIRED FIELDS AND SET DEFAULT FIELD VALUES

It is important that the most critical fields in a table do not contain blanks. You decide to review the Animals table and set the required value to Yes for important fields. You also establish default values for fields that usually repeat. Refer to Figure 5.17 as you complete Step 1.

Step h: Default value of Cat appears for New record

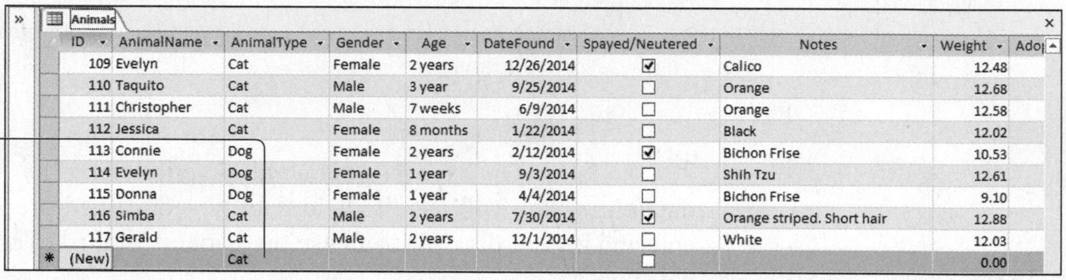

FIGURE 5.17 Default Value for AnimalType Field

ID	AnimalName	AnimalType	Gender	Age	DateFound	Spayed/Neutered	Notes	Weight	Adop
109	Evelyn	Cat	Female	2 years	12/26/2014	☑	Calico	12.48	
110	Taquito	Cat	Male	3 year	9/25/2014	☐	Orange	12.68	
111	Christopher	Cat	Male	7 weeks	6/9/2014	☐	Orange	12.58	
112	Jessica	Cat	Female	8 months	1/22/2014	☐	Black	12.02	
113	Connie	Dog	Female	2 years	2/12/2014	☑	Bichon Frise	10.53	
114	Evelyn	Dog	Female	1 year	9/3/2014	☐	Shih Tzu	12.61	
115	Donna	Dog	Female	1 year	4/4/2014	☐	Bichon Frise	9.10	
116	Simba	Cat	Male	2 years	7/30/2014	☑	Orange striped. Short hair	12.88	
117	Gerald	Cat	Male	2 years	12/1/2014	☐	White	12.03	
(New)		Cat				☐		0.00	

a. Open *a05h1Tommys*. Click the **FILE tab**, click **Save As**, click **Save Database As**, and then verify Access Database is selected under *Database File Types*. Click **Save As** and save the file as **a05h1Tommys_LastFirst**.

When you save files, use your last and first names. For example, as the Access author, I would name my document *a05h1Tommys_CameronEric*.

> **TROUBLESHOOTING:** Throughout the remainder of this chapter and textbook, click Enable Content whenever you are working with student files.

b. Open the Animals table in Design view.

c. Click the **AnimalName field** in the design grid.

d. Click in the **Required field** in the Field Properties pane. Click the arrow on the right side of the Required property box and select **Yes** from the list.

An entry in the AnimalName field is now required for each animal.

e. Click the **AnimalType field** in the table design grid.

f. Click **Default Value** in the Field Properties pane and type **Cat**.

Because most of the animals in the shelter are cats, you set the default value to Cat. You now need to test the changes you made to the table design.

g. Click **Save** on the Quick Access Toolbar. If you get a warning about testing the data integrity rules, click **Yes**.

h. Switch to the Datasheet view of the Animals table. Look at the new record row to ensure that the AnimalType is displayed as Cat by default. See Figure 5.17.

i. Click in the **Gender field** of the New record row and type **Female**. Type **2 months** in the **Age field**, 8/11/2014 in the **DateFound field**, **Very shy. Black and White** in the **Notes field**, **3** in the **Weight field**, and **$25** in the **AdoptionFee field**. The AnimalName, Spayed/Neutered, Adopted, OwnerName, OwnerPhone, and DateOfAdoption fields should be left blank.

To test data validation rules, you have left a required field blank.

j. Press **Tab** until you get an error message.

An error message appears indicating that you must enter a value in the AnimalName field. This is because you made the AnimalName field a required field, so every record must contain a value in that field.

k. Click **OK**, click in the **AnimalName field** for the new record you just typed, and then type **Pepper** in the **AnimalName field**. Click the next record to save the new record. Notice you no longer see an error.

STEP 2 ≫ SET A VALIDATION RULE AND GENERATE VALIDATION TEXT

One issue Tommy reported was that people accidentally entered incorrect adoption fees. You add a validation rule and validation text to enforce this rule. Refer to Figure 5.18 as you complete Step 2.

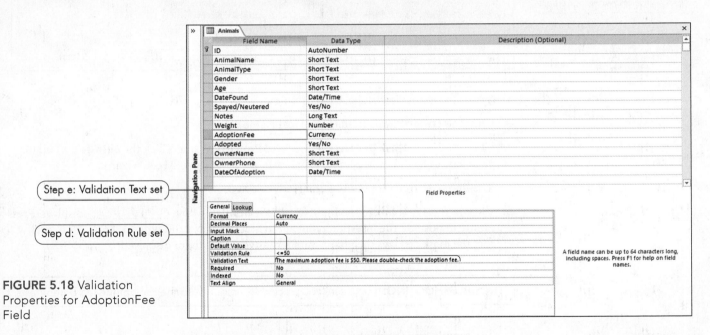

FIGURE 5.18 Validation Properties for AdoptionFee Field

a. Switch to Design view of the Animals table.

b. Click the **AdoptionFee field** in the table design grid.

c. Click the **Validation Rule property** in the Field Properties pane.

The maximum adoption fee is $50. You will establish a rule that notifies the user if a value greater than $50 is entered in the AdoptionFee field.

d. Type **<=50** in the **Validation Rule property box**.

e. Click the **Validation Text property** and type **The maximum adoption fee is $50. Please double-check the adoption fee.**

When a user enters an adoption fee that is too high, a message appears telling the user to modify the entry.

f. Compare your settings to Figure 5.18 and save the changes. Click **Yes** in response to the message about changed data integrity rules.

Access tests the data in the table to make sure that none of the adoption fees are too high.

g. Switch to the Datasheet view of the Animals table.

h. Click in the **AdoptionFee field** of the first record. Replace the current value with **51** and press **Tab**.

You receive an error message stating the maximum adoption fee is $50.

i. Click **OK** in the error message box. Change the first record to **20** for the AdoptionFee field. Press **Tab**.

As $20 is an acceptable value, you do not receive an error message.

STEP 3 ≫ USE THE INPUT MASK WIZARD

You decide to add an input mask to the phone number field so that all users follow a consistent data entry format. Refer to Figure 5.19 as you complete Step 3.

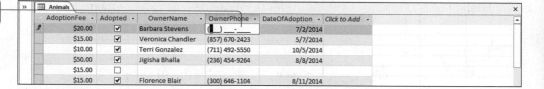

Steps c–f: Input mask applied to OwnerPhone field

FIGURE 5.19 Input Mask Applied to Phone Number Field

a. Switch to Design view of the Animals table.

b. Click the **OwnerPhone field** in the Field Name column.

c. Click the **Input Mask property** in the Field Properties pane. Click the **ellipsis (…)** on the right side of the Input Mask property box to open the Input Mask Wizard.

The Phone Number input mask is already selected.

d. Click in the **Try It box** of the Input Mask Wizard dialog box. (___) ___-____ displays. Press **Home** to position the insertion point at the first character and type **5556667777** to verify that the mask displays the phone numbers as you want them displayed.

> **TROUBLESHOOTING:** Make sure you place the cursor just to the right of the left parenthesis.

The sample data entry works fine.

e. Click **Next** twice.

You accept the mask with the default placeholder character.

f. Click the **With the symbols in the mask option**. Click **Next** and click **Finish**.

g. Save the table. Switch to the Datasheet view of the Animals table.

The phone numbers display in the preset format with parentheses and hyphens.

h. Type your phone number into the first record to test the input mask. Your entry should resemble Figure 5.19. Press **ESC** to return the record to its original state.

STEP 4 » CREATE A LOOKUP FIELD

Rather than typing in the name of an option (from a list of options) and risk the possibility of a misspelled or invalid animal type, you decide to create a lookup field that enables the volunteers to choose from a list.

a. Switch to Design view of the Animals table.

b. Click the **AnimalType field**.

c. Click the **Data Type arrow** and choose **Lookup Wizard** from the list.

   The Lookup Wizard launches.

d. Verify that the *I want the lookup field to get the values from another table or query* option is selected. Click **Next**.

e. Click **Table: Types of Animals** and click **Next**.

   This table was prefilled with animal types.

f. Double-click **AnimalType** to move it to the Selected Fields box. Click **Next**.

g. Click the arrow in the first sort box and select **AnimalType**. Click **Next**.

h. Adjust the column width so AnimalType is visible, if necessary. Click **Next**.

i. Verify that *AnimalType* is the label for the lookup column. Click **Finish**. Click **Yes** to save the table.

   The Lookup Field has now been established.

j. Switch to the Datasheet view of the Animals table. Add a new animal using the following data, pressing **Tab** between each entry. Note that once you enter an AnimalName, you are given an ID automatically:

AnimalName	Marco
Gender	Male
Age	2 months
DateFound	8/14/2014
Spayed/Neutered	Yes
Notes	Parakeet. Yellow and blue
Weight	0.2
AdoptionFee	$50

   The AnimalType, Adopted, OwnerName, OwnerPhone, and DateOfAdoption fields should be left blank.

   TROUBLESHOOTING: If you make a mistake in the middle of entering and start again, the ID automatically skips a number. Do not try to fix the ID; just add the record again using the next sequential number.

   ---

k. Click the **AnimalType field** for Marco. Select **Bird** from the menu.

   The lookup field gives you a menu of animal types. The default is Cat from Step 1.

l. Close the Animals table.

STEP 5 >> MODIFY A LOOKUP FIELD

After a few days of testing, you decide to modify the table containing the lookup values for the lookup field. Volunteers have pointed out they do not accept snakes, but they do accept rabbits, which are not listed as an option. Refer to Figure 5.20 as you complete Step 5.

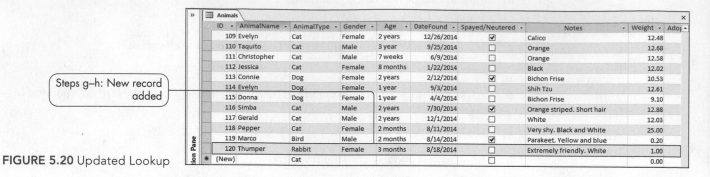

Steps g–h: New record added

FIGURE 5.20 Updated Lookup

a. Open the Types of Animals table in Datasheet view.

b. Delete the Snake record.

c. Add a new row with **Rabbit** as the AnimalType.

d. Close the *Types of Animals* table.

e. Open the Animals table in Datasheet view.

f. Add a new record to the table. Accept the default ID and enter **Thumper** as the value for the **AnimalName field**.

g. Select the menu for AnimalType. Notice that Snake is no longer an option, but Rabbit is. Select **Rabbit** for the AnimalType.

h. Enter the rest of the data below, leaving any fields not mentioned blank:

Gender	Female
Age	3 months
DateFound	8/18/2014
Spayed/Neutered	No
Notes	Extremely friendly. White.
Weight	1
AdoptionFee	$25

i. Save and close all open tables.

j. Keep the database open if you plan to continue with Hands-On Exercise 2. If not, close the database and exit Access.

Data Analysis Using Advanced Select Queries

In a previous chapter, you used some basic query techniques to extract data from your database. Extracting and manipulating data is the center of the database experience, one of the major reasons to use a database rather than a spreadsheet.

Aside from extracting information more effectively, you may also want to be more efficient. Creating a group of queries to extract information from one table is not a bad thing, but imagine for a moment a database with dozens of tables. If you have many queries for each of the tables, it becomes more difficult to manage. You may spend time recreating queries you have already created, for example. You can apply special conditions that enable you to make a query more versatile. This may remove the need for you to create multiple similar queries with minor differences in the criteria.

One of the reasons people choose Excel over Access is a perceived lack of built-in functions. However, Access does include a number of functions through the Expression Builder (as discussed in a previous chapter). You have the ability to create advanced functions, similar to Excel, while being able to enjoy the benefits of a database software package.

In this section, you will learn advanced select queries including parameter queries and advanced functions in the Expression Builder.

Creating a Parameter Query

Access provides a variety of query types to help business owners make decisions. To determine how many pets of a certain animal type were adopted at Tommy's this year, you could construct a query with the relevant fields, and then enter Cat into the Criteria row of the AnimalType field. You could save the query as Cat Adoptions. If you wanted to see the same information for dogs, you could copy the first query, rename the copy as Dog Adoptions, and then enter Dog into the Criteria row of the AnimalType field. This process could be repeated for other animal types as needed. However, you might ask yourself if there is a better way to handle this situation. The answer is yes—using a parameter query.

A *parameter query* is a select query where the user provides the criterion at run time. A parameter query provides flexibility that other queries do not. It enables you to create a query for one situation and then expand it into a query for unlimited situations.

Create a Parameter Query to Provide Flexibility

A parameter query reduces your development time because you can use the query repeatedly without modifying the design as only the criterion changes. The parameter query is not different from the queries you have used before—it is still a select query. However, it is unique in the way it asks the user to respond before completing its execution.

Suppose the alumni relations office at Passaic County Community College, in Paterson, New Jersey, contacts alumni to keep them connected to the college after graduation. For example, when college events—sporting events, theater events, musical presentations, and so forth—are in a certain geographical area, the college contacts the alumni in the area. Akira Yamamoto, professor of communication, might need a list of the alumni in the same city as her next off-campus production. Each time a new event is scheduled, the query criterion would have to be changed—unless a parameter query is created. A parameter query would prompt the user to Enter City, and after Akira enters a city, the list of alumni would appear. The alumni office can then mail an announcement (or send an e-mail) to inform the Passaic alumni about the event. Parameter queries enable you to create a more versatile select query.

Creating a parameter query is similar to creating most other query types. The major difference is in the criteria. To create a parameter query, do the following:

STEP 1 »
1. Click Query Design in the Queries group on the CREATE tab.
2. Choose a table that contains the records that you want included in the query.

3. Drag the relevant fields from the table to the query design grid.
4. Click inside the Criteria row of the field that you need to filter, but instead of entering the criteria, type a text phrase enclosed in brackets [ ] that you want to appear in a dialog box. The text should instruct the user what to do, such as [Enter the City] or [Enter State Abbreviation] or [Enter Type of Animal], as shown in Figure 5.21. When a user runs the query, this text appears as a prompt in the Enter Parameter Value dialog box (see Figure 5.22).

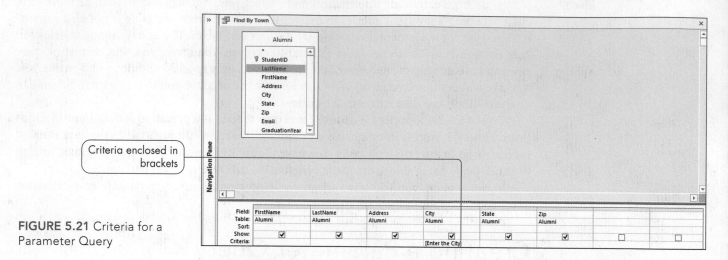

Criteria enclosed in brackets

FIGURE 5.21 Criteria for a Parameter Query

5. If you need additional parameters for other fields, move to the Criteria row for the next field and type the user instructions in brackets in that field.
6. Save the query as you normally would.

In the Passaic County Community College example, you could create a query based on the Alumni table. Then you would add all the fields relevant to the mailing address (name, address, city, state, ZIP) to the design grid. If you want to find all the alumni from a specific city, type [Enter the City] in the Criteria of the City field. You will be prompted as shown in Figure 5.22. Figure 5.23 shows the results after *Paterson* is typed into the Enter Parameter Value dialog box.

FIGURE 5.22 Parameter Query Prompt

City value for all records is Paterson

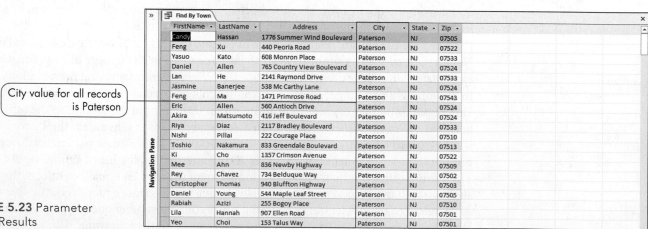

FIGURE 5.23 Parameter Query Results

In an earlier chapter, you learned about advanced operators such as Between and Like. These can be added to a parameter query to extend the capabilities even more.

When multiple parameters are involved, Access asks for the information starting from the left and moving to the right. You can also use multiple parameters within a single criteria selection. For example, if you want to see events with certain date ranges, you could use the Between operator. Type *Between [Enter Start Date] And [Enter End Date]* into the criteria of the EventDate column. This expression generates two dialog boxes, one for the starting date and one for the ending date. After the user supplies the date criteria by typing them in the Enter Parameter Value dialog box, Access uses the responses to create a criteria expression as if it were typed into the Criteria row of the query. For example, if you enter 6/1/2014 when prompted for the starting date and 6/30/2014 as the ending date, Access interprets that as *Between #6/1/2014# And #6/30/2014#*. Recall that Access encloses date fields with the # character. Also recall that the Between operator is inclusive; that is, saying *between 6/1/2014 and 6/30/2014* includes any events on 6/1/2014 and 6/30/2014.

You can also use the Like operator to create a parameter query. The Like operator enables you to significantly expand your match criteria. Instead of searching for an exact match, you can use the Like operator as you did in an earlier chapter. For example, if you were to set the parameter to *[Enter City]* for a City field, you could revise the criterion to allow users to enter the partial name of a city. The new criterion would be *Like [Enter Partial City] & '*'* (use single quotation marks around the *), as shown in Figure 5.24. This new expression enables you to enter P at the prompt, and Access finds all cities that begin with P. The results, shown in Figure 5.25, include Paterson, Pompton Lakes, and Passaic.

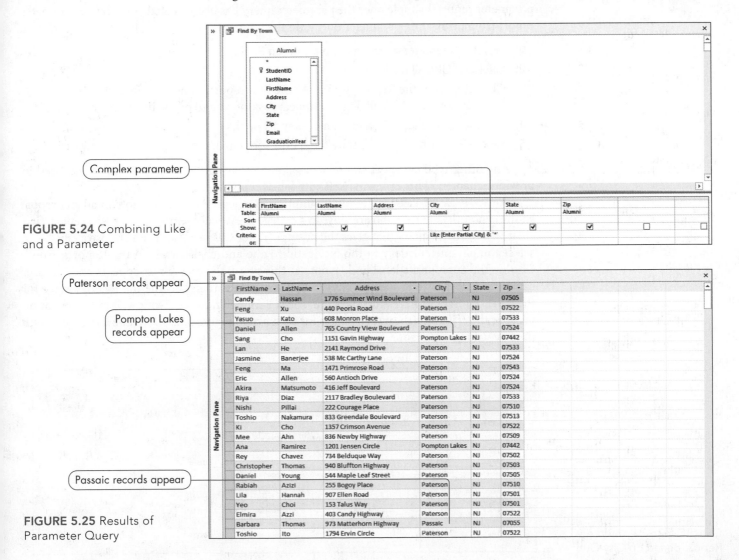

FIGURE 5.24 Combining Like and a Parameter

FIGURE 5.25 Results of Parameter Query

When a parameter query contains multiple parameter questions, Access provides a Query Parameters window to organize and keep track of these multiple parameters. To display the Query Parameters window, do the following:

1. Switch to Layout or Design view.
2. Display the DESIGN tab.
3. Click Parameters in the Show/Hide group.
4. In the first Parameter row, type the name of the parameter excluding the brackets [ ]. Use the Data Type column to specify what data type is stored in the parameter's field. When you run the query, the Parameter dialog boxes appear in the order they are listed in the Query Parameters window.

Create a Parameter Report

The effectiveness of parameter queries can be extended to reports. By creating a report based on a parameter query, you automatically receive the benefits of a parameter query—adding flexibility that enables a user to control the content of the report. A report based on a parameter query becomes an effective management tool for any organization. The creation of a parameter report is simple once the parameter query has been created. To create a parameter report from an existing parameter query, do the following:

1. Select a parameter query in the Navigation Pane.
2. Click the CREATE tab.
3. Click Report in the Reports group. As the new report is being created, the familiar Enter Parameter Value dialog box appears asking you to enter the criterion.
4. Enter a value, click OK, and then the report opens in Layout view.
5. Save the report. Note each time the report is opened, it prompts you for new criteria.

Any other type of report can be created as well using the same process as you used in previous chapters. This can work well with labels reports.

For example, at Passaic County Community College, Akira wants to run a label report so she can notify alumni who are close to a college theatrical event. To create this report, first create a parameter query that gives the prompt [Enter City] so Akira can choose a city. Next, select the parameter query in the Navigation Pane and click Labels in the Reports group. Choose the appropriate label and layout. At this point, the dialog box appears and the user can enter Paterson (or whatever city). The query results then become the record source for the label report, and Access displays the labels. Parameter queries work well in this situation because the criterion (the city) changes for each event. Figure 5.26 shows the City query with the city value of Paterson.

FIGURE 5.26 Parameter Report Based on City Query

TIP | Add a Parameter to an Existing Report

Often, database design evolves over time. Even after careful planning and implementation, a database may have incomplete requirements or may be designed by a less experienced database designer. If you have a report that is perfectly formatted and laid out but you want to add parameters, it can be done even if the original design did not call for it.

To do so, create a parameter query as demonstrated earlier. Open the report in Layout or Design view and open the Property Sheet. Locate and click the Record Source property. Type the new query name that you created in place of the table name currently shown. Save the report changes and the next time you run the report, the Enter Parameter Value dialog box will appear.

Using Advanced Functions in the Expression Builder

As shown in an earlier chapter, the Expression Builder is a powerful tool enabling you to create mathematical functions. You used the Pmt function to calculate a periodic payment for a loan. However, over 125 built-in functions exist in Access. Although most users are just familiar with the ones they use on a daily basis, searching the Web or using Microsoft Help may be useful to find assistance with unfamiliar functions. As you gain experience with Access functions, you may remember functions and their parameters and just type them in. To start, you will likely use the Expression Builder.

TIP | Renaming Columns

From a previous chapter, recall that the default titles for calculated columns are names like Expr1. To fix this, you can add any name you like (without spaces) before the expression, followed by a colon (:).

Use the Date Function

You performed date arithmetic in an earlier chapter. However, you started with a fixed date for the arithmetic. This is not always realistic. You may want to run the same query over and over and, based on the current date, perform some sort of calculation. To do so, you can use the *Date function*, which calculates the current date. The Date function takes no parameters. For example, you could calculate days since a student's last payment using the Date function and subtracting the last PaymentDate from it. The Date function also is commonly used as a default value for date fields.

STEP 2 Date()

The Date function can be typed in manually or entered through the Expression Builder. In the Expression Builder, it can be found by double-clicking Functions. Then click Built-In Functions, followed by Date/Time, in the Expression Categories section of the Expression Builder. Date appears in the Expression Values portion of the Expression Builder, as shown in Figure 5.27.

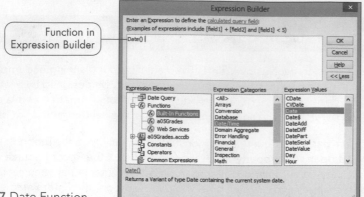

Function in
Expression Builder

FIGURE 5.27 Date Function

TIP | Default a Date Field to Today

You can type Date() in the Default Value property to insert the current date when a new record is added. This type of default value is useful for fields like Date of Entry, Date Record Added, and Order Date.

Use the Round Function

The *Round function* returns a number rounded to a specific number of decimal places. You may not want to round to the nearest number necessarily. You can round to a different number of decimal places by changing the precision parameter. If you leave the precision parameter blank, Access assumes the nearest whole number.

In the Expression Builder, the Round function is in the Math category of Built-In Functions. It has the following syntax:

Round(expression, precision)

Going back to our previous example, Akira Yamamoto, the communication professor, has her final grades in an Access database. She generally rounds her grades before she submits them to the registrar's office.

Akira has set up a query to do this for her. She used the Expression Builder to do so. See Figure 5.28. Notice the main function is written as Round([Grade]). As you saw in an earlier chapter, the parameters appear between the brackets. In this case, the Round function requires one parameter. Rounding to a whole number, a student with an 89.25 would receive an 89, but a student with an 83.95 would end up with an 84 for the class. See Figure 5.29 to see results.

Function with parameter
in Expression Builder

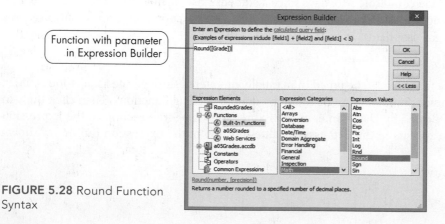

FIGURE 5.28 Round Function Syntax

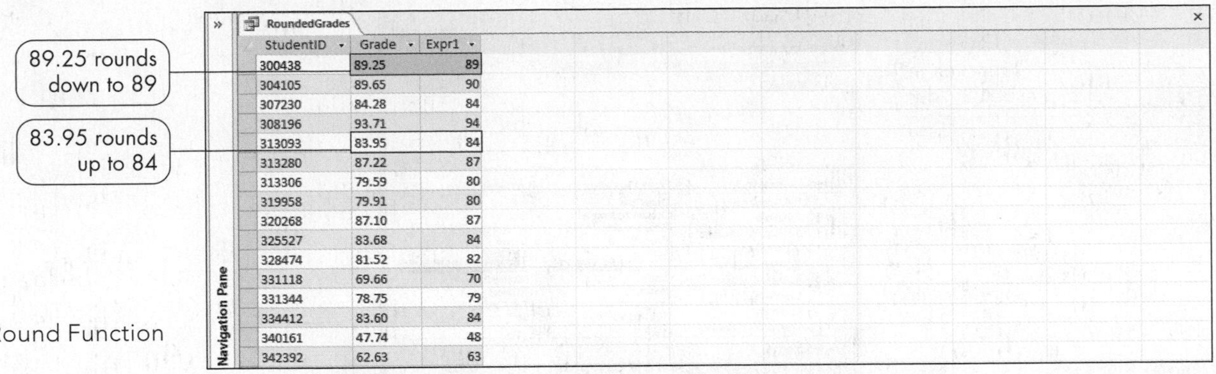

FIGURE 5.29 Round Function Results

The callouts read:
- 89.25 rounds down to 89
- 83.95 rounds up to 84

StudentID	Grade	Expr1
300438	89.25	89
304105	89.65	90
307230	84.28	84
308196	93.71	94
313093	83.95	84
313280	87.22	87
313306	79.59	80
319958	79.91	80
320268	87.10	87
325527	83.68	84
328474	81.52	82
331118	69.66	70
331344	78.75	79
334412	83.60	84
340161	47.74	48
342392	62.63	63

The precision element is important in determining how to round. If you choose a precision of zero (or leave it blank), the value of the field is rounded to a whole number. If you choose a precision of 1, it is rounded to the first decimal place, and so on. Precision cannot be a negative number. Here are some examples of the Round function in practice:

- Round(500.554) would return 501. Because no parameter exists, Access assumes nearest integer, which is 501.

- Round(500.554,0) would return 501. We have given a parameter of zero decimal places, so it returns 501.

- Round(500.554,1) would return 500.6. A parameter of 1 rounds to the first decimal place.

- Round(500.554,2) would return 500.55. A parameter of 2 rounds to two decimal places.

Use the IsNull Function

The *IsNull function* checks whether a field has no value. You learned in an earlier chapter that null essentially means an absence of value. IsNull checks if a field has no value assigned. For example, you may have a Date/Time field. Instead of trying to determine what an absence of a value is for a Date/Time field, you can simply use IsNull. This can be useful in comparisons (to be discussed shortly) or as part of a query. In the Expression Builder, the IsNull function can be found in the Math category of Built-In Functions.

STEP 3 » IsNull(expression)

For example, Akira is preparing to send a mailing to a list of students. However, some of the students in the database, as you may have noticed in an earlier example, do not have street addresses listed. This may happen when a student moves and does not inform the college. If no address exists, a label is unnecessary. In this case, Akira can use an IsNull function to determine if each person has a street address. In this case, the function would be IsNull([Address]).

When the IsNull function is added to a query, it displays one of two values. Access determines "is this value null"? If the value is null, it displays –1. If the value is not null—that is, it has a value—the function displays 0. Figure 5.30 shows the syntax of the function in the Expression Builder, and Figure 5.31 shows the results.

IsNull is frequently paired with some sort of condition. For example, you could display only null values by typing –1 in the condition row. You could display non-null values by setting a condition of 0.

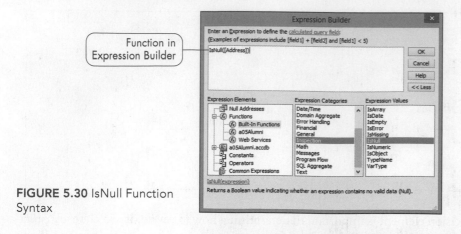

FIGURE 5.30 IsNull Function Syntax

Function in Expression Builder

Null addresses have a value of −1

Non-null addresses have a value of 0

FIGURE 5.31 IsNull Function Results

Create Conditional Output with the IIf Function

Another common function used in Access is the *IIf function*, which evaluates an expression and displays one value when the expression is true and another value when the expression is false. When creating an IIf statement, you will find three options that need to be filled in: the expression (the question you are asking Access to check), the true part (what to do if the expression is yes), and the false part (what to do if the expression is false). The expression in this case is a statement that can be evaluated to true or false. You can find the function through the Expression Builder in the Program Flow category of Built-In Functions.

IIf (expression, truepart, falsepart)

The important piece of the IIf function is the expression, which involves some sort of comparison. In your day-to-day life, you are constantly performing IIf statements. Based on the weather, you make a decision on whether to carry an umbrella. In that case, you check the weather. If the weather is rainy, you bring the umbrella. If the weather is not rainy, you leave the umbrella at home.

Another example in your daily life might have to do with traffic. If too much traffic exists on Route 3, take Route 21. If it is 7:00 AM, get up; otherwise, do not. If you are thirsty, get a glass of water; otherwise, do not. The commonality here is that some sort of condition determines the action. In the case of any condition, it is something that can be evaluated as yes or no.

You can perform six types of comparisons, as you saw in an earlier chapter. The six comparison operators are equal (=), not equal (<>), greater than (>), less than (<), greater than or equal to (>=), and less than or equal to (<=). As you do with queries, you can use these comparison operators in an IIf statement.

The expression must evaluate as yes (or true) or no (or false) only. For example, *Balance >= 10000* or *City = "Sarasota"* are valid expressions because they can be evaluated as true or false. Either the balance is greater than or equal to 10000 or it is not; either the city is Sarasota or it is not. *DateListed + 90* is not a valid criterion for the IIf function because this expression is a calculation, not a comparison. Access evaluates the expression, determines whether it is true or false, then performs one action if the expression is true and another if the expression is false. For example, if accounts with balances of $10,000 or more earn

3.5% interest, whereas accounts with balances below $10,000 earn only 1.5% interest, the following IIf function could be created: IIf (Balance>=10000, .035, .015).

The IIf function can also evaluate text values. For example, to classify a list of students based on whether they are in or out of the state of New Jersey, you could create the following IIf function: IIf([State]="NJ", "In State", "Out of State"). Figure 5.32 shows the expression syntax in the Expression Builder, and Figure 5.33 shows the results.

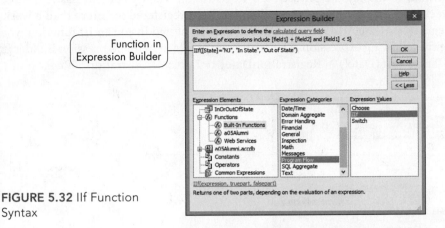

Function in Expression Builder

FIGURE 5.32 IIf Function Syntax

Non-NJ addresses display *Out of State*

NJ addresses display *In State*

FIGURE 5.33 IIf Function Results

TIP Using Comparison Operators

To create an expression with a *greater than or equal to* comparison operator, type the two operators >=. To create an expression with a *less than or equal to* comparison operator, type the two operators <=. Both of these comparison operators require two operators, and they must be typed in the correct order with the equal sign in the second position.

Notice that when you say one number is not equal to another, you are effectively saying it is either less than or greater than that number. Hence, you type <> to represent *not equal to*.

It would be easier to read if you could use ≥, ≤, or ≠, but you do not have those keys on your keyboard.

Nesting Functions

As with Excel, you may wish to combine functions. For example, if you had to find the square root of a number, you might want to first make sure the number is positive by using the absolute value function. If you were trying to perform this on a field named Hypotenuse, you would end up with the following formula: Sqr(Abs([Hypotenuse])). Using one function within another function is known as *nesting functions*. The combination of parentheses and brackets may be hard to read, but sometimes combining functions is the only way to accomplish a task. IIf functions are one function often used in as a nested function.

Combine IIf with Other Expressions

Suppose you want to display the phrase New Registration when a student has registered in the last week, and Registered when a student has been registered for more than a week. Using the RegistrationDate field and the Date() function nested inside an IIf function, you would create the following expression. The expression is shown in the Expression Builder in Figure 5.34. It reads: IIf (Date() – [RegistrationDate] <=7, "New Registration", "Registered").

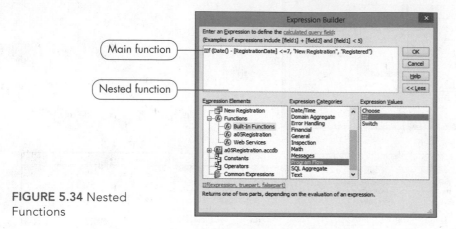

FIGURE 5.34 Nested Functions

The expression Date() – [RegistrationDate]<=7 evaluates each student and determines if the number of days since the student registered is less than or equal to 7. When the expression is true, the function displays New Registration. When the expression is false, the function displays Registered. The results of the function are shown in Figure 5.35. For that example, the date it is run is 8/31/2016.

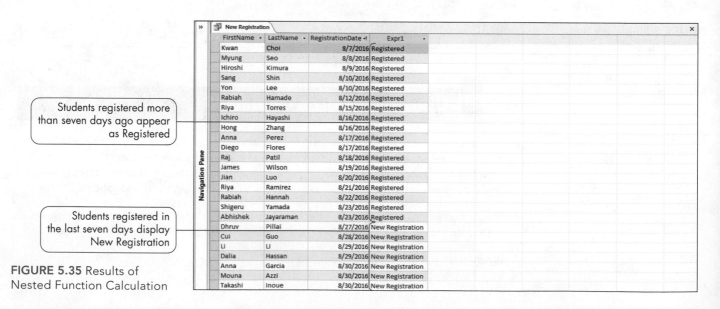

FIGURE 5.35 Results of Nested Function Calculation

This IIf statement includes one function, math, and a comparison inside of it. This may be a little difficult to read, but to get the full benefit of Access it is often necessary to nest functions.

Use Nested IIf Functions

Experienced Access users sometimes need to create nested IIf functions. This happens when two conditions are not sufficient to evaluate an expression. For example, the function IIf (Date() – [RegistrationDate] <=7, "New Registration", "Registered") was used based on two conditions existing.

Let us say a third status is needed, with the following conditions:

- If a student has registered in the past 2 days, mark as Brand New Registration.
- If a student has registered in the past 2 to 7 days, mark as New Registration.
- If a student has been registered for more than 7 days, mark as Registered.

The IIf statement to accomplish this would read as follows:

IIf (Date() – [RegistrationDate] <=2, "Brand New Registration", IIf (Date() – [RegistrationDate] <=7, "New Registration", "Registered"))

Access would process this as follows:

1. Subtract the RegistrationDate from today's date. If it is less than or equal to 2, display *Brand New Registration*.
2. If that is not the case, subtract the RegistrationDate from today's date. If it is less than or equal to 7, display *New Registration*. Note that Access has already determined it is not less than or equal to 2 with the first condition, so only registrations between 2 and 7 days old display *New Registration*.
3. If neither of those things are true, the student has been registered for more than 7 days, so display *Registered*.

Performing Date Arithmetic

Working with dates in Access can be challenging, especially when performing date arithmetic. This can be even more problematic if your output will contain multiple formats for the United States, Europe, and Asia. Each has its own method of formatting dates. Fortunately, Access has some built-in functions to help work with dates and date arithmetic.

Date formatting affects the date's display without changing the actual underlying value in the table. All dates and times in Access are stored as the number of days that have elapsed since December 31, 1899. For example, January 1, 1900, is stored as 1, indicating one day after December 31, 1899. If the time were 9:00 PM on November 20, 2010, no matter how the date or time is formatted, Access stores it as 40502.875. The 40502 represents the number of days elapsed since December 31, 1899, and the .875 reflects the fraction of the 24-hour day that has passed at 9:00 PM. Because dates are stored by Access as sequential numbers, you can calculate the total numbers of hours worked in a week if you record the starting and ending times for each day. Using *date arithmetic*, you can create expressions to calculate lapsed time, such as a person's age based on birth date or the number of years since a person's start at a college.

Identify Partial Dates with the DatePart Function

Using a date function, you can isolate a portion of the date that is of interest to you. The date math you have worked with thus far included basic subtraction of one date from another. However, you may not always just want to get the number of days between two dates. Assume you are working at a company that plans on giving all employees who started working for the company 10 or more years ago a slight longevity pay increase. Using date subtraction could work. However, your criteria would then be a number of days, and modifications might be difficult for someone who might need to perform a similar query in the future.

STEP 4 >> Another way to accomplish this would be to extract only the year portion of the date. The *DatePart function* is an Access function that examines a date and returns a portion of the date, and it works well for this case. DatePart returns a numeric value for the interval you have selected. You can find this function through the Expression Builder in the Date/Time category of Built-In Functions.

DatePart(interval, date, *firstdayofweek*, *firstweekofyear*)

Assuming the query is run in 2016, you would want the query to find anyone who has a HireDate in 2006 or earlier. If you could find just the year portion of the HireDate, you could easily subtract it from 2016 and only add a raise when the difference is greater than or equal to 10 years. The first part of this operation would be to extract the year from the HireDate, which can be done using DatePart: DatePart("yyyy", [HireDate]). Figure 5.36 shows the expression syntax in the Expression Builder, and Figure 5.37 shows the results.

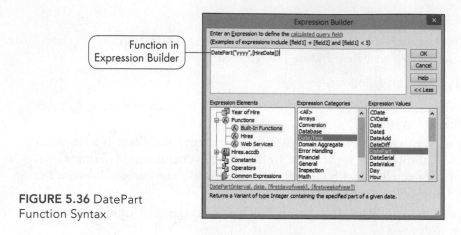

FIGURE 5.36 DatePart Function Syntax

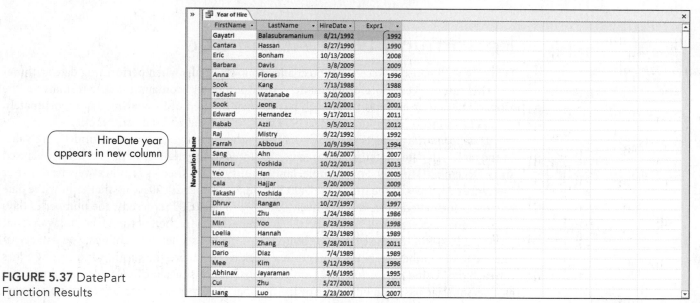

FIGURE 5.37 DatePart Function Results

DatePart is not only used to extract the year; it can also be used to extract the month, day, and a number of other intervals as well. You could use this function, for example, to find all employees who started in the current month (say, January), and send them a card thanking them for being with the company another year.

The function always returns a numeric value, so if you extract the month, you get a number from 1 (representing January) through 12 (December). If you extract the weekday, you get a number from 1 (representing Sunday) through 7 (Saturday).

Table 5.1 shows the DatePart function parameters.

TABLE 5.1 Using the DatePart Function

Function Portion	Explanation	
«interval»	The first argument, the interval, describes the portion of the date that you wish to return. You can use any of the following:	
	"yyyy"	Year
	"q"	Quarter
	"m"	Month
	"y"	Day of year
	"d"	Day
	"w"	Weekday
	"ww"	Week
	"h"	Hour
	"n"	Minute
	"s"	Second
«date»	The second argument, the date, tells Access where to find the Date/Time information.	
«firstdayofweek»	*Optional.* A constant that specifies the first day of the week. If not specified, Sunday is assumed.	
«firstweekofyear»	*Optional.* A constant that specifies the first week of the year. If not specified, the first week is assumed to be the week in which January 1 occurs.	

Here are some examples of the DatePart function being used on a date field named HireDate. For these examples, assume HireDate is 8/31/2017.

TABLE 5.2 Evaluating the DatePart Function

Function Portion	Resulting Value	Explanation
DatePart("yyyy",[HireDate])	2017	August 31, 2017, has a year of 2017.
DatePart("q",[HireDate])	3	Quarter 3 is July, August, and September.
DatePart("m",[HireDate])	8	August is the 8th month of the year.
DatePart("y",[HireDate])	243	August 31 is the 243rd day of the year.
DatePart("w",[HireDate])	4	August 31, 2017, is a Thursday.
DatePart("ww",[HireDate])	35	August 31, 2017, is in the 35th week of the year.

 TIP Displaying Month or Day Names

The numbers for months or days may be hard to read and not intuitive. However, a function to help with that exists. It makes sense to nest the results of your DatePart function within another function. If you want to specifically display the day of the week, the function WeekDay(«expression») would display the day of the week as a word. So, WeekDay(1) would return Sunday. Likewise, the function MonthName(«expression») would return the name of the month. For example, MonthName(3) would return March. This may make it easier for you to read.

Apply Criteria and Grouping to DatePart Results

Like any other field, a calculated field using DatePart can have criteria applied for it. For example, similar to our previous example, we could extract the month for our HireDate:

DatePart("m", [Employees]![HireDate])

If this were added as a field, it would display a number from 1 through 12 in the column. If you wanted to only display employees hired in April, for example, you would type the number 4 in the Criteria row. Upon running the query, you get a list of employees hired in April, regardless of the year.

In a previous chapter, you learned how to group by fields. This operation works well with the DatePart function. For example, if you wanted to see how many employees were hired by month, you could use the same example as before:

DatePart("m", [Employees]![HireDate])

Next, click the Totals button on the Query Tools Design tab, and then select Group By for this field. You would then add another field (HireDate, in this case) as the second column, and then set the Group By for that field to Count. You would end up with a list of months (1 through 12, representing January through December), each followed by the number of employees hired in that year.

In Hands-On Exercise 2, you will practice creating a parameter query. You will use advanced Expression Builder functions to perform calculations. You will perform date arithmetic as well.

Quick Concepts

1. What is the advantage to creating a parameter query? *p. 597*

2. What are two common uses for the Date function? *p. 601*

3. What does the IsNull function do? *p. 603*

4. Why is the expression a critical component of the IIf function? *p. 604*

5. Which function would you use if you needed to display just the year portion of a date? *p. 607*

Hands-On Exercises

Watch the Video
for this Hands-
On Exercise!

MyITLab®
HOE2 Training

2 Data Analysis Using Advanced Select Queries

After applying data validation rules to the tables, you will perform some advanced queries against the database. You will create a parameter query, use advanced Expression Builder functions, and use date arithmetic to manipulate the data.

Skills covered: Create a Parameter Query • Use Date and Round Functions • Use IIf and IsNull Functions • Perform Date Arithmetic

---

STEP 1 >> CREATE A PARAMETER QUERY

Tommy is hoping to create a query that will enable the volunteers to input the animal type and display all animals matching. He is hoping to also create a report based on that query. In addition, he would like to create a query to display all animals adopted in a certain date range. Refer to Figure 5.38 as you complete Step 1.

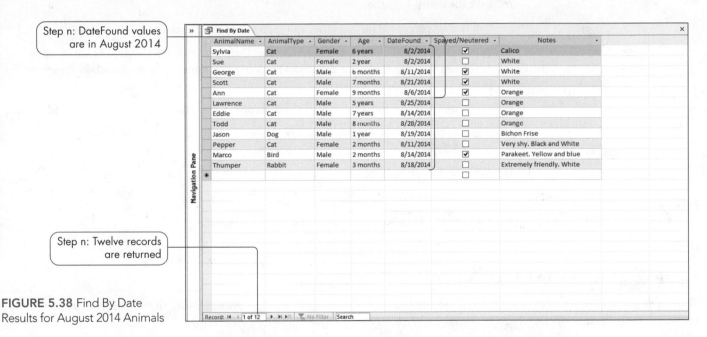

Step n: DateFound values are in August 2014

Step n: Twelve records are returned

FIGURE 5.38 Find By Date Results for August 2014 Animals

a. Open *a05h1Tommys_LastFirst* if you closed it at the end of Hands-On Exercise 1 and save it as **a05h2Tommys_LastFirst**, changing *h1* to *h2*.

b. Create a query using Query Design. Double-click the **Animals table** to add it to the query. Click **Close**.

c. Double-click each of the following fields to add them to the query: **AnimalName**, **AnimalType**, **Gender**, **Age**, **DateFound**, **Spayed/Neutered**, and **Notes**.

d. Type **[Enter Animal Type]** in the Criteria row for the AnimalType field.

e. Save the query as **Find Animal Type**. Run the query.

   You are prompted to enter an animal type in a box labeled Enter Animal Type.

> **TROUBLESHOOTING:** If you are not prompted to Enter Animal Type, ensure your criterion for the AnimalType field is enclosed in brackets exactly as shown in step d.

f. Enter **Bird** at the prompt and click **OK**.

All nine birds in the database are displayed.

> **TROUBLESHOOTING:** If you get no results, ensure you typed [Enter Animal Type] in the correct field's criteria.

g. Close the Find Animal Type query.

h. Double-click the **Find Animal Type query** to run the query again. Enter **Cat** when prompted. Verify 86 records are displayed and close the Find Animal Type query.

i. Right-click the **Find Animal Type query** and select **Copy**. Right-click in a blank area of the Navigation Pane and select **Paste**. Name the query **Find By Date** and click **OK**.

j. Open the Find By Date query in Design view.

k. Remove the criterion from the AnimalType field.

l. Type **Between [Enter Start Date] and [Enter End Date]** on the Criteria row for the DateFound field.

m. Save the query. Run the query.

You will be prompted for one date, and then for a second date.

n. Type **8/1/2014** when prompted to Enter Start Date and click **OK**. Type **8/31/2014** when prompted to Enter End Date and click **OK**. Verify 12 animals are displayed, as shown in Figure 5.38 and close the query.

o. Click the **Find Animal Type query**. Click **Report** in the Reports group on the CREATE tab.

A report based on the Find Animal Type query is created, and you are prompted to Enter Animal Type.

p. Type **Bird** when prompted.

The same nine records displayed earlier appear in report form.

q. Save the report as **Animal Report** and close the report.

STEP 2 ≫ USE DATE AND ROUND FUNCTIONS

Tommy has some modifications to the database that you can achieve using advanced functions. You will assist him by setting a default date and rounding animal weights. Refer to Figure 5.39 as you complete Step 2.

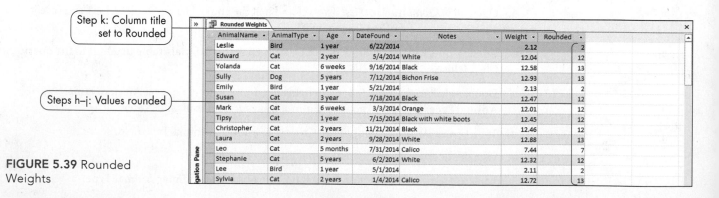

FIGURE 5.39 Rounded Weights

a. Open the Animals table in Design view. Click the **DateFound field**.

b. Add **Date()** to the Default Value in Field Properties.

The default value for all new records is the current date.

c. Switch to Datasheet view. Save the changes when prompted. Scroll to the new record at the bottom of the table.

The first blank record has a default value of your current date. Note if you are working on this before 2014, your default date may be before some of the other dates.

d. Close the Animals table.

e. Create a new query using Query Design. Double-click the **Animals table** in the Show Table dialog box. Click **Close**.

f. Double-click the **AnimalName**, **AnimalType**, **Age**, **DateFound**, **Notes**, and **Weight fields** to add them to the query.

g. Click in the top row of the first column after the Weight field.

You will create a new column to round the Weight field.

h. Click **Builder** in the Query Setup group. Double-click **Functions**. Click **Built-In Functions** and click **Math** in the *Expression Categories* section of the Expression Builder.

i. Double-click **Round** in the *Expression Values* section.

Round(«number», «precision») displays in the Expression Builder.

j. Remove *«number», «precision»* from the expression and replace it with **Weight**.

Round(Weight) displays in the Expression Builder.

k. Click **OK**. Replace *Expr1* in your new column with **Rounded**. Run the query. Check the Rounded column against the Weight column to make sure animal weights are rounded to the nearest whole number. See Figure 5.39.

l. Save the query as **Rounded Weights** and close the query.

STEP 3 ≫ USE IIF AND ISNULL FUNCTIONS

Tommy hopes to find data entry errors in his database. Due to the sheer number of volunteers, he has noticed mistakes in the database, and he would like an automated query to find any pets that are listed as adopted but do not have an owner name. You will help him to accomplish this by nesting an IsNull function inside an IIf function. Refer to Figure 5.40 as you complete Step 3.

Step h: Column named ErrorCheck

Steps d–g: IIf function created

AnimalName	AnimalType	Adopted	OwnerName	OwnerPhone	DateOfAdoption	ErrorCheck
Leslie	Bird	☑	Barbara Stevens	(351) 962-5300	7/2/2014	Ok
Edward	Cat	☑	Veronica Chandler	(857) 670-2423	5/7/2014	Ok
Yolanda	Cat	☑	Terri Gonzalez	(711) 492-5550	10/5/2014	Ok
Sully	Dog	☑	Jigisha Bhalla	(236) 454-9264	8/8/2014	Ok
Susan	Cat	☑	Florence Blair	(300) 646-1104	8/11/2014	Ok
Christopher	Cat	☑	Stephanie Campbell	(351) 991-2011	12/19/2014	Ok
Leo	Cat	☑				Error
Stephanie	Cat	☑	Bernard Lane	(555) 433-4650	6/13/2014	Ok
Lee	Bird	☑	Tom Lyons	(351) 521-8818	5/29/2014	Ok
Marcus	Bird	☑	Joshua Harris	(998) 284-2499	8/6/2014	Ok
Judy	Cat	☑	Julie Cross	(300) 853-8707	1/17/2014	Ok
Rachel	Cat	☑	Ernest Hicks	(300) 871-1069	2/16/2014	Ok
Linda	Cat	☑	Juan Mckinney	(857) 820-9476	1/11/2014	Ok
Stephanie	Cat	☑	Gail Cole	(958) 734-2955	12/28/2014	Ok
Jill	Cat	☑				Error
Stephen	Cat	☑	Susan Gutierrez	(424) 750-3842	4/4/2014	Ok
Pearl	Bird	☑	Sarah Williamson	(822) 960-9675	10/15/2014	Ok
Rosemary	Cat	☑	Henry Snyder	(976) 828-7453	8/10/2014	Ok

FIGURE 5.40 Results of IIf Function

a. Create a new query in Query Design. Double-click the **Animals table**. Click **Close**. Double-click the **AnimalName**, **AnimalType**, **Adopted**, **OwnerName**, **OwnerPhone**, and **DateOfAdoption fields** to add them to the query.

You will use a combination of an IIf and IsNull function to find animals that are listed as adopted but do not have owners listed.

b. Type **Yes** in the Criteria row of the Adopted field.

You will limit your query results to animals that are listed as adopted.

c. Click in the top row of the first blank column following the DateOfAdoption column. Click **Builder**.

d. Double-click **Functions**. Click **Built-In Functions** and click **Program Flow** in the *Expression Categories* section of the Expression Builder. Double-click **IIf**.

IIf(«expression», «truepart», «falsepart») displays in the Expression Builder.

e. Click **«expression»**. Press **Delete**. Click **Inspection** in the *Expression Categories* section of the Expression Builder. Double-click **IsNull**.

IIf(IsNull(«expression») , «truepart», «falsepart») displays in the Expression Builder.

f. Click **«expression»**. Type **OwnerName**.

IIf(IsNull(OwnerName) , «truepart», «falsepart») displays in the Expression Builder.

g. Click **«truepart»**. Type **"Error"**. Click **«falsepart»**. Type **"Ok"**.

IIf(IsNull(OwnerName) , "Error", "Ok") displays in the Expression Builder.

h. Click **OK**. Replace *Expr1* with **ErrorCheck**. Run the query and compare the results to Figure 5.40.

The first Error message appears for Animal #7 (Leo). Notice Leo is listed as adopted but has no owner. Tommy can now review his records and fix the errors.

i. Save the query as **Data Entry Check**. Close the query.

STEP 4 ≫ PERFORM DATE ARITHMETIC

Tommy has been asked by a local animal control agency to provide a list of all animals that have been found in the month of January in any year. The agency is hoping to use this information to determine whether to add more part-time workers for January. You will need to help him get a list of all animals the shelter has collected during *any* January.

a. Create a new query in Query Design. Double-click the **Animals table**. Click **Close**. Double-click the **AnimalType**, **Gender**, **Age**, **DateFound**, **Weight**, and **Notes fields** to add them to the query.

b. Click the top row of the first blank column after the Notes field. Click Builder.

c. Double-click **Functions**. Click **Built-In Functions** and click **Date/Time** in the *Expression Categories* section of the Expression Builder. Double-click **DatePart**.

DatePart(«interval», «date», «firstdayofweek», «firstweekofyear») displays in the Expression Builder.

d. Click **«firstdayofweek»** and press **Delete**. Repeat the process for **«firstweekofyear»**. Remove the extra commas as well.

DatePart(«interval», «date») displays in the Expression Builder.

e. Click **«interval»**. Type **"m"**. Click **«date»**. Type **DateFound**.

DatePart("m",DateFound) now appears in the Expression Builder.

f. Click **OK**. Replace *Expr1* with **Month**.

g. Run the query. Examine the new column.

The new column now contains a number corresponding to the number of the month of the year (for example, 1 for January and 12 for December).

h. Switch to Design view. Enter **1** in the Criteria row for the newly created column and run the query.

The five animals found in the month of January appear.

i. Save the query as **January Animals**. Close the query.

j. Close the database and exit Access. Submit the database based on your instructor's directions.

Chapter Objectives Review

After reading this chapter, you have accomplished the following objectives:

1. **Establish data validation.**
   - Establish required fields: Required fields cannot be left blank, and existing records do not have to be updated if you set this property.
   - Set default field values: Automatically enters a value in a field, which is useful if a majority of new records have the same value.
   - Set a validation rule and generate validation text: Validation rules limit the type or range of data that can be entered, and validation text provides more information when the user violates a validation rule.

2. **Create an input mask.**
   - Use the Input Mask Wizard: Input masks specify the exact format of the data entry. You can use the wizard to create common input masks such as Social Security number and phone number.

3. **Create and modify a lookup field.**
   - Create a lookup field: A field with a number of repeated values may be better suited as a lookup field, which provides the user with a finite list of values to choose from in a menu.
   - Modify a lookup field by adding and deleting values: Lookup field options are usually in a separate table, so changes can be performed in that table.

4. **Create a parameter query.**
   - Create a parameter query to provide flexibility: A parameter query is a select query where the user provides the criterion at run time. It enables you to create a query for one situation and then expand it into a query for unlimited situations.

   - Create a parameter report: Base a report on a query with parameters, and the same option to enter parameters is available. Used to extend the effectiveness of the query to a report.

5. **Use advanced functions in the Expression Builder.**
   - Use the Date function: Calculates the current date. Takes no parameters.
   - Use the Round function: Return a number rounded to a specific number of decimal places. Different precision levels are available by changing the precision parameter.
   - Use the IsNull function: Checks whether a field has no value.
   - Create conditional output with the IIf function: Evaluates an expression and displays one value when the expression is true and another value when the expression is false. The expression involves some sort of comparison that can be evaluated as yes or no. You can perform six types of comparisons: equal (=), not equal (<>), greater than (>), less than (<), greater than or equal to (>=), and less than or equal to (<=).
   - Nesting functions: Using one function within another function is known as nesting functions.

6. **Perform date arithmetic.**
   - Identify partial dates with the DatePart function: DatePart enables you to isolate part of a date (day of the week, week number, month, year, etc.).
   - Apply criteria and grouping to DatePart results: A calculated field using DatePart can have criteria applied for it. Grouping also works well with the DatePart function.

Key Terms Matching

Match the key terms with their definitions. Write the key term letter by the appropriate numbered definition.

a. Data validation
b. Date arithmetic
c. Date formatting
d. Date function
e. DatePart function
f. IIf function
g. Input mask
h. Input Mask Wizard

i. IsNull function
j. Lookup field
k. Lookup Wizard
l. Nesting functions
m. Parameter query
n. Round function
o. Validation rule

1. _____ A set of constraints or rules that help control how data is entered into a field. **p. 582**

2. _____ Restricts the data values that can be entered into a field. **p. 584**

3. _____ Enables you to restrict the data being input into a field by specifying the exact format of the data entry. **p. 585**

4. _____ Creates the menu of finite values by asking you six questions and using your answers to create the options list. **p. 588**

5. _____ Provides the user with a finite list of values to choose from in a menu. **p. 587**

6. _____ Frequently used to generate data restrictions for a field based on responses to a few questions. **p. 585**

7. _____ A select query where the user provides the criterion at run time. **p. 597**

8. _____ Calculates the current date. **p. 601**

9. _____ Returns a number rounded to a specific number of decimal places. **p. 602**

10. _____ Checks whether a field has no value. **p. 603**

11. _____ Evaluates an expression and displays one value when the expression is true and another value when the expression is false. **p. 604**

12. _____ Using one function within another function. **p. 606**

13. _____ Used to create expressions to calculate lapsed time. **p. 607**

14. _____ Affects the date's display without changing the actual underlying value in the table. **p. 607**

15. _____ An Access function that examines a date and returns a portion of the date. **p. 607**

Multiple Choice

1. Which of the following is not an example of a data validation technique?

   (a) Descriptive field names
   (b) Lookup fields
   (c) Default values
   (d) Input masks

2. To make a field required, you should:

   (a) Set the Required property in the Form Wizard.
   (b) Add an input mask.
   (c) Set the Required property in the Field Properties pane in the table's Design view.
   (d) Click the Required/Default command in the Table Design group.

3. Which field data type enables users to choose from a list of options while entering data?

   (a) Lookup field
   (b) Validation text
   (c) Input mask
   (d) Parameter

4. The string of characters !\(999") "000\-0000;0;_ represents which of the following?

   (a) Lookup field
   (b) Validation text
   (c) Input mask
   (d) Parameter

5. To alter the number of options in a lookup field, you should:

   (a) Add, change, or delete the records in the lookup table.
   (b) Add an input mask.
   (c) Change the validation text for the lookup field.
   (d) Delete the lookup field.

6. A parameter query enables you to:

   (a) Specify criteria for a field when you run the query.
   (b) Find and display specific parts of a date, for example the year.
   (c) Restrict the data a user enters into a field, such as requiring the data to appear as a phone number.
   (d) Perform mathematical operations, such as rounding.

7. Which of the following statements about the Round function is false?

   (a) The Round function has two parameters: the value you want to round and the precision.
   (b) A Round function with a precision of 1 rounds to the nearest integer.
   (c) A Round function without a precision parameter returns an integer.
   (d) Round(210.45,0) would return 210.

8. Which of the following statements is false?

   (a) The IsNull function works on date fields.
   (b) IsNull returns True if there is no value and False if there is a value.
   (c) A null value means that the value is zero for any type of field.
   (d) All of the above are true.

9. Which of the following is not a valid condition for an IIf function?

   (a) Age >= 17
   (b) TodaysDate – 90
   (c) City <> "Paterson"
   (d) All of the above are valid.

10. Which of the following cannot be extracted by the DatePart function?

   (a) Hours
   (b) Month
   (c) Years
   (d) All of the above can be extracted.

Practice Exercises

1 Physicians Center

The Paterson Physician Center has asked you to improve their data entry process. They want to create a form to enroll new physicians. Because the data entry personnel sometimes misspell the members' specializations, you decide to create a lookup table. If all of the specialty areas are entered uniformly, a query of the data will produce accurate results. Before you create the form, you decide to apply some of the data validation techniques you learned. You will also create a parameter query to assist a doctor in finding potential new volunteers. This exercise follows the same set of skills as used in Hands-On Exercise 1 in the chapter. Refer to Figure 5.41 as you complete this exercise.

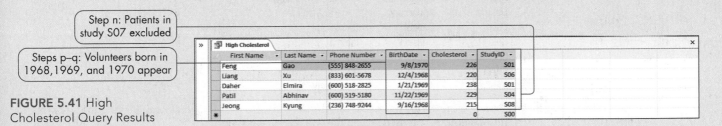

FIGURE 5.41 High Cholesterol Query Results

a. Open *a05p1Physicians*. Save the database as **a05p1Physicians_LastFirst**.

b. Open the Physicians table in Design view.

c. Click **FirstName** in the table design grid and change the Required property to **Yes** in the Field Properties pane. Do the same for the LastName, State, PhoneNumber, and Specialization fields.

d. Save the table. Click **Yes** in response to all error messages that say *Data integrity rules have been changed* and *Existing data violates the new setting*.

e. Click the **PhoneNumber field** in the table design grid and click the **Input Mask** in the Field Properties in the bottom section of the window. Click **…** on the right of the Input Mask field to start the Input Mask Wizard.

f. Click **Next** twice to accept the default mask and placeholder character.

g. Change the third screen to store data *With the symbols in the mask*. Click **Next**.

h. Click **Finish** on the final screen. Save the table and switch to Datasheet view.

i. Click the **Phone Number column** of the first record. Delete the existing phone number, type your phone number, and then press **Tab** to check for errors. Press **Esc** to exit the new record without saving.

j. Switch to Design view. Click the **Specialization field**. Change the Data Type box to **Lookup Wizard**.

k. Respond to the wizard as follows.

- Select **I want the lookup field to get the values from another table or query**. Click **Next**.
- Select **Table: Specialization** as the lookup table. Click **Next**.
- Double-click **Specialization** in the Available Fields box to move it to the Selected Fields box. Click **Next**.
- Click the arrow of the first sort box and select **Specialization**. Click **Next**.
- Widen the column by dragging the right border to the right so all data is displayed. Click **Next**.
- Click **Finish** to accept the default table name.
- Click **Yes** to save the table.

l. Switch to Datasheet view. Click in the **Specialization field** and click the arrow to verify the new lookup field is working. For each physician, click the **Specialization arrow** and select the correct specialization as listed below. Once you have completed that, close the table.

First Name	Last Name	Specialization
Takeo	Yamada	Obstetrics
Qiturah	Hamade	Hematology
Kazuo	Yamaguchi	General Medicine
Farrah	Hariri	Cardiology
Guo	Sun	Internal Medicine
Arun	Jayaraman	Exercise Physiology
Donald	Anderson	General Medicine
Pola	Dallah	Cardiology
Cala	Hussein	Internal Medicine
Charles	Smith	Hematology
Kwan	Cho	Internal Medicine
Nabila	Azizi	Cardiology

m. Create a new query based on the Volunteers table. Select the **FirstName, LastName, PhoneNumber, BirthDate, Cholesterol**, and **StudyID fields**.

n. Change the Criteria row for the StudyID field to read **<>7** so that the query excludes patients already in Study S07.

o. Change the Criteria row for the Cholesterol field to read **>200** so only patients with high cholesterol are displayed. Ensure the criteria appears on the same row as the StudyID criteria.

p. Change the criterion for the BirthDate field to read **Between [Start Date] and [End Date]** so the user is able to enter a start and end date. Ensure the criterion is on the same row as the StudyID and Cholesterol criteria.

q. Run the query. You will be prompted for a Start Date and End Date. Enter **1/1/1968** as the Start Date and **12/31/1970** as the End Date. You should see exactly five results. Save the query as **High Cholesterol**. See Figure 5.41.

r. Close the database. Close Access. Submit based on your instructor's directions.

2 Technical Support

Passaic County Technology Services (PCTS) provides technical support for a number of local companies. The human resources manager, Dora Marquez, has requested your assistance in creating a parameter query, a query that summarizes the calls by day of the week, and a query that rounds the hours a technician worked on a call. This exercise follows the same set of skills as used in Hands-On Exercise 2 in the chapter. Refer to Figure 5.42 as you complete this exercise.

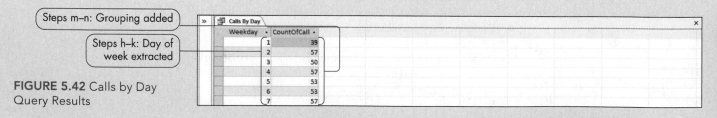

Steps m–n: Grouping added

Steps h–k: Day of week extracted

FIGURE 5.42 Calls by Day Query Results

a. Open the database *a05p2PCTS* and save the database as **a05p2PCTS_LastFirst**.

b. Open the Calls table in Design view and click the **OpenedDate field**. Under *Field Properties*, change the default value to read **Date()** so the current date appears as the default. Change the field to **Required**. Save the table.

c. Switch to Datasheet view. Click **No** when prompted to test the existing data with the new rules. Click the **Last record button** at the bottom of the datasheet to verify the new record (marked with a *) shows today's date as the default value. Close the table.

d. Open the Calls By Type query in Design view. Click in the Criteria row of the CallTypeID field.

e. Type **[Enter Number of Call Type]** and run the query. Enter **1** when prompted to *Enter Number of Call Type*. Verify 29 records are displayed and save and close the query.

f. Create a new query in Query Design. Add the CallID from the Calls table.

g. Click **Insert Columns** in the Query Setup group of the Query Tools Design tab to insert a new column before the CallID field. Click in the top row of the newly inserted column and click **Builder** to launch the Expression Builder.

h. Double-click **Functions**. Click **Built-in Functions**. Click **Date/Time** and double-click **DatePart**.

i. Click **«interval»**. Type **"w"** in place of the interval. Ensure you include the quotes.

j. Click **«date»**. Type **OpenedDate** in place of the date.

k. Delete «firstdayofweek», «firstweekofyear», and the extra commas from the expression. The expression now reads *DatePart("w",OpenedDate)*.

l. Click **OK**. Replace *Expr1* that appears before the DatePart function with the word **Weekday**.

m. Click **Totals** in the Show/Hide group of the Query Tools Design tab.

n. Change the **Total row** for CallID to Count and run the query. Your results should show that Sunday (weekday 1) has the lowest volume of calls. Save the query as **Calls By Day** and close the query. See Figure 5.42.

o. Open the Customer Billing query in Design view. Click the first empty column (following the HoursLogged column) and launch Builder. Double-click **Functions**. Click **Built-in Functions**. Click **Math** and double-click **Round**.

p. Click **«number»** and replace it with **HoursLogged**. Click **«precision»** and replace it with **0**. Run the query and ensure the new column lists only whole numbers. Save and close the query.

q. Open the Call Status query in Design view. Click the top row of the OpenOrClosed column and click **Builder**.

r. Replace *[expression]* with **IsNull(ClosedDate)**, ensuring you do not delete the existing comma. Click **OK**.

s. Run the query. Notice the cases with no ClosedDate are listed as Open in the OpenOrClosed column, while the cases with a ClosedDate are listed as Closed. Save and close the query.

t. Close the database. Close Access. Submit based on your instructor's directions.

Mid-Level Exercises

1 Hotel Chain

You are the general manager of a large hotel chain. Your establishment provides a variety of guest services ranging from rooms and conferences to weddings. Your staff need to improve their data entry accuracy, so you have decided to move to Microsoft Access and implement several data validation techniques. You also will take advantage of Access's Expression Builder to help analyze data.

a. Open *a05m1Hotel*. Save the database as **a05m1Hotel_LastFirst**.

b. Open the Members table in Design view. Add a phone number input mask to the Phone field. Save and close the table.

c. Open the Location table in Design view. Change the Required property for the City and Address fields to **Yes**.

d. Convert the Last Renovation field to a Lookup Wizard. Look the values up in the Renovation table. Save and close the Location table.

e. Open the Orders table in Design view. Add a validation rule that requires the value of the NumInParty field to be less than or equal to 75. Set validation text to **Party sizes cannot exceed 75.** then save and close the Orders table.

f. Create a copy of the Average By Day query. Name the new query **Average By Month**.

DISCOVER

g. Replace the day grouping with a grouping by month. Use the appropriate formula with the correct parameters to achieve this. Display the name (e.g., January) for the month instead of the number (e.g., 1). Name the column **Month**.

h. Run the query. Save the query.

i. Create a copy of the Average By Month query. Name the new query **Average By Month and Year**.

j. Add a second grouping field so the results are grouped by month and year. Run the query. Verify your results show both an April 2017 average as well as an April 2018 average. Name the new field **Year**. Sort by Year in ascending order. Save and close the query.

k. Close the database. Close Access.

l. Submit based on your instructor's directions.

2 Northwind Traders

ANALYSIS CASE

You are the office manager of the Northwind Traders specialty food wholesaler. You need to modify the company's Access database to help produce more reliable information. You create a lookup customers form in which data cannot be modified by users. You also create queries and reports to validate data.

a. Open *a05m2Traders*. Save the database as **a05m2Traders_LastFirst**.

b. Open the Employees table in Design view. Add a phone number input mask to the HomePhone field.

c. Change the TitleOfCourtesy field to be a lookup field. Find values in the TitleOfCourtesy table. Sort by the TitleOfCourtesy field. Accept the default name. Save and close the table.

d. Open the TitleOfCourtesy table in Datasheet view. Add the titles **Sr.**, **Sra.**, and **Srta.** on separate lines, as the company has hired a Spanish-speaking representative and may hire more. Save and close the table. If you get a warning that data may be lost, click **OK**.

e. Open the Employees table in Datasheet view. Scroll to record 10 for Claudia Mendiola. Select **Srta.** for her TitleOfCourtesy by selecting it from the menu. Close the table.

DISCOVER

f. Open the Customers table in Design view. Add an input mask to the CustomerID field so the field must be five nonnumeric characters in all uppercase.

g. Switch to Datasheet view. Locate the record for *Around the Horn*. Change the name of the company to **London Specialties**. Attempt to change the CustomerID to **99999**. If your input mask is working correctly, you will not be able to type it.

h. Change the CustomerID for London Specialties to **LONSP**. Close the table.

i. Create a copy of the Shipments By Vendor query. Name the query **Shipments By Vendor and Year**. Open the query in Design view.

j. Add a new field before Company Name. Calculate the year from the ShippedDate field and ensure the totals row is set to Group By. Name the column **Year**.

k. Add a parameter to the Year column so the user can enter a year at runtime and see one year's results at a time. Prompt the user to Enter Year. Save and close the query.

l. Open the Revenue query in Design view. Create a new field named **Net** that calculates the difference between Revenue and TotalCost. Round the Net field to the nearest dollar.

m. Add a new field to the Revenue query that displays *Profit* when the value of the Net field is greater than zero and *Loss* when it is less than or equal to zero. Name the field **ProfitOrLoss**.

n. Save and close the query.

★ **o.** Open Microsoft Word and open the *a05m2Traders* document from your data files. Save the document as **a05m2Traders_LastFirst**. Use the queries you created and modified to answer the questions found in the Word document. Save and close the document.

p. Close the database. Close Access.

q. Submit based on your instructor's directions.

3   Willow Insurance Agency

Your team works together as database consultants. You have been contracted to assist the Willow Insurance Agency modify their Access database to produce more reliable information. You will individually make a copy of the database and implement what you believe are appropriate changes. You will then meet as a group, compare databases, and write a recommendation to the Willow Insurance Agency summarizing suggested changes.

a. Divide the tables in the Willow Insurance Agency database among your group members. The three tables found in the database are Employees, Location, and Titles. If you have three group members, each member chooses one table. If you have two members, one member should choose the Employees table, and the other should choose the Location and Titles tables.

b. Open *a05m3Willow* individually. Save the database as **a05m3Willow_LastFirst**.

c. Open Microsoft Word. Open *a05m3WillowAnalysis*. Save the file as **a05m3WillowAnalysis_LastFirst**.

d. Open your assigned table(s) in Design view. Examine the current data validation for each field where it exists. Is there an input mask? Is there a default value? Is there a validation rule? Are the fields required? Is there a lookup field?

e. Make changes to your assigned table(s) in the Access database, implementing what you feel are the appropriate data validation for each field. Save all changes and close the database.

f. Record whether you feel changes are suggested for each field and what changes you recommend in the Word document. Save and close the document.

g. Meet as a group once all group members have completed their analysis. Create a new Access database named **a05m3Willow_GroupName**. Import the updated tables from each group member's database. If you made changes such as adding a lookup field, ensure you import any tables you created as well.

h. Combine your Word documents into one document, showing the analysis for each table. Save the file as **a05m3WillowAnalysis_GroupName**. Ensure you fill in the team member names at the top of the Word document.

i. Discuss the results as a group. If the group feels any changes are necessary, adjust the Word document and the database to reflect these changes. Save all changes.

j. Exit Access and Word. Submit the four files—your individual analysis and database, as well as the group analysis and database—based on your instructor's directions.

Using Unfamiliar Functions

RESEARCH CASE

This chapter introduced you to some advanced Builder functions. You will use the Internet to find an unfamiliar function and also use a familiar function in a way you did not in this chapter. Open *a05b2Builder*. Save the database as **a05b2Builder_LastFirst**.

(1) Use a search engine to find out how to combine text values in Access using an expression. Using the information from the Internet, create a query based on the Customers table that combines the LastName and FirstName fields into one field that displays the last name, followed by a comma and a space, followed by the first name (e.g., Harris, Donald). Display the Phone field as the second column. Alphabetize by the created field. Save the query as **Phone List** and close the query.

(2) Create a query to display the name of the month (not the number) and sum of the balance for all accounts opened in each month (regardless of the year). *Hint:* The total balance for October should be $9,000.00, which will require some sort of grouping. Name the calculated column MonthOpened. Sort by the SumOfBalance field in descending order. Resize columns so all values are displayed. Save the query as **Total Balance By Month** and close the query.

Close the database. Close Access. Submit based on your instructor's directions.

Fixing a Query

DISASTER RECOVERY ✚

Anthony Carmelo, a co-worker in the Finance Department, has asked for your help with an Access query he is working on. The company gives all employees a 1 percent raise to their salary every five years they have been with the company. With your help, he was able to calculate the raise using a combination of Access functions. He is running the query on 1/1/2018, and it correctly grants a longevity increase for any employees who started in 2013, 2008, 2003, 1998, 1993, and 1998. He notices employees who left the company at some point are also being granted raises. Open the *a05b3Longevity* database and save it as **a05b3Longevity_LastFirst**. Open the Longevity Bonus query. Anthony is certain that he needs to add something to the Still Active field to check if the employee is still active; that is, that the employee does not have an end date.

He has most of the query working, but he cannot figure out how to ensure the EndDate field is empty in the StillActive field. The current expression, *IIf([EndDate]=Null,"Yes","No")*, always displays *No*. He believes if you can help him fix this expression to do what he is intending, the query will work. Change the StillActive field so it displays *Yes* for employees without an EndDate and *No* for employees with an EndDate.

Save and close the query, and close the database. Close Access. Submit based on your instructor's directions.

Job Search

SOFT SKILLS CASE S

FROM SCRATCH

Amy Lee, human resources director for Moody Training, has a spreadsheet containing job applicants. She needs help converting the spreadsheet to a database and then performing some operations on the database.

(1) Start Access and create a new, blank desktop database. Save the file as **a05b4Applicants_LastFirst**. Import the Excel spreadsheet *a05b4Applicants*. Ensure that Access knows the first row contains column headings. Accept default data types. Select the SSN field as the primary key and save the table as **Applicants**.

(2) Amy would like a menu of degree types rather than having to type in B.S., B.A., and other degree types. Use the skills learned in this chapter to turn the HighestDegreeType field into a lookup field. Note: Seven degree types exist in the database that need to appear in the menu.

(3) Amy would like new records to have a default DateOfApplication set to today's date automatically and the SSN field to have an appropriate input mask applied to it.

(4) Amy noticed some applicants did not provide their degree. She would like a query (rather than a filter) to find the first name, last name, and e-mail address for all applicants with null degree names so they can be contacted via e-mail for clarification. She would like the query saved as **Missing Degrees**.

Close the database. Close Access. Submit based on your instructor's directions.

You work as the database manager at Replacements, Ltd., located in Greensboro, North Carolina. Replacements, Ltd., has the world's largest selection of old and new dinnerware, including china, stoneware, crystal, glassware, silver, stainless steel, and collectibles. Your task is to add validation rules, create a form that data entry associates can use to add new items to the inventory, and create a new table to classify merchandise as china, crystal, or flatware. You will also use queries and reports to analyze existing data.

Database File Setup and Add New Table

You need to copy an original database file, rename the copied file, and then open the copied database to complete this capstone exercise. After you open the copied database, you will create a new table that will be the source for a lookup.

a. Open *a05c1Replace* and save it as **a05c1Replace_LastFirst**.

b. Use Design view to create a new table. Add **ProductLineID** as the first field name, with data type AutoNumber; add **ProductLineDescription** as the second field name, with data type Short Text and field size 10. Ensure ProductLineID is set as the primary key. Save the table and name it **Product Lines**. Add three records: **China**, **Flatware**, and **Crystal**. Close the table.

Establish Data Validation

You need to edit the Inventory table design to validate data. Specifically, you will set the ProductLineID and SKU fields to Required. You will also set a validation rule requiring OnHandQty to contain a value of 0 or higher.

a. Open the Inventory table in Design view.

b. Set the OnHandQty and ProductLineID fields to **Required**.

c. Establish a validation rule for the OnHandQty field that requires the value to be greater than or equal to zero.

d. Create validation text for the OnHandQty: **The value of this field must be 0 or greater.**

e. Save the table. Switch to Datasheet view and test the data with the new rules.

f. Change the OnHandValue in the first record to **–3**. The validation text appears.

g. Press **Esc** to restore the original OnHandValue value. Close the Inventory table.

Create an Input Mask

To help keep data input consistent, you will add input masks to the Phone fields in the Employees and Customer tables.

a. Open the Employees table in Design view.

b. Add a phone number input mask for the Phone field.

c. Save and close the table.

d. Open the Customer table in Design view.

e. Add a phone number input mask for the Phone field.

f. Save and close the table.

Create and Modify a Lookup Field

Create a lookup field in the Inventory table for ProductLineID. Use the new table you created previously as the source for the values in the lookup field.

a. Open the Inventory table in Design view.

b. Change the Data Type of the ProductLineID field to **Lookup Wizard**. Use the Product Lines table for the values in the lookup field, select both fields in the table, accept the default sort, hide the key field from the user, and then accept the default name *ProductLineID*.

c. Save the table. Switch to Datasheet view.

d. Change the product line to **Crystal** in the first record and click the second record. If the record updates successfully, change the first record back to **China**.

e. Close the table.

Create a Parameter Query

You need to modify an existing query to add a parameter so employees doing data entry can quickly get a list of inventory below a certain level.

a. Open the Find Low Quantities query in Design view.

b. Add criteria for the OnHandQty field. The user should be prompted to Enter Threshold. The query should display all results that are less than or equal to the threshold but greater than or equal to 1.

c. Run the query. Enter **2** when prompted to Enter Threshold. You should have two results.

d. Save and close the query.

Use Advanced Functions in the Builder

You will modify the Rounded Prices query to round retail values for items in the inventory. You will also create a query to display employees in need of a performance review.

a. Open the Rounded Prices query in Design view.

b. Create a new column to round the Retail price of each item to the nearest dollar. Name the field **RoundedRetail**.

c. Create a new column to display **Luxury** for all items that have a RoundedRetail value of $100 or more and **Everyday** for items that are less than $100. Name the field **Class**.

d. Run the query. Ensure the correct values appear.

e. Save and close the query.

f. Open the Overdue Reviews query in Design view.

g. Add a new column to determine if an employee's performance review is overdue. If the employee's DateOfLastReview is null, it should display **Overdue**. If not, it should display nothing. Name the column **ReviewStatus**.

h. Add criteria of **Overdue** to the column you just created, so only the employees who are Overdue display.

i. Run the query. Ensure only employees with null DateOfLastReview display.

j. Save and close the query.

Perform Date Arithmetic

Modify an existing query displaying daily totals to display monthly totals instead.

a. Open the Order Totals By Month query in Design view.

b. Change the first column so that instead of grouping by the order date, you group by the month. Use the DatePart function to extract the month from the date. Name the column **MonthNumber**.

c. Run the query. The first line should read 5 (as the month, representing May), with a total of $5,405.89.

d. Save and close the query.

e. Close the database. Close Access. Submit based on your instructor's directions.

Action and Specialized Queries

Moving Beyond the Select Query

OBJECTIVES   AFTER YOU READ THIS CHAPTER, YOU WILL BE ABLE TO:

1. Determine when to use an action query p. 630

2. Update data with an update query p. 632

3. Add records to a table with an append query p. 635

4. Create a table with a make table query p. 638

5. Delete records with a delete query p. 639

6. Summarize data with a crosstab query p. 649

7. Find duplicate records with a query p. 653

8. Find unmatched records with a query p. 655

CASE STUDY | Replacement China, Inc.

Replacement China, Inc., is an international firm that sells china, crystal, and flatware replacement pieces. You are the database administrator for Replacement China, Inc., and need to perform several database management operations. The most urgent is the need to increase retail prices for a key manufacturer, Spode China, by 5 percent. You will use an update query to make this price increase; you will create other action queries to make additional changes to the firm's database.

Before you run the action queries, you decide to make a backup copy of the database. If a problem exists with any of the queries, you will be able to easily recover from the error by reverting to the backup copy. In addition to backing up the database as a precaution, you need to develop a method of verifying that each action query works properly. One method of verifying an action query is to check the values before running the update query and again after running it, ensuring that the values are updated properly.

You will also create another special type of query known as the crosstab query; a crosstab query will summarize data in the Replacement China, Inc., database and help the managers evaluate the sales and other company statistics. Finally, you will create two queries that will reveal tables with missing data and tables with duplicate data.

Action Queries

When you create a query, by default you are creating a select query. You begin your query design by selecting the necessary tables and then selecting the required fields to add to the query design grid. Select queries provide a subset of the data that answers most questions that users ask about the data in their databases. A select query is also flexible; you can update the underlying table data if you see an error or discover a blank field value. Another advantage of a select query is that you can create a query for one condition—for example, banquet sales in Boston hotels—and then copy the query, rename the copy, and change the criteria to extract data for a second city, for example, Miami.

Access provides four additional query types—update, append, make table, and delete—that you can use to add, edit, or delete data. The four queries are collectively referred to as action queries. An *action query* adds, edits, or deletes data in a database. You use these queries to update records that meet certain criteria, to append records to a table, to make a new table, and to delete specific records from a table. Because action queries change data, Access gives a warning when you attempt to run one. Access warns you that you are about to change data in the specified number of records and gives you a chance to cancel the changes.

TIP | Database Administrator Career

A database administrator (DBA) helps manage databases, including performing backups, security checks, and upgrades to keep data both safe and accessible. According to the U.S. Department of Labor (www.bls.gov/ooh/computer-and-information-technology/database-administrators.htm), you need a bachelor's degree in Management Information Technology, Information Systems, or Computer Science to work in this field. This Web site also contains salary information.

In this section, you will learn about action queries and how they are used to maintain databases. Specifically, you will create the following types of action queries: update, append, make table, and delete.

Determining When to Use an Action Query

Four main action queries can be used to maintain a database:

- **Update query.** An update query is used to update or change data automatically based on criteria that you specify. Rather than modifying data manually or using the find and replace tool, the update query is fast and accurate.

- **Append query.** An append query is used for adding records to an existing table. Records can be selected from various sources, such as external databases and spreadsheets. Rather than entering data manually or performing multiple copy-and-paste operations to a table, the append query is an automated process.

- **Make Table query.** A make table query automatically creates a new table from data that already exist in a database. You can create the new table in the current or another database. For example, a make table query can use criteria to make a table that archives older records that need to be stored outside of the current table. The process is automated and saves the trouble of tedious copy-and-paste operations. A make table query overwrites existing data in a table of the same name.

- **Delete query.** A delete query removes records from a table based on criteria that you specify. For example, after a make table query is run to create records in another table, you may want to remove those same records from the current table. The delete query saves the chore of having to locate and delete records manually.

The Replacement China, Inc., database, like most Access databases, requires some type of regular maintenance—usually performed by the DBA or another person assigned to these tasks. For example, customer orders that were entered last month but not filled might now be outdated. Over time, those outdated orders must be dealt with so they are not just taking up space in the database. One way to handle this type of outdated data is to move it from the primary order table to an inactive order table. You can accomplish this task using a make table query, an append query, and a delete query. First, design a make table query to create an inactive orders table based on existing data, create an append query to add future outdated orders to the inactive orders table, and then create a delete query to remove the outdated orders from the primary order table.

Another condition that exists in the Replacement China, Inc., database (and many Access databases) is null (i.e., blank) values in numeric data fields. In a list of products, each with a cost and a retail price, it is not uncommon for one of the fields to contain a null value. Access does not always calculate properly when a null is in the list of values. It is usually better to enter the value zero rather than have a null value. When null values exist, you can use an update query to replace null values with a zero. First, find all the records with null values using a select query, and then create an update query that will replace the null values with zeros. This is a good alternative to a manual or some other filter-and-replace operation. Once the update query has been created, it can be used on a regular basis to remedy this condition.

Recognize the Benefits of an Action Query

One situation that requires an action query is when an end user is required to enter the same information into many records. For example, at Replacement China, Inc., if all of the customers who had Julia as their sales representative are now going to be handled by Susan, then Julia will need to be replaced by Susan for each of her customers. An employee could complete this task manually, or you could create an action query and replace "Julia" with "Susan" automatically. To handle this situation, create a select query that lists all the customers who have Julia as their sales representative. Next, change the select query to an update query and enter Susan as the new sales representative. Run the update query, and the task is finished! Once an update query has been created, it can be used repeatedly or modified to handle different situations.

A student database in a college is another situation where an Access designer needs to use action queries. When students enroll in a school or program, they are classified as current students and are entered into the Students table. After graduation, the school likely moves them to a Graduates table. An append query is the easiest way to move records from one table to another. Create a select query to select all the records from the Students table in which the graduation date is not blank (i.e., the student *has* a graduation date). Change the select query to an append query, specify the Graduates table as the *append to* table, and then run the query. The students are now in the Graduates table. Use a delete query to remove the students from the Students table (to avoid storing duplicate data).

Back Up a Database When Testing an Action Query

STEP 1 » Action queries locate and alter data that meet specific criteria. You cannot undo updates or deletions performed with an action query. Therefore, you should exercise caution when executing an action query. Before running an action query, it is best to back up the entire database. This provides you with some insurance in case you need to recover from a mistake. After the backup is made, you usually want to create a simple select query first to test your criteria and determine which data will be modified, appended, or deleted before switching to an action query. Once you run an action query, you are committing yourself to an irreversible change.

Updating Data with an Update Query

An *update query* changes the data values in one or more fields for all records that meet specific criteria. For example, the phone company announces that all of your customers in a specific area code will now have a different area code. You construct an update query to identify records of all customers who live in the specific area code and then change their existing area code to the new area code. Another example might be in a database storing information about student athletes and their academic eligibility. At the end of each semester, you would create an update query to identify all academically eligible athletes based on their grade point average (GPA). All athletes with a GPA of 2.5 or higher would be updated to eligible.

Create a Select Query Before Running an Update Query

Prior to updating data in a table, you may first want to locate the records that need to be modified. For example, you discover that one or more orders have a missing order date—key information required to process the order. To find other orders with a missing order date, you would first create a select query.

To create a select query, do the following:

1. Click Query Design in the Queries group on the CREATE tab.
2. Add the order data table to the query design and add all fields to the query design grid.
3. Add Is Null to the criterion of the order date field, as shown in Figure 6.1.
4. Run the query to see how many orders have a missing order date, as shown in Figure 6.2.

You could then ask a customer service employee to research the orders with missing dates, perhaps by talking with user 8580, the employee who entered the orders.

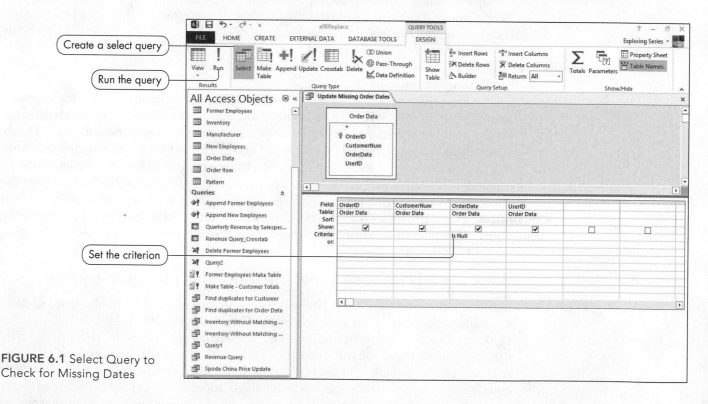

FIGURE 6.1 Select Query to Check for Missing Dates

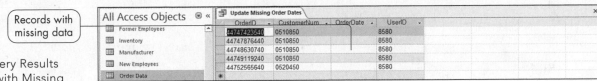

FIGURE 6.2 Query Results
Show Records with Missing
Dates

Records with missing data

Convert a Select Query to an Update Query

STEP 2 » Your goal is to update records with a missing order date. Once the records with a missing order date are found by a select query, you decide to convert it to an update query and insert the current date into any record with a blank order date so that the orders can be processed.

To create the update query, do the following:

1. View the select query in Design view (as shown in Figure 6.1).
2. Click Update in the Query Type group.
3. Enter the new value into the Update To row. In the missing order date example, type the Date() function into the Update To row of the OrderDate field (as shown in Figure 6.3).
4. Click Run in the Results group. (If you want to verify which records the update query will affect before running the query, test the query as described in the next section.)

The current date is inserted into the OrderDate field for all records with a missing order date.

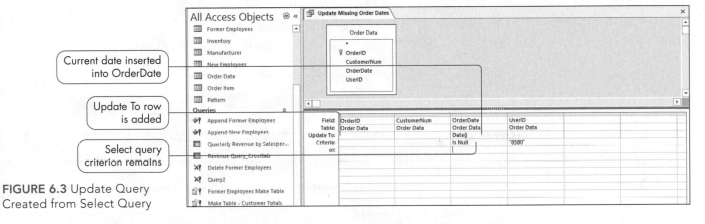

Current date inserted into OrderDate

Update To row is added

Select query criterion remains

FIGURE 6.3 Update Query Created from Select Query

Test an Update Query

STEP 3 » You can test an update query (before clicking Run) and verify that the correct records will be updated by switching to Datasheet view first. Once an update query is run, you cannot undo the action, so it is important to view the eligible records beforehand.

To test an update query before running it, do the following:

From Design view, click View in the Results group and click Datasheet view.

Datasheet view will look different than usual—most of the columns that were showing in the Datasheet view of the select query are no longer showing in the Datasheet view of the update query (see Figure 6.4). Only the column and records that conform to the Update To criteria are showing. You can use this information to evaluate the number of records that will be updated when you run the update query. Look at the number of records shown in the navigation bar at the bottom of the Datasheet view. If the number of records is what you expect, then it is safe to run the update query.

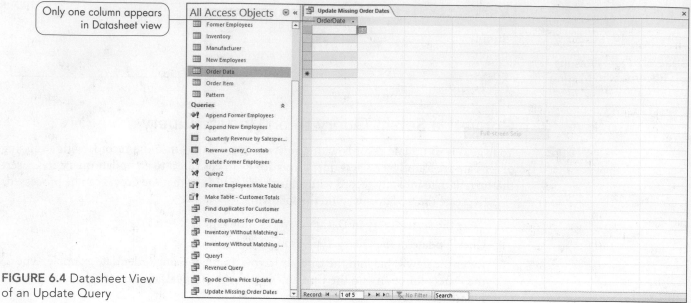

FIGURE 6.4 Datasheet View of an Update Query

To run the update query, do the following:

1. Return to the query Design view.
2. Verify that Update is selected in the Query Type group.
3. Click Run in the Results group. The five records will have the current date inserted into the order date field, after you click Yes to the Access message *Are you sure you want to update these records?* (as shown in Figure 6.5).
4. Click Yes to the warning message and the update query executes.

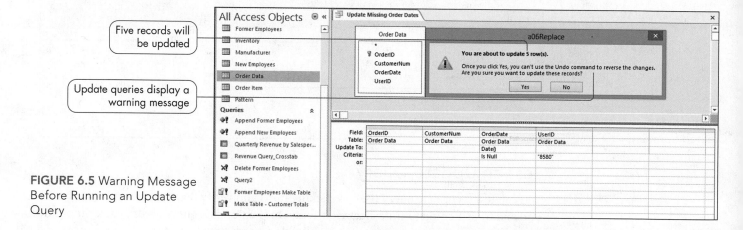

FIGURE 6.5 Warning Message Before Running an Update Query

TIP Add a New Field Before Running an Update Query

Backing up the database prior to running an update query is the best precaution. Additionally, there may be times when adding a new field to a table may be a practical option. For example, if you are reducing the values of retail prices by 15 percent, you lose the original prices after changing them with an update query. To avoid this, add a new field to the table named Retail Original (for example). Then create an update query that updates the Retail Original field with the current retail price. Next, run the update query to decrease the current retail prices by 15 percent. Now you have both the original retail price (Retail Original) and the new retail price (Retail New).

Verify an Update Query

Running an action query from Design view does not display a view of the results; Access simply returns you to the query design window. No records (with the new data) are displayed. One way to test the results would be to create a query to locate the updated records. Click Select in the Query Type group and modify the query's criteria to select the updated data. In the sample database, we inserted the current date into the missing order date fields. You would change the order date criterion from Is Null to today's date and run the query to view the corrected records.

Another method is to try to locate the original records prior to their being updated and discovering that those records no longer exist in their original state. In the example, you could select orders for User (employee) 8580 where the order dates are null. With Is Null as the criterion in the order date field, enter 8580 in the User ID criteria row and run the query. The query results show that there are no longer records for this user with missing (null) order dates (as shown in Figure 6.6).

FIGURE 6.6 Verify the Data After an Update Query

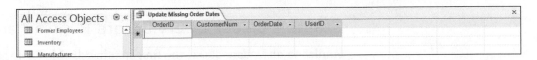

TIP Do Not Rerun Action Queries

After you run an action query, it might appear that nothing has happened except that the warning box disappears. You might be tempted to click Run again—but you should not; you may find that data is changed again unnecessarily. For example, if you created an update query to lower the sale price of all products by 15 percent, entering *[Sale Price]* * .85 into the Update To row for the sale price field would work correctly. However, running the query a second time would lower the price an additional 15 percent from the current price. In this case, the total reduction would be a 27.75 percent discount (lower than the intended 15 percent).

Adding Records to a Table with an Append Query

STEP 4 >>
Another type of action query is the append query. An *append query* copies records from one or more tables (the source) and adds them to an existing table (the destination). The appended records appear in the destination table in primary key order, or they are added to the bottom of the table if no primary key exists. If any appended record violates the primary key rule or another rule created for the destination table, the record is rejected. For example, you might use an append query to copy employee records in the Replacement China, Inc., database. Suppose the company hires new employees each week. The company may place new hires into a Candidates table until the background checks are complete. Once the checks are completed, the candidates can be appended to the Employees table and then deleted from the Candidates table. Moving records from one table to another can be accomplished with the combination of an append query and a delete query. Append queries are frequently used in conjunction with delete queries. If you use an append query to copy a record from one table to another, the original record still exists. The same data is now stored in two different places—a practice that must be avoided in a database. After the criteria for an append query are established, you can reuse the same criteria to create a delete query and delete the records from the source table. This is a common practice when working with append queries.

Often, organizations store the active records (today's or this week's activities) in one table and then append them to a more permanent table after they are completed. The tables involved with an append query—the source and destination—usually contain the same field names. In most cases, the data types of the source fields must match the data types of the destination fields. The rules for appending are as follows:

- Data types of the fields in both tables must match in most cases; however, some exceptions to this rule exist.
- All the normal rules for adding a new record to the destination table apply. For example, the records are not added if a value is missing in the source table when the field is required in the destination table.
- If a field from the source table does not exist in the destination table, Access leaves a blank in the Append To row, and you will need to manually specify the destination field name (or just delete the unneeded source field from the query design grid). If the destination table has non required fields that are not in the source table, the record appends, and the missing field values are blank.
- The destination table should not contain an AutoNumber field. An AutoNumber in the source table should append to a Number field in the destination table.

Create a Select Query Before Running an Append Query

Similar to an update query, the first step in creating an append query is to create a select query. You can use one or multiple tables for the data source. Next, select the fields you want to append from the table(s) to the query design grid. Enter the criteria to filter only the records you want to append. For example, if Replacement China, Inc., wanted to move its former employees from the Employees table to the Former Employees table, it could create a select query, and then add criteria to find employees where the termination date is not null. The results of this query are shown in Datasheet view in Figure 6.7.

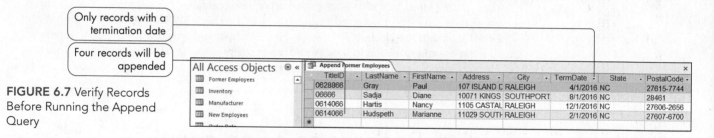

FIGURE 6.7 Verify Records Before Running the Append Query

Set Append To Fields in an Append Query

After you verify that the correct records are selected, switch to Design view, and then change the select query to an append query.

To convert the select query to an append query, do the following:

1. In Design view, click Append in the Query Type group.
2. Select the destination table using the table name arrow and click OK.

Figure 6.8 shows the Append dialog box that displays, in which you specify the destination table.

When you change to an append query, Access removes the Show row in the query design grid and adds the Append To row in its place. If the fields in the source and destination tables are the same, Access automatically inserts the correct field names into the Append To row, as shown in Figure 6.9.

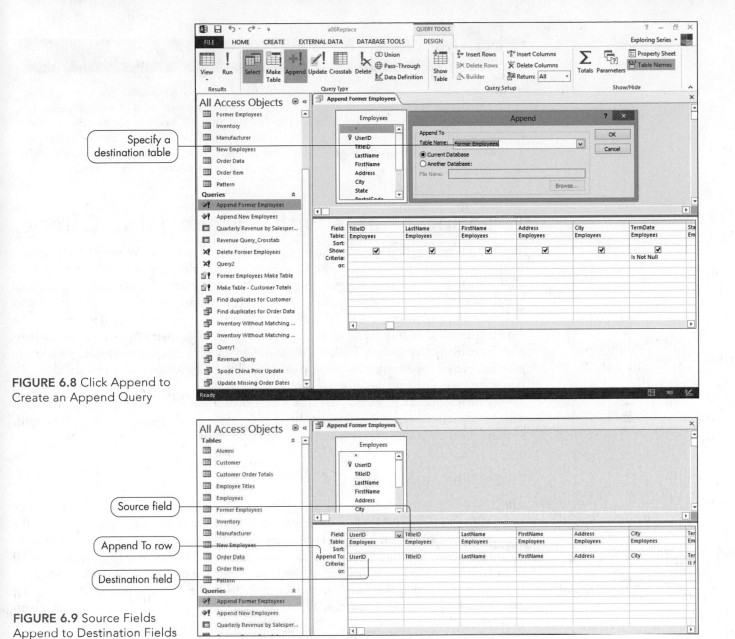

FIGURE 6.8 Click Append to Create an Append Query

Specify a destination table

FIGURE 6.9 Source Fields Append to Destination Fields

Source field

Append To row

Destination field

Run an Append Query

If you need to verify the records to be appended, you can click View in the Results group to double-check in Datasheet view. After verifying the records, switch back to Design view.

To run an append query, do the following:

1. In Design view, click Run in the Results group. You will receive a warning message telling you that you are about to append the number of records selected, as shown in Figure 6.10.

2. Click Yes to continue. As with all the action queries, you cannot undo the action after it is run.

3. Save and close the append query (if required).

4. Open the destination table and verify that the appended records are in the table.

Four rows will be appended

Append query warning message

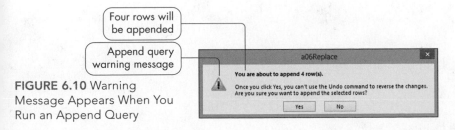

FIGURE 6.10 Warning Message Appears When You Run an Append Query

When an Append Query Does Not Append

If Access cannot append the records to the destination table, a message appears explaining the reasons why the append query failed. If the primary key value of a record you are attempting to append already exists in the destination table, you will not be able to add the record that is causing the key violation. When this failure occurs, close the message box and examine the source and destination tables. Locate the records that have duplicate primary key values and determine the best way to handle necessary changes.

Creating a Table with a Make Table Query

The third type of action query is the make table query. A *make table query* selects records from one or more tables and uses them to create a new table. Suppose that your school has a large database that stores information about students. The database has information about the classes students are registered for each term, their majors, and their emergency contact information. The Business and Technology Department needs to know the names of the students enrolled in its programs. You can use a make table query to extract the Business and Technology Department student data and then use it to create a new table. Subsequent searches can be done on the new table, reducing the response time required by searching the larger database that contains all student records.

At Replacement China, Inc., the sales manager may want to know the total year-to-date orders for each customer. You could create a make table query that would insert this information into a new table—Customer Order Totals, for example.

Create a Make Table Query

STEP 5 ≫ The process of creating a make table query is very similar to creating an append query. The difference is that a make table query creates the structure of the table and then adds the records to the table. An append query requires the destination table to exist first; otherwise, it cannot append additional records. You can use the make table query to copy some or all records from a source table to a destination table even if the destination table does not exist. If the destination table exists and you run the make table query, Access prompts you before it deletes the original table. If you click Yes, Access deletes the source table and replaces it with data specified by the make table query.

To create a make table query, do the following:

1. Create a select query; specify the tables and field names that you want to add to the new table to the query design window.
2. Specify the criteria that will result in selecting the correct records for your new table.
3. In Design view, click Make Table in the Query Type group.
4. Specify the table name that you want to create in the Table Name box.
5. Click OK.

Figure 6.11 displays the setup for a make table query that will copy aggregate order data to a new table.

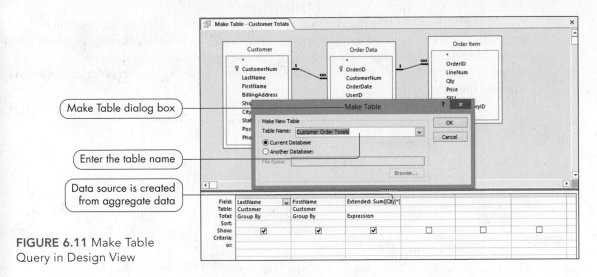

Make Table dialog box

Enter the table name

Data source is created from aggregate data

FIGURE 6.11 Make Table Query in Design View

Test and Run a Make Table Query

As with the other action queries, you should preview the datasheet prior to running the query to verify that the records are those that you intend to insert into a new table.

To test and run a make table query, do the following:

1. Click View in the Results group to view the records in Datasheet view.
2. After you verify that the records are correct, click View again to return to Design view.
3. Click Run in the Results group and Access displays a warning telling you that you are about to append records to a new table.
4. Click Yes and the new table is created.
5. Open the new table and verify the records are correct.
6. Save and close the query (if required).

If you run the same make table query at a later date, the first table is replaced with a new, up-to-date table.

Deleting Records with a Delete Query

STEP 6 ▶▶ The final type of action query is the delete query. A ***delete query*** selects records from a table, and then removes them from the table. Sometimes it is necessary to identify and delete data in a database. However, it should always be done with caution. For example, if you copy the Replacement China, Inc., database inactive customers from the Customers table to the Inactive Customers table using an append query, you will want to delete those records from the Customers table. Take precautions prior to running a delete query. If you create a backup copy of the database prior to running a delete query, you can always recover from an error.

Create a Delete Query

The delete query begins the same way as all of the other action queries, with a select query.

To create a delete query, do the following:

1. Create a select query; specify the tables and field names that you want to remove from the table in the query design window.
2. Specify the criteria in the fields that will result in deleting the correct records from your table.
3. In Design view, click Delete in the Query Type group.

At Replacement China, Inc., there may be times when they need to remove orders that were incorrectly entered on a specific date. Figure 6.12 shows the criterion to delete the orders that were placed on 6/10/2016. If you fail to specify a criterion, Access deletes all the records in the Orders table. Access displays a warning message and enables you to avoid running the delete query.

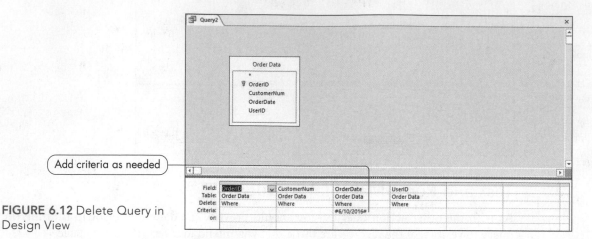

Add criteria as needed

FIGURE 6.12 Delete Query in Design View

Test and Run a Delete Query

As with the other action queries, always view the records to be deleted in Datasheet view prior to running the delete query. After you verify the number of records in the datasheet, run the query.

To run the delete query, do the following:

1. Switch to Design view, if you were testing the query in Datasheet view.
2. Click Run in the Results group to run the query and delete the records.
3. Click Yes when the warning message appears. Verify the results of the delete query by opening the table to confirm that the records were deleted.
4. Save and close the query (if required).

TIP Action Query Icons

Access denotes the action queries differently from select queries by displaying a specific icon for each action query type in the Navigation Pane (see Figure 6.13). This may prevent users from accidentally running an action query and getting unexpected results. For example, if an update query is created to increase prices by 10 percent, running the query a second time would increase those prices again. Exercise caution when running action queries.

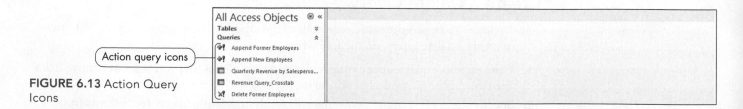

Action query icons

FIGURE 6.13 Action Query Icons

You will experiment with creating and running action queries in Hands-On Exercise 1 using the data from Replacement China, Inc. You will run an update query to identify all of the products in inventory from a specified manufacturer and increase their prices by

5 percent. You will use an append query to add new employees to the Employees table. Next, you will make a table containing the employees who are no longer with the firm. You will use a delete query to remove the employees from the Employees table who no longer work for Replacement China, Inc.

Quick Concepts

1. What is a benefit of creating an append query? *p. 630*

2. What is a potential disadvantage of running an update query? *p. 634*

3. What is a good strategy for handling mistakes that can occur while running action queries? *p. 634*

1 Action Queries

Several maintenance tasks are required at Replacement China, Inc. Before work begins, you decide to back up the database to make it easy to recover from a mistake. Each task requires an action query. After you create and run each query, you verify the changes by checking the records in the modified table.

Skills covered: Back Up a Database When Testing an Action Query • Create an Update Query • Test an Update Query • Create an Append Query • Create a Make Table Query • Create a Delete Query

---

STEP 1 ≫ BACK UP A DATABASE WHEN TESTING AN ACTION QUERY

Create a backup copy of the Replacement China, Inc., database before you create any action queries. If you make a mistake along the way, revert to the original file and start again. Refer to Figure 6.14 as you complete Step 1.

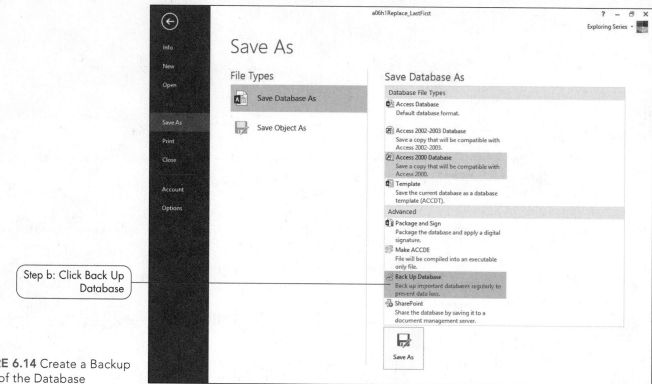

Step b: Click Back Up Database

FIGURE 6.14 Create a Backup Copy of the Database

a. Open *a06h1Replace*. Click **Save As** on the FILE tab, click **Save As**, and then type **a06h1Replace_LastFirst**. Click **Save**.

> **TROUBLESHOOTING:** Throughout the remainder of this chapter and textbook, click Enable Content whenever you are working with student files.

> **TROUBLESHOOTING:** If you make any major mistakes in this exercise, you can close the file, repeat step a above, and then start over.

b. Click **Save As** on the FILE tab, and double-click **Back Up Database**.

Before you execute an action query, it is recommended that you make a backup copy of the entire database first. If a problem occurs, you can use the backup copy to recover.

c. Click **Save** to accept the default file name for the backup copy of the *a06h1Replace_LastFirst_date* database.

A backup copy of the database now exists in your default folder.

d. Verify the backup file exists in your default folder.

STEP 2 ≫ CREATE AN UPDATE QUERY

One of your manufacturers, Spode China, has increased its prices for the upcoming year. You decide to increase your retail prices as well. You create an update query to increase the retail price by 5 percent but only for items that are supplied by Spode China. Refer to Figure 6.15 as you complete Step 2.

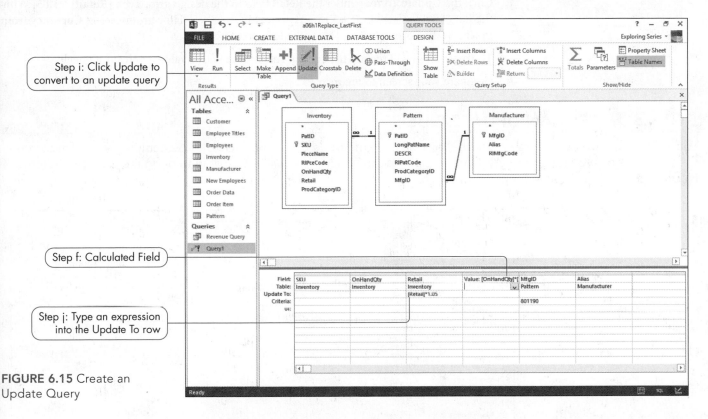

FIGURE 6.15 Create an Update Query

a. Click **Query Design** in the Queries group on the CREATE tab.

The Show Table dialog box opens.

b. Double-click the **Inventory**, **Pattern**, and **Manufacturer tables** to add these tables to the query design space. Close the Show Table dialog box.

c. Add the SKU, OnHandQty, and Retail fields from the Inventory table, MfgID field from the Pattern table, and Alias field from the Manufacturer table to the design grid. Type **801190** in the **Criteria row** of the MfgID column.

You added the criteria to select only Spode China pieces to update the prices. The MfgID for Spode China is 801190.

d. Switch to Datasheet view and verify the correct records are selected.

The results include 1,129 Spode China records.

e. Switch to Design view. Click the **MfgID column** and click **Insert Columns** in the Query Setup group.

A new blank column appears between Retail and MfgID.

f. Type **Value: [OnHandQty]*[Retail]** in the first row of the new blank column. Click **Property Sheet** in the Show/Hide group. Select **Currency** from the list in the Format box and close the Property Sheet.

You created a calculated field so that you can check the total value of the inventory before and after the update.

g. Switch to Datasheet view. Click **Totals** in the Records group. Advance to the last record.

h. Click in the **Total row** of the Value column, click the arrow, and then select **Sum**.

The total of the Value column is $911,415.88. The value after the update should be $956,986.67 (911,415.88 × 1.05).

i. Click **View** to return to Design view. Click **Update** in the Query Type group.

You changed the query type from a select to an update query. The Sort and Show rows are replaced by the Update To row in the grid.

j. Click the **Update To row** under the Retail field in the design grid. Type **[Retail] * 1.05**. With the Retail field selected, click **Property Sheet** in the Show/Hide group. Select **Currency** from the list in the Format box and close the Property Sheet.

The expression will replace the current retail value with a value 5 percent higher.

k. Compare your screen to Figure 6.15.

STEP 3 ≫ TEST AN UPDATE QUERY

You created an update query to increase the retail price of Spode China products by 5 percent, but you want to verify the values before you run the query. Once you update the prices, you will not be able to undo the changes. Refer to Figure 6.16 as you complete Step 3.

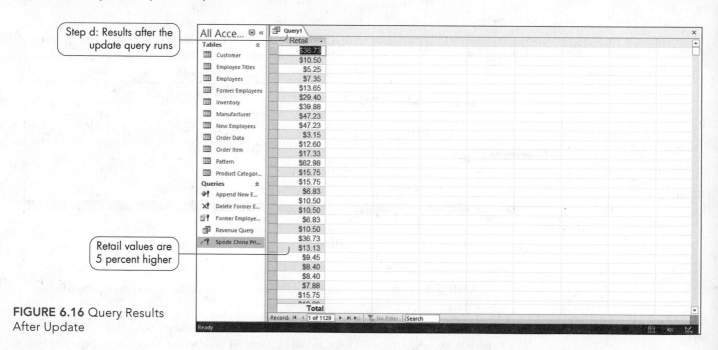

FIGURE 6.16 Query Results After Update

a. Switch to Datasheet view and examine the records before running the query.

You should see a list of retail prices ($34.98, $10.00, $5.00, $7.00, etc.) but no other columns. Access only displays the columns that have a value in the Update To row. These are the current prices that will be updated.

b. Click **View** to return to Design view.

c. Click **Run** in the Results group to execute the query. Click **Yes** in response to the *You are about to update 1129 row(s)* warning.

Although it may seem as though nothing happened, your prices have changed.

d. View the results in Datasheet view.

The first four retail prices are now $36.73, $10.50, $5.25, and $7.35, as shown in Figure 6.16. These prices are 5 percent higher than the original retail prices you saw in step a above.

e. Return to Design view. Click **Select** in the Query Type group.

f. Switch to Datasheet view.

The prices in the Retail column reflect the updated prices, and the bottom of the Retail column is now $956,986.67, which verifies that the update query worked correctly.

g. Return to Design view.

h. Click **Update** in the Query Type group to change back to an update query. Save the query as **Spode China Price Update**. Close the query.

The query icon in the Navigation Pane indicates the query is an update query.

STEP 4 ≫ CREATE AN APPEND QUERY

Replacement China, Inc., hired several new employees who were placed into the New Employees table for a 30-day probation period. The probation period is over, and now you need to add them to the Employees table. Refer to Figure 6.17 as you complete Step 4.

Step i: Append query will add four records

FIGURE 6.17 New Employees to Be Appended to the Employees Table

> **TROUBLESHOOTING:** You could make a backup copy of the database to revert back to in the event of an error. You backed up the database at the beginning of this exercise, but you may want another backup in case the append query causes a problem. If you complete this step on the same day as you completed the last step, Access adds_(1) to the end of the backup file name to distinguish it from the earlier file name.

a. Open the New Employees table in Datasheet view. Add yourself as a new record. Type **8966000** in the **UserID field**; **0626266** in the **TitleID field**; your last name, first name, address, city, state, postal code, and phone number in the respective name fields; and **9/11/2016** in the **HireDate field**.

b. Close the New Employees table.

c. Open the Employees table and note the total records in the navigation bar at the bottom of the window.

The navigation bar shows 115 current employees.

d. Close the Employees table.

e. Click **Query Design** in the Queries group on the CREATE tab. Double-click the **New Employees table**. Close the Show Table dialog box.

You have begun to create a select query.

f. Click **Append** in the Query Type group.

You need to change the query design to an append query to add the newly hired employees to the Employees table. The Append dialog box opens, prompting you to supply the destination table name.

g. Click the **Table Name arrow** and select **Employees**. Verify the Current Database option is selected and click **OK**.

The Append To row appears on the design grid, ready for you to add fields. You need all of the fields in the New Employees table added to the Employees table.

h. Double-click the title bar of the New Employees table in the top portion of the Design view window. All of the fields are selected. Drag the selected fields to the first field box in the design grid.

i. Click **View** in the Results group and preview the data you are about to append.

You should see 4 rows and 10 fields, as shown in Figure 6.17.

j. Click **View** in the Views group to return to Design view.

k. Click **Run** in the Results group to run the query. Click **Yes** in response to the *You are about to append 4 row(s)* warning.

l. Open the Employees table. Sort the table in descending order (Newest to Oldest) by the HireDate field and make sure the four newest records were added.

The Employees table should now contain a total of 119 employees. Your own name should be one of the top four records.

m. Click the **Query1 tab** and click **Save** on the Quick Access Toolbar. Save the query as **Append New Employees**. Close the open objects. Save the design of the New Employees table.

The query icon in the Navigation Pane indicates the query is an append query.

STEP 5 ≫ CREATE A MAKE TABLE QUERY

Replacement China, Inc., needs to create a Former Employees table for all employees who are no longer with the company. The records of these former employees are currently stored in the Employees table. You need to move them to a Former Employees table. Refer to Figure 6.18 as you complete Step 5.

Step j: Nine records added to the Former Employees table

FIGURE 6.18 Use Make Table to Create a New Table

a. Click **Query Design** in the Queries group on the CREATE tab.

b. Double-click the **Employees table** to add it to the query. Close the Show Table dialog box.

Some of the employees listed in the Employees table no longer work for Replacement China, Inc. You need to retain this information but do not want these records included in the Employees table; the records will be stored in the archived Former Employees table.

c. Double-click the title bar of the Employees table in the top portion of the Design view window to select all the fields. Drag the selected fields to the first field box in the design grid.

d. Type **Is Not Null** in the **Criteria row** of the TermDate field.

This criterion will select only those employees with a value in the termination date field.

e. Display the results in Datasheet view.

You should find that nine employees are no longer with the company. These are the employees you want to move to a new table using a make table query.

f. Click **View** to switch back to Design view.

g. Click **Make Table** in the Query Type group.

The Make Table dialog box opens and asks that you name and provide storage location information for the new table. You want to archive this data, but the new table can reside in the same database.

h. Type **Former Employees** in the **Table Name box**. Make sure the Current Database option is selected. Click **OK**.

i. Click **Run** in the Results group to run the query. Click **Yes** in response to the *You are about to paste 9 row(s) into a new table* warning.

j. Examine the Navigation Pane to make sure that the new Former Employees table exists. Open the Former Employees table to verify the nine former employees are present, as shown in Figure 6.18. Close the table.

> **TROUBLESHOOTING:** If your table did not come out properly, delete the query and the newly created table. You can try this query again by beginning from Step 5b. Be sure to check that the correct criterion is entered to locate employees with termination dates.

k. Save the query as **Former Employees Make Table**.

The query icon in the Navigation Pane indicates the query is a make table query.

l. Close the query.

STEP 6 ≫ CREATE A DELETE QUERY

You moved the former employees from the Employees table to the Former Employees table in the Replacement China, Inc., database. Now you need to delete the former employees from the Employees table. It is not a good practice to have the same data stored in two different tables. Refer to Figure 6.19 as you complete Step 6.

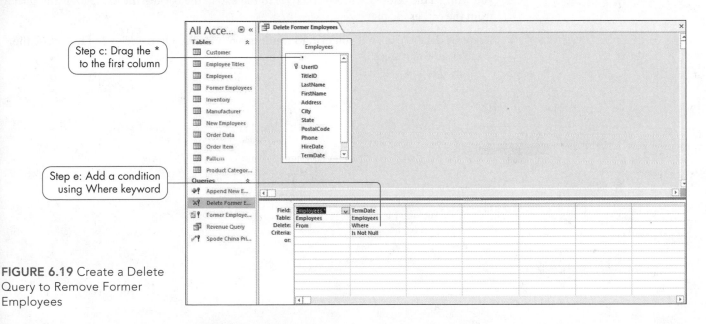

FIGURE 6.19 Create a Delete Query to Remove Former Employees

a. Click **Query Design** in the Queries group on the CREATE tab.

b. Double-click the **Employees table** in the Show Table dialog box to add it to the query. Close the Show Table dialog box.

c. Drag the * from the Employees table to the first column of the query design grid.

The * field only takes up one column in the design grid. The * field represents all the fields in the Employees table. This is a shortcut for adding all of the fields to the design grid in one step rather than one by one.

d. Drag the **TermDate field** from the Employees table to the second column of the query design grid.

You need to add the TermDate a second time to use it to set the criteria for the select query.

e. Type **Is Not Null** in the **Criteria row** for the TermDate field. Click **View** to switch to Datasheet view.

You created a select query to make sure you have correctly identified the nine records for deletion prior to changing it to a delete query. Nine records are shown in Datasheet view.

f. Switch to Design view. Click **Delete** in the Query Type group.

The Delete row now contains From in the Employees.* column and Where in the TermDate column. This delete query will delete all records in the Employees table that have a termination date.

g. Click **Run** in the Results group. Click **Yes** in response to the *You are about to delete 9 row(s) from the specified table* warning.

You deleted the nine former employees from the Employees table.

h. Save the query as **Delete Former Employees**. Close the query.

i. Open the Employees table and verify that the total employees has been reduced from 119 to 110. Close the table.

j. Click **Compact & Repair Database** on the FILE tab.

k. Click **Save As** on the FILE tab, and double-click **Back Up Database**. Name the backup **a06h1Replace_LastFirst_date_(1)**.

You just created a backup of the database you used to complete Hands-On Exercise 1. The *a06h1Replace_LastFirst* database remains open. If you complete this step on the same day as you worked the last step, Access adds_(1) to the end of the backup file name to distinguish it from the earlier file name.

l. Keep the database open if you plan to continue with Hands-On Exercise 2. If not, close the database and exit Access.

Queries for Special Conditions

This section will improve your overall effectiveness with a database by introducing you to three types of queries that are used for special conditions.

A crosstab query calculates data using a sum, average, or other function and groups the results by two sets of values. In this section, you will learn how to construct a crosstab query that displays aggregate data in a row-and-column format where each row and column presents values that you select from your database. An unmatched record is a record in one table without a matching record in a related table. A duplicate record is one where the same information is entered extraneously in a table, usually by data entry error. You will also create two special queries: one to find unmatched records and one to find duplicate records.

Summarizing Data with a Crosstab Query

STEP 1 » You can present aggregate data to the user with a crosstab query. A ***crosstab query*** summarizes a data source into a grid of rows and columns; the intersection of each row and column displays the aggregate data. A crosstab query is usually created to show trends in values (e.g., sales) over time. For example, to evaluate the sales force at Replacement China, Inc., you might want to construct a crosstab query to examine the revenue generated by each salesperson over a specific period of time. The salespersons' names would be listed along the left side of the grid (the rows). The name of each quarter (or month, for example) would be listed along the top of the grid (the columns). The intersection of the rows and columns displays the total or average revenue for each salesperson for each quarter (or month) of the year. This intersecting cell is the heart of the crosstab query. Crosstab queries can be based on a table or a query.

Group and Summarize Data

The grouping in a crosstab query comes from the definitions of row and column headings. ***Row headings*** display field names along the left side of a crosstab query. ***Column headings*** display field names along the top of a crosstab query. The summarizing or aggregating data in a crosstab query is displayed at the intersection of the rows and columns. The type of data that is displayed depends on which aggregate function you choose when you create the crosstab query—count, sum, and average are a few examples. If you want to know the quarterly sales for each salesperson for the current year, use salesperson as the row heading, the order date as the column heading, and the total quarterly sales in dollars as the intersecting values. When you assign a date field to the column heading, Access gives you an option for summarizing by year, quarter, month, or date. You can also add rows to give the crosstab query additional levels of grouping.

> **TIP** Choosing a Data Source for a Crosstab Query
>
> Crosstab queries work best when you select a data source that has at least two grouping fields. For example, if you want to evaluate a baseball team's performance over the past five years, you could create a crosstab query. The rows could list the category of the game—preseason, conference, nonconference—and the columns could list each of the past five years. The intersection of each category with each year would give you the count of the games won. If you wish to break down the crosstab query even further, you could add the Home/Away field to the rows—the data would be grouped first by game category, and then by home/away games. Then, the query could provide some additional information about the team's effectiveness while playing at home or away.

Use the Crosstab Query Wizard

You will almost always use the Crosstab Query Wizard to build a crosstab query, although it can be built from scratch using the query design grid. As with any query wizard, you first need to identify the source of the data that will be the basis of the crosstab query. Unlike other queries, you can only reference one object (table or query) as the data source in a crosstab query. Therefore, if you want to use fields stored in different tables, you must first combine the required data in a query. Once the data are combined in a single source, you can create the crosstab query.

To create a crosstab query, do the following:

1. Click the Query Wizard in the Queries group on the CREATE tab.
2. When the New Query dialog box appears, select Crosstab Query Wizard.
3. Click OK, as shown in Figure 6.20.

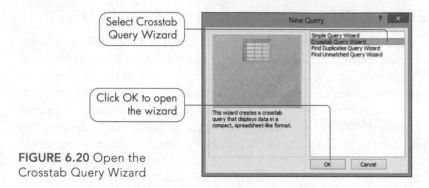

FIGURE 6.20 Open the Crosstab Query Wizard

4. Identify the data source and click Next. You can display tables, queries, or a combination of both by selecting the appropriate view (see Figure 6.21).
5. In the next step, shown in Figure 6.22, identify up to three row heading fields. To make a selection, double-click the field name or click the > button. Click Next. Access limits the number of row heading fields to three and the number of column headings to one. You can have as many aggregate fields as you want, but more than two or three makes the crosstab query difficult to read.
6. Select the field for the column headings, as shown in Figure 6.23. Click Next.
7. If the field contains date data, the next window will ask for the date interval (see Figure 6.24). Click Next. In this example, the sales data for each salesperson will be summarized by quarter.
8. Choose the field to use in a calculation at the intersection of each row and column; then choose what type of aggregate function to apply, such as Avg, Count, or Sum. Click Next. Figure 6.25 shows the result of selecting the Revenue field and the Sum function.
9. Name the query and provide information on how you want to view the new query (see Figure 6.26).
10. Close the query.

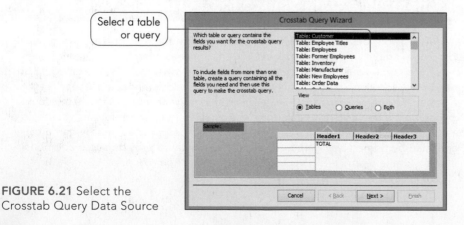

FIGURE 6.21 Select the Crosstab Query Data Source

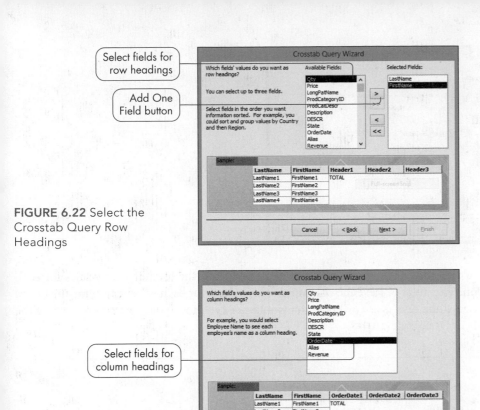

FIGURE 6.22 Select the Crosstab Query Row Headings

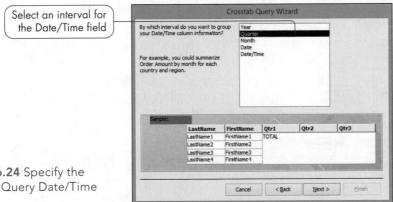

FIGURE 6.23 Select the Crosstab Query Column Heading

FIGURE 6.24 Specify the Crosstab Query Date/Time Interval

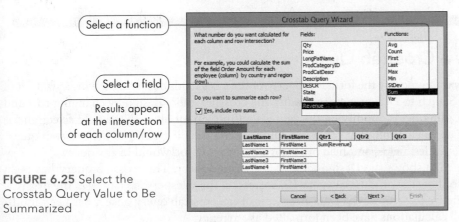

FIGURE 6.25 Select the Crosstab Query Value to Be Summarized

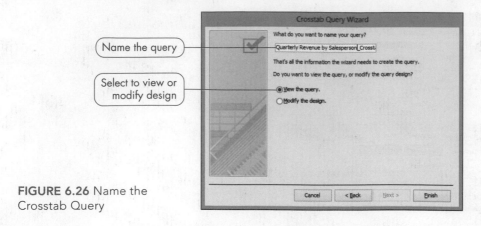

FIGURE 6.26 Name the Crosstab Query

Name the query

Select to view or modify design

Figure 6.27 shows the results of a crosstab query with the total quarterly sales for each salesperson. The Total of Revenue column displays totals for each salesperson for the entire year. To format the results as currency, you would need to modify the format property of the sales fields in Design view.

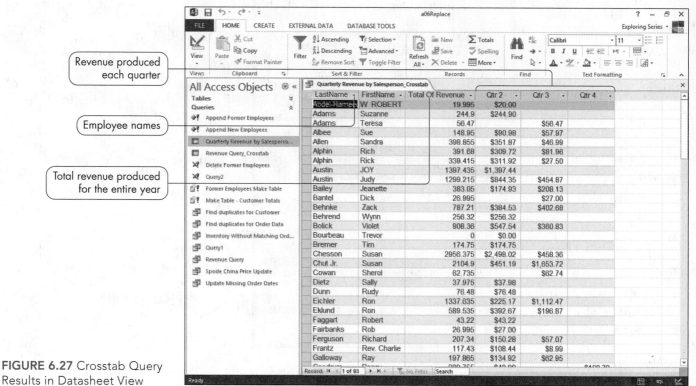

Revenue produced each quarter

Employee names

Total revenue produced for the entire year

FIGURE 6.27 Crosstab Query Results in Datasheet View

Modify a Crosstab Query

STEP 2 You may want to modify the format property of the sales fields or change the organization of the query. Switch to Design view to modify the crosstab query design by changing row and column heading fields, modifying the aggregate function, or altering the field selection for the aggregate calculation. You can add additional row heading fields to the crosstab query. Modify properties, fields, and field order for a crosstab as you would in any query.

Figure 6.28 shows the Design view of a crosstab query. The crosstab query has been modified to show the product category IDs instead of the salesperson's names as the first row heading. Figure 6.29 shows the Datasheet view of the crosstab query once it has been modified, and all calculations have been formatted as currency.

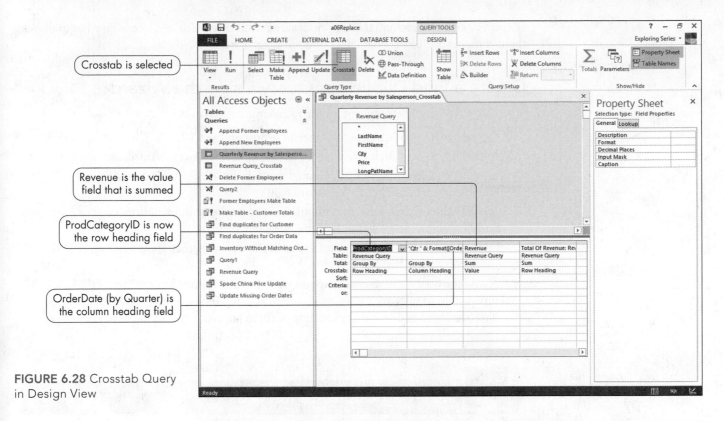

Crosstab is selected

Revenue is the value field that is summed

ProdCategoryID is now the row heading field

OrderDate (by Quarter) is the column heading field

FIGURE 6.28 Crosstab Query in Design View

FIGURE 6.29 Edited Crosstab Query in Datasheet View

ProdCatego	Total Of Revenue	Qtr 1	Qtr 2	Qtr 3
1	$31,114.33	$23.00	$18,198.41	$12,892.93
2	$26,744.52	$88.29	$14,471.53	$12,184.70
3	$15,026.88	$49.49	$7,878.41	$7,098.97

Finding Duplicate Records with a Query

If two records with the same name and address are in a table, that may indicate a duplicate entry. You might expect Access to restrict a user from entering a record into a table with the same name and address; however, because many tables use unique values as the ID number for each record, as long as the ID is different, a user would be able to enter one, two, three, or more records with the same name and address. Access can create a query to display records that are potential duplicate records, for example, a duplicated order.

Sometimes data is entered more than once by mistake. However, not all duplicated data in a database is the result of an error. Some duplication occurs naturally. For example, the CustomerID field is the unique identifier in the Customer table; no two customers can have the same ID number. However, the CustomerID field also appears as a foreign key field in the Orders table. Because of the one-to-many relationship between the Customer table and the Orders table, the CustomerID can repeat in the Orders table. One customer may place many orders. Repeating data values in a foreign key on the many side of a one-to-many relationship is standard database design—duplication is expected.

Additionally, some data values repeat naturally in a table. The city field will contain many records with duplicating values. The LastName field may contain records with the same name, such as Smith, Lee, or Rodriguez. These duplicated data values are not errors. Not all duplicated data values are problematic; however, there may be occasions when you will need to find and manage unwanted duplicates.

Use a Find Duplicate Records Query

STEP 3 You can use a *find duplicates query* to help identify duplicate values in a table. If you inherit a poorly designed database and are unable to enforce referential integrity between tables, you can run a find duplicates query to identify the duplicate values in the primary key field candidate. Once you identify the problem records, you can fix or eliminate them and then attempt to enforce referential integrity. Finding duplicate fields and knowing what to do with them remains one of the challenges of good database design.

Create a Find Duplicates Query Using the Wizard

To create a find duplicates query, do the following:

1. Click the Query Wizard in the Queries group on the CREATE tab.
2. In the New Query dialog box, select Find Duplicates Query Wizard, and then click OK.
3. Select the table or query that contains the data source for your query, such as Customer, and click Next (see Figure 6.30).
4. Identify the field or fields that might contain duplicate information, such as LastName and FirstName, as shown in Figure 6.31. Click Next.
5. Select additional fields you want to see in the query results, shown in Figure 6.32. Click Next.
6. Name the query and decide how you want to view it initially (see Figure 6.33). Click Finish. The results are shown in Figure 6.34. The first two records for Susan Agner have the same address; therefore, one of them should probably be removed.
7. Close the query.

Deleting Duplicate Records

Use caution when deleting duplicate records. For example, if two customers in a table have the same exact details but unique ID (primary key) fields, records (such as orders) may be stored using both customer IDs. Be sure to ensure that when you delete the duplicated customer record, you do not delete associated orders in a related table. Associate the orders with the customer record that you are keeping.

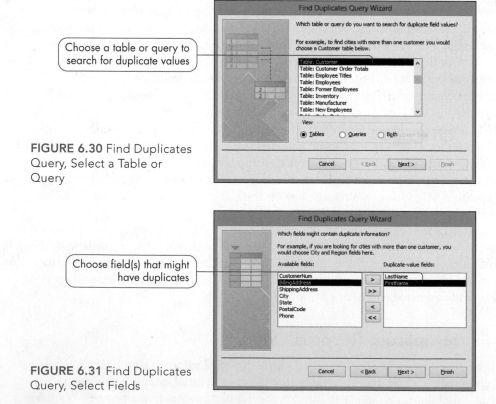

Choose a table or query to search for duplicate values

FIGURE 6.30 Find Duplicates Query, Select a Table or Query

Choose field(s) that might have duplicates

FIGURE 6.31 Find Duplicates Query, Select Fields

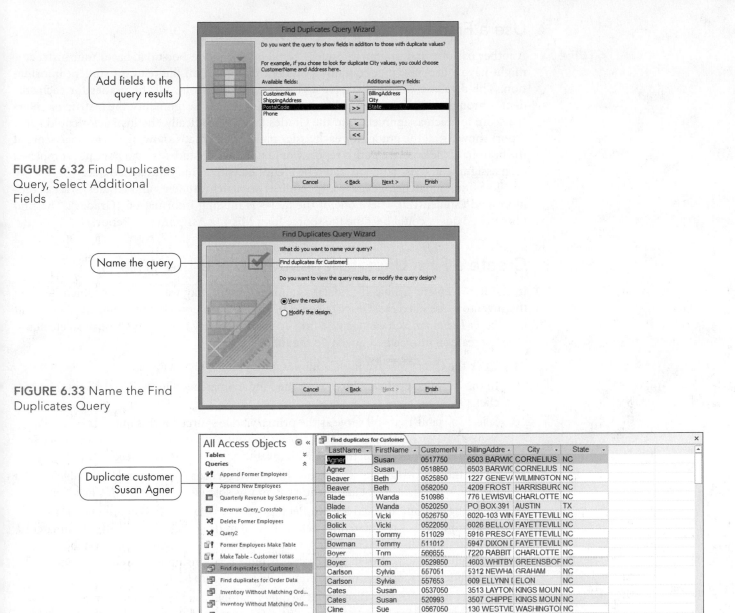

FIGURE 6.32 Find Duplicates Query, Select Additional Fields

FIGURE 6.33 Name the Find Duplicates Query

FIGURE 6.34 Duplicate Customers

Finding Unmatched Records with a Query

It is possible for a company to run reports that show which customers did *not* place an order in the past week, or in the previous month, or in the past 12 months, or ever. No matter how a company decides to handle this group of customers, it could be useful to know how many customers who receive their catalog have never placed an order. Access comes with a special query wizard that helps you find these customers. A *find unmatched query* compares records in two related tables and displays the records found in one table but not the other.

Use a Find Unmatched Query

STEP 4 » Another use of a find unmatched query could be in a grade-book database. Your instructor might have a database that contains a Student table with all the relevant student information. The database would also have a Grades table that holds all the grades for each student. Throughout the semester, as students complete their assignments, the instructor enters the score for each assignment into the Grades table. Periodically, the instructor could run a report showing all the grades for each assignment and perhaps showing the average score at the bottom of the report. But this report would not include students who have not completed each assignment; these students could be identified with a find unmatched query.

The find unmatched query would require two tables (Students and Grades) with a common field (StudentID) where one of the tables is missing information (Grades). The find unmatched query could become the source for a Missing Assignments Report.

Create a Find Unmatched Query Using the Wizard

In the Replacement China, Inc., database, management may want to know which items in the inventory are obsolete. *Obsolete could be defined as items that the company stocks that have never been sold.* You can create a find unmatched query to identify these obsolete items. To create an unmatched query, do the following:

1. Click the Query Wizard in the Queries group on the CREATE tab.
2. In the New Query dialog box, select the Find Unmatched Query Wizard, and then click OK.
3. Select the table that will serve as the primary table source for this query (see Figure 6.35). Click Next. The first table is the one with the records you want to see in the results—for example, the one with inventory items that have never sold.
4. Select the second table that contains the related records—for example, the table that can show whether or not an inventory item was sold (see Figure 6.36). Click Next.
5. Click the appropriate field in each field list, if necessary. Click Matching Fields to determine what is the matching field you want to use. Click Next. The find unmatched query only works if the two tables share a common field. Usually, the two tables are related to each other in a relationship, but a relationship is not required. Access automatically recognizes the common field (see Figure 6.37).
6. Identify which fields to display in the query output. Use the One Field arrow to move the fields you want from the *Available fields* box to the *Selected fields* box, as shown in Figure 6.38. Click Next. In this case, three fields have been selected for the query.
7. Name the query (see Figure 6.39), and then click Finish to view the results.

Figure 6.40 displays the query results.

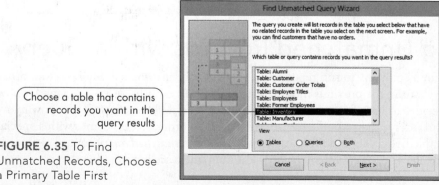

Choose a table that contains records you want in the query results

FIGURE 6.35 To Find Unmatched Records, Choose a Primary Table First

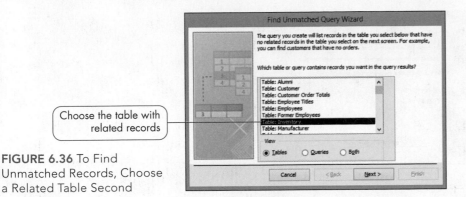

Choose the table with related records

FIGURE 6.36 To Find Unmatched Records, Choose a Related Table Second

The results will show which items in the inventory have no sales. These items can be returned to the manufacturer, discounted in order to sell them, or used as a write-off.

TIP ## Which Table Do I Choose First?

The first screen of the Find Unmatched Query Wizard asks you *Which table or query contains records you want in the query results?* Choosing this first table is not always an easy task. Select the table that contains records that may be unmatched. The second screen asks, *Which table or query contains the related records?* When you choose the second table, choose a table that shares a common field with the first one. If the two tables have more than one common field candidate, you will need to carefully select which fields you want Access to use. If you make a mistake, delete the query, start over, and then try reversing the order of the two tables.

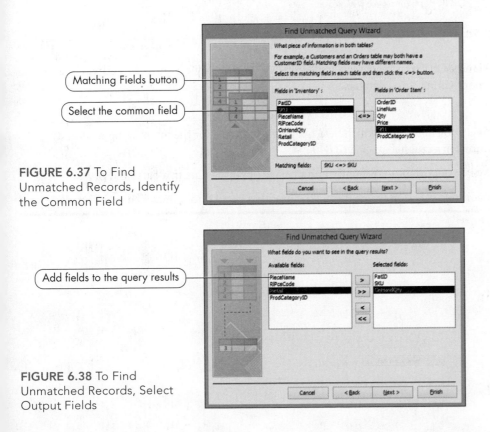

Matching Fields button

Select the common field

FIGURE 6.37 To Find Unmatched Records, Identify the Common Field

Add fields to the query results

FIGURE 6.38 To Find Unmatched Records, Select Output Fields

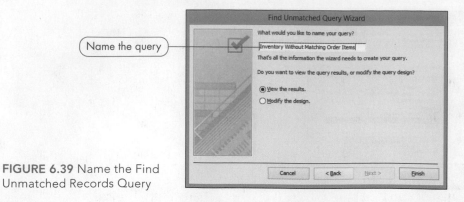

Name the query

FIGURE 6.39 Name the Find Unmatched Records Query

Inventory items that have not sold

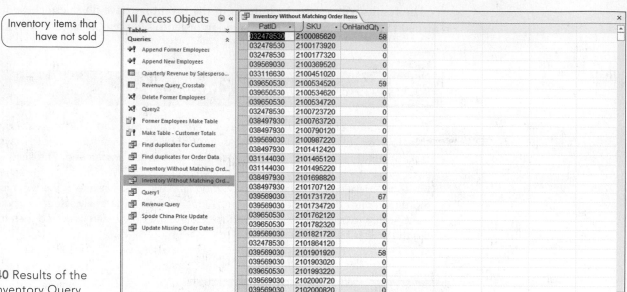

FIGURE 6.40 Results of the Obsolete Inventory Query

In Hands-On Exercise 2, you will improve your querying skills as you work with the Replacement China, Inc., database.

Quick Concepts

1. How do you determine which field is a good candidate for the intersecting rows and columns in a crosstab query? *p. 649*

2. Why is it important to recognize and manage duplicate data in a database? *p. 653*

3. What is one situation where it could be useful to run a find unmatched query? *p. 655*

Hands-On Exercises

Watch the Video for this Hands-On Exercise!

MyITLab® HOE2 Training

2 Queries for Special Conditions

Replacement China, Inc., has asked you to review their database and make a few improvements. You decide to create a crosstab query to help them look up employee information more easily. You also summarize their revenue data by state to help them analyze sales history. Finally, you check for unmatched data and duplicate data using the built-in query tools.

Skills covered: Use the Crosstab Query Wizard • Edit a Crosstab Query • Create a Find Duplicate Records Query Using the Wizard • Create a Find Unmatched Query Using the Wizard

STEP 1 ≫ USE THE CROSSTAB QUERY WIZARD

You need to analyze the revenue generated by each salesperson at Replacement China, Inc. You decide to break down the results by state. This type of summary can be accomplished using a crosstab query. Refer to Figure 6.41 as you complete Step 1.

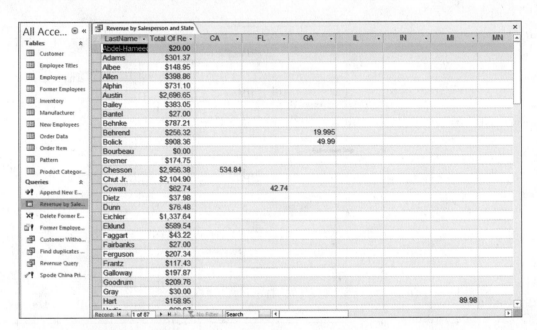

FIGURE 6.41 Crosstab Query Results

a. Open *a06h1Replace_LastFirst* if you closed it at the end of Hands-On Exercise 1. Click **Save As** on the FILE tab, click **Save As**, and then type **a06h2Replace_LastFirst**, changing *h1* to *h2*. Click **Save**.

b. Click **Query Wizard** in the Queries group on the CREATE tab.

c. Select the **Crosstab Query Wizard**. Click **OK**.

The Crosstab Query Wizard opens..

d. Click **Queries** in the *View* section of the Crosstab Query Wizard dialog box. Select **Query: Revenue Query**. Click **Next**.

You selected the Revenue query as the data source that contains revenue by salesperson and state for the crosstab query.

e. Double-click the **LastName field** in the Available Fields box to move it to the Selected Fields box. Click **Next**.

You selected the LastName field as the row heading. The query summarizes the data for each salesperson's last name.

f. Click the **State field** to select it as the column heading. Click **Next**.

You selected the State field as the column heading.

g. Click the **Revenue field** in the Fields box to select it as the summarizing field. Click **Sum** in the Functions box to specify which aggregate function to perform. Click **Next**.

You directed the crosstab query to show you the sum of revenue for each salesperson and for each state.

h. Change the query name to **Revenue by Salesperson and State**. Make sure the *View the query* option is selected. Click **Finish**.

i. Examine the results.

The data shows the sum of revenue for each salesperson in each state. However, the results are cumbersome to view. You will edit the crosstab query in the next step.

STEP 2 ≫ EDIT A CROSSTAB QUERY

The sales reps at Replacement China, Inc., would like to change the column heading field from State to ProdCategoryID. This will help the sales reps identify the sales for each product category and also reduce the number of columns in the crosstab query. Refer to Figure 6.42 as you complete Step 2.

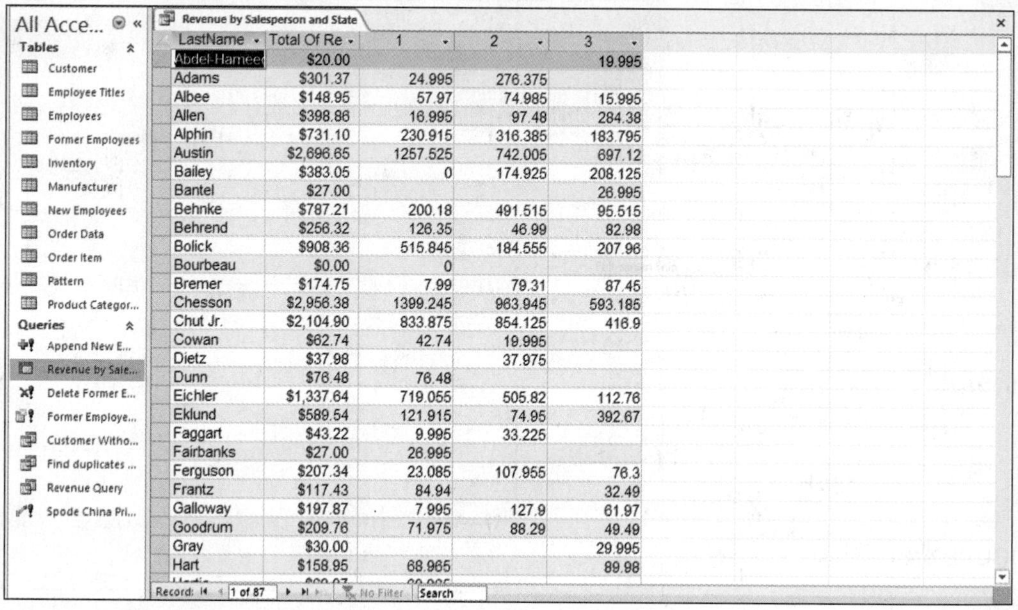

FIGURE 6.42 Revised Crosstab Query Results

a. Switch to Design view.

b. Click the arrow in the Field row of the State column in the query design grid and select **ProdCategoryID**.

The columns now show the product category IDs rather than the state names, reducing the number of columns.

c. Click in the **Total of Revenue field**, open the Property Sheet, and then change the Format field property on the General tab to **Currency**. Close the Property Sheet.

d. Click **Run** in the Results group to see the new results. Double-click the right border of the *Total of Revenue* column so all of the data displays.

e. Save the changes and close the query.

One of the data entry employees believes duplicate entries are present in the Pattern table. You create a query to look for duplicates in the LongPatName field in the Pattern table. If duplicates do exist, the company will need to move all orders to one Pattern and then delete the other Pattern. Refer to Figure 6.43 as you complete Step 3.

Step e: Two duplicates exist in the LongPatName field

FIGURE 6.43 Results of the Find Duplicate Records Query

a. Click **Query Wizard** on the CREATE tab and select **Find Duplicates Query Wizard** to create a find duplicates query. Click **OK**.

b. Click **Table: Pattern** (scroll down, if necessary). Click **Next**.

c. Double-click the **LongPatName** in the Available fields box to move it to the Duplicate-value fields box. Click **Next**.

d. Click >> to move the rest of the fields in the table from the Available fields box to the Additional query fields box. Click **Next**.

e. Click **Finish** to accept the default name, *Find duplicates for Pattern*, and the option to view the results.

The query runs and opens in Datasheet view. It contains four records showing two duplicate LongPatName fields.

f. Save the query. Close the query.

STEP 4 ≫ CREATE A FIND UNMATCHED QUERY USING THE WIZARD

The Marketing Manager at Replacement China, Inc., asked you to identify the customers who have not placed orders. You create a find unmatched query to find the customers who have no records in the Order Data table. Someone from the Marketing Department will contact these customers and offer them an incentive to place an order. Refer to Figure 6.44 as you complete Step 4.

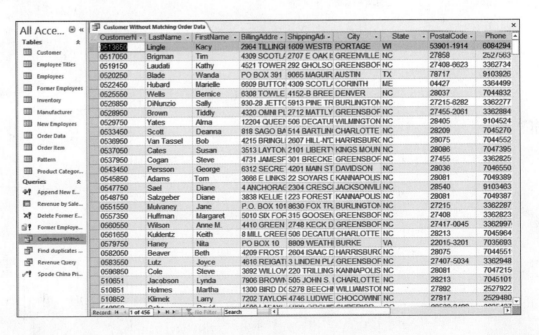

FIGURE 6.44 Customers Who Have Not Ordered

a. Click **Query Wizard** in the Queries group on the CREATE tab. Select the **Find Unmatched Query Wizard** in the New Query dialog box and click **OK**.

You need to create a find unmatched query to find the customers who have not placed an order.

b. Click **Table: Customer** to select the Customer table. Click **Next**.

You selected the Customer table as the first table. You will select the Order Data table next so you can find customers who have not ordered.

c. Click **Table: Order Data** and click **Next**.

You selected the Order Data table as the second table so you can find customers who have not ordered.

d. Click **Next** at the next screen.

Access identifies the common field (CustomerNum) that exists in both tables.

e. Click **>>** to add all of the fields to the query. Click **Next**.

f. Click **Finish** to accept the default name and the option to view the results.

456 customers have not placed an order.

g. Save the query. Close the query.

h. Click **Compact & Repair Database** on the FILE tab.

i. Close the database. Close Access.

j. Submit based on your instructor's directions.

Chapter Objectives Review

After reading this chapter, you have accomplished the following objectives:

1. **Determine when to use an action query.**
   - Recognize the benefits of an action query: Action queries add, edit, or delete the data in a database. These four queries—update, append, make table, and delete—are used for updating records that meet certain criteria, for appending records to a table, for making a new table, and for deleting specific records from a table.
   - Back up a database when testing an action query: Action queries change data in your database, so it is important to back up your database in case it needs to be restored.

2. **Update data with an update query.**
   - Create a select query before running an update query: Create a select query to define the fields and criteria to be used in your update query.
   - Convert a select query to an update query: An update query changes the data values in one or more fields for all records that meet a specific criterion. The update query defines precisely how field values will be updated.
   - Test an update query: View the update query in Datasheet view to determine which records will be affected before you run it.
   - Verify an update query: Open the table to determine the results of the updates.

3. **Add records to a table with an append query.**
   - Create a select query before running an append query: Create a select query to define the fields and criteria to be used in your append query.
   - Set Append To fields in an append query: An append query selects records from one or more tables and adds them to another table. The append query will define precisely how fields and records will be appended.
   - Run an Append Query: If you need to verify the records to be appended, you can click View in the Results group to double-check in Datasheet view.

4. **Create a table with a make table query.**
   - Create a make table query: A make table query selects records from one or more tables and uses them to create a new table.

   - Test and run a make table query: View the make table query in Datasheet view to determine which records will be added to the new table before you run it.

5. **Delete records with a delete query.**
   - Create a delete query: A delete query selects records from a table and then removes them from the table.
   - Test and run a delete query: View the delete query in Datasheet view to determine which records will be deleted from the table before you run it.

6. **Summarize data with a crosstab query.**
   - Group and summarize data: A crosstab query summarizes a data source into a grid of rows and columns; the intersection of each row and column displays valuable aggregate data.
   - Use the Crosstab Query Wizard: The wizard guides you through the steps of creating the crosstab query, including setting the row and column headings.
   - Modify a crosstab query: In Design view, you can modify the row/column headings of the query, format fields, and summarize the data in different ways.

7. **Find duplicate records with a query.**
   - Use a find duplicate records query: The Find Duplicates Query Wizard is used to help identify duplicated values in a table. However, not all duplicated data in a database are the result of an error.
   - Create a find duplicates query using the wizard: The wizard guides you through the steps of creating the query, including identifying which fields to search for duplicated data.

8. **Find unmatched records with a query.**
   - Use a find unmatched query: The Find Unmatched Query Wizard creates a query that compares records in two related tables and returns the records found in one table but not the other.
   - Create a find unmatched query using the wizard: The wizard guides you through the steps of creating the query, including identifying which fields to search for unmatched data.

Key Terms Matching

Match the key terms with their definitions. Write the key term letter by the appropriate numbered definition.

- **a.** Action query
- **b.** Append query
- **c.** Column headings
- **d.** Crosstab query
- **e.** Delete query
- **f.** Find duplicates query
- **g.** Find unmatched query
- **h.** Make table query
- **i.** Row headings
- **j.** Update query

1. _____ A query that selects records from one or more tables (the source) and adds them to an existing table (the destination). **p. 635**

2. _____ A query that compares records in two related tables, and then displays the records found in one table but not the other. **p. 655**

3. _____ A query that summarizes a data source into a few key rows and columns; the intersection of each row and column displays aggregate data. **p. 649**

4. _____ A query that selects records from one or more tables and uses them to create a new table. **p. 638**

5. _____ The field names displayed along the left side of a crosstab query. **p. 649**

6. _____ A query that selects records from a table and then removes them from the table. **p. 639**

7. _____ The field name displayed at the top of a crosstab query. **p. 649**

8. _____ A query that adds, updates, or deletes data in a database. **p. 630**

9. _____ A query that changes the data values in one or more fields for all records that meet specific criteria. **p. 632**

10. _____ A query that helps you identify repeated values in a table. **p. 653**

Multiple Choice

1. Which one of the following tasks could not be completed with an action query?

   (a) Deleting records from a table

   (b) Updating records in a table

   (c) Displaying data based on a value entered at run time

   (d) Creating a new table based on a group of selected records

2. Which statement is true about action queries?

   (a) Users use action queries more frequently than database administrators.

   (b) You can run an action query as many times as you like.

   (c) A delete query is not an action query.

   (d) Action queries should be executed with caution because you cannot undo their changes.

3. Which query below is used as a basis to create the other three?

   (a) Select query

   (b) Update query

   (c) Delete query

   (d) Append query

4. Your company merged with another company, and now the two customer lists are combined into one table. Because the two companies had many of the same customers, the customer table now contains many duplicate customers with different account numbers. What is the best way to resolve this problem?

   (a) Delete duplicate customers manually.

   (b) Create a select query showing all customers in alphabetical order and then run a delete query to delete every other record.

   (c) It will not affect overall performance of the database to have duplicated records, so leave the table as is.

   (d) Use a find duplicates query to locate duplicate customers. Delete one of the duplicates.

5. Why is it important to monitor how many times an update query is executed?

   (a) Update queries are capable of changing values (such as prices) more than one time.

   (b) Update queries can be used to delete records from your tables.

   (c) It is not important; you can always undo the results of an update query.

   (d) An update query can erase your table and create a new one in its place.

6. Which statement is true about action queries?

   (a) An append query is usually run after an update query.

   (b) A delete query is usually run before an update query.

   (c) A delete query is usually run after an append query.

   (d) Make table queries are usually constructed from an update query.

7. Why would you use an update query?

   (a) Because users need to be able to select records based on varied selection criteria

   (b) To determine which records may need to be deleted from the database

   (c) To summarize the data in a firm's database to help managers evaluate their financial position

   (d) To increase retail prices in a firm's database

8. How do you create a crosstab query?

   (a) Click Crosstab Query on the Create tab.

   (b) Click Query Wizard and select Crosstab Query Wizard for the query type.

   (c) Click Crosstab Query on the Database Tools tab.

   (d) Create a select query and convert it to a crosstab query.

9. What is an unmatched record?

   (a) A record that contains the primary key in the one table

   (b) A record that requires deletion when running a delete query

   (c) A duplicated record that cannot be connected to a parent record

   (d) A record in one table without a matching record in a related table

10. What is the best way to find students who have not attended a certain class?

    (a) Create a select query of attendance and compare the results to the student roster.

    (b) Create a select query of attendance and use the query to create an update query.

    (c) Create a select query of attendance for the students in the class. Then create a find duplicates query using the attendance table.

    (d) Create a find unmatched query using the student and attendance tables.

Practice Exercises

1 National Bank

You are the DBA for a national bank. The bank has decided to decrease mortgage loans by a half percent. You use an update query to modify the mortgage rates. In addition, you decide to move all mortgages from the loans table to a new mortgages table. You delete the mortgages from the loans table after they are moved. This exercise follows the same set of skills as used in Hands-On Exercise 1 in the chapter. Refer to Figures 6.45 and 6.46 as you complete this exercise.

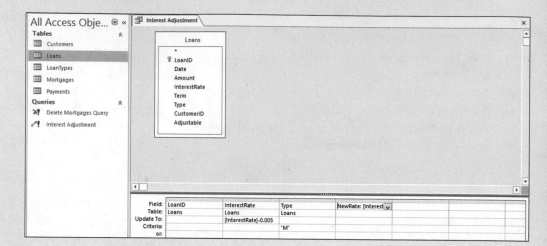

FIGURE 6.45 Update Query to Decrease Rates by 0.50 Percent

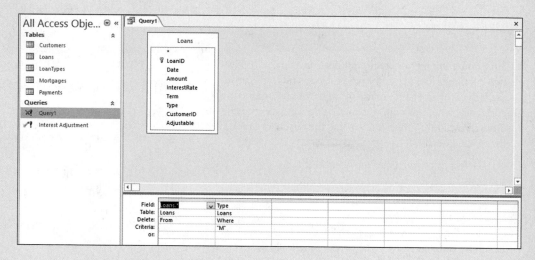

FIGURE 6.46 Query Design to Delete Mortgages from Loans Table

a. Open *a06p1Bank*. Click **Save As** on the FILE tab, click **Save As**, and then type **a06p1Bank_LastFirst**. Click **Save**.

b. Click **Query Design** in the Queries group on the CREATE tab. Double-click the **Loans table** in the Show Table dialog box to add it to the query. Close the Show Table dialog box.

c. Double-click the **LoanID**, **InterestRate**, and **Type fields**. Click **Run** in the Results group. Save the query as **Interest Adjustment**.

d. Switch to Design view. Type **M** in the **Criteria row** of the Type column.

   Entering *M* in the Criteria row of the Type column will isolate only those loans that are mortgages.

e. Click in the **Field row** of the fourth column and type **NewRate: [InterestRate] - 0.0050**. Press **Enter**.

   You have created a new field with the calculation for the new interest rate, which decreases by 0.50 percent.

f. Click **Property Sheet** in the Show/Hide group with the calculated field column selected. Change the Format property to **Percent**. Close the Property Sheet.

g. Click **Run** in the Results group and examine the results of the NewRate calculated field.

h. Switch to Design view. Click **Update** in the Query Type group. Click in the **Update To row** of the InterestRate field and type **[InterestRate] - 0.0050**.

The update query changes the existing interest rates to the lower interest rates calculated in the NewRate field. Compare your query design to Figure 6.45.

i. Click **View** in the Results group to verify that 12 records will be updated. Switch back to Design view.

j. Click **Run** in the Results group. Click **Yes** in response to the Warning box. Save and close the query.

k. Open the Loans table and verify the Mortgage loan interest rates are 0.50 percent lower. Close the table.

l. Click **Query Design** in the Queries group on the CREATE tab. Double-click the **Loans table** in the Show Table dialog box. Close the Show Table dialog box.

m. Double-click the title bar of the Loans table to select all the fields and drag them to the first column in the design grid.

n. Click **Run** in the Results group to run the query.

o. Switch back to Design view. Type **M** in the **Criteria row** of the Type column. Click **Run** in the Results group to run the query.

You only want to see the mortgages in the query results.

p. Switch back to Design view. Click **Make Table** in the Query Type group and type **Mortgages** as the new table name. Accept the default setting of Current Database and click **OK**.

q. Switch to Datasheet view to verify that only the 12 mortgage loans will be affected.

r. Switch to Design view. Click **Run** in the Results group. Click **Yes** in response to the Warning box.

s. Double-click the **Mortgages table** in the Navigation Pane. Verify that the 12 mortgages are in the table. Close the table.

t. Click **Delete** in the Query Type group on the DESIGN tab to change the make table query to a delete query.

u. Delete all the columns in the query design grid except the Type column.

The Type column contains the criterion you need for the delete query.

v. Drag the *** field** from the Loans table to the first column in the query design grid.

Compare your query design to Figure 6.46.

w. Click **Run** in the Results group. Click **Yes** in response to the Warning box.

x. Save the query as **Delete Mortgages Query**. Close the query.

y. Compact and repair the database. Close the database. Close Access.

z. Submit based on your instructor's directions.

2 Break Room Suppliers, Inc.

Break Room Suppliers, Inc., is a small service organization that provides coffee, tea, and snacks to local businesses. You have been asked to review the database and create several queries; these queries can be run periodically by the owner. This exercise follows the same set of skills as used in Hands-On Exercises 1 and 2 in the chapter. Refer to Figures 6.47 and 6.48 as you complete this exercise.

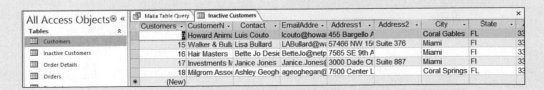

FIGURE 6.47 Inactive Customers Table

FIGURE 6.48 Crosstab Query Showing Profit for Each City

City	Total Of Re	2/1/2016	2/11/2016	2/12/2016	2/14/2016	2/19/2016	2/20/2016
Coconut Grove	$582.00						
Coral Springs	$392.75						$118.50
Miami	$1,812.88	$301.50	$114.00	$50.13	$201.75	$34.00	$42.50

All Access Objects
Tables
- Customers
- Inactive Customers

Profit Summary_Crosstab

a. Open *a06p2Coffee*. Click **Save As** on the FILE tab, click **Save As**, and then type **a06p2Coffee_LastFirst**. Click **Save**.

b. Double-click the **Sales Reps table** to open it. Replace *Your_Name* with your name. Close the table.

c. Click **Query Wizard** in the Queries group on the CREATE tab. Click **Find Unmatched Query Wizard**, click **OK**, and then answer the wizard questions as follows:
  - Select **Table: Customers** as the first table. Click **Next**.
  - Select **Table: Orders** as the second table. Click **Next**.
  - Accept the CustomerID field as the common field. Click **Next**.
  - Click >> to move all of the fields in the Available fields box to the Selected fields box. Click **Next**.
  - Accept *Customers Without Matching Orders* as the query name and click **Finish** to display the four inactive customers. Leave the Customers Without Matching Orders query open.

d. Switch to Design view. Click **Make Table** in the Query Type group and follow these steps:
  - Type **Inactive Customers** in the **Table Name box**. Click **OK**.
  - Click **View** in the Results group to verify that four customers are shown.
  - Click **View** to return to Design view.
  - Click **Run** in the Results group to run the make table query.
  - Click **Yes** in response to the Warning box.
  - Click **Save As** on the FILE tab, click **Save Object As**, and then click **Save As**. Save the copy of the query with the name **Make Table Query**. Click **OK**.

e. Open the Inactive Customers table to verify that the four records have been archived. Close the table.

f. Ensure the Customers Without Matching Orders query is open. Click the **DESIGN tab**, click **Delete** in the Query Type group, and then follow these steps:
  - Right-click the **Orders table** and select **Remove Table**.
  - Type **9 Or 15 Or 16 Or 17** into the **Criteria row** of the CustomerID column.
  - Click **View** in the Results group to verify that four customers are shown.
  - Click **View** to return to Design view.
  - Click **Run** in the Results group to run the delete query.
  - Click **Yes** in response to the Warning box.
  - Click **Save As** on the FILE tab, click **Save Object As**, and then click **Save As**. Save the copy of the query with the name **Delete Inactive Customers Query**.
  - Close the query.

  You have deleted the inactive customers (IDs 9, 15, 16, and 17) from the Customers table.

g. Create a copy of the Delete Inactive Customers Query and rename it as **Append Inactive Customers Query**.
  - View the query in Design view.
  - Click **Append** in the Query Type group. Append to Inactive Customers and click **OK**.
  - Delete the existing criterion and type **5** into the **Criteria row** of the CustomerID column.
  - Click **View** in the Results group to verify that one customer is shown.
  - Click **View** to return to Design view.
  - Click **Run** in the Results group to run the append query.
  - Click **Yes** in response to the Warning box.
  - Save and close the query.

  You have appended CustomerID 5 to the Inactive Customers table, as shown in Figure 6.47. Note that because CustomerID is an AutoNumber field in the Inactive Customers table, the record will be renumbered when appended to that table.

h. Click **Query Wizard** in the Queries group on the CREATE tab. Click **Crosstab Query Wizard**, click **OK**, and then follow these steps:

- Click **Queries** in the *View* section.
- Click **Query: Profit Summary**. Click **Next**.
- Click **City** and click > to select it as the Row heading. Click **Next**.
- Click **OrderDate** to select it for the Column heading. Click **Next**.
- In the next screen, click **Date** and click **Next**.
- Click **Revenue** as the calculated field and click **Sum** as the aggregate function. Click **Next**.
- Click **Finish** to accept *Profit Summary_Crosstab* as the query name and view the query results. Compare your results to Figure 6.48.
- Save and close the query.

i. Click **Query Wizard** in the Queries group on the CREATE tab. Click **Find Duplicates Query Wizard**, click **OK**, and then follow these steps:

- Click **Table: Customers**. Click **Next**.
- Click **Contact** and click > to search for duplicates in this field. Click **Next**.
- Click >> to indicate you want to see all the additional fields. Click **Next**.
- Type **Find contact duplicates in Customers** as the query name. Click **Finish**.
- Close the query.

j. Compact and repair the database.

k. Close the database. Close Access.

l. Submit based on your instructor's directions.

Mid-Level Exercises

1 Northwind Traders

Northwind Traders is a small international specialty foods distribution firm. Management has decided to close their North and South American operations and concentrate on their European markets. They have asked you to update certain customer records and to move all deactivated customers to another table. Once you move the records, you will delete them from the original table. Refer to Figure 6.49 as you complete this exercise.

FIGURE 6.49 Deactivated Customers Table Created with Action Queries

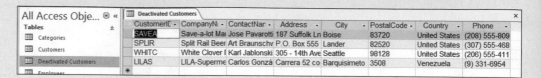

a. Open *a06m1Exporters*. Click **Save As** on the FILE tab, click **Save As**, and then type **a06m1Exporters_ LastFirst**. Click **Save**.

b. Create a select query based on all of the fields from the Customers table. Add criteria to show only customers in the USA. Run the query.

c. Change the query to an update query that replaces all instances of *USA* with **United States**. Run the query. Save the query as **Update US Customers**. Close the query.

d. Create a make table query that is based on all of the fields in the Customers table. Name the new table **Deactivated Customers**. Add criteria to select only United States customers. Run the query and save it as **Make Table Query**. Close the query.

e. Make a copy of the Make Table Query in the Navigation Pane and name the copy **Append Query**. Right-click the new **Append Query** and select **Design View** from the list.

f. Change the query type to **Append**. Append records to the Deactivated Customers table. Change the criteria of the Country field to **Venezuela**. Run the query. Save and close the query.

g. Make a copy of the Append Query in the Navigation Pane and name the copy **Delete Query**. Right-click the new **Delete Query** and choose **Design View** from the list.

h. Change the query type to **Delete**. Change the Country criteria to **United States Or Venezuela**. Delete all the columns in the query design grid except the Country column. Run the query. Save and close the query. Open the Deactivated Customers table to view the records added by the make table and append queries. Close the table.

i. Close the database. Close Access.

j. Submit based on your instructor's directions.

2 Hotel Chain

ANALYSIS CASE

You are assisting the general manager of a large hotel chain. You need to perform several tasks for the general manager including calculating the total revenue for each service for each city. You also need to find duplicate names in the members table. Refer to Figures 6.50 and 6.51 as you complete this exercise.

FIGURE 6.50 Crosstab Query Displays Revenue by Service and City

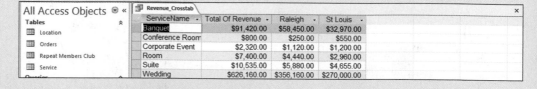

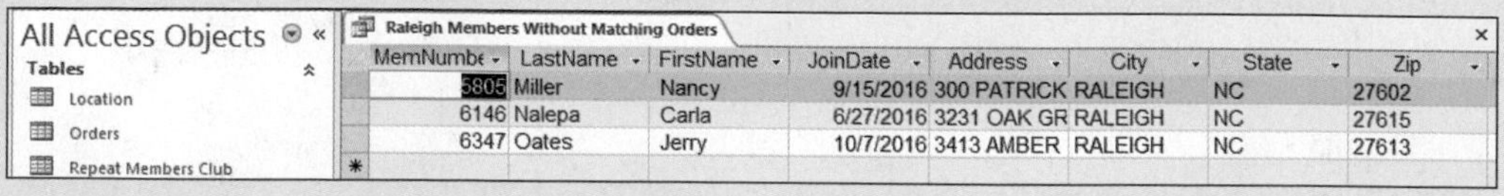

FIGURE 6.51 Raleigh Members Without Matching Orders

a. Open *a06m2Rewards*. Click **Save As** on the FILE tab, click **Save As**, and then type **a06m2Rewards_LastFirst**. Click **Save**.

b. Create a crosstab query based on the Revenue query. Use the ServiceName field for the row heading, the City field for the column heading, and the Revenue field for the column and row intersection. Sum the Revenue field. Save the query as **Revenue_Crosstab**.

c. Format the Revenue and Total of Revenue crosstab values as **Currency**. Run the query. Compare your results to Figure 6.50. Save and close the Revenue_Crosstab query.

DISCOVER

d. Create a copy of the Revenue_Crosstab query and save it as **Revenue_Crosstab2**.

e. Modify the query so that the City field is the row heading and the ServiceName field is the column heading. Run the query, save the query, and close it.

f. Create a find unmatched query that displays repeat members from Raleigh. Records from the Repeat Members Club table should display in the results. Include all fields from the table. Test the query and save it as **Raleigh Members Without Matching Orders**. Compare your results to Figure 6.51. Print the results of the query and submit to your instructor.

g. Create a copy of the Raleigh Members Without Matching Orders query and save it as **Charlotte Members Without Matching Orders**.

h. Modify the query so that Charlotte members who have not used any hotel services are displayed in the results.

i. Create a find duplicates query that displays any locations that have the same city and address. Display the LocationID field as an additional field in the query. Run the query and save it as **Find Duplicate Locations**.

j. Change the Address for LocationID 15 to **Downtown**, in the query results. Close the query.

k. Close the database. Close Access.

l. Submit based on your instructor's directions.

3 | Car Dealership

COLLABORATION CASE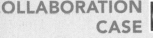

You have been asked to modify a car dealership database that tracks employee data, sales records, and vehicle information. You and your team will identify new hires in the database and move them to a separate table. You will summarize data in the database and locate unmatched records. Refer to Figure 6.52 as you complete this exercise.

FIGURE 6.52 Vehicles Without Matching Sales Agreements

VehicleID	VehicleYear	VehicleMake	VehicleModel	VehicleColor	VehicleCos	VehicleSalePrice	Veh
1000	2013	Honda	Accord	Gray	$25,000.00	$26,999.00	
1002	2013	Honda	Accord	Red	$23,500.00	$27,500.00	
1003	2012	Honda	Accord EX	Black	$24,900.00	$28,950.00	
1004	2011	Honda	Civic	White	$11,300.00	$14,500.00	
1007	2012	BMW	325i	White	$25,000.00	$32,000.00	
1008	2013	BMW	528i	Black	$28,000.00	$35,900.00	
1009	2010	BMW	M3	Red	$25,900.00	$31,500.00	
(New)							

a. Open *a06m3Collaboration*. Click **Save As** on the FILE tab, click **Save As**, and then type **a06m3Collaboration_GroupName**. As a team, study the existing database and the relationships between the tables. Open each table and study the data that you will be working with.

Assign the following two tasks to a team member:

b. Create a select query based on all of the fields from the Employees table. Add criteria to show only employees whose Active status is No. Run the query.

c. Convert the select query a make table query. Name the new table **Hires Not Activated**. Run the query and save it as **Make Table Query_LastFirst**. Close the query. Open the Hires Not Activated table to verify the results.

Assign the following three tasks to a team member:

d. Set the Active status of Employee ID 3 (Jim Delsor) to **No** in the Employees table. Close the table.

e. Make a copy of the Make Table Query_LastFirst in the Navigation Pane and name the copy **Append Query_LastFirst**. Right-click the new append query and choose **Design View** from the list.

f. Change the query type to **Append**. Append records to the Hires Not Activated table. Modify the criteria to select Employee ID 3 and delete the existing criterion. Run the query. Save and close the query.

Assign the following two tasks to a team member:

g. Make a copy of the Append Query_LastFirst in the Navigation Pane and name the copy **Delete Query_LastFirst**. Right-click the new delete query and choose **Design View** from the list.

h. Change the query type to **Delete**. Modify the criteria to show only employees whose Active status is No and delete the existing criterion. Run the query. Save and close the query. Open the Employees table and note that the inactive employees are deleted.

Assign the following two tasks to a team member:

i. Create a crosstab query based on the Available Inventory query. Use the VehicleMake field for the row heading, the VehicleYear field for the column heading, and the VehicleSalePrice field for the column and row intersection. Average the VehicleSalePrice field. Save the query as **Available Inventory_Crosstab_LastFirst**.

j. Set the caption of the Total Of VehicleSalePrice: [VehicleSalePrice] field to **Average Sale Price**. Save and close the query.

k. Collaborate with your team to determine what would be the best way to portray vehicles that have no sales agreement. Create an unmatched query to view these records, and include all of the fields from the Vehicles table. Accept the default query name. Finish and then close the query.

l. Compact and repair the database. Close the database. Exit Access. Submit the database based on your instructor's directions.

Beyond the Classroom

Find Duplicate Data in a Database

RESEARCH CASE

In this chapter, you learned about the difference between valid and invalid duplicates in a database. Go to www.microsoft.com and search for **duplicate data in Access 2013**. Locate the article *Find duplicate records with a query* that discusses the Find Duplicates Query Wizard. Read through the article and write a brief summary of your findings in a Word document; save the file as **a06b2Duplicate_LastFirst**. Close the document. Submit based on your instructor's directions.

Prohibit Duplicate Append

DISASTER RECOVERY

Northwind Traders is an international specialty foods distributor that relies on an Access 2013 database to process its orders. A make table query moved all the owners from the Customers table to a new Customer Owners table. A colleague converted the make table query to an append query and ran it again (expecting it would not add another set of records). Unfortunately, it did add a second set of owners to the table, and now every owner is duplicated. What is the best way to fix this problem? You need to retain the append query and run it once in a while in case a new owner was added to the database. Running the append query should not add any duplicate records to the Customer Owners table. Open *a06b3Food* and save it as **a06b3Food_LastFirst**. Correct the problem in the table. When you are finished, compact, repair, and close your database. Submit based on your instructor's directions.

Cover Letters and Resume Tips

SOFT SKILLS CASE

You want to determine how many of the new employees in your database have no resumes on file with the Human Resources Department. You decide to create a make table query with their personal information so that they can be contacted by HR. Open *a6b4Resumes*. Save a copy of the database as **a6b4Resumes_FirstLast**. Create the query based on the New Employees table and include the following fields: FirstName, LastName, Email, DateOfHire, and ResumeOnFile (in that order). Hide the ResumeOnFile field in the query results. Set the query to create a table named **Missing Resume**. Save the query as **Missing Resume_Make Table**. Run the query to create the table and close the query. Close the database. Exit Access. Submit the database *a6b4Resumes_FirstLast* based on your instructor's directions.

Capstone Exercise

Northwind Traders is a small international gourmet foods whole-saler. You will update the database by increasing the price of all of the beverage and dairy products. You will make a table of discontinued products. You will also summarize profits by salesperson and category and identify products that have no orders.

Database File Setup

Open the original database file, save a copy with a new file name, and then open the copied database to complete this capstone exercise.

a. Open *a06c1Prices* and save it as **a06c1Prices_LastFirst**.

Identify and Update Selected Category Prices

Create a select query to identify all of the products in the beverage and dairy categories, and then create an update query to increase their prices.

a. Create a select query that includes the CategoryID and CategoryName from the Categories table and the UnitPrice and ProductName fields from the Products table. Run the query and note the CategoryIDs for Beverages and Dairy.

b. Add the appropriate CategoryID criterion to limit the query output to only Beverages.

c. Convert the query to an update query. Update the UnitPrice for beverages only by increasing it by 5 percent. View the query in Datasheet view prior to running it to make sure you are updating the correct records. Return to Design view and run the query.

d. Update the UnitPrice for dairy products only by increasing it by 4 percent. View the query in Datasheet view prior to running it to make sure you are updating the correct records. Return to Design view and run the query.

e. Save the query as **Update Prices**. Close the query.

Create a New Table

Identify the discontinued products and create a new table to store them.

a. Create a select query that identifies all of the discontinued products. Include all fields from the Products table.

b. Convert the select query to a make table query.

c. Name the new table **Discontinued Products**. Run the query.

d. Save the query as **Make Discontinued Products Table**. Close the query.

e. Make a copy of the Make Discontinued Products Table query and save it as **Append Discontinued Products Table**. Open the Append Discontinued Products Table query in Design view. Convert the make table query to an append query. The query will append to the Discontinued Products table.

f. Modify the criteria to append Boston Crab Meat as a product, using the SupplierID from the Products table. Run the query, save it, and then close it.

g. Make a copy of the Append Discontinued Products Table query and save it as **Delete Discontinued Products**. Open the Delete Discontinued Products query in Design view. Convert the append query to a delete query.

h. Modify the criteria to delete the discontinued products, as well as the record for Boston Crab Meat using its SupplierID (*Hint:* There will be two criteria). Run, save, and close the query.

Calculate Summary Statistics

Create a crosstab query that shows profits by salesperson and category.

a. Open the Profit query in Design view and add the **LastName field** from the Employees table to the last column of the design grid. Run, save, and close the query.

b. Use the query wizard to create a crosstab query based on the Profit query that shows total profit by LastName (row heading) and CategoryName (column heading). Name the query **Profit_Crosstab**.

c. Modify the query to display **CategoryName** as a row heading field and **LastName** as a column heading field. Run, save, and close the query.

Create a Find Unmatched Query

a. Create a query to find out if any of the products have no current order details. Add all of the fields from the Products table to the results.

b. Save the query as **Products With No Orders**. Run the query and close it.

c. Close the database. Close Access.

d. Submit based on your instructor's directions.

Advanced Forms and Reports

CHAPTER 7

Moving Beyond the Basics

Yuri Arcurs/Shutterstock

OBJECTIVES   AFTER YOU READ THIS CHAPTER, YOU WILL BE ABLE TO:

1. Restrict edits in a form p. 676
2. Create a drop-down menu p. 678
3. Set the tab order p. 681
4. Use subforms p. 682
5. Use advanced controls p. 691
6. Use sections p. 695

CASE STUDY | Technical Services

Yellowstone County Technical Services is a small company that provides technical support for a number of businesses in Yellowstone County, Montana. As one of the company's supervisors, you have been tasked with updating the customer tracking database to expand the input and output capabilities of the system.

In your experience with the company, you have seen some of the common errors users make when performing data entry and have also seen what is effective and what is not effective in forms. In addition, you have seen which reports users utilize and have heard suggestions about changes they would like made.

Creating a database is difficult, but updating a database and making it more user-friendly can be the difference between a tool that is accepted and a tool that is rejected. As any good database administrator realizes, being proactive and helping users prevent errors is critical. In addition, finding ways to extract more information from the same amount of data is important as well. Being able to interpret and present the information in a database so management can use it can be what makes or breaks your career as a database administrator.

In your role as supervisor, you also want to lead your technicians by example, and implementing improvements in your database is a good start. After implementing the changes, you can use the database as a case study to train your technicians in effective database design.

Advanced Forms

For basic database solutions, a simple form created with the Form tool will handle most needs. However, at times you need to go beyond the basics. For example, you can create a form that enables users to look up information but not change it, thereby providing a measure of security. You do not have to worry about users accidentally changing data. You can change a field to a lookup field, finding values in another table or a list of values. However, there may be times where you do not need the lookup in the table but would like it in a form. This can be done through the use of a combo box. Another part of improving data entry is making a form easy to navigate. Sometimes when you tab through a form, you may not end up in the desired field. You can change the tab order in a form to make data entry more efficient. You can also create and manipulate subforms, which show related records from other tables. Part of your goal when administering a database is to make the database simple and powerful, and forms provide that functionality. You will use Design view to make most of the changes in this chapter.

Restricting Edits in a Form

One method of protecting data in a database is to restrict casual users from editing the data. Casual users may need access to the data to look up information such as a person's address or phone number or to review the details of an order. However, the people who need to look up information may be people you do not want adding, editing, and deleting records. When too many users make changes to the data, the data can become unreliable and difficult to maintain. If only a select group of users is allowed to enter and edit data, maintaining the integrity of the data is much easier.

Most databases have data entry forms. For example, a customer form might be created in a bank's database to enable customer information to be entered. If a mistake is made, data entry personnel can find the record with the mistake and fix the error. The form does not require permission or a password to make an edit. Perhaps other employees at the bank also need to look up information—for example, a phone number to contact a customer. The person making these calls will need to look up the phone number of a customer without making any changes to the data. When users need to look up information without making changes, it is best to create a copy of the original form and then restrict editing on the copy. A form that enables users to view but not change data is a *read-only form*. Incorporating read-only forms in a database helps avoid accidental changes to data. You may ask why you would create a read-only form instead of simply creating a report. Remember that forms are preferred because they show one record at a time, and they enable searches.

In addition to setting the form so data cannot be changed, you as the designer have two other questions to answer. Do you want to allow users to delete records using this form? Do you want to allow users to add new records using this form? Even if a form has restricted editing, it still enables adding and deleting records. These options can be switched off as well.

Create a Read-Only Form

To create a read-only form, do the following:

STEP 1 »

1. Open the form in Layout view.
2. Click the Property Sheet in the Tools group on the DESIGN tab.
3. Select Form in the *Selection type* box at the top of the Property Sheet.
4. Click the Allow Edits property on the Data tab.
5. Change the Allow Edits property to No, as shown in Figure 7.1.
6. Change the Allow Additions and Allow Deletions properties to No (if desired).
7. Switch to Form view to test the form.

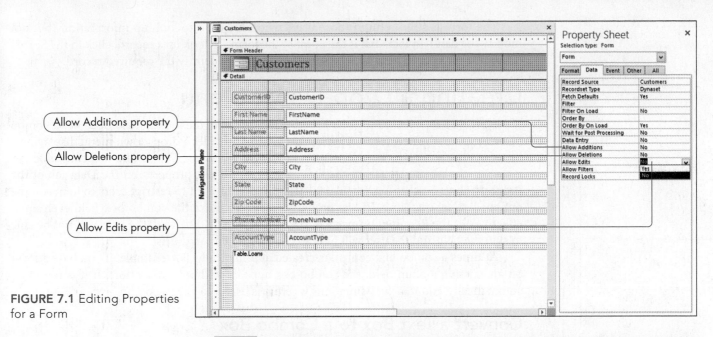

- Allow Additions property
- Allow Deletions property
- Allow Edits property

FIGURE 7.1 Editing Properties for a Form

> **TIP** **Change the Title for Read-Only Forms**
>
> It is suggested that you change the form title and name to indicate it is read-only. Otherwise, you can frustrate users who might open the form and wonder what they are doing wrong!

To test the changes to the form, switch to Form view, and then attempt to change the data in the first record. If you attempt to change the address, for example, nothing happens. In addition, if you changed the Allow Additions and Allow Deletions properties to No, you can see the results of this change when you attempt to click Delete in the Records group on the Home tab—Delete is no longer available. Normally, you add a record in a form by clicking the *New (blank) record* button in the navigation bar at the bottom of the form window. However, because the Allow Additions property is set to No, the option has been disabled. Figure 7.2 shows a read-only form. You will notice it is not obvious it is read-only. Editing the form title to indicate it is read-only will help.

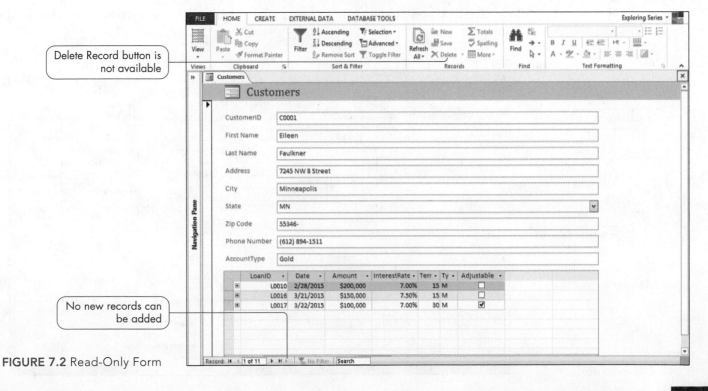

- Delete Record button is not available
- No new records can be added

FIGURE 7.2 Read-Only Form

The form is still useful to those users who only need to look up information (but not modify the data). In fact, that is the point of the form. To look up a record, click in the Search box in the navigation bar and type some key words to identify the required record.

Creating a Drop-Down Menu

If you create a form based on a table with a lookup field, the lookup field becomes a combo box control on the new form. A **combo box control** provides a drop-down menu displaying a list of options from which the user can choose a single value. The combo box control forces a user to choose an item from the list if the Limit To List property on the Data tab of the Property Sheet is set to Yes (the default). If you do not want to restrict users to items on the options list, set the Limit To List property to No. To make the combo box field even more effective, set the Required property of the underlying field to Yes—the user will not be able to skip the field and the user will have to choose an item on the list.

At times a combo box control is created automatically. For example, if you base a form on an existing lookup field, the combo box appears without extra effort. If it is not done automatically, you may find situations where it is useful to have a combo box.

Convert a Text Box to a Combo Box

At times, a text box on a form should be converted to a combo box. This can happen when the data you are collecting may not appear to contain repeating data at first. As you enter transactions over time, you may realize that a field does have repeating data and that a combo box may be appropriate. The desire to make input easier for the user should be weighed against creating a drop-down menu that is too long. For example, the state field will sometimes be a combo box. Fifty states and the District of Columbia make up the United States, and you may prefer not to have a drop-down menu containing 51 items. However, if the customers that are entered in your database are located in only a subset of the 50 states, you may be able to include a subset of the states.

Before you convert a text box to a combo box, you should first create a new table and enter the values for the option list, much like you do for lookup fields. Then, do the following:

STEP 2 >>

1. Open the form in Design view (or Layout view) and right-click the text box you want to convert.
2. From the shortcut menu, click the Change To option and select Combo Box, as shown in Figure 7.3.

The field now displays with an arrow on the right side of the text box. It does not yet do anything, however.

FIGURE 7.3 Changing a Text Box to a Combo Box

Customize a Converted Combo Box

Once you have converted a text box to a combo box, you still have changes to make to enable the options. For example, you likely want to ensure that users can only enter values appearing on the menu. Though optional, these enable you to help improve data entry. Figure 7.4 shows three properties you can set to customize a combo box, and Figure 7.5 shows how a combo box appears in form view. To set a source for a combo box, do the following:

1. Switch to Design view of the form.
2. Click the Property Sheet in the Tools group on the DESIGN tab.
3. Select a Row Source on the Data tab.
4. Switch to Form view to test the combo box.

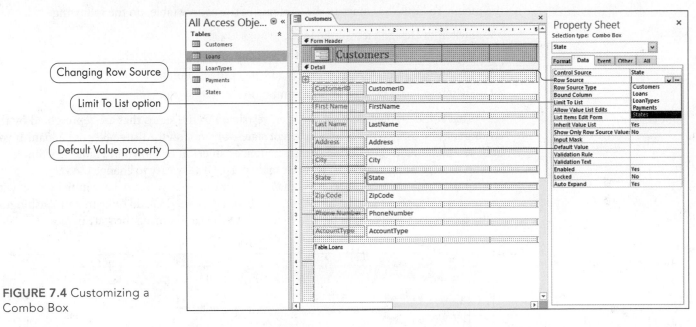

FIGURE 7.4 Customizing a Combo Box

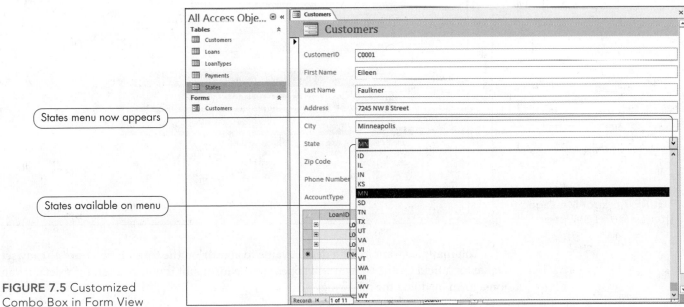

FIGURE 7.5 Customized Combo Box in Form View

There are 16 items by default on a combo box menu. If your list contains more than 16 items, users will have to scroll to find the appropriate value. If you prefer to increase this number, switch to Layout or Design view, click the text box for your combo box field, and ensure that the Property Sheet is displayed. If not, on the Form Design Tools Design tab in the Tools group, click Property Sheet. Find the property named List Rows on the Format tab and change the number from 16 to a more appropriate number.

As described earlier, you may want to ensure your users only enter values that exist in the menu. To limit the values to the contents of the source table, do the following:

1. Switch to Design view of the form.
2. Click the Property Sheet in the Tools group on the DESIGN tab.
3. Change the Limit To List property to Yes on the Data tab.
4. Switch to Form view to test the combo box.

What if the available states have been restricted to the states that are represented by the customers, and a customer from a different state—one not on the list—takes out a loan? If you have set the Limit To List option, Access generates an error, as shown in Figure 7.6. Similar to lookup fields, storing values in a separate table makes it very easy to change the values allowed in a combo box if the values ever need changing. For example, you may have initially dealt with customers in Idaho, Montana, and Wyoming. If you ever need to add Oregon and Washington to the combo box, you can simply add new rows to the table storing the state names.

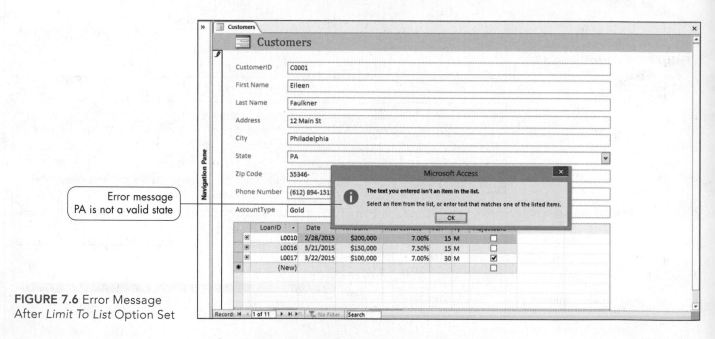

Error message
PA is not a valid state

FIGURE 7.6 Error Message After *Limit To List* Option Set

You may also want to set a default value to appear on the form. If you have already set a value for a field on the table, it will appear in the form, but if not, you can set a default value on a form by doing the following:

1. Switch to Design view of the form.
2. Click the Property Sheet in the Tools group on the DESIGN tab.
3. Enter a Default Value on the Data tab.
4. Switch to Form view to test the combo box.

Setting the Tab Order

When entering data into a table, users press Tab to advance from one field to the next. Data cannot be entered out of order unless you click a field with the mouse instead of pressing Tab. The *tab order* is the sequential advancing in a form from one field or control to the next when you press Tab. When working with forms, the designer must remember to check the tab order before delivering the form to the end users; when a form is created, the initial tab order is not necessarily the order that is most useful to the user.

Set the Tab Order

STEP 3»

Sometimes, Access sets the tab order in a way that makes little sense. You may enter data in the first field, hit Tab, and end up in the bottom text box. This is something that frustrates users but is easily fixed. The first step you should take if this occurs is to have Access automatically set the tab order. To automatically set the tab order in a form, do the following:

1. Switch to Design view.
2. Click Tab Order in the Tools group on the DESIGN tab. This displays the Tab Order dialog box showing all the controls in each section of the form, as shown in Figure 7.7.
3. Click Detail to display the tab order for the fields.
4. Click Auto Order if the form has a Stacked layout and you want to enter data from top to bottom.
5. Click OK to accept the changes.

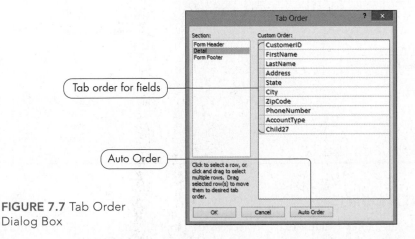

FIGURE 7.7 Tab Order Dialog Box

Access does its best to set the tab order properly, but at times it does not work as you might require. For example, Auto Order does not work well if you have a two-column form. If you need to create a customized tab order, do the following:

1. Switch to Design view.
2. Click Tab Order in the Tools group on the DESIGN tab.
3. Click Detail to display the tab order for the fields.
4. Click the field selector to the left of a field name, release the mouse, and then drag the field to the desired position in the tab order. For example, if two fields are next to each other but in the wrong order, click the second field, release the mouse, and then drag the second field on top of the first one.
5. Click OK to accept the changes.

Remove a Tab Stop

At times, you want the tab order to skip a field completely. For example, if you add a calculated field to the form, you would not want to stop at this field. Calculated fields do not require data entry. Another example occurs when you have an AutoNumber field as the primary key. Your user does not need to add data there, so it should not have a tab stop.

To remove the Tab Stop property of a field, do the following:

1. Switch to Layout view (or Design view).
2. Click the field you want to remove.
3. Click Property Sheet in the Tools group on the DESIGN tab stop.
4. Click the Other tab in the Property Sheet.
5. Locate the Tab Stop property and change the property setting to No, as shown in Figure 7.8.
6. Return to Form view and test the change by pressing Tab to advance through the fields on the form. The field you modified should be skipped when you press Tab.

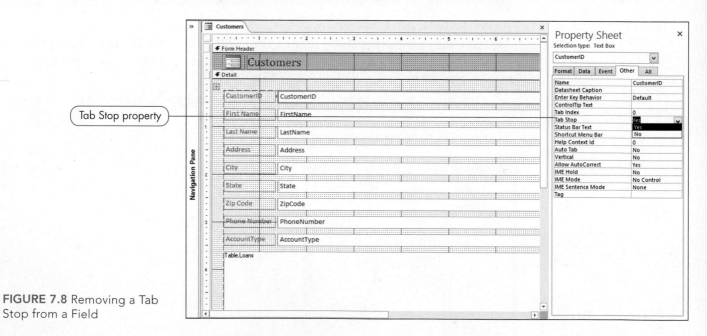

FIGURE 7.8 Removing a Tab Stop from a Field

Using Subforms

Relationships between tables usually exist in Access databases, which can lead to more complicated forms. How should you display records from related tables? Commonly, the main form displays records from a related table using a *subform*. Subforms are generally laid out in a tabular fashion and are used when a relationship exists between two tables, as shown in Figure 7.9.

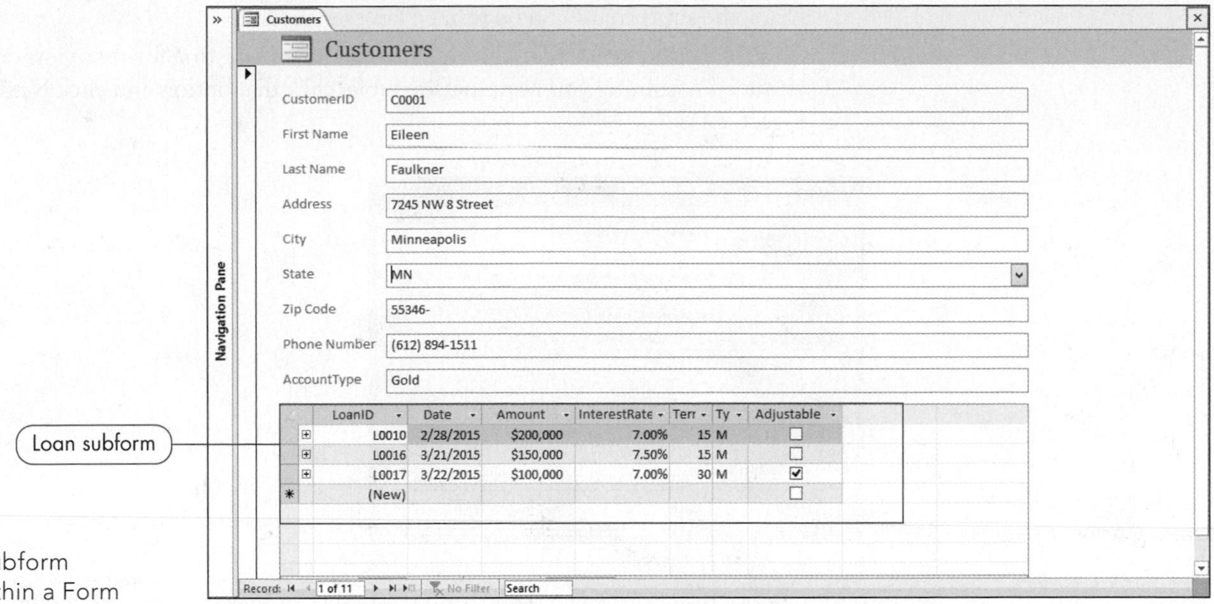

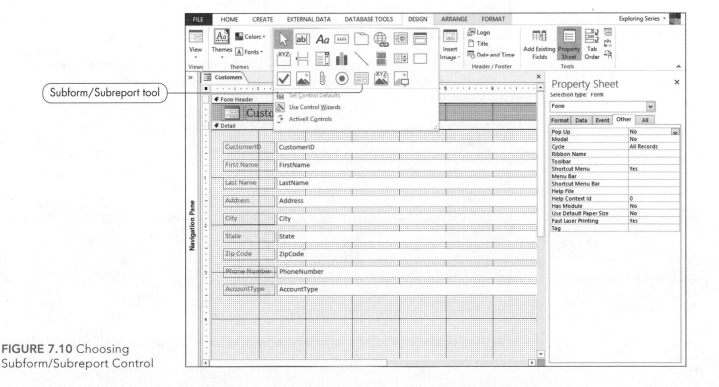

FIGURE 7.9 Subform Appearing Within a Form

Loan subform

Subforms are created by the Form tool automatically. They also can be created by the Form Wizard. If a relationship exists and you choose fields from two different tables using the Form Wizard, it automatically assumes you want a form with a subform. You can also manually add a subform to any form using the Subform/Subreport tool. To manually add a subform using the Subform/Subreport tool, do the following, assuming a relationship exists between the two tables:

STEP 4 ≫

1. Open the form in Design view.
2. Click the Subform/Subreport tool in the Controls group on the DESIGN tab, as shown in Figure 7.10. Depending on your screen resolution, you may need to click More.

FIGURE 7.10 Choosing Subform/Subreport Control

Subform/Subreport tool

3. Draw the subform. It can be resized later as needed.
4. Choose the source for the subform. You can use an existing form or view data in a table or query. Assuming you want to use a table, click that option and click Next, as shown in Figure 7.11.

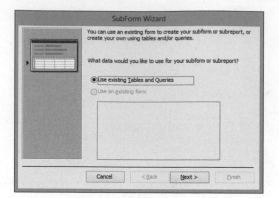

FIGURE 7.11 SubForm Wizard: Choosing Source

5. Choose the appropriate fields from the table (or query) source, as shown in Figure 7.12. Click Next.

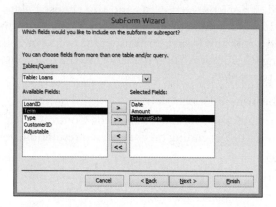

FIGURE 7.12 SubForm Wizard: Choosing Fields

6. Assuming a relationship exists between the two tables, you will be shown a connection between the tables. Choose the relationship you want to use, as shown in Figure 7.13. Click Next.

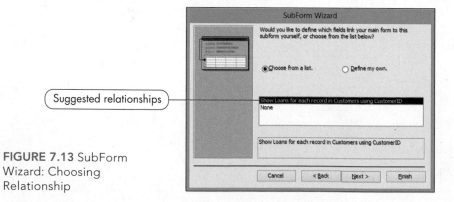

Suggested relationships

FIGURE 7.13 SubForm Wizard: Choosing Relationship

7. Accept the default name or create your own name for the subform. Click Finish. Your results will resemble Figure 7.14.

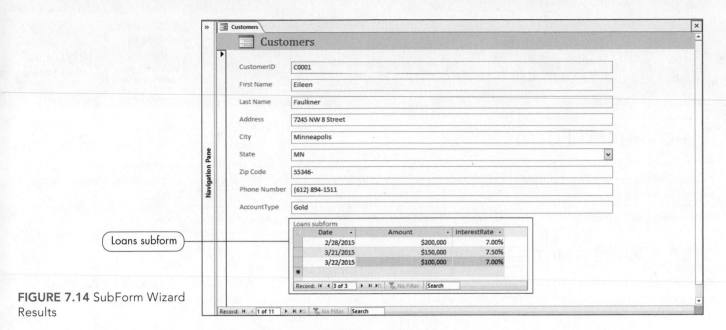

Loans subform

FIGURE 7.14 SubForm Wizard Results

You can change the size of the subform or the size of the fields in the subform as necessary. It will display in tabular fashion. The changes are easier to make in Layout view, as you can see the data as it appears in the subform.

Quick Concepts ✓

1. Why create a read-only copy of a form? ***p. 676***

2. What does a combo box control do? ***p. 678***

3. What is one reason the Auto Order option of the tab order may not work? ***p. 681***

4. What does a subform do? ***p. 682***

Hands-On Exercises

1 Advanced Forms

You have decided to create a lookup form for customer data. You will also create a form with a drop-down menu to enable users to help record customer call satisfaction. You will repair an old form that has problems with tab ordering. You will also create a form with a subform.

Skills covered: Restrict Edits in a Form • Create a Drop-Down Menu • Set the Tab Order • Use Subforms

STEP 1 ≫ RESTRICT EDITS IN A FORM

You have decided to use the Form tool to create a Customers form. This form will enable you to look up customer information. You will make this read-only so you do not accidentally make errors when looking up information. Refer to Figure 7.15 as you complete Step 1.

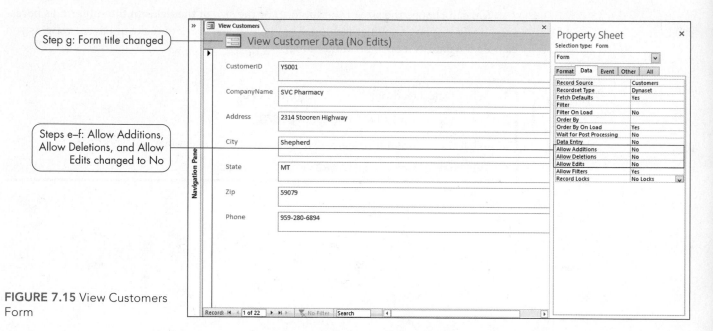

FIGURE 7.15 View Customers Form

a. Open *a07h1Yellowstone* and save it as **a07h1Yellowstone_LastFirst**.

b. Select the **Customers table** in the Navigation Pane. Click the **CREATE tab** and click **Form** in the Forms group.

   Access creates a new form based on the Customers table. The form opens in Layout view, ready to edit.

c. Click anywhere in the subform at the bottom of the window, click the border of the subform, and then press **Delete** to delete the subform.

> **TROUBLESHOOTING:** If you are prompted to confirm deleting of records, press No and ensure you have clicked the border before pressing Delete.

d. Click **Property Sheet** on the DESIGN tab in the Tools group if it is not already displayed.

   The Property Sheet displays on the right side of your screen.

e. Click the **Data tab**, if necessary. Click in the **Allow Edits box**, which currently displays *Yes*, and click the drop-down menu at the right. Change the value to **No**.

f. Repeat step e to change the **Allow Additions** and **Allow Deletions property values** to **No**. Close the Property Sheet.

g. Change the title of the form to **View Customer Data (No Edits)**. Compare your results to Figure 7.15.

h. Switch to Form view.

i. Attempt to type in the **CompanyName box**.

You should not be able to change the field value.

j. Attempt to add and delete a record.

You should not be able to add or delete a record.

k. Click **Save** in the Quick Access Toolbar and save the form as **View Customers**. Close the form.

STEP 2 ≫ CREATE A DROP-DOWN MENU

You will use the Form tool to create an Access form to help manage customer call data. This form will enable you to record customer data. You will implement this using a drop-down menu. Refer to Figure 7.16 as you complete Step 2.

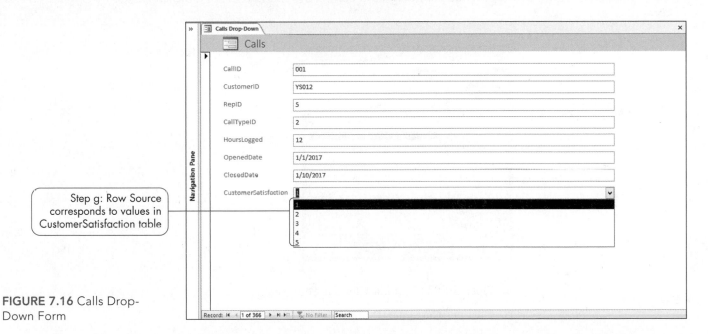

Step g: Row Source corresponds to values in CustomerSatisfaction table

FIGURE 7.16 Calls Drop-Down Form

a. Select the **Calls table** in the Navigation Pane. Click the **CREATE tab** and click **Form** in the Forms group.

Access creates a new form based on the Calls table.

b. Right-click the **CustomerSatisfaction text box**, click the **Change To option**, and then select **Combo Box**.

The CustomerSatisfaction text box changes to a combo box with an arrow on the right side of the box.

c. Click **Property Sheet** on the DESIGN tab in the Tools group if it is not already displayed.

d. Click the **Row Source property** on the Data tab of the Property Sheet, click the arrow, and then select **Satisfaction Results**.

e. Click the **Limit To List property** and change the value to **Yes**.

f. Switch to Form view.

g. Click in the **CustomerSatisfaction field**. Notice an arrow now appears on the right of the box. Click the arrow and notice values of 1, 2, 3, 4, and 5 appear, as shown in Figure 7.16.

h. Type the value **6** for the **CustomerSatisfaction field** and press **Tab**.

Access will display an error message that the text you entered is not a value on the list.

TROUBLESHOOTING: If Access does permit the value to be entered, ensure you set the Limit To List property to Yes.

---

i. Click **OK**. Change the value for the first record's CustomerSatisfaction field to **2** and press **Tab**.

The value will save properly.

j. Save the form as **Calls Drop-Down**, and close the form.

STEP 3 ≫ SET THE TAB ORDER

The users of the current Edit Customers report have reported problems with the tab order. You will fix the tab order. You will also fix an old form so that the tabs appear in the correct order and remove a tab stop. Refer to Figure 7.17 as you complete Step 3.

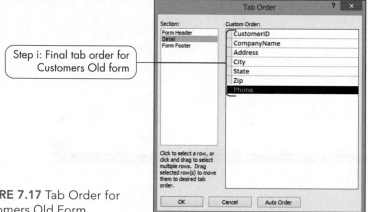

FIGURE 7.17 Tab Order for Customers Old Form

a. Open the Edit Customers form in Form view.

b. Click the **CustomerID box**. Press **Tab**.

When you press Tab, Access brings you to the State field.

c. Press **Tab** five more times, noticing where the cursor moves each time.

The fields are not displayed in a logical order.

d. Switch to Design view and click **Tab Order** in the Tools group on the DESIGN tab.

e. Click **Detail** and click **Auto Order**. Click **OK**.

Because this is a Stacked Layout form, Access changes the tab order so it moves down one field at a time.

f. Switch to Form view. Press **Tab** six times and verify that the tab order progresses in a logical order. Save and close the form.

g. Open the Customers Old form in Form view. Press **Tab**.

The form moves to the Phone field. You will switch the tab order so Phone appears last.

h. Switch to Design view. Click **Tab Order** in the Tools group on the DESIGN tab. Click **Detail** and click **Auto Order**.

Notice *Phone* is now at the beginning of the tab order, which is not the logical location for it.

i. Click the **Row Selector** to the left of the Phone field. Drag the **Phone field** beneath the Zip field. Your tab order should match Figure 7.17. Click **OK**.

j. Click the **CustomerID field**. Display the Property Sheet.

k. Click the **Other tab** in the Property Sheet. Locate the Tab Stop property and change the property setting to **No**.

You will no longer be able to access the CustomerID field by pressing Tab.

l. Switch to Form view. Tab through the fields, ensuring the fields display in the correct order and that pressing Tab does not bring you to the CustomerID field.

m. Save and close the form.

STEP 4 ≫ USE SUBFORMS

The Edit Customers form does not display the related call information for each customer. You will modify it so the subform containing the information appears. Refer to Figure 7.18 as you complete Step 4.

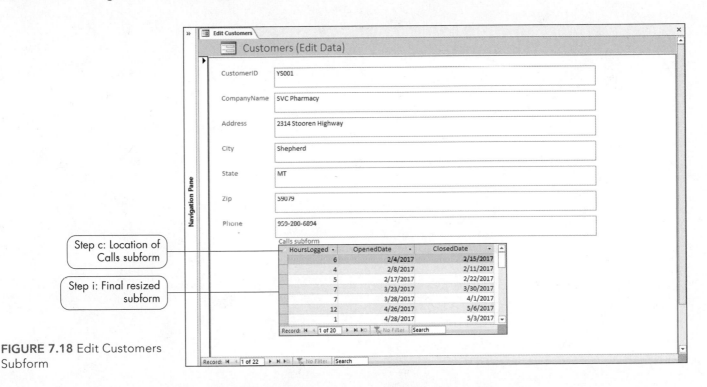

FIGURE 7.18 Edit Customers Subform

a. Open the Edit Customers form in Design view.

b. Click the **Subform/Subreport tool** in the Controls group on the DESIGN tab. If it is not visible, you may need to scroll or click the **More button** at the bottom-right of the Controls box.

c. Draw a box in the location shown in Figure 7.18. The size does not matter, as it will be resized later.

The Subform Wizard dialog box displays.

d. Select **Use existing Tables and Queries** and click **Next**.

e. Click the **Tables/Queries arrow** and select Table: **Calls**. Double-click the **HoursLogged, OpenedDate**, and **ClosedDate fields**. Click **Next**.

f. Click **Next** to accept the default relationship.

g. Accept the default Calls subform name and click **Finish**.

h. Switch to Layout view. Notice the Calls subform appears at the bottom of the screen.

i. Resize the subform and the fields to be approximately the size shown in Figure 7.18.

j. Save and close the form.

k. Keep the database open if you plan to continue with Hands-On Exercise 2. If not, close the database and exit Access.

Controls and Sections

As you work with tools to create and modify forms and reports, you will often need to switch between the three views in Access—Form or Report view, Layout view, and Design view. You use Layout view to perform most changes, but Design view gives you, as a designer, a higher level of control.

To lay out forms and reports, to display fields, and to display field labels, you use basic controls such as text boxes and labels. However, other types of controls exist. You can add formatting controls as well as controls that perform calculations using the same functions found in the Expression Builder.

In this section, you will examine the different form and report sections. As you learn how to create forms and reports, placing fields and labels in the correct section will become a habit. You may have to use trial and error at first, switching between different views until the form or report is working correctly.

The overlap between forms and reports will be easy to see. The same functionality applies to both, so the skills you use in forms can be applied to reports and vice versa.

Using Advanced Controls

Whether you are dealing with a form or report, some features are common to both. A number of common controls are available. When you use the form and report wizards to create basic objects, the resulting forms and reports contain a number of controls that you did not add yourself.

Both forms and reports have a text box control, which displays the data found in record source (often, a table). Although the term *text box* may imply it only displays Short Text values, it can display numeric data, currency, and dates, depending on the field's data type.

The label control is a word or phrase to describe the data associated with a text box. For a field in a form or report, the label control defaults to the caption you set for a field. If you have not set a caption for a field, the label will default to the field name.

Forms and reports also have layout controls. The layout control keeps the fields together in an orderly fashion, enabling you to move fields without having to worry about lining fields up.

Identify Control Types

Both label controls and text box controls are known as **bound controls**. A bound control is a control that is connected to a field in a table or query. Outside of computers, the term *bound* can refer to two objects tied together, so you can see where this term comes from. A bound control changes each time a new record is displayed, as the value is dynamic.

Forms and reports also contain **unbound controls**. An unbound control is a control not tied to a specific field. Generally, this refers to decorative elements, such as the title of the report. An unbound control stays the same as you switch between records. Some other examples of unbound controls are lines, pictures, and other non-data-related elements.

 TIP | **Remove the Tab Stop from Unbound Controls**

In most cases, you will want to remove the tab stop from an unbound control. Unbound controls do not require data entry, so there is no reason for the cursor to stop on them.

A *calculated control* contains an expression that generates a calculated result. Calculated controls can also be applied to forms or reports and include aggregate functions such as Sum, Min, Max, and Average. These are basic calculated controls. More advanced calculated controls can contain a combination of functions, constants, and field names from the record source. Figure 7.19 shows each of these types of controls.

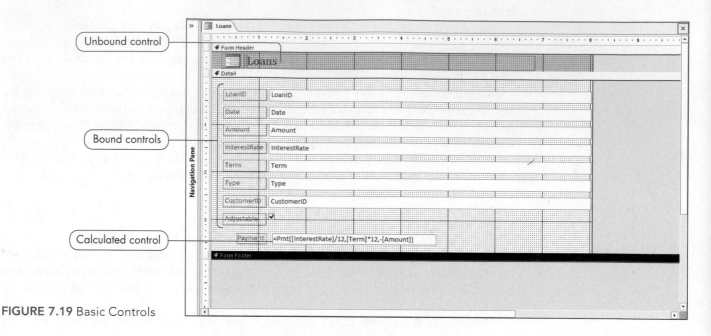

FIGURE 7.19 Basic Controls

Despite having the name *control* in the name, bound, unbound, and calculated controls are not found on the Controls group on the Design tab, which is available in Layout or Design view. Each of these is a category of controls. Recall a text box control is an example of a bound control because it is connected to a field.

Add Emphasis to a Form or Report

When using the Form or Report tools to create an automatic form or report, you have a number of default controls. The title, the form/report icon, and each field are examples. In addition, the form or report has a layout control.

If you want to add emphasis to your form or report, the Line control and Rectangle control are two options. The Line control will allow you to insert a line into your form or report, and the Rectangle will allow you to add a rectangle. After inserting these into an object, you can modify the shape to have a different line color, line thickness, and line type (such as dashed or dotted), and in the case of rectangles you can change the fill color. You will only find these options in Design view; they are not available in Layout view. To add a line or rectangle shape to a form or report, do the following:

STEP 1 >> 1. Switch to Design view.

STEP 2 >> 2. Click the DESIGN tab.

3. In the Controls group, select the Line or Rectangle control, as shown in Figure 7.20. You may need to click More or scroll to see this, depending on your screen configuration.

4. In the form or report, drag the mouse from the desired start point to the desired end point.

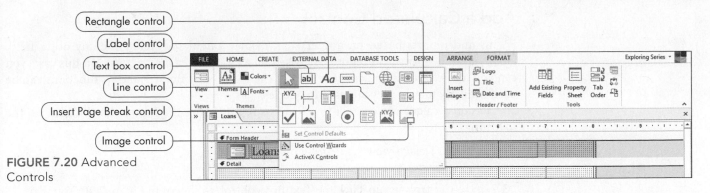

FIGURE 7.20 Advanced Controls

Your line or rectangle will appear. Once you have added a line or rectangle, you can format it by doing the following:

1. Switch to Design view.
2. Click the line or rectangle you wish to format.
3. Click the FORMAT tab.
4. In the Control Formatting group, choose the Shape Outline menu to change the color, thickness, and line type for the rectangle or line. Choose Shape Fill to add a fill color to a rectangle.

Add Text and Images to a Form or Report

Both forms and reports have the option to include text and images.

In addition to the existing label controls, you may wish to add some sort of explanatory text to a form or report. Instead of (or in addition to) a validation rule, you can add text providing guidance for your users. As this text is not tied to a specific field and is unchanging, it is considered a label. To add text to a form or report, do the following:

1. Switch to Design view.
2. Click the DESIGN tab.
3. In the Controls group, click the Label control, as shown in Figure 7.20. You may need to click More or scroll to see this, depending on your screen configuration.
4. Drag the mouse from the desired start point to the desired end point.
5. Type the text you would like to appear in the label.

Images can be useful especially when dealing with corporate forms and reports. Companies commonly use the same logo and colors on official publications. When creating a form or report, you can insert an image file containing the company logo or any other image. Often, the image is inserted in the Form Header or Report Header, so it displays once when printed or viewed on the screen. The Form Header and Report Header will be discussed further in this chapter. To add an image to a form or report, do the following:

1. Switch to Design view.
2. Click the DESIGN tab.
3. In the Controls group, click the Image control, as shown in Figure 7.20. You may need to click More or scroll to see this, depending on your screen configuration.
4. Drag the mouse from the desired start point to the desired end point. The Insert Picture dialog box appears.
5. Browse to the location containing the image and click Open.
6. Resize the image control as necessary.

Add a Calculated Control

Forms and reports based on a query can display calculated fields like any other field. However, some forms and reports are based on a table rather than a query. In this case, you can add a calculated field using a text box. The Expression Builder and its functions can be used similarly to how they are used in queries.

To add a calculated control to a form or report using the Expression Builder, do the following:

1. Switch to Design view.
2. Click the DESIGN tab.
3. In the Controls group, click the Text Box control, as shown in Figure 7.20. You may need to click More or scroll to see this, depending on your screen configuration.
4. Drag the mouse from the desired start point to the desired end point. The word *Unbound* appears in the text box. Access also displays a label by default. You can choose to delete or modify the label as necessary.
5. Display the Property Sheet.
6. Click the Data tab on the Property Sheet and click the Ellipsis (...) found next to the Control Source property to open the Expression Builder.
7. Create the desired expression.

Note that if you are comfortable with functions, you do not have to use the Expression Builder. You could simply type the formula into the text box, preceded by an equal sign. For example, you could type =Date() to show the current date.

If you want to format the results of the function (for example, change the number of decimal places for a numeric field), do the following:

1. Switch to Design view.
2. Click the text box you wish to format.
3. Click Property Sheet on the DESIGN tab in the Tools group.
4. To change the format, click the Format property on the Property Sheet's Format tab. To change decimal places for a numeric field, click the Decimal Places property.

Fix Layout Errors After Adding Controls

When dragging a new text box label to a report, you may find it puts the label in the same row as the data rows. If this happens, you can click Tabular Layout in the Table group of the Arrange tab while both the label and text box controls are selected.

Add a Page Break Control

Pagination can be important for forms and reports. Instead of being unsure where a page will break when printed, you can add a page break at a certain location. To add a page break to a form or report, do the following:

1. Open the report in Design view.
2. On the DESIGN tab, click the Insert Page Break control, as shown in Figure 7.20. You may need to click More or scroll to see this, depending on your screen configuration.
3. Click the mouse in the section of the form or report where you want the page break. When you click the Insert Page Break control, the mouse pointer changes to a crosshair with a small report (even in forms) icon.
4. After you click the form or report, a series of six dots appears on the left margin.

To remove a page break, click the six dots and press Delete.

Using Sections

A *section* is a part of a form or report that can be manipulated separately from other parts of a form or report. Basic forms have three sections, and basic reports contain five sections. Sections are visible in Design view. Each section can be collapsed or expanded as needed.

Identify the Default Sections

STEP 3»

STEP 4»

One section common to forms and reports is the **Form Header** (for forms) or the **Report Header** (for reports). The *Form Header* section and the *Report Header* section are similar in that they are headers that display one time at the top of each form or report. This section contains the title by default. Column headings (labels) are also located in this section for reports as well as some types of forms. When a form or report is printed, the Form Header or Report Header displays only once immediately before the first record appearing on a printout.

Similarly, the **Form Footer** and **Report Footer** sections are footers that display one time at the bottom of the form or report. This section is left blank by default for forms and may contain some sort of aggregate function (such as Count) for a report. When a form or report is printed the Form Header or Form Footer appears once, in this case after the final record, regardless of the number of pages.

Another default section is the **Page Header** section. The Page Header is a header that appears once at the top of each page in a form or report. This is more commonly used for reports, as they are designed for printing. Page Headers are switched off by default for forms but can be switched on as necessary.

The **Page Footer** is a footer that appears once at the bottom of each page in a form or report. As with the Page Header, the Page Footer is much more common on reports. The Page Footer is also switched off by default for forms.

The distinction between the Form/Report and Page headers and footers can be confusing at first. If you had a 10-page form or report, each page would display a Page Header, while only the first page would display the Form/Report Header. Likewise, the same report would display the Page Footer on each page while displaying the Form/Report Footer once after the final record.

The **Detail section** displays the records in the record source. The *Detail* section displays in between the headers and footers sections in both forms and reports. Figure 7.21 shows the various form sections in Design view, and Figure 7.22 shows them as they appear when printed. Figure 7.23 shows the report sections in Design view, and Figure 7.24 shows them as they appear when printed.

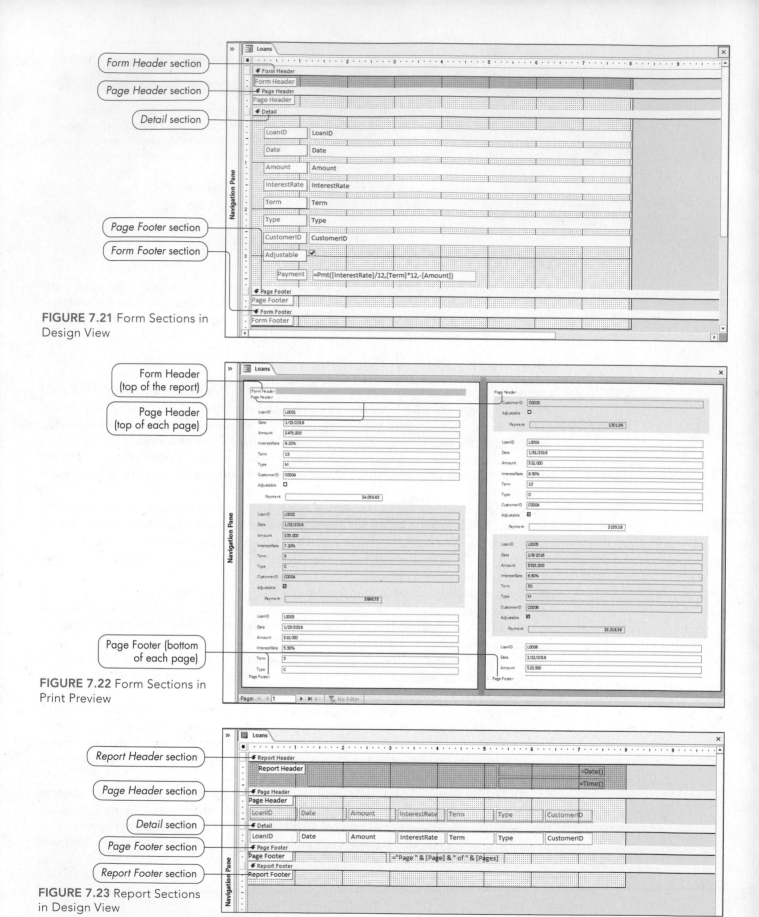

FIGURE 7.21 Form Sections in Design View

FIGURE 7.22 Form Sections in Print Preview

FIGURE 7.23 Report Sections in Design View

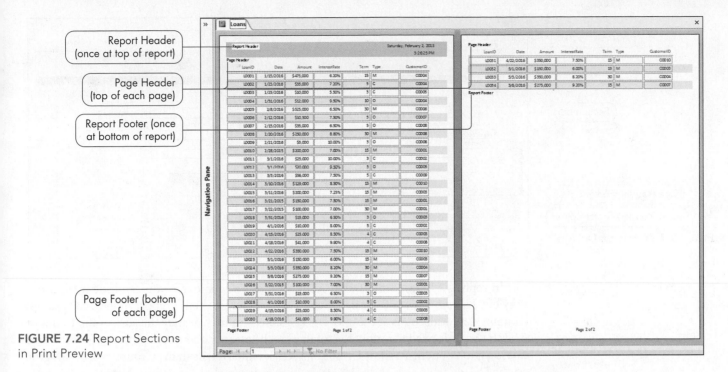

FIGURE 7.24 Report Sections in Print Preview

Report Header (once at top of report)

Page Header (top of each page)

Report Footer (once at bottom of report)

Page Footer (bottom of each page)

Show, Hide, and Resize Sections

Forms and reports display the *Detail* and *Form/Report Header* and *Footer* sections by default. Reports also include the Page Header/Footer by default. Right-clicking a blank area of the form or report enables you to switch on or off sections. Note that when you switch a section off, it deletes all controls in the section. The header and footer sections are tied together; if you remove the Form or Report Header, the Form or Report Footer also disappears. See Figure 7.25 for an illustration in Form Design view and Figure 7.26 for Report Design view.

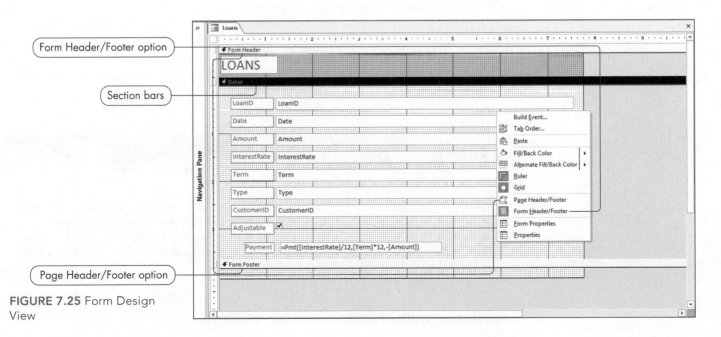

Form Header/Footer option

Section bars

Page Header/Footer option

FIGURE 7.25 Form Design View

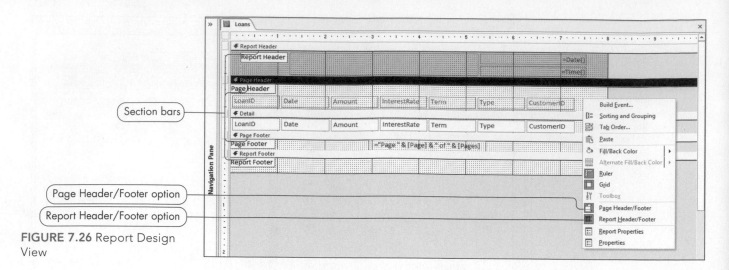

Section bars

Page Header/Footer option

Report Header/Footer option

FIGURE 7.26 Report Design View

In reports, although the *Detail* section cannot be removed, you can hide it from Print Preview, Layout view, and Design view. This is helpful when a report output, for example, contains data with totals at the end. For example, you may display the sum of the values in a field. If you only need to output the totals of each category and not the values of every record, this is a good option. To show Details only, click Hide Details in the Grouping & Totals group on the Design tab. Click Hide Details again to redisplay hidden details. Note that this option is not available for forms.

Within a form or report, you may want to change the height or width of portions of a section. The width is a global property. You cannot change the width of one section without changing it for the entire object. However, you can change the height of each section independently. In Figures 7.25 and 7.26, each gray *section bar* marks the top boundary of a section. Section bars appear gray in these figures, but they can appear in different colors based on your Office setup. You can expand or collapse the space between report sections by moving your mouse over the section bar and dragging to the desired location. The top bar denotes the top boundary of the header. The bottom bar displays the top boundary of the footer. The grid-like area under the bars shows the space allotted to that section. If you decide that the allotted space for a particular section is not needed, you can collapse that section fully so that the section bars are touching. The section remains in the report's design but will not take up any room on the Print Preview or the printed page.

TIP Footer Confusion

In Design view, the *Form Footer* or *Report Footer* section is located below the *Page Footer* section. However, in Print Preview, the Form Footer or Report Footer is positioned above the Page Footer. This may cause some confusion at first; however, the *Form Footer* or *Report Footer* section will be needed to produce grand totals at the end of a report. The Form Footer or Report Footer will only appear one time—at the end of a form or report.

Add a Group Header/Footer to Reports

The Report Wizard and the Group & Sort button are used to add grouping to a report. In addition to the five main sections previously listed, you can also add a custom *Group Header* and *Group Footer* section to a report. Because you cannot add grouping to forms, you will not have the option to add a Group Header or Footer to a form. To add a Group Header, do the following:

1. Switch to Layout view.
2. Click the Group & Sort button on the Grouping & Totals group of the DESIGN tab.
3. Click *Add a group* in the *Group, Sort, and Total* pane at the bottom of the screen.
4. Select the field to group by.
5. Note that even though you have done most work in this chapter in Design view, doing the grouping in Layout view saves you a few steps.

Once you have added grouping, a **Group Header** section appears just above the *Detail* section in Design view, along with the name of the field by which you are grouping. This section appears once each time the grouping field value changes, and the group header prints with the new value. For example, in a Loan report grouped by Type, the group header prints once for each Type, with the loans of that type following. If you select the Type field as a custom group, the section is named Type Header, as shown in Figure 7.27.

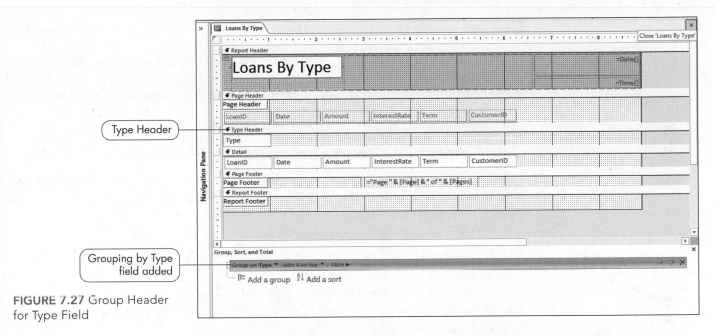

FIGURE 7.27 Group Header for Type Field

A **Group Footer** section does not show by default. It appears just below the *Detail* section in Design view, but only when you select this option in the *Group, Sort, and Total* pane. As with the Group Header, the Group Footer appears once for each distinct value in the grouping field. To display the Group Footer, do the following:

1. Switch to Layout or Design view.
2. Click the More arrow on the *Group, Sort, and Total* pane
3. Switch the option that currently reads *without a footer section* to *with a footer section*, as shown in Figure 7.28.

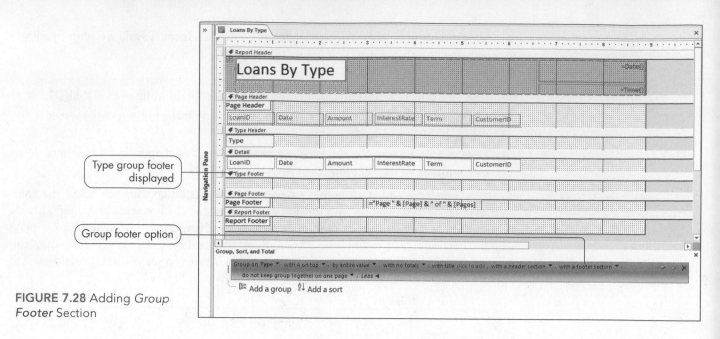

FIGURE 7.28 Adding *Group Footer* Section

The group footer is useful for totaling the data at the end of each group. If a group of physicians is part of a major practice, it would be good to know how many physicians are assigned to each specialization. The group footer could display the count of physicians for each specialization.

Add Totals to a Group Footer/Report Footer

Often, reports require totals at the group level and/or at the grand total level. For example, the Physicians Report might contain a count of physicians in each Specialization group and again at the end of the report.

To add totals to a report, do the following:

1. If you have not done so, create the group section required for the totals.
2. Switch to Design view.
3. Click the More arrow on the *Group, Sort, and Total* pane
4. Switch the option that currently reads *without a footer section* to *with a footer section*, as shown in Figure 7.29.

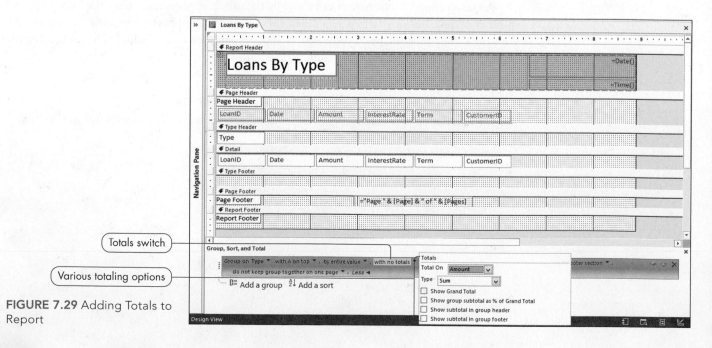

FIGURE 7.29 Adding Totals to Report

5. Select the appropriate total option. Figure 7.30 shows the count (Count Records) for the LoanID field added to the Type Footer and Report Footer.

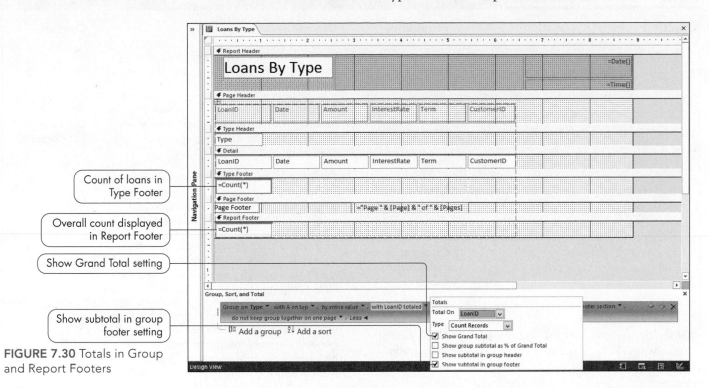

Count of loans in Type Footer

Overall count displayed in Report Footer

Show Grand Total setting

Show subtotal in group footer setting

FIGURE 7.30 Totals in Group and Report Footers

TIP Add a Page Break to a Group Footer

A page break is commonly used in a group footer. Doing so causes each group to print on a separate page. For example, if you had a report grouped by customer, the report would print each customer's data on a separate page (rather than continuing with the next customer on the same page). This type of report is useful when the information is distributed to each customer. In the case that a customer's information takes up more than one page, the page break is inserted after each customer's information.

REFERENCE Sections

Section	Location	Frequency	Usage	Default
Form/Report Header	Top of the form/report	Once	May include the form/report title, the company's name and logo, and the run date and time.	On
Page Header	Top of each page	Once per page	Generally contains the column headings in reports. In a multipage report, the labels repeat at the top of each page to provide continuity.	On (reports) Off (forms)
Group Header (reports only)	At the start of each new group	At the start of each group	Available in reports only. Prints the value of each unique instance for a grouped field. A report grouped by state would print up to 50 unique state names.	Off
Detail	Middle	Once per record in the record source	Repeats for each record in the record source. If there were 500 records in the record source, the form or report would have 500 detail listings.	On
Group Footer (reports only)	At the end of each group	At the end of each group	Available in reports only. Repeats for each record in the record source. This section generally mirrors the group header. May be used to provide aggregate statistics for each group.	Off
Page Footer	Bottom of each page	Once per page	Generally used to print page numbers.	On (reports) Off (forms)
Form/Report Footer	End of the form/report	Once	Often used to print grand totals or other aggregate information for the records.	On

Quick Concepts

1. What is the difference between controls in forms and controls in reports? *p. 691*

2. What is the difference between a bound control and an unbound control? *p. 691*

3. What is the purpose of a calculated control? *p. 692*

4. List the five default sections of a report. *p. 695*

5. What do the Group Header and Footer do? *pp. 698–699*

Hands-On Exercises

2 Controls and Sections

You have decided to modify reports to add calculations, and to modify the different header and footer sections of forms and reports to improve the print and on-screen readability.

Skills covered: Use Advanced Controls in Forms • Use Advanced Controls in Reports • Use Sections in Forms • Use Sections in Reports

STEP 1 ≫ USE ADVANCED CONTROLS IN FORMS

You will be making changes to an existing form and a calculated control to determine if a call is Open or Closed. Refer to Figure 7.31 as you complete Step 1.

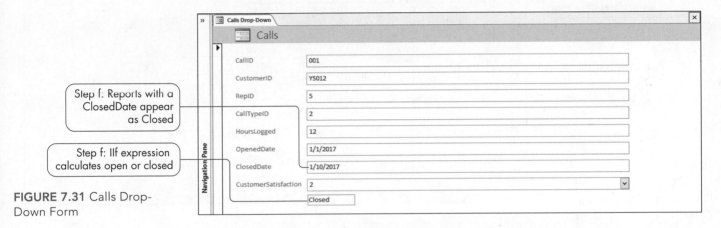

FIGURE 7.31 Calls Drop-Down Form

a. Open *a07h1Yellowstone_LastFirst* if you closed it at the end of Hands-On Exercise 1. Save the database as **a07h2Yellowstone_LastFirst**, changing *h1* to *h2*.

b. Open the Calls Drop-Down form in Design view.

c. Drag the end of the *Detail* section (appearing right above the Form Footer) to about 4" on the vertical toolbar.

d. Click **Text Box** in the Controls group on the DESIGN tab. Click beneath the last control in the form to insert the control. It should be placed approximately where it appears in Figure 7.31.

> **TROUBLESHOOTING:** If you are unable to see the Text Box control, click the More button in the Controls group and select the Text Box control.

e. Display the Property Sheet. Click the **Data tab** on the Property Sheet, click in the **Control Source box**, and then click the **Ellipsis (…)** found next to the Control Source property.

f. Type **IIf(IsNull([ClosedDate]),"Open","Closed")** in the **Expression Builder**. Click **OK**.

This expression displays Open when the ClosedDate is null (in other words, when no value exists in the ClosedDate field) and Closed otherwise.

g. Delete the label for the new control. The control has a default name of *Text* followed by a two-digit number.

h. Switch to Form view. Ensure the first few records display *Closed*. Click the **Last Record Navigation button** and ensure the last record in the table has a value of *Open*.

i. Save and close the form.

STEP 2 >> USE ADVANCED CONTROLS IN REPORTS

You will make changes to an existing report to display the number of days each call has been open. Refer to Figure 7.32 as you complete Step 2.

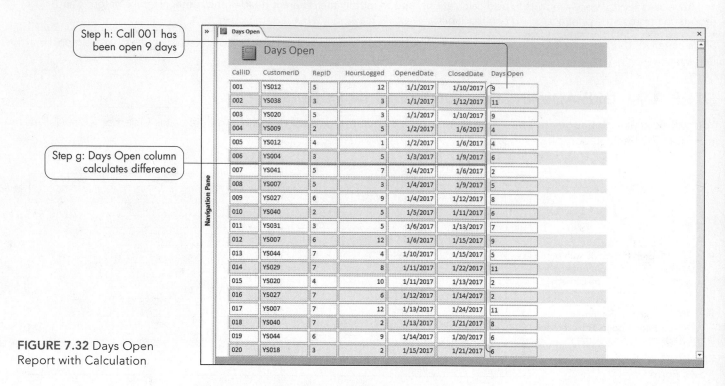

FIGURE 7.32 Days Open Report with Calculation

a. Open the Days Open report in Design view.

b. Click the **Text Box control** in the Controls group on the DESIGN tab. Click to the right of the ClosedDate text box in the *Detail* section of the report to add a new field.

> **TROUBLESHOOTING**: If you are unable to see the Text Box control, click the More button in the Controls group and select the Text Box control.

c. Click the **Tabular button** in the Table group on the ARRANGE tab.

The new field lines up after the final column in the report.

d. Click the **label control** for the new column. Delete the existing text and type **Days Open**.

e. Click in the **text box control** for the new column. Display the Property Sheet.

f. Click the **Data tab** on the Property Sheet and click **Control Source**. Click the **Ellipses (. . .)** to launch the Expression Builder.

g. Type =**[ClosedDate]-[OpenedDate]** in the **Expression box**. Click **OK**.

h. Switch to Report view. Verify the calculation correctly displays the number of days each call was open, as shown in Figure 7.32.

i. Save and close the report.

You will adjust an existing form by adding a logo to the form header and adding a page header. Refer to Figure 7.33 as you complete Step 3.

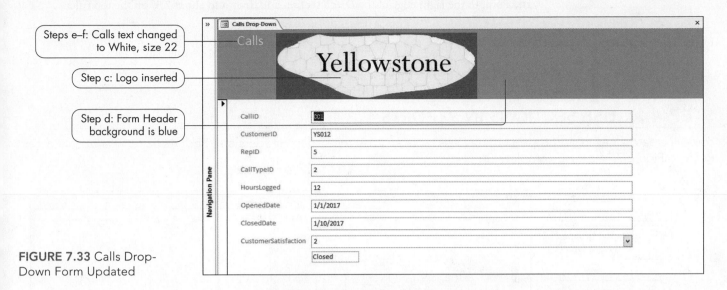

Steps e–f: Calls text changed to White, size 22

Step c: Logo inserted

Step d: Form Header background is blue

FIGURE 7.33 Calls Drop-Down Form Updated

a. Open the Calls Drop-Down form in Design view.

b. Click the **form logo** in the *Form Header* section and press **Delete**.

The form logo disappears.

c. Click the **Image control** in the Controls group on the DESIGN tab. Click to the right of the word *Calls* in the Form Header. Browse to the location of your data files and select **a07h2Logo**.

A logo for Yellowstone appears in the report header.

d. Click the grey background of the Form Header. Click the **Shape Fill arrow** in the Control Formatting group on the FORMAT tab. Select **Blue, Accent 1** (first row, fifth column).

e. Click the **Calls label**. Click the **Font Color arrow** in the Font group on the FORMAT tab. Select **White, Background 1**. Recall you can see the names for each color by pointing to a color and waiting for the ScreenTip to appear.

f. Click the **Font Size arrow** in the Font group on the FORMAT tab. Change the size to **22**.

g. Switch to Form view and compare your form to Figure 7.33.

h. Switch to Design view. Right-click a blank area and select **Page Header/Footer**.

A *Page Header* section appears above the *Detail* section, and a *Page Footer* section appears below the *Detail* section.

i. Click the **Label control** in the Controls group on the DESIGN tab. Click the left side of the Page Footer. Type **Created by First Last**, replacing *First* with your first name and *Last* with your last name.

j. Switch to Form view.

The page footer is not displayed because it will only appear when printed.

k. Click the **FILE tab** and click **Print**. Click **Print Preview**.

The footer should appear on each page. You will notice the form is too wide to fit on one page left to right. When printed, this might lead to extra pages.

l. Switch to Design view. Click the **CallID text box** and change the width to **5.5"** on the top ruler.

All other controls resize as well.

m. Point to the right edge of the *Detail* section and drag it to about 7.5" on the top ruler.

n. Click the **FILE tab** and click **Print**. Click **Print Preview**.

As a printed page in Portrait is 8.5" wide, this will now fit on one page wide.

o. Click **Close Print Preview** and save and close the form.

STEP 4 ≫ USE SECTIONS IN REPORTS

You will create a new report based on the Calls table and use the Group Headers and Footers to summarize the data. Refer to Figure 7.34 as you complete Step 4.

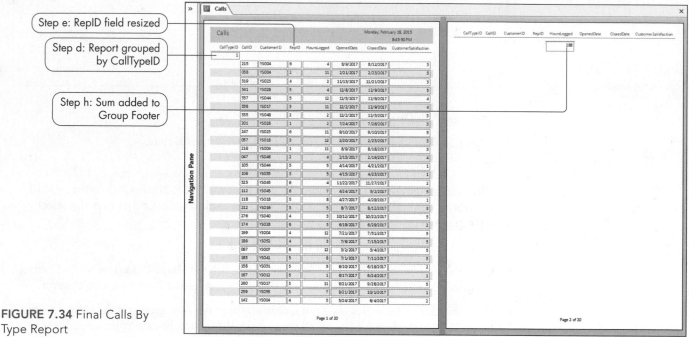

Step e: RepID field resized

Step d: Report grouped by CallTypeID

Step h: Sum added to Group Footer

FIGURE 7.34 Final Calls By Type Report

a. Click the **Calls table**. Click the **Report tool** on the Reports group of the CREATE tab.

b. Delete the report icon from the Report Header.

c. Click **Group & Sort** in the Grouping & Totals group on the DESIGN tab if it is not already displayed.

The *Group, Sort, and Total* pane appears at the bottom of the report.

d. Click **Add a group** in the *Group, Sort and Total* pane and select **CallTypeID**.

The report will be grouped by the type of call.

e. Resize the RepID field width so it takes up only as much room as necessary.

The report should fit on one page, left to right.

f. Switch to Design view.

Notice a CallTypeID Header appears between the *Page Header* and *Detail* sections.

g. Click the **More arrow** in the *Group, Sort, and Total* pane. Click the **without a footer section arrow** and switch to **with a footer section**.

A CallTypeID footer appears between the *Detail* and *Page Footer* sections.

h. Click the **HoursLogged text box**. Click **Totals** in the Grouping & Totals group on the DESIGN tab and select **Sum**.

A Sum function appears in both the CallTypeID Footer and the Report Footer.

i. Resize the CallTypeID Footer and Report Footer to be about 1" tall.

j. Resize the text boxes for the new sum fields to be about double the current height.

k. Click the **Insert Page Break control** in the Controls group on the DESIGN tab. Click the bottom of the CallTypeID Footer.

Six small dots appear on the left of the CallTypeID Footer.

l. Display the report in Print Preview.

TROUBLESHOOTING: If you get an error message stating *The section width is greater than the page width, and there are no items in the additional space, so some pages may be blank.*, try making the rows slightly less tall.

All calls with a CallTypeID appear on page 1, with a total of 188 hours appearing on page 2. Scroll to page 4 and notice a total of 208 hours for all calls with a CallTypeID of 2. Your results should resemble Figure 7.34.

m. Save the report as **Calls By Type** and close the report.

n. Exit Access. Submit based on your instructor's directions.

Chapter Objectives Review

After reading this chapter, you have accomplished the following objectives:

1. **Restricting edits in a form.**
   - Create a read-only form: Read-only forms enable users to view but not change data to help prevent erroneous data entry.

2. **Creating a drop-down menu.**
   - Convert a text box to a combo box: A combo box control provides a drop-down menu that displays a list of options from which the user can choose a single value.
   - Customize a converted combo box: Information can be looked up in a table or, less commonly, added manually. You can restrict to only the provided values using the Limit To List option.

3. **Setting the tab order.**
   - Set the tab order: Tab enables users to advance from one field to the next in a form. The tab order is the sequential advancing in a form from one field or control to the next when you press Tab. Changing the tab order may become useful in some instances.
   - Remove a tab stop: Tab stops can be removed from any field. Oftentimes, they are removed from fields that do not require data entry.

4. **Using subforms.**
   - Form can display records from a related table using a subform.
   - Subforms are generally laid out in a tabular fashion and are used when a relationship exists between two tables.

5. **Using advanced controls.**
   - Identify control types: Label controls and text box controls are known as bound controls. A bound control is a control that is connected to a field in a table or query. An unbound control is a control not tied to a specific field, often decorative elements such as titles, lines, pictures, and other decorative objects.
   - Add emphasis to a form or report: The Line and Rectangle controls are among the options to add emphasis.
   - Add text and images to a form or report: Text can be added using a Label control, and images can be added using the Image control.

   - Add a calculated control: A calculated control is placed inside a text box that contains an expression that generates a calculated result and can contain functions, constants, or field names from the record source. Calculated controls can use the Expression Builder to help create complex expressions.
   - Fix layout errors after adding controls: When adding controls, you may need to add them to a layout to maintain a consistent layout.
   - Add a page break control: You can specify exactly where to add a page break using the Page Break control.

6. **Using sections.**
   - Identify the default sections: A section is a part of a form or report that can be manipulated separately from other parts of the form or report. They are viewable in Design view. The *Form Header* section and the *Report Header* section are headers that display one time at the top of each form or report. The Form Header and Report Header appear only once on printouts immediately before the first record appearing on a printout. *Form Footer* and *Report Footer* sections are footers that display one time at the bottom of the form or report. When a form or report is printed the Form Header and Form Footer appear once regardless of the number of pages. The Page Header is a header that appears once at the top of each page in a form or report. The Page Footer is a footer that appears once at the bottom of each page in a form or report. The *Detail* section displays the records in the record source.
   - Show, hide, and resize sections: You can show any missing section by right-clicking and selecting the missing section. Most sections can be hidden.
   - Add a Group Header/Footer to reports: The *Group Header* section appears just above the *Detail* section in Design view, along with the name of the field by which you are grouping. The *Group Header* section appears once each time the grouping field value changes. The *Group Footer* section appears just below the *Detail* section in Design view. Group Headers and Footers are only available in reports.
   - Add totals to a Group Footer/Report Footer: Group Footers (hidden by default) are commonly used for totals.

Key Terms Matching

Match the key terms with their definitions. Write the key term letter by the appropriate numbered definition.

a.	Bound control	**j.**	Page Header
b.	Calculated control	**k.**	Read-only form
c.	Combo box control	**l.**	Report Footer
d.	*Detail* section	**m.**	Report Header
e.	Form Footer	**n.**	Section
f.	Form Header	**o.**	Section bar
g.	Group Footer	**p.**	Subform
h.	Group Header	**q.**	Tab order
i.	Page Footer	**r.**	Unbound control

1. _____ A form that enables users to view but not change data. **p. 676**

2. _____ Provides a drop-down menu displaying a list of options from which the user can choose a single value. **p. 678**

3. _____ The sequential advancing in a form from one field or control to the next when you press Tab. **p. 681**

4. _____ Records displayed that are related to records in a main form. **p. 682**

5. _____ A control that is connected to a field in a table or query. **p. 691**

6. _____ A control not tied to a specific field. **p. 691**

7. _____ A control containing an expression that generates a calculated result. **p. 692**

8. _____ Part of a form or report that can be manipulated separately from other parts of the form or report. **p. 695**

9. _____ A header that displays once at the top of each form. **p. 695**

10. _____ A header that displays once at the top of each report. **p. 695**

11. _____ A footer that displays one time at the bottom of a form. **p. 695**

12. _____ A footer that displays one time at the bottom of a report. **p. 695**

13. _____ A header that appears once at the top of each page in a form or report. **p. 695**

14. _____ A footer that appears once at the bottom of each page in a form or report. **p. 695**

15. _____ Displays the records in the record source. **p. 695**

16. _____ Marks the top boundary of a section in a form or report. **p. 698**

17. _____ Appears just above the *Detail* section in Design view, along with the name of the field by which you are grouping. Appears once each time the grouping field value changes. **p. 699**

18. _____ Appears just below the *Detail* section in Design view. Appears once each time the grouping field value changes. **p. 699**

Multiple Choice

1. A form that is read-only enables you to:
   - (a) Change formatting.
   - (b) Change data.
   - (c) View records.
   - (d) All of the above

2. A combo box enables you to:
   - (a) Add a drop-down menu.
   - (b) Perform calculations.
   - (c) Add headers to a form.
   - (d) Create a read-only form.

3. Which of the following statements about tab order is false?
   - (a) Tab order can be automatically assigned.
   - (b) Fields can have their tab stop removed.
   - (c) Tab order can be arranged in any order you want.
   - (d) None of the above

4. Which of the following would most likely not be a subform?
   - (a) A list of patients for a doctor
   - (b) A list of orders for each customer
   - (c) A list of employees for a location
   - (d) A list of birth mothers for a child

5. A control connected to a field in a table or query is a(n):
   - (a) Bound control.
   - (b) Calculated control.
   - (c) Rectangle control.
   - (d) Unbound control.

6. A control containing =*Date()* is most likely to be a(n):
   - (a) Bound control.
   - (b) Calculated control.
   - (c) Rectangle control.
   - (d) Unbound control.

7. Which statement is false about controls?
   - (a) The *Detail* section displays the values of records.
   - (b) A label control is used for text, such as titles.
   - (c) A calculated field is created with a text box control.
   - (d) Forms cannot display calculated controls.

8. Which of the following prints once per report?
   - (a) Form Header
   - (b) Group Header
   - (c) Page Header
   - (d) Report Header

9. Which of the following prints on every page of a form?
   - (a) Form Header
   - (b) Group Header
   - (c) Page Header
   - (d) Report Header

10. Which of these is not available in an Access form?
    - (a) *Detail* section
    - (b) *Group Header* section
    - (c) *Form Header* section
    - (d) *Page Footer* section

Practice Exercises

1 La Vida Mocha

  You are helping La Vida Mocha, a small coffee supply store, migrate to Access. You will help them add data validation and create two forms, one for data entry and one for viewing data. This exercise follows the same set of skills as used in Hands-On Exercises 1 and 2 in the chapter. Refer to Figure 7.35 as you complete this exercise.

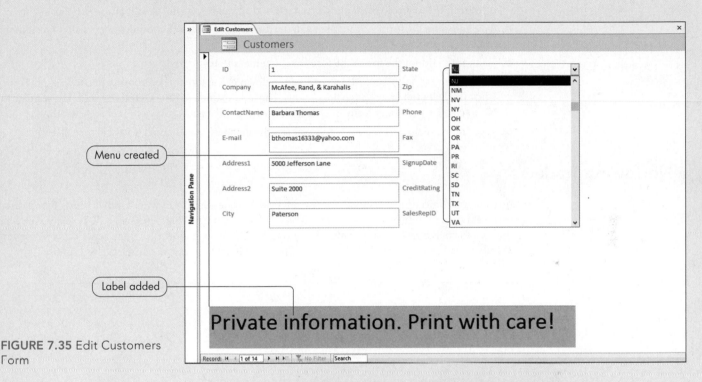

FIGURE 7.35 Edit Customers Form

a. Open Access and create a new database named **a07p1Coffee_LastFirst**.

b. Import the text file *a07p1States* into the database. Name the field **StateName** and choose the StateName field as the primary key. Save the table as **State**. Accept all other default properties.

c. Import the text file *a07p1Customers* into the database. Ensure you check the **First Row Contains Field Names option**, accept default field names, and choose **ID** when asked to select a primary key. Name the table **Customers**.

d. Click the **Customers table** in the Navigation pane. Click **Form** in the Forms group on the CREATE tab. Save the form as **Edit Customers**.

e. Right-click the **State text box**, select **Change To**, and then select **Combo Box**. Click the **Property Sheet button** in the Tools group on the DESIGN tab.

f. Change the **Row Source property** to **State**. Change the **Limit To List property** to **Yes**. Switch to Form view.

g. Change the City for the first customer to **Paterson**, the State to **NJ**, and the Zip to **07505**. You may notice the tab order does not work correctly for this form.

h. Switch to Design view. Click **Tab Order** in the Tools group on the DESIGN tab. Click the **Row Selector** to the left of the State field and drag it below the City field. Click **OK**.

i. Drag the **section bar** below the Form Footer down to approximately 1" on the vertical ruler.

j. Click the **Label control** in the Controls group on the DESIGN tab. Click in the top-left corner of the *Form Footer* section. Type the text **Private information. Print with care!** in the label.

k. Click the border of the label you created in step j to select the entire control. Click the **Font Size menu** in the Font group on the FORMAT tab. Change the font size for the Label control to **36**. Resize the control so all information is displayed on one line.

l. Click the **Font Color menu** in the Font group on the FORMAT tab. Select the **Black, Text 1 color** in the first row.

m. Click the **Background Color menu** in the Font group on the FORMAT tab. Select the **Gold, Accent 4 color** in the first row. Switch to Form view and compare your form to Figure 7.35.

n. Save and close the form. Create a copy of the form named **View Customers**. Open View Customers in Design view.

o. Change the title at the top of the form to **Customers (View Only)**.

p. Display the Property Sheet. Ensure the drop-down at the top of the Property Sheet displays *Form*. Click the **Data tab** and change the options **Allow Additions**, **Allow Deletions**, and **Allow Edits** to **No** to create a read-only form. Switch to Form view and ensure you cannot change data.

q. Save and close the form. Exit Access. Submit the database based on your instructor's directions.

2 Northwind Traders

You are a technical supervisor at Northwind Traders. The technician who handles most Access tasks just went on paternity leave, and he was unable to address user changes before going on leave. You will create a form and report based on user requests. This exercise follows the same set of skills as used in Hands-On Exercises 1 and 2 in the chapter. Refer to Figure 7.36 as you complete this exercise.

FIGURE 7.36 Products Report

a. Open *a07p2Traders*. Save the database as **a07p2Traders_LastFirst**.

b. Open the Products by Category form in Design view.

c. Use the section bar to increase the size of the *Detail* section to about 5" vertically.

d. Click the **Subform/Subreport tool** in the Controls group on the DESIGN tab. Click below the top-left corner of the Description label.

e. Answer the Subform Wizard as follows:

- Select **Use existing Tables and Queries** and click **Next**.
- Select **Table:Products** from the Tables/Queries list. Double-click the **ProductName**, **QuantityPerUnit**, **UnitPrice**, **UnitsInStock**, and **UnitsOnOrder fields**. Click **Next**.
- Select the default relationship (show Products for each record in Categories using CategoryID). Click **Next**.
- Accept the default name of *Products subform*. Click **Finish**.

f. Switch to Layout view. Resize the columns in the subform so all fields are displayed.

g. Save and close the form.

h. Open the Products report in Layout view. Click **Group & Sort** in the Grouping & Totals group on the DESIGN tab. Click **Add a group** in the *Group, Sort and Total* pane. Select **CompanyName**. Notice the CompanyName field is not wide enough to display all values.

i. Switch to Design view. Change the width of the CompanyName field (displayed in the CompanyName Header) to **4"** on the horizontal ruler.

j. Click the **Text Box control** in the Controls group on the DESIGN tab. Click to the right of the ProductCost box.

k. Click **Tabular** in the Table group on the ARRANGE tab.

l. Click in the label for the control created in step j. Change the text in the label from the existing text (which should be *Text* followed by two numbers) to **Net**.

m. Click the text box for the new field and type =**UnitPrice-ProductCost** in the box.

n. Display the Property Sheet by clicking the **Property Sheet button** in the Tools group on the DESIGN tab.

o. Click the **Format button** on the Property Sheet. Change the format to **Currency** and change the **Decimal Places property** to **2**.

p. Switch to Report view. Compare your report to Figure 7.36.

q. Save and close the report.

r. Close the database. Exit Access.

s. Submit based on your instructor's directions.

Mid-Level Exercises

1 Red Cliffs City Hotels

ANALYSIS CASE

You are the general manager of a large hotel chain. You track revenue by categories: hotel rooms, conference rooms, and weddings. You need to create a form that includes a drop-down menu for the state and the company logo in the header, uses the company colors, and has a correct tab order. You also plan on modifying a report so it displays the number of years that each customer has been a member.

a. Open *a07m1Rewards*. Save the database as **a07m1Rewards_LastFirst**.

b. Select the **Members table** and create a form using the Form tool. Save the form as **Maintain Members**.

c. Switch to Design view. Change the State text box to a combo box.

d. Change the Row Source to **States**.

e. Delete the form logo and the label control (containing the word *Members*) from the *Form Header* section.

f. Insert an Image control in the top-left corner of the *Form Header* section. Insert the **a07m1Logo** file.

DISCOVER

g. Change the background color of the *Detail* section to the orange color found in the first row (*Orange, Accent 6*). Note: Select all the labels by drawing a box around them in Design view. Change the font color of the labels to **Black, Text 1**. Change the border width of the labels to **4 pt** and the border color to **Blue, Accent 1**.

h. Switch to Form view. Ensure the form appears correctly. Verify the tab order works as expected by pressing **Tab** to visit each field. Save and close the form.

i. Open the Members By State report in Design view.

j. Add a formula in the **Time as Member box** to determine the number of years they have been a member. Use **#12/31/2017#** as the current date (recall dates must be surrounded by # signs), subtract the MemberSince field, and divide the result by **365**.

k. Change the format of the formula you created in step k to display as **Standard format** with 1 decimal place.

l. Add grouping by the State field. Ensure you remove the State label from the Page Header.

m. Switch to Report view. Ensure the values displayed make sense. For example, member Melissa Remaklus been a member since 11/8/2006, so she has been a member for slightly more than 11 years (assuming it is 12/31/2017).

n. Save and close the report.

o. Open the *a07m1Analysis* document in Word and save as **a07m1Analysis_LastFirst**. Use the database objects you created to answer the questions. Save and close the document.

p. Close the database. Exit Access. Submit based on your instructor's directions.

2 Replacement Parts

You are working as a stockperson in the warehouse for Replacement Parts. You have been given an internship in the information technology department. You have been tasked with making modifications to the company's database. As you are hoping to move from being a stockperson to being a member of the technology staff, you want to impress and go above and beyond what has been asked of you.

a. Open *a07m2Replace*. Save the database as **a07m2Replace_LastFirst**.

b. Create a new form based on the Employees table. Save the form as **Employees Lookup**.

c. Delete the subform. Change the form to be read-only, ensuring users cannot add, delete, or edit records.

d. Change the title in the Form Header to **Employees (Lookup Only)**. Save and close the form.

e. Open the Customer Orders report in Design view.

f. Insert the **a07m2Logo image** in the Report Header to the right of the Customer Orders text.

g. Display the Group Footer. Display the sum of the Qty field in the Group Footer. Add a label that displays **Total Qty Ordered** to the left of the Qty sum.

h. Add a new Text Box control after the Price field. Click **Tabular** in the Table group on the ARRANGE tab.

i. Change the label for the new control to **Line Total**. Add a formula in the text box to multiply the Qty field by the Price field.

j. Change the format of the Line Total to **Currency**.

k. Use the Line control to add a horizontal line at the bottom of the *Group Footer* section.

l. Switch to Report view and ensure the Total Qty Ordered values appear correctly. Switch to Design view.

DISCOVER

m. Add a Sparse Dots border to the Total Qty Ordered text boxes. Add a Special Effect of **Shadowed**. Save and close the report.

n. Exit Access. Submit the database based on your instructor's directions.

3 Ramos Hospital

OLLABORATION CASE

You are working for a local hospital in the information technology department. The founder, Waynet Ramos, has asked your team to help her put together some forms and reports. As she is very busy, she is hoping your team can independently develop some reports and work together to implement and revise them. After discussions with her, you realize she is asking for grouped reports.

a. Waynet needs a report based on which doctors are assigned to each patient, a report showing all medications and who they are prescribed to, and a report showing each patient with the medications they are on. Each group member will create one report.

b. Open Access and open *a07m3Ramos* individually. Save the file as **a07m3Ramos_LastFirst**. Each of you will create your report in an individual database.

c. Create a report using the Report Wizard based on the appropriate tables. Add grouping as necessary.

d. Save the report as **LastFirst**, replacing *Last* and *First* with your last and first names.

e. Make the report as attractive and useful as possible. You may want to perform tasks such as adding subtotals to the group or report footer, changing sorting, removing or add a layout control, changing formatting options, and changing the background color. Modify the report, save the changes, and then exit Access.

f. Meet as a group. Open *a07m3Ramos* and save the file as **a07m3Ramos_GroupName**.

g. Import the report from each of your databases.
   Your *a07m3Ramos_GroupName* file will now have one report for each student.

h. Examine the reports each of you created.

i. Work with your group to improve the reports as necessary. Ensure that you take a critical eye to what your group members came up with and help them improve their report.

j. Save the changes and close all reports. Ensure each student has a copy of the final *a07m3Ramos_GroupName* database.

k. Exit Access and submit both the *a07m3Ramos_GroupName* and *a07m3Ramos_LastFirst* databases based on your instructor's directions.

Beyond the Classroom

Create a Tabbed Form

RESEARCH CASE

Cindy Livesey has a Web site at LivingRichWithCoupons.com where she posts coupon deals. She also has a coupon database that she maintains in Access, which she uses to keep track of her own stockpile. Cindy has contacted you, as one of the users of her Web site, to assist her in organizing the way she inputs coupons. Open the *a07b2Coupons* database and save it as **a07b2Coupons_LastFirst**.

1. Research tabbed forms in Access help or on the Internet. You will create a form based on the Products table, with a tabbed form below. The tabbed form will have two tabs. One tab should display the contents of the related Coupon table as a subform, and the second tab should display the Stockpile Information table. Save the form as **Coupon Reference**.

2. Cindy would like a field on the Stockpile Information tab to display *Yes* when it is time to restock and *No* when it is not. You can accomplish this by inserting a text box field and using the IIf function, displaying *Yes* when the NumberInStockpile is less than the RestockNumber field.

Close the database and close Access. Submit based on your instructor's directions.

Products Database

DISASTER RECOVERY

A new hire for your company is performing data entry for company products. Her system crashed, and the information technology department was able to restore the database from an old backup. She has asked you for help in fixing the database. She has noticed a few problems with the Products Ordered form:

1. The form's tab order does not work properly.

2. The Total On-Hand Value at the top of the page is used to display a value and no longer does. It used to display with two decimal places and no dollar sign. In addition, a lot of extra space exists at the top of the screen between the title and data.

3. The form no longer displays the current date and time at the top right of each page when printed.

4. The subform field widths are too small.

Open *a07b3Food* and save it as **a07b3Food_LastFirst**. Repair the errors above and save and close the database. Submit based on your instructor's directions.

Health Care Privacy

SOFT SKILLS CASE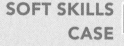

The Woodland Park Hospital is working on a database system to keep track of patients, illnesses, and the doctor assigned to treat the patient. As the technology lead on this project, the group evaluating the database would like your thoughts on how to implement forms and reports. The evaluating committee will be looking at the HIPAA Protected Health Information (PHI) regulation when deciding whether your solution is acceptable. Create forms and reports as specified below and examine the HIPAA PHI regulations. In addition, consider what information you think should be available for each type of user. Open *a07b4Medications* and save it as **a07b4Medications_LastFirst**. Create forms and reports to meet the following specifications. Choose only the fields that you think each group needs based on your research.

1. Doctors need a report showing patient information. Save the report as **Doctor Patient List** and ensure the report title is *Doctor Patient List* as well.

2. Nurses need a report showing medications, doses, and room numbers for each patient. Save the report as **Medications By Room** and change the report title to **Medications by Room**.

3. Front-desk personnel want to enter new patients using a form. Save the form as **Intake**.

4. The hospital needs to provide statistics about how many people are hospitalized with each type of illness to various agencies. Save the report as **Illness Statistics** and change the report title to **Illness Statistics** as well.

Exit Access. Submit the database based on your instructor's directions.

Capstone Exercise

The Human Resources department has asked you to assist them in updating the database they have been using. They need to create a form that can be used to find information but not change information. They have an existing form that they would like to enhance, and they need to be able to present supervisors with a list of employees who report to them. You will assist them in these tasks.

Database File Setup

You will save a copy of the original database and open the database to complete this capstone exercise.

a. Open *a07c1Prices*.

b. Save the database as **a07c1Prices_LastFirst**.

Restrict Edits in a Form

You will create a form to view employees. Use the Form tool to create the form, and then switch the form to be read-only.

a. Select the Employees table and use the Form tool to create a new form.

b. Change the title to **View Employees**.

c. Delete the Orders subform.

d. Change the **Allow Edits**, **Allow Additions**, and **Allow Deletions** settings to **No**.

e. View the form and data in Form view.

f. Save the form as **View Employees** and close the form.

Create a Drop-Down Menu and Set Tab Order

You will modify an existing form to implement a drop-down menu and fix the tab order.

a. Create a new table named **Countries**. Rename the default ID field to **Country** and change the data type to **Short Text**. Enter two records, **UK** and **USA**. Close the table.

b. Open the Update Employees form in Design view.

c. Change the Country field to a combo box.

d. Set the Row Source to **Countries** and the Limit To List property to **Yes**.

e. Fix the tab order so the Postal Code field comes before the Country field. Save and close the form.

Use Controls and Sections

You have been asked to add some privacy information to the bottom of the View Employees form and make some design changes. You have also been asked to create a report for managers that shows the name of all employees who work for them and calculates the number of years the employees have been employed at the company.

a. Open the View Employees form in Design view. Add a new label control in the left-side of the Form Footer that displays the text **Personnel information is considered private and printouts should be shredded after use**.

b. Change the font color to **Black, Text 1** and bold the text.

c. Save and close the form.

d. Create a new report based on the Employees table using the Report Wizard. Select the **FirstName, LastName, HireDate**, and **HomePhone fields**. Select all other default options.

e. Switch to Layout view. Add grouping by the ReportsTo field.

f. Switch to Design view. Display the Group Footer. Display the count of the First Name field in the Report Footer.

g. Add an Insert Page Break control at the bottom of the ReportsTo footer.

h. Resize the Home Phone field so the right side lines up with the 6" on the horizontal ruler.

i. Add a new Text Box control to the right of the Home Phone box. Use the Tabular button in the Table group on the ARRANGE tab to place it correctly.

j. Change the label for the field to **Years Employed**.

k. Add a formula in the text box to calculate the number of years the employee has been employed, assuming the current date is #12/31/2017#. Format the field as **Standard** with 1 decimal place.

l. Close and save the report. Close the database. Exit Access.

m. Submit based on your instructor's directions.

Get Connected

CHAPTER 8

Exchanging Data Between Access and Other Applications

OBJECTIVES AFTER YOU READ THIS CHAPTER, YOU WILL BE ABLE TO:

1. Create a Hyperlink field p. 720
2. Add an Attachment field p. 722
3. Add attachment controls to forms and reports p. 725
4. Export data to Excel p. 735
5. Export data to Word p. 739
6. Export data to a PDF or XPS document p. 742

7. Export objects to another Access database p. 745
8. Link to an Access table p. 756
9. Link to an Excel spreadsheet p. 759
10. Import an Excel spreadsheet p. 762
11. Import a text file p. 765

CASE STUDY | Property Management Data Exchange

The Blackwood Maintenance Service (BMS) is a property management company located in Pineville, North Carolina. The owners would like to attract new customers by expanding the services they offer. Many of the properties that are maintained by BMS belong to residents' associations.

Your task is to contact the board members of each association and ask them if you can send information about the new services. You will also ask permission to send the homeowners a flyer by regular mail.

After contacting each association, you send the association manager a list of the new services that BMS can offer the homeowners. You also need to create a list of homeowners who BMS will contact by mail. You can prepare the information in a variety of ways, so you need to ask each association its preferred format. Information will also be sent to BMS in a variety of formats, and you will need to incorporate the new data into the database.

Connecting Access to External Files

In many cases, it is necessary or desirable to connect to data that exists apart from an Access database. Access provides several ways that you can access data, Web sites, or files from within your database. Access supports a *hyperlink* data type that enables you to quickly link to any file on your computer or to any Web page on the Internet. The data you enter as a hyperlink can be a path to any file on your computer, the location of a Web page on an intranet, an e-mail address, or a URL. A *uniform resource locator (URL)* is the location of a Web site or Web page on the Internet. When you click a hyperlink field value while in Datasheet view, Access launches the program required to display the file or Web page.

If you have a database that contains a Customers table, you can add a hyperlink field to store the Web site address of each customer. When you need information about the customer—the address, phone number, or contact information—you can quickly access the customer Web site by clicking the hyperlink. If the hyperlink is an e-mail address, Access launches a new e-mail window and automatically adds the customer's e-mail address into the To field. You can also link to an Excel spreadsheet that contains a list of the most recent invoices for the customer.

Access also offers you the option of attaching files to a record in a database through an attachment field. An attachment field enables you to attach multiple files of different types. Rather than links that direct you outside of your database, attachments are stored within the database file itself. No limit exists as to the number of files you can attach. For customers, you could attach a photo of the president or CEO, or a photo of a key contact that you work with. You can also attach other document formats, such as Word documents, including contracts or specifications for a product, or scanned documents that are in PDF format.

Users can easily interact with these documents by double-clicking on the appropriate attachment field. A dialog box appears with options to add, remove, open, or save a file. Choose the appropriate file, and then choose the action you want to take.

In this section, you will create a hyperlink field to store Web site addresses. In addition, you will learn how to attach photos and documents to records. Finally, you will learn how to attach files and use an attachment control in forms and reports.

Creating a Hyperlink Field

STEP 1 If you were working in a Customers table, you could add a Hyperlink field in Design view of the table to store the customers' Web sites. Figure 8.1 shows the hyperlink data type selection for the field name CustomerWebsite. After you add the hyperlink field, save the changes and switch to Datasheet view, where you can add the URLs, as shown in Figure 8.2.

Add a Hyperlink Field in Design View

To add a Hyperlink field in Access, do the following:

1. Open the table in Design view and add the new field name to the table.
2. Select Hyperlink from the Data Type list.
3. Save the changes and switch to Datasheet view.
4. Add the data values to the new hyperlink field.
5. Click a hyperlink value and Access launches the appropriate program, such as a Web browser or Excel, and enables you to interact with the file.
6. If you make any changes to the file, save the changes within the host application. For example, if you launch an Excel spreadsheet from within Access, you can make changes to the spreadsheet and then save your changes in Excel.

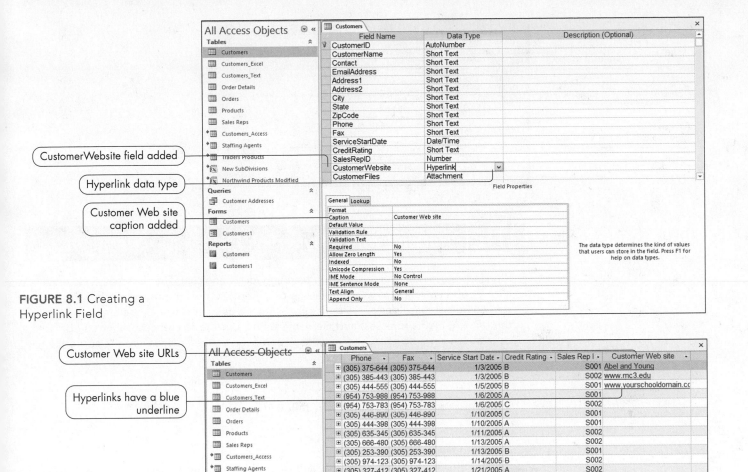

CustomerWebsite field added

Hyperlink data type

Customer Web site caption added

FIGURE 8.1 Creating a Hyperlink Field

Customer Web site URLs

Hyperlinks have a blue underline

FIGURE 8.2 Hyperlink Fields

Edit a Hyperlink in Datasheet View

STEP 2 When you attempt to edit a hyperlink by clicking it, you may accidentally launch the software application instead of just editing the hyperlink value.

To edit a hyperlink value, do the following:

1. Right-click the hyperlink field.
2. Point to *Hyperlink*.
3. Select Edit Hyperlink. The Edit Hyperlink dialog box displays as shown in Figure 8.3. Several options exist in the dialog box; however, the two options that are most commonly used are the *Text to display* box and the Address box.
4. In the *Text to display* box, change the *Text to display* value to modify what the user sees when he or she views the data in Datasheet view (for a table), Form view (for a form), or Print Preview (for a report).
5. In the Address box, enter the actual address that Access uses to locate and launch a file and open it with the appropriate software.
6. Click ScreenTip to create a ScreenTip that will display when you point your mouse over the hyperlink text. This is similar to the ScreenTips that appear when you hover your mouse over commands on the Ribbon.
7. Click OK.

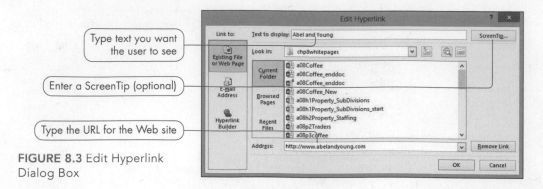

Type text you want the user to see

Enter a ScreenTip (optional)

Type the URL for the Web site

FIGURE 8.3 Edit Hyperlink
Dialog Box

TIP **Working with a Hyperlink Field**

Working with hyperlink fields can be frustrating for an end user. The user may accidentally click to open a program when he or she only wants to edit the hyperlink. For this reason, some database designers define hyperlink fields as text fields. Users can still store the URLs, e-mail addresses, and file name paths, but the references will not automatically launch any software. Users must copy and paste the references into the appropriate application.

To remove a hyperlink field, do the following:

1. Right-click the hyperlink field.
2. Point to *Hyperlink*.
3. Select Remove Hyperlink. Access will remove the current hyperlink without asking for confirmation.

Other options for manipulating a hyperlink field exist in the shortcut list that displays when you right-click a hyperlink; however, editing and removing a hyperlink field are the most commonly used.

Adding an Attachment Field

STEP 3» An Access database is primarily used to store and analyze data and to retrieve information. This data is usually typed directly into the tables or entered using an Access form. Sometimes you may want to store a reference to an external file—an image, a scanned document, an Excel spreadsheet, a PDF document—and then be able to open that file from within Access. These situations can be handled by adding an attachment field to a table. An *attachment field* is similar to an attachment in an e-mail; you can use an Access attachment to attach multiple files of any format and then launch those files from within Access. The files are actually copied into the database itself. Keep in mind that Access is not able to analyze the data within these external files; Access can only open the files. To review the documents, you need to use another program.

The size of your database grows when you attach files. Some file types are compressed by Access when you attach them (such as Excel and Word), and other file types increase the database size byte for byte (such as JPEG and other photo formats). You can monitor the increase in size using these steps:

1. Compact the database.
2. Check the size of the database file.
3. Add the file attachment.
4. Check the size of the database file again.

If the database grows too large, you can remove some attachments (such as JPEGs), resize the files, and reattach the files in a smaller format. JPEG attachments are one of the leading causes for "bloating" in an Access database. Remember to compact your database after you add and remove attachments.

Add an Attachment Field in Design View

If you were working with a Customers table and you wanted to store a photo of the owner, the office building, and the master contract in Access, in Design view you could add a new field named CustomerFiles and select the data type *Attachment*, as shown in Figure 8.4. Save the changes, and then switch to Datasheet view so you can add the files to the new attachment field. A paperclip icon with the number of files attached is shown in the New Attachment column. All records, except record 6, show (0) attachments because no files are attached yet (see Figure 8.5).

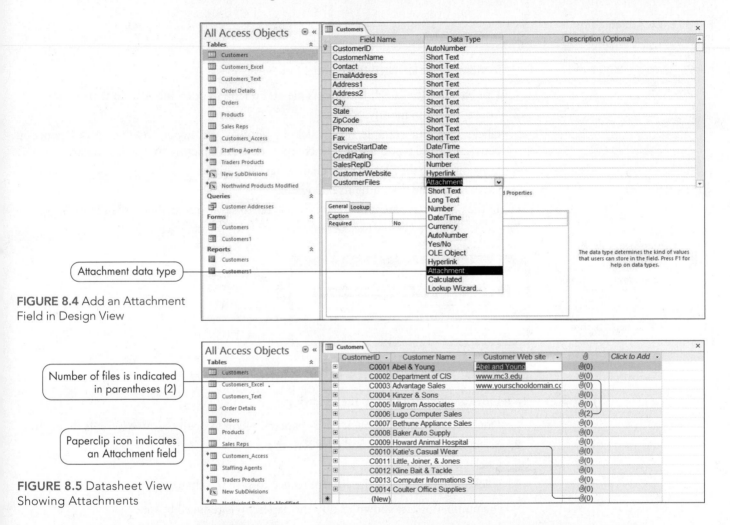

FIGURE 8.4 Add an Attachment Field in Design View

Attachment data type

Number of files is indicated in parentheses (2)

Paperclip icon indicates an Attachment field

FIGURE 8.5 Datasheet View Showing Attachments

Add or Edit Attachments in Datasheet View

STEP 4 Suppose you have a database that stores all the customer information for your business. You want to store a photo of the owner, a photo of the exterior of the main building, a map with directions to the business, and a Word document containing the price structure for each company. The directions file was created using Google Maps and then saved as a PDF document. You can attach all of the files relating to each customer's record.

To attach a file to a record, do the following:

1. Double-click the attachment field's paperclip icon to open the Attachments dialog box, shown in Figure 8.6.
2. Click Add to add the first attachment.
3. Use the Choose File dialog box to locate and select the file.

4. Click Open to attach the file to the record.

5. Click Add again to add the next file and each additional file. In the previous example, you would need to click Add four times to add the two photos, the map, and the price structure document.

6. Click OK to close the Attachments dialog box. The paperclip icon would now show that (4) files are attached to the current record.

7. Click the record below the current record to save the attached files.

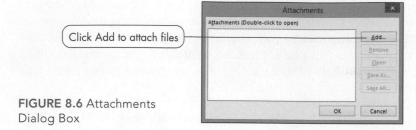

Click Add to attach files

FIGURE 8.6 Attachments Dialog Box

To view or edit attached files, do the following:

1. Double-click the attachment field's paperclip icon to open the Attachments dialog box.

2. Select the file to modify.

3. Click Open. For example, if you click the photo of the owner, and then click Open, you can modify the photo using your computer's default picture manager software.

4. Save and close the file once the change has been made.

5. Click OK in the Attachments dialog box.

6. In the Save Attachment dialog box, click Yes to save your changes (see Figure 8.7).

7. Click the record below the current record to save the changes.

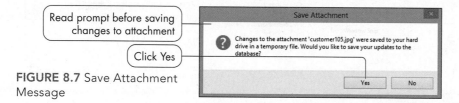

Read prompt before saving changes to attachment

Click Yes

FIGURE 8.7 Save Attachment Message

Remove Attachments in Datasheet View

STEP 5 » To remove an attached file, do the following:

1. Double-click the attachment field's paperclip icon to open the Attachments dialog box.

2. Select the file to remove and click Remove.

3. Click OK.

4. Click the record below the current record to save the changes.

The number of files shown next to the paperclip is reduced by one.

TABLE 8.1	Using the Attachments Dialog Box
Add	Click to add one or more files to a record.
Remove	Click to remove previously attached files.
Open	Click to launch the appropriate application and open the file. If you try to close the Attachments dialog box with the file open, you will receive a warning that your changes may not be saved. If you are sure you have saved your changes, click OK. You will receive a message that the changes were saved to your hard drive in a temporary file. Access asks if you would like to save your updates to the database (see Figure 8.7).
Save As	Use to save the attached file to a local storage location. You must remember to add it back into the database if you make changes.
Save All	Save all of the attachments in a record to a local, temporary folder.

Adding Attachment Controls to Forms and Reports

STEP 6 In a form or report, you can interact with attachments using an attachment control. An ***attachment control*** is a control that lets you manage attached files in forms and reports. In a form, the attachment control enables you to add, edit, and delete attachments the same way you can in a table. If the attachment is a photo, the control displays the photo as you navigate through the records. If the attachment is a document, you will only see an icon representing the application that was used to create the file. When you click an attachment control in Form view, the Attachment toolbar displays arrows that enable you to advance through the attachments. The Attachment toolbar also has a paperclip icon that you can click to open the Attachments dialog box. This dialog box is the same one that opens when you click an attachment field in a table.

In a report, the attachment field displays the first file only in Print Preview. If the first attachment is a photo, the control displays the photo; if the first file is a document, an icon representing the application is displayed. The Attachment toolbar does not appear in Print Preview. To see the Attachment toolbar and advance through multiple attachments in a report, close Print Preview, and then switch to Report view. Report view enables you to advance through multiple attachments. In a form, switch to Form view to work with the Attachment toolbar.

Add an Attachment Control to a Form

To add an attachment control to a form, do the following:

1. Open the form in Layout view.
2. Click Add Existing Fields in the Tools group on the DESIGN tab.
3. In the Field List, the attachment field appears as a parent field with three child fields. The expand symbol (+) enables you to expand and collapse the child fields.
4. Drag the parent field name to the form, and then drop it in the desired location, as shown in Figure 8.8. Access adds the bound attachment control and the associated label to the form.
5. Resize the bound control, if necessary, to ensure that the images display correctly.
6. Save your changes, and then switch to Form view to view your changes (see Figure 8.9).
7. Return to Layout view for additional modifications if necessary.

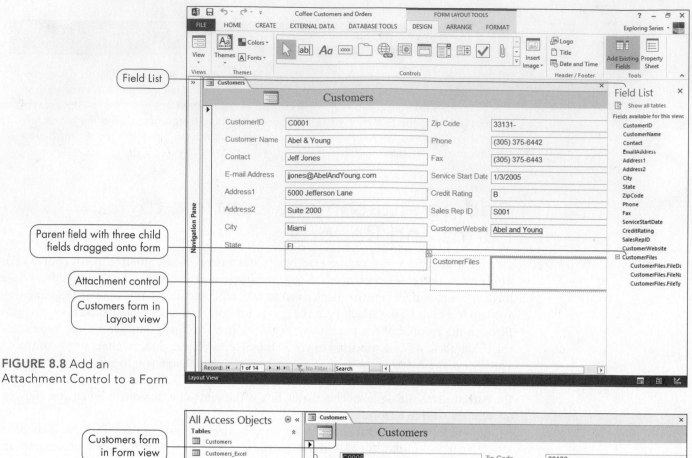

FIGURE 8.8 Add an Attachment Control to a Form

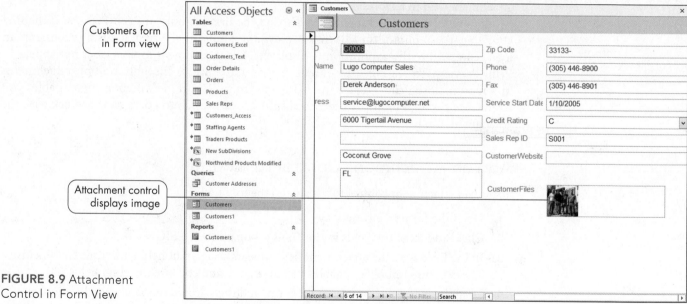

FIGURE 8.9 Attachment Control in Form View

Add an Attachment Field to a Report

STEP 7 To add an attachment field to an existing report, do the following:

1. Open the report in Layout view.
2. Click Add Existing Fields in the Tools group on the DESIGN tab.
3. Drag the parent field name to the report, and then drop it in the desired location.
4. When the attachment control is in place, click the control to view the Attachment toolbar, as shown in Figure 8.10. Attachments can also be viewed in Report view of the report.

5. Using the Attachment toolbar, click the *next* and *previous* arrows to advance from one attachment to the next, or click the paperclip icon to open the Attachments dialog box. You should reduce the size of the attachment control in a report because a report usually displays multiple records on one page. If a user needs a larger view of a thumbnail, he or she can always review the photo in Layout view by opening the Attachments dialog box.

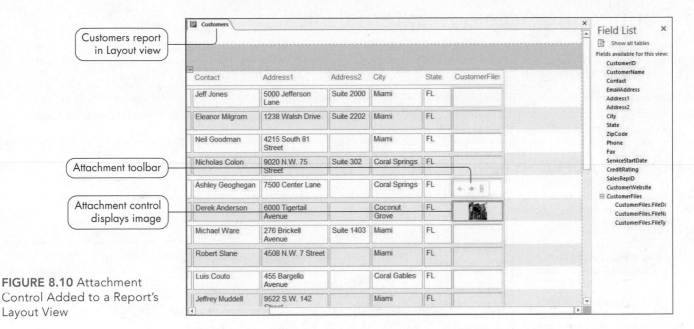

Customers report in Layout view

Attachment toolbar

Attachment control displays image

FIGURE 8.10 Attachment Control Added to a Report's Layout View

In Hands-On Exercise 1, you will work with the database from the Blackwood property management company. You will add and edit a Hyperlink field that will link properties to the appropriate school district's Web page. You will create and use an Attachment field (some with multiple attachments) in an Access table, and you will add attachment controls to a form and a report.

Quick Concepts

1. What is the major difference between a linked file and an attachment? *p. 720*

2. What is a potential disadvantage of storing attachments in your databases? *p. 722*

3. In which view of a report is the Attachment toolbar available? *p. 725*

Hands-On Exercises

Watch the Video
for this Hands-
On Exercise!

MyITLab®
HOE1 Training

1 Connecting Access to External Files

Blackwood Maintenance Service wants to add a link to a Web site for each subdivision and a link to the school district that each subdivision resides in. You will also add a photo of each property that BMS now serves. Finally, you will add a photo and related documents to the record of each BMS agent.

Skills covered: Add a Hyperlink Field in Design View • Edit a Hyperlink in Datasheet View • Add an Attachment Field in Design View • Add or Edit Attachments in Datasheet View • Remove Attachments in Datasheet View • Add an Attachment Control in Layout View • Add an Attachment Field in a Form or Report

STEP 1 ≫ ADD A HYPERLINK FIELD IN DESIGN VIEW

Create a new field that will link to a Web site for each subdivision served by Blackwood. Also add a link to the school district Web site for each subdivision. Refer to Figure 8.11 as you complete Step 1.

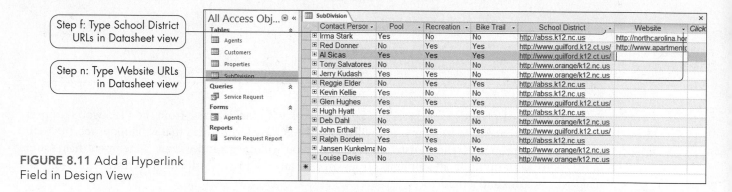

Step f: Type School District URLs in Datasheet view

Step n: Type Website URLs in Datasheet view

FIGURE 8.11 Add a Hyperlink Field in Design View

a. Open *a08h1Property*. Click the **FILE tab**, click **Save As**, click **Save As**, and then type **a08h1Property_LastFirst**. Click **Save**.

> **TROUBLESHOOTING:** Throughout the remainder of this chapter and textbook, click Enable Content whenever you are working with student files. If you make any major mistakes in this exercise, you can close the file, open *a08h1Property* again, and then start this exercise over.

b. Open the Agents table and replace *Your_Name* with your name in both the FirstName and LastName fields. Close the Agents table.

c. Open the SubDivision table in Design view. In the blank row below the BikeTrail field name, type **SchoolDistrict**. Click the **Data Type arrow** and select **Hyperlink**.

d. Type **School District** in the **Caption property box** in the Field Properties window in the bottom portion of the Table Design view.

e. Save the changes to the table. Switch to Datasheet view.

You are ready to add the school districts' Web site addresses to the new hyperlink field.

f. Type **http://abss.k12.nc.us** into the **School District field** for records 1, 6, 7, 9, and 12.

Fair Brook, North Point, Red Canyon, The Links, and The Pines are all located in the Alamance-Burlington School System.

g. Type **http://www.guilford.k12.ct.us** into the **School District field** for records 2, 3, 8, and 11.

King's Forest, Dale, Seeley Lake, and The Orchards are in the Guilford District.

h. Type **http://www.orange.k12.nc.us** into the **School District field** for the remaining records (records 4, 5, 10, 13, and 14).

The remaining subdivisions are in the Orange County School District.

> **TROUBLESHOOTING:** If you make a mistake, do not click in the School District field to correct it. Instead, click in the BikeTrail column and press Tab to select the field that contains an error. Retype the information.

i. Test the accuracy of the URLs by clicking the **School District hyperlink** in records 1 and 2. If the security window appears, click **Yes** to continue.

The browser opens and the school district's Web site opens. Close the browser window.

j. Widen the School District field so all the data is displayed, and then compare your screen to Figure 8.11.

k. Switch to Design view.

l. Type **Website** in the first blank field under *School District*. Select **Hyperlink** as the data type.

You added a second hyperlink field for each community's Web site.

m. Save the changes to the table. Switch to Datasheet view.

You are ready to add the community Web site addresses to the new hyperlink field.

n. Type **http://northcarolina.hometownlocator.com/nc/catawba/fairbrook.cfm** into the **Website field** of record 1.

This hyperlink points to the nearby community.

o. Type **http://www.apartmentguide.com/neighborhoods/North-carolina-Greensboro-Kings-Forests** into the **Website field** of record 2.

This hyperlink lists information about the surrounding community.

STEP 2 ≫ EDIT A HYPERLINK IN DATASHEET VIEW

You realized that you entered an incorrect URL for the Guilford schools. The current URL links point to schools in Connecticut, not in North Carolina. You will fix the links in this step so that the URL links to schools in North Carolina. Refer to Figure 8.12 as you complete Step 2.

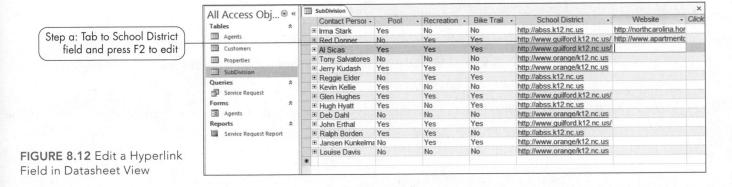

FIGURE 8.12 Edit a Hyperlink Field in Datasheet View

a. Click in the **BikeTrail column** of record 2 and press **Tab** to select the School District field. Press **F2** and edit the link so it reads **http://www.guilford.k12.nc.us**.

The *ct* segment of the hyperlink was changed to *nc*. The hyperlink is enclosed with pound signs (#), which Access uses to activate the link when clicked.

b. Click in the **BikeTrail column** of record 3 to save your changes. Test the new hyperlink by clicking the **School District field** in record 2, *http://www.guilford.k12.nc.us*.

The link now points to the correct school district. Close the browser window. You will use another method to edit the remaining Guilford URLs.

c. Right-click the **http://www.guilford.k12.ct.us** hyperlink in record 3, point to *Hyperlink*, and then select **Edit Hyperlink** from the shortcut menu.

The Edit Hyperlink dialog box opens.

d. Change the *ct* segment of the hyperlink to **nc** in the Address field at the bottom of the dialog box. Click **OK** to accept your changes and press the down arrow to save your changes.

The Text to display changes.

e. Test the modified URL by clicking **http://www.guilford.k12.nc.us hyperlink** in record 3.

The link now points to the correct school district. Close the browser window.

f. Edit the remaining Guilford URLs (change *ct* to **nc**) using the Edit Hyperlink dialog box. Compare your results to Figure 8.12.

g. Close the SubDivision table.

STEP 3 ≫ ADD AN ATTACHMENT FIELD IN DESIGN VIEW

BMS has collected photos of its properties for the past several years. The photos are stored in a folder where employees can access them as needed. The owners have asked you to create an attachment field so you can attach each photo to its corresponding property. Refer to Figure 8.13 as you complete Step 3.

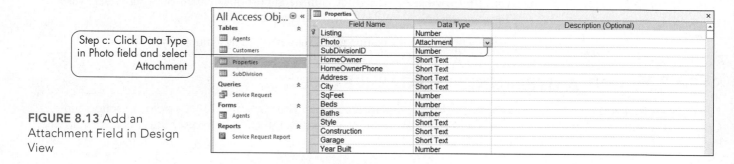

FIGURE 8.13 Add an Attachment Field in Design View

a. Open the Properties table in Design view.

You will add an attachment field that enables you to attach the photos of the properties.

b. Click the **SubDivisionID field row selector** and click **Insert Rows** in the Tools group.

A new row is added between Listing and SubDivisionID.

c. Type **Photo** in the **Field Name column** and select **Attachment** as the data type.

d. Save the changes to the table design. Switch to Datasheet view.

The new attachment field displays a paperclip symbol with a (0), indicating no attachments are on any of the property records.

STEP 4 ≫ ADD OR EDIT ATTACHMENTS IN DATASHEET VIEW

In this step, you will attach the photos to the corresponding properties. Having these photos attached to the properties enables the agents to access them when working with the property owners. You will add 13 photos now and the other photos later. Refer to Figure 8.14 as you complete Step 4.

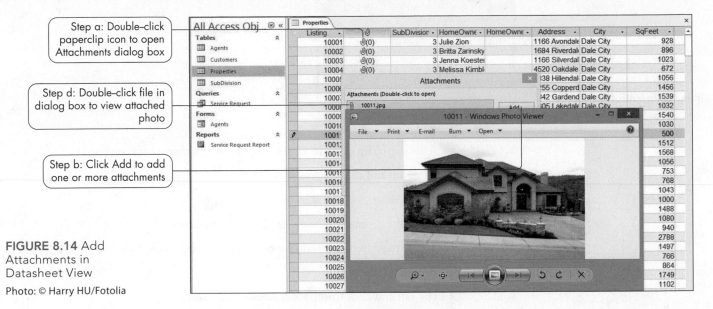

Step a: Double-click paperclip icon to open Attachments dialog box

Step d: Double-click file in dialog box to view attached photo

Step b: Click Add to add one or more attachments

FIGURE 8.14 Add Attachments in Datasheet View

Photo: © Harry HU/Fotolia

a. Double-click the **paperclip icon** in the Photo field in the record for listing 10011 to open the Attachments dialog box.

b. Click **Add**. Locate the *10011.jpg* photo found in the a08h1Photos folder. Double-click the file to add it to the Attachments dialog box.

   The file displays in the Attachments dialog box.

c. Click **OK** to close the Attachments dialog box, and then click the record for listing 10012 to save the record.

d. Double-click the **paperclip** in record 11 to open the Attachments dialog box again. Double-click the *10011.jpg* photo to open your computer's default photo software.

   Compare your screen to Figure 8.14.

e. Close the photo software and click **OK** in the Attachments dialog box.

f. Double-click the **paperclip** in listing 10043.

g. Click **Add** in the Attachment dialog box, and then locate and attach photo *10043.jpg* to the record. Click **OK**.

h. Double-click the **paperclip** in listing 10067 and attach photo *10067.jpg* to the record.

i. Add the corresponding photos to the following records: 10865, 10888, 10899, 10935, 10968, 11028, 11042, 11118, 11141, and 11171.

j. Select the record for listing 10025. Double-click the **paperclip** to open the Attachments dialog box. Click **Add** and add photo *10025a.jpg* to the Attachments dialog box. Before clicking OK to attach the photo, click **Add** in the Attachments dialog box to add a second attachment to the record. Double-click *10025b.jpg* to add it to the Attachments dialog box. Click **OK** to add both photo attachments to the record. Click the record for listing 10026 to save the record.

STEP 5 ➤➤ REMOVE ATTACHMENTS IN DATASHEET VIEW

One of the properties was sold, and the new owners are not going to use BMS to manage their property. You decide to remove the photos from this property. Refer to Figure 8.15 as you complete Step 5.

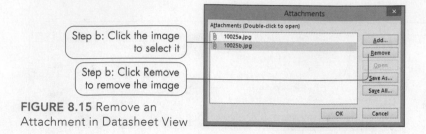

Step b: Click the image to select it

Step b: Click Remove to remove the image

FIGURE 8.15 Remove an Attachment in Datasheet View

a. Double-click the **paperclip** in listing 10025 to open the Attachments dialog box.

b. Click the first photo and click **Remove**.

c. Click the second photo and click **Remove**.

Both photos have been removed from the Attachments dialog box.

d. Click **OK** to close the Attachments dialog box and click the record below to save the record.

e. Close the Properties table.

f. Click the **FILE tab** and click **Compact & Repair Database**.

You decide to compact the database because adding and removing attachments can increase the size of the database.

STEP 6 ➤➤ ADD AN ATTACHMENT CONTROL IN LAYOUT VIEW

BMS asks you to create a report showing the properties with an outstanding service request. You decide to include a photo of each property, but only a thumbnail will appear in the report. Refer to Figure 8.16 as you complete Step 6.

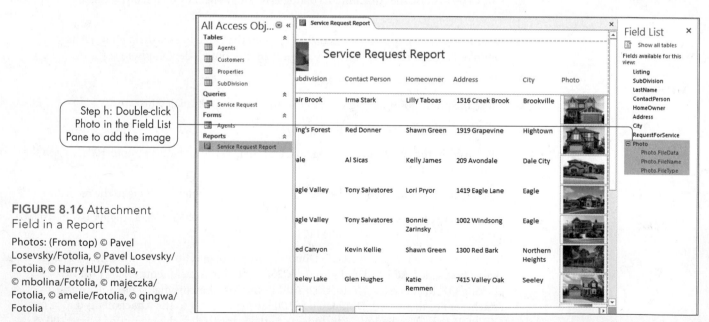

Step h: Double-click Photo in the Field List Pane to add the image

FIGURE 8.16 Attachment Field in a Report

Photos: (From top) © Pavel Losevsky/Fotolia, © Pavel Losevsky/Fotolia, © Harry HU/Fotolia, © mbolina/Fotolia, © majeczka/Fotolia, © amelie/Fotolia, © qingwa/Fotolia

a. Open the Service Request query in Design view. Change the criterion from *Your_name* to your last name.

b. Switch to Datasheet view and examine the query results.

Thirteen properties display with you as the manager. The Photo field is missing; you must return to Design view to add it to the query design.

c. Switch to Design view.

d. Drag the **Photo field** from the Properties table and drop it into the first blank column in the query design grid.

> **TROUBLESHOOTING:** If you drag one of the three child fields, delete the column and try again. Make sure you add the parent photo field, the field with a (+) or (−) symbol to its left.

e. Switch to Datasheet view and examine the query results again. Save and close the query.

f. Double-click **Service Request Report** and switch to Layout view.

g. Click **Add Existing Fields** in the Tools group.

h. Click **Brookville** to select the City column. Double-click **Photo** in the Field List pane to add the field to the right side of the report.

> **TROUBLESHOOTING:** If you double-click one of the three child fields, click Undo and try again. Make sure you double-click the parent photo field, the field with a (+) or (−) symbol to its left.

The Photo field becomes the last column on the right of the report. Most of the photos are positioned on the right side of the right margin line. You will resize the other columns to reduce the layout width to one page.

i. Click **Add Existing Fields** in the Tools group to close the Field List window. Reduce the width of the Listing column by dragging the right border of the Listing column heading to the left.

j. Reduce the width of the City column until no photos are positioned on the second page.

k. View the report in Print Preview.

All the fields now fit onto one page.

l. Click **Close Print Preview** in the Close Preview group. Save and close the report.

STEP 7 ›› USE AN ATTACHMENT FIELD IN A FORM OR REPORT

Blackwood wants to add a photo of each agent to the database. They also want to attach the latest performance evaluation to each employee's record. Refer to Figure 8.17 as you complete Step 7.

FIGURE 8.17 Attachment Field in a Form

Photo: © Rido/Fotolia

a. Open the Agents table in Design view. Add a field named **RelatedFiles** in the first blank row under *CellPhone*. Select **Attachment Data Type**. In the *Field Properties* section, type **Photo and Related Files** in the **Caption property**.

You added an attachment field to store the photo and performance review for each agent.

b. Save the table changes, and then switch to Datasheet view.

You need to attach a photo and a Word file for each employee.

c. Double-click the **paperclip** in the first record, for Juan Rosario. The Attachments dialog box opens. Click **Add**. Locate and open the *a08h1Agents* folder. Find and double-click *juan.jpg* to attach it. Click **OK** to close the Attachments dialog box and click another record to save the current record.

The paperclip now shows that (1) file is attached to Juan's record. Next, add a photo and a Word file to Kia Hart's record.

d. Double-click the **paperclip** in Kia Hart's record to open the Attachments dialog box. Click **Add**. Locate the *kia.jpg* photo and attach it to the record by double-clicking the file. Click **Add** again and attach the document *Kia Hart Performance Evaluation*. Click **OK** to close the Attachments dialog box and click another record to save the current record.

Kia's record should indicate (2) attachments.

e. Attach the remaining agents' photos to their records. Use the photo named *your_name* for your photo. Attach the *Your_Name Performance Evaluation* document to your record as well. Close the table.

f. Open the Agents form in Design view. Click the **ID field** to activate the Layout Selector (the small square with a cross inside, located to the left of the first field).

You will move all the fields to the right.

g. Click **Layout Selector** and drag the fields as a group to the right.

Use Figure 8.17 (the completed form) as a guide as you reposition the fields.

h. Click **Add Existing Fields** in the Tools group to open the Field List.

i. Drag the **RelatedFiles field** to the left of the fields you just moved.

The field is added to the left side of the form. You need to reposition the label and the control separately.

j. Move the **RelatedFiles control** to the top of the form using the small solid square at the top-left of the control. Resize the control using Figure 8.17 (the completed form) as a guide.

> **TROUBLESHOOTING:** If the label follows the attachment control, release the mouse and try again. Verify you are dragging the attachment using the small solid square.

k. Drag the **Photo and Related Files label** to the bottom of the control, as shown in Figure 8.17. Click the **FORMAT tab** and click **Center** in the Font group to center align the label text.

l. Switch to Form view. Click **Next record** in the Navigation bar to advance to record 2, Kia Hart's record.

This record has two attachments. The Word file displays as an icon, and the photo is not displayed.

m. Double-click the **Word icon** to open the Attachments dialog box. Click **Open**. Kia's overall rating is *Good*. Close the Word file. Click **Kia.jpg** and click **Open**. Close the photo file. Click **OK** in the Attachments dialog box.

n. Click the **Attachment control** to activate the Attachment toolbar. Click the **green arrow** to display the next attachment.

Kia's photo displays.

o. Click **Next record** in the Navigation bar to advance to your record. Double-click the Attachment control to open the Attachments dialog box. Click each attachment and click **Open** to view each file. Close the Attachments dialog box when you are finished.

p. Save and close the form.

q. Click the **FILE tab** and click **Compact & Repair Database**.

r. Keep the database open if you plan to continue with Hand-On Exercise 2. If not, close the database and exit Access.

Exporting Data to Office and Other Applications

Using Access to collect and store data, to extract information, and to analyze information is useful for any organization. The accounting department of a company will always need to track sales, inventory, materials, and labor so it can report the financial statements to management each month. Access can handle this task. In addition, the sales department will need to process orders and track profitability based on each order and on categories of products. Access can handle this task as well. If management wants to know who its best customers are based on sales for the current year, Access can provide this information, too, using a query and a report.

But what happens when this information must be shared with the other departments or with other companies? How can the accountants deliver database information to others who might not be familiar with using Access or even have the software? One way to deliver information is via hard copies. However, this does not work if the recipient wants to manipulate the data him- or herself to analyze it further from a different angle. A common way to distribute data stored in an Access database is to export the data to another application.

In this section, you will learn how to export Access data to Excel and Word. Because these two applications are part of the Microsoft Office Suite, exporting from Access is straightforward. In addition to exporting to Excel and Word, this section will show you how to create a PDF or XPS document and how to export objects from one Access database to another Access database.

Exporting Data to Excel

Exporting data from Access to Excel is generally uncomplicated because the data in Access is usually structured in a manner that Excel understands. However, a few special situations exist when exporting to Excel; these situations will be discussed in the section that follows.

Select a Record Source to Export to Excel

If the record source you want to export to Excel is a table, such as the Customers table shown in Figure 8.18, then the export-to-Excel process is fast and easy. When you export a table to Excel, the field names become the column headings and the table records become the rows in the Excel spreadsheet.

To export a table to Excel, do the following:

1. Select the table in the Navigation Pane (or open the table first).
2. Click Excel in the Export group on the EXTERNAL DATA tab. Access opens the Export – Excel Spreadsheet dialog box to guide you through the export process.
3. Specify the file name and destination and the format for the exported file. Specify whether to export the data with formatting and layout. This option preserves most formatting and layout information applied in Access. Otherwise, the file opens using default Excel formatting.
4. Specify if you want to open the destination file after the export operation is complete. This option opens the resulting file. Otherwise, you would need to open it from within its application.
5. Specify if you want to export only the selected records (if you have selected one or more records in the datasheet).
6. Click OK.

When you export a table from Access, all of the columns and all the records in the table are exported, even if the table is open and not all of the data is visible (as shown in Figure 8.18). The end result is a new Excel worksheet containing all of the columns and all of the records in the Customers table, as shown in Figure 8.19.

FIGURE 8.18 Customers Table in Access Before Exporting to Excel

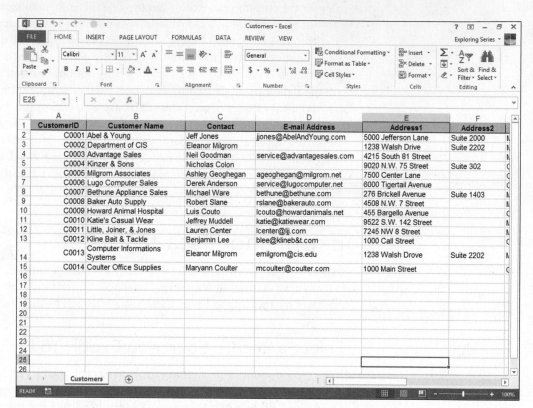

FIGURE 8.19 Customers Table Exported to Excel

STEP 1 ≫   If you want to export only a subset of the Customers table, you can filter a table or select specific records before exporting. Alternatively, you could create a query to then export to Excel. For example, if you only need the address fields for customers in a certain zip code, you can create a query and then save it. Select the query, and then export the query records to Excel.

Export a Query to Excel

To export a query to Excel, do the following:

1. Select the query in the Navigation Pane (or open the query first).
2. Click Excel in the Export group on the EXTERNAL DATA tab. Access opens the Export – Excel Spreadsheet dialog box (shown in Figure 8.20) to guide you through the export process.
3. Specify the file name and destination and the format for the exported file.
4. Specify whether to export the data with formatting and layout.
5. Specify if you want to open the destination file after the export operation is complete (see Figure 8.21).
6. Specify if you want to export only the selected records (if you have selected one or more records in the datasheet).
7. Click OK.

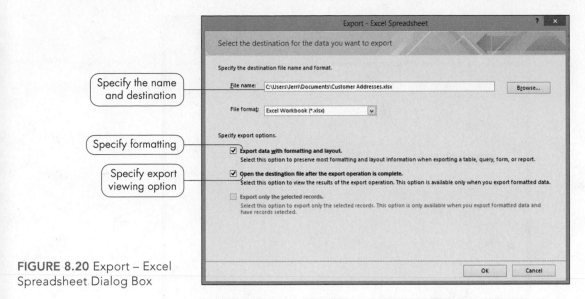

FIGURE 8.20 Export – Excel Spreadsheet Dialog Box

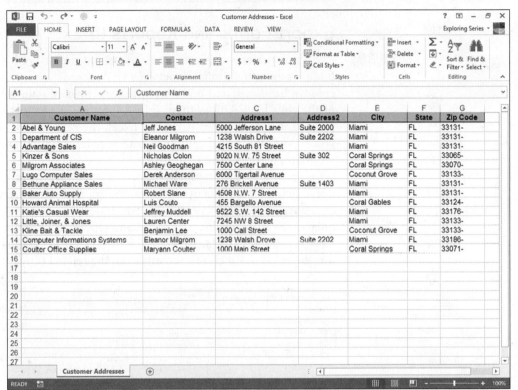

FIGURE 8.21 Customer Addresses Query Exported to Excel

The Excel spreadsheet will display. Once you are finished reviewing the exported Excel spreadsheet, and then return to the Access window, one final screen requires a response. In Figure 8.22, Access asks you, *Do you want to save these export steps?* Click the *Save export steps* check box if you want to repeat the same export process at a later time. Saving export steps is useful if you need to repeatedly export the same query. The saved steps are stored under Saved Exports in the Export group.

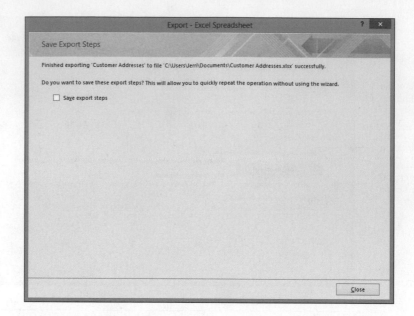

FIGURE 8.22 Save Export
Steps Dialog Box

Export Forms and Reports to Excel

STEP 2 » Exporting tables and queries to Excel usually yields predictable and consistent results. The main reason is the similarity between an Access datasheet and an Excel worksheet. Both have column headings, and both have multiple rows of data below the column headings. Most of the cells have data in them (blank cells are the exception). However, when you export forms and reports from Access to Excel, the results can be unpredictable. For example, if you export a form that contains Customers information and a subform showing the Orders for each customer, the Customers data exports but the Orders (subform data) does not. Furthermore, if you attempt to export a grouped report in Access, the grouping in Excel may not match the grouping in the Access report. You can either accept the results from the form or report, or redo the export using the underlying record source. The underlying tables and queries are more reliable than forms and reports. Figure 8.23 shows an Access form based on Customers and the related Orders for each customer. Figure 8.24 shows the same form after it is exported to Excel. The records from the related (Orders) table do not display.

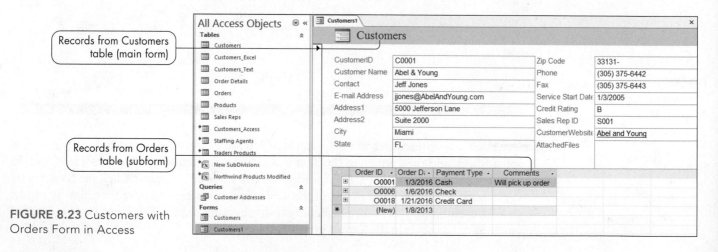

FIGURE 8.23 Customers with
Orders Form in Access

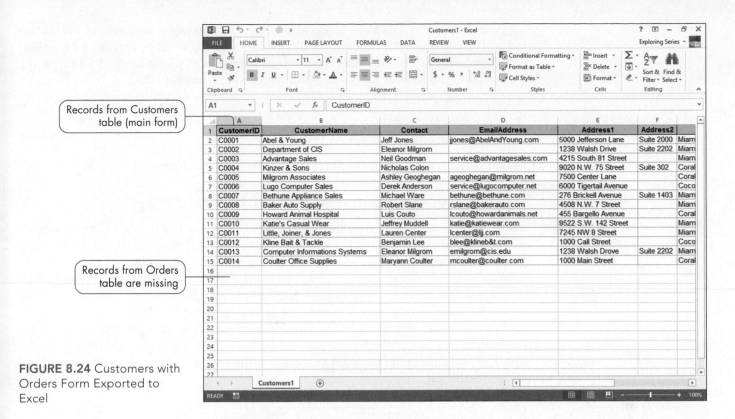

FIGURE 8.24 Customers with Orders Form Exported to Excel

TIP **When to Export to Excel**

Several reasons exist for Access users to export data to Excel. One is to take advantage of Excel's charting capabilities. Another reason is to test different scenarios with the data and to analyze the results. This type of analysis enables managers to predict future trends. Manipulating data in Excel is preferable to changing data in Access. You want the raw data in Access to stay the same! A final reason for exporting to Excel is to be able to distribute the Access data to users who do not have Access or who do not know how to use Access.

Exporting Data to Word

Exporting data from Access to Word is similar to exporting data to Excel, except that you are not able to analyze the data as you can in Excel. Once the data is exported to Word, you will most likely use the data as is for reporting purposes rather than for analysis. Although you can modify the data in the table cells, those changes do not update the totals or other calculated fields (as they do in Excel).

The objects you select to export from Access to Word should have a tabular layout—tables, queries, and tabular reports fit this description. Although other object types do export to Word, the results are unpredictable and poorly formatted. If you are uncertain about which type of objects to export to Word, select any object in Access and export it to Word to see if it is properly formatted. If the data is usable, you can keep the Word document. If the data is not what you wanted, just close the file without saving and try again with a different layout.

When you export an object from Access to Word, Access creates a file in the RTF format. *Rich Text Format (RTF)* is a format that enables documents created in one software application to be opened with a different software application. The RTF format was introduced in 1987 by Microsoft and is now supported by Windows, Macintosh, open source, Unix, and other environments. RTF is a useful format for basic formatted text documents such as instruction manuals, résumés, letters, and other documents. These documents support special text formatting such as bold, italic, and underline. RTF documents also support left-, center-, and right-justified text. Furthermore, font specifications and document margins are supported in RTF documents.

When you export data from Access to Word, the RTF format is used and the file's extension will be .rtf. If you double-click the file, Windows opens Word by default and then displays the contents of the file. Word is the default software application for the RTF extension.

To convert an RTF file to a Word document, do the following:

1. From within Word, click the FILE tab.
2. Click Save As.
3. Change the *Save as type* to Word Document.

From that point forward, the document retains the Word format.

Select a Record Source to Export to Word

STEP 3>>

Similar to exporting to Excel, exporting Access tables and queries to Word is much simpler (as compared to exporting forms and reports). For example, if you need to add the Products table from an Access database into a Word document, as shown in Figure 8.25, the export-to-Word process is fast and easy. When you export a table to Word, Access creates an RTF file and inserts a table into the document. For the Products table, the field names become the column headings and the records become the table rows in the RTF file.

You can export tabular reports to Word; Access preserves the report's grouping aggregate functions. Some of the formatting may be lost. Columnar forms and reports do not export to Word properly; however, you can test the export of these objects to see if they produce usable data.

FIGURE 8.25 Product Data in Access

Export Tables and Queries to Word

Exporting tables and queries to Word is similar to exporting tables and queries to Excel.
To export a table or query to Word, do the following:

1. Select the table or query in the Navigation Pane (or open the table or query first) and click the EXTERNAL DATA tab.
2. Click the More button in the Export group.
3. Select Word. Access opens the Export – RTF dialog box (shown in Figure 8.26) to guide you through the export process.

4. Specify the file name, destination, and format for the exported file.
5. Specify if you want to open the destination file after the export operation is complete (see Figure 8.26).
6. Specify if you want to export only the selected records (if you have selected one or more records in the datasheet).
7. Click OK.

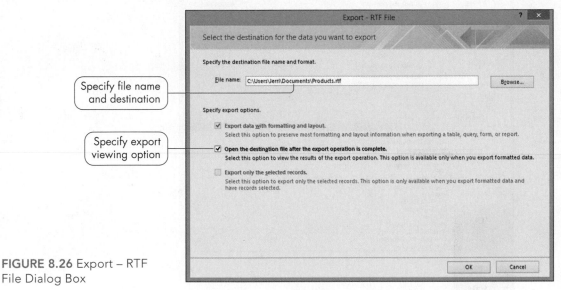

FIGURE 8.26 Export – RTF File Dialog Box

Modify an RTF File in Word

STEP 3» After you export an Access table to an RTF file, you can edit the file in Word and add additional text to the Products table content. If you need to send the products list to a few vendors to check current prices, you can insert a few blank lines above the Products table and type the To, From, and Subject lines as shown in Figure 8.27. Because the Products table was inserted at the top of the page, to insert lines above the table, click immediately before the first value in the first cell of the table and press Enter three times. The table moves down to make room for the To, From, and Subject lines. Type the rest of the information and save the document.

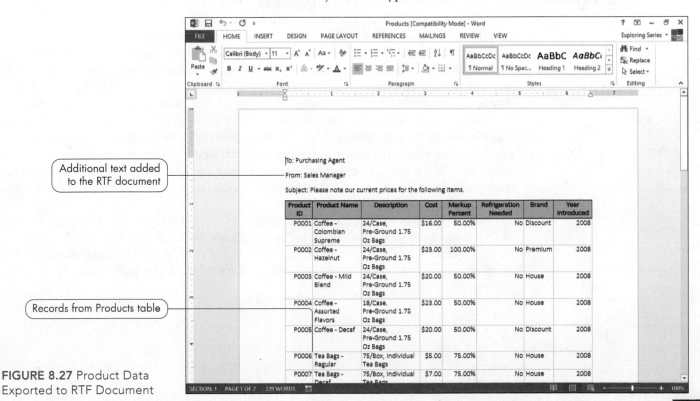

FIGURE 8.27 Product Data Exported to RTF Document

When you save an RTF file, you might want to change the file type to Word Document so that you can take full advantage of Word's features and formatting tools.

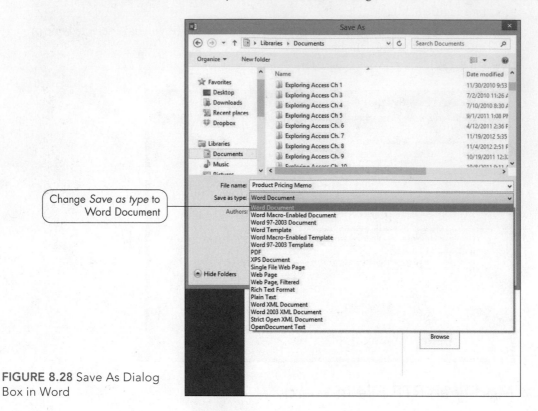

Change *Save as type* to Word Document

FIGURE 8.28 Save As Dialog Box in Word

Exporting Data to a PDF or XPS Document

Exporting data from Access to a PDF or XPS document is similar to exporting data to Word, except that you are not able to edit the exported documents. When you export from Access to Word or Excel, you can modify the exported files. This is not the case with PDF and XPS documents.

STEP 4 »

Two main reasons exist for exporting to a PDF or XPS document. First, these documents do not require purchase of a commercial software application to view the information. Both PDF and XPS documents can be opened by their respective document readers. Both readers are available as free downloads to users. ***Portable Document Format (PDF)*** is a file format created by Adobe Systems in 1993 for document exchange independent of software application and operating system environment. PDF documents can be viewed with Adobe Reader, which is available online at http://get.adobe.com/reader/. Windows Reader, an alternative to Adobe Reader, may be preinstalled with your operating system. ***XML Paper Specification (XPS)*** is a file format developed by Microsoft and designed to display a printed page onscreen identically on any computer platform. The XPS format is considered an alternative to PDF. An XPS document can be viewed with the XPS Viewer, which may be preinstalled with your operating system; otherwise it is available as a free download online at www.microsoft.com/whdc/xps/viewxps.mspx.

Second, neither PDF nor XPS documents can be modified after they are created. The recipient cannot modify a document (a contract, quote, or letter) that should only be revised by the creator. If a document contains errors or needs to be revised for another reason, the recipient must contact the sender and ask for the changes to be made using the original software.

Select an Object to Export

Tables, queries, forms, and reports can all be exported to a PDF or XPS document. However, the number of pages should be checked when the objects are exported. If you attempt to export one record in a form, you will be surprised to find the results contain all the records in the record source. Reports tend to be a good choice for creating PDF and XPS documents, particularly if they do not need modification or data analysis.

Export to a PDF or XPS Document

To export to a PDF or XPS document, do the following:

1. Select the object that you want to export and click the EXTERNAL DATA tab.
2. Click PDF or XPS in the Export group. The Publish as PDF or XPS dialog box opens, as shown in Figure 8.29.
3. Select the folder where the document should be saved, type the name of the exported document, and then select the document type, either PDF or XPS Document.
4. Click the *Open file after publishing* check box.
5. Click Publish to create the document.

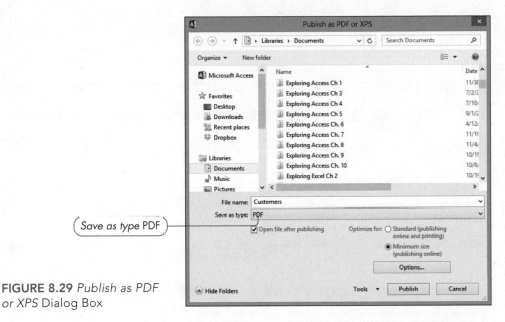

FIGURE 8.29 *Publish as PDF or XPS* Dialog Box

A document opens using the reader associated with the document type (PDF or XPS). The document contains multiple pages if the source has multiple pages. If the document is too wide, then two pages may be required to display one page of data. See Figure 8.30 as an example of a PDF document and Figure 8.31 as an example of an XPS document.

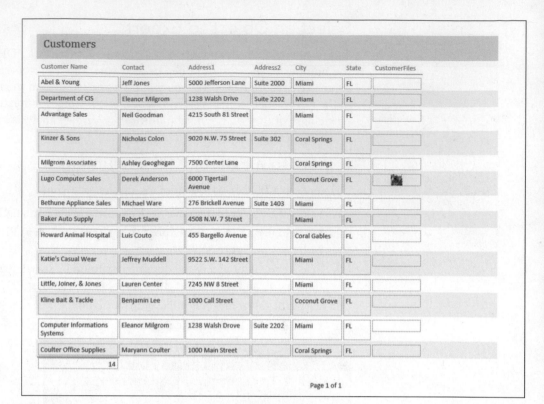

FIGURE 8.30 PDF Document Created from an Access Report

Customers						
Customer Name	Contact	Address1	Address2	City	State	CustomerFiles
Abel & Young	Jeff Jones	5000 Jefferson Lane	Suite 2000	Miami	FL	
Department of CIS	Eleanor Milgrom	1238 Walsh Drive	Suite 2202	Miami	FL	
Advantage Sales	Neil Goodman	4215 South 81 Street		Miami	FL	
Kinzer & Sons	Nicholas Colon	9020 N.W. 75 Street	Suite 302	Coral Springs	FL	
Milgrom Associates	Ashley Geoghegan	7500 Center Lane		Coral Springs	FL	
Lugo Computer Sales	Derek Anderson	6000 Tigertail Avenue		Coconut Grove	FL	
Bethune Appliance Sales	Michael Ware	276 Brickell Avenue	Suite 1403	Miami	FL	
Baker Auto Supply	Robert Slane	4508 N.W. 7 Street		Miami	FL	
Howard Animal Hospital	Luis Couto	455 Bargello Avenue		Coral Gables	FL	
Katie's Casual Wear	Jeffrey Muddell	9522 S.W. 142 Street		Miami	FL	
Little, Joiner, & Jones	Lauren Center	7245 NW 8 Street		Miami	FL	
Kline Bait & Tackle	Benjamin Lee	1000 Call Street		Coconut Grove	FL	
Computer Informations Systems	Eleanor Milgrom	1238 Walsh Drove	Suite 2202	Miami	FL	
Coulter Office Supplies	Maryann Coulter	1000 Main Street		Coral Springs	FL	
14						

Page 1 of 1

XPS documents are viewed with the XPS Viewer

FIGURE 8.31 XPS Document Created from an Access Report

Customers_XPS.xps - XPS Viewer

File ▼   Permissions ▼   Signatures ▼   Find

Customers						
Customer Name	Contact	Address1	Address2	City	State	CustomerFiles
Abel & Young	Jeff Jones	5000 Jefferson Lane	Suite 2000	Miami	FL	
Department of CIS	Eleanor Milgrom	1238 Walsh Drive	Suite 2202	Miami	FL	
Advantage Sales	Neil Goodman	4215 South 81 Street		Miami	FL	
Kinzer & Sons	Nicholas Colon	9020 N.W. 75 Street	Suite 302	Coral Springs	FL	
Milgrom Associates	Ashley Geoghegan	7500 Center Lane		Coral Springs	FL	
Lugo Computer Sales	Derek Anderson	6000 Tigertail Avenue		Coconut Grove	FL	
Bethune Appliance Sales	Michael Ware	276 Brickell Avenue	Suite 1403	Miami	FL	
Baker Auto Supply	Robert Slane	4508 N.W. 7 Street		Miami	FL	
Howard Animal Hospital	Luis Couto	455 Bargello Avenue		Coral Gables	FL	
Katie's Casual Wear	Jeffrey Muddell	9522 S.W. 142 Street		Miami	FL	
Little, Joiner, & Jones	Lauren Center	7245 NW 8 Street		Miami	FL	
Kline Bait & Tackle	Benjamin Lee	1000 Call Street		Coconut Grove	FL	

TIP   Viewing XPS Documents

XPS documents can be viewed with your browser (e.g., Internet Explorer) or Windows Reader if the XPS Viewer has not been installed. XPS documents are not as widely used and distributed as PDF documents. For that reason, PDF documents are the preferred format when exporting this type of document from Access.

Exporting Objects to Another Access Database

STEP 5 »

After you create a database for one organization, you may be able to use the structure of some objects in a different database. For example, many business databases require an Employees table, a Customers table, and an Orders table. Companies also need a data-entry form for each of those three tables. There may be common reports that could also be exported from one database to another—for example, an Employee List report and a Customer List report. Exporting objects from one Access database to another saves time because you do not have to create the objects (tables, forms, reports) from scratch. You do not have to set the field names and data types (which Access refers to as the definition). You may have to modify the imported objects slightly to match the requirements of the new database.

When you export tables to another database, the Export dialog box asks if you want to export the data along with the definition. Usually, you will not want the data exported to the new database. After the tables are successfully exported, you can delete unwanted fields and add new fields to create the table structure you need for the new organization. Forms and reports need to be modified as well. Open the forms and reports in Layout view, and then delete any fields that were removed from the underlying tables. Add any new fields to the forms and reports that were added to the tables. You are now ready to populate the new tables either by adding data directly into the tables or by entering data using the forms.

Export Tables to Another Database

Before you can export a table to another database, you must first create the new database (or export the table to an existing database).

To create the new database, do the following:

1. Start Access and click *Blank desktop database* to create a new database.
2. Specify the location and type the name of the new database. You will have to navigate to the location of the new database when you export a table.
3. Click Create.
4. Close the blank target database.

To export a table from one database to another, do the following:

1. Select the table in the Navigation Pane.
2. Click the EXTERNAL DATA tab.
3. Click Access in the Export group.
4. The Export – Access Database dialog box appears (see Figure 8.32).
5. Click Browse to locate the destination file, click the file to select it, and then click Save.
6. Click OK to proceed to the next dialog box, shown in Figure 8.33. The second dialog box asks for the name of the table (you can accept the default name) and whether to export the Definition and Data or Definition Only.
7. Click OK in the second dialog box; the table is then exported to the destination database.
8. Return to the Access window. Close the Save Export Steps window without saving the steps.

To verify that the exported table is now in the destination database, locate and open the destination database. In the Navigation Pane, locate the exported table. Double-click the table to open it. After you verify the table was exported correctly, close the table, and then close the database. Return to the original database and export the next object.

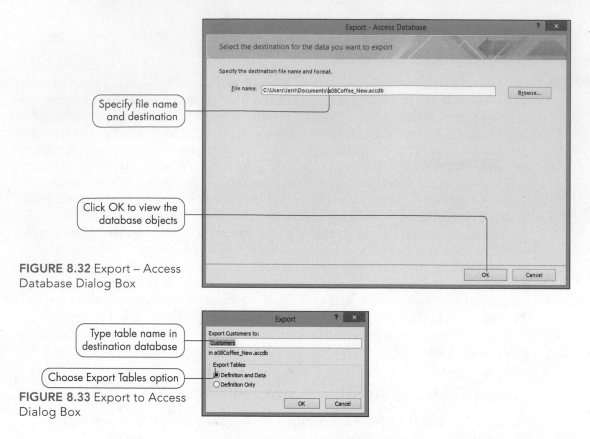

Specify file name and destination

Click OK to view the database objects

FIGURE 8.32 Export – Access Database Dialog Box

Type table name in destination database

Choose Export Tables option

FIGURE 8.33 Export to Access Dialog Box

Export Other Objects to Another Database

STEP 6》 To export other objects from one Access database to another, do the following:

1. Select the object (query, form, or report) in the Navigation Pane.
2. Click the EXTERNAL DATA tab.
3. Click Access in the Export group. The Export – Access Database dialog box appears (see Figure 8.32).
4. Click Browse to locate the destination file, click the file to select it, and then click Save.
5. Click OK to proceed to the next dialog box, shown in Figure 8.34. The second dialog box asks for the name of the object (you can accept the default name or type a new name).
6. Click OK in the second dialog box; the table is then exported to the destination database.
7. Return to the Access window. Close the Save Export Steps window without saving the steps.

Verify that the exported object is in the destination database by opening the destination database. In the Navigation Pane, locate the exported object. After you verify the object was exported correctly, return to the original database, and then open the original database to export the next object.

In Hands-On Exercise 2, you will export table data to Excel and export query data into Word using the same real estate database you used for Hands-On Exercise 1. You will also export data to a PDF document and export objects from the real estate database to another database. Verify that the objects were exported successfully by opening the destination database.

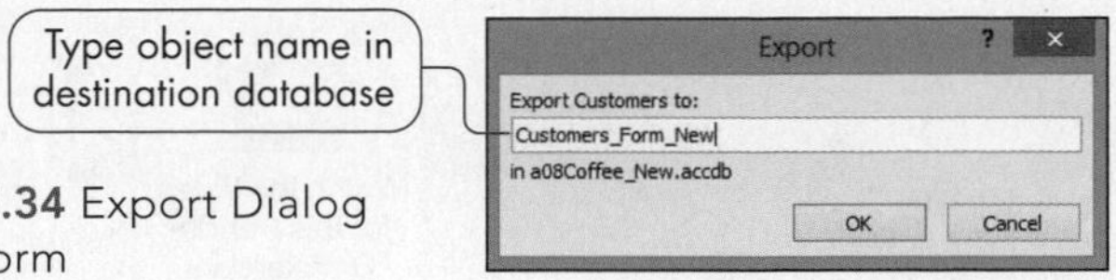

Type object name in destination database

FIGURE 8.34 Export Dialog Box for Form

Quick Concepts ✓

1. What is one advantage to exporting Access data to Excel? *p. 735*

2. Why would you want to have an Access report exported to PDF format? *p. 742*

3. Why would you decide to export the definition of a table to a different database, but not the data? *p. 745*

Hands-On Exercises

2 Exporting Data to Office Applications

Blackwood Maintenance Service wants to contact the homeowners from the subdivisions they serve to tell them about their new services. You will create several formats, depending on the preference of the subdivision contact person. Some prefer an Excel spreadsheet, some prefer a Word document, one prefers PDF, and one prefers data in an Access table.

Skills covered: Export a Query to Excel • Export a Report to Excel • Export a Query to Word and Modify an RTF File in Word • Export to a PDF or XPS Document • Export a Table to Another Database • Export a Form to Another Database

---

STEP 1 ›› EXPORT A QUERY TO EXCEL

Create a new query that lists all the homeowners in The Woodlands subdivision and export it to an Excel spreadsheet. Refer to Figure 8.35 as you complete Step 1.

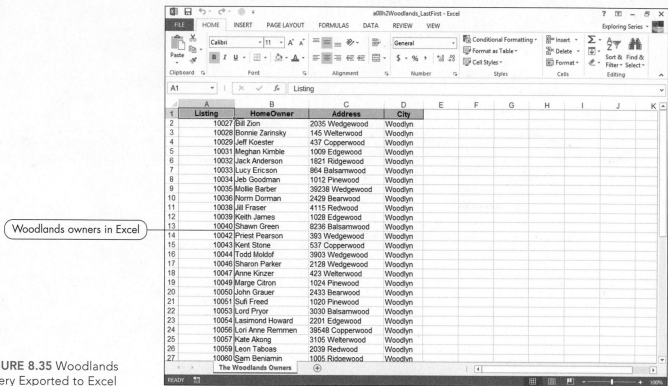

Woodlands owners in Excel

FIGURE 8.35 Woodlands Query Exported to Excel

a. Open *a08h1Property_LastFirst* if you closed it at the end of Hands-On Exercise 1. Click the **FILE tab**, click **Save As**, click **Save As**, and then type **a08h2Property_LastFirst**, changing the *h1* to *h2*.

TROUBLESHOOTING: If you did not complete Hands-On Exercise 1, go back and complete it now. When you are finished, continue with Hands-On Exercise 2. If you make any major mistakes in this exercise, you can close the file, open *a08h1Property_LastFirst* again, and then start this exercise over.

---

b. Click the **CREATE tab** and click **Query Design** in the Queries group. Add the Properties table to the query design and close the Show Table dialog box.

c. Double-click the **SubDivisonID, Listing, HomeOwner, Address,** and **City fields** to add them to the query design grid.

d. Type **14** into the **Criteria row** of the SubDivisionID field. Uncheck the **Show check box.** Save the query as **The Woodlands Owners.**

You entered 14 in the Criteria row, which represents The Woodlands subdivision.

e. Run the query and widen the columns of the query so all the data values are visible.

When you export to Excel, the columns show all the data if the column widths are wide enough in Access.

f. Click the **EXTERNAL DATA tab** and click **Excel** in the Export group. Click **Browse** to choose the export location. Type **a08h2Woodlands_LastFirst** in the **File name box.** Click **Save.**

> **TROUBLESHOOTING:** If you inadvertently click Excel in the Import & Link group, cancel the dialog box and click Excel in the Export group.

g. Click the **Export data with formatting and layout** and **Open the destination file after the export operation is complete check boxes** in the Export – Excel Spreadsheet dialog box. Click **OK.**

A new Excel spreadsheet window opens showing The Woodlands owners' data.

> **TROUBLESHOOTING:** If you attempt to create an Excel file that already exists, Access warns you and asks you, *Do you want to replace the existing one?* If you attempt to create an Excel file that is already open, Access displays a warning, *Microsoft Office Access can't save the output data…* Close the open Excel file and try again.

h. Click **Microsoft Access** on the taskbar to return to Access. Click **Close** to close the Save Export Steps dialog box without saving.

i. Close the query. Save the query if you are asked.

j. Close the workbook and close Excel.

You need to send the Service Request Report to one of the BMS subcontractors. You will export the report to Excel. Refer to Figure 8.36 as you complete Step 2.

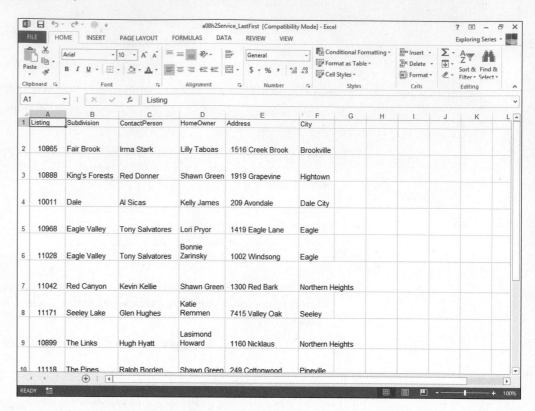

FIGURE 8.36 Report Exported to Excel

a. Double-click the **Service Request Report** in the Navigation Pane to open it.

   You will export this report to Excel.

b. Click the **EXTERNAL DATA tab**.

c. Click **Excel** in the Export group.

d. Click **Browse**. Choose a location to save the export file. Change the file name to **a08h2Service_LastFirst**. Click **Save**. Click the **Open the destination file after the export operation is complete check box** in the Export – Excel Spreadsheet dialog box. Click **OK**.

   A new Excel spreadsheet window opens, showing the Service Request Report data. The photos are missing, and the report title was deleted.

e. Click **Microsoft Access** on the taskbar to return to Access. Click **Close** to close the Save Export Steps dialog box without saving.

   Compare the Excel report with your report in Access.

f. Close the report.

g. Close the workbook and close Excel.

You will need to create a query showing all homes with a tile roof built in or before 1997; these roofs may need to be repaired or replaced. Export the query results to Word. Modify the exported document to include the typical memo elements. Refer to Figure 8.37 as you complete Step 3.

Step h: Press Enter in Word document, and type to modify the RTF file

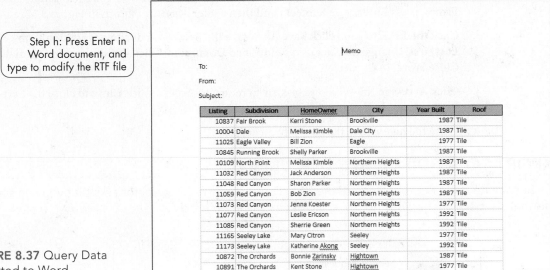

Memo

To:

From:

Subject:

Listing	Subdivision	HomeOwner	City	Year Built	Roof
10837	Fair Brook	Kerri Stone	Brookville	1987	Tile
10004	Dale	Melissa Kimble	Dale City	1987	Tile
11025	Eagle Valley	Bill Zion	Eagle	1977	Tile
10845	Running Brook	Shelly Parker	Brookville	1987	Tile
10109	North Point	Melissa Kimble	Northern Heights	1987	Tile
11032	Red Canyon	Jack Anderson	Northern Heights	1987	Tile
11048	Red Canyon	Sharon Parker	Northern Heights	1987	Tile
11059	Red Canyon	Bob Zion	Northern Heights	1987	Tile
11073	Red Canyon	Jenna Koester	Northern Heights	1977	Tile
11077	Red Canyon	Leslie Ericson	Northern Heights	1992	Tile
11085	Red Canyon	Sherrie Green	Northern Heights	1992	Tile
11165	Seeley Lake	Mary Citron	Seeley	1977	Tile
11173	Seeley Lake	Katherine Akong	Seeley	1992	Tile
10872	The Orchards	Bonnie Zarinsky	Hightown	1987	Tile
10891	The Orchards	Kent Stone	Hightown	1977	Tile

FIGURE 8.37 Query Data Exported to Word

a. Click the **CREATE tab** and click **Query Design** in the Queries group. Add the Properties table and the SubDivision table to the query design and close the Show Table dialog box.

b. Double-click the fields **Listing**, **HomeOwner**, **City**, **YearBuilt**, and **Roof** in the Properties table and drag **SubDivision** from the SubDivision table to the second column in the query design grid.

The other fields shift to the right to make room for the SubDivision field.

> **TROUBLESHOOTING:** If you inadvertently add the SubDivision field to the last column of the query design grid, point over the thin gray bar above the field name and when the downward-pointing arrow appears, click to select the column. Point in the selected column and click and drag to move the column into the correct position.

c. Type **Tile** in the **Criteria row** of the Roof column and type **<=1997** in the **Criteria row** of the YearBuilt column.

You only want to see properties with a tile roof that were built on or before 1997.

d. Save the query as **Properties Built on or Before 1997**.

e. Run the query. Widen the columns of the query so all the data values are visible.

When you export to Word, the columns show all the data if the column widths are wide enough in Access and the total width of the exported table does not exceed the Word document width.

f. Click the **EXTERNAL DATA tab**, click the **More button** in the Export group, and then select **Word** from the displayed list.

You will use the list of properties to create a memo to send to the roofer so he can inspect the roofs for damage.

g. Click **Browse** to choose a location to save the export file. Type **a08h2Sub_LastFirst** in the **File name box**. Click **Save**. Click the **Open the destination file after the export operation is complete check box** in the Export – RTF File dialog box. Click **OK**.

A new Word window opens, showing the Properties Built on or Before 1997 data.

> **TROUBLESHOOTING:** If you attempt to create a Word file that already exists, Access warns you and asks you, *Do you want to replace the existing one?* If you attempt to create a Word file that is already open, Access displays a warning, *Microsoft Office Access can't save the output data...* Close the open Word file and try again.

h. Press **Enter** one time in Word, type **Memo**. Press **Enter** and type **To:**. Press **Enter**, type **From:**, press **Enter**, type **Subject:**, and then center *Memo*, as shown in Figure 8.37.

i. Click the **FILE tab** and click **Save As** to save the new Word document as **a08h2Sub_LastFirst**. Change the *Save as type* to **Word Document**. Click **OK** in the warning dialog box. Close Word.

j. Click **Access** in the Windows taskbar to return to Access. Click **Close** to close the Save Export Steps dialog box without saving.

k. Close the query. Save the query if you are asked.

STEP 4 ›› EXPORT TO A PDF OR XPS DOCUMENT

You need to send the Service Request Report to one of the BMS contractors. The contractor asks that you send him the report in a PDF format file because he does not own Microsoft Office. Refer to Figure 8.38 as you complete Step 4.

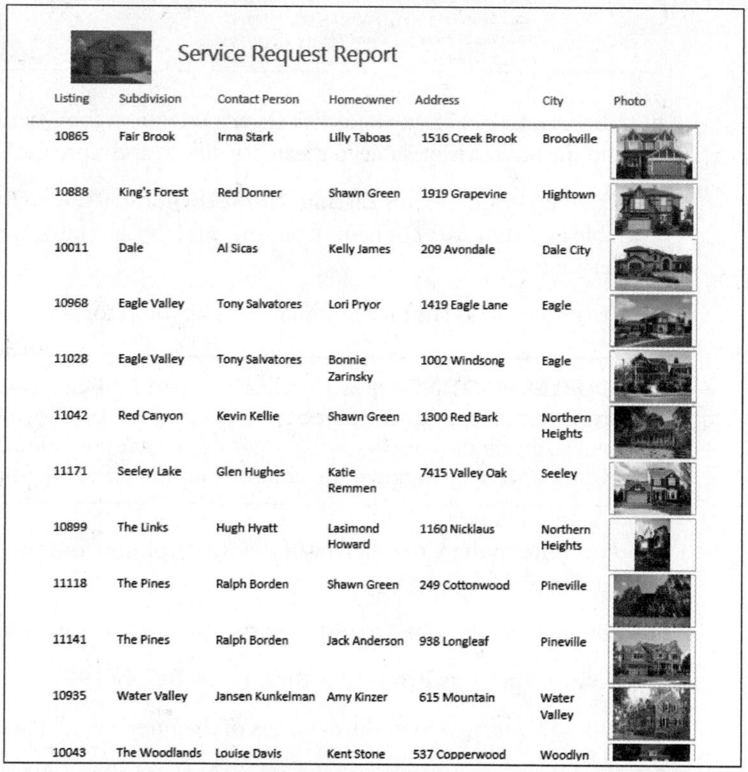

Service Request Report

Listing	Subdivision	Contact Person	Homeowner	Address	City	Photo
10865	Fair Brook	Irma Stark	Lilly Taboas	1516 Creek Brook	Brookville	
10888	King's Forest	Red Donner	Shawn Green	1919 Grapevine	Hightown	
10011	Dale	Al Sicas	Kelly James	209 Avondale	Dale City	
10968	Eagle Valley	Tony Salvatores	Lori Pryor	1419 Eagle Lane	Eagle	
11028	Eagle Valley	Tony Salvatores	Bonnie Zarinsky	1002 Windsong	Eagle	
11042	Red Canyon	Kevin Kellie	Shawn Green	1300 Red Bark	Northern Heights	
11171	Seeley Lake	Glen Hughes	Katie Remmen	7415 Valley Oak	Seeley	
10899	The Links	Hugh Hyatt	Lasimond Howard	1160 Nicklaus	Northern Heights	
11118	The Pines	Ralph Borden	Shawn Green	249 Cottonwood	Pineville	
11141	The Pines	Ralph Borden	Jack Anderson	938 Longleaf	Pineville	
10935	Water Valley	Jansen Kunkelman	Amy Kinzer	615 Mountain	Water Valley	
10043	The Woodlands	Louise Davis	Kent Stone	537 Copperwood	Woodlyn	

FIGURE 8.38 Service Request Report Exported to PDF

Photos: (Left) © Pavel Losevsky/Fotolia; (Right, from bottom) © qingwa/Fotolia, © Maisna/Fotolia, © pics721/Fotolia, © Nomad_Soul/Fotolia, © Pavel Losevsky/Fotolia

a. Select the **Service Request Report** in the Navigation Pane.

You will use this report to create a PDF document.

b. Click the **EXTERNAL DATA tab** and click **PDF or XPS** in the Export group.

c. Navigate to the folder where you are saving your files.

d. Change the file name to **a08h2Service_LastFirst** and select **PDF** for the *Save as type*. Click **Publish**.

A new PDF document is created in the folder where you are saving your files.

e. Click **Close** to close the Save Export Steps dialog box without saving.

f. Close the report.

STEP 5 ≫ EXPORT A TABLE TO ANOTHER DATABASE

Blackwood's landscaping contractor asked you for a list of all properties for which BMS provides landscaping services. Because his office manager knows Access, he asks you to send him the information in an Access database. Refer to Figure 8.39 as you complete Step 5.

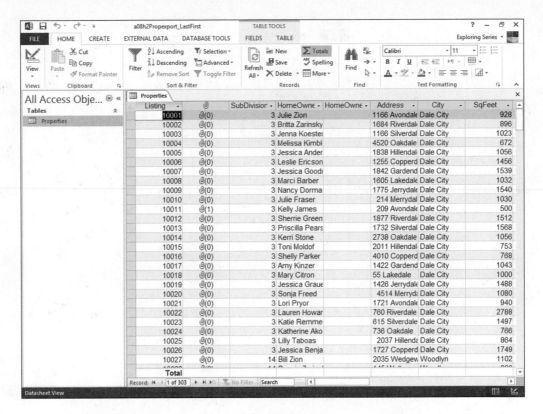

FIGURE 8.39 Destination Database with the Properties Table

a. Close the *a08h2Property_LastFirst* database, if necessary. Open the *a08h2Propexport* database. Save it as **a08h2Propexport_LastFirst** in the folder where you are saving your solution files. Verify that this database does not contain any tables. Close *a08h2Propexport_LastFirst*. Open *a08h2Property_LastFirst*. Select, but do not open, the **Properties table** in the Navigation Pane.

b. Click the **EXTERNAL DATA tab** and click **Access** in the Export group.

The Export – Access Database dialog box appears.

c. Click **Browse** to locate the destination database file. Select the *a08h2Propexport_LastFirst* database and click **Save**. When you return to the Export – Access Database dialog box, click **OK**.

The Export dialog box displays, asking for additional information about the table you are exporting.

d. Confirm that *Properties* is in the *Export Properties to* box. Accept the **Definition and Data option**. Click **OK**.

You are sending the properties data to the landscaping contractor, and he will need all of the properties data.

e. Click **Close** to close the Save Export Steps dialog box without saving.

The table should have been exported, and next you want to verify that it is in the destination database.

f. Close *a08h2Property_LastFirst*. Locate *a08h2Propexport_LastFirst* and open the database. Open the Properties table.

Compare your findings to Figure 8.39.

g. Close the *a08h2Propexport_LastFirst* database.

h. Open the *a08h2Property_LastFirst* database.

STEP 6 ≫ EXPORT A FORM TO ANOTHER DATABASE

The landscaping contractor would like you to send him a form to make it easier to work with the properties data. You will use the Form Tool to quickly make a form with stacked layout. You will export the form to the same destination database as in Step 5. Refer to Figure 8.40 as you complete Step 6.

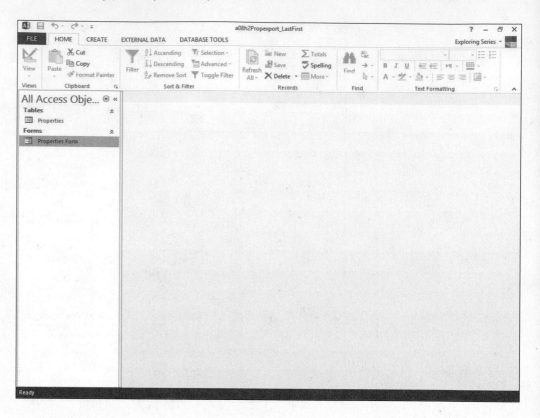

FIGURE 8.40 Destination Database with the Properties Form

a. Click to select the **Properties table** in the Navigation Pane in the *a08h2Property_LastFirst* database.

b. Click the **CREATE tab** and click **Form** in the Forms group.

   Access creates a new stacked layout form based on the Properties table.

c. Reduce the width of the Listing control by clicking on the right border and dragging it to the left. Reduce the width by 50%.

d. Select the last four fields (text box and label)—**DateServiceStarted**, **RequestForService**, **SellingAgent**, and **ListingAgent**—one at a time and press **Delete** to delete the fields from the form.

e. Save the form as **Properties Form**. Close the form. Select the **Properties Form** in the Navigation Pane.

f. Click the **EXTERNAL DATA tab** and click **Access** in the Export group.

   The Export – Access Database dialog box appears.

g. Click **Browse** to locate the destination database file. Select the *a08h2Propexport_LastFirst* database and click **Save**. When you return to the Export – Access Database dialog box, click **OK**.

   The Export dialog box appears, asking you to type the name of the form you are exporting.

h. Confirm that *Properties Form* is in the *Export Properties Form to* box. Click **OK**.

   You accept the default name Properties Form.

i. Click **Close** to close the Save Export Steps dialog box without saving.

The form should have been exported, and next you want to verify that it is in the destination database.

j. Close the *a08h2Property_LastFirst* database. Locate *a08h2Propexport_LastFirst* and open the database. Verify the Properties Form is in the database.

Compare your screen to Figure 8.40.

k. Open the form to view the data.

l. Close the form.

m. Click the **FILE tab** and click **Compact & Repair Database**.

n. If you plan to continue with Hands-On Exercise 3, close the database but keep Access open.

Importing Data into Access

In the previous section, you learned about the benefits of exporting information from Access to Excel, from Access to Word, from Access to PDF or XPS, and from one Access database to another Access database. Sometimes you need the opposite process—*importing* data into Access, which enables you to copy external data into your database without linking it to its source file. A variety of data formats can be imported into Access. You will learn how to import the three most common formats: Access, Excel, and text.

When you work with Access, most of the data entry is achieved by typing directly into the tables or forms. However, at times, you may want to import Access database objects from another database into your Access database. If the other objects are tables, you can import the table from the other database into your database and then append that data to your tables. When you append the data to your tables, you may only need a subset of the fields, and you may also use criteria to limit the number of records you append. Create a form or a report based on the imported data if you plan to use the information as stand-alone data (with no connection to the other tables in the database).

You may also receive data in an Excel spreadsheet that can be imported directly into your Access database. Once the data is imported into Access, you can append that data to another table and consequently save a lot of data-entry time. Alternatively, you can use the imported Excel data as a stand-alone table; a stand-alone table can be used to create other objects—queries, forms, or reports.

You may also want to import and use text files in your Access databases rather than typing the data that originates from this type of source file.

In this section, you will learn how to link data from one Access database to another. You will also learn to access data in Excel when using Access by creating a link to and importing an Excel worksheet. Finally, you will learn how to import data into Access using a Text file.

Linking to an Access Table

When a table in another database is relevant to your database, two options are available. One is that you can import the table from the external database into your database; the other is to create a link to a table in another Access database. Importing a table from an external database increases the size of your database; the table could be so large that your database may run less efficiently. *Linking* lets you connect to a table without having to import the table data into your database. You can only link to the tables in another Access database; you cannot link to queries, forms, reports, macros, or modules.

When you link to a table in another Access database, Access creates a new table, called a *linked table*, which maintains a connection to the source table. You cannot change the structure of a linked table in the destination database (e.g., you cannot add or delete a field in a linked table, and you cannot modify the data type of a field). Any changes you make to the data in the source database are reflected in the linked table in the destination database, and vice versa.

A link to an Access table enables edits to the table in the source database from within the destination database. This is in contrast to a link to an Excel spreadsheet. You cannot edit a linked spreadsheet from within Access. The ability to link to Access tables is important because databases are sometimes intentionally split so that nontable objects reside in one database, whereas tables reside in another. To join the two databases, links are created from the database *without* tables to the database *with* tables. Users can add, delete, and edit data (in the linked tables) as if the tables resided in the first database (when they actually reside in the second).

Examine the Tables in the Source Database

STEP 1 ⟫ Before you link to tables in another Access database, it is best to examine the tables in the source database first. To examine the Access tables, open the source database—the same way you open any Access database—and examine the data in the table(s). Double-click the table that contains the information you need, as shown in Figure 8.41. Make sure the contents, field names, and other elements are correct prior to linking to the table.

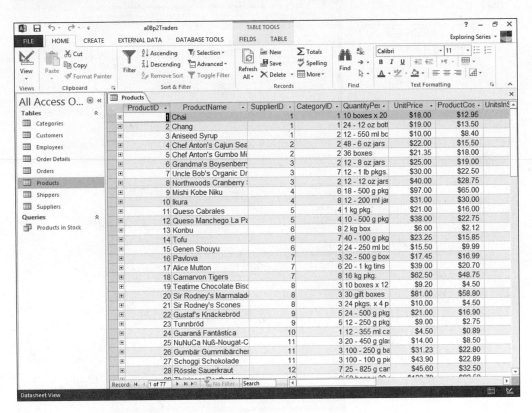

FIGURE 8.41 Products Table in External Database

If the data in the source table looks like it is generally compatible with a table in your database, you can add the linked data to your table. To add the new data into your existing table, you can append all or only a subset of the new table records to your table. You accomplish this by creating an append query based on the linked Access table. An append query is a special query that adds records to an existing table.

Link to an Access Table

STEP 2 ⟫ After you examine the data in the source table—the data you want to link to Access—you are ready to create a link from within your Access database.

To link to an Access table in another database, do the following:

1. Click the EXTERNAL DATA tab.
2. Click Access in the Import & Link group. The Get External Data – Access Database dialog box opens, as shown in Figure 8.42.
3. Click *Link to the data source by creating a linked table*.
4. Click Browse to locate the Access database you want to link to.
5. Click the file to select it and click Open to specify this file as the source of the data.
6. Click the *Link to the data source by creating a linked table* option and click OK. The Link Tables dialog box appears, as shown in Figure 8.43.
7. Select the table you want to link to and click OK. Click Select All if the database contains multiple tables and you want to link to all of them.

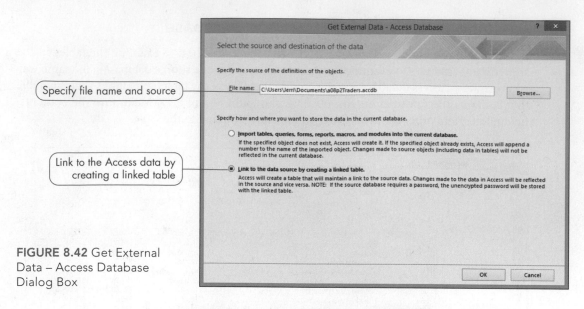

Specify file name and source

Link to the Access data by
creating a linked table

FIGURE 8.42 Get External
Data – Access Database
Dialog Box

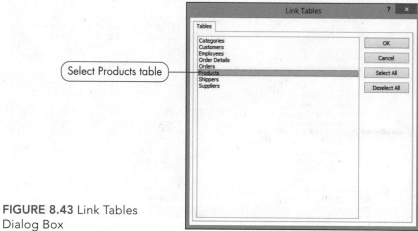

Select Products table

FIGURE 8.43 Link Tables
Dialog Box

Once the link is created, you will see a special arrow icon next to the table name in the Navigation Pane that indicates the table is linked to an Access table (see Figure 8.44). Because the name of the linked table, Products, is the same as that of a table that already exists in your Access database, Access adds the number 1 to the end of the table name. Therefore, Access renames the linked table Products1. If you link to another table with the same name, Products, Access renames the third table Products2. To distinguish the linked Products table from the existing Products table, the second table could be renamed (as Traders Products, for example), as shown in Figure 8.45.

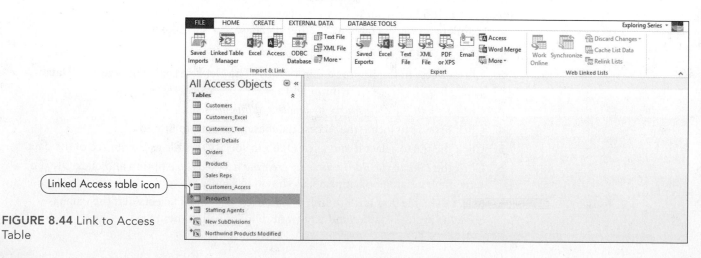

Linked Access table icon

FIGURE 8.44 Link to Access
Table

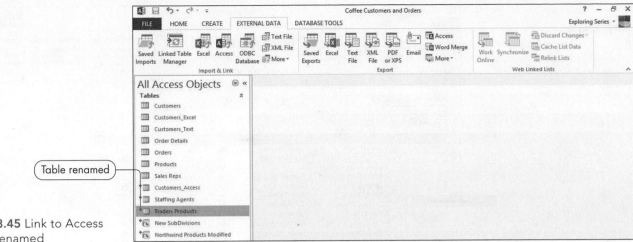

FIGURE 8.45 Link to Access Table—Renamed

Table renamed

Linking to an Excel Spreadsheet

If you have an Access database and you want to import data from an Excel spreadsheet that contains information related to your database, you have three options. You can manually enter the information contained in the spreadsheet into the database tables; you can create a link from Access to Excel that enables you to update tables or create reports based on the data in the Excel spreadsheet; or you can import the data into your Access database to manipulate the data prior to appending it to the tables.

Linking and importing may appear to produce the same results; however, some differences do exist with regard to the resulting size of the database and the ability to modify data. Linking enables you to view the Excel data without increasing the size of the Access database. Importing a large Excel worksheet may increase the Access database substantially (linking to the same spreadsheet does not affect the size of the Access file). Importing an Excel sheet enables you to modify the data prior to appending it to a table. Linking does not enable you to update data from within Access; if errors exist in the worksheet, you must correct the errors in Excel and redisplay the linked table in Access.

Verify the Format of an Excel Spreadsheet

You find that some new property subdivisions are opening in your region, and you may want to target them for new business. You have obtained a spreadsheet that contains initial details, and you want to add the new data to your database. First open the spreadsheet in Excel and examine the data, as shown in Figure 8.46.

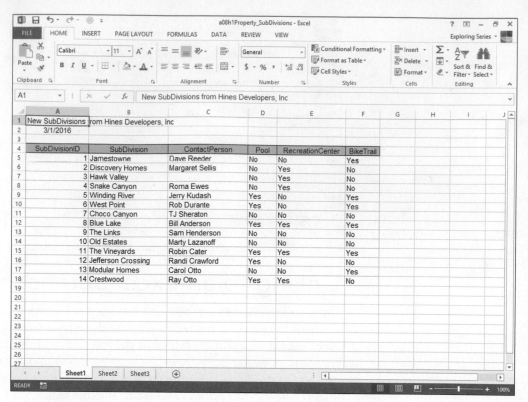

FIGURE 8.46 Property SubDivisions Spreadsheet to Import into Access

STEP 3 Before linking to the spreadsheet, you want to be sure the data is organized so that the import will be successful. The data should be in continuous rows and columns with no blank rows, columns, or extraneous explanatory text. Ideally, the column headings and data formats should be an exact match to those in your database and in the same order, particularly if you are planning to merge the linked spreadsheet into an existing table. The data in the Excel spreadsheet contains titles in cells A1 and A2 and a blank row in row 3. These first three rows will not import properly and should be deleted prior to importing the data. However, it is a good idea to create a backup copy of the original spreadsheet before deleting the rows. This enables you to look up the original data in case this information is needed at another time. In the sheet to be linked, delete the title and blank rows, then save and close the Excel spreadsheet. The results should match those shown in Figure 8.47.

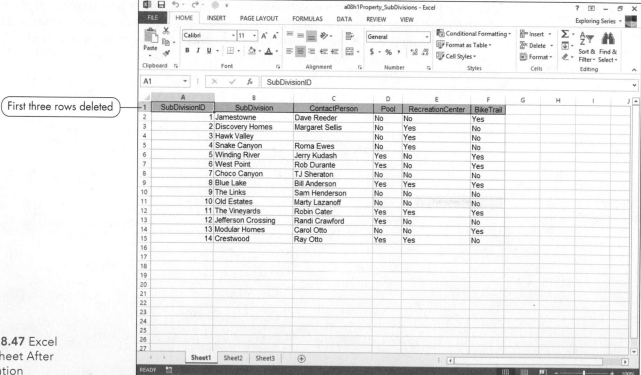

FIGURE 8.47 Excel Spreadsheet After Modification

Link to an Excel Spreadsheet

STEP 4 ≫ After you modify the Excel spreadsheet so the data will properly link to Access, you are ready to create a link from within Access.

To link the Excel spreadsheet to Access, do the following:

1. Click the EXTERNAL DATA tab and click Excel in the Import & Link group. The Get External Data – Excel Spreadsheet dialog box launches as shown in Figure 8.48.
2. Click Browse to locate the Excel file you want to link to, click the file to select it, and then click Open to specify this file as the source of the data.
3. Click the *Link to the data source...* option and click OK. The Link Spreadsheet Wizard launches as shown in Figure 8.49.
4. Select the worksheet from the list of worksheets shown at the top of the dialog box and click Next.
5. Click First Row Contains Column Headings and click Next. The column headings of the Excel spreadsheet become the field names in the Access table.
6. Enter the new table name in the Linked Table Name box, as shown in Figure 8.50, and click Finish.

Because Access can only link to one sheet at a time, you might have to create multiple links, one for each worksheet. Make sure you label the links with descriptive names.

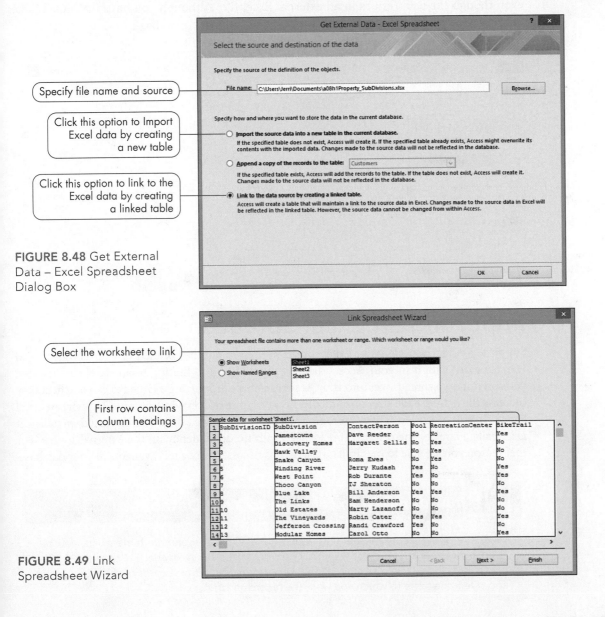

FIGURE 8.48 Get External Data – Excel Spreadsheet Dialog Box

FIGURE 8.49 Link Spreadsheet Wizard

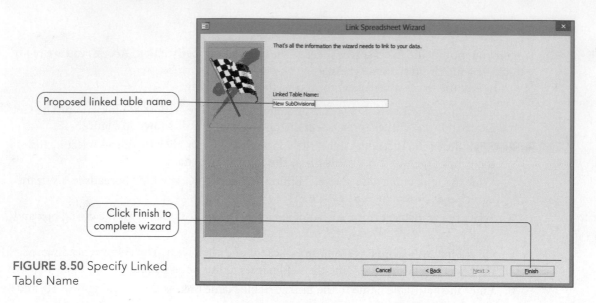

Proposed linked table name

Click Finish to complete wizard

FIGURE 8.50 Specify Linked Table Name

Once the link is created, you will see a special arrow icon next to the table name in the Navigation Pane that indicates the table is linked to the Excel file (see Figure 8.51). Double-click the table name and the table opens. The data looks similar to data in the other tables, even though the data resides in an external Excel file. Although you have the linked table open in Access, you can still open the file in Excel (and vice versa).

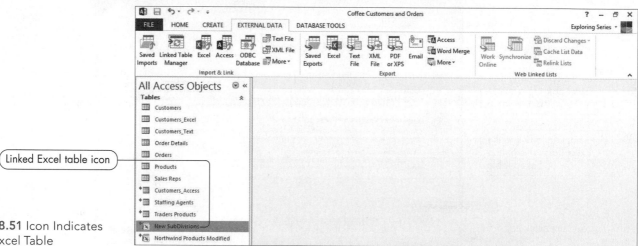

Linked Excel table icon

FIGURE 8.51 Icon Indicates Linked Excel Table

Importing an Excel Spreadsheet

Suppose you receive data in an Excel spreadsheet from another branch of your company and want to work with it in your Access database. In addition to linking to an Excel spreadsheet, you can import a spreadsheet into your Access database. Importing a large Excel worksheet may increase the database file size substantially; however, one reason why you would import an Excel spreadsheet is because you have more control over the imported data. The imported spreadsheet is actually a copy of the original spreadsheet, with no dependency on the external source. For that reason you are able to manipulate the data as necessary once it is available in your database.

TIP Appending Excel Data to Your Database

When importing a spreadsheet into your database, if a comparable table exists, you can choose to append a copy of the Excel records to the table. In the Get External Data – Excel Spreadsheet dialog box, click the *Append a copy of the records to the table* option and select the table to which you want the records added.

Examine the Spreadsheet Before Importing

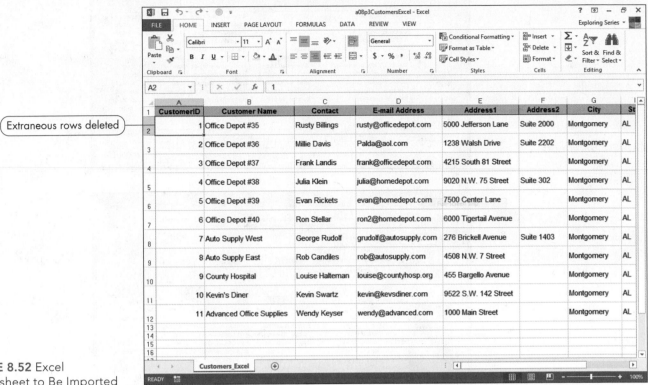

STEP 5 >>

Always examine the Excel spreadsheet (as shown in Figure 8.52) before attempting to import it into Access. You want to be sure there are no extra rows of data that do not comply with the format of an Access table. You also need to delete any blank rows to ensure that the data to import is continuous and check that the column headings appear in the first row of the spreadsheet.

FIGURE 8.52 Excel Spreadsheet to Be Imported

Import a Spreadsheet into Access

After you examine the Excel spreadsheet to determine that the data will properly import to Access, you are ready to create the imported table.

To import the Excel spreadsheet to Access, do the following:

1. Click the EXTERNAL DATA tab.
2. Click Excel in the Import & Link group. The Get External Data – Excel Spreadsheet dialog box launches as shown in Figure 8.48.
3. Click Browse to locate the Excel file you want to import, click the file to select it, and then click Open to specify this file as the source of the data.
4. Click the *Import the source data...* option and click OK. The Import Spreadsheet Wizard launches.
5. Select the worksheet from the list of worksheets shown at the top of the dialog box (if necessary) and click Next.
6. Click the First Row Contains Column Headings check box and click Next two times (see Figure 8.53). The column headings of the Excel spreadsheet become the field names in the Access table.
7. Click the *Choose my own primary key* option if the imported data has a field that is acceptable as a primary key (as shown in Figure 8.54) and click Next. Access sets the value in the first column of the spreadsheet (for example, CustomerID) as the primary key field of the table. You can also allow Access to set the primary key if no value that is eligible to be a key field exists, or to set no primary key at all.
8. Enter the new table name in the Import to Table box, as shown in Figure 8.55, and click Finish.
9. Click Close when prompted to Save Import Steps.

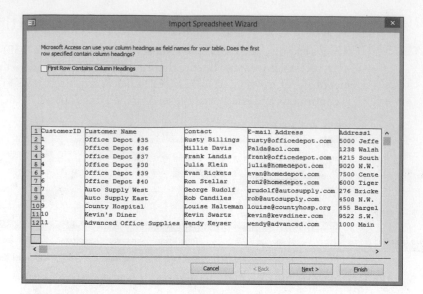

FIGURE 8.53 Import Spreadsheet Wizard

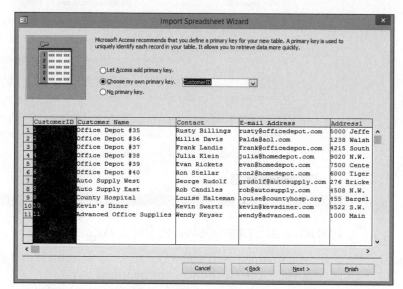

FIGURE 8.54 Choose My Own Primary Key Option

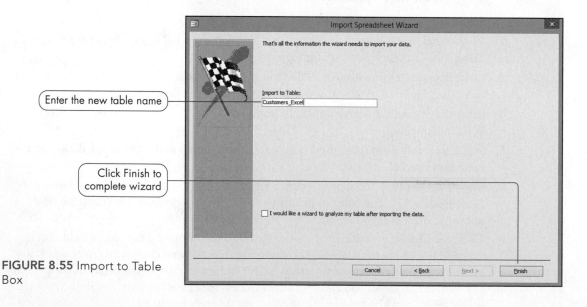

Enter the new table name

Click Finish to complete wizard

FIGURE 8.55 Import to Table Box

Importing a Text File

In the preceding examples, you learned how to link to a table in another Access database and to link to and import an Excel spreadsheet. In this example, you will import a text file directly into your existing Access database. *Text files* are common methods of exchanging information between two computer systems. Text files are usually created by computer software, not manually by humans, and usually contain consistent formatting.

The two most common text file types are comma-separated values (CSV) and fixed-length files. *CSV text files* use a comma to separate one column from the next column, enabling the receiving software to distinguish one set of field values from the next. *Fixed-length text files* allocate a certain number of characters for each field. A fixed-length file containing company data might contain the fields Company Name with 25 characters allocated, Address with 20 characters allocated, City with 20 characters allocated, Region with 2 characters allocated, and Postal Code with 10 characters allocated. Any values with fewer than the allocated characters have spaces added to the end of the value, and any value that is longer than its allocated characters is cut off at the position where the characters exceed the maximum allowed.

Examine the Text File Before Importing

STEP 6 >> If you receive a text file that needs to be imported into Access, you should examine the file first before performing the import routine. You need to confirm that the contents of the text file are relevant to your database. Also, verify that the format of the file is consistent and that the fields and data values correspond to your Access tables. A text file of the CSV type usually has a .csv extension. If you double-click a CSV file, Excel, the default software application associated with CSV files, opens the file. You can examine the file using Excel. To see the file in its native format, right-click the file, click *Open with*, and then click Notepad from the shortcut menu.

For example, suppose the file NewCustomers.csv contains a list of new prospects for your company. Rather than open the file using the default software, Excel, you could open the file in Notepad to view the comma-separated text.

To open the CSV file in Notepad, do the following:

1. Right-click the file in File Explorer.
2. Point to *Open with*.
3. Click Notepad. The file opens in Notepad, as shown in Figure 8.56.

The data contains field names in the first row—Customer ID, Customer Name, Contact, and so forth—with data values starting in the second row. Each row contains commas separating one column from the next.

New customers in a CSV text file

FIGURE 8.56 CSV File Opened with Notepad

Import a Text File into Access

STEP 7 ▶ After you examine the data in the CSV file you are ready to import the data into your Access database.

To import a text file into an Access database, do the following:

1. Click the EXTERNAL DATA tab.
2. Click Text File in the Import & Link group. The Get External Data – Text File dialog box launches, as shown in Figure 8.57.
3. Click Browse to locate the CSV file you want to import (e.g., NewCustomers.csv), click the file to select it, and then click Open to specify this file as the source of the data.
4. Click the *Import the source data into a new table...* option and click OK. The Import Text Wizard dialog box appears as shown in Figure 8.58.
5. Click Next to proceed through the questions in the wizard.
6. Click the *First row contains field names* check box and click Next two times.
7. Click the *Choose my own primary key* option and click Next. Access sets the value in the first field name of the text file, if it is acceptable, as the primary key field of the table. You can also allow Access to set the primary key if no value that is eligible to be a key field exists, or to set no primary key at all.
8. Enter the new table name in the *Import to Table* box and click Finish.
9. Click Close when shown the Save Import Steps prompt. The new table appears in the Navigation Pane, as shown in Figure 8.59.

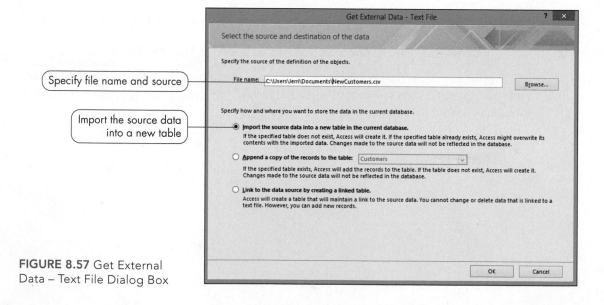

Specify file name and source

Import the source data into a new table

FIGURE 8.57 Get External Data – Text File Dialog Box

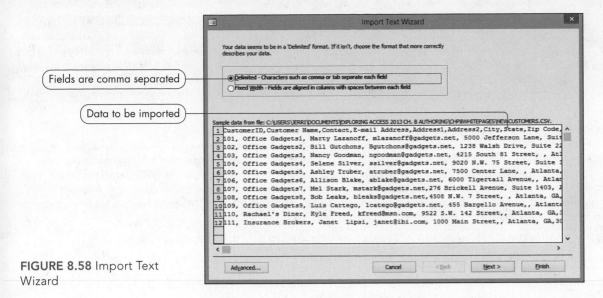

Fields are comma separated

Data to be imported

FIGURE 8.58 Import Text Wizard

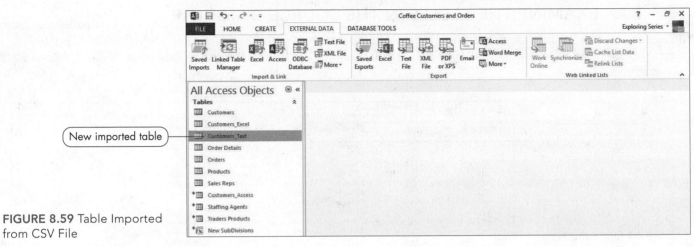

New imported table

FIGURE 8.59 Table Imported from CSV File

Quick Concepts ✓

1. What would be a benefit of importing a spreadsheet into your database rather than linking it? *p. 762*

2. Why is it important to examine a spreadsheet before importing it into Access? *p. 763*

3. How is the data organized in a CSV file? *p. 765*

Hands-On Exercises

Watch the Video
for this Hands-
On Exercise!

MyITLab®
HOE3 Training

3 Importing Data into Access

Blackwood Maintenance Service is adding additional subdivisions to its portfolio. It will need several new employees to manage the new subdivisions—you will review the list of agents provided in an Access database and link it to the BMS database. BMS has obtained some subdivision information in an Excel spreadsheet, which you will link and import to the database. Another spreadsheet containing potential properties to be inspected also needs to be imported. Finally, BMS purchased a list of properties that might need its services. You need to import the CSV list into the current database.

Skills covered: Examine the Tables in the Source Database • Link to an Access Table • Verify the Format of an Excel Spreadsheet • Link to an Excel Spreadsheet • Examine and Import a Spreadsheet into Access • Examine the Text File Before Importing • Import a Text File into Access

STEP 1 » EXAMINE THE TABLES IN THE SOURCE DATABASE

BMS needs to hire additional agents. It received an Access database from a staffing company with a list of possible agents. You will need to review the data first before you add the data to the Blackwood database. Refer to Figure 8.60 as you complete Step 1.

Step b: Staffing Agents records

All Access Obj...	Staffing Agents					
Tables	ID	FirstName	LastName	Title	CellPhone	Click to Add
Staffing Agents	1 Heidi	Fargo	Agent	501-224-0000		
	2 Alexis	Dunbar	Broker	515-224-0001		
	3 Kevin	Mast	Agent	510-224-0022		
	4 Chew Chee	Hoot	Agent	509-224-0003		
	5 Matt	Hoot	Agent	510-224-0004		
	6 Carlita	Sanchez	Broker	515-223-0005		
	7 Fred	Thomas	Agent	501-224-0300		
	8 Maribel	Febus	Agent	501-224-0302		
	9 Connie	Wilson	Agent	501-224-0402		
	10 Lynda	Hudson	Broker	501-224-0403		
	11 Rich	Berardi	Agent	501-224-0502		
	12 Chris	Jones	Agent	501-224-0506		
	13 Dana	Humes	Broker	501-224-0628		
	* (New)					

FIGURE 8.60 Open the New Database and Table

a. Open the *a08h3Propstaff* database file.

Access opens the *a08h3Propstaff* database, and the staffing agents table displays in the Navigation Pane.

b. Open the Staffing Agents table in Datasheet view.

Thirteen agents are in the table.

c. Close the Staffing Agents table. Click the **FILE tab**, click **Save As**, click **Save As**, and then type **a08h3Propstaff_LastFirst**. Save the database in the folder where you are saving your solution files. Close the database.

STEP 2 » LINK TO AN ACCESS TABLE

After examining the data from the staffing company, Blackwood wants to link the data to its database. You will create a link to the table in the staffing database; you will then append the data into the Agents table in the Blackwood database. Refer to Figure 8.61 as you complete Step 2.

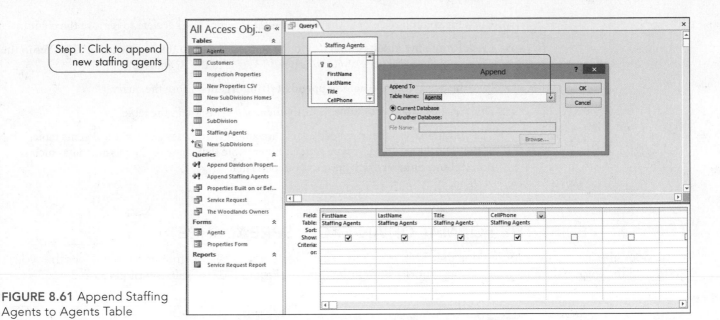

Step I: Click to append new staffing agents

FIGURE 8.61 Append Staffing Agents to Agents Table

a. Open *a08h2Property_LastFirst*. Click the **FILE tab**, click **Save As**, click **Save As**, and then type **a08h3Property_LastFirst**, changing the *h2* to *h3*.

> **TROUBLESHOOTING:** If you did not complete Hands-On Exercises 1 and 2, go back and complete them now. When you are finished, continue with Hands-On Exercise 3.

b. Click the **EXTERNAL DATA tab** in the *a08h3Property_LastFirst* database and click **Access** in the Import & Link group.

c. Click **Browse** to locate the *a08h3Propstaff_LastFirst* database. Click the file to select it and click **Open**.

d. Select the **Link to the data source… option** and click **OK**.

e. Select the **Staffing Agents table** in the Link Tables dialog box and click **OK**.

You created a link to the Staffing Agents table in the staffing database.

f. Double-click the **Staffing Agents table** in the Navigation Pane.

You are now prepared to add the new agents to the Agents table so that all of the agents can be merged into one table.

g. Close the Staffing Agents table.

h. Click the **CREATE tab** and click **Query Design** in the Queries group. Add Staffing Agents to the query design and close the Show Table dialog box.

You created a select query, which you will convert to an append query.

i. Double-click the title bar of the Staffing Agents table to select all the fields. Drag the fields to the query design grid.

j. Switch to Datasheet view.

The new staffing agents are listed as expected.

k. Switch back to Design view.

l. Click **Append** in the Query Type group and select **Agents** using the Table Name arrow. Click **OK**.

The *Append to* row appears in the query design grid with the corresponding field names listed. Some of the new IDs are the same as the existing IDs. You decide to remove the ID field from the append query.

m. Click the column selector at the top of the ID column. Press **Delete** to remove the column.

n. Click **Run** in the Results group to add the staffing agents to the Agents table. Click **Yes** in the message that says you are about to append 13 rows to the Agents table.

o. Save the query with the name **Append Staffing Agents**. Close the query.

p. Double-click the **Agents table** to verify the new agents are in the table.

The ID numbers of the appended agents are automatically assigned by the Agents table, as the ID field has the data type AutoNumber. Note that some of the missing data, such as home phone numbers, will need to be added later.

q. Close the table.

STEP 3 ➤ VERIFY THE FORMAT OF AN EXCEL SPREADSHEET

You will open the list of new subdivisions that BMS received in an Excel spreadsheet format and decide whether you want to add the information to your existing subdivision table. Refer to Figure 8.62 as you complete Step 3.

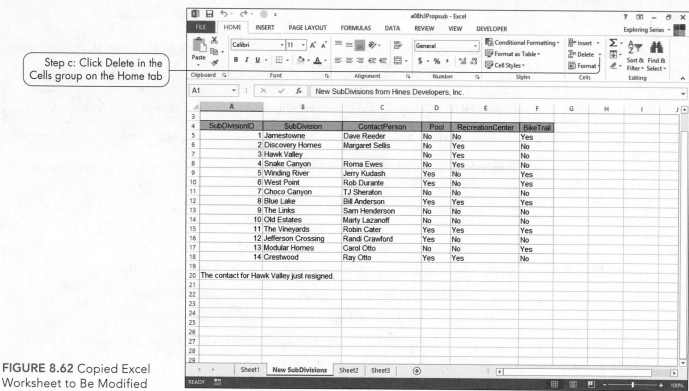

FIGURE 8.62 Copied Excel Worksheet to Be Modified

a. Open the Excel workbook *a08h3Propsub*. Click the **FILE tab**, click **Save As**, click **Save As**, click **Browse** to navigate to correct folder, click enter the file name **a08h3Propsub_LastFirst**, and then click Save.

You need to decide if the data will fit into the existing subdivision table and whether the data is formatted properly and does not contain extraneous rows.

b. Click **Enable Editing** in the Excel window, if necessary. Right-click the **Sheet1 tab**. Select **Move or Copy**. Select **Sheet2** in the *Before sheet:* box and click the **Create a copy check box**. Click **OK**. Double-click the copied sheet tab, rename the worksheet **New SubDivisions**, and then press **Enter**.

The new worksheet is the second worksheet.

c. Click the **New SubDivisions tab**, if necessary. Select the first three rows of the worksheet. Click **Delete** in the Cells group on the HOME tab, as shown in Figure 8.62.

The first row of a spreadsheet must contain column headings that can be recognized as field names by Access.

d. Click **cell A17**, which contains *The contact for Hawk Valley just resigned*. Press **Delete**.

There should not be any data after the last row of formatted data.

e. Save and close the workbook, and exit Excel.

The Excel spreadsheet can now be linked to the Access database.

STEP 4 ›› LINK TO AN EXCEL SPREADSHEET

You decide to create a link to the new subdivisions worksheet. You will then import the data into your Access database. You will use the linked worksheet to create a new table in the database. If the linked Excel spreadsheet is updated later, you could run the Make Table query to overwrite the table with the new data. Refer to Figure 8.63 as you complete Step 4.

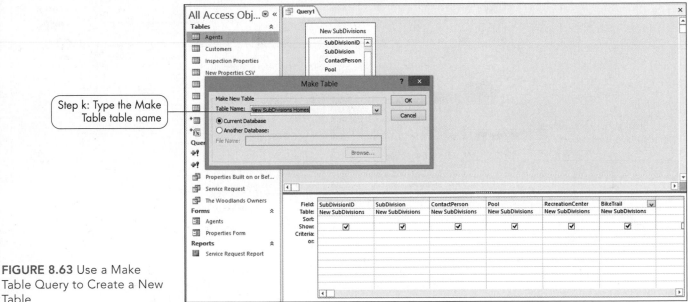

FIGURE 8.63 Use a Make Table Query to Create a New Table

a. Click **Access** in the Windows taskbar and click the **EXTERNAL DATA tab.**

b. Click **Excel** in the Import & Link group.

c. Click **Browse** to locate the spreadsheet *a08h3Propsub_LastFirst*. Click **Open**.

d. Select the **Link to the data source… option** and click **OK**.

e. Select **New SubDivisions** in the Show Worksheets box of the Link Spreadsheet Wizard. Click **Next**.

You chose the revised worksheet for the link.

f. Click the **First Row Contains Column Headings check box**. Click **Next**.

g. Accept the name *New SubDivisions* for the Access linked table name. Click **Finish**. Click **OK** in the message box that appears.

The Excel linked icon appears next to the New SubDivisions table.

h. Click the **CREATE tab** and click **Query Design** in the Queries group. Add the New SubDivisions table to the query design and close the Show Table dialog box.

You decide to create a new table from the linked spreadsheet using a Make Table query.

i. Add all the fields from the New SubDivisions table to the query design grid. Switch to Datasheet view to examine the records.

j. Switch back to Design view.

k. Click **Make Table** in the Query Type group. Type **New SubDivisions Homes** in the **Table Name box**, as shown in Figure 8.63. With the Current Database option selected, click **OK**. Click **Run** in the Results group and click **Yes** to the warning message. Close the Make Table query without saving the changes.

The Excel spreadsheet data is now an Access table.

STEP 5 ›› EXAMINE AND IMPORT A SPREADSHEET INTO ACCESS

Blackwood received an Excel spreadsheet containing a list of potential new properties to be inspected. You need to examine the data prior to adding it to BMS's database; for now, the imported data will be used as a stand-alone table. Refer to Figures 8.64 and 8.65 as you complete Step 5.

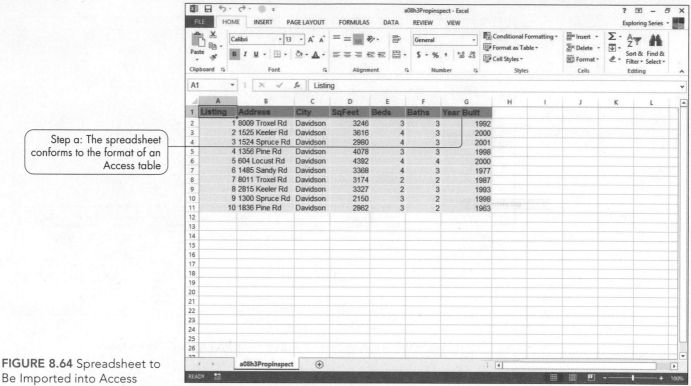

Step a: The spreadsheet conforms to the format of an Access table

FIGURE 8.64 Spreadsheet to Be Imported into Access

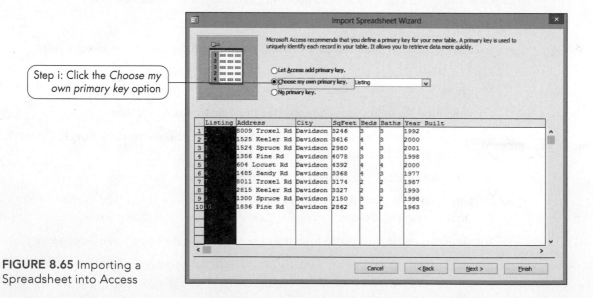

Step i: Click the *Choose my own primary key* option

FIGURE 8.65 Importing a Spreadsheet into Access

a. Open the *a08h3Propinspect* workbook.

The spreadsheet conforms to the format of an Access table, so you do not need to make any changes to it at this time.

b. Close the workbook and exit Excel without making any changes to the file.

c. Click **Access** in the Windows taskbar and click the **EXTERNAL DATA tab**.

d. Click **Excel** in the Import & Link group.

e. Click **Browse** to locate the spreadsheet *a08h3Propinspect*. Click **Open**.

f. Select the **Import the source data into a new table in the current database option** and click **OK**.

g. Ensure *First Row Contains Column Headings* is checked and click **Next** in the Import Spreadsheet Wizard.

The first row of the spreadsheet contains column headings that will be used as the field names for the Access table.

h. Click **Next**.

i. Click the **Choose my own primary key option** and click **Next**.

Access sets the value in the first column of the spreadsheet, Listing, as the primary key field of the table.

j. Enter the new table name, **Inspection Properties**, in the *Import to Table* box and click **Finish**.

k. Click **Close** in the Save Import Steps dialog box.

The imported table appears in the Navigation Pane.

STEP 6 ≫ EXAMINE THE TEXT FILE BEFORE IMPORTING

Blackwood wants to add additional properties to its database. You want to examine the data prior to adding it to the database. The new data is in a text file. Refer to Figure 8.66 as you complete Step 6.

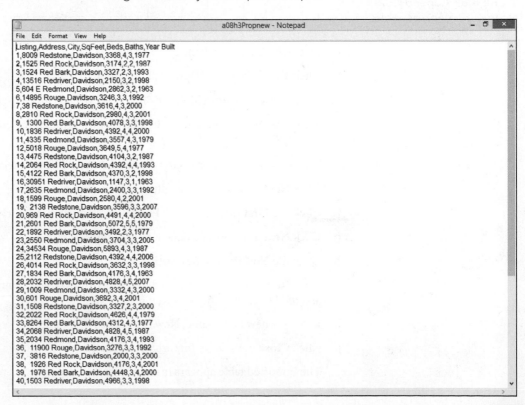

FIGURE 8.66 CSV File Opened in Notepad

a. Open *a08h3Propnew.csv*.

b. Exit Excel without making any changes to the file.

c. Right-click the *a08h3Propnew.csv* file in File Explorer, choose **Open with**, and then click **Notepad** from the shortcut menu.

You decide to examine the file in its native format using Notepad. The file has consistent formatting for importing into Access.

d. Close Notepad.

STEP 7 ≫ IMPORT A TEXT FILE INTO ACCESS

The BMS owners want to import and then append these properties to the Properties table in the Blackwood database. The Listing values will have to be modified when the data is appended so that they are higher than the existing values in the table. Refer to Figure 8.67 as you complete Step 7.

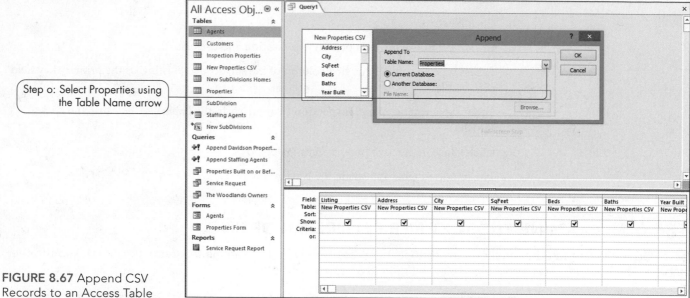

FIGURE 8.67 Append CSV Records to an Access Table

a. Return to Access. Click the **EXTERNAL DATA tab**.

b. Click **Text File** in the Import & Link group.

c. Click **Browse** to locate the *a08h3Propnew.csv* file. Click **Open**.

d. Select the **Import the source data into a new table in the current database option** and click **OK**.

The Import Text Wizard starts. Delimited should be selected by default.

e. Click **Next** to accept the default options in this dialog box.

f. Click the **First Row Contains Field Names check box**. Click **Next**.

g. Click **Next** to accept the default field options in this dialog box.

h. Click the **No Primary Key option**. Click **Next**.

When the records are appended into an existing table in your database, a unique value is assigned to each of the imported records.

i. Enter the new table name, **New Properties CSV**, in the *Import to Table* box and click **Finish**.

j. Click **Close** in the Save Import Steps dialog box.

The imported table appears in the Navigation Pane.

k. Click the **CREATE tab** and click **Query Design** in the Queries group. Add **New Properties CSV** to the query design and close the Show Table dialog box.

You created a select query, which you will convert to an append query.

l. Double-click the title bar of the New Properties CSV table to select all the fields. Drag the fields to the query design grid.

m. Switch to Datasheet view.

The new properties are listed as expected.

n. Switch to Design view.

o. Click **Append** in the Query Type group and select **Properties** using the Table Name arrow. Click **OK**.

The *Append to* row appears in the design grid with the corresponding field names listed. The new listing values need to be modified so they conform to the format of the existing listings. You decide to add 11300 to each new listing number using a calculated field.

p. Select the **Listing field name** in the first column. Type the calculated field: **Listing2: [Listing] + 11300**.

q. Switch to Datasheet view to see the results of the calculated field.

All of the listing values are now higher than the listing numbers of the existing properties.

r. Switch to Design view.

s. Click **Run** in the Results group to add the new (Davidson) properties to the Properties table.

t. Click **Yes** in response to the *You are about to append 58 row(s)* message.

u. Save the query with the name **Append Davidson Properties**. Close the query.

v. Click the **FILE tab** and click **Compact & Repair Database**.

w. Close the database. Exit Access.

x. Submit *a08h3Property_LastFirst* based on your instructor's directions.

Chapter Objectives Review

After reading this chapter, you have accomplished the following objectives:

1. **Create a hyperlink field.**
   - Add a hyperlink field in Design view: A hyperlink in a table or form launches the appropriate software and enables you to interact with the file.
   - Edit a hyperlink field in Datasheet view: Edit a hyperlink value if it navigates to an incorrect Web page, file, or location.

2. **Add an attachment field.**
   - Add an attachment field in Design view: An attachment field stores a reference to an external file, and you can open that file from within Access.
   - Add or edit attachments in Datasheet view: Manage your attachments from the datasheet using the Attachments dialog box.
   - Remove attachments in Datasheet view: Attachments can be removed using the Attachments dialog box.

3. **Add attachment controls to forms and reports.**
   - Add an attachment control to a form: An attachment control lets you manage attached files in forms.
   - Add an attachment field to a report: You can also manage attached files in reports. In a report, only the first file displays in Print Preview, and you have to navigate to the others.

4. **Export data to Excel.**
   - Select a record source to export to Excel: Tables, queries, forms, and reports can all be exported to Excel if their formats are compatible with spreadsheets.
   - Export a query to Excel: Tables and queries tend to export well to Excel as their datasheet formats are compatible with spreadsheets.
   - Export forms and reports to Excel: Subforms or grouped data may not export or display correctly.

5. **Export data to Word.**
   - Select a record source to export to Word: Data that has been exported to Word cannot always be modified or analyzed.
   - Export tables and queries to Word: Export objects that have a tabular layout (e.g., tables and queries).
   - Modify an RTF file in Word: When an object is exported to Word, Access creates a file in Rich Text Format that opens in Word by default.

6. **Export data to a PDF or XPS document.**
   - Select an object to export: You are not able to edit the data exported to a PDF or XPS document.
   - Export to a PDF or XPS document: PDF and XPS documents can be opened by their respective readers.

7. **Export objects to another Access database.**
   - Export tables to another database: After you create a table for one database, you may be able to use it again (definition or both definition and data) for your next database.
   - Export other objects to another database: There may be common queries, forms, or reports that could also be exported from one database to another.

8. **Link to an Access table.**
   - Examine the tables in the source database: Ensure that the data and format are relevant to your database.
   - Link to an Access table: Linking lets you connect to a table without having to import the table data into your database.

9. **Link to an Excel spreadsheet.**
   - Verify the format of an Excel spreadsheet: Ensure that the data will display properly in Access; delete extraneous or blank rows.
   - Link to an Excel spreadsheet: Create a link from Access to Excel that enables you to view Excel data in Access.

10. **Import an Excel spreadsheet.**
    - Examine the spreadsheet before importing: Ensure that the data will display properly in Access.
    - Import a spreadsheet into Access: Import the data into your Access database to evaluate it before appending it to the tables.

11. **Import a text file.**
    - Examine the text file before importing: Ensure that the data is eligible to be separated into columns and is consistent from row to row.
    - Import a text file into Access: You are able to manipulate the data after it is imported into Access without changing the original text file.

Match the key terms with their definitions. Write the key term letter by the appropriate numbered definition.

a. Attachment control
b. Attachment field
c. CSV text file
d. Fixed-length text file
e. Hyperlink
f. Importing

g. Linking
h. Portable Document Format (PDF)
i. Rich Text Format (RTF)
j. Text file
k. Uniform resource locator (URL)
l. XML Paper Specification (XPS)

1. _____ A file format developed by Microsoft and designed to display a printed page onscreen identically on any computer platform. **p. 742**

2. _____ Uses a comma to separate one column from the next column, enabling the receiving software to distinguish one set of field values from the next. **p. 765**

3. _____ Data type that enables you to quickly link to any file on your computer or to any Web page on the Internet. **p. 720**

4. _____ A common method of exchanging data between two computer systems. **p. 765**

5. _____ The location of a Web site or Web page on the Internet. **p. 720**

6. _____ Process that enables you connect to a table without having to import the table data into your database. **p. 756**

7. _____ A format that enables documents created in one software application to be opened with a different software application. **p. 739**

8. _____ This process may result in increasing the size of the Access database substantially. **p. 756**

9. _____ A file format created by Adobe Systems for document exchange independent of software application and operating system environment. **p. 742**

10. _____ Similar to an attachment in an e-mail; you can use it to attach multiple files of any format and then launch those files from within Access. **p. 722**

11. _____ Allocates a certain number of characters for each field. **p. 765**

12. _____ A control that lets you manage attached files in forms and reports. **p. 725**

Multiple Choice

1. Which statement about hyperlink fields is false?

    (a) Hyperlinks can launch Web pages on the Internet.

    (b) Hyperlinks can launch Excel spreadsheets.

    (c) Editing a hyperlink must be done in Design view.

    (d) Hyperlinks can be modified using the right-click option.

2. Which statement about attachments is true?

    (a) You can attach only one file per record in a table.

    (b) You can use attachment files in forms and reports, but you must first define them in the table.

    (c) Attached photos display as thumbnails in queries.

    (d) Attachment files do not increase the size of an Access database.

3. You need to attach an employee's most recent performance review to her record in the Employees table. What is the correct action?

    (a) Open the Employees table, add an OLE field, and then attach the document to the employee's record in Datasheet view of the table.

    (b) Open the Employees table, add an attachment field, and then attach the document to the employee's record in Design view of the table.

    (c) Open the Employees table, add an attachment field, and then attach the document to the employee's record in Datasheet view of the table.

    (d) Open the Employees table, add a hyperlink field, and then attach the document to the employee's record in Datasheet view of the table.

4. What is the primary difference between an imported table and a linked table?

    (a) Data in an imported table can be modified from Access; data in a linked table cannot be modified.

    (b) Both types increase the size of the database.

    (c) Users cannot create queries with a linked table.

    (d) The data in imported tables resides inside the database; the data in linked tables resides outside the database.

5. You have exported an Access table to Excel because:

    (a) You cannot create reports in Access.

    (b) It can be analyzed by a user who does not know Access or own the software.

    (c) Data cannot be sorted or filtered in Access.

    (d) The Access database has grown too large.

6. What is the default format when you export data to Word?

    (a) PDF

    (b) RTF

    (c) DOC

    (d) DOCX

7. What is the main difference between a PDF document and an XPS document?

    (a) PDF does not require reader software to open the documents.

    (b) PDF documents can be opened with an Internet browser.

    (c) XPS documents show a replica of what the printed document looks like.

    (d) One format was created by Adobe (PDF) and the other by Microsoft (XPS).

8. You have imported an Excel spreadsheet named *Inventory* into your database. It displays in the Navigation Pane as

    (a) The Inventory table.

    (b) The Inventory form.

    (c) The Inventory report.

    (d) A linked table.

9. Which type of objects can be exported from one database to another?

    (a) Tables only

    (b) Tables and queries

    (c) All objects

    (d) Reports only

10. Importing a text file

    (a) Requires the Import Wizard.

    (b) Can only be done with a CSV file.

    (c) Is limited to files with 999 rows or less.

    (d) Is similar to importing a Word file.

1 Houston Bank Customer Updates

As database administrator for Houston Bank, your manager wants you to attach photos of the customers to the records in the Customers table. You will create an attachment field in the Customers table and then attach the photos to each record. You will also create an e-mail field for the customers and add your own e-mail address to the table. This exercise follows the same set of skills as used in Hands-On Exercise 1 in the chapter. Refer to Figure 8.68 as you complete this exercise.

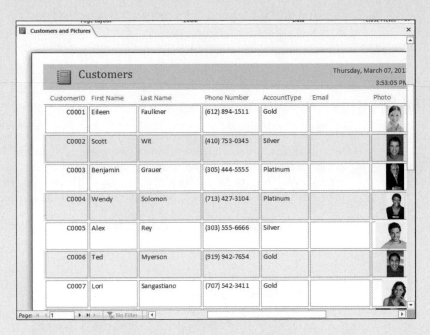

FIGURE 8.68 Hyperlink and Attachment Control in a Report

Photos: (From top) Fotolia, Fotolia, © carlos Restrepo/Fotolia, © Paul Hill/Fotolia, © Rido/Fotolia, Fotolia, © Rido/Fotolia

a. Open *a08p1Bank*. Click the **FILE tab**, click **Save As**, click **Save As**, and then type **a08p1Bank_ LastFirst**. Click **Save**.

b. Open the Customers table in Datasheet view and replace *Your_Name* with your name. Switch to Design view.

c. Type **Email** in the first blank row of the Field Name column. Select **Hyperlink** as the Data Type.

d. Add another field, **Photo**, under *Email*, and then select **Attachment** as the Data Type.

e. Save the table. Switch to Datasheet view.

f. Type your e-mail address into the Email column of the eighth record.

g. Double-click the **paperclip** in the first record. Click **Add** in the Attachments dialog box. Locate and open the *a08p1Customer_photos* folder. Double-click the file named *C0001.jpg* to attach it to the record and click **OK** in the Attachments dialog box.

h. Double-click the **paperclip** in the second record. Click **Add**. Double-click the file named *C0002.jpg* to attach it to the record and click **OK**.

i. Repeat until all of the records have photos attached. Use either the provided picture for record 8 or attach a photo of yourself.

j. Click the **CREATE tab** and click **Report** in the Reports group to create a new report.

k. Modify the report in Layout view. Delete the Address, City, State, and Zip Code columns by clicking each column heading, pressing **Shift**, clicking the first text box below it, and then pressing **Delete**. Delete the empty columns by clicking the column heading of each one and pressing **Delete**.

l. Shrink the remaining columns so all of the fields will fit on one page. Display the report in Print Preview to verify that all columns fit on one page.

TROUBLESHOOTING: If empty columns remain in the report in Layout view, click the empty column heading of each one and press Delete. If the report does not fit onto one page, switch to Design view and drag the page numbers text box to the left. Then reduce the width of the report grid until the report fits on one page.

m. Save the report as **Customers and Pictures**. Close the report. Close the Customers table.

n. Click the **FILE tab** and click **Compact & Repair Database**.

o. Close the database. Exit Access.

p. Submit based on your instructor's directions.

2 International Gourmet Traders

The International Gourmet Traders is a small specialty foods distribution firm. Management wants to send its current product line list to several new potential suppliers. You will need to create several output formats for the product line list so that the new suppliers can receive the information in any one of the following formats: Excel, Word, PDF, or Access. This exercise follows the same set of skills as used in Hands-On Exercise 2 in the chapter. Refer to Figure 8.69 as you complete this exercise.

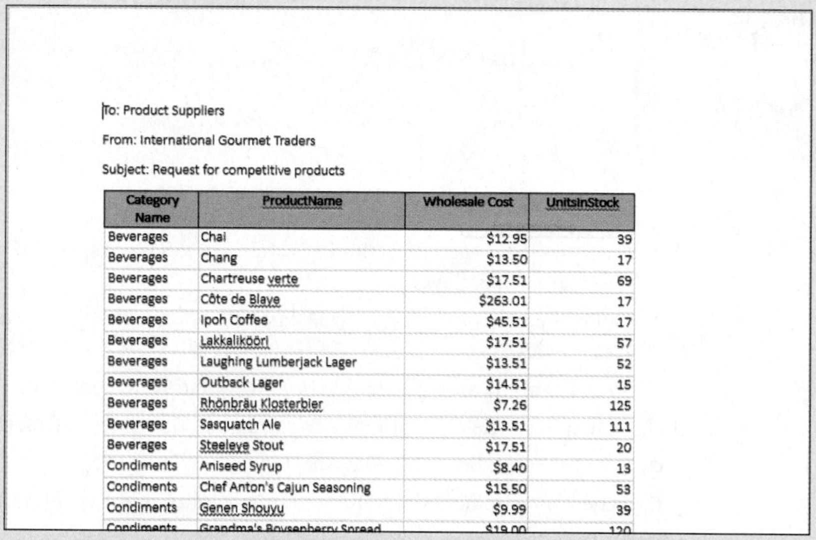

To: Product Suppliers

From: International Gourmet Traders

Subject: Request for competitive products

Category Name	ProductName	Wholesale Cost	UnitsInStock
Beverages	Chai	$12.95	39
Beverages	Chang	$13.50	17
Beverages	Chartreuse verte	$17.51	69
Beverages	Côte de Blaye	$263.01	17
Beverages	Ipoh Coffee	$45.51	17
Beverages	Lakkalikööri	$17.51	57
Beverages	Laughing Lumberjack Lager	$13.51	52
Beverages	Outback Lager	$14.51	15
Beverages	Rhönbräu Klosterbier	$7.26	125
Beverages	Sasquatch Ale	$13.51	111
Beverages	Steeleye Stout	$17.51	20
Condiments	Aniseed Syrup	$8.40	13
Condiments	Chef Anton's Cajun Seasoning	$15.50	53
Condiments	Genen Shouyu	$9.99	39
Condiments	Grandma's Boysenberry Spread	$19.00	120

FIGURE 8.69 Product Pricing Request in Word Format

a. Open *a08p2Traders*. Click the **FILE tab**, click **Save As**, click **Save As**, and then type **a08p2 Traders_LastFirst**. Click **Save**.

b. Open the Current Product Line query, examine the records in Datasheet view, and then close the query. Verify that the Current Product Line query is selected in the Navigation Pane before you complete each step below.

c. Export the product information to an Excel format as follows:

- Click the **EXTERNAL DATA tab**.
- Click **Excel** in the Export group.
- Click **Browse** to open the File Save dialog box.
- Navigate to the location where you are saving your files.
- Type **a08p2Prodline_LastFirst** as the file name.
- Verify that the *Save as type* is set as Excel Workbook.
- Click **Save** to return to the Export – Excel Spreadsheet dialog box.
- Click the **Export data with formatting…** and **Open the destination file… check boxes.**
- Click **OK**.

- Verify that the data exported correctly to Excel and exit Excel. (The Excel file is automatically saved.)
- Click **Close** in the Save Export Steps dialog box in Access.

d. Export the product information to a Word format as follows:

- Click the **EXTERNAL DATA tab**.
- Click the **More button** in the Export group and select **Word** from the list.
- Click **Browse** to open the File Save dialog box.
  - Navigate to the location where you are saving your files.
  - Type **a08p2Prodline_LastFirst** as the file name.
  - Verify that the *Save as type* is set as Rich Text Format.
  - Click **Save** to return to the Export – RTF File dialog box.
- Click the **Open the destination file… check box**.
- Click **OK**.
- Verify that the data exported correctly to Word, press **Enter**, and then type the To, From, and Subject lines as shown in Figure 8.69.
- Click the **FILE tab** and click **Save As**.
- Navigate to the location where you are saving your files and type **a08p2Prodline_LastFirst** as the file name.
- Change the file type to Word Document.
- Click **Save**. Click **OK** in the compatibility message box.
- Close the Word document.
- Click **Close** in the Save Export Steps dialog box in Access.

e. Export the product information to a PDF format as follows:

- Click the **EXTERNAL DATA tab**.
- Click **PDF or XPS** in the Export group.
- Navigate to the location where you are saving your files.
- Type **a08p2Prodline_LastFirst** as the file name.
- Verify that the *Save as type* is set to PDF.
- Click **Publish**.
- Verify that the data exported correctly. Navigate to where you are saving your files in File Explorer and double-click the file to open it in your reader software.

> **TROUBLESHOOTING:** If all of the columns do not fit onto one page, return to the Current Product Line query and reduce the column widths. Publish to PDF again.

- Close the reader program.
- Click **Close** in the Save Export Steps dialog box in Access.

f. To export the product information to another Access database, follow these steps:

- Open the Current Product Line query in Design view.
- Click **Make Table** in the Query Type group to create a new table.
- Type **Products to Export** in the **Table Name box**, and with the Current Database option selected, click **OK**.
- Click **Run** in the Results group.
- Click **Yes** in response to the *You are about to paste 68 rows* message.
- Click the **FILE tab**, click **Save As**, click **Save Object As**, and then click **Save As**.
- Type **Make Table Products in Stock** as the query name and click **OK**. Close the query.
- Select the **Products to Export table** in the Navigation Pane and click the **EXTERNAL DATA tab**.
- Use File Explorer to locate and open *a08p2Prodstock*. Save it as **a08p2Prodstock_LastFirst**.
- Close *a08p2Prodstock_LastFirst* and return to the *a08p2Traders_LastFirst* database.
- Click **Access** in the Export group.
- Click **Browse** in the Export – Access Database dialog box.
  - Locate and select the *a08p2Prodstock_LastFirst* file.
  - Click **Save** to return to the Export – Access Database dialog box.

- Click **OK**.
- Click **OK** to accept the *Products to Export* table name and the *Definition and Data* option.
- Click **Close** in the Save Export Steps dialog box.

g. Click the **FILE tab** and click **Compact & Repair Database**.

h. Close the database.

i. Open the *a08p2Prodstock_LastFirst* database. Verify that the table exported correctly.

j. Close the database. Exit Access.

k. Submit based on your instructor's directions.

3 Break Room Suppliers, Inc.

Break Room Suppliers, Inc., provides coffee, tea, beverages, and snacks to businesses in its area. In an effort to expand their business, the owners have purchased several customer-prospect lists. You will need to link and import the prospect lists into Access so the owners can determine how best to use them in their database. You will also import an Excel spreadsheet containing newly developed sales rep information. This exercise follows the same set of skills as used in Hands-On Exercise 3 in the chapter. Refer to Figure 8.70 as you complete this exercise.

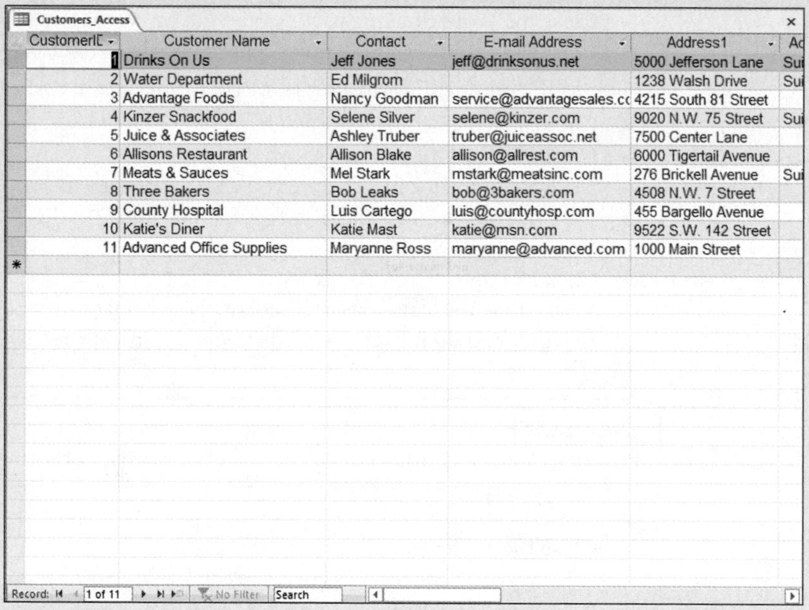

Customers_Access

CustomerID	Customer Name	Contact	E-mail Address	Address1	Ad
1	Drinks On Us	Jeff Jones	jeff@drinksonus.net	5000 Jefferson Lane	Su
2	Water Department	Ed Milgrom		1238 Walsh Drive	Su
3	Advantage Foods	Nancy Goodman	service@advantagesales.cc	4215 South 81 Street	
4	Kinzer Snackfood	Selene Silver	selene@kinzer.com	9020 N.W. 75 Street	Su
5	Juice & Associates	Ashley Truber	truber@juiceassoc.net	7500 Center Lane	
6	Allisons Restaurant	Allison Blake	allison@allrest.com	6000 Tigertail Avenue	
7	Meats & Sauces	Mel Stark	mstark@meatsinc.com	276 Brickell Avenue	Su
8	Three Bakers	Bob Leaks	bob@3bakers.com	4508 N.W. 7 Street	
9	County Hospital	Luis Cartego	luis@countyhosp.com	455 Bargello Avenue	
10	Katie's Diner	Katie Mast	katie@msn.com	9522 S.W. 142 Street	
11	Advanced Office Supplies	Maryanne Ross	maryanne@advanced.com	1000 Main Street	

Record: 1 of 11 No Filter Search

FIGURE 8.70 Customers Imported from Another Access Database

a. Open *a08p3Coffee*. Click the **FILE tab**, click **Save As**, click **Save As**, and then type **a08p3Coffee_LastFirst**. Click **Save**.

b. Click the **EXTERNAL DATA tab** and click **Excel** in the Import & Link group.

c. Click **Browse** in the Get External Data – Excel Spreadsheet dialog box and locate the file *a08p3Custexcel*.

d. Select the file and click **Open** to return to the Get External Data dialog box.

e. Click the **Link to the data source by creating a linked table option**. Click **OK**.

f. Click the **First Row Contains Column Headings check box**. Click **Next**.

g. Confirm **Customers_Excel** is the Linked Table Name. Click **Finish**. Click **OK** in the message box.

h. Double-click the **Customers_Excel table** in the Navigation Pane to view the customer records. Close the table.

i. Click the **EXTERNAL DATA tab** and click **Excel** in the Import & Link group.

j. Click **Browse** in the Get External Data – Excel Spreadsheet dialog box and locate the file *a08p3Repsexcel*.

k. Select the file and click **Open** to return to the Get External Data dialog box.

l. Click the **Import the source data into a new table in the current database option**. Click **OK**.

m. Click the **First Row Contains Column Headings check box**. Click **Next** two times.

n. Click the **Choose my own primary key option**. Click **Next**.

o. Confirm **Sales Reps** is the *Import to Table* name. Click **Finish**. Click **Close** in the Save Import Steps dialog box.

p. Double-click the **Sales Reps table** in the Navigation Pane to view the records. Close the table.

q. Click **Access** in the Import & Link group on the EXTERNAL DATA tab.

r. Click **Browse** in the Get External Data – Access Database dialog box and locate the file *a08p3Custaccess*.

s. Select the file and click **Open** to return to the Get External Data dialog box.

t. Click the **Link to the data source by creating a linked table option**. Click **OK**.

u. Click **Customers_Access** in the Link Tables dialog box. Click **OK**.

v. Double-click the **Customers_Access table** in the Navigation Pane to view the customer records. Close the table.

w. Click **Text File** in the Import & Link group on the External Data tab.

x. Click **Browse** in the Get External Data – Text File dialog box and locate the file *a08p3Custtext.csv*.

y. Select the file and click **Open** to return to the Get External Data dialog box. Verify that the *Import the source data into a new table in the current database* option is selected. Click **OK**.

z. Click **Next** when the Import Text Wizard appears.

aa. Click the **First Row Contains Field Names check box**. Click **Next**.

bb. Click **Next** to confirm the field options.

cc. Click the **No primary key option** in the next dialog box. Click **Next**.

dd. Change the *Import to Table* name to **Customers_Text**. Click **Finish**. Click **Close** in the Save Import Steps dialog box. Close the window.

ee. Double-click the **Customers_Text table** in the Navigation Pane to view the customer records. Close the table.

ff. Click the **FILE tab** and click **Compact & Repair Database**.

gg. Close the database. Exit Access.

hh. Submit based on your instructor's directions.

Mid-Level Exercises

1 Morrison Arboretum

ANALYSIS CASE

The Morrison Arboretum at NC University wants to add a few new features to its database. They want to add photos of the plants to the Plant Descriptions table and a hyperlink field that points to a Web site that describes each plant. You also need to create a report showing the plant names, the corresponding hyperlinks, and the plant photos. You will export this report to Word, but because you notice that the photos will not export to Word, you will publish the report as a PDF document to distribute via e-mail to members. Finally, you will export a query to Excel to be used as a mailing list. Refer to Figure 8.71 as you complete this exercise.

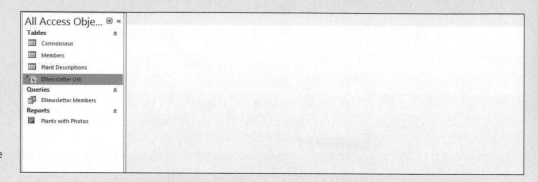

FIGURE 8.71 Navigation Pane with Report and Linked Table

a. Open the file *a08m1Arbor*. Save it as **a08m1Arbor_LastFirst**.

b. Create a new hyperlink field named **PlantLink** in the Plant Descriptions table below the PlantName field.

c. Create a new attachment field named **Picture** in the Plant Descriptions table below the PlantLink field.

DISCOVER

d. Visit Wikipedia.org and perform a search on **viburnum**. Copy the URL and paste it into the correct PlantLink field in Datasheet view.

e. Use the Attachments dialog box to add the appropriate photo for each plant. The photos are in the folder named *a08m1Plant_Photos*.

f. Create a basic report based on the Plant Descriptions table. Set the title of the report as **Plants with Links and Pictures**.

★ g. Center the report title text in the control and delete the logo to the left of the title control. Save the report as **Plants with Photos**. Close the report. Export the *Plants with Photos* report to Word and save the document as **a08m1Plants_LastFirst**. Note that no pictures were exported and close Word. Close the Save Export Steps dialog box without saving the export steps. Write a short paragraph in Word that discusses why it could be useful to save the export steps. Use Access Help as necessary to research this feature. Save the document as **a08m1Exports_LastFirst**.

h. Publish the report in PDF format and save the document as **a08m1Plants_LastFirst**. View the PDF report in your reader program, note that the pictures were exported, and then close the reader. Close the Save Export Steps dialog box without saving the export steps.

i. Export the query ENewsletter Members to Excel to use as mailing list and save the workbook as **a08m1Email_LastFirst**. Review the exported data and close Excel. Close the Save Export Steps dialog box without saving the export steps. Import the Excel spreadsheet back into the database as a linked table named **ENewsletter List**, using the first row headings as field names.

j. Open the ENewsletter List table and close the table. Compact and repair the database.

k. Close the database. Exit Access.

l. Submit based on your instructor's directions.

ANALYSIS CASE As the database manager of a hotel chain, you monitor the services ordered using a summary query. The hotel chain's manager asks you to send him a summary of the Raleigh location orders as an Excel spreadsheet. He also asks you to export the Repeat Members Club table to a different database. Several hotels in Los Angeles are for sale, and you decide to import their order data to determine their activity levels. Refer to Figure 8.72 as you complete this exercise.

FIGURE 8.72 Navigation Pane with Linked and Imported Data

a. Open *a08m2Hotel* and save it as **a08m2Hotel_LastFirst** in the folder where you are saving your files. Open *a08m2Hotelexport*. Save the database as **a08m2Hotelexport_LastFirst**. Close *a08h2Hotelexport_LastFirst* and return to the *a08m2Hotel_LastFirst* database.

b. Export the Repeat Members Club table to another Access database, *a08m2Hotelexport_LastFirst*. Verify that the table was exported correctly and return to the *a08m2Hotel_LastFirst* database. Do not save the export steps.

c. Modify the *Summary by ServiceID* query so that it displays only orders from location 3 (which is Raleigh). Save, run, and then close the query. Export the query to Excel and save the workbook as **a08m2Raleighorders_LastFirst** in the folder where you are saving your solution files.

d. Review the exported data and close Excel. Do not save the export steps. Import the Excel spreadsheet back into the database as a linked table named **Raleigh Property Updates**, with the first row headings as field names. Open the Raleigh Property Updates table and close the table. Do not save the import steps.

e. Open *a08m2Ordersexcel.xslx*. Exit Excel and return to *a08m2Hotel_LastFirst*. Import the Excel spreadsheet as a table named *Orders_Excel* with the first row as column headings and OrderID as the primary key field. Do not save the import steps.

f. Open *a08m2Ordersaccess*. Close *a08m2Ordersaccess* and return to *a08m2Hotel_LastFirst*. Create a link to the *Orders_Access* table in the *a08m2Ordersaccess* database. Do not save the import steps.

g. Open *a08m2Orderstext.csv*. Exit Excel and return to *a08m2Hotel_LastFirst*. Import the data as **Orders_Text** from the *a08m2Orderstext.csv* text file using the first row headings as field names and **OrderID** as the primary key field into the database. Do not save the import steps.

⭐ h. Save a copy of the file *a08m2Orderstext* as **a08m2Orderstext_LastFirst** with the text file format (.txt). Edit the file using the Notepad program to delete the first record, *OrderID 4001*, and reimport the modified text file into your database as **Orders_Text**. Overwrite the original table when prompted. Write a short paragraph in Word that explains why it is important to edit a text file before it is imported into Access. Save the document as **a08m2Orderstext_LastFirst**.

i. Compact and repair the database. Close the database. Exit Access.

j. Submit based on your instructor's directions.

COLLABORATION CASE

You have been asked to modify a loan-tracking database that tracks customer data, loan records, and payment information. You and your team will modify and import a spreadsheet and a text file into the database. You will add a hyperlink field that will store an e-mail address for each customer. You will then use imported data to create a query in the database, create a report based on the query, and then export the report to a Word document. Refer to Figure 8.73 as you complete this exercise.

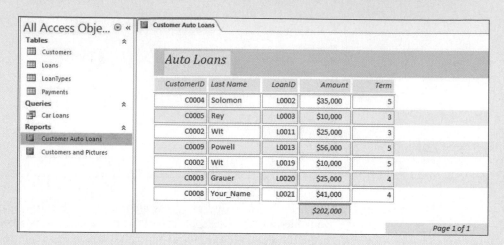

FIGURE 8.73 Customer Auto Loans Report Includes Imported Data

a. Open *a08m3Collaboration* and save it as **a08m3Collaboration_GroupName**. As a team, study the existing database and the relationship between the Customers and Loans tables. You will add two new tables to the database by importing external data.

Assign the next two tasks to a team member.

b. Open the text file named *a08m3LoanTypes.txt* and save a copy of the file as *a08m3LoanTypes_LastFirst.txt*. Modify the text file so that instead of the existing separators, commas will specify where the values should be separated. Save your changes.

c. Create a table in the database by importing the modified text file named *a08m3LoanTypes_LastFirst.txt*. Use the first row of the file as field names and **Type** as the primary key and name the table **LoanTypes**. Accept all other default options. Do not save the import steps.

Assign the next two tasks to a team member.

d. Open the workbook named *a08m3Payments* and save a copy of the file as *a08m3Payments_LastFirst*. Modify the workbook so that it will import properly to an Access database. Save your changes.

e. Create a new table in the database by importing the workbook named *a08m3Payments_LastFirst*. Use the first row of the worksheet as column headings, ensure that PaymentID is set as the primary key, and them import the table as **Payments**. Accept all other default options. Do not save the import steps. Change the field size of the LoanID field to Long Integer. If a warning message appears, proceed with the change and then save and close the table.

Assign the next two tasks to a team member.

f. Add a Hyperlink field named **EmailAddress** below the PhoneNumber field in the Customers table.

g. Enter your own first and last names and your personal e-mail address in the appropriate fields for record C0008. Remove the existing attachment from the Photo field and add your own personal photo. Close the table.

Assign the next two tasks to a team member.

h. Add the LoanTypes and Payment tables to the Relationships window. Create a relationship between the Loans and Payments table, enforcing referential integrity. Create a relationship between LoanTypes and Loans, enforcing referential integrity. Save and close the Relationships window.

i. Create a query in Design view. Add the Customers, Loans, and LoanTypes tables to the query window. Add the following fields in this order: CustomerID, LastName, LoanID, Amount, Term, and LoanName. Set the criteria so that customers who have car loans will display in the results. Run the query, save it as **Car Loans**, and then close it.

j. Collaborate with your team to determine what would be the best way to portray the Car Loans query results in a report. Create the report and format it appropriately. Adjust the column widths so that they all fit within the page but the data is still visible. Delete the LoanName column and the Date and Time fields from the report.

k. Switch to Design view and move the page numbering control to the left so that its right edge is just inside the 7-inch mark on the horizontal ruler. Drag the right edge of the report to the left so that it is just inside the 7-inch mark on the ruler. View the report in Print Preview; the report should consist of one page.

l. Modify the report title as **Auto Loans** and delete the logo to the left of the title, if necessary

m. Save the report as **a08m3CustomerAutoLoans_LastFirst** and close the report. Export the report as a Word document using the same name and save it as a Word document. Close the report and exit Word. Do not save the export steps.

n. Compact and repair the database. Close the database. Exit Access. Submit the database and documents based on your instructor's directions.

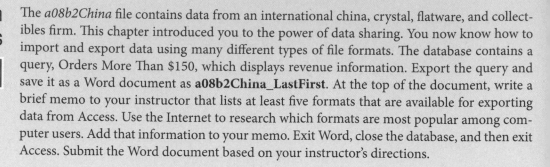

Exporting from Access

RESEARCH CASE

The *a08b2China* file contains data from an international china, crystal, flatware, and collectibles firm. This chapter introduced you to the power of data sharing. You now know how to import and export data using many different types of file formats. The database contains a query, Orders More Than $150, which displays revenue information. Export the query and save it as a Word document as **a08b2China_LastFirst**. At the top of the document, write a brief memo to your instructor that lists at least five formats that are available for exporting data from Access. Use the Internet to research which formats are most popular among computer users. Add that information to your memo. Exit Word, close the database, and then exit Access. Submit the Word document based on your instructor's directions.

Exporting to Word

DISASTER RECOVERY

Your colleague needs you to export a report from Access to Word to provide him with the most recent sales data. Open *a08b3Real*. Export the Sales Report to Word. Save the Word document as **a08b3Real_LastFirst**. Compact, repair, and then close the database. Exit Access. Submit the Word document based on your instructor's directions.

Workplace Etiquette

SOFT SKILLS CASE [S]

You want to determine how many of the new employees in the *a08b4Etiquette* database require a workplace etiquette in-service. Open *a08b4Etiquette*. Modify the Require Etiquette Inservice query so that only employees who have *not* had etiquette training display in the results. Export the query results to Excel. Save the Excel workbook as **Require Etiquette Inservice_LastFirst**. Close Excel. Compact, repair, and then close the database. Exit Access. Submit the Excel workbook based on your instructor's directions.

Capstone Exercise

You work as an associate database manager at Replacement China, Inc. This firm specializes in finding difficult-to-replace, no-longer-manufactured china, crystal, silver, and collectibles. You need to add a hyperlink field that will store a URL for each manufacturer's Web site. The HR department manager wants to store a photo and the most recent performance review for each employee. You also need to export select inventory items in three different formats. Finally, you will import information from Excel, Access, and text files. Compact and repair the database and make a backup of it when you are finished.

Database File Setup

Make a copy of the original database file, rename the copy, and then open the copy. After you open the copied database, you will replace an existing employee's name with your name.

a. Open *a08c1Replace* and save it as **a08c1Replace_LastFirst**.

b. Open the Employees table.

c. Navigate to record 21 and replace *Your_Name* with your name. Save the record and close the table.

Create Attachment and Hyperlink Fields

Add a hyperlink field to the Manufacturer table to store each company's Web site address. Add an attachment field to the Employees table to store the employee's performance reviews and photos.

a. Create a new field in the Manufacturer table after RlMfgCode named **Website** with the Hyperlink data type. Save the table.

b. Switch to Datasheet view, add the Web site **http://www.lenox.com** to the Lenox China record (7), and then add **http://www.waterford.com** to the Waterford Crystal record (14). Click each link to make sure it launches a browser and locates the appropriate Web site. Close the table.

c. Create a new field in the Employees table after HireDate named **Files** with the Attachment data type. Save the table.

d. Switch to Datasheet view and use the Find command to locate the record for UserID 822680. Add the Word document named *822680.doc* and the picture file named *822680.jpg* to the Files field. The files you need are in the a08c1Reviews folder. Additional attachments will be added in the future.

e. Create a basic form based on the Employees table that will open in Layout view. Delete the subform. Navigate to the record for UserID 822680 (record 21) and use the Attachment toolbar to display the Word document and the picture file.

f. Save the form as **Employees**. Close the form and the table.

Export a Filtered Table to Excel, Word, and PDF

You need to filter the Inventory table and then export the records to three formats: Excel, Word, and PDF. This information will be used to get prices on items that have no on-hand quantity.

a. Use *Filter by Selection* to display records in the Inventory table where the Category equals *Crystal*. Filter the records further to display Crystal where the OH (on-hand) value equals *0* (three records will display). Leave the filtered table open for the next three steps.

b. Export the filtered records to an Excel file. Save the file as **a08c1Crystal_LastFirst**. Do not save the export steps.

c. Export the same filtered records to a Word file. Press **Enter** one time and add the title **Crystal with 0 on hand** to the Word file. Save the file as a Word document with the name **a08c1Crystal_LastFirst**. Do not save the export steps.

d. Export the filtered records to a PDF document. Save the file as **a08c1Crystal_LastFirst**. Do not save the export steps.

e. Close the Inventory table without saving the changes.

Import and Link Data from Excel, Access, and a Text File

You need to import new customer records from Excel and Access. You also will import customer records from a text file.

a. Create a linked table in the database by importing the workbook named *a08c1Customers*. Use the first row of the Customers1 worksheet as row headings and accept all other default options.

b. Create a linked table in the database by importing the Customers2 table from the database named *a08c1Customers*.

c. Create a table in the database by importing the text file named *a08c1Textcust.csv*. Use the first row of the file as field names, **CustomerNum** as the primary key, and name the table **Customers Text**. Accept all other default options.

d. Compact and repair the database.

e. Close the database. Exit Access.

f. Submit based on your instructor's directions.

Fine-Tuning the Database

Yuri Arcurs/Shutterstock

CHAPTER 9

Analyzing and Improving Database Performance

CASE STUDY | The Metropolitan Zoo

Your job as the information manager of the Metropolitan Zoo is to maintain the records for all of the animals at the zoo. The zoo maintains its records in an Access 2013 database, which you have been using for the past two months. The database was created by a former employee who learned about Access by taking a night course at a local community college. The forms and reports have been working well, according to Director of Field Programs, Selene Platt. Selene has worked at the Metropolitan Zoo for 27 years, and she provides you with the information about each animal. She hired you to help with the daily upkeep of the database; she also wants to evaluate the design and performance of the database.

Your tasks include entering new animals, updating changes to existing records, and archiving records for animals that leave the zoo. As you work with the Access database and become familiar with the tables, the table relationships, the data-entry forms, and the reports, you start to look for ways to improve the performance of the database. You also look for ways to protect the data that already exists in the database. These improvements will help you complete the daily tasks of the database; they may also help your boss, Selene, get faster and more reliable results from the database.

Database Normalization

In an earlier chapter, you used common sense to determine which fields to include in each table. The process changes when you deal with a more complex system. Database designers generally start by performing customer interviews, reviewing existing documents, examining existing files, and applying their own knowledge to create a list of potential fields. They then identify potential primary keys and divide the fields into tables. They then go through a process to refine the tables and remove issues. *Normalization* is the formal process of deciding which fields should be grouped together into which tables. Experienced database designers may instinctively create tables that follow the rules of normalization. Less experienced designers generally use the process of normalization to guide them in the process of creating the database. The benefits of normalization are:

- Minimization of data redundancy
- Improvement of referential integrity enforcement
- Ease of maintaining data (add, update, delete)
- Accommodation of future growth of a database

Though this sounds straightforward, it can present challenges. Many colleges and universities have multiple graduate-level database classes to train future database designers in this process.

Following the rules of normalization while creating tables in Access helps you design tables that are free from anomalies. An *anomaly* is an error or inconsistency within a database. Many times, these errors occur when you add, edit, and delete data. Assume a spreadsheet is keeping track of company orders, one order per row. Repeat customers would lead to multiple references to the same customer. Mixed in among thousands of orders, we might have the following information for customer Faten Bader:

9/1/15	Faten Bader	West Paterson, NJ	#456789	3	$12.50
9/10/15	Faten Bader	West Paterson, NJ	#894561	1	$2.95
9/25/15	Faten Bader	West Paterson, NJ	#981156	1	$.95

Faten may call in and change her address, saying her town name changed from West Paterson to Woodland Park, and this introduces an update problem (anomaly). How does the database know which record to update—the first, the second, the third, or all three? A user might try to update the records manually, but this might produce an anomaly as well if only one or two of the three records are changed. If the town's name has changed, should it change for all other customers?

In this section, you will learn the first three rules of normalization. These rules are known as *normal forms* and indicate the current state of a table. The first three normal forms are referred to as first normal form (1NF), second normal form (2NF), and third normal form (3NF). By definition, a table cannot be in 2NF unless it is already in 1NF, and it cannot be in 3NF unless it is in 2NF.

A table that meets 1NF criteria is better than a table that does not. Similarly, a table that meets 2NF criteria is better than a table that is in 1NF, and a table that meets 3NF criteria is better than a table that is in 2NF. There are five normal forms; however, the majority of database designs only require the first three normal forms.

Verifying First Normal Form

STEP 1 » First normal form is the first rule to identify and correct. It can be demonstrated by using an Excel spreadsheet that contains information about authors, books, and publishers (see Figure 9.1). In the spreadsheet, Dan Brown is listed as an AuthorName in column C; the titles of the books that Brown authored are listed on row 5 in column D. The remaining fields contain additional information related to the books. This example would not pass the

1NF test because column D—including the books that Brown authored—has multiple values in a single cell. Brown, the author, is listed once, and the books he wrote are listed in one cell. Even titles on two lines in the same cell are considered multiple values in one cell. If this Excel spreadsheet were imported into Access, the corresponding Access table with repeating groups would be as shown in Figure 9.2. This table shows the same condition with repeating values in the Title field. Repeating groups are not allowed in a normalized table.

Two values in the same cell →

	A	B	C	D	E	F	G	H	I	J	K
1	ISBN	AuthorID	AuthorName	Title	Publisher	PubYear					
2	9781401208417	ALMO01	Alan Moore	V for Vendetta	DC Comics	2005					
3	9780767931557	BEME01	Ben Mezrich	The Accidental Billionaires	Anchor Books	2009					
4	0809400774	DABR02	Dale Brown	American Cooking: The Northwest	Time Life	1970					
5	0312995423 / 9780593054277	DABR01	Dan Brown	Digital Fortress / The Lost Symbol	St. Martin / Doubleday	1998 / 2009					
6	0805029648 / 9780399154379	DABA01	Dave Barry	Bad Habits / History of the Millenium (So Far)	Henry Holt & Co. / G. P. Putnam's Sons	1987 / 2007					
7	9780307405807	DOSA01	Douglas Sarine	The Ninja Handbook	Three Rivers Press	2008					
8	9781572439597	JAST01	Jayson Stark	The Stark Truth	Triumph Books	2007					
9	0380788624	NEST01	Neal Stephenson	Cryptonomicon	Perennial	1999					
10	9780345517951	ROJA01	Ron Jaworski	The Games that Changed the Game	ESPN Books	2010					

FIGURE 9.1 Excel Spreadsheet with Repeating Groups

Two values in the same record →

ISBN	AuthorID	AuthorName	Title	Publisher	PubYear	Click to Add
9781401208417	ALMO01	Alan Moore	V for Vendetta	DC Comics	2005	
9780767931557	BEME01	Ben Mezrich	The Accidental Billionaires	Anchor Books	2009	
0809400774	DABR02	Dale Brown	American Cooking: The Northwest	Time Life	1970	
031299542397 80593054277	DABR01	Dan Brown	Digital Fortress The Lost Symbol	St. Martin Doubleday	1998 2009	
080502964897 80399154379	DABA01	Dave Barry	Bad Habits History of the Millenium (So Far)	Henry Holt & Co. G. P. Putnam's Sons	1987 2007	
9780307405807	DOSA01	Douglas Sarine	The Ninja Handbook	Three Rivers Press	2008	
9781572439597	JAST01	Jayson Stark	The Stark Truth	Triumph Books	2007	
0380788624	NEST01	Neal Stephenson	Cryptonomicon	Perennial	1999	
9780345517951	ROJA01	Ron Jaworski	The Games that Changed the Game	ESPN Books	2010	

FIGURE 9.2 Access Table with Repeating Groups

We define *first normal form (1NF)* as a table that contains no repeating groups or repeating columns. In the book example, the Title column might be replaced with Title1, Title2, and Title3. This might appear to correct the repeating groups problem because each cell contains one piece of information; however, this type of design still violates 1NF and must be corrected. In this example, it is still difficult to find data efficiently.

TIP **Multivalued Data Types in Access**

Access enables you to create a multivalued field using the Lookup Wizard data type. This data type enables you to enter multiple values into a single field for one record. This data type may appear to break the rules of 1NF, but remember that multivalued fields are handled with special invisible tables Access creates in the background. Although multivalued fields can be useful at times, remember to avoid them if you plan to upgrade to a more powerful database (e.g., SQL Server) in the future.

There are several problems with tables that have repeating groups—it is difficult to add new entries, it is difficult to update existing entries, and it is difficult to properly extract information when running queries. For example, if you want see the information for *Digital Fortress*, you could create a filter or query searching for those results. However, Access considers them to be part of the same record, and you would also see the book *The Lost Symbol*. As a matter of fact, when you attempt to filter your data (as shown in Figure 9.3), you would immediately notice the two book names listed as one piece of data. Similar problems would exist with queries searching for a specific book. In other words, there is no easy way to only show the information for *Digital Fortress*. This occurs because all the books by one author are contained in the same record.

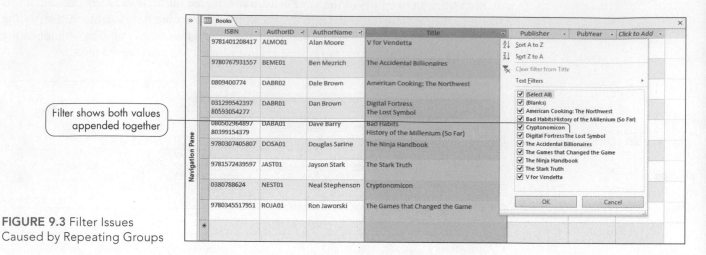

Filter shows both values appended together

FIGURE 9.3 Filter Issues Caused by Repeating Groups

To fix a table that has repeating groups, simply make sure each unique piece of information is on a separate row. Any columns should have the missing information added, even if this leads to repetition. You would need to do this in Excel before importing to Access, or alternately add rows in Access and separate the repeating data into individual rows.

Figure 9.4 shows the Books table in Access after it has been put into first normal form; the single Brown row has been split into two rows, and the books by the same author have been separated. Now each book has its own record.

At this point, although the table is in 1NF, it still has redundancy issues. In fact, we have introduced redundancy into our table. However, because normalization is a process, further normalization will remove the introduced redundancies.

Two records created from original

FIGURE 9.4 Books Table in First Normal Form

The following situations may violate 1NF:

- Multiple values in the same field separated by commas or some other identifier
  - An Authors field listing **Poatsy, Krebs, Cameron, and Williams** is a violation of 1NF.
  - An Address2 field listing **Paterson, NJ 07501** is a violation of 1NF.
  - A Teaching field that contains the following values for the same class, on two lines is a violation of 1NF:
    Cameron
    Siegel
- Multiple columns in the same record containing the same sort of data
  - A table with an Author1 field set to **Poatsy**, Author2 field set to **Krebs**, Author3 field set to **Cameron**, and Author4 field set to **Williams** is a violation of 1NF.

Our focus will be on the more obvious examples, such as multiple values in the field separated by commas or values on separate lines.

Verifying Second Normal Form

STEP 2>> A table is in ***second normal form (2NF)*** if it meets 1NF criteria and all non-key fields are functionally dependent on the entire primary key. ***Functional dependency*** occurs when the value of one field is determined by the value of another. A ***non-key field*** is any field that is not part of the primary key. Therefore, a table with a single-field primary key is usually in 2NF. Because many tables have a single-field primary key, 2NF often requires no changes to a table. However, some tables have a ***composite key***, a primary key that is made of two or more fields. Tables with a composite key may require some changes.

Most bookstore databases contain information about location and quantity in stock. Therefore, we have expanded the earlier example to include three extra fields, as shown in Figure 9.5. For the purposes of this example, assume the bookstore has two locations, one in Paterson and one in Wanaque. Because this more realistic version of the table has the location added, a problem now exists. Notice in Figure 9.5 that the ISBN cannot be the primary key for this table because the same book (with the same ISBN) can appear in both locations. In this case, a good option is to use a combination of two fields as the primary key. The composite key for this table would be ISBN plus the location, which uniquely identifies each row.

Because this table has a composite key, you need to ensure all fields are functionally dependent on the entire primary key. To find out the number of books on hand for any specific title, you need to know both the ISBN and the location. Likewise, to find the aisle in which a book is stored, you would need both the ISBN and the location. However, a book's title is independent of the location. Regardless of whether it is in Paterson or Wanaque, the book with an ISBN of 0312995423 is always *Digital Fortress.* The same goes for the rest of the fields. Notice in Figure 9.5 that all the information related to the book *Digital Fortress* is repeated—the AuthorName, Title, Publisher, and PubYear. One data-entry error can lead to inconsistent data.

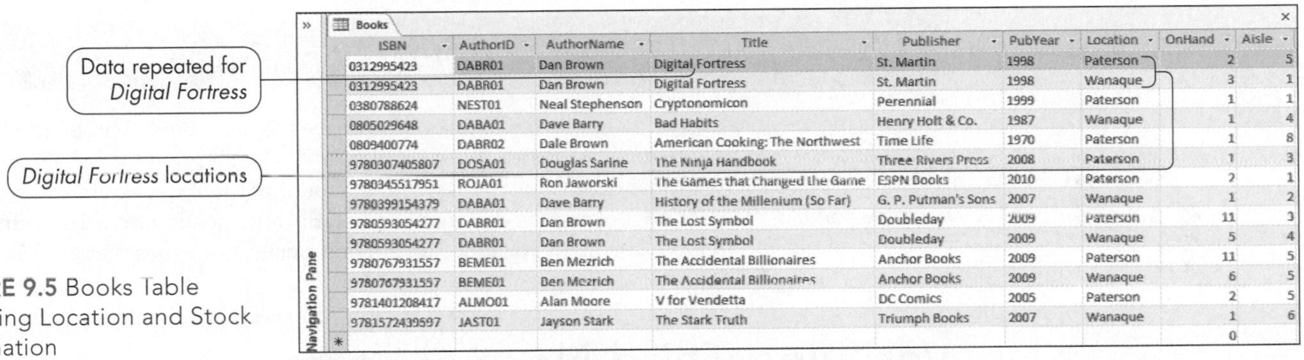

ISBN	AuthorID	AuthorName	Title	Publisher	PubYear	Location	OnHand	Aisle
0312995423	DABR01	Dan Brown	Digital Fortress	St. Martin	1998	Paterson	2	5
0312995423	DABR01	Dan Brown	Digital Fortress	St. Martin	1998	Wanaque	3	1
0380788624	NEST01	Neal Stephenson	Cryptonomicon	Perennial	1999	Paterson	1	1
0805029648	DABA01	Dave Barry	Bad Habits	Henry Holt & Co.	1987	Wanaque	1	4
0809400774	DABR02	Dale Brown	American Cooking: The Northwest	Time Life	1970	Paterson	1	8
9780307405807	DOSA01	Douglas Sarine	The Ninja Handbook	Three Rivers Press	2008	Paterson	1	3
9780345517951	ROJA01	Ron Jaworski	The Games that Changed the Game	ESPN Books	2010	Paterson	2	1
9780399154379	DABA01	Dave Barry	History of the Millenium (So Far)	G. P. Putman's Sons	2007	Wanaque	1	2
9780593054277	DABR01	Dan Brown	The Lost Symbol	Doubleday	2009	Paterson	11	3
9780593054277	DABR01	Dan Brown	The Lost Symbol	Doubleday	2009	Wanaque	5	4
9780767931557	BEME01	Ben Mezrich	The Accidental Billionaires	Anchor Books	2009	Paterson	11	5
9780767931557	BEME01	Ben Mezrich	The Accidental Billionaires	Anchor Books	2009	Wanaque	6	5
9781401208417	ALMO01	Alan Moore	V for Vendetta	DC Comics	2005	Paterson	2	5
9781572439597	JAST01	Jayson Stark	The Stark Truth	Triumph Books	2007	Wanaque	1	6
*							0	

FIGURE 9.5 Books Table Including Location and Stock Information

If you look up the ISBN 0312995423, whether in this database, on an online bookstore such as Amazon, or in a Barnes & Noble retail store, you should always find the same title, publisher, and author name of the book. Therefore, the title, publisher, and author name are functionally dependent on the ISBN, not the combination of ISBN and location. In other words, these fields are each characteristics of the book.

Amazon may have the same book in its inventory as our bookstore in Paterson, but the book's location, the number on hand, and the aisle will be different or possibly not present. This is because the location, number on hand, and the aisle are not characteristics of the book. Instead, these are characteristics of the book as it exists in a bookstore.

Second normal form tells you that when fields are functionally dependent upon part of a primary key, you need to remove those fields from the table. Most of the time, this results in new tables, though it is possible to move fields into another existing table.

To resolve the problem, you need to create two tables. The first table you will name Books. The Books table should contain the fields ISBN, AuthorID, AuthorName, Title, Publisher, and PubYear. The primary key of this table is ISBN. See Figure 9.6.

FIGURE 9.6 Books Table in Second Normal Form

The second table you will name Stock. This table contains the fields ISBN, Location, OnHand, and Aisle, as shown in Figure 9.7. The primary key for this table is a composite key, the combination of ISBN and Location.

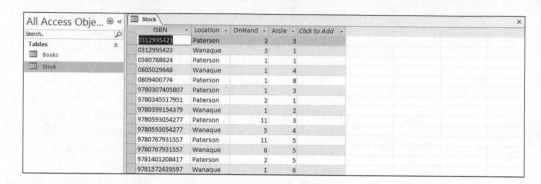

FIGURE 9.7 Newly Created Stock Table

Notice that the data, once divided into two tables, has less repetition of book information.

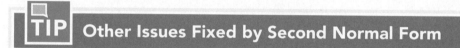

TIP | Other Issues Fixed by Second Normal Form

For simplicity's sake, this example has focused on composite key issues. There are other situations in which 2NF may require changes. In Figure 9.5, just adding an AutoNumber field labelled as the primary key would not solve the issue that the ISBN would still determine some of the information, and the combination of ISBN and location would determine some of the information. Examples will focus on the composite key issues that 2NF fixes.

Verifying Third Normal Form

STEP 3 ≫ A table is in *third normal form (3NF)* if it meets 2NF criteria and no transitive dependencies exist. *Transitive dependencies* occur when the value of one non-key field is functionally dependent on the value of another non-key field. AuthorName in the example is dependent on AuthorID and, therefore, is an example of a transitive dependency. Whenever you know the AuthorID, the AuthorName is automatically known. Therefore, to conform to 3NF, AuthorName must be moved to another table, as shown in Figure 9.8. The new table contains two fields: AuthorID and AuthorName. The Books table can now reference the author using the AuthorID field, as shown in Figure 9.9. The Books table is in 3NF because the transitive dependency was removed. In effect, moving to 3NF requires some work, as a new table often needs to be created and data moved. For a large database, this may require creation of a Make Table query (see the *Action Queries* section of this textbook for more information). In the worst case, this could require large amounts of tedious data entry. However, the trade-off is less repeated data, which leads to fewer anomalies. For example, if you had a typographical error for an author's name (say, Steven King instead of Stephen King), you would only need to change the spelling in one place to correct it.

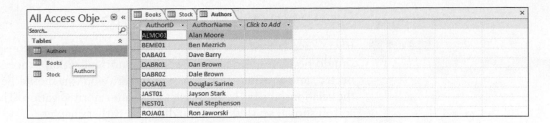

FIGURE 9.8 Newly Created Author Table

FIGURE 9.9 Books Table in Third Normal Form

Another way to handle a conversion to 3NF is to delete fields that may not be necessary. In this specific case, you probably want to keep the AuthorID. In other cases, ask yourself if there is an extra field that can be eliminated. Table 9.1 presents a summary of the three normal forms covered in this chapter.

TABLE 9.1	**Normalization Summary**	
Form	**What It Does**	**Notes**
First Normal Form	Removes repeating groups	Introduces redundancy, which is fixed by later normal forms.
Second Normal Form	Removes dependencies on part of a composite primary key	Commonly an issue when a table has a composite key. If the primary key is a single field, a table is usually in 2NF. Changes usually result in added tables.
Third Normal Form	Removes dependencies on any field that is not a primary key	Changes usually result in new tables.

TIP City, State, ZIP, 3NF?

For most locations in the United States, if you have the ZIP code, you can look up the city and state. This might lead you to believe that this is a transitive dependency. However, on some rare occasions this is not true. For example, the ZIP code 42223 covers parts of Christian County, Kentucky, and Montgomery County, Tennessee. In this case, the same ZIP code not only crosses county borders, it also crosses state lines! Note that in this case, this oddity has to do with an army base that crosses state borders. Due to issues such as these, it is safe to consider a database with the city, state, and ZIP in the same table to be in 3NF.

On the other hand, if you have two customers who live in North Brunswick, NJ, one person doing data entry might type it into the database as North Brunswick and the other may abbreviate it as N Brunswick. If you created a filter or query to locate all towns listed as North Brunswick, only one of those two customers would appear. The argument for putting ZIP in a separate table is to avoid issues such as that.

Creating Relationships

STEP 4 » If you have created new tables, you will need to create relationships between the tables. This should be done after completion of the normalization process. The tables should be connected, and the Enforce Referential Integrity option should be checked. Figure 9.10 shows the relationships in the Books database after normalization. This is not done automatically, so you should set this up as you did in an earlier chapter.

Creating relationships can also be a way to test your normalization. Normalization should not result in data loss, so if you cannot create a relationship between the tables, there is likely an issue with the way you have normalized.

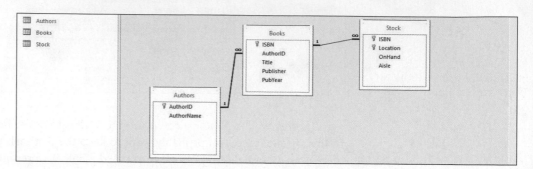

FIGURE 9.10 Relationships in Books Database

In Hands-On Exercise 1, you will work with the Metropolitan Zoo's database to make sure its tables are normalized. The database has been functioning for over two years, so you will have to preserve the existing data when you modify any table. Your boss will work with you to determine which information is important and which data can be discarded.

Quick
Concepts

1. What is the purpose of normalizing a database? *p. 792*

2. What problems does first normal form fix? *p. 793*

3. What problems does second normal form fix? *p. 795*

4. What problems does third normal form fix? *p. 796*

Hands-On Exercise

Watch the Video for this Hands-On Exercise!

MyITLab® HOE1 Training

1 Database Normalization

Your job at the Metropolitan Zoo has been fun and challenging. You have been making daily updates to the zoo's database with the help of your boss, Selene Platt. Based on your understanding of the rules of normalization, you decide to recommend some design changes to the database.

Skills covered: Verify First Normal Form • Verify Second Normal Form • Verify Third Normal Form • Create Relationships

STEP 1 » VERIFY FIRST NORMAL FORM

Your boss has asked you to review the table structure to see if any changes should be made. You decide to apply the rules of normalization to the Animals table, starting with 1NF—eliminate any repeating groups. Refer to Figures 9.11–9.13 as you complete Step 1.

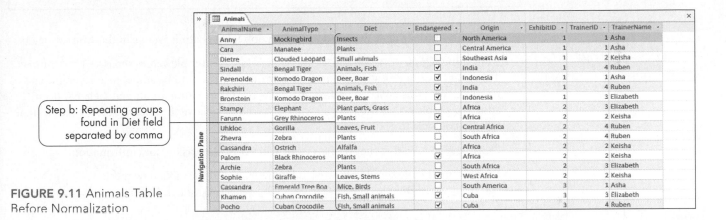

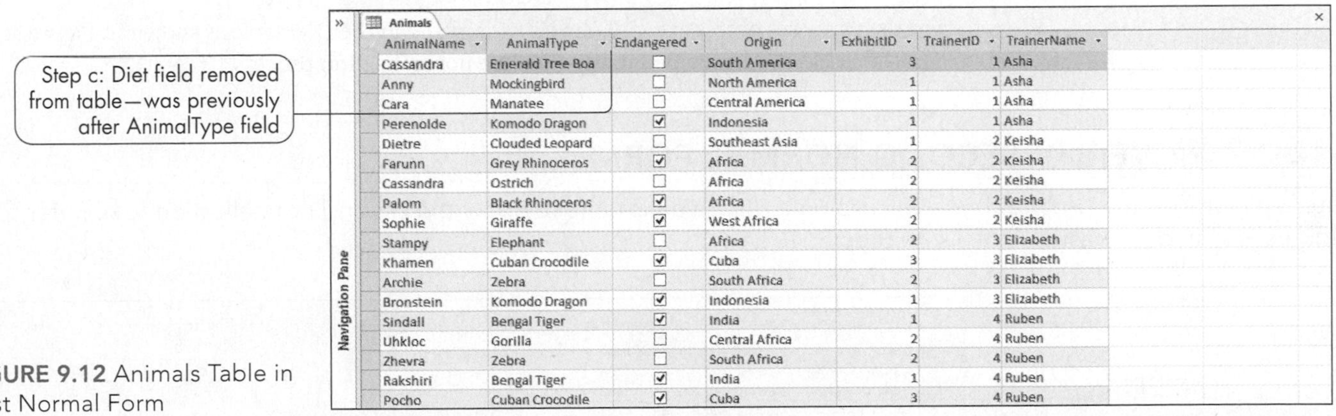

Step b: Repeating groups found in Diet field separated by comma
Animals
Navigation Pane

AnimalName	AnimalType	Diet	Endangered	Origin	ExhibitID	TrainerID	TrainerName
Anny	Mockingbird	Insects	☐	North America	1	1	Asha
Cara	Manatee	Plants	☐	Central America	1	1	Asha
Dietre	Clouded Leopard	Small animals	☐	Southeast Asia	1	2	Keisha
Sindall	Bengal Tiger	Animals, Fish	☑	India	1	4	Ruben
Perenolde	Komodo Dragon	Deer, Boar	☑	Indonesia	1	1	Asha
Rakshiri	Bengal Tiger	Animals, Fish	☑	India	1	4	Ruben
Bronstein	Komodo Dragon	Deer, Boar	☑	Indonesia	1	3	Elizabeth
Stampy	Elephant	Plant parts, Grass	☐	Africa	2	3	Elizabeth
Farunn	Grey Rhinoceros	Plants	☑	Africa	2	2	Keisha
Uhkloc	Gorilla	Leaves, Fruit	☐	Central Africa	2	4	Ruben
Zhevra	Zebra	Plants	☐	South Africa	2	4	Ruben
Cassandra	Ostrich	Alfalfa	☐	Africa	2	2	Keisha
Palom	Black Rhinoceros	Plants	☑	Africa	2	2	Keisha
Archie	Zebra	Plants	☐	South Africa	2	3	Elizabeth
Sophie	Giraffe	Leaves, Stems	☑	West Africa	2	2	Keisha
Cassandra	Emerald Tree Boa	Mice, Birds	☐	South America	3	1	Asha
Khamen	Cuban Crocodile	Fish, Small animals	☑	Cuba	3	3	Elizabeth
Pocho	Cuban Crocodile	Fish, Small animals	☑	Cuba	3	4	Ruben

FIGURE 9.11 Animals Table Before Normalization

Step c: Diet field removed from table—was previously after AnimalType field
Animals
Navigation Pane

AnimalName	AnimalType	Endangered	Origin	ExhibitID	TrainerID	TrainerName
Cassandra	Emerald Tree Boa	☐	South America	3	1	Asha
Anny	Mockingbird	☐	North America	1	1	Asha
Cara	Manatee	☐	Central America	1	1	Asha
Perenolde	Komodo Dragon	☑	Indonesia	1	1	Asha
Dietre	Clouded Leopard	☐	Southeast Asia	1	2	Keisha
Farunn	Grey Rhinoceros	☑	Africa	2	2	Keisha
Cassandra	Ostrich	☐	Africa	2	2	Keisha
Palom	Black Rhinoceros	☑	Africa	2	2	Keisha
Sophie	Giraffe	☑	West Africa	2	2	Keisha
Stampy	Elephant	☐	Africa	2	3	Elizabeth
Khamen	Cuban Crocodile	☑	Cuba	3	3	Elizabeth
Archie	Zebra	☐	South Africa	2	3	Elizabeth
Bronstein	Komodo Dragon	☑	Indonesia	1	3	Elizabeth
Sindall	Bengal Tiger	☑	India	1	4	Ruben
Uhkloc	Gorilla	☐	Central Africa	2	4	Ruben
Zhevra	Zebra	☐	South Africa	2	4	Ruben
Rakshiri	Bengal Tiger	☑	India	1	4	Ruben
Pocho	Cuban Crocodile	☑	Cuba	3	4	Ruben

FIGURE 9.12 Animals Table in First Normal Form

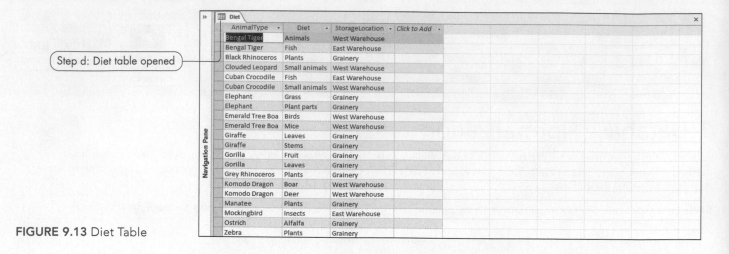

Step d: Diet table opened

FIGURE 9.13 Diet Table

a. Open *a09h1Zoo*. Save the database as **a09h1Zoo_LastFirst**.

> **TROUBLESHOOTING:** If you make any major mistakes in this exercise, you can close the *a09h1Zoo_LastFirst* file and repeat the exercise.

b. Open the Animals table in Datasheet view. Look for repeating groups in the Animals table.

Examining Figure 9.11, you can see the Diet field has multiple values separated by commas. This qualifies as a repeating group. This information needs to be added to a new table and removed from this table. For simplicity's sake, the information for animal diets has been added to a table called Diet, so you will only need to remove the Diet field from the Animal table to conform to 1NF.

c. Delete the Diet field in the Animals table. Click **Yes** when asked for confirmation.

Your Animals table should now match Figure 9.12, and the table now meets 1NF criteria. You deleted the Diet field because it contained repeating values. Repeating values violate 1NF.

d. Open the Diet table in Datasheet view.

For the purposes of this exercise, the data is already in the Diet table as shown in Figure 9.13. This table has been provided to expedite the normalization process.

STEP 2 ≫ VERIFY SECOND NORMAL FORM

After you remove the Diet field, you will examine the Animals table to apply the second normalization rule. Refer to Figures 9.14 and 9.15 as you complete Step 2.

Step b: Origin field

Step b: Endangered field

FIGURE 9.14 Animal Information Table

Step d: Origin and Endangered fields removed

AnimalName	AnimalType	ExhibitID	TrainerID	TrainerName
Anny	Mockingbird	1	1	Asha
Archie	Zebra	2	3	Elizabeth
Bronstein	Komodo Dragon	1	3	Elizabeth
Cara	Manatee	1	1	Asha
Cassandra	Emerald Tree Boa	3	1	Asha
Cassandra	Ostrich	2	2	Keisha
Dietre	Clouded Leopard	1	2	Keisha
Farunn	White Rhinoceros	2	2	Keisha
Khamen	Cuban Crocodile	3	3	Elizabeth
Palom	Black Rhinoceros	2	2	Keisha
Perenolde	Komodo Dragon	1	1	Asha
Pocho	Cuban Crocodile	3	4	Ruben
Rakshiri	Bengal Tiger	1	4	Ruben
Sindall	Bengal Tiger	1	4	Ruben
Sophie	Giraffe	2	2	Keisha
Stampy	Elephant	2	3	Elizabeth
Uhkloc	Gorilla	2	4	Ruben
Zhevra	Zebra	2	4	Ruben

FIGURE 9.15 Animals Table in Second Normal Form

a. Switch to Design view, if necessary, for the Animals table. Notice this table has a composite key. Examine the Animals table to look for any non-key fields that are not functionally dependent on the entire primary key.

The primary key for this table is a composite key. Notice in Figure 9.12 that there are two animals named Cassandra, so the combination of AnimalName and AnimalType is the only way to uniquely identify any animal. As there is a composite key in this table, you must check to make sure it is in 2NF.

Origin, Diet, and Endangered are all determined by AnimalType and are attributes of a type of animal, not a specific animal. ExhibitID, TrainerID, and TrainerName are attributes of a specific animal.

b. Open the Animal Information table in Datasheet view. Note this table includes the Origin and Endangered fields as well as other fields regarding animals. See Figure 9.14.

In reality, you may have to create a separate table for this information, but this table is provided to avoid tedious data entry.

c. Close the Animal Information table.

d. Examine the Animals table. This table is not in 2NF because some fields are dependent on part of the primary key. Delete the Origin and Endangered fields, clicking **Yes** in response to the warning.

You delete these two fields because they are not functionally dependent on the entire primary key.

e. Save the Animals table. Switch to Datasheet view.

Your table should match Figure 9.15.

All the remaining fields are functionally dependent on the entire primary key. Therefore, the table now meets 2NF criteria.

STEP 3 ≫ VERIFY THIRD NORMAL FORM

The final step to improve the zoo's Animals table is to apply 3NF: the value of a non-key field cannot be functionally dependent on the value of another non-key field.

a. Switch to the Datasheet view for the Animals table. Look for any non-key field values that are functionally dependent on another non-key field value.

TrainerName (non-key) is functionally dependent on TrainerID (non-key). If you know the TrainerID, you automatically know the TrainerName. For example, if you enter value 1 for the TrainerID, then the trainer's name will always be Asha. A Trainers table already exists.

b. Switch to Design view in the Animals table.

c. Delete the TrainerName field, clicking **Yes** in response to the warning.

You delete the TrainerName field because it is functionally dependent on the TrainerID field and therefore is not allowed in the Animals table. Normally, this would then require you to set up a new table, but as you already have a Trainers table, you can simply delete the TrainerName field. Note that this may not always be the case.

d. Save and close the Animals table.

The table now meets 3NF criteria.

STEP 4 » CREATE RELATIONSHIPS

You will now create relationships for the tables in the database. Because there are three tables with the AnimalType field, there may be some confusion as to how to establish the proper relationships between tables to ensure proper database function.

a. Click **Relationships** in the Relationships group on the DATABASE TOOLS tab to show the Relationships window.

> **TROUBLESHOOTING:** If all the tables are not closed, you will get a warning about tables being locked. If you receive this warning, exit the Relationships window, close all open tables, and repeat step a.

b. Click **Show Table**. Add each of the four tables to the layout and close the Show Table dialog box.

c. Drag the **AnimalType field** from the Animal Information table to the AnimalType field in the Animals table.

The Animals and Animal Information tables are related by the common AnimalType field.

d. Select the **Enforce Referential Integrity** and **Cascade Update Related Fields options**. Click **Create** to create this relationship.

e. Repeat steps c and d to connect the AnimalType field in the Animal Information table to the AnimalType field in the Diet table.

You may also notice the Animals and Trainers tables are not yet linked. You are leaving these tables unlinked intentionally.

f. Save the relationships and close the Relationships window.

g. Keep the database open if you plan to continue with Hands-On Exercise 2. If not, close the database and exit Access.

Built-In Analysis and Design Tools

A supervisor asks you to create a survey in the database to store suggestions from visitors about their experience while visiting the zoo. Then another department hears about the survey and asks you to add their items to the survey. As new tables, queries, forms, and reports are added to the database, its performance may decline. This slower performance may be due to the fact that Access databases are often created by users—sales managers, accountants, scientists, and production managers—who lack formal training about how to design an Access database. For example, a scientist who creates a database with 10 tables might not understand how to join the tables to produce efficient results.

Even if a database is in 3NF, deficiencies that cause the database to perform poorly may exist. For example, even though the rules of normalization dictate how to design tables, setting relationships may be applied incorrectly. This affects performance. Some IT administrators may try to compensate for a poorly designed database by migrating to an enterprise-level Database Management System (DBMS), such as Microsoft SQL Server or Oracle.

Moving to a DBMS may have a positive net effect on the speed of processing; however, the design problems that existed in Access will still exist. It is best to resolve the design issues first (in Access) and then evaluate whether Access can handle the processing demands of the database. If it can, other reasons to use Access rather than move to an enterprise-level DBMS may exist. These reasons include wizards to help create tables, forms, and reports and a graphical user interface (GUI) that is intuitive to Access users. Also, Access can run on a desktop computer and does not require its own dedicated server as enterprise-level DBMS programs do. Another reason is cost. Microsoft SQL Server and Oracle are much more expensive than Access. If you recommend migrating to one of those solutions, it is best to be sure it is worth the investment.

Sometimes, you can fix problems using the built-in Access tools. For example, you can split an Access database into two database files. If a number of users are accessing the same database, splitting the database may improve performance. One file would contain all the tables and reside on a server, while the other would reside with each user. Users could create their own queries, forms, and reports on their local machines but still access the same data everyone else is using. This could save your company money, which is always a plus.

Access provides three useful tools that database administrators can use to improve the performance of a database—the Database Documenter tool, the Performance Analyzer tool (found as the Analyze Performance icon), and the Table Analyzer tool (found as the Analyze Table icon). In this section, you will learn how to use these three tools, which can be found in the Analyze group on the Database Tools tab, as shown in Figure 9.16. Also in this section, you will learn how to split an Access database into two databases using the Database Splitter tool. The Database Splitter tool is shown in Figure 9.16 on the Database Tools tab, in the Move Data group, with the name Access Database.

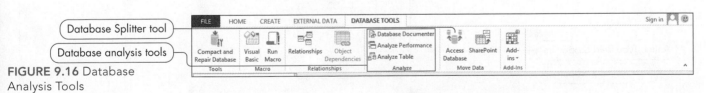

FIGURE 9.16 Database Analysis Tools

Using the Database Documenter Tool

STEP 1 ▶▶ The *Database Documenter* creates a report that contains detailed information for each selected object. When you run the Database Documenter, you can specify which object group you want to see and which specific objects within the selected group you want to document. The Documenter creates a report showing the field names, data types, properties, indexes, and permissions for each of the selected tables. If you run the Documenter for the entire zoo database, the report generated is between 15 and 20 pages long. In other words, the important information can get lost, so it is important to choose only the information you want to see. A common use for the Database Documenter is to verify and update the properties of one object using a printout of the properties of another similar object.

Start the Database Documenter

To use the Database Documenter, click Database Documenter in the Analyze group on the Database Tools tab. The Documenter dialog box opens so that you can select objects to include in the report (see Figure 9.17). Each tab in the Documenter dialog box represents a database object that can be documented. After you select the objects you want to analyze, click OK to generate the report.

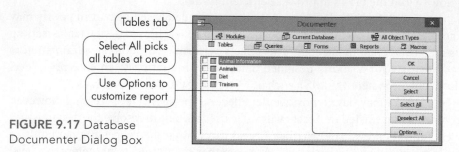

FIGURE 9.17 Database Documenter Dialog Box

The Documenter creates a report that contains detailed information about the tables and other selected objects in your database; the report opens in Print Preview mode, as shown in Figure 9.18. This shows a large amount of detail about the table and fields, likely more than you need for the type of analysis you are performing. Access enables you to specify which items to include and which to skip. To select the items to be included, click Options, as shown in Figure 9.17. Once you click Options, the Print Table Definition dialog box displays; using the options available, specify which items you want to see on the report. For example, if you want to minimize the information on the report, uncheck all the *Include for Table* items, select the second option in the *Include for Fields* section, and then select nothing in the *Include for Indexes* section (see Figure 9.19). The result is a report that is 4 or 5 pages long, as compared to 20 pages when all the items were checked.

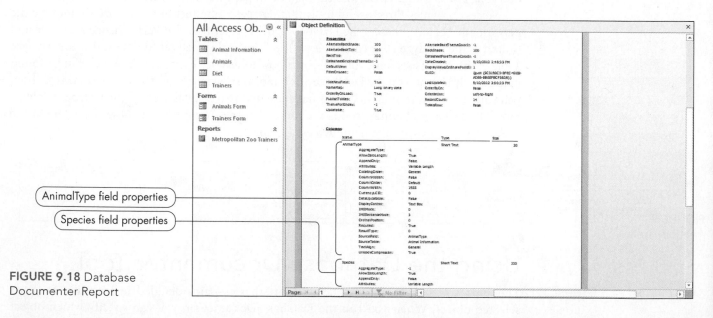

FIGURE 9.18 Database Documenter Report

Although the Documenter starts in Print Preview mode, also notice on the Print Preview tab options to save the report in a number of formats, including as a PDF or XPS file. This is especially useful if you need to share the results of a report with someone else electronically. See Table 9.2 for more details about the Database Documenter options.

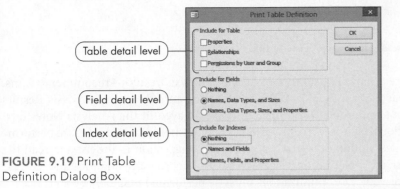

FIGURE 9.19 Print Table Definition Dialog Box

TABLE 9.2 Database Documenter Options

Option	Function
Include for Table: Properties	Options for table properties, including coloring, number of records, and date of last update.
Include for Table: Relationships	Documents table relationships, including which fields are common between tables and type of relationship, such as one to many.
Include for Table: Permissions by Users and Group	Shows permissions for the tables based on users and/ or groups. If your database does not have user-based permissions, this is not worth leaving checked.
Include for Fields: Nothing	Includes no detail about the fields in the selected tables.
Include for Fields: Names, Data Types, and Sizes	Includes field names, data types and field sizes for each field in the selected tables.
Include for Fields: Names, Data Types, Sizes, and Properties	Includes field names, data type, and field size for each field in the selected tables and options such as whether a zero-length value (or null value) is allowed, column width, and text alignment. This makes the report much longer.
Include for Indexes: Nothing	Includes no detail about the indexes in the selected tables.
Include for Indexes: Names and Fields	Includes the names of all indexes and the fields with which they are associated.
Include for Indexes: Names, Fields, and Properties	Includes the names of all indexes, the fields they are associated with, and the index properties, including the number of distinct index values and whether the index is required and must be unique. This makes the report much longer.

Using the Performance Analyzer Tool

STEP 2 >> The Database Documenter is useful for listing the properties of each object in a database. However, the Documenter does not identify any flaws in the design of the database. To evaluate the design of the database, you can use the Performance Analyzer. The *Performance Analyzer* evaluates a database and makes recommendations for optimizing the database. Figure 9.20 shows the Performance Analyzer dialog box, where you can select what you would like to analyze.

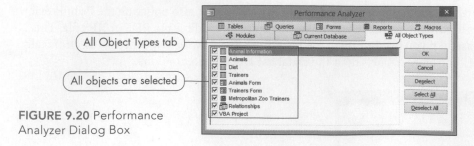

All Object Types tab

All objects are selected

FIGURE 9.20 Performance Analyzer Dialog Box

The Performance Analyzer lists three kinds of analysis results—recommendations, suggestions, and ideas (see Figure 9.21). When you click an item in the Analysis Results list, information about the proposed optimization is displayed in the Analysis Notes box. Suggestion optimizations have potential trade-offs that you should consider before performing them. To view a description of the trade-offs, click a suggestion in the list and read the information in the Analysis Notes box. Access can perform recommendations and suggestions automatically for you; idea optimizations must be performed manually by you.

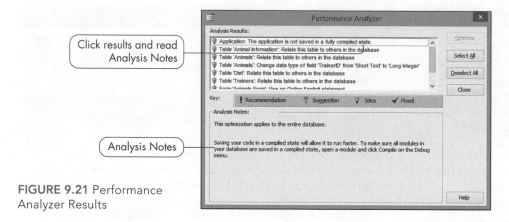

Click results and read Analysis Notes

Analysis Notes

FIGURE 9.21 Performance Analyzer Results

Start the Performance Analyzer

To launch the Performance Analyzer, click Analyze Performance in the Analyze group on the Database Tools tab (refer to Figure 9.16) to display the Performance Analyzer dialog box shown in Figure 9.20. The Tables tab is selected by default. There are tabs for Queries, Forms, Reports, Macros, Modules, Current Database, and All Object Types. Often, the tables are the cause of slowdowns in databases, so the Tables tab is usually the first place to start analyzing performance. Performing searches using queries on poorly designed tables can result in performance issues. The Performance Analyzer attempts to find these issues.

If users inform you that the database generally runs slowly (e.g., reports take a long time to complete), you might choose to analyze the All Object Types tab in an attempt to improve performance. It is possible that forms and reports can have issues as well.

After you select objects for analysis and click OK in the Performance Analyzer dialog box, the dialog box displays an Analysis Notes box, as shown in Figure 9.21. The analysis results in three different types of potential solutions. An Analysis Note provides a brief description of a potential problem and its possible solution. Table 9.3 shows more detail about the three result types you may see if you run the Performance Analyzer.

TABLE 9.3	Performance Analyzer Result Types
Recommendation	Read the Analysis Notes, click the specific recommendation, and then click Optimize. The item's icon changes to Fixed after optimization.
Suggestion	Read the Analysis Notes, click the specific suggestion, and then click Optimize. The item's icon changes to Fixed after optimization.
Idea	Read the Analysis Notes and determine how you will manually implement this idea into your database. Access does not optimize ideas, as these materially change the database design. These require manual changes.

You optimize the database by clicking the result items and then clicking Optimize after you read the Analysis Notes. On occasion, you will find that an optimization results in a trade-off that affects your database in ways you might not consider. For example, changing an existing field named TrainerID with a data type of Short Text to a data type of Long Integer may erase existing data that does not fit the new data type. You may have TrainerIDs that are nonnumeric, and these would be erased from the database. However, changing data types as recommended does improve performance.

Also note that the Performance Analyzer does not catch all problems. Though a useful tool, the Performance Analyzer may miss some issues, so think of this tool as a supplement to your own analysis, not a replacement for it.

 TIP **Back Up Database Before Optimizing It**

Before optimizing your database by using the recommendations, suggestions, and ideas of the Performance Analyzer, it is best to back up your database. That way, you can revert back to the copy if the optimization yields unexpected results. It is also a good practice to read the Analysis Notes before executing any of the analysis recommendations or suggestions.

Add an Index

An item that appears frequently in the Analysis Notes box is *Add an index*. This is a simple change to a field (or fields) in a table that could improve performance when implemented. An **index** reduces the time it takes to run queries and reports. It is similar to the index in the back of this textbook. Generally, you should add an index to any field that will be searched often. For example, in a college database, a student's name would likely be indexed, but not a phone number. However, in a cell phone service provider's database, a phone number would probably be indexed because customer service representatives might use it to find a customer.

On one hand, for reports and queries with a large record source, adding an index can save substantial time. On the other hand, adding more indexes to a table can decrease database performance because each time you add a new record to a database the index must be sorted. In a large database, this may result in a longer wait time before a record is saved. A database of the size of the zoo database may not need an index, but in a larger project this is a common suggestion.

Using the Table Analyzer Tool

STEP 3 The **Table Analyzer** analyzes the tables in a database and normalizes them for you. Normalizing an existing table involves splitting a table into smaller, related tables, with each table focused on a single topic of information, as you did in the first section of this chapter.

As stated earlier, a normalized database has a number of advantages over an unnormalized one. First, updating information is faster and easier because fewer data changes are required.

Second, only the minimum information is stored; therefore, the database is smaller. Finally, a normalized database holds more reliable data because data is stored in only one place.

Although the Table Analyzer helps you create a normalized database, you may want to modify the decisions the Table Analyzer makes if you have database design experience. You can rename tables, split tables, rearrange fields in tables, and create relationships between tables. You can modify Table Analyzer decisions during every step of the normalization process.

Start the Table Analyzer

To start the Table Analyzer, click Analyze Table in the Analyze group on the Database Tools tab. Step one of the Table Analyzer Wizard opens with an explanation of the pitfalls of duplicating information. The output from this process should be tables that pass through normalization, resulting in the creation of additional tables in your database. The Table Analyzer Wizard explains problems for which it will search, describes how it will attempt to fix problems it identifies, and asks you to identify a table for analysis. You can take some control of the process by deciding which fields should be included in new tables created by the Table Analyzer Wizard, or you can choose to let the wizard decide on your behalf.

You could advance through the entire Table Analyzer Wizard accepting the defaults, but this is uncommon. The wizard will offer suggestions, but it is best to think about whether they make sense in your database. It is best to run the Table Analyzer before you attempt any normalization. If you have already created tables and have an incomplete normalization, you may not get a solid recommendation.

Step Through the Table Analyzer Wizard

If you choose to let the Table Analyzer Wizard normalize the tables in your database, the Table Analyzer Wizard runs through the following process:

Step 1. The Table Analyzer Wizard asks you to choose a table (see Figure 9.22). The wizard then breaks the table into a set of smaller tables. Each of these smaller tables contains the minimum set of information that should be grouped together.

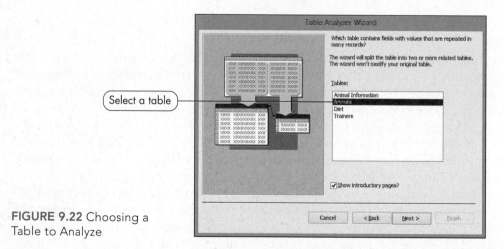

FIGURE 9.22 Choosing a Table to Analyze

Step 2. You can direct the wizard to decide what fields go in what tables, as shown in Figure 9.23. The other option is for you to decide how to divide the table into smaller tables. Access makes a recommendation, but if you prefer, you can do the breakdown yourself.

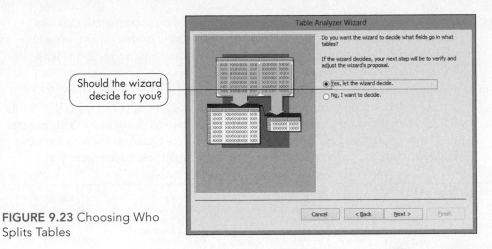

FIGURE 9.23 Choosing Who Splits Tables

Step 3. If you tell the wizard to decide for you, the wizard divides the table and creates relationships that control how the new tables are linked, as shown in Figure 9.24. These relationships enforce referential integrity (data consistency) with cascading updates. The wizard does not automatically add cascading deletes to the relationships because of the risk that you may accidentally delete large portions of data. You can rename the tables in this step. If you prefer to set the cascading deletes option, you must do so yourself.

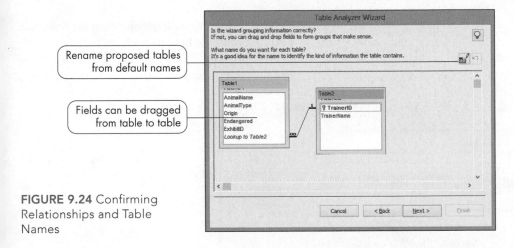

FIGURE 9.24 Confirming Relationships and Table Names

Step 4. The wizard proposes tables and fields, and asks you to confirm the primary keys in each table, as shown in Figure 9.25.

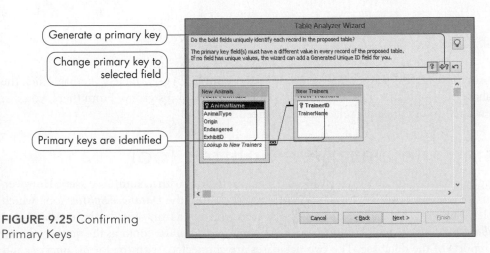

FIGURE 9.25 Confirming Primary Keys

Step 5. In the next step, the wizard searches the new tables for inconsistent data (for example, the same customer with two different phone numbers) and presents a list of records that you can change or accept. If there are no problems with inconsistent data, this step does not appear.

Step 6. Finally, you can choose to create a query that simulates the original table. The wizard first backs up the original table and renames it by appending "_OLD" to its name. Then the wizard creates a query using the original table name. This ensures that any existing forms or reports based on the original table work with the new table structure as well. The results of the wizard might resemble Figure 9.26.

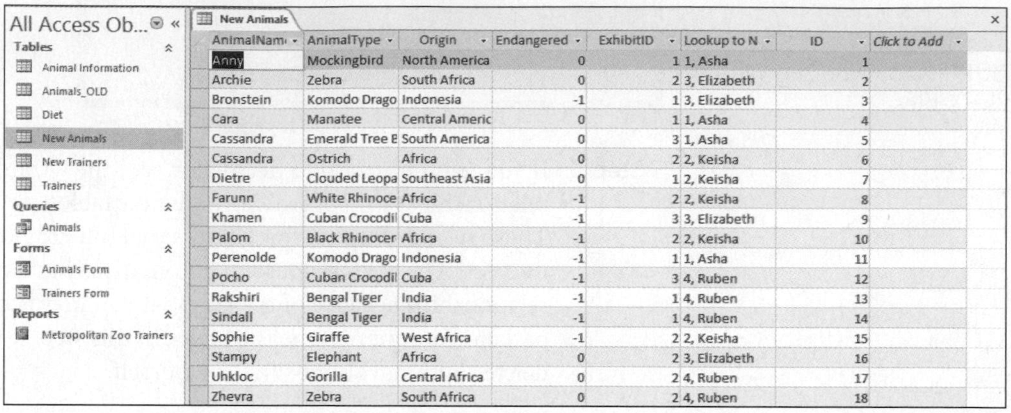

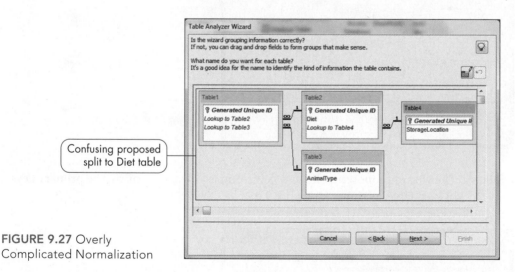

AnimalName	AnimalType	Origin	Endangered	ExhibitID	Lookup to N	ID	Click to Add
Anny	Mockingbird	North America	0	1	1, Asha	1	
Archie	Zebra	South Africa	0	2	3, Elizabeth	2	
Bronstein	Komodo Drago	Indonesia	-1	1	3, Elizabeth	3	
Cara	Manatee	Central Americ	0	1	1, Asha	4	
Cassandra	Emerald Tree B	South America	0	3	1, Asha	5	
Cassandra	Ostrich	Africa	0	2	2, Keisha	6	
Dietre	Clouded Leopa	Southeast Asia	0	1	2, Keisha	7	
Farunn	White Rhinoce	Africa	-1	2	2, Keisha	8	
Khamen	Cuban Crocodi	Cuba	-1	3	3, Elizabeth	9	
Palom	Black Rhinocer	Africa	-1	2	2, Keisha	10	
Perenolde	Komodo Drago	Indonesia	-1	1	1, Asha	11	
Pocho	Cuban Crocodi	Cuba	-1	3	4, Ruben	12	
Rakshiri	Bengal Tiger	India	-1	1	4, Ruben	13	
Sindall	Bengal Tiger	India	-1	1	4, Ruben	14	
Sophie	Giraffe	West Africa	-1	2	2, Keisha	15	
Stampy	Elephant	Africa	0	2	3, Elizabeth	16	
Uhkloc	Gorilla	Central Africa	0	2	4, Ruben	17	
Zhevra	Zebra	South Africa	0	2	4, Ruben	18	

FIGURE 9.26 New Animals Table

As you can see from Figure 9.27, the underlying tables may look messier than the ones you created through normalization. However, if you do not know how to perform normalization, or if the database is straightforward, the analyzer tool would be preferable. Either way, it is important to check the tables Access recommends and not just accept them without viewing.

FIGURE 9.27 Overly Complicated Normalization

After the Table Analyzer Wizard is finished, examine the new table structure. Click the Database Tools tab and click Relationships in the Relationships group. From there, you can review and modify the table relationships as needed.

Using the Database Splitter Tool

STEP 4 » A single-file Access database may work fine for a small office with a handful of users. However, when the number of users grows beyond that, you can use the *Database Splitter* tool, which enables you to split a database into two files: a back-end and a front-end database. A *back-end database* contains the tables of the database. A *front-end database* contains the queries, forms, and reports of the database. The two databases are connected, with the forms, queries, and reports stored in the front-end database and the tables stored in the back-end database. You could then have multiple front-end databases using one back-end database.

The main reason to split an Access database is to improve development and maintenance. When a developer works with a single-file Access database, all users must exit the database while the developer makes changes. This can be inefficient for the developer and disruptive for the users. The front end of a split database can be modified while users continue to work. Once the changes to the front end are completed, the new file is distributed to the users (to replace the existing front-end database file).

This approach offers other advantages as well. Splitting the database may improve the speed at which the database processes data and returns results. A report that takes two minutes to display in a single-file database may take only one minute in a split database. There are many other reasons to support splitting a database into two files, as outlined in Table 9.4. The back-end database is typically placed on a server, and a front-end database is placed on each individual user's computer. The front-end database contains links to the tables in the back end.

TABLE 9.4 Reasons to Split an Access Database into Two Files	
Improved Performance	The performance of the database usually improves because only the data is sent across the network—not the queries, forms, reports, macros, and modules.
Greater Data Availability	When only the data is sent across the network, database edits are completed more quickly, which makes the data available quicker.
Enhanced Security	If you store the back-end database on a server, you can use the server's security features to help protect your data. Because users access the back-end database by using linked tables, it is less likely that intruders can obtain unauthorized access to the data.
Improved Reliability	If a user encounters a problem and the database closes unexpectedly, any database file corruption is usually limited to the front-end database. Because the user only accesses data in the back-end database by using linked tables, the back-end database file is much less likely to become corrupted. In addition, servers are generally backed up in a business environment; a client machine may not be.
Flexible Development Environment	Because each user works with a separate copy of the front-end database, each user can independently develop queries, forms, reports, and other database objects without affecting other users. Also, developers can distribute an updated version of the front-end database without affecting the data in the back-end database.

Start the Database Splitter

The Database Splitter is not identified by name on the Access Ribbon. To start the Database Splitter, click the Database Tools tab and click Access Database in the Move Data group. The first screen explains what the Database Splitter Wizard does and gives a brief summary of the benefits of a split database. The Database Splitter starts as shown in Figure 9.28.

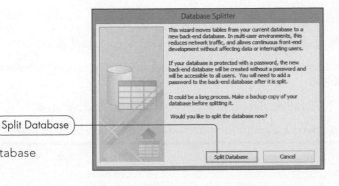

Split Database

FIGURE 9.28 Database Splitter Wizard

In the next step, the wizard asks you to name the new back-end database. Designate the database name and location for the back-end database or just accept the default file name that Access suggests—the original name plus the suffix "be" for "back-end" (see Figure 9.29).

Work with the Front-End Database

After Access creates the back end, the front-end database remains open. The tables that existed in the original database have been replaced with linked tables with the same table names. Linked tables have an arrow icon to indicate they are linked to another Access database (see Figure 9.30). When you point to a table name, a ScreenTip shows the path to the physical table to which your front-end database is linked. As you add data to the linked tables using the front-end database, the data becomes available to other users of the back-end tables.

Note that if you use the front-end database on a different machine, or if you move the files into a different folder, you may get an error stating the file path is not valid. The back-end database is generally stored on a networked server, so this is not an issue in the real world unless the file is moved on the server.

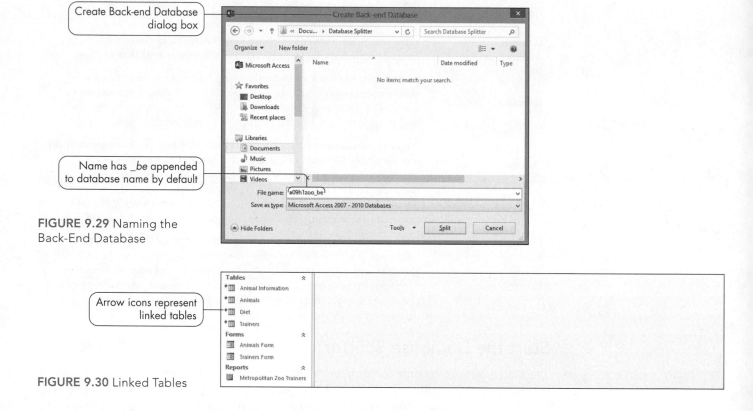

Create Back-end Database dialog box

Name has _be appended to database name by default

FIGURE 9.29 Naming the Back-End Database

Arrow icons represent linked tables

FIGURE 9.30 Linked Tables

In Hands-On Exercise 2, you will use the built-in analysis and design tools to analyze a database. You will also split a database into a front end and a back end.

Quick Concepts

1. Describe three reasons to use the Database Documenter tool. **p. 803**

2. Define the three possible analyzer result types the Performance Analyzer tool might propose. **p. 806**

3. How does the Table Analyzer tool make you more productive? **p. 807**

4. Why would a database administrator choose to split a database? **p. 810**

Hands-On Exercise

2 Built-In Analysis and Design Tools

The Metropolitan Zoo database has been working well, but you decide to examine the database to see if more improvements can be made. You use the built-in tools to analyze the database; you also decide to split the database into two files. Before you begin, you make a copy of the database so the original format will be safe in case you make a mistake.

Skills covered: Use the Database Documenter Tool • Use the Performance Analyzer Tool • Use the Table Analyzer Tool • Use the Database Splitter Tool

---

STEP 1 ≫ USE THE DATABASE DOCUMENTER TOOL

You will create a report with the Database Documenter to show information on relationships. You will save this report as a PDF file. Refer to Figure 9.31 and Figure 9.32 as you complete Step 1.

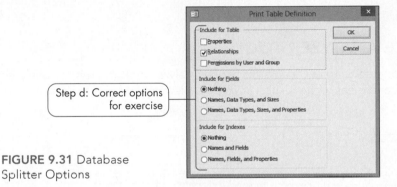

Step d: Correct options for exercise

FIGURE 9.31 Database Splitter Options

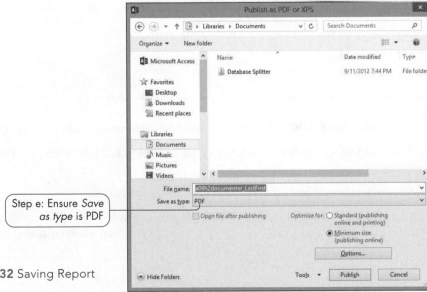

Step e: Ensure *Save as type* is PDF

FIGURE 9.32 Saving Report as PDF

a. Open *a09h1Zoo_LastFirst* if you closed it at the end of Hands-On Exercise 1. Save the database as **a09h2Zoo_LastFirst**, changing *h1* to *h2*. Click **Save**.

b. Click **Database Documenter** in the Analyze group on the DATABASE TOOLS tab. Click the **All Objects Types tab**.

c. Click **Select All** on the All Object Types tab and click **Options**.

d. Check the **Relationships box** in the *Include for Table* section. Uncheck checkboxes for *Properties* and *Permission by User and Group*, if necessary. Click **Nothing** in the *Include for Fields* section and click **Nothing** in the *Include for Indexes* section. Your dialog box should resemble Figure 9.31. Click **OK**. Click **OK** to run the report.

You have changed the options so only the required information is present in the report.

e. Select **PDF or XPS** in the Data group on the PRINT PREVIEW tab. Select **PDF** as the option for *Save as type* and type **a09h2ZooDocumenter_LastFirst** for the file name. Click **Publish** to save the file, as shown in Figure 9.32.

This enables you to save the report.

> **TROUBLESHOOTING:** After saving the report, it may open in Adobe Reader or Adobe Acrobat. If this happens, close the program and return to Access.

f. Click **Close** on the next screen, which asks you if you want to save the steps.

g. Click **Close Print Preview** in the Close Preview group to close the report.

STEP 2 ›› USE THE PERFORMANCE ANALYZER TOOL

To evaluate the performance of the zoo database, you decide to run the Performance Analyzer tool. You run the analyzer and then review the recommendations, suggestions, and ideas in the results. You will implement some of the results. Refer to Figure 9.33 as you complete Step 2.

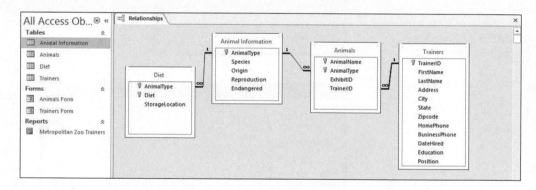

FIGURE 9.33 Final Relationships for Zoo Database

a. Click the **DATABASE TOOLS tab** and click **Analyze Performance** in the Analyze group.

b. Click the **All Object Types tab**, click **Select All**, and then click **OK** to start the Performance Analyzer.

The results window displays ideas to improve the zoo database.

c. Review the results of the Performance Analyzer and take note of the idea regarding relating Trainers to another table. Click **Close** to close the Performance Analyzer dialog box.

You decide to establish relationships between the Trainers and Animals tables.

d. Click **Relationships** in the Relationships group on the DATABASE TOOLS tab and create a relationship between the Trainers and Animals tables, using the common field TrainerID. Ensure the Enforce Referential Integrity and Cascade Update Related Fields options are set.

Your relationships should now match Figure 9.33. The tables may appear in a different order or of a different height in your database.

e. Save and close the Relationships window.

f. Repeat the procedure in steps a and b above to run the Performance Analyzer again and see if the results are different this time.

The idea to relate tables is gone.

g. Close the Performance Analyzer dialog box.

STEP 3 ≫ USE THE TABLE ANALYZER TOOL

You decide to test the design of the tables in the zoo database. To do this, you will open an older version of the database, run the Table Analyzer, and then compare the results to the current database. Refer to Figure 9.34 as you complete Step 3.

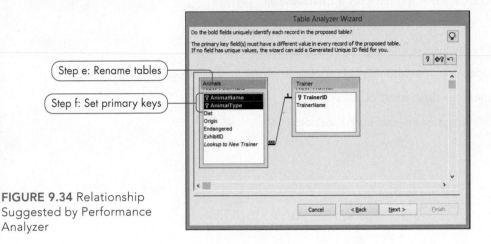

FIGURE 9.34 Relationship Suggested by Performance Analyzer

a. Open *a09h2ZooAnalyzer*. Save the database as **a09h2ZooAnalyzer_LastFirst**.

b. Click the **DATABASE TOOLS tab** and click **Analyze Table** in the Analyze group.

The Table Analyzer Wizard starts.

c. Click **Next** twice.

Access shows a screen asking you to select tables.

d. Select the **ZooAnimals table**. Click **Next** twice.

The ZooAnimals table has been split into three tables.

e. Click the **Rename Table icon**, type **Animals** as the name of Table1, and then click **OK**. Select **Table2** and use the same steps to rename Table2 **Animal Information**. Select **Table3** and rename it **Trainers**. Click **Next**.

f. Click the **AnimalID field** in the Animals table and click the **Set Unique Identifier icon** to set the primary key. Click the **AnimalType field** in the Animal Information table and use the same process to set the primary key. Click **Next**.

Note that Access correctly identified the primary key for the Trainers table, so there is no need to set that manually.

g. Select the **No, don't create the query option** and click **Finish**. Click **OK** in response to the warning message.

This normalization is similar to the one you did in Hands-On Exercise 1, but it did not fix the repeating groups issue in the Diet field. However, if you had no understanding of normalization, using the Table Analyzer helps achieve the goal of reducing data redundancies.

h. Close the database.

i. Submit based on your instructor's directions.

You decide to split the zoo database to see if the performance of the database improves. You use the Database Splitter to divide the database into a front-end and a back-end file.

a. Open *a09h2Zoo_LastFirst*. Save the database as **a09h2ZooSplit_LastFirst**.

The new database is displayed.

b. Click the **DATABASE TOOLS tab** and click **Access Database** in the Move Data group.

The Database Splitter Wizard starts.

c. Click **Split Database**. Accept *a09h2ZooSplit_LastFirst_be* as the file name and click **Split**.

The Database Splitter splits the database into two files.

d. Click **OK**.

The database is split successfully.

e. Open the tables and the other objects to verify the database is working properly.

f. Close the database. Close Access.

g. Submit based on your instructor's directions.

Database Security

Computer security can be defined as the protection of data from unauthorized access, change, or destruction and can be divided into two general categories: physical security and logical security. Physical security involves protecting assets you can touch, such as computers, storage devices, backup tapes, and the office safe. Logical security protects the information that resides on the physical devices, including databases and other computer software. Security measures need to be taken to protect your assets against both physical and logical threats.

Database security is a specialty within computer security that protects a database application from unintended use. Unintended use includes unauthorized viewing of data, unauthorized copying and selling of data, malicious attacks, destruction of data by employees, and inadvertent mistakes made by employees.

In this section, you will learn several techniques available in Access to keep your database application safe. These techniques include:

- Creating a navigation form.
- Encrypting and password protecting a database.
- Digitally signing and publishing the database.
- Saving a database as an ACCDE file.

Creating a Menu System

Most database users prefer a menu system for opening and closing forms and reports, especially forms and reports that are used every day. This can be accomplished using a *navigation form*, which is a tabbed menu system that ties the objects in the database together so that the database is easy to use. The interface displays a menu enabling a nontechnical person to open the various objects within the database and to move easily from one object to another. The form is quite powerful, but it is also easy to create. When you create a navigation form, you simply drag and drop forms and reports onto tabs. An added benefit of a navigation form is that it can be easily converted to a Web form if the Access database is deployed on a company intranet or on the Internet. Navigation forms have the look and feel of a web form.

TIP | Switchboards: Another Menu System

Navigation forms were introduced in Access 2010. Before that point, users would use a switchboard to do what the navigation form accomplishes. If you are using a database that is more established, you may find a switchboard as the primary method of interacting with the database rather than a navigation form.

Microsoft removed the Switchboard Manager from the Ribbon when it introduced navigation forms. If you ever need to create or manage a switchboard, follow these steps to display the Switchboard Manager:

1. Click the FILE tab and click Options.
2. Click Customize Ribbon.
3. Select All Commands from the *Choose commands from* option. See Figure 9.35.
4. Scroll down until you see Switchboard Manager.
5. Select Switchboard Manager.
6. On the right, expand the Database Tools group.
7. Click Database Tools.
8. Click New Group.
9. Rename *New Group* as Switchboard.
10. Click Switchboard (Custom).
11. Click Add. The Switchboard Manager is added to the Ribbon as shown in Figure 9.36.

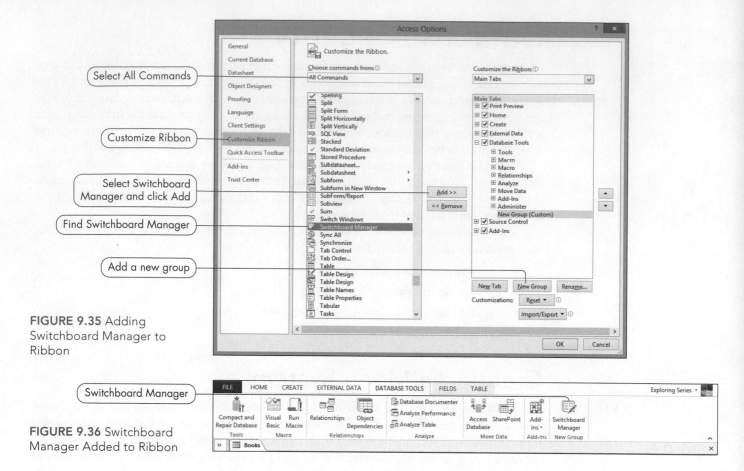

FIGURE 9.35 Adding Switchboard Manager to Ribbon

Select All Commands

Customize Ribbon

Select Switchboard Manager and click Add

Find Switchboard Manager

Add a new group

Switchboard Manager

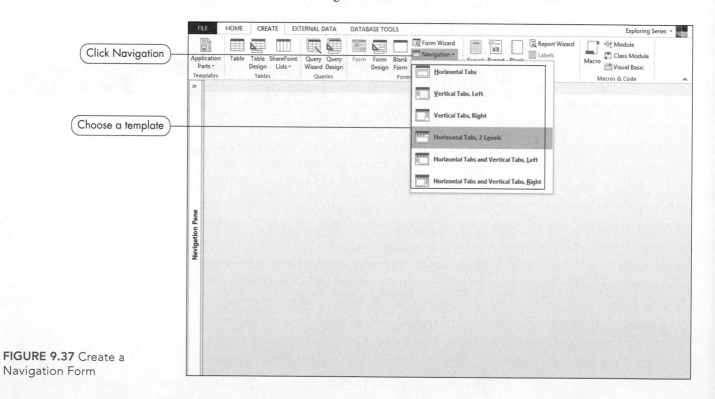

FIGURE 9.36 Switchboard Manager Added to Ribbon

To create a navigation form, click the Create tab and click Navigation in the Forms group. Select one of the six preset templates (as shown in Figure 9.37) and Access creates the basic structure of the navigation form.

Click Navigation

Choose a template

FIGURE 9.37 Create a Navigation Form

Create a Navigation Form

For example, choose the first template on the list, Horizontal Tabs, and Access creates a navigation form with [Add New] at the top-left corner of the page. Drag an object from the Navigation Pane onto [Add New], and Access displays the object in the main viewing area, as shown in Figure 9.38. Drag the next object from the Navigation Pane onto [Add New] and Access displays that object. Continue adding the remainder of the objects you want on the navigation form. Switch to Form view and click each tab to view and test each object (see Figure 9.38). Save and close the form.

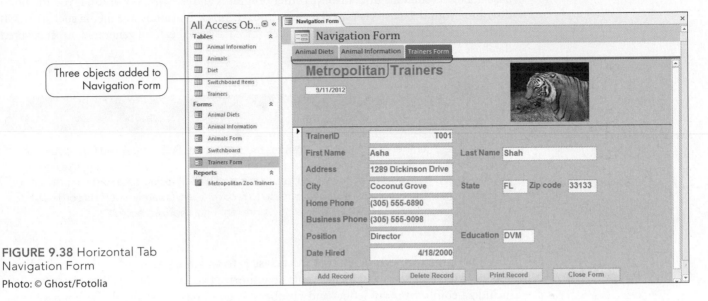

FIGURE 9.38 Horizontal Tab Navigation Form

Photo: © Ghost/Fotolia

Start a Navigation Form Automatically

To start the navigation form automatically when the database starts, click the File tab and click Options. Click Current Database and select the name of the navigation form using the Display Form option, as shown in Figure 9.39. Click OK to close the Access Options window.

Note that any form, not only a navigation form, can be set to display automatically. Also note that this applies to the current database, so each database can have different forms set to launch on startup.

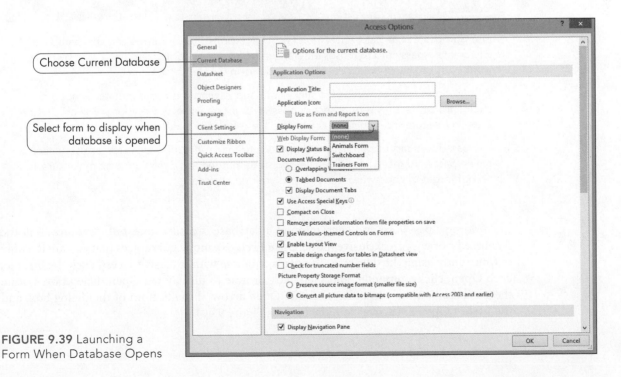

FIGURE 9.39 Launching a Form When Database Opens

Encrypting and Password Protecting a Database

STEP 2 >> Access 2013 incorporates encryption methods to help keep your databases secure. *Encryption* is the process of altering digital information using an algorithm to make it unreadable to anyone except those who possess the key (password). As the point of encryption is to protect your data, you need to choose a password when setting up encryption. Encrypting a database makes its contents unreadable to other programs and is especially useful if you intend to distribute your database via e-mail or store your database on removable media such as a USB flash drive. Because millions of secret codes (or passwords) can be generated, an encrypted database is difficult to break.

TIP Lost Your Password?

There are a number of software applications that attempt to find a password for a database. However, the more secure the password, the longer it takes to recover. It may take days or weeks for a password to be recovered, but that is better than losing data permanently. Also keep in mind that the same tool you can use to recover a legitimately lost password can be used by anyone, so a strong password helps prevent unauthorized access.

One of the methods to encrypt a database is to assign a password to the file. Adding a password to an Access database prevents unauthorized access to the file. Passwords typically include a combination of letters and numbers. A good password should be impossible for unauthorized users to guess. For example, use at least eight characters that combine uppercase and lowercase letters, numbers, and symbols to make the password more difficult for others to guess. An example of a weak password is Eric1999 (the author's name and year of graduation). A stronger password is Exp2013@r$. Be sure to record the passwords you assign to your database.

TIP Password Security

The purpose of the password is to keep unauthorized users from using the database. If you create a password that uses letters, numbers, and symbols, make sure your own password does not keep you from accessing your own data!

Writing down the password on a sticky note and leaving it on your monitor is not a good choice for protecting a truly secure password. If you write down your passwords, store them in a secure location such as a locked file cabinet or a safe.

You can download or purchase a client tool to manage your passwords or use a secure online password manager. Of course, tools like that require a password, so make sure you do not forget the password that protects your passwords.

Adding a password and encryption to a database is easily done, but it requires that the database be opened in exclusive mode. *Open Exclusive* mode guarantees that you are the only one currently using the database. To open a database with exclusive access, click the File tab, click Open, click Computer, and then click Browse to display the Open dialog box. Locate the database you want to open, click the Open arrow at the bottom of the dialog box, and then select Open Exclusive from the list (see Figure 9.40).

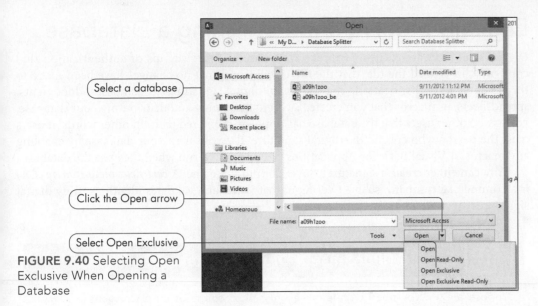

Select a database

Click the Open arrow

Select Open Exclusive

FIGURE 9.40 Selecting Open Exclusive When Opening a Database

After opening a database in exclusive mode, you are ready to assign a password. To accomplish this, click the File tab, click Info, and then click *Encrypt with Password*, as shown in Figure 9.41. The Set Database Password dialog box opens so that you can enter and verify a password. The database is encrypted when you click OK in the Set Database Password dialog box. Once you have set the password, close the database and then open it again without exclusive access. When you open the database, the Password Required dialog box appears. You must type the correct password and click OK to open the database.

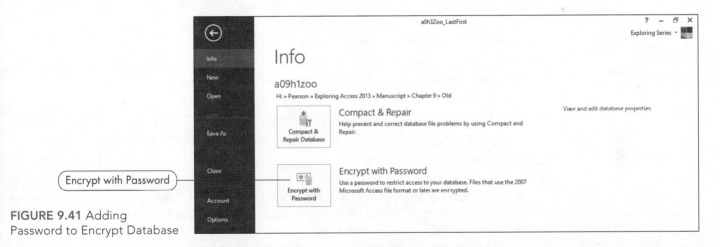

Encrypt with Password

FIGURE 9.41 Adding Password to Encrypt Database

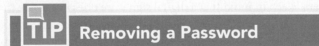

Removing a Password

If you want to remove a password, you must open the database using the Open Exclusive option. Click the File tab, click Info, and then click Decrypt Database. In the Unset Database Password dialog box, type the password and click OK. The database password has been removed. You need the database password to do this, of course.

Digitally Signing and Publishing a Database

 Digital signatures are electronic, encryption-based, secure stamps of authentication that confirm who created the file, that the file is valid, and that no changes have been made to the file after its authentication. You can apply digital signatures to databases, documents, spreadsheets, or macros that you create. By digitally signing and distributing your database, you assure other users that the database has not been tampered with. In other words, if users trust the person who created the digital signature, they can trust your database by enabling any macros or Visual Basic for Applications (VBA) code to run when they use the database.

You can either create a signature yourself or purchase one. A **certification authority (CA)** is a commercial company, such as VeriSign, that issues and validates identities using digital signatures for a fee.

TIP | Should I Purchase a Digital Signature?

Choose a CA if you need high-level security. Most countries have stringent laws that regulate CAs so that purchasers can be sure that their digital signatures are valid. Many software manufacturers purchase digital signatures, so when you install their software, you are shown the name of the software publisher. As only the publisher can digitally sign the software, the signature enables users to trust the source of software.

Digital signatures are also used in banking and other fields. If you have a need to assure others that you are the sender of a file and it has not been tampered with, a digital certificate might be a better choice than self-certification. Having an independent group verifying your identity and preventing digital forgeries may be worth the cost.

Use the SelfCert Tool

If you do not have a security certificate from a commercial vendor, you can create one by using the SelfCert tool (included with Microsoft Office).

To create a self-signed certificate, complete the following:

1. From the Start screen, type *Digital Certificate for VBA Projects*. Click the tool to start it.
2. Type a name for the new certificate into the *Your certificate's name* box.
3. Click OK twice.

If the Digital Certificate for VBA Projects tool does not appear on the Start screen, it is possible it was not installed to the Start screen. If not, use File Explorer to navigate to the following location: C:\Program Files\Microsoft Office\Office15. In that folder, double-click SelfCert.exe and complete steps 2 and 3 above.

You can attach your certificate to a database immediately before you distribute it to your users. Keep in mind that a digital signature does not prove that you own the database. By use of a timestamp, it can prove that you were the last person to modify it. You provide the timestamp information to others when you distribute, or publish, your database. By examining the timestamp on your database, you can prove that it has or has not been modified since you applied your signature. A **timestamp** is a combination of the date and time that is encrypted as part of the digital signature. For a timestamp to be truly valid to others, it must be passed through a timestamping service provider. Again, this can be a commercial entity or a server located on your network. Further discussion of this process is outside the scope of this textbook.

Apply a Digital Signature

You can digitally sign and publish your database simultaneously from within Access 2013. To digitally sign and publish your database, click the File tab, click Save As, and then double-click *Package and Sign*. If the Select Certificate dialog box opens, select an existing certificate and click OK. The database is packaged and converted to the .accdc file format and digitally signed with your certificate.

Saving a Database as an ACCDE File

STEP 4 » Access 2013 enables the use of the file extension .accde. Creating an *Access Database Executable (ACCDE)* file will remove all VBA source code, prohibit users from making design and name changes to forms or reports within the database, and prohibit users from creating new forms and reports. Users can execute the VBA code, but they cannot modify it. The ACCDE file type was first introduced in Access 2007.

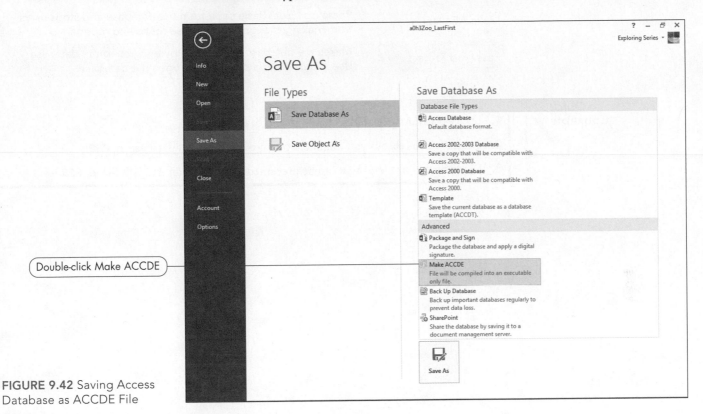

Double-click Make ACCDE

FIGURE 9.42 Saving Access Database as ACCDE File

Create an ACCDE File

You can create a database with the .accde file extension within Access 2013. This is a simple process that saves your existing database with the new file extension, making a copy of the last saved edition of your database. To create an ACCDE file, click the File tab, click Save As, and then double-click Make ACCDE (see Figure 9.42). The Save As dialog box opens. The *File name* box displays the same main name as the original database with the .accde extension. The *Save as type* box displays *ACCDE File (*.accde)*. Click Save to save the database with the .accde file format. Note you cannot create an ACCDE file unless you have clicked the Enable Content button. As ACCDE files can cause potentially dangerous code to be executed, you first need to assure Access the file is trustworthy.

If you do not have exclusive use of the database before you convert the database to the .accde file format, you receive a message telling you that another user has the database open. The process stops.

Keep the Original Database File Safe

When the database has been converted to .accde, it cannot be converted back to its source format (.accdb). Therefore, keep your original database—the database as it existed when it was converted to the .accde file format—in a safe place. This backup is needed if one or more of its objects (forms, reports, or VBA code) needs to be changed. Without your original database, you would not be able to make these changes. You would be forced to create the database again. Users would not be able to alter the design of forms and reports, nor would they be able to change the VBA code.

In Hands-On Exercise 3, you will practice all of the security measures discussed in this section. Table 9.5 recaps the highlights from this section.

TABLE 9.5 Security Measures and Their Intended Results	
Digital Signature	Provides proof to others of when you last modified the database. Not very secure without password protection.
Make ACCDE	Removes Visual Basic code from the database and stops users from making changes to database forms and reports.
Password Protect	Makes the database unreadable by encrypting the database. Users must enter a password to open the database.

Quick Concepts

1. List two advantages of a navigation form. *p. 817*

2. Describe two reasons you might choose to digitally sign a database. *p. 822*

3. Describe the problems that can be prevented by creating an ACCDE file. *p. 823*

Hands-On Exercise

3 Database Security

Management has asked you for a plan to protect the database from accidental deletes, intrusions, and theft. You decide to put several safety and security measures into action, including the addition of a password to protect against unauthorized use of the database.

Skills covered: Create a Menu System • Encrypt and Password-Protect a Database • Digitally Sign and Publish a Database • Save a Database as an ACCDE File

---

STEP 1 ≫ CREATE A MENU SYSTEM

You decide to create a navigation form to make it easier to open the daily forms and reports. You ask the employees which objects they use the most, and then add them to the navigation form. You decide to use the Horizontal Tabs template. Refer to Figure 9.43 as you complete Step 1.

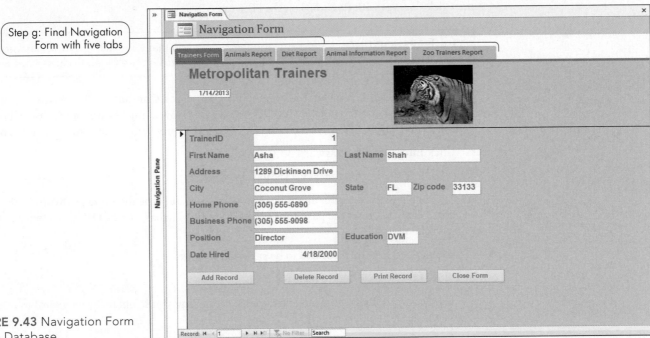

FIGURE 9.43 Navigation Form in Zoo Database

a. Open *a09h2Zoo_LastFirst*. Save the database as **a09h3Zoo_LastFirst**, changing *h2* to *h3*.

b. Select the **Animals table** and create a basic report using the Report tool. Save the report as **Animals Report**. Close the report.

c. Repeat step b to create a report based on the Diet table. Save the report as **Diet Report**. Close the report.

d. Repeat step b to create a report based on the Animal Information table. Save the report as **Animal Information Report**. Close the report.

e. Click the **CREATE tab** and click **Navigation** in the Forms group. Select the **Horizontal Tabs option** (the first item on the list).

   A new Horizontal Tabs navigation form appears in the workspace.

f. Drag the **Trainers Form** from the Navigation Pane to [Add New].

g. Repeat step g to add Animals Report, Diet Report, Animal Information Report, and Zoo Trainers Report, in that order.

> **TROUBLESHOOTING:** If the Field List appears and covers your form, you can close it.

h. Switch to Form view and test the navigation form by clicking each tab.

Compare your results to Figure 9.43.

i. Save and close the navigation form with the default name.

STEP 2 ≫ ENCRYPT AND PASSWORD-PROTECT A DATABASE

Selene asked you to add a password to the database. Several new employees have just been hired, and she wants to restrict their access to the database for the first six weeks. You discuss the password with Selene and decide to use a combination of letters, numbers, and symbols. Refer to Figure 9.44 as you complete Step 2.

Step f: Password masked by asterisks

FIGURE 9.44 Database Password Established

a. Click **Encrypt with Password** on the FILE tab.

> **TROUBLESHOOTING:** A message appears telling you that you must have the database open for exclusive use. Close the file and open it again using the Open Exclusive option.

b. Click **OK**. Click **Close Database** on the FILE tab. Click **Computer**. Click **Browse**. Locate the *a09h3Zoo_LastFirst* database, click the **Open arrow** at the bottom of the dialog box, and then select **Open Exclusive** from the list. Refer to Figure 9.40 if you cannot find this option.

c. Click **Encrypt with Password** on the FILE tab.

This time the warning message should not appear.

d. Type the password **exploring** in the **Password box** and type the same password in the **Verify box**. Click **OK** to set the password and encrypt the database. Click **OK** in response to the warning message.

You need to test the password to be sure that it works.

e. Close the database and open it again.

The Password Required dialog box opens, prompting you to enter the password to open the database.

f. Type **exploring** in the **Enter database password box** and click **OK**.

STEP 3 ≫ DIGITALLY SIGN AND PUBLISH A DATABASE

You suggest to Selene that she add a digital signature to the database. You explain that the database content will be trusted when users from other departments start to use it. Refer to Figure 9.45 as you complete Step 3.

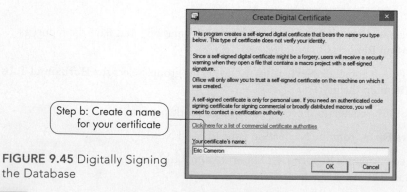

Step b: Create a name for your certificate

FIGURE 9.45 Digitally Signing the Database

a. Type **Digital Certificate for VBA Projects** in the **Start screen**. Click the tool to start it.

> **TROUBLESHOOTING:** If Digital Certificate for VBA Projects is not linked on your Start screen, use File Explorer to browse to the C:\Program Files\Microsoft Office\Office15 folder. Double-click SelfCert.exe.

b. Type your full name in the **Your certificate's name box** and click **OK**.

The *Your Name Success* dialog box appears, confirming that you successfully created a new certificate.

c. Click **OK**.

d. Click **Save As** on the FILE tab, and double-click **Package and Sign**.

e. Select the certificate you created in step b, if prompted. Click **OK**.

A new ACCDC file name is suggested using the current database.

f. Click **Create** to accept the new database name with the attached certificate.

A digitally signed database is created in the background; the original database remains open.

STEP 4 ≫ DIGITALLY SIGN A DATABASE

You decide to make the database more secure digitally signing it and saving it as an ACCDE file. This type of file prohibits the zoo employees from making changes by mistake (or intentionally). Refer to Figure 9.42 as you complete Step 4.

a. Click **Save As** on the FILE tab, and then double-click **Make ACCDE**.

The Save As dialog box opens. The default *Save as type* is ACCDE File (*.accde), and the suggested file name is *a09h3Zoo_LastFirst.accde*.

> **TROUBLESHOOTING:** If your file extensions are hidden, your file name will not show *accde* on the end of the file. Make sure the *Save as type* is ACCDE File.

b. Click **Save** to create the *a09h3Zoo_LastFirst.accde* database file.

c. Click **Close** on the FILE tab.

d. Locate and open the *a09h3Zoo_LastFirst.accde* file you created.

You are prompted for the database password. After you type the password, click Open if a security notice appears.

e. Test the ACCDE file by opening the Animals Form. Right-click the **ANIMALS FORM tab** and observe that *Design View* and *Layout View* are is missing from the shortcut menu.

f. Close the form.

g. Close the file and exit Access.

h. Submit based on your instructor's directions.

Chapter Objectives Review

After reading this chapter, you have accomplished the following objectives:

1. **Verify first normal form**
   - The first step to normalizing a table, which removes repeating groups.

2. **Verify second normal form**
   - Requires 1NF. Criteria is that all non-key fields must be functionally dependent on the entire primary key. If no composite key exists, the table is often in 2NF.

3. **Verify third normal form**
   - Requires 2NF. Removes transitive dependencies, or dependencies on non-key fields.

4. **Create relationships**
   - After normalization, relationships exist between your tables. If a table cannot be connected to others, there is likely a problem with your normalization.

5. **Use the Database Documenter tool**
   - Start the Database Documenter: Database Documenter creates a report containing detailed information for each selected object. Database Documenter can be run on specific objects (for example, only tables, or only forms and reports). Users can select varying levels of detail.

6. **Use the Performance Analyzer tool**
   - Start the Performance Analyzer: Performance Analyzer evaluates a database and makes optimization recommendations.
   - Add an index: Performance Analyzer may recommend adding an index, which will speed up searches such as queries or filters.

7. **Use the Table Analyzer tool**
   - Start the Table Analyzer: The Table Analyzer guides the user through the normalization process. This is a great tool for users with no experience with normalization.
   - Step through the Table Analyzer Wizard: The wizard enables you to split tables, rename newly created tables, rearrange fields in the new tables, and create relationships.

8. **Use the Database Splitter tool**
   - Start the Database Splitter tool: The Database Splitter tool is useful when the number of database users grows beyond a few. The tool splits a database into two files—a front-end database containing queries, forms, and reports, and a back-end database containing tables. Splitting a database may improve the speed of data processing. The back-end database is generally on a server.
   - Work with the front-end database: The front-end database is typically on each user's machine. The front-end database enables users to create their own queries, forms, and reports if necessary. The front end links to back-end tables, which can be shared between users.

9. **Create a menu system**
   - Create a Navigation form: Navigation forms help users open important forms and reports quickly. Choose one of six prebuilt layouts. Drag and drop forms and reports directly on tabs. A navigation form can be easily converted to a Web form.
   - Starting a Navigation form automatically: Navigation forms can start automatically when a database opens to help provide guidance to users.

10. **Encrypt and password-protect a database**
    - Encryption alters digital information using an algorithm, making it unreadable without the key (secret code). Encrypted databases are very difficult to break in to. Encryption is suggested especially if a database is sent via e-mail or put on removable storage such as a USB drive.

11. **Digitally sign and publish a database**
    - Use the SelfCert tool: SelfCert creates a personal signature. The signature can be applied to databases as well as other Office files.
    - Apply a digital signature: Once a certificate is created, it can be applied to a database. Doing so creates an ACCDC file, indicating it has been digitally signed.

12. **Save a database as an ACCDE file**
    - Create an ACCDE file: An ACCDE file is an executable form of the database—objects such as forms, reports, and VBA code cannot be changed. Saving as an ACCDE file adds an extra layer of protection.
    - Keep the original database file safe: Once created, an ACCDE file does not let you modify objects (forms, reports, and VBA code), so the original ACCDB must be kept safe. If the ACCDB file disappears, you will have to recreate your database objects.

Key Terms Matching

Match the key terms with their definitions. Write the key term letter by the appropriate numbered definition.

a. Access Database Executable (ACCDE)
b. Anomaly
c. Back-end database
d. Certification authority (CA)
e. Composite key
f. Database Documenter
g. Database Splitter
h. Digital signatures
i. Encryption
j. First normal form (1NF)

k. Front-end database
l. Functional dependency
m. Navigation form
n. Non-key field
o. Normalization
p. Performance Analyzer
q. Second normal form (2NF)
r. Table Analyzer
s. Third normal form (3NF)
t. Transitive dependencies

1. _____ A commercial company, such as VeriSign, that issues and validates identities using digital signatures for a fee. **p. 822**

2. _____ A file that has had all VBA source code removed, prohibits users from making design and name changes to forms or reports within the database, and prohibits users from creating new forms and reports. **p. 823**

3. _____ A tabbed menu that ties the objects in the database together so that the database is easy to use. **p. 817**

4. _____ A primary key that is made up of two or more fields. **p. 795**

5. _____ A tool that creates a report containing detailed information for each selected object. **p. 803**

6. _____ An error or inconsistency that occurs when you add, edit, and delete data. **p. 792**

7. _____ Analyzes the tables in a database and normalizes them for you. **p. 807**

8. _____ Any field that is not part of the primary key. **p. 795**

9. _____ Contains the queries, forms, and reports of the database. **p. 810**

10. _____ Contains the tables of the database. Often stored on a server or network location. **p. 810**

11. _____ Electronic, encryption-based, secure stamps of authentication that confirm who created the file, that the file is valid, and that no changes have been made to the file after its authentication. **p. 822**

12. _____ Enables you to split a database into two files—a back-end database, which contains the data tables, and a front-end database. **p. 810**

13. _____ Evaluates a database and then makes recommendations for optimizing the database. **p. 805**

14. _____ Occur when the value of one non-key field is functionally dependent on the value of another non-key field. **p. 796**

15. _____ Satisfied when a table contains no repeating groups or repeating columns. **p. 793**

16. _____ Satisfied when a table meets 2NF criteria and no transitive dependencies exist. **p. 796**

17. _____ Satisfied when a table that meets 1NF criteria and all non-key fields are functionally dependent on the entire primary key. **p. 795**

18. _____ The formal process of deciding which fields should be grouped together into which tables. **p. 792**

19. _____ The process of altering digital information using an algorithm to make it unreadable to anyone except those who possess the key (or secret code). **p. 820**

20. _____ When the value of one field is determined by the value of another. **p. 795**

Multiple Choice

1. Which of the following statements about normalization is false?

   (a) A database in 3NF must also be in 1NF.

   (b) There are only three normal forms.

   (c) Normalization reduces redundancy.

   (d) The Table Analyzer can help normalize tables.

2. A table is considered the most normalized when it is in which form?

   (a) 2NF

   (b) 1NF

   (c) 3NF

   (d) Unnormalized

3. Normalization can be defined as:

   (a) Eliminating repetition of data.

   (b) Adding a layer of security to a database.

   (c) Transforming tables into forms.

   (d) A database with multiple tables.

4. The Performance Analyzer:

   (a) Lists the properties of every object in the database.

   (b) Locates places where the database can be optimized.

   (c) Searches for rows of repeating data and suggests design changes to improve performance.

   (d) Is a wizard that provides step-by-step instructions on the creation of tables and forms.

5. The Database Documenter:

   (a) Lists the properties of every object in the database.

   (b) Locates places where the database can be optimized.

   (c) Searches for rows of repeating data and suggests design changes to improve performance.

   (d) Is a wizard that provides step-by-step instructions on the creation of tables and forms.

6. The Table Analyzer:

   (a) Lists the properties of every object in the database.

   (b) Locates places where the database can be optimized.

   (c) Normalizes a database.

   (d) Is a wizard that provides step-by-step instructions on the creation of tables and forms.

7. Which of the following describes a digital signature?

   (a) A scanned copy of the database owner's signature

   (b) Provided by Microsoft when you purchase Office 2013

   (c) Provides a timestamp that can help prove who last modified the database

   (d) An e-mail that details who last made changes to the attached database

8. Which of the following is true about encrypted databases?

   (a) Database encryption alters the contents of the database so that it cannot be opened without a password.

   (b) Encrypted databases can be broken into with ease.

   (c) The contents of encrypted databases cannot be modified.

   (d) Databases can be encrypted but not have a password assigned.

9. Which password is strongest?

   (a) MyAuntSally

   (b) Ginger125

   (c) Mypassword11

   (d) 5*m6notX

10. You open a database with exclusive access. What can other users do?

    (a) Other users can open the database and make changes to it.

    (b) Other users cannot open the database when it is already open with exclusive access.

    (c) No rules apply. Exclusive access is a database setting that can be turned on or off.

    (d) Other users can open but cannot modify the database.

Practice Exercises

1 | Info Labs

Info Labs, a clinical studies company in Mississippi, employs 14 employees; most employees fall in the categories of manager, account rep, or trainee. The employee database holds information about each employee, including their salary and gender, their title, and their location. You have been asked to review the database to see if the employee table was designed properly. This exercise follows the same set of skills as used in Hands-On Exercises 1 and 2 in the chapter. Refer to Figure 9.46 as you complete this exercise.

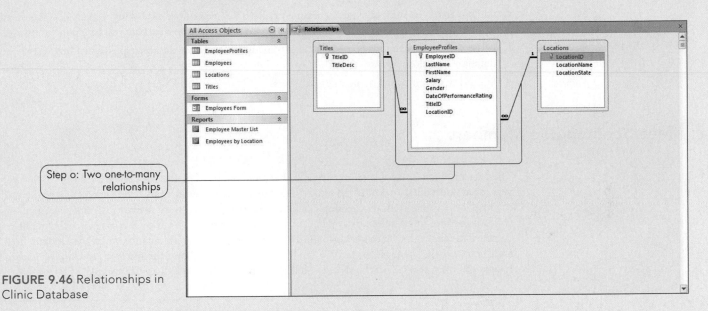

FIGURE 9.46 Relationships in Clinic Database

a. Open *a09p1Clinic*. Save the database as **a09p1Clinic_LastFirst**.

b. Open the Employees table in Datasheet view and examine the data. Determine if the data meets the three normalization rules: 1NF, 2NF, and 3NF.

c. Close the Employees table. You decide to use the Table Analyzer for help with normalizing the Employees table.

d. Click **Analyze Table** in the Analyze group on the DATABASE TOOLS tab. When the first wizard screen appears, click **Next** twice.

e. Select the **Employees table** when the *Which table contains fields with values that are repeated in many records* screen appears. Click **Next** twice.

f. Verify the Employees table has been split into three tables on the next screen.

g. Click **Table1**, click the **Rename Table icon**, and then type **Employee Profiles** as the new name of this table. Click **OK**.

h. Click **Table2**, click the **Rename Table icon**, and then type **Locations** as the new name of this table. Click **OK**.

i. Click **Table3**, click the **Rename Table icon**, and then type **Titles** as the new name of this table. Click **OK**.

j. Click **Next**.

k. Click **LocationID** in the Locations table and click the **Set Unique Identifier icon** to set LocationID as the primary key.

l. Click **EmployeeID** in the EmployeeProfiles table and click the **Set Unique Identifier icon** to set EmployeeID as the primary key.

m. Click **Next**. Select the **No, don't create the query option**. Click **Finish**. Click **OK** when the information message appears.

n. Review the new tables and confirm that the Analyzer moved fields from the Employees table into the two new lookup tables. Close all the tables.

o. Click **Relationships** on the DATABASE TOOLS tab in the Relationships group. Click **All Relationships** to reveal the relationships created by the Table Analyzer. Close the Relationships window and click **No**.

p. Click **Info** on the FILE tab, and click **Encrypt with Password**. Access displays the message *You must have the database open for exclusive use*. Click **OK**. Close the database. Use the Open Exclusive option to open the database.

q. Click **Info** on the FILE tab, and click **Encrypt with Password**. Use **exploring** as the password, in all lowercase letters. Click **OK**. Click **OK** in response to the *Row level locking will be ignored* message.

r. Close the database and reopen it. Type **exploring** in the **Enter database password box**. Close the database and close Access.

s. Submit based on your instructor's directions.

2 Metropolitan Zoo Members

The Metropolitan Zoo invites its patrons to become members of the zoo. For a donation of $50 per year for an individual, or $100 for a family membership, members are entitled to special discounts and member-only promotions. For example, when the pygmy hippos were delivered to the zoo, members were allowed to observe their arrival before the rest of the public. Your task is to review the members database to review the tables for normalization errors, check the performance, to create a lookup field, and then save the database as an ACCDE file. This exercise follows the same set of skills as used in Hands-On Exercises 1–3 in the chapter. Refer to Figures 9.47 and 9.48 as you complete this exercise.

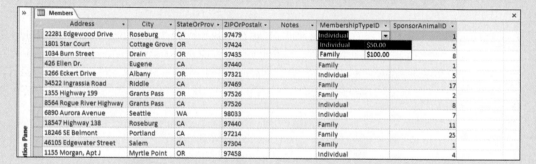

FIGURE 9.47 Lookup Field in Membership Table

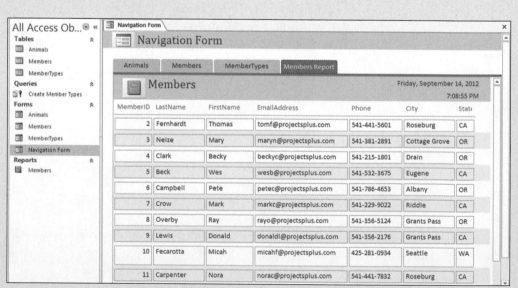

FIGURE 9.48 Navigation Form in Members Database

a. Open *a09p2Members*. Save the database as **a09p2Members_LastFirst**.

b. Open the Members table and examine the data. Determine if the data meets the three normalization rules: 1NF, 2NF, and 3NF.

c. Close the Members table. You decide to normalize the table manually.

d. Click **Query Design** in the Queries group on the CREATE tab. Add the Members table to the query design and close the Show Table dialog box.

e. Add the MembershipTypeID, MembershipTypeName, and MembershipDonation fields to the query design grid. Run the query. Take note of the repeating rows of data.

f. Switch to Design view. Click **Totals** in the Show/Hide group to eliminate the duplicate rows. Run the query. Only the unique rows show in the results.

g. Switch to Design view. Click **Make Table** in the Query Type group and type **MemberTypes** in the **Table Name box**. Click **OK**. Click **Run** in the Results group to create the MemberTypes table. Click **Yes** to the warning message. You created a second table (MemberTypes) to help normalize the Members table.

h. Save the query as **Create Member Types**. Close the query.

i. Open the MemberTypes table in Design view. Set the MembershipTypeID field as the primary key. Save and close the table.

j. Open the Members table in Design view and use the Lookup Wizard to join the Members table to the MemberTypes table in a relationship. Complete the following steps:

- Change the MembershipTypeID Data Type to *Lookup Wizard*.
- Click **Next** in the first Lookup Wizard step, select the **MemberTypes table** in the next step, and then click **Next**.
- Click the >> **button** to include all fields in the Lookup field. Click **Next** three times.
- Click **Finish** and click **Yes** to save the table. The two tables are now joined using the MembershipTypeID field.

k. Switch to Datasheet view. Click the **MembershipTypeID field** in the first row and verify the Lookup field is working. Next, you will delete the redundant fields in the Members table.

l. Switch to Design view. Select the **MembershipTypeName** and **MembershipDonation fields**. Click **Delete Rows** in the Tools group. Click **Yes** to confirm the deletion. Save and close the table.

m. Create a basic form using the Form button for each of the three tables in the database using the Form tool. Delete any subforms that appear automatically.

n. Create a basic report based on the Members table using the Report tool. Include MemberID, LastName, FirstName, EmailAddress, Phone, City, and StateOrProvince, in that order.

o. Use these four new objects to create a navigation form using the Horizontal Tabs template (see Figure 9.45). Edit the fourth tab and change the caption to **Members Report**. Close the Navigation Pane. Switch to Form view and test the new navigation form. Close the navigation form.

p. Click the **DATABASE TOOLS tab** and click **Analyze Performance**. Click the **All Object Types tab**, click **Select All**, and then click **OK**. The first idea in the Results window suggests you save your application as an MDE file, which is called ACCDE in Access 2013.

q. Close the Results dialog box.

r. Click **Save As** on the FILE tab, and double-click **Make ACCDE**. Click **Save**. The ACCDE file is saved in the same location as the original file with the same name, *a09p2Members_LastFirst*.

s. Close the database and close Access.

t. Submit based on your instructor's directions.

1 The Computer Store

ANALYSIS CASE

The Computer Store, based in Florida, sells computer products to individuals and businesses. You have been hired to assist with the daily computer operations, including management of the order processing database. Your assignment is to analyze the database, create a front end for the users, and transfer the tables to a back-end database. After splitting the database, you recommend a navigation form to open the database objects. Refer to Figure 9.49 as you complete this exercise.

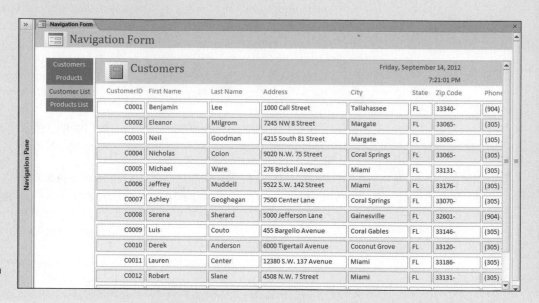

FIGURE 9.49 Navigation Form in Computers Database

a. Open *a09m1Computers*. Click **Save Database As** on the FILE tab, and type **a09m1Computers_ LastFirst**. Click **Save**.

b. Open the Database Documenter. Click **Options** and ensure none of the Include for Table items are selected. Select the **Names, Data Types, and Sizes option** in the *Include for Fields* section and select nothing in the *Include for Indexes* section. Click **OK**. Click the **Customers check box** and click **OK**. In the generated report, take note of the Size (the third column) of each field. Notice the values for the ZipCode and PhoneNumber field sizes in the Customers table. Close the generated report after viewing it.

c. Open the Customers table in Design view and increase the field size to an appropriate size. The field size should be large enough to accommodate all data but small enough so users can not enter extra characters. Save and close the table.

d. Click **Access Database** in the Move Data group and click **Split Database** to split the database into a front-end and a back-end database. Keep the default back-end name, which adds the suffix *be* to the current database name. The front-end Navigation Pane shows linked table icons, similar to those in Figure 9.30.

e. Open the Customers table and type your name as the next customer. Close the table. Open the back-end database and verify your name is in the Customers table. Close the back-end database.

> **TROUBLESHOOTING:** If you use the front-end database on another machine, you may get an error stating the file path is not valid. Use the techniques learned in a previous chapter to link the front-end database to the back-end database.

f. Open the front-end database again and create three objects: a Customers form using the Customers table, a Products form using the Products table, and a Customer List report using the Customers table.

g. Create a navigation form using the Vertical Tabs, Left template. Add the Customers form, followed by the Products form, followed by the Customer List report, followed by the Products List report.

h. Test the navigation form in Form view (compare to Figure 9.49). Save and close the form.

i. Add the navigation form to the Display Form option in the Access Options page so the navigation form opens when the database opens. Test the feature by closing and opening the database. Refer to Figure 9.37 if necessary.

j. Close the database.

k. Submit based on your instructor's directions.

2 Boats for All Seasons

The owners of Boats for All Seasons would like to improve their database. They would like to add some additional forms and reports and also modify their main table. They are having a problem because customers who bought boats from them years ago are returning to purchase again. The owners are unsure how to record a second transaction for the same customer. After the modifications are completed, they would like you to create a navigation form and also make suggestions for making the database more secure. Refer to Figure 9.50 as you complete this exercise.

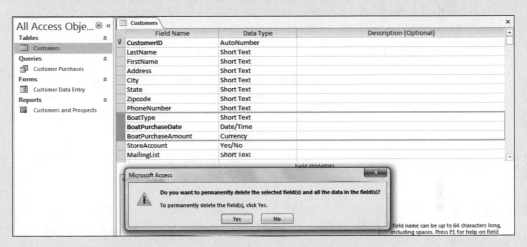

FIGURE 9.50 Deleting Redundant Fields in Customers Table

a. Open *a09m2Boats*. Save the database as **a09m2Boats_LastFirst**.

b. Open the Customers table and review the contents of the table. Make a list of any problems that may cause data-entry errors. Does the table need to be normalized? You will split the customers table into two tables: the Customers table and the BoatPurchases table.

c. Open the Customer Purchases query and examine the results. The owners are trying to use this query to enter purchases. They are confused because the boat purchase data is comingled with the Customers table. Also, some of the customers are still prospects and have not even purchased a boat yet. You will fix the problem in the steps below.

d. Modify the Customer Purchases query so it only shows fields with values. Run the query. Your query should list only customers who purchased a boat (56 records).

e. Switch to Design view. Click **Make Table** and type **BoatPurchases** in the **Table name box**. Click **OK**. Run the query and click **Yes** at the warning. Save and close the query.

f. Open the BoatPurchases table in Design view and change the CustomerID Data Type to **Number**. Save the table and switch to Datasheet view. Sort the records by CustomerID, locate the three customers who purchased more than one boat (Billingslea, Mcdowell, and Windon), and then update their CustomerIDs so that both purchases show the smaller ID. For example, change the second Billingslea CustomerID from *62* to **2**.

g. Change the CustomerID field in the BoatPurchases table to a Lookup Wizard displaying CustomerID, LastName, and FirstName, sorted by LastName and then by FirstName. Hide the key column. Save the table and click **Yes** at the prompt. Your field should show the customer LastName and FirstName when you click in the CustomerID field.

h. Switch to Datasheet view. Verify that the name in column 1 matches the names in columns 2 and 3. If it does, switch to Design view and delete the **LastName** and **FirstName fields**. These two fields were for reference only until you verified the data matched the column 1 data. Save and close the BoatPurchases table.

i. Open the Customers table in Design view and delete the **BoatType**, **BoatPurchaseDate**, and **BoatPurchaseAmount fields**. This information is not needed in the Customers table because it now exists in the BoatPurchases table.

j. Save the table and switch to Datasheet view. Sort the table by Ascending LastName. Locate the three customers who purchased more than one boat (Billingslea, Mcdowell, and Windon) and delete the three duplicate records with the larger CustomerID. For example, delete the second Billingslea record with a CustomerID of *62*.

k. Close the database and reopen it using the Open Exclusive option. Encrypt the database with a password of **exploring**.

l. Create a new form and a new report using the BoatPurchases table.

m. Use the information in the *Add the Switchboard Manager* section to create a switchboard using the Switchboard Manager. Add the Boat Purchases form, the Boat Purchases report, the Customer Data Entry form, and the Customers and Prospects report to the switchboard. Modify the Access options so the switchboard automatically opens when the database opens. Close and reopen the database to test the switchboard.

n. Click **Save As** on the FILE tab, and make an ACCDE file. The ACCDE file is saved in the same location as the original file.

o. Close the database and close Access.

p. Submit based on your instructor's directions.

3 Normalizing a Database

COLLABORATION CASE

The Specialty Foods, Ltd., company has a large database that has not been normalized. The company's recent hires have been given the task of trying to normalize the database.

a. Open the *a09m3Orders* database and save it as **a09m3Orders_GroupName**. (This step should be completed by only one person in your group. Replace *GroupName* with the name or number assigned to your group by your instructor.)

b. Examine the contents of the CustomerOrders table. Create a list of fields in the database. This database, with over 2,100 rows of information, contains a large amount of redundancy. Some companies, Specialty Foods included, create a database and do not normalize until the amount of data becomes unmanageable.

c. Each member of the group should take the list of fields, examine them separately, and create an initial guess as to what the final tables will look like. Be sure to identify potential primary keys for each table.

d. Come together as a group and discuss your proposals. Reach a consensus on the final design. Put this aside for the moment.

e. Each student should separately attempt to convert the database from the unnormalized state to 1NF.

f. Come together as a group and discuss your proposals. Reach a consensus on the design after 1NF. Be sure to identify primary keys. Open Microsoft Word and open *a09m3Normalization*. Record your proposal in the section labeled *First Normal Form* and save it as **a09m3Normalization_ GroupName**. For example, the table titles shown in Figure 9.46 would be described like this:

Table Name: Titles

Fields: TitleID, TitleDesc

Primary Key: TitleID

g. Attempt to convert the database from the 1NF group settled on in step f to 2NF. Do this separately.

h. Come together as a group and discuss your proposals. Reach a consensus on the design after 2NF. Be sure to identify primary keys. Record the proposal in the *a09m3Normalization_GroupName* document in the section labeled *Second Normal Form*.

i. Each student should separately attempt to convert the database from the 2NF the group settled on in step h to 3NF.

j. Come together as a group and discuss your proposals. Reach a consensus on the design after 3NF. Be sure to identify primary keys. Record the proposal in the *a09m3Normalization_GroupName* document in the section labeled *Third Normal Form*.

k. Run the Analyze Table tool in Access on the CustomerOrders table. Name the tables appropriately. Accept the default primary keys proposed. Do not create a query when prompted. Examine the tables created and the relationships between the tables. Discuss as a group what (if anything) differs between your proposal and that proposed by Access. In the *a09m3Normalization_GroupName* document in the *Comparison* section, summarize the differences and attempt to explain why Access has different results than your proposal. Given the choice, would you use your proposal or the one provided by Access? Why?

l. Exit Word. Exit Access. Submit the Word document and the Access database based on your instructor's directions.

Beyond the Classroom

Switchboard Versus Navigation Form

RESEARCH CASE

Your company uses an Access 2013 database to store its customer and sales information. The Accounting Department uses and maintains this database. Three other departments—Marketing, Sales, and Production—also need access to the database. Some users have asked for a switchboard, and others have asked for a navigation form. The accounting department does not have experience with creating either of these forms. Your assignment is to do online research to determine which menu system is better for your company: a switchboard or a navigation form. Create a Word document named **a09b2Switchboard_LastFirst**, giving a brief summary of the two menu systems and recommending which one is better for the company.

Troubleshoot: ACCDE File Errors

DISASTER RECOVERY

Keith Hernandez, the manager of a local collectibles store, has contacted you about a database issue he has. His former technology support person set up a database for him on his USB flash drive. When he brought the file home, he was shown the following error:

> *The database was created with the 32-bit version of Access. Please open it with the 32-bit version of Microsoft Access.*

He tried then recreating the ACCDE from his home machine, but when he brought it to work, he was given the following error:

> *The database was created with the 64-bit version of Access. Please open it with the 64-bit version of Microsoft Access.*

Keith is frustrated and is hoping you can find out if there is a way for him to create an Access Database Executable that works on both the 32-bit and 64-bit versions of the program. If there is no way to do this, he is hoping you might have recommendations on how he should work with these ACCDE files. Write up your findings in a Word document and save it as **a09b3Collect_LastFirst**. Note he does not want you to fix the issue; he is just interested in finding out if this can be done or not. Keith has provided you with *a09b3Collect* (the original database), *a09b3Collect64* (which works on 64-bit editions of Access but not 32-bit editions), and *a09b3Collect32* (which works on 32-bit editions of Access but not 64-bit editions). However, you should only submit the final Word document to your instructor.

Interview Questions

SOFT SKILLS CASE

You are a database administrator at a large company. The company is hiring a new entry-level database administrator, and your supervisor, Keith Mast, has asked you to draft questions to be asked during the interview. Specifically, he would like questions that an entry-level person should be expected to answer. You have decided you will ask them a question about normalization, another about database performance, a third about splitting databases, and a fourth about encryption. Your boss has asked to see the questions (and ideal answers) before the interview. Create a new Word document named **a09b4Interview_LastFirst**. Create the four questions you would ask an interviewee to explain during an interview, and provide optimal answers for the four questions. Submit based on your instructor's directions.

Capstone Exercise

Your company handles room registration, speaker coordination, and other functions for national conferences that are held at your campus throughout the year. The sales department mails schedules to speakers and building coordinators. The speaker database was modified by unauthorized personnel, and some of the changes need to be reversed. For example, all of the relationships were deleted; they need to be recreated. You have been asked to analyze the database, fix the relationships, and make the database more secure to avoid this situation in the future. The database tables may already be normalized; however, you need to examine the tables to verify this.

Restore Database Relationships

You open the original database and use Save As to create a copy of the original.

a. Open *a09c1NatConf* and save the database as **a09c1NatConf_LastFirst**.

b. Open each table in the database and look for normalization errors.

c. Open the Relationships window. Notice there are currently no relationships.

d. Add the Speakers, SessionSpeaker, Sessions, and Rooms tables to the Relationships window. Restore relationships by dragging the primary key from the primary table onto the foreign key of a related table.

e. Enforce *Referential Integrity* and *Cascade Update Related Fields* for each relationship you create.

f. Save the changes and close the Relationships window.

Analyze Database Performance

You want to verify that the database performs properly when it is used in a production environment. Run Performance Analyzer and take note of the recommendations, suggestions, and ideas in the analysis results.

a. Open the Performance Analyzer dialog box, click the **All Object Types tab**, click **Select All**, and then click **OK**.

b. Verify that the first item on the list (an idea) suggests creating an MDE file, which is called ACCDE in Access 2013. You will create an ACCDE file later.

c. Verify the third item on the list (an idea) suggests you change the data type of RoomID in the Sessions table from *Short Text* to **Long Integer**. You decide not to make this change.

> **TROUBLESHOOTING:** If changing the data type of RoomID is not the third idea, ensure you set the options properly in step a.

d. Close the Performance Analyzer.

Split the Database

Splitting the database by creating a back end and a front end enables users to customize their individual front-end databases; the back end (the tables) remains safe and secure.

a. Split the database, accepting the default back-end name *a09c1NatConf_LastFirst_be*. The front-end copy of the database remains open.

b. Look for the linked tables in the front-end copy of the database.

Create the Navigation Form

You need to create a navigation form that displays a new form and the three reports in the database. Add the navigation form to the Display Form option to make the navigation form appear whenever the database opens.

a. Create a new form based on the Speakers table.

b. Save the form as **Add or Edit Speakers**.

c. Create a navigation form based on the Horizontal Tabs template.

d. Drag the new **Add or Edit Speakers form** to the first tab position.

e. Drag the reports to fill the next three tab positions.

f. Switch to Form view and test the navigation form. Save the navigation form with the default name and close it.

g. Set the database to open the navigation form when the database opens. This setting can be found in Options on the FILE tab. Click the **Current Database tab** and update the Display Form option.

h. Test the navigation form by closing and then reopening the database.

Encrypt the Database with a Password and Create the ACCDE File

Make sure you have the database open with exclusive access before completing these steps. You need to encrypt the front-end database with a password. In addition, you want to convert the front-end database to the ACCDE file format.

a. Display the Set Database Password dialog box.

b. Set the database password to **exploring**. Type the same password in both text boxes. Click **OK** at the next prompt.

c. Close and reopen the database to test the password.

d. Convert the front-end database to an ACCDE file format. A new database file with extension .accde is created in the background.

e. Close the database. Close Access.

f. Submit based on your instructor's directions.

CHAPTER 10

Using Macros and SQL in Access

Advanced Techniques

OBJECTIVES AFTER YOU READ THIS CHAPTER, YOU WILL BE ABLE TO:

1. Understand the purpose of a macro p. 842
2. Create a stand-alone macro p. 843
3. Use the Macro Designer p. 844
4. Attach an embedded macro to an event p. 845
5. Identify when to use a data macro p. 855
6. Create an event-driven data macro p. 855
7. Create a named data macro p. 856
8. Understand the fundamentals of SQL p. 865
9. Interpret an SQL SELECT statement p. 866
10. Use an SQL SELECT statement as a record source p. 868

CASE STUDY | Retirement Plan Helps Retain Employees

Terry Jackson, owner of Sunshine Therapy Club in Chicago, Illinois, offers her full-time employees a generous benefits package. In addition to a health care plan, paid vacation, and paid holidays, she also offers a 401k retirement plan to all full-time employees who have been employed for at least 90 days. Employees can contribute a percentage of their wages to 401k accounts and receive a tax deduction on their federal, state, and local tax returns. Employees can set the amount of their contribution anywhere between 1% and 15% of their weekly pay. For employees who have been with the company for at least one year, the company will match the employees' contributions up to 5%.

You have been asked to assist Associate Director Nancy Williams with verifying the accuracy of the Sunshine employee data and the employee contributions and ensuring that they fall within the plan guidelines. For example, only employees who have worked for the company at least one year are eligible for the company match. In addition, the plan must meet the minimum standard of employee participation. Terry would also like to receive a weekly report that shows the contribution per employee and the total contribution for the week. She would also like to see the company match per employee and the total company match for the week.

You decide to use macros and data macros to verify the plan is in compliance each week rather than wait until the end of a quarter or year. Any problems can then be corrected immediately. Data macros will also be utilized to verify data entry and alert the user if data is outside the normal plan parameters. You will also construct several SQL statements to use as the record source for several reports.

Macro Design

Access provides developers with a variety of built-in tools to create tables, queries, forms, and reports. However, sometimes a developer needs to have more control over how the objects in a database behave individually or in relation to other objects. This type of functionality can be accomplished through programming code. Access provides two methods of programming—creating macros and creating procedures using Visual Basic for Applications (VBA). In general, it is easier to create a macro than a VBA procedure because Access includes an automated tool for creating macros, the Macro Designer. VBA will not be covered in detail in this chapter; however macros can be converted to VBA without having to write any complex programming code whatsoever.

In this section, you will learn how to create two types of macros: stand-alone macros and embedded macros. You will also learn how Access creates macros for you when you add a command button to a form.

Understanding the Purpose of a Macro

STEP 1 »

A *macro* is a series of actions that can be programmed to automate tasks. Macros can be used to automate a repetitive task or perform a specific action. You can use macros to group a series of commands and instructions into a single command to accomplish repetitive or routine tasks automatically. After you create a macro, you initiate all its tasks by running the macro. For example, if you import the same Excel workbook data into Access each week, you could create a macro to help you accomplish this task. Or you might want to add a button to a form to run the same report each week. Access creates macros automatically for you when you add certain controls to a form or report, for example, if you create a command button in a form to run a report or print a customer order. Access uses embedded macros to enable the buttons to function.

Access supports two categories of macros: stand-alone macros and embedded macros. A *stand-alone macro* is a database object that you create and use independently of other controls or objects. Stand-alone macros display as objects in the Navigation Pane. Figure 10.1 shows three stand-alone macros.

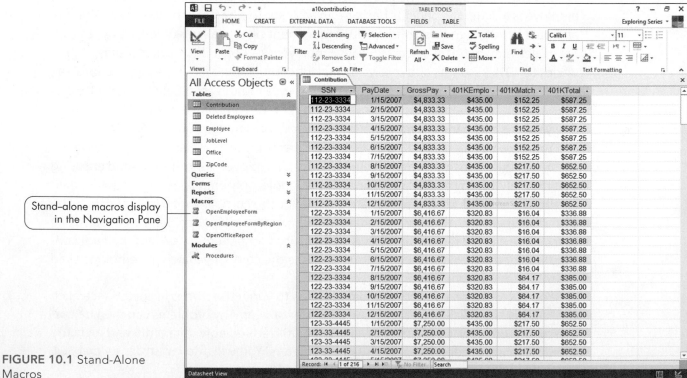

Stand–alone macros display in the Navigation Pane

FIGURE 10.1 Stand-Alone Macros

An *embedded macro* is a macro that executes when an event attached to a control or object occurs. An *event* occurs when a user enters, edits, or deletes data; events also occur when users open, use, and close forms and reports. After Update is an example of an event attached to a control. After Update is triggered each time you enter (update) data into a field on a form. On Close is another example of an event attached to an object. Whenever you close a form or a report, the On Close event is triggered and Access executes the steps stored in the macro associated with the On Close event.

Another common use of an embedded macro is to validate the data in a field or a record. When a user enters data into a field, the After Update event is activated. You can attach an embedded macro to the After Update event and evaluate the data entered to verify that it falls within a set of parameters. For example, if a user enters a series of 401k contributions, a macro could verify that the amounts are positive values and that the contributions are equal to or less than 15% of an employee's salary.

Table 10.1 summarizes the two macro types supported by Access.

TABLE 10.1 Access Macro Types

Macro Type	Description
Stand-alone macro	A macro that is a separate object in the Access database. A stand-alone macro displays in the Navigation Pane and can be run independently. Stand-alone macros are also available to any control or object in the database.
Embedded macro	A macro that is embedded in a specific object or control. An embedded macro does not display in the Navigation Pane. Use an embedded macro when only one object needs to run the macro.

Creating a Stand-Alone Macro

STEP 2》 A stand-alone macro, as stated earlier, displays as an object in the Navigation Pane and can be run independently of other objects. You use the Macro Designer to create a stand-alone macro.

To create a macro using the Macro Designer, do the following:

1. Click the CREATE tab.
2. Click Macro in the Macros & Code group. The Macro Designer is displayed, as shown in Figure 10.2. In this figure, the Navigation Pane is on the left, the build-a-macro area is in the middle, and the Action Catalog is on the right. The Action Catalog can be used as a reference as you design a macro; you can also locate an action in the Action Catalog and double-click it (or drag it) to add it to the macro.
3. Specify the arguments you want for the action or actions you added to the macro.
4. When you finish building the macro, click Save.
5. Type a descriptive name for the macro. The macro name will display in the Navigation Pane, as shown in Figure 10.1.
6. To run a stand-alone macro, double-click the macro name in the Navigation Pane.

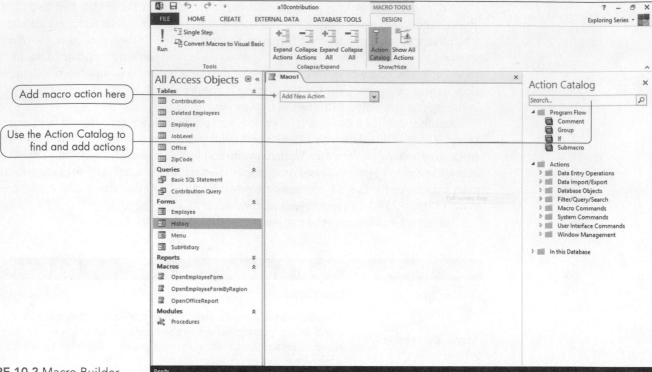

Add macro action here

Use the Action Catalog to find and add actions

FIGURE 10.2 Macro Builder

To edit an existing stand-alone macro using the Macro Designer, do the following:

1. Right-click the macro name in the Navigation Pane.
2. Select Design View from the shortcut menu.
3. After modifying, adding, or deleting macro actions, save and close the macro.

Using the Macro Designer

STEP 3 ▶

The *Macro Designer* enables you to create and edit macros. Macro Designer was designed to make it easier to create macros, to modify macros, and to add or delete actions from macros. You can use any of the following four methods for adding actions to a macro with the Macro Designer:

- Click the Add New Action arrow and choose the action you want to add to your macro.
- Type the action name directly into the Add New Action box; Access autocompletes the action name as you type.
- Locate an action in the Action Catalog and double-click it to add it to the macro.
- Drag the action from the Action Catalog into the macro.

Access executes the actions in the order in which you list them.

Next, specify the arguments you want for the action or actions you added to the macro. An *argument* is a variable, constant, or expression that is needed to produce the output for an action. For example, you may want to add a MessageBox action to the macro to display a message to users when the macro runs. The MessageBox action contains four arguments, one of which is required. To see a short description of each argument, point to the argument box, and Access displays a short explanation of the argument. The MessageBox action contains the arguments Message, Beep, Type, and Title, as shown in Figure 10.3.

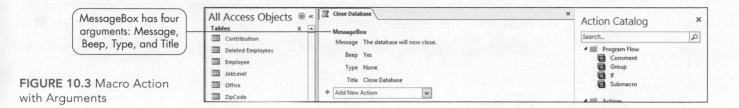

FIGURE 10.3 Macro Action with Arguments

You can also create an action by dragging a database object from the Navigation Pane to an empty row in the Macro Designer. If you drag a table, query, form, or report to the Macro Designer, Access adds an action that opens the table, query, form, or report. If you drag a macro to the Macro Designer, Access adds an action that runs the macro. Figure 10.4 shows the results of dragging the Employee form from the Navigation Pane into a new macro.

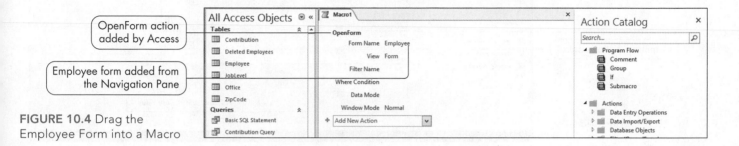

FIGURE 10.4 Drag the Employee Form into a Macro

Attaching an Embedded Macro to an Event

STEP 4 Embedded macros are always attached to an event of a control on a form or report, or to an event of the form or report object itself.

Access provides two methods to create an embedded macro. First, you can use a wizard, such as the Command Button Wizard, and let Access create the macro for you. Or you can add a macro to an existing control manually by clicking the ellipsis (…) in the event box of the control or object you are manipulating. When you add a macro to an event (such as the On Click event of a button), Access embeds a macro in the object or control as shown in Figure 10.5. Regardless of which method you use, the Event tab in the object's Property Sheet enables you to open and edit the embedded macro. Figure 10.5 shows how an embedded macro displays in the Property Sheet for a control.

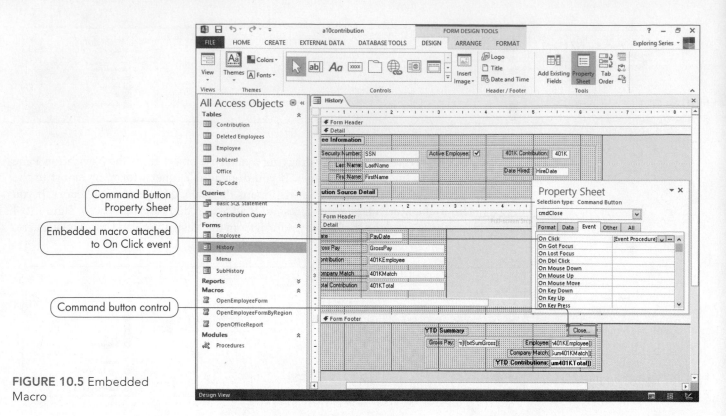

Command Button Property Sheet

Embedded macro attached to On Click event

Command button control

FIGURE 10.5 Embedded Macro

To attach an embedded macro, first open the form or report in Design view. You can attach a macro to an event using one of two methods. The first method is by adding a command button control that automatically creates an embedded macro for you. The command button control creates an embedded macro automatically using the Command Button Wizard. After the wizard is finished, an embedded macro is inserted into the On Click event property of the button. The second method is to attach an embedded macro to an event.

STEP 5 >> To attach an embedded macro to an event, do the following:

1. Open the object in Design view and open the Property Sheet.
2. Click the control you want to add the macro to and click in the desired event property box on the Event tab. When you click in an event property box, the ellipsis (…) displays on the right side of the box, as shown in Figure 10.6.
3. Click the ellipsis (…), click Macro Builder, and then click OK.

The Macro Designer opens, and you can add actions using the same methods you used for the stand-alone macro. For example, you can create a macro to compute employee 401k contributions. The macro can display a message after the 401k Contribution is selected, informing the employee (or the user) the amount that will be deducted each paycheck (by displaying the 401k Contribution Percent *times* the weekly Salary).

TIP **Editing an Embedded Macro**

To edit an embedded macro, open the form or report in Design view. Next, open the Property Sheet, and then click the event property that contains the embedded macro. Click the ellipsis (…), and Access opens the Macro Designer and displays the actions associated with the macro. Modify the embedded macro, click Save, and then close when finished. The macro remains embedded in the object.

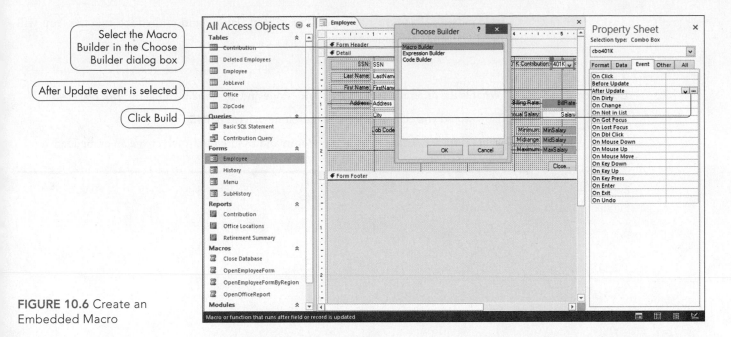

FIGURE 10.6 Create an Embedded Macro

> **TIP** **Converting a Macro to VBA**
>
> Although VBA is not covered in this textbook, it is helpful to know that macros can be converted to VBA. At times, VBA may be a better choice for automating an Access object, as VBA enables more complex functionality. However, rather than creating VBA code from scratch, you can convert an existing macro to VBA and then modify the VBA code as needed.
>
> To convert a stand-alone macro to VBA, open the macro in Design view. While in Design view, click Convert Macros to Visual Basic in the Tools group on the Design tab, as shown in Figure 10.7. A new module is created with the VBA required to perform the same automated tasks as the original macro. The module displays in the Navigation Pane of the database.

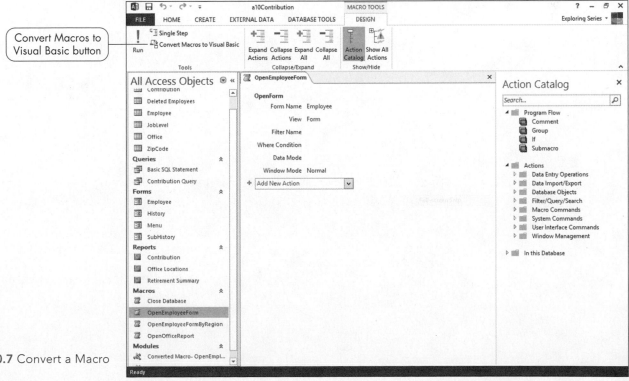

FIGURE 10.7 Convert a Macro to VBA

In Hands-On Exercise 1, you will create stand-alone and embedded macros. You will also practice using the Macro Designer.

Quick Concepts

1. What is the difference between a stand-alone and an embedded macro? *pp. 842–843*

2. How would you edit an existing stand-alone macro? *p. 845*

3. What is the advantage of using the Command Button control to create an embedded macro? *p. 846*

Hands-On Exercises

1 Macro Design

You were hired to help Nancy administer the 401k plan at Sunshine Therapy Club. After you examine the design of the database, you decide to use stand-alone and embedded macros to open the forms and reports that Nancy uses to administer the plan. Because macros are powerful and can accidentally harm a database, you decide to make a copy of the original database and work with the copy.

Skills covered: Understand the Purpose of a Macro • Create a Stand-Alone Macro • Use the Macro Designer • Attach an Embedded Macro to an Event • Attach an Embedded Macro to a Report Event

STEP 1 >> UNDERSTAND THE PURPOSE OF A MACRO

Because this is your first time working with the Sunshine Therapy Club database, you examine the current database by opening each table in Datasheet view. Next, you will open the Relationships window to see which tables are related. You will also open the forms and reports that are used frequently and determine that a macro can be created to open several objects automatically. Refer to Figure 10.8 as you complete Step 1.

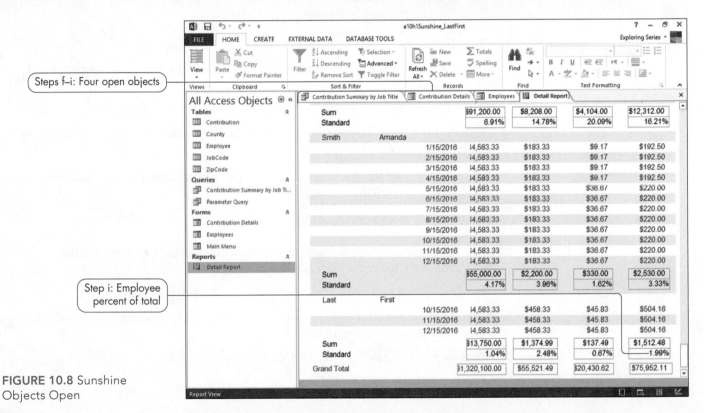

FIGURE 10.8 Sunshine Objects Open

a. Open *a10h1Sunshine*. Click the **FILE tab**, click **Save As**, click **Save As**, and then type **a10h1Sunshine_LastFirst**. Click **Save** and click **Enable Content**.

> **TROUBLESHOOTING:** If you make any major mistakes in this exercise, you can close the file and start over.

b. Open the Employee table in Datasheet view and examine the records. Open the Contribution table and examine the records. Open the remaining tables and examine the records. Close all tables.

You examine the data in each table to get acquainted with the database. The Contribution table contains the 401k contributions for each employee. The Employee table contains personal information for each employee.

c. Click the **DATABASE TOOLS tab** and click **Relationships** in the Relationships group to open the Relationships window.

You examine the table relationships to help you understand the data entry rules of the database. The Employee table contains a unique Social Security number (SSN) for each employee. The Contribution table contains an SSN field, but multiple contributions can be entered for each SSN.

d. Close the Relationships window. Open the Employee table and add your data as a new record to the table. Type the following data when you enter your record:

SSN	999-99-9999 *(do not type the dashes)*
LastName	*your last name*
FirstName	*your first name*
Gender	*your gender*
Other fields	*the same data as Amanda Smith's record*

e. Close the Employee table.

f. Open the Contribution Summary by Job Title query and review the contributions by job title.

Terry will use this information to track which employees are participating in the plan.

g. Open the Contribution Details form and scroll to the bottom of the data. Add three new entries using the following data:

SSN	PayDate	GrossPay	EmployeeContribution	CompanyMatch
999-99-9999	10/15/2016	$4,583.33	$458.33	$45.83
999-99-9999	11/15/2016	$4,583.33	$458.33	$45.83
999-99-9999	12/15/2016	$4,583.33	$458.33	$45.83

h. Open the Employees form. Advance to your record by clicking **Last record** in the Navigation Bar. Change the **HireDate** to today's date.

The HireDate will be used later to calculate the length of employment.

i. Open the Detail Report. Locate your record (the last record of the report) and find your Emp Total percent. Your contribution is 1.99%.

j. Compare your database to Figure 10.8. Close all open objects.

STEP 2 » CREATE A STAND-ALONE MACRO

Nancy would like to easily open the four objects that are used every day. You create a stand-alone macro to automatically open the four objects used in Step 1. Refer to Figure 10.9 as you complete Step 2.

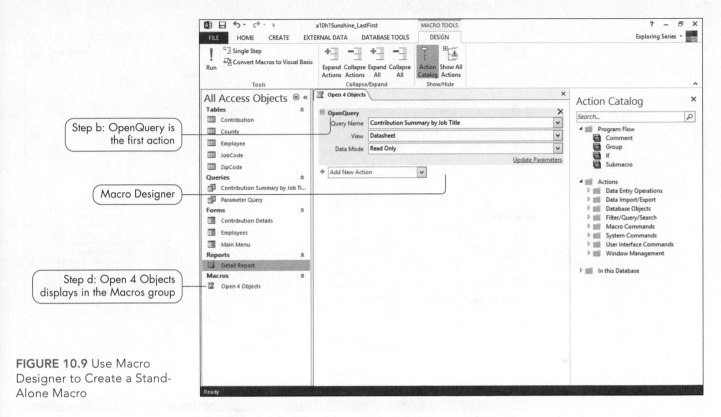

FIGURE 10.9 Use Macro Designer to Create a Stand-Alone Macro

a. Click the **CREATE tab** and click **Macro** in the Macros & Code group.

The Macro Designer opens.

b. Click the **Add New Action arrow** and select **OpenQuery** from the list of options.

The OpenQuery arguments are displayed. The OpenQuery action will open a query automatically.

c. Click the arrow at the end of each box and select the following arguments:

Query Name Contribution Summary by Job Title
View Datasheet *(default)*
Data Mode Read Only

d. Save the macro as **Open 4 Objects**. Close the macro.

The Open 4 Objects macro now displays in the Macros Group in the Navigation Pane.

e. Double-click the **Open 4 Objects macro** to run it.

Only one object, the *Contribution Summary by Job Title* query, opens.

f. Close the query.

You created and tested a stand-alone macro in the previous step. Because the macro works correctly so far, you decide to edit the macro and add the other three objects. All four objects will open when you run the Open 4 Objects macro. Refer to Figure 10.10 as you complete Step 3.

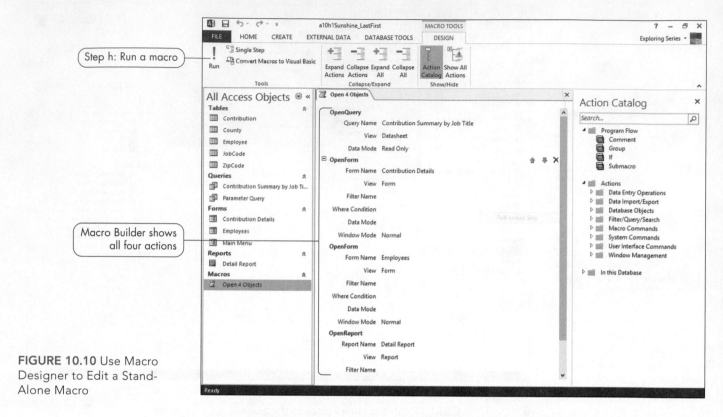

FIGURE 10.10 Use Macro Designer to Edit a Stand-Alone Macro

a. Right-click the **Open 4 Objects macro** in the Navigation Pane and select **Design View** from the shortcut menu.

The Macro Designer opens.

b. Click in the **Add New Action box** and type **OpenForm**. Press **Enter**.

You can type any action into the Add New Action box or select an action from the list. When you type an action, AutoComplete is enabled so you only have to type the first few letters of the action. The OpenForm arguments are displayed.

c. Select the following arguments:

Form Name	Contribution Details
View	Form *(default)*
Window Mode	Normal *(default)*

The remaining arguments can be left blank.

d. Click in the **Add New Action box** and type **OpenForm**. Press **Enter**.

The OpenForm arguments are displayed for the second form.

e. Select the following arguments:

Form Name	Employees
View	Form *(default)*
Window Mode	Normal *(default)*

The remaining arguments can be left blank.

f. Click in the **Add New Action box**, click the **Add New Action arrow**, and then click **OpenReport**.

The OpenReport arguments are displayed for the report.

g. Select the following arguments:

Report Name	Detail Report
View	Report *(default)*
Window Mode	Normal *(default)*

The remaining arguments can be left blank. You have added an OpenQuery, two OpenForms, and one OpenReport action to the macro.

h. Save the macro. Click **Run** in the Tools group on the DESIGN tab.

The Open 4 Objects macro runs and opens the four objects one after the other.

i. Close the four objects and close the macro.

STEP 4 ›› ATTACH AN EMBEDDED MACRO TO AN EVENT

You created a stand-alone macro. Next, you will create an embedded macro attached to a control on a form. You will add a command button to the main menu with an embedded macro; the macro will open the Parameter Query when the button is clicked. The Parameter Query will prompt the user to enter a minimum salary and then display employees who earn at least that amount. Refer to Figure 10.11 as you complete Step 4.

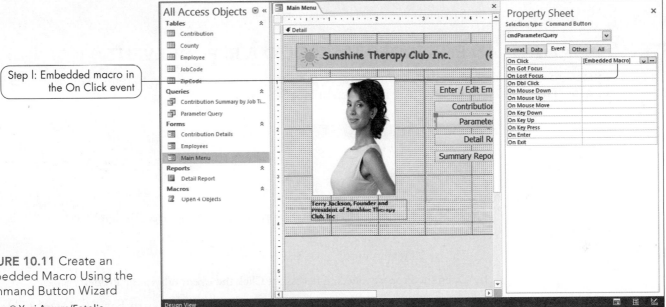

Step I: Embedded macro in the On Click event

FIGURE 10.11 Create an Embedded Macro Using the Command Button Wizard

Photo: © Yuri Arcurs/Fotolia

a. Double-click **Parameter Query** in the Navigation Pane. When prompted, enter **70000** and press **Enter**. Close the query.

The query displayed employees who earn at least $70,000.00.

b. Right-click the **Main Menu form** in the Navigation Pane and select **Design View** from the shortcut menu.

The Main Menu opens in Design view.

c. Click the **Button control** in the Controls group on the FORM DESIGN TOOLS DESIGN tab and click in the space between the Contribution Details and Detail Report buttons.

The Command Button Wizard opens.

d. Select **Miscellaneous** from the Categories list and select **Run Query** from the Actions list. Click **Next**.

e. Click **Parameter Query** and click **Next**.

f. Select the **Text option** and type **Parameter Query** as the display text. Click **Next**.

g. Type **cmdParameterQuery** as the name for the button. Click **Finish**.

h. Click **Property Sheet** in the Tools group on the DESIGN tab with the button selected. On the Format tab in the Property Sheet, set the button width to **2.25"** and the height to **.25"**. Click the **Font Size arrow** to select **12**. Leave the Property Sheet open. Click and drag the **Parameter Query button** so that its left edge is aligned with the left edge of the buttons above and below it.

i. Switch to Form view and click **Parameter Query**.

The query opens and asks for the minimum salary amount.

j. Type **70000** and press **Enter**.

The query results display all the employees with a salary of at least $70,000.

k. Close the query and switch to the Design view of the Main Menu form. Click **Parameter Query** (if necessary) and click the **Event tab** in the Property Sheet.

The embedded macro displays in the On Click event.

l. Click the **ellipsis (…)** on the right side of the On Click property. The Macro Designer opens and enables you to modify the embedded macro. Close the Macro Designer.

m. Save and close the Main Menu form.

STEP 5 ›› ATTACH AN EMBEDDED MACRO TO A REPORT EVENT

Terry asks you to prompt the employees each time they run the Detail Report. She wants to remind them to give the report to her every Friday. Refer to Figure 10.12 as you complete Step 5.

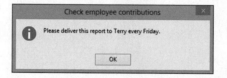

FIGURE 10.12 Message Appears When the Report Opens

a. Right-click the **Detail Report** in the Navigation Pane and select **Design View** from the shortcut menu.

The Detail Report opens in Design view.

b. Open the Property Sheet, if necessary. Click the **Event tab** on the Property Sheet.

c. Click the **ellipsis (…)** on the right side of the On Open property box. The Macro Builder option should be selected by default. Click **OK**.

The Macro Designer opens and enables you to create an embedded macro.

d. Click the **Add New Action arrow** in the Add New Action box and click **MessageBox**.

The MessageBox arguments are displayed.

e. Type **Please deliver this report to Terry every Friday.** (include the period) in the **Message box**.

f. Verify that *Yes* is in the Beep box. Select **Information** in the Type box. Type **Check employee contributions** in the **Title box**.

g. Save and close the macro. With the report in Design view, click **View** and click **Print Preview** in the Views group to test the macro.

A message displays immediately, reminding you to give the report to Terry every Friday.

h. Click **OK**, close Print Preview, and then save and close the report.

i. Keep the database open if you plan to continue with Hands-On Exercise 2. If not, close the database and exit Access.

Data Macros

A data macro executes a series of actions when a table event occurs or whenever a named data macro is executed. A table event occurs naturally as users enter, edit, and delete table data. *Data macros* attach programming logic to tables; they also enable organizations to apply business logic to a database. Business logic describes the policies and procedures established by an organization. For example, you may want a macro to compare the values in two different fields when data is entered and perform an action as a result. When a form is based on a table that contains a data macro, the form contains the same business logic and the same results of the data macro as the table.

Data macros, like stand-alone macros and embedded macros, use the Macro Designer. The actions available in the Macro Designer are different for data macros than for stand-alone or embedded macros; however, the user interface is the same for each macro type. If you become proficient in creating one type of macro, you will be proficient in creating the other types as well.

In this section, you will learn data validation techniques using data macros. You will learn how to create event-driven data macros and named data macros. You will also see the similarity between data macros and other macros, and identify when to use which type.

Identifying When to Use a Data Macro

STEP 1 You can use data macros to validate and ensure the accuracy of data in a table. You learned how to use a validation rule to apply business logic to one field in a table. However, when business logic requires the comparison of two or more fields to intercept data entry errors, you need to use a data macro. In the case study, you might want to validate a contribution rate (field 1) based on an employee's position (field 2) and an employee's hire date (field 3). To automate this type of business logic easily, a data macro is required.

A few examples of when you might add a data macro to a table are as follows:

- Verifying that a customer has no outstanding invoices before placing a new order
- Keeping a log of any changes made to a specific table
- Sending a confirmation e-mail when a contributor makes a donation
- Maintaining a backup table

Data macros can only be used with table events. You cannot use a data macro with other objects; however, as stated earlier, a form based on a table that contains a data macro inherits the logic of the table. Two main types of data macros exist—event-driven data macros and named data macros. Event-driven data macros are triggered by table events; named data macros can be run from anywhere in the database. After you practice adding a few data macros, you will begin to see the power they add to a database.

Creating an Event-Driven Data Macro

STEP 2 Table events occur naturally as users enter, edit, and delete table data. Event-driven data macros, such as After Delete or Before Change, can be programmed to run before or after a table event occurs.

To attach a data macro to a table event, do the following:

1. Open the table you want to add the data macro to in Design view.
2. Click Create Data Macros in the Field, Record & Table Events group on the DESIGN tab, as shown in Figure 10.13.

3. Click the event to which you want to attach the macro. For example, to create a data macro that runs before you save a record, click Before Change.

4. Add macro actions using the Macro Designer. If a macro was previously created for this event, Access displays the existing macro actions.

5. Save and close the macro.

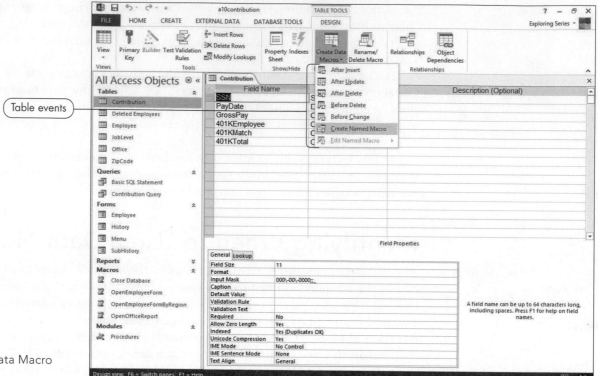

FIGURE 10.13 Data Macro Events

STEP 3 ▶▶

In order to test the effect of a data macro, open the table to which the macro was added, and then add, delete, or update a record in order to trigger the macro. For example, if you attached a macro to the Before Change event, open the table, modify the data, and then advance to the next record to save the changes and to trigger the Before Change event. The data macro will run and execute the actions you created.

Creating a Named Data Macro

STEP 4 ▶▶

In addition to creating data macros that are triggered by events, Access enables you to create named data macros. You can access these macros from anywhere in the database, including running them from within another macro.

To create a named data macro, do the following:

1. In Design view, click Create Data Macros in the Field, Record & Table Events group and select Create Named Macro from the list (see Figure 10.14).

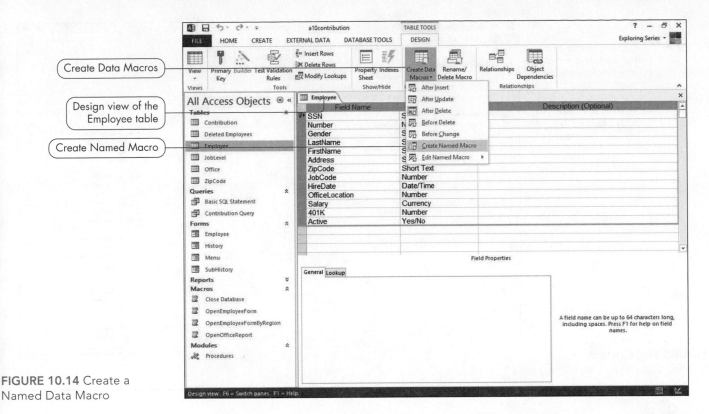

FIGURE 10.14 Create a Named Data Macro

- Create Data Macros
- Design view of the Employee table
- Create Named Macro

The Macro Designer displays so you can create the macro logic (see Figure 10.15). After you create a named data macro, save the macro with a descriptive name, such as DataMacro-Email. You will then be able to run the data macro from inside another macro using the RunDataMacro action. Figure 10.16 shows a data macro attached to the After Update event of the Employee table. The macro sends an e-mail to the database administrator each time the Employee table is updated. The data macro could also be attached to an event in an employees form that is dependent on the Employee table.

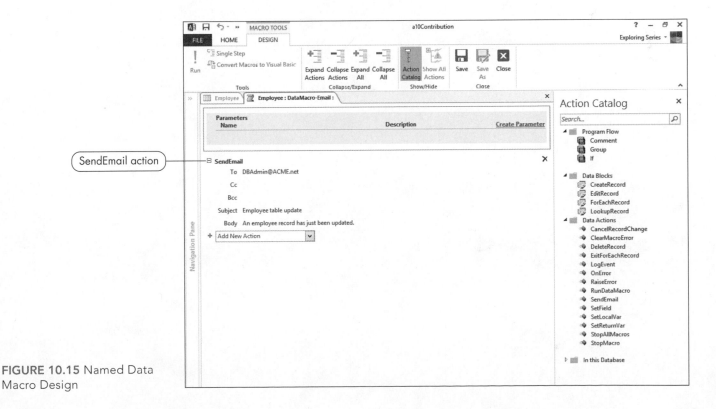

- SendEmail action

FIGURE 10.15 Named Data Macro Design

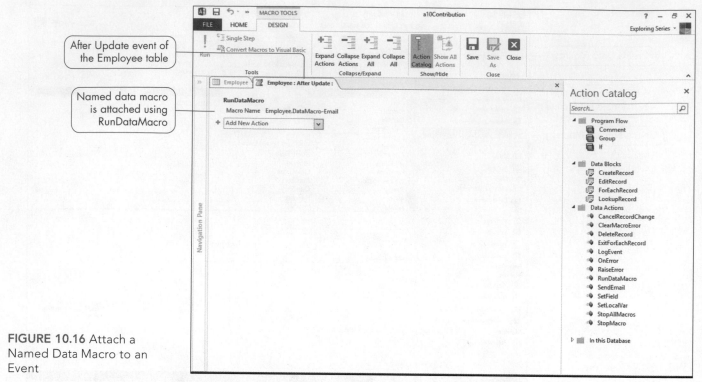

After Update event of the Employee table

Named data macro is attached using RunDataMacro

FIGURE 10.16 Attach a Named Data Macro to an Event

Quick Concepts

1. When does a data macro run? *p. 855*

2. Why would you use a data macro? Name a specific reason. *p. 855*

3. When does an event-driven macro run? *p. 855*

2 Data Macros

You decide to demonstrate the power of data macros to Terry and Nancy. You will show them how data macros help reduce data entry errors by intercepting and changing incorrect data before it is added to a table. Although data macros are only created from within tables, you will demonstrate that named data macros can also be used with other objects in the database. You will create a named data macro in a table to send an e-mail, and then attach the same named data macro to a form.

Skills covered: Identify When to Use a Data Macro • Create a Before Change Data Macro • Test and Modify a Data Macro • Create a Named Data Macro • Attach a Named Data Macro to a Form

STEP 1 ≫ IDENTIFY WHEN TO USE A DATA MACRO

Certain tasks are completed manually, which lend themselves to using a data macro. A data macro will save time, and if set up correctly will never fail. In this exercise, you will identify an opportunity to create a data macro in the Employee table. Refer to Figure 10.17 as you complete Step 1.

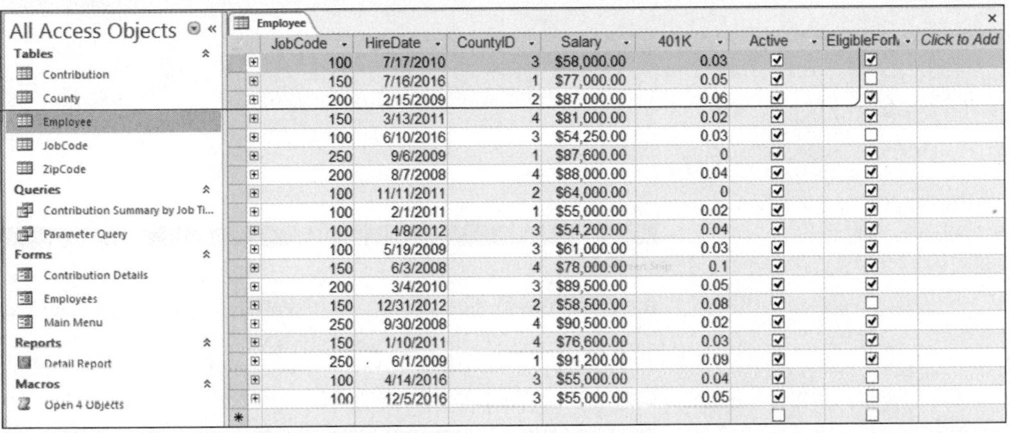

Step e: Add and update the EligibleForMatch field

FIGURE 10.17 Identify When to Use a Data Macro

a. Open *a10h1Sunshine_LastFirst* if you closed it after completing Hands-On Exercise 1. Click the **FILE tab**, click **Save As**, click **Save As**, and then type **a10h2Sunshine_LastFirst**, changing *h1* to *h2*. Click **Save**.

b. Open the Employee table in Design view.

c. Add a new field, **EligibleForMatch**, with data type **Yes/No**, to the table. Save the table.

You will use the new field to indicate which employees are eligible for the company 401k matching contribution.

d. Switch to Datasheet view.

e. Update the first 10 records to indicate whether or not they are eligible for the company match. If an employee has been employed for at least one year, check the **EligibleForMatch check box**.

> **TROUBLESHOOTING:** Ensure that your own record contains today's date as the date of hire. As you have only joined the organization today, you will not be eligible for the company match.

Next, you will create a data macro to update the EligibleForMatch field. A data macro will update the EligibleForMatch check box each time a record changes.

STEP 2 ≫ CREATE A BEFORE CHANGE DATA MACRO

The EligibleForMatch check box can be updated automatically by a data macro based on the HireDate because the same eligibility rule applies to all employees. To eliminate the possibility of entry errors, you will use the Before Change event to update the eligibility of an employee automatically. Refer to Figure 10.18 as you complete Step 2.

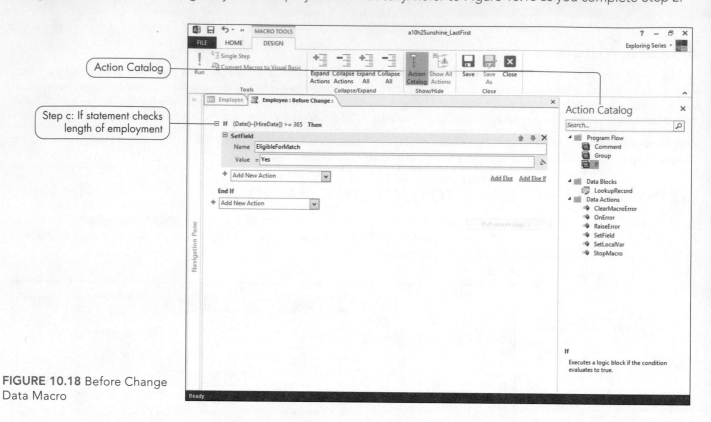

FIGURE 10.18 Before Change Data Macro

a. Switch to Design view. Click **Create Data Macros** in the Field, Record & Table Events group on the DESIGN tab and click **Before Change**.

The Macro Designer displays.

b. Drag the **If statement** from the Program Flow folder in the Action Catalog to the Add New Action box in the Macro.

The structure of the If statement is added to the macro.

c. Type **(Date() – [HireDate]) >= 365** in the **Conditional expression box**.

The expression determines if the employee has been employed at least one year (or 365 days) by subtracting the employee's hire date from today's date and then evaluating that difference to determine if it is greater than or equal to 365. If true, the macro will set the value of the EligibleForMatch field to Yes.

d. Select **SetField** from the Add New Action arrow within the If action.

The SetField arguments are added to the macro.

e. Type **el** in the **Name box** (and Access displays *EligibleForMatch*, the field name it predicts you are looking for). Press **Tab** to accept the EligibleForMatch field.

f. Type **yes** in the **Value box**.

Access checks the EligibleForMatch check box if the length of employment expression evaluates to true.

g. Save and close the macro. Save the Employee table.

STEP 3 ›› TEST AND MODIFY A DATA MACRO

You decide to test the Before Change macro using the rest of the employee records (11–19). Change one field in each record in order to trigger the Before Change event and verify the macro correctly updates the EligibleForMatch check box. You will also add an extra condition to the If statement in the macro that will update the check box if the employee is not eligible for the match. Refer to Figure 10.19 as you complete Step 3.

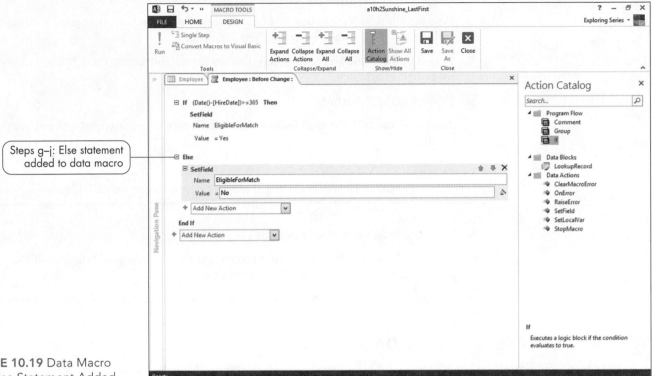

FIGURE 10.19 Data Macro with Else Statement Added

a. Switch to Datasheet view.

   To test the accuracy of the data macro, you will retype the 401k (percent) for records 11 through 19 in order to trigger the Before Change event. The macro automatically selects the EligibleForMatch check box for the appropriate records. Later, when new records are added to the table, the macro will run each time a record is entered.

b. Type **0.03** in the **401K column** of record 11 (Sally Keller). Click in the **401K column** of row 12.

   Because employee Sally Keller was hired on 5/19/2009, she is eligible for the 401k match. The data macro checks the check box.

c. Type **0.1** in the **401K column** of record 12. Click in the **401K column** of row 13.

   Because employee Samantha Jackson was hired on 6/3/2008, she is eligible for the 401k match. The data macro checks the check box.

d. Repeat the process for the remaining records.

   You wonder if the macro would uncheck an employee with an incorrectly checked EligibleForMatch check box. You decide to test the data macro for this condition.

e. Click the **EligibleForMatch check box** for your record and press ⬇ to trigger the macro.

   You realize that the check box remains checked even though you are not eligible. You decide to modify the data macro to update the check box if the employee is not eligible for the match.

f. Switch to Design view. Click **Create Data Macros** in the Field, Record & Table Events group on the TABLE TOOLS DESIGN tab and click **Before Change**.

The Macro Designer displays showing the If statement you set up earlier.

g. Click the **If statement** and click the **Add Else hyperlink** to add the Else statement.

You will add another SetField statement to uncheck the EligibleForMatch check box when employees are employed for less than one year.

h. Type **s** in the **Add New Action box** (and Access displays *SetField*, the action it thinks you are looking for). Press **Tab** to accept the SetField action.

i. Type **el** in the **Name box** (and Access displays *EligibleForMatch*). Press **Tab** to accept the field EligibleForMatch.

j. Type **no** in the **Value box**.

Access will uncheck the eligible check box if the length of employment expression evaluates to false.

TROUBLESHOOTING: Access attempts to add the Now function when you type no. Press Esc.

---

k. Save the macro. Close the macro. Save the Employee table.

l. Switch to Datasheet view, locate your record, and then change your proposed 401K contribution to **0.05**. Press ↓ to save your change.

The check box is unchecked by the data macro because you are not eligible for the match.

STEP 4 ≫ CREATE A NAMED DATA MACRO

Terry wants to be notified when any changes are made to the Employee table. You decide to create a named data macro that will send an e-mail to her whenever a change is made to the Employee table. Refer to Figure 10.20 as you complete Step 4.

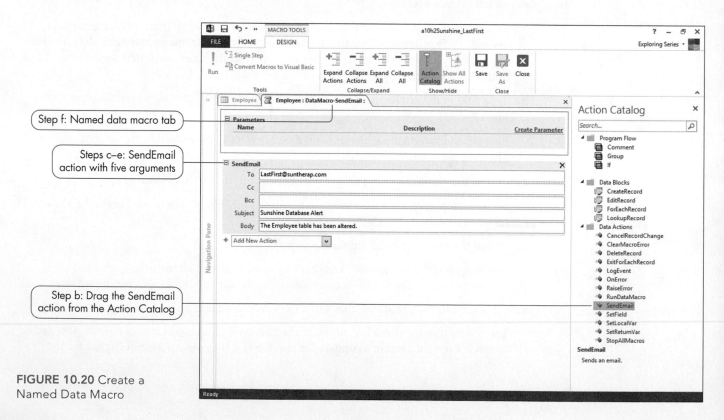

FIGURE 10.20 Create a Named Data Macro

a. Switch to Design view. Click **Create Data Macros** and click **Create Named Macro** in the Field, Record & Table Events group on the TABLE TOOLS DESIGN tab.

The Macro Designer displays.

b. Drag the **SendEmail action** from the Data Actions folder in the Action Catalog to the Add New Action box.

The SendEmail action and its five arguments are added to the macro.

c. Type your e-mail address in the **To argument box**. Skip the Cc and Bcc arguments.

> **TROUBLESHOOTING:** Your instructor may provide you with an alternate e-mail address to complete this step.

d. Type **Sunshine Database Alert** in the **Subject argument box**.

e. Type **The Employee table has been altered.** (include the period) in the **Body argument box**.

f. Save the macro as **DataMacro-SendEmail**. Close the macro.

g. Save the Employee table. Close the table.

STEP 5 ≫ ATTACH A NAMED DATA MACRO TO A FORM

You will attach the named data macro to a form event because many updates to the Employee table will be done through the Employees form. You decide to use the After Update event as the trigger for the send e-mail macro. Refer to Figure 10.21 as you complete Step 5.

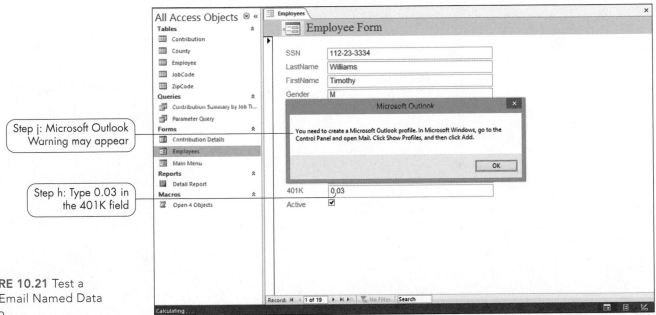

Step j: Microsoft Outlook Warning may appear

Step h: Type 0.03 in the 401K field

FIGURE 10.21 Test a SendEmail Named Data Macro

a. Open the Employees form in Design view.

b. Click **After Update** on the Event tab of the Property Sheet.

The ellipsis (…) displays on the right side of the After Update event.

c. Click the **ellipsis (…)**, click **Macro Builder** if necessary, and then click **OK**.

The Macro Designer displays.

d. Click the **Add New Action arrow** and select the **RunDataMacro action** from the list.

e. Select **Employee.DataMacro-SendEmail** using the Macro Name arrow.

f. Save and close the macro.

g. Save the Employees form and switch to Form view.

h. Type the existing 401k percent in the **401K field** of the first record (Timothy Williams).

i. Press **Tab** twice to advance to the second employee.

As soon as you move to the second employee, the After Update event is triggered and the SendEmail macro is activated. Access attempts to send an e-mail using the parameters you typed in Step 4.

TROUBLESHOOTING: If an e-mail client is not set up on the computer you are using, you may have to cancel this step and stop the macro. When your computer is correctly configured to send the e-mail, the macro will run as expected.

---

j. Click **OK** if you receive the warning message shown in Figure 10.21. Click **OK** again and click **Stop All Macros**.

If the warning message was not received as shown in Figure 10.21, click **Allow**. Check your e-mail after a few minutes to see if you received the Sunshine Database Alert message.

k. Save and close the form.

l. Keep the database open if you plan to continue with Hands-On Exercise 3. If not, close the database and exit Access.

Structured Query Language

Until now, whenever you wanted to ask a question about the data in a database, you created a query using the query Design view. The query Design view enables you to select the tables you need and select the required fields from those tables. You can also add criteria and sorting in the query design grid. Whenever you create a query using the query Design view, you create a Structured Query Language (SQL) statement simultaneously. Access stores the SQL statement in the background. In this section, you will learn the basics of SQL, the correlation between query Design view and SQL view, and how to use an SQL statement in forms and reports.

Understanding the Fundamentals of SQL

STEP 1▶ **Structured Query Language (SQL)** is the industry-standard language for defining, manipulating, and retrieving the data in a database. SQL was developed at IBM in the early 1970s. Since then, Microsoft has developed its own version of SQL for Microsoft Access, which varies slightly from the industry-standard SQL language. Although you can use SQL to create and modify tables, this section will be limited to the retrieval of data. All of the queries you created so far in this textbook were created using the query Design view; however, they could have been created using SQL. In fact, all Access queries use an SQL statement—behind the scenes—to extract data from tables.

When you learn SQL, you are learning the data retrieval and data manipulation language of all the industry-leading databases—SQL Server, Oracle, and Sybase, to name a few. If you learn SQL in Access, your skills will be useful when you work in these other database environments. SQL is also used to extract data from a Web database.

Figure 10.22 shows a basic query that was created using the query Design view. This query extracts all records from the Contribution table for the employee with SSN 456667778. Figure 10.23 shows the results in Datasheet view; the results contain 12 records. You can switch to SQL view to examine the statements generated by any query you create. To switch to SQL view from any query view, click the View arrow, and then select SQL View (see Figure 10.23).

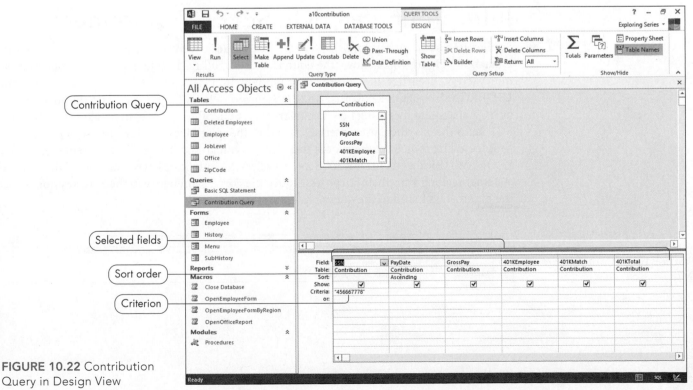

FIGURE 10.22 Contribution Query in Design View

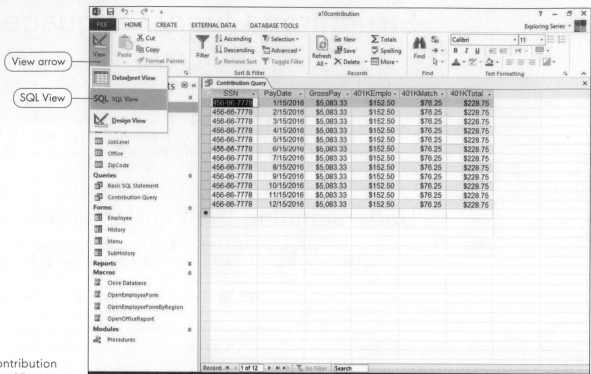

FIGURE 10.23 Contribution Query in Datasheet View

SQL View

When you are working with queries in Access, you can switch to SQL view using three methods. You can click the View arrow and select SQL View from the list of options, you can right-click the query tab and select SQL View from this list, or, from the open query, you can click the small SQL icon at the bottom right of the Access window.

Interpreting an SQL SELECT Statement

STEP 2 ▶▶

Similar to a select query, an **SQL SELECT statement** is used to retrieve data from tables in a database. Figure 10.24 shows the equivalent SQL SELECT statement of the Contribution query created earlier in Design view (shown in Figure 10.22). The words shown in UPPERCASE are SQL keywords. An **SQL keyword** defines the purpose and the structure of an SQL statement. Learning how to construct an SQL SELECT statement takes time because SQL lacks the graphical user interface found in the query Design view. To use SQL, you will first learn the four basic keywords found in a typical SQL SELECT statement—SELECT, FROM, WHERE, and ORDER BY. Table 10.2 lists the four basic keywords of an SQL SELECT statement, along with their purposes. Notice the correlation between the SQL keywords and the parameters found in the query Design view.

FIGURE 10.24 Contribution Query in SQL View

Keyword	Purpose
	TABLE 10.2 Four Basic Keywords of an SQL SELECT Statement and Their Purposes
Keyword	**Purpose**
SELECT	Specifies the fields to include in the query
FROM	Specifies the table or tables where the fields can be found
WHERE	Sets the criteria for the rows in the results
ORDER BY	Determines how the rows will be sorted

Dissect an SQL SELECT Statement: SELECT and FROM Keywords

The **SELECT keyword** instructs Access to return the specific fields from one or more tables (or queries). When a query or expression containing a SELECT statement is executed, Access searches the specified table (or tables), extracts the designated data, and displays the results. The **FROM keyword** specifies the table (or tables) that will be searched. In Figure 10.24, the SQL statement begins as follows:

SELECT Contribution.SSN, Contribution.PayDate, Contribution.GrossPay,

Contribution.[401KEmployee], Contribution.[401KMatch],

Contribution.[401KTotal]

FROM Contribution

In the statement above, field names are listed after the SELECT statement and are separated by commas. If two fields from two different tables have the same name, the table name prefix followed by a dot is required. In the above example, *Contribution.* appears before each field name because the same field names appear in other tables in the database. Some field names, such as 401KEmployee, 401KMatch, and 401KTotal, are enclosed by brackets [ ] when a field name has a leading numeric character. In the above example, the FROM command is instructing Access to pull data from the Contribution table.

Instead of specifying the individual field names in SQL, you can use the asterisk character (*) to select all of the fields in a table. For example, the following SELECT statement returns all fields and records from the Contribution table and displays the results in a datasheet:

SELECT *

FROM Contribution;

Dissect an SQL Statement: WHERE Keyword

After you select the tables and fields using SELECT and FROM, you can then filter the resulting records using the WHERE keyword. The **WHERE keyword** specifies the criteria that records must match to be included in the results. If your query does not include the WHERE keyword, the query will return all records from the table(s). In Figure 10.24, the SQL statement contains the following clause:

WHERE (((Contribution.SSN)="456667778"))

In this example, the WHERE clause specifies that only records with SSN equal to 456667778 will display in the results. Because the SSN field is a text field, the quotes are required around the SSN criterion.

Dissect an SQL Statement: ORDER BY Keyword

Typically, you want the query results to be arranged in a particular order. The ***ORDER BY keyword*** is used to sort the records by a certain field in either ascending or descending order. The ORDER BY clause must be added to the end of an SQL statement after the WHERE clause. In Figure 10.24, the SQL statement contains the following clause:

ORDER BY Contribution.PayDate;

In the statement above, the ORDER BY clause sorts the records in ascending order by PayDate. To sort in descending order, add DESC to the end of the ORDER BY clause. To sort the above records beginning with the most recent pay date, the statement would become as follows:

ORDER BY Contribution.PayDate DESC;

Learn Advanced SQL Statements

The easiest way to learn more advanced SQL statements is to create Access queries in Design view and then view the SQL statement in SQL view. Although some statements might seem complex at first, the more you work with SQL, the easier it will become to understand SQL statements. You will begin to recognize that each SQL statement contains a shared syntax. For example, most SQL statements begin with SELECT and end with a semicolon (;).

Action queries can also be translated into SQL statements. Update queries, Append queries, Make Table queries, and Delete queries each have their equivalent SQL keywords and syntax. For example, suppose you wanted to add all the records in Figure 10.23 to a new table named Archive. To do this, you would create a Make Table query. The equivalent SQL statement would be:

SELECT Contribution.SSN, Contribution.PayDate, Contribution.GrossPay,

Contribution.[401KEmployee], Contribution.[401KMatch],

Contribution.[401KTotal] INTO Archive

FROM Contribution

WHERE (((Contribution.SSN)="456667778"))

ORDER BY Contribution.PayDate;

Using an SQL SELECT Statement as a Record Source

When you create a form or a report in Access, the first step is to choose a record source in the Navigation Pane. The record source can be either a table or a query, depending on the complexity of the data. The next step is to click the Create tab and choose the Form tool, Report tool, or another tool so that Access can create the new object. A sample report based on the Contribution table is shown in Figure 10.25.

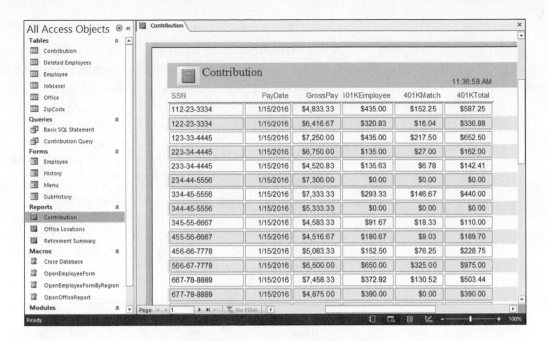

FIGURE 10.25 Contribution Report Created with Contribution Table

Create an SQL Record Source for a Report

Based on the information you learned about SQL in this section, you should be able to create an SQL record source for a report. You know that the basic structure of an SQL statement is as follows:

SELECT field names

FROM table name

WHERE specified criteria must be met

ORDER BY field name;

STEP 3 The sample Contribution report, as shown in Figure 10.25, contains all of the records from the Contribution table; therefore no WHERE clause is required. The records are not sorted in a different order than the SSN order found in the Contribution table, so no ORDER BY clause is needed. Based on this information, the SQL statement for the record source of the Contribution report is as follows:

SELECT *

FROM Contribution;

Add an SQL Record Source to a Report

Now that you know the SQL record source for the Contribution report, you can replace the existing record source (the Contribution table) with the SQL statement. The following are reasons for using an SQL statement for a record source:

- You can create a form or report without creating a new query (because the record source is contained in the object).

- It is easier to transfer a form or report to another database (because the record source is contained in the object).

- You can construct the record source of a report at run-time using VBA (based on user input).

To replace a report's record source, do the following:

1. Open the report in Design view and open the Property Sheet.
2. Select Report using the Selection arrow at the top of the Property Sheet.
3. Click the DATA tab and click in the Record Source property box.
4. Delete the existing value (for example, Contribution) from the Record Source and type the SQL statement, such as *SELECT * FROM Contribution;* in its place, as shown in Figure 10.26.
5. Click View in the Views group on the DESIGN tab to display the Contribution report in Print Preview to test the change.

For example, in the sample Contribution report, you could open the report in Design view, and then open the Property Sheet. Locate the Record Source property on the Data tab, and then paste the SQL statement from the Contribution query (as shown in Figure 10.24) into the Record Source property box. View the report in Print Preview, as shown in Figure 10.27.

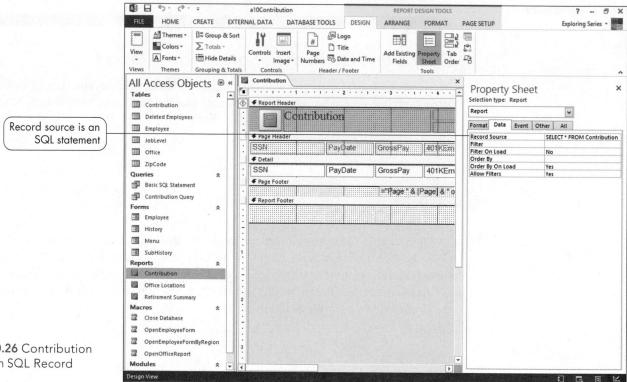

FIGURE 10.26 Contribution Report with SQL Record Source

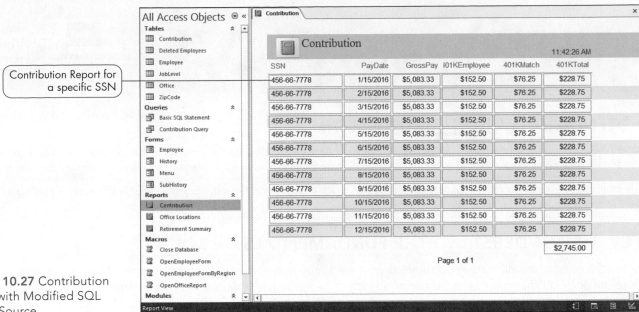

FIGURE 10.27 Contribution Report with Modified SQL Record Source

Copy an SQL Statement from SQL View

The query discussed earlier, shown in Figure 10.22, contains SSN criteria and is sorted by PayDate. When you switch the query to SQL view, as shown in Figure 10.24, the SQL statement is displayed. Because the SQL statement is in text format, you can copy the statement and paste it into the record source of a report.

> **TIP A Lengthy SQL Statement**
>
> When you paste an SQL statement into a record source, it might appear that the statement will not fit into the property box. However, the Record Source property can hold most SQL statements, including those statements that are very long. Use Shift+F2 to open the Zoom window to view or paste a lengthy SQL statement.

Quick Concepts

1. What is the purpose of Structured Query Language (SQL)? *p. 865*
2. What is the purpose of the SQL SELECT statement? *p. 866*
3. Why would you use an SQL statement as a record source for a report? *p. 869*

3 Structured Query Language

SQL will only be used in the Sunshine database in special circumstances. You suggest to Nancy that you use an SQL statement for the record source of two reports. You explain that an SQL statement can be used in place of a table or query record source.

Skills covered: Understand the Fundamentals of SQL • Create a Query and View the Equivalent SQL Statement • Using an SQL SELECT Statement as a Record Source

---

STEP 1 >> UNDERSTAND THE FUNDAMENTALS OF SQL

You need a query that will display employees who are social workers, and you have decided to try creating it in SQL before making any changes to the Sunshine objects. You create a new query, and then immediately switch to SQL view, where you can practice writing an SQL statement. Refer to Figure 10.28 as you complete Step 1.

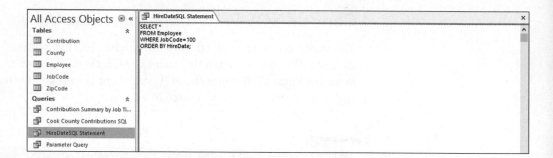

FIGURE 10.28 Basic SQL Statement

a. Open *a10h2Sunshine_LastFirst* if you closed it at the end of Hands-On Exercise 2. Click the **FILE tab**, click **Save As**, click **Save As**, and then type **a10h3Sunshine_LastFirst**, changing *h2* to *h3*. Click **Save**.

b. Click the **CREATE tab** and click **Query Design** in the Queries group.

The Show Table dialog box displays.

c. Close the Show Table dialog box without adding any tables.

You will create a query using SQL statements rather than the usual query design interface.

d. Click **SQL** in the Results group.

The abbreviated SELECT statement displays in the SQL window.

e. Move the insertion point after *SELECT* and before the semicolon (;). Complete the following SQL statement in the SQL window and click **Run** in the Results group.

SELECT *
FROM Employee;

The records for all 19 employees are displayed in the results. All fields from the Employee table also display.

f. Click the **View arrow** and select **SQL View** from the list of options.

The current SQL statement displays in the SQL window.

g. Move the insertion point before the semicolon (;), revise the SQL statement as shown below, and then click **Run**.

SELECT *
FROM Employee
WHERE JobCode = 100;

You added a WHERE clause to extract only the employees who are social workers (JobCode = 100). Only eight employees are displayed in the results.

h. Click the **View arrow** and select **SQL View**. Move the insertion point before the semicolon (;), revise the SQL statement as shown below, and then click **Run**.

SELECT *
FROM Employee
WHERE JobCode = 100
ORDER BY HireDate;

The same eight employees are displayed in the results, except now they display in HireDate order.

i. Save the query as **HireDateSQL Statement**. Close the query.

STEP 2 ≫ CREATE A QUERY AND VIEW THE EQUIVALENT SQL STATEMENT

You need to create a query that will show all the 401k contributions for Cook County employees. You want to see the equivalent SQL statement after you create the query in Design view first. Refer to Figure 10.29 as you complete Step 2.

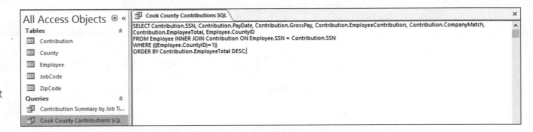

FIGURE 10.29 SQL Statement to Extract Cook County Contributions

a. Click the **CREATE tab** and click **Query Design** in the Queries group.

The Show Table dialog box displays.

b. Add the Contribution and Employee tables to the Query design using the Show Table dialog box and close the Show Table dialog box.

c. Add all the fields from the Contribution table to the query design grid. Add the CountyID field from the Employee table. Run the query.

All the fields of all 219 contributions are displayed in the results. You need to add the criterion for Cook County.

d. Switch to Design view and type **1** in the **CountyID criteria row**. Run the query.

The numeral 1 is the Cook County ID and is used as the criterion for the search. Forty-eight contributions now display in the results. You need to sort the results by descending EmployeeTotal amount.

e. Switch to Design view and select **Descending** from the EmployeeTotal sort row. Run the query.

The same 48 contributions are now displayed in descending EmployeeTotal order.

f. Switch to SQL view to see the equivalent SQL statement.

You learned how to create a query in Design view first and viewed the equivalent SQL statement in SQL view.

g. Save the query as **Cook County Contributions SQL**. Close the query.

STEP 3 ➤ USING AN SQL SELECT STATEMENT AS A RECORD SOURCE

Terry asks you to create an employee report sorted by the JobCode field. You decide to create the report based on the Employee table using the Report tool. You will then replace the Employee table record source with an SQL statement. Refer to Figure 10.30 as you complete Step 3.

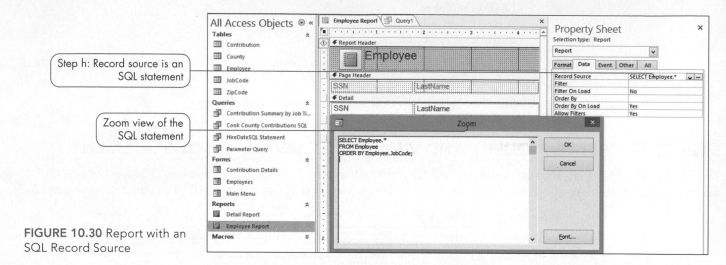

FIGURE 10.30 Report with an SQL Record Source

a. Click the **Employee table**, click the **CREATE tab**, and then click **Report** in the Reports group.

Access creates a new tabular layout report.

b. Switch to Design view, open the Property Sheet, select the report, and then verify that the Record Source on the Data tab for the new report says *Employee*. Close the Property Sheet.

c. Click the **CREATE tab** and click **Query Design** in the Queries group.

The Show Table dialog box displays.

d. Add the Employee table to the query design using the Show Table dialog box. Close the Show Table dialog box.

e. Add the * field from the Employee table to the query design grid. Run the query.

Nineteen employees are displayed in the results.

f. Switch to Design view and add the JobCode field to the query design grid. Uncheck the **Show box** for JobCode and select **Ascending** from the JobCode sort row. Run the query.

The same 19 employees are displayed in Job Code order.

g. Switch to SQL view and copy the statement in the SQL window.

h. Click the **EMPLOYEE tab** and open the Property Sheet. Delete the existing Record Source and paste the SQL statement you copied into the box. Press **Shift+F2** and compare your statement to Figure 10.30.

i. Close the Zoom dialog box and open the report in Print Preview to test the new record source.

Because the report contains all the fields for the 19 employees, the report does not fit onto one page; however, you can leave the report as is.

j. Save the report as **Employee Report** and close it.

k. Close the query without saving it.

Chapter Objectives Review

After reading this chapter, you have accomplished the following objectives:

1. **Understand the purpose of a macro.**
   - Understanding the purpose of a macro: A macro is an Access object that enables you to execute an action or series of actions based on the status of a button, a form, or a report. A macro can be run to accomplish repetitive or routine tasks automatically.

2. **Create a stand-alone macro.**
   - Creating a stand-alone macro: A stand-alone macro displays as an object in the Navigation Pane and can be run independently of other objects. You use the Macro Designer to create a stand-alone macro. To run a stand-alone macro, double-click the macro name in the Navigation Pane.

3. **Use the Macro Designer.**
   - Using the Macro Designer: The Macro Designer is a tool in Access that makes it easier to create and edit macros. The user interface simplifies the tasks of adding actions and parameters while building macros.

4. **Attach an embedded macro to an event.**
   - Attaching an embedded macro to an event: Embedded macros are always attached to an event of a control on a form or report, or to an event of the form or report object itself. They can only be run from within the object itself.
   - Attach an embedded macro to a report event: You can create a control that automatically creates an embedded macro for you (such as the command button control) or attach an embedded macro to an event by clicking the ellipsis (…) in the Property Sheet. A command button can be placed on a report that will print the report, close it, or close the database automatically.

5. **Identify when to use a data macro.**
   - Identifying when to use a data macro: Data macros are only used with table events. You might add a data macro to a table to verify that a customer has no outstanding invoices before placing a new order, to keep a log of any changes made to a specific table, or to send a confirmation e-mail when a contributor makes a donation. A form based on a table that contains a data macro inherits the logic of the table.

6. **Create an event-driven data macro.**
   - Creating an event-driven macro: Event-driven data macros are triggered when a table event, such as After Delete or Before Change, occurs.

   - Testing and modifying a data macro: To attach a data macro to a table event, open the table you want to add the data macro to (in Design view) and click Create Data Macros in the Field, Record & Table Events group on the Design tab; to modify a data macro, reopen the macro and edit as needed.

7. **Create a named data macro.**
   - Creating a named data macro: You can access these macros from anywhere in the database. You can run the named data macro from inside another macro using the RunDataMacro action.
   - Attaching a named data macro to a Form: A named data macro can be run from within a form, for example, after a record is updated, an e-mail can be automatically generated.

8. **Understand the fundamentals of SQL.**
   - Understanding the fundamentals of SQL: Structured Query Language (SQL) is the industry-standard language for defining, manipulating, and retrieving the data in a database. In fact, all Access queries use an SQL SELECT statement—behind the scenes—to extract data from tables.

9. **Interpret an SQL SELECT statement.**
   - Interpreting an SQL SELECT statement: When you view an SQL SELECT statement in SQL view, the words shown in UPPERCASE are SQL keywords. An SQL keyword defines the purpose and the structure of an SQL statement. The four basic keywords found in a typical SQL SELECT statement are SELECT, FROM, WHERE, and ORDER BY.

10. **Use an SQL SELECT statement as a record source.**
    - Creating a query and viewing the equivalent SQL statement: Once a query is created using Design view, the SQL statements can be viewed by switching to SQL view. A correlation exists between each SQL statement and a query parameter.
    - Using an SQL statement as a record source: You can also use an SQL SELECT statement as the record source for a form or a report rather than a table or a query. Locate the Record Source property of the form or report and either type an SQL statement into the property box or copy and paste a statement from the SQL view window.

Key Terms Matching

Match the key terms with their definitions. Write the key term letter by the appropriate numbered definition.

a. Argument
b. Embedded macro
c. Event
d. Data macro
e. FROM keyword
f. Macro
g. Macro Designer

h. ORDER BY keyword
i. SELECT keyword
j. SQL keyword
k. SQL SELECT statement
l. Stand-alone macro
m. Structured Query Language (SQL)
n. WHERE keyword

1. _____ A series of actions that can be programmed to automate tasks. **p. 842**

2. _____ Database object that you create and use independently of other controls or objects. **p. 842**

3. _____ Occurs when a user enters, edits, or deletes data; also occurs when a user opens, uses, or closes a form or report. **p. 843**

4. _____ A macro that executes when an event attached to a control or object occurs. **p. 843**

5. _____ User interface that enables you to create and edit macros. **p. 844**

6. _____ A variable, constant, or expression that is needed to produce the output for an action. **p. 844**

7. _____ The industry-standard language for defining, manipulating, and retrieving the data in a database. **p. 865**

8. _____ Defines the purpose and the structure of an SQL statement. **p. 866**

9. _____ Block of text that is used to retrieve data from the tables in a database. **p. 866**

10. _____ The keyword that specifies the table (or tables) that will be searched. **p. 867**

11. _____ The keyword that instructs Access to return the specific fields from one or more tables. **p. 867**

12. _____ The keyword that is used to sort the records by a certain field in either ascending or descending order. **p. 868**

13. _____ The keyword that specifies the criteria that records must match to be included in the results. **p. 867**

14. _____ Executes a series of actions when a table event occurs. **p. 855**

Multiple Choice

1. Which statement about macros is false?

   (a) Access supports embedded macros.

   (b) Macros can be used with tables.

   (c) The Macro Designer makes it easier to create macros.

   (d) All macros display in the Navigation Pane.

2. Which tool automatically creates an embedded macro?

   (a) Macro Designer

   (b) Command Button Wizard

   (c) Report Wizard

   (d) Form Wizard

3. Which statement is true about a stand-alone macro?

   (a) A stand-alone macro is created with the Macro Designer.

   (b) Stand-alone macros exist outside the database.

   (c) Stand-alone macros contain VBA code.

   (d) Stand-alone macros can only be used in a table.

4. Which of these is a variable, constant, or expression that is needed to produce the output for a macro action?

   (a) Command

   (b) Statement

   (c) Argument

   (d) Event

5. Which statement is false for a named data macro?

   (a) It must be created in a table.

   (b) It cannot be attached to an event.

   (c) It can be modified using the Macro Designer.

   (d) It can be referenced using RunDataMacro.

6. Which is not a valid event?

   (a) Before Update

   (b) On Close

   (c) If Open

   (d) After Insert

7. Which statement is not true about SQL?

   (a) It was invented originally by Microsoft.

   (b) When you create a query, SQL is created automatically.

   (c) SELECT statements retrieve data from tables.

   (d) SQL lacks a graphical user interface.

8. Which SQL keyword returns a subset of the table records based on criteria?

   (a) SELECT

   (b) FROM

   (c) WHERE

   (d) ORDER BY

9. Which character is required at the end of an SQL statement?

   (a) >

   (b) :

   (c) "

   (d) ;

10. Which of the following is not a valid record source for a report?

    (a) A query

    (b) A SELECT statement

    (c) A table

    (d) A macro

1 Advertising Specialists, Inc.

Advertising Specialists, Inc., is a leading advertising agency with offices in Atlanta, Chicago, Miami, and Boston. The company has asked you to create a new form named Chicago Employees that only contains employees in Chicago. You have also been asked to create a menu that users can use to open the three reports and one form. First, you will create a macro that opens the Switchboard Manager (the feature that enables you to create a menu system). However, you will then decide to use the Form Design to create a menu manually instead. This exercise follows the same set of skills as used in Hands-On Exercises 1 and 3 in the chapter. Refer to Figure 10.31 as you complete this exercise.

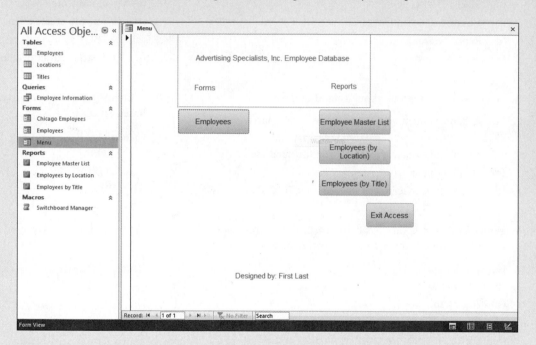

FIGURE 10.31 Menu Created with Command Buttons

a. Open *a10p1Advertise*. Click the **FILE tab**, click **Save As**, click **Save As**, and then type **a10p1Advertise_LastFirst**. Click **Save**.

b. Open the Employees table and add yourself as a new record. Type **88888** as your EmployeeID. Type your last name, first name, and gender. Use the same values as the previous record (Marder) to complete the remaining fields. Close the table.

c. Open the Employees form in Design view. Click the **FILE tab**, click **Save As**, click **Save Object As**, and then click **Save As**. Type **Chicago Employees** in the **Save As dialog box** and click **OK**.

d. Open the Property Sheet, click the **Data tab**, and then click the **Record Source property**. Press **Shift+F2** to see a zoom view of the record source property.

e. Type **Select * From Employees Where LocationID="L03";** in the **Record Source property** to replace the Employees table with an SQL statement. Include the ending semicolon (;).

f. Click **OK** and save the form. Switch to Form view. Advance through all the records to verify that only Chicago (L03) employees are showing. Close the form.

g. Add the Switchboard Manager to the database by creating a macro as follows:
   • Click the **CREATE tab** and click **Macro**.
   • Type **RunMenuCommand** in the **Add New Action box**. Press **Enter**.
   • Type **SwitchboardManager** in the **Command box**.
   • Save the macro as **Switchboard Manager**.
   • Close the Macro Designer.

h. Double-click the **Switchboard Manager macro** in the Navigation Pane. The Switchboard Manager starts, but you decide not to create a switchboard. When the warning message displays, click **No** to close the dialog box.

   You decide to use Form Design and create a menu manually.

i. Click the **CREATE tab** and click **Form Design** in the Forms group.

j. Add the following labels, using Figure 10.31 as a guide:
- A title label: **Advertising Specialists, Inc. Employee Database**
- A subtitle label: **Forms**
- A subtitle label: **Reports**

k. Use the Command Button Wizard to add the following buttons, using Figure 10.31 as a guide:
- A button to open the Employees form. Set the text to display on the button as **Employees** and name the button **cmdEmployees**. Adjust the button position and size as shown.
- A button to open the Employee Master List report. Set the text to display on the button as **Employee Master List** and name the button **cmdMasterEmployee**. Adjust the button position and size as shown.
- A button to open the Employees by Location report. Set the text to display on the button as **Employees (by Location)** and name the button **cmdEmployeesLocation**. Adjust the button position and size as shown.
- A button to open the Employees by Title report. Set the text to display on the button as **Employees (by Title)** and name the button **cmdEmployeesTitle**. Adjust the button position and size as shown.

l. Add the following button, using Figure 10.31 as a guide:
- A button to quit the application. Set the text to display on the button as **Exit Access** and name the button **cmdExitAccess**. Adjust the button position and size as shown.

m. Add the following design elements, using Figure 10.31 as a guide:
- A rectangle surrounding the title and the subtitle labels.
- A label at the bottom of the report: **Designed by** *your name*.

n. Save the form with the name **Menu**.

o. View the Menu form in Form view. Click each button to test the functionality. Click the **Exit Access button** to test it; if Access closes, then your testing is complete.

p. Close Access.

q. Submit based on your instructor's directions.

2 | Reliable Insurance, Inc.

Reliable Insurance, Inc., has decided to raise the salary of any employee with a good performance rating by 5%. You will create a data macro to help them implement this new policy. The company also creates a spreadsheet containing all employees from location L01 (Atlanta). The spreadsheet is faxed to the corporate office each month. The office manager would like to automate this process with a macro. This exercise follows the same set of skills used in Hands-On Exercises 1 and 2 in the chapter. Refer to Figure 10.32 as you complete this exercise.

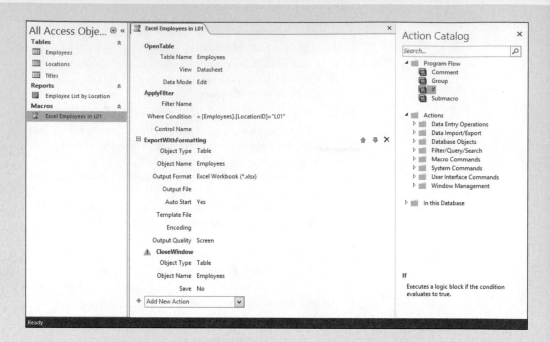

FIGURE 10.32 Macro to Export Data to Excel

a. Open *a10p2Reliable*. Click the **FILE tab**, click **Save As**, click **Save As**, and then type **a10p2Reliable_LastFirst**. Click **Save**.

b. Open the Employees table and add yourself as a new record. Type **88888** as your EmployeeID. Type your last name, first name, and gender. Type **L01** for your location. Use the same values as the previous record (Marder) to complete the remaining fields.

c. Switch to Design view and add a new field under the Salary field, called **SalaryAdjusted**, with data type **Currency**. Save the table.

d. Click **Create Data Macros** in the Field, Record & Table Events group and click the **Before Change event**. The Macro Designer opens. Follow these steps:

   • Drag the **If statement** from the Program Flow folder in the Action Catalog to the Add New Action box in the Macro.
   • Type [**Performance**] = "**Good**" in the **Conditional expression box**.
   • Select **SetField** using the Add New Action arrow.
   • Type **SalaryAdjusted** in the **Name box**.
   • Type [**Salary**]*1.05 in the **Value box**.
   • Click the **Add Else command**.
   • Select **SetField** using the Add New Action arrow.
   • Type **SalaryAdjusted** in the **Name box**.
   • Type [**Salary**] in the **Value box**.
   • Save the Data Macro.
   • Close the Data Macro.
   • Save the table.

e. Switch to Datasheet view. Retype **Good** in the **Performance field** of the third employee (Johnson). Press ⬇ to move to the next record and activate the data macro.

   The new increased salary displays in the SalaryAdjusted field.

f. Repeat the process for all Good employees and upgrade your performance from Average to Good and press ⬇. Close the table.

g. Click the **CREATE tab** and click **Macro** in the Macros & Code group to open the Macro Designer. You will create a macro to show employees with location L01.

h. Click in the **Add New Action box** and type **OpenTable**. Press **Enter**.

i. Add the following arguments:

Table Name	Employees
View	Datasheet *(default)*
Data Mode	Edit *(default)*

j. Click in the **Add New Action box** and type **ApplyFilter**. Press **Enter**.

k. Add the following arguments:

Filter Name	*(blank)*
Where Condition	[Employees].[LocationID]="L01"
Control Name	*(blank)*

l. Save the macro as **Excel Employees in L01**. Click **Run** in the Tools group to test the macro results so far. If the macro is working, the Employees table should open with only the L01 employees displayed. Close the filtered Employees table.

m. Click in the **Add New Action box** and type **ExportWithFormatting**. Press **Enter**.

n. Add the following arguments:

Object Type	Table *(default)*
Object Name	Employees
Output Format	Excel Workbook (*.xlsx)
Output File	*(optional: enter a file name and path)*
Auto Start	Yes
Template File	*(blank)*
Encoding	*(blank)*
Output Quality	Screen

o. Click in the **Add New Action box** and type **CloseWindow**. Press **Enter**.

p. Add the following arguments:

Object Type	Table
Object Name	Employees
Save	No

q. Save the macro. Close the macro. Run the macro by double-clicking the macro name in the Navigation Pane. The results should export the L01 employees to an Excel spreadsheet (you must designate the location if you left the Output File blank above). Close the spreadsheet, and the macro closes the Employees table.

r. Close Access.

s. Submit based on your instructor's directions.

1 Northwind Exporters

ANALYSIS CASE

Northwind Exporters provides specialty foods to businesses around the world. You have been asked to filter the orders form so that each employee can see only his or her orders. You will also filter a report using an SQL statement. Refer to Figure 10.33 as you complete this exercise.

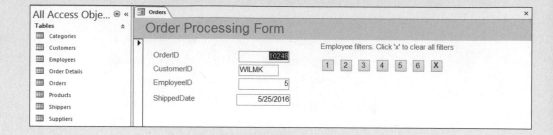

FIGURE 10.33 Filtering with an Embedded Macro

a. Open *a10m1Exporters*. Click the **FILE tab**, click **Save As**, click **Save As**, and then type **a10m1Exporters_LastFirst**. Click **Save**.

b. Open the Employees table and note that nine employees are shown. Close the table.

c. Open the Orders form. Advance through the orders using the Navigation Bar at the bottom of the form. Notice that the EmployeeID value is different for each order. Switch to Design view.

d. Add the first button to the form as shown in Figure 10.33. Click **Cancel** when the Command Button Wizard displays. Open the Property Sheet. Set the caption of the command button to **1**. Set the size of the button to **.25"** high and **.25"** wide.

   You are planning to create an embedded macro to filter the order records for Employee ID 1 when the command button is clicked.

e. Click the new **1 button** and in the Property Sheet, click the **On Click event**. Click the **ellipsis (...)** and with Macro Builder selected, click **OK** when the Choose Builder dialog box displays.

   The Macro Designer displays.

f. Type **ApplyFilter** in the **Add New Action box**. Type **[EmployeeID]=1** in the **Where Condition box**. Save and close the macro.

g. Switch to Form view and notice the total orders (50) as indicated in the Navigation Bar at the bottom of the form. Click **1** and notice the total orders (4) for EmployeeID 1 in the Navigation Bar. Advance through the orders, and then verify the EmployeeID is 1 for each order.

h. Switch to Design view, copy the **1 button**, paste it to the right of button 1, and then set **2** as the caption. In the Property Sheet, with button 2 selected, click the **On Click event**, and then click the **ellipsis (...)**. Modify the Where Condition box so it reads **2** instead of *1*. Test the new button in Form view.

i. Add buttons 3 to 6 using the same method as in step h.

DISCOVER

j. Create a seventh button with the caption **X** to remove the filters so all the orders will display in the form. Test each new button in Form view when finished and save the form.

k. Select the seven buttons. Click **Align** in the Sizing & Ordering group on the ARRANGE tab to align the tops of the seven buttons. Increase the horizontal spacing between the buttons so that about two dots of space remain between them. Save and close the form.

l. Open the Customers report and take note of the range of countries represented.

m. Switch to Design view. Open the Property Sheet, select the report, and then, on the DATA tab, click the **Record Source property**. Type **SELECT * FROM Customers WHERE Country = [Enter a country];** in the record source in place of the Customers table.

n. Save the report. Switch to Print Preview and type **USA** in the **Enter Parameter Value dialog box**. Click **OK** and close the report. Close Access.

o. State why you think it might be important to create a report that enables you to make selections according to the country code. Write a brief paragraph or two stating your reasons in a Word document and submit it to your instructor with the file name *a10m1Exporters.docx*.

p. Submit based on your instructor's directions.

2 Payroll Service, Inc.

 **ANALYSIS CASE**

Payroll Service, Inc., provides payroll services to mid-sized businesses in Massachusetts, Illinois, Colorado, and California. You have been assigned to help the company set up business logic rules using macros and data macros. Your first task is to restrict the number of exemptions an employee can claim (based on marital status). You begin by restricting single employees to only one exemption. You will also create a macro that will e-mail the current list of employees to the main office. The main office needs the list in HTML format. Finally, you will create an SQL record source for a report. Refer to Figure 10.34 as you complete this exercise.

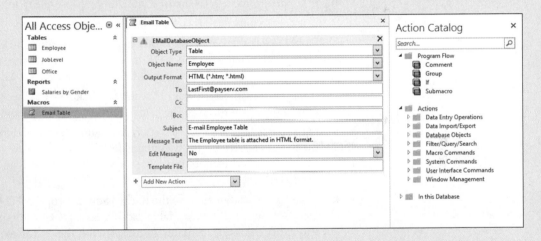

FIGURE 10.34 Stand-Alone Macro Sends a Database Object

a. Open *a10m2Salaries*. Click the **FILE tab**, click **Save As**, click **Save As**, and then type **a10m2Salaries_LastFirst**. Click **Save**.

b. Open the Employee table in Design view. Click **Create Data Macros** in the Field, Record & Table Events group and click the **Before Change event**.

The Macro Designer displays.

c. Drag the **If statement** from the Program Flow folder in the Action Catalog to the Add New Action box in the macro.

- Type **[MaritalStatus] = "single"** in the **Conditional expression box**.
- Select **SetField** from the Add New Action arrow.
- Type **Exemptions** in the **Name box**.
- Type **1** in the **Value box**.
- Save the Data Macro.
- Close the Data Macro.
- Save the table.

d. Switch to Datasheet view. In the first record, type **2** in the **Exemptions field**. Press ↓ to move to the second row to trigger the Before Change event and the data macro. The number *2* changes to *1*. Repeat the test on the second record. Close the table.

e. Click the **CREATE tab** and click **Macro** in the Macros & Code group to open the Macro Designer.

f. Click in the **Add New Action box** and type **EmailDatabaseObject**. Press **Enter**.

g. Add the following arguments:

Object Type	Table *(default)*
Object Name	Employee
Output Format	HTML (*.htm; *.html)
To	*your e-mail address*
Cc	*(blank)*
Bcc	*(blank)*
Subject	E-mail Employee Table
Message Text	The Employee table is attached in HTML format.
Edit Message	No
Template File	*(blank)*

h. Save the macro with the name **Email Table**. Close the macro.

The macro now displays in the Navigation Pane.

i. Double-click the **Email Table macro**. The macro runs and attempts to send the Employee table as an attachment. Click **OK** if you receive the Microsoft Outlook warning message, as shown in Figure 10.21. Click **OK** again and click **Stop All Macros**.

If the warning message was not received, click **Allow**. Check your e-mail after a few minutes to see if you received the E-mail Employee Table message.

DISCOVER j. Open the Salaries by Gender report in Design view. Open the Property Sheet and verify the Record Source property contains *Employee*. Determine from the database which job code refers to which job title. Note the job code for Associate Consultant and the data type for this field.

★ k. Type an SQL statement into the Record Source property. The report should include all records from the Employee table except Associate Consultants. Switch to Print Preview and verify the report contains 10 records with the overall average salary of $79,650.00. Save the report.

l. Close the report. Close Access.

m. Submit based on your instructor's directions.

3 | Loan Analysis

COLLABORATION CASE

In the following exercise, you will create a data macro to send an e-mail message if the loan for a customer is set to Adjustable. Then you will modify the SQL record source for a query to change its criterion. Finally, you will modify a report based on the modified query.

a. Open *a10m3Collaboration* and save it as **a10m3Collaboration_GroupName**. As a team, study the existing database and the relationship between the Customers and Loans tables.

Assign the following tasks to a team member:

b. Open the Loans table in Design view. Create an embedded After Update data macro. Create an If statement that will determine if the loan is set to Adjustable. If true, send an e-mail to yourself with the following information:

Subject: **Adjustable vs. Fixed Rates**

Body: **Please check our recently lowered fixed interest rate for this loan**.

Save and close the macro.

c. View the Loans table in Datasheet view. Save the table when prompted. In the record for L0001, set the Adjustable field to *Yes* by clicking in the check box and pressing [↓] to update the record. The update causes an e-mail to be sent to you if your computer is configured to do so. Otherwise, click **OK** in the Microsoft Outlook message box. Close the Loans table.

Assign the following task to a team member:

d. Open the Car Loans query in SQL view. Set the criterion so that the query displays mortgage loans. Return to Design view, observe the change, and then run the query. Save and close the query, and then rename it as **Mortgage Loans**.

Assign the following tasks to a team member:

e. Open the Customers table. For Customer C0008, add your first and last names and e-mail address to the table. Close the table.

f. Rename the Customer Auto Loans report as **Customer Mortgage Loans**. Open the report.

g. Collaborate with your team to determine what would be the best way to portray the Customer Mortgage Loans report. Make any design changes you see fit. Modify the report title to **Mortgage Loans**. Sort the records first by Last Name and then by Amount in ascending order.

h. View the report in Print Preview; the report should consist of one page. Save and close the report. Export the report as a Word document using the same name and save it as a Word document. Close the report and exit Word. Do not save the export steps.

i. Close the database. Exit Access. Submit the database and documents based on your instructor's directions.

Beyond the Classroom

Advanced SQL

RESEARCH CASE

Find a Web site that will teach you some additional SQL statements. Research the correct keywords to join two tables together. For example, find out how to list all of the fields and records from the Orders table and add the Customer Name field from the Customers table in the first column of the query results. Open the *a10b2Orders* database, save it as **a10b2Orders_LastFirst**, and then practice creating the SQL statements. Create a query in SQL view that performs the required task and save it as Orders by Customer. Submit the database *a10b2Orders_LastFirst* based on your instructor's directions.

Troubleshoot: Fix a Macro

DISASTER RECOVERY

Open the *a10b3Bonus* database and save the database as **a10b3Bonus_LastFirst**. A macro named Macro—Open Objects was created to open the Employees table, the Employees Form, and the Employees Report. The macro is not working properly; the third object does not display at all, and the first two objects are read-only—you want them to open in edit mode. Analyze the macro, diagnose the problems, and then fix the problems. Save and run the macro to ensure that it works properly. Submit the database *a10b3Bonus_LastFirst* based on your instructor's directions.

Meetings

SOFT SKILLS CASE **S**

You want to determine how many of the new employees in your database will attend orientation meetings on specific dates. You decide to create a command button to run a macro from a form that will display query results with meeting attendees. Open *a10b4Meetings*. Save a copy of the database as **a10b4Meetings_LastFirst**. In the New Employees Data Entry form, create a command button that will open the Orientation Meeting query. Place the button at the 5" mark on the horizontal ruler, aligned with the top of the SSN control. Set the caption of the button as **Run Orientation Meeting** and name the button **cmdOrientation**. Set the width of the button to **1.75"**. Test the button in Form view. When prompted, enter the meeting date of **11/5/2018**. Close the query. Save and close the form, and close the database. Exit Access. Submit the database *a10b4Meetings_LastFirst* based on your instructor's directions.

Capstone Exercise

You are employed at Specialty Foods, Ltd., a small international gourmet foods distributor. The company has asked you to modify the database and improve the reliability of the data entry process. You decide to create a few macros and also add a menu for the common forms and reports. You will also modify the record source of one of the reports.

Database File Setup

a. Open *a10c1Specialty*, click the **FILE tab**, click **Save As**, click **Save As**, and then type **a10c1Specialty_LastFirst**. Click **Save**.

Create an Event-Driven Data Macro

A new field, ExpectedShipDate, was added to the Orders table. You will populate this new field when a new order is added using a Data Macro.

a. Open the Orders table in Datasheet view, observe the data, and then switch to Design view.

b. Create a data macro attached to the Before Change event.

c. Use the SetField Action to populate the ExpectedShipDate in the table. The ExpectedShipDate will always be 10 days after the OrderDate.

d. Save the macro. Close the macro. Save the table.

Test the Data Macro

Change a value in the first record, and then move to the second record to trigger the macro.

a. Switch to Datasheet view of the Orders table.

b. Retype the OrderDate in the first record (Order No 10248) and press ⬇. The macro will be triggered and automatically fill in the ExpectedShipDate with a date 10 days after the OrderDate.

c. Repeat the test on the second and third records (10249 and 10250). Close the table.

Create a Menu Form

Create a menu form using the Form Design view. Add three command buttons for the three forms in the database, and then add three command buttons for the three reports in the database.

a. Open the Main Menu form in Design view.

b. Add three buttons below the Forms label that will open the three forms in the database: Enter Customers, Enter Employees, and Enter Suppliers (in that order). Set the

first one at the 2" mark on the vertical ruler and the 1" mark on the horizontal ruler. Set the height of the button to **0.5"** and the width to **1"**. The first button should have the caption **Enter Customers** with the button named as **cmdEnterCustomers**.

c. Repeat the same procedure for Enter Employees and Enter Suppliers, setting each button immediately below the one before it.

d. Add three buttons below the Reports label that will print preview the three reports in the database: Employees, Orders, and Products (in that order). Set the first one at the 2" mark on the vertical ruler and the 4" mark on the horizontal ruler. Set the height of the button to **0.5"** and the width to **1"**. The first button should have the caption **Employees** with the button named as **cmdEmployees**.

e. Repeat the same procedure for Orders and Products, setting each button immediately below the one before it.

f. Save the form, switch to Form view, and then test the buttons. Close all objects except the Main Menu form.

g. Switch to Design view, add an **Exit button** that exits Access to the top-right corner of the form, at the 0" mark on the vertical ruler and the 5" mark on the horizontal ruler, with a height of **0.5"** and a width of **1"**. Name the button **cmdExit**.

h. Apply the **Slice theme** to the Main Menu form only. Save the form, switch to Form view, and then test the Exit button. Reopen the database.

Add an SQL Statement as a Record Source

You need to modify the records in the Employees report. Modify the record source so that only employees with a Sales position display in the report.

a. Open the Employees report in Design view. Open the Property Sheet and click the **Record Source box**.

b. Type an SQL statement into the Record Source property of the report. The statement should select all fields (*) for employees with the Sales Representative title. Save the report.

c. Test the report in Print Preview and close the report. Close Access.

d. Submit based on your instructor's directions.

Infographics

Creating Text Charts, Tables, and Graphs

OBJECTIVES AFTER YOU READ THIS CHAPTER, YOU WILL BE ABLE TO:

1. Create a poster or a banner p. 892
2. Draw a table p. 893
3. Create a table structure p. 894
4. Format table components p. 902
5. Change table layout p. 905
6. Share information between applications p. 906
7. Identify chart types and elements p. 913
8. Create and insert a chart p. 916
9. Switch row and column data p. 918
10. Change a chart type p. 925
11. Change the chart layout p. 925
12. Format chart elements p. 926

CASE STUDY | Healthy Living: Antioxidants

The county health department is sponsoring a health fair, and you have been invited to present a session on antioxidants. Studies show there is a correlation between eating food rich in antioxidants and better overall health, so you want to share this information with others.

You prepare a poster that quickly and efficiently communicates the message that antioxidants promote good health and invites participants to enter the room for more information. After preparing the poster, you work on the PowerPoint presentation and decide to present information about top foods rich in antioxidants in tables so the information is neatly organized. Finally, you decide to add a graph displaying the antioxidant levels in "superfoods" and format a graph displaying the top 20 common food sources of antioxidants.

Text-Based Charts

In today's electronic environment, information is readily and quickly available, which makes it easy to feel overwhelmed. Common infographics that aid you in organizing and understanding information include text-based charts and statistical charts and graphs. **Text-based charts** primarily arrange and organize information with text to illustrate relationships among words, numbers, and/or graphics. These charts communicate relationships both verbally and visually. Statistical charts and graphs use points, lines, circles, bars, or other shapes to visually communicate numerical relationships, such as changes in time or comparisons.

Posters, large printed items that are displayed to advertise or publicize, and hanging signs printed on paper, vinyl, or cloth are used for advertising and publicizing. Both can be created in PowerPoint as text-based charts. Tables are another common type of text-based chart. Though text can communicate a message by its appearance (typeface, color, size, style, contrast), it can also communicate a message by how it is positioned or arranged. Therefore, when you design a text-based chart you need to carefully plan how the information is arranged within the chart and fully utilize formatting tools. Figure 5.1 shows an example of a text-based chart—a banner that has been printed locally on vinyl for durability. Once created in PowerPoint, a text-based chart can be uploaded to an online printing service to be mounted on foam backing for display or printed to use as handouts. Both can be delivered by the printing service for distribution at a function or event.

Event advertisement

FIGURE 5.1 Common Use for Text-Based Charts
Photo: Domas Balys/Fotolia

Figure 5.2 shows a PowerPoint table template illustrating a classic example of a relationship between numbers. This example, a simple multiplication table, is used to teach multiplication in an elementary school classroom. The table shows the product derived when a number in the column heading is multiplied by a number in the row heading. Notice that the intersection of the first row and the first column shows the multiplication operator.

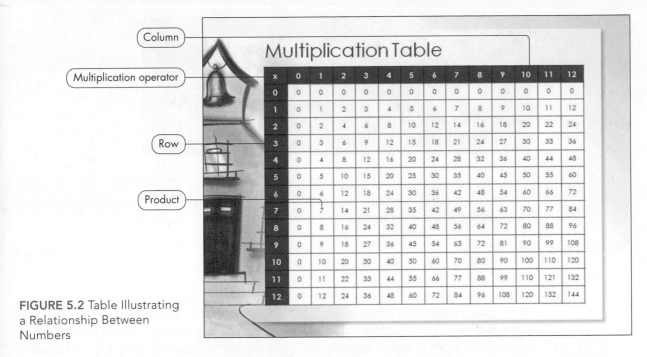

FIGURE 5.2 Table Illustrating a Relationship Between Numbers

Figure 5.3 shows another PowerPoint table template. This example illustrates a more complex relationship. Text, color, and font size, along with cell shading and arrow graphics, are used to guide the viewer through the process.

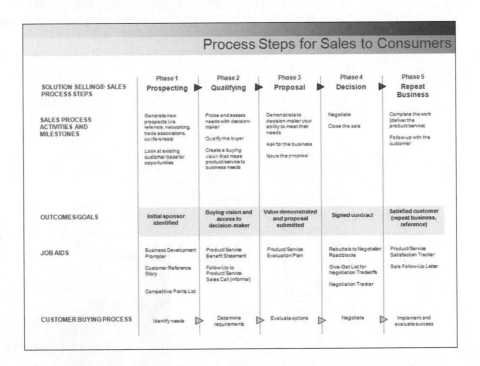

FIGURE 5.3 Table Illustrating a Complex Relationship Between Steps in a Process

Figure 5.4 displays an attention-grabbing banner announcing a local sporting event. For large banners or for posters printed on material other than paper, you can send your file to a commercial printing service.

In this section, you will learn how to create a poster and a banner. You will also learn how to create and draw a table in a slide. Finally, you will learn how to design a table to effectively communicate and organize your ideas.

Creating a Poster or a Banner

Although graphic professionals use other tools for professional print jobs, you can create banners or posters with PowerPoint. You create the poster or banner on a single slide. An important part of planning for a poster or banner is to consider how you will print the slide because this often determines how you format the single slide. Consider the printer when determining margins. Printers have margins beyond which text and graphics will not print. For commercial printing, it is important to identify all specifications, such as width and height of the finished product, not just margins. Also, when printing wide-format banners or posters, the printer may not support large-sized sheets of paper. If your printer does not support banner- or poster-sized paper, you can submit the file to a local or online printing service.

STEP 1 ➤➤ Use the Page Setup command to design the size of your poster or banner. With the Page Setup command, you can create documents that range from wide-format text-based documents, such as posters and banners, to small banners that appear at the tops of Web pages. The poster in Figure 5.5 is a standard size for uploading to an online printing service. The page setup for this poster, 17" × 22", also displays in the figure.

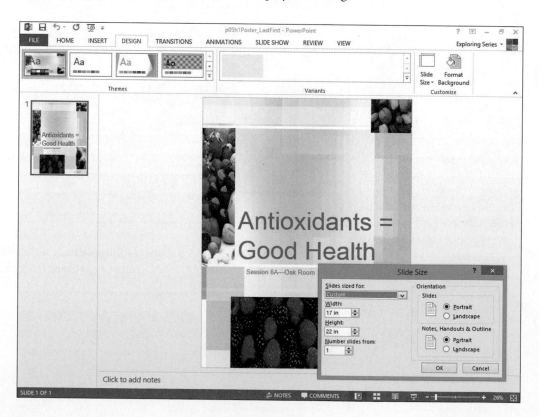

FIGURE 5.5 17" × 22" Poster
Created in PowerPoint

After opening PowerPoint and opening a file, you can access the Page Setup command on the Ribbon. To use the Page Setup command, do the following:

1. Click the DESIGN tab.
2. Click Slide Size in the Customize group.
3. Select Custom Slide Size.
4. Click the first option, the *Slides sized for* arrow, and click to select the slide size based upon the desired output.
5. Next, use the Width and Height spin arrows to further adjust the size or, if a desired option is not available in the *Slides sized for* box, to create a custom-sized output.
6. On the right side of the Slide Size dialog box, choose the orientation for Slides and for Notes, Handouts & Outline based upon the desired output.
7. If you have chosen Custom and clicked OK, you may be prompted to adjust content or scale. Choose Maximize or Ensure Fit based upon the desired output.

> **TIP** Web Page Banners
>
> The Banner option in the *Slides sized for* area is 8" × 1"—an ideal size for a Web banner that displays across the top of a Web page.

Drawing a Table

Tables are a form of text-based chart that organizes information into a highly structured grid (up to 75 rows and columns). Because tables are such a common way to present information, they can be created in PowerPoint, Word, Excel, and Access. If you create a table in Word, Excel, or Access, you can then insert it into a PowerPoint slide. Previously, you inserted a table by using the Insert feature to automatically create a table grid. In this section, you create tables by manually drawing the grid.

 If the table design requires multiple cell heights and widths or diagonal borders, using the Pencil tool to draw the table can save time.

To draw a table, do the following:

1. Click the INSERT tab and click the *Add a Table* arrow in the Tables group.
2. Select Draw Table.
3. Drag the pencil to define the outer table boundary.
4. Click Draw Table in the Draw Borders group on the TABLE TOOLS DESIGN tab.
5. Drag the pencil to draw the column and row borders inside the table.
6. Click Eraser in the Draw Borders group on the TABLE TOOLS DESIGN tab and drag the eraser across the border between the two cells you wish to join.
7. Press Esc to finish drawing your table.

> **TIP** Distribute Table Space Equally
>
> You do not need to be exact when drawing a table because the Layout tab includes buttons that distribute the width of the columns or the height of the rows so that they are uniformly spaced. To distribute columns or rows, select the cells you want to equalize and click Distribute Columns or Distribute Rows in the Cell Size group on the Layout tab.

Creating a Table Structure

Think carefully about the structure of a table before you create it to maximize the impact of the data it will contain. Tables should convey essential facts that supplement the message in the presentation but should omit distracting details. The table should be easy to understand and consistent with other objects in the presentation.

STEP 3 » A table needs a title to communicate its purpose. Keep the title short, but ensure that it gives enough information to accurately identify the table's purpose. Use a subtitle to give further information about the purpose, if necessary, but it should be in a smaller font size. The top row of the table body usually contains *column headers* to identify the contents of the columns. Column headers should be distinguishable from cell contents. Set the headers off by using color, bold font, italics, or a larger font than you use for the table body cells. Make sure that the font size of the column headers is not larger than the title and subtitle.

TIP | Merge Cells to Create a Title Row

To create a title row that stretches across several cells, select the cells to merge, and then click Merge Cells in the Merge group on the Layout tab. You can also use the Eraser tool on the Table Tools Design tab to erase the border between the cells or right-click selected cells and click Merge Cells.

The first column of a table, or the *stub column*, typically contains the information that identifies the data in each row. The last row of a table can be used for totals, a note, or source information. Use a smaller font size for the note or source, but make sure it is still large enough to be readable.

You can use table and cell borders to help clarify the information. Typically, horizontal borders are used to set off the title and subtitle from the headings and to set off headings from the table body. Vertical borders help define the columns. Figure 5.6 shows a basic table structure with the table elements identified. Bold is used to emphasize the table title and column headings. Font sizes vary depending on the table element, but the note or source-information row uses the smallest font size. One of the columns is shaded in blue and one of the rows is shaded in pale pink to help identify the differences. This is for illustration purposes only—this is not a table style. The intersection of the column and row, or the cell, is shaded in purple. The table is boxed, or surrounded by borders, and borders surround each cell. A heavier border is used to set off the title information from the column headings, the column headings from the body of the table, and the note information from the rest of the table.

Table Title		
Subtitle		
Stub Heading	**Column Heading**	**Column Heading**
Stub (Row Heading)	cell	
Stub (Row Heading)		
Stub (Row Heading)		
Stub (Row Heading)		
Note or Source Information		

FIGURE 5.6 Table Elements

Format Table Elements

The formatting of table elements is no longer as rigid as in years past unless you are preparing a table to adhere to specific guidelines such as American Psychological Association (APA) style. If this is the case, be sure to check a style guide for the style requirements and format the table per the guidelines. Otherwise, use type size, type style (bold, italics), alignment, or color to distinguish the table elements from one another. Remember to use design effects to clarify, not decorate.

Simplify Table Data

Table data on a slide should be as simple as possible to convey the message. Just as you limit text in bullets, limit the number of entries in tables to keep the font size large enough to read. For example, rather than listing 30 items in a table, list the top 5. Consider providing the audience with a printed Word table if you want them to have a list of all 30 items.

Another way to simplify data is to shorten numbers by rounding them to whole numbers. An alternative to this is to show numbers with a designation stating that the number is in thousands or millions. How you align the numbers in a cell depends on the type of data the cell contains. For example, numbers that do not have a decimal point can be right-aligned, or they can align on the decimal point if one exists. Occasionally you may have to left-align or center text in other columns. Generally speaking, however, you want to keep the alignment consistent throughout the table.

Change Row Height, Column Width, and Table Size

The row height or column width can be changed to accommodate information or to call attention to a cell, row, or column. For example, title rows are often taller than the rows containing body cells. To quickly adjust row height or column width, position the pointer over the target border of a row or column until the pointer changes into a sizing pointer and drag the border to adjust the row or column to the desired height or width. For a more precise change, use the Table Row Height or Table Column Width features in the Cell Size group on the Layout tab. You can also adjust the size by clicking the spin box arrows or by entering an exact size in the box.

You can resize the table manually by dragging a corner or middle sizing handle. Dragging the top- or bottom-middle handles changes the table height, whereas dragging the left- or right-middle handles changes the table width. Dragging a corner handle while holding down Shift sizes the table in both the vertical and horizontal directions simultaneously. To set a specific size for the table, specify Height or Width in the Table Size group of the Table Tools Layout tab.

Align Text Within Cells, Rows, and Columns

The Alignment group on the Layout tab includes features that not only align the contents of a cell horizontally and vertically but also change the direction of the text by rotating it or changing its orientation. You can even change the margins inside the cell. First, select the text you want to align in a single cell, row, or column. Then, to align text, click one of the alignment buttons in the Alignment group on the Layout tab. To align text horizontally, select Align Left, Center, or Align Right. To align vertically, select Align Top, Center Vertically, or Align Bottom.

To change the direction of the text within a cell, row, or column, click Text Direction and select from the options. To rotate the text, select *Rotate all text 90 degrees* (text positioned vertically facing to the right) or select *Rotate all text 270 degrees* (text positioned vertically facing to the left). To change the text orientation from horizontal to vertical for each individual character, select Stacked.

You can change internal margins from a default of 0.05" for top and bottom margins and 0.1" for left and right margins to no margins, narrow margins, and wide margins. To change the cell margins, click Cell Margins in the Alignment group and click an option from the Cell Margins gallery. Click Custom Margins at the bottom of the gallery to set each margin individually. Figure 5.7 shows a table with text rotated 270 degrees within a column.

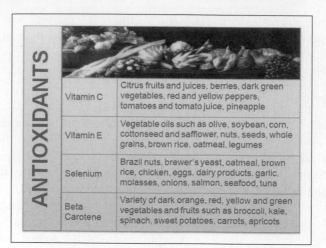

FIGURE 5.7 Rotated Text Within a Column

Table titled **ANTIOXIDANTS** (text rotated within the left column):

Vitamin C	Citrus fruits and juices, berries, dark green vegetables, red and yellow peppers, tomatoes and tomato juice, pineapple
Vitamin E	Vegetable oils such as olive, soybean, corn, cottonseed and safflower, nuts, seeds, whole grains, brown rice, oatmeal, legumes
Selenium	Brazil nuts, brewer's yeast, oatmeal, brown rice, chicken, eggs, dairy products, garlic, molasses, onions, salmon, seafood, tuna
Beta Carotene	Variety of dark orange, red, yellow and green vegetables and fruits such as broccoli, kale, spinach, sweet potatoes, carrots, apricots

Quick **Concepts**

1. What type of relationships in the displayed data do statistical charts or graphs communicate? *p. 890*

2. Explain how text-based charts show relationships. *p. 890*

3. List the purposes of a table title and subtitle. *p. 894*

896   CHAPTER 5 • Infographics

Hands-On Exercises

Watch the Video
for this Hands-
On Exercise!

1 Text-Based Charts

You prepare a poster that visitors at the county health fair can see as they walk by the room in which you are presenting. After preparing the poster, your focus turns to the work on the PowerPoint presentation that will be delivered. Information about top foods rich in antioxidants will be presented and neatly organized in tables.

Skills covered: Create a Poster • Draw a Table • Create Table Structure

STEP 1 ≫ CREATE A POSTER

The poster you prepare will be displayed outside your room to communicate the simple message that antioxidants promote good health. You also want the poster to follow the same design as the antioxidant slide show already created, so you use the slide-show title slide as the basis for the poster and resize it to a standard poster size. Finally, you print a scaled-down version of the poster as a record of the presentation. Refer to Figure 5.8 as you complete Step 1.

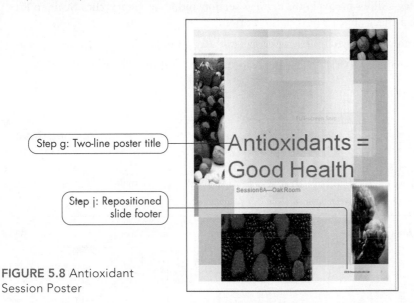

FIGURE 5.8 Antioxidant Session Poster

a. Open *p05h1Poster* and save it as **p05h1Poster_LastFirst**.

> **TROUBLESHOOTING:** If you make any major mistakes in this exercise, you can close the file, open *p05h1Poster* again, and then start this exercise over.

b. Create a handout header with your name and a handout footer with your instructor's name and your class. Include the current date.

c. Click the **DESIGN tab**, click **Slide Size** in the Customize group, and then select **Custom Slide Size**.

d. Select the existing number for *Width* and change it to **17**.

e. Select the existing number for *Height* and change it to **22**.

The *Slides sized for* box changes to Custom. Orientation changes to portrait for the *Slides* option and the *Notes, Handouts & Outline* option because the height of the slide is now greater than its width.

f. Click **OK**. Click **Maximize** and note the change in orientation.

The Maximize options scale the slide to show the entire slide. The Ensure Fit option scales the slide to fit in the window.

g. Select the **title placeholder** and type **Antioxidants = Good Health**.

h. Change the font size of the title placeholder to **144 pt**.

The session title is split into two lines. It is important to use a font large enough to be viewed easily by health-fair participants.

i. Create a slide footer that reads **2016 County Health Fair**. Click **Apply**.

By default, the slide footer is positioned at the bottom center of the slide, which makes it very difficult to read.

j. Click the **footer placeholder** to select it. Hold down **Shift** to constrain the movement horizontally and drag the slide footer border straight across to the right side of the poster so that it is positioned under the picture of the artichokes with the right border of the placeholder on the edge of the slide.

This new position increases the readability of the footer.

k. Click the **FILE tab** and click **Print**.

The Preview display may show only a portion of the poster because the poster size is larger than the typical printer paper size.

l. Click the **Full Page Slides arrow** in the *Settings* section and, if necessary, click **Scale to Fit Paper** to ensure a check appears next to this option.

The poster can now be printed to the paper size in the printer.

m. Save and close the file, and submit based on your instructor's directions.

STEP 2 ≫ DRAW A TABLE

With the poster done, you open the Antioxidants = Healthy Living slide show you want to use during your health-fair presentation. You have sketched out a plan for an antioxidant table that lists a vitamin or mineral and some foods that include this antioxidant type. You realize that because of the varied columns and rows, the most efficient way to create the table is to draw it. Refer to Figure 5.9 to see the table structure that will result when you complete Step 2.

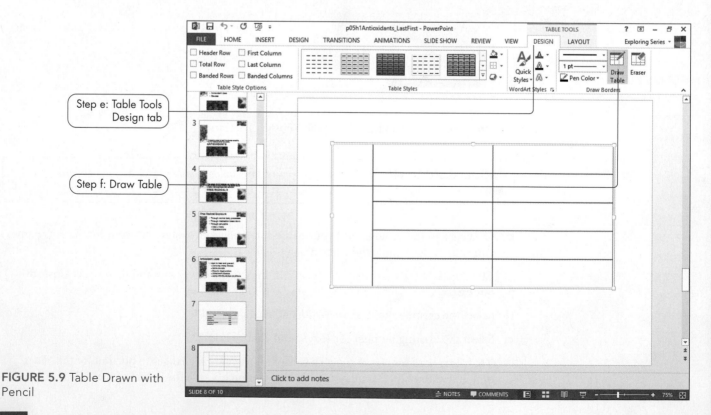

FIGURE 5.9 Table Drawn with Pencil

a. Open *p05h1Antioxidants* and save it as **p05h1Antioxidants_LastFirst**

b. Create a handout header with your name and a handout footer with your instructor's name and your class. Include the current date.

c. Click the **VIEW tab** and click the **Ruler check box** in the Show group to display the ruler, if necessary.

The horizontal and vertical rulers display for use in creating a table.

d. Click **Slide 7** to create a new slide after Slide 7. Click the **HOME tab**, click the **New Slide arrow**, and then click **Blank**.

e. On new Slide 8, click the **DESIGN tab** and click **Format Background** in the Customize group. Click the **Hide background graphics check box** in the Format Background pane. Close the Format Background pane.

f. Click the **INSERT tab**, click **Table** in the Tables group, and then select **Draw Table**.

The pointer changes to a pencil.

g. Use the ruler as a guide to draw a table starting at 4" to the left of the zero mark on the horizontal ruler and 2.5" above the zero mark on the vertical ruler. End the table at 4" to the right of the zero mark on the horizontal ruler and 2.5" below the zero mark on the vertical ruler.

The outer border of the table is created.

h. Click the **TABLE TOOLS DESIGN tab**, if necessary, and click **Draw Table** in the Draw Borders group.

i. Drag the pencil down to create a column border, beginning at approximately 1" on the horizontal ruler. Release the mouse button as soon as you see the complete border appear.

Inches are measured from the top-left edge of the table.

> **TROUBLESHOOTING:** If a new table is created in this step, you may have dragged the pencil outside of the table boundaries. Click Undo on the Quick Access Toolbar and select Draw Table in the Draw Borders group on the Table Tools Design tab. Beginning inside the table borders, drag the pencil straight down and release it when you see the complete border.

j. Drag a row border beginning from the first column right border to the right boundary of the table approximately 1" from the top boundary.

k. Drag three more row borders without worrying whether the rows are exactly the same height at this time.

Your table now contains five rows to the right of the first column.

l. Split the new rows of the table into two columns by dragging a vertical border.

Your table now contains three columns.

m. Press **Esc** to deactivate the table-drawing mode.

n. Select the center cell and the right cell in the top row, click the **LAYOUT tab**, and then click **Distribute Columns** in the Cell Size group.

The width of the selected cells is distributed equally.

o. Select all five rows that were created by drawing the four borders in steps j and k.

p. Click **Distribute Rows** in the Cell Size group.

The height of the selected cells is distributed equally.

q. Select the center column and click **Center** in the Alignment group.

Any text typed into the center column is centered horizontally in the cells.

r. Select the center and right columns and click **Center Vertically** in the Alignment group.

Any text typed into the two right column cells is centered vertically.

s. Save the presentation.

You save the table and will add the content in Hands-On Exercise 2.

STEP 3 ≫ CREATE TABLE STRUCTURE

You review the Antioxidants = Healthy Living slide show and note that the table on Slide 7 does not include a title row or column headings. Without this information, the data in the table are meaningless. You create structure in the table by adding a row for a title and by adding headers to the columns. Refer to Figure 5.10 as you complete Step 3.

Step g: Table title row added and formatted

Step l: Column headers added and formatted

Top Five Foods Rich in Antioxidants	
Food	**Antioxidants** **mmol/serving**
Blackberries	5746
Walnuts	3721
Strawberries	3584
Artichokes, prepared	3559
Cranberries	3125

FIGURE 5.10 Added Title Row and Column Headers

a. On Slide 7, select the table. Click the **TABLE TOOLS DESIGN tab** and click **Draw Table** in the Draw Borders group.

b. Drag the pencil horizontally through the blank row at the top of the table.

A new row is created above *Blackberries*. You now have two blank rows available that you can use to create and format the table title and column headings.

> **TROUBLESHOOTING:** If a new table is created in this step instead of a new row, click Undo on the Quick Access Toolbar and drag the pencil through the row without touching the border of the existing table.

c. Press **Esc** to exit Draw Table mode and select both cells in the top row of the table.

d. Click the **LAYOUT tab** and click **Merge Cells** in the Merge group.

The selected cells merge into one cell for the table title. The table title is formatted with a white font color for emphasis.

e. Type the title **Top Five Foods Rich in Antioxidants** in the title row.

The wording of the title now clearly defines the table's purpose.

f. Click **Center** in the Alignment group and click **Center Vertically** in the Alignment group.

g. Change the Height value in the Cell Size group to **0.6"**.

The Cell Size group is located in the center of the Ribbon. Be careful to not use the Table Size group on the right end of the Ribbon.

h. Select the title and change the font size to **24 pt**. Click the **TABLE TOOLS DESIGN tab**, click the **Text Effects arrow** in the WordArt Styles group, point to *Shadow*, and then click **Offset Diagonal Bottom Right** (the first option under *Outer*) to add a text shadow.

The formatting of the title enhances the title message.

i. Type **Food** in the left cell of the blank row 2 and press **Tab**. Type **Antioxidants mmol/ serving** in the right cell of the blank row 2.

j. Select the column headings in row 2 and apply bold.

The column heading for the second column wraps to fit the text on two lines in the cell.

k. Click the **LAYOUT tab** and click **Center** in the Alignment group.

l. Click **Center Vertically** in the Alignment group.

m. Save the presentation. Keep the presentation open if you plan to continue with the Hands-On Exercise 2. If not, close the presentation and exit PowerPoint.

Table Design

After you create a table, you may find that its appearance or structure must be modified to ensure the tabular information can be quickly read and understood. In this section, you will learn how to set a background fill; change table borders and effects; insert and delete columns and rows; and adjust text within cells, rows, and columns—all with the goal of making information meaningful to the audience.

Because tables may be created in other software applications, you may choose to import or paste the table into PowerPoint and modify it. In this section, you will learn how to share information between applications.

Formatting Table Components

To change the appearance of a table, you may choose to apply formatting to table components, such as the header or total rows, or use the tools in the Table Style Options group on the Table Tools Design tab. You can change table components using a *table style*, a combination of formatting choices for table components based on the theme of the presentation.

STEP 1》 Whether you choose to format and customize the individual style options or apply a full table style, you should understand the different types of formatting available. Table 5.1 shows what is formatted when a table style is applied to a table component.

TABLE 5.1	Table Components and Table Style Formatting Options
Header Row	Formats the row used for the table title or column headers
Total Row	Formats the last row in the table and displays column totals
First Column	Formats the stub (first column) differently than other columns
Last Column	Formats the last column differently than the other columns
Banded Rows	Formats even rows differently than odd rows
Banded Columns	Formats even columns differently than odd columns

To apply a style option to a selected table, click the check box next to the style option name in the Table Style Options group on the Table Tools Design tab. To apply a table style from the Table Styles gallery that impacts all of the formatting options based on the theme of the presentation, click the More button in the Table Styles group. This gallery displays the Best Match for Document at the top of the gallery along with Light, Medium, and Dark styles. Note that at the bottom of the Quick Styles gallery there is an option to clear the table of all styles. It does not remove individual attributes such as bold if those attributes were applied separately, however. Figure 5.11 shows the Table Styles group and the Table Quick Styles gallery.

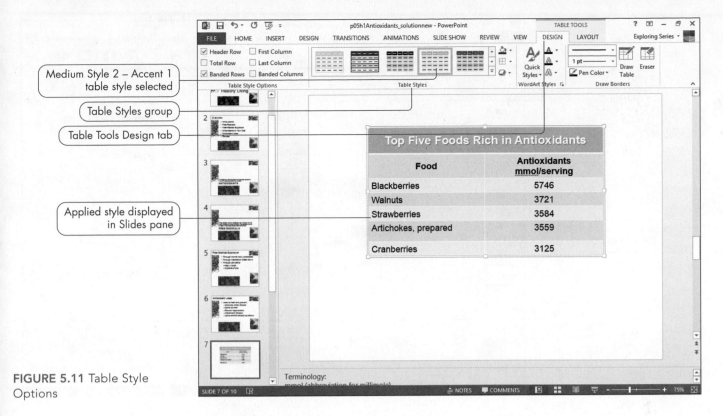

FIGURE 5.11 Table Style Options

Set a Background Fill

To add an interesting element to the background of the table or selected cells, you can change the background fill style. To change the background fill style, do the following:

1. Select the cells in which you want a background change.
2. Click the TABLE TOOLS DESIGN tab.
3. Click the Shading arrow in the Table Styles group.
4. Select from Theme, Standard Colors, Picture, Gradient, Texture, or Table Background or use the eyedropper tool to pick a color from another object.

Another way to change these background attributes is to right-click in the cell or selected cells in which you want the background change and click Format Shape to display the Format Shape pane. The main advantage of using the right-click method is that the Format Shape pane enables you to choose multiple options including shape and text options, which are not available through the Table Styles group.

You can easily add a picture as the background attribute. To add a picture background to a table cell, do the following in the Format Shape pane:

1. Right-click the cell and select Format Shape.
2. If necessary, click Shape Options.
3. Click the Fill & Line button and click the *Picture or texture fill* option.
4. Click Online under *Insert picture from*.
5. Enter a keyword to search for the picture you want to insert. Locate the picture and click Insert.
6. Click Close to close the Format Shape pane.

You can also insert a clip art image or photo by clicking File instead of clicking Online. The Insert Picture dialog box opens. Navigate and locate the desired image and click Insert (alternatively, double-click the image file). Click Close. Figure 5.12 has an added column to the left of the Food column that uses a picture of berries from Microsoft's Clip Art as a background fill for the top food listing and displays the Format Shape pane options.

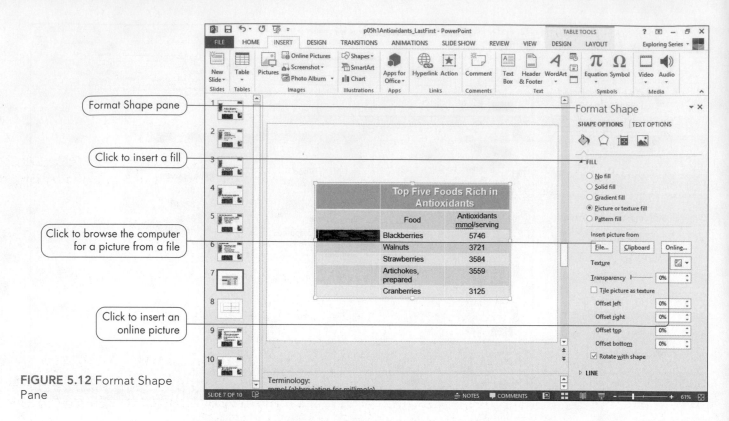

Labels (left to right pointing into figure):
- Format Shape pane
- Click to insert a fill
- Click to browse the computer for a picture from a file
- Click to insert an online picture

FIGURE 5.12 Format Shape Pane

Change Table Borders

Change border style, weight, and color by using the pen options located in the Draw Borders group on the Table Tools Design tab. The Pen Style option changes the style of the line used to draw borders and includes options for dotted and dashed lines. The Pen Weight option changes the width of the border, and the Pen Color option changes the color of the border.

After selecting the style, weight, and color of a border, click the border you want to change with the pencil. You can also drag to create additional borders with the pencil. If you have multiple borders to change, however, it is faster to use the Borders button in the Table Styles group on the Table Tools Design tab. Select the cell or cells you want to affect, or select the entire table. You can choose to have no border; all cells bordered; only outside borders; only inside borders; just a top, bottom, left, or right border; inside horizontal or vertical borders; or diagonal down or up borders.

Apply a Table Special Effect

Special effects may be added to a cell, selected cells, or a table. To apply one of the effects, click Effects in the Table Styles group on the Table Tools Design tab. Three effects options include Cell Bevel, Shadow, and Reflection. Pointing to one of these options opens that effect's gallery. As with other galleries, you can preview the effects on the selected cells or the table to view the impact of the effects before committing to a choice. The gallery also includes a No option for each effect that removes any previously applied effects. Figure 5.13 shows four tables: the original table with the default style settings, a table with the Riblet bevel effect applied to all cells, a table with the Perspective Diagonal Upper Left shadow effect, and a table showing a Full Reflection, touching reflection style.

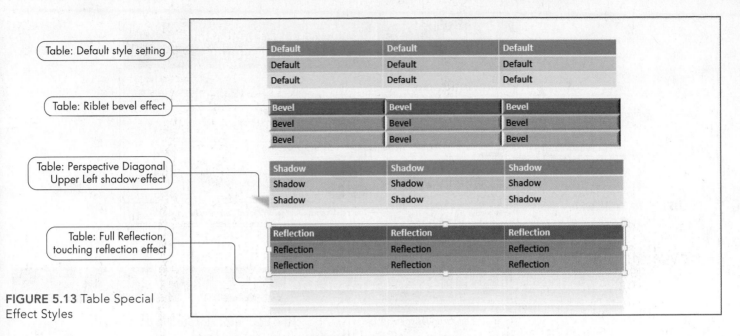

Table: Default style setting

Table: Riblet bevel effect

Table: Perspective Diagonal Upper Left shadow effect

Table: Full Reflection, touching reflection effect

FIGURE 5.13 Table Special Effect Styles

Changing Table Layout

After creating a table, or even while creating it, you can use the tools on the Table Tools Layout tab to change the layout of the table by inserting or deleting columns and rows. View Gridlines is also included on the Layout tab in the Table group, which is a toggle button that enables you to show or hide the table gridlines.

Insert Columns and Rows

STEP 2 ⟫ You can add a row or a column to your table. To control where the row appears, click in a cell next to where you want to add the new row. Click Insert Above or Insert Below in the Rows & Columns group on the Layout tab. If you want the new row to appear at the bottom of a table, click in the last cell of the table and press Tab. The process is similar for inserting a column to the left or right of an existing column: click in a cell next to where you want the new column, and then click Insert Left or Insert Right in the Rows & Columns group on the Layout tab. As an alternative to using the Layout tab, you can right-click in a selected cell, click Insert on the context menu that displays, and then click one of the insert columns or insert rows options.

Delete Columns and Rows

To delete selected columns and rows, click Delete in the Rows & Columns group on the Layout tab and click Delete Columns, Delete Rows, or Delete Table. You can also right-click in selected cells, click Delete on the Mini toolbar, and then click Delete Columns, Delete Rows, or Delete Table. Figure 5.14 displays two tables: an original table and the same table after modifications. The theme style was changed. The modified table no longer contains a top row with a picture fill. A column was added to the left, and a clip art image was inserted in each of the resulting cells. Finally, a row was added to the bottom of the table so source information could be included.

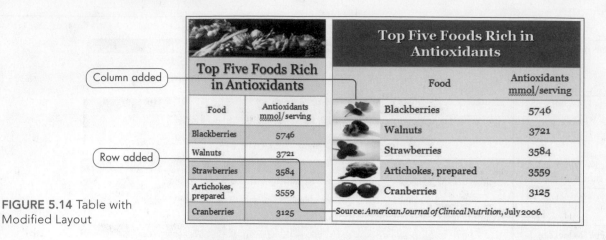

 Column added

Row added

FIGURE 5.14 Table with Modified Layout

> **TIP** **Use the Eraser Tool**
>
> You can quickly merge cells by clicking the Eraser tool located in the Draw Borders group on the Table Tools Design tab, and then use the Eraser tool to click the border you want to remove.

Sharing Information Between Applications

PowerPoint's table features can handle simple tables well, but if a table requires calculations, create it in Excel to take advantage of Excel's powerful data features. After creating the table, you can embed the Excel worksheet in a presentation slide as an object or link the slide to the Excel worksheet or a Word table. ***Object linking and embedding (OLE)*** lets you insert an object created in one application into a document created in another application.

STEP 3 Linking an object differs from embedding an object. To understand the differences, you need to understand four key terms used in the object linking and embedding process (see Table 5.2).

TABLE 5.2	Object Linking and Embedding Key Terms
Key Term	**Definition**
Source application	The application you used to create the original object, such as Word or Excel
Destination application	The application into which the object is being inserted, such as PowerPoint
Source file	The file that contains the original table or data that is used or copied to create a linked or embedded object, such as a Word document or an Excel worksheet
Destination file	The file that contains the inserted object, such as a PowerPoint presentation with an Excel worksheet embedded in it

If you create a table in Excel and paste it into a PowerPoint slide, Excel is the source application and PowerPoint is the destination application. The Excel file containing the table is the source file for the object. Once you insert the table object into PowerPoint, the PowerPoint presentation is the destination file. The simplest way to transfer any object is to copy it within the source application, and then paste it into the destination application. This embeds the copied object into the application.

An ***embedded object*** becomes a part of the destination file, and, once inserted, the object is no longer a part of the source file. An embedded object does not maintain a connection to the source file or source application in which the object was created. For example, a cell range of data copied from Excel and pasted into PowerPoint results in a table object displaying the data that can be edited as a table. Changes to the table data in PowerPoint do not change the source cells within the original Excel file. The PowerPoint table tool options appear on the Ribbon when the data is selected in PowerPoint, and the table is treated as any other table of data.

In the case of a chart created in Excel, the default option to paste creates a linked object. You would need to choose the option to paste as a picture to embed the chart into PowerPoint without a link to the source file. The PowerPoint Ribbon would display picture tool options. Figure 5.15 shows a PowerPoint presentation with an embedded table. It is important to note that if you edit the embedded table, the source document (an Excel document in this example) is *not* changed.

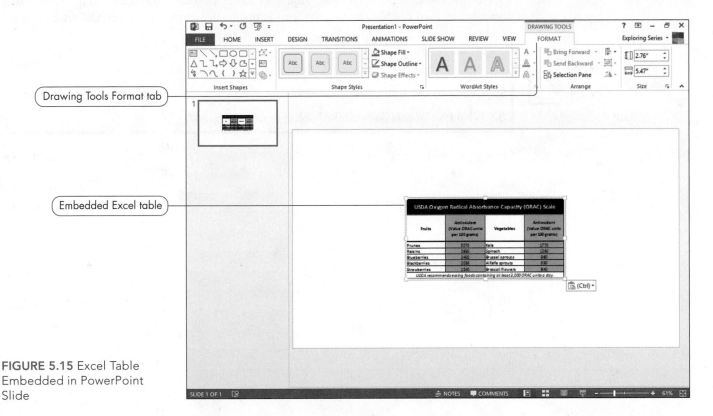

FIGURE 5.15 Excel Table Embedded in PowerPoint Slide

If you link an object, the information is stored in the source file, and the object in the destination file is updated when you modify it in the source file. When you double-click a linked object, the source application opens, and you are actually editing the source file. The changes you make in the source file display in PowerPoint. The **linked object** stores the data in the source file. The destination file stores only the location of the source file while displaying a picture or representation of the linked data from the source file. The representation in PowerPoint is only a shortcut to the source file so that changes to the source file are reflected and updated in the presentation. One advantage of linking is a smaller file size because PowerPoint stores only the link to the data needed to display the information. Another advantage is the data only needs to be changed once in the source file, and any files linked to that source file automatically update the information. However, there may be times when it is not desirable to update the data, in which case an embedded object is the desired method.

To embed a new object, do the following:

1. Open the source file.
2. Select and copy the object or data.
3. Click to make the destination PowerPoint file active and click at the insertion point.
4. Paste the object into PowerPoint.

To link a previously created object, do the following:

1. Open the source file.
2. Select and copy the object or data.
3. Click to make the destination PowerPoint file active and click at the insertion point.
4. Click the Paste arrow and click Paste Special.
5. In the Paste Special dialog box, check the *Paste link* option, choose the object type in the As box, such as a Microsoft Excel Worksheet Object, and then click OK.

Alternatively, you can link an object into PowerPoint by using the Object button in the Text group on the Insert tab. From the Insert Object dialog box, choose the *Create new* option, which links to a new file, or choose the *Create from file* option, which enables navigating (Browse) to an existing file. The *Display as icon* option displays an icon in the PowerPoint presentation, and double-clicking the icon launches the source file. Click OK when you are finished.

Quick Concepts

1. What Ribbon tab provides table formatting options? *p. 902*
2. Define an embedded object. *p. 906*
3. What type of data does a linked object represent? *p. 907*

Hands-On Exercises

Watch the Video for this Hands-On Exercise!

MyITLab®
HOE2 Training

2 Table Design

You continue revising the county health fair antioxidants presentation to make the information in the tables easy to read and to enhance their appearance.

Skills covered: Format Table Components • Change Table Layouts • Share Information Between Applications

STEP 1 » FORMAT TABLE COMPONENTS

You enhance the table on Slide 7 by changing the table style to a clean, clear style. You add a column to the table, and then format the cells in the column to include pictures of the food mentioned in the middle column. As a final step, you add a row to the table so that you can acknowledge a source. Refer to Figure 5.16 as you complete Step 1.

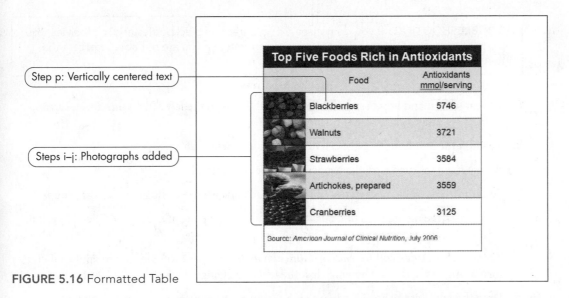

Step p: Vertically centered text

Steps i–j: Photographs added

FIGURE 5.16 Formatted Table

a. Open the *p05h1Antioxidants_LastFirst* slide show, if necessary. Save the slide show as **p05h2Antioxidants_LastFirst**, changing the *h1* to *h2*.

b. On Slide 7, select the table. Click the **TABLE TOOLS DESIGN tab**, click the **More button** in the Table Styles group, and then select **Medium Style 1 - Accent 4** (first row, fifth column, Medium category).

   Medium Style 1 - Accent 4 includes a Header Row style and a Banded Rows style. The black font color can be easily read.

TIP Control Table Style Options

The Table Style Options group in the Table Tools Design tab is where you can turn on or turn off the various style options that control table styles.

c. Click in any of the cells in the first column, click the **LAYOUT tab**, and then click **Insert Left** in the Rows & Columns group.

   A new column is inserted to the left of the Food column.

d. Select both cells in the top row and click **Merge Cells** in the Merge group.

e. Click in the new left column, click in the **Width box** in the Cell Size group, type **1.2**, and then press **Enter** to apply the change. Change the width of the middle column to **3"** and the width of the right column to **2"**.

f. Select the last five rows of the table (exclude the title and column heading rows), click in the **Height box** in the Cell Size group, and then type **.75**.

g. Click in the cell to the left of *Blackberries* and right-click.

h. Click **Format Shape** to open the Format Shape pane, click **Fill & Line** (image of bucket), if necessary, and then click **Fill** to open the fill options. Click the **Picture or texture fill option** if necessary.

A texture appears in your cell.

i. Click **Online** to open the Insert Picture dialog box, type **blackberries** in the **Office.com Clip Art Search box**, and then press **Enter**. Select the photograph of the blackberries and raspberries (see Figure 5.16) that appears in the search results and click **Insert** to close the Insert Picture dialog box. Close the Format Shape pane.

TROUBLESHOOTING: If you do not see a photograph of blackberries and raspberries, you may not have Internet access. Substitute a clip art image if you are not able to access the Internet.

---

j. Repeat steps h and i to insert photographs in the cells to the left of *Walnuts*, *Strawberries*, *Artichokes*, and *Cranberries*.

k. Position the pointer in the last cell of the table and press **Tab**.

A new row is created with the properties of the row above it.

l. Select the cells in the newly created last row and click **Merge Cells** in the Merge group.

m. Right-click the merged cell to display the Format Shape pane, if necessary. Click **No Fill** in the Format Shape pane and click **Close**.

n. Type **Source:** *American Journal of Clinical Nutrition*, **July 2006**. Be sure to apply italic formatting to the text as shown. Select the text and change the font size to **14 pt**.

o. Drag the table (at the border edge) to reposition to the approximate vertical center of the slide.

p. Select **rows 3 through 8** and click **Center Vertically** in the Alignment group on the LAYOUT tab.

q. Save the presentation.

STEP 2 >> CHANGE TABLE LAYOUTS

As you work with the design of the tables in your slide show, you often find that changing the structure of a table requires that you change the formatting of a table and vice versa. Each choice you make entails making further choices as you refine the presentation. In this exercise, you continue refining the tables in your antioxidants presentation. Refer to Figure 5.17 as you complete Step 2.

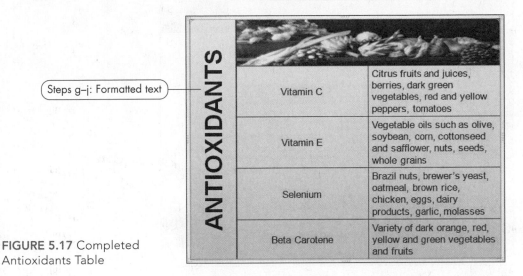

Steps g–j: Formatted text

FIGURE 5.17 Completed Antioxidants Table

a. Select the table on Slide 8. Click the **TABLE TOOLS DESIGN tab**, click the **More button** in the Table Styles group, and then click **Themed Style 1 - Accent 4** (first row, fifth column, *Best Match for Document* category).

b. Click **Eraser** in the Draw Borders group and click the vertical border that splits row 1 into two cells. (Do not click the border that divides columns 2 and 3 for the remaining rows.) Press **Esc**.

The border disappears, and the cells merge into one.

c. Click in the top row. Click the **Shading arrow** in the Table Styles group and click **Picture**.

d. Click **Browse** in the Insert Picture dialog box, locate and select *p05h2Fruits.jpg*, and then click **Insert**.

The image is resized to fit the row.

e. Click the **LAYOUT tab**, change the row height to **1.2"**, and then press **Enter**.

f. Enter the remaining data, as shown in Figure 5.17, without worrying about the text size or position.

g. Click in **column 1**, click **Text Direction** in the Alignment group, and then click **Rotate all text 270°**.

h. Click **Center Vertically** in the Alignment group.

i. Select the **Antioxidants text** in column 1, change the font size to **44 pt**, and then click **Center** for the alignment. Click the **TABLE TOOLS DESIGN tab**. Click **Effects** in the Table Styles group and click **Shadow** and **Offset Bottom** (under *Outer*).

j. Click the **First Column option** in the Table Style Options group.

Activating the First Column table style bolds the text in the first column and creates a bold black border between the first column and the remaining columns.

k. Drag the table to the approximate vertical and horizontal center of the slide.

l. Save the presentation.

STEP 3 >> SHARE INFORMATION BETWEEN APPLICATIONS

You have an Excel file that contains data for the USDA Oxygen Radical Absorbance Capacity (ORAC) Scale that you want to include in the presentation. Rather than re-create this information, you insert a linked copy of the table in your presentation. Refer to Figure 5.18 as you complete Step 3.

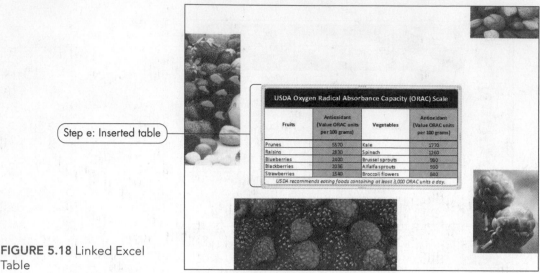

Step e: Inserted table

FIGURE 5.18 Linked Excel Table

a. Create a new slide after Slide 8 using the Blank layout.

b. Open *p05h2Orac.xlsx* and save the file as **p05h2Orac_LastFirst.xlsx**.

c. Select the **range A1:D8** to select all the table data in the Excel file. Click **Copy** in the Clipboard group on the HOME tab (or press **Ctrl+C**).

d. Click the PowerPoint file on the Windows taskbar to make the presentation the active file. Click the **Paste arrow** in the Clipboard group on the HOME tab and click **Paste Special**.

e. Click the **Paste link option** in the Paste Special dialog box. Click **Microsoft Excel Worksheet Object** in the As box, if necessary, and then click **OK**.

A copy of the Excel table is inserted into your presentation. The copy is a shortcut link to the original data file so that changes to the source data file are reflected in your presentation.

f. Close the Excel file. Double-click the table object in the presentation.

The source application, the Microsoft Excel file, opens for editing.

g. Select **row 2** in Excel, click the **Font Color arrow**, and then select **Red** under *Standard Colors*.

The column headings in the linked table change to reflect the editing you performed in Excel.

h. Observe the color change to the column headings in the presentation. Save the changes in the Excel file. Close Excel.

i. Save the presentation. Keep the presentation open if you plan to continue with the Hands-On Exercise 3. If not, close the presentation and exit PowerPoint.

Statistical Charts and Graphs

Statistical charts and graphs help you communicate numerical relationships more effectively than using words to describe them. A chart or graph can compare data and show trends or patterns. Summarizing information in a chart or graph helps your audience understand and retain your message.

In this section, you will identify chart types and elements. Then you will learn how to create and insert a chart in a slide.

Identifying Chart Types and Elements

PowerPoint includes tools to create professional-looking charts. You can even save your chart as a template so you can apply the same formatting to new charts of the same type. When you create a chart using PowerPoint, you enter the information in an Excel workbook. The Excel worksheet you use to create the chart is then embedded in your presentation.

Whereas the term *chart* can refer to visual displays of information such as tables, maps, lists, SmartArt diagrams, and others, the term *graph* is specific to a chart that displays a relationship between two sets of numbers plotted as data points with coordinates on a grid. These two terms have become synonymous and are used interchangeably now. Microsoft Office applications use the term *chart* to describe the charts and graphs provided for your use.

Before beginning to create a chart, think about the information you are presenting and determine what message you want to convey using a chart. Are you representing changes over time? Are you comparing or summarizing data? Are you representing a single series or multiple series? What type of chart will your audience understand quickly?

Select Basic Chart Types

Each of the basic chart types has appropriate uses. Choose the type that portrays your message most effectively. The chart should be clear and easy to read and should present enough detail to provide the audience with an understanding of your message without overwhelming people with detail. Generally, audiences can easily understand the commonly used charts, such as pie, line, column, and bar charts.

Office includes a wide variety of charts: column charts, line charts, pie charts, bar charts, area charts, XY (scatter) charts, stock charts, surface charts, doughnut charts, bubble charts, and radar charts. The most common purposes of some of these charts are listed in Table 5.3. For greater detail on the available chart types, including chart subtype information, enter chart types in the Search box for PowerPoint Help and click the hyperlink for Available chart types.

TABLE 5.3   Reference Chart Purposes

Type	Series Type	Purpose	Sample Chart
Pie chart	Single-series	Use to show proportions of a whole. Slices are proportioned to show the relative size of each piece. Information is from data arranged in only one column or row.	
Doughnut chart	Multi-series	Use to show the relationship of parts to a whole like a pie chart but can contain more than one data series. The doughnut contains a hole in the center. Information is from data arranged only in columns or rows.	
Column chart	Single- or multi-series	Use to show data changes over a period of time or comparisons among items. Information is arranged in columns or rows and is used to plot the chart using a horizontal and a vertical axis. Categories are typically organized along the horizontal axis and values along the vertical axis. The information is displayed in vertical columns. Shapes other than vertical bars can be used for the columns, including 3-D bars, cylinders, cones, and pyramids.	
Line chart	Single- or multi-series	Use to display a large number of data points over time. Ideal for showing trends over equal time intervals such as months, quarters, or years. Information is arranged in columns or rows on a worksheet and set against a common scale. Category information is distributed evenly along the horizontal axis, and all value information is distributed evenly along the vertical axis. The information is displayed as individual points linked by lines.	
Bar chart	Single- or multi-series	Use to show comparisons between items. Information is arranged in columns or rows on a worksheet the same as in a column chart, but the bars stretch horizontally instead of vertically.	
Area chart	Single- or multi-series	Use to emphasize the magnitude of change over time. Draws attention to the total value across a trend. Basically, a line graph with the area below the plotted lines filled in. Information is arranged in columns or rows on a worksheet.	
XY (scatter) chart	Single- or multi-series	Use to show the relationships among the numeric values in several data series, or plot two groups of numbers as one series of XY coordinates. This shows distributions, groupings, or patterns. A scatter chart plots two variables, one of which is plotted on the horizontal (X) scale and one of which is plotted on the vertical (Y) scale.	

Type	Series Type	Purpose	Sample Chart
Stock chart	Single- or multi-series	Use to show fluctuations or the range of change between the high and low values of a subject over time. Commonly used to show fluctuation of stock prices, but can be used for fluctuations in temperature or scientific data. Data must be arranged in columns or rows in a specific order on the worksheet. To create a simple high-low-close stock chart, data must be arranged with High, Low, and Close entered as column headings, in that order.	
Surface chart	Single- or multi-series	Use to plot a surface using two sets of data. Colors indicate areas that are in the same range of values. Information is arranged in columns or rows on a worksheet. This is similar to a line graph but with a dimensional effect added.	
Bubble chart	Single- or multi-series	Use to show relationships like an XY (scatter) chart, but uses three values instead of two. The third value determines the size of the bubble. Bubble charts should not be used to show absolute quantities, as the scales are relative. Information is arranged in columns on the worksheet so that X values are listed in the first column and corresponding Y values and bubble size values are listed in adjacent columns.	
Radar chart	Multi-series	Use to compare the aggregate values of three or more variables represented on axes starting from the same point, like the spokes on a wheel. Enables you to use multiple criteria. Information is arranged in columns or rows on a worksheet.	

Identify Chart Elements

When you enter the data for your table in an Excel workbook, the cells that contain numeric values are called data points. A ***data series*** contains the data points representing a set of related numbers. The data series can be a ***single-series data series*** (representing only one set of data) or a ***multiseries data series*** (representing data for two or more sets of data). For example, you would plot the profits for a store in Destin, Florida, on a single-series chart, and the profits for stores in Destin, Fort Walton Beach, and Pensacola, Florida, on a multi-series chart.

A pie chart is an example of a single-series chart. With the whole represented as a circle, a pie chart shows the proportional relationship of each segment to the whole. A fill may be applied to each segment, or slice, or applied to the entire pie. A ***label*** identifies data in a chart—for example, in a pie chart, the label identifies the slices in the pie. The slices can be labeled with the series name, category name, value, or percentage. The labels can be centered, positioned inside a slice, positioned outside of the slice, or positioned according to the Best Fit option, which is based on the amount of text inside the label. Leaders are lines used to connect the label to the slice of pie. Though it is preferable to have the labels within a pie slice, often they do not fit. In that case, leaders become necessary to avoid possible confusion. Exploded pie charts emphasize data by separating, or exploding, a slice or slices from the pie.

Figure 5.19 shows a pie chart with a single series—the assets of a charitable foundation. The chart includes a title and labels indicating the category names and the percentage each slice of the pie contributes to the total. The Trusts slice is exploded for emphasis. The ***chart area*** (the chart and all of its elements) is bounded by the placeholder borders, whereas the ***plot area*** (the area representing the data) is defined by a bounding box comprised of single lines.

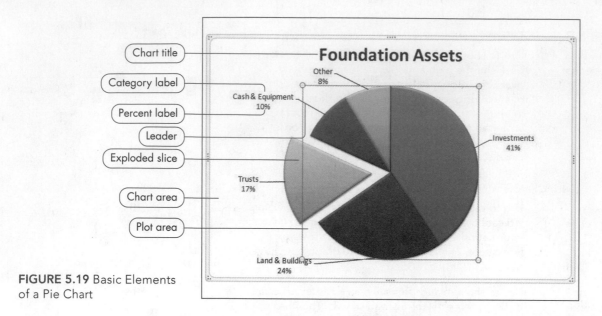

FIGURE 5.19 Basic Elements of a Pie Chart

The remaining chart types available in Office are plotted on a coordinate system and may be single-series or multiseries charts. The chart is created by plotting data points between two reference lines, or scales, called axes. The *X-axis* is the horizontal axis and usually contains the category information, such as products, companies, or intervals of time. The *Y-axis* is the vertical axis and usually contains the values or amounts. Three-dimensional charts have a third axis, the *Z-axis*, used to plot the depth of a chart. Axes can be given titles to describe what the data represent. Note that some chart types, such as pie charts, do not have axes.

Gridlines, lines that extend from the horizontal or vertical axes, can be displayed to make the chart data easier to read and understand. Tick marks are short lines on the axes that mark the category and value divisions. Data points plotted on the chart are indicated by data markers, or graphical representations such as bars, dots, or slices that can be enhanced with lines, filled areas, or pictures. To help identify the data series, a *legend* assigns a format or color to each data series and then displays that information with the data series name. Legends are only necessary for multiseries charts. Figure 5.20 shows the basic elements of a column chart.

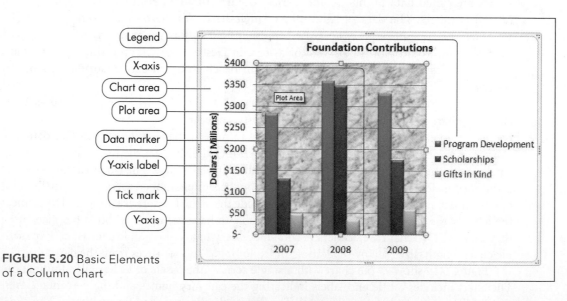

FIGURE 5.20 Basic Elements of a Column Chart

Creating and Inserting a Chart

To create a chart, start by clicking the Chart icon in a content placeholder or by clicking the Insert tab, and then clicking Chart in the Illustrations group. The Insert Chart dialog box opens with two panes. The left pane contains the chart types, and the right pane contains chart styles, or subtypes, and a preview of the selected chart type. Figure 5.21 displays the default chart type, a column chart, in the left pane and the default chart style, Clustered Column, in the right pane.

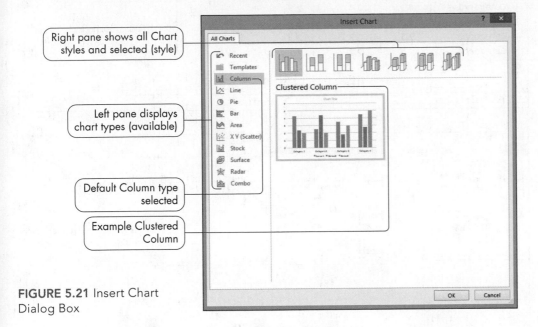

FIGURE 5.21 Insert Chart Dialog Box

STEP 1

STEP 3

After selecting the chart type and style, click OK. Microsoft Excel opens with a worksheet containing sample data, and the PowerPoint presentation contains a chart based on the sample data. The title of the Excel workbook is *Chart in Microsoft PowerPoint*. Replace the sample data with your own data, and the PowerPoint chart updates to reflect the updated information. The Excel worksheet contains a grid of rows and columns. When you type in a cell, you replace the sample data, and your data point is created in your chart. When you enter the data, you might need to change the row heights or column widths to fit the data. If pound signs display (#####) in a cell, it means there is not enough room in the cell to display the data. To increase the width of the column, position the pointer on the line to the right of the column heading, and then double-click to adjust the column width automatically. To resize the chart data range, drag the bottom-right corner of the range. When you finish entering the data, click the Close (X) button in Excel and view the chart embedded in PowerPoint.

> **TIP** Delete the Sample Chart Data
>
> To quickly delete the sample data in a chart, click the Select All button (the intersection between the column designations and the row designations), which is located in the top left of the worksheet. This selects all of the cells in the worksheet. Once they are selected, press Delete on the keyboard.

If you close Excel and then need to edit the data the chart is based upon, click the chart, click the Chart Tools Design tab, and then click Edit Data in the Data group. The Excel worksheet reopens so you can edit your data. When you are done editing, click the Close button on the Excel worksheet to return to PowerPoint. Figure 5.22 shows an Excel worksheet, and Figure 5.23 shows the associated chart created in PowerPoint.

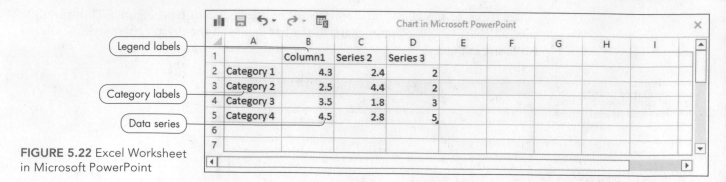

Legend labels

Category labels

Data series

FIGURE 5.22 Excel Worksheet
in Microsoft PowerPoint

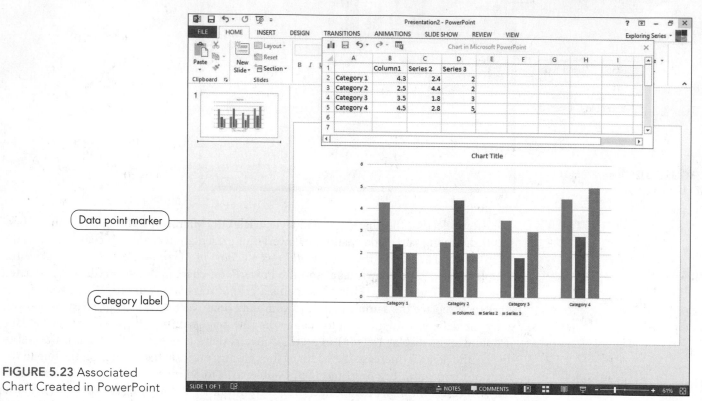

Data point marker

Category label

FIGURE 5.23 Associated
Chart Created in PowerPoint

Switching Row and Column Data

By default, a chart is plotted based on the series data displayed in the columns of the
worksheet and the column headings displayed in the legend. Because of this, the chart in
Figure 5.23 emphasizes the changes in each category over three series. You can switch the
emphasis if you want to emphasize the changes by year rather than by category. To do so,
click Switch Row/Column in the Data group on the Design tab in PowerPoint.

STEP 2

The chart shown in Figure 5.23 is at its most basic level. Charts should be modified
and formatted to ensure that the chart conveys the intended message. For example, without
a descriptive title or labels, it is impossible to tell the purpose of the chart or what the amounts
represent. In Hands-On Exercise 3, you create a basic pie chart and a column chart, and
then in the next section, you explore modifications and formatting changes that complete
your chart.

Quick Concepts ✓

1. Statistical charts and graphs are used to communicate what type of data? *p. 913*

2. List the type of data relationships represented by a column chart. *p. 914*

3. A pie chart is used to represent what type of data? *p. 914*

Watch the Video for this Hands-On Exercise!

MyITLab®
HOE3 Training

3 Statistical Charts and Graphs

Although antioxidants are available in common foods, some foods are referred to as superfruits because of the high level of antioxidants per serving. You want to show the audience at the county health fair a comparison of the antioxidant levels in a top "common" food and some of the superfruits. You create a chart to illustrate this comparison and also create a chart to show the ideal percentage of each food group in an average diet.

Skills covered: Create and Edit a Basic Column Chart • Switch the Row and Column Data • Create a Basic Pie Chart

---

STEP 1 ≫ CREATE AND EDIT A BASIC COLUMN CHART

You create a clustered column chart to compare the antioxidant levels in foods. While proofreading the chart, you notice an incorrect amount and a missing fruit, so you edit the chart. Refer to Figure 5.24 as you complete Step 1.

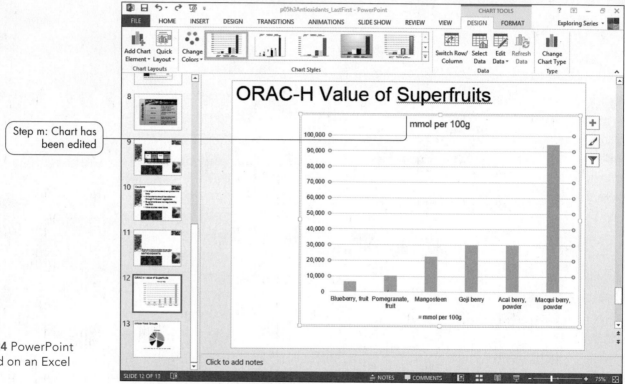

FIGURE 5.24 PowerPoint Chart Based on an Excel Worksheet

a. Open the *p05h2Antioxidants_LastFirst* slide show, if necessary. Save the slide show as **p05h3Antioxidants_LastFirst**, changing the *h2* to *h3*.

b. Insert a new slide after Slide 11 using the Title and Content layout.

c. On the new Slide 12, type **ORAC-H Value of Superfruits** in the **title placeholder**. Click outside the title placeholder.

d. Click the **DESIGN tab**, click **Format Background** in the Customize group, and then click the **Hide background graphics option** in the Format Background pane. Close the Format Background pane.

> **TROUBLESHOOTING:** If you do not see the *Hide background graphics* option, you may have clicked the text placeholder after step c. You cannot be in either the title placeholder or the text placeholder for this option to display.

e. Click the **Insert Chart icon** on the slide. Note the default setting of Column chart, Clustered Column subtype, in the Insert Chart dialog box. Click **OK**.

Excel opens with sample data.

f. Replace the worksheet data with the following data:

	mmol per 100g
Blueberry, fruit	6,500
Mangosteen	22,500
Goji berry	10,000
Acai berry, powder	30,000
Macqui berry, powder	94,500

g. Drag the bottom-right corner of the chart data range to resize the range to fit the data you just entered and exclude any remaining sample data.

Series 2 and Series 3 of the sample data are not needed, and the data do not display on the PowerPoint chart once you resize the range to fit the data. If you want to clean up the source data file, the unwanted sample Series 2 and Series 3 data can be deleted.

h. Close the Excel worksheet and return to PowerPoint.

i. Click the **CHART TOOLS DESIGN tab**, if necessary, and click the **Edit Data arrow** in the Data group. Click **Edit Data in Excel 2013**. Maximize the Excel window.

Excel opens, displaying the chart data again.

j. Click the **row 3 indicator** (Mangosteen row), right-click, and then click **Insert**.

A new row 3 is inserted above the original row 3.

> **TROUBLESHOOTING:** The entire row 3 must be selected to see the Insert command after you right-click. If you just select the cell, your options are to move cells up or down.

k. Type **Pomegranate, fruit** in **cell A3**, press **Tab**, and then type **10,500**.

l. Click in **cell B5**, type **30,000**, and then press **Enter**.

m. Close the Excel worksheet and return to PowerPoint.

n. Save the presentation.

> **TROUBLESHOOTING:** If you close the presentation and then open it at a later time, a Microsoft PowerPoint Security Notice opens because of the linked table on Slide 9. Click Update Links to retrieve the latest information.

STEP 2 ≫ SWITCH THE ROW AND COLUMN DATA

After evaluating the graph, you decide that you want the list of superfruits in the legend. You will swap the data from a single-series data set to a multiseries data set. Refer to Figure 5.25 as you complete Step 2.

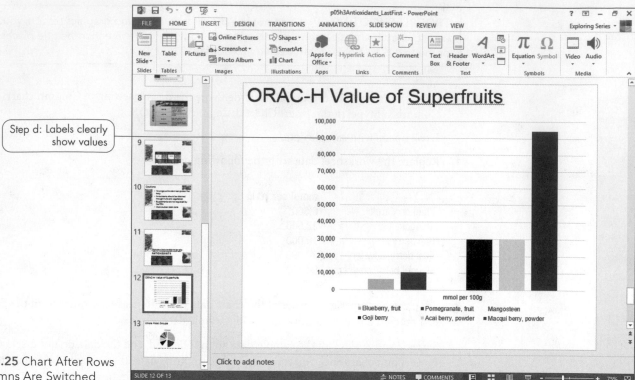

FIGURE 5.25 Chart After Rows and Columns Are Switched

a. Select the chart (if necessary).

b. Click **Select Data** in the Data group on the CHART TOOLS DESIGN tab.

The Select Data Source dialog box opens, as does Excel. The Legend Entries (Series) pane shows the *mmol per 100g* series entry, and the Horizontal (Category) Axis Labels display the food category.

c. Click **Switch Row/Column**.

The Legend Entries (Series) pane now displays the food categories, and the Horizontal (Category) Axis Labels pane now displays the *mmol per 100g* entry (see Figure 5.26).

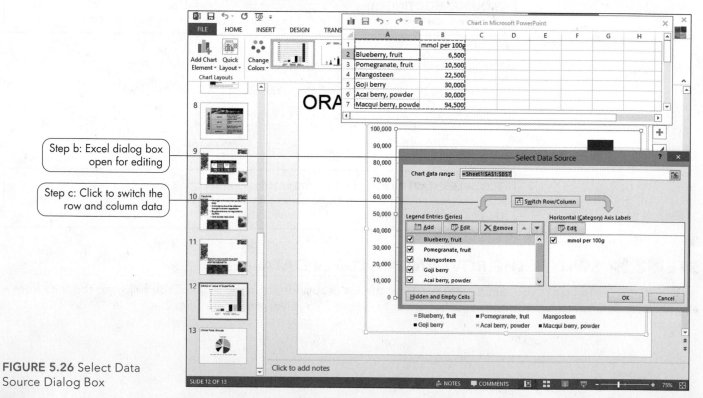

FIGURE 5.26 Select Data Source Dialog Box

> **d.** Click **OK** and close the Excel worksheet.
>
> The data markers (bars) now clearly show that *Maqui berry, powder* exceeds the other superfruit ORAC-H values. Two of the markers display the same color, so a modification is necessary. You will correct this problem in Hands-On Exercise 4.
>
> **e.** Save the presentation.

STEP 3 ≫ CREATE A BASIC PIE CHART

Because antioxidants are available from so many different food sources, you decide that, as part of the summary, you will discuss the ideal percentage of each food group in an average diet. As you discuss each food group, you will suggest foods in that group that contain antioxidants. You create a basic pie chart displaying the food groups as an aid for this discussion. Refer to Figure 5.27 as you complete Step 3.

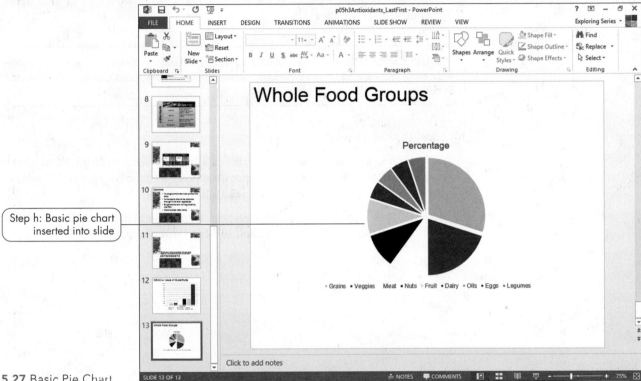

FIGURE 5.27 Basic Pie Chart

> **a.** Create a new slide after Slide 12 using the Title Only layout.
>
> **b.** Type **Whole Food Groups** in the **title placeholder**. Click outside of the title placeholder.
>
> **c.** Click the **DESIGN tab**, click **Format Background** in the Customize group, and then click the **Hide background graphics** option in the Format Background pane. Close the Format Background pane.
>
> **d.** Click the **INSERT tab** and click **Chart** in the Illustrations group.
>
> The Insert Chart dialog box opens.
>
> **e.** Click **Pie** in the left pane and click **OK**.
>
> The default pie chart type is automatically selected, and Excel opens with sample pie chart data.

f. Enter the following data for your pie chart in Excel.

	Percentage
Grains	30
Veggies	20
Meat	10
Nuts	10
Fruit	10
Dairy	5
Oils	5
Eggs	5
Legumes	5

Because a pie chart is a single-series chart, only one data series (Percentage) is entered.

g. Drag the bottom-right corner of the chart data range to resize the range to fit the data you just entered, if necessary.

> **TROUBLESHOOTING:** If you close Excel before resizing the range, not all the categories will display. Click Edit Data in the Data group on the Chart Tools Design tab to reopen Excel and resize the range to fit all categories.

h. Close the Excel worksheet.

A basic pie chart is displayed in PowerPoint. The chart needs to be modified because duplicate colors exist, and the white slice disappears into the background. You will make these modifications in Hands-On Exercise 4.

i. Save the presentation. Keep the presentation open if you plan to continue with Hands-On Exercise 4. If not, close the presentation and exit PowerPoint.

Chart Modification

Charts should be modified and formatted to ensure that the message is conveyed quickly and accurately. Adding a chart title or subtitle, axis titles, data labels, or a legend can help clarify the message, but you must balance the need for clarity with the need for simplicity. This can be a challenge, so ask a classmate or coworker to review your chart and describe their understanding of what your message is.

In addition, review your chart data to see if the numbers can be shortened by showing them as thousands, millions, or other values. If you shorten the numbers on the value axis (Y-axis), you must include an axis label identifying the axis as "in thousands" or "in millions." If you want your audience to see the actual data upon which the chart is based, you can show the data table with or without a legend.

In this section, you will learn how to change a chart type, change a chart layout, and format chart elements.

Changing a Chart Type

After creating the chart, you can experiment with other chart types to see which chart type conveys the message most effectively. For example, you may find that due to the number of bars created by the data, your column chart is cluttered and difficult to read. Changing the chart type to a line chart may show the same information in a clean, easy-to-understand format.

Changing the chart subtype may be enough to emphasize the desired point. Each of the chart types available includes subtypes or variations. Changing the subtype can give the chart a totally different look or can change the purpose of the chart dramatically. The variations include changing from 2-D formatting to 3-D formatting, stacking the data, changing the marker shape, and exploding slices, to name a few.

STEP 1 »   To change the chart type or subtype, do the following:

1. Select the chart.
2. Click the CHART TOOLS DESIGN tab.
3. Click Change Chart Type in the Type group.
4. Click the chart type you want from the left pane or the chart subtype from the right pane.
5. Click OK.

Changing the Chart Layout

Each chart type has predefined layouts that you can quickly apply to your chart. Although you can change each element of the layout individually by manually selecting a style for the individual elements, using a predefined layout keeps your charts consistent and maintains a professional feel to your presentation. To apply a predefined layout, select your chart and click the Chart Tools Design tab. Click Quick Layout in the Chart Layouts group and select the desired layout.

STEP 2 »   To change the layout manually, click the Chart Tools Design tab. Click Add Chart Element in the Chart Layouts group, choose the chart element you want to change, and then select one of the predefined options or click More Options at the bottom of the list. For example, the legend can be moved to predefined locations in the chart. Figure 5.28 shows a sample chart with the legend located at the bottom of the chart.

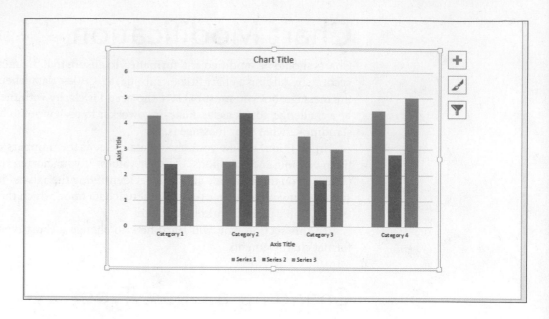

FIGURE 5.28 Chart with Legend Located at the Bottom of the Chart

1. Select the chart.
2. Click the DESIGN tab.
3. Click Add Chart Element.
4. Click Legend.
5. Click Bottom.

A chart layout generally includes a title, axis titles, and a legend. You can modify each of these elements manually by clicking each element from the Add Chart Element options.

PowerPoint determines the measurement or increments on the chart's Y-axis automatically based on the data entered in the worksheet. However, you can change the measurement used—but be careful when changing the measurements of the axes. Changing the Y-axis measurement to a smaller increment can exaggerate the data peaks and valleys displayed in the chart. Changing the measurements to larger increments can flatten or smooth out the data peaks and valleys. Additionally, when the measurements use Excel's Auto feature, they automatically adjust if you make changes to the data to which the maximum and minimum values need to adapt. By contrast, manual measurements do not adapt unless manual readjustments are applied; thus, changes to the Excel data may also require additional changes to the axis measurements for the chart.

To change the chart axis, click the Design tab and click Add Chart Element in the Chart Layouts group. Click Axes, select the axis options you wish to change, and then make the desired changes.

Formatting Chart Elements

To change chart elements such as the fill of a bar in a bar chart, select the element by either clicking it or choosing the element from the list available when you click the Chart Elements arrow in the Current Selection group on the Format tab. You can change shape fills, outline styles, and shape effects on the chart objects just as you changed shapes in SmartArt. After selecting the element, choose Shape Fill, Shape Outline, or Shape Effects from the Shape Styles group on the Format tab.

STEP 3 ››

To make multiple formatting changes to an element, click Format Selection in the Current Selection group on the Format tab. This opens the Format pane for the element you have selected. Depending on that element, you can change the fill, border color, border styles, shadow, and 3-D format simply by clicking options such as Fill & Line, Effects, or Series, and choosing the formatting in the Format pane.

Quick Concepts ✓

1. How can you ensure that a chart conveys your message quickly and accurately? *p. 925*

2. Why would you want to use a predefined layout for your chart? *p. 925*

3. Name three components of a chart's layout. *p. 926*

Hands-On Exercises

 Watch the Video for this Hands-On Exercise!

 MyITLab® HOE4 Training

4 Chart Modification

In your final review of the county health fair presentation, you modify the charts you have created to change a chart type for ease of reading and to correct problems with chart layouts and elements.

Skills covered: Change a Chart Type • Change a Chart Layout • Format Chart Elements

STEP 1 >> CHANGE A CHART TYPE

The chart on Slide 12 contains data about the amount of antioxidants per 100 grams of superfruit. You decide to convert the chart into a bar chart so that the viewer can read down a list to quickly identify the superfruit providing the most antioxidants. Refer to Figure 5.29 as you complete Step 1.

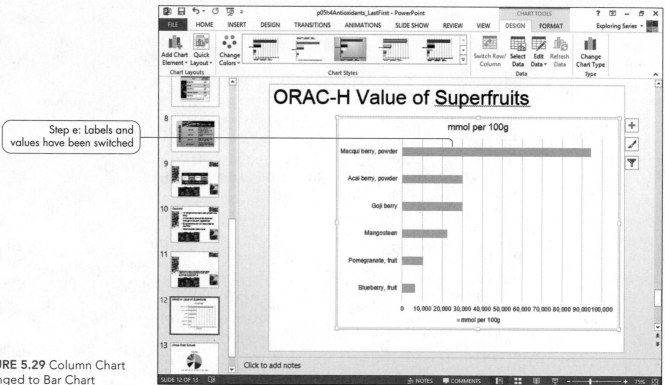

FIGURE 5.29 Column Chart Changed to Bar Chart

a. Open *p05h3Antioxidants_LastFirst*, if necessary. Save the presentation as **p05h4Antioxidants_LastFirst**, changing the *h3* to *h4*.

b. On Slide 12, select the chart.

c. Click the **CHART TOOLS DESIGN tab** and click **Change Chart Type** in the Type group.

d. Select **Bar** as the chart type and accept the default subtype. Click **OK**. Reselect the chart if necessary.

The column chart type changes to the bar chart type.

e. Click **Select Data** in the Data group, click **Switch Row/Column**, click **OK**, and then close Excel.

The superfruits are listed down the vertical axis, and the values are displayed along the horizontal axis. The legend displays but is unnecessary because of the chart title.

> **TROUBLESHOOTING:** If you do not see the superfruits listed down the vertical axis, click the Add Chart Element button in the Chart Layouts group on the CHART TOOLS DESIGN tab. Click Axes and click Primary Vertical.

f. Save the presentation.

STEP 2 ≫ CHANGE A CHART LAYOUT

You decide that including data labels would help the county health fair viewers understand the data. You change the layout of the bar chart so that the labels are easily added and also decide to change the fill of the bars by applying a style to make them more visible when projected. Refer to Figure 5.30 as you complete Step 2.

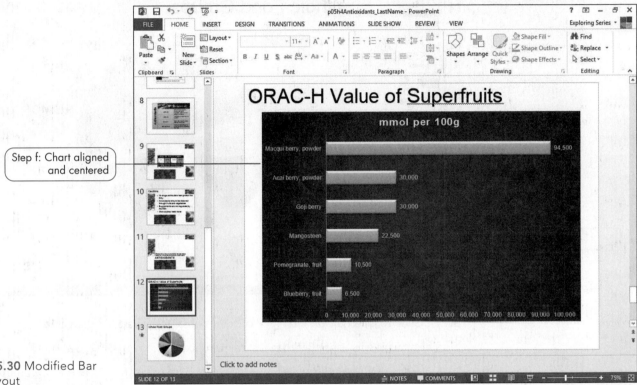

FIGURE 5.30 Modified Bar Chart Layout

a. On Slide 12, select the chart, if necessary.

b. Click the **CHART TOOLS DESIGN tab**, click **Quick Layout** in the Chart Layouts group, and then click **Layout 2**.

Layout 2 puts data labels at the outside ends of the bars and removes the horizontal axis. Layout 2 also moves the legend underneath the chart title. The legend is unnecessary and will be addressed in the next instruction.

c. Click **Add Chart Element** in the Chart Layouts group, click **Legend**, and then select **None**.

The legend is deleted.

d. Click **More** in the Chart Styles group on the CHART TOOLS DESIGN tab and click **Style 7**.

A dark background is applied to make the chart more readable and to add contrast.

e. Click the border of the chart if necessary, click the **FORMAT tab**, and then change the width of the chart to **9"** in the Size group.

f. Click **Align Objects** in the Arrange group and click **Align Middle**. Click **Align Objects** again and click **Align Center**.

g. Save the presentation.

STEP 3 ≫ FORMAT CHART ELEMENTS

After reviewing the pie chart on Slide 13, you decide several elements of the chart need to be formatted. The white slice blends with the background, so the color style of the chart needs to be changed. You also want the category name and percentage on the inside end of each pie slice. Finally, because you want to discuss each food group with the county health fair attendees, you apply an animation to bring the slices in one at a time. Refer to Figure 5.31 as you complete Step 3.

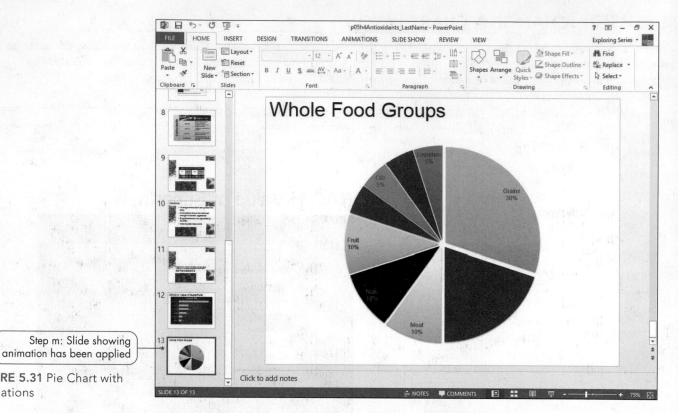

Step m: Slide showing animation has been applied

FIGURE 5.31 Pie Chart with Animations

a. On Slide 13, select the **pie chart** and click the border to activate the chart area.

The chart is selected rather than just the pie slices.

b. Click the **FORMAT tab** and change the height of the chart to **6.7"** in the Size group.

The change in the chart height moves part of the chart off the slide.

c. Click **Align Objects** in the Arrange group and click **Align Bottom**. Click **Align Objects** again and click **Align Center**.

The bottom chart border aligns with the bottom of the slide.

d. Click any slice of the pie and click **Quick Layout** in the Chart Layouts group on the CHART TOOLS DESIGN tab.

Clicking a slice of the pie once selects all slices of the pie.

TROUBLESHOOTING: If you double-click a pie slice, the Format Data Point pane opens. Click Close and the pie slice is selected.

---

e. Click **Layout 1** (first row, first column) in the Quick Layout group.

The category name and the percentage now appear at the end of each pie slice. Because of the color scheme, some labels are not visible.

f. Click the **CHART TOOLS DESIGN tab**, click **More** in the Chart Styles group, and then click **Style 5** (first row, fifth column). Click one of the data labels on a pie slice once to select all the data labels. Click the **FORMAT tab**, click the **Text Fill arrow** in the WordArt Styles group, and then click **Red** under *Standard Colors*.

The text is changed to a theme style that coordinates with the presentation. The previous black text color was difficult to see on some of the slices, but the red color makes it easier to read the text on all the slices.

g. Select the legend on the bottom of the pie chart and press **Delete**.

The legend is unnecessary when data labels are used.

h. Select the title *Percentage* at the top of the chart and press **Delete**.

The title is unnecessary because the percent symbol appears next to the percentage displayed on each pie slice.

i. Click the **ANIMATIONS tab**, click **More** in the Animation group, and then click **Zoom** (Entrance category).

j. Click **Effect Options** in the Animation group.

The Effect Options gallery opens.

k. Click **Slide Center** in the Vanishing Point category.

l. Click **Effect Options** again and click **By Category** in the Sequence category.

m. Click **Preview** in the Preview group.

Each pie slice now individually zooms out from the center of the pie when the slide show plays.

n. Save and close the file, and submit based on your instructor's directions.

Chapter Objectives Review

After reading this chapter, you have accomplished the following objectives:

1. **Create a poster or a banner**
   - Text-based charts convey relationships among words, numbers, or graphics.
   - Posters and banners are specialized text-based charts.
   - Poster and banner files can be uploaded to an online printing service or delivered to a local printing company to be printed on special-sized paper.

2. **Draw a table**
   - Tables are text-based charts that organize information, making it possible to more easily see relationships among words, numbers, or graphics.
   - Tables can be inserted by specifying the number of columns and rows needed or by drawing the table.
   - When you have multiple cell heights and widths, drawing a table can be an efficient method to use.

3. **Create a table structure**
   - Make the table data as simple as possible to convey your message.
   - Change row height, column width, and table size to accommodate your information or call attention to it.
   - Align text within cells, rows, and columns to enhance the readability of the data.

4. **Format table components**
   - Set a background fill to add interest to the background of a table using the background fill style.
   - You can easily change border style, weight, and color.
   - You can add special effects to a cell, selected cells, or a table.

5. **Change table layout**
   - You can insert rows above or below an existing row, or insert columns to the left or right of an existing column.
   - You can delete rows or columns to change the overall layout of a table.

6. **Share information between applications**
   - Tables created in Word or Excel can be embedded in or linked to a PowerPoint presentation.
   - Embedding creates a larger file than linking because linking simply places a copy of the table into the presentation and all editing takes place in the source application.

   - Other objects, such as charts, can also be linked to or embedded in a presentation.

7. **Identify chart types and elements**
   - Choose the type of chart that best portrays your message.
   - The chart area is made up of the chart and all its elements.
   - The plot area contains the data.

8. **Create and insert a chart**
   - PowerPoint charts are based on Excel worksheets.
   - Information is entered into a worksheet and plotted to create the PowerPoint presentation.
   - The Insert Chart dialog box enables you to select the chart type and the chart style you want to use.

9. **Switch row and column data.**
   - Switch row and column data to change emphasis.
   - Charts should be modified and formatted to ensure that the chart conveys the intended message.

10. **Change a chart type**
    - Each chart type organizes and emphasizes data differently.
    - You can experiment with chart styles after creating a chart. Select the one that conveys the intended message of the chart.

11. **Change the chart layout**
    - Use a predefined layout to keep your charts consistent and maintain a professional feel for your presentation.
    - You can also edit the layout manually by choosing from chart title and axis title options, legend options, data label options, data table options, and axes and gridline options and by changing backgrounds in chart elements.

12. **Format chart elements**
    - The shape style (fill, outline, and effects) can be changed for individual chart elements.
    - You can also use the Format Selection option to affect a current selection, which enables you to choose from fill, border color, border styles, shadow, and 3-D format options.

Key Terms Matching

Match the key terms with their definitions. Write the key term letter by the appropriate numbered definition.

a. Bar chart
b. Chart area
c. Column chart
d. Data series
e. Destination file
f. Embedded object
g. Gridline
h. Label
i. Legend
j. Line chart

k. Linked object
l. Multiseries data series
m. Object linking and embedding (OLE)
n. Pie chart
o. Single-series data series
p. Source file
q. Stub column
r. Text-based chart
s. X-axis
t. Y-axis

1. _____ The file that contains an inserted object, such as a PowerPoint presentation with an Excel worksheet embedded in it. **p. 906**

2. _____ A part of the destination file that is updated when the source file is updated because the information is stored in the source file but displayed as the object in the destination file. **p. 907**

3. _____ A chart that shows a relationship between words, numbers, and/or graphics and arranges and organizes information by text. **p. 890**

4. _____ A data series representing data for two or more sets of data. **p. 915**

5. _____ A part of the destination file that, once inserted, no longer maintains a connection to the source file or source application in which the object was created. **p. 906**

6. _____ The horizontal axis, which usually contains the category information, such as products, companies, or intervals of time. **p. 916**

7. _____ A type of chart used to show comparisons among items, where the information is displayed horizontally. **p. 914**

8. _____ A line that extend from the horizontal or vertical axes and that can be displayed to make the chart data easier to read and understand. **p. 916**

9. _____ A type of chart used to show proportions of a whole. **p. 914**

10. _____ A feature that enables you to insert an object created in one application into a document created in another application. **p. 906**

11. _____ A type of chart used to show changes over time or comparisons among items where the information is displayed vertically. **p. 914**

12. _____ A data series representing only one set of data. **p. 915**

13. _____ The first column of a table that typically contains the information that identifies the data in each row. **p. 894**

14. _____ A chart element found in multiseries charts that helps identify the data series, assigns a format or color to each data series, and then displays that information with the data series name. **p. 916**

15. _____ The vertical axis, which usually contains the values or amounts. **p. 916**

16. _____ The file that contains the original table or data that is used or copied to create a linked or embedded object, such as a Word document or an Excel worksheet. **p. 906**

17. _____ A chart element that identifies data in the chart. **p. 915**

18. _____ The chart and all of its elements, bounded by the placeholder borders. **p. 915**

19. _____ A type of chart used to display a large number of data points over time. **p. 914**

20. _____ A chart element that contains the data points representing a set of related numbers. **p. 915**

Multiple Choice

1. The graphical representation you would use to communicate a relationship between numerical data such as a comparison in sales over years is a:

   (a) Photograph.

   (b) Statistical chart or graph.

   (c) SmartArt diagram.

   (d) Text-based chart.

2. A stub column is the:

   (a) Title that appears at the top of a table describing the table contents.

   (b) Data points representing a set of related numbers.

   (c) First column of the table.

   (d) Last row of the table.

3. What is the chart element that identifies data in the chart?

   (a) Gridline

   (b) Legend

   (c) Label

   (d) Data series

4. A PowerPoint slide displaying a table object that is a copy or representation of a file stored in Excel that does not get updated displays what type of object?

   (a) Embedded object

   (b) Linked object

   (c) Included object

   (d) Outsourced object

5. Which of the following is not a true statement regarding creating charts for display in a PowerPoint presentation?

   (a) When you create a chart in PowerPoint, you use an Excel worksheet to enter the data you wish to plot.

   (b) When you create a chart in PowerPoint, you use an Access database to enter the data you wish to plot.

   (c) You can create a chart by clicking the chart icon in a content placeholder.

   (d) You can paste a copy of an Excel chart into a PowerPoint slide by using the Paste Special command.

6. The purpose of a legend is to identify:

   (a) The type of information defined by the X-axis.

   (b) The type of information defined by the Y-axis.

   (c) The chart type.

   (d) What marker colors and patterns represent.

7. To represent the portion of time you spend studying versus the time you spend on other activities in a day, which chart type should you use to show their proportions relative to a 24-hour time period?

   (a) Pie

   (b) Radar

   (c) Line

   (d) Column

8. To show the growth of student enrollment at your college over the past 20 years, the best choice for your chart type would be:

   (a) Pie.

   (b) Bar.

   (c) Line.

   (d) Column.

9. To compare the sales of three sales representatives for the past two years, the best choice for your chart type would be:

   (a) Pie.

   (b) Column.

   (c) Line.

   (d) Doughnut.

10. What is the name of the table object that is part of the destination file and is updated when the source file is updated?

    (a) Linked object

    (b) Embedded object

    (c) Multiseries data series

    (d) X-axis

Practice Exercises

1 Coffee Club Poster

You are designing a poster to advertise the Saturday Morning Coffee Club at the 1st and Main Coffee House. The poster will be stapled to bulletin boards and placed in the store to remind customers of the event. The owner wants the poster to be simple but eye-catching, so you decide to create a poster that announces the ongoing event with general information. Once the poster is designed, you plan to take the file to a local print shop for reproduction, but before doing so you need a copy for the owner to review. You print a copy scaled to fit a standard 8.5" × 11" page. This exercise follows the same set of skills as used in Hands-On Exercise 1 in the chapter. Refer to Figure 5.32 as you complete this exercise.

Event advertisement

FIGURE 5.32 Scaled Advertising Poster

a. Begin a new presentation using the Retrospect theme and save it as **p05p1CoffeeClub_LastFirst**.

b. Create a handout header with your name and a handout footer with the file name, your instructor's name, and your class. Include the current date.

c. Click **Layout** in the Slides group on the HOME tab and click **Picture with Caption**.

d. Click the **DESIGN tab**, click **Slide Size** in the Customize group, and then select **Custom Slide Size** to open the Slide Size dialog box.

e. Select the existing number for *Width* and type **17**.

f. Select the existing number for *Height* and type **22**. Note that the *Slides sized for* option now displays *Custom* as its paper size and the Orientation is now set to *Portrait* for Slides and for Notes, Handouts & Outlines. Click **OK** and click **Maximize**.

g. Click the **INSERT tab** and click **Online Pictures**. Locate a picture online and click **Insert**. Drag the picture as needed to make it fit the placeholder.

h. Click the picture, if necessary, and click **More** in the Picture Styles group on the PICTURE TOOLS FORMAT tab.

i. Click **Simple Frame, Black** in the Picture Styles group.

j. Click the **title placeholder** and type the following information. Press **Enter** after each line (see Figure 5.32).

Saturday Morning Coffee Club at

1st and Main Coffee House

k. Click the **text placeholder** and type the following information. Press **Enter** after each line (see Figure 5.32).

Join us each Saturday for Coffee and Tea specials.

Local artists, authors, or musicians will present their current works!

9:00 a.m.–12:00 noon

l. Click the **FILE tab**, click **Print**, click the **Full Page Slides arrow**, and then click **Handouts, 1 Slide**.

m. Click the **1 Slide arrow** and click **Scale to Fit Paper**, if necessary. Click **Print**.

The poster prints on the size of paper loaded in the printer. Because desktop printers generally have a nonprintable region, the poster may have a white border surrounding it. Because you printed a handout instead of the full-page slide, the header and footer further reduce the size of the poster.

n. Save and close the file, and submit based on your instructor's directions.

2 Garden Club Presentation

Gardening is a seasonal activity. Each season demands specific tasks to be completed, depending on the climate zone. Some gardens require bulbs to be planted a few seasons prior to the bloom period, and some plants can be added to the garden once spring has arrived. You have been asked to create a presentation explaining this planning process. This exercise follows the skills practiced in Hands-On Exercise 2. Refer to Figure 5.33 as you complete this skill.

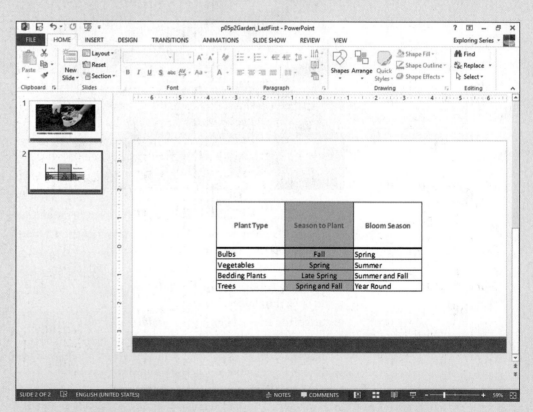

FIGURE 5.33 Planning Your Garden Activities Presentation

Photo: JackF/Fotolia

a. Open *p05p2Garden* and save the presentation as **p05p2Garden_LastFirst**.

b. Create a handout header with your name and a handout footer with your instructor's name and your class. Include the current date.

c. Open *p05p2Activities.xlsx* and save the file as **p05p2Activities_LastFirst.xlsx**.

d. Select the **range A2:C6** to select all the table data in the Excel file. Click **Copy** in the Clipboard group on the HOME tab (or press **Ctrl+C**).

e. Click the PowerPoint file on the Windows taskbar to make the presentation the active file. Click **Slide 2**. Click the **Paste arrow button** in the Clipboard group on the HOME tab and click **Paste Special**.

f. Click the **Paste link option** in the Paste Special dialog box. Click **Microsoft Excel Worksheet Object** in the As box, if necessary, and click **OK**.

g. Close the Excel file. Double-click the table object in the presentation.

h. Select **row 2** in Excel, click the **Font Color arrow**, and then select **Blue** under *Standard Colors*.

i. Observe the color change to the column headings in the presentation. Save the changes in the Excel file and close Excel.

j. Drag the bottom-right corner of the table to enlarge the table in the presentation. Click the **FORMAT tab** and click **Align Objects** in the Arrange group. Click **Align Center** and click **Align Middle**. Save and close the file, and submit based on your instructor's directions.

3 Savings Chart

FROM SCRATCH

No matter what stage of life you are in—a student, a recent college graduate, a newlywed, a new parent, or a retiree—you may want to create a savings account to help you reach some kind of goal. One way to accomplish this is to determine the amount you need, and then break it down into regular contributions necessary to reach your goal amount. A key idea to remember is that the more time you give your money to grow, the less money you have to invest. In this exercise, you begin a presentation on savings by creating a chart. This exercise follows the same set of skills as used in Hands-On Exercises 3 and 4 in the chapter. Refer to Figure 5.34 as you complete this exercise.

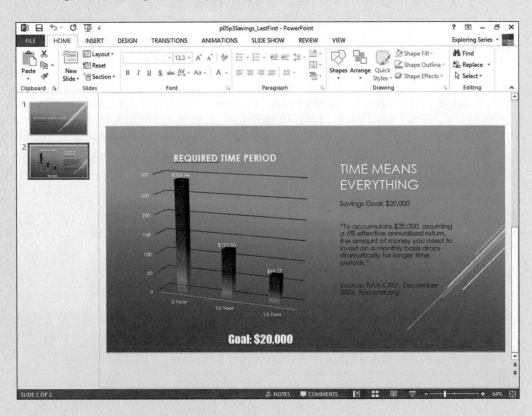

FIGURE 5.34 Savings Presentation

a. Create a new presentation based on the Slice template available in the New Presentation window. Save the presentation as **p05p3Savings_LastFirst**.

b. Create a handout header with your name and a handout footer with your instructor's name and your class. Include the current date.

c. Create a title slide, if necessary. Type **Putting Time to Work** as the title and **Saving for the Future** as the subtitle.

d. Add a new slide using the *Content with Caption* layout.

e. Click the **title placeholder** and type **Time Means Everything**. Select the text and increase the font size to **32 pt**.

f. Click the **text placeholder** on the right side of the slide below the title and type **Savings Goal: $20,000**.

g. Press **Enter** twice and type **"To accumulate $20,000, assuming a 6% effective annualized return, the amount of money you need to invest on a monthly basis drops dramatically for longer time periods."**

h. Size the text placeholder to change the height to **3.5"**. Click to place the insertion point at the end of the last sentence typed. Press **Enter** twice and type **Source: TIAA-CREF, December 2006, tiaa-cref.org**.

i. Click the **Insert Chart icon** in the *Click to add text* placeholder on the left side of the slide.

j. Click **OK** to insert the default Clustered Column chart.

k. Clear the current sample data. Enter the following information and resize the chart data range as needed to fit the data entered. Close Excel.

	Required Time Period
5-Year	286.44
10-Year	122.50
15-Year	69.37

l. Click **More** in the Chart Styles group and click **Style 9**.

m. Click **Add Chart Element** in the Chart Layouts group, click **Legend**, and then select **None**.

n. Click **Add Chart Element** in the Chart Layouts group, click **Data Labels**, and then click **Outside End**.

o. Click one of the data labels at the top of a bar to select all labels and click the **FORMAT tab**. Click **Format Selection** in the Current Selection group. In the Format Data Labels pane, click the **Label Options icon** under the LABEL OPTIONS tab heading. Click **Number** in the bottom pane options to expand it. Click the list arrow under *Category* and click **Currency**. Close the pane.

p. Insert a new text box positioned beneath the X-axis and type **Goal: $20,000** Resize and reposition the text box as necessary. Change the font to **Impact, 28 pt**.

q. Select the chart, click **Change Chart Type** in the Type group on the CHART TOOLS DESIGN tab, and then click **3-D Clustered Column** in the Column category. Click **OK**.

r. Save and close the file, and submit based on your instructor's directions.

Mid-Level Exercises

1 School Spirit Banner

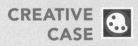

CREATIVE CASE

FROM SCRATCH

You belong to a student organization that prepares posters and banners for school activities. Next Saturday, your team, the Tazewell Tigers, faces the Ukiah Lions at Jefferson Field. You prepare a banner for this event. Refer to Figure 5.35 as you complete this exercise.

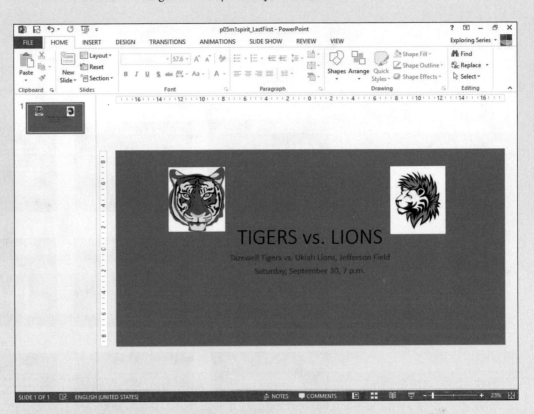

FIGURE 5.35 Example of a School Spirit Banner

a. Save a blank presentation as **p05m1Spirit_LastFirst**.

b. Create a handout header with your name and a handout footer with your instructor's name and your class. Include the current date.

c. Create a custom page size of 36" × 18", a standard size for small banners.

d. Type **TIGERS vs. LIONS** as the slide title using the font of your choice.

e. Create a two-line subtitle. Type **Tazewell Tigers vs. Ukiah Lions, Jefferson Field** as the first line of the subtitle. Type **Saturday, September 30, 7 p.m.** as the second line of the subtitle.

 f. Insert the clip art images of your choice to represent the Tigers and the Lions. If you want, you may replace the tiger and lion mascots with the mascots of your choice, making sure you also change the team names in the subtitle.

g. Arrange the clip art and placeholders on the page as you see fit. Make any other changes such as additional text and a background change as desired.

h. Save and close the file, and submit based on your instructor's directions.

You put together a presentation for a successful retail store owned by three close friends. They wish to expand their operation by requesting venture capital. Instead of creating PowerPoint tables, you decide to link to a worksheet that already contains sales data. Refer to Figure 5.36 as you complete this exercise.

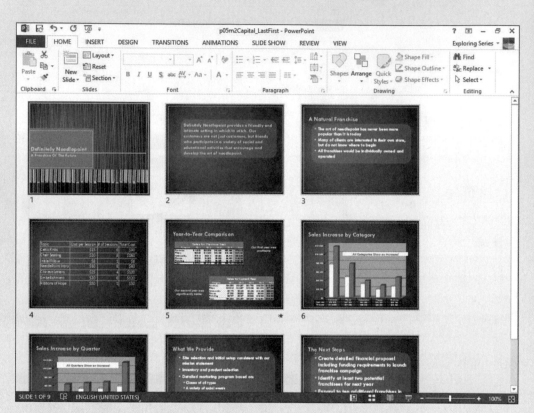

FIGURE 5.36 Microsoft Excel Objects in a Presentation

Photo: toey19863/Fotolia

a. Open *p05m2Capital* and save it as **p05m2Capital_LastFirst**.

b. Create a handout header with your name and a handout footer with your instructor's name and your class. Include the current date.

c. Open the *p05m2Sales* Excel workbook and save it as **p05m2Sales_LastFirst**.

d. Copy the data in the Previous Year tab for the range A1:F8 in Excel, switch to PowerPoint, and then paste the data as a picture on Slide 5. Change the table size height to **2"**. Drag the worksheet object to the left of the text *Our first year was profitable* and under the slide title.

e. Copy the data in the Current Year tab for the range A1:F8 in Excel, switch to PowerPoint, and then paste the data to the same slide (Slide 5), keeping the source formatting. Change the table size by locking the aspect ratio and change the table height to **2"**. Drag the worksheet object to the right of the text *Our second year was significantly better*.

f. Copy the *Increase by Category* Excel chart and paste (with Use Destination Theme & Embed Workbook selected) to Slide 6 in the presentation. Resize the chart area height to **5.5"**. Reposition the chart below the slide title. Change the font size for the vertical axis and the horizontal data table axis to **12 pt** and the font color to **White, Text 1**.

g. Copy the *Increase by Quarter* Excel chart and paste (with Use Destination Theme & Embed Workbook selected) to Slide 7 in the presentation. Size the chart area height to **5.5"**. Reposition the chart below the slide title. Change the vertical and horizontal data table axis font size to **12 pt** and the font color to **White, Text 1**.

DISCOVER

h. Use PowerPoint's Insert Object feature to create a new object on Slide 4: a new Microsoft Excel Worksheet. Create the following table in Excel cells A1:D8 and use a formula in cell D2 to calculate the *Cost per Session × # of Sessions* for Celtic Knits. Auto fill the formula down to cell D8 to copy the formula for the range D2:D8 (to allow enable Excel to figure the total cost of the class for each topic). Format column D as **Currency**.

Topic	Cost per Session	# of Sessions	Total Cost
Celtic Knits	$15	6	=PRODUCT(B2:C2)
Chair Seating	$20	8	
Initial Pillow	$8	1	
NeedlePoint Intro	$10	8	
Chinese Letters	$25	4	
Embellishment	$20	6	
Ribbons of Hope	$50	1	

i. Resize the Excel window to fit the data cell range. Resize the columns to fit data by double-clicking the right column border. Change the font size to **16 pt** and change the font color to **White, Background 1**.

j. Exit Excel and size the new Excel object to a width of **8.25"** in PowerPoint. Resize columns widths as necessary.

k. Apply **Align Center** and **Align Middle** to the new Excel object.

l. Save and close the file, and submit based on your instructor's directions.

3 Social Networking for Businesses

COLLABORATION CASE

You and a classmate have been assigned to create a presentation about a subject that interests you personally. Together, you have decided to create the presentation about the use of social networking in business. Create a new presentation using the Ion theme available in the Themes palette and save it as **p05m3Social_LastFirst**. Each of you must research two different types of social networking that are often used. Find as much information as you can about how companies use social networking to communicate with their customers and the number of customers or users that each social network has in a least four major countries.

Create the following slides: (1) a Title slide, (2) two Content with Caption slides, and (3) a Picture with Caption slide. Create a title and subtitle as appropriate on the Title slide. Briefly describe each of the social-network advertising options and add a descriptive chart or table for the two types of social networking on the Content with Caption slides. Finally, summarize your social networking research and add an image that enhances your presentation on the final slide in the presentation.

Beyond the Classroom

Winter Sports
RESEARCH CASE

FROM SCRATCH

You decide to get away next week and indulge in your favorite winter sports—snowboarding and skiing. You research current daily snowfall and the price of a lift ticket at your favorite winter location. Because you are also studying charting in your Basic Computer Applications class, you decide to practice your charting skills by creating a line graph showing the new snowfall for the past seven days at your favorite location. You also create a bar chart showing the price of full-day lift tickets. You may choose to add additional slides, if desired.

Visit any site on the Internet you choose and gather the data you need to complete the charts. Create a presentation, and then save it as **p05b2Winter_LastFirst**. Enter the data for each of the charts in worksheets, and then format the charts in an attractive, easy-to-read format. Create a handout header with your name and a footer with your instructor's name and class. Include the date. Apply appropriate titles and labels as needed to ensure that the chart is easily and accurately understood. Include a slide that lists the resources you used for the data. Save and close the file, and submit based on your instructor's directions.

Chart Improvements
DISASTER RECOVERY

The presentation *p05b3Tips* includes four charts that confuse the message they are supposed to deliver. In some cases, the wrong chart type has been applied, and in others the formatting of the chart is distracting. In the Notes pane of each slide, design tips are given that you can read to help you identify the errors in the chart. Open the file and immediately save it as **p05b3Tips_LastFirst**. Read the notes associated with each slide, and then edit the chart on the slide so it incorporates the tips. Make all modifications necessary to create a professional, easy-to-understand chart. Even if you do not complete this exercise, you should read the design tips in this slide show. Save and close the file, and submit based on your instructor's directions.

Job Search Strategies
SOFT SKILLS CASE **S**

Research the profession you are most interested in pursuing after graduation, and then create a presentation. One slide should outline two key job-search strategies for your chosen profession. Another slide should illustrate some data for expected job growth in the profession as an embedded chart or table. The last slide should provide a typical job description or want ad for your profession. Save and close the presentation, and submit based on your instructor's directions.

Capstone Exercise

A Kiss of Chocolate is a successful spa and lounge dedicated to the appreciation of chocolate and its benefits. The operation has been so successful in its five years of operation that the owners opened two additional locations and are now considering franchising. They are meeting with officers of a franchising corporation, which offers strategic corporate, management, and marketing services for franchisers. The franchising representatives have asked for an overview of the services and products of A Kiss of Chocolate, sales for this year and last year, a year-to-year comparison, and charts showing the increase. The owners of A Kiss of Chocolate ask for your help in preparing the presentation for the meeting.

Create a Poster

The owners of A Kiss of Chocolate have reserved a meeting room at a local conference center. They want a large, foam-backed poster on an easel next to the conference room door. They ask you to prepare the poster, and then they will have a local company print it.

a. Open *p05c1Spaposter* and save it as **p05c1Spaposter_ LastFirst**.

b. Create a handout header with your name and a handout footer with the file name, your instructor's name, and your class. Include the current date.

c. Change the width of the page to **17"** and the height of the page to **22"** in the Page Setup dialog box. Click **OK**. Click **Maximize**.

d. Type **Gardenia Room, 9 a.m.** in a new text box.

e. Change the default text color to **Light Yellow, Text 2**. Apply bold to the text.

f. Position the left top edge of the new text box at 1" horizontal and 10" vertical positions from the top left corner.

g. Print a copy of the poster as a handout, one per page, using the *Scale to Fit Paper* option.

h. Save and close the file, and submit based on your instructor's directions.

Create a Day Spa Packages Table

Some slides of the A Kiss of Chocolate slide show have been created, including an introduction to the spa, products available for sale in the gift store, services available in the spa, and chocolate desserts and drinks available in the lounge. Now you insert a table showing the packages available in the Day Spa.

a. Open *p05c1Spashow* and save it as **p05c1Spashow_ LastFirst**.

b. Create a new slide following Slide 4 using the *Title and Content* layout.

c. Type the title **Day Spa Packages**.

d. Create a four-column, five-row table. Do not worry about width or height of rows or columns.

e. Type the following column headings: **Package**, **Length**, **Cost**, **Services**.

f. Fill in the table using the following information (the table will exceed the slide, but you will format the table to fit in the next step):

A Kiss of Chocolate	1.5 hours	$160	Spa Rain Shower, Full-Body Mint Chocolate Exfoliation, 45-Minute Peppermint-Chocolate Massage
A Chocolate Hug	1.5 hours	$160	Hot Stone Treatment with Warm Raspberry-Chocolate Oil, Hydrating Body Wrap, 45-Minute Peppermint-Chocolate Massage
The Chocolate Dip	2 hours	$175	Mint-Chocolate Soufflé Body Mask, Full-Body Mint Chocolate Exfoliation, Hydrating Body Wrap, Raspberry-Chocolate Shower
Chocolate Decadence	3 hours	$300	Hot Stone Treatment with Warm Raspberry-Chocolate Oil, Raspberry-Chocolate Shower, Full-Body Mint Chocolate Exfoliation, Mint-Chocolate Soufflé Body Mask, 50-Minute Peppermint-Chocolate Massage

Modify Table Structure and Format Table

The table structure needs to be modified so the table fits on the slide. You also format the table to obtain the desired appearance.

Size the table and apply a table style. Refer to Figure 5.37 while completing this step.

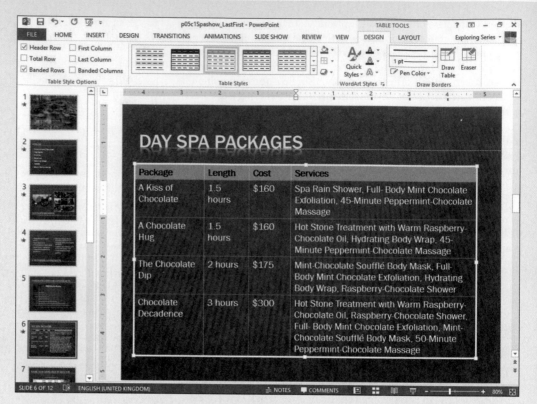

FIGURE 5.37 Day Spa Packages Table

Photos: (Slide 1) happysunstock/
Fotolia, (Slide 3, left) gtranquillity/
Fotolia, (Slide 3, right) BeTa-Artworks/
Fotolia

a. Change the table structure by dragging the first three column borders until they closely fit the column headings.

b. Set the table size to a height of **5.01"** and a width of **9"**.

c. Apply the **Light Style 2 - Accent 1 table style** (second row, second column, Light category) to the table.

d. Arrange the table so that it is centered horizontally on the slide and does not block the slide title.

Link Excel Tables and Charts

A Kiss of Chocolate's owners have tables and charts showing sales figures for this year and the previous year. These figures show that all three branches of A Kiss of Chocolate have increased revenue and profit each year, and the charts emphasize the data. Refer to Figure 5.38 while completing this step.

a. Create a Title Only slide after Slide 5 and type **Sales Have Increased at Each Spa** as the title.

b. Open the *p05c1Spasales* workbook in Excel, save it as **p05c1Spasales_LastFirst.xlsx**, and then move to the worksheet containing the sales data for the previous year. Copy the data and paste it into Slide 6 of the presentation. Change the Paste options to **Keep Source Formatting**.

c. Repeat step b to paste the worksheet data for the current year into Slide 6.

d. Size the two worksheets on Slide 6 to a height of **2.5"** and a width of **8"**.

e. Arrange the two tables attractively on the slide.

f. Create a Title Only slide after Slide 6 and type **All Stores Show an Increase** as the title of the new Slide 7. Link the *Increase by Store* Excel chart to the new slide.

g. Size the chart to a height of **4.5"** and a width of **7.5"**.

h. Align the chart in the center of the slide.

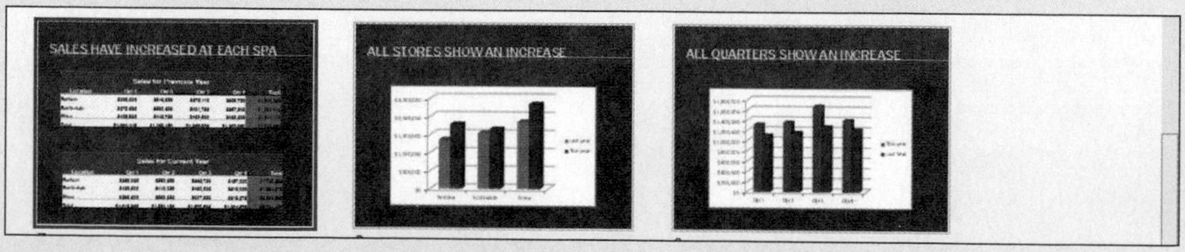

FIGURE 5.38 Linked Excel Sales Data

i. Create a Title Only slide after Slide 7 and type **All Quarters Show an Increase** as the title of the new Slide 8. Link the *Increase by Quarter* Excel chart to the new slide.

j. Size the chart to a height of **4.5"** and a width of **7.5"**.

k. Align the chart in the center of the slide.

Create a Bar Chart

Because you serve dark and milk chocolate desserts and drinks in the Chocolate Lounge, you decide to add a slide to support the idea that chocolate intake may be healthy. You create a bar chart to show the amount of antioxidants in a serving of chocolate in comparison to other foods that contain antioxidants.

a. Create a *Title and Content* slide after Slide 4 and type **Chocolate Contains Antioxidants** as the title of the new Slide 5.

b. Create a bar chart using the default Clustered Bar type with the following data:

Dark Chocolate	9080
Cocoa	8260
Prunes	5570
Milk Chocolate	3200
Raisins	2830
Blueberries	2400
Blackberries	2036
Strawberries	1540

c. Add **ORAC Units per Serving** for the title. Size the chart to a height of **5"** and a width of **8.5"**.

d. Align the chart in the center of the slide

Modify and Format a Bar Chart

You modify and format the bar chart to improve the appearance. Refer to Figure 5.39 while completing this step.

a. Remove the legend.

b. Apply **Chart Style 7** to the chart.

c. Click **Add Chart Element** in the Chart Layouts group, select **Data Labels**, and choose **More Data Label Options**.

d. Click **Number**, set the options to **General**.

e. Add a **Glow Shape Effect** to the plot area series using the **Orange, 8 pt glow, Accent color 1**.

f. Save and close the file, and submit based on your instructor's direction.

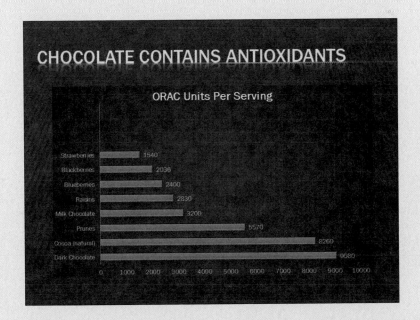

FIGURE 5.39 Chocolate Antioxidants Bar Chart

Interactivity and Advanced Animation

Engaging the Audience

1. Insert and use hyperlinks p. 948
2. Add action buttons p. 952
3. Use a trigger p. 955
4. Apply multiple animations to an object p. 966
5. Apply a motion path animation p. 967
6. Specify animation settings and timing p. 970
7. Animate text p. 972
8. Use the Animation Pane p. 973

CASE STUDY | Teaching Aids

As the teaching assistant for a computer literacy instructor, you prepare numerous teaching aids to help students. You modify a presentation in a quiz format to help students review charts and graphs. The existing presentation includes slides that display a question and a list of choices. You insert sound action buttons so that if a student answers correctly, the student hears applause; if the student answers incorrectly, the student hears feedback indicating it is an incorrect choice. You add action buttons for students to use to navigate through the presentation and hyperlinks to open a reference table and an assignment. You include your e-mail address in the slide show in case the students need to contact you.

After modifying the Charts and Graphs presentation, you modify a presentation designed to help the computer literacy students understand PowerPoint's advanced animation features. You create animation examples for students to view.

Hyperlinks and Action Buttons

A typical PowerPoint presentation is a *linear presentation*. In a linear presentation, each slide is designed to move one right after another, and the viewer or audience progresses through slides, starting with the first slide and advancing sequentially until the last slide is reached. If you add *interactivity*, or the ability to branch nonsequentially, to another part of the presentation based on decisions made by a viewer or audience, you create a *non-linear presentation*. Adding interactivity by involving your audience in your presentation helps capture interest and retain attention. The flexibility and spontaneity of a non-linear presentation typically frees you to become more conversational with the audience, which leads to even more interaction.

You can add interactivity by creating *hyperlinks* that branch to slides or other locations containing additional information or by adding *action buttons*. An action button is a ready-made button designed to serve as an icon that can initiate an action when clicked, pointed to, or run over with the mouse. Figure 6.1 demonstrates the linear versus non-linear navigation options in a presentation. In the non-linear slide show, Slide 1 could include a menu option enabling the viewer to choose any of the remaining five slides, and the remaining slides could be designed to enable the viewer to navigate back to the first slide or to other related slides.

In this section, you will add interactivity to a slide show by adding hyperlinks, action buttons, and a trigger.

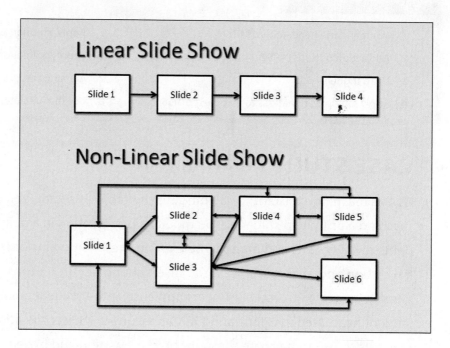

FIGURE 6.1 Linear Versus Non-Linear Navigation Options in a Presentation

Inserting and Using Hyperlinks

You can insert a hyperlink to enable a presenter to tailor the flow and content of a presentation based on audience questions or to enable single viewers to navigate through a slide show at their own pace, visiting the slides desired to gain more information in areas of interest or to review as needed. To activate a hyperlink, display the presentation in Slide Show view or Reading view and position the mouse pointer over a hyperlink; the mouse pointer becomes a hand pointer. If the hyperlink is attached to text, the text color will be different from regular text and the text will be underlined. Click the hyperlink and you jump to a new location. The first time you click a hyperlink, the color of the hyperlink changes so that you know the link has been accessed previously. The colors assigned to the unused link and the used link are set by the theme you have applied to your slide show.

PowerPoint enables you to attach a hyperlink to any selected object such as text, shapes, images, charts, and even SmartArt or WordArt. The hyperlink can link to a(n):

- Existing file
- Web page
- Slide in the open presentation
- New document
- E-mail address

Regardless of where you want the user to be able to move, the process for inserting a hyperlink is similar. To insert a hyperlink, do the following:

1. Select the object or text you want the link attached to.
2. Click the INSERT tab.
3. Click Hyperlink in the Links group.
4. Click the type of link you want in the *Link to* pane on the left side of the Insert Hyperlink dialog box.
5. Select and add any additional desired options and information related to the link location you selected.
6. Click OK.

TIP | Using Other Methods to Insert Hyperlinks

You can also use the keyboard shortcut Ctrl+K or you can right-click the selected object or text and select Hyperlink from the shortcut menu to open the Insert Hyperlink dialog box.

Link to an Existing File or Web Page

When the Insert Hyperlink dialog box opens, *Link to Existing File or Web Page* is the default selection. If you are attaching the *link to* text and you selected the text before opening the dialog box, the text appears in the *Text to display* box at the top of the dialog box. If you did not pre-select text, the word to the right of the insertion point displays. You can delete any text that appears and enter the text you want to display on your slide in this box.

Often, hyperlinks link to Web pages. At the bottom of the dialog box is an Address box where you enter the ***uniform resource locator (URL)***, or Web address, of the Web page you wish to link to. If you know the URL, you can type it in the box, but it is better to copy and paste a link to avoid errors caused by misspelling or incorrect punctuation.

If you do not know the URL, you can find it in one of several ways. If you visited the page recently, click Browsed Pages to show a list of the Web sites you have recently visited. Click the address from the list of URLs shown. You can also click *Browse the Web* (located below the *Text to display* box) to open your browser and navigate to the desired Web page. When you locate the page, click the PowerPoint icon on the Windows taskbar to return to PowerPoint. The URL displays in the Address box in the Insert Hyperlink dialog box. Lastly, you can copy the URL from the Web page address box by selecting the address and pressing Ctrl+C, closing the browser, and then pasting the URL in the Address box by pressing Ctrl+V.

Figure 6.2 shows how you would create a link to the Yellowstone National Park Web site. The text is selected so that a link to the Web site giving information about the park can be attached. The Insert Hyperlink dialog box is open and recently browsed pages are displayed. The hyperlink to the National Park Service Web site is shown in the Address box.

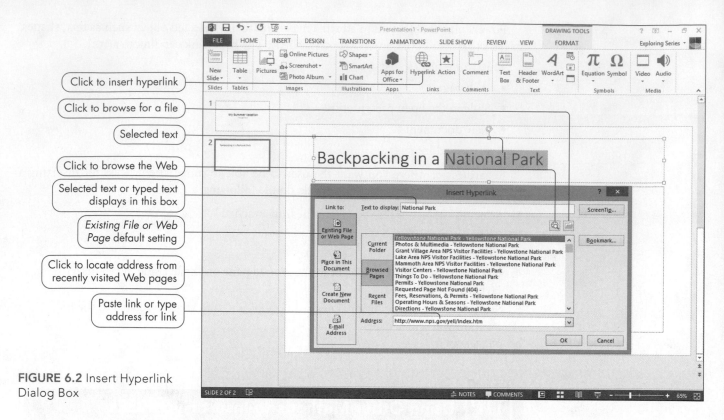

FIGURE 6.2 Insert Hyperlink Dialog Box

Labels in figure:
- Click to insert hyperlink
- Click to browse for a file
- Selected text
- Click to browse the Web
- Selected text or typed text displays in this box
- *Existing File or Web Page* default setting
- Click to locate address from recently visited Web pages
- Paste link or type address for link

If you want to link to a file stored on your computer or other storage device, from the Insert Hyperlink dialog box, click Current Folder, Recent Files, or *Browse for File* to navigate to the location of the desired file. If you know the exact file name and location, you can type it in the dialog box instead of browsing to locate the file. When you click the link during your presentation, the application in which the file was created opens and your file displays.

> **TIP Linking Picture Files**
>
> What if you have a company logo that you want to use in all presentations you create? Every time you insert the logo, the picture file is embedded multiple times in a presentation, wasting storage space on your drive. Rather than embed the picture, you can create a picture link to keep your PowerPoint file sizes much smaller. To create a picture link, click the Insert tab and click Pictures in the Images group. Browse for the picture you want and, instead of clicking Insert, click the Insert arrow and select *Link to File*. PowerPoint inserts a link to the picture instead of embedding the picture file in your slide show. The link stores the entire path to the file, the location of the picture, and the picture size. Always save your objects to the same folder and storage device where you store your presentation. Then, link to that location so that the link will not be broken when you present. If you ever change the logo, you replace the old logo file with the new logo file in the same location and with the same file name. When a presentation is opened that is linked to the picture, the new logo appears, so you do not have to replace the logo in every presentation.

Link to a Slide in the Open Presentation

Sometimes, you may want to create a link to another slide in a presentation. For example, you may create a menu of topics that are covered in the presentation. When you click a menu option, the presentation jumps to the slide containing the related content. Each topic slide should also include a link back to the menu. You can use links to branch to the slides that focus on your audience's anticipated questions or comments.

To create a link to another slide in the presentation, select *Place in This Document* from the Insert Hyperlink dialog box. The list of slides in the slide show displays. Select the slide to which you wish to link and click OK to close the dialog box (see Figure 6.3).

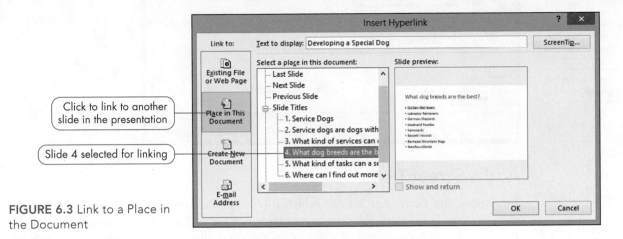

FIGURE 6.3 Link to a Place in the Document

Link to a New Document

In a training presentation, you may find it helpful to open a program and demonstrate a feature. Clicking the Create New Document option in the Insert Hyperlink dialog box enables you to do this. Use this option to create a hyperlink to a new PowerPoint presentation or other document. Browse to locate a file using the Change button or enter a file name and designate the location for the new presentation. You can specify whether you want to open the new presentation immediately for editing or to edit later. Figure 6.4 shows the options for creating a new presentation with the file name *Abilities* and opening it for immediate editing.

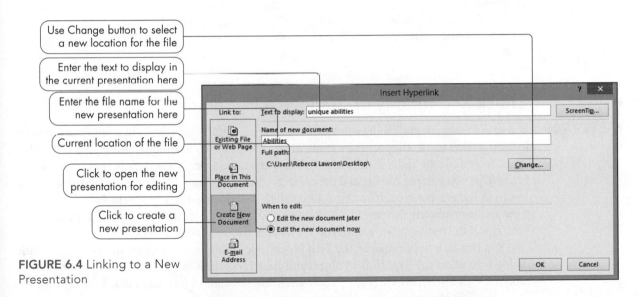

FIGURE 6.4 Linking to a New Presentation

Link to an E-Mail Address

STEP 1 » To add an e-mail link to a slide, select the E-mail Address option in the Insert Hyperlink dialog box and type the address in the *E-mail address* box. As you type, the protocol designator *mailto:* is automatically added before the e-mail address. Creating an e-mail link enables your viewer to contact you for more information and is especially helpful if you post your presentation on the Web. You can add any text on the slide, such as *Contact me for further information*, by typing it on the slide and selecting it or by typing the text in the *Text to display* box. Add a subject for the e-mail to help you identify incoming mail. Alternatively, you can type your e-mail address directly on the slide, and PowerPoint automatically formats it as a link for you. Figure 6.5 displays the *E-mail address* options in the Insert Hyperlink dialog box.

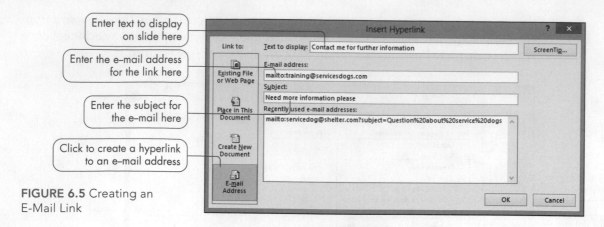

Enter text to display on slide here

Enter the e-mail address for the link here

Enter the subject for the e-mail here

Click to create a hyperlink to an e-mail address

FIGURE 6.5 Creating an E-Mail Link

Add a ScreenTip

Sometimes, the viewer needs more information to determine the purpose of the hyperlink object or text. To help a viewer determine whether or not to click a hyperlink, use a ScreenTip. When you or your viewer rolls the mouse over the hyperlink, the *ScreenTip* appears with the additional information.

To add a ScreenTip to a hyperlink, click ScreenTip in the Insert Hyperlink dialog box. The Set Hyperlink ScreenTip dialog box opens. Type the text you want to display in the box.

TIP Adding Definitions to Technical Terms

ScreenTips are an excellent way to define technical or new terms in a presentation. To use a ScreenTip in this manner, select the term in the text on your slide, click the Insert tab, and then click Hyperlink in the Links group. Link to *Place in This Document* and select the slide you are currently in. Finally, click ScreenTip and type the definition for the word you selected.

Check and Modify or Remove a Hyperlink

STEP 7» Before delivering or publishing a presentation, test each of the hyperlinks in a presentation view to see if it takes you to the proper location. This is the preferred technique, although you can also check hyperlinks by right-clicking the link and selecting Open Hyperlink. Check to see if the ScreenTips you entered display and are correct. Close each linked location, and make sure you return to the presentation. If you find a hyperlink that does not link properly, leave Slide Show view and immediately fix the link so you do not forget to do it later. Once you have edited the link, repeat the testing process until you are assured that every link works.

You can edit hyperlinks in the Edit Hyperlink dialog box. To open the Edit Hyperlink dialog box, select the hyperlinked object and click Hyperlink in the Links group on the Insert tab. You can also press Ctrl+K or right-click the selected object and click Edit Hyperlink. Once the Edit Hyperlink dialog box opens, you can modify the existing hyperlink.

To remove a hyperlink, click Remove Link in the Edit Hyperlink dialog box or right-click the selected object and click Remove Hyperlink from the shortcut menu. If you delete the object to which a hyperlink is attached, the hyperlink is also deleted.

Adding Action Buttons

Another way to add interactivity is by using an action button that, when you click, point to, or run the mouse over it, initiates an action. Action buttons can contain shapes such as arrows and symbols. In addition to being a hyperlink to another location, action buttons can display information, movies, documents, sound, and the Help feature. *Custom buttons* can be created and set to trigger unique actions in a presentation. Action buttons are excellent tools for navigating a slide show and are especially useful if you want to create a presentation for a *kiosk*, an interactive computer terminal available for public use, such as on campus, at a mall, or at a trade show. An interactive slide show is perfect for a kiosk display.

 TIP | **Using Action Buttons for Navigation**

Slide Show view includes default action buttons on the bottom-left of a slide that return to the previous slide, advance to the next slide, activate a pen tool, open Slide Sorter view, zoom, or display a shortcut menu. If your presentation will be used by multiple users with varied skill levels, you may want to use the default buttons. If, however, you wish to provide your users with additional choices, you may want to create custom buttons.

Table 6.1 lists the 12 different ready-made action buttons that PowerPoint includes in the Shapes gallery.

TABLE 6.1 PowerPoint Ready-Made Action Buttons

Action Button Icon	Name	Default Button Behavior
◁	Back or Previous button	Moves to previous slide
▷	Forward or Next button	Moves to next slide
◁|	Beginning button	Moves to the first slide in the slide show
|▷	*End button*	Moves to the last slide in the slide show
🏠	*Home button*	Moves to the first slide of the slide show by default but can be set to go to any slide
ⓘ	Information button	Can be set to move to any slide in the slide show, a custom show, a URL, another presentation, or another file in order to reveal information
↩	Return button	Returns to previous slide view regardless of the location in the slide show
🎬	*Movie button*	Can be set to play a movie file
📄	Document button	Can be set to load a document in the application that was used to create it
🔊	Sound button	Can be set to play a sound when clicked
?	*Help button*	Can be set to open the Help feature or a Help document
☐	Custom button	Can be set to move to a slide in the slide show, a custom show, a URL, another PowerPoint presentation, a file, or a program; also can be set to run a macro, add an action to an object, or play a sound

To insert an action button, do the following:

STEP 3 » 1. Click the INSERT tab.
STEP 4 » 2. Click Shapes in the Illustrations group. The Shapes gallery can also be accessed from the HOME tab by clicking Shapes in the Drawing group.
 3. Click the action button you want in the *Action Buttons* section of the Shapes gallery.
STEP 5 » 4. Click the desired location to create the button on the slide (or click and drag to control the button size).

5. Select the Mouse Click or Mouse Over tab in the Action Settings dialog box.
6. Select desired options in the Action Settings dialog box.
7. Click OK.

Figure 6.6 shows the Action Buttons displayed in the Shapes gallery with the action button designed to return to the beginning of the slide show selected.

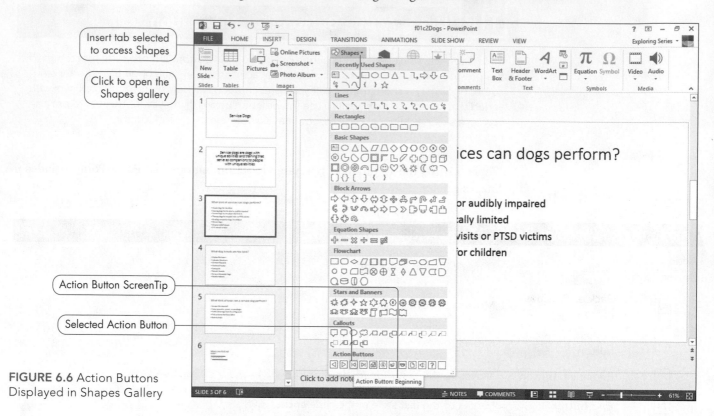

FIGURE 6.6 Action Buttons Displayed in Shapes Gallery

Attaching Actions to Objects

Actions can be associated with any object, not just an action button. Select an object, click the Insert tab, and then click Action in the Links group. The Action Settings dialog box opens so that you can select the type of action and how you want the action to be initiated.

When you release the mouse button after creating an action button, the Action Settings dialog box opens. Click the *Mouse Click or Mouse Over* tab to select how to initiate the action. Regardless of which method you select, the action options are the same. You can choose to have the action button hyperlink to another location in the slide show, a Custom Show, a URL, another PowerPoint presentation, or another file. An action button can even initiate a new program. To link to a specific slide in the slide show, click the *Hyperlink to* arrow and select a slide from the list. To have the action button run a specific program, click *Run program* and browse to locate the program you wish to open. You can also program the action button to run a macro or to add an action to an object. Figure 6.7 shows the settings for an action button that returns to the first slide.

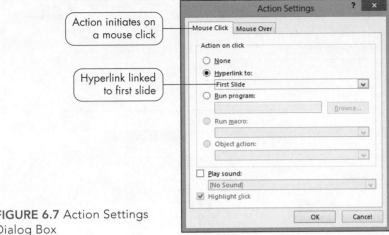

Action initiates on
a mouse click

Hyperlink linked
to first slide

FIGURE 6.7 Action Settings
Dialog Box

TIP | **Returning to the Last Slide Viewed**

The Return action button returns you to the last slide you viewed, regardless of its location in the presentation. The Previous button takes you to the slide preceding the slide you are currently viewing.

Add Sound to an Object

Sound can be added to a hyperlink attached to an object to capture your audience's attention or to add emphasis to the subject of the link. To attach a sound to a hyperlink, click the *Play sound* check box in the Action Settings dialog box. Click the *Play sound* arrow and select the sound you want to play when the object is clicked or moused over during the show. To assign a sound file you have saved to your computer, scroll to the bottom of the list, click Other Sound, browse for the sound, and then select it.

Using a Trigger

Another way to introduce interactivity into your presentation is through the use of a trigger. A ***trigger*** launches an animation that takes place when you click an associated object or a bookmarked location in a media object. An ***animation*** is an action used to draw interest to an object in a presentation. For example, you can use text as a trigger. The trigger is set up so when you click the text, an image appears. Triggers are a fun way to add interactivity to presentations—the viewer clicks a trigger to see a surprise element. Remember this key point about triggers: a trigger must use animation.

Figure 6.8 displays a slide with a trigger. The Animation Pane is open on the right side of the slide and shows the object and the animation or action associated with the trigger. The trigger is attached to the words *Thank you*. The slide is interactive because the viewer initiates the process by clicking the trigger.

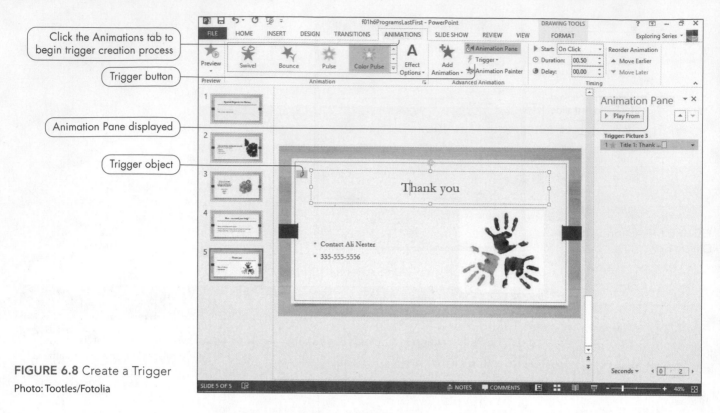

Click the Animations tab to begin trigger creation process

Trigger button

Animation Pane displayed

Trigger object

FIGURE 6.8 Create a Trigger

Photo: Tootles/Fotolia

To set up a trigger, do the following:

1. Select the object that will serve as the trigger.
2. Click the ANIMATIONS tab.
3. Add the animation effect of your choice from the Animation group.
4. Click Trigger in the Advanced Animation group.
5. Select the *On Click of* or *On Bookmark* option to determine how the animation is triggered.
6. Select the object or bookmark that will launch the animation from the displayed list.

 TIP Using Games for Quizzes

Microsoft includes a Quiz Show template that includes sample quiz layouts such as True or False, Multiple Choice, and more. You can locate it by searching the templates available. You can also go to the Internet and use a search engine to search for *PowerPoint Games*. Create a storyboard to plan the slides you will need for the quiz and the interactive elements required by your plan. A standard quiz presentation would probably contain slides to introduce the test, directions, questions, feedback slides, and an ending slide.

The answers to the questions would link to the feedback slides, and the *correct* feedback slide would link to the next question. The *incorrect* feedback slide would link to the same question slide so the viewer could try again.

Quick Concepts

1. What is a presentation that enables the user to progress through the slides using action buttons and hyperlinks? *p. 948*
2. What are the main advantages of adding an e-mail link to a presentation? *p. 951*
3. Which type of event is a trigger used to launch in a presentation? *p. 955*

Hands-On Exercises

Watch the Video for this Hands-On Exercise!

MyITLab®
HOE1 Training

1 Hyperlinks and Action Buttons

One of your responsibilities as a teaching assistant is to provide materials for a computer literacy class. You create a presentation to help students review charts and graphs in a quiz format. Students answer questions and receive feedback on whether they selected a "correct" or "incorrect" answer. Students can also open a reference guide and an assignment from the presentation.

Skills covered: Insert and Edit an E-Mail Hyperlink • Add an Action to a Clip Art Object • Create and Edit Sound Action Buttons • Create Action Buttons for Navigation • Create a Custom Action Button • Insert and Use Hyperlinks • Test Hyperlinks

STEP 1 >> INSERT AND EDIT AN E-MAIL HYPERLINK

The following table displays the storyboard used in creating the Charts and Graphs Review presentation. The storyboard notes all interactive elements you want to include in the presentation. You will modify this slide show to add the interactive elements. You will begin by inserting your e-mail address so that, if necessary, a student could contact you with questions. Refer to the table below to add the following interactive elements to the slides in the presentation.

Slide	Content	Interactive Element
1	Title Slide	None
2	Directions	• E-mail hyperlink
		• Four navigation buttons: Beginning, Back or Previous, Forward or Next, End
3	Speaker Test	Clip art object with sound action attached
4	Question One	• Four sound action buttons (one for each answer)
		• Chart with animation trigger
		• Four navigation buttons: Beginning, Back or Previous, Forward or Next, End
5	Question Two	• Four sound action buttons (one for each answer)
		• Chart with animation trigger
		• Four navigation buttons: Beginning, Back or Previous, Forward or Next, End
6	Ending Slide	• Existing file hyperlink
		• Four navigation buttons: Beginning, Back or Previous, Forward or Next, End

a. Open *p06h1Review* and save it as **p06h1Review_LastFirst**.

> **TROUBLESHOOTING:** If you make any major mistakes in this exercise, you can close the file, open *p06h1Review* again, and then start this exercise over.

b. Create a handout header with your name and a handout footer with your instructor's name and your class. Include the current date.

c. On Slide 2, position the insertion point after the colon following *contact*, press the **Spacebar**, type your e-mail address, and then press the **Spacebar**.

Because PowerPoint recognizes the format of an e-mail address, it creates an automatic hyperlink to your e-mail.

d. Right-click your e-mail address and click **Edit Hyperlink**.

e. Click in the **Subject box**, type **Charts and Graphs Review Question**, and then click **OK**.

f. Save the presentation.

Because the quiz review slide show uses audio cues to indicate whether a student answers the question correctly, it is important for the student to have a working headset. You will create an action attached to a clip art image of a headset so the student can test to see if his or her headset is working. Refer to Figure 6.9 as you complete Step 2.

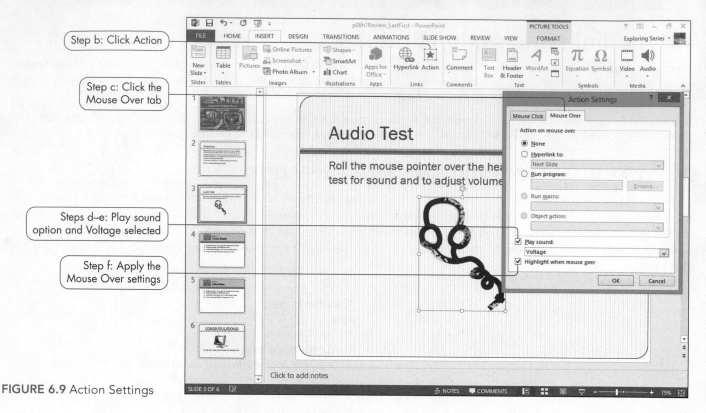

FIGURE 6.9 Action Settings

a. On Slide 3, select the **headset picture** and click the **INSERT tab**.

b. Click **Action** in the Links group.

The Action Settings dialog box opens so that you can assign an action to the selected clip art image.

c. Click the **Mouse Over tab**, if necessary.

By selecting the Mouse Over tab, you assign any applied actions to occur when the mouse moves over the selected object.

d. Click the **Play sound check box** and click the **list arrow**.

PowerPoint includes a variety of sounds you can attach to objects, or you can select the Other Sound option and browse to locate a sound you have saved.

e. Click **Voltage**.

f. Click the **Highlight when mouse over check box**, if necessary, and click **OK**.

With this option selected, the clip art image will be surrounded by a border when the mouse rolls over the top of it, which makes it easy to note the mouse-over area.

TROUBLESHOOTING: You will not be able to hear the voltage sound or see the highlight border unless you are in Slide Show view.

---

g. Save the presentation.

STEP 3 >> CREATE AND EDIT SOUND ACTION BUTTONS

You will create action buttons next to the answers on each of the question slides so that when clicked, the action button will play an audio response letting the student know whether he or she selected the correct answer. Refer to Figure 6.10 as you complete Step 3.

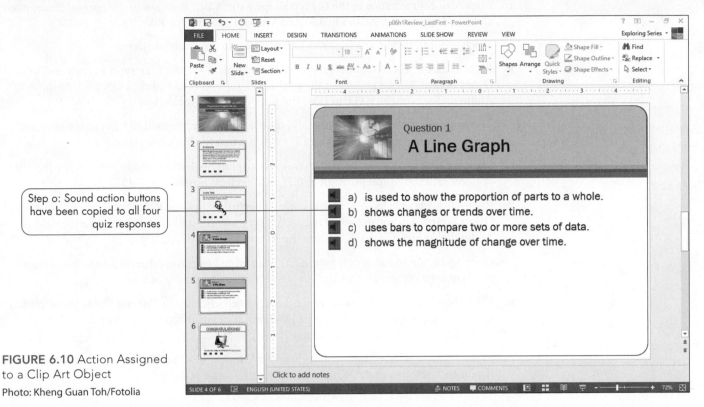

Step o: Sound action buttons have been copied to all four quiz responses

FIGURE 6.10 Action Assigned to a Clip Art Object

Photo: Kheng Guan Toh/Fotolia

a. On Slide 4, click the **INSERT tab** and click **Shapes** in the Illustrations group.

The Shapes gallery opens, and the action buttons display at the bottom of the gallery.

b. Click **Action Button: Sound**.

The Shapes gallery closes, and the pointer becomes a crosshair pointer.

c. Click in an empty portion of the slide to create the button.

Do not worry about the size or position of the button at this time. You will adjust both in a later step. The Action Settings dialog box opens to the Mouse Click tab.

d. Click the **Play sound arrow** and select **Other Sound**.

e. Locate and select the *p06h1Incorrect.wav* file.

The sound file is assigned to the action button. Because this is not the correct answer, the viewer hears *Incorrect* when the button is clicked.

f. Click **OK** to close the Add Audio dialog box and click **OK** in the Action Settings dialog box.

The action button now has sound attached to it, and the sound plays when the presentation is viewed in the Slide Show view and the Reading view.

g. Click the **FORMAT tab** with the action button still selected and click the **Size Dialog Box Launcher** in the Size group. Set **Height** to **0.35"** and **Width** to **0.35"**.

h. Click **Position** in the Format Shape pane and set **Horizontal position** to **0.5"** and **Vertical position** to **2.5"**.

i. Keep the sound action button selected and press **Ctrl+D** three times.

Three duplicates of the original sound action button are created. It is easier to edit duplicates than to re-create the button because the duplicates are already sized. The last duplicate created is now selected, so you will edit it first.

j. Click **Size & Properties** in the Format Shape pane. Click **Position** in the Format Shape pane and set **Horizontal position** to **0.5"** and **Vertical position** to **3.9"**.

The last duplicate you made moves into position to the left of answer *d*.

k. Right-click the selected button and click **Hyperlink**. Click the **Play sound arrow** and select **Other Sound**. Locate and select the *p06h1TryAgain.wav* file and click **OK** to close the Add Audio dialog box. Click **OK** to close the Action Settings dialog box.

The sound action button has been edited to play a different sound file. Because this is not the correct answer, the viewer hears *Try Again* when the button is clicked.

l. Click the third sound action button from the top. In the Format Shape pane, in the Position options, set **Horizontal position** to **0.5"** and **Vertical position** to **3.43"**.

m. Right-click the selected button and click **Hyperlink**. Click the **Play sound arrow** and select **Other Sound**. Locate and select the *p06h1Sorry.wav* file and click **OK** to close the Add Audio dialog box. Click **OK** to close the Action Settings dialog box.

Once again, the sound action button has been edited to play a different sound file. Because this is not the correct answer, the viewer hears *Sorry* when the button is clicked.

n. Click the second sound action button from the top, click in the **Format Shape pane**, click in the **Position options**, and then set **Horizontal position** to **0.5"** and **Vertical position** to **2.97"**. Click **Close** to close the Format Shape pane.

o. Right-click the selected button and click **Hyperlink**. Click the **Play sound arrow**, click **Applause**, and then click **OK** to close the Action Settings dialog box.

This is the correct answer, so the viewer hears applause when the button is clicked.

p. Hold down **Shift** and click to select the four sound action buttons. Press **Ctrl+C** to copy them to the Clipboard. Click **Slide 5** and press **Ctrl+V** to paste the buttons on Slide 5. Click away from the selected buttons to deselect them.

It is fastest to copy, paste, and edit the buttons to additional slides, although the sound action buttons will need to be repositioned.

q. On Slide 5, select the top sound action button (the sound action button for answer *a*), right-click, and then click **Hyperlink**. Click the **Play sound arrow**, select **Applause**, and then click **OK** to close the Action Settings dialog box.

This is the correct answer, so the viewer hears applause when the button is clicked.

r. Select the second sound action button (the sound action button for answer *b*), right-click, and then select **Hyperlink**. Click the **Play sound arrow** and select **Other Sound**. Select the *p06h1Incorrect.wav* file and click **OK** to close the Add Audio dialog box. Click **OK** to close the Action Settings dialog box.

s. Save the presentation.

You want navigation buttons with consistent placement on the slides in your slide show. You will create the buttons on one slide, and then copy and paste them to other slides. Refer to Figure 6.11 and the below table as you complete Step 4.

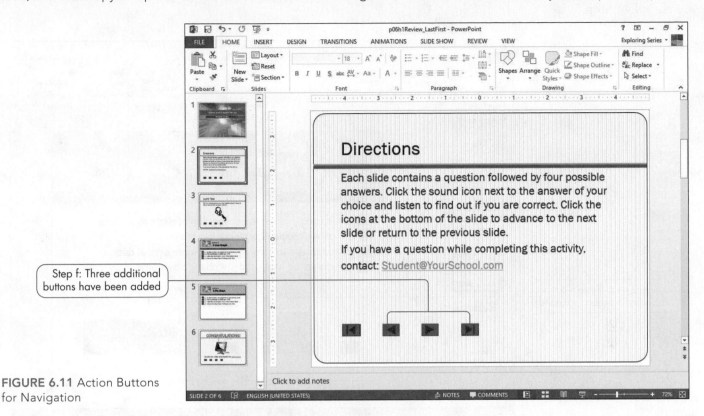

FIGURE 6.11 Action Buttons for Navigation

a. On Slide 2, click the **INSERT tab**, click **Shapes** in the Illustrations group, and then click **Action Button: Beginning** from the Action Buttons category of the Shapes gallery.

b. Click anywhere on the slide to create the action button.

 The Action Settings dialog box opens, and the Beginning action button is preset to hyperlink to the first slide.

c. Click **OK**. Keep the button selected, click the **FORMAT tab** if necessary, click the **Size Dialog Box Launcher** in the Size group, and then click **Size**, if necessary.

d. Set **Height** to **0.35"** and **Width** to **0.5"**.

e. Click **Position** in the Format Shape pane and set **Horizontal position** to **0.92"** and **Vertical position** to **6.25"**.

f. Create three additional buttons using the default settings in the Action Settings dialog box and the information included in the following table:

Action Button	Height	Width	Horizontal Position	Vertical Position
Back or Previous	0.35"	0.5"	2.11"	6.25"
Forward or Next	0.35"	0.5"	3.27"	6.25"
End	0.35"	0.5"	4.46 "	6.25"

g. Select and copy the four action buttons.

h. Paste the action buttons on Slides 3 through 6.

i. Save the presentation.

You want to provide students with the option of opening a Charts and Graphs Reference Guide before answering quiz questions. You will create a customizable action button for students to click to open the guide. Refer to Figure 6.12 as you complete Step 5.

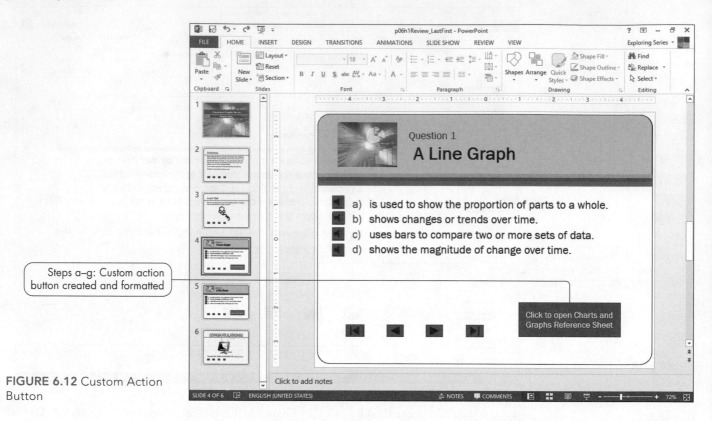

Steps a–g: Custom action button created and formatted

FIGURE 6.12 Custom Action Button

a. On Slide 4, click the **INSERT tab**, if necessary, click **Shapes** in the Illustrations group, and then click **Action Button: Custom**.

b. Click the bottom right on the slide to create an action button.

c. Click **Hyperlink to** on the Mouse Click tab in the Action Settings dialog box, click the arrow, scroll down, and then select **Other File**.

d. Locate and select the *p06h1Guide.docx* file and click **OK** to close the *Hyperlink to Other File* dialog box. Click **OK** to close the Action Settings dialog box.

e. Type **Click to open Charts and Graphs Reference Sheet** inside the selected custom action button.

f. Click the **FORMAT tab** if necessary, click the **Size Dialog Box Launcher** in the Size group, and then set **Height** to 1" and **Width** to 3".

g. Click **Position** in the Format Shape pane and set **Horizontal position** to 6" and **Vertical position** to 5.58". Click **Close**.

h. Click the border of the button object to select the entire object and text, press **Ctrl+C** to copy the custom action button, and then paste it to Slide 5.

i. Save the presentation.

After completing the review quiz, you want the students to complete an assignment on charts and graphs. To include interactivity, you will add a ScreenTip to a clip art picture that instructs the student to click the picture. You will create a hyperlink to an existing file using text in a text box. Finally, you will create a trigger that launches the text. Refer to Figure 6.13 as you complete Step 6.

FIGURE 6.13 Slide 6 Triggers and Hyperlink

a. On Slide 6, select the monitor picture.

b. Click the **INSERT tab** and click **Hyperlink** in the Links group.

c. Click **Place in This Document** and click **Slide 6**.

   You are linking the monitor picture to the same location in the document so that you have access to the ScreenTip option.

d. Click **ScreenTip**, type **Click Me!** in the Set Hyperlink ScreenTip dialog box, and then click **OK**.

   The ScreenTip displays when the presentation is viewed in the Slide Show or Reading View.

e. Click **OK** to close the Insert Hyperlink dialog box.

f. Select the word *assignment* in the text box.

g. Click the **INSERT tab** if necessary and click **Hyperlink**.

h. Click **Existing File or Web Page**, click the **Browse for File button**, locate and insert *p06h1Assignment*, and then click **OK**.

i. Verify that the address for the *p06h1Assignment* file appears in the Address box and click **OK**.

   The word *assignment* is underlined, indicating it is a hyperlink.

j. Click to select the text box border, if necessary, and click the **ANIMATIONS tab**.

k. Click **Fly In** in the Animation group.

   With an animation assigned, the Trigger option is available.

l. Click **Trigger** in the Advanced Animation group, point to *On Click of*, and then click **Picture 9**.

   Picture 9 (the monitor clip art) triggers the text animation when clicked in the Slide Show or Reading View.

m. Save the presentation.

STEP 7 ≫ TEST HYPERLINKS

Although it is always important to view a slide show while you are developing it to ensure it plays correctly, it is critical that a slide show with hyperlinks, action buttons, and triggers be viewed and all interactive components tested. You test the *Charts and Graphs* slide show before getting approval from your supervisor to create additional questions. Refer to Figure 6.14 as you complete Step 7.

Step a: The completed presentation is ready to be shown as a slide show

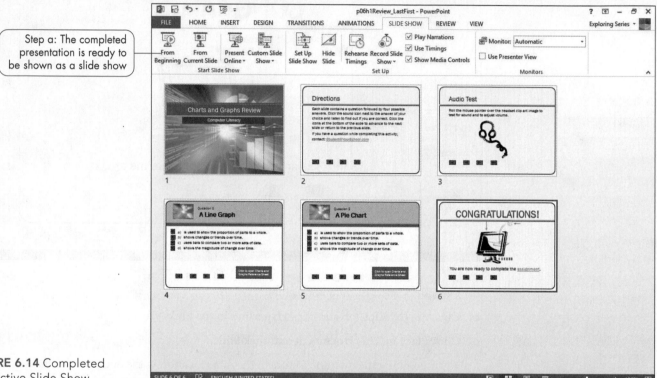

FIGURE 6.14 Completed Interactive Slide Show

a. Click the **SLIDE SHOW tab** and click **From Beginning** in the Start Slide Show group.

b. Advance to Slide 2 and click the e-mail hyperlink. Close the e-mail screen without saving.

> **TROUBLESHOOTING:** When testing sounds, you may need to adjust your volume to hear the sounds playing. You may want to use a headset if you are in a public computer lab.

c. Click the **Forward or Next action button** to move to Slide 3. Point to the headset clip art image.

> **TROUBLESHOOTING:** You will not be able to hear the Voltage sound or see the highlight border unless you are in Slide Show view. If the Voltage sound does not play when you mouse over it, exit the slide show and right-click the clip art image of the headset. Click Hyperlink, click the Mouse Over tab, and then check *Play sound.* Select Voltage from the list of sounds and click OK. Return to Slide Show mode.

d. Continue advancing through the slides in the presentation using the action buttons for navigation. Be sure to test each button.

> **TROUBLESHOOTING:** If any of the action buttons do not work, exit the slide show. In any slide, right-click the action button. Click Edit Hyperlink and check the slide showing in the *Hyperlink to:* box. If no slide is showing or if the wrong slide is showing, click the arrow and select the right slide from the list. Click OK. Copy the button and paste it on all other slides containing the button. Return to Slide Show mode.

e. On Slide 4, click each of the sound action buttons. Answer *b* should play the applause sound. The remaining sound action buttons should play a sound that indicates the choice of answer was incorrect.

> **TROUBLESHOOTING:** If any of the sound action buttons play the wrong sound, exit the slide show. Select the sound action button that plays the wrong sound, right click, and then click Hyperlink. Change the linked sound to the correct choice. Return to Slide Show mode.

f. On Slides 4 and 5, click **Click to open Charts and Graphs Reference Sheet** to open the Word document. Close the document after opening.

> **TROUBLESHOOTING:** If the Word document did not open, exit the slide show. Right-click the custom action button and click Hyperlink. Click the *Browse for File* button and locate and insert *p06h1Guide.docx*. Click OK twice. Return to Slide Show mode.

g. On Slide 5, click each of the sound action buttons. Answer *a* should play the applause sound. The remaining sound action buttons should play a sound that indicates the choice of answer was incorrect.

> **TROUBLESHOOTING:** If any of the sound action buttons plays the wrong sound, follow the Troubleshooting instructions in step e.

h. On Slide 6, point to the clip art image to view the ScreenTip.

> **TROUBLESHOOTING:** If the ScreenTip does not display, exit the slide show, right-click the image, and then click Edit Hyperlink. Click *Place in This Document*, click Slide 6, and then click ScreenTip. Type Click Me!, if necessary. Click OK twice. Return to Slide Show mode.

i. Click the image to trigger the text box animation.

> **TROUBLESHOOTING:** If the text box does not fly onto the slide, exit the slide show. Select the text box, click the Animations tab, and then check to see if the Fly In animation is assigned. Then, click Trigger in the Advanced Animation group, click *On Click of*, and then check to see if *Picture 9* is selected. Return to Slide Show mode.

j. Click **assignment** to ensure the *Charts and Graphs* assignment opens. Close the document after opening.

> **TROUBLESHOOTING:** If Word does not open and display the *p06h1Assignment.docx* file, exit the slide show. Right-click the assignment hyperlink and click Edit Hyperlink. Click the *Browse for File* button and locate and select *p06h1Assignment*. Click OK twice.

k. Save and close the file, and submit it based on your instructor's directions.

Advanced Animation

In the previous section, you used an animation trigger to control the flow of information on a slide. By fully utilizing the different types of animations and animation options, you can engage the audience's interest and direct their focus to important points in your presentation. Carefully plan animations, however, to ensure they enhance the message of the slide. Used indiscriminately, animations can be distracting to the audience.

Table 6.2 shows PowerPoint's four animation types. Each of these animation types has properties, effects, and timing that can be modified.

TABLE 6.2	PowerPoint Animation Types
Type	**Content**
Entrance	Controls how an object moves onto or appears on a slide
Emphasis	Draws attention to an object already on a slide
Exit	Controls how an object leaves or disappears from a slide
Motion Paths	Controls the movement of an object from one position to another along a predetermined path

In this section, you will apply multiple animations to an object, modify a motion path, specify animation effects, set animation timing, control the flow of text, and fine-tune your animations using the Animation Pane.

Applying Multiple Animations to an Object

Multiple animations can be applied to an object. For example, you could apply an entrance animation that causes your company logo to fly onto a title slide, an emphasis animation that causes the logo to grow and shrink, a motion animation that causes the logo to move in a circle, and an exit animation that causes the logo to fly off the slide. You can control the timing of the animations as well as the trigger that starts the animation sequence. This complex set of animations may not be necessary, but it shows the power of the animation effects. Keep in mind, though, when you use too many animations on one object or slide, the result can be distracting and take away from the message of the object or slide.

Figure 6.15 shows multiple animations applied to a slide. Numbered animation tags indicate the order in which the animations will play.

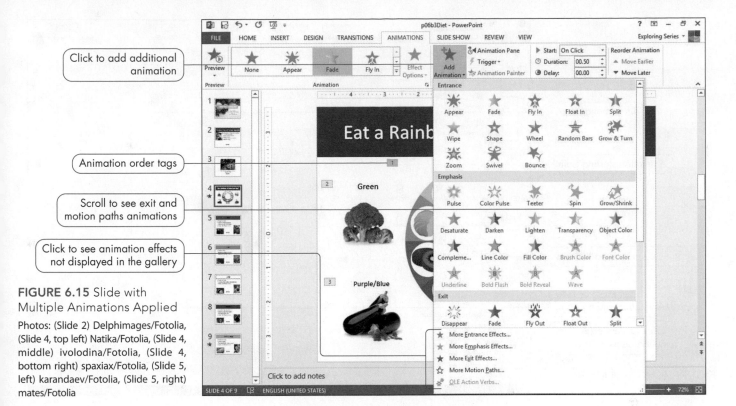

Click to add additional animation

Animation order tags

Scroll to see exit and motion paths animations

Click to see animation effects not displayed in the gallery

FIGURE 6.15 Slide with Multiple Animations Applied

Photos: (Slide 2) Delphimages/Fotolia, (Slide 4, top left) Natika/Fotolia, (Slide 4, middle) ivolodina/Fotolia, (Slide 4, bottom right) spaxiax/Fotolia, (Slide 5, left) karandaev/Fotolia, (Slide 5, right) mates/Fotolia

STEP 1 ≫

To add multiple animations, do the following:

1. Select the object and click the ANIMATIONS tab.
2. Apply an animation from the Animation gallery.
3. Click Add Animation in the Advanced Animation group.
4. Click an animation to apply it to the object.
5. Continue adding animations as needed.

Animation sequences should be checked as you create them to make sure they respond in the way you expect. At any time, click Preview in the Preview group to see the animation sequence in Normal view. You can also check the sequence in the Slide Show or Reading View.

Applying a Motion Path Animation

Because the eye is naturally drawn to motion, using a motion path (a predetermined path that an object follows as part of an animation) to animate an object can capture and focus a viewer's attention on key objects or text. Motion paths are linear, curved, or follow a predetermined shape. PowerPoint includes a variety of interesting motion paths such as arcs, waves, hearts, and stars. You can even draw a custom path for the object to follow.

To apply a motion path animation, do the following:

1. Select the object and click the ANIMATIONS tab.
2. Click the More button in the Animation group.
3. Scroll down to the Motion Paths category.
4. Click a motion path animation to apply it to the selected object.

Once you have applied the motion path animation to an object, the motion path appears as a dotted line on the slide. A small arrow indicates the starting point for the animation, and a red arrow with a line indicates the ending point. If it is a closed path like a circle, only the starting point displays. Figure 6.16 displays a leaf clip art image with the Turns motion path animation applied.

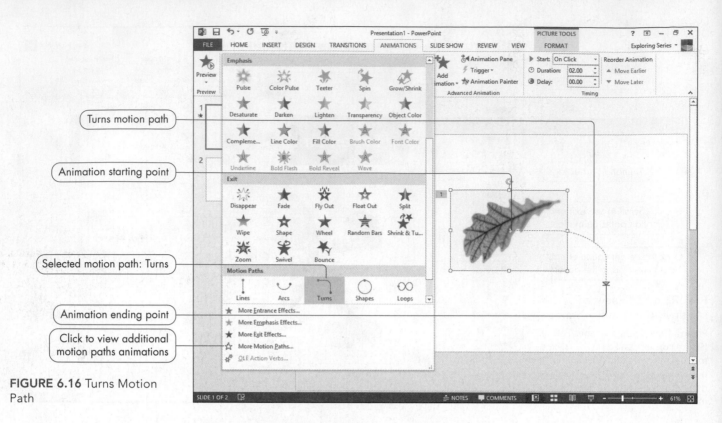

Turns motion path

Animation starting point

Selected motion path: Turns

Animation ending point

Click to view additional motion paths animations

FIGURE 6.16 Turns Motion Path

Create a Custom Path

STEP 2 A ***custom path*** is an animation path that can be created freehand instead of following a preset path. To draw a path in the direction and the length you determine rather than in a standard path available in the Animation gallery, select the Custom Path animation from the Animation gallery. Position the crosshair pointer in the approximate center of the object you wish to animate and drag in the direction you want the object to follow. The crosshair pointer becomes a Pencil tool that you drag until you have the desired path. Double-click to end the path.

By default, a custom path animation uses the Scribble option, which enables you to draw the path by using the mouse like a pencil. Click Effect Options in the Animation group to draw a curved or straight path. Figure 6.17 shows a custom path animation drawn using the Scribble option.

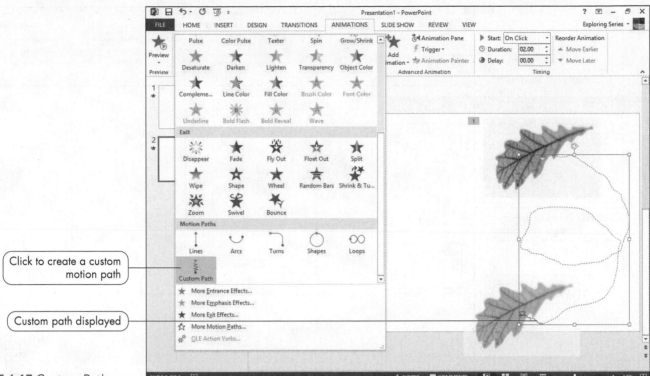

FIGURE 6.17 Custom Path

Whether you apply one of PowerPoint's motion paths or create your own, you can resize, move, or rotate the path using the same methods you use to edit a shape. To use a motion path, you choose More Motion Paths in the Animation gallery. Figure 6.18 shows a clip art image with the Stairs Down motion path applied.

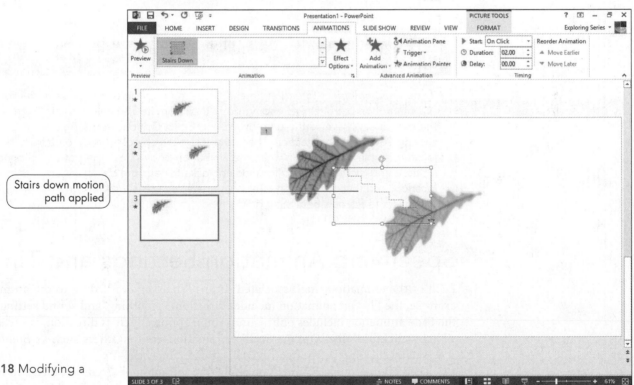

FIGURE 6.18 Modifying a Path

If you want to reshape the motion path, you must display the points that create the path. Once the points are displayed, drag a point to its new location. The path automatically adjusts. Figure 6.19 shows a custom path animation with its points displayed.

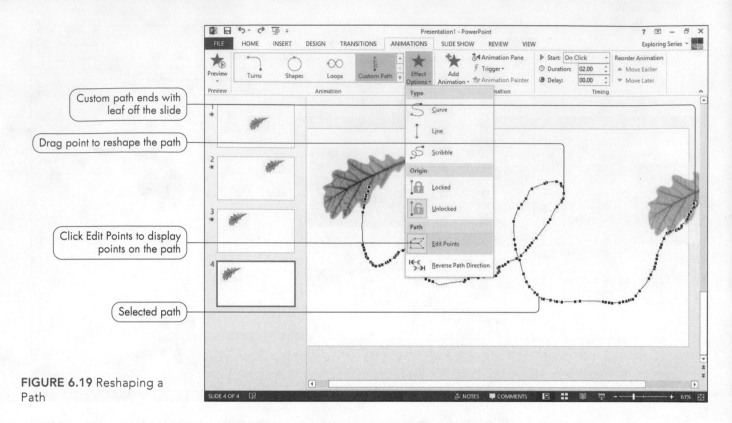

FIGURE 6.19 Reshaping a Path

Labels in figure:
- Custom path ends with leaf off the slide
- Drag point to reshape the path
- Click Edit Points to display points on the path
- Selected path

To display the points, select the path, click Effect Options in the Animation group, and then click Edit Points. Drag points on the path as needed. You can add or delete points by right-clicking the path to display the editing menu and then clicking Add Point or Delete Point.

TIP   Reversing a Custom Path

If you need an object to end at an exact location on a slide, it may be easier for you to draw a motion path from its ending point than from its beginning point. Once you have the path drawn, reverse the path by clicking Effect Options in the Animation group and clicking Reverse Path Direction. Then, to prevent the object from jumping from its original location to the new location when the animation begins, lock the path by clicking Effect Options and clicking Locked. If you do not lock the path, the object will show at its original location, and then its position after being reversed, causing a jerky motion. Finally, drag the object to the new beginning point.

Specifying Animation Settings and Timing

Each of the animations has associated settings that vary according to the animation. For example, the Fly Out animation includes direction, smoothing, and sound settings, whereas the Fade animation includes only sound. Some options, such as direction, are readily accessible by clicking Effect Options in the Animation group. Others such as *Bounce end* are accessed by clicking the Animation Dialog Box Launcher.

The Left motion path animation applied to the automobile clip art image in Figure 6.20 utilizes the *Smooth start* and *Smooth end* settings. The *Smooth start* and *Smooth end* settings enable an object to accelerate and decelerate along its motion path. In this figure, the clip art image speeds up at the beginning of the animation and slows down as it nears the end of its path. The automobile disappears after animating because the *After animation* setting is set to Hide After Animation.

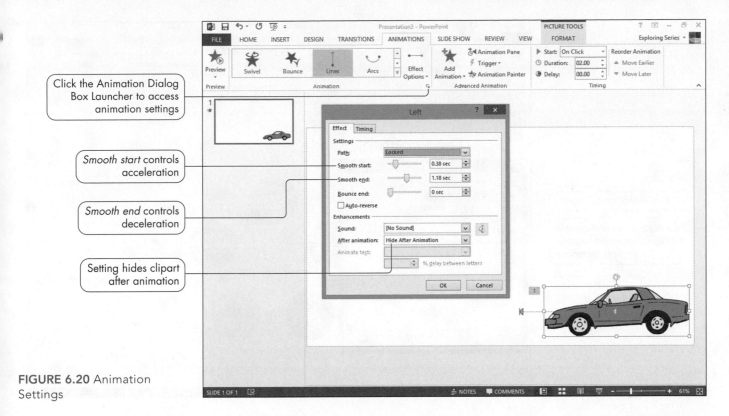

Click the Animation Dialog Box Launcher to access animation settings

Smooth start controls acceleration

Smooth end controls deceleration

Setting hides clipart after animation

FIGURE 6.20 Animation Settings

STEP 3 ≫ Attaching timing settings to animations frees you from constantly advancing to the next object and lets you concentrate on delivering your message. Previously, you have set timing options in the Timing group on the Animations tab, and that is the quickest way to set the method for starting an animation, to set the duration of an animation, and to set the delay. The Animation Dialog Box Launcher also provides access to these settings, but the dialog box it opens gives you several additional settings. You can set the number of times an animation is repeated, set the animation to rewind when it is done playing, and determine how the animation is triggered on the Timing tab of the dialog box. Figure 6.21 shows a SmartArt object with a motion path applied. In addition to animating a SmartArt object as one object, you can select individual shapes that make up the SmartArt object and animate them individually. The Circle dialog box is open, showing the Timing tab options available for the selected SmartArt object.

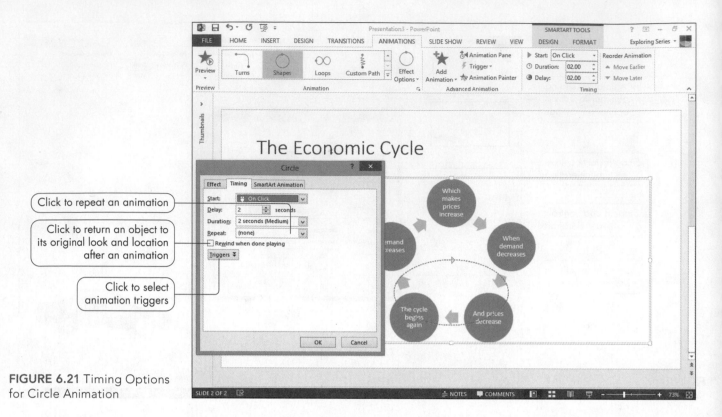

Click to repeat an animation

Click to return an object to
its original look and location
after an animation

Click to select
animation triggers

FIGURE 6.21 Timing Options
for Circle Animation

Animating Text

Although animating non-bulleted text in placeholders and text boxes uses the same method as other objects, bullet text has additional options available. These options help you keep audience attention and can keep the audience from reading ahead. You can bring text onto the slide by animating the text as one object, animating all paragraphs to come in together, and by sequencing the text animation by text outline level. A paragraph in PowerPoint can be a line of text, several lines of text or even a blank line. Whenever you press Enter to move the cursor to a new line, you create a new paragraph.

STEP 4≫   To determine the animation sequence of bullet text, do the following:

1. Select the text and click the ANIMATIONS tab.
2. Apply an animation effect.
3. Click Effect Options in the Animation group.
4. Select the desired text grouping option from the Sequence list.

To assign animations beyond the first level, click the Animation Dialog Box Launcher and click the Text Animation tab. Click the *Group text* arrow and animate text up to five outline levels. Figure 6.22 shows text animated by first-level paragraphs.

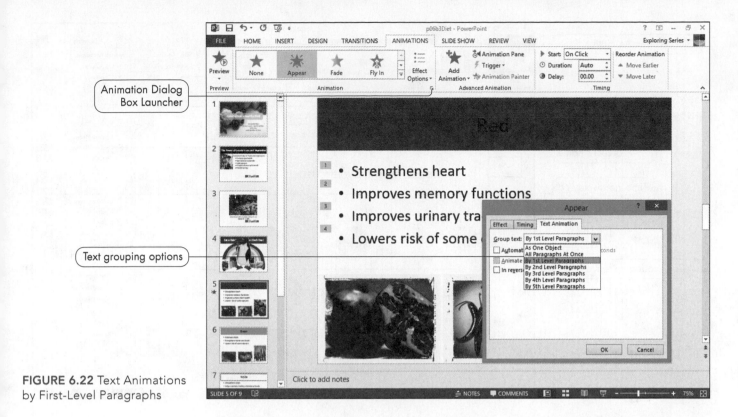

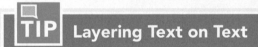

Text grouping options

FIGURE 6.22 Text Animations by First-Level Paragraphs

TIP — Layering Text on Text

When following the 7×7 per slide text guideline, which suggest using no more than seven lines with seven words on a slide, you may find that you have more text to display on a slide than there is room available. If this happens, create two text boxes. Animate the first text box, and then click the Animation Dialog Box Launcher. Click the *After animation* arrow and click Hide After Animation. Select the second text box and animate using the Appear animation. Set the animation to play *After previous*.

Using the Animation Pane

STEP 5 » As you work with complex animations, it is helpful to view the Animation Pane. The Animation Pane is similar to a summary of animation effects used. The display begins with a tag indicating how the animation starts. A *0* tag indicates the animation starts with the previous animation. A numbered tag indicates the animation begins with a mouse click, and the number indicates the animation order. No tag indicates that the animation automatically starts after the previous animation. Office 2013 has a new feature where animation effects are color-coded. For example, green indicates an entrance animation and red indicates an exit animation. An emphasis animation is coded yellow, and a motion path is coded blue.

An icon displays to the right of the tag that represents the type of animation effect applied. Next, a portion of the name of the animated object displays. Finally, a timeline displays the duration of an animation as a bar that can be used to adjust timing. To open the Animation Pane, click the Animations tab and click Animation Pane in the Advanced Animation group. To adjust animation timing, drag the edge of the animation bar. Figure 6.23 shows a slide with animated objects with the Animation Pane open.

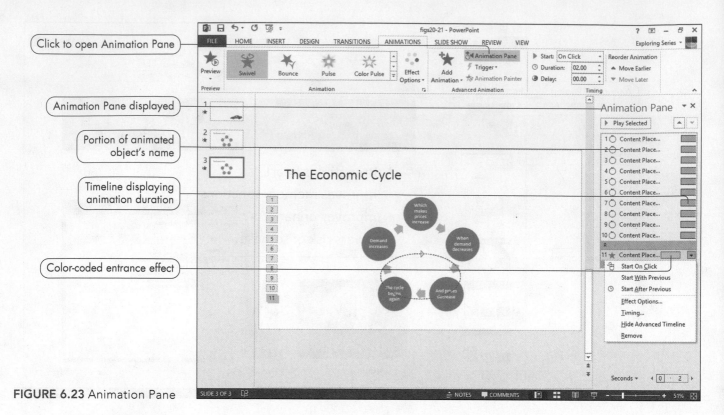

FIGURE 6.23 Animation Pane

Labels on figure:
- Click to open Animation Pane
- Animation Pane displayed
- Portion of animated object's name
- Timeline displaying animation duration
- Color-coded entrance effect

Quick **Concepts** ✓

1. Which animation effect does an Entrance animation type apply to an object? *p. 966*

2. How will applying a motion path to an object or text enhance your presentation? *p. 967*

3. What animation effects are edited and controlled in the Animation Pane? *p. 973*

Hands-On Exercises

Watch the Video for this Hands-On Exercise!

MyITLab®
HOE2 Training

2 Advanced Animation

In your role as the teaching assistant for the computer literacy class, you begin modifying a presentation designed to help the students understand PowerPoint's animation features. You create examples of animation for students to view.

Skills covered: Apply Multiple Animations to an Object • Create and Modify a Custom Motion Path • Specify Animation Settings and Timing • Animate Text and SmartArt • Use the Animation Pane to Modify Animations

STEP 1 >> APPLY MULTIPLE ANIMATIONS TO AN OBJECT

To illustrate an example of multiple animations applied to one object, you apply an entrance, emphasis, motion, and exit animation to a clip art image. After testing the animations, you use the Animation Pane to select and modify the animations. Refer to Figure 6.24 as you complete Step 1.

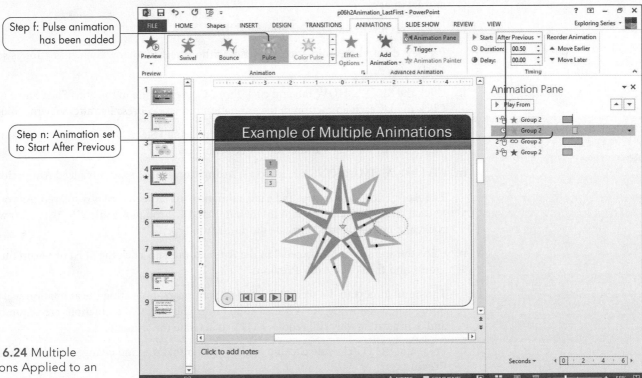

FIGURE 6.24 Multiple Animations Applied to an Object

a. Open *p06h2Animation* and save it as **p06h2Animation_LastFirst**.

> **TROUBLESHOOTING:** If you make any major mistakes in this exercise, you can close the file, open *p06h2Animation* again, and then start this exercise over.

b. Create a handout header with your name and a handout footer with your instructor's name and your class. Include the current date.

c. On Slide 4, select the **star clip art image** and click the **ANIMATIONS tab**.

d. Click the **More button** in the Animation group and click **Grow & Turn** in the Entrance category.

The Grow & Turn animation previews, and an animation tag numbered 1 is assigned to the clip art image.

e. Click **Add Animation** in the Advanced Animation group.

f. Click **Pulse** in the Emphasis category.

The Pulse animation previews and an animation tag numbered 2 is assigned to the clip art image.

g. Click **Add Animation** in the Advanced Animation group.

h. Scroll down the Animation gallery and click **Loops** in the Motion Paths category.

The Loops animation previews, the Loops motion path displays, and an animation tag numbered 3 is assigned to the clip art image.

i. Click **Add Animation** in the Advanced Animation group.

j. Scroll down the Animation gallery and click **Shrink & Turn** in the Exit category.

The Shrink & Turn animation previews, and an animation tag numbered 4 is assigned to the clip art image.

k. Click **Preview** in the Preview group.

Preview displays the animation sequence without regard to how each animation is set to start.

l. Click the **SLIDE SHOW tab** and click **From Current Slide** in the Start Slide Show group. Click to play each animation in the animation sequence. Press **Esc** after viewing Slide 4.

Because the animations were created using the default Start: On Click timing option, you must click to start each animation in the sequence.

m. Click the **ANIMATIONS tab** and click **Animation Pane** in the Advanced Animation group.

The Animation Pane opens, and each animation in the sequence is displayed. As you point to each animation, the animations are numbered 1 through 4, indicating they start with a click, and color-coded to indicate the animation type.

n. Click the animation numbered **2** in the Animation Pane, click the **Start arrow** in the Timing group, and then click **After Previous**.

The number next to the second animation disappears, indicating the animation will activate immediately following the previous animation. The next two animations are renumbered 2 and 3, indicating they still require a click to activate the animation.

o. Press and hold **Ctrl** while clicking the last two animations and change their timings to **After Previous**.

The Animation Pane now indicates that the first animation requires a click to start. All of the numbers have disappeared, which indicates the remaining animations in the sequences will play after the previous animation is completed.

p. Test the animation sequence in Slide Show view to ensure that the animations play correctly.

q. Close the Animation Pane.

r. Save the presentation.

STEP 2 ⟫ CREATE AND MODIFY A CUSTOM MOTION PATH

The next example of an animation in the presentation is a custom path motion animation. You will create a motion path to move a clip art image around the slide, and then you will copy the image and path to another slide and modify the path to smooth it. Refer to Figure 6.25 as you complete Step 2.

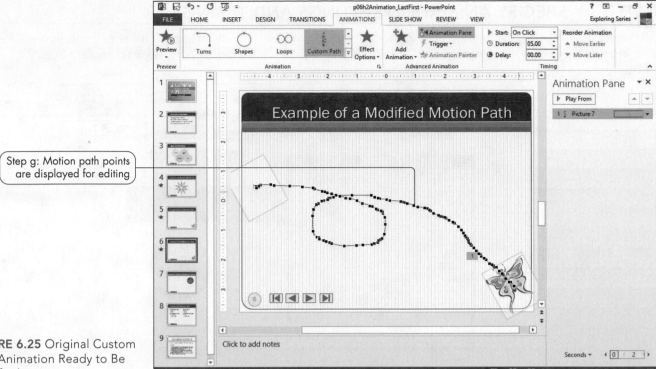

Step g: Motion path points are displayed for editing

FIGURE 6.25 Original Custom Path Animation Ready to Be Modified

a. On Slide 5, select the **butterfly clip art image**.

b. Click the **ANIMATIONS tab**, if necessary, and click the **More button** in the Animation group.

c. Click **Custom Path** in the Motion Paths category.

d. Click in the approximate center of the butterfly and drag the **Pencil tool** in a loop and off the left side of the slide. Refer to Figure 6.25. Double-click to end the path.

The animation previews, and when the preview finishes, you see the path with its green starting point and red ending point.

e. Select **02.00** in the Duration box in the Timing Group and type **05.00**.

Increasing the duration increases the amount of time it takes to complete the animation.

f. Copy the clip art image and paste the copy on Slide 6 using the **Use Destination Theme paste option**.

The clip art image and its associated animation are pasted on Slide 6.

g. On Slide 6, click the **Animations tab**, if necessary, click the path, click **Effect Options** in the Animation group, and then click **Edit Points**.

The points that create the motion path appear.

h. Click a point on the path and drag the point to a new position.

The path reshapes based on the new point position.

i. Click a point on the path, right-click, and then click **Delete Point**.

> **TROUBLESHOOTING:** If you press Delete on the keyboard, the entire path disappears. Click Undo on the Quick Access Toolbar and repeat step i.

j. Continue to delete any points that cause a jerky animation motion, or right-click any point causing a jerky motion, and select **Smooth Point**.

k. Save the presentation.

STEP 3 >> SPECIFY ANIMATION SETTINGS AND TIMING

To illustrate how changing animation settings and timing can help an animation appear more realistic, you will modify the animation settings and timing of a basketball clip art image. Refer to Figure 6.26 as you complete Step 3.

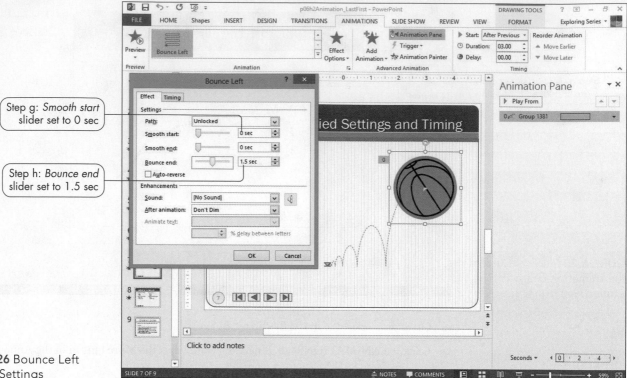

FIGURE 6.26 Bounce Left Animation Settings

a. On Slide 7, click the **basketball clip art image** to select it.

b. Click the **ANIMATIONS tab**, if necessary, click the **More button**, and then click **More Motion Paths**.

c. Click **Bounce Left** in the *Lines_Curves* section and click **OK**.

d. Click the red ending point of the animation. When the double-headed arrow displays, drag it to the left to extend the distance the animation will cover.

> **TROUBLESHOOTING:** Be sure the mouse displays as the double-headed arrow before dragging the red ending point of the animation. Otherwise, you will move the entire animation instead of extending the distance the animation will cover.

e. Click the **Duration up arrow** in the Timing group until the duration time is set at **03.00**.

   The animation will now take three seconds to complete.

f. Click the **Animation Dialog Box Launcher** in the Animation group to show additional animation effect options.

   The Bounce Left dialog box opens.

g. Drag the **Smooth start slider** to **0 sec**.

   The animation now starts at a higher speed rather than starting slowly and speeding up.

h. Drag the **Bounce end slider** to **1.5 sec** and click **OK**. (The *Smooth end* setting automatically becomes 0 sec.)

   The animation begins to slow after 1.5 seconds.

i. Click **Preview** in the Preview group.

j. Save the presentation.

STEP 4 ≫ ANIMATE TEXT AND SMARTART

You want to demonstrate how to control the flow of information to the computer literacy students. To do so, you will animate text and a SmartArt diagram. You will apply the Appear animation effect on text content placeholders so that students will not be distracted by movement and can concentrate on reading the text. You will apply a Shape entrance animation so that the animation shape matches the circle shapes used in the SmartArt. Refer to Figure 6.27 as you complete Step 4.

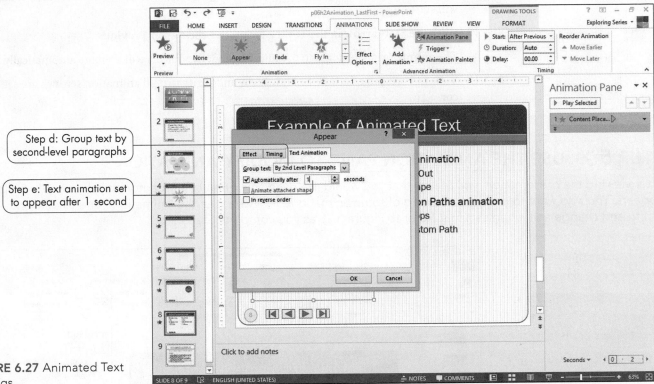

FIGURE 6.27 Animated Text Settings

a. On Slide 8, click the **left content placeholder** to select it.

Selecting text enables you to apply an animation; selecting the content placeholder is faster.

b. Click **Appear** in the *Entrance* section of the Animation group.

Animation 1 and 2 tags appear next to the first and second first-level bullets and their associated second-level bullets.

c. Click the **Animation Dialog Box Launcher**, click the **After animation arrow**, and then click the last color option.

Text that has been viewed dims to the new color after viewing.

d. Click the **Text Animation tab** in the Appear dialog box, click the **Group text arrow**, and then select **By 2nd Level Paragraphs**.

First-level text and second-level text will animate one at a time.

e. Click **Automatically after**, select **0**, type **1**, and then click **OK**.

The animation tags change to 0, indicating that they will start automatically. Preview displays the text entering, pausing for 1 second, and then dimming when the next animated text appears.

f. Click the **left content placeholder**, if necessary, click **Animation Painter**, and then click the **right content placeholder**.

The animation timing and settings are copied to the placeholder.

g. On Slide 3, select the SmartArt diagram.

h. Click the **More button** in the Animation group and click **Shape** in the *Entrance* section.

Preview displays a Circle animation that begins at the edges of the SmartArt and moves inward to complete the shape.

i. Click **Effect Options** in the Animation group and click **Out** in the *Direction* section.

j. Click **Effect Options** in the Animation group and click **One by One** in the *Sequence* section.

Animation tags 1 through 4 appear, indicating that each object will animate individually and will start on a mouse click.

k. Click the **Start arrow** in the Timing group and click **After Previous**.

The animation tag changes to 0, indicating that the objects will animate automatically.

l. View the presentation in Slide Show view and verify that all animation settings are set correctly.

m. Save the presentation.

STEP 5 ≫ USE THE ANIMATION PANE TO MODIFY ANIMATIONS

After viewing the presentation, you realize that you would like each animation to start automatically when the slide appears. You also want to modify the timing of some animations. You will open the Animation Pane to efficiently locate and change animation settings. Refer to Figure 6.28 as you complete Step 5.

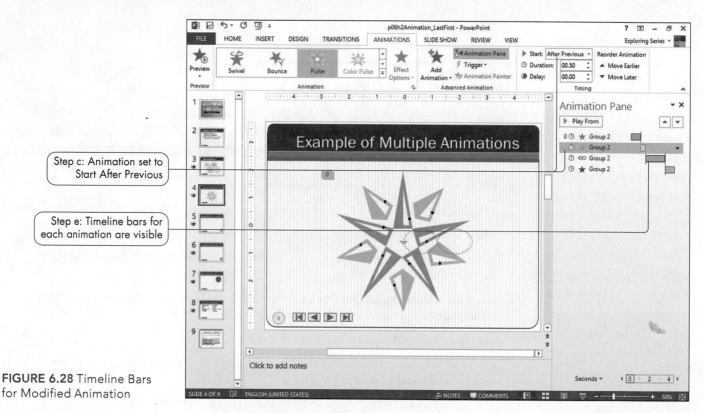

Step c: Animation set to Start After Previous

Step e: Timeline bars for each animation are visible

FIGURE 6.28 Timeline Bars for Modified Animation

a. Click the **ANIMATIONS tab** and click **Animation Pane** in the Advanced Animation group.

b. On Slide 4, click the **star clip art image** and notice the Animation Pane.

All animations in the Animation Pane are selected. The animation 1 tag next to the first bullet indicates that this animation plays first and requires a mouse click to launch.

c. Click the first animation in the Animation Pane to select it and click the **Start arrow** in the Timing group. Click **After Previous**.

The animation 1 tag changes to a 0.

d. Repeat step c for Slides 5 through 7.

e. On Slide 4, drag the left border of the Animation Pane to the left until the timeline bar next to each animation is visible.

The timeline bars show that each animation starts immediately after the preceding animation. The loop animation takes longer to complete than the other three animations.

f. Drag the right edge of the timeline bar for the second animation to the right until the ScreenTip displays *End: 2.6s*.

The Pulse animation duration is increased.

TROUBLESHOOTING: Be sure the mouse displays as the double-headed arrow with vertical lines in the middle. A plain double-headed arrow will not work for this task.

---

g. Click the last animation to select it, click the **Start arrow**, and then click **With Previous**.

The beginning point for the third and fourth animations align so they begin at the same time.

h. Position the pointer over the fourth animation timeline bar and drag the bar so that it begins at **3.2s**. Drag the right edge of the bar to **5.5s**.

The time the animation starts and the duration of the animation is changed.

i. Click the first animation and click **Play From** in the Animation Pane to test the animation.

j. View the presentation in Slide Show view.

k. Save and close the file, and submit it based on your instructor's directions.

Chapter Objectives Review

After reading this chapter, you have accomplished the following objectives:

1. **Insert and use hyperlinks.**
   - Hyperlinks connect two locations and can be used to add interactivity to a slide show.
   - Clicking a hyperlink takes the viewer to another slide in a slide show, to an existing file, to a Web page on the Internet, to another program, or to the screen to begin an e-mail.
   - ScreenTips can be added to hyperlinks to offer the viewer additional information.
   - Hyperlinks can be attached to any object.
   - Hyperlinks can be activated by a mouse click or a mouse over.

2. **Add action buttons.**
   - Actions are instructions to PowerPoint to perform a task such as jumping to another slide, playing a sound, or opening another program.
   - You can attach actions to any object or use an action button—a pre-made icon with actions attached.
   - Action buttons are typically used to navigate a slide show (Back or Previous button, Forward or Next button, Beginning button, End button, Home button, and Return button) or to display some type of information (Information button, Movie button, Document button, Sound button, and Help button).
   - Activate an action button with a mouse click or a mouse over.

3. **Use a trigger.**
   - A trigger is an animation option that controls when an event takes place.
   - In order for the event to take place, a viewer must click an object that has an animation trigger attached.

4. **Apply multiple animations to an object.**
   - You can apply more than one animation effect to an object.
   - Multiple animations direct the flow of information or enhance the message of a slide.

5. **Apply a motion path animation.**
   - In a motion path animation, an object follows a predetermined path to capture and focus a viewer's attention.
   - Motion paths can be linear, curved, or follow a predetermined shape.
   - Creating a Custom path motion path enables you to draw a path in any direction and of any length.
   - Add, delete, and move points on a motion path to edit it.

6. **Specify animation settings and timing.**
   - Animation settings vary according to the animation type and are modified using the Animations tab or the Animation dialog box associated with the selected animation effect.
   - Attaching timings to animations frees you from constantly advancing to the next object and lets you concentrate on delivering your message.

7. **Animate text.**
   - Animating text controls the flow of information to the audience.
   - You can bring text onto the slide by animating the text as one object, by animating all paragraphs to come in together, or by sequencing the text animation by text outline level.

8. **Use the Animation Pane.**
   - The Animation Pane provides a summary of animation effects used.
   - Tags indicate how an animation starts; the type of animation effect applied; a portion of the name of the animated object; and a timeline with bars that displays the start, end, and duration of animations.

Key Terms Matching

Match the key terms with their definitions. Write the key term letter by the appropriate numbered definition.

a. Action button
b. Animation
c. Custom button
d. Custom path
e. Emphasis
f. End button
g. Entrance
h. Exit
i. Help button
j. Home button

k. Hyperlink
l. Interactivity
m. Kiosk
n. Linear presentation
o. Motion path
p. Movie button
q. Non-linear presentation
r. ScreenTip
s. Trigger
t. Uniform resource locator (URL)

1. _____ The ability to branch or interact based on decisions made by a viewer or audience. **p. 948**

2. _____ Additional information that displays as you mouse over an object, such as a hyperlink. **p. 952**

3. _____ An action button that can be set to trigger unique actions in the presentation. **p. 952**

4. _____ A ready-made button designed to serve as an icon to which an action can be assigned. **p. 948**

5. _____ Progress through a presentation according to choices made by the viewer that determine which slide comes next. **p. 948**

6. _____ An interactive computer terminal available for public use. **p. 953**

7. _____ A predetermined path that an object follows as part of an animation. **p. 966**

8. _____ An action used to draw interest to an object in a presentation. **p. 955**

9. _____ The address of a resource on the Web. **p. 949**

10. _____ Progress through a presentation sequentially, starting with the first slide and ending with the last slide. **p. 948**

11. _____ A PowerPoint animation type that draws attention to an object already on a slide. **p. 966**

12. _____ An action button that moves to the last slide in the presentation. **p. 953**

13. _____ A connection or link that branches to another location. **p. 948**

14. _____ A PowerPoint animation type that controls how an object moves onto or appears on a slide. **p. 966**

15. _____ An action button that can be set to play a movie. **p. 953**

16. _____ An animation path that can be created freehand instead of following a preset path. **p. 968**

17. _____ An action button set to move to the first slide in the presentation. **p. 953**

18. _____ A PowerPoint animation type that controls how an object leaves or disappears from a slide. **p. 966**

19. _____ Launches an animation that takes place when the user clicks on an associated object or bookmark location in a media object. **p. 955**

20. _____ An action button that can be set to open a document with instructions or help information. **p. 953**

Multiple Choice

1. The term used for a connection from one location to another is:

   (a) Hyperlink.

   (b) Trigger.

   (c) Motion path.

   (d) Object.

2. When you click an object on the slide or when you launch an animation with a bookmark in a video and an animation effect occurs, which of the following is used?

   (a) Hyperlink

   (b) Mouse over

   (c) Action button

   (d) Trigger

3. Which of the following refers to an interactive slide show?

   (a) Sequential presentation

   (b) Linear presentation

   (c) Non-linear presentation

   (d) Abstract presentation

4. To create an action button, which tab do you click to start the process?

   (a) INSERT

   (b) DESIGN

   (c) SLIDE SHOW

   (d) VIEW

5. An alternate method for inserting or editing a hyperlink in a presentation is:

   (a) Press Ctrl+V.

   (b) Right-click the object and select Hyperlink.

   (c) Press F7.

   (d) Click the VIEW tab and choose Web Layout.

6. Which of the following is a true statement regarding multiple animations?

   (a) To add a second animation, click the INSERT tab and click Add Animation.

   (b) Multiple animations can be added to shape objects but not text objects.

   (c) Individual animations that are part of an animation sequence display in the Animation Pane.

   (d) All of the above.

7. Which of the following animation effects would enable you to change its direction setting?

   (a) Grow/Shrink

   (b) Fly In

   (c) Pulse

   (d) Appear

8. Attaching a timing setting to animations enables the presenter to more effectively:

   (a) Concentrate on delivering the message.

   (b) Close the presentation at the end.

   (c) Change timing during the presentation on the fly.

   (d) All of the above.

9. The Animation Pane includes which of the following symbols?

   (a) The letter T representing text that is animated on the slide

   (b) A direction arrow indicating the direction of the assigned animation

   (c) A clock representing whether the animation starts automatically or requires a mouse click

   (d) A symbol representing the type of animation assigned

10. Which of the following is not a type of PowerPoint animation?

    (a) Evolving

    (b) Exit

    (c) Entrance

    (d) Motion path

Practice Exercises

1 Copyright and the Law

The IT manager of your company has observed some violations of software copyright in the organization. He immediately removed the offending software but feels that perhaps it is a lack of understanding about copyright rather than deliberate theft. He has asked you, as a company trainer, to prepare and deliver a presentation about basic copyright principles for company employees. You will create a custom action button, attach sound actions, and create navigation buttons. You will link to an existing Word document with a Microsoft End User License Agreement as a sample. You will also include a link to the Microsoft volume licensing site. You will edit a hyperlink that links to a Web site with further information about copyright and copyright protection. Finally, you will add an Appear entrance animation that groups text by second-level paragraphs so the presenter can discuss each level as needed. The exercise follows the same set of skills as used in Hands-On Exercises 1 and 2 in the chapter. Refer to Figure 6.29 as you complete this exercise.

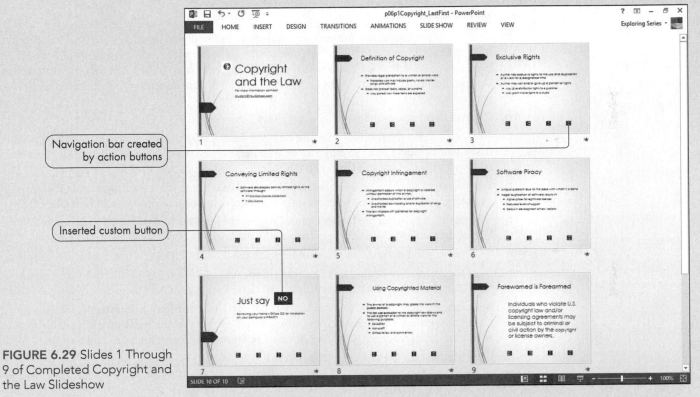

FIGURE 6.29 Slides 1 Through 9 of Completed Copyright and the Law Slideshow

a. Open *p06p1Copyright* and save it as **p06p1Copyright_LastFirst**.

b. Create a handout header with your name and a handout footer with your instructor's name and your class. Include the current date.

c. On Slide 1, position the insertion point after the colon following *contact* on the Title slide, press **Enter**, type your e-mail address, and then press **Spacebar**.

d. On Slide 7, click the **INSERT tab**, click **Shapes** in the Illustrations group, and then click **Action Button: Custom**. Click to create a button in the top right of the slide. You will size and position the button in a later step.

e. Click the **Play sound check box** on the Mouse Click tab in the Actions Settings dialog box, click the **Play sound arrow**, and then click **Other Sound**.

f. Locate and select *p06p1No.wav* and click **OK** twice.

g. Click the **FORMAT tab**, if necessary. Click the **Size Dialog Box Launcher** in the Size group and set **Height** to 1" and **Width** to 1.5". Click **POSITION** in the Format Shape pane and set **Horizontal position** to 6.25" and **Vertical position** to 1.42".

h. Type **NO** in the action button. Select the text, apply bold, and then change the font size to **40 pt**.

i. On Slide 2, click the **INSERT tab**, click **Shapes** in the Illustrations group, and then click **Action Button: Beginning**. Click to create a button near the bottom of the slide. Click **OK** to accept the default action settings.

j. Click the **FORMAT tab**, if necessary, and click the **Size Dialog Box Launcher** in the Size group to return to the Size options in the Format Shape pane. Size the button to **0.35"** by **0.35"** and position the button at a horizontal position of **6.4"** and a vertical position of **6.5"** (if necessary, refer to step g instructions). Close the dialog box.

k. Click the **FORMAT tab**, if necessary, click **Shape Fill** in the Shape Styles group, and then click **Orange, Accent 2, Lighter 60%** (third row, sixth column).

l. On Slide 2, click the **Shapes More button** in the Insert Shapes group on the FORMAT tab to create action buttons for *Back or Previous*, *Forward or Next*, and *End* (three more buttons). Repeat steps j through k to accept the default action settings for each button. Size the buttons and change the Shape Fill (step k), but do not worry about the button positions. You will position the buttons in the next step.

m. Select the left-facing arrow **Action Button: Back or Previous** and position it at **3"** horizontally and **6.5"** vertically from the top-left corner. Select the right-facing arrow **Action Button: Forward or Next** and position it at **4.7"** horizontally and **6.5"** vertically from the top-left corner. Select **Action Button: End** and position it at **8.1"** horizontally and **6.5"** vertically from the top-left corner. Close the Format Shape pane.

n. Copy all four buttons and paste them on Slides 3 through 10.

o. On Slide 4, select the text *End User License Agreement*. Click the **INSERT tab** and click **Hyperlink** in the Links group. Click **Existing File or Web Page**, if necessary, click **Browse for File**, locate and select *p06p1Eula.docx*, and then click **OK** twice.

p. Select the text *Site License*. Click **Hyperlink** in the Links group, click **Existing File or Web Page**, if necessary, and then type **www.microsoftvolumelicensing.com** in the **Address box**. Click **OK**.

q. On Slide 10, right-click the **United States Copyright hyperlink** and click **Edit Hyperlink**. Edit the Web address to **http://www.loc.gov/copyright** and click **OK**.

r. On Slide 2, select the **content placeholder**, click the **ANIMATIONS tab**, and then click **Appear**.

s. Click the **Animation Dialog Box Launcher** in the Animation group and click the **Text Animation tab**. Click the **Group text arrow**, click **By 2nd Level Paragraphs**, and then click **OK**.

t. Select the content placeholder on Slide 2, double-click **Animation Painter** in the Advanced Animation group, and then click each content placeholder in the remaining slides to copy the animation settings to each. Click the **Animation Painter button** to toggle it off when done.

u. View the presentation and test each hyperlink.

v. Save and close the file. Submit based on your instructor's directions.

2 GeGo Power!

You work in the lab of a food products company and have created several formulations of a nutritious new hot drink. You conducted a series of focus groups to study and determine consumer preferences. The focus group study also sought to determine whether consumers would be inclined to give up their morning coffee in favor of the new drink, code name "GeGo." You now want to present the results of the study to the food products company officials in the hopes they will agree to test it in the local college market in the fall. You will create a presentation that will include a study summary revealing the focus group preferences. You want to include the option to see detailed results for those who want to see them. You realize that creating a button as a trigger for the results is an excellent option. In this exercise, you will use a clip art image as the trigger button to animate the table. Finally, you will add animation. The exercise follows the same set of skills as used in Hands-On Exercise 2 in the chapter. Refer to Figure 6.30 as you complete this exercise.

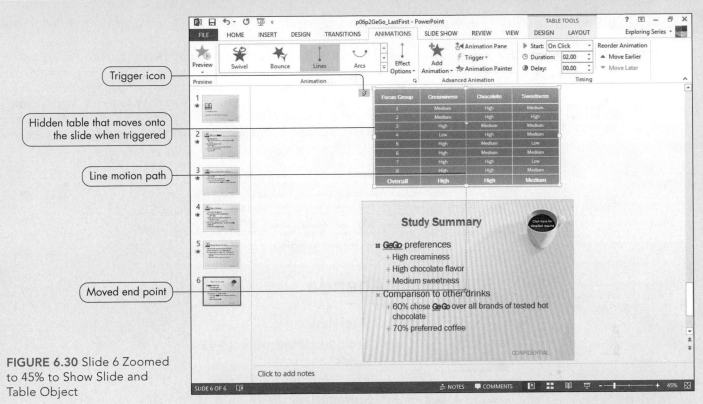

Trigger icon

Hidden table that moves onto the slide when triggered

Line motion path

Moved end point

FIGURE 6.30 Slide 6 Zoomed to 45% to Show Slide and Table Object

a. Open *p06p2GeGo* and save it as **p06p2GeGo_LastFirst.**

b. Create a handout header with your name and a handout footer with your instructor's name and your class. Include the current date.

c. On Slide 1, click the outside border of the **GeGo logo**, click the **ANIMATIONS tab**, click the **More button** in the Animation group, and then click **Zoom** under Entrance.

d. Click the **More button** in the Animation group, click **More Motion Paths**, click **Vertical Figure 8** in the *Special* section, and then click **OK.**

e. Click the **Start arrow** in the Timing group and click **With Previous.**

f. On Slide 2, click the **content placeholder** and click **Fade.**

g. Select the **content placeholder** again, double-click **Animation Painter** in the Advanced Animation group, and then click each of the **content placeholders** on Slides 3 through 5. Click the **Animation Painter** in the Advanced Animation group to turn off the feature when done.

h. On Slide 6, click the **VIEW tab**, click **Zoom** in the Zoom group, type **45%**, and then click **OK.**

   With the view reduced, a portion of a table containing the focus group results is visible at the top of the design window.

i. Click the table to select it, click the **ANIMATIONS tab**, and then click the **More button** in the Animation group.

j. Click **Lines** in the Motion Paths category to apply the animation to the table.

k. Click the red end when the double-headed arrow appears, press and hold **Shift** to constrain movement to a straight line, and then drag the red end arrow to the top of the letter *d* in the word *drinks* on the slide.

   The table descends and covers the text when triggered.

l. Click the table. Click **Trigger** in the Advanced Animation group, point to *On Click of*, and then click **Group 7.**

   Group 7 is the grouping of the hot chocolate clip art and the text box reading *Click here for detailed results.*

m. View the presentation. When Slide 6 appears, click the **hot chocolate clip art** to trigger the table animation.

n. Save and close the file, and submit it based on your instructor's directions.

1 Creative Presentation

CREATIVE CASE

FROM SCRATCH

The presentation in Figure 6.31 was created using a Microsoft Office Online template, *Presentation on brainstorming*. Because it is a presentation template, it includes suggested text to jump-start the creative process. In this exercise, you will download the template and modify it. You will add a navigation bar using custom action buttons that link to the related slides. As an alternative method for navigating, you will change the agenda items to hyperlinks that link to the associated slide. Finally, you will animate text using the animation effects and settings you select. Refer to Figure 6.31 as you complete this exercise.

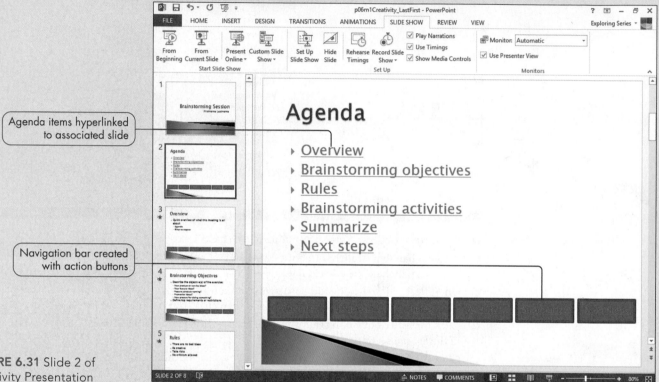

FIGURE 6.31 Slide 2 of Creativity Presentation

a. Access the New Presentation pane. Search for the *Presentation on brainstorming* template. Choose the first template in the row of options. Save the presentation as **p06m1Creativity_LastFirst**.

b. Create a handout header with your name and a handout footer with your instructor's name and your class. Include the current date.

c. On Slide 1, replace the subtitle *Your Name* with your own name.

d. On Slide 2, create a Custom Action button and click **Cancel** to bypass the Actions Setting dialog box at this time. Resize the button height to **0.59"** and **1.5"** wide. Change the Shape Fill to **Blue** (under *Standard Colors*).

e. Change the Shape Outline color to Theme Color **Indigo, Accent 5** (first row, ninth column).

f. Type **Agenda** in the action button, select the text, and then change the font size to **16 pt**.

g. Duplicate the button five times. Change the label of the duplicate buttons to **Objectives**, **Rules**, **Activity**, **Summarize**, and **Next Steps**. Position the buttons just above the slide bottom accents with Agenda as the first button and the remaining buttons listed in the order above. With all six buttons selected, align bottom and distribute the buttons horizontally.

h. Select the text on each action button and add a hyperlink to **Place in This Document** to the slide title to correspond to each of the action button titles you just created.

i. Copy the buttons and paste them on Slides 3 through 8.

j. On Slide 2, select **Overview** and add a hyperlink to Slide 3. Rather than create a return button, use the Return navigation button on the bottom left of the slide.

k. On Slide 2, continue adding hyperlinks for each agenda item to its associated slide.

l. Add the animation effects and settings you choose to the text in the presentation using a minimum of one each of the following animations: entrance, emphasis, exit, and motion path.

m. View the presentation and make any needed changes using the Animation Pane. Adjust or add additional animations, if desired.

n. Save and close the file. Submit it based on your instructor's directions.

2 Patient Assessment Flow Chart

In this exercise, you will create hyperlinks for a patient assessment flow chart for the Fire and Rescue Academy. Your task is to turn each shape in the flow chart into a clickable button with an action assigned. When clicked, the button will link to its associated slide. You will create a button to return the viewer to the flow chart after viewing a slide. You will assign a mouse-over action to a clip art image that plays the sound of an ambulance. Finally, you will add triggers to launch a sequence of animated images. Refer to Figure 6.32 as you complete this exercise.

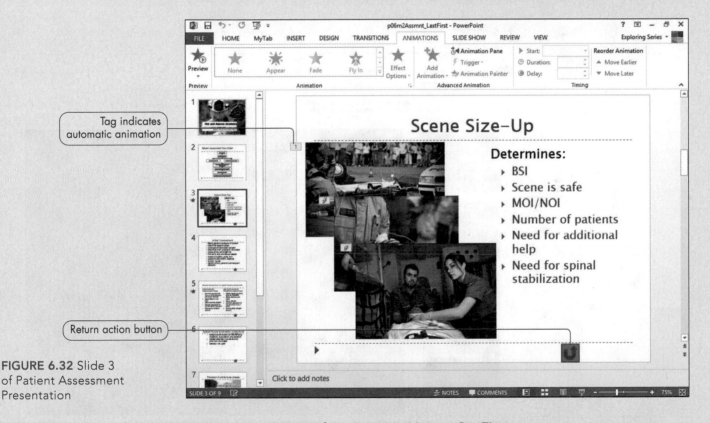

FIGURE 6.32 Slide 3 of Patient Assessment Presentation

a. Open *p06m2Assmnt* and save it as **p06m2Assmnt_LastFirst**.

b. Create a handout header with your name and a handout footer with your instructor's name and your class. Include the current date.

c. On Slide 2, select **Scene Size-Up** and add a hyperlink for the label to Slide 3.

d. Continue converting each shape label text in the Patient Assessment Flow Chart into a hyperlink to the associated slide. Note that the Focused Assessment and the Rapid Trauma Assessment labels share a common slide, Slide 5. Each of these two button labels, therefore, must link to Slide 5.

e. Enable the viewer to move quickly back to the flow chart slide by doing the following: on Slide 3, create an Action Button: Return that links to Slide 2. Resize the button to **0.5"** high by **0.5"** wide. Position it horizontally at **7.5"** from the top-left corner and vertically at **7"** from the top-left corner. Copy the button to Slides 4 through 9.

f. On Slide 7, insert a mouse-over action that plays the *p06m2Ambulance.wav* audio clip for the ambulance picture.

g. Create an animation sequence for the images in Slide 3. All animations should fly in from the left. The top picture should start on click. Clicking the first image should trigger the appearance of the middle image. Clicking the middle image should trigger the appearance of the bottom image.

h. On Slide 5, use the Animation Pane to reorder the animations. The *Focused Assessment* subtitle currently appears last but should appear first, followed by its associated bullet points. The *Rapid Trauma Assessment* subtitle should appear next, followed by its associated bullet points.

i. Test each of the buttons and triggers you created in Slide Show view.

j. Edit any buttons that do not link correctly.

k. Save and close the file. Submit it based on your instructor's directions.

3 Internet History Game

COLLABORATION CASE

FROM SCRATCH

You have been assigned to work with one or more other classmates to develop an interactive PowerPoint game on some aspect of Internet history. You should begin by searching for a Microsoft PowerPoint quiz template. The quiz needs to have a variety of question types such as short answer, true/false, or another question type. Because everyone's schedule is varied, you should use either your Outlook account, another e-mail account, or SkyDrive to pass the presentation file. Save the quiz as **p06m3Quiz_GroupName**. Refer to Figure 6.33 as you complete this exercise.

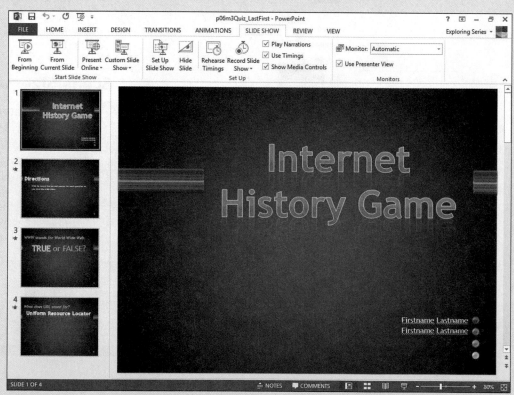

FIGURE 6.33 Interactive Game

- It will be helpful to create a storyboard to plan the slides you will need for the game and the interactive elements required by your plan.
- The first slide should contain the name of the game, your first and last names, and your partners' first and last names.
- Be sure to include a slide that gives directions for the game.
- The question slides should use animation to reveal the answers when a trigger is performed.
- Pass the presentation to the next student so that he or she can perform the same tasks, and so on.
- After all students have contributed to the presentation, submit the file as directed by your instructor.

Beyond the Classroom

Professionalism

RESEARCH CASE

FROM SCRATCH

Many professions have support organizations that are created to serve the membership and to enhance the professional growth of the members. Laurie Brems, president of the Utah Business and Computer Educators, created a slide to show Utah business educators two professional routes available for them. Following one route, educators join state and national career and technical education organizations. Following the other route, educators join the state and national business education organizations. Joining both sets of organizations ensures a business educator the greatest support network possible.

Research the professional organizations available to you in your field of interest. Create a slide that shows professional organizations from a minimum of two routes you could choose to pursue for your field of interest to illustrate the professional path(s) available to you. Include hyperlinks to the organizations. Include additional information on this slide or on additional slides in the slide show. Animate the path as desired and use the Animation Pane to adjust the duration of the animations, if necessary. Save the presentation as **p06b2Professional_LastFirst**. Create a handout header with your name and a handout footer with your instructor's name and your class. Include the current date.

Colorful Diet = Healthy Diet Presentation

DISASTER RECOVERY

You are part of a group assigned to create a presentation on healthy eating. Your group was given one hour in a computer lab to prepare, so first you sketched out a storyboard, and then you divided responsibilities. One member of the group researched the benefits of eating fruits and vegetables, and two members created the design of the presentation, including locating pictures. As information was located, it was typed into the presentation.

Open *p06b3Diet* and save it as **p06b3Diet_LastFirst**. Create a handout header with your name and a handout footer with your instructor's name and your class. Include the current date. Check the presentation design to ensure all aspects display properly and that the introduction slide, body slides, and conclusion slide appear in the correct order. Test hyperlinks, action buttons, and triggers to ensure they link properly. Edit any hyperlinks that do not link correctly. Resize the action buttons and distribute them horizontally. Apply entrance, emphasis, motion path, and exit animations to the pictures on Slide 9. Make other changes to the slide show as desired. Finally, carefully proofread the text and check the images. Remove cartoon-style images so the design is consistent.

Answering Tough Interview Questions

SOFT SKILLS CASE

FROM SCRATCH

Create a presentation that will help other students prepare to answer tough interview questions. Create a slide that lists at least five tough interview questions. Insert suggested responses to each question on a separate slide, and then create a hyperlink from the question to the slide with the appropriate answer. Apply other interactivity and advanced animations to enhance the presentation. Save and close the presentation, and submit it based on your instructor's directions.

Capstone Exercise

As a volunteer in the Campus Health Center, you are often asked to prepare presentations to run at various kiosks located around campus. The presentations vary, but all have the goal of educating students about health and safety issues. This week, you were asked to prepare a presentation based on information about the Cycle of Abuse provided to the center from the local city police department Crime Advocate Program. Refer to Figure 6.34 as you complete this capstone exercise.

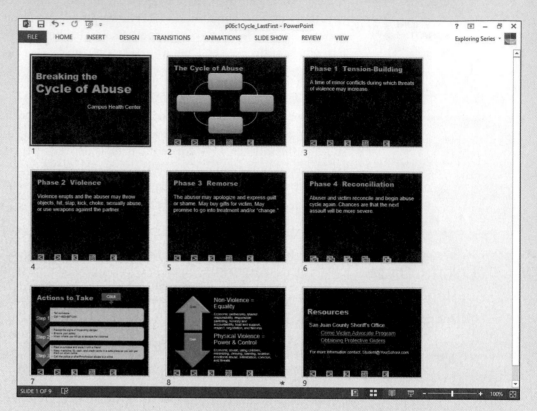

FIGURE 6.34 Animated Action Buttons and Triggers

Adding an E-Mail Address, a Web Page Hyperlink, and a Link to an Existing File

In this exercise, you will include a hyperlink to the Web site of the Crime Victim Advocate Program on the Resource slide of the presentation. You will also create a link to a Word document containing information about obtaining a protective order. You will include your e-mail address for contact information.

a. Open *p06c1Cycle* and immediately save it as **p06c1Cycle_LastFirst**.

b. Create a handout header with your name and a handout footer with your instructor's name and your class. Include the current date.

c. On Slide 9, create a hyperlink that links the text *Crime Victim Advocate Program* to http://www.sanjuancounty.org/victim_advocate.htm. Include the ScreenTip **Click to read additional information**.

d. Link the text *Obtaining Protective Orders* to the Word document *p06c1Order*.

e. Position the insertion point after the colon and space following *contact*, type your e-mail address, and then press **Spacebar**.

f. Save the presentation.

Attaching Actions to Shapes and Creating a Navigation Bar

You want to add interactivity to the slide show by enabling the viewer to click a shape in the cycle illustration on Slide 2 and then jump to a slide giving detail about the related phase. You also want the viewer to be able to easily navigate between slides, so you create a navigation bar.

a. On Slide 2, insert an action for the Tension shape so that when it is clicked, the viewer is sent to the Phase 1 Tension-Building slide.

b. Select each of the remaining shapes and convert them to action buttons that link to the appropriate slide.

c. Create an Action Button: Beginning link to Slide 2 (The Cycle of Abuse) and size it to **0.5"** high and **0.5"** wide. Set the horizontal position at **3.47"** and the vertical position at **7"**.

d. Create the following action buttons and size them to **0.5"** high and **0.5"** wide.

- Action Button: Back or Previous to a horizontal position of **0.59"** and vertical position of **7"**.
- Action Button: Return to a horizontal position of **4.96"** and vertical position of **7"**.

- Action Button: Forward or Next to a horizontal position of **0.59"** and vertical position of **7"**.
- Action Button: End

e. Set the position for Action Button: End to a horizontal position of **6.75"** and a vertical position of **7"**.

f. Copy the action buttons and paste them to Slides 3 through 9.

g. Save the presentation.

Create Animations, Action Buttons, and Triggers

To emphasize the message that physical violence equates to power and control, you will animate the information on Slide 8, convert the clip art into buttons, and then attach sound to the buttons. You will also apply a trigger to the SmartArt in Slide 7 so the viewer clicks to bring the next piece of information onscreen.

a. On Slide 8, apply a **Float In animation** to the Physical Violence = Power & Control text box. Set the animation to start **With Previous**.

b. Apply a **Fly In animation** to the *down arrow* clip art. Adjust the Effect Options so the arrow flies in **From Top**. Set the animation to start **After Previous**.

c. Apply a **Float In animation** to the *Non-Violence = Equality* text box. Set the animation to start **After Previous**.

d. Apply a **Fly In animation** to the *up arrow* clip art. Set the animation to start **After Previous**.

e. Attach a **Play sound action** to the *up arrow* clip art and set the action to play the **Chime sound**.

f. Attach a **Play sound action** to the *down arrow* clip art and set the action to play the **Explosion sound**.

g. Set a trigger to the *down arrow* clip art so that it is launched when the Physical Violence = Power & Control text box appears.

h. On Slide 7, apply a **Wipe entrance animation** to the SmartArt. Adjust the Effect Options so the steps flow from the top down and appear one by one.

i. On Slide 7, trigger the SmartArt animation using Down Arrow Callout 4.

j. Save the presentation.

Testing Hyperlinks, Action Buttons, and Triggers

Before publishing the Cycle of Abuse presentation, you know it is critical to check all hyperlinks, action buttons, and triggers to ensure they are working correctly. If a link does not work, exit the slide show and edit the link immediately so you are not relying on your memory when editing.

a. View the slide show from the beginning.

b. Click the **Tension shape** to test the action button to see if it successfully jumps to the Phase 1 Tension-Building slide.

c. Click **Action Button: Back or Previous** to see if it returns you to Slide 2.

d. Click the **Violence shape** to test the action button to see if it successfully jumps to the Phase 2 Violence slide.

e. Click **Action Button: End** to see if it successfully jumps to the Resources slide.

f. Click the **Crime Victim Advocate Program hyperlink** to see if it jumps to the San Juan County Victim Advocacy Program site. Close the browser.

g. Click the **Obtaining Protective Orders hyperlink** to see if it opens the Protective Orders information sheet. Close the browser.

h. Click **Action Button: Beginning** to see if it jumps to the menu on Slide 2.

i. Click the **Reconciliation shape** to test the action button to see if it jumps to the Phase 4 Reconciliation slide.

j. Click **Action Button: Forward or Next**.

k. Click **Click trigger** on Slide 7 until you have advanced through all steps.

l. Click the **Action Button: Forward or Next** to view Slide 8.

m. Click each arrow and listen to the associated sounds.

n. Press **Esc**.

o. Save and close the file. Submit it based on your instructor's directions.

Customization

CHAPTER 7

Customizing PowerPoint and the Slide Show

OBJECTIVES AFTER YOU READ THIS CHAPTER, YOU WILL BE ABLE TO:

1. Set PowerPoint options p. 996
2. Customize the Ribbon p. 999
3. Use Combine Shapes commands p. 1002
4. Modify handout and notes masters p. 1010
5. Modify a slide master p. 1012

6. Save a slide master as a template p. 1018
7. Create a custom slide show p. 1029
8. Run and navigate a custom slide show p. 1031
9. Designate and display hidden slides p. 1031

CASE STUDY | Survival Solutions

You are the owner of Survival Solutions, a store that provides family emergency preparation supplies. You believe that preparation provides peace of mind before, during, and after an emergency. Because of your knowledge about family emergency planning and communication, you are often invited to be a guest speaker. The two topics on which you are invited to present most often are "Emergency Preparedness" and "What to Do Before, During, and After a Disaster."

To make it easier and more time efficient when you create presentations, you modify PowerPoint's settings and personalize the Ribbon to take advantage of shape tools not on the Ribbon by default. You then use the tools to create a logo for Survival Solutions. To help create recognition for your business, you modify the slide masters that control the layout and appearance of handouts, notes, and slides. You add the new logo, and then change the theme colors to match your logo colors. Finally, you create a custom show from a presentation you have used in the community so that you can have flexibility on topics based on audience request. You also control the detail displayed to the audience by hiding and unhiding slides.

PowerPoint Customization

You can become a PowerPoint power user by setting PowerPoint's options to meet your individual needs and by modifying PowerPoint's working environment to include customized tabs. Changing the default PowerPoint options can help you work more productively and smoothly, while adding a personalized tab that contains the features you use most to the Ribbon enables you to work with less effort.

In this section, you will learn how to set general options for working with PowerPoint, change how PowerPoint corrects and formats your text, customize how you save your documents, and use other more advanced options. You will also learn how to customize the Ribbon by adding a new tab containing commands that are not available on the default Ribbon. Finally, you will use the new commands to create a logo.

Setting PowerPoint Options

PowerPoint provides you with a broad range of settings that enable you to customize **PowerPoint Options** to meet your needs. To access the options, click the File tab to display the Backstage view and select Options (see Figure 7.1) to open the PowerPoint Options dialog box. Although this discussion will highlight many of the settings, you should spend time exploring all the options.

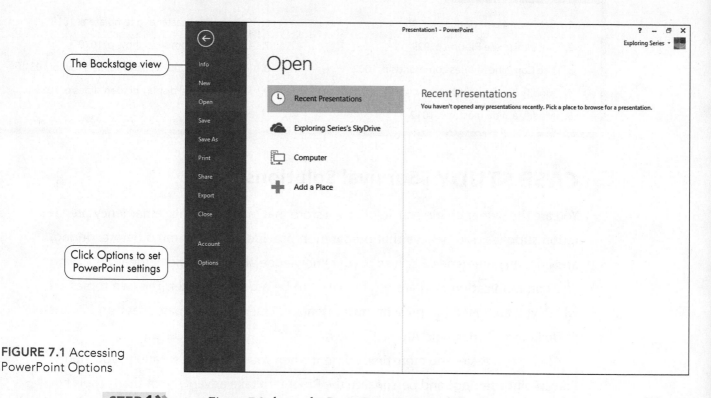

FIGURE 7.1 Accessing PowerPoint Options

STEP 1 ≫ Figure 7.2 shows the PowerPoint Options dialog box with General options displayed.

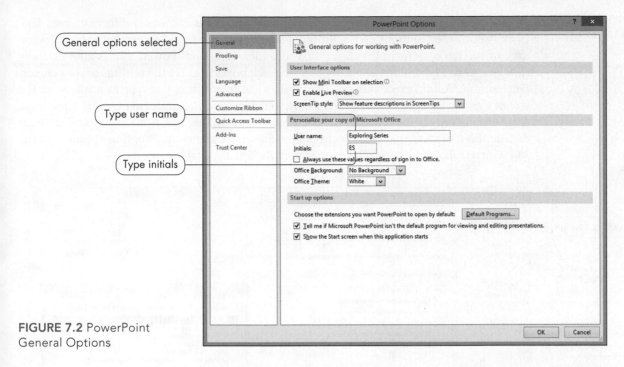

General options selected

Type user name

Type initials

FIGURE 7.2 PowerPoint General Options

Each of the sections can help you customize your presentations.

- *User Interface options* enable you to determine whether to show the Mini Toolbar when text is selected, use Live Preview, and determine how ScreenTips display.

- *Personalize your copy of Microsoft Office* enables you to specify your name and initials. You should add your user name and initials the first time you work with PowerPoint because when you work with others on presentations, your identifying information is used to identify your comments and is included in the presentation information if you created the presentation or were the last person to modify it. Figure 7.3 shows the user's name as the author in the Backstage view Info tab because *User name* was set in General options.

- *Start up options* also enable you to specify a program choice when starting PowerPoint.

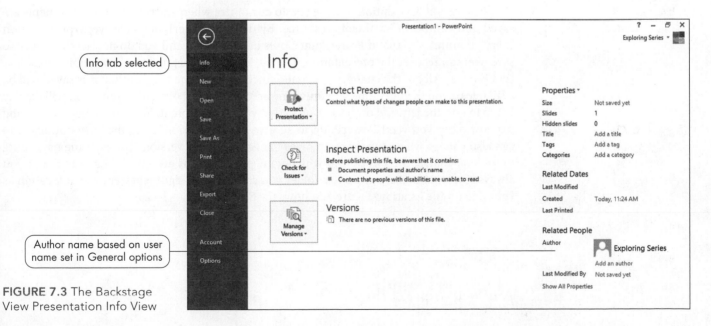

Info tab selected

Author name based on user name set in General options

FIGURE 7.3 The Backstage View Presentation Info View

STEP 2 »

Proofing options enable you to change how PowerPoint corrects and formats your text. Click AutoCorrect Options on the Proofing tab to open the AutoCorrect dialog box. Review each of the tab options in the dialog box to understand what PowerPoint is automatically changing as you type. Then select or deselect check boxes to apply the settings of your choice. For example, AutoCorrect automatically resizes the font of text you type as a title to fit the size of the title text placeholder. If you want the title text to be uniform on every slide, click the AutoFormat As You Type tab in the AutoCorrect dialog box if necessary and deselect the *AutoFit title text to placeholder* check box. Figure 7.4 shows the Proofing options and the AutoCorrect dialog box with the AutoFormat As You Type tab open.

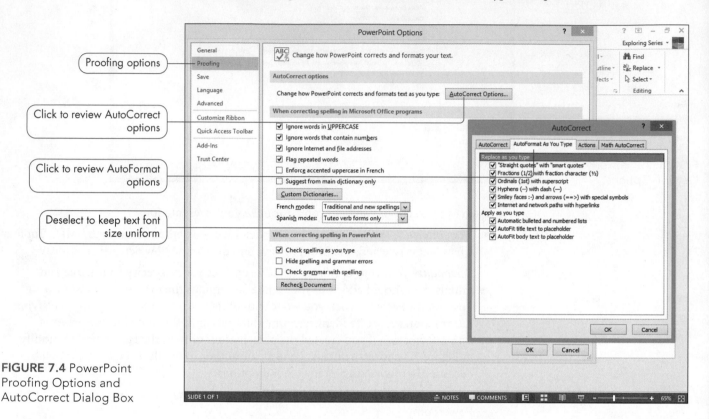

FIGURE 7.4 PowerPoint Proofing Options and AutoCorrect Dialog Box

PowerPoint Save options enable you to customize when and where your documents are saved and can be an invaluable resource. By default, PowerPoint saves your presentation every 10 minutes so that if PowerPoint closes unexpectedly and you do not have a chance to save, you can recover the presentation. The file extension assigned to a PowerPoint presentation is *.pptx*. All but the changes you made since the last time the AutoRecover saved will be available to you the next time you open PowerPoint. The recovered presentation will display in a pane on the left side of the screen so that you can restore it. You can change the setting for how often you want PowerPoint to save your presentation using the Save options. You can also change where the program saves the AutoRecover version. To save time navigating to folders, change the location to which your presentations are saved. For example, if you always save your presentations to a folder you created for assignments, enter that location as your default file location. Figure 7.5 shows the Save options.

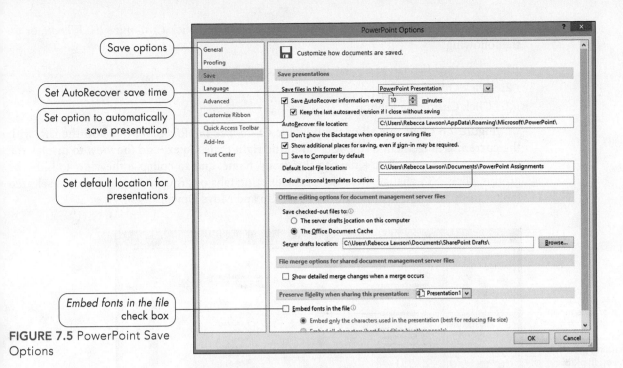

Save options

Set AutoRecover save time

Set option to automatically save presentation

Set default location for presentations

Embed fonts in the file check box

FIGURE 7.5 PowerPoint Save Options

TIP Embed Fonts

To ensure that you have the font you need when you work on a presentation on another computer, or to ensure others reviewing and editing a presentation have access to any TrueType font you used while creating a presentation, embed the fonts in your presentation. TrueType fonts are scalable fonts supported by Windows that display and print smoothly at any point size. Click Save in the PowerPoint Options dialog box and click the *Embed fonts in the file* check box. Select the *Embed only the characters used in the presentation* option or the *Embed all characters* option. Embedding fonts increases the file size of a presentation.

Language options enable you to set the Office language used for editing, display, Help, and ScreenTips. Advanced options enable you to set your preferences for editing, cutting, copying, pasting, sizing and quality of images, setting chart data point properties, setting display options, working in Slide Show view, and printing, as well as several general options. For example, in the *Editing options* section, you can change the number of *undos* (which reverses your last action) from the default of 20 to any number from 3 to 150. The more you increase the number of undo levels, however, the more of your computer's RAM (random access memory) is used to store the undo history. If you set your undo levels to a high number, you may experience a computer slowdown.

Customizing the Ribbon

The *Customize Ribbon tab* in the PowerPoint Options dialog box enables you to create a personal tab on the Ribbon as well as modify the settings of any tab. Ribbon customization enables you to include features that are not available on the standard Ribbon. By creating a custom tab, you have access to these features as well as the features you use most often. In addition to creating a new tab, you can change the order of the tabs, change the order of the groups that appear within the tabs, and create new groups within a tab.

STEP 3 ≫   To customize the Ribbon, right-click the Ribbon and click *Customize the Ribbon*, or do the following:

1. Click the FILE tab to display the Backstage view.
2. Click Options.
3. Click Customize Ribbon.

Figure 7.6 shows the all of the possible *Customize the Ribbon* options on the left, with the current arrangement of the Ribbon in the right pane. To expand the view to display the groups within a tab, click + next to the group name, and to collapse the view to hide the groups, click -. To change the order of the existing tabs or groups, drag and drop a selected tab or group to a new position or use Move Up and Move Down.

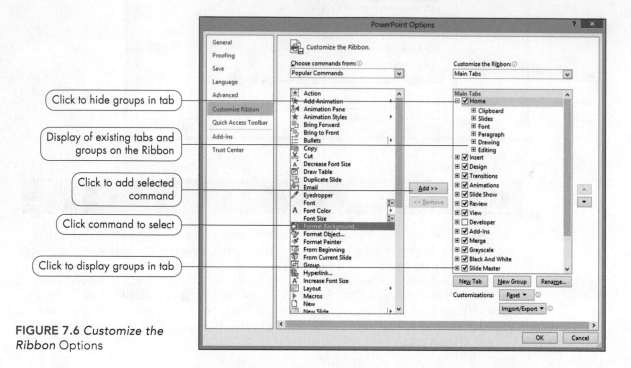

FIGURE 7.6 *Customize the Ribbon* Options

Click to hide groups in tab

Display of existing tabs and groups on the Ribbon

Click to add selected command

Click command to select

Click to display groups in tab

 Restore the Ribbon

You can restore the Ribbon to its original arrangement by clicking Reset and clicking *Reset all customizations*. Reset also enables you to reset individual Ribbon tabs.

Add a New Tab

To have access to the commands you use most, add a new tab to the Ribbon and add frequently used commands. In the *Customize the Ribbon* window, select the tab you want the new tab to appear after and click New Tab. The new tab is created and named *New Tab (Custom)*. The new tab also contains a new group named *New Group (Custom)*. To add additional groups, click New Group. You can rename tabs or groups by clicking Rename or by right-clicking the tab and selecting *Rename*. When you rename a group, you can select a colorful symbol to represent the contents of the group. Figure 7.7 shows that a new tab containing a new group has been created.

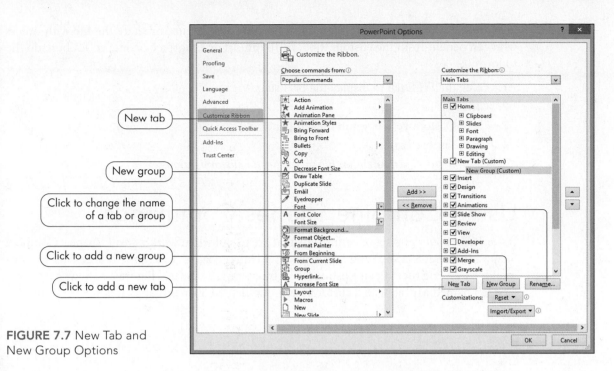

New tab

New group

Click to change the name
of a tab or group

Click to add a new group

Click to add a new tab

FIGURE 7.7 New Tab and
New Group Options

Add Commands to a Group

To add commands to an existing tab or group or to a newly created tab, click a command name on the left and click Add. Popular commands that you can add are displayed in the default view, but you can click the *Choose commands from* arrow to choose from additional commands and macros. For example, instead of using the arrow keys on the keyboard to nudge an object (move in small, precise increments), you can add the nudge commands to a group in a personalized tab. Figure 7.8 displays a customized tab with added nudge commands.

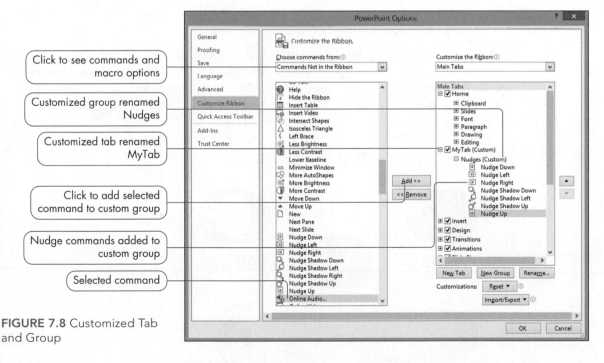

Click to see commands and
macro options

Customized group renamed
Nudges

Customized tab renamed
MyTab

Click to add selected
command to custom group

Nudge commands added to
custom group

Selected command

FIGURE 7.8 Customized Tab
and Group

After customizing the Ribbon to maximize your productivity, you can export it as an exported Office User Interface (UI) customization file, which uses the extension

.exportedUI. Then import the file to other computers you use or share the file with others who can benefit from the custom Ribbon. To import or export a customized Ribbon, do the following:

1. Click the FILE tab to display the Backstage view.
2. Click Options.
3. Click Customize Ribbon in the left pane.
4. Click Import/Export.
5. Click *Import customization file* or *Export all customizations*.

Using Combine Shapes Commands

PowerPoint includes a set of commands that are useful when working with shapes: Combine Shapes, Intersect Shapes, Subtract Shapes, and Union Shapes. You can only access these commands by adding them to an existing tab or by creating a new tab. Figure 7.9 shows a customized tab named MyTab with a customized group named Shapes that includes the commands.

FIGURE 7.9 Custom Shapes Group Including Shape Commands

STEP 4»

Using the Combine Shapes commands enables you to create complex shapes by joining shapes in four ways: Combine, Intersect, Subtract, or Union.

- *Combine* removes the overlapping area of two shapes.
- *Intersect* removes any area that is not overlapped.
- *Subtract* removes the shape of the second selected object from the area of the first object.
- *Union* joins selected overlapping objects so they become one shape. The shape takes on the formatting of the first shape selected.

Figure 7.10 displays two original circles that have been duplicated and joined using each of the above methods. In each case, the red circle was selected first so that the joined objects are all formatted with a red fill. The dotted outlines have been added to indicate the original areas and are not part of the result.

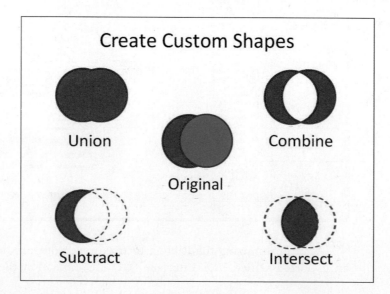

FIGURE 7.10 Combined Shapes

Quick Concepts ✓

1. What are some advantages of setting PowerPoint options? *p. 996*

2. You are working on a shared computer. How can you restore the Ribbon to its default setting? *p. 1000*

3. How can you access the Combine Shapes commands? *p. 1002*

Hands-On Exercises

1 PowerPoint Customization

You decide to modify several of PowerPoint's settings to meet your needs. Because you want to create a new logo for your store, you also create a custom Ribbon tab and add the Combine Shapes commands. You then use the Combine Shapes commands to create a logo for Survival Solutions.

Skills covered: Create User Name and Initials • Set Advanced and Proofing Options • Create a New Tab • Use Combine Shapes Commands

STEP 1 >> CREATE USER NAME AND INITIALS

Because you plan on working with others on several presentations, you decide to personalize your copy of Microsoft Office by adding your name and your initials. Refer to Figure 7.11 as you complete Step 1.

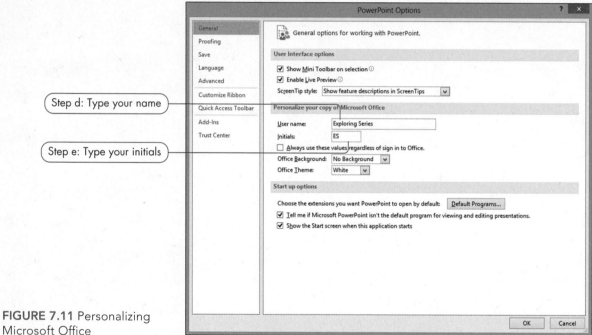

FIGURE 7.11 Personalizing Microsoft Office

a. Open the *p07h1Preparedness* presentation and save it as **p07h1Preparedness_LastFirst.**

> **TROUBLESHOOTING:** If you make any major mistakes in this exercise, you can close the file, open *p07h1Preparedness* again, and then start this exercise over.

b. Create a handout header with your name and a handout footer with your instructor's name and your class. Include the current date.

c. Click the **FILE tab** and click **Options**.

The PowerPoint Options dialog box opens.

d. Type your name in the **User name box**, if necessary.

e. Type your initials in the **Initials box**, if necessary.

f. Keep the PowerPoint Options dialog box open for the next step.

TROUBLESHOOTING: If you are working in a public lab, you should restore the Ribbon to its original arrangement after making changes to the Ribbon as part of these exercises.

STEP 2 ›› SET ADVANCED AND PROOFING OPTIONS

You decide to turn off background printing. Background printing enables you to continue working as you print but increases the print response time. Also, you use your company name, Survival Solutions, in most of the presentations you create. To minimize the chances for a typographical error, you set AutoCorrect to replace the initials "ss" with Survival Solutions. Finally, to improve the spelling checker results, you activate the *Check grammar with spelling* feature so the correct usage of words can be identified. Refer to Figure 7.12 as you complete Step 2.

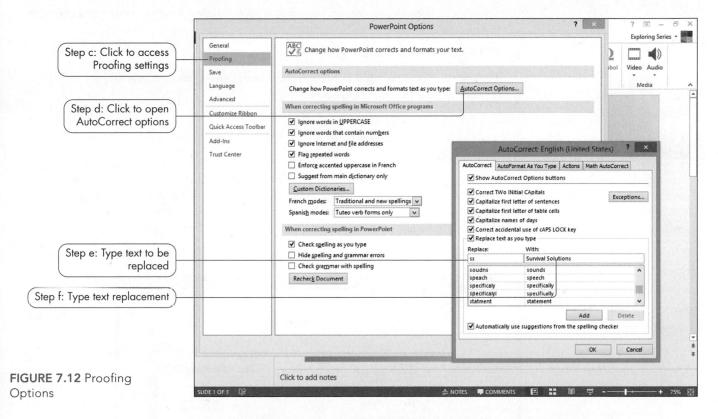

FIGURE 7.12 Proofing Options

a. Click **Advanced** in the left pane of the PowerPoint Options dialog box.

b. Scroll until you see the *Print* section and click the **Print in background check box** to deselect it if necessary.

The *Print in background* option is deselected.

c. Click **Proofing** in the left pane of the PowerPoint Options dialog box.

d. Click **AutoCorrect Options** and click the **AutoCorrect tab**, if necessary.

The AutoCorrect tab in the AutoCorrect dialog box opens.

e. Type **ss** in the **Replace box**.

f. Type **Survival Solutions** in the **With box** and click **OK**.

Because you are only adding one text replacement, you click OK. If you wanted to add additional text replacements, you would click Add and click OK when all replacements are made.

g. Select the **Proofing tab**, if necessary. Click the **Check grammar with spelling check box** to select it if necessary and click **OK**.

The PowerPoint Options dialog box closes, and you return to Slide 1 of the presentation.

h. Click the **title placeholder**. Type **ss** and press **Spacebar** in the **title placeholder**.

Survival Solutions replaces the original placeholder text.

> **TROUBLESHOOTING:** If the text is not replaced, do the following: click the File tab, click Options, click Proofing, and then click AutoCorrect Options. Make sure the *Replace text as you type* check box is selected. Repeat steps d through f.

i. Type the following after *Survival Solutions* in the **title placeholder: is the write place for getting prepared.**

A wavy line displays underneath the word *write*, indicating it is the wrong word choice in this context.

j. Right-click **write** and select **right**.

The incorrect word is replaced, and the sentence is now grammatically correct.

k. Save the presentation.

STEP 3 ≫ CREATE A NEW TAB

You decide to use PowerPoint shapes to create a new logo for Survival Solutions. Because you want to combine the shapes, and because you know that you cannot access the Combine Shapes tools from the standard Ribbon, you will create a new tab customized to include a group with the Combine Shapes tools. After creating the custom tab, you will modify it to include a command to make shapes available from the new tab. Refer to Figure 7.13 as you complete Step 3.

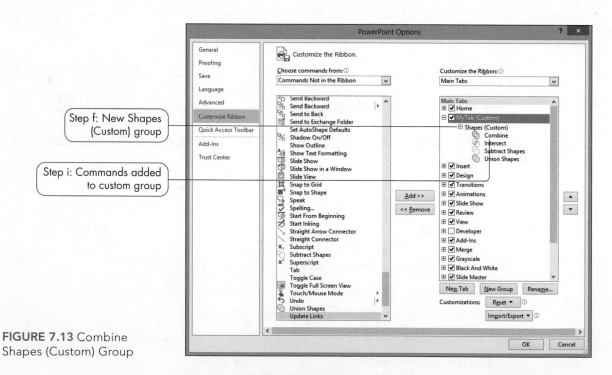

FIGURE 7.13 Combine Shapes (Custom) Group

a. Click the **FILE tab**, click **Options**, and then click **Customize Ribbon** in the PowerPoint Options dialog box.

The *Customize the Ribbon* options display in the PowerPoint Options dialog box, with the Home tab selected in the Main Tabs list.

b. Click **New Tab**.

A new tab is created in the Main Tabs list and positioned between the Home tab and the Insert tab. The tab is named *New Tab (Custom)* and contains a new group named *New Group (Custom)*.

> **TROUBLESHOOTING:** If the new tab is positioned elsewhere, click Reset, select *Reset all customizations*, and then click Yes. Repeat step b. As an alternative, you can select the new tab and click the Move Up and Move Down arrows to reposition the new tab.

c. Select **New Tab (Custom)**, click **Rename**, type **MyTab** in the **Display name box**, and then click **OK**.

The new tab displays as *MyTab (Custom)*.

d. Select **New Group (Custom)** and click **Rename**.

The Rename dialog box opens.

e. Click the **Key icon** (third row, seventh column) in the *Symbol* section; do not close the Rename dialog box.

You can display icons on the Ribbon to make it smaller if you want. Also, icons will display if your monitor has a low screen resolution setting. In either of these cases, a key icon will represent the new custom group.

f. Type **Shapes** in the **Display name box** and click **OK**.

The group displays as *Shapes (Custom)*.

g. Click the **Choose commands from arrow** and click **Commands Not in the Ribbon**.

h. Scroll down the list of commands, click **Combine Shapes**, and then click **Add**.

Combine Shapes is added to MyTab (Custom) in the Shapes (Custom) group.

i. Add the following commands to MyTab (Custom) in the Shapes (Custom) group:

- Intersect Shapes
- Subtract Shapes
- Union Shapes

j. Click **OK** to close the PowerPoint Options dialog box.

k. Click the **MyTab tab** and note that the Shapes group contains four buttons.

> **TROUBLESHOOTING:** The buttons are dimmed until two shapes are selected.

l. Right-click the **Ribbon** and click **Customize the Ribbon** so you can begin the process to insert another command on the Ribbon.

The PowerPoint Options dialog box opens.

m. Click **Shapes (Custom)** to select the group.

n. Click **Shapes** in the Popular Commands list and click **Add**.

The Shapes (Custom) group expands, and *Shapes* displays at the bottom of the list of commands contained in the group.

o. Drag **Shapes** above *Combine*.

Shapes is the first command in the reordered list.

p. Click **OK** and view the Shapes group.

The group now contains five commands.

q. Save the presentation.

STEP 4 » USE COMBINE SHAPES COMMANDS

After practicing using the Combine Shapes commands, you will create a new logo for Survival Solutions. You will save the new logo so that you can use it in presentations. Refer to Figure 7.14 as you complete Step 4.

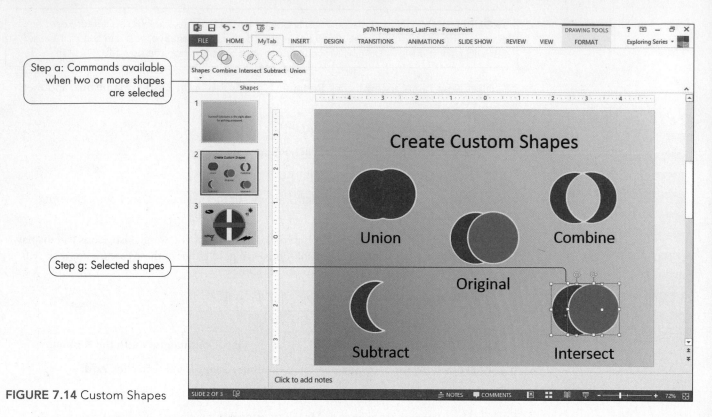

FIGURE 7.14 Custom Shapes

a. On Slide 2, select the **red circle** above the *Union* label, press and hold **Shift**, and then click the **blue circle** above the *Union* label.

The selection contains two objects.

b. Click **Union** in the Shapes group.

The circles join and become a single shape with a red fill.

TROUBLESHOOTING: If the new shape is blue, the blue circle was selected first. Click Undo on the Quick Access Toolbar, click outside the circles, and then repeat steps a and b.

---

c. Select the **red circle** above the *Combine* label, press and hold **Shift**, and then click the **blue circle** above the *Combine* label.

d. Click **Combine** in the Shapes group.

The overlapping area of the two circles is cut out, making the background visible.

e. Select the **red circle** above the *Subtract* label, press and hold **Shift**, and then click the **blue circle** above the *Subtract* label.

f. Click **Subtract** in the Shapes group.

The overlapping area of the blue circle is cut from the red circle, creating a crescent shape.

g. Select the **red circle** above the *Intersect* label, press and hold **Shift**, and then click the **blue circle** above the *Intersect* label.

h. Click **Intersect** in the Shapes group.

The overlapping area is retained and other areas are cut from the shape.

i. On Slide 3, select the **green circle**, press and hold **Shift**, and then click the **blue circle** to add it to the selection.

j. Click **Combine** in the Shapes group.

The overlapping area of the two circles is cut out, which reveals a yellow circle that had been hidden by the shapes.

k. Select the **red rectangle**, press and hold **Shift**, and then click the vertical **yellow rectangle** to add it to the selection. Click **Union** in the Shapes group to form a red cross. Select the **green circle**, click the **FORMAT tab**, and then click **Bring Forward**.

The green circle moves to the front and becomes a border for the logo.

l. Select the **black jagged line shape** in the bottom-right corner, press and hold **Shift**, and then click the adjacent **yellow jagged line shape** to add it to the selection.

TROUBLESHOOTING: If the yellow shape is difficult to select, click the View tab and click Zoom. Change the zoom setting to 200% and drag the vertical scroll button to the bottom of the vertical scroll bar and the horizontal scroll button to the far right of the horizontal scroll bar. Perform step m and click *Fit to Window* in the Zoom group.

---

m. Click **Intersect** in the Shapes group on the MyTab tab.

The intersection of the shapes is a thin jagged black line.

n. Copy the jagged line and paste and position it under the first line to represent the shaking that might occur during an earthquake.

o. Click a jagged line, press and hold **Shift**, and then click the other jagged line to add it to the selection. Click the **FORMAT tab** and click **Group** in the Arrange group two times.

p. Size the group to **1.3"** high by **1.85"** wide.

q. Select the **black cloud shape**, press and hold **Shift**, and then click the **yellow lightning shape** to add it to the selection.

r. Click **Subtract** in the Shapes group on the MyTab tab.

The lightning shape is subtracted from the cloud shape.

s. Drag each of the four black disaster symbols onto the yellow circle, one in each quadrant.

t. Press **Ctrl+A** to select all objects in the logo and group the objects.

The group includes the large green circle and its boundary box and sizing handles, the red cross and its boundary box and sizing handles, and each of the four disaster symbols with their boundary boxes and sizing handles. If a blank box displays on the lower left side of the slide, delete it.

u. Right-click the selected group and select **Save as Picture**. Navigate to where you are saving your student data files and type **p07h1SSLogo_LastFirst** in the **File name box**.

v. Click the **Save as type arrow**, click **PNG Portable Network Graphics Format (*.png)**, and then click **Save**.

w. Save and close the presentation, and exit PowerPoint. Submit the files as directed by your instructor.

x. Restore the Ribbon to its original arrangement if you are working in a public lab.

Master Basics

Customize a PowerPoint presentation, and you will be putting your unique creative ideas to work. Although you want to customize your slides, you still want a consistent look throughout the presentation. *Masters* control the layouts, background designs, and color combinations for handouts, notes pages, and slides, giving the presentation a consistent appearance. By changing the masters, you make selections that affect the entire slide show and the supporting materials. This is more efficient than changing each slide in the presentation. The design elements you already know about, such as themes and layouts, can be applied to each type of master. Masters control the consistency of your presentations, notes, and handouts. Slide masters can be reused in other presentations.

In this section, you learn how to modify masters. Specifically, you will learn how to customize the layout and formatting of handouts, notes, the slide master, and slide layouts controlled by the slide master.

TIP | Fresh Start

Modifications to masters can be made at any time as you create the presentation, but it is best to begin with a blank presentation. This gives you a clean workspace, enabling you to concentrate on the design of your slide show, handouts, and notes.

Modifying Handout and Notes Masters

You can print handouts and notes pages of your presentation. The handouts printout displays thumbnails of the slides for audience use. The notes pages printout displays individual slides with notes and is typically used by the presenter. You might want to customize these types of printouts to display all the information you want in the position that is most advantageous.

Customize the Handout Master

The *handout master* contains the design information about the layout and formatting of audience handout pages. The handout master controls the orientation of the page; the number of slides per page; and the layout of fields such as the header, footer, date, and page number. To modify the handout master, click the View tab and click Handout Master in the Master Views group.

STEP 1 ▶ Click Handout Orientation in the Page Setup group to change the orientation of the handouts from portrait to landscape. You can select the number of slides you want to appear on the handouts in the Page Setup group on the Handout Master tab. Click Slides Per Page in the Page Setup group to select the number of slide thumbnails you want to print per handout page. You can also print the presentation outline from this option. Figure 7.15 shows an open handout master with *6 Slides* selected.

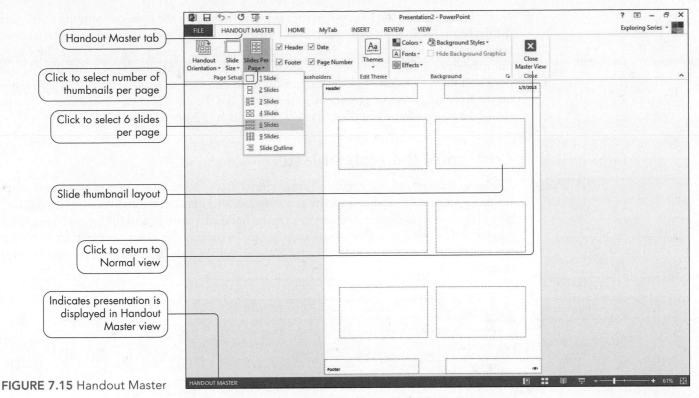

Handout Master tab

Click to select number of thumbnails per page

Click to select 6 slides per page

Slide thumbnail layout

Click to return to Normal view

Indicates presentation is displayed in Handout Master view

FIGURE 7.15 Handout Master

On the handout master, you modify the header, date, footer, or page number fields using the Placeholders group. You can omit any of these fields from the handout by deselecting the field's check box in the Placeholders group. Initially, the placeholders for the header and date fields are at the top of the page. The footer and the page number field placeholders are at the bottom of the page. You can move each placeholder by dragging it to a new location. In Figure 7.16, the date placeholder is moved to the bottom of the page. The footer is moved to the top of the page, and the page number is removed. Although the term *footer* implies that the location is always at the bottom of a page or slide, sometimes PowerPoint slide templates reposition footers at the top or on the sides.

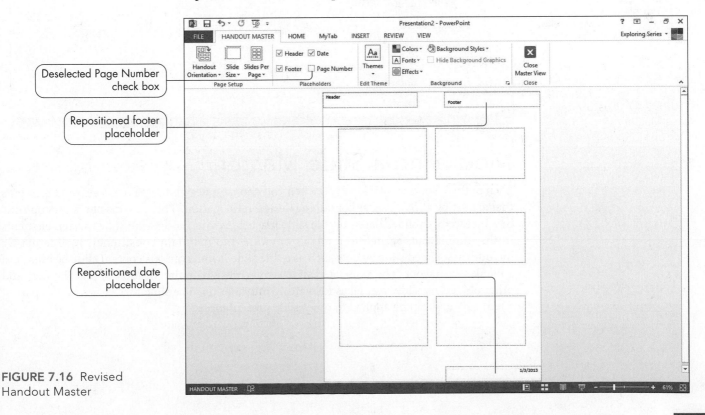

Deselected Page Number check box

Repositioned footer placeholder

Repositioned date placeholder

FIGURE 7.16 Revised Handout Master

You can modify the handout master even further using the options from the other tabs displayed on the Ribbon. For example, if you want to have a company logo on each handout page, click the Insert tab and click Pictures in the Images group. As you revise the handout master, keep in mind that the handouts are to supplement your presentation. Audience members appreciate handouts that are uncluttered and easy to read, as they often take notes on the handouts that you give them. After modifying the master, click Close Master View in the Close group on the Handout Master tab to return to Normal view.

Customize the Notes Master

STEP 2 » The *notes master* contains design information for notes pages. Often, the speaker uses notes pages to prepare for and deliver the presentation and may occasionally distribute detailed notes pages to an audience. You can specify the fields, the format, and the layout of the notes master just as you did with the handout master. To modify the notes master, click the View tab and click Notes Master in the Master Views group. Figure 7.17 shows a customized notes master.

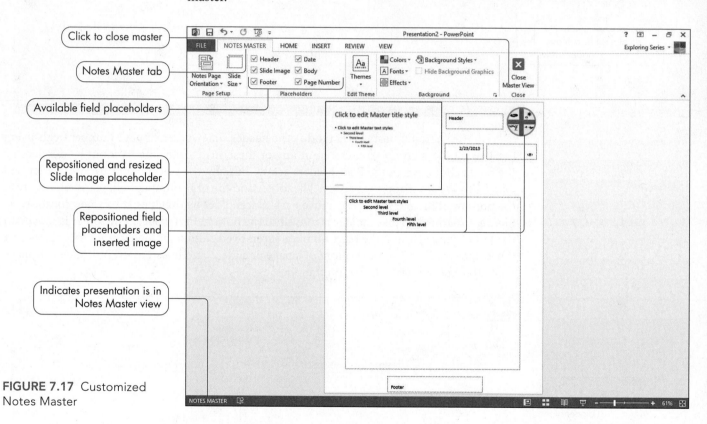

FIGURE 7.17 Customized Notes Master

Modifying a Slide Master

Each of the layouts available to you when you choose a design theme has consistent elements that are set by a *slide master* containing design information. The slide master is the top slide in a hierarchy of slides based on the slide master. As you modify the slide master, elements in the slide layouts related to it are also modified to maintain consistency. A slide master includes associated slide layouts such as a title slide layout, various content slide layouts, and a blank slide layout. The associated slide layouts designate the location of placeholders and other objects on slides as well as formatting information. The slide master is saved as part of a template and can be applied to other slide presentations.

If you want your presentation to contain two or more themes, insert a slide master for each theme. For example, you may use a different theme for different sections of the slide show. Click the View tab and click Slide Master in the Master Views group. Click Themes in the Edit Theme group and select a Built-In theme or browse for a custom theme you have saved. The theme is applied to the existing slide master and its associated layouts. Then click below the last slide layout in the Thumbnail pane. Click Themes in the Edit Theme group and select a Built-In theme or browse for a saved theme. A new slide master and its associated slide layouts are created using the new theme.

STEP 3 » To modify a slide master or slide layout based on a slide master, do the following:

1. Click the VIEW tab.
2. Click Slide Master in the Master Views group.
3. Click the slide master at the top of the list or click one of the associated layouts.
4. Make modifications.
5. Click Close Master View in the Close group on the SLIDE MASTER tab.

In Slide Master view, the slide master is the larger, top slide thumbnail shown in the left pane. The Title Slide Layout is the second slide in the pane. The number of slides following it varies depending upon the template. Figure 7.18 shows the default Office Theme Slide Master and its related slide layouts. The ScreenTip for the slide master indicates it is used by one slide because the slide show is a new slide show comprised of a single title slide.

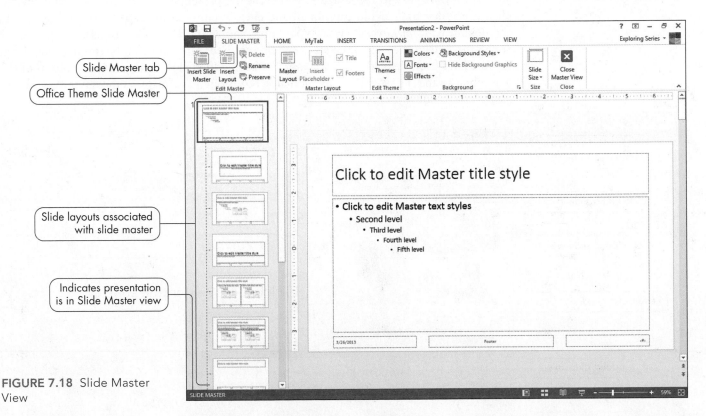

FIGURE 7.18 Slide Master View

The slide master is the most efficient way of setting the fonts, color scheme, and effects for the entire presentation. To set these choices, click the slide master thumbnail in the left pane to display the slide master. The main pane shows the placeholders for title style, text styles, a date field, a footer field, and a page number field. Double-click the text in the Master title style or any level of text in the Master text styles placeholder and modify the font appearance. You can also make adjustments to the footer, date, and page number fields.

You can move and size the placeholders on the slide master. The modifications in position and size are reflected on the associated slide layouts. This may conflict with some of the slide layout placeholders, however. The placeholders can be moved on the individual slide layouts as needed.

> **TIP Slide Master Headers and Footers**
>
> As you modify the footer, date, and slide numbers on the slide master, it appears as if the information is added to the slide. This is not the case—the slide master contains formatted field placeholders and not actual information. To insert header and footer text while in the slide master, click the Insert tab and click Header & Footer in the Text group. An alternative method is to make the selections as you build the presentation in Normal view.

Delete and Add Slide Layouts

STEP 4 ▶

If you only need a limited number of layouts, delete the extras to save file size. Click the slide layout thumbnail you wish to delete and click Delete in the Edit Master group on the Slide Master tab. The Title Slide Layout cannot be deleted, but all other layouts can be removed. You can preserve a slide layout within the master even if it is not used in the presentation by clicking Insert Slide Master and clicking Preserve. If you want to add a slide layout, click Insert Layout in the Edit Master group. You should rename added slide layouts so that they are easy to recognize as you build the presentation. To rename a slide layout, click the added slide layout thumbnail and click Rename in the Edit Master group. Select the default *Custom Layout* name, type a new name, and then click Rename. Figure 7.19 shows the slide master with the Parallax theme applied. All but two of the original associated layouts have been deleted. A new layout has been added and displays at the bottom of the Thumbnail pane. The Rename Layout dialog box is open and displays the name PowerPoint assigns new slide layouts.

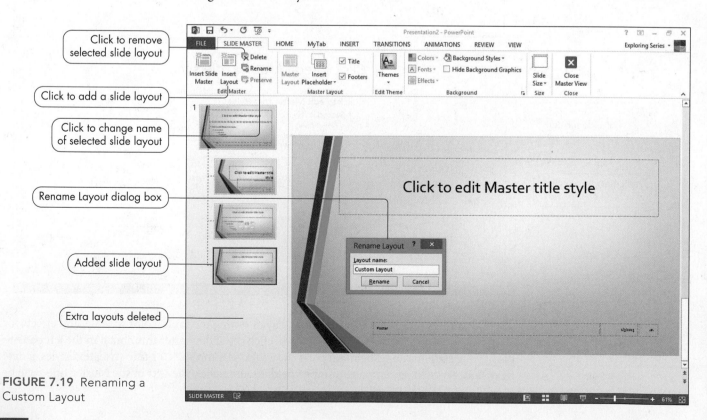

FIGURE 7.19 Renaming a Custom Layout

You can add, remove, and size placeholders on a slide layout as needed. To add a placeholder to a selected layout, click Insert Placeholder or click the Insert Placeholder arrow in the Master Layout group on the Slide Master tab. Clicking Insert Placeholder enables you to drag to create a standard content placeholder containing content buttons anywhere on the slide. Clicking the Insert Placeholder arrow enables you to create specific types of placeholders (see Figure 7.20). Once you select a type of placeholder, you can continue adding this type by clicking Insert Placeholder. To change the type, click the Insert Placeholder arrow and make a selection from the list.

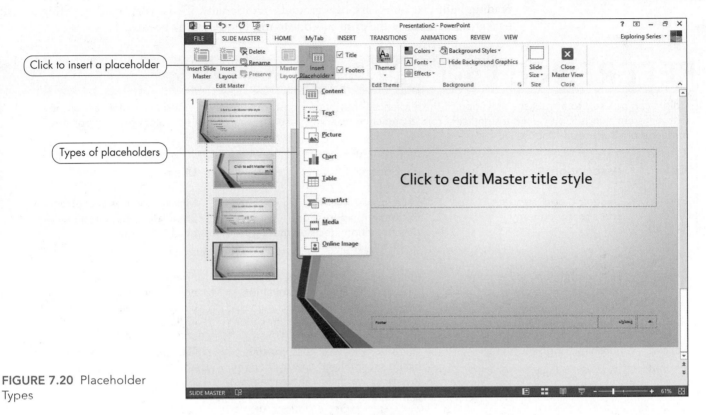

FIGURE 7.20 Placeholder Types

You may access the tabs and add objects such as images, SmartArt, shapes, and sounds. Animations can be applied to the objects, or transitions can be added to slide layouts. Elements added on a slide layout, such as a bullet list layout, appear on every slide in the presentation that uses that layout.

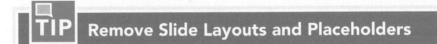

TIP **Remove Slide Layouts and Placeholders**

Select the slide thumbnail first. Click Delete in the Edit Master group on the Slide Master tab to delete the entire slide layout. If you want to remove placeholders from a slide layout, click the placeholder border and press Delete.

Customize the Slide Master Color Theme

Creating custom colors adds a creative touch to a presentation. Using the custom colors in the slide master ensures that the slide layouts maintain continuity. For example, after adding a logo to the slide master, you can use the logo colors on elements of the slide master. The associated slide layouts use the same colors.

Consider your audience and the message of your presentation as you select colors on your slide master. Look at things around you to come up with color combinations. Other PowerPoint presentations that you may see—in addition to magazines, Web sites, and other graphically designed materials—will give you a good idea of what colors work well together.

Certain color combinations work well together, and other combinations are hard to read when they are placed together. Look for combinations that provide high contrast. Think of your favorite team colors, and you are probably thinking about high-contrast color combinations. If black-and-white printouts are made for the audience, then the choice of colors for the text should provide even more contrast so the handouts are legible. Generally, the slides will be easiest to read when a dark text is placed on a lighter background. You see many presentations where the background is dark and the text is light. In making color choices, you need to consider your audience. Some members of your audience may have problems reading light text on a dark background. Additionally, if cost is an issue, printing a dark background increases the print cost due to the amount of ink needed.

REFERENCE Color Associations

Colors can be used to attract the attention of the audience. They have a powerful effect on emotions. Colors are associated with different things. Color plays a significant role in audience response. Use this chart to select colors that support the message of your presentations.

Color	Associations	Emotions	Uses
Red	Danger, blood, strength, courage, fire, energy	Love, power, passion, rage, excitement, aggression, determination, decision making, romance, longing	Make a point or gain attention. Stimulate people into making quick decisions.
Orange	Fall, warmth, fun, joy, energy, creativity, tropics, heat, citrus fruit	Pleasure, excitement, strength, ambition, endurance, domination, happiness, enthusiasm, playfulness, determination, success, stimulation	Emphasize happiness and enjoyment. Stimulate thought. Ensure high visibility. Highlight important elements.
Yellow	Sunshine, bright, warnings	Cheerful, joy, happiness, warmth, optimism, intellect, energy, honor, loyalty, cowardice, lightheartedness, jealousy	Gain a positive response. Gain attention.
Green	Nature, calm, refreshing, money, growth, fertility	Tranquility, growth, safety, harmony, freshness, healing, restive, stability, hope, endurance, envy, jealousy	Present a new idea. Suggest safety. Promote "green" products.
Blue	Sea, sky, peace, calm, cold, impersonal, intellect, masculine, expertise, integrity	Truth, dignity, trust, wisdom, loyalty, harmony, stability, confidence, calming, tranquility, sincerity, healing, understanding, melancholy, belonging	Build trust and strength. Promote cleanliness. Suggest precision. Suppress diet.
Violet	Wealth, royalty, sophistication, intelligence, spirituality, wisdom, dignity, magic, feminine	Power, stability, luxury, extravagance, creativity, frustration, gloom, sadness	Promote children's products. Gain respect and attention.
Black	Formal, mystery, death, evil, power, elegant, prestigious, conservative, the unknown	Authority, boldness, seriousness, negativity, strength, seductiveness, evil	Emphasis. Contrast with bright colors. Ease of reading.
White	Snow, cleanliness, safety, simplicity, youth, light, purity, virginity	Perfection, distinction, enlightenment, positivity, successful, faith	Emphasis. Suggest simplicity. Promote medical products.
Gray	Neutral, science, architecture, commerce, cold	Easy-going, original, practical, solid	Complement other colors. Unify colors. Bring focus to other colors.
Brown	Earth, richness, masculine, harvest, fall	Conservative, steady, dependable, serious, stability	Build trust.

Colors convey meanings to your audience. Write the word *hot* in blue letters, and your audience will be confused. Write *hot* in red or orange, and the audience will grasp what you are trying to say. Certain colors evoke feelings. Blue, green, and violet are cool, relaxing colors. Yellow, orange, and red are invigorating, warm, action colors. If your presentation is long, using a warm color will quickly wear your audience out. The reference table shows common colors, associations people make with the colors, and emotions that are linked with the colors.

STEP 5 » *Color themes* are combinations of 12 colors used for the text, lines, background, and graphics in a presentation. Color themes contain four text and background colors, six accent colors, and two hyperlink colors. Standard Office color themes may not include the color combinations that are used by your school, business, or other organization. You can customize your own color scheme in this case.

As you focus your attention on creating your own color scheme for the slide master, you have 16 million colors from which to choose. You may change any of the 12 colors used in a color theme to customize it to your needs. Avoid making each of the 12 colors completely different—choose one color family, use different shades of the colors in the family, and add two or three accent colors. Select colors that work well together. Use light and dark shades of the same color within your color scheme for a unified, professional appearance.

To customize the color theme for a slide master, do the following:

1. Click the VIEW tab.
2. Click Slide Master in the Master Views group.
3. Click the slide master thumbnail in the Slides pane.
4. Click Colors in the Background group.
5. Select a Built-In color theme or select Customize Colors.

If you select Customize Colors, the Create New Theme Colors dialog box opens showing the current theme colors. A preview of how the colors are applied on a slide is shown in a Sample pane. Click the color box next to the name of the color element that you want to change and choose a Theme color, a Standard color, or More Colors. Figure 7.21 displays the Create New Theme Colors dialog box.

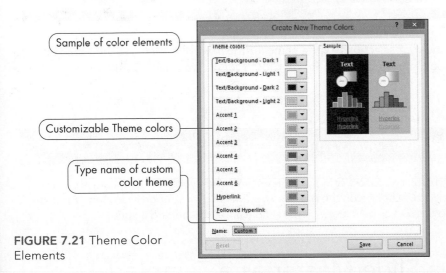

FIGURE 7.21 Theme Color Elements

The Colors dialog box that displays when you select More Colors offers two tabs for selecting colors. The Standard tab contains 127 colors and 14 shades of white to black. The Custom tab enables you to make selections based on the **RGB** color model, where numbers are assigned to red, green, or blue, and the mixture of red, green, or blue light creates a color representation. A zero for each represents black. The number 255 for each of the colors in the model represents white. The RGB model uses 16 million colors. Using this system, you can match any color where you know the three RGB numbers. A similar color model, **HSL**, balances hue, saturation, and luminosity to produce a color. The numbers for black and white are represented the same way as in the RGB model.

Figure 7.22 shows the Custom tab in the Colors dialog box with the RGB color model selected. Drag the crosshairs in the Color box to the color family you wish to use, for instance green. The slider to the right of the Color box is used to select the shade of that color. If you know the RGB number, you can use the spin boxes to increase or decrease the numbers, or you can type the numbers into the boxes for each of the colors. After selecting the color, click OK to place that color into the theme. The Sample box in the Create New Theme Colors dialog box displays the current color and the new color. As you make changes to the theme element colors, look at the Sample to get an idea of how your color scheme will look on the slide.

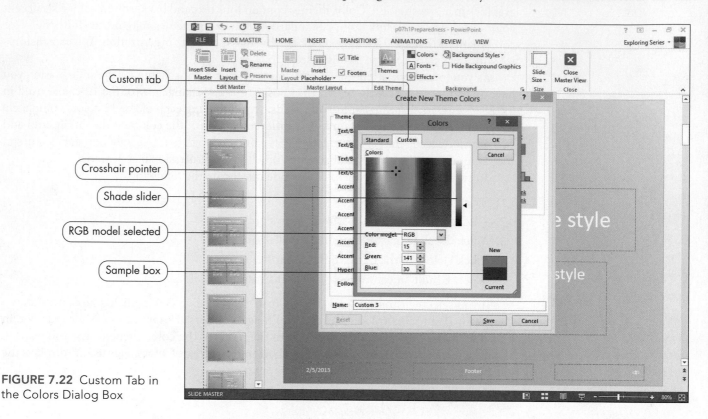

FIGURE 7.22 Custom Tab in the Colors Dialog Box

After making your selections, type a name for the new color theme in the Name box and click Save. Click Close Master View in the Close group if you have finished modifying the slide master.

TIP **Monitor and Projector Differences**

Monitors and projectors show colors in different ways. To avoid surprises, always test your presentation color schemes on the projector you will use for your presentation. If you are unable to do this, keep your color scheme simple and use standard colors.

Saving a Slide Master as a Template

STEP 6 ≫ After you modify a slide master, save the file as a template. PowerPoint saves the master as a template with an extension of *.potx* and retains the changes in the file. You can then reuse the slide master with any presentation.

To save the file as a presentation template, do the following:

1. Determine the location for your saved template.
2. Click the FILE tab and click Save As.
3. Type a file name in the *File name* box.

4. Click the *Save as type* arrow.

5. Click PowerPoint Template and click Save.

To use your custom presentation template, do the following:

1. Click the FILE tab and click Open.

2. If you saved the template to the default location, click Custom Office Templates, select your template, and then click Open.

3. If you saved the template to another location, click Open, navigate to the location, select your template, and then click Open.

Quick Concepts

1. What are the benefits of using masters? *p. 1010*

2. Explain the importance of color use in your presentation. *p. 1016*

3. Monitors and projectors show color in different ways. Explain how you can ensure your presentation color schemes work for both environments. *p. 1018*

2 Master Basics

Because you deliver many presentations to local groups on emergency preparedness, you decide to customize a master for handouts and notes that includes your logo and contact information. Then you create a slide master and several slide layouts that you can use for presentations so people identify your business when they see your presentations and advertising.

Skills covered: Modify Handout Master • Modify Notes Master • Modify a Slide Master • Delete and Add Slide Layouts • Create a Custom Color Theme • Use the Slide Master and Template

---

STEP 1 ≫ MODIFY HANDOUT MASTER

At the beginning of your presentations, you will give your audience a handout of your presentation that shows four slides per page because you want the audience to have room to write notes below the slide thumbnails. For identification purposes and to save time in the future, you decide to modify the master so it includes your logo and business name. You will also reposition the date field placeholder so it appears below the header. Refer to Figure 7.23 as you complete Step 1.

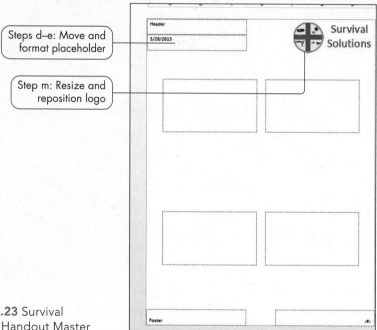

FIGURE 7.23 Survival Solutions Handout Master

a. Create a new blank presentation and save it as **p07h2Survival_LastFirst**.

b. Click the **VIEW tab** and click **Handout Master** in the Master Views group.

The Handout Master tab opens and the master displays.

c. Click **Slides Per Page** in the Page Setup group and select **4 Slides**.

Four slide placeholders appear on the handout for positioning purposes. You will still need to pick the number of placeholders you want to print when you are ready to print the handouts.

d. Drag the **date placeholder** immediately below the header placeholder.

e. Click the **HOME tab**, click the **date placeholder**, and then click **Align Left** in the Paragraph group.

The Header field and the content of the date placeholder align on the left.

f. Click the **INSERT tab** and click **WordArt** in the Text group.

g. Click **Fill - Blue, Accent 1, Shadow** (first row, second column).

h. Type **Survival**, press **Enter**, and then type **Solutions**.

i. Select the text, click **Text Fill** in the WordArt Styles group, and then click **Red** in the Standard Colors category.

The text is now red.

j. Change the font size to **28 pt**.

k. Drag the WordArt to the top-right corner of the handout so that the top and right borders of the WordArt align with the top and right edges of the page.

l. Click the **INSERT tab**, click **Pictures** in the Images group, and then navigate to the location where you saved the logo you created in Hands-On Exercise 1 (*p07h1SSLogo_LastFirst*) or in your data files (*p07h2SSLogo*). Click the logo and click **Insert**.

m. Resize the logo to **1"** high by **1"** wide and drag the logo to the left of the business name.

n. Select the logo, press **Ctrl** while selecting the WordArt, and then click the **HOME tab**. Click **Copy** in the Clipboard group.

The logo and WordArt are saved together as an item to the Clipboard so that you can paste it in other locations.

o. Click the **Clipboard Dialog Box launcher** to open the Clipboard. View the copied selection in the Clipboard to ensure it was saved. Close the Clipboard.

> **TROUBLESHOOTING:** If the logo and WordArt do not appear in the Clipboard, select both objects, and then press Ctrl+C. When the copy appears in the Clipboard, close the Clipboard.

p. Click the **FILE tab** and click **Save As**. Click **Computer** and click **Browse**. Click the **Save as type arrow** and select **PowerPoint Template**. Navigate to the location where you are saving your files and name the file **p07h2SurvivalTemplate_LastFirst**. Click **Save**.

STEP 2 ≫ MODIFY NOTES MASTER

Sometimes the notes you add to your slides are very detailed and take a great deal of space. PowerPoint automatically resizes the font to fit the text to the page, which can make the text difficult to read. You will change the notes master to provide more space for notes and add your logo and business name. Refer to Figure 7.24 as you complete Step 2.

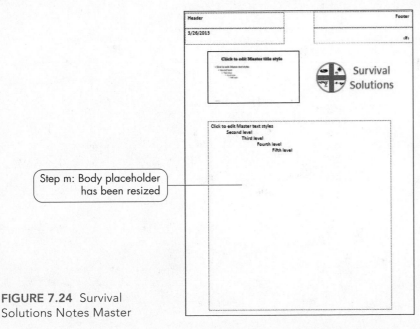

FIGURE 7.24 Survival Solutions Notes Master

a. Click the **VIEW tab** and click **Notes Master** in the Master Views group.

The Notes Master tab opens and the notes master displays.

b. Click the **Slide Image placeholder**, click the **FORMAT tab**, and then click the **Size Dialog Box Launcher**. Scale the placeholder to 50% of its current size.

The placeholder reduces in size to 1.69" high by 3" wide.

c. Click **Position**. If necessary, change the **Horizontal position** to **0.75"**, change the **Vertical position** to **1.25"** from the Top Left Corner, and then click **Close**.

d. Drag the **date placeholder** beneath the header placeholder.

e. Click the **HOME tab** and click **Align Left** in the Paragraph group.

The header information and the date are left aligned.

f. Drag the **footer placeholder** to the top right of the page.

g. Right-click the **footer placeholder** and select **Format Shape**.

The Format Shape pane opens.

h. Click **TEXT OPTIONS**, click **Textbox**, change the **Vertical alignment** to **Top**, and then click **Close**.

i. Click **Align Right** in the Paragraph group.

j. Drag the **page number placeholder** beneath the footer placeholder.

k. Click the **Clipboard Dialog Box Launcher** to open the Clipboard. Select both the logo and WordArt in the list, click the arrow, and then click **Paste**. Close the Clipboard.

The objects are pasted on the Notes page.

l. Drag the logo and WordArt so they are approximately centered in the white space to the right of the Slide Image placeholder.

m. Select the **body placeholder** (the placeholder containing the text levels), click the **FORMAT tab**, and then resize the placeholder to **6.25"** high and **6"** wide.

n. Drag the **body placeholder** up until it fits on the page.

o. Click the **NOTES MASTER tab** and click **Close Master View** in the Close group.

p. Save the template.

STEP 3 ≫ MODIFY A SLIDE MASTER

To help create the identity of your business and to build recognition for your store, you will create a Survival Solutions slide master. You will include the logo you created on the slide master and a photograph of your store on the Title Slide Master. Refer to Figure 7.25 as you complete Step 3.

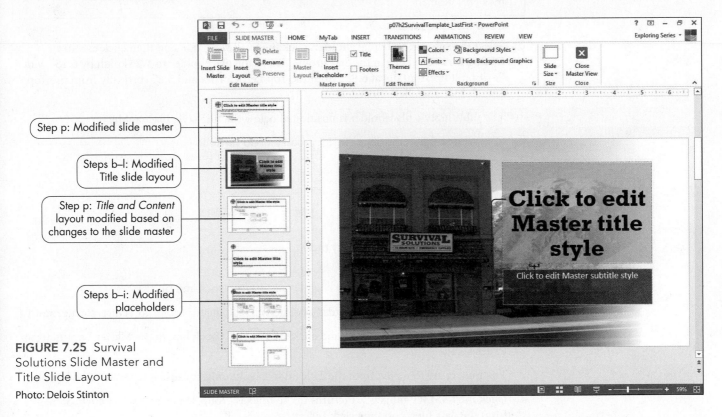

FIGURE 7.25 Survival Solutions Slide Master and Title Slide Layout

Photo: Delois Stinton

a. Click the **VIEW tab** and click **Slide Master** in the Master Views group.

The Slide Master tab opens with the Title Slide Layout selected in the thumbnails list.

> **TROUBLESHOOTING:** If you closed the template after the previous step, you will need to open the file.

b. Select the **title style placeholder**, click the **FORMAT tab**, and then click the **Size Dialog Box Launcher** in the Size group.

The Format Shape pane opens.

c. Resize the placeholder so it is **3.6"** high by **6.15"** wide.

d. Click **Position**, if necessary. Set the **Horizontal position** to **6.88"** from the Top left Corner and the **Vertical position** to **0.87"** from the Top Left Corner and click **Close**.

The placeholder moves to the right side of the slide.

e. Click the **FORMAT tab** if necessary, click **Shape Fill** in the Shape Styles group, and then do the following:

- Click **More Fill Colors**.
- Click the **Custom tab**.
- Type **206** in the **Red box**.
- Type **172** in the **Green box**.
- Type **152** in the **Blue box**.
- Type **40** in the **Transparency box**.
- Click **OK**.

The placeholder fill changes to a semitransparent fill.

f. Click the **HOME tab**, change the font to **Rockwell**, and then change the font size to **60**, if necessary. Change the font style to **Bold**.

> **TROUBLESHOOTING:** If Rockwell is not available, select any serif font available, such as Times New Roman.

g. Select the **subtitle style placeholder**, click the **FORMAT tab**, and then click the **Size Dialog Box Launcher** in the Size group. Resize the placeholder to **1.25"** high by **6.15"** wide. Position it horizontally at **6.88"** from the Top Left Corner and **4.8"** vertically from the Top Left Corner and click **Close**.

The subtitle style placeholder is positioned below the title style placeholder.

h. Click **Shape Fill** in the Shape Styles group and do the following:

- Click **More Fill Colors**.
- Click the **Custom tab**.
- Type **128** in the **Red box**.
- Type **47** in the **Green box**.
- Type **53** in the **Blue box**.
- Type **20** in the **Transparency box**.
- Click **OK**.

The placeholder fill changes to a slightly transparent brick-red fill.

i. Click the **HOME tab**, select the text, and then change the font color to **White, Background 1**.

j. Click the **SLIDE MASTER tab** and click the **Footers check box** in the Master Layout group to deselect it.

The footers are removed from the Title Slide Layout only because it is the selected layout.

k. Click the **INSERT tab**, click **Pictures** in the Images group, locate and select *p07h2Store.png* from the data files, and then click **Insert**.

l. Press ← on the keyboard once to nudge the picture to the left. Click the **Send Backward arrow** in the Arrange group on the FORMAT tab and click **Send to Back**.

The picture is positioned behind the two placeholders.

m. Click **Title Slide Layout**. Click **Hide Background Graphics** in the Background group. Select the picture and change its horizontal position to **0.63"** and vertical position to **0"**.

n. Click the **Office Theme Slide Master thumbnail**, which is located at the top of the thumbnail list.

The slide master is selected, and changes made to it will be reflected in associated slide layouts.

o. Select the **title style placeholder** and change the size to **1.38"** high by **10.55"** wide. Position it horizontally at **1.86"** and vertically at **0.42"** from the Top Left Corner.

p. Click the **HOME tab** and change the font to **Rockwell** and the font style to **Bold**, if necessary.

q. Click the **Clipboard Dialog Box launcher** to open the Clipboard. Point to the logo and WordArt in the list, click the arrow, and then click **Paste**. Delete the WordArt so only the logo remains on the slide. Close the Clipboard.

> **TROUBLESHOOTING:** If the logo and WordArt are no longer available, click the View tab, click Handout Master in the Master Views group, copy just the logo, and then return to the Slide Master view. Paste the logo on the slide master.

r. Deselect the **Lock Aspect Ratio checkbox** on the Format Picture pane. Make the following size and position modifications to the logo:

- Height: **1"**
- Width: **1"**
- Horizontal position: **0.25"** from the Top Left Corner
- Vertical position: **0.25"** from the Top Left Corner

s. Save the template.

STEP 4 >> DELETE AND ADD SLIDE LAYOUTS

Several of the slide layouts associated with the Office Theme Slide Master you are modifying are not needed, so you will delete them. You will need a layout that includes a picture placeholder in the bottom-right corner of the slide that you will use to put pictures of supplies, however, so you create a custom layout. Refer to Figure 7.26 as you complete Step 4.

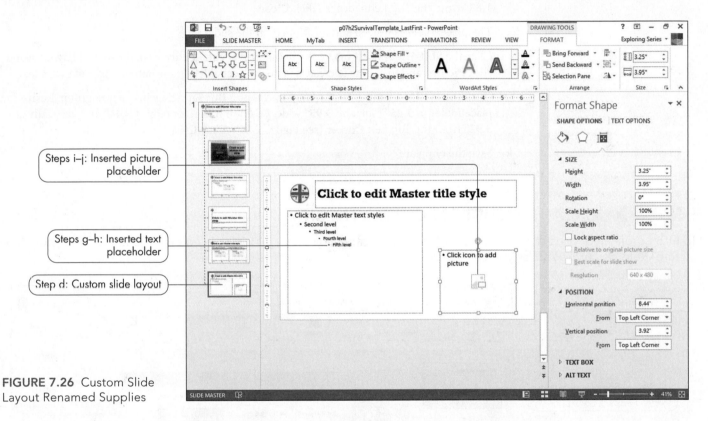

FIGURE 7.26 Custom Slide Layout Renamed Supplies

a. Click **Two Content Layout** in the thumbnail list of layouts associated with the slide master.

The Two Content layout displays.

b. Select **Delete** in the Edit Master group on the SLIDE MASTER tab.

The Two Content layout is deleted and the Comparison Layout, the next layout in the list, displays.

c. Delete the following layouts:

- Title Only
- Blank
- Content with Caption
- Picture with Caption
- Title and Vertical Text
- Vertical Title and Text

The slide master and four associated layouts remain (Title Slide, Title and Content, Section Header, and Comparison).

d. Select the last layout in the thumbnail list and click **Insert Layout** in the Edit Master group.

A new layout, Custom Layout, appears at the bottom of the list of layout thumbnails, and the slide displays in the Slide pane. The layout includes title and footers placeholders.

e. Click **Rename** in the Edit Master group and type **Supplies** in the **Layout name box** in the Rename Layout dialog box. Click **Rename**.

The name of the new layout is changed to *Supplies*.

f. Click the **Footers check box** in the Master Layout group to deselect it.

The footers at the bottom of the slide layout are removed.

g. Click the **Insert Placeholder arrow** in the Master Layout group, click **Text**, and then drag to create a text placeholder on the left side of the slide.

h. Click the **FORMAT tab** and click the **Size Dialog Box launcher** in the Size group. Resize the placeholder to **5.33"** high and **7.02"** wide. Position it horizontally at **0.42"** and vertically at **1.83"** from the Top Left Corner. Click **Close**.

The placeholder is resized and positioned on the slide.

i. Click the **SLIDE MASTER tab**, click the **Insert Placeholder arrow** in the Master Layout group, click **Picture**, and then drag to create a picture placeholder on the bottom-right of the slide.

j. Click the **FORMAT tab** and click the **Size Dialog Box launcher** in the Size group. Resize the placeholder to **3.25"** high and **3.95"** wide. Position it horizontally at **8.44"** and vertically at **3.92"** from the Top Left Corner (see Figure 7.26). Click **Close**.

k. Save the template.

STEP 5 ≫ CREATE A CUSTOM COLOR THEME

To further refine your custom master, you will create a custom color theme using the colors in your logo and your store picture. Refer to Figure 7.27 as you complete Step 5.

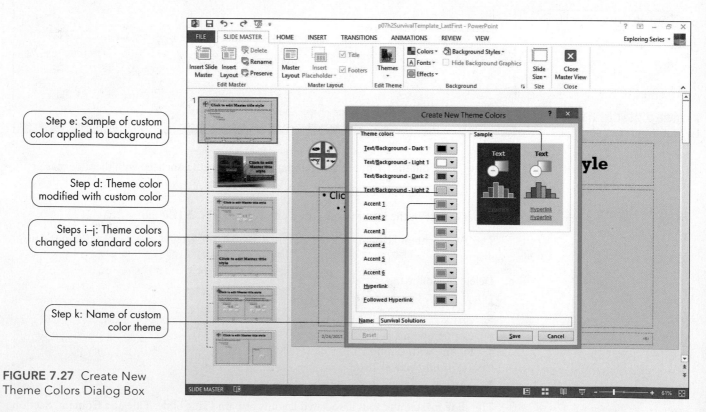

Step e: Sample of custom color applied to background

Step d: Theme color modified with custom color

Steps i–j: Theme colors changed to standard colors

Step k: Name of custom color theme

FIGURE 7.27 Create New Theme Colors Dialog Box

a. Click the **Office Theme Slide Master thumbnail** at the top of the thumbnail list.

b. Click **Colors** in the Background group.

c. Click **Customize Colors**.

The Create New Theme Colors dialog box displays the theme colors used in the Office Theme that your slide master has been using.

d. Click the **Text/Background - Light 2 arrow** and click **More Colors**.

The Colors dialog box opens with the Custom tab active.

e. Type **193** in the **Red box**, type **231** in the **Green box**, type **250** in the **Blue box**, and then click **OK**.

The Create New Theme Colors dialog box opens the custom color in the color box and in the sample.

f. Click **Save** and click **Background Styles** in the Background group.

Note that the four text and background colors from the color theme display within the 12 thumbnails, and the thumbnails in the second column show the custom color you created.

g. Click **Style 2** (first row, second column) to apply the custom color to the slide master.

h. Click **Colors** in the Background group, right-click **Custom 1**, and then select **Edit**.

The custom color theme you created opens so you can make additional modifications.

i. Select the **Accent 1 color box** and select **Green** in the Standard Colors category.

j. Select the **Accent 2 color box** and select **Red** in the Standard Colors category.

k. Type **Survival Solutions** in the **Name box** and click **Save**.

l. Click **Close Master View** in the Close group.

m. Save the template.

STEP 6 ≫ USE THE SLIDE MASTER AND TEMPLATE

To test the masters you created, you will insert slides from a Survival Solutions slide show you previously presented to a community group. You will view the slide show, and then you will preview the handout master and the notes master. Refer to Figure 7.28 as you complete Step 6.

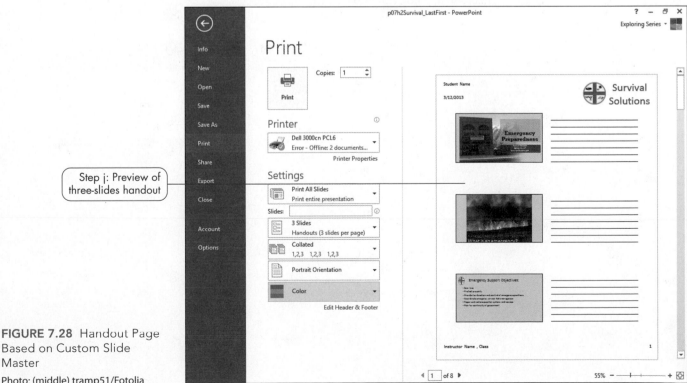

FIGURE 7.28 Handout Page Based on Custom Slide Master

Photo: (middle) tramp51/Fotolia

a. Click the **New Slide arrow** in the Slides group and select **Reuse Slides**.

The Reuse Slides task pane opens.

b. Click **Browse** in the Reuse Slides task pane and select **Browse File**.

c. Locate and select *p07h2Plan.pptx* and click **Open**.

The 24 added slides appear as thumbnails in the Reuse Slides pane.

d. Right-click any of the slides in the list and select **Insert All Slides**. Close the Reuse Slides pane.

The slides appear in the Slides pane with the slide master you created.

e. Click the **FILE tab**, click **Save As**, locate and select *p07h2Survival_LastFirst*, making sure you are saving it as a PowerPoint Presentation (.pptx file) and not as a PowerPoint Template (.potx file), and then click **Save**. Click **Yes** to confirm that you want to replace the existing file of the same name.

You will save the file using the original presentation file name so you do not overwrite the template you created. You want to be able to use the template with other presentations.

f. Create a *Notes and Handouts* header with your name and a footer with your instructor's name and your class. Include the current date.

g. Delete Slide 1.

The empty title slide is deleted, and the title slide from the inserted presentation becomes the new Slide 1.

h. Click the **VIEW tab** and click **Reading View** in the Presentation Views group. View the slide show and note the various layouts used.

i. Click the **FILE tab**, click **Print**, and then click **Full Page Slides**.

j. Click **3 Slides** in the *Handouts* section. View the preview of the handout.

k. Click **3 Slides** and click **Notes Pages** in the *Print Layout* section.

l. Scroll to view the notes for each slide.

m. Save the presentation. Keep PowerPoint open if you plan to continue with Hands-On Exercise 3. If not, exit PowerPoint.

Custom Shows

Custom shows are composed of a subset of slides assembled for a presentation. Often, a main show is developed and a number of different presentations based on the main show are created. For instance, you may plan for a 40-minute presentation only to find out at the last minute that your time has been cut to 25 minutes. Rather than show all of the slides in the presentation, moving quickly past less important slides, you can create a custom show using only the critical slides. You can also create multiple custom slide shows in a presentation that are linked so that the presentation pulls slides from each. Custom shows enable you to focus your presentation to the needs of your audience.

An alternative to creating a custom show is to designate hidden slides in a slide show. If you only have a few slides to reserve in case they are needed later, hidden slides are an alternative to creating a custom show. As you give your presentation, you can reveal hidden slides within the sequence based on your audience needs and the time constraint. You can also use hidden slides to reveal increasingly detailed slides and complex concepts as needed, or you can skip the slides without the audience being aware that you are skipping material. You will experiment with hiding slides and revealing them as you display a slide show.

In this section, you will learn how to create multiple custom shows from a single presentation and how to run and navigate a custom slide show. Finally, you will designate and display hidden slides.

Creating a Custom Slide Show

In *basic custom shows*, you select slides from one presentation and then group them to create other presentations, enabling you to adapt a single presentation to a variety of audiences. If your original presentation contains 10 slides, you might designate the first, third, eighth, and tenth slides for one custom show and the first, fifth, and sixth slides for another. The original presentation contains all of the slides needed in the custom shows.

STEP 1 ≫ To create a custom show, do the following:

1. Click the SLIDE SHOW tab.
2. Click Custom Slide Show in the Start Slide Show group.
3. Select Custom Shows.
4. Click New.
5. Type a name in the *Slide show name* box.
6. Click the slide you want to include in the custom show and click Add.
7. Continue adding slides and click OK.
8. Repeat Steps 4 through 7 to create additional custom shows.

Figure 7.29 shows the Custom Shows dialog box and the Define Custom Show dialog box that opens when you click New. The dialog boxes have been rearranged so they are both visible. The slides in the original presentation are listed in the left pane of the Define Custom Show dialog box and are identified by the slide number and the title of the slide. The slides in the custom show are listed in the right pane and are numbered based on their position in the new show.

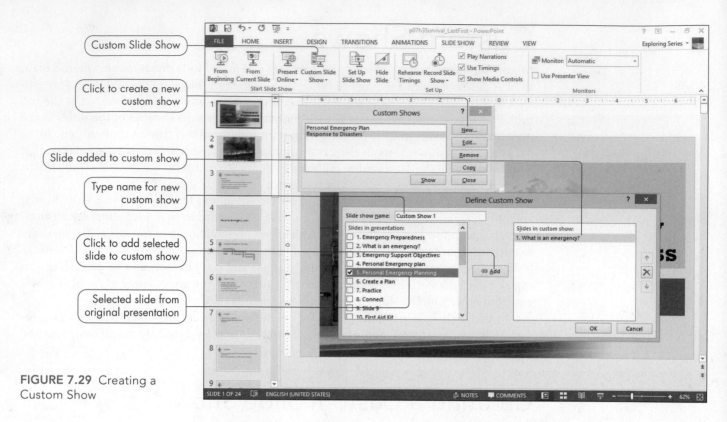

Labels on figure:
- Custom Slide Show
- Click to create a new custom show
- Slide added to custom show
- Type name for new custom show
- Click to add selected slide to custom show
- Selected slide from original presentation

FIGURE 7.29 Creating a Custom Show

Hyperlinked custom shows connect a main custom show to other custom shows using hyperlinks. For example, you might be giving a presentation to a group of potential students who are exploring college majors. One slide in your presentation could have links to parts of your slide show that discuss individual majors. After you quickly poll your audience, you find that everyone is interested in hearing you talk about the nursing major, while half are interested in the business major, and only one or two people want to hear about the other programs. As you present the hyperlinked show, you can decide whether to branch to the supporting shows containing other program information or not. To create a hyperlinked custom show, all of the slides must be in the same presentation. This presentation is then divided into custom shows. A hyperlinked custom show might include 10 slides from the main presentation, 3 slides from another part of the show, and 5 slides from yet another.

Create the main custom slide show, as previously described, by opening the presentation and selecting the slides that will be in the main show. Name this custom show with a unique name, such as Proposal_Links, so that you will be able to identify it later as the show that contains the hyperlinks. Create the supporting custom slide shows, as described, by selecting slides from the presentation and naming each show with a different name.

> ## TIP | Main Custom Show
>
> Name the basic custom slide show with the word *Main* or *Major* as part of the name to make it easy to identify. For instance, a cooking hyperlinked custom show might be called Main Vegetable Presentation. The supporting custom slide shows might be named Cooking Beans, Peeling Tomatoes, or Roasting Vegetables.

After you create all of the custom shows, click the Home tab to return to the original presentation, if necessary. Use the Slide Thumbnail pane to select the slide in the main custom slide show that contains the hyperlinks.

1. Select the text or other object that you plan to click to view the supporting slides.
2. Click the INSERT tab and click Hyperlink in the Links group.

3. Click *Place in This Document* in the Insert Hyperlink dialog box, as shown in Figure 7.30.

4. Scroll to the bottom of the slide list where the Custom Shows list begins and click the name of the support slide show. A preview of the first slide in that show will appear in the Slide preview box.

5. Click the *Show and return* check box so that the supporting slide show will return to the main show after all of the slides have been shown.

6. Repeat these steps to set up the remaining hyperlinks.

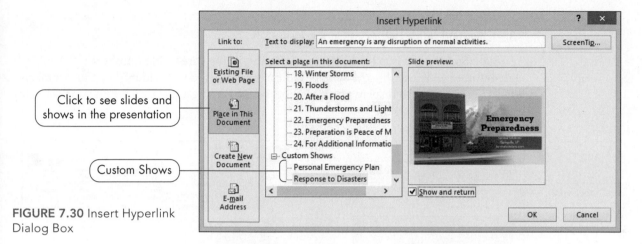

FIGURE 7.30 Insert Hyperlink Dialog Box

Running and Navigating a Custom Slide Show

STEP 3 › The presentation file must be saved so that the custom show remains a subset of it. Then display the custom show from the beginning or at any time while showing the main show. To show the basic custom slide show from the beginning, do the following:

1. Open the presentation and click the SLIDE SHOW tab.
2. Click Custom Slide Show.
3. Click the name of the custom show you wish to present.

The show will begin automatically. To show the custom show during the display of the main show, right-click and select Custom Show. Then, select the title of the custom show you wish to display.

To show the hyperlinked presentation, do the following:

1. Open the presentation.
2. Click the SLIDE SHOW tab.
3. Click Custom Slide Show.
4. Select the name of the main custom slide show.

The custom presentation will begin. When a slide is reached that contains a hyperlink, click the hyperlink and continue through the supporting slides. Advance through all of the supporting slides and return to the main custom slide. Select another hyperlink if one appears on this slide or continue displaying the slides in the main custom slide show.

Designating and Displaying Hidden Slides

Although custom shows fit many needs, in some cases you may prefer to skip detailed slides in the main presentation and only show them if the audience requests additional information. Hiding slides within the sequence of the presentation depends on your ability to anticipate what your audience might ask. For example, a presentation on budgeting might include slides that speak of the budgeting process as a concept. Your audience might ask to see some actual numbers plugged into a budget. If you anticipate this question, you can create a slide with this information and hide it within the presentation. During the presentation, if no one asks to see numbers in a budget, you continue through the slide show. But if someone asks, you can show the hidden slide, and then continue through the presentation. The next time you make a presentation, the slide will again be hidden.

STEP 2》 To hide a slide, do the following:

1. Select the slide you want to hide in the Slide Sorter view or in the Slides pane in Normal view.
2. Click the SLIDE SHOW tab.
3. Click Hide Slide in the Set Up group.

Slide Sorter view is active in Figure 7.31, displaying three slide numbers followed by a slide number with a slash—the symbol indicating that a slide is hidden. The thumbnail also appears grayed out. To display a hidden slide, select it in the Slide Thumbnail pane and click Hide Slide again.

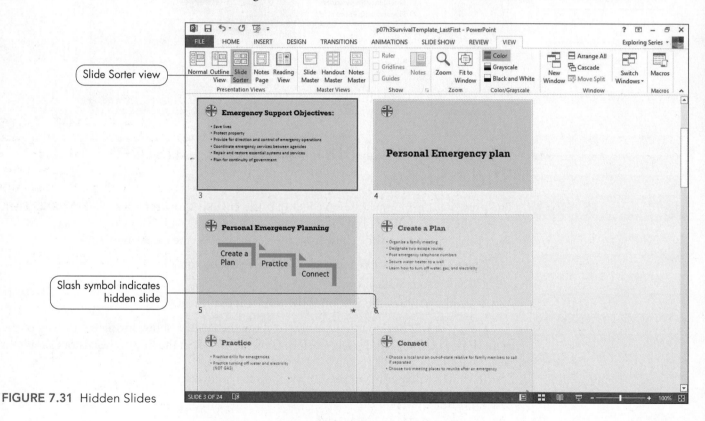

FIGURE 7.31 Hidden Slides

During the presentation, when you arrive at the location of the hidden slide, you reveal the slide by pressing H.

TIP   Display a Specific Slide in Slide Show View

While in Slide Show view, if you know the slide number of a hidden slide, type the number on the keyboard and press Enter to display it. Any slide in the slide show, not just hidden slides, can be quickly displayed using this method.

As you print your slide presentation, you may decide to print the hidden slides or not. The Backstage Print view contains a check box to designate whether to print the hidden slides. It is a good idea to print the hidden slides on the notes pages for the presenter. This way, as the speech is being delivered, the presenter is reminded of the hidden slide and its content.

Quick Concepts

1. What is the main advantage of creating a custom show? *p. 1029*

2. Explain why you might want to create a hyperlinked custom show. *p. 1030*

3. You decide that you want to be alerted to any hidden slides as you give your presentation. How can you print hidden slides? *p. 1033*

3 Custom Shows

The main slide show for Survival Solutions was designed so that you can create custom shows based on it to allow flexibility while presenting. You can present a custom show on how to prepare for emergencies or a custom show on responses to specific disasters depending upon audience questions and feedback. The slide show also contains several general slides that can be followed up with reserved slides containing greater detail. You will hide the detail slides and then practice navigating custom shows and displaying hidden slides.

Skills covered: Create a Custom Slide Show • Designate and Display Hidden Slides • Run and Navigate a Custom Slide Show

STEP 1 ≫ CREATE A CUSTOM SLIDE SHOW

You create two custom slide shows based on the main Survival Solutions presentation so that you can select the show that best meets your audience's interests. Refer to Figure 7.32 as you complete Step 1.

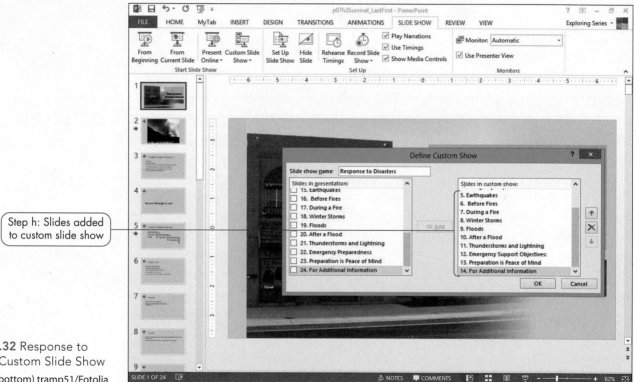

Step h: Slides added to custom slide show

FIGURE 7.32 Response to Disasters Custom Slide Show

Photo: (left, bottom) tramp51/Fotolia

a. Open *p07h2Survival_LastFirst*, if necessary, and save the presentation as **p07h3Survival_LastFirst**, changing *h2* to *h3*.

> **TROUBLESHOOTING:** Be sure you start with the correct file. Start with the Survival file, not the SurvivalTemplate file.

b. Click the **SLIDE SHOW tab** and click **Custom Slide Show** in the Start Slide Show group.

c. Select **Custom Shows** and click **New**.

The Define Custom Show dialog box opens.

d. Type **Personal Emergency Plan** in the **Slide show name box**.

e. Select **Slides 1 through 14** and **Slides 23** and **24**. Click **Add**.

Slides 1 through 14, 23, and 24 are added to the custom show. The slides are renumbered in the custom show.

> **TROUBLESHOOTING:** If you select the wrong slide, click the name of the slide on the right side of the Define Custom Show dialog box and click Remove.

f. Click **OK**.

g. Click **New** and type **Response to Disasters** in the **Slide show name box**.

h. Add the following slides in this order: 1, 2, 14, 22, 15 through 21, 3, 23, and 24.

i. Click **OK** and click **Close**.

j. Save the presentation.

STEP 2 ›› DESIGNATE AND DISPLAY HIDDEN SLIDES

To allow for differing presentation times and audience interest, you will hide slides showing detailed personal emergency planning (Slides 6–8) and storage recommendations (Slides 10–13). If time allows, you will display these slides.

a. Select the **Slide 6 thumbnail**.

b. Click the **SLIDE SHOW tab**, if necessary, and click **Hide Slide** in the Set Up group.

A slash appears through the number for the slide in the Slides tab.

c. Hide Slides 7, 8, and 10 through 13.

> **TROUBLESHOOTING:** If you hide a slide by mistake, select the slide and click Hide Slide in the Set Up group on the Slide Show tab again.

d. Click the **VIEW tab** and click **Slide Sorter** in the Presentation Views group.

Slide Sorter view displays the Hide Slide symbol on Slides 6 through 8 and 10 through 13.

e. Click **Normal**. Save the presentation.

STEP 3 ›› RUN AND NAVIGATE A CUSTOM SLIDE SHOW

To check slide order and practice displaying custom slide shows and hidden slides, you view the Personal Emergency Plan custom show.

a. Click the **SLIDE SHOW tab** and click **Custom Slide Show**.

b. Select **Personal Emergency Plan**.

c. Advance through the presentation until you reach the *Personal Emergency Planning* SmartArt diagram.

d. Click **H** on the keyboard.

Slide 6 displays, followed by Slides 7 and 8, all of which are part of a hidden sequence of slides. Then the next nonhidden slide displays, and the slide show advances through all remaining nonhidden slides. If additional hidden slides follow after this sequence, they can be displayed by pressing H on the keyboard, as in step d.

e. Advance to the end of the presentation and exit the slide show.

f. Save and close the file, and submit based on your instructor's directions.

Chapter Objectives Review

After reading this chapter, you have accomplished the following objectives:

1. **Set PowerPoint options.**
   - Set PowerPoint's options to meet your individual needs and maximize your productivity.
   - You can set options such as general working environment preferences, proofing, saving, working with languages, customizing, and many more.

2. **Customize the Ribbon.**
   - Customize the Ribbon to efficiently access PowerPoint features.
   - Create custom tabs with new groups displaying the features you use most often in one location, or move buttons and groups within the existing groups.

3. **Use Combine Shapes commands.**
   - PowerPoint includes a set of commands that are useful when working with shapes: Combine, Intersect, Subtract, and Union.
   - Combine removes the overlapping area of two shapes.
   - Intersect removes any area that is not overlapped.
   - Subtract removes the shape of the second selected object from the area of the first object.
   - Union joins selected overlapping objects so they become one shape.
   - You can only access these commands by adding them to an existing tab or by creating a new tab.

4. **Modify handout and notes masters.**
   - Masters control the consistency of your presentations, notes, and handouts.
   - A handout master controls the layout and formatting of audience handout pages.
   - The notes master controls the design information for notes pages.
   - You can customize these masters so that your printouts provide the information you want to display in the position that is most advantageous.

5. **Modify a slide master.**
   - A slide master controls the design elements and slide layouts associated with the slides in a presentation.
   - Slide layouts include a title slide layout, various content slide layouts, and a blank slide layout.
   - The layout designates the location of placeholders and other objects on the slide as well as formatting information.

6. **Save a slide master as a template.**
   - After you modify a slide master, you can save the file as a template so that you can reuse the slide master with any presentation.
   - PowerPoint saves the master as a template with an extension of .potx and retains the changes in the file.

7. **Create a custom slide show.**
   - Once a slide show is developed, you can create a number of custom slide shows based on subsets of slides from the original show.
   - Creating custom shows enables you to keep all the shows you need for various audiences within one file.
   - You can display the custom show that relates to your audience's interests.

8. **Run and navigate a custom slide show.**
   - Display a custom show from its beginning, at any time while showing the main show, or by clicking a hyperlink.
   - To show the basic custom slide show from the beginning, open the presentation, click the Slide Show tab, click Custom Slide Show, and then click the name of the custom show you wish to present. The show begins automatically.
   - To show the custom show during the main slide show, right-click and select Custom Show. Then select the title of the custom show you wish to display.
   - To display a hyperlinked custom slide show, click a link on a slide displayed during the main slide show.

9. **Designate and display hidden slides.**
   - You can create and hold slides on reserve in anticipation of audience questions. You can then hide the slide with the reserved or detailed information until the appropriate time during the presentation.
   - While presenting in Slide Show view, display a hidden slide by pressing H on the keyboard.

Key Terms Matching

Match the key terms with their definitions. Write the key term letter by the appropriate numbered definition.

a. Basic custom show
b. Color theme
c. Combine
d. Custom show
e. Customize Ribbon tab
f. Handout master
g. HSL
h. Hyperlinked custom show
i. Intersect

j. Master
k. Notes master
l. PowerPoint Options
m. .potx
n. .pptx
o. RGB
p. Slide master
q. Subtract
r. Union

1. _____ A grouped subset of the slides in a presentation. **p. 1029**

2. _____ A color model in which the numeric system refers to the hue, saturation, and luminosity of a color. **p. 1017**

3. _____ A Combine Shapes command that removes the shape of the second selected object from the area of the first object. **p. 1002**

4. _____ The top slide in a hierarchy of slides that contains design information for the slides. **p. 1012**

5. _____ The file extension assigned to a PowerPoint template. **p. 1018**

6. _____ A numeric system for identifying the color resulting from the combination of red, green, and blue light. **p. 1017**

7. _____ Contains the design information for audience handout pages. **p. 1010**

8. _____ Consists of the color combinations for the text, lines, background, and graphics in a presentation. **p. 1017**

9. _____ A Combine Shapes command that joins selected overlapping objects so they become one shape. **p. 1002**

10. _____ Begins with a main custom show and uses hyperlinks to link between other shows. **p. 1030**

11. _____ A broad range of settings that enable you to customize the environment to meet your needs. **p. 996**

12. _____ A Combine Shapes command that removes any area that is not overlapped. **p. 1002**

13. _____ The file extension assigned to a PowerPoint presentation. **p. 998**

14. _____ Contains the design information for notes pages. **p. 1012**

15. _____ A single presentation file from which you can create separate presentations. **p. 1029**

16. _____ Contains design information that provides a consistent look to your presentation, handouts, and notes pages. **p. 1010**

17. _____ A tab in the PowerPoint Options dialog box that enables you to create a personal tab on the Ribbon that includes features that are not available on the standard Ribbon. **p. 999**

18. _____ A Combine Shapes command that removes the overlapping area of two shapes. **p. 1002**

Multiple Choice

1. Which of the following options can be changed in the General options within PowerPoint Options?

   (a) Image Size and Quality

   (b) User name

   (c) AutoCorrect

   (d) Customize Ribbon

2. Which of the following statements is not true regarding customizing the Ribbon?

   (a) All available PowerPoint commands are displayed on the default Ribbon.

   (b) Custom tabs and groups can be added to the Ribbon.

   (c) Tabs and groups can be renamed.

   (d) Commands can be removed from one tab and added to another.

3. The Intersect Shapes command performs which of the following functions?

   (a) Unites selected overlapping objects so they become one shape

   (b) Removes the overlapping area of two selected shapes

   (c) Removes the shape of a second selected object from the area of the first selected object

   (d) Removes any area of two selected objects that is not overlapped

4. By default, notes masters contain:

   (a) Three slide thumbnails per page.

   (b) Only a slide thumbnail and note text.

   (c) A note text, date, header, and footer.

   (d) A header, date, slide thumbnail, note text, footer, and page number.

5. Which of the following is not a true statement regarding a slide master?

   (a) A slide master controls the position of the slide thumbnail in handouts and note pages.

   (b) A slide master saved as a template can be used with multiple presentations.

   (c) A slide master is the top slide in a hierarchy of slides that stores design information and slide layouts.

   (d) A presentation can contain more than one slide master.

6. Which of the following is not a true statement about slide layouts associated with a slide master?

   (a) Slide layouts can be renamed or deleted.

   (b) Slide layouts contain the same theme (color scheme, fonts, and effects) as the slide master.

   (c) Slide layouts cannot be modified by adding additional placeholders.

   (d) Slide layouts can use either portrait or landscape orientation.

7. Custom slide shows are:

   (a) Multiple presentation files with slides copied from a main presentation file.

   (b) Subsets of slides saved in a presentation file.

   (c) Shows with a modified slide master.

   (d) Shells for building presentations.

8. Custom slide shows cannot contain:

   (a) Slides that are not a part of the original presentation.

   (b) Hyperlinks to other slide shows.

   (c) Hidden slides.

   (d) More than 10 slides.

9. Custom slide shows can be viewed using all of the following methods except by:

   (a) Clicking the SLIDE SHOW tab, clicking Custom Slide Show, and then clicking the name of the custom show.

   (b) Right-clicking in Slide Show view, selecting Custom Show, and then selecting the name of the custom show.

   (c) Pressing Ctrl+C while in Slide Show view and selecting the name of the custom show.

   (d) Clicking a hyperlink on a slide while in Slide Show view.

10. Which of the following statements is not true about hidden slides?

    (a) A hidden slide does not show when you advance from one slide to another when displaying a slide show.

    (b) A hidden slide is created using Hide Slide in the Set Up group on the SLIDE SHOW tab.

    (c) A hidden slide cannot be used during a custom slide show.

    (d) A hidden slide can be revealed when displaying a slide show by pressing H.

1 Mountain Biking Presentation

You are preparing a presentation to a local youth group about mountain bike safety and general mountain biking rules of the trail. You want the title slide to include a mountain scene with a mountain bike popping up on a trail. To begin, you will change PowerPoint options to include an AutoCorrect phrase for efficiency and to change the AutoRecover time to five minutes. You will modify the Ribbon structure you created in Hands-on Exercise 1 to add positioning features. You will use PowerPoint's Combine Shapes feature to complete the mountain scene, and then you will add and position a clip art image of a mountain bike. Finally, you will enter sample text in the title slide text and a content slide so you can view the finished handouts and notes masters. This exercise follows the same set of skills used in Hands-On Exercise 1. Refer to Figure 7.33 as you complete this exercise.

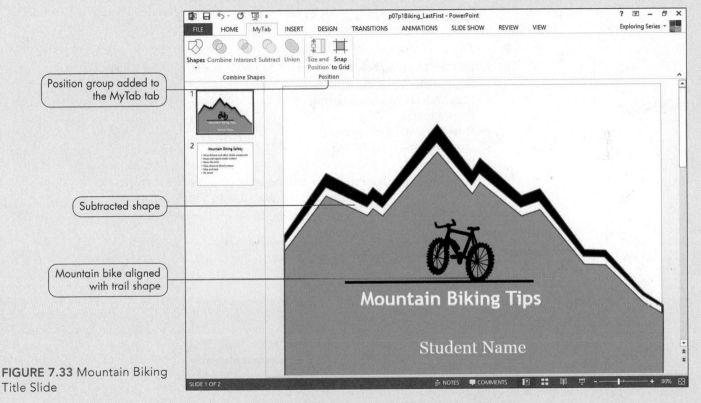

FIGURE 7.33 Mountain Biking Title Slide

a. Open *p07p1Biking* and save it as **p07p1Biking_LastFirst.pptx**.

b. Create a handout header with your name and a handout footer with the file name, your instructor's name, and your class. Include the current date.

c. Click the **FILE tab**, click **Options**, and then click **Proofing**.

d. Click **AutoCorrect Options** and click the **AutoCorrect tab**, if necessary. Type **mb** in the **Replace box** and type **Mountain Biking** in the **With box**. Click **OK**.

e. Click **Save** in the left pane, select the number in the *Save AutoRecover information every* box, and then type **5**.

f. Click **Customize Ribbon** and click **MyTab (Custom)**.

> **TROUBLESHOOTING:** If you do not have a tab named MyTab (Custom), complete Hands-On Exercise 1, Step 3.

g. Click **New Group** and click **Rename**. Type **Position** in the **Display name box** and click **OK**.

h. Select **Size and Position** in the Popular Commands list and click **Add**.

i. Click the **Choose commands from arrow** and select **Commands Not in the Ribbon**.

j. Select **Snap to Grid** and click **Add**. Click **OK**.

k. Select the **black mountain shape**, press and hold **Shift**, and then click the **orange shape** to add it to the selection. Click the **MyTab tab** and click **Subtract** in the Combine Shapes group. A jagged white line now exists where the orange shape was cut out of the black mountain shape.

l. Click the **INSERT tab**, click **Online Pictures**, type **mountain bike** in the **Office.com Clip Art box**, and then press **Enter**. Insert the clip art image shown in Figure 7.33 or another image if it is not available.

m. Drag the back wheel of the mountain bike clip art as close to the straight black trail line as possible. If the grid setting does not enable you to align the back tire with the trail, click the **MyTab tab** and click **Snap to Grid** in the Position group to deactivate it. Drag the image until the back wheel aligns with the trail line. Resize the image as desired.

n. Click in the **title placeholder** and type **mb Tips**. AutoCorrect replaces *mb* with *Mountain Biking*.

o. Type your name in the **subtitle placeholder**.

p. Add a new slide using the *Title and Content* layout.

q. Click in the **title placeholder** and type **mb Safety**. Type the following bulleted points:
   - **Wear a helmet and use other safety equipment.**
   - **Keep your speed under control.**
   - **Know the trail.**
   - **Slow down on blind corners.**
   - **Stop and look.**
   - **Be smart.**

r. Click the **FILE tab**, click **Print**, click **Full Page Slides**, and then click **Notes Pages**. View the Notes Pages preview. Click **Notes Pages** and click **Handouts 4 Slides Horizontal**.

s. Save and close the file, and submit based on your instructor's directions.

2 Sunshine Buildings

FROM SCRATCH

Your manager prepared a presentation discussing the positive features of building a home using the services of Sunshine Builders. You have been asked to modify the handouts so that the printouts have two slides per page and contain the date, company name and logo, and page number. The manager would also like the company name and logo on the slides. Because your manager will be using this same format in the future, you will save the masters as a template. This exercise follows the same set of skills as used in Hands-On Exercise 2. Refer to Figure 7.34 as you complete this exercise.

FIGURE 7.34 Handout Master

a. Open a new blank presentation and save it as **p07p2Sunshine_LastFirst.pptx**.

b. Click the **VIEW tab** and click **Handout Master** in the Master Views group.

c. Click **Slides Per Page** in the Page Setup group and select **4 Slides**.

d. Deselect the **Header check box** in the Placeholders group.

e. Select the **Page Number placeholder**, click the **MyTab tab**, and then click **Size and Position** in the Position group.

f. Set the following in the Format Shape pane and close the pane:
   - Size: Height **0.5"**, Width **1"**.
   - Position: Horizontal **3.25"** from the Top Left Corner, Vertical **9.5"** from the Top Left Corner.
   - Text Box: Vertical alignment **Top Centered**.

g. Drag the **date placeholder** to the bottom-right corner of the page, aligning its bottom border with the bottom edge of the page and the right border with the right edge of the page.

h. Click the **INSERT tab**, click **WordArt** in the Text group, click **Fill - Gold, Accent 4, Soft Bevel** (first row, fifth column), and then type **Sunshine Builders**. Drag the WordArt to the top-left corner of the page, aligning its top border with the top edge of the page and the left border with the left edge of the page.

i. Click the **INSERT tab**, click **Online Pictures** in the Images group, type **solar panel** in the **Office .com Clip Art box**, and then press **Enter**. Insert the image shown in Figure 7.34.

j. Click the **MyTab tab** and click **Size and Position** in the Position group. Set the following in the Format Picture pane and close the pane:
   - Size: Height **0.75"**, Width **0.75"**.
   - Position: Horizontal **5.75"** from the Top Left Corner, Vertical **0.1"** from the Top Left Corner.

k. Select the WordArt and clip art image, click the **HOME tab**, and then click **Copy** in the Clipboard group.

l. Click the **VIEW tab** and click **Notes Master** in the Master Views group. Deselect the **Header** and **Date check boxes** in the Placeholders group.

m. Click the **HOME tab** and click the **Clipboard Dialog Box launcher** to open the Clipboard. Point to the WordArt and clip art in the list, click the arrow, and then click **Paste**. Deselect the objects. Close the Clipboard.

n. Select the WordArt, change the font size to **48 pt**, and then drag the placeholder upward until it aligns with the left edge of the slide and is centered in the available vertical white space above the slide thumbnail.

o. Select the clip art image, click the **MyTab tab**, and then click **Size and Position** in the Position group. Set the following in the Format Picture pane and close the pane:
   - Size: Height **0.6"**, Width **0.6"**.
   - Position: Horizontal **5.75"** from the Top Left Corner, Vertical **0.25"** from the Top Left Corner.

p. Click the **VIEW tab**, click **Slide Master** in the Master Views group, and then paste the WordArt and the clip art on the Office Theme Slide Master.

q. Drag the WordArt and clip art to the top-left corner of the slide so the top border of the selection touches the top of the slide and the left border of the selection touches the left border of the slide. Close the Clipboard.

r. Select the **Master title styles placeholder**, set the following in the Format Shape pane, and then close the pane:
   - Size: Height **1.25"**, Width **8"**.
   - Position: Horizontal **1.33"** from the Top Left Corner, Vertical **1.08"** from the Top Left Corner.

s. Select the **Master text placeholder**, set the following in the Format Shape pane, and then close the pane:
   - Size: Height **4.3"**, Width **8"**.
   - Position: Horizontal **1.33"** from the Top Left Corner, Vertical **2.42"** from the Top Left Corner.

t. Click the **FILE tab** and click **Save As**. Click **Computer** and click **Browse**. Click the **Save as type arrow** and select **PowerPoint Template**. Navigate to the location where you save your solution files and name the file **p07p2SunshineTemplate_LastFirst**. Click **Save**.

u. Close the slide master. On Slide 1, type **Build Your Dream Home** in the **title placeholder** and your name in the **subtitle placeholder**. Type the following text in the notes pane: **Sunshine Builders is well known as one of the premier custom home builders in the Valley area. If innovative design, distinctive quality, and impressive value are important to you, we are your builder!**

v. Create a handout header with your name and a handout footer with the file name, your instructor's name, and your class. Include the current date.

w. Create a new slide using the *Title and Content* layout. Type **Floor Plans** in the **text placeholder** and enter the following as bullets: **Ashville**, **Berkeley**, **Cassidy**, **Drayton**, **Grayson**.

x. Add the following text in the notes pane: **One of the most exciting parts of your home-building experience is selecting your floor plan. Our floor plans reflect today's design trends.**

y. Click the **FILE tab**, click **Print**, and then click **Full Page Slides**. Click **Notes Pages** and note the preview of the printed notes pages. Click **Notes Pages** and click **2 Slides (Handouts)**. Note the preview of the handout.

z. Click **Save As**, locate *p07p2Sunshine_LastFirst.pptx*, and then click **Save**, being careful not to save the presentation over the template file. Close the file, and submit based on your instructor's directions.

3 Luxury Estates Presentation

You are a realtor selling luxury country estates. This week, you have appointments with two potential customers, so you will create a presentation using recent photographs and information about the estates you personally selected as being the most suitable. You will create custom shows for each customer including a slide personalizing the show and slides highlighting the estates. You will hide slides with cost information on each estate so they can be shown if the customer expresses an interest in the property. This exercise follows the same set of skills as used in Hands-On Exercise 3. Refer to Figure 7.35 as you complete this exercise.

FIGURE 7.35 Luxury Estates Presentation

Photos: (Slide 1) xy/Fotolia, (Slide 5, left) pics721/Fotolia, (Slide 5, right) Iriana Shiyan/Fotolia

a. Open *p07p3Luxury* and save it as **p07p3Luxury_LastFirst**.

b. Create a handout header with your name and a handout footer with your instructor's name and your class. Include the current date.

c. Click the **SLIDE SHOW tab** and click **Custom Slide Show** in the Start Slide Show group. Select **Custom Shows** and click **New**.

d. Type **Roberts** in the **Slide show name box**.

e. Select **Slides 1, 2, 4, 5, 6, 10, 11, 12**, and **19**, click **Add**, and then click **OK**.

f. Click **New** and type **Lewis** in the **Slide show name box**.

g. Select **Slides 1, 3, 7, 8, 9, 13, 14, 15, 16, 17, 18**, and **19**, click **Add**, and then click **OK**. Click **Close**.

h. Select **Slides 6, 9, 12, 15**, and **18** in the Slides pane and click **Hide Slide** in the Set Up group.

i. Click the **SLIDE SHOW tab** if necessary, click **Custom Slide Show** in the Start Slide Show tab, and then click **Roberts**.

j. Advance to Slide 5 and press **H** on the keyboard to reveal Slide 6, which is a hidden slide. Advance to the end of the presentation and exit. Repeat with the Lewis show. Advance to Slide 8 and press **H** on the keyboard to reveal Slide 9, which is a hidden slide.

k. Save and close the file, and submit based on your instructor's directions.

Mid-Level Exercises

1 Family Reunion

CREATIVE CASE

FROM SCRATCH

You are creating a PowerPoint presentation for a family reunion and have asked family members to provide a picture labeled with names, recent family information, and the connection to your great-grandfather. You will modify PowerPoint options and the Ribbon to put the tools you need on one tab, and then combine shapes to create a family logo. You will include the logo on the handout, notes, and slide masters to create a theme. You will also modify the slide master with your preferences for a font scheme and color scheme and create three new slide layouts. You will save your work as a template so others may use it.

a. Open a blank presentation and save it as **p07m1Reunion_LastFirst.pptx**.

b. Set PowerPoint options to save AutoRecover information every **15 minutes** (Save option) and to set the default target output to **150 ppi** (Advanced option), if necessary.

c. Customize the Ribbon to put the buttons you use most on one custom tab with groups. You can modify the MyTab tab you created in previous exercises or reset the Ribbon to its original state and create a new tab with groups.

d. Click the **Title box** and type **Our Family Reunion**. Click the **subtitle box** and add your name. Search for a clip art image using a key term such as *family* to use as your logo. After finding your logo, position it in the bottom-right corner of the slide. Copy it to the Clipboard.

e. Modify the handout and notes masters to include your logo in the position of your choice. Make at least one change to the placeholders (e.g., location, font, size) and make any other changes.

f. Display the slide master. Create a new Color theme by modifying at least two theme colors. Then, create a new Font theme by selecting a new Heading font.

g. Select the **Title Slide Layout** and insert and position a 4" by 6" picture placeholder on the slide for your great-grandfather's image. Apply a **Shape Style** as desired. Rearrange or reformat the title and subtitle placeholders to fit on the empty area of the slide.

h. Replace the title text with **Enter Great-Grandfather's Name**. Replace the subtitle text with **Enter reunion date, time, and location**.

i. Remove the date and page number placeholders from the title slide layout. Make additional design changes as desired.

j. Replace the text in the footer placeholder with your family name and the word *Reunion*. Use the *Header and Footer* dialog box on the INSERT tab to apply the footer to the title slide layout only.

k. Delete all other slide layouts. Insert a new slide layout named **Family Information**.

l. Remove the footer, date, and page number placeholders from the Family Information slide layout. Add a text placeholder that fills the blank space of the slide.

m. Copy the Family Information slide and paste it on the Slide Thumbnail pane. Rename the slide layout **Family Relationship**.

n. Remove the title and text placeholders on the Family Relationship slide layout. Insert a SmartArt placeholder that fills the blank space of the slide. Select the SmartArt options you desire.

o. Add animations and transitions as desired.

p. Click the **FILE tab** and click **Save As**. Click the **Save as type arrow** and select **PowerPoint Template**. Navigate to where you are saving your files. Name the file **p07m1ReunionTemplate_LastFirst**, and then click **Save**.

q. Click the **Slide Master tab** and click **Close Master View** in the Close group.

r. Create a Title slide, a Family Information slide, and a Family Relationship slide using your own family information and photo or using a clip art family image and an imaginary family.

s. Create a handout header with your name and a handout footer with your instructor's name and your class. Include the current date.

t. Save the file as **p07m1Reunion_LastFirst.pptx**, being careful to save over the presentation file and not the template file. Close the presentation and submit based on your instructor's directions.

2 PTA Fundraising Shows

The PTA at the elementary school has quarterly meetings where discussions focus on plans for fundraising throughout the year. At the beginning of the year, all of the plans are put into a presentation. Two presentations cover the plans for each fundraising project. The slides contain the project description, dates, and committee assignments. One slide details the budget and is hidden during the general member meeting and displayed to the PTA board meeting. You create two custom shows that contain the title slide, the slides pertaining to the most recent project and the next project, the budget slide, and a thank-you slide.

a. Open *p07m2PTA* and save it as **p07m2PTA_LastFirst**.

b. Create a handout header with your name and a handout footer with your instructor's name and your class. Include the current date.

c. Create a custom show named **Fall Projects** using Slides 1 through 6 and 9 through 11.

d. Create a custom show named **Winter Projects** using Slides 1, 2, and 5 through 11.

e. Hide Slide 10.

f. Display the Fall Projects custom show. Show the hidden slide.

g. Display the Winter Projects custom show. Show the hidden slide.

DISCOVER

h. Use the Set Up Slide Show dialog box to display the Winter Projects custom slide show. Also set the Laser pointer color to **green**.

i. Display the entire presentation. Use the Laser pointer to draw attention to details on slides.

j. Save and close the file, and submit based on your instructor's directions.

3 Red Cliff City Agenda

OLLABORATION CASE

As the administrative clerk for the mayor of the city, you are responsible for preparing a PowerPoint agenda presentation for every city council meeting. Because this is a task that encompasses several departments, you rely on other administrative clerks to provide pertinent information. The title slide includes meeting details, and each agenda item is listed on a single slide with the name of the person responsible for the discussion of this item. Another type of slide contains additional resources related to the agenda item, such as text, graphics, or SmartArt. You will create a slide master template so that the structure of the presentation is prepared. You will create the design of the slide master to match the city's colors and include the city logo. Each administrative clerk is responsible for providing information to you. This can be accomplished using Outlook or SkyDrive. After saving the master as a template named **p07m3AgendaTemplate**, all you will have to do prior to the meeting is to put the information in the presentation using the template. Save the file as **p07m3Agenda_LastFirst**. Submit both files based on your instructor's directions.

Nurse Presentation

RESEARCH CASE

FROM SCRATCH

As a nurse practitioner with the Lindenberg Health Department, you spend a few hours each week talking to small groups. One week you might talk to senior citizens, and the next week you may be presenting to the faculty of the elementary school. Popular topics in the winter are colds, flu, bronchitis, and pneumonia. Most groups request information on the symptoms of these illnesses and ways to prevent getting them. After your research, you develop a presentation that contains information that will be useful to all of these groups. Use your knowledge of slide masters to create appropriate layouts. Use illustrations, images, sounds, video, animation, and transitions as appropriate. You realize that elementary school students probably are not interested in bronchitis and pneumonia, so create a custom slide show on colds and flu for this audience. Save your presentation file as **p07b2Nurse_LastFirst.pptx**.

Templates Gone Haywire

DISASTER RECOVERY ➕

Your 14-year-old brother has been working on a presentation for his science class. He tried revising a design template but has become confused. His handouts print with a blue background, he gets blank pages when he tries to view notes pages, and the animation and transitions he applied create a mixed-up jumble of words and graphics flying all over the screen. You sit down with him and help him with the templates. You correct the handout master so that the background is white. You revise the notes page master so the placeholders necessary to display the header, slide image, and body appear, as well as the footer and page number. You make adjustments to the animations and transitions so they enhance the slide show rather than distract the audience. Open *p07b3Corrections*, make the necessary revisions, and then save it as **p07b3Corrections_LastFirst**.

Planning and Managing Your Career

SOFT SKILLS CASE Ⓢ

FROM SCRATCH

You will create a customized presentation that will help other students plan for and manage their careers. Create a slide that lists at least three common strategies for planning and managing careers. Suggest responses for each strategy on a separate slide, and then create a custom show for three different planning scenarios. Save and close the presentation, and submit based on your instructor's directions.

Capstone Exercise

As a volunteer docent at the Bayside Park Conservatory, you learned about plants and their care. You have specialized knowledge of exotic plants and roses. You have studied both in classes at the university. The volunteer supervisor recently observed you as you led a group through the conservatory. She approached you and requested that you speak at various gardening guild meetings throughout the state. In this capstone exercise, you will create a custom presentation demonstrating the skills learned in this chapter.

Set PowerPoint Options and Customize the Ribbon

The computer you are assigned to use while at the conservatory is one you have not used before. The person using it before you had set custom options and made Ribbon changes. You decide to change the PowerPoint Options to fit your needs, reset the Ribbon to its original state, and then customize the Ribbon to meet your needs.

a. Create a new blank presentation and save it as **p07c1Gardening_LastFirst**.

b. Create a slide footer that reads **www.bayparkconservatory .org**. Include a slide number on all slides. Do not include the slide footer and slide number on the Title slide.

c. Create a handout header with your name and a handout footer with the instructor's name and your class. Include the current date.

d. Set PowerPoint General options to include your user name and initials, if necessary.

e. Set PowerPoint Save options to AutoRecover information every 5 minutes, to keep the last autosaved version if you close without saving, and to embed fonts.

f. Reset all customizations on the Ribbon.

g. Add a custom group following the Drawing group in the HOME tab. Name the custom group **Combine Shapes**.

h. Include the following buttons from the *Commands Not in the Ribbon* list in the Combine Shapes group: Combine Shapes, Intersect Shapes, Subtract Shapes, and Union Shapes.

Combine Shapes

To add interest to the title slide, create a custom shape to frame an image of flowers in the garden.

a. Create a Round Same Side Corner Rectangle shape with the following specifications:

- Picture Fill: *p07c1Garden.jpg*.
- Size: Height **1.61"**, Width **8.5"**.
- Position: Horizontal **2.42"** from the Top Left Corner, Vertical **2.33"** from the Top Left Corner.

b. Create a Flowchart: Delay shape using the following specifications:

- Size: Height **5"**, Width **1.42"**.
- Rotation: **270°**.
- Position: Horizontal **5.96"** from the Top Left Corner, Vertical **−0.88"** from the Top Left Corner.

c. Join the rectangle shape and the flowchart shape using Union.

d. Copy the two shapes to the Clipboard.

Modify Masters and Save the Template

You decide that the frame you created belongs on the Title Slide Master. You will cut the frame from the title slide and paste it on the Title Slide Master. Then you will change the Color theme, format the master title style as WordArt, and modify the master subtitle text. Next, you will modify the handout master and the notes master. You will save the presentation as a template for reuse with other presentations.

a. Cut the frame group from the Title slide, switch to Slide Master view, and then paste the frame and flower image on the Title Slide Master.

b. Apply the **Cambria font theme**.

c. Apply the **Blue Warm color theme**. Then modify the theme by creating new theme colors using the following specifications:

Element	Red	Green	Blue
Text/Background - Dark 1	0	24	0
Text/Background - Light 1	242	242	242
Text/Background - Dark 2	0	72	0
Text/Background - Light 2	250	250	250
Accent 1	103	133	153
Accent 6	251	211	181
Hyperlink	150	210	225
Followed Hyperlink	85	5	80

d. Change the text in the title placeholder to **Place title here**.

e. Change the text in the subtitle placeholder to **Place docent name and e-mail address here**.

f. Format the slide background style using Style 5.

g. Select the **Office Theme Slide Master** and insert *p07c1Rose.png*. Align the bottom edge of the rose border with the top border of the page number placeholder.

h. Apply an **Appear animation** to the title placeholder.

i. Delete all slide layouts except for Title Slide Layout and insert two new slide layouts.

j. Select the first slide layout and rename it **Information**.

k. Replace the text in the title placeholder with **Place title here**.

l. Fill the blank portion of the slide layout with a text placeholder.

m. Select the second slide layout and rename it **Photograph**.

n. Replace the text in the title placeholder with **Place plant name here**.

o. Fill the blank portion of the slide layout with a picture placeholder.

p. Delete the bullet from the picture placeholder and replace the word *Picture* with **Place photograph here**.

q. Hide *Background Graphics* on the Title Slide Master and the Photograph Layout.

r. Apply the **Doors transition** to the Title Slide Master.

s. Switch to the Handout Master view and move the footer placeholder immediately below the header placeholder. Move the page number placeholder immediately below the date placeholder.

t. Insert *p07c1Rose.png* and modify it using the following specifications:

- Size: Height **0.71"**, Width **0.83"**.
- Position: Horizontal **3.33"** from the Top Left Corner, Vertical **0.12"** from the Top Left Corner.

u. Switch to Notes Master view and type **Slide** before the number field in the **page number placeholder**.

v. Close the Notes Master view and save the presentation as a template named **p07c1GardeningTemplate_LastFirst**.

w. Add slides to the presentation by reusing all of the slides in *p07c1Flowers.pptx*.

x. Save the presentation as **p07c1Gardening_LastFirst**, saving over the presentation you began at the beginning of this exercise. Be careful not to save over the template you created.

Set Up and Display Custom Shows

You will create two custom slide shows using a single presentation. Both will contain a title slide, information slides, and photograph slides specific to the slide show.

a. Create a custom show named **Rose Presentation** and use Slides 1, 2, 4 through 8, and 14 through 17.

b. Create a custom show named **Tropical Plants Presentation** and use Slides 1, 3, 9 through 11, and 15 through 17.

c. Display the Rose Presentation custom show.

d. Display the Tropical Plants Presentation custom show.

e. Save the presentation and close the file.

Collaboration and Distribution

CHAPTER 8

Collaborating, Preparing, Securing, and Sharing a Presentation

Konstantin Chagin/Shutterstock

OBJECTIVES | AFTER YOU READ THIS CHAPTER, YOU WILL BE ABLE TO:

1. Work with comments and annotations p. 1050

2. Show, hide, and print markup p. 1052

3. Compare and merge presentations p. 1054

4. View presentation properties p. 1055

5. Check a presentation for issues p. 1063

6. Protect a presentation p. 1066

7. Select a presentation file type p. 1076

8. Save and share a presentation p. 1082

CASE STUDY | The Harbor Business Center

ACSL Development is a large, internationally owned commercial real estate development company specializing in developing properties to serve as business hubs with access to cutting-edge technology. The centers are designed to meet the demands of leading global companies. You are an intern working for the vice president of marketing, Susil Akalushi. Susil has asked you to prepare a presentation under her supervision. The presentation must describe ACSL's latest project, the Harbor Business Center, a $58.5 million, mixed-use project offering luxurious new office space that includes multiperson office suites and one-, two-, or four-person offices. Office suites are finished to a high standard with imported tile, stylish décor, and a sense of spaciousness and comfort. They include state-of-the-art communication technology. Monthly leases offer fully customizable office space, 24-hour access to the office 365 days a year, high security, access to state-of-the-art meeting facilities, and on-site banking and global messenger services. The project is centrally located two blocks from the city harbor area and one block from the state and federal courthouses.

After completing the presentation, you send it to Susil for her review. She reviews your presentation and sends it back to you with comments regarding the changes you need to make. You make the requested changes and prepare the presentation for sharing with other company employees by protecting the presentation and checking it for issues. You package the presentation so that it can be burned to a CD.

Presentation Collaboration

Collaboration is a process by which two or more individuals work together to achieve an outcome or goal. Many times, a presentation results from the collaborative efforts of a team of people. Collaborating with others in a presentation sparks the creativity and problem-solving skills of all group members, which makes the final project a better project than one in which one individual has sole responsibility. Today's technology enables you to collaborate easily with others, and Office 2013 applications include features to facilitate this process.

In this section, you will learn how to add comments, edit comments, print comments, and delete comments. You will learn how to add annotations while displaying a presentation and how to save the annotations. You will merge and compare presentations and review and manage the changes made by others. You will also view presentation properties.

Working with Comments and Annotations

After you have created your PowerPoint presentation, you may want to route it to others for review. After receiving your presentation, the *reviewer* examines the presentation and can add *comments* (text notes attached to the slide) or *annotations* (markings written or drawn on a slide for additional commentary or explanation while displaying a slide show presentation) or make additional changes. A presentation or document with comments and annotations contains *markup*. When the reviewer returns the presentation to you, you determine the changes you wish to make based on the markup in the presentation.

Add Comments

Think of comments as onscreen sticky notes that you can insert and remove as needed. You can insert comments to remind yourself of revisions you want to make or as reminders of where you are as you develop the project. If you distribute the presentation to others for review, they can add comments with suggestions. Start by clicking the Review tab and clicking New Comment in the Comments group. The Comments pane opens, and you insert a comment on the slide by typing it in a comment box. The name of the person inserting the comment is included along with the date and the reviewer's account icon. If nothing is selected, the comment icon is positioned at the top left of the slide but may be dragged to any location on the slide. If you select text or an object, or position the insertion point within text before you insert the comment, the comment icon appears next to the text or object. The Comments pane lists comments in the order they are added to the slide. To move from one comment to another, use the Previous and Next buttons in the Comments pane. You can add a new comment by clicking the New button.

 TIP **Delete All Comments**

To delete all of the comments on the current slide, click the Delete arrow in the Comments group and click *Delete All Comments and Ink on This Slide*. To delete all of the comments in the presentation, click the Delete arrow and then *Delete All Comments and Ink in This Presentation*.

STEP 1 ≫

As you review comments, you can choose to incorporate any suggestions you agree with or to ignore any you do not wish to incorporate. Usually, you would delete a comment after your decision. This helps you determine where you are in the review process. If you are part of a work group, you may choose to leave the comments for others to see, and you may choose to reply to existing comments. To insert a comment, do the following:

1. Click the REVIEW tab.
2. Click New Comment in the Comments group. The Comments pane opens.
3. Type the comment in the comment box.
4. Click outside the box to close it.

To reply to a comment, do the following:

1. Click the comment that you want to reply to.
2. Click in the Reply text box and type your reply.
3. Press Tab when you are finished.

When you open a presentation that has new comments, a pop-up displays to alert you to the comments. To view a comment, click the comment icon on the slide or Comments on the status bar at the bottom of the screen to show the Comments pane. Comments do not display during Slide Show mode. If you want to edit an existing comment, click the comment to select it. If more than one comment is located on the slide, the fill of the selected comment icon changes color to indicate it is the active comment. Otherwise, the comment icon is simply outlined. Then click inside the comment text box in the Comments pane and edit the comment. Delete a comment by clicking Delete in the comment box or by selecting it and clicking Delete in the Comments group on the Review tab. Figure 8.1 shows the Comments pane and a slide with an open comment.

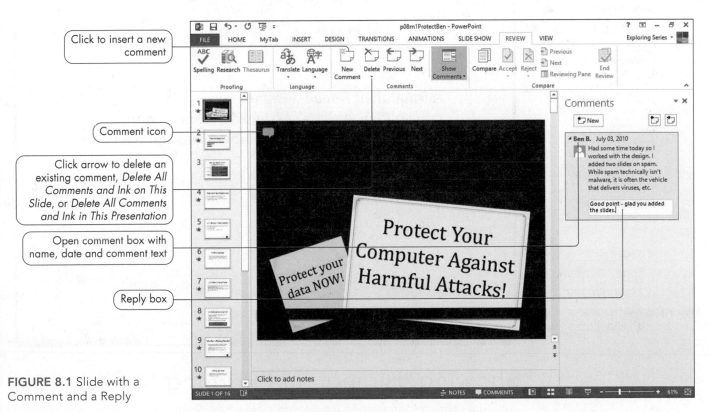

FIGURE 8.1 Slide with a Comment and a Reply

Insert Annotations

Annotations are written or drawn on a slide for additional commentary or explanation while a slide show is displayed, similar to the way a sports commentator may draw a play during the broadcast of a football game. To add an annotation while playing a slide show, right-click a slide, select Pointer Options, and then select Pen or Highlighter. Pen creates a thin line, and Highlighter creates a thick line. Drag the mouse (or your finger or stylus on a touch screen) to draw or write on the slide. To turn off the pen or highlighter, right-click, select Pointer Options, select Arrow Options, and then select Automatic. When you exit the slide show, you will be prompted to keep or discard the ink annotations.

> ### TIP Use a Mouse as a Laser Pointer
>
> You can use your mouse as a laser pointer while displaying a presentation. This calls your audience's attention to the portion of the slide you want to emphasize without creating ink markup (annotations). To use a laser pointer, start the presentation in either Slide Show view or Reading view, press and hold Ctrl, hold down the left mouse button, and then drag the mouse to make the laser pointer appear on the slide. When you release the left mouse button, the laser pointer disappears. You can also right-click the mouse, point to Pointer Options, and then click Laser Pointer. To remove the laser pointer, return to Pointer Options and click Laser Pointer again.

Figure 8.2 shows a slide displaying in Slide Show view with the Pointer Options open and displaying annotations made with the pen and highlighter.

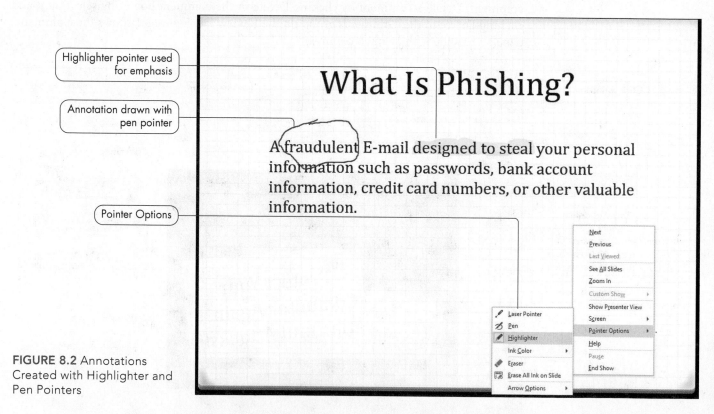

FIGURE 8.2 Annotations Created with Highlighter and Pen Pointers

Showing, Hiding, and Printing Markup

STEP 2 ❯❯ A comment or saved annotation is only visible if you have Show Markup active. Show Markup is in the Show Comments arrow in the Comments group of the Review tab. Show Markup is a toggle that displays or hides inserted comments and saved annotations. Figure 8.3 displays the active Show Markup command. The slide is displayed in Normal view. The annotations still display because they were kept when the slide show ended.

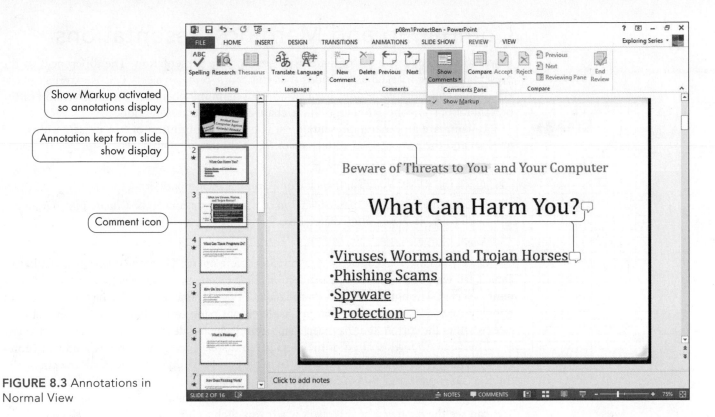

FIGURE 8.3 *Annotations in Normal View*

Because it is sometimes easier to review comments and annotations in print format, you may choose to print the comments and annotations that have been stored on your slides. When you choose to print comments and annotations (markup), the comments print on a separate page from the slides that display the annotations. To print comments and ink markup, click the File tab and click Print. Select Full Page Slides (or whatever layout is desired) and if your slide show contains comments or annotations, the *Print Comments and Ink Markup* option is active. This option is grayed out if the presentation does not contain comments or annotations. Figure 8.4 displays the *Print Comments and Ink Markup* option.

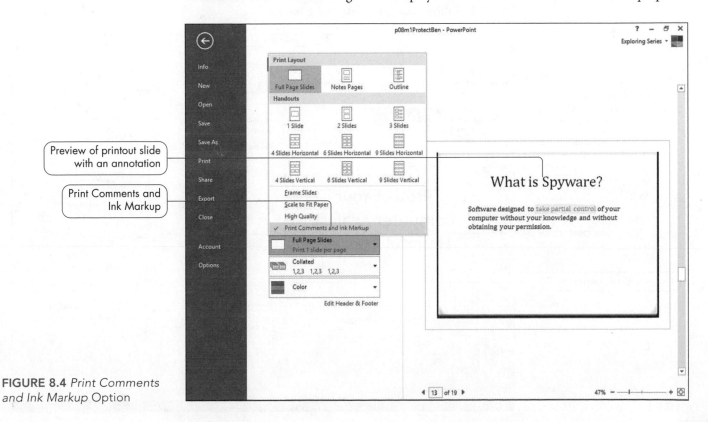

FIGURE 8.4 *Print Comments and Ink Markup Option*

Comparing and Merging Presentations

PowerPoint enables you to compare two versions of a presentation. The differences in the presentations are marked as revisions that you can accept or reject. This is extremely beneficial in a collaborative project because after all team members submit their version of the presentation, someone can merge all the changes into one presentation.

STEP 3 » To compare and merge presentations, you need a minimum of two presentations: the original and the presentation with changes. Then do the following:

1. Open the original presentation.
2. Click the REVIEW tab and click Compare in the Compare group.
3. Locate and select the changed version of the presentation in the *Choose File to Merge with Current Presentation* dialog box.
4. Click Merge.

Once you have clicked Merge, the Revisions pane opens. The pane opens, by default, to a Details tab with two sections. The top section, *Slide Changes*, lists the changes to the slide currently selected. The bottom section, *Presentation Changes*, lists any slides that have been added or removed from the original presentation. The Revisions pane also includes a Slides tab that indicates whether the current slide has been changed and which slide contains the next set of changes.

The *Slide Changes* section of the Details tab displays icons and abbreviated text representing changes to objects on the slide. To accept an individual change, click the change in the Revisions pane and click Accept in the Compare group. You can also click the icon representing the object on the slide and select a check box in the Revisions checklist that opens. You can see the change that will result when you click a check box. To accept all changes on the current slide, click the Accept arrow in the Compare group on the Review tab and click *Accept All Changes to This Slide* or *Accept All Changes to the Presentation*.

If you accept a change and then decide you no longer want the change, click Reject in the Compare group. Any changes that you do not accept are discarded when you complete the review. To complete the review, click End Review in the Compare group. Figure 8.5 shows the Revisions pane with the Details tab selected. The *Slide Changes* section shows changes for slide properties on the current slide. The *Presentation Changes* section shows two changes in the presentation. All changes made in the slide are displayed in the Revisions check box on the slide. In this case, two slides were inserted.

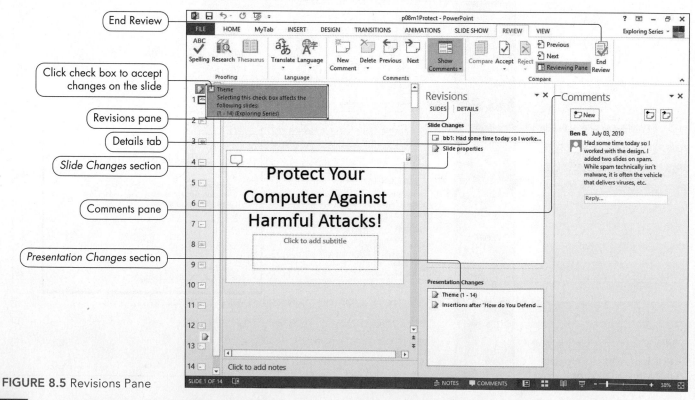

FIGURE 8.5 Revisions Pane

Viewing Presentation Properties

STEP 4 » To view the original author(s) of a presentation and its creation date, or to see who last modified the presentation and when the modification took place, view the presentation properties. The presentation properties (*document properties* or *metadata*) are the attributes about a presentation that describe it or identify it. In addition to the author and modifier properties, you can view many details such as the title, file size, keywords, and statistics. Some of the properties are created and updated automatically, and some are created by the user. The presentation properties help you organize and search for your presentations.

To view presentation properties, click the File tab to display the Backstage Info view. The panel on the right side of the screen displays some properties. Click Show All Properties at the bottom of the panel to see all properties. You can change document properties not automatically set by PowerPoint by clicking the property box and typing the change. Figure 8.6 displays the properties for a presentation on protecting your computer.

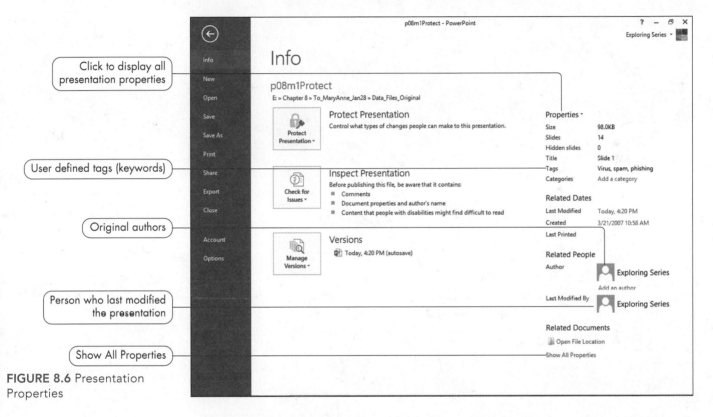

FIGURE 8.6 Presentation Properties

To set multiple document properties, click the Properties arrow in the right pane and click Show Document Panel. The Document Properties panel appears above the selected slide in Normal view. The Author and Title properties are entered automatically but can be changed. The words you type in the Keywords property box display as tags when you display the Properties panel in the Info view in the Backstage view. Figure 8.7 displays the Document Properties panel for a presentation on protecting your computer.

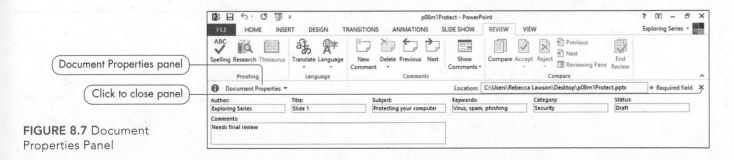

FIGURE 8.7 Document Properties Panel

Quick Concept ✓

1. Explain how comments can be edited or deleted. *p. 1051*
2. How can you print comments and ink markup? *p. 1053*
3. Why is it beneficial to be able to compare two versions of a presentation? *p. 1054*

Hands-On Exercises

Watch the Video for this Hands-On Exercise!

MyITLab®
HOE1 Training

1 Presentation Collaboration

You review the Harbor Business Center presentation and add comments and annotations. You print a copy of the presentation, comments, and ink markup for your records. When the presentation is returned to you by the reviewer, you compare and merge the presentations. Finally, you view and edit the presentation properties.

Skills covered: Insert Annotations and a Comment • Show, Hide, and Print Markup • Compare and Merge Presentations • View and Change Presentation Properties

STEP 1 >> INSERT ANNOTATIONS AND A COMMENT

You have completed the Harbor Business Center presentation, and you are ready to send it to Susil for her review. Before sending it to her, you review the presentation in Slide Show view. You have a question about the data as you watch the presentation, so you add annotations to mark the location that raised your question. Then you ask the questions as comments in the presentation. Refer to Figure 8.8 as you complete Step 1.

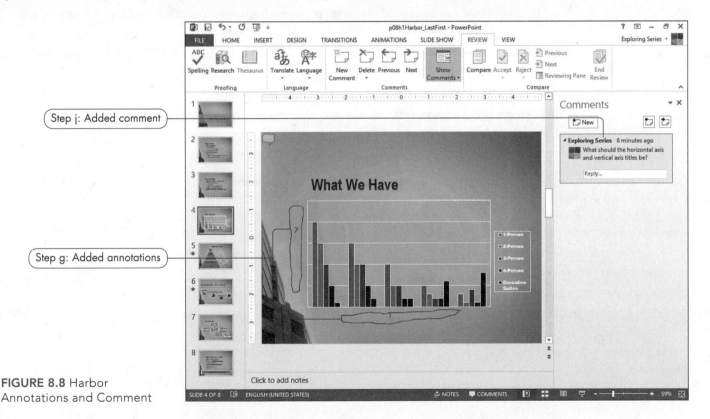

FIGURE 8.8 Harbor Annotations and Comment

a. Open the *p08h1Harbor* presentation and save it as **p08h1Harbor_LastFirst**.

The Harbor Business Center presentation opens. It has formatting problems that will be addressed in a later step.

> **TROUBLESHOOTING:** If you make any major mistakes in this exercise, you can close the file, open *p08h1Harbor* again, and then start this exercise over.

b. Create a handout header with your name and a handout footer with your instructor's name and your class. Include the current date.

c. Click the **FILE tab**, click **Options**, and then type your name in the **User name box** if necessary. Type your initials in the **Initials box** if necessary and click **OK**.

Figures in this chapter display the initials *ES* for "Exploring Series," and it is also used as the name.

> **TROUBLESHOOTING:** If your school lab has a software program installed to protect software and hardware settings from being changed, you will need to reset your user name and initials each time you log in.

d. Click the **SLIDE SHOW tab** and click **From Beginning** in the Start Slide Show group.

e. Click three times to advance to the fourth slide, titled *What We Have*. Note that no vertical or horizontal axis titles exist to describe what the columns in the chart represent.

> **TROUBLESHOOTING:** If you advance too far and display the next slide, right-click, and select See All Slides in the shortcut menu. Then select 4 *What We Have*.

f. Right-click the slide, point to *Pointer Options*, and then select **Pen**.

g. Draw a circle around the location where a horizontal axis title would typically appear and draw a question mark within the circle.

h. Draw a circle around the location where a vertical axis title would typically appear and draw a question mark within the circle.

i. Press **Esc** and click **Keep** to save the ink annotations.

j. Click the **REVIEW tab** and click **New Comment** in the Comments group.

A comment icon appears in the top-left corner of Slide 4. A new comment box opens with your name in the Comments pane,

k. Type **What should the horizontal axis and vertical axis titles be?** in the **comment box**.

l. Save the presentation.

STEP 2 ≫ SHOW, HIDE, AND PRINT MARKUP

You view the slide with the markup showing, and then you hide the markup. You also preview the comment and the annotations printouts in Print Preview. Refer to Figure 8.9 as you complete Step 2.

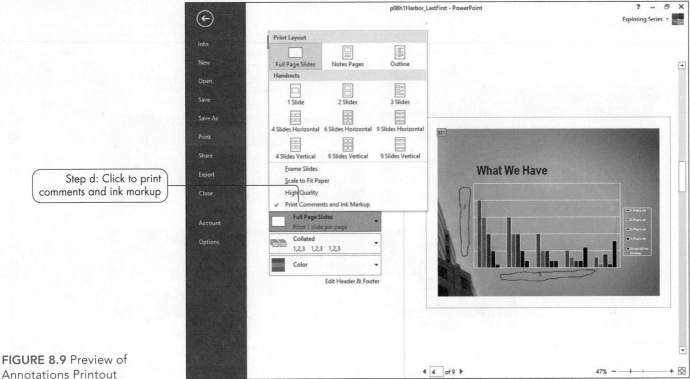

Step d: Click to print comments and ink markup

FIGURE 8.9 Preview of Annotations Printout

a. Click the **REVIEW tab** if necessary and click the **Show Comments arrow** in the Comments group. Click **Show Markup** to deselect it.

Clicking Show Markup toggles the feature off so the comment and the annotations no longer display.

b. Click **Show Comments** in the Comments group and click **Show Markup** so that it is now checked.

The comment and the annotations display again.

c. Click the **FILE tab** and click **Print**.

d. Click the **Full Page Slides arrow** and note that *Print Comments and Ink Markup* is checked. Click outside the dialog box to close it.

The annotations on Slide 4 display and will print if Slide 4 is printed. In the top-left corner of the slide, the initials of the person who made the comment is displayed.

> **TROUBLESHOOTING:** If *Print Comments and Ink Markup* is not selected, click the check box.

e. Click **Next Page** in the navigation control at the bottom center of the Backstage Print view to advance to page 581.

Page 581 displays the comment on Slide 4.

f. Save the presentation.

Susil has returned her version of the Harbor Business Center presentation. You merge her presentation with your original, and then accept and reject changes. You remove all remaining comments, and then save the merged version of the presentation. Refer to Figure 8.10 as you complete Step 3. Although you will not access this particular view, it is used here to illustrate the final presentation.

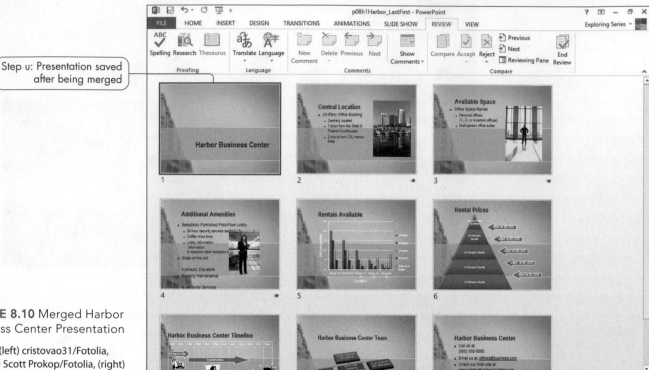

Step u: Presentation saved after being merged

FIGURE 8.10 Merged Harbor Business Center Presentation

Photos: (left) cristovao31/Fotolia, (middle) Scott Prokop/Fotolia, (right) bst2012/Fotolia

a. Click the **REVIEW tab** and click **Compare** in the Compare group.

The *Choose File to Merge with Current Presentation* dialog box opens.

b. Navigate to your student data files, select *p08h1HarborAkalushi*, and then click **Merge**.

The Revisions pane opens with the Details tab active. The first slide of the presentation displays in Normal view. The *Slide Changes* section displays one item, a comment from Susil. The *Presentation Changes* section shows two changes to the presentation: a theme change on Slides 1 through 8 and insertions after "Harbor Business Center." The Comments pane also opens. One comment from Susil exists.

c. Click the icon in the *Slide Changes* section, if necessary, and read the comment on the slide.

The comment box is open, and Susil's comment displays.

d. Click **Theme (1–8)** in the *Presentation Changes* section.

The Revisions box attached to the thumbnail of Slide 1 in the Slides tab opens and indicates the theme change made by Susil, which impacts Slides 1 through 8.

e. Click **Accept** in the Compare group.

A checked icon appears next to the Theme (1–8) item in the *Presentation Changes* section, indicating the change was accepted. A check mark also appears above the Slide 1 thumbnail in the Slides tab.

f. Select **Insertions after "Harbor Business Center"** in the *Presentation Changes* section.

A Revisions box displays between Slide 1 and Slide 2 that reads *Inserted "Central Location" (Susil Akalushi)*.

g. Click the **Inserted "Central Location" (Susil Akalushi) check box** above Slide 2 in the Slides pane.

A new Slide 2 is added to the presentation using the slide Susil created. A check mark also appears on the slide thumbnail in the Slides tab indicating a change was made. A check appears next to the Slide 2: Central Location item in the *Presentation Changes* section indicating the change was accepted.

h. Click the **Accept arrow** in the Compare group and select **Accept All Changes to the Presentation**.

All changes to the presentation by Susil are made.

i. Click the **SLIDE SHOW tab** and click **From Beginning** in the Start Slide Show group. Advance through the slides in the presentation. Press **Esc**.

j. Click **Slide 8** and click the **SLIDES tab** in the Revisions pane.

A thumbnail of Slide 8 displays in the Revisions pane.

k. Click the **Slide 8 thumbnail check box** in the Revisions pane to deselect it. Note that the organization chart is a SmartArt style that displays in 3D format.

l. Click the **Slide 8 thumbnail check box** again. Click the **REVIEW tab** and click the **Reject arrow** in the Compare group. Select **Reject All Changes to This Slide**.

All changes to Slide 8 are rejected.

m. Click the **DETAILS tab** in the Revisions pane and select **Rectangle 2: Who We Are**. Click **All changes to Rectangle 2**. Click the **Reject arrow** in the Compare group. Click **Reject All Changes to This Slide**.

The title changes from *Harbor Business Center Team* to *Who We Are* because you rejected Susil's changes.

n. On Slide 1, select the comment in the *Slide Changes* section of the DETAILS tab in the Revisions pane. Click **Delete** in the Comments group.

o. Click **Next** in the Comments group.

The *Slide Changes* section of the Details tab displays the two comments and three changes in Slide 5.

p. Read a comment and click **Next** in the Comments group. Read the next comment and click **Next** again in the Comments group.

The presentation advances to Slide 9.

q. Read the comment on Slide 9 regarding animating the content placeholders on Slides 2 through 4.

r. On Slide 2, select the **content placeholder**, click the **ANIMATIONS tab**, and then click **More** in the Animation group. Click **Wipe** in the Entrance category. Click **Effect Options** in the Animation group and click **From Left**. Click the **Start arrow** in the Timing group and select **After Previous**.

s. Deselect the **content placeholder** and select it again to enable the Animation Painter feature. Double-click **Animation Painter** in the Advanced Animation group and copy the content placeholder animation to the content placeholders on Slides 3 and 4. Deselect the **Animation Painter**.

t. Click the **REVIEW tab**, click the **Delete arrow** in the Comments group, and then click **Delete All Comments and Ink in This Presentation**. Click **Yes** and close the Revisions and Comments panes.

u. Save the presentation. If you get a message about ending the review, click **Save** again.

STEP 4 ≫ VIEW AND CHANGE PRESENTATION PROPERTIES

To help you organize your presentation files and to help you and Susil locate the file through the Windows Search feature, you create document properties. Refer to Figure 8.11 as you complete Step 4.

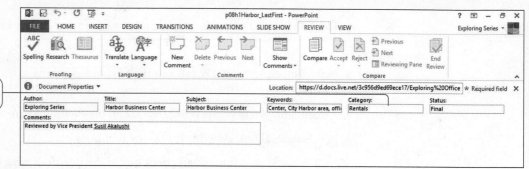

Step f: Properties added to Document Properties Panel

FIGURE 8.11 Document Properties Panel

a. Click the **FILE tab** and note the properties that are displayed on the right side of the Backstage Info view.

b. Click **Add a tag** next to the Tags property and type **Center**.

Center becomes a keyword that you can use to search for the presentation.

c. Click **Show All Properties** at the bottom of the Properties pane and note the additional properties that display.

d. Click **Properties** at the top of the Properties pane and click **Show Document Panel**.

The Document Properties Panel displays below the Ribbon and includes the following properties: Author, Title, and Keywords (Center).

e. Click in the **Subject box** and type **Harbor Business Center**.

f. Add the properties shown in the following table:

Type of Property	Property Information
Keywords	City Harbor area, office suites, space available
Category	Rentals
Status	Final
Comments	Reviewed by Vice President Susil Akalushi

> **TROUBLESHOOTING:** Be sure to keep the keyword *Center* from the merged presentation.

g. Click **Close the Document Information Panel** in the top-right corner of the panel.

h. Save the presentation. Keep the presentation open if you plan to continue with Hands-On Exercise 2. If not, close the presentation and exit PowerPoint.

Preparation for Sharing and Presentation Security

Once you complete a slide show, you can present it or distribute it to others to view. If you want to distribute the presentation to others, take advantage of PowerPoint's tools for preparing and securing a presentation for distribution. In addition to the ability to add and remove document properties that was covered in the previous section, these two collections of tools enable you to do the following:

- Check the content of the presentation for accessibility issues.
- Run a compatibility check to identify features that viewers using previous versions are not able to see.
- Mark the presentation as final and make it read only.
- Add a password.
- Allow people viewing rights but restrict their rights to edit, copy, and print.
- Attach a digital signature.

To access these features, click the File tab to display the Backstage Info view as shown in Figure 8.12.

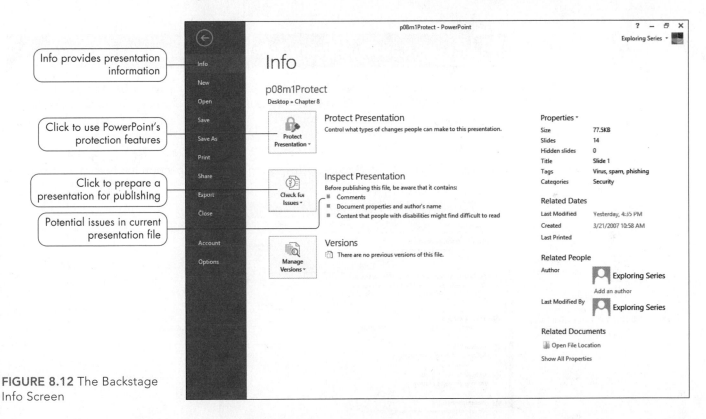

FIGURE 8.12 The Backstage Info Screen

In this section, you will learn how to inspect a presentation for issues before sharing and to secure a presentation for distribution.

Checking a Presentation for Issues

While adding details to the presentation properties helps you organize and locate your presentations, you may not wish other people to have access to that data. Your presentation may also contain content that someone with disabilities cannot view or someone using an earlier version of PowerPoint cannot view. The *Check for Issues* commands enable you to uncover issues that may cause difficulties for viewers.

Access Document Inspector

To check for hidden and personal data in the presentation or in its properties, use the *Document Inspector*. You can search the following content areas:

- Comments and Annotations
- Document Properties and Personal Information
- Custom XML Data
- Invisible On-Slide Content
- Off-Slide Content
- Presentation Notes

STEP 1 ≫

To use the Document Inspector, do the following:

1. Click the FILE tab to display the Backstage Info view.
2. Click Check for Issues.
3. Select Inspect Document.
4. Click the check box next to the content that you wish to inspect.
5. Click Inspect.
6. Review the results in the Document Inspector dialog box.
7. Click Remove All next to the types of content you want to remove from your presentation and click Close.

TIP Be Cautious Using Document Inspector

If you remove hidden content from your presentation, you may not be able to restore it with the Undo command. To be safe, make a copy of your presentation and use the copy when using the Document Inspector.

Figure 8.13 shows the Document Inspector after an inspection has been performed.

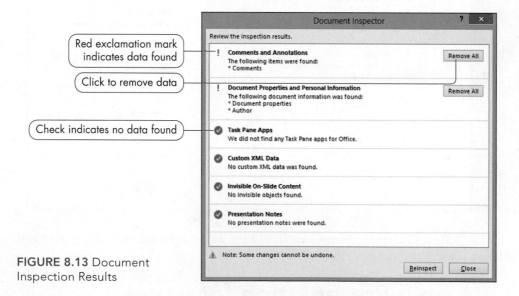

FIGURE 8.13 Document Inspection Results

Check Accessibility

Because you want your presentation to be accessible for users with varying challenges when you distribute it, you should use the Accessibility Checker before sharing it. The *Accessibility Checker* helps you identify and resolve problems with accessibility issues in your presentation. *Accessibility* in PowerPoint refers to the ease with which a person with physical challenges is able to access and understand a presentation. To fix some of the issues the Accessibility Checker identifies, you may have to change, reformat, or update your content.

The Accessibility Checker locates accessibility issues and assigns them to one of three categories:

- *Error*: Issues where content is unreadable. For example, no **alternative text (alt text)** means a text-based description of an image is not available.

- *Warning*: Issues where content is difficult to read. For example, a table is difficult to read because of complex formatting.

- *Tip*: Issues that may or may not make content difficult to read. For example, the order in which text should be read is unclear due to the order of objects on a slide.

To use the Accessibility Checker, do the following:

1. Click the FILE tab to access the Backstage Info view.
2. Click Check for Issues.
3. Select Check Accessibility.
4. Review and fix the issues in the Accessibility Checker pane that opens on the right side of the Normal view.

The Accessibility Checker pane enables you to find and fix the issues in the presentation. It is divided into two sections. The top section lists the inspection results and is divided into Errors, Warnings, and Tips. The bottom section describes why an issue should be fixed and provides a link to more information about making documents accessible. Figure 8.14 shows the Accessibility Checker pane with two errors displayed in the *Inspection Results* section along with a Warning and a Tip.

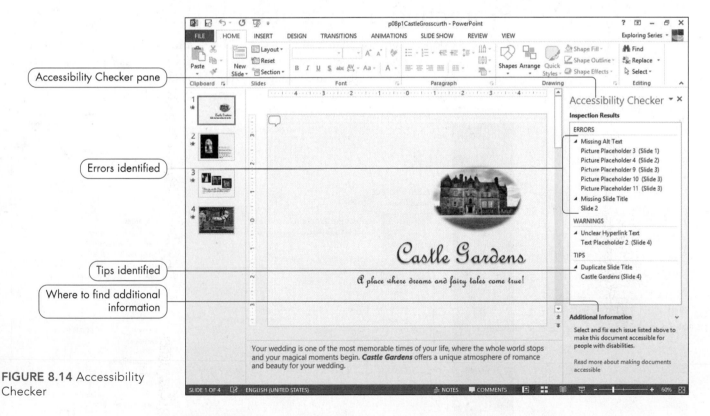

FIGURE 8.14 Accessibility Checker

Check Compatibility

Whenever you share your presentation with others, you need to consider what software they are using. If they are using an earlier version of PowerPoint, they may not be able to see or use some of the features available in PowerPoint 2013. You can check your presentation for features not supported by earlier versions of PowerPoint by activating the **Compatibility Checker**.

The Microsoft PowerPoint Compatibility Checker dialog box appears and warns you about features you used in your presentation that may be lost or degraded when you save the presentation to an earlier format for distribution.

STEP 2 »

To use the Compatibility Checker, do the following:

1. Click the FILE tab to access the Backstage Info view.
2. Click Check for Issues.
3. Select Check Compatibility.
4. Read any messages that are generated and see what action to take.

Figure 8.15 displays the Microsoft PowerPoint Compatibility Checker dialog box with a warning about the compatibility of a SmartArt diagram with PowerPoint 97–2003 applications.

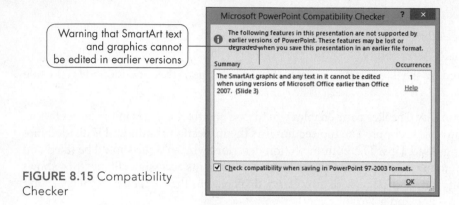

Warning that SmartArt text and graphics cannot be edited in earlier versions

FIGURE 8.15 Compatibility Checker

Protecting a Presentation

Anyone can open, copy, or change any part of a presentation unless you protect its integrity by using PowerPoint's Protect Presentation features. You can make a presentation read only; require a password; restrict the editing, copying, or printing; or add a digital signature. Figure 8.16 displays the Protect Presentation features available in PowerPoint.

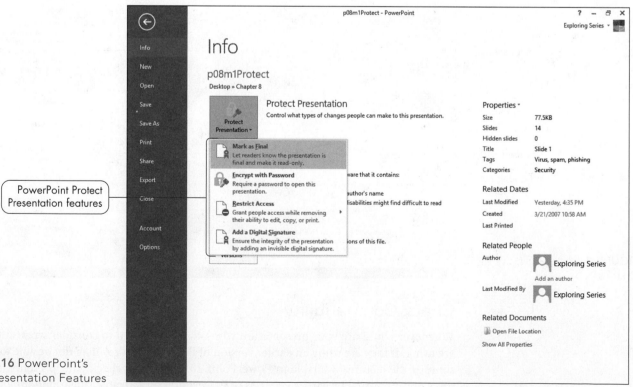

PowerPoint Protect Presentation features

FIGURE 8.16 PowerPoint's Protect Presentation Features

Mark as Final

After you prepare your presentation for distribution, you can mark it as a final version. This feature deactivates most PowerPoint tools and converts the presentation to read-only format. Doing this allows viewers to watch your presentation but not to edit it unless they turn off the *Mark as Final* feature—which is easy to remove if changes are needed. A *Mark as Final* designation lets your viewers know they are viewing a finished presentation.

STEP 4 » To mark a presentation as final, do the following:

1. Click the FILE tab to access the Backstage Info view.
2. Click Protect Presentation.
3. Select *Mark as Final*.
4. Click OK in the warning message box that appears stating *This presentation will be marked as final and then saved*.
5. Click OK in the PowerPoint information message box (see Figure 8.17).

FIGURE 8.17 *Mark as Final* Information Box

A *Marked as Final* message bar appears below the Ribbon and a *Marked as Final* icon displays on the status bar. If you wish to make changes, however, you can click Edit Anyway on the warning bar. You can also turn off final status by clicking the File tab, clicking Protect Presentation, and then clicking *Mark as Final*. Figure 8.18 shows a presentation marked as final.

FIGURE 8.18 Presentation Marked as Final

Protect with a Password

Use *encryption* to protect the privacy of your presentation by converting the presentation into unreadable scrambled text that needs a password to be opened. Set a password on your presentation to prevent other people from opening or changing your presentation. Once you set a password, you can change it or remove it only if you know the original password.

STEP 3 » To encrypt a presentation with a password, do the following:

1. Click the FILE tab to access the Backstage Info view.
2. Click Protect Presentation.
3. Select *Encrypt with Password*.
4. Type a password in the Encrypt Document dialog box.
5. Reenter the password in the Confirm Password dialog box and click OK.

You are prompted to reenter the password as a security measure to ensure you enter the password with no typographical errors. This is critical because if you type the password incorrectly or forget the password, you will not be able to open your presentation or change the password. Also be careful about what you type in capital letters and what you type low-ercase. Passwords are intentionally case sensitive. Avoid creating passwords using dictionary words, words spelled backwards, common misspellings, and abbreviations. Do not use sequences or repeated characters such as 123456, 33333, or abcdef. Never use personal information such as your name, birthday, or driver's license number. See the reference table for Microsoft's recommendations for creating a strong password for online safety. These guidelines can help you set a pattern for all passwords you use.

REFERENCE Password Tips

Tip	Background	Example
Think of a sentence or two about something meaningful to you. Use about 10 words.	Creating a sentence about something meaningful will help you remember the password.	King is an English Bulldog. He is my best friend. *10 words*
Turn your sentence into a row of letters.	Using the first letter of each word will help you remember the password.	kiaebhimbf *10 characters*
Add complexity.	Make some of the letters uppercase. For example, make only the letters in the first half or last half of the alphabet uppercase.	kiaebhiMbf *10 characters*
Add length with numbers.	Put two numbers that are meaningful to you between sentences.	kiaeb18hiMbf *12 characters*
Add length with punctuation.	Put a punctuation mark at the beginning of the password	!kiaeb18hiMbf *13 characters*
Add length with symbols.	Put a symbol at the end of the password.	!kiaeb18hiMbf& *14 characters*

Source: www.microsoft.com/security/online-privacy/passwords-create.aspx

Another method you can use to set a password for your presentation is to click the File tab, select Save As, select Browse, select Tools, and then select General Options. If you use this method to encrypt your document, you have more options. You can set one password to open the presentation and a different password to modify the presentation. You can also remove automatically generated personal information when you save. This does not, however, remove properties you have added. After setting it, a password takes effect the next time you open the presentation. When you attempt to open the presentation, the Password dialog box opens. Enter the password and click OK to open the presentation.

Restrict Access

Office 2013 uses an *information rights management (IRM)* feature to help businesses restrict the access of others to sensitive information such as financial records and employee data. In PowerPoint, IRM restricts presentations, templates, shows, and themes from being forwarded, edited, printed, or copied without authorization. It can also set an expiration date for a presentation so that it can no longer be viewed after a selected date. Using the IRM feature enables you to allow unrestricted access to your presentation or to specify the restrictions you want enabled, such as the permissions an individual user must possess to view the presentation.

IRM uses a server to authenticate the credentials of people who create or receive presentations with restricted permissions. Microsoft provides free access to the IRM service for users with a Microsoft account. To access the Restrict Permission feature, click the File tab, click Protect Presentation, point to Restrict Access, and then click *Connect Rights Management Servers and get templates*. The default is Unrestricted Access, but if you select either Restricted Access or Manage Credentials, a Service Sign-Up dialog box appears giving you information about IRM with a hyperlink you can click to learn more about information rights management. You can also click *Yes, I want to sign up for this free service from Microsoft* or *No, I do not want to use this service from Microsoft*.

TIP | To Obtain a Microsoft Account

Create your credentials for a Microsoft account, and you will have access to many more services than just IRM. Your Microsoft account, formerly referred to as a Windows Live ID, enables you to log in to such sites and services as SkyDrive, MSN Messenger, MSN Hotmail, MSN Music, and other sites. To sign up for a Microsoft account, visit https://signup.live.com/signup.aspx.

Add a Digital Signature

A *digital signature* is an invisible, electronic signature stamp that is encrypted and attached to a certificate. The certificate is attached to the presentation. This is similar to signing a paper document. If you want those with whom you share your presentation to be able to verify the authenticity of your digital signature, you can obtain a digital ID from a Microsoft partner. You can also create your own digital ID; however, it will only enable you to verify that a presentation has not been changed on the computer on which you have saved the presentation.

To create your own digital signature, do the following:

1. Click the FILE tab to access the Backstage Info view.
2. Click Protect Presentation.
3. Select *Add a Digital Signature*, read the Microsoft PowerPoint Information dialog box, and then click Yes.
4. Choose among the Available Digital ID providers found on the Microsoft Office Web site. Each will have a different method to get the digital ID, so follow the onscreen steps to complete the process.

Adding a digital signature should be the last step you perform when preparing the document because, if you make any changes after the signature is added, your signature is invalidated.

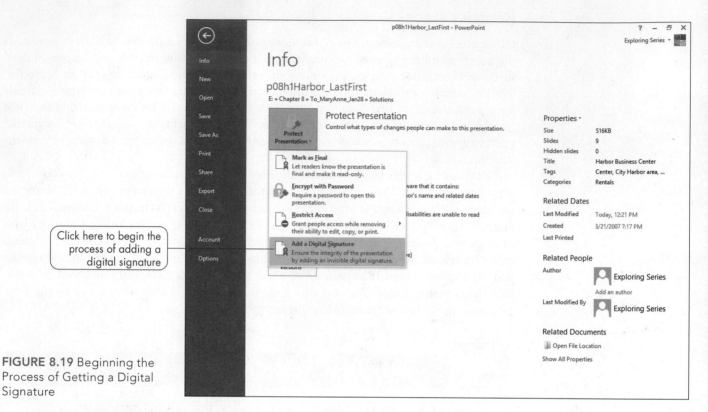

Click here to begin the process of adding a digital signature

FIGURE 8.19 Beginning the Process of Getting a Digital Signature

Quick
Concept ✓

1. Which areas of content can be searched using the Document Inspector? *p. 1064*

2. Explain why you should use the Accessibility Checker. *p. 1064*

3. What does the Compatibility Checker do? *p. 1065*

4. Describe two methods that can be used to set a password for your presentation. *p. 1068*

Hands-On Exercises

2 Preparation for Sharing and Presentation Security

Now that you have incorporated Susil Akalushi's changes in the Harbor Business Center presentation, you prepare the presentation for sharing with other company employees. You check the presentation for issues and protect the presentation.

Skills covered: Inspect the Presentation • Check for Compatibility • Set and Remove a Password • Mark as Final

STEP 1 ≫ INSPECT THE PRESENTATION

Before you send the presentation out to other ACSL Development employees, you use the Document Inspector to check the document for information that you may not want others to view. Refer to Figure 8.20 as you complete Step 1.

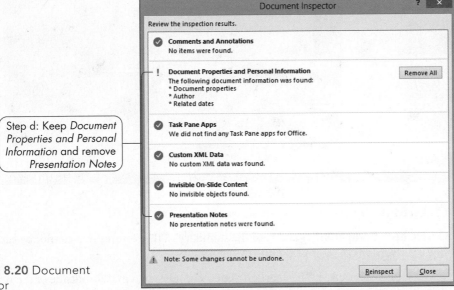

FIGURE 8.20 Document Inspector

a. Open *p08h1Harbor_LastFirst*, if necessary and save the presentation as **p08h2Harbor_LastFirst**, changing **h1** to **h2**.

b. Click the **FILE tab**, click **Check for Issues**, and then select **Inspect Document**.

The Document Inspector dialog box opens and displays a list of items the inspector will search for.

c. Click **Inspect**.

No comments or annotations were found because you removed them in Hands-On Exercise 1. Document properties and personal information were found, as well as presentation notes.

d. Keep the Document Properties and Personal Information and click **Remove All** in the *Presentation Notes* section.

Because *p08h2Harbor_LastFirst* is a duplicate of *p08h1Harbor_LastFirst*, it is a convenient method to create a copy for distribution that has changes from the original document.

e. Click **Close**.

f. Save the presentation.

Some of the ACSL Development employees still use Office 2003 because the company has not updated software in all departments to the latest version of Office. You check the Harbor Business Center presentation's compatibility with the earlier versions of Office. Refer to Figure 8.21 as you complete Step 2.

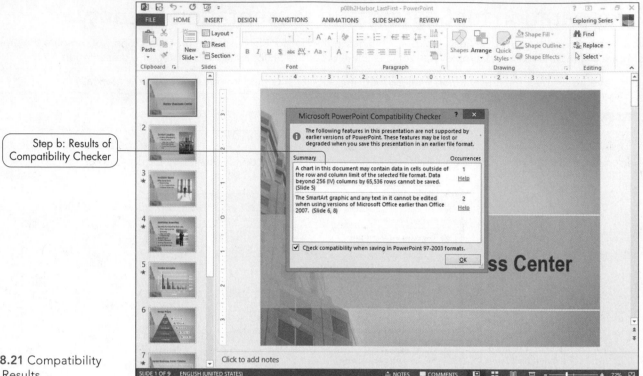

FIGURE 8.21 Compatibility Checker Results

a. Click the **FILE tab** and click **Check for Issues**.

b. Click **Check Compatibility** and read the summary of the features that cannot be supported in earlier versions of Microsoft Office.

Two issues are identified. The chart on Slide 5 contains data in cells outside of the row and column limit, and Slides 6 and 8 contain SmartArt graphics that cannot be edited when using versions of Microsoft Office earlier than Office 2007.

> **TROUBLESHOOTING:** A compatibility pack may download as part of this step.

c. Click **OK**.

Compatibility issues have been identified, but nothing has been changed.

d. Save the presentation.

To secure the Harbor Business Center presentation, you add a password to the file. Then, to make it easier for Susil to access the file, you use the Save As General Options to remove the password and set a new one. Refer to Figure 8.22 as you complete Step 3.

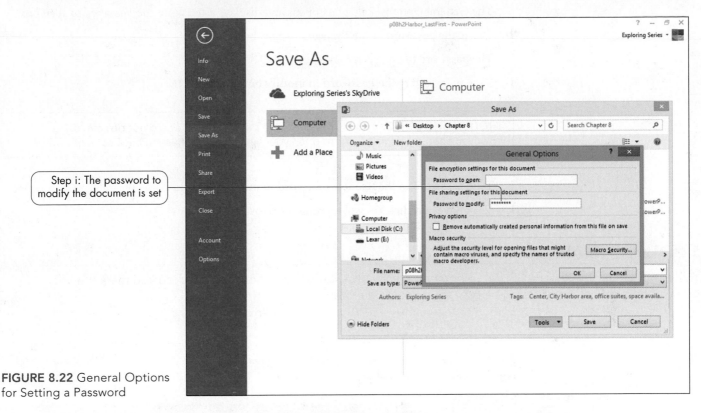

> Step i: The password to modify the document is set

FIGURE 8.22 General Options for Setting a Password

a. Click the **FILE tab**, click **Protect Presentation**, and then click **Encrypt with Password**.

   The Encrypt Document dialog box opens.

b. Type **h@Rb0R!c3nT3R?** and click **OK**.

> **TROUBLESHOOTING:** This is a secure password created from the name of the project, Harbor Center, and created using uppercase and lowercase letters and numbers and symbols from the top and bottom keyboards. It is 14 characters long.

c. Type **h@Rb0R!c3nT3R?** when you are prompted to reenter the password and click **OK**.

   The *Protect Presentation* section changes to a yellow color and reads *A password is required to open this presentation.*

> **TROUBLESHOOTING:** If you typed the two passwords differently, you receive a warning that the passwords did not match and that the password was not created. Repeat the process until the passwords match. Never copy a password and paste it into the duplicate password box because if you copy and paste a typographical error, you will not be able to open the file or remove the password.

d. Save and close *p08h2Harbor_LastFirst* and reopen the presentation.

   The Password dialog box opens.

e. Type **h@Rb0R!c3nT3R?** in the **Password dialog box** and click **OK**.

   The Harbor Business Center presentation opens.

f. Click the **FILE tab** and click **Save As**. Click **Browse** to navigate to the location where you saved the presentation.

The Save As dialog box opens.

g. Click **Tools** just to the left of the Save button in the dialog box and click **General Options**.

The General Options dialog box opens and displays asterisks in the *Password to open* box.

h. Delete the password in the *Password to open* box.

The password to open is removed.

i. Type **password** in the **Password to modify box** and click **OK**.

> **TROUBLESHOOTING:** This is a very insecure password and would not be safe. It will, however, enable your instructor to open your file and verify that you have set a password.

j. Type **password** in the **Reenter password to modify box** and click **OK**.

k. Click **Save** and click **Yes** when prompted to overwrite.

STEP 4 ≫ MARK AS FINAL

You want the employees of ACSL Development to know that the presentation is finished, so you mark the presentation as final. Refer to Figure 8.23 as you complete Step 4.

FIGURE 8.23 Harbor Business Center Presentation Marked as Final

a. Click the **FILE tab** and click **Protect Presentation**.

> **TROUBLESHOOTING:** If you closed the presentation after Step 3, the Password dialog box appears prompting you to enter the password to modify the presentation. If you do not enter the password, the presentation opens as a read-only version.

b. Select **Mark as Final** and click **OK** in the Microsoft PowerPoint Information dialog box that appears indicating that the presentation will be marked as final and then saved.

c. Click **OK** in the additional Microsoft PowerPoint Information dialog box indicating that the document has been marked final.

A *Marked as Final* message bar appears below the Ribbon and reads *An author has marked this presentation as final to discourage editing.*

d. Click the **HOME tab**.

The Ribbon appears over the message bar (*Marked as Final*). Most features have been greyed out, preventing the user from making changes.

e. Save and close the file, and submit based on your instructor's directions.

Presentation Sharing

You spent a great deal of time creating a professional presentation that delivers your message—now how will you deliver that message to your audience? Will you present it, or will you distribute it to your audience? If you are going to distribute it, what file format will you use? What distribution methods are available?

PowerPoint includes multiple distribution options using a variety of file formats. Among the variety of methods you can use to distribute your presentation are burning it to a CD or DVD, presenting it on the Web, delivering it on a network location, or printing the presentation in an image format. These methods may require different file formats. In this section, you will save your presentation using several file types and examine PowerPoint's distribution options.

Selecting a Presentation File Type

By default, PowerPoint saves a presentation in the .pptx file format, an open format that uses *eXtensible Markup Language (XML)*. XML is a set of encoding rules that creates a file format that is designed to provide maximum flexibility when storing and exchanging structured information. Microsoft Office moved to the use of XML file formats with Office 2007 and continues its use with Office 2013. Among the many benefits of XML are more compact files, improved damaged-file recovery, better privacy and control over personal information, better integration, and easier detection of documents that contain macros.

Change File Type

While you can change the file type of a PowerPoint presentation using the Save As feature, you may find it helpful to use Export to determine the file type you wish to use. Export includes a Change File Type option that provides a list of commonly used file types and a description of the file type to help you determine if it is appropriate for your needs. To change a file type using this method, do the following:

1. Click the FILE tab and click Export.
2. Click Change File Type (see Figure 8.24).
3. Select a file format from the *Presentation File Types*, *Image File Types*, or *Other File Types* sections.
4. Click Save As at the bottom of the list.
5. Navigate to the location where you want to store the file, type a file name in the *File name* box, and then click Save.

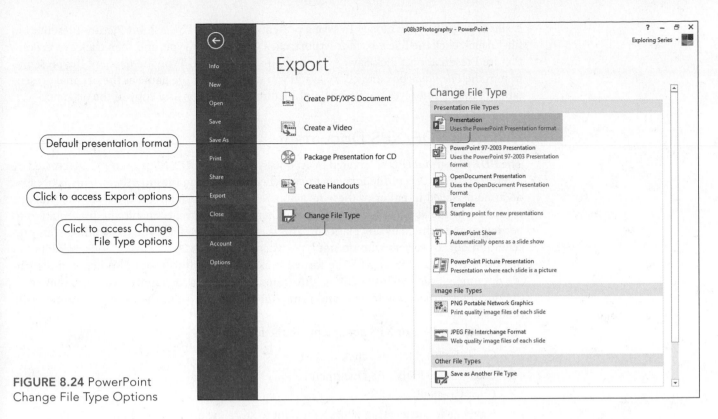

FIGURE 8.24 PowerPoint Change File Type Options

One option in the Change File Type list enables you to save a presentation as an *OpenDocument presentation (*.odp)*, a presentation that conforms to the OpenDocument standard for exchanging data between applications. This standard is an open XML-based format used in both free software and in proprietary software, such as Microsoft Office 2013, that seeks to make records and documents accessible across platforms and applications. Some PowerPoint 2013 features are fully supported when saved as an OpenDocument presentation, but others may be only partially or not at all supported. Be sure to save your presentation in a PowerPoint 2013 format before saving as an OpenDocument presentation to ensure that you have a backup of the original format if needed.

After creating a presentation, you may want to save the individual slide or slides as graphic images. You can save each slide or all slides in the presentation as PNG Portable Network Graphics (*.png) image(s) that use lossless compression and provide print-quality image files of each slide. You can also save each slide or all slides in the presentation as JPEG File Interchange Format (*.jpg) image(s) that use a lossy format, which makes the file size small and makes the files good for Web-quality images. To save a presentation slide(s) as an image file(s), do the following:

1. Click the FILE tab and click Export.
2. Click Change File Type.
3. Select PNG Portable Network Graphics (*.png) or JPEG File Interchange Format (*.jpg) from the Image File Types list.
4. Click Save As at the bottom of the list.
5. Navigate to the location where you want to store the file, type a file name in the *File name* box, and then click Save.

Create a PowerPoint Picture Presentation

STEP 1» PowerPoint 2013 has the PowerPoint Picture Presentation option. This option *flattens* (converts all objects on a slide to a single layer) the content of each slide and then saves the slides in the .pptx presentation format. By converting each slide into an image, the slides become harder for others to modify. In addition, the presentation file size is much smaller and it is easier to e-mail or download. To save a presentation in the PowerPoint Picture Presentation file format, click the File tab, click Export, click Change File Type, and then click PowerPoint Picture Presentation. Click Save As at the bottom of the list. Type the name of the presentation in the *File name* box and click Save. If you use the same file name as the original presentation, PowerPoint saves the PowerPoint Picture Presentation as a copy of the original.

Create a PDF/XPS Document

The *PDF file format (PDF)* (created by Adobe Systems) and *XPS file format (XPS)* (created by Microsoft) are excellent file formats to use when distributing files to others. This is because documents saved in either of these formats are fixed file formats—they retain their format regardless of the application used to create them. These formats enable the presentation to be viewed and printed by any platform. This is extremely helpful if you are sending your presentation out to viewers who do not have Microsoft Office 2013. Saving your presentation or document in a PDF or XPS file format makes it difficult to modify. When you distribute documents such as instructions, directions, legal forms, or reports, you probably want the document to be easy to read and print, but you do not want the document to be easily modified.

To create a PDF or XPS document, do the following:

1. Click the FILE tab and click Export.
2. Click Create PDF/XPS Document.
3. Click Create PDF/XPS.
4. Navigate to the location where you want to store the document when the *Publish as PDF or XPS* dialog box appears and type a file name in the *File name* box.
5. Select the *Optimize for Standard (publishing online and printing)* or *Minimize size (publishing online)* option.
6. Click Publish.

Create a Video

Take advantage of the excitement of video by converting your presentation into a dynamic video! PowerPoint 2013 includes an option for converting your presentation content into video that you can share with anyone. PowerPoint outputs your presentation as a Windows Media Video (WMV) video clip and includes all recorded timings and narrations, if used in the presentation; all slides that are not hidden; and all animations, transitions, and media.

Before creating a video, create your presentation and record any narration and timings you want as part of the video. You can use your mouse as a laser pointer to draw a viewer's attention to objects on your slides. Save the presentation. Then, to convert your presentation to a video, do the following:

1. Click the FILE tab and click Export.
2. Click *Create a Video*.
3. Click *Computer & HD Displays* to display video quality and size options and select the desired option.
4. Click *Don't Use Recorded Timings and Narrations* and click *Use Recorded Timings and Narration* if you wish to use any recorded timings and narration or laser pointer movements.
5. Click the *Seconds to spend on each slide* spin arrows to change the default time of 5 seconds if you are not using recorded timings and narrations.
6. Click Create Video.
7. Navigate to the location where you want to store the video when the Save As dialog box appears and type a file name in the *File name* box.
8. Click Save.

Before you determine the video quality and size for the presentation, you need to determine the output for the video. If you plan on the presentation video being displayed on a computer or high definition (HD) display, you need to create a high-quality video (960 × 720 pixels). This creates a large file size. If you plan to upload the video to the Internet or burn it to a DVD, you need to create a medium-quality video (640 × 480 pixels). This creates a moderate file size. If you plan on the video being played on a portable device, you need to create a low-quality video (340 × 240 pixels). This creates the smallest file size, but text would be difficult to read. Figure 8.25 displays the *Create a Video* options with the default setting for computer and HD displays.

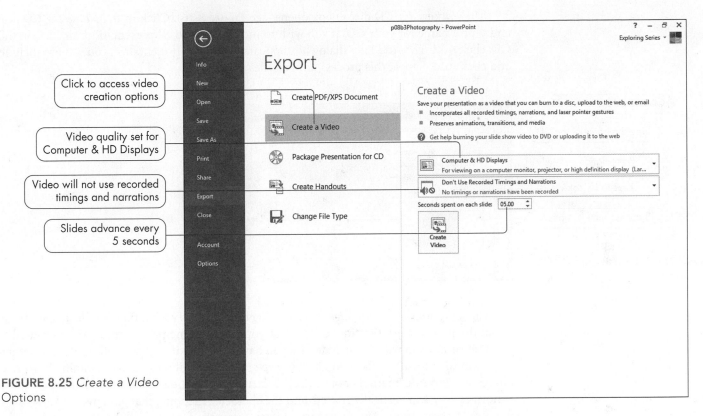

FIGURE 8.25 *Create a Video Options*

The length of time it takes to create a video depends on the content in the presentation and the length and quality of the video. The presentation will be recorded in real time, so it may take several hours to record. You can monitor the progress of the recording on the status bar. To play the video, locate and double-click the file.

Package Presentation for CD

STEP 2》 *Package Presentation for CD* is a PowerPoint feature that enables you to copy your presentation to a CD or a storage location such as a hard drive, a network location, or a USB device. You can save the fonts you used, linked and embedded items, and a special PowerPoint Viewer. After you have packaged your presentation for CD, you can then distribute it to others, who do not even need to have PowerPoint installed on their computers to view it because the PowerPoint Viewer is part of the package. You may package your presentation on a CD for your personal use, too. If you are presenting at another location and are unsure of the system you will be using to present, you can package your presentation and carry the CD with you. At the new location, you simply play the presentation without worrying about whether the computer you are using to present has PowerPoint installed.

To package your presentation, do the following:

1. Save the presentation you want to package.
2. Insert a CD into the CD drive if you want to copy the presentation to a CD. Omit this step if you are copying the presentation to a folder on a USB device, a hard drive, or to a network location.
3. Click the FILE tab and click Export.
4. Click *Package Presentation for CD*.
5. Click *Package for CD* in the right pane.

The *Package for CD* dialog box opens (see Figure 8.26). Click in the *Name the CD* box and type a name for your CD. If you wish to include additional presentations or files on the CD, click Add. The Add Files dialog box appears. Select the presentation you want to include and click Add. Repeat this process until all files are added.

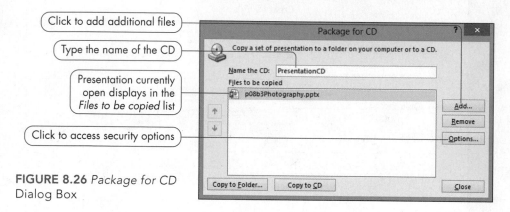

FIGURE 8.26 *Package for CD Dialog Box*

Click Options in the *Package for CD* dialog box to specify what files will be included and to set the privacy and security options that you want for the presentation. You can choose whether or not you want to include files you have linked to in the presentation and whether you want to embed TrueType fonts. **TrueType fonts** are digital fonts that contain alphabetic characters and information about the characters, such as the shape of the character, how it is horizontally and vertically spaced, and the character mapping that governs the keystrokes you use to access them. This is important if you want the font to display as the font designer created it and as you used it in the presentation. If you have used a nonstandard font in your presentation, you cannot be sure the computer on which you are going to display your presentation has the same font. If it does not have the same font, the computer substitutes another font, which can create havoc in your presentation design. If you embed the TrueType fonts you used in your presentation, you will have a larger file, but you can be sure that your presentation displays fonts accurately.

To ensure the security and privacy of your presentation, the *Package for CD* options also enable you to set a password for opening the presentation and a second password for modifying the presentation. You can also check the option to inspect the presentation for inappropriate or private information and remove it, a feature you explored earlier in this chapter. After setting the options you want, click OK. Figure 8.27 displays the Options dialog box.

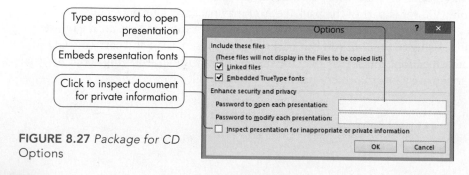

FIGURE 8.27 *Package for CD Options*

Once you have selected the options you want, click either *Copy to Folder* or *Copy to CD*. If you click *Copy to Folder*, you can copy the files to a new folder on your hard drive or a storage location such as a USB drive. You can create a name for the folder, browse to the location you wish to store the folder, and then copy the presentation to that location. If you click *Copy to CD*, for security purposes, you are asked if you want to include linked files. If you trust the linked files, click Yes. At that point, you see instructions for writing to your CD writer. These instructions vary depending on the device you use to burn CDs.

After you have packaged your presentation for CD and distributed it, the individual receiving the CD simply places the CD in his or her CD drive, and the CD loads and displays your presentation. If you included more than one presentation on the CD, the presentations load and display in the order in which you added them to the CD. This is the default setting for *Package for CD*. If the presentation was packaged to a folder, locate and open the folder and double-click the presentation name. This starts the Viewer, and a screen displays with a list of the presentations you packaged. Click the presentation you wish to display and click Open.

Create Handouts in Microsoft Word

In addition to the excellent handouts you can create in PowerPoint, you can prepare handouts in Word. When you create your audience handouts through Word, you can take advantage of all of Word's word-processing tools. In addition, you are given several helpful layouts not available in PowerPoint. For example, when you create notes page handouts in PowerPoint, the handouts consist of a thumbnail of the slide at the top of the page with its related notes beneath it—one slide per sheet of paper. If you have many slides, this can be an inefficient use of paper. By sending your presentation to Word, you can select a layout that puts thumbnails of the slides on the left side of the page and the related notes on the right side. Depending on the length of your notes, you may fit several slides per sheet of paper. This saves paper but can be time-consuming, as Word has to create a table and insert the slides and notes in the table cells. Figure 8.28 shows a notes page in PowerPoint, and Figure 8.29 shows its counterpart in Word.

FIGURE 8.28 PowerPoint
Notes Page
Photo: Patryk Kosmider/Fotolia

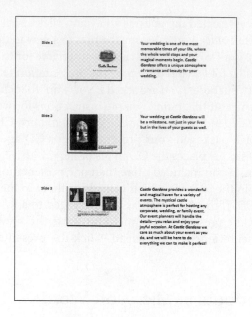

FIGURE 8.29 Word Notes Page

To create handouts in Word, do the following:

1. Click the FILE tab and click Export.
2. Select Create Handouts.
3. Click Create Handouts in the right pane.
4. Click the layout you want for your handouts in the *Send to Microsoft Word* dialog box (see Figure 8.30).
5. Click OK.

Click to select desired layout

Click to create a link between the Word document and the presentation

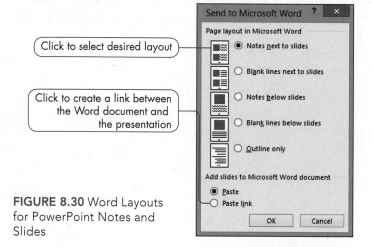

FIGURE 8.30 Word Layouts for PowerPoint Notes and Slides

The *Send to Microsoft Word* dialog box includes an option to paste a link between the Word document and the presentation so that changes you make in either one are reflected in the other. After you click OK in the dialog box, Microsoft Word opens and displays your presentation in the page layout you selected. When you are done making changes in Word and done printing the handout, click Close to quit Word.

Saving and Sharing a Presentation

A variety of methods exist for sharing a presentation to others, depending on your audience and how you want to connect with them. You can share the presentation by using e-mail, inviting people to SkyDrive to view or collaborate on it, getting a Sharing Link, using the Present Online feature, or publishing the slides.

Send Using E-Mail

One easy-to-use method for distributing a presentation is to send it by e-mail. If your default e-mail client is Outlook, Windows Mail, or Outlook Express, you can send the presentation file directly from PowerPoint. Recipients receive the presentation as an attachment to the e-mail.

To e-mail a presentation from PowerPoint, do the following:

1. Click the FILE tab and click Share.
2. Click Email.
3. Click *Send as Attachment* or another send option (see Figure 8.31).
4. Type or select the e-mail addresses of the recipient(s) in the To box that opens in your default e-mail application.
5. Change the subject line from the name of the presentation if you want and add a message informing the recipient(s) of your purpose for sending the presentation.
6. Click Send.

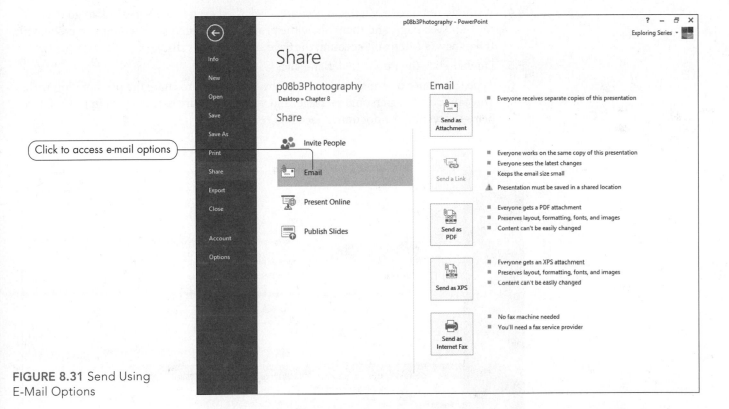

FIGURE 8.31 Send Using E-Mail Options

If you do not use Outlook, Windows Mail, or Outlook Express as your default e-mail client and want to send your presentation via e-mail, do the following:

1. Save the presentation in the file type that meets your needs and close the presentation.
2. Open your e-mail client.
3. Click Attach, locate the file, and then attach the file to the e-mail.
4. Type or select the e-mail addresses of the recipient(s) in the To box.
5. Change the subject line to the subject you want and add a message informing the recipient(s) of your purpose for sending the presentation.
6. Click Send.

Invite People to SkyDrive

STEP 3 You can use PowerPoint to send your presentation to *SkyDrive*, an app used to store, share, and access files and folders. SkyDrive is part of Microsoft's *Windows Live* online services designed to help users communicate and collaborate, and it currently provides 7 GB of free online storage for photos and documents. SkyDrive enables you to store, access, and share your files from anywhere with Internet access—no need to carry a USB or external drive with you! When you share a presentation stored in SkyDrive, you can share a link to SkyDrive with others rather than sending an attachment. This enables you to maintain a single version of the presentation and enables others to edit the presentation in their browsers. To log in to SkyDrive, you will need a Microsoft account and password. If you use Hotmail, Messenger, or Xbox Live, you already have a Microsoft account.

To send a presentation to the Web using SkyDrive, do the following:

1. Click the FILE tab and click Share.
2. Click Invite People. Click Save To Cloud.
3. Click *User name*'s SkyDrive on the Save As pane. Then click Browse.
4. If you do not have a Microsoft account, click the Learn More hyperlink to go the sign-up Web page, and then follow the prompts to create your account and credentials. If you have a Microsoft account, the Save As dialog box displays (see Figure 8.32).
5. Double-click the Public folder and click Save.
6. Type the names or e-mail addresses of those you want to share the presentation with. You can include a personal message, and you can require users to sign in to SkyDrive before accessing the document (see Figure 8.33).
7. Click Share.

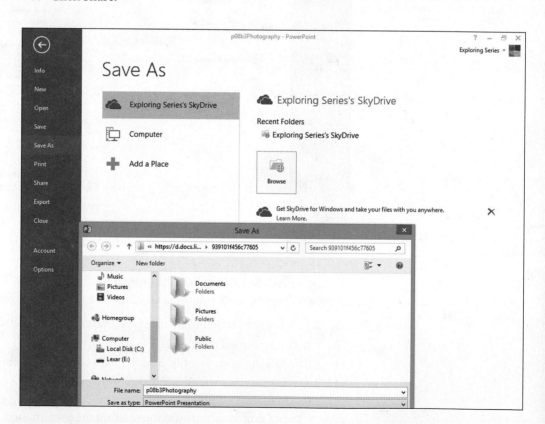

FIGURE 8.32 Saving to SkyDrive

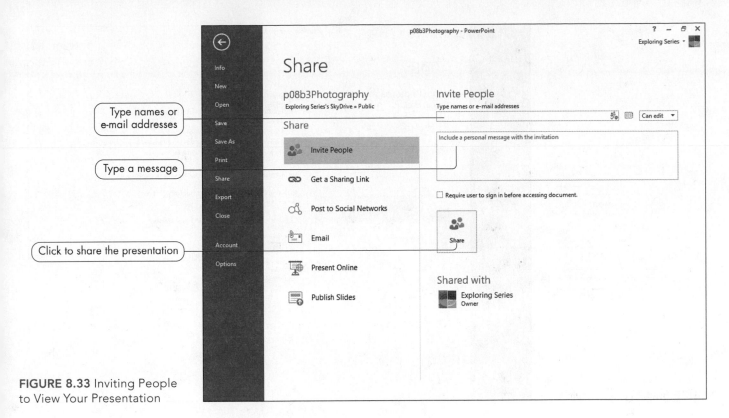

FIGURE 8.33 Inviting People to View Your Presentation

Present Online

It is possible for you to use *Present Online*, or transmit a presentation over the Internet to invited participants who are in different locations. To do this, you use a Microsoft account to log into the Office Presentation Service, a free service provided by Microsoft for PowerPoint users. To share the presentation, you send the URL for the presentation to your invited participants, and they watch your presentation on their Internet browser at the same time you deliver it.

To broadcast a presentation, do the following:

1. Click the FILE tab and click Share.
2. Click Present Online.
3. Click the Present Online button in the right pane (see Figure 8.34).
4. Sign in using your Microsoft account if prompted to do so.
5. Click Copy Link and share the link with participants via an instant messenger program or e-mail. Click *Send in Email* to send the link through Outlook, Windows Mail, or Outlook Express.
6. Click Start Presentation.
7. Advance through the slide show and exit the slide show when you have displayed all slides.
8. Click File and click Close to end the online presentation. When warned that everyone viewing the presentation will be disconnected if you continue, click End Online Presentation (see Figure 8.35).

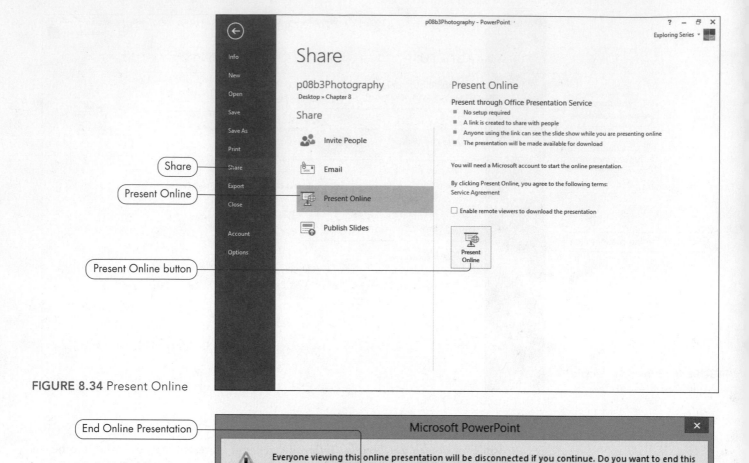

Share

Present Online

Present Online button

FIGURE 8.34 Present Online

End Online Presentation

FIGURE 8.35 Ending an Online Presentation

Publish Slides

You can share and reuse individual PowerPoint slides by storing them in a slide library on a server or at a SharePoint site.

In an office environment, you may have access to a Microsoft **SharePoint library** (a location on a SharePoint site where you can store and manage files you add to the library) or a **SharePoint workspace** (a copy of a SharePoint site for offline use). Access to a SharePoint site enables collaboration between team members on a project and provides additional services unavailable in PowerPoint. All SharePoint team members are able to save to and obtain files from a centralized browser-based location, depending on their permissions. A SharePoint site is generally found in a corporate environment, but check with your instructor or lab manager to see whether a SharePoint site is available for your use.

Using SharePoint for collaborating enables you to do the following:

- Store your presentations in a document workspace.
- Save and reuse presentations in a PowerPoint slide library so team members have access to each other's work.
- Have online discussions as presentations are being developed.
- Track the progress of a presentation using workflow.

SharePoint enables work teams to work together on a presentation, share files, and discuss presentations in progress. The workspace provides a set of icons to make sharing and updating documents easy. Slides can be saved directly to a slide library that has been created and published slides are available to team members for reuse in other presentations. The slides are available from the Reuse Slides pane. Finally, SharePoint sites provide for workflow management by monitoring the start, progress, and completion of a presentation review process.

You and your coworkers can access the slide library and do the following:

- Add slides to the slide library.
- Reuse slides in the slide library in a presentation.
- Track changes made to slides in the slide library.
- Locate the latest version of a slide in the slide library.
- Receive e-mail notifications when slides in the slide library are changed.

To publish slides from the current presentation to a slide library or a SharePoint site, do the following:

1. Click the FILE tab and click Share.
2. Click Publish Slides.
3. Select slides that you want to publish in the *Publish slides* dialog box. Click Browse to select a slide library where you want the presentation saved.
4. Click Select and click Publish.

Quick Concept

1. Explain when you might want to change file types for a presentation. Discuss two different file types you would use. *p. 1077*

2. What are the benefits of saving a presentation using PowerPoint Picture Presentation? *p. 1077*

3. What is the difference between sharing a presentation in SkyDrive and sending the presentation as an attachment? *p. 1084*

Hands-On Exercises

Watch the Video for this Hands-On Exercise!

MyITLab®
HOE3 Training

3 Presentation Sharing

You want to share the Harbor Business Center presentation with an associate. You decide to save the presentation as a PowerPoint Picture Presentation to flatten the content to a single image per slide, and to invite your associate to view the presentation on SkyDrive. You also package the presentation to a folder so that others can watch the presentation on most computers.

Skills covered: Create a PowerPoint Picture Presentation • Package a Presentation • Share by Inviting People

STEP 1 ≫ CREATE A POWERPOINT PICTURE PRESENTATION

You want to save the Harbor Business Center presentation as a PowerPoint Picture Presentation so each slide is flattened as an image, making it more difficult to modify. Refer to Figure 8.36 as you complete Step 1.

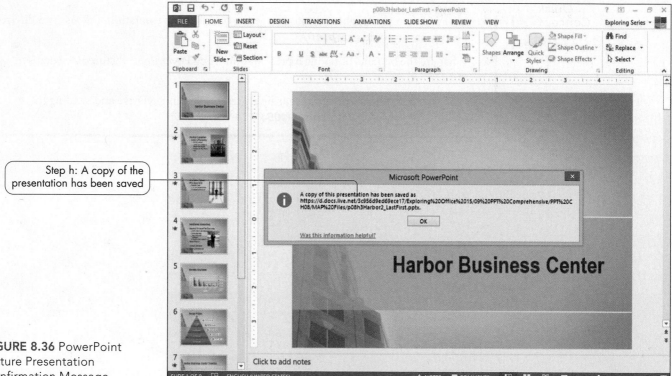

Step h: A copy of the presentation has been saved

FIGURE 8.36 PowerPoint Picture Presentation Confirmation Message

a. Use File Explorer to make a copy of *p08h2Harbor_LastFirst*. Rename the copied presentation **p08h3Harbor_LastFirst**.

> **TROUBLESHOOTING:** If you open *p08h2Harbor_LastFirst* and try to save it as another file name, PowerPoint removes the digital signature and the *Marked as Final* designation. You need to preserve those settings so that your instructor can verify that you completed Hands-On Exercise 2.

b. Open *p08h3Harbor_LastFirst* and type **password** when prompted to enter the password to modify or open as read only. Click **OK**.

You protected the presentation with a password in Hands-On Exercise 2.

c. Click **Edit Anyway** on the *Marked as Final* message bar.

The *Marked as Final* message bar is removed, and the status bar no longer contains the Digital Signature and *Marked as Final* icons.

d. Click the **FILE tab**, click **Export**, and then click **Change File Type**.

A list of file types display in the right pane, the Change File Type pane.

e. Click **PowerPoint Picture Presentation** and click **Save As** at the bottom of the pane.

A Save As dialog box displays.

f. Change the presentation to **p08h3HarborPicture_LastFirst**, adding *Picture* to the file name. Click **Save**.

A Microsoft PowerPoint dialog box displays indicating a copy of the presentation has been saved and giving the full path and file name of the copy.

g. Click **OK**.

The dialog box disappears and the *p08h3Harbor_LastFirst* presentation is onscreen.

h. Save *p08h3Harbor_LastFirst* and leave it open.

STEP 2 ❯❯ PACKAGE A PRESENTATION

You use the *Package a Presentation for CD* feature to package the Harbor Business Center presentation.

a. Open *p08h3Harbor_LastFirst*, if necessary.

> **TROUBLESHOOTING:** If you closed *p08h3Harbor_LastFirst* while completing the previous step, you will need to type password in the Password dialog box and click OK.

b. Click the **FILE tab** and click **Export**.

The Export options display in the Backstage view.

c. Click **Package Presentation for CD** and click **Package for CD** in the right pane.

The *Package for CD* dialog box appears. The default name assigned by PowerPoint, *PresentationCD*, displays and the presentation file name is shown in the *Files to be copied* list.

d. Type **Harbor Business** in the **Name the CD box**.

e. Click **Copy to Folder**.

The *Copy to Folder* dialog box displays the name of the folder and the location in which it will be saved.

f. Click **Browse**, navigate to the location where you save your solution files, and then click **Select**.

g. Click **OK** and then click **Yes** to include linked files.

File Explorer opens and displays the PresentationPackage folder, an AUTORUN.INF file (the instruction file that starts the presentation when a CD is inserted), and the presentation file.

h. Close File Explorer and close the *Package for CD* dialog box.

i. Leave *p08h3Harbor_LastFirst* open for the next step.

STEP 3 » SHARE BY INVITING PEOPLE

You want to share the presentation by inviting your associate (your instructor) to see it at SkyDrive. Refer to Figure 8.37 as you complete Step 2.

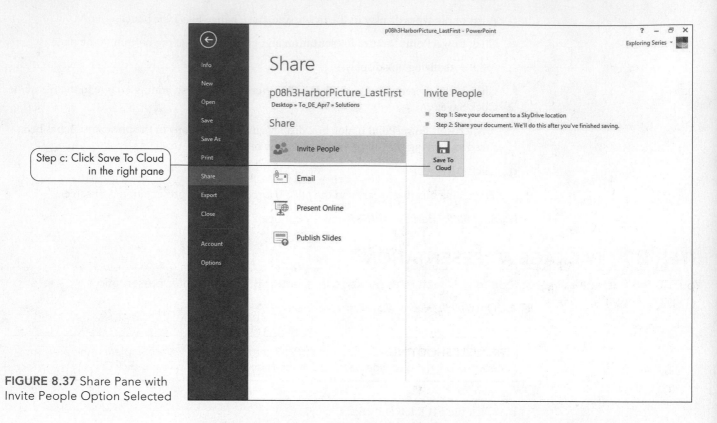

Step c: Click Save To Cloud in the right pane

FIGURE 8.37 Share Pane with Invite People Option Selected

TROUBLESHOOTING: You will not be able to do this step if you do not have a Microsoft account. To obtain a Microsoft account, refer to the Tip that appears just before the beginning of Hands-On Exercise 2.

---

a. Open *p08h3HarborPicture_LastFirst* if necessary.

b. Click the **FILE tab** and click **Share**.

c. Click **Invite People** and click **Save To Cloud** in the right pane.

   The Save As pane opens where you can choose to save the presentation in SkyDrive.

d. Click **User Name's SkyDrive** on the Save As pane. Click **Browse**.

e. Double-click the **Public folders** and click **Save**.

f. Type the names or e-mail addresses of those you want to share the presentation with. Make sure the *Require user to sign in before accessing the document* check box is not checked.

g. Click **Share** as directed by your instructor.

h. Save and close the file, and submit based on your instructor's directions

Chapter Objectives Review

After reading this chapter, you have accomplished the following objectives:

1. Work with comments and annotations.

- To facilitate the collaboration process, PowerPoint provides tools that team members can use to review a presentation.
- The Review tab contains the Comments group, which has tools for adding a new comment on a slide, for editing or deleting existing comments, and for moving between comments.
- While displaying a slide show, a team member can add ink annotations, such as highlighting or drawings, and save the annotations.

2. Show, hide, and print markup.

- When the annotations are saved, they display on the slides in Normal view, or when comments have been added to a slide, the slide shows the markup.
- The Show Markup button is located in the Comments group on the Review tab and can be toggled on or off to be hidden or displayed.
- You can keep a record of markups made to a presentation by printing the comments and ink annotations. Comments will print on a separate page for each slide, whereas annotations print on the slide for which they were created.

3. Compare and merge presentations.

- PowerPoint 2013 enables you to compare two versions of a presentation.
- The differences in the presentations are marked as revisions that you can accept or reject.

4. View presentation properties.

- PowerPoint automatically stores data about your documents as document properties.
- It automatically stores the name of the author creating the presentation, as well as data such as the number of slides in the show and the number of words.
- You can add additional properties such as a subject, keywords, status, and comments that can be used to search for and locate documents.

5. Check a presentation for issues.

- Before distributing the slideshow, you can use the Inspect Document feature to find the document properties and strip out the properties you do not want others to see.
- The Check Accessibility feature checks a presentation for issues that people with disabilities may find hard to read.
- The Compatibility Checker inspects the presentation for features not supported by earlier versions of PowerPoint.

6. Protect a presentation.

- To indicate that the presentation is completed, use the *Mark as Final* feature.
- For security and privacy reasons, you may want to encrypt a presentation and set a password to open a document or modify a document.
- IRM prevents presentations or other documents from being forwarded, edited, printed, or copied without your authorization.
- Add a digital signature to your presentation if you want to authenticate it. To authenticate your presentation to others, you must sign up with a third-party signature service. You can create a personal digital signature for your use to authenticate that a presentation has not been modified since you last worked on it.

7. Select a presentation file type.

- PowerPoint includes many options for saving a document based on your needs and the needs of your audience.
- The file types are available in the Save As feature, but accessing the Change File Type option provides you with a list of commonly used file types and a description of the file type to help you determine if it is appropriate for your needs.

8. Save and share a presentation.

- You have a variety of methods for sending a presentation to others. The method of distribution you select depends on your audience and how you want to connect with them.
- You can send the presentation to your audience using e-mail, save the presentation to the Web or to a SharePoint location, transmit the presentation using the Present Online service, or publish the slides to a slide library.

Key Terms Matching

Match the key terms with their definitions. Write the key term letter by the appropriate numbered definition.

a. Accessibility
b. Accessibility Checker
c. Alternative text (alt text)
d. Comment
e. Compatibility Checker
f. Digital signature
g. Document Inspector
h. Document property
i. Encryption
j. eXtensible Markup Language (XML)

k. Markup
l. Metadata
m. OpenDocument presentation (.odp)
n. Present Online
o. Reviewer
p. SharePoint workspace
q. SkyDrive
r. TrueType font
s. Windows Live
t. XPS file format (XPS)

1. _____ A Microsoft service that enables the transmission of a presentation in real time over the Internet to a remote audience. **p. 1085**

2. _____ An app used to store, share, and access files and folders. **p. 1084**

3. _____ A digital font that contain alphabetic characters and information about the characters, such as the shape, spacing, and character mapping of the font. **p. 1080**

4. _____ A presentation that conforms to the OpenDocument standard for exchanging data between applications. **p. 1077**

5. _____ Comments and ink annotations appearing in a presentation. **p. 1050**

6. _____ Aids in identifying and resolving accessibility issues in a presentation. **p. 1064**

7. _____ Checks for features in a presentation that are not supported by earlier versions of PowerPoint. **p. 1065**

8. _____ Protects the contents of your presentation by converting it into unreadable scrambled text that needs a password to be opened. **p. 1068**

9. _____ A set of encoding rules that create a file format that is designed to provide maximum flexibility when storing and exchanging structured information. **p. 1076**

10. _____ Detects hidden and personal data in the presentation. **p. 1064**

11. _____ In PowerPoint, refers to the ease with which a person with physical challenges is able to access and understand a presentation. **p. 1064**

12. _____ An invisible, electronic signature stamp that is encrypted and attached to a certificate that can be added to a presentation. **p. 1069**

13. _____ Data that describes other data. **p. 1055**

14. _____ A copy of a SharePoint site that can be used while offline. **p. 1086**

15. _____ A text-based description of an image. **p. 1065**

16. _____ A text note attached to the slide. **p. 1050**

17. _____ Someone who examines the presentation and provides feedback. **p. 1050**

18. _____ An electronic file format created by Microsoft that preserves document formatting and is viewable and printable on any platform. **p. 1078**

19. _____ A group of online services provided by Microsoft that are designed to help users communicate and collaborate. **p. 1084**

20. _____ An attribute, such as an author's name or keyword, that describes a file. **p. 1055**

Multiple Choice

1. The process whereby a team works together to accomplish a goal is referred to as which of the following?

    (a) Unification

    (b) Collusion

    (c) Collaboration

    (d) Deliberation

2. Which of the following is an Adobe electronic file format that preserves document formatting?

    (a) PDF

    (b) XPS

    (c) PDX

    (d) XML

3. Markup may consist of all of the following except:

    (a) Comments inserted by the presentation creator.

    (b) Annotations.

    (c) Comments inserted by a reviewer.

    (d) Passwords created for opening and modifying a presentation.

4. Which of the following statements regarding comments in a presentation is not true?

    (a) Comments are printed on a separate page than the slide.

    (b) Comments display as a small icon that may be clicked on to open so the comment text can be read.

    (c) Comments display in the bottom-right side of the presentation by default but may be dragged to any location.

    (d) Comments print when Show Markup on the REVIEW tab is selected.

5. Which of the following document properties is not created automatically by PowerPoint but can be added?

    (a) Number of slides in the presentation

    (b) Location of the presentation

    (c) Keywords

    (d) Date the presentation was created

6. Which of the following is not checked by the Document Inspector?

    (a) Comments and annotations

    (b) Version compatibility

    (c) Document properties and personal information

    (d) Presentation notes

7. Which of the following is a true statement regarding passwords?

    (a) One password may be set to open a document, and a second password may be set to modify a document.

    (b) Mary_Sept18_1990 is a more secure password than M@ryO9LB_L99O.

    (c) A password can only be set through the *Prepare for Sharing* feature.

    (d) If you forget a password you have created, contact www.microsoft.com for a tool that will restore your document without a password.

8. Which of the following may be packaged with your presentation when you use the *Package for CD* feature?

    (a) All TrueType fonts used in the presentation

    (b) Any files linked to the presentation

    (c) A PowerPoint Viewer

    (d) All of the above

9. All of the following statements about creating handouts in Microsoft Office Word are true except:

    (a) Create Handouts is available from the REVIEW tab.

    (b) Creating handouts in Microsoft Word enables you to use word-processing features to format the handouts.

    (c) Word provides layouts not available in PowerPoint.

    (d) A link can be pasted between PowerPoint and Word so changes can update in either document when made.

10. When merging presentations, the Reviewing pane does which of the following?

    (a) Displays a list of all comments and annotations created in the presentation

    (b) Lists features in the presentation that are not supported by earlier versions of PowerPoint

    (c) Lists changes to the slide currently selected and any slides that have been added or removed in the presentation

    (d) Enables you to add a digital signature to ensure the integrity of the presentation

Practice Exercises

1 Castle Gardens

Castle Gardens provides wedding packages that include the use of fabulous gardens or a castle great hall, a wedding planner, pewter tableware, old English décor, photography, and videography. You create a PowerPoint presentation advertising Castle Gardens and submit it to the owner, Ms. Grosscurth, for review. She reviewed the slides, added comments, and made changes. You merge the presentations and accept and reject changes. You view the presentation and highlight words and phrases you think create the emotional appeal of Castle Gardens and you keep the ink annotations when you exit Slide Show view. You print a copy of the comments and annotations to create a record of the changes you made and hide the markup. This exercise follows the same set of skills as used in Hands-On Exercise 1 in the chapter. Refer to Figure 8.38 as you complete this exercise.

FIGURE 8.38 Castle Gardens Presentation

Photos: (Slide 2) Jon Turner/Fotolia, (Slide 3, left) gmg9130/Fotolia, (Slide 3, middle) ilfotokunst/Fotolia, (Slide 3, right) Mat Hayward/Fotolia, (Slide 4) Pefkos/Fotolia

a. Open *p08p1Castle* and save it as **p08p1Castle_LastFirst**. Click the **FILE tab**, click **Options**, and then change the user name to your name and the initials to your initials (if necessary). Click **OK**.

b. Create a handout header with your name and a handout footer with your instructor's name and your class. Include the current date.

c. On Slide 1, click the **REVIEW tab** and click **New Comment** in the Comments group. Type **Ms. Grosscurth, this is the beginning of the presentation we discussed. Please review it and make suggestions for changes. Thanks!**

d. Save the presentation and click **Compare** in the Compare group.

e. Navigate to your student data files, select *p08p1CastleGrosscurth*, and then click **Merge**.

f. On Slide 1, select and read the first comment in the *Slide Changes* section displayed in the DETAILS tab of the Revisions pane, the comment requesting that Ms. Grosscurth review the presentation.

g. Click **Delete** in the Comments group.

h. Click **Insertions at beginning of presentation** in the *Presentation Changes* section. Click **All slides inserted at this position** in the Slides pane. Select and read the next comment in the *Slide Changes* section, the comment requesting that you change the color tone of the castle picture.

i. Select the image of the castle and click the **FORMAT tab**. Click **Color** in the Adjust group. Click **Temperature: 4700 K** in the *Color Tone* section.

j. Click the **REVIEW tab**, click **Next** two times in the Comments group, and then read the comment on Slide 2. Click **Next** in the Comments group.

k. On Slide 3, read the comment, select the text *The castle*, and then type **Castle Gardens**.

l. Click **Next** two times in the Comments group and read the comment for Slide 4 at the top of the *Slide Changes* section.

m. Click the **Accept arrow** in the Compare group and click **Accept All Changes to the Presentation**. All of the changes are accepted, but the comments remain.

n. Close the Revisions pane. Close the Comments pane.

o. Click the **SLIDE SHOW tab** and click **From Beginning** in the Slide Show group.

p. On Slide 1, right-click anywhere on the slide, point to *Pointer Options*, and then select **Highlighter**. Highlight the following words in the presentation, selecting the highlighter on each slide:

Slide #	Words to Highlight
1	dreams, fairy tales
2	wishes came true
3	most lavish wedding

q. Exit the presentation and click **Keep** in the Microsoft PowerPoint dialog box asking if you want to keep your ink annotations.

r. Click the **FILE tab**, click **Print**, and then click **Full Page Slides**. Click **4 Slides Horizontal** in the *Handouts* section. Note the annotations display on the print preview.

s. Drag the vertical scroll bar down and note that comments from all four slides display.

t. Click the **REVIEW tab**, click the **Show Comments arrow**, and then click **Show Markup** to toggle the display of the markup off.

u. Save and close the file, and submit based on your instructor's directions.

2 Martin Luther King Jr. Commemoration Flyer

You are part of a student council committee working on the annual Martin Luther King Jr. Commemoration. You have created a one-page flyer that can be e-mailed to students and also printed and handed out in the Student Center. In this exercise, you change the presentation properties, check the presentation for issues, save the presentation as a PDF file to preserve the formatting and image when printing, and then create handouts in Microsoft Word. This exercise follows the same set of skills as used in Hands-On Exercises 2 and 3 in the chapter. Refer to Figure 8.39 as you complete this exercise.

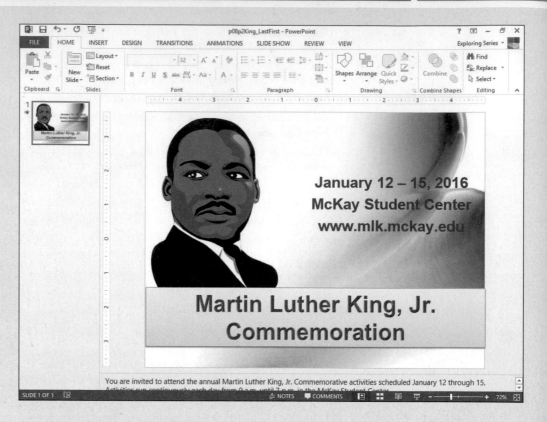

FIGURE 8.39 Accessibility Issues in Flyer

Photo: BasheeraDesigns/Fotolia

a. Open *p08p2King* and then save it as **p08p2King_LastFirst**.

b. Create a handout header with your name and a handout footer with your instructor's name and your class. Include the current date.

c. Click the **FILE tab**, click **Properties** in the right pane, and then click **Show Document Panel**. Make the following changes to the properties:

Property	Change
Title	Martin Luther King Jr. Commemoration
Subject	Annual MLK Commemoration Flyer
Keywords	Martin Luther King Jr., Commemoration, Flyer, MLK, Ad, civil rights
Category	Civil rights
Comments	Flyer to be mailed, and printed and distributed in the Student Center

d. Close the Document Properties panel.

e. Click the **FILE tab**, click **Check for Issues**, and then click **Check Accessibility**.

f. Note the Accessibility Checker shows two errors and one tip for making the document more accessible. Click **Picture 4 (Slide 1)** in the *Inspection Results* section of the Accessibility Checker and read why this error needs to be fixed and how to fix the error in the *Additional Information* section.

g. Click the picture of Martin Luther King Jr., if necessary, and click the **Format tab**. Click the **Size dialog box launcher**.

h. Click **Alt Text** in the Format Picture pane and type the following:

Alt Text	Text-Based Representation
Title	Martin Luther King Jr.
Description	This is an image of Martin Luther King Jr., an African American leader in the civil rights movement, an activist, and an American clergyman.

i. Click **Close** in the Format Picture Pane. Leave the Accessibility Checker open.

j. Click **Slide 1** in the *Errors* section of the *Inspection Results* section of the Accessibility Checker and read why this error needs to be fixed and how to fix the error in the *Additional Information* section.

k. Click in the **title placeholder** and type **Martin Luther King Jr. Commemoration**.

l. Click **Slide 1** displayed under *Tips* in the *Inspection Results* section of the Accessibility Checker and read the tip on why reordering the objects on the slide can benefit the comprehension of someone who cannot view the slide.

m. Click the **HOME tab**, click **Arrange** in the Drawing group, and then select **Selection Pane**. Ensure **Title 1** is selected and click the **Re-order up arrow** twice so that the title will be read first by a text reader. Select **Subtitle 2** and click the **Re-order up arrow** once so that the subtitle will be read next by a text reader. Close the Selection pane and the Accessibility Checker pane.

n. Click the **FILE tab**, click **Export**, and then click **Create PDF/XPS Document**, if necessary.

o. Click **Create PDF/XPS** in the right pane, navigate to the folder containing your files, and then click **Publish**.

p. Close Adobe Acrobat Reader or Adobe Acrobat.

q. Click the **FILE tab**, click **Export**, and then click **Create Handouts**.

r. Click **Create Handouts** in the right pane.

s. Click **Notes below slides**. Click **OK**.

t. Delete Slide 1 in the top-left corner when Word opens. Navigate to where you are saving your files and save the document as **p08p2KingHandout_LastFirst**. Close Word.

u. Save the presentation, and submit based on your instructor's directions.

Mid-Level Exercises

1 | Protecting Your Computer Training Presentation

As an employee of your company's IT department, you sometimes prepare technology training materials. You are currently preparing a presentation on threats to computer security and computer safety tips. You ask Ben, a colleague in human resources, to review the presentation and insert comments with suggestions. Because the presentation is password protected, you share the password with him. When he returns the presentation, you merge and compare the presentations and decide which suggestions to incorporate. Then you prepare the presentation for distribution and select a presentation file type.

a. Open *p08m1Protect* and save it as **p08m1Protect_LastFirst**.

b. Create a handout header with your name and a handout footer with your instructor's name and your class. Include the current date.

c. Use Protect Presentation to encrypt the presentation with a password for opening. Use Th>3@t$ as the password.

d. On Slide 1, create a comment that reads **Ben, please review the presentation and make suggestions. Do I need to add anything? Thank you.**

e. Compare and merge *p08m1ProtectBen* with the open *p08m1Protect_LastFirst*.

f. Note that the Revisions pane lists two changes in the *Presentation Changes* section. Accept both of the presentation changes: *Theme (1-14)* and *Insertions after "How do You Defend Against Spyware."*

g. Starting with Slide 1, advance one by one through the comments on each slide using Next in the Comments group. Read each of the comments and make the following changes based on the comments:

Slide	Comment	Change
2	bb2	Link the *Viruses, Worms, and Trojan Horses* bullet to Slide 3.
2	bb3	Remove the *Protection* bullet.
2	bb4	Change slide titles to sentence case (the first letter of the sentence is capitalized, with the rest being lowercase unless requiring capitalization for a specific reason) on all slides except Slide 1. (Tip: Use Change Case in the Font group of the Home tab.)
5	bb5	Find and replace all occurrences of *E-mail* with *e-mail*. (Tip: Use Match Case)

h. Check the spelling in the presentation. Change all occurrences of *trojan* to **Trojan**. Ignore the suggestion for *OnGuard*.

i. View the presentation in Slide Show view. Annotate Slide 13, the *What is spam?* slide, by highlighting *spam* in the title to remind you to add a Spam hyperlink to the menu slide. Keep the ink annotations when you exit the slide show. On Slide 2, add **Spam** to the bulleted list and hyperlink it to Slide 13.

j. View the Print Preview for Handouts (4 slides Horizontal per page). Scroll through Print Preview and note the comments. Print as directed by your instructor.

k. Run the Compatibility Checker to check for features not supported by earlier versions of PowerPoint. Note that the SmartArt graphic on Slide 3 and any text in it cannot be edited when using versions of Microsoft Office earlier than Office 2007. Depending on the transition effect you selected, the transition effect may not be viewable using any earlier version of PowerPoint.

l. Change the file encryption settings for the presentation in General Options. Delete the password in the *Password to open* box.

m. Save the presentation and use the Export option Change File Type to save a version of the file to a PowerPoint Show so that it automatically opens as a slide show. Use the name **p08m1ProtectShow_LastFirst**.

n. Close the Revisions and Comments panes if necessary. Make the following changes to the properties:

Property	Change
Title	Protect Your Computer Against Harmful Attacks
Subject	Computer Safety
Keywords	Computer safety, viruses, worms, Trojan horses, spam
Category	Training
Comments	Presentation for Employee Education Program. Reviewed by Ben B.

o. Accept all changes and end the review. Close both of the presentations, and submit based on your instructor's directions.

2 Impressionist Artists

You have been refining a presentation on impressionist artists for your Nineteenth Century Art class. In this exercise, you prepare the presentation for distribution, create a handout in Microsoft Word, and then package the presentation. Finally, you present the presentation online to classmates who will be unable to be in class the day you present.

a. Open *p08m2Impressionism* and save it as **p08m2Impressionism_LastFirst**.

b. Create a handout header with your name and a handout footer with your instructor's name and your class in the presentation. Include the current date.

c. Inspect the presentation for hidden metadata or personal information. Check every type of information, including off-slide content.

d. Remove Document Properties and Personal Information. Do not remove presentation notes.

e. Run the Compatibility Checker to check for features not supported by earlier versions of PowerPoint. Note that earlier versions cannot change the shape and text in Slides 1 and 3.

f. Create handouts in Microsoft Word with notes next to the slides. Insert your name, instructor's name, and class in a header and print as directed by your instructor. Save the Word handout as **p08m2Handout_LastFirst**.

g. Use the *Package Presentation for CD* feature to copy the presentation and media links to the folder where you have saved your solution files. Name the CD **Impres_LastFirst**.

h. Create a Microsoft account so that you can access the Office Presentation Service.

i. Use your Microsoft account to log into the Office Presentation Service.

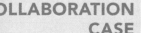
DISCOVER

j. Send an e-mail sharing the link for the online presentation with your instructor and start the slide show. After viewing the presentation, end the online presentation.

k. Save and close the file, and submit based on your instructor's directions.

3 Rescue Pets

COLLABORATION CASE
CREATIVE CASE

You and your friends volunteer at the local animal shelter each week. You have been asked to put together a short presentation about some of the success stories for matching animals with loving families. The presentation will be used to solicit donations, to recruit more volunteers, and to attract more adoptive families. You and your friends can use SkyDrive or pass the presentation among group members as an attachment using your Outlook accounts.

a. Open *p08m3Pets* and save it as **p08m3Pets_LastFirst**.

b. Add your name on the title slide. Create a handout header with your name and a handout footer with your instructor's name and your class in the presentation. Include the current date.

c. Add one slide with a description and a photo of a pet.

d. Save the presentation and pass it to the next student so that he or she can perform the same tasks. Continue until all group members have created a slide in the presentation.

e. Inspect the presentation by inspecting the document and running the Accessibility Checker and the Compatibility Checker. Correct all errors.

f. Create and publish a PDF of the presentation. Name the PDF **p08m3PetsHandout_LastFirst**. Close Adobe Acrobat Reader or Adobe Acrobat.

g. Use the *Package Presentation for CD* feature to copy the presentation and media links to the folder where you have saved your solution files. Name the CD **PetsCD_LastFirst**.

h. Save and close the files, and submit based on your instructor's directions.

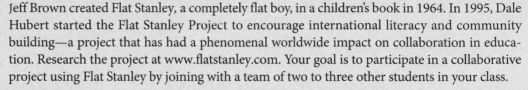

Flat Stanley Team Project

RESEARCH CASE →

Jeff Brown created Flat Stanley, a completely flat boy, in a children's book in 1964. In 1995, Dale Hubert started the Flat Stanley Project to encourage international literacy and community building—a project that has had a phenomenal worldwide impact on collaboration in education. Research the project at www.flatstanley.com. Your goal is to participate in a collaborative project using Flat Stanley by joining with a team of two to three other students in your class.

Each team member must create a Flat Stanley, or download the Flat Stanley template from the Web site. Team members should journal Flat Stanley's activities for several days by recording them with a digital camera. Create a presentation using your images. Send the presentation to your teammates via e-mail so they can add comments, annotations, and their own Flat Stanley images. When they return the presentation to you, compare and merge the documents. Accept and reject changes as needed to create a cohesive presentation of Flat Stanley's activities. Insert a handout header with your name and a handout footer with your instructor's name and your class. Include the current date. Create presentation properties that could help you locate the presentation, if needed. Inspect the document and remove anything that appears except the properties. Check the compatibility of the presentation with earlier versions of PowerPoint. Save the presentation as a PowerPoint Show. Present the slide show online to your teammates, or package the presentation to a folder including all links. Save the presentation as **p08b2FlatStanley_LastFirst**. Submit to your instructor as directed.

Photography Class Project

DISASTER RECOVERY

As a project for your Art Appreciation class, you contacted a local photographer, Katherine Hulce, and asked her to share several of her digital images with you. The photographer gave you permission to use her images but retained the copyright. You created a presentation to introduce her work and e-mailed the presentation to her. She returned the presentation with some added images, annotations, comments, and changes.

Open *p08b3Photography* and save it as **p08b3Photography_LastFirst**. Compare and merge the presentation with *p08b3PhotographyHulce*. Accept all changes to the presentation and end the review. As you view each slide, you notice two other photographers are mentioned on Slide 2. Change the slide title to singular and delete their names, leaving only Katherine Hulce's information. Run the Document Inspector to ensure no other photographers' information is included. Remove all comments, annotations, document properties, and personal information. Create a handout header with your name and a handout footer with your instructor's name and your class. Include the current date. Add the photographer's name as key words in the presentation properties. Save the presentation and resave it as a PowerPoint Picture Presentation with the name **p08b3PhotographyShow_LastFirst**. Mark the presentation as final and submit as directed by your instructor.

E-Mail Etiquette

SOFT SKILLS CASE S

Create a brief presentation that explores proper e-mail etiquette. Include a comment asking for feedback and suggestions for improvement on the last slide. Add keywords to the presentation properties. Run the Accessibility Checker and fix issues as needed. Save the presentation as **p08b4Etiquette_LastFirst**.

Compare your presentation with a classmate's presentation. Make any modifications needed. Save this version of the presentation as a PowerPoint Show as **p08b4EtiquetteShow_LastFirst**. Submit both files to your instructor as directed.

Capstone Exercise

You just returned from your first visit to New York City. Your sister combined your digital images into a memories slide show and e-mailed it to you. She wants you to review the presentation and make suggestions. After you make suggestions, she incorporates the suggestions in her slides and then returns the presentation for you to compare and merge. After accepting the changes, you prepare the presentation for distribution.

Create Annotations and Comments, Hide Markup

You open the presentation your sister sent to you and add annotations on some slides and make a comment.

a. Open the *p08c1NewYork* presentation and save it as **p08c1NewYork_LastFirst**.

b. Create a handout header with your name and a handout footer with your instructor's name and your class. Include the current date.

c. Play the slide show from the beginning. On Slide 2, change your pointer options to **Pen** and circle the existing text by using the mouse. Continue advancing through the slide show, circling any existing text until you reach the end of the presentation.

d. When you reach the end of the presentation, keep the ink annotations as a reminder of changes you want to suggest.

e. On Slide 1, create a comment that reads **Hey Sis, Why don't you use this spot to identify where we were? That's a picture of Battery Park on the southern tip of Manhattan.** Drag the comment balloon so it is next to the vertical text placeholder.

f. Save the presentation.

Merge Presentations

You compare and merge your sister's presentation with the presentation you created. Your sister made the changes you suggested and removed all comments and annotations from her copy.

a. Compare and merge the onscreen *p08c1NewYork_LastFirst* presentation with *p08c1NewYorkMichelle*.

b. Accept all changes and end the review.

c. Close the Revisions and the Comments panes.

Inspect the Presentation and Check Compatibility

You inspect the presentation to ensure that only the metadata you want is retained. You run the Compatibility Checker to see which features you used that are not supported by earlier versions of PowerPoint.

a. Inspect the presentation for hidden metadata or personal information. The Document Inspector locates document properties and presentation notes. Do not remove these items. Close the Document Inspector.

b. Run the Compatibility Checker to see which features you used that are not supported by earlier versions of PowerPoint. Slides 11 and 12 have shapes with text that cannot be edited (WordArt) if you save the presentation in an earlier file format. You do not need to make changes for the earlier version as part of this exercise.

Package the Presentation

You are ready to package the presentation to a folder so that it can be uploaded to the family Web site.

a. Package the presentation for CD with **NY2016_LastFirst** as the name.

b. Copy the presentation to the folder where you store your files. Include the linked files in your package.

c. Close File Explorer and save the presentation.

Mark as Final

In addition to packaging your presentation and burning it to a CD, you plan to indicate that this presentation is complete. You mark the presentation as final.

a. Mark the presentation as **Final**.

b. Verify the presentation has been marked as final by checking the status bar for the *Marked as Final* icon.

c. Save and close the file. Submit all files as directed by your instructor.

Word Application Capstone Exercise

You are an intern with the Hospitality Industry Professionals Association (HIPA), which hosts a conference for its members every year at different locations in this country. This year, the conference will be held July 20–22 in Miami, Florida. One of your responsibilities is to create a document that provides a description of HIPA and the conference, the conference agenda, and a form for members to calculate conference expenses. You will apply several Word features to make the document look more professional. Then, you will insert several form controls into the Calculate Your Expenses table and create a macro to align the document. After you create the Agenda bookmark, you will create hyperlinks to this bookmark, the About HIPA bookmarks, and also to a Web site. Restrict the editing to allow filling in forms so that members can only type in description and expense into the Expenses table. Finally, you will create and insert a digital signature into the document.

Save a Template as a Word Document and Combine Two Documents

You will open a Word template and save it as a Word document. Then you will combine this saved document with the content from another Word file to create the Conference document.

a. Start Word. Open the Word template file named *w00c2ConferenceTemplate.dotx*.

b. Save a copy of the template as a Word document with the file name **w00c2Original.docx**.

c. Combine the contents of the *w00c2Original.docx* and the *w00c2Revised.docx* documents into a new document.

d. Accept all changes in the combined document.

e. Save the combined document as **w00c2Conference_LastFirst.docx**.

f. Close all documents except for *w00c2Conference_LastFirst.docx*.

Insert a Continuous Section Break and a Column Break

You want to format the document to have two columns below the masthead. Therefore, you will insert a continuous section break near the beginning of the document and change the column layout. Also, you want the column content to look balanced on the page, so you will insert a column break on the first page.

a. Position the insertion point immediately to the left of the *Description* heading and insert a Continuous section break.

b. Change the layout of the section starting with the *Description* heading to two equal columns, with a line between.

c. Change the left and right margins to **0.75"**.

d. Position your insertion point immediately to the left of the paragraph that begins *In addition to* and insert a column break.

Copy and Paste a Link to a Spreadsheet File

You will copy and paste the content of a spreadsheet file to the Word document. But you also want to maintain the link so that the data in the Word document can be updated when you make changes to the spreadsheet file.

a. Open the *w00c2Fields.xlsx* spreadsheet file.

b. Copy the **range A1:B8** to the Clipboard.

c. Click the Word document on the taskbar.

d. Paste the copied Excel data as a linked Microsoft Office Excel Worksheet Object in the first blank paragraph of the Word document, below the paragraph that begins *The Hospitality Industry*.

e. Center the object in the left column.

f. Close the spreadsheet file.

Insert a WordArt Object and Format a Paragraph

You will improve the appearance of the document with a masthead created using WordArt, format a selected paragraph, and use shading.

a. Insert a WordArt object at the beginning of the document by doing the following steps:

- Position the insertion point to the left of the text *About HIPA* and insert a Gradient Fill - Aqua, Accent 1, Reflection WordArt.
- Type **HIPA 2016 Conference** as the text for the WordArt.
- Change the width of the WordArt to **6.47"** and the height to **1.6"**.
- Change the font size to **48 pt**.
- Change the wrapping style of the WordArt object to **Top and Bottom**.

b. Format a paragraph with shading and a border by following the steps below:

- Select the paragraph beginning *In addition to*.
- Apply a **Blue, Accent 1, Lighter 80% shading** to the selected paragraph.
- Set the border width to **1 pt**.
- Set the border color to **Blue, Accent 1, Darker 50%**.

Insert a Logo, a SmartArt Graphic, and Group Objects

A logo will help to improve the visibility of the association, so you want to insert a logo below the first heading of the document. You will continue to improve the appearance of the document by using a SmartArt graphic and by grouping four stars together.

a. Insert a logo for HIPA by implementing the following steps:

- Position the insertion point immediately to the left of the text *The Hospitality Industry* under the *Description* heading.
- Insert the *w00c2Logo.png* file.
- Resize the logo's height to **1.5"**. The width will automatically change to 1.05".
- Apply the **Tight wrapping style** to the picture.

b. Insert a Vertical Curved List SmartArt graphic by doing the following steps:

- Position your insertion point in the first blank paragraph below the paragraph that begins *A few of the main reasons*.
- Insert a Vertical Curved List SmartArt graphic.
- Type the following text into the three shapes (from top to bottom):

  Educational Opportunities

  In-person Networking

  Inspiration and Innovation
- Change the height of the three shapes in the SmartArt graphic to **0.5"**.

c. Select the four star shapes immediately below the newly created SmartArt graphic and group them together.

Create and Insert Subdocuments

You will highlight a portion of the text in the Conference document and convert the selected text into a subdocument. The conference agenda is in another file so you will insert the content of the conference agenda into the document that you are currently working on.

a. Switch to Outline view to create and insert subdocuments.

b. Select the heading *Calculate Your Expenses* and the table that follows it.

c. Click **Show Document** and click **Create** to create a subdocument.

d. Select the **Agenda heading** and insert the subdocument *w00c2Agenda.docx* into the current document.

e. Agree to rename the style in the subdocument, when prompted. Note: The original *Agenda* heading will be replaced when the subdocument is inserted.

f. Unlink all subdocuments since you prefer to have the files' content in the document that you are currently working on.

g. Close Outline view.

Insert a Header, and Apply a Document and a Font Theme

You want to include a header, which will display the title of the document and the date that you are preparing the document. You will then apply a document theme and a font theme to the document so that all the features in the Word document are color-coordinated.

a. Insert the header building block named *Retrospect*.

b. Type **Conference Information** in the **Title field**.

c. Type **1/1/2016** in the **Date field**.

d. Apply the **Retrospect theme** to the document.

e. Apply the **Office font theme** to the document.

f. Apply a page background color that uses the **Newsprint texture fill effect**.

Insert Form Fields

You want to insert several form fields into the document. For instance, you want to use a Date Picker content control for date, a Drop-Down List content control to list item choices available to members, a Text Form field to display the individual amount, and another Text Form field to calculate the Total Expenses incurred for the conference.

a. Show the Developer tab on the Ribbon.

b. Turn on Design Mode.

c. Insert a Date Picker Content Control in the table on page 3, in the cell immediately below *Date*.

d. Insert a Drop-Down List content control in the same table, in the cell immediately below *Type of Expense*.

e. Set the properties for the drop-down list to display **Type of Expense** as the title. Enter **Type** in the **Tag box**.

f. Add the following items to the list in the order given:

Transportation

Lodging

Meals

Misc.

a. Insert the Legacy control, Text Form Field in the table, in the cell below *Amount*.

b. Set the properties of the text form field to be a number, the default number to **0**, and the format to **#,##0**. Replace the contents of the Bookmark box with **Amt1** and select the option to **Calculate on exit**.

c. Insert the Legacy control, Text Form Field in the cell to the right of *Total Expenses*.

d. Set the properties of the text form field to be a calculation, the expression to **=SUM(ABOVE)**, and the format to **$#,##0.00;($#,##0.00)**.

e. Turn off Design Mode.

Create a Macro

A macro can be very useful if you need to repeat a certain set of specified tasks regularly. You will practice your macro skills by creating a macro to align the adjustment of the document and then editing the macro using the Visual Basic editor.

a. Create a new macro by doing the following steps:
- Select **Record Macro**.
- Name the macro **Alignment**.
- Type the description of the macro as **Change document alignment** (no period). While recording the macro, be sure to follow the steps exactly as specified. Do not switch between windows in between steps.
- Press **Ctrl+A** to select the entire document.
- Press **Ctrl+E** to change the alignment of the entire document to center.
- Stop recording the macro.

b. Edit the macro by completing the following steps:
- Open the Alignment macro in the Visual Basic Editor.
- Edit the text *Selection.ParagraphFormat.Alignment = wdAlignParagraphCenter* to read **Selection.ParagraphFormat.Alignment = wdAlignParagraphLeft**.
- Save the macro.

c. Copy the entire Alignment macro from the Sub statement to the End Sub statement inclusive to the Clipboard.

d. Click the Word document and paste the code into the last line of this Word document.

e. Run the Alignment macro.

Insert Bookmarks and Hyperlink

Bookmarks and hyperlinks will help members to move quickly from one part of the document to another. You want to create a new bookmark and then hyperlink the newly created bookmark and an existing bookmark to the right place. You will also add a Web site link to the document for easier access to the conference Web site.

a. Create a bookmark to the left of the *Conference Agenda* heading on page 2, using **Agenda** for the name of the bookmark.

b. Create a hyperlink from the word *Agenda*, at the top of page 1, to the Agenda bookmark.

c. Create a hyperlink from the text *About HIPA* to the About bookmark.

d. Select the text *Web site* on page 1, at the bottom of the paragraph that begins *The Hospitality Industry*, and create a hyperlink to the Web page http://www.hipa .conference.net. (Note: This link does not actually open a live Web site.)

Restrict Editing

You do not want the members to make any editorial changes to the document, but at the same time, you want them to be able to enter the data pertaining to their conference expenses.

a. Click the **REVIEW tab** and restrict editing in the document by checking the **Limit formatting to a selection of styles check box**.

b. Allow filling in forms as the only type of editing in the document.

c. Start enforcing protection, leaving the password boxes blank.

Create a Digital Certificate and Add a Digital Signature

Finally, you will create a digital certificate using the name Conner Lee and add a digital signature to the document before you send it out to the members as an e-mail attachment.

a. Create a digital certificate for **Conner Lee**. (Hint: Search for the *SELFCERT.EXE* file in File Explorer.)

b. Add a digital signature to the document for Conner Lee. Note that you may have to change the signature to select Conner Lee.

c. Type **verify integrity of contents** (no period) in the **Purpose for signing this document box**.

d. Click **Yes** to use the certificate if a warning that the certificate cannot be verified is displayed.

e. Ignore any references to Invalid Signatures that may be displayed in the Backstage view after this step is completed.

f. Save and close the document, and exit Word.

g. Submit the *w00c2Conference_LastFirst.docx* document as directed.

Excel Application Capstone Exercise

In this project, you will update a workbook to display bank transactions as a PivotTable. You will filter the PivotTable, format the values, display the values as calculations, and create a PivotChart using this data. Additionally, you will sort and subtotal data, create one- and two-variable data tables, and use Goal Seek and Scenario Manager to calculate possible mortgage payments. You will format grouped worksheets, set up validation rules, and create mathematical, logical, and lookup functions. You will also import a text file and XML data and manipulate the imported text. Finally, you will modify the document properties, insert a comment, and mark the workbook as final.

Database File Setup

a. Open the file named *e00c1Transactions,* click the **FILE tab**, click **Save As**, and then type **e00c1Transactions_LastFirst**. Click **Save**.

Calculate Totals and Create Pivot Table

a. Make the the JuneTotals worksheet active. Sort the data in the **range A3:E16** in ascending order by Category. At each change in Category, use the Sum function to add subtotals to the data in column E. Accept all other defaults. Collapse the outline to show the grand total and Category subtotals only.

b. Create a PivotTable in **cell F1** on the Annual Exp worksheet using the data in the range A1:D17. Add the Expense field to the PivotTable as the row label, add the Amount field as the value, and then add the Year field as the column label. Change the format of the values in the PivotTable to **Accounting** with no decimal places and set columns F:J to **Auto Fit Column Width**.

c. Add the Category field to the Report Filter area of the PivotTable. Filter the data so that only expenses in the Variable category are displayed. Display the values as percentages of the grand total.

d. Insert a Year slicer in the worksheet and use the slicer to filter the data so that only data from 2013 is displayed. Change the height of the slicer to **2"** and reposition it so that the top-left corner aligns with the top-left corner of cell I2.

e. Create a PivotChart based on the data in the PivotTable using the pie chart type. Change the chart title text to **Variable Expenses** and remove the legend. Add data labels to the Outside End position displaying only the category names and leader lines. Reposition the chart so that the top-left corner aligns with the top-left corner of cell F13.

Perform What-If Analysis

a. Make the Home Loan worksheet active. In **cell A10**, enter a reference to the monthly payment from column B. Create a one-variable data table in the **range A9:H10** using the interest rate from column B as the Row input cell.

b. Enter a reference to the monthly payment from column B in **cell A12**. Create a two-variable data table in the **range A12:H16**, using the interest rate from column B as the Row input cell and the term in months from column B as the Column input cell.

c. Perform a Goal Seek analysis to determine what the down payment in column B needs to be if you want the monthly payment in column B to be $2,000. Accept the solution.

d. Create a scenario named **Maximum** using cells B2, B3, B5, and B6 as the changing cells. Enter these values for the scenario: **280000, 24000, .075**, and **360**, respectively. Show the results and close the Scenario Manager. Undo the last change.

Perform Lookup Functions and Conditional Math

a. Make the June2015 worksheet active. In **cell I7**, sum the values in the range E7:E24 if the purchase in column C is groceries; in **cell I8**, average the values in the range E7:E24 if the purchase in column C is groceries; and in **cell I9**, calculate the number of times groceries were purchased during the month.

b. Calculate the total amount spent on groceries using a credit card in **cell I11**, calculate the average spent on groceries using a credit card in **cell I12**, and then calculate the number of times groceries were purchased using a credit card during the month in **cell I13**.

c. Nest an AND function within an IF function in **cell F7** to determine if the transaction was paid using a credit card and the amount of the transaction is less than –100. If both conditions are met in the AND function, the function should return the text *Flag*. For all others, the function should return the text *OK*. Copy the function down through cell F24.

d. Use the INDEX function in **cell E4** to identify the transaction amount that aligns with the position in cell C4. Type **5** for the column_num and use the range A7:F24 as the array argument.

Perform Advanced Filtering and Database Functions

a. Make the June2015 worksheet active. Filter the data in the **range A6:E24** using the criteria in the range A27:E28. Set the filter to copy the data to the range A31:E31. In **cell I17**, use the DAVERAGE function to determine the average amount spent for transactions meeting the criteria in the range A27:E28.

Group and Fill Across Worksheets

a. Group the June2015 and JuneTotals worksheets together. Fill the contents and formatting from the range A1:F1 on the JuneTotals worksheet across the grouped worksheets. Ungroup the worksheets. In **cell I19** on the June2015 worksheet, insert a reference to cell E26 on the JuneTotals worksheet.

Create Data Validation

a. Make the June2015 worksheet active. Create a validation rule for the range D7:D24 to only allow values in the list from the range I21:I24. Create an error alert for the selected range that will display after invalid data is entered. Using the Stop style, enter **Invalid Entry** as the title and type **Please select a valid method.** (include the period) as the error message.

Specialized Functions

a. Make the CarLoan worksheet active. In **cell G10**, use the CUMPRINC function to calculate the cumulative principle paid on the car loan. Use the data in the range E4:E6 when entering the first three arguments in the function. Reference cell A10 as the start and end period arguments. Enter **0** as the type argument. Modify the function to convert the results to a positive value. Make the row references absolute in all arguments, except for the end period. Copy the formula down through cell G19.

Import Data

a. Open the downloaded, tab-delimited text file *eV2_stocks.txt* in Excel using a data format of general. You do not need to create a connection to the original data file. Copy the **range A1:F5** and close the text file. Paste the copied range onto the Stocks worksheet in **cell A3**.

b. Make the Stocks worksheet active. Separate the text in the first column into two columns using the asterisk (*), as the delimiter. Insert a function in **cell A3** that will display the text in cell A9 with initial capitalization only.

c. Import the downloaded XML file *eV2_highclose.xml* into the Stocks worksheet in **cell A11**. Open the XML file in Notepad and find and replace all instances of the text *General Electric* with **General Electric Co** (no period). Save the XML document and close Notepad. Refresh the XML data on the Stocks worksheet.

Apply Workbook Theme and Cell Style

a. Apply the **Frame theme** to the workbook. Apply the cell style **Accent1** to cells **A3** and **D3** on the CarLoan worksheet.

Finalize Workbook

a. Set the Author property of the workbook to **Exploring Excel Student** and set the Title property to **Personal Finances**.

b. Change your user name to **Exploring Excel Student**. On the CarLoan worksheet, insert the comment **Updated on 7/17/2015** in **cell A1**. Mark the workbook as final.

c. Ensure that the worksheets are correctly named and placed in the following order in the workbook: JuneTotals, June2015, AnnualExp, HomeLoan, CarLoan, and Stocks. Close the workbook and exit Excel. Submit the workbook as directed.

Access Application Capstone Exercise

In this project, you will add fields to a table and set data validation rules. You will also import a text file into a database, design advanced queries, and create a navigation form. Additionally, you will use SQL to modify a record source and create an embedded macro to automate opening a report.

Database File Setup

a. Start Access. Open the file named *a00c2Drivers*, click the **FILE tab**, click **Save As**, click **Save As**, and then type **a00c2Drivers_LastFirst**. Click **Save**.

Import a Text File into the Database and Modify the Table

a. Create a table in the database by importing the delimited text file named *Insurance_Text.txt*. Use the first row of the file as field names, use **InsuranceID** as the primary key, and then name the table **InsuranceCos_Text**. Accept all other default options.

b. Create a new field in the Agency Info table after *InsPhone* named **Web site** with the **Hyperlink data type**. Save the table. In Datasheet view, add the Web site **http://William_Smith.com** to the William Smith record (1).

c. Create a new field in the Agency Info table after *Web site* named **AgentPhoto** with the **Attachment data type**. Save the table. In Datasheet view for Record 1 (William Smith), add the picture file named *a00c2WmSmith.jpg* to the AgentPhoto field.

d. Set the validation rule of the InsuranceCo field to accept the values **AS**, **NAT**, or **SF** only. Set the validation text to read **Please enter AS, NAT, or SF.** (include the period).

e. Make InsuranceCo a lookup field in the Agency Info table. Set the lookup to get values from the InsuranceID field in the InsuranceCos_Text table. Accept the default label and save the table. In Datasheet view, click in any InsuranceCo cell and click the arrow to view the options. Close the table.

Create Queries to Analyze, Update, and Delete Records

a. Create a new query using Design view. From the Insurance table, add the DriverID, AutoType, TagID, and TagExpiration fields (in that order). Save the query as **Missing Tag Dates**.

b. Switch to Design view of the same query and set the criteria in the TagExpiration field to find null values. Run the query (two records will display). Save and close the query.

c. Change the query type to **Update** and set the criteria to update drivers whose class is *Minor* to *Junior*. Run the query (eight records will update). Save the query as **Driver Class_Update** and close the query. View the updates in the Drivers table and close the table.

d. Create a new query using Design view. From the Drivers table, add the Class field. Save the query as **Driver Class_Delete**.

e. Change the query type to **Delete** and set the criteria to delete drivers whose class is *Special*. Run the query (one record will delete). Save and close the query. View the changes in the Drivers table and close the table.

Create a Query to Prompt for Data

a. Create a new query using Design view. From the Insurance table, add the DriverID, AutoType, AutoYear, and TagID fields (in that order). Save the query as **Auto Year_Parameter**.

b. Set the criteria in the Auto Year field to display the prompt as **Enter the auto year:** and run the query. In the prompt, enter **2007** and click **OK** to view the results (two records). Close the query.

Use the Performance Analyzer

a. Use the Performance Analyzer to analyze the Drivers table. Note the idea to change the data type of the Weight field from Short Text to Long Integer. In the Drivers table, set the data type of the Weight field to **Number (Long Integer)** and save and close the table.

Create a Navigation Form

a. Create a Navigation form based on the Vertical Tabs, Left template. Drag and drop the Drivers form onto the first tab of the form. Drop the Insurance form onto the second tab.

b. Drag and drop the Drivers report onto the third tab of the Navigation form. View the form in Form view, click each of the tabs, and then save the form as **Navigator**. Close the form.

Add an SQL Statement as a Record Source and Create an Embedded Macro

a. Open the Drivers report in Design view. Modify the record source of the report using a SQL statement to select all Drivers records with a Class of **Adult**. Print Preview the report (eight records will display). Save and close the report.

b. Open the Drivers form in Design view, click to add a command button at the intersection of the six-inch mark on the horizontal ruler and the three-inch mark on the vertical ruler.

c. Set the command button to open the report named *Drivers*. Use the default picture as the button. Set the name and the caption of the button to **Open Drivers Report**. Save the form. View the form in Form view and click the command button.

d. Close all database objects, close the database, and then exit Access. Submit the database as directed.

PowerPoint Application Capstone Exercise

As a member the IPC International Photo Conference Committee, you have been asked to help create a presentation for the upcoming Conference & Expo at the Boston Bailey Expo Center. Some of the slides will be printed as posters and displayed at the conference. Charts will be used to highlight last year's worldwide workshops and total attendees, and a table will display the workshop schedule for the Boston conference. You will also apply some animations, insert hyperlinks, and work with the slide master.

Presentation Creation

a. Start PowerPoint. Open *p00ac2IPC* and save the file as **p00ac2IPC_LastFirst**.

b. Change Slide Size to **On-screen Show (16:10)** and **Ensure Fit**.

Design a Table and Change the Table Layout

a. On Slide 2, insert a table with 3 columns and 5 rows. Add the following information to the table:

Left Column	Middle Column	Right Column
Capturing the Moment	9:00 AM	12:00 PM
Giving Your Images the Edge	10:30 AM	1:00 PM
From Stills to Motion	12:00 PM	3:30 PM
Social Media	2:00 PM	4:30 PM
Wedding Techniques	4:00 PM	7:00 PM

b. Insert a new top row to the table. Add the following information to the new row:

Left Column	Middle Column	Right Column
WORKSHOP	START	END

c. Add a new first column to the table. Merge all the cells in the first column and format the cell in the first column with a picture fill using the downloaded *p00ac2Snapshot.jpg* file.

d. Center all of the text in the table vertically and horizontally. Apply the **Convex bevel effect** to all cells of the table except for the picture. Change the height of the table to **4.5"**.

Create and Insert a Chart, Change a Chart Type, and Change the Chart Layout

a. On Slide 3, insert the chart found in the downloaded Excel file *p00ac2Workshops* as an object to the slide. Change the height of the object to **4.5"** and center it on the slide.

b. On Slide 4, insert a Clustered Column chart. When Excel opens, resize the chart data range to A1:B6. Delete the contents of the cells in columns C and D. Replace the remaining content in the Excel worksheet with the following data:

Cell A2: CTM
Cell A3: GYITE
Cell A4: FSTM
Cell A5: SM
Cell A6: WT
Cell B1: Attendees
Cell B2: 9,673
Cell B3: 11,412
Cell B4: 6,591
Cell B5: 4,809
Cell B6: 9,177

Close Excel.

c. On Slide 4, change the chart to a *Line with Markers* chart. Apply the **Layout 8 layout style** to the chart. Format the data labels to display to the right of the data points.

Insert and Use a Hyperlink and Add an Action Button

a. On Slide 6, insert a hyperlink from the text *IPCzone.org* to the Web page **http://www.ipczone.org**. Add the ScreenTip **Click for additional information** to the hyperlink.

b. Click at the end of the next line, *E-mail us at*, add a space, and then type **ipczone@domain.net**, followed by a space.

c. On the next line, insert a hyperlink from the text *Download Registration Materials* to the downloaded Word document *p00ac2Registration*.

d. On Slide 6, insert an Action Button: Beginning shape by clicking in the bottom-left corner of the slide. Set the action button to link to Slide 2 (Workshop Schedule) when clicked. Align the action button with the left and bottom borders of the slide.

Apply a Motion Path Animation and Specify Animation Settings and Timings

a. On Slide 5, apply a **Fly In entrance animation** to the text placeholder on the left. Set the effect options so that the text flies in from the top left. Set clicking the picture on the bottom left (Picture 3) as the trigger for the animation and set the Start to **After Previous**.

b. On the same slide, apply the **Fly In entrance animation** to the text placeholder on the right. Set the Effect Options so that the text flies in from the top right. Set clicking the picture on the bottom right (Picture 2) as the trigger for the animation and set the Start to **After Previous**.

c. On the same slide, add an action to each of the two pictures on the bottom so that when they are clicked, the Camera sound is played.

d. On Slide 6, apply the **Diagonal Down Right motion path** to the picture of the ink pen.

Customize the Ribbon

a. Create a custom tab to the right of the HOME tab. Name the tab **Shapes**. Name the group in the tab **Combine Shapes**. Include the following buttons from the *Commands Not in the Ribbon* list in the Combine Shapes group: Combine, Intersect, Subtract, and Union.

Use Combine Shape Commands

a. Switch to Slide Master view. There are three shapes in the top-left corner of the top-level Slide Master. Combine the three shapes. Remove the slide number placeholder from the slide.

Modify a Slide Master, Handout, and Notes Master

a. Apply the **Century Gothic-Palatino font theme** to the Slide Master. Apply the **Red Orange color theme** to the Slide Master. Beginning with the Comparison Layout, delete the remaining slide layouts.

b. Switch to Handout Master view. Change the page setup to **2 Slides** per page. Delete the Header placeholder.

c. Switch to Notes Master view. Type **Page** followed by a space before the number field in the **page number placeholder**. Close the Notes Master view.

Hide Slides and Create a Custom Slide Show

a. Hide Slides 3 and 4 in the presentation.

b. Create a new custom slide show named **Boston Show** using Slides 1, 2, 5, 7, and 6 (in that order). Start the custom show from the beginning.

Work with Comments and Annotations

a. On Slide 2, use the Highlight tool with the default color to highlight the words *Social Media* in the table. Disable the highlight tool and proceed through the presentation to the Registration slide.

b. On the Registration slide, change the ink color to **Blue** and use the Pen tool to draw a line connecting the pen tip next to the slide title to the bottom-right edge of the *n* in *Registration*. Exit the slide show and save the annotations that you've made.

c. Insert the comment **I'm not sure we need Slides 3 and 4** on Slide 3.

Check a Presentation for Issues and Protect a Presentation

a. Run the Compatibility Checker to see which features you used that are not supported by earlier versions of PowerPoint, but do not make any changes as a result.

b. Mark the presentation as final.

c. Save the presentation. Close the presentation and exit PowerPoint. Submit the presentation as directed.

Glossary

.potx The file extension assigned to a PowerPoint template.

.pptx The file extension assigned to a PowerPoint presentation.

3-D formula The file extension assigned to a PowerPoint presentation

Access Database Executable (ACCDE) A file that has had all VBA source code removed, prohibits users from making design and name changes to forms or reports within the database, and prohibits users from creating new forms and reports.

Accessibility Refers to the ease with which a person with physical challenges is able to access and understand a presentation.

Accessibility Checker (Excel) A tool that detects issues that could hinder a user's ability to use a workbook. (PowerPoint) Aids in identifying and resolving accessibility issues in a presentation.

Accounting Number Format A number format that displays $ on the left side of a cell and formats values with commas for the thousands separator and two decimal places.

Action button A ready-made button designed to serve as an icon that can initiate an action when clicked, pointed to, or moused over.

Action query A query that adds, updates, or deletes data in a database.

Active cell The current cell in a worksheet. It is indicated by a dark green border onscreen.

ActiveX control A form element designed for use in Office 2007 or later versions and that requires a macro to work.

Add-in A program that can be added to Excel to provide enhanced functionality.

Alternative text (alt text) A text-based description of an image.

Analysis ToolPak An add-in program that contains tools for performing complex statistical analysis, such as ANOVA, Correlation, and Histogram.

AND function A logical function that returns TRUE when all arguments are true and FALSE when at least one argument is false.

Animation An action used to draw interest to an object in a presentation; a movement that controls the entrance, emphasis, exit, and/or path of objects in a slide show.

Annotation A written note or drawing on a slide for additional commentary or explanation that is added while displaying a slide show presentation.

Anomaly An error or inconsistency within a database that occurs when you add, edit, or delete data.

ANOVA ANOVA stands for Analysis of Variance and is a statistical tool that compares the means between two data samples to determine if they were derived from the same population.

Append query A query that selects records from one or more tables (the source) and adds them to an existing table (the destination).

Area chart A chart type that emphasizes magnitude of changes over time by filling in space between lines with color.

Argument A variable, constant, or expression that is needed to produce the output for a function or action.

Attachment control A control that enables you to manage attached files in forms and reports.

Attachment field Use an Access attachment to attach multiple files of any format to an individual record; attached files can be launched from Access.

AVERAGEIF function A statistical function that calculates the average of values in a range when a specified condition is met.

AVERAGEIFS function A statistical function that returns the average (arithmetic mean) of all cells that meet multiple criteria.

Back-end database Contains the tables of the database.

Background (Word) A color, design, image, or watermark that appears behind text in a document or on a Web page. (Excel) An image that appears behind the worksheet data onscreen; it does not print.

Bar chart A type of chart used to show comparisons among items where the information is displayed horizontally.

Basic custom show A single presentation file from which you can create separate presentations.

Binding constraint A constraint that Solver enforces to reach the target value.

Blog The chronological publication of personal thoughts and Web links.

Bookmark A feature that provides an electronic marker for a specific location in a document, enabling you to find that location quickly.

Bound control A control that is connected to a field in a table or query.

Bubble chart A chart type that shows relationships among three values by using bubbles to show a third dimension.

Building Block A predefined object to insert quickly and easily for frequently used document components, such as a disclaimer, company address, logo, or cover page.

Calculated control A control containing an expression that generates a calculated result.

Calculated field A user-defined field that performs an arithmetic calculation based on other fields in a PivotTable.

Cell style A set of formatting options applied to worksheet cells to produce a consistent appearance for similar cells within a worksheet.

Certification authority (CA) A commercial company, such as VeriSign, that issues and validates identities by using digital signatures for a fee.

Changing variable cell A cell containing a variable whose value changes until Solver optimizes the value in the objective cell.

Chart area The chart and all of its elements, bounded by the placeholder borders.

Check box form field Consists of a box that can be checked or unchecked.

Collaboration A process that occurs when multiple people work together to achieve a common goal by using technology to edit the contents of a file.

Color theme Consists of the color combinations for the text, lines, background, and graphics in a presentation.

Column chart A type of chart used to show changes over time or comparisons among items where the information is displayed vertically.

Column header The text in the top row of the table that identifies the contents of the column.

Column heading The field name displayed at the top of a crosstab query.

Columns area The region in which to place a field that will display labels to organize data vertically in a PivotTable.

Combine (Word) A feature that integrates all changes from multiple authors or documents into one single document. (PowerPoint) A Combine Shapes command that removes the overlapping area of two shapes.

Combo box control Provides a drop-down menu displaying a list of options from which the user can choose a single value.

Comma separated values (CSV) file A text file that uses commas to separate text into columns and a newline character to separate data into rows.

Comment (Excel) (1) A notation attached to a cell to pose a question or provide commentary. (2) A line that documents programming code; starts with an apostrophe and appears in green in the VBA Editor. (PowerPoint) A text note attached to the slide.

Comment indicator A colored triangle in the top-right corner of a cell to indicate that the cell contains comments.

Compare A Word feature that evaluates the contents of two or more documents and displays markup balloons showing the differences between the two documents.

Compatibility Checker A tool that detects features that are not supported by earlier versions of the program.

Composite key A primary key that is made of two or more fields.

CONCATENATE function A text function that joins two or more text strings into one text string.

Constraint A limitation that imposes restrictions on a spreadsheet model as Solver determines the optimum value for the objective cell.

CORREL function A statistical function that calculates the correlation coefficient of two data series.

COUNTIF function A statistical function that counts the number of cells in a range when a specified condition is met.

COUNTIFS function A statistical function that applies criteria to cells across multiple ranges and counts the number of times all criteria are met.

Covariance Measure of how to sample sets of data vary simultaneously.

Criteria Range An area that is separate from the data table and specifies the conditions used to filter the table.

Crosstab query A query that summarizes a data source into a few key rows and columns.

CSV text file A file that uses a comma to separate one column from the next column, enabling the receiving software to distinguish one set of field values from the next.

CUMIPMT A financial function that calculates cumulative interest for specified payment period.

CUMPRINC A financial function that calculates cumulative principal for specified payment periods.

Curriculum Vitae (CV) Similar to a resume, displays your skills, accomplishments, job history, or other employment information, and is often used by academics.

Custom button An action button that can be set to trigger unique actions in a presentation.

Custom path An animation path that can be created freehand instead of following a preset path.

Custom show A grouped subset of the slides in a presentation.

Customize Ribbon tab A tab in the PowerPoint Options dialog box that enables you to create a personal tab on the Ribbon that includes features that are not available on the standard Ribbon.

Data macro A macro that executes a series of actions when a table event occurs.

Data mining The process of analyzing large volumes of data to identify patterns and trends.

Data range property A setting that controls the format, refresh rate, and other characteristics of a connection to external data.

Data series A chart element that contains the data points representing a set of related numbers.

Data validation A set of constraints or rules that require that rules be followed in order to allow data to be entered.

Database Documenter A tool that creates a report that contains detailed information for each selected object.

Database function A function that analyzes data for selected records in a table.

Database Splitter Enables you to split a database into two files: a back-end database and a front-end database.

Date arithmetic The process of adding or subtracting one date from another, or adding or subtracting a constant from a date.

Date formatting Affects the date's display without changing the actual underlying value in the table.

Date function Calculates the current date.

Date Picker Displays a calendar that the user can navigate on an electronic form and click rather than typing in a date.

DatePart function An Access function that examines a date and returns a portion of the date.

DAVERAGE function A database function that averages values in a database column based on specified conditions.

DCOUNT function A database function that counts the cells that contain a number in a database column based on specified conditions.

Delete query A query that selects records from a table and then removes them from the table.

Delimiter A character, such as a comma or tab, used to separate data in a text file.

Design Mode Enables you to view and select the control fields to allow for modifications to the control field layout or options.

Desktop publishing The merger of text with graphics to produce a professional-looking document.

Destination application The application that created the document into which the object is being inserted.

Destination file A file that contains a pointer to the source file.

Detail section Displays the records in the record source.

Digital certificate An attachment to a file that guarantees the authenticity of the file, provides a verifiable signature, or enables encryption.

Digital signatures Electronic, encryption-based, secure stamps of authentication that confirm who created the file, that the file is valid, and that no changes have been made to the file after its authentication.

DMAX function A database function that identifies the highest value in a database column based on specified conditions.

DMIN function A database function that identifies the lowest value in a database column based on specified conditions.

Document Inspector A tool that detects hidden and personal data in a workbook to remove.

Document property An attribute, such as an author's name or keyword, that describes a file.

Document theme A set of coordinating fonts, colors, and special effects that gives a stylish and professional look.

Doughnut chart A chart type that shows proportions to a whole and can contain more than one data series.

Drawing canvas A frame-like area that helps you keep parts of your drawing together.

Drop cap A large capital letter at the beginning of a paragraph.

Drop-down list Enables the user to choose from one of several existing entries.

DSUM function A database function that adds values in a database column based on specified conditions.

Editing restriction Specifies limits for users to modify a document.

Element An XML component, including the start tag, an end tag, and the associated data.

Embed The process of importing external data into an application but not maintaining any connection to the original data source.

Embedded macro A macro that executes when an event attached to a control or object occurs.

Embedded object A part of the destination file that once inserted, no longer maintains a connection to the source file or source application in which the object was created.

Embedding Imports an object into a document from its original source and allows editing directly in the document without changing the source data file.

Emphasis A PowerPoint animation type that draws attention to an object already on a slide.

Encryption The process of altering digital information by using an algorithm to make it unreadable to anyone except those who possess the key (or secret code).

End button An action button that moves to the last slide in the presentation.

End tag An XML code that indicates the end of an element and contains the element's name preceded by a slash character, such as </Rent>.

Entrance A PowerPoint animation type that controls how an object moves onto or appears on a slide.

Error alert A message that appears when the user enters invalid data in a cell containing a validation rule.

Event Occurs when a user enters, edits, or deletes data; events also occur when users open, use, or close forms and reports.

Exit A PowerPoint animation type that controls how an object leaves or disappears from a slide.

Expanded outline Displays the slide number, icon, title, and content of each slide in Outline view.

Extensible Characteristics that indicate that XML can be expanded to include additional data.

eXtensible Markup Language (XML) A data-structuring standard that enables data to be shared across applications, operating systems, and hardware.

File Transfer Protocol (FTP) A process that uploads files from a PC to a server or from a server to a PC.

Fill The interior space of an object.

Filters area The region in which to place a field so that the user can then filter the data by that field in a PivotTable or PivotChart.

Find duplicates query A query that helps you identify repeated values in a table.

Find unmatched query A query that compares records in two related tables, and then displays the records found in one table, but not the other.

First normal form (1NF) Satisfied when a table contains no repeating groups or repeating columns.

Fixed-length text file A file that allocates a certain number of characters for each field.

Fixed-width text file A text file that stores data in columns that have a specific number of characters designated for each column.

Flash Fill A feature that fills in data or values automatically based on one or two examples you enter using another part of data entered in a previous column in the dataset.

Flatten To convert all objects on a slide to a single layer.

Form control Helps a user complete a form by displaying prompts such as drop-down lists and text boxes.

Form Footer A footer that displays one time at the bottom of a form.

Form Header A header that displays once at the top of each form.

Form template A document that defines the standard layout, structure, and formatting of a form.

Formatting restriction Ensures that others do not modify formatting or styles in a document.

Formula auditing Tools to enable you to detect and correct errors in formulas by identifying relationships among cells.

FREQUENCY function A statistical function that determines the number of occurrences of numerical values in a dataset based on predetermined bins.

FROM keyword Specifies the table (or tables) that will be searched in an SQL Select Statement

Front-end database Contains the queries, forms, and reports of the database.

Functional dependency When the value of one field is determined by the value of another.

FV function A financial function that calculates the future value of an investment given a fixed interest rate, a term, and periodic payments.

Goal Seek A tool that identifies the necessary input value to obtain a desired goal.

Grid An underlying, but invisible, set of horizontal and vertical lines that determine the placement of major elements.

Gridline A line that extends from the horizontal or vertical axes and that can be displayed to make the chart data easier to read and understand.

Group Footer Appears just below the *Detail* section in Design view. Appears once each time the grouping field value changes.

Group Header Appears just above the *Detail* section in Design view, along with the name of the field by which you are grouping. Appears once each time the grouping field value changes.

Grouping (Word) The process of combining selected objects so they appear as a single object. (Excel) (1) The process of joining rows or columns of related data into a single entity so that groups can be collapsed or expanded for data analysis. (2) The process of selecting worksheets to perform the same action at the same time.

Handout master Contains the design information for audience handout pages.

Help button An action button that can be set to open a document with instructions or help information.

Hierarchy Indicates levels of importance in a structure.

Histogram A tabular display of data frequencies organized into bins.

History worksheet A specially created worksheet through the Change Tracking feature that lists particular types of changes made to a workbook.

HSL A color model in which the numeric system refers to the hue, saturation, and luminosity of a color.

Hyperlink An electronic marker that points to a different location within the same document, another document, or displays a different Web page.

Hyperlinked custom show Begins with a main custom show and uses hyperlinks to link between other shows.

HyperText Markup Language (HTML) Uses codes to describe how a document appears when viewed in a Web browser.

IFERROR function A logical function that checks a value and returns the result if possible or an error message.

IIf function Evaluates an expression and displays one value when the expression is true and another value when the expression is false.

Importing The process of inserting data from one application or file into another.

Index Reduces the time it takes to run queries and reports.

INDEX function A lookup & reference value or reference to a value within a range.

Information Rights Management (IRM) Services designed to help control who can access documents containing sensitive or confidential information.

Input mask Enables you to restrict the data being input into a field by specifying the exact format of the data entry.

Input Mask Wizard Frequently used to generate data restrictions for a field based on responses to a few questions.

Input message A description or instructions for data entry.

Interactivity The ability to branch or interact with a presentation based on decisions made by a viewer or audience.

Internet A network of networks that connects computers anywhere in the world.

Intersect A Combine Shapes command that removes any area that is not overlapped.

IPMT function A financial function that calculates periodic interest for a fixed-term, fixed-rate loan or investment.

IsNull function Checks whether a field has no value.

Keyword A special programming syntax used for a specific purpose that appears in blue in the VBA Editor.

Kiosk An interactive computer terminal available for public use.

Label A chart element that identifies data in the chart.

Layering The process of placing one object on top of another.

Legacy form field A form element that is created or used in Word 2003 and later. When used in a later version of Word, the document must be opened in Compatibility Mode.

Legal blacklining The comparing of two documents and the displaying of the changes between the two documents using Word.

Legend A chart element found in multiseries charts used to help identify the data series, assigns a format or color to each data series and then displays that information with the data series name.

Line chart A type of chart used to display a large number of data points over time.

Linear presentation A presentation where each slide is designed to move one right after another, starting with the first slide and advancing sequentially until the last slide is reached.

Linked object A part of the destination file that is updated when the source file is updated because the information is stored in the source file but displayed as the object in the destination file.

Linking (Word) The process of importing an object from another program, but the object retains a connection to the original data file. (Excel) The process of connecting cells between worksheets. (Access) A process that enables you to connect to a table without having to import the table data into your database.

Loan amortization table A schedule showing monthly payments, interest per payment, amount toward paying off the loan, and the remaining balance for each payment.

Locked Cell A cell that prevents users from making changes to that cell in a protected worksheet.

Logic error An error that occurs when a formula adheres to syntax rules but produces inaccurate results.

Lookup field Provides the user with a finite list of values to choose from in a menu.

Lookup Wizard Creates the menu of finite values by asking you six questions and using your answers to create the options list.

LOWER function A text function that converts all uppercase letters to lowercase.

Macro A set of instructions that executes a specific task or series of keystrokes that complete a repetitive task using only a button click or keyboard shortcut.

Macro Designer The user interface that enables you to create and edit macros.

Macro Recorder A tool that records a series of commands in the sequence performed by a user and converts the commands into programming syntax.

Macro-Enabled Document Adds the extension .docm to the file and stores VBA macro code in the document to enable execution of a macro.

Make table query A query that selects records from one or more tables and uses them to create a new table.

Mark as Final Creates a read-only file and also sets the property to Final on the status bar.

Markup Comments and ink annotations appearing in a presentation.

Master Contains design information to control the layouts, background designs, and color combinations for handouts, notes pages, and slides, giving the presentation a consistent appearance.

Master document A document that acts like a binder for managing smaller documents.

Masthead The identifying information at the top of a newsletter or other periodical.

MATCH function A lookup & reference function that identifies a searched item's position in a list.

Metadata Pieces of data, such as a keyword, that describe other data, such as the contents of a file.

Module A VBA module is a file that stores Sub procedures and Functions. Modules can be created and viewed in the VBA Editor.

Motion path A predetermined path an object follows as part of an animation.

Movie button An action button set to play a movie.

Multiseries data series A data series representing data for two or more sets of data.

Navigation Form A tabbed menu system that ties the objects in the database together so that the database is easy to use.

Navigation Pane Enables you to navigate through a document by viewing headings, viewing pages, and browsing the results of your last search.

Nesting functions Using one function within another function.

Newline character A character that designates the end of a line and starts data on a new line or row in a text file.

Nonbinding constraint A constraint that does not restrict the target value that Solver finds.

Non-key field Any field that is not part of the primary key.

Non-linear presentation A presentation that progresses according to choices made by the viewer or audience that determine which slide comes next.

Normal form A rule of normalization that indicates the current state of a table.

Normal template The framework that defines the default page settings for all new blank Word documents.

Normalization The formal process of deciding which fields should be grouped together into which tables.

NOT function A logical function that returns TRUE if the argument is false and FALSE if the argument is true.

Notes master Contains the design information for notes pages.

NPER function A financial function that calculates the number of periods for an investment or loan.

NPV function A financial function that calculates the net present value of an investment with periodic payments and a discount rate.

Object A variable that contains both data and code and represents an element of Excel.

Object linking and embedding (OLE) A feature that enables you to insert an object created in one application into a document created in another application.

Objective cell The cell that contains the formula-based value that you want to maximize, minimize, or set to a value in Solver.

One-variable data table A data analysis tool that provides various results based on changing one variable.

Open Exclusive A mode that guarantees that you are the only one currently using the database.

OpenDocument presentation (*.odp) A presentation that conforms to the OpenDocument standard for exchanging data between applications.

Optimization model A model that finds the highest, lowest, or exact value for one particular result by adjusting values for selected variables.

OR function A logical function that returns TRUE if any argument is true and returns FALSE if all arguments are false.

ORDER BY keyword Used to sort the records by a certain field in either ascending or descending order in an SQL Select Statement.

Outline A hierarchical structure of data organized so that groups can be expanded to show details or collapsed to show high-level structure.

Package Presentation for CD Copies a presentation, its fonts and embedded items, and a PowerPoint Viewer to a CD or folder for distribution.

Page Footer A footer that appears once at the bottom of each page in a form or report.

Page Header A header that appears once at the top of each page in a form or report.

Parameter query A select query where the user provides the criterion at run time.

PDF file format (PDF) A more secure electronic file format created by Adobe Systems that preserves document formatting and is viewable and printable on any platform.

PERCENTILE.EXC function A statistical function that returns the percentile of a range excluding the 0 or 100% percentile.

PERCENTILE.INC function A statistical function that returns the percentile of a range including the 0 or 100% percentile.

PERCENTRANK.EXC function A statistical function that identifies a value's rank as a percentile, excluding 0 and 1, of a list of values.

PERCENTRANK.INC function A statistical function that identifies a value's rank as a percentile between 0 and 1 of a list of values.

Performance Analyzer Evaluates a database and then makes recommendations for optimizing the database.

Personal Macro Workbook A hidden workbook stored in the XL Start folder that contains macros and opens automatically when you start Excel.

Pie chart A type of chart used to show proportions of a whole.

PivotChart A graphical representation of data in a PivotTable.

PivotTable An interactive organization of data that consolidates and aggregates data by categories that can be sorted, filtered, and calculated.

PivotTable Fields task pane A window that enables a user to specify what fields are used from a dataset and how to organize the data in columns, rows, values, and filters.

Placeholder A field or block of text used to determine the position of objects in a document.

Plot area The region containing the graphical representation of the values in the data series.

Population A dataset that contains all the information you would like to evaluate.

PowerPivot A PivotTable functionality in which two or more related tables can be used to extract data into a PivotTable.

PowerPoint Options A broad range of settings that enable you to customize the environment to meet your needs.

PPMT function A financial function that calculates the principal payment for a specified payment period given a fixed interest rate, term, and periodic payments.

Precedent cell A cell that is referenced by a formula in another cell.

Present Online A Microsoft service that enables the transmission of a presentation in real time over the Internet to a remote audience.

Procedure A named sequence of statements that execute as one unit.

PROPER function A text function that capitalizes the first letter in a text string and any other letters in text that follow any character other than a letter.

Pull quote A phrase or sentence taken from an article to emphasize a key point.

PV function A financial function that calculates the present value of an investment.

Quartile A value used to divide a range of numbers into four equal groups.

QUARTILE.EXC function A statistical function that identifies the value at a specific quartile, exclusive of 0 and 4.

QUARTILE.INC function A statistical function that identifies the value at a specific quartile.

Radar chart A chart type that compares the aggregate values of three or more variables represented on axes starting from the same point.

RANK.AVG function A statistical function that identifies the rank of a value, providing an average ranking for identical values.

RANK.EQ function A statistical function that identifies the rank of a value, omitting the next rank when tie values exist.

RATE function A financial function that calculates the periodic rate for an investment or loan.

Read-only form A form that enables users to view but not change data.

Record macro The process of creating a macro.

Refresh The process of updating data in Excel to match current data in the external data source.

Relationship A connection between two or more tables using a common field, such as an ID field.

Report Footer A footer that displays one time at the bottom of a report.

Report Header A header that displays once at the top of each report.

Reverse A technique that uses light text on a dark background.

Reviewer Someone who examines the presentation and provides feedback.

RGB A numeric system for identifying the color resulting from the combination of red, green, and blue light.

Rich Text Format (RTF) A file format that enables documents created in one software application to be opened with a different software application.

Round function Returns a number rounded to a specific number of decimal places.

Row heading The field names displayed along the left side of a crosstab query.

Rows area The region in which to place a field that will display labels to organize data horizontally in a PivotTable.

Run macro The process of playing back or using a macro.

Run time error A software or hardware problem that prevents a program from working correctly.

Sample A smaller portion of the population that is easier to evaluate.

Scenario A set of values that represent a possible situation.

Scenario Manager A tool that enables you to define and manage scenarios to compare how they affect results.

Scenario summary report A worksheet that contains the scenarios, their input values, and their respective results from using Scenario Manager.

ScreenTip An object that the viewer can mouse over to obtain additional information about a hyperlink.

Second normal form (2NF) Satisfied when a table meets 1NF criteria and all non-key fields are functionally dependent on the entire primary key.

Section Part of a form or report that can be manipulated separately from other parts of the form or report.

Section bar Marks the top boundary of a section in a form or report.

SELECT keyword Determines which fields will be included in the results of an SQL Select Statement.

Shared workbook A file that enables multiple users to make changes at the same time.

SharePoint library A location on a SharePoint site where you can store and manage files you add to the library.

SharePoint workspace A copy of a SharePoint site that can be used while offline.

Sidebar Supplementary text that appears along side the featured information.

Signature line Enables the user of the file to digitally sign the file.

Single-series data series A data series representing only one set of data.

SkyDrive A central storage location in which you can store, access, and share files via an Internet connection.

Slicer A window listing all items in a field so that the user can click button to filter data by that particular item or value.

Slicer caption The text or field name that appears as a header or title at the top of a slicer to identify the data in that field.

Slide master The top slide in a hierarchy of slides based on the master that contains design information for the slides.

Solver An add-in application that manipulates variables based on constraints to find the optimal solution to a problem.

Source application The application used to create the original object.

Source file The file that contains the original table or data that is used or copied to create a linked or embedded object, such as a Word document or an Excel worksheet.

Split bar A vertical or horizontal line that frames panes in a worksheet and enables the user to resize the panes.

Splitting The process of dividing a worksheet window into resizable panes to enable viewing separate parts of a worksheet at the same time.

SQL keyword Defines the purpose and the structure of an SQL statement.

SQL SELECT statement Used to retrieve data from the tables in a database.

Stand-alone macro A macro that can be used independently of other controls or objects.

Standard deviation A statistic that measures how far the data sample is spread around the mean.

Start tag An XML code that indicates the starting point for an element and contains the element's name, such as <Rent>.

Stock chart A chart type that shows fluctuations or the range of change between the high and low values of a subject over time.

Structured Query Language (SQL) The industry-standard language for defining, manipulating, and retrieving the data in a database.

Stub column The first column of a table that typically contains the information that identifies the data in each row.

Sub Procedure Command lines written in the VBA Editor that have the ability to perform actions in Excel.

Subdocument A smaller document that is a part of a master document.

Subform Records displayed that are related to records in a main form.

SUBSTITUTE function A text function that substitutes new text for old text in a text string.

Substitution value A value that replaces the original value of a variable in a data table.

Subtotal An aggregate calculation, such as SUM or AVERAGE, that applies for a subcategory of related data within a larger dataset.

SUBTOTAL function A math or trig function that calculates the total of values contained in two or more cells; the first argument in the function specifies which aggregate function applies to the values in the range specified by the second argument.

Subtract A Combine Shapes command that removes the shape of the second selected object from the area of the first object.

SUMIF function A statistical function that calculates the total of a range of values when a specified condition is met.

SUMIFS function A statistical function that adds the cells in a range that meet multiple criteria.

Surface chart A chart type that displays trends using two dimensions on a continuous curve.

Synchronous scrolling Enables you to simultaneously scroll through both documents in Side by Side view at the same time.

Syntax error An error that occurs when formula construction rules are violated.

Tab order The sequential advancing in a form from one field or control to the next when you press Tab.

Tab-delimited file A text file that uses tabs to separate data.

Table Analyzer Analyzes the tables in a database and normalizes them for you.

Table style A combination of formatting choices for table components available to you that are based on a theme.

Template (Word) A partially completed document containing preformatted text or graphics. (Excel) A predesigned workbook that incorporates formatting elements, such as themes and layouts, and may include content that can be modified. A template is used as a model to create similar workbooks.

Text box A graphical object that contains text.

Text content control Used to enter any type of text into a form.

Text file A data file that contains letters, numbers, and symbols only; it does not contain formatting, sound, or video.

Text pane A special pane that opens up for entering text when a SmartArt diagram is selected.

Text-based chart A chart that shows a relationship between words, numbers, and/or graphics that primarily arranges and organizes information by text.

Theme A collection of design choices that includes colors, fonts, and special effects used to give a consistent look to a document, workbook, database form or report, or presentation.

Theme color Represents coordinated colors for the current text and background, accents, and hyperlinks.

Theme effect Includes lines, fill effects, and 3-D effects such as shadowing, glows, and borders to incorporate into a document theme.

Theme font Contains a coordinating heading and body text font for each different theme.

Third normal form (3NF) Satisfied when a table meets 2NF criteria and no transitive dependencies exist.

Thumbnail A small picture of each page in your document that displays in the Navigation Pane.

Timestamp A combination of the date and time that is encrypted as part of the digital signature.

Tracer arrow A colored line that indicates relationships between precedent and dependent cells.

Track Changes A collaboration feature that records certain types of changes made in a workbook.

Transitive dependency Occurs when the value of one non-key field is functionally dependent on the value of another non-key field.

Trigger An object that launches an animation that takes place when you click an associated object or a bookmarked location in a media object.

TrueType font A digital font that contain alphabetic characters and information about the characters, such as the shape, spacing, and character mapping of the font.

Two-variable data table A data analysis tool that provides results based on changing two variables.

Unbound control A control not tied to a specific field.

Ungrouping (Word) Breaks a grouped object into separate individual objects. (Excel) The process of deselecting worksheets that are grouped.

Uniform resource locator (URL) The location of a Web site or Web page on the Internet.

Union A Combine Shapes command that joins selected overlapping objects so they become one shape.

Update query An action query that changes the data values in one or more fields for all records that meet specific criteria.

UPPER function A text function that converts text to uppercase letters.

User exception An individual or group that is allowed to edit all or specific parts of a restricted document.

Validation criteria Rules that dictate the data to enter in a cell.

Validation rule Prevents invalid data from being entered into a field.

Values area The range in which to place a field that will display aggregates, such as SUM, for categories of data in a PivotTable.

Variable A value that you can change to see how that change affects other values.

Variance A descriptive statistics tool that determines the summation of the squared deviations divided by the amount of the sample – 1.

View Side by Side Enables you to display two documents on the same screen.

Visual Basic Editor The Office application used to create, edit, execute, and debug macros using programming language.

Visual Basic for Applications (VBA) A programming language that is built into Microsoft Office.

Watch Window A window that enables you to view formula calculations.

Web page Any document that displays on the World Wide Web.

Web query A data connection that links an Excel worksheet to a particular data table on a Web page.

Web server A computer system that hosts pages for viewing by anyone with an Internet connection.

What-if analysis The process of changing variables to observe how changes affect calculated results.

WHERE keyword Specifies the criteria that records must match to be included in the results of an SQL Select Statement.

Windows Live A group of online services provided by Microsoft that are designed to help users communicate and collaborate.

WordArt A Microsoft Office feature that creates decorative text that can be used to add interest to the text used in a document.

Worksheet reference A pointer to a cell in another worksheet.

Workspace file A document that specifies the window settings for a workbook.

World Wide Web (WWW) A very large subset of the Internet that stores Web page documents.

X Y (scatter) chart A chart type that shows a relationship between two variables using their X and Y coordinates. One variable is plotted on the horizontal X-axis, and the other variable is plotted on the vertical Y-axis. Scatter charts are often used to represent data in educational, scientific, and medical experiments.

X-axis The horizontal axis and usually contains the category information, such as products, companies, or intervals of time.

XML declaration A statement that specifies the XML version and character encoding used in the XML document.

XML Paper Specification (XPS) A file format developed by Microsoft and designed to display a printed page onscreen identically on any computer platform.

XPS file format (XPS) An electronic file format created by Microsoft that preserves document formatting and is viewable and printable on any platform.

Y-axis The vertical axis and usually contains the values or amounts.

Z-axis The axis used to plot the depth of a chart.

Index